the omnibus book of

britishand **american** hitsingles 1960-1990

the omnibus book of

britishand american hitsingles 1960-1990

by dave mcaleer

OMNIBUS PRESS
LONDON · NEW YORK · SYDNEY

© **1990 omnibus press**
(A Division of Book Sales Limited)

Edited by **chris charlesworth**
Cover designed by **monica chrysostomou**
Cover art direction **lisa pettibone**
Book designed by **peter dolton**
Picture research by **paul giblin**

All pictures supplied by **lfi** and **pictorial press**

ISBN 0.7119.2180.6
Order No. OP45889

Exclusive distributors:

Book Sales Limited,
8/9 Frith Street,
London W1V 5TZ, UK.

Music Sales Corporation
225 Park Avenue South,
New York, NY 10003, USA.

Music Sales Pty Ltd.,
120 Rothschild Avenue,
Rosebery, NSW 2018, Australia.

To the Music Trade only:
Music Sales Limited,
8/9 Frith Street,
London W1V 5TZ, UK.

Design and production in association with
book production consultants, 47 Norfolk Street, Cambridge
Typeset by **cambridge photosetting services**
Printed in England by **william clowes ltd**, Beccles, Suffolk

INTRODUCTION

The aim of this book is to list together for the first time the 6,000+ Top 10 British and American hits made by over 2,000 stars who have charted in the last three decades and also to present fact packed biographies of all of these artists.

When compiling and researching the information for use in the book I tried to include all of an artist's career high spots and cover the periods before and after their chart life. In most cases I have compared their success on both sides of the Atlantic and where possible have included some lesser known facts.

One of the main aims of this book is to make record buyers on both sides of the Atlantic more aware of each other's stars and musical tastes during the rock era. Now that for the first time all the biggest transatlantic hits can be found in the same book, it will hopefully help answer many of those questions that occasionally crop up like how successful is Jason Donovan in the US or how many UK hits did Paul Revere have?

The book includes every Top 10 hit made after 1960 plus every Top 10 made by the artists included back to 1955 (the start of the rock era). I included only the Top 10s so that you could be sure every record here was a genuine 100% smash hit. The reason for starting in 1960 is simply that before then transatlantic hits were almost totally one-way traffic from the US to the UK. In the 50s a British act thought themselves honoured if their UK hit was even released in the US never mind if it sold!

For the record it was on Jan 18, 1964, (The Beatles first chart entry) when the US really opened its doors to UK acts and in less than 16 months UK acts held nine of the Top 10 places on the US chart! Rather than being a flash in the pan, as thought by many at the time, UK acts have continued to regularly score Stateside and in April 1984 they held 40 of the Top 100 slots!

Obviously the slant of the book is towards the hit singles an artist has achieved but where relevant we also include the most important LP related facts. These often offer a clearer picture of an artist's true stature.

You may be surprised to find that many records that mean a lot to you were probably never even heard by people of similar musical tastes on the other side of the Atlantic. It's also interesting to note that many top stars had to wait years before getting their first hit on both sides of the Atlantic. This book will have served a useful purpose if it inspires you to search out some of the records you missed – as you can be certain of finding many real gems amongst them.

You will also see from the book that success very seldom comes overnight and that in most cases artists really have to pay their dues before getting their often short taste of success. Also, after a last hit an act seldom gives up the business and often their persistence pays off again. So remember there are hundreds of past hit acts still out there working and recording and keeping their fingers crossed that you will buy their new records and return them to that so important Top 10!

CHART POSITIONS & BIOGRAPHY DATA

The chart positions used are the ones most respected at the time by record buyers, namely Billboard (Hot 100/Best Sellers only – not Juke Box or Disc Jockey charts) in the US and New Musical Express in the UK up until Jan 1, 1964, and from then on the chart used by Record Retailer/Record Mirror/Music Week and the BBC. Therefore you will see for instance that The Beatles did top the recognised chart with 'Please Please Me'. The period covered is January 1, 1960, to December 31, 1989.

For the first time **Peak dates** (i.e. the date that the record sold its most copies and reached the height of its popularity) are used for each record rather than the less important (and easier to compile) entry date as used in other books.

All references to R&B/soul/black music (the name changed over the years) or country, modern rock, A/C (adult contemporary), easy listening, dance, club play and jazz refer to the Billboard US charts. References to Indie charts mean one off the recognised Indie singles charts in the UK.

For pre-1952 hits please note that all chart positions referred to are American as no UK record charts existed before that date and that in the few weeks where no UK charts were available to the public the charts that were made available to the industry only have been used.

Where known the **Original versions** or the **First hit versions** of songs are listed in brackets after the title with the **Year** and the **Country** (if not a chart record in both) it charted.

All top 10 hits UK or US list their **Equivalent US/UK chart placing** in brackets. If there is no equivalent chart placing listed then that record did not enter the US Top 100 or the UK Top 30 (up to 1.1.64), 50 (up to 6.5.78) or 75. This does not mean it was not a hit elsewhere in the world and neither do the words US-only or UK-only that often occur in the biographies. These again are simply comparing the two largest record markets in the world.

Where possible we have also included:

Every known record label that an **act has recorded on.**
Every group an artist has been in and **all the names a group has used.**
Forgotten follow ups to those **one-hit wonders** and **best forgotten** later **cash-in** attempts to chart again.
Top 10 hits written (or co-written) or produced by top 10 acts for other artists.
Name session musicians & singers who have appeared on other artists' records.
Records that entered the chart in high positions and **numerous records that made big jumps up the chart.**
The **names** of **all groups' lead singers** and **every act's home town.**

There are also thousands of references to:

The **total number of single & LP chart entries in the US & UK.**
Trivia records set by **acts** and **singles**, i.e. the longest, shortest, biggest, fastest etc etc etc.
Film credits, award winners, gold & platinum records. Plus much much more trivia!!

ABBREVIATIONS/OFTEN USED WORDS & PHRASES

Prod. = Producer
Comp. = Composer
Writ. = Writer
Co-writ. = Co-writer

Vid. = Video
Rel. = Released
Arr. = Arranger
(ex.) = The group/s the act was in previously.
(Number) = the peak chart position
Inc. = Including
Trad.= Traditional song
MOR = Middle of The Road
AOR = Adult Orientated Rock
R'n'R = Rock'n'Roll
R&B = Rhythm & Blues
45 = single record
NME = New Musical Express (UK pop magazine)
RM = Record Mirror (UK pop magazine)
MM = Melody Maker (UK pop magazine)

WORDS & PHRASES

GRAMMY = The American Record Industry Awards
BRITS = The British Record Industry Awards
R'n'R Hall of Fame = Recent US organisation formed to honour the most important and influential acts in rock.
From the film = from the film of the same name as the title listed.
American Music Awards = Another very important yearly US award.
Ivor Novello Award = A Top UK music publishers' award to songwriters.
Black music = the current US name for music played on radio stations aimed mainly at a black listening audience. The name replaced soul music which replaced R&B which replaced race music which replaced The Harlem Hit Parade.
UK Gold records = A UK only million seller (rare occurrence).
(name) in brackets = persons real (not stage) name.
Hit or Charter = chart entry anywhere in the US Top 100 or UK 30/50/75
was on = recorded on the following labels.
(when used after song titles) With = Act mentioned after 'with' was listed first on label.
(when used after song titles) And = Act mention after 'And' listed second on label.
Feat. = Featuring

LABEL ABBREVIATIONS

ABC PARA = ABC PARAMOUNT
ATLANTIC/COT = ATLANTIC/COTILLION
ATLANTIC/HANS = ATLANTIC/HANSA
BLANCO Y = BLANCO Y NEGRO
BOILING P. = BOILING POINT
CANADIAN AM. = CANADIAN AMERICAN
CADET CON. = CADET CONCEPT
CBS ASSOC = CBS ASSOCIATED
DE CONST = DE CONSTRUCTION
DELICIOUS VIN. = DELICIOUS VINYL
EMI AM = EMI AMERICA
EMI MAN = EMI MANHATTAN
FOOD FOR = FOOD FOR THOUGHT
FORBIDDEN = FORBIDDEN FRUIT
FOURTH & B. = FOURTH & BROADWAY
FRATERN. = FRATERNITY
MERCIFUL RELE = MERCIFUL RELEASE

ORIGINAL S. = ORIGINAL SOUND
PAISLEY = PAISLEY PARK
PENNY F = PENNY FARTHING
POWER E = POWER EXCHANGE
PYE DISCO D. = PYE DISCO DEMAND
REALLY = REALLY USEFUL
REGAL ZONO= REGAL ZONOPHONE
RHYTHM K = RHYTHM KING
SCOTTI BROTHE = SCOTTI BROTHERS
TETRAGRAM = TETRAGRAMMATON
TOTAL EXPER. = TOTAL EXPERIENCE

THE AUTHOR

Dave McAleer has worked in the record business on both sides of the Atlantic for over 25 years. He has headed International record companies, run successful production, promotion, marketing and management companies and had over ten years as a top A&R man. He discovered several of the acts included in this book and has worked with scores of them. He has also written for numerous US & UK magazines on all areas of rock, pop, black music and country.

For 35 years his No. 1 hobby has been records and the collecting of information and trivia concerning them and during this time he has put together one of the largest libraries of record information in the world. He was also the founder of the 'Music Business Trivia League', the industry quiz league that preceded all the radio and TV pop quizzes.

He is always looking for more information and would love to hear from any readers with additions and amendments to this book.

THANKS

I would like to thank the music papers and all their writers plus numerous authors whose works I have studied over the years. I would also like to thank several record trivia collectors and many recording artists and producers who have passed on information that I have used herein – not to mention those without whose work the book would not physically have been finished. This list includes but is not limited to Alley Cat, Billboard, Bim Bam Boom, Blues & Soul, Derek Brecknock, British Hit Singles & Albums, Fred Bronson, Cashbox, Chris Charlesworth, Mike Clifford, Country Music People, Luke Crampton, Tony Cummings, Rick Davies, Fred Dellar, Pete Frame, Charlie Gillett, Goldmine, Paul Grien, James Hamilton, Phil Hardy, Brian Henson, Alan Hood, Terry Hounsome, Tony Jasper, John Javna, Alan Jones, Hugh Jones, Brian Justice, Dave Laing, Barry Lazell, Bob MacDonald, Melody Maker, Colin Morgan, Bert Muirhead, Joseph Murrells, Music Master, Music Week, New Musical Express, Norm N. Nite, Now Dig This, Stephen Nugent, Big Al Pavlow, Paul Pelletier, Jon Philibert, Record Business, Record Mirror, Record World, Daffyd Rees, Clive Richardson, Rolling Stone, Bob Shannon, Shout, Smash Hits, Stak-O-Wax, Roger St. Pierre, Steve Sullivan, John Tobler, Marcia Vance and Joel Whitburn with extra special thanks to Billie McAleer.

BRITISH CHARTS PRE 1964 – © NME BRITISH CHARTS 1964–1983 © MUSIC WEEK. Compiled by Gallup.
BRITISH CHARTS 1983–1989 © BPI. Compiled by Gallup.
US CHART INFORMATION COURTESY OF 'BILLBOARD' MAGAZINE.

A

ABBA

Scandinavia's most successful transatlantic recording act and composers. Members Bjorn Ulvaeus & Benny Andersson recorded as Bjorn & Benny and in The Hep Stars in the early 70s before teaming with Agnetha (who recorded solo on Cupol in 68) and Frida to form the biggest selling mixed group of all time. They had nine UK No 1 singles and eight No. 1 UK LPs. They broke up in 1982.

WATERLOO	1(2)	04 MAY 74	EPIC
(Eurovision song contest winner first Swedish No.1)			
S.O.S. *(US No. 15)*	6	25 OCT 75	EPIC
MAMMA MIA *(US No. 32)*	1(2)	31 JAN 76	EPIC
FERNANDO *(US No. 13)*	1(4)	08 MAY 76	EPIC
DANCING QUEEN *(Jumped from 16 to 1)*	1(6)	04 SEP 76	EPIC
MONEY MONEY MONEY *(US No. 56)*	3	11 DEC 76	EPIC
(At the time they had Nos.1 & 2 on UK LP chart)			
KNOWING ME KNOWING YOU	1(5)	02 APR 77	EPIC
(Top UK record 77) (US No. 14)			
THE NAME OF THE GAME *(US No. 12)*	1(4)	05 NOV 77	EPIC
TAKE A CHANCE ON ME	1(2)	18 FEB 78	EPIC
SUMMER NIGHT CITY	5	07 OCT 78	EPIC
CHIQUITITA *(US No. 29)*	2	10 FEB 79	EPIC
DOES YOUR MOTHER KNOW *(US No. 19)*	4	12 MAY 79	EPIC
ANGEL EYES/VOULEZ VOUS *(US No. 64/80)*	3	11 AUG 79	EPIC
GIMME GIMME GIMME (A MAN AFTER MIDNIGHT)	3	10 NOV 79	EPIC
I HAVE A DREAM	2	22 DEC 79	EPIC
THE WINNER TAKES IT ALL	1(2)	09 AUG 80	EPIC
SUPER TROUPER *(Last of 9 UK No. 1s) (US No. 45)*	1(3)	29 NOV 80	EPIC
LAY ALL YOUR LOVE ON ME	7	25 JUL 81	EPIC
ONE OF US	3	26 DEC 81	EPIC
WATERLOO	6	24 AUG 74	ATLANTIC
(Highest placed Eurovision song of all time in US)			
DANCING QUEEN	1(1)	09 APR 77	ATLANTIC
TAKE A CHANCE ON ME	3	08 JUL 78	ATLANTIC
THE WINNER TAKES IT ALL	8	14 MAR 81	ATLANTIC

RUSS ABBOT

UK comedian, TV personality and ex member of The Black Abbots on Cannon in 77. He was on EMI in 80 and later had two UK-only Top 20s, the other being his follow-up 'All Night Holiday' (20).

ATMOSPHERE	7	26 JAN 85	SPIRIT

GREGORY ABBOTT

New York born ex English school teacher hit in the UK and US with his first single on Columbia. His follow up was 'I Got The Feelin' (It's Over)'.

SHAKE YOU DOWN	6	13 DEC 86	CBS
SHAKE YOU DOWN	1(1)	17 JAN 87	COLUMBIA
(Topped US black chart 12 weeks before)			

ABC

Group from Sheffield (UK). Members Mark White and Stephen Singleton were in Vice Versa and recruited stylish Martin Fry (then editor of Fanzine Modern Drugs) to front the act that became ABC. Regular charters on both sides of the Atlantic since 82, they signed with Parlophone (UK) and MCA (US) in 89.

POISON ARROW *(US No. 25)*	6	20 MAR 82	NEUTRON
THE LOOK OF LOVE (PT.1) *(US No. 18)*	4	12 JUN 82	NEUTRON
ALL OF MY HEART	5	25 SEP 82	NEUTRON
BE NEAR ME *(Topped US Dance chart) (UK No. 26)*	9	16 NOV 85	MERCURY
WHEN SMOKEY SINGS *(UK No. 11)*	5	19 SEP 87	MERCURY
(About Smokey Robinson (in US Top 10 same time))			

PAULA ABDUL

L.A. based singer/dancer who won five MTV awards including 'Choreographer Of The Year' in 87 for her work with Janet Jackson. She also worked on the Jacksons' stage show amongst others. In 89 she had three consecutive US No 1s, won many video awards and her 'Forever Girl' LP sold five million.

STRAIGHT UP	3	08 APR 89	VIRGIN
STRAIGHT UP	1(3)	11 FEB 89	VIRGIN
(MTV Award Best Female video of 89)			
FOREVER YOUR GIRL *(UK No. 24)*	1(2)	20 MAY 89	VIRGIN
COLD HEARTED	1(1)	02 SEP 89	VIRGIN
(Was 'B' of her first No. 1 "Straight Up")			
(IT'S JUST) THE WAY YOU LOVE ME	3	02 DEC 89	VIRGIN
(Was her first chart entry – was US No. 88 in 88)			

COLONEL ABRAMS

Detroit born Colonel (his real name) recorded for Polydor in 77 in the group 94 East with Prince. He was often seen on UK TV in the mid 80s but oddly never made the US Top 100. His follow up was 'I'm Not Gonna Let You (Get The Best of Me)'.

TRAPPED	3	19 OCT 85	MCA

FATHER ABRAHAM – FOR HIT DETAILS SEE THE SMURFS

ACE

Sheffield (UK) born Paul Carrack, who first recorded with Warm Dust in 70, joined ex members of Mighty Baby and Warm Dust to form Ace. Follow up to their transatlantic Top 20 was 'Rock & Roll Runaway'. Paul later had chart records as a soloist and with Squeeze and Mike & The Mechanics.

HOW LONG *(UK No. 20)*	3	31 MAY 75	ANCHOR
(Song about departing group member Terry Comer)			

Also see Paul Carrack/Squeeze/Mike & The Mechanics

AD LIBS

Quintet from Newark with lead vocals from Mary Ann Thomas. They were previously known as The Creators and followed their US hit with 'He Aint No Angel'. They were later on Interphon in 65, Karen in 66, AGP in 66, Philips in 67, Vando, Capricorn and Share in 68 and Capitol in 70.

THE BOY FROM NEW YORK CITY	8	27 FEB 65	BLUE CAT

ADAM & THE ANTS

Original group formed by London based ex Bazooka Joe member Adam (Stuart Goddard). They were on Decca and Do-it and signed to CBS after Adam's co-writer Marco Pironi joined. They were the Top UK act of 81 but their flamboyant pirate image and 'Ant music' did not sell in the US.

DOG EAT DOG	4	08 NOV 80	CBS
ANTMUSIC	2	17 JAN 81	CBS
YOUNG PARISIANS	9	31 JAN 81	DECCA
(Had been group's first release on Decca in 78)			
KINGS OF THE WILD FRONTIER	2	14 MAR 81	CBS
(At this time act had 5 singles & 2 LPs on UK chart)			
STAND AND DELIVER	1(5)	09 MAY 81	CBS
PRINCE CHARMING *(Entered UK chart No. 2)*	1(4)	19 SEP 81	CBS
ANT RAP *(Entered UK chart No. 9)*	3	09 JAN 82	CBS

Also see Adam Ant

ADAM ANT

Adam went solo at the height of Adam & The Ants fame and quickly scored his only US hit. In the UK he notched up a few more hits, turned to acting, then re-entered the UK Top 20 in 90 on MCA.

GOODY TWO SHOES *(US No. 12)*	1(2)	12 JUN 82	CBS
FRIEND OR FOE	9	02 OCT 82	CBS
PUSS 'N BOOTS	5	12 NOV 83	CBS

Also see Adam & The Ants

BRYAN ADAMS

Canadian rock singer/songwriter/guitarist first attracted attention with the disco/dance record 'Let Me Take You Dancing' in 79. Three years later 'Lonely Nights' started his long string of US chart records which included seven solo top 20s and one 'It's Only Love' with Tina Turner (15).

STRAIGHT FROM THE HEART (UK No. 51)	10	28 MAY 83	A&M
RUN TO YOU (Biggest UK hit No. 11)	6	19 JAN 85	A&M
HEAVEN (UK No. 38)	1(2)	22 JUN 85	A&M
SUMMER OF '69 (UK No. 42)	5	31 AUG 85	A&M

AEROSMITH

New Hampshire (US) band formed in 70 and fronted by charismatic Steve Tyler. They first hit (US) with 'Dream On' in 73. Despite over a dozen US hit singles and 11 gold LPs the band did not make the UK Top 20 single or LP chart until 89.

DREAM ON (Originally made No. 59 in 73)	6	10 APR 76	COLUMBIA
WALK THIS WAY	10	29 JAN 77	COLUMBIA
(Revived by Run DMC 86 with Steve Tyler guesting)			
ANGEL (UK No. 69)	3	30 APR 88	GEFFEN
LOVE IN AN ELEVATOR (UK No. 13)	5	28 OCT 89	GEFFEN

AFTER THE FIRE

UK band led by Andy Piercy were formed in 74 and recorded an LP in 78 on their own Rapid label for a Christian music following. First charted in UK in 79 with 'One Rule For You' (40th). They had a few flops before scoring with a cover of Falco's German hit. Follow up was 'Dancing In The Shadows'.

DER KOMMISSAR (UK No. 47)	5	30 APR 83	EPIC

A-HA

The first Norwegian act to top the transatlantic charts and the most successful act yet from that country. The trio formed in 82 by Morten, Mags and Pal are known for their award winning videos and were one of the top teen appeal acts in the UK in 86/87.

TAKE ON ME (First released in UK Oct 84)	2	26 OCT 85	WARNER
(An earlier version was top in Norway previously)			
THE SUN ALWAYS SHINES ON T.V. (US No. 20)	1(2)	25 JAN 86	WARNER
TRAIN OF THOUGHT	8	19 APR 86	WARNER
HUNTING HIGH AND LOW	5	21 JUN 86	WARNER
I'VE BEEN LOSING YOU	8	11 OCT 86	WARNER
CRY WOLF (US No. 50)	5	05 JAN 87	WARNER
THE LIVING DAYLIGHTS (From James Bond Film)	5	11 JUL 87	WARNER
STAY ON THESE ROADS	5	02 APR 88	WARNER
TAKE ON ME	1(1)	19 OCT 85	WARNER

AIR SUPPLY

Australian based duo Russell Hitchcock and UK born Graham Russell had Australian hits in the 70s and toured the US with Rod Stewart in 77 (they were on Columbia then). In the US their first seven chart records all made the Top 5 – a great achievement – but in the UK they never made the Top 10.

LOST IN LOVE	3	03 MAY 80	ARISTA
ALL OUT OF LOVE (UK No. 11)	2	13 SEP 80	ARISTA
EVERY WOMAN IN THE WORLD	5	31 JAN 81	ARISTA
THE ONE THAT YOU LOVE	1(1)	25 JUL 81	ARISTA
HERE I AM			
(JUST WHEN YOU THOUGHT I WAS OVER YOU)	5	21 NOV 81	ARISTA
SWEET DREAMS	5	20 MAR 82	ARISTA
EVEN THE NIGHTS ARE BETTER (UK No. 44)	5	04 SEP 82	ARISTA
MAKING LOVE OUT OF NOTHING AT ALL	2	08 OCT 83	ARISTA
(Jim Steinman wrote & prod this & No. 1 that week)			

JEWEL AKENS

Texan Jewel (parents wanted a girl) worked with Eddie Cochran in the 50s and had been in Eddie & The Four Tunes, Jewel & Eddie (Daniels), The Four Dots (on Freedom) and Astro-Jets before his hit. He also recorded on Silver, RTV, Capeheart, Crest, Colgems, Paula and Minasa. Follow up was the similar sounding 'Georgie Porgie'.

THE BIRDS AND THE BEES (UK No. 29)	3	2 MAR 65	ERA

MORRIS ALBERT

Brazilian Morris started in a group called The Thunders. Before charting in the UK and US his one-off transatlantic toptenner was huge in South America. He followed with 'She's My Girl'.

FEELINGS	4	18 OCT 75	DECCA
FEELINGS	6	25 OCT 75	RCA

ALESSI

Photogenic New York duo Billy & Bobby Alessi who followed their UK hit with 'Sad Songs', but surprisingly never charted again there. They had a small US hit in 82 on Qwest.

OH LORI	8	30 JUL 77	A&M

ALIVE & KICKING

New York sextet fronted by Pepe Cardona and Sandy Toder (only girl in the group). Their sole US Top 40 hit was written and produced by Tommy James (who recorded the song himself in 79) and arranged by Jimmy Wisner (see Kokomo). The follow up was 'Just Let It Come'. Member Bruce Sudano later married Donna Summer.

TIGHTER, TIGHTER	7	08 AUG 70	ROULETTE

ALL ABOUT EVE

London based goth band formed in 85 and featuring Julianne Reagan and Mark Price (known in UK as the boy in the old Hovis bread ads). They recorded on their own Eden label (sometimes with help from The Mission's Wayne Hussey) and perfected an 80s hippy sound and image but have yet to score in US.

MARTHA'S HARBOUR		10	20 AUG 88	MERCURY

DONNA ALLEN

Former cheerleader from Florida has so far achieved more pop success in the UK than her homeland where her sales to date have mainly been in the black music field.

SERIOUS (US No. 21)	8	06 JUN 87	PORTRAIT
JOY AND PAIN (Maze 80 R&B hit)	10	01 JUL 89	BCM

ALLISONS

London born John Alford and Bob Day became overnight UK stars when their own composition came second in the Eurovision song contest. The first UK duo to top the UK chart had two more UK-only Top 40s. They re-appeared with an Xmas LP in 78 and John worked with P.J. Proby on one of P.J.'s unsuccessful comebacks.

ARE YOU SURE	1(2)	05 MAR 61	FONTANA

ALLMAN BROTHERS BAND

Floridians Duane & Gregg Allman (previously in The House Rockers, Allman Joys and Hourglass) formed the first big Southern rock band The Allman Brothers in 69 and scored eight US-only Top 40 LPs. Duane, who also played on many soul hits, died in 71. Greg was still charting in the 80s.

 RAMBLIN' MAN   2   13 OCT 73   CAPRICORN

MARC ALMOND

Marc was in Soft Cell in 79 and then Marc & The Mambas and Marc & Friends in 82 before guesting with Bronski Beat. His 14th solo single was a million seller and Gene Pitney's first UK No. 1 but it did not sell in the US.

I FEEL LOVE (With BRONSKI BEAT)		3	11 MAY 85	FORBIDDEN
(Inc. 'Love To Love You Baby' & *'Johnny Remember Me')*				
SOMETHING'S GOTTEN HOLD OF MY HEART		1(4)	28 JAN 89	PARLOPHONE
(Featuring GENE PITNEY – song was hit for *Gene in 67)*				

Also see Soft Cell

HERB ALPERT

L.A. trumpeter and co-writer of 'Wonderful World' and 'Only 16' in the 50s. Recorded for Andex in 59 as Herbie Alpert Sextet and on RCA in 61 and Dot in 62 as Dore Alpert. First hit with his second release on own A&M label and in April 66 had four LPs in the US Top 10 together. He is still a good seller with strong dance and black music base and has recently sold A&M for $300 million.

SPANISH FLEA *(US No. 27)*		3	05 FEB 66	PYE INT.
(As Herb Alpert & The Tijuana Brass)				
THIS GUY'S IN LOVE WITH YOU		2	07 SEP 68	A&M
THE LONELY BULL (As The Tijuana Brass)		6	08 DEC 62	A&M
A TASTE OF HONEY		7	27 NOV 65	A&M
(As Herb Alpert & The Tijuana Brass)				
THIS GUY'S IN LOVE WITH YOU		1(4)	22 JUN 68	A&M
RISE *(UK No. 13)*		1(2)	20 OCT 79	A&M
DIAMONDS *(Feat. JANET JACKSON) (UK No. 27)*		5	20 JUN 87	A&M

ALPHAVILLE

German trio Frank Mertens, Marian Gold and Bernhard Lloyd. Their German No. 1 'Forever Young' was also a small US hit.

BIG IN JAPAN *(US No. 66)*   8   22 SEP 84   WEA INT.

ALTERED IMAGES

Glasgow (UK) band, named after a design company and fronted by singer/actress Clare Grogan. First hit was the controversial 'Dead Pop Stars'. Their cute pop sound and image met with no success in the US. Clare formed Universal Love School in 89.

HAPPY BIRTHDAY		2	31 OCT 81	EPIC
I COULD BE HAPPY		7	16 JAN 82	EPIC
DON'T TALK TO ME ABOUT LOVE		7	02 APR 83	EPIC

ALTHIA AND DONNA

Jamaican Reggae duo Althia Forest (then 17) and Donna Reid (18) were the first black female duo to top the UK charts, which they did with their sole UK hit. They quickly joined Virgin Records but had no further chart action.

 UPTOWN TOP RANKING   1(1)   04 FEB 78   LIGHTNING

AMAZULU

Female group who were also on Towerbell in 83 and EMI in 87. They started as a reggae act but later specialised in updating US oldies like 'Don't You Just Know It', 'Mony Mony' and 'Montego Bay' not to mention their biggest hit. They had little US success. Annie Amazulu signed to Imperative in 89.

 TOO GOOD TO BE FORGOTTEN   5   28 JUN 86   ISLAND
(Chi-Lites 74 UK hit)

AMBROSIA

L.A. trio formed in 70 by David Pack, Burleigh Drummond and Joe Puerta. They originally recorded on Sceptre in 73 and first hit on 20th Century in 75. The two-times Grammy nominees never hit in the UK. David Pack recorded solo and in another trio with Michael McDonald and James Ingram in 86.

HOW MUCH I FEEL		3	18 NOV 78	WARNER
BIGGEST PART OF ME		3	07 JUN 80	WARNER

AMEN CORNER

Septet formed in Wales in 66 and fronted by Andy Fairweather-Low, became one of the UK's top acts of the late 60s but failed to chart in US. Group split in 69 and Andy had solo hits until 75.

BEND ME SHAPE ME		3	17 FEB 68	DERAM
(Originally by US act The Models)				
HIGH IN THE SKY		6	07 SEP 68	DERAM
(IF PARADISE IS) HALF AS NICE *(Jumped 19-1)*		1(2)	15 FEB 69	IMMEDIATE
HELLO SUSIE		4	12 JUL 69	IMMEDIATE

Also see Andy Fairweather-Low

AMERICA

US acoustic trio of Dewey Bunnell, Gerry Beckley and Dan Peek, all sons of UK based US servicemen, formed in 69. They first hit in the UK but despite string of US hit singles and LPs they never made UK Top 40 singles again.

HORSE WITH NO NAME		3	22 JAN 71	WARNER
A HORSE WITH NO NAME		1(3)	25 MAR 72	WARNER
I NEED YOU		9	01 JUL 72	WARNER
VENTURA HIGHWAY *(UK No. 43)*		8	09 DEC 72	WARNER
TIN MAN		4	09 NOV 74	WARNER
LONELY PEOPLE		5	08 MAR 75	WARNER
SISTER GOLDEN HAIR		1(1)	14 JUN 75	WARNER
YOU CAN DO MAGIC *(UK No. 59)*		8	16 OCT 82	CAPITOL

AMERICAN BREED

Chicago quartet led by Gary Liozzo were originally called Gary & The Nitelites on MGM. Their biggest US hit was their fourth release on Acta. The group recorded for Dunwich in 67 and Paramount in 70 and evolved into Ask Rufus, then simply Rufus and had chart records with Chaka Khan.

BEND ME, SHAPE ME *(UK No. 24)*   5   27 JAN 68   ACTA
(Original by The Models – co-written Scott English)

Also see Chaka Khan/Rufus

ED AMES

Born Ed Urick he was the only member of the top 50s group The Ames Brothers to have solo US chart records. He first recorded with the Boston quartet in 1948 and appeared as Mingo in the 50s TV show Daniel Boone.

MY CUP RUNNETH OVER *(from I Do, I Do)*   8   25 MAR 67   RCA

ANGRY ANDERSON

Bald singer/actor who was with Australian rock band Rose Tattoo and appeared in films Mad Max 3 and Rasputin had a surprise UK hit with the love theme from the Aussie soap opera Neighbours. Follow up was 'Calling'.

 SUDDENLY   3   10 DEC 88   FOOD FOR

BILL ANDERSON

South Carolina born 'Whispering Bill' first recorded for TNT (58) and was a top country singer and writer in the 60s & 70s scoring 37 country Top 10s including seven No. 1s. He later hosted US TV quiz show Fandango and was on Southern Tracks (82) and Swanee (85).

 STILL *(Top US Country record of 63)*   8   08 JUN 63   DECCA
(One of three of his songs covered in UK by Ken Dodd)

CARL ANDERSON – SEE GLORIA LORING FOR HIT DETAILS

LAURIE ANDERSON

Unique Chicago performer had a UK hit with the indescribable eight minute single (from her seven hour work 'United States') which was first on the One-Ten label. The record did not get radio support in the US where she remains a cult figure. Follow up was 'Big Science'. Her performances incorporate sculpture, film, mime and lighting effects.

 O SUPERMAN *(Took only two weeks to hit No. 2)*   2   24 OCT 8   WARNER

LYNN ANDERSON

Raised in San Francisco she is the daughter of country singer/writer Liz Anderson. Her only transatlantic Top 10 was her second 45 on Columbia, a cover of a Joe South song, which was later sampled by Kon Kan on 'I Beg Your Pardon'. She was top female country act of 71 and still gets country hits to add to her 60.

 ROSE GARDEN   3   27 MAR 71   CBS
ROSE GARDEN   3   13 FEB 71   COLUMBIA

CHRIS ANDREWS

Romford (UK) born songwriter turned singer penned hits for Sandie Shaw and Adam Faith before writing his Top 10 hit and the follow up 'To Whom It Concerns' (UK 13). In a 65 UK Poll he was voted No. 2 'Best Newcomer'. He re-appeared on Pye in 69 and Epic in 77.

YESTERDAY MAN   3   13 NOV 65   DECCA
(No. 94 US-Top in Germany and European Gold Record)

ANEKA

Scottish housewife Mary Sandeman had her sole UK Top 40 hit with this novelty which incidentally was rejected by her Japanese label for being 'too Chinese'. She followed it with 'Little Lady' and turned Japanese again in 83 with 'Rose Rose I Love You', this time with no chart result.

JAPANESE BOY   1(1)   29 AUG 81   HANSA

ANGELS

New Jersey trio Phyllis & Barbara Allbut and Linda Jansen first recorded as The Starlets in 60 on Astro. First hit was 'Til' in 61 (US 14) and after Peggy Santiglia replaced Linda they hit No. 1 with a song composed by The Strangeloves. They later recorded on Cameo, RCA, Tollie, Ascot, and Bell.

 MY BOYFRIENDS BACK *(UK No. 28)*   1(3)   31 AUG 63   SMASH

ANIMALS

Newcastle (UK) based quintet originally called The Alan Price Combo were popular both in the UK & US with their anglicised R&B music. Act re-formed in 76 & 83 (when they toured with The Police). Alan and singer Eric Burdon had high charting solo records too. Eric signed to Stripped Horse (US) in 88. Bassist Chas Chandler went on to manage Jimi Hendrix and Slade.

HOUSE OF THE RISING SUN   1(1)   11 JUL 64   COLUMBIA
(Recorded in 20 mins – returned to No. 11 UK in 82)
I'M CRYING *(US No. 19)*   8   17 OCT 64   COLUMBIA
DON'T LET ME BE MISUNDERSTOOD   3   27 FEB 65   COLUMBIA
(US No. 15 – song originally by Nina Simone)
BRING IT ON HOME TO ME   7   01 MAY 65   COLUMBIA
(US No. 32 – Sam Cooke 62 US hit)
WE'VE GOT TO GET OUT OF THIS PLACE   2   14 AUG 65   COLUMBIA
(US No. 13 – co-written by Barry Mann)
IT'S MY LIFE *(US No. 23)*   7   13 NOV 65   COLUMBIA
DON'T BRING ME DOWN   6   25 JUN 66   DECCA
(US No. 12 – co-written by Carole King)
SAN FRANCISCAN NIGHTS   7   18 NOV 67   MGM
(As Eric Burdon & The Animals)

HOUSE OF THE RISING SUN   1(3)   05 SEP 64   MGM
(Trad. song – first Top 10 for prod. Mickie Most)
SEE SEE RIDER *(Chuck Willis 57 hit)*   10   22 OCT 66   MGM
SAN FRANCISCAN NIGHTS   9   30 DEC 67   MGM
(Above two releases as Eric Burdon & The Animals)

Also see Eric Burdon

ANIMOTION

US quintet originally led by Astrid Plane and Bill Wadhams. Lead vocalist Cynthia Rhodes (Mrs Richard Marx) took over on latest hit. They were also on Casablanca in 86.

OBSESSION   5   15 JUN 85   MERCURY
OBSESSION   6   04 MAY 85   MERCURY
ROOM TO MOVE   9   06 MAY 89   POLYDOR

PAUL ANKA

Ottawa born singer/composer whose first record was 'I Confess' in 56 at age 15 with noted doo-wop group The Jacks. He was the youngest transatlantic chart regular in the 50s. Acts who have hits with his songs include Donny Osmond, Buddy Holly, Tom Jones, Freddie & The Dreamers, Frank Sinatra ('My Way'), and he even had three songs on the country chart in the same week. He also recorded for RCA, Barnaby, Buddah, Fame, Epic and Columbia.

DIANA   1(9)   30 AUG 57   COLUMBIA
(UK Gold – first solo by a teenager to top chart)
I LOVE YOU BABY *(US No. 97)*   3   13 DEC 57   COLUMBIA
YOU ARE MY DESTINY   6   07 MAR 58   COLUMBIA
(ALL OF A SUDDEN) MY HEART SINGS *(US No. 15)*   10   13 MAR 59   COLUMBIA
LONELY BOY   3   28 AUG 59   COLUMBIA
PUT YOUR HEAD ON MY SHOULDER   7   20 NOV 59   COLUMBIA
(YOU'RE) HAVING MY BABY *(Feat. ODIA COATES)*   6   26 OCT 74   UA

DIANA *(About his baby sitter Diana Ayoub)*   1(1)   09 SEP 57   ABC PARA
YOU ARE MY DESTINY   9   24 FEB 58   ABC PARA
LONELY BOY   1(4)   13 JUL 59   ABC PARA
PUT YOUR HEAD ON MY SHOULDER   2   18 OCT 59   ABC PARA
IT'S TIME TO CRY *(UK No. 28)*   4   27 DEC 59   ABC PARA
PUPPY LOVE   2   04 APR 60   ABC PARA
MY HOME TOWN   8   04 JUL 60   ABC PARA
DANCE ON LITTLE GIRL   10   10 JUL 61   ABC PARA
(YOU'RE) HAVING MY BABY *(Feat. ODIA COATES)*   1(3)   24 AUG 74   UA
ONE MAN WOMAN/ONE WOMAN MAN *(-do-)*   7   25 JAN 75   UA
I DON'T LIKE TO SLEEP ALONE   8   24 MAY 75   UA
TIMES OF YOUR LIFE   7   07 FEB 76   UA

ANNETTE

Annette Funicello joined the 'Mouseketeers' in 55 and became the most famous of them all. After a couple of flops she scored her biggest hit and followed it with another nine US-only chart entries over the next two years. In the early 60s she appeared in a series of popular beach movies.

TALL PAUL		7	23 FEB 59	DISNEYLAND
(Original by fellow Mousketeer Judy Harriet)				
O DIO MIO		10	28 MAR 60	VISTA

APOLLO 100

UK project masterminded by pianist Tom Parker and including top session men Vic Flick and Clem Cattini. 'Mendelssohns 4th (2nd Movement)' (US No. 94) was the follow up. They also revived unsuccessfully 'Telstar' (Clem had played on the Tornados No. 1).

JOY (Based on 'Jesu, Joy Of Man's Desiring')	6	26 FEB 72	MEGA

APPLEJACKS

Solihull (UK) group previously known as The Crestas and The Jaguars and featuring ex Sunday School teacher Megan Davies and Al Jackson. They also made the UK-only Top 30 with 'Like Dreamers Do' and 'Three Little Words'.

TELL ME WHEN	7	18 APR 64	DECCA

ARCADIA

Short lived Duran Duran spin-off featuring Simon Le Bon, Nick Rhodes and Roger Taylor only had one transatlantic Top 20 single.

ELECTION DAY *(Narration Grace Jones)*	7	02 NOV 85	ODEON
ELECTION DAY	6	14 DEC 85	CAPITOL

Also see Duran Duran

ARCHIES

Cartoon session group created by Don Kirshner (of The Monkees fame) for much hyped US TV show based on the comic book (started in 1941) and fronted by top session man Ron Dante (see Cuff Links). Their first hit was also a UK No. 1 despite the fact that the TV show was not seen there.

SUGAR SUGAR *(Co-written by Andy Kim)*	1(8)	25 OCT 69	RCA
(Jumped 11-1, Dante recorded disco version in 75)			
SUGAR SUGAR *(Top US single 69)*	1(4)	20 SEP 69	CALENDAR
(Originally written for & rejected by The Monkees)			
JINGLE JANGLE	10	07 FEB 70	KIRSHNER

ARGENT

UK group evolved from The Zombies fronted by Rod Argent and including Russ Ballard (from Adam Faith's band The Roulettes and Unit Four + 2). Their follow up was 'Tragedy' and they had two further UK-only Top 40s. Rod scored later as San Jose and co-produced Tanita Tikaram while Russ wrote hits for other acts.

HOLD YOUR HEAD UP	5	01 APR 72	EPIC
(Originally released in 6½ min version in 71)			
HOLD YOUR HEAD UP	5	26 AUG 72	EPIC

Also see Zombies/San Jose

JOAN ARMATRADING

Better known in the UK/US for her LPs – Joan was born in the Caribbean and raised in Birmingham (UK). She first recorded on Cube and signed with A&M a year later. She had another UK-only Top 20 with 'Drop The Pilot' (11).

LOVE AND AFFECTION	10	13 NOV 76	A&M

LOUIS ARMSTRONG

'Satchmo' was born in New Orleans in 1900 and died 71 years later. He has the longest chart span in the US having first charted in 1926 and last made the Top 40 in 1988 (with 'Wonderful World' his UK No. 1 20 years earlier). He is also the oldest person to top either the US or UK charts. 'What a Wonderful World' was used in the soundtrack for Good Morning Vietnam.

THEME FROM THE THREEPENNY OPERA	8	11 MAY 56	PHILIPS
(US No. 20 – a.k.a. 'Mack the Knife')			
HELLO, DOLLY! *(From the musical)*	4	27 JUN 64	LONDON
WHAT A WONDERFUL WORLD	1(4)	27 APR 68	HMV
(US No. 32 in 88 – Top UK single of 68)			
HELLO, DOLLY!	1(1)	09 MAY 64	KAPP
(The first US No. 1 after The Beatles Invasion!)			

EDDY ARNOLD

Born in Tennessee and nicknamed 'The Tennessee Ploughboy' he is the top all time country artist, with an amazing 136 chart records between 1945 and 1983. He was elected to the Country Hall Of Fame in 66. His only pop Top 20 record came with his 17th (of 23) country chart toppers.

MAKE THE WORLD GO AWAY	8	02 APR 66	RCA
MAKE THE WORLD GO AWAY	6	25 DEC 65	RCA

STEVE ARRINGTON

Dayton, Ohio (US) native was lead vocalist of Slave from 78 to 82 when he formed Steve Arrington's Hall of Fame on Konglather. In 85 he went solo and was most successful in the UK; his biggest US hit was 'Dancin' in The Key of Life' (68). He joined EMI in 87.

FEEL SO REAL	5	18 MAY 85	ATLANTIC

ARRIVAL

Seven piece Liverpool group fronted by Dyan Burch had been singing semi-pro for some years before scoring their two UK-only Top 20s – the other being 'I Will Survive' (16). They later recorded for CBS and Kaleidoscope.

FRIENDS	8	31 JAN 70	DECCA

ARROWS

US/UK trio fronted by Bronx born Alan Merrill (Laura Nyro's cousin) who had previously had three solo heavy rock LPs out in Japan. They had a UK childrens TV series and had another UK-only Top 40 hit with 'My Last Night With You'. Their flop fourth single 'I Love Rock'n'Roll' was a No. 1 in 82 by Joan Jett.

A TOUCH TOO MUCH	8	22 JUN 74	RAK

ART OF NOISE

Initially planned as a faceless instrumental act by UK session players Anne Dudley, J.J. Jeczalik and Gary Langan. Their first hit came on the US black music chart with their second release 'Beat Box' in 84. They feature guest performers on most singles.

CLOSE (TO THE EDIT)	8	23 FEB 85	ZTT
PETER GUNN *(US No. 50 & No. 2 US Dance chart)*	8	12 APR 86	CHINA
(Feat. DUANE EDDY – who had a hit with it in 59)			
KISS *(Featuring TOM JONES – US No. 31)*	5	05 NOV 88	CHINA
(Prince 86 hit-MTV video award winner 89)			

ASHFORD & SIMPSON

Soulful singer/songwriters Nick Ashford & Valerie Simpson were staff writers at the Motown production factory during the sixties. They first recorded as Valerie & Nick in 64 and in 73 had the first of more than 30 black music chart records. They have also written Top 20 hits for acts like Chaka Khan, Diana Ross and Marvin Gaye.

 SOLID *(US No. 12)*   3   16 FEB 85   CAPITOL

ASHTON, GARDNER & DYKE

UK sextet fronted by Tony Ashton, Roy Dyke (both ex Remo 4) and Kim Gardiner who were first on Polydor in 69. George Harrison and Eric Clapton (Tony thought up the name Derek & The Dominoes for him) guested on an LP for the act who had a one-off hit, which Tom Jones covered in the US. Follow up was 'Can You Get it'.

 RESURRECTION SHUFFLE *(US No. 40)*   3   20 FEB 71   CAPITOL

ASIA

UK supergroup comprising Steve Howe, Geoff Downes, Carl Palmer and John Wetton; they had variously been in Yes, ELP, UK, Buggles, King Crimson, Uriah Heep and Roxy Music. In the US their debut LP was No. 1 for nine weeks and their second also made the Top 10. They were less successful in the UK and broke up in 85.

 HEAT OF THE MOMENT *(UK No. 46)*   4   26 JUN 82   GEFFEN
DON'T CRY *(UK No. 33)*   10   17 SEP 83   GEFFEN

Also see Yes/ELP/Buggles

ASSEMBLY

A one-off UK hit from Vince Clarke (ex-Depeche Mode and Yazoo), producer Eric Radcliffe and Feargal Sharkey (ex-Undertones).

 NEVER NEVER   4   26 NOV 83   MUTE

ASSOCIATES

Dundee (Scotland) band included Billy McKenzie and Alan Rankine who were originally known as the Absorbic Ones. Recorded on Double Hip and MCA in 79 and Fiction and Situation Two in 80 before starting their own label in 82. They broke up in 85. Alan recorded on Virgin in 87, Billy on Circa in 89 without notable success but retaining the name The Associates.

 PARTY FEARS TWO   9   27 MAR 82   ASSOCIATES

ASSOCIATION

California sextet formed by ex-Mother of Invention Terry Kirkham and Gary Alexander. Formerly called Men they recorded for Jubilee in 65 and Davon in 66. Group's second Valiant single started a string of US-only Top 20s. They later recorded on Columbia, Mums, Elektra and RCA and were still touring on 'oldies' shows in 89.

 ALONG COMES MARY   7   16 JUL 66   VALIANT
(It was thought that Mary referred to Marijuana)
CHERISH   1(3)   24 SEP 66   VALIANT
WINDY   1(4)   01 JUL 67   WARNER
NEVER MY LOVE   2   14 OCT 67   WARNER
EVERYTHING THAT TOUCHES YOU   10   02 MAR 68   WARNER

RICK ASTLEY

Merseyside born ex truck driver had previously been in Give Way and FBI. Discovered by Peter Waterman (S.A.W.) he was on the No. 1 by Ferry Aid and dueted in Rick & Lisa before scoring first of a string of transatlantic Top 10s. In 87/88 he won many awards including Top US dance act.

NEVER GONNA GIVE YOU UP *(Top UK single 87)*   1(5)   29 AUG 87   RCA
WHENEVER YOU NEED SOMEBODY   3   07 NOV 87   RCA
(Original by O'Chi Brown in 86 – No. 1 US Dance)
WHEN I FALL IN LOVE/MY ARMS KEEP
MISSING YOU *(Entered at No. 2)*
(Nat 'King' Cole 57 UK hit)   2   12 DEC 87   RCA
TOGETHER FOREVER   2   12 MAR 88   RCA
SHE WANTS TO DANCE WITH ME   6   15 OCT 88   RCA
TAKE ME TO YOUR HEART   8   10 DEC 88   RCA
HOLD ME IN YOUR ARMS   10   25 FEB 89   RCA

NEVER GONNA GIVE YOU UP   1(2)   12 MAR 88   RCA
(Top selling US 12" of 88)
TOGETHER FOREVER   1(1)   18 JUN 88   RCA
(Only act in 80s with first 2 rels. No. 1s US)
IT WOULD TAKE A STRONG MAN   10   17 SEP 88   RCA
SHE WANTS TO DANCE WITH ME   6   25 FEB 89   RCA

ASWAD

UK reggae band including Brinsley Forde signed to Island (76) and had reggae No. 1 with 'Back To Africa'. Later on Grove (80), CBS (81) and Simba (83) before hitting No. 1 with their 23rd single, an old Tina Turner 'B' side and their third UK-only hit. Follow up song was a Bucks Fizz 'B' side 'Give a Little Love' (UK 11).

 DON'T TURN AROUND   1(2)   26 MAR 88   MANGO

ATLANTA RHYTHM SECTION

Georgia based sextet included two members of the hit act Classics IV, J.R. Cobb and Dean Daughtry. Act first recorded for Decca in 72 and cut two LPs for MCA before their first hit. They had seven US-only Top 40s and their sole UK charter was 'Spooky' (48), an old Classics 1V hit. Act re-formed on Epic in 89.

SO IN TO YOU   7   30 APR 77   POLYDOR
IMAGINARY LOVER   7   03 JUN 78   POLYDOR

Also see Classics 1V

ATLANTIC STARR

Formed in New York in 76 out of three local groups by the Lewis Brothers Wayne, Jonathan and David. Their first chart record was 'Stand Up' in 78. Original lead singer Sharon Bryant went solo, with success in 89, and was replaced in 84 by Barbara Weathers who was featured on their two Transatlantic Top Tens.

SECRET LOVERS   10   12 APR 86   A&M
ALWAYS *(Vocal Barbara & David Lewis)*   3   25 JUL 87   WARNER

SECRET LOVERS   3   22 MAR 86   A&M
ALWAYS   1(1)   13 JUN 87   WARNER

ATOMIC ROOSTER

Formed by ex Crazy World of Arthur Brown members Vincent Crane (co-writer of 'Fire') and Carl Palmer, who joined ELP shortly after. They had two UK-only Top 20s – the other being 'Tomorrow Night' (11). Chris Farlowe joined in 72. They were also on Pegasus, Mooncrest, Dawn, Decca and Polydor. Crane died in 89.

 DEVIL'S ANSWER   4   07 AUG 71   B&C

BRIAN AUGER – SEE JULIE DRISCOLL FOR HIT DETAILS

PATTI AUSTIN

New Yorker and god-daughter of her producer Quincy Jones and Dinah Washington. She had a lot of unsuccessful records on Coral in 65 and first hit the black chart with 'Family Tree' on UA in 69. Thanks to plays on 'General Hospital' her small 82 duet hit took her to the top in 83. She joined GRP in 89.

BABY COME TO ME (Duet with JAMES INGRAM) (UK No. 11 – was US No.73 in 82) (Took record 23 weeks to No. 1)		1(2)	19 FEB 83	QWEST

AVERAGE WHITE BAND

Scottish sextet originally called the Scots of St. James were formed in 72 and recorded for MCA in 73. Their first hit was a US No. 1 and they notched up another four Top 40's in the US (3 in the UK). They joined RCA in 78 and Alan Gorrie who formed them went solo on A&M in 85. In 89 they re-appeared on Polydor UK without singer/guitarist Hamish Stuart who had joined Paul McCartney's band.

PICK UP THE PIECES		6	22 MAR 75	ATLANTIC
PICK UP THE PIECES		1(1)	22 FEB 75	ATLANTIC
CUT THE CAKE		10	21 JUN 75	ATLANTIC

AVONS

The Avon Sisters, actually two sisters in-law Valerie & Eileen Murtagh, were discovered at the 58 BBC Radio Exhibition. They added Ray Adams in 59 and had some UK-only chart records covering US hits. Valerie went on to write hits for other acts.

SEVEN LITTLE GIRLS SITTING IN THE BACK SEAT (Paul Evans 59 hit)	3	06 JAN 60	COLUMBIA

CHARLES AZNAVOUR

The top French entertainer had his second million seller (the first was 'La Mama' in 63) with this song that he wrote especially for the UK TV series The Seven Faces Of Woman. In the US without the TV exposure it failed to chart.

SHE (2 Weeks to No. 1) (First Solo French act to top chart)	1(4)	29 JUN 74	BARCLAY

AZTEC CAMERA

Five piece Scottish band fronted by East Kilbride's Roddy Frame. Act was originally on Postcard in 81 and then Rough Trade in 82 before joining WEA in 83 in a well publicised deal. They were regulars on the UK Indie chart before hitting with 'Oblivious' in 83. Despite US tours band has not taken off there as yet.

SOMEWHERE IN MY HEART	3	11 JUN 88	WEA

B

ERIK B – FOR HIT DETAILS SEE JODY WATLEY

B-52'S

Quirky mixed quintet named after the bouffant hairstyles of singers Kate Pierson and Cindy Wilson. Formed in 77 in Georgia they quickly won a transatlantic cult following scoring three US Top 40 LPs and seeing their 'Rock Lobster' chart in the UK in both 79 (37) & 87 (12). Their first Top Ten single and LP came in 89.

LOVE SHACK (UK Top 10 in 90) (UK Top 40 in 90 - prod. Don Was of Was (Not Was))	3	18 NOV 89	REPRISE

B.V.S.M.P.

Miami trio Calvin Williams, Percy Rodgers and Frederick Byrd's European million seller gave them a one-off UK hit. Follow up was 'Any Time'.

I NEED YOU (It flopped when originally released in March 88)	3	20 AUG 88	DEBUT

BABYFACE

Kenny 'Babyface' Edmonds was half of the top US production team in 88/89 (with L.A. Reid) with 12 Top 10s in just over two years and five in the Top 40 in the same week not to mention 12 black music No. 1s in two years. He had been in successful group Deele since 83, recorded solo since 86 and saw his 89 LP go gold.

IT'S NO CRIME	7	28 OCT 89	SOLAR

BACCARA

The German based duo of Maria Mendiola and Mayte Mateos were not only the first Spanish act to top the UK chart but also the first female duo to do it. They worked together as dancers in Madrid since 73 but never charted again after these two UK hits. They were on Loading Bay records in 89.

YES SIR I CAN BOOGIE (Sold over 3 million)	1(1)	29 OCT 77	RCA
SORRY I'M A LADY	8	11 FEB 78	RCA

BURT BACHARACH

The most successful (non performing) writer during the rock years was born in Kansas City and had his first No. 1 (UK) in 58 with 'The Story of My Life' (followed immediately by another – 'Magic Moments'). He has had scores of Transatlantic Top 10s as a writer but this was his only hit as an artist.

TRAINS AND BOATS AND PLANES	4	26 JUN 65	LONDON

BACHELORS

Brothers Declan & John Stokes formed this Irish trio with Con Cluskey in the late 50s and recorded in 60. Even though they were a MOR orientated act they became one of the more successful UK acts in the first British invasion of the US charts. They later recorded on Galaxy in 77 and President in 81 and broke up in 84.

CHARMAINE (Mantovani 51 hit)	6	22 MAR 63	DECCA
DIANE (At the time act had 2 in UK Top 10)	1(1)	22 FEB 64	DECCA
I BELIEVE (US No. 33 – Frankie Laine 53 hit)	2	09 MAY 64	DECCA
RAMONA (Gene Austin 28 hit)	4	04 JUL 64	DECCA
I WOULDN'T TRADE YOU FOR THE WORLD	4	11 SEP 64	DECCA
NO ARMS COULD EVER HOLD YOU (US No. 27)	8	02 JAN 65	DECCA
MARIE (US No. 15)	9	19 JUN 65	DECCA
THE SOUND OF SILENCE (Only UK hit of the Simon & Garfunkel song)	3	16 MAR 66	DECCA
DIANE (Nat Shilkret hit 28)	10	20 JUN 64	LONDON

BACHMAN-TURNER OVERDRIVE

Canadian rock band led by Randy Bachman and Fred Turner. Randy had fronted the hit group Guess Who before forming this act, who first recorded as Brave Belt for Reprise in 71. Their fifth single for Mercury gave them their only Transatlantic Top 10. In 77 Randy went solo and the group re-appeared on Compleat in 85.

 YOU AIN'T SEEN NOTHIN' YET | 2 | 21 DEC 74 | MERCURY
(Cut as joke about Randy's stuttering Brother Gary)

 YOU AIN'T SEEN NOTHIN' YET | 1(1) | 09 NOV 74 | MERCURY

Also see Guess Who

BAD COMPANY

UK supergroup featuring vocalist Paul Rodgers and drummer Simon Kirke (both ex Free), Mick Ralphs (ex Mott The Hoople) and Boz Burrell (ex King Crimson). Their first LP hit No. 1 in the US (3 UK) and they became transatlantic chart regulars until 79. They split up and reformed often in the 80s and were still collecting US Platinum LPs in 89.

CAN'T GET ENOUGH *(UK No. 15)* | 5 | 02 NOV 74 | SWAN SONG
FEEL LIKE MAKIN' LOVE *(UK No. 20)* | 10 | 20 SEP 75 | SWAN SONG

BAD ENGLISH

Supergroup formed by ex-members of The Babys and Journey fronted by John Waite and including Neil Schon and Jonathan Cain. They first charted in the US with 'Forget Me Not' and their second chart single went right to the top there.

WHEN I SEE YOU SMILE *(UK No. 61)* | 1(2) | 11 NOV 89 | EPIC

BAD MANNERS

The North London ska/2-Tone band's music never dented the charts in the US but in the UK the act fronted by the outrageous Buster Bloodvessel (Doug Trendle) had a dozen hits in three years. They starred in the film 'Dance Craze' and had other releases on Portrait in 85 and Blue Beat in 89.

SPECIAL BREW | 3 | 08 NOV 80 | MAGNET
CAN CAN *(Famous old French song)* | 3 | 04 JUL 81 | MAGNET
WALKIN' IN THE SUNSHINE | 10 | 17 OCT 81 | MAGNET
MY GIRL LOLLIPOP (MY BOY LOLLIPOP) | 9 | 14 AUG 82 | MAGNET
(Originally by Barbie Gaye in 56)

BADFINGER

UK quartet charted in the US as The Iveys before having a trio of Transatlantic Top 10s. They also had some US success on Elektra in 79 and Radio in 81. Members Pete Ham and Tom Evans (who wrote Nilsson's 'Without You') committed suicide before the act won an 11 year battle over unpaid royalties.

COME AND GET IT *(Composed Paul McCartney)* | 4 | 31 JAN 70 | APPLE
NO MATTER WHAT | 5 | 06 FEB 71 | APPLE
DAY AFTER DAY | 10 | 26 FEB 72 | APPLE

COME AND GET IT | 7 | 18 APR 70 | APPLE
NO MATTER WHAT | 8 | 05 DEC 70 | APPLE
DAY AFTER DAY | 4 | 05 FEB 72 | APPLE

JOAN BAEZ

The New York born 'Queen of Folk music' signed to Vanguard after appearing at the 59 Newport Folk Festival. Like her male counterpart Bob Dylan, she is really an LP act but had some chart singles starting with the US No. 90 hit 'We Shall Overcome' in 63. She was later on RCA, MCA, A&M and Portrait and Gold Mountain.

THERE BUT FOR FORTUNE | 8 | 07 AUG 65 | FONTANA
THE NIGHT THEY DROVE OLD DIXIE DOWN | 6 | 06 NOV 71 | VANGUARD
(Composed by Robbie Robertson of The Band)

THE NIGHT THEY DROVE OLD DIXIE DOWN | 3 | 02 OCT 71 | VANGUARD

PHILIP BAILEY

Denver born vocalist with the very successful Earth, Wind & Fire since 71. His biggest hit without them was the only Transatlantic Top Ten by two singing drummers (The drum Phills!). Collins is a member of Genesis and a solo star. It was their second single as a duo and they wrote and produced it together.

EASY LOVER (And Phil Collins) | 1(4) | 23 MAR 85 | CBS
EASY LOVER (And Phil Collins) | 2 | 02 FEB 85 | COLUMBIA

Also see Earth Wind & Fire

ADRIAN BAKER

London session singer/writer and jingle producer and one time Beach Boy (he joined his favourite group once on a tour). Later under the name Gidea Park he had two more UK-only Top 40s with medleys of Beach Boys and Four Seasons hits. He was also on MCA in 78, Mix Factory in 85 and Ariola in 89.

SHERRY *(Four Seasons 62 hit)* | 10 | 16 AUG 75 | MAGNET

ANITA BAKER

Detroit born Anita was the singer in Chapter 8 from 76-84. Her initial success came with the black music hit 'Angel' in 83. Label trouble halted her career until 86 when she hit big with the Grammy winning 'Rapture' LP in both the US & UK.

SWEET LOVE *(UK No. 13)* | 8 | 01 NOV 86 | ELEKTRA
GIVING YOU THE BEST THAT I GOT *(UK No. 55)* | 3 | 10 DEC 88 | ELEKTRA

GEORGE BAKER SELECTION

Top Dutch singer (real name Johannes Bouwens) first charted (US) in 70 with 'Little Green Bag' (21). He followed his biggest hit, which was the Top US Easy Listening hit of 76, with 'Baby Blue' and tried to repeat the formula with 'Wild Bird'.

PALOMA BLANCA | 10 | 11 OCT 75 | WARNER
(US No. 26 – UK cover by Jonathan King got No. 5 UK)

LONG JOHN BALDRY

The 6'7" London based singer was part of the early UK R&B scene. He sang with Alexis Korner, Cyril Davies, Steampacket (with Rod Stewart) and Bluesology (with Elton John). Strangely his biggest hits were with MOR styled ballads. He had US hits on Warner in 71 and EMI in 79.

LET THE HEARTACHES BEGIN | 1(2) | 25 NOV 67 | PYE
(Second No. 1 in row for writers Macaulay & Mcleod)

MARTY BALIN

Ohio singer had two singles on Challenge in the early 60s, was in the acoustic trio The Town Criers and was a founder member of Jefferson Airplane in 65. He is the only member to achieve a Top 40 solo hit.

HEARTS | 8 | 08 AUG 81 | EMI AM.

Also see Jefferson Airplane/Starship

14

KENNY BALL & HIS JAZZMEN

The Essex (UK) born trumpeter was a leading light in the UK trad music boom of the early 60s. Like Lonnie Donegan (who discovered him) he was one of the few UK acts to score in the US before The Beatles.

 **MIDNIGHT IN MOSCOW** (He also had 'Red Square' & 'From Russia With Love') 5 15 DEC 61 PYE JAZZ
MARCH OF THE SIAMESE CHILDREN (US No. 88) 1(1) 07 MAR 62 PYE JAZZ
THE GREEN LEAVES OF SUMMER (US No. 87) 8 06 JUL 62 PYE JAZZ
SUKIYAKI (Original by Kyu Sakamoto) 10 22 FEB 63 PYE JAZZ
MIDNIGHT IN MOSCOW (Based on Russian song 'Padmeskoveeye Vietchera') 2 17 MAR 62 KAPP

MICHAEL BALL

UK singer/actor who appeared in the Andrew Lloyd Webber musical 'Aspects of Love' (the cast LP was a UK No.1) which his UK hit and the follow up came from. Follow up was 'The First Man You Remember'. Michael and the show opened on Broadway in 90.

LOVE CHANGES EVERYTHING 2 25 FEB 89 REALLY

HANK BALLARD & THE MIDNIGHTERS

Detroit R&B act were one of the top acts of 54 with controversial hits like 'Work With Me Annie' and 'Sexy Ways'. R'n'R Hall of Famer Hank wrote and cut the original of 'The Twist' in 58 (No.16 R&B) and had his biggest pop hits in 60. He had no UK chart entries and finally made a successful live debut there in 86.

FINGER POPPIN' TIME (He re-recorded this on People in 72) 7 15 AUG 60 KING
LETS GO, LET'S GO, LET'S GO 6 21 NOV 60 KING

BALTIMORA

Singer from Northern Ireland (real name Jimmy McShane) recorded Europe's biggest novelty hit of 85 hit in Italy. His previous experience included singing backing vocals on Dee D. Jackson's 'Automatic Lover'. Follow up was 'Living In The Background'.

TARZAN BOY (US No.13) 3 07 SEP 85 COLUMBIA

BANANARAMA

The most successful UK female group both in the UK & US. Original line up was Sarah Dallin, Siobhan Fahey (Dave Stewart's wife) and Keren Woodward. Their first release 'Aie A Mwana' missed but thanks, in part, to Fun Boy Three they soon started their long string of hits. Siobhan later formed Shakespears Sister.

IT AIN'T WHAT YOU DO IT'S THE WAY THAT YOU DO IT (Released as Fun Boy Three & Bananarama) 4 13 MAR 82 CHRYSALIS
REALLY SAYING SOMETHING (And FUN BOY THREE – Velvelettes 65 US Hit) 5 01 MAY 82 DERAM
SHY BOY (US No. 83) 4 24 JUL 82 LONDON
NA NA HEY HEY KISS HIM GOODBYE (Steam 69 hit) 5 19 MAR 83 LONDON
CRUEL SUMMER 8 06 AUG 83 LONDON
ROBERT DE NIRO'S WAITING (US No. 95) 3 31 MAR 84 LONDON
VENUS (Shocking Blue 69 hit) 8 12 JUL 86 LONDON
LOVE IN THE FIRST DEGREE/MR. SLEAZE (US No. 48 – 'B' was by Stock, Aitken & Waterman) 3 31 OCT 87 LONDON
I WANT YOU BACK (First with Jacquie O'Sullivan who replaced Siobhan) 5 30 APR 88 LONDON
HELP (Beatles hit 65) (Charity record with UK comics Lananeeneenoonoo) 3 11 MAR 89 LONDON
CRUEL SUMMER 9 29 SEP 84 LONDON
VENUS 1(1) 06 SEP 86 LONDON
I HEARD A RUMOUR (UK No. 14) 4 26 SEP 87 LONDON

Also see Shakespears Sister

BAND AID

The UK's biggest selling single ever (3.6 million) was the first Top 10 charity record and was arguably the most important pop record ever made. A 38 piece group put together by Bob Geldof and Midge Ure, it included many top UK stars and led to the 'Live Aid' shows which raised over £50 million pounds for Ethiopian relief.

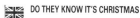 **DO THEY KNOW IT'S CHRISTMAS** (US No. 13) (Only act with no chart record to enter at No. 1) 1(5) 15 DEC 84 MERCURY
DO THEY KNOW IT'S CHRISTMAS (with new 'B') 3 21 DEC 85 MERCURY

BAND AID II

Like its predecessor the last UK No. 1 of the 80's also entered in that position and the money raised from it went to Ethiopian relief. This SAW production featured stars like Kylie Minogue, Jason Donovan, Bros, Cliff Richard, Bananarama and Wet Wet Wet.

DO THEY KNOW IT'S CHRISTMAS 1(3) 23 DEC 89 PWL

BANDWAGON – SEE JOHNNY JOHNSON

BANGLES

L.A. female quartet led by Susanna Hoffs were formed in 81 as The Colours, who became The Bangs on Down Kiddie in 81 and on Posh Boy before becoming The Bangles on IRS. With help from Prince their third for Columbia started a string of hits and they became the first girl group in the 80s to have a transatlantic No. 1.

 MANIC MONDAY 2 15 MAR 86 CBS
WALK LIKE AN EGYPTIAN 3 15 NOV 86 CBS
ETERNAL FLAME 1(4) 15 APR 89 CBS
MANIC MONDAY (Composer Prince also wrote US No. 1 in same week) 2 19 APR 86 COLUMBIA
WALK LIKE AN EGYPTIAN (Top US single 87) 4 20 DEC 86 COLUMBIA
HAZY SHADE OF WINTER (UK No. 11 – From film 'Less Than Zero') 2 06 FEB 88 DEF JAM
IN YOUR ROOM (UK No. 35) 5 07 JAN 89 COLUMBIA
ETERNAL FLAME 1(1) 01 APR 89 COLUMBIA

BARBRA & NEIL – SEE BARBRA STREISAND/NEIL DIAMOND

BARDO

UK's Eurovision entry for 82 was by two young veterans of the stage Sally Ann Triplett who had been in previous Eurovision entry Prima Donna ('Love Enough For Two') and Stephen Fischer who has been in Red Hot and had turned down a chance to be in Bucks Fizz. It was their only hit.

ONE STEP FURTHER 2 01 MAY 82 EPIC

BOBBY BARE

Ohio singer was on Capitol in 56 and Trey in 59 and his first hit was credited to the act on the 'B' side. Whilst he was A&R man for Fraternity he wrote the music for the film 'Teenage Millionaire' and recorded with The All American Boys. He was a major country act in the 60s and has had 70 country hits.

 ALL AMERICAN BOY (Credited to 'B' side act Bill Parsons) 2 01 FEB 59 FRATERN.
500 MILES AWAY FROM HOME 10 16 NOV 63 RCA

J.J. BARRIE

UK based singer, manager and one time comedian was born Barrie Authors in Canada. He had a one-off UK hit with a cover of a No. 1 country song. He also recorded on MCA, RCA, Monarch, Magic and Starblend and EMI. His other releases included 'So Long Bing' and a duet with soccer manager Brian Clough.

 NO CHARGE (Melba Montgomery 74 US Hit) 1(1) 05 JUN 76 POWER

BARRON KNIGHTS

Duke D'Mond fronted this humorous UK quintet from Leighton Buzzard who first recorded for Fontana (62) and were on Columbia (63). Their anglicised version of The Four Preps parody style gave them UK-only hits for 19 years. They also recorded on Penny Farthing (74), Tavern (72), Towerbell (84), Spartan (85), WEA (86) and Big Wave (89).

CALL UP THE GROUPS	3	08 AUG 64	COLUMBIA
POP GO THE WORKERS	5	01 MAY 65	COLUMBIA
MERRIE GENTLE POPS	9	08 JAN 66	COLUMBIA
LIVE IN TROUBLE	7	19 NOV 77	EPIC
A TASTE OF AGGRO	3	23 DEC 78	EPIC

JOHN BARRY SEVEN

Born in York (UK) his group were regulars on UK's first real TV Pop show '6-5 Special'. Their first release was 'Zip Zip' in 57 and they first hit with the theme from 'Juke Box Jury' ('Hit and Miss'). He relocated to the US and has worked consistently in film music and is best known for his James Bond movie scores.

WALK DON'T RUN (cover of Ventures US hit)	6	21 OCT 60	COLUMBIA

LEN BARRY

Philadelphia's Len Borisoff was in The Bosstones and was leader of successful Philly group The Dovells. He followed his first solo 'Lip Sync' with two transatlantic hits. He also scored in the US as Electric Indian ('Keem-O-Sabe') and later wrote many soul and dance hits and was on Buddah in 72 and Paramount in 73.

1-2-3	3	04 DEC 65	BRUNSWICK
LIKE A BABY (US No. 27)	10	12 FEB 66	BRUNSWICK
1-2-3 (in 68 he cut '4-5-6' on Amy)	2	20 NOV 65	DECCA

Also see The Dovells

TONI BASIL

L.A. dancer/singer/actress first known for her choreography on US TV shows 'Shindig' and 'Hullabaloo' and in the film American Grafitti. She recorded on A&M in 66 and had the world's first simultaneously released LP and video LP in 81 'Word of Mouth'. She recorded for Virgin in 84.

MICKEY (Her third release on label)	2	06 MAR 82	RADIAL
MICKEY (Song originally called 'Kitty' by Racey)	1(1)	11 DEC 82	CHRYSALIS

FONTELLA BASS

Native of St. Louis, worked with Oliver Sain and Little Milton and recorded for Prann, Bobbin and Sonja before hitting in a duet with Bobby McClure. 'Recovery' the follow up to her Top 20 hit also charted on both sides of the Atlantic. She also recorded for Paula in 72 and Gusto in 80 and was with The Art Ensemble of Chicago. She is the sister of black music star David Peaston.

RESCUE ME (UK No. 11)	4	20 NOV 65	CHECKER

SHIRLEY BASSEY

Welsh songstress/entertainer is one of UK's most successful ever female singers. Her first single was 'Burn My Candle' in 56 and she has had 28 more UK hits since then, not to mention a record 28 chart albums in the UK. Her sole US Top 40 hit was surprisingly one of her smaller UK successes. As a performer she still packs them in both in the UK & US.

BANANA BOAT SONG (Harry Belafonte 57 hit)	8	29 MAR 57	PHILIPS
KISS ME HONEY HONEY KISS ME	3	06 FEB 59	PHILIPS
AS I LOVE YOU	1(4)	20 FEB 59	PHILIPS
AS LONG AS HE NEEDS ME (from 'Oliver')	2	21 OCT 60	COLUMBIA
YOU'LL NEVER KNOW (Dick Haymes 43 hit)	4	09 JUN 61	COLUMBIA
REACH FOR THE STARS/CLIMB EV'RY MOUNTAIN	1	01 SEP 61	COLUMBIA
I'LL GET BY (Ruth Etting 29 hit)	6	15 DEC 61	COLUMBIA
WHAT NOW MY LOVE	10	12 OCT 62	COLUMBIA
I (WHO HAVE NOTHING) (Ben E. King 63 US hit)	4	01 NOV 63	COLUMBIA
SOMETHING (Beatles 69 hit composed by George Harrison)	4	15 AUG 70	UA
FOR ALL WE KNOW	6	16 OCT 71	UA
GOLDFINGER (UK No. 21 from the film)	8	27 MAR 65	UA

MIKE BATT

UK writer/producer/artist was the man behind The Wombles string of hits. He also wrote big hits for Alvin Stardust, Art Garfunkel and Cliff Richard. Oddly none of these or his sole hit as an act charted in the US. His follow up was 'House of Clowns'. In 89 he cut an LP with Justin Hayward.

SUMMERTIME CITY (With New Edition)	4	20 SEP 75	EPIC

ALSO SEE THE WOMBLES

BAY CITY ROLLERS

Scottish group fronted by Les McKeown originally called The Saxons and re-named after a town in Utah. It took three years of recording before 'Rollermania' took over the UK. They were the biggest act in the UK since The Beatles, and US hits came in 76 (when they were on the wane at home), but by 79 the group and their tartan image were passé, and their music forgotten. They shortened their name to The Rollers in 81 without success. Les was in the 90 UK Eurovision contest.

KEEP ON DANCING (Prod. by Jonathan King – Originally by Aventis 63)	9	30 OCT 71	BELL
REMEMBER (SHA-LA-LA)	6	09 MAR 74	BELL
SHANG-A-LANG	2	25 MAY 74	BELL
SUMMERLOVE SENSATION	3	24 AUG 74	BELL
ALL OF ME LOVES ALL OF YOU	4	26 OCT 74	BELL
BYE BYE BABY (Top UK record 75 – 4 Seasons 65 US Hit)	1(6)	22 MAR 75	BELL
GIVE A LITTLE LOVE (Entered at No. 7)	1(3)	19 JUL 75	BELL
MONEY HONEY	3	06 DEC 75	BELL
LOVE ME LIKE I LOVE YOU	4	01 MAY 76	BELL
I ONLY WANNA BE WITH YOU (US No. 12 – Dusty Springfield 64 hit)	4	25 SEP 76	BELL
SATURDAY NIGHT (UK flop in 73 first sung on Howard Cossell's show)	1(1)	03 JAN 76	ARISTA
MONEY HONEY	9	03 APR 76	ARISTA
YOU MADE ME BELIEVE IN MAGIC	10	13 AUG 77	ARISTA

BAZUKA

US instrumental session group put together by Tony Camillo. The record did not happen in the UK. Follow up was 'Love Explosion'.

DYNOMITE (Featuring TONY CAMILLO)	10	02 AUG 75	A&M

BEACH BOYS

The most successful and consistent US pop group on both sides of the Atlantic. They recorded as Kenny & The Cadets on Randy, first charted with 'Surfin'' (US No. 118) in 62 on Candix and soon became the leaders of the surf music movement. They took until late 64 to score in the UK and since then they have achieved an enviable list of transatlantic hit LPs and singles. Their style, master-minded by principal songwriter/erratic genius Brian Wilson is known worldwide.

I GET AROUND	7	29 AUG 64	CAPITOL
BARBARA ANN (Regents 61 US Hit) (Vocals inc. Jan & Dean and Glen Campbell)	3	12 MAR 66	CAPITOL
SLOOP JOHN B (Trad song-Lonnie Donegan 60 UK hit)	2	21 MAY 66	CAPITOL
GOD ONLY KNOWS (US No. 39)	2	27 AUG 66	CAPITOL

GOOD VIBRATIONS	1(2)	19 NOV 66	CAPITOL
(Return UK No. 18 in 76 – Glen Campbell ld. guitar)			
THEN I KISSED HER (Crystals 63 hit)	4	27 MAY 67	CAPITOL
HEROES AND VILLAINS (US No. 12)	8	09 SEP 67	CAPITOL
DO IT AGAIN (US No. 20)	1(1)	31 AUG 68	CAPITOL
I CAN HEAR MUSIC (US No. 24)	10	12 APR 69	CAPITOL
BREAK AWAY (US No. 24)	6	12 JUL 69	CAPITOL
COTTONFIELDS (Trad song)	5	20 JUN 70	CAPITOL
LADY LYNDA	6	21 JUL 79	CARIBOU
WIPEOUT (With THE FAT BOYS) (US No. 12)	2	12 SEP 87	URBAN
🇺🇸 SURFIN' U.S.A.	3	25 MAY 63	CAPITOL
(UK No. 28 – based on 'Sweet Little 16' – Chuck Berry)			
SURFER GIRL (written about Judy Bowles)	7	14 SEP 63	CAPITOL
BE TRUE TO YOUR SCHOOL	6	21 NOV 63	CAPITOL
FUN, FUN, FUN	5	21 MAR 64	CAPITOL
I GET AROUND	1(2)	04 JUL 64	CAPITOL
WHEN I GROW UP (TO BE A MAN) (UK No. 27)	9	17 OCT 64	CAPITOL
DANCE, DANCE, DANCE (UK No. 24)	8	19 DEC 64	CAPITOL
HELP ME, RHONDA (UK No. 27)	1(2)	29 MAY 65	CAPITOL
CALIFORNIA GIRLS (UK No. 26)	3	28 AUG 65	CAPITOL
BARBARA ANN	2	05 FEB 66	CAPITOL
SLOOP JOHN B	3	07 MAY 66	CAPITOL
WOULDN'T IT BE NICE	8	17 SEP 66	CAPITOL
GOOD VIBRATIONS	1(3)	10 DEC 66	CAPITOL
(90 hours recording cost $50,000-a record at time)			
ROCK AND ROLL MUSIC	4	14 AUG 76	BROTHER
(UK No. 36 – Chuck Berry 57 US Hit)			
KOKOMO (UK No. 25)	1(1)	05 NOV 88	ELEKTRA
(Their first US No. 1 for 22 years)			

BEASTIE BOYS

King Ad-Rock, MCA and Mike D make up this notorious New York trio. Booed off Madonna's US tour in 85, they hit the Indie charts on Rat Cage in 86 and later joined Def Jam. They were the Top New US Act of 87 and were the first Rap act to top the US charts. The trio incurred bad press on both their US and UK tours and amidst legal battles joined Capitol in 89.

🇬🇧 SHE'S ON IT	10	01 AUG 87	DEF JAM
🇺🇸 (YOU GOTTA) FIGHT FOR YOUR RIGHT (TO PARTY)	7	07 MAR 87	DEF JAM
(UK No. 11)			

BEAT

Birmingham (UK) group were one of the top exponents of the UK craze for ska/2-Tone music. Shortly after their biggest hit the band split with Dave Wakeling forming General Public, and Andy Cox and David Steele launching the far more successful Fine Young Cannibals with Roland Gift.

🇬🇧 TEARS OF A CLOWN/RANKING FULL STOP	6	12 JAN 80	2 TONE
(Miracles 70 hit – In US act called English Beat)			
HANDS OFF-SHE'S MINE	9	15 MAR 80	GO FEET
MIRROR IN THE BATHROOM	4	17 MAY 80	GO FEET
(UK's first digitally recorded single to be released)			
TOO NICE TO TALK TO	7	17 JAN 81	GO FEET
CAN'T GET USED TO LOSING YOU	3	28 MAY 83	GO FEET
(Andy Williams 63 hit)			

BEATLES

John Lennon, Paul McCartney, George Harrison and Ringo Starr are the world's all time top group. At times they had the top five US singles (and the top nine in Canada!) and three of the top four US LPs. They often had the UK's top two singles and even had the top four UK CDs long after their collective career was over, not to mention five in the UK Top 20 singles or 13 in the US 100 simultaneously. They had 21 US No. 1s & 18 in the UK plus 15 US No. 1 LPs and 12 in the UK. Not bad for an act that most experts on both sides of the Atlantic in 63 thought would not make it in the US. But it is the timeless quality of the music behind these statistics, the consistency and freshness of their work, that continues to entrance generation after generation.

🇬🇧 PLEASE PLEASE ME	1(2)	20 FEB 63	PARLOPHONE
FROM ME TO YOU (US No. 41 in 64)	1(6)	26 APR 63	PARLOPHONE
(Top UK record 63 – entered at No. 6)			
TWIST AND SHOUT E.P. (Isley Brothers 62 hit)	4	09 AUG 63	PARLOPHONE
SHE LOVES YOU (Entered at No. 2)	1(4)	06 SEP 63	PARLOPHONE

I WANT TO HOLD YOUR HAND	1(6)	06 DEC 63	PARLOPHONE
(Entered at No. 1 – sold million 3 days UK – a record)			
CAN'T BUY ME LOVE (Entered at No. 1)	1(3)	04 APR 64	PARLOPHONE
A HARD DAY'S NIGHT	1(3)	25 JUL 64	PARLOPHONE
I FEEL FINE	1(5)	12 DEC 64	PARLOPHONE
TICKET TO RIDE	1(3)	24 APR 65	PARLOPHONE
HELP!	1(3)	07 AUG 65	PARLOPHONE
DAY TRIPPER/WE CAN WORK IT OUT	1(5)	18 DEC 65	PARLOPHONE
PAPERBACK WRITER	1(2)	25 JUN 66	PARLOPHONE
YELLOW SUBMARINE/ELEANOR RIGBY	1(4)	20 AUG 66	PARLOPHONE
(12th No. 1 in a row)			
PENNY LANE/STRAWBERRY FIELDS FOREVER	2	04 MAR 67	PARLOPHONE
ALL YOU NEED IS LOVE	1(3)	22 JUL 67	PARLOPHONE
HELLO GOODBYE	1(7)	09 DEC 67	PARLOPHONE
MAGICAL MYSTERY TOUR (DOUBLE E.P.)	2	30 DEC 67	PARLOPHONE
LADY MADONNA	1(2)	30 MAR 68	PARLOPHONE
HEY JUDE (Jumped from 21-1)	1(2)	14 SEP 68	APPLE
GET BACK	1(6)	26 APR 69	APPLE
(Featuring BILLY PRESTON – entered at 1)			
BALLAD OF JOHN AND YOKO	1(3)	14 JUN 69	APPLE
SOMETHING/COME TOGETHER	4	22 NOV 69	APPLE
('A' composed by George Harrison)			
LET IT BE (From the film)	2	14 MAR 70	APPLE
YESTERDAY (First time released in UK)	8	03 APR 76	APPLE
BEATLES MOVIE MEDLEY	10	03 JUL 82	PARLOPHONE
LOVE ME DO (re-issue)	4	30 OCT 82	PARLOPHONE

🇺🇸 I WANT TO HOLD YOUR HAND	1(7)	01 FEB 64	CAPITOL
(Reviewed in US as 'Surf on the Thames sound')			
PLEASE PLEASE ME	3	14 MAR 64	VEE JAY
(When first released in US act spelled Beattles)			
SHE LOVES YOU	1(2)	21 MAR 64	SWAN
TWIST AND SHOUT (Returned to US chart 88)	2	04 APR 64	TOLLIE
CAN'T BUY ME LOVE (No. 1 in record 2 weeks)	1(5)	04 APR 64	CAPITOL
DO YOU WANT TO KNOW A SECRET	2	09 MAY 64	VEE JAY
(Not rel. in UK – hit there for Billy J. Kramer)			
LOVE ME DO	1(1)	30 MAY 64	TOLLIE
P.S. I LOVE YOU	10	06 JUN 64	TOLLIE
A HARD DAY'S NIGHT (From the film)	1(2)	01 AUG 64	CAPITOL
I FEEL FINE	1(3)	26 DEC 64	CAPITOL
SHE'S A WOMAN	4	26 DEC 64	CAPITOL
(Last of 11 Top 10s in year – which is still a record)			
EIGHT DAYS A WEEK (45 not released in UK)	1(2)	13 MAR 65	CAPITOL
TICKET TO RIDE	1(1)	22 MAY 65	CAPITOL
HELP! (From the film)	1(3)	04 SEP 65	CAPITOL
YESTERDAY	1(4)	09 OCT 65	CAPITOL
(The most played song ever on US radio)			
WE CAN WORK IT OUT	1(3)	08 JAN 66	CAPITOL
DAY TRIPPER	5	22 JAN 66	CAPITOL
NOWHERE MAN (45 not released in UK)	3	26 MAR 66	CAPITOL
PAPERBACK WRITER	1(2)	25 JUN 66	CAPITOL
YELLOW SUBMARINE (From the film)	2	17 SEP 66	CAPITOL
STRAWBERRY FIELDS FOREVER	8	01 JAN 67	CAPITOL
(In 84 Yoko gave the old folks home £250,000)			
PENNY LANE	1(1)	18 MAR 67	CAPITOL
ALL YOU NEED IS LOVE	1(1)	19 AUG 67	CAPITOL
HELLO GOODBYE	1(3)	30 DEC 67	CAPITOL
LADY MADONNA	4	20 APR 68	CAPITOL
HEY JUDE (Top US single of 70s)	1(9)	28 SEP 68	APPLE
GET BACK (Featuring BILLY PRESTON)	1(5)	24 MAY 69	APPLE
(Above 2 entered at No. 10 – this 15th Top 5 in row)			
BALLAD OF JOHN AND YOKO	8	12 JUL 69	APPLE
COME TOGETHER/SOMETHING	1(1)	29 NOV 69	APPLE
LET IT BE	1(2)	11 APR 70	APPLE
(Entered US chart at No. 6 – an all time record)			
THE LONG AND WINDING ROAD (Not rel. UK)	1(2)	13 JUN 70	APPLE
GOT TO GET YOU INTO MY LIFE (Not rel. UK)	7	24 JUL 76	CAPITOL

Also see John Lennon/Paul McCartney/George Harrison/Ringo Starr

BEATMASTERS

London crew Paul, Manda and Richard use different performers on their projects. In 89, the one time jingle writers, became one of the UK's (no US pop success yet) most consistent acts. Rapper on their second hit was in youth custody for house burglary at time of hit and had police escort to and from Top of the Pops TV show.

 ROK DA HOUSE (Featuring The COOKIE CREW) | 5 | 06 FEB 88 | RHYTHM KING
(An indie chart hit seven months earlier)
WHO'S IN THE HOUSE (Featuring MERLIN) | 8 | 29 APR 89 | RHYTHM KING
HEY D.J./I CAN'T DANCE (TO THAT MUSIC...)/
SKA TRAIN (Featuring BETTY BOO) | 7 | 02 SEP 89 | RHYTHM KING

BEAU BRUMMELS

First UK influenced US group to hit after the British Invasion of 64 were led by Sal Valentino. This San Francisco act were produced by Sly Stone (Sly & The Family Stone) and the first of their two US-only Top 20s was 'Laugh Laugh'. They folded in 68 and briefly returned in 75. Sal later recorded solo and with Stoneground.

JUST A LITTLE | 8 | 05 JUN 65 | AUTUMN

BEAUTIFUL SOUTH

Splinter group from The Housemartins included Paul Heaton and Dave Hemmingway (who had joined them in 87). They are tipped to have a bright UK future but as yet have not scored in the US.

SONG FOR WHOEVER | 2 | 08 JUL 89 | GO DISCS
YOU KEEP IT ALL IN | 8 | 07 OCT 89 | GO! DISCS
(Featuring vocalist Braina Corrigan)

Also see The Housemartins

GILBERT BECAUD

Famous French singer/songwriter/entertainer who composed such hits as 'It Must be Him' (Vikki Carr), 'The Day That The Rains Came Down' (Jane Morgan) and the oft recorded 'Let It Be Me'.

A LITTLE LOVE AND UNDERSTANDING | 10 | 10 MAY 75 | DECCA

JEFF BECK – SEE DONOVAN FOR HIT DETAILS

ROBIN BECK

Florida session singer who worked with Leo Sayer, George Benson, Alice Cooper, David Bowie, Luther Vandross and Chaka Khan. Her first one for Mercury was 'Suddenly' in 79. Follow up to her hit was 'Save Up All Your Tears'. She was launched in the US with a hard metal image in 89 and her hit was re-issued there in 90.

 THE FIRST TIME (Co-written by Tommy Boyce) | 1(2) | 19 NOV 88 | MERCURY
(Fifth Coco-Cola ad to be a hit & 2nd No. 1)

BEE GEES

The Manchester (UK) born Gibb brothers have been top transatlantic stars for over 20 years. Booed off on their first UK shows (with Fats Domino) they have since had five UK No.1s and four songs they wrote (inc. three records they produced) took turns at No. 1 in the US. Also their LP 'Saturday Night Fever' sold 25 million and was a US No. 1 for a record 24 weeks.

 MASSACHUSETTS (US No. 11) | 1(4) | 14 OCT 67 | POLYDOR
WORLD (Not released in US) | 9 | 09 DEC 67 | POLYDOR
WORDS (US No. 15) | 8 | 02 MAR 68 | POLYDOR
I'VE GOTTA GET A MESSAGE TO YOU | 1(1) | 07 SEP 68 | POLYDOR
FIRST OF MAY (US No. 37) | 6 | 15 MAR 69 | POLYDOR
DON'T FORGET TO REMEMBER (US No. 73) | 2 | 20 SEP 69 | POLYDOR
RUN TO ME (US No. 16) | 9 | 19 AUG 72 | POLYDOR
JIVE TALKIN' | 5 | 26 JUL 75 | RSO
YOU SHOULD BE DANCING | 5 | 11 SEP 76 | RSO
HOW DEEP IS YOUR LOVE | 3 | 10 DEC 77 | RSO
STAYIN' ALIVE | 4 | 04 MAR 78 | RSO
NIGHT FEVER | 1(2) | 29 APR 78 | RSO
TOO MUCH HEAVEN | 3 | 09 DEC 78 | RSO
TRAGEDY (Entered at No. 7) | 1(2) | 03 MAR 79 | RSO
YOU WIN AGAIN | 1(4) | 17 OCT 87 | WARNER
(US No. 75 – 60th hit the Gibb Brothers had written)
I'VE GOTTA GET A MESSAGE TO YOU | 8 | 28 SEP 68 | ATCO
I STARTED A JOKE | 6 | 08 FEB 69 | ATCO
LONELY DAYS (UK No. 33) | 3 | 30 JAN 71 | ATCO
HOW CAN YOU MEND A BROKEN HEART | 1(4) | 07 AUG 71 | ATCO
JIVE TALKIN' | 1(2) | 09 AUG 75 | RSO
(Song written in car started life as 'Drive Talkin'')
NIGHTS ON BROADWAY | 7 | 13 DEC 75 | RSO
YOU SHOULD BE DANCING | 1(1) | 04 SEP 76 | RSO
LOVE SO RIGHT (UK No. 41) | 3 | 20 NOV 76 | RSO
HOW DEEP IS YOUR LOVE | 1(3) | 24 DEC 77 | RSO
(Written for Yvonne Elliman)
STAYIN' ALIVE | 1(4) | 04 FEB 78 | RSO
NIGHT FEVER | 1(8) | 18 MAR 78 | RSO
TOO MUCH HEAVEN | 1(2) | 06 JAN 79 | RSO
TRAGEDY | 1(2) | 24 MAR 79 | RSO
LOVE YOU INSIDE OUT (UK No. 13) | 1(1) | 09 JUN 79 | RSO
ONE (UK No. 71) | 7 | 30 SEP 89 | WARNER

ARCHIE BELL & THE DRELLS

Texas act recorded on East-West and Ovid before joining Atlantic. First recorded their No. 1 in 64 and had UK Top 20s with 'Here I Go Again' and 'Soul City Walk' (both US misses). They were also on Glades, TSOP, WMOT, Philly Int., Becket and Nightmare. Later in their career they worked out of Philadelphia.

TIGHTEN UP (Was 'B' side when released) | 1(2) | 18 MAY 68 | ATLANTIC
I CAN'T STOP DANCING | 9 | 24 AUG 68 | ATLANTIC

MAGGIE BELL – SEE B.A. ROBERTSON FOR HIT DETAILS

WILLIAM BELL

Born in Memphis as William Yarborough he worked with Rufus Thomas and The Del Rios in the 50s. He was part of the Stax family from 62 and notched up 18 black music hits between 66-86. He also recorded for Kat Family and his own Wilbe label.

PRIVATE NUMBER (With JUDY CLAY) (US No. 75) | 8 | 25 JAN 69 | STAX
TRYIN' TO LOVE TWO | 10 | 30 APR 77 | MERCURY

BELLAMY BROTHERS

David Bellamy's first success came as writer of Jim Stafford's 'Spiders & Snakes'. He worked with brother Howard in the band Jericho before recording on Warner as a solo artist. When Howard joined him they scored two transatlantic Top 40s and the first of over three dozen country hits (including 10 No. 1s) so far.

LET YOUR LOVE FLOW | 7 | 05 JUN 76 | WARNER
(Originally recorded as a solo by David)
IF I SAID YOU HAD A BEAUTIFUL BODY (US No. 39) | 3 | 29 SEP 79 | WARNER
LET YOUR LOVE FLOW | 1(1) | 01 MAY 76 | WARNER

LA BELLE EPOQUE

Integrated French based female trio had a one-off UK hit with an old Los Bravos song. They also had a small US hit a year later with the follow up 'Miss Broadway'.

BLACK IS BLACK | 2 | 15 OCT 77 | HARVEST

BELLE STARS

Seven piece UK female group who specialised in reviving US hits like 'The Clapping Song' and 'Mockingbird'. In 84 they became a trio with just Miranda, Sarah Jane and Leslie remaining. Their first UK charter 'Iko Iko' (old James Crawford/Dixie Cups hit) made No.14 in US in 89 after it was used in the film Rain Man.

	SIGN OF THE TIMES *(First original song they recorded)*	3	12 FEB 83	STIFF

BELLS

Canadian based sextet fronted by UK born Jakki Ralph. First scored in North America with 'Fly Little White Dove Fly' before getting their biggest US-only hit with their Canadian No. 1.

	STAY AWHILE	7	08 MAY 71	POLYDOR

BELMONTS – SEE DION FOR HIT DETAILS

PAT BENATAR

Born Pat Andrejewski in New York, she was the most successful female rock star of the 80s. She first scored in 79 and has notched up three Top 5 US LPs to date. It took until 85 for her to debut in the UK Top 20.

	HIT ME WITH YOUR BEST SHOT	9	20 DEC 80	CHRYSALIS
	LOVE IS A BATTLEFIELD *(UK No. 17 in 85)*	5	10 DEC 83	CHRYSALIS
	WE BELONG *(UK No. 22)*	5	05 JAN 85	CHRYSALIS
	INVINCIBLE *(Theme from the film 'The Legend of Billie Jean')*	10	14 SEP 85	CHRYSALIS

CLIFF BENNETT & THE REBEL ROUSERS

One of the best pre-Beatles UK acts who could really perform R&B and rock'n'roll. Possibly lack of good original songs stopped their progress. Bennett appeared again on Korkova in 80.

	ONE WAY LOVE *(Drifters 64 US Hit)*	9	31 OCT 64	PARLOPHONE
	GOT TO GET YOU INTO MY LIFE *(Beatles song)*	6	17 SEP 66	PARLOPHONE

GEORGE BENSON

Well respected jazz guitarist in the 60s he worked with Wes Montgomery and recorded as a soloist on Prestige, Columbia, A&M and CTI before making 'commercial' records for Warner in 76. He has won various Grammys and topped the UK LP chart in 85.

	GIVE ME THE NIGHT *(First UK Top 20 with his 5th chart entry)*	7	16 AUG 80	WARNER
	LOVE X LOVE *(US No. 61)*	10	25 OCT 80	WARNER
	IN YOUR EYES	7	15 OCT 83	WARNER
	THIS MASQUERADE *(Grammy winner for Record of the Year)*	10	28 AUG 76	WARNER
	ON BROADWAY *(Drifters 63 US Hit)*	7	10 JUN 78	WARNER
	GIVE ME THE NIGHT	4	27 SEP 80	WARNER
	TURN YOUR LOVE AROUND *(UK No. 29)*	5	06 FEB 82	WARNER

BROOK BENTON

Velvet voiced singer/composer (real name Ben Peay). Recorded on Okeh in 55 and Epic and Vik before getting the first of his 49 US hits (including 18 Gold records). He also recorded for RCA, Reprise, MGM, Stax, Brut, All Platinum, Olde World and Polydor with little UK sales and unfortunately died in 1988 (age 56).

	IT'S JUST A MATTER OF TIME *(Brook's song was a Country No. 1 in 70 & 89)*	3	05 APR 59	MERCURY
	SO MANY WAYS	6	22 NOV 59	MERCURY
	BABY (YOU GOT WHAT IT TAKES)	5	21 MAR 60	MERCURY
	A ROCKIN' GOOD WAY *(And DINAH WASHINGTON for above two)*	7	27 JUN 60	MERCURY

KIDDIO *(Top US R&B Record 60)* *(UK No. 29 – first recorded by Teddy Randazzo)*	7	19 SEP 60	MERCURY
THE BOLL WEEVIL SONG *(UK No. 28)*	2	10 JUL 61	MERCURY
HOTEL HAPPINESS	3	19 JAN 63	MERCURY
RAINY NIGHT IN GEORGIA *(Comp. Tony Joe White)* *(Made him first act to have Top 5s in 3 decades)*	4	07 MAR 70	COTILLION

BERLIN

L.A. based trio (previously a sextet) formed by John Crawford and fronted by Terri Nunn. Originally on IRS they first hit with the controversial 'Sex (I'm a...)'. They followed their Transatlantic No. 1 with 'Like Flames' and as yet have been unable to reach the heights again.

	TAKE MY BREATH AWAY *(from film 'Top Gun')* *(The 9th No. 1 for producer Giorgio Moroder)*	1(4)	08 NOV 86	CBS
	TAKE MY BREATH AWAY	1(1)	13 SEP 86	COLUMBIA

ELMER BERNSTEIN

Conductor and composer of numerous film scores. He had his only US Top 20 in 56 with the theme from The Man With The Golden Arm and he was still writing film scores in 89.

	STACCATO'S THEME *(from TV show 'Johnny Staccato')*	4	15 JAN 60	CAPITOL

CHUCK BERRY

The first guitar playing, songwriting rock 'n' roll star who is often considered to be rock's premier poet and most influential guitarist. His 12-bar blues licks have been emulated by rockers for three decades. He starred in many films, played for the President, had 27 US hits, was one of the first acts in the R'n'R Hall of Fame, has been jailed twice and has 'duck walked' on stage to packed audiences for 35 years.

	MEMPHIS TENNESSEE *(His 17th UK single and only his 2nd Top 20 hit)*	8	08 NOV 63	PYE INT
	NO PARTICULAR PLACE TO GO	3	13 JUN 64	PYE INT.
	MY DING-A-LING *(Banned in UK)*	1(4)	25 NOV 72	CHESS
	MAYBELLENE	5	10 SEP 55	CHESS
	SCHOOL DAY *(UK No. 24)*	3	13 MAY 57	CHESS
	ROCK & ROLL MUSIC	9	09 DEC 57	CHESS
	SWEET LITTLE SIXTEEN *(UK No. 16)*	2	17 MAR 58	CHESS
	JOHNNY B. GOODE *(Chuck's song was a Country No. 1 in 69)*	9	26 MAY 58	CHESS
	NO PARTICULAR PLACE TO GO	10	11 JUL 64	CHESS
	MY DING-A-LING *(Originally recorded by Dave Bartholomew in 52)*	1(2)	21 OCT 72	CHESS

DAVE BERRY

Born Dave Grundy in Sheffield (UK) he adopted his stage name from his hero Chuck Berry. His slinky stage act was unique (later updated by another UK-only star Alvin Stardust) but his songs were usually cover versions of US hits. His chart debut was with Chuck Berry's 'Memphis Tennessee'. He joined CBS in 72.

	THE CRYING GAME	5	04 SEP 64	DECCA
	LITTLE THINGS *(Bobby Goldsboro 65 US Hit)*	6	01 MAY 65	DECCA
	MAMA *(B.J. Thomas 66 US Hit)*	5	24 SEP 66	DECCA

MIKE BERRY

UK singer/actor recorded on Decca in 61 and first hit with the controversial 'Tribute To Buddy Holly' (whom he sounded like). He returned to the UK-only Top 10 after 17 years by which time he had became a well known TV actor. He was also on York in 73, Rak in 75, Lightning in 79, Switchback in 85 and Breakheart in 87.

	DON'T YOU THINK IT'S TIME *(With The OUTLAWS – A Joe Meek production)*	6	01 FEB 63	HMV
	SUNSHINE OF YOUR SMILE *(Prod. by Chas Hodges – John McCormack 16 hit)*	9	06 SEP 80	POLYDOR

NICK BERRY

UK actor/singer and star of the UK soap opera EastEnders. He was the first soap star to get a UK No. 1.

 EVERY LOSER WINS *(Jumped from 66-4)* | 1(3) | 18 OCT 86 | BBC

BIG COUNTRY

Scots group formed by Stuart Adamson (ex-Skids). First release 'Harvest Home' failed but their distinctive sound led to a run of UK hits including three top 3 LPs with 'Steeltown' hitting No. 1. In the US they had a Top 20 LP and 45 ('In A Big Country' No. 17).

FIELDS OF FIRE (400 MILES) *(US No. 52)*	10	16 APR 83	MERCURY
CHANCE	9	01 OCT 83	MERCURY
WONDERLAND *(US No. 86)*	8	28 JAN 84	MERCURY
LOOK AWAY	7	26 APR 86	MERCURY

BIG FUN

Scottish based trio, Phil Cheswick, Jason John and Mark Gillespie. Their second release on Jive, an S.A.W. production, gave them their first UK hit and they were voted Best New Group of 89 in the teen magazine Smash Hits.

BLAME IT ON THE BOOGIE *(Mick Jackson/Jacksons 78 hit)*	4	09 SEP 89	JIVE
CAN'T SHAKE THE FEELING	8	09 DEC 89	JIVE

BARRY BIGGS

Jamaican reggae singer has had six UK-only chart entries the biggest two were revivals of Blue Magic songs (the other being 'Three Ring Circus' – UK 22) He has also recorded for Hoss, Mobiliser, Afrik, Starlight, Trojan and Revue.

SIDE SHOW	3	22 JAN 77	DYNAMIC

ACKER BILK

Somerset (UK) born clarinettist Mr. Acker Bilk & His Paramount Jazz Band (as they were known in the UK) were at the forefront of the UK trad jazz boom of 60/61. When he added strings (Leon Young String Chorale) he had a US No. 1 and was Top Instrumentalist of 62 there. He made a brief return to the UK charts in 76.

SUMMER SET	9	04 MAR 60	COLUMBIA
BUONA SERA *(Old Louis Prima song)*	8	27 JAN 61	COLUMBIA
THAT'S MY HOME	8	01 SEP 61	COLUMBIA
STRANGER ON THE SHORE *(UK million seller – originally title 'Jenny')*	1(1)	05 JAN 62	COLUMBIA
ARIA *(Billed as Acker Bilk, His Clarinet & Strings)*	5	18 SEP 76	PYE
STRANGER ON THE SHORE	1(1)	26 MAY 62	ATCO

BILLY JOE & THE CHECKMATES

The only xylophone led hit was a Maxwell House TV jingle by Billy Joe Hunter & his group. They made other singles including the novelty 'Clair De Looney' but never hit again.

PERCOLATOR (TWIST)	10	17 MAR 62	DORE

JANE BIRKIN & SERGE GAINSBOURG

Londoner Jane and French singer/actor/composer Serge had a two million selling one-off with the sexiest record of the 60s. Originally recorded by Brigitte Bardot, it was banned in most countries including the UK. They later recorded 'La Deca Danse' and Serge wrote Jimmy Somerville's 89 hit 'Comment Te Dire Adieu'.

 JE T'AIME...MOI NON PLUS *(First foreign language No. 1 – US No. 58)* | 1(1) | 11 OCT 69 | FONTANA/MAJOR

ELVIN BISHOP

Oklahoma born guitarist was a founder member of The Paul Butterfield Blues band (he spent three years with them). He recorded for Fillmore in 69 and Epic before having the first of his successes in 74 with 'Travelin Shoes' (US No. 61).

 FOOLED AROUND AND FELL IN LOVE *(UK No. 34 – Vocal by Mickey Thomas)* | 3 | 22 MAY 76 | CAPRICORN

BLACK

As a trio, then a duo they recorded for Wonderful and Eternal and saw their first two releases on WEA fail. Then as a soloist Liverpool's Colin Vearncombe had the first of his UK only hits and was voted Top New Act in an 87 record paper poll.

SWEETEST SMILE	8	18 JUL 87	A&M
WONDERFUL LIFE *(Was on Red Rhino & Ugly Man in 76 & reached No. 72)*	8	05 SEP 87	A&M

BILL BLACK'S COMBO

Memphis born Bill was Elvis' bass player in his Sun Records days. His distinctive combo which included top session men Reggie Young and Carl McVoy had 18 US hits (one in UK) and were the most played instrumental group in the US in 60. He died in 65, aged 39.

WHITE SILVER SANDS *(Don Rondo 57 hit-song orig. called 'If I Knew')*	9	25 APR 60	HI

CILLA BLACK

Priscilla White was the hat check girl at the famous Cavern Club in Liverpool and her first single 'Love Of The Loved' (UK No. 35) was written for her by friends Lennon & McCartney. She has had 20 UK hits (3 US) and is now a top TV personality in the UK hosting top rated shows.

ANYONE WHO HAD A HEART *(Dionne Warwick 64 Hit)*	1(2)	07 MAR 64	PARLOPHONE
YOU'RE MY WORLD *(US No. 26)*	1(4)	30 MAY 64	PARLOPHONE
IT'S FOR YOU *(US No. 76)*	7	04 SEP 64	PARLOPHONE
YOU'VE LOST THAT LOVIN' FEELIN' *(Righteous Brothers 64 hit)*	2	30 JAN 65	PARLOPHONE
LOVE'S JUST A BROKEN HEART	5	05 FEB 66	PARLOPHONE
ALFIE *(from the film) (US No.95)*	9	07 MAY 66	PARLOPHONE
DON'T ANSWER ME	6	02 JUL 66	PARLOPHONE
STEP INSIDE LOVE *(Her theme song)*	8	13 APR 68	PARLOPHONE
SURROUND YOURSELF WITH SORROW	3	29 MAR 69	PARLOPHONE
CONVERSATIONS	7	16 AUG 69	PARLOPHONE
SOMETHING TELLS ME (SOMETHING IS GONNA HAPPEN TONIGHT)	3	25 DEC 71	PARLOPHONE

JEANNE BLACK

California country orientated singer who specialised in 'answer records'. She had another US-only hit with 'Oh How I Miss You Tonight' (US No. 63) her answer to 'Are You Lonesome Tonight'.

HE'LL HAVE TO STAY *(Answer record to Jim Reeves 'He'll Have To Go')*	4	30 MAY 60	CAPITOL

BLACK BOX

Italian act comprising of Daniele Davoli, Valerio Semplici, Mirko Limoni and singer/model Catherine Quinol. Their UK No. 1 included sampled vocals from Loleatta Holloway's 'Love Sensation'. The act had no success in their homeland in the 80s.

 RIDE ON TIME *(First Italian based act No. 1 in UK-Top record 89)* | 1(6) | 09 SEP 89 | DE CONSTR.

BLACKBYRDS

Sextet, including Allan Curtis Barnes, Keith Killgo and Joseph Hall III was formed by Detroit Jazz trumpeter Donald Byrd, who also produced them. They have had 6 US (1 UK) chart entries.

 WALKING IN RHYTHM   6   10 MAY 75   FANTASY

BLACKFOOT SUE

Midlands (UK) based foursome featuring singer Tom Farmer and his identical twin brother Dave. They had played together since 66 and had Robert Plant stand in occasionally. Previously with UA they had a second UK-only hit with 'Sing Don't Speak' (35).

 STANDING IN THE ROAD   4   09 SEP 72   JAM

BLACK LACE

Originally comprised of Alan Barton and Colin Routh and formed for the Eurovision contest in 79 when they charted with 'Mary Anne'. They had a run of three UK-only Top 10s with their Euro sounding party records. Dean Michael replaced Colin in 86 after he had some bad publicity. The new duo were still charting in 89.

SUPERMAN (GIOCA JOUER)	9	22 OCT 83	FLAIR
AGADOO	2	18 AUG 84	FLAIR
DO THE CONGA	10	22 DEC 84	FLAIR

BLACK SABBATH

UK heavy metal giants formed in 67 as Polka Tulk and then called Earth. First single covered Crow's 'Evil Woman'. Members have included Ozzy Osbourne, Ronnie James Dio, Ian Gillan and Tony Iommi and recently Cozy Powell. They have had over a dozen big US/UK hit LPs and are still charting.

PARANOID   4   10 OCT 70   VERTIGO
(It returned to No. 14 UK in 80)

Also see Cozy Powell/Gillan/Ozzy Osbourne

BLACK SLATE

Jamaican sextet featuring Keith Drummond, had some success with 'Sticks Man' on Slate in 77. They mixed reggae and Brit-funk on their self-composed and produced UK hit. Follow up was 'Boom Boom' (UK no. 51). They were also on Top Ranking in 82.

 AMIGO   9   11 OCT 80   ENSIGN

BAND OF THE BLACK WATCH

Scottish bagpipe band had a surprise UK hit and Top 20 LP. Their follow up was Laurel & Hardy's theme 'Dance Of The Cuckoos' and they also recorded 'Highland Hustle' in the disco era.

 SCOTCH ON THE ROCKS   8   18 OCT 75   SPARK

BLANCMANGE

UK duo Neil Arthur and Stephen Luscombe's own brand of easily digestible pop started with 'God's Kitchen' in 82. They also had three hit LPs but only US charter was a Dance No. 2 with 'Lose Your Love'/'Ave Maria'. Steve later formed West India Company.

LIVING ON THE CEILING	7	27 NOV 82	LONDON
BLIND VISION	10	21 MAY 83	LONDON
DON'T TELL ME	8	05 MAY 84	LONDON

BILLY BLAND

North Carolina native's first hit with two Chicken records (a dance craze) in 56 'Chicken In The Basket' and 'Chicken Hop' and he scored his only transatlantic Top 20 on the same label four years later. Follow up was 'You Were Born To be Loved'.

 LET THE LITTLE GIRL DANCE   7   16 MAY 60   OLD TOWN
(Composed by Carl Spencer of The Halos)

MARCIE BLANE

Brooklyn born Marcie, the daughter of a musician and one time music teacher, had another US-only chart entry with her follow up 'What Does A Girl Do' (No. 82) and she tried unsuccessfully to repeat the formula later with 'Bobby Did' – it didn't.

 BOBBY'S GIRL   3   01 DEC 62   SEVILLE

• BLONDIE

One of the world's top acts of 79-81, fronted by Debbie Harry, who had previously been with Wind In The Willows in 68 and The Stilettos. The group initially called Angel & The Snakes first hit in the UK on Private Stock. After five UK and four US No. 1s they split in 82 and Debbie later returned to the Top 10 as a soloist.

DENIS (Randy & The Rainbows 63 hit they later recorded it as 'Debbie')	2	18 MAR 78	CHRYSALIS
(I'M ALWAYS TOUCHED BY YOUR) PRESENCE DEAR	10	27 MAY 78	CHRYSALIS
HANGING ON THE TELEPHONE (original by The Nerves)	5	02 DEC 78	CHRYSALIS
HEART OF GLASS (Entered at No. 6 – UK gold record) 79	1(4)	03 FEB 79	CHRYSALIS
SUNDAY GIRL (2 weeks to No. 1 – jumped 10-1)	1(3)	26 MAY 79	CHRYSALIS
DREAMING (Entered at No. 7) (US No.27)	2	06 OCT 79	CHRYSALIS
ATOMIC (US No.39 – entered No. 3 UK)	1(2)	01 MAR 80	CHRYSALIS
CALL ME	1(1)	26 APR 80	CHRYSALIS
THE TIDE IS HIGH (Last of 5 No. 1s – entered at No. 5)	1(2)	15 NOV 80	CHRYSALIS
RAPTURE (First White Rap hit-Sax Tom Scott)	5	31 JAN 81	CHRYSALIS
HEART OF GLASS	1(1)	28 APR 79	CHRYSALIS
CALL ME (Top US single 80)	1(6)	19 APR 80	CHRYSALIS
THE TIDE IS HIGH (Comp. John Holt and Originally by The Paragons)	1(1)	31 JAN 81	CHRYSALIS
RAPTURE	1(2)	28 MAR 81	CHRYSALIS

BLOOD SWEAT & TEARS

Jazzy rock band formed in 67 by ex Blues Project pianist Al Kooper, who left in 69 to be replaced by UK born singer David Clayton Thomas. They scored 10 US chart singles and 10 LPs (1 single & 3 LPs in UK) in the next seven years. Thomas also recorded as a soloist on MCA, Decca, Columbia, Tower, Roulette, Atco and RCA.

YOU'VE MADE ME SO VERY HAPPY (UK No.35 – Brenda Holloway 67 US hit)	2	12 APR 69	COLUMBIA
SPINNING WHEEL	2	05 JUL 69	COLUMBIA
AND WHEN I DIE (Laura Nyro song)	2	29 NOV 69	COLUMBIA

BLOODSTONE

Kansas city sextet, previously known as The Sinceres, found that working with UK producer Mike Vernon gave them their big break and their third single on London became the first of five Top 10 US black music hits for them. They were also on Epic in 77, Motown in 79 and T-Neck in 82.

 NATURAL HIGH (UK No. 40)   10   21 JUL 73   LONDON

BOBBY BLOOM

Singer/songwriter started as a member of The Imaginations (on Music Makers). He recorded for Kapp, Kama Sutra and Map City before co-writing his biggest transatlantic hit with Jeff Barry. He also co-wrote Tommy James No. 1 'Mony Mony'. He died in a shooting accident in 74.

MONTEGO BAY	3	03 OCT 70	POLYDOR
MONTEGO BAY	8	28 NOV 70	L&R/MGM

BLOW MONKEYS

UK group, named after the jazz slang for sax players, fronted by Dr. Robert (Howard). First recorded for Parasol in 82, joined RCA in 84 and first hit with their seventh single 'Digging Your Scene' (UK 12/US 14) in 86. They are regular UK chartmakers and Robert also had a hit duet in the UK with Kym Mazelle.

IT DOESN'T HAVE TO BE THAT WAY	5	14 FEB 87	RCA

Also see Robert Howard

BARRY BLUE

Singer/songwriter originally recorded for Decca in 71 as Barry Green and had five UK-only Glitter Rock hits. His band became The Rubettes and he concentrated on writing and producing having hits with Heatwave, Cheryl Lynn and Five Star amongst others.

(DANCING) ON A SATURDAY NIGHT	2	01 SEP 73	BELL
DO YOU WANNA DANCE	7	24 NOV 73	BELL

BLUEBELLS

Formed in Glasgow and featuring the McCluskey brothers Dave & Ken. Their second release on London 'Cath' charted and 'I'm Falling' gave them the first of their two UK-only top 20s. They released their last record (All I am) in 85 and broke up in 87. The McCluskey brothers subsequently released an album of folk songs.

YOUNG AT HEART	8	28 JUL 84	LONDON

BLUE MAGIC

The 70s Philadelphia group with the 50s Doo-Wop feel are led by high pitched tenor Ted Mills. They scored 13 US-only black music hits between 73-83 the biggest of these 'Sideshow' and 'Three Ring Circus' (US No. 36) were UK hits by Barry Biggs. They started on Liberty in 69 and joined Def Jam's OBR label in 89.

SIDESHOW	8	10 AUG 74	ATCO

BLUE MINK

UK based multi-racial group fronted by Roger Cook and US vocalist Madeline Bell. Roger who is one of the UK's most successful ever song writers co-wrote all the groups UK hits. Only US charter was with 'Our World' (64th). Roger later had solo records and has been one of Nashville's most successful writers in the 80s.

MELTING POT	3	10 JAN 70	PHILIPS
GOOD MORNING FREEDOM	10	25 APR 70	PHILIPS
(Co-writer Albert Hammond)			
BANNER MAN	3	26 JUN 71	REGAL ZONO
RANDY	9	28 JUL 73	EMI

Also see David & Jonathan

BLUES IMAGE

Florida based group led by Mike Pinera and including Welsh bass player Malcolm Jones. They played on both sides of the Atlantic before getting their sole US hit. Follow up was 'Gas Lamps And Clay'. When the group broke up Mike joined Iron Butterfly.

RIDE CAPTAIN RIDE	4	11 JUL 70	ATCO

BLUES MAGOOS

New York based psychedelic quintet fronted by Peppy Thielman were originally called The Bloos Magoos. They recorded for Verve Folkways and Ganim and their second single for Mercury was their one big US hit. Peppy unsuccessfully organised a new Blues Magoos in the 70s and joined The Alessi Brothers in Barnaby Bye.

(WE AIN'T GOT) NOTHIN' YET	5	11 FEB 67	MERCURY

BLUE SWEDE

Bjorn Skifs & Blabus was the name they used in their native Sweden. They were the first Scandinavian act to top the US chart but their unusual versions of old hits did not sell in the UK.

HOOKED ON A FEELING *(B.J. Thomas 68 US Hit)*	1(1)	06 APR 74	EMI
NEVER MY LOVE *(Association 67 US Hit)*	7	19 OCT 74	EMI

BOB & EARL

Bobby Relf and Earl Nelson started recording together as The Voices in 55. Bobby had been a solo act on Dot, Cash and Flair and Earl had recorded on Ebb and Class and also had hits under the name Jackie Lee and as lead singer of The Hollywood Flames. The duo later recorded for Mirwood, UNI, Loma and Tip.

HARLEM SHUFFLE *(US No. 44 in 63)*	7	03 MAY 69	ISLAND
(They re-recorded it on White Whale 69)			

BOB & MARCIA

Jamaican duo Bob Andy & Marcia Griffiths had two UK-only Top 20s with reggae revivals of US songs – the other being 'Pied Piper' (11). Marcia later made solos for Epic, Solomonic and Island and first made the US chart in 89 with 'Electric Boogie' on Mango.

YOUNG GIFTED AND BLACK	5	04 APR 70	HARRY J.
(Nina Simone 69 US Hit – Boris Gardiner played bass)			

HAMILTON BOHANNON

Georgia born musician played drums for Stevie Wonder in the mid 60s and was an arranger for various Motown acts before going solo in 74. He had half-a-dozen UK chart entries and 19 US black music hits but never got higher than 98 on their pop chart. He later recorded for Mercury, Phase 11 and Handshake.

DISCO STOMP	6	05 JUL 75	BRUNSWICK

MARC BOLAN – SEE T-REX FOR HIT DETAILS

BOMB THE BASS

Brainchild of UK club DJ Tim Simenon. First single entered UK chart at No. 5 equalling the all time record for a new artist. Group uses guest vocalist/rappers and gave Merlin (Justin Boreland) his first hit. In the US their only chart records to date have been in the dance field.

BEAT DIS *(US Dance No. 1)*	2	27 FEB 88	MISTER-RON
MEGABLAST/DON'T MAKE ME WAIT	6	03 SEP 88	MISTER-RON
(Vocals by Merlin & Antonia and 'B' by Lorraine)			
SAY A LITTLE PRAYER	10	03 DEC 88	RHYTHM KING
(Featuring Maureen – Dionne Warwick 67 US Hit)			

BON JOVI

New Jersey heavy rock band led by Jon Bon Jovi (real name Bongiovi) were one of the world's top selling acts of the late 80s. Their first hit was 'Runaway' in 84, produced by then hot dance producer Tony Bongiovi. They really broke through with the US nine million selling LP 'Slippery When Wet' and its No. 1 singles. They headlined the 'Moscow Music Peace Festival' in 89.

LIVIN' ON A PRAYER		4	06 DEC 86	VERTIGO
YOU GIVE LOVE A BAD NAME (UK No. 14)		1(1)	29 NOV 86	MERCURY
(First Metal single to top US chart)				
LIVIN' ON A PRAYER		1(4)	14 FEB 87	MERCURY
BAD MEDICINE (UK No. 17)		1(2)	19 NOV 88	MERCURY
BORN TO BE MY BABY (UK No. 22)		3	18 FEB 89	MERCURY
I'LL BE THERE FOR YOU (UK No. 18)		1(1)	13 MAY 89	MERCURY
LAY YOUR HANDS ON ME (UK No. 18)		7	29 JUL 89	MERCURY
LIVING IN SIN (UK No. 35)		9	16 DEC 89	MERCURY

GARY US BONDS

Virignia born Gary Anderson called himself US Bonds as a gimmick and his distinctive sound gave him eight US & two UK hits in the 60s. He wrote many 70s soul hits and later producer Bruce Springsteen gave him three more charters. He also recorded on Skydisc, Prodigal, MCA, EMI, Botanic, Sue, Atco and Bluff City.

QUARTER TO THREE		7	25 AUG 61	TOP RANK
(Based on 'A Night With Daddy G' – Church Street 5)				
NEW ORLEANS (UK No. 16)		6	28 NOV 60	LEGRAND
QUARTER TO THREE		1(2)	26 JUN 61	LEGRAND
SCHOOL IS OUT		5	04 SEP 61	LEGRAND
DEAR LADY TWIST		9	24 FEB 62	LEGRAND
TWIST, TWIST SENORA		9	12 MAY 62	LEGRAND

BONEY M

Produced by Fred Farian in Germany, this mixed quartet of West Indian origin (Marcia, Liz, Maizie and Bobby) were named after an Australian TV detective show. They were one of the UK's top acts in the late 70s but never really broke in US. They re-appeared with little success on Carrere in 86 and Imperative in 89.

DADDY COOL		6	05 FEB 77	ATLANTIC
(US No. 65 – the first hit released on 12")				
SUNNY (Bobby Hebb 66 hit)		3	16 APR 77	ATLANTIC
MA BAKER (US No. 96)		2	30 JUL 77	ATLANTIC
BELFAST		8	17 DEC 77	ATLANTIC
RIVERS OF BABYLON/BROWN GIRL IN THE RING		1(5)	13 MAY 78	ATLANTIC/HAN
(US No. 30 – 2 million in UK & Top UK record 78)				
RASPUTIN		2	21 OCT 78	ATLANTIC/HAN
MARY'S BOY CHILD-OH MY LORD (US No. 85)		1(3)	09 DEC 78	ATLANTIC/HAN
(UK Gold as was original Harry Belafonte 57 hit)				
PAINTER MAN (Creation 66 UK hit)		10	10 MAR 79	ATLANTIC/HAN
HOORAY HOORAY IT'S A HOLI-HOLIDAY		3	12 MAY 79	ATLANTIC/HAN

GRAHAM BONNETT

He was 50% of The Marbles who had been voted most promising group of 68 and had also recorded as a soloist on DJM in 74 and Ringo in 77. His recognisable voice was also heard as a member of Rainbow before notching up his biggest solo hit. He shortly after joined The Michael Schenker group but left six months later.

NIGHT GAMES		6	18 APR 81	VERTIGO

Also see Marbles/Rainbow

BONZO DOG DOO-DAH BAND

Quirky UK band fronted by Neil Innes and Viv Stanshall. Their humorous 1920's orientated music was first heard on Parlophone in 66 and UK success came when when they joined Liberty. Neil has worked mainly with ex-Monty Python comedians since group split.

I'M THE URBAN SPACEMAN (Prod. Paul McCartney)		5	21 DEC 68	LIBERTY

BOOGIE BOX HIGH

A project masterminded by George Michael's brother Andros and released on his own label. Rumour has it that George was also featured on their hit which they followed with 'Gave It All Away'. They signed with SBK in 89.

JIVE TALKIN' (Bee Gees 75 hit)		7	01 AUG 87	HARDBACK

BOOKER T. & THE M.G.'S

Instrumental quartet formed from Stax Records session men and featuring Booker T Jones and guitar wizard Steve Cropper. Their unique sound resulted in 15 US hits and four in the UK in the soulful 60s. They had an unsuccessful comeback in the 70s. Jones later had hits producing acts like Willie Nelson and Bill Withers. Their 'Soul Limbo' is BBC TV's cricket theme.

TIME IS TIGHT		4	21 JUN 69	STAX
GREEN ONIONS (Used in film 'Quadrophenia')		7	26 JAN 80	ATLANTIC
(Follow ups included 'Mo' Onions')				
GREEN ONIONS (UK hit 18 years later)		3	29 SEP 62	STAX
(1st called 'Behave Yourself' – A & B titles changed)				
HANG 'EM HIGH (From the film)		9	08 FEB 69	STAX
TIME IS TIGHT		6	03 MAY 69	STAX

BOOMTOWN RATS

Now best known as the group 'Sir' Bob Geldof fronted, the Rats started as The Nightlife Thugs and were one of the top UK groups in the late 70s with five UK-only Top 10s in 17 months. The band continued until Bob became completely involved in his charity work. His solo career from 86 onwards met with less success.

LIKE CLOCKWORK		6	15 JUL 78	ENSIGN
RAT TRAP		1(2)	18 NOV 78	ENSIGN
I DON'T LIKE MONDAYS (US No.73 – Jumped 15-1)		1(4)	28 JUL 79	ENSIGN
(Song about Brenda Spencer who shot 11 people)				
SOMEONE'S LOOKING AT YOU		4	16 FEB 80	ENSIGN
BANANA REPUBLIC		3	06 DEC 80	ENSIGN

DEBBY BOONE

Grand daughter of 40s country star Red Foley, daughter of 50s pop star Pat Boone and daughter-in-law of Rosemary Clooney. Started in The Boones with her three sisters. Her sole US Top 40 hit spent a record time at No. 1. Her follow up was 'California' and she is now a successful gospel music artist.

YOU LIGHT UP MY LIFE		1(10)	15 OCT 77	WARNER
(From the film – originally by Kasey Cisyk)				

PAT BOONE

He and Elvis were the top transatlantic acts of the late 50s. His first releases on Republic in 53 failed but soon he started a record run of 207 consecutive weeks in the US Top 40 (many of his hits being 'safe' cover versions of R&B records). He won many polls including World's Top Singer. He is now a Christian music act.

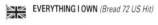

AIN'T THAT A SHAME *(Fats Domino 55 hit)*		7	09 DEC 55	LONDON
I'LL BE HOME *(Flamingos 56 US Hit)*		1(5)	15 JUN 56	LONDON
FRIENDLY PERSUASION *(From the film)*		3	25 JAN 57	LONDON
DON'T FORBID ME		2	08 MAR 57	LONDON
LOVE LETTERS IN THE SAND *(Top UK record of 57)*		2	16 AUG 57	LONDON
REMEMBER YOU'RE MINE/ THERE'S A GOLDMINE IN THE SKY		5	01 NOV 57	LONDON
APRIL LOVE *(From the film)*		7	14 FEB 58	LONDON
IT'S TOO SOON TO KNOW *(Orioles 48 hit)*		7	25 APR 58	LONDON
A WONDERFUL TIME UP THERE		2	16 MAY 58	LONDON
SUGAR MOON *(Collins & Harlan 10 hit)*		6	18 JUL 58	LONDON
JOHNNY WILL *(US No.35 – comp. Paul Evans)*		4	27 DEC 61	LONDON
SPEEDY GONZALES		2	03 AUG 62	LONDON
AIN'T THAT A SHAME		2	17 SEP 55	DOT
AT MY FRONT DOOR (CRAZY LITTLE MAMA) *(Eldorados 55 US Hit)*		8	25 NOV 55	DOT
I'LL BE HOME		6	24 MAR 56	DOT
I ALMOST LOST MY MIND *(UK No. 14 – Ivory Joe Hunter 56 US Hit)*		2	07 JUL 56	DOT
FRIENDLY PERSUASION/CHAINS OF LOVE		9	20 OCT 56	DOT
DON'T FORBID ME		3	09 FEB 57	DOT
WHY BABY WHY *(UK No. 17)*		5	13 APR 57	DOT
LOVE LETTERS IN THE SAND *(Ted Black 31 hit)*		1(5)	03 JUN 57	DOT
REMEMBER YOU'RE MINE/ THERE'S A GOLDMINE IN THE SKY		10	23 SEP 57	DOT
APRIL LOVE/ WHEN THE SWALLOWS COME BACK TO CAPISTRANO		1(2)	16 DEC 57	DOT
A WONDERFUL TIME UP THERE/ IT'S TOO SOON TO KNOW		4	10 MAR 58	DOT
SUGAR MOON/CHERIE I LOVE YOU		10	26 MAY 58	DOT
MOODY RIVER *(UK No. 14)*		1(1)	19 JUN 61	DOT
SPEEDY GONZALES		6	28 JUL 62	DOT
(His 38th Top 40 – banned by some Mexican stations)				

KEN BOOTHE

Jamaican reggae star whose follow up 'Crying Over You'(No.11) was also a UK-only Top 20. Ken also recorded on Cactus, Greensleeves, Camel, Green Door, Lord Koos, Ashanti, Dynamic, Taxi, Germaine, Live & Love, Tads, Small Acts, Silverman and Tapper Zukie.

EVERYTHING I OWN *(Bread 72 US Hit)*		1(3)	26 OCT 74	TROJAN

BOSTON

Tom Scholz led group from Boston, featuring Brad Delp's vocals. They had instant success with their 10 million selling debut LP 'Boston' and its singles. They were sued for $20 million by label for slow delivery of LP 'Third Stage' in 83. When released in 86 it went to No. 1 in US in three weeks and reached 37 in UK.

MORE THAN A FEELING *(UK No. 22)*		5	25 DEC 76	EPIC
DON'T LOOK BACK *(UK No. 43)*		4	07 OCT 78	EPIC
AMANDA		1(2)	08 NOV 86	MCA
WE'RE READY		9	14 FEB 87	EPIC

PERRY BOTKIN JR. – SEE BARRY DeVORZON FOR HIT DETAILS

JUDY BOUCHER

St. Vincent born reggae artist who moved to the UK when she was 15. Her hit was released in 86 and only took off when used on Breakfast TV by UK aerobics star 'Mad' Lizzie. Follow up 'You Caught My Eye' was also a UK-only Top 20 hit (18).

CAN'T BE WITHOUT YOU TONIGHT		2	25 APR 87	ORBITONE

BOW WOW WOW

Managed by mastermind Malcolm McLaren and fronted by 15 year old Annabella Lwin. The act that once included Boy George saw their first record 'C30, C60, C90 Go' fail but they attracted lots of publicity as it was the UK's first cassette only release and because Annabella was photographed semi-naked. Group broke up in 82 and she went solo unsuccessfully.

GO WILD IN THE COUNTRY *(Their 6th chart hit)*		7	20 MAR 82	RCA
I WANT CANDY *(Strangeloves 65 US Hit)*		9	26 JUN 82	RCA

DAVID BOWIE

One of rock's true originals. Before charting he recorded with The King Bees, The Manish Boys, as Davy Jones & The Lower Third and as a soloist. He had to wait three years for hit two but since then he's spent more time on the UK LP chart than any other UK male and he's had 20 UK Top 10 LPs (with 10 on the chart in one week) and eight in the US, plus 30 singles in the UK Top 20 (8 US). Often called rock's greatest chameleon, Bowie stays ahead of the pack by predicting, not following, trends.

SPACE ODDITY *(Took over 6 years from first entry to get No. 1)*		5	01 NOV 69	PHILIPS
STARMAN *(US No. 65)*		10	29 JUL 72	RCA
THE JEAN GENIE *(US No. 71)*		2	13 JAN 73	RCA
DRIVE-IN SATURDAY		3	05 MAY 73	RCA
LIFE ON MARS		3	14 JUL 73	RCA
THE LAUGHING GNOME *(Re-issue)*		6	13 OCT 73	DERAM
SORROW		3	03 NOV 73	RCA
REBEL REBEL *(US No. 64-entered at No. 6)*		5	02 MAR 74	RCA
KNOCK ON WOOD *(US 'B' side)*		10	12 OCT 74	RCA
SPACE ODDITY *(Re-issue)*		1(2)	08 NOV 75	RCA
GOLDEN YEARS		8	20 DEC 75	RCA
SOUND AND VISION *(US No. 59)*		3	26 MAR 77	RCA
BOYS KEEP SWINGIN'		7	02 JUN 79	RCA
ASHES TO ASHES *(entered at no. 4)*		1(2)	23 AUG 80	RCA
FASHION *(US No. 70)*		5	22 NOV 80	RCA
UNDER PRESSURE (With QUEEN) *(US No. 29) (Was No. 1 in 2 weeks)*		1(2)	21 NOV 81	RCA
PEACE ON EARTH/LITTLE DRUMMER BOY *(And BING CROSBY – Age gap between duo of 40 years)*		3	25 DEC 82	RCA
LET'S DANCE *(Entered at No. 5)*		1(3)	09 APR 83	EMI AM.
CHINA GIRL *(Entered at No. 8)*		2	18 JUN 83	EMI AM.
MODERN LOVE *(US No.14 – entered at No. 8)*		2	08 OCT 83	EMI AM.
BLUE JEAN		6	29 SEP 84	EMI AM.
DANCING IN THE STREET (with MICK JAGGER) *(Entered at No. 1 – the first time either act done this)*		1(4)	07 SEP 85	EMI AM.
ABSOLUTE BEGINNERS *(US No. 53 – entered at No. 8)*		2	22 MAR 86	VIRGIN
FAME *(UK No. 17)*		1(2)	20 SEP 75	RCA
GOLDEN YEARS		10	03 APR 76	RCA
LET'S DANCE *(His biggest transatlantic hit)*		1(1)	21 MAY 83	EMI AM.
CHINA GIRL		10	27 AUG 83	EMI AM.
BLUE JEAN		8	03 NOV 84	EMI AM.
DANCING IN THE STREET *(Money to 'Live Aid') (with MICK JAGGER – names reversed on label in US)*		7	12 OCT 85	EMI AM.

BOX TOPS

Successful late 60s group from Memphis fronted by Alex Chilton and including Rick Allen (ex-Gentrys). They achieved seven Top 40s in the US and three in the UK. They later recorded for Bell in 70, Hi in 72 and Stax in 74. After their demise Alex, who is still recording, formed Big Star and became a cult figure.

THE LETTER		5	21 OCT 67	STATESIDE
THE LETTER *(Top US single 67)*		1(4)	23 SEP 67	MALA
CRY LIKE A BABY		2	27 APR 68	MALA

BOY GEORGE

Flamboyant front man of the 80s group Culture Club. He started in the business as Lieutenant Lush and surprisingly missed the US chart with his UK No. 1. To date his biggest US solo charter was 'Live My Life' (40). In 89 he had a black music Top 5 and also recorded as Jesus Loves You.

| | EVERYTHING I OWN | 1(2) | 14 MAR 87 | VIRGIN |
| | (Bread 72 hit and UK No. 1 for Ken Boothe) | | | |

Also see Culture Club

BOY MEETS GIRL

Singer/song writing duo of George Merrill and Shannon Rubican who penned 'How Will I Know' and 'I Wanna Dance With You' for Whitney Houston and 'Let's Hear It For The Boy' for Deniece Williams. They were on A&M in 85 and wrote their big hit for Whitney (but she rejected it). Follow up was 'Bring Down The Moon'.

| | WAITING FOR A STAR TO FALL | 9 | 21 JAN 89 | RCA |
| | WAITING FOR A STAR TO FALL | 5 | 17 DEC 88 | RCA |

TOMMY BOYCE & BOBBY HART

US singer/songwriting duo had 4 US-only Top 40s and claim their songs (including Top 10s for The Monkees, Jay & The Americans and Showaddywaddy) have sold over 40 million. As soloists Tommy has been on Colpix, Dot, R-Dell, Wow, MGM and RCA and Bobby has been on Infinity, DCP, Chelsea, Era, Radio, Bamboo, Ariola and Warner.

| | I WONDER WHAT SHE'S DOING TONIGHT | 8 | 24 FEB 68 | A&M |

BOYS CLUB

Minneapolis duo of Gene Hunt and Joe Pasquale. Gene had previous success in The Jets and Joe was in King's English (one of the Jam & Lewis roster of acts). So far they have had the one US hit.

| | I REMEMBER HOLDING YOU | 8 | 14 JAN 89 | MCA |

BOYSTOWN GANG

US West Coast mixed trio, fronted by Jackson Moore, whose Hi-Nrg style appealed more to the UK dance crowd. They first charted with 'Ain't No Mountain High Enough – Remember Me (Medley)'. They followed their hit with the Motown song 'Signed Sealed Delivered'.

| | CAN'T TAKE MY EYES OFF YOU | 4 | 28 AUG 82 | ERC |
| | (Andy Williams 68 hit – originally released in 81) | | | |

BILLY BRAGG

Left wing London singer/writer started in punk band Riff Raff on Chiswick. First solo LP was on Utility and later on Go! Discs. The 'Between The Wars E.P.' was the first of his two UK Top 20s (15). His first 45 'A New England' was a Top 10 when revived by Kirsty MacColl. The No. 1 was a charity record for 'Child Helpline' taken from 'Sgt Pepper Knew My Father', a charity album on which various 80s acts covered all the songs from The Beatles' 'Sgt Pepper' LP in the same order.

| | SHE'S LEAVING HOME/WITH A LITTLE HELP FROM | | | |
| | MY FRIENDS (Double 'A' with WET WET WET) | 1(3) | 21 MAY 88 | HELPLINE |

LAURA BRANIGAN

New York born singer and actress' first record for Atlantic was 'Tell Him' in 75. Eight years later she had twin Transatlantic Top 10s with Euro sounding dance hits which included her Grammy nominee 'Gloria'. She has also appeared in TV shows like Chips.

	GLORIA (Original by Dario Balden Bembo)	6	05 FEB 83	ATLANTIC
	SELF CONTROL (German No. 1)	5	01 SEP 84	ATLANTIC
	GLORIA	2	27 NOV 82	ATLANTIC
	(Prod. Greg Mathieson also had US No. 1 same week)			
	SOLITAIRE	7	21 MAY 83	ATLANTIC
	SELF CONTROL	4	30 JUN 84	ATLANTIC

LOS BRAVOS

Four Spaniards and a German who were previously well known in Spain as Mike (Kogel) & The Runaways. Their big international hit was recorded in the UK and they followed it there with 'I Don't Care' (No. 16) and in the US with 'Going Nowhere' which it and the group then did.

| | BLACK IS BLACK | 2 | 30 JUL 66 | DECCA |
| | BLACK IS BLACK | 4 | 01 OCT 66 | PARROT |

BREAD

Very successful 70s AOR rock group started as Pleasure Faire (UNI). Members included top writers David Gates (prev. on East West, Mala, Robbins, Del-Fi, Jads, Planetary, GSP, London and Vee Jay) and James Griffin (who'd been on Dot, Atco, Imperial, Reprise and Viva). The influential foursome who had four Top 20 LPs in both the US & UK split in 73 and briefly re-united in 76.

	MAKE IT WITH YOU	5	12 SEP 70	ELEKTRA
	MAKE IT WITH YOU	1(1)	22 AUG 70	ELEKTRA
	IT DON'T MATTER TO ME	10	14 NOV 70	ELEKTRA
	BABY I'M A WANT YOU (UK No. 14)	3	27 NOV 71	ELEKTRA
	EVERYTHING I OWN (UK No. 32)	5	04 MAR 72	ELEKTRA
	(Song was UK No. 1 twice by Ken Booth & Boy George)			
	IF (Song was UK No. 1 for Telly Savalas)	4	15 MAY 72	ELEKTRA
	LOST WITHOUT YOUR LOVE (UK No. 27)	9	19 FEB 77	ELEKTRA

BREAK MACHINE

New York dance music trio consisting of brothers Lindsay & Lindell Blake and Cortez Jordan. This energetic act introduced break dancing to the majority of the UK public via their TV spots. In their homeland they had little chart action.

| | STREET DANCE (US No. 105) | 3 | 17 MAR 84 | RECORD SHACK |
| | BREAK DANCE PARTY | 9 | 26 MAY 84 | RECORD SHACK |

BREAKFAST CLUB

Five piece New York based dance music band which includes Madonna's producer Steve Bray and once contained the lady herself. They followed their hit with 'Kiss & Tell'.

| | RIGHT ON TRACK | 7 | 30 MAY 87 | MCA |

BREATHE

UK trio led by David Glasper. Their first release was 'Don't Tell Me Lies' in Jan 86, which was a hit when re-issued. They are currently more successful in the US where they had a smash hit before charting in their homeland.

	HANDS TO HEAVEN	4	03 SEP 88	SIREN
	HANDS TO HEAVEN	2	06 AUG 88	A&M
	HOW CAN I FALL	3	03 DEC 88	A&M
	DON'T TELL ME LIES (UK No. 45)	10	18 MAR 89	A&M

WALTER BRENNAN

The late actor and three time Oscar winner had a left field US hit when aged 68 about a man and his mule, which had originally been written for Johnny Cash. He was perhaps best known as 'Grandpa' in the 50s US TV series 'The Real McCoys'.

	OLD RIVERS	5	26 MAY 62	LIBERTY

BREWER AND SHIPLEY

Folk/rock singers Mike Brewer and Tom Shipley, who were on A&M in 68, had a US hit about 'tokes'. Their follow up was 'Tarkio Road' (US 55). They recorded for Capitol in 74, Mercury in 78 and later moved to a commune in Missouri.

	ONE TOKE OVER THE LINE	10	10 APR 71	KAMA SUTRA

BRIAN & MICHAEL

UK duo Brian Burke & Michael Coleman had a one-off UK hit with a song about the painter Lowry. Follow up was 'Evensong'.

	MATCHSTALK MEN AND MATCHSTALK CATS (Featuring The St. Winifred's School Choir)	1(3)	08 APR 78	PYE

BRICK

Atlanta quintet, which included Jimmy Brown, combined disco and jazz. Formed in 72 they first charted with 'Music Matic' on Main Street in 76 and had four Top 10 Soul hits between 76 & 81.

	DAZZ (UK No.36) (A re-mix was released on Magic City in 87)	3	29 JAN 77	BANG

EDIE BRICKELL & NEW BOHEMIANS

Folk/rock sextet based in Texas. Edie saw them at a club and simply joined them on stage. The group signed to Geffen in 86 and hit with their Welsh recorded LP 'Shooting Rubber Bands At The Sky' which also included their follow up 'Circle'.

	WHAT I AM (UK No. 31)	7	04 MAR 89	GEFFEN

ALICIA BRIDGES

Atlanta based disco singer had a Grammy nomination for her biggest hit. She also charted with the follow up 'Body Heat' (US 86) but never returned to the top end of the chart.

	I LOVE THE NIGHT LIFE (DISCO 'ROUND) (UK No. 32)	5	23 DEC 78	POLYDOR

BRIGHOUSE AND RASTRICK BRASS BAND

A very well known brass band in the North of England had a left field UK hit with a traditional West of England folk song. Their follow up was 'Barwick Green'.

	THE FLORAL DANCE (No. 2 for 6 weeks)	2	10 DEC 77	TRANSATLANTIC

SARAH BRIGHTMAN

UK singer/actress who is married to top composer Andrew Lloyd Webber. She has made the UK-only Top 10 in five different duets. She was also on Whisper in 81, RCA in 84 and CBS in 89.

	I LOST MY HEART TO A STARSHIP TROOPER (And HOT GOSSIP)	6	09 DEC 78	ARIOLA
	PIE JESU (And PAUL MILES-KINGSTON)	3	30 MAR 85	HMV
	THE PHANTOM OF THE OPERA (And STEVE HARLEY)	7	08 FEB 86	POLYDOR

	ALL I ASK OF YOU (With CLIFF RICHARD)	3	25 OCT 86	POLYDOR
	THE MUSIC OF THE NIGHT/ WISHING YOU WERE SOMEHOW HERE AGAIN (With MICHAEL CRAWFORD)	7	14 DEC 87	POLYDOR

JOHNNY BRISTOL

North Carolina born artist started in the duo Johnny & Jackey (Beavers) in the early 60s. He joined Motown as a writer/producer and had hits with Stevie Wonder, The Supremes, Edwin Starr and Jr. Walker. During his solo career he also produced or wrote hits for The Osmonds, Johnny Mathis and Amii Stewart.

	HANG ON IN THERE BABY (He re-recorded it in a duet with Alton McClain)	3	28 SEP 74	MGM
	HANG ON IN THERE BABY	8	05 OCT 74	MGM

BRONSKI BEAT

UK trio formed in 83 originally featuring the distinctive high voice of Jimmy Somerville (with Steve Bronski & Larry Steinbachek). Jimmy was replaced in 85 by John Foster who left a year later. They had UK hit in 89 featuring 50s star Eartha Kitt.

	SMALLTOWN BOY (US No. 48 – US Dance No. 1)	3	23 JUN 84	FORBIDDEN
	WHY?	6	06 OCT 84	FORBIDDEN
	I FEEL LOVE (And MARC ALMOND)	3	11 MAY 85	FORBIDDEN
	HIT THAT PERFECT BEAT	3	18 JAN 86	FORBIDDEN

Also see Jimmy Somerville

BROOKLYN BRIDGE

Act was originally an 11 piece group (an amalgamation of The Del Satins and The Rhythm Method) with lead vocalist Johnny Maestro, who had previously had US hits both as a solo act and as leader of The Crests. The group, who still do shows, had seven US hits. Oddly none of Johnny's many hits charted in the UK.

	WORST THAT COULD HAPPEN (Originally recorded by Fifth Dimension)	3	01 FEB 69	BUDDAH

DONNIE BROOKS

Born Johnny Faircloth in Texas this pop/MOR singer previously recorded as Johnny Faire (on Fable and Surf), Johnny Jordan (on Jolt) and Dick Bush. He had three US-only hits and was later on Reprise, DJ, Yardbird, Challenge, Happy Tiger and Midsong Int.

	MISSION BELL	7	05 SEP 60	ERA

ELKIE BROOKS

Lancashire (UK) born singer started recording on Decca in 64 then for HMV and NEMS again without success before joining groups Da Da and Vinegar Joe (with Robert Palmer). With help from top writers Leiber & Stoller she finally broke through in the UK-only and has had many successful singles and LPs there since 77. The sister of Billy J. Kramer, she has become a respected MOR stylist.

	PEARL'S A SINGER (Originally by Dino & Sembello)	8	07 MAY 77	A&M
	SUNSHINE AFTER THE RAIN	10	01 OCT 77	A&M
	NO MORE THE FOOL (Composed by Russ Ballard)	5	17 JAN 87	LEGEND

BROS

Originally a trio with twins Matt & Luke Goss and Craig Logan (who left in 89). This top teen appeal act saw their first single 'I Owe You Nothing' fail (a No. 1 when re-issued) and their next temporarily banned for chart hyping but this did not stop them scoring six UK-only Top 5s, breaking video sales records, selling out tours and winning numerous UK music awards. By 90 their star was fading.

WHEN WILL I BE FAMOUS (US No. 83)		2	06 FEB 88	CBS
DROP THE BOY		2	26 MAR 88	CBS
I OWE YOU NOTHING		1(2)	25 JUN 88	CBS
(Released in 3 different sleeves)				
I QUIT (Entered at No. 4)		4	17 SEP 88	CBS
CAT AMONG THE PIGEONS/SILENT NIGHT		2	03 DEC 88	CBS
(Entered at No. 2)				
TOO MUCH (Entered at No. 2)		2	29 JUL 89	CBS
CHOCOLATE BOX (Entered at No. 9)		9	07 OCT 89	CBS
SISTER		10	30 DEC 89	CBS

BROTHER BEYOND

The UK group fronted by Nathan Moore had their first single produced by Don Was of Was (Not Was) in 86. They then had three small hits and became one of the UK's top teen attractions when they got together with the S.A.W. team whose songs and productions have helped give them a run of UK-only successes.

THE HARDER I TRY		2	03 SEP 88	PARLOPHONE
HE AIN'T NO COMPETITION		6	19 NOV 88	PARLOPHONE

BROTHERHOOD OF MAN

The name was first used in 1970 for a UK session group put together by Tony Hiller and fronted by Tony Burrows. They were on Dawn in 74 and in 76 they became a mixed quartet and represented the UK in the 76 Eurovision Song contest. This new act which included singer/songwriters Martin Lee and Lee Sheriden won the contest and afterwards had a string of UK-only hits.

UNITED WE STAND (US No. 13)		10	28 FEB 70	DERAM
SAVE YOUR KISSES FOR ME		1(6)	27 MAR 76	PYE
(US No. 27 – UK Gold and Top UK record 76)				
OH BOY		8	16 APR 77	PYE
ANGELO		1(1)	20 AUG 77	PYE
FIGARO		1(1)	11 FEB 78	PYE

BROTHERS

Five London based brothers, originally from Mauritius, led by Clarel Bayou. They were winners on TV talent show Opportunity Knocks and managed to get a one-off UK Top 10 hit.

SING ME		8	26 FEB 77	BUS STOP
(Winning song in Opportunity Knocks competition)				

BROTHERS FOUR

Four fraternity brothers from the University of Washington who had their only Top 20 hit with their second release on Columbia. They also recorded the original version of 'The Green Leaves of Summer' (UK hit for Kenny Ball). They recorded for Fantasy in 69.

GREENFIELDS (UK No.26)		2	18 APR 60	COLUMBIA

BROTHERS JOHNSON

Singers/musicians/composers George & Louis Johnson from L.A. After a spell in Billy Preston's God Squad they were spotted by producer Quincy Jones who helped the duo notch up 17 black music hits (including nine Top 20s).

STOMP!		6	05 APR 80	A&M
I'LL BE GOOD TO YOU		3	10 JUL 76	A&M
(They were on Quincy Jones' 89 revival of this)				
STRAWBERRY LETTER 23 (UK No.35)		5	24 SEP 77	A&M
STOMP!		7	24 MAY 80	A&M

CRAZY WORLD OF ARTHUR BROWN

Yorkshire born Arthur had a one-off Top 10 in 68 with his second release. Their outrageous act (based on Screamin' Jay Hawkins') soon became passé. Also in the group were Carl Palmer and Vincent Crane who left to form Atomic Rooster. Arthur joined Gull in 74.

FIRE		1(1)	17 AUG 68	TRACK
FIRE		2	19 OCT 68	TRACK

BOBBY BROWN

Boston born Grammy winning singer who originally hit as a member of the successful group New Edition. His first solo charter was 'Girlfriend' a black music No. 1 in 86. In 88 his music first hit the peaks of the US pop chart and a year later he was the hottest male singer in the UK too. He was also the youngest male to top the US LP chart for 26 years.

MY PREROGATIVE		6	25 FEB 89	MCA
EVERY LITTLE STEP		6	27 MAY 89	MCA
ON OUR OWN		4	22 JUL 89	MCA
(Entered at No. 8 – from 'Ghostbusters 11')				
DON'T BE CRUEL (UK No. 13)		8	15 OCT 88	MCA
(One of 2 songs in Top 10 together with same title)				
MY PREROGATIVE		1(1)	14 JAN 89	MCA
(Above 2 both No. 1s on black chart				
3 months before)				
RONI (UK No. 21)		3	18 MAR 89	MCA
EVERY LITTLE STEP		3	10 JUN 89	MCA
ROCK WIT'CHA (UK No. 33)		7	04 NOV 89	MCA

Also see New Edition

JAMES BROWN

Known as 'Soul Brother No. 1', 'The Godfather of Funk' and 'The Hardest Working Man In Show Business'. This Georgia born superstar who first recorded in 56 has had a record 116 black music hits (94 US Top 100 pop). His stage act is legendary and has inspired acts like The Rolling Stones, Prince and Terence Trent D'Arby. Sadly the most sampled man in dance music and the most influential black act of all time was jailed in 88.

LIVING IN AMERICA		5	15 FEB 86	SCOTTI BROS
(His first UK Top 10 – he has only had 3 Top 20s)				
PAPA'S GOT A BRAND NEW BAG (UK No.25)		8	04 SEP 65	KING
I GOT YOU (I FEEL GOOD) (UK No.29)		3	18 DEC 65	KING
IT'S A MAN'S MAN'S MAN'S WORLD (UK No. 13)		8	04 JUN 66	KING
COLD SWEAT (Pt. 1)		7	26 AUG 67	KING
(Considered by many to be the first Funk record)				
I GOT THE FEELIN'		6	27 APR 68	KING
(All above US hits with The Famous Flames)				
SAY IT LOUD-I'M BLACK AND I'M PROUD		10	19 OCT 68	KING
(Top R&B record 68 – backing vocals The 4 Jewels)				
LIVING IN AMERICA (From the film 'Rocky 1V')		4	01 MAR 86	SCOTTI BROS

JOE BROWN & THE BRUVVERS

Cockney singer/guitarist was part of the UK R'n'R stable run by manager Larry Parnes. He was a popular live act even before his run of 11 UK-only hits started. He was later on Pye, MCA, Ammo, Pinnacle, Bell, Vertigo, Power Exchange, Solid Gold, Parlophone, TFI, and BBC. His daughter Sam is now a chart artist.

A PICTURE OF YOU		1(1)	06 JUL 62	PICCADILLY
(Covered in the US by Paul Evans and Kalin Twins)				
IT ONLY TOOK A MINUTE		9	04 JAN 63	PICCADILLY
THAT'S WHAT LOVE WILL DO		3	08 MAR 63	PICCADILLY
(Covered in US by Bobby Goldsboro)				

PETER BROWN

Chicago singer and keyboard player who first hit with 'Do Ya Wanna Get Funky With Me' (US 18/UK 43). He later recorded on RCA and Columbia (including a duet with Betty Wright).

DANCE WITH ME		8	08 JUL 78	DRIVE

SAM BROWN

Daughter of 60s UK star Joe Brown. Had done sessions for acts like Adam Ant, Dexy's Midnight Runners and Spandau Ballet. 'Stop' was a small UK hit, then a European smash and it re-charted in the UK. Follow up was Marvin Gaye's 'Can I Get A Witness' (UK 15).

 STOP *(US No. 65 – Had peaked 52 UK in 88)*   4   04 MAR 89   A&M

JACKSON BROWNE

German born multi-talented artist who has worked with acts like The Eagles (he co-wrote 'Take It Easy'), Nitty Gritty Dirt Band and Warren Zevon and had his songs recorded by numerous hit acts. His only UK Top 40 was 'Stay' (12). He does a lot of work for Amnesty International and performed at The Nelson Mandela concert.

 DOCTOR MY EYES   8   06 MAY 72   ASYLUM
SOMEBODY'S BABY   7   16 OCT 82   ASYLUM

TOM BROWNE

New York based jazz trumpeter who previously played with The Fatback Band in 76. He topped the black music chart with his UK Pop hit. Follow up was 'Thighs High'.

 FUNKIN' FOR JAMAICA (N.Y.)   10   16 AUG 80   ARISTA

BROWNS

Distinctive Arkansas country music trio consisting of Jim Ed Brown and his sisters Maxine & Bonnie. They started in the late 40s and first charted with 'Looking Back To See' in 54 and their ninth country hit was a transatlantic Top 10. Maxine and Jim Ed both went solo in 65 and he strung together 51 country hits.

 THE THREE BELLS   6   16 OCT 59   RCA
(Les Compagnons De La Chanson 52 hit)

THE THREE BELLS   1(4)   24 AUG 59   RCA
THE OLD LAMPLIGHTER *(Sammy Kaye 46 hit)*   5   02 MAY 60   RCA

BROWNSVILLE STATION

Michigan rock trio fronted by 'Cub' Koda. Recorded for Warner and Polydor in 70 and had the first of seven US chart records in 72 (many being covers). Their biggest hit was later successfully revived by Motley Crue. They were later on Hideout and Private Stock and Koda recorded three LPs on Baron and is now a rock journalist and DJ.

SMOKIN' IN THE BOYS ROOM *(UK No. 27)*   3   19 JAN 74   BIG TREE

DAVE BRUBECK QUARTET

Well respected jazz quartet led by Dave Brubeck (born Dave Warren in California). He was one of the best known jazz performers of the late 50s/early 60s when he had his unexpected hit (it had flopped when first released two years before). He followed it with 'It's A Raggy Waltz'.

TAKE FIVE *(US No. 25)*   6   03 NOV 61   FONTANA

TOMMY BRUCE & THE BRUISERS

Cockney singer who specialised in singing standards in a style not dissimilar to the Big Bopper. He released many other records but never repeated the success of his first UK hit.

 AIN'T MISBEHAVIN' *(Fats Waller 29 hit)*   2   01 JUL 60   COLUMBIA

ANITA BRYANT

A former 'Miss Oklahoma' who came third in the 'Miss America' competition, she recorded for Davis in 56 and in 58. A year later she had her first hit 'Till There Was You' (US 30) and she became one of the US

top MOR female acts in the early 60s. Both her hits were later recorded by Marie Osmond.

PAPER ROSES *(UK No. 25)*   5   13 JUN 60   CARLTON
IN MY LITTLE CORNER OF THE WORLD   10   29 AUG 60   CARLTON

PEABO BRYSON

Born in South Carolina he started with The Upsetters and Moses Dillard & The Tex Town Display. He first recorded in 65 and has had over three dozen black music hits to date including duets with Natalie Cole, Roberta Flack, Melissa Manchester and Regina Belle. He was also on Bang, Bullet, Atlantic, Arista and MCA.

 TONIGHT I CELEBRATE MY LOVE   2   17 SEP 83   CAPITOL
IF EVER YOU'RE IN MY ARMS AGAIN   10   18 AUG 84   ELEKTRA

B.T. EXPRESS

Eight man band formed in 72 in Brooklyn and previously called The King Davis (their managers name) House Rockers, The Madison Street Express and Brooklyn Trucking Express. They had many US hits and their work was often sampled in the late 80s. They were later on Columbia (76), Coast to Coast (81) and King Davis (85).

 DO IT ('TIL YOU'RE SATISFIED)   2   16 NOV 74   ROADSHOW
EXPRESS   4   29 MAR 75   ROADSHOW
(UK No. 34 – both tracks were black music No. 1s)

LINDSEY BUCKINGHAM

He was in the San Franciscan group Fritz before he and fellow group member Stevie Nicks set up Buckingham Nicks and recorded for Polydor. They both joined Fleetwood Mac to everyone's mutual advantage in 75 and he stayed with the multi-platinum act until 1988.

 TROUBLE *(UK No. 31)*   9   16 JAN 82   ASYLUM

Also see Fleetwood Mac

BUCKINGHAMS

Illinois quartet led by Dennis Tufano. Recorded as The Falling Pebbles on Alley Cat and as The Centuries on Spectra Sound. Their fourth release on the USA label was a US No. 1 and the first of five US-only Top 20s. Dennis and group member Carl Giamarese later recorded as a duo and the group re-appeared on Red label in 85.

 KIND OF A DRAG   1(2)   18 FEB 67   USA
DON'T YOU CARE   6   13 MAY 67   COLUMBIA
MERCY, MERCY, MERCY   5   12 AUG 67   COLUMBIA
(Cannonball Adderly 67 US hit)

BUCKNER & GARCIA

Atlanta's Jerry Buckner & Gary Garcia had a one-off US hit with this novelty about the arcade game. They tried to follow it with tracks like 'Do The Donkey Kong' and 'E.T. I Love You'. They had a US charter later as Willis 'The Guard' and Vigorish.

PAC-MAN FEVER   9   27 MAR 82   COLUMBIA

BUCKS FIZZ

Mixed quartet formed for the 81 Eurovision song contest were one of the UK's top acts of the early 80s. Members Cheryl Baker (now a UK TV personality), Mike Nolan (badly injured in a coach crash), Jay Aston (later replaced by Shelley Preston in 85) and Bobby G (Gubby) became stars in the UK but had no US success.

MAKING YOUR MIND UP   1(3)   18 APR 81   RCA
LAND OF MAKE BELIEVE   1(2)   16 JAN 82   RCA
MY CAMERA NEVER LIES   1(1)   17 APR 82   RCA
NOW THOSE DAYS ARE GONE   8   17 JUL 82   RCA
IF YOU CAN'T STAND THE HEAT   10   15 JAN 83   RCA
WHEN WE WERE YOUNG   10   25 JUN 83   RCA
NEW BEGINNING (MAMBA SAYRA)   8   28 JUN 86   POLYDOR

BUFFALO SPRINGFIELD

Named after a steamroller, they were one of the most influential groups of the 60s and included noteworthies Stephen Stills, Neil Young, Richie Furay and part time members Jim Messina and David Crosby. The volatile group, who never charted in the UK, folded in 68 and the members went on to greater things.

 FOR WHAT IT'S WORTH   7   25 MAR 67   ATCO

JIMMY BUFFETT

Unique song stylist/composer who has made his home in Florida, originally recorded for Andy Williams' Barnaby label. He and his Coral Reefers Band are still regular US LP chart makers but as yet they have had No. UK chart placings.

 MARGARITAVILLE   8   23 JUL 77   ABC

BUGGLES

UK duo Trevor Horn and Geoff Downes first worked together in Tina Charles backing band. Their initial joint project was an instant No. 1 in the UK and was the first song heard on MTV in the US. In 80 they both joined Yes for a year then Geoff helped form Asia and Trevor became one of the UK's most successful producers.

VIDEO KILLED THE RADIO STAR   1(1)   20 OCT 79   ISLAND

B.BUMBLE & THE STINGERS

Group supposedly led by William Bumble but more likely to be West Coast session men including Kim Fowley and Ernie Freeman ('Raunchy' in 57). Their debut was 'Bumble Boogie' and other classical pieces given their rock treatment became 'Bee Hive', 'Apple Knocker', and 'Dawn Cracker'. They later re-appeared on Mercury and 20th Century.

NUT ROCKER *(US No. 23 – back to UK No. 19 in 72)*   1(1)   09 MAY 62   TOP RANK
(Originally by Jack B. Nimble & The Quicks)

ERIC BURDON & WAR

After leaving The Animals Eric teamed with L.A. funk band Night Shift then re-named War. Their records were US-only successes and they parted in 71 with the group going on to greater things.

 SPILL THE WINE   3   22 AUG 70   MGM

Also see The Animals/War

JOHNNY BURNETTE

Johnny was a Memphis trucker and singer before Elvis (being on Von in 53). His trio cut some classic R'n'R on Coral in 56 and he also wrote hits for Ricky Nelson. In the 50s he was on Jox, Gothic, Infinity, Vee Jay, Imperial and Freedom. Before his untimely death in 64, this transatlantic pop/rock star, was also on Chancellor, Capitol, Sahara, Reprise and Magic Lamp.

DREAMIN' *(US No.11 – Composed Barry DeVorzon)*   3   18 NOV 60   LONDON
YOU'RE SIXTEEN   4   10 FEB 61   LONDON
(song originally recorded as 'You're 13')

YOU'RE SIXTEEN   8   26 DEC 60   LIBERTY
(Comp. Sherman brothers who wrote 'Mary Poppins')

ROCKY BURNETTE

Memphis born son of Johnny Burnette was born in the year Johnny started recording (53). He originally recorded for Curb before joining EMI. His first LP was appropriately called 'The Son of Rock'n'Roll'. To date he has only had one US hit.

 TIRED OF TOEIN' THE LINE   8   26 JUL 80   EMI AM.

KATE BUSH

Probably the UK's most distinctive and talented female singer/songwriter and one who has yet to really score in the US. She was the first female to top the UK singles chart with her own song and was the first UK female to top the LP chart and also the first to enter the LP chart at No. 1 (which she has done twice). Her productivity moves at a snail's pace.

 WUTHERING HEIGHTS *(Inspired by the book)*   1(4)   11 MAR 78   EMI
MAN WITH THE CHILD IN HIS EYES *(US No. 85)*   6   08 JUL 78   EMI
KATE BUSH ON STAGE E.P.   10   13 OCT 79   EMI
BABOOSHKA *(Jumped from 63-16)*   5   02 AUG 80   EMI
RUNNING UP THAT HILL   3   31 AUG 85   EMI
(US No. 30 – Entered UK at No. 9)
DON'T GIVE UP *(With PETER GABRIEL - US No. 72)*   9   15 NOV 86   VIRGIN

JERRY BUTLER

He charted first as leader of The Impressions in 58 and was a US-only (only) chart regular until 83 having 58 black music entries and 39 pop ones. Amongst his successes were the original hits of 'Make It Easy on Yourself' and 'Moon River'. He also recorded on Philly Int, Motown, Fountain and CTI.

HE WILL BREAK YOUR HEART   7   05 DEC 60   VEE JAY
(Later a hit for Dawn as 'He Don't Love You')
LET IT BE ME *(And BETTY EVERETT)*   5   07 NOV 64   VEE JAY
(Originally by Jill Corey in 57)
ONLY THE STRONG SURVIVE   4   19 APR 69   MERCURY

MAX BYGRAVES

UK comic, entertainer and MOR singer who first recorded on Decca in 50. He is best known in the UK-only for a series of 'Sing-a-long' LPs in the 70s (oddly his first record in this vein in 56 flopped) when he had a record five Top 20 LP's in 15 months. He also holds the UK chart span record having been in the very first singles chart in 52 and in the Top 5 LPs in 89 – 37 years.

MEET ME ON THE CORNER   2   06 JAN 56   HMV
YOU NEED HANDS/TULIPS FROM AMSTERDAM   3   04 JUL 58   DECCA
(Covered in US by Eydie Gorme)
JINGLE BELL ROCK *(Bobby Helms 57 hit)*   7   01 JAN 60   DECCA
FINGS AIN'T WHAT THEY USED T'BE   2   01 APR 60   DECCA

CHARLIE BYRD – SEE STAN GETZ FOR HIT DETAILS

GARY BYRD & GB EXPERIENCE

New York DJ and songwriter was recording Rap (spoken word) in the 70s on Real Thing ('Are You Ready For Black Power'), RCA and Atlantic. He had a one-off UK hit which he co-wrote and produced with Stevie Wonder. He later had a radio DJ show in the UK.

 THE CROWN *(first 12" only single to chart)*   6   30 JUL 83   MOTOWN

BYRDS

The first US group to make it after the British invasion of 64 had a great influence on rock, folk and country music. First known as The Jet Set then The Beefeaters they had recorded previously on Scholastic and Elektra. Members included Chris Hillman, Roger McGuinn, David Crosby, Gene Clark and Gram Parsons, the former two having much recent country chart action.

MR. TAMBOURINE MAN   1(2)   24 JUL 65   CBS
(first by writer Bob Dylan & Ramblin' Jack Elliott)
ALL I REALLY WANT TO DO *(Bob Dylan song)*   4   04 SEP 65   CBS
MR. TAMBOURINE MAN *(First Folk/Rock hit)*   1(1)   26 JUN 65   COLUMBIA
TURN! TURN! TURN!   1(3)   04 DEC 65   COLUMBIA

C

FANTASTIC JOHNNY C

Johnny Corley is the real name of this South Carolina soul singer who had a US hit with this dance record. He followed it with 'Got What You Need' and later recorded on Kama Sutra in 70.

BOOGALOO DOWN BROADWAY	7	23 DEC 67	PHIL L.A. OF
(He later unsuccessfully recorded 'Cool Broadway')			

C.C.S.

Short for The Collective Consciousness Society, a very large group, sometimes with more than 25 members, put together by the 'father of UK R&B' Alexis Korner and producer Mickie Most and featuring vocalist Peter Thorup. They had five UK Top 40s and their only US hit was a version of Led Zeppelin's 'Whole Lotta Love' (No. 58).

WALKIN'	7	10 APR 71	RAK
TAP TURNS ON THE WATER	5	01 OCT 71	RAK

MONTSERRAT CABALLE – SEE FREDDIE MERCURY FOR HIT DETAILS

SUSAN CADOGAN

UK reggae singer had two UK-only Top 40s the second being 'Love Me Baby' (22). She was later on Hawkeye, C & E and Solid Gold.

HURT SO GOOD *(Originally by Katie Love)*	4	03 MAY 75	MAGNET

JOHN CAFFERTY & THE BEAVER BROWN BAND

Rhode Island (US) rockers who found US fame playing on the soundtrack of 'Eddie & The Cruisers' when it was shown on HBO cable TV. The band who formed in 80 have often charted in the US and can also be heard in the 89 movie Eddie & The Cruisers II.

ON THE DARK SIDE *(Reached 64 in 83)*	7	27 OCT 84	SCOTTI BROS
(Originally released as by Eddie & The Cruisers)			

BOBBY CALDWELL

New York born singer/songwriter/musician has written for acts like Dionne Warwick, Natalie Cole and Robert Flack. His big US hit was issued on red heart shaped plastic for Valentines day. He later recorded for Polydor in 81 and MCA in 84.

WHAT YOU WON'T DO FOR LOVE	9	24 MAR 79	CLOUDS

CAMEO

Act masterminded by talented all rounder Larry Blackmon. He had previously been in East Coast, with Gwen Guthrie, before forming The New York Players who turned into Cameo in 76. They were a 13 piece and are now a trio and have had 30 black music hits and many hit LPs but as yet have only had one transatlantic Top 10.

WORD UP *(18th UK single)*	3	27 SEP 86	CLUB
WORD UP	6	22 NOV 86	ATLANTA ART

ANDY CAMERON

Scottish entertainer who had a one-off chart record with his own song which was a tribute to the Scottish soccer team.

ALLY'S TARTAN ARMY	6	01 APR 78	KLUB

GLEN CAMPBELL

Top early 60s guitar and vocals session man turned country star. He played on many hits and sang on chart records for The Beach Boys and The Crickets. As a soloist he recorded for Capeheart, Ceneco and first charted on Crest in 61. It was not until 67 (69 UK) that his decade as one of the world's top MOR acts started. He is still a country chart regular with over 70 hits to his credit.

WICHITA LINEMAN	7	08 MAR 69	EMBER
ALL I HAVE TO DO IS DREAM			
(With BOBBIE GENTRY)			
(Everly Brothers 58 hit)	3	17 JAN 70	CAPITOL
HONEY COME BACK *(US No. 19)*	4	06 JUN 70	CAPITOL
IT'S ONLY MAKE BELIEVE *(Conway Twitty 58 hit)*	4	12 DEC 70	CAPITOL
RHINESTONE COWBOY	4	08 NOV 75	CAPITOL
(Original by Larry Weiss – US Top Country record 75)			
WICHITA LINEMAN	3	11 JAN 69	CAPITOL
GALVESTON *(UK No. 14)*	4	12 APR 69	CAPITOL
IT'S ONLY MAKE BELIEVE	10	31 OCT 70	CAPITOL
RHINESTONE COWBOY	1(2)	06 SEP 75	CAPITOL
SOUTHERN NIGHTS	1(1)	30 APR 77	CAPITOL

JUNIOR CAMPBELL

William 'Junior' Campbell was a member of UK hitmakers Marmalade. His first solo fell by the wayside but he did achieve two UK-only Top 20s, the other being' 'Sweet Illusion' (15). He also recorded for Rocket in 76.

HALLELUJAH FREEDOM	10	11 NOV 72	DERAM

CANNED HEAT

Much respected L.A. blues/rock quartet led by huge singer and blues buff Bob Hite. Discovered at the Monterey Pop Festival in 67 they were equally popular in US & UK until the end of the blues boom in the early 70s. The act later recorded with John Lee Hooker, Little Richard and even The Chipmunks. Sadly key members Hite and Al Wilson died.

ON THE ROAD AGAIN *(US No. 16)*	8	21 SEP 68	LIBERTY
LET'S WORK TOGETHER	2	21 FEB 70	LIBERTY
(US No. 26 – Original by Wilburt Harrison)			

FREDDY CANNON

Before 59 Boston born Freddy Picariello worked as Freddy Carmen (his label changed his name without asking) and did session work which included playing on The G-Clef's first hit. For a few years the hits rolled in for 'Boom Boom' as he was known and he last charted (US) in 81 in a duet with The Belmonts (Mia sound).

WAY DOWN YONDER IN NEW ORLEANS	3	12 FEB 60	TOP RANK
(Peerless Quartet 22 hit)			
TALLAHASSEE LASSIE	6	28 JUN 59	SWAN
(UK No. 17 – written by his mother)			
WAY DOWN YONDER IN NEW ORLEANS	3	11 JAN 60	SWAN
PALISADES PARK	3	23 JUN 62	SWAN
(UK No. 22 – composed Chuck Barris, US TV host)			

JIM CAPALDI

Singing drummer with UK band Traffic. In the US his highest chart record was 'That's Love' (28). He later recorded for Polydor, RSO, Carrerre and WEA.

LOVE HURTS *(US No. 97)*	4	29 NOV 75	ISLAND

Also see Traffic

CAPITOLS

Detroit soul group led by Sam George. Their big US hit was written by member Don Norman and was originally intended as the 'B' side. They later tried unsuccessfully to repeat the formula with records like 'Cool Pearl' and 'Cool Jerk 68'. Sam was murdered in 82.

🇺🇸	COOL JERK *(Released in UK as by 3 Caps)*	7	02 JUL 66	KAREN

CAPRIS

The New York group (led by Nick Santamaria) recorded on Sabre and then Planet where they first cut their big hit in 58. It flopped then and the group broke up in 59. It was re-discovered in 61 and was a US smash so the group re-united and had a few small hits. They re-appeared again in 82 and cut 'There's a Moon Out Again' on Ambient Sound.

🇺🇸	THERE'S A MOON OUT TONIGHT	3	27 FEB 61	OLD TOWN

TONY CAPSTICK

Sheffield (UK) entertainer/comedian/actor who had previously had folk albums released on Rubber had a double sided UK one-off hit. One side was his version of a Hovis TV advert and the other featured The Carlton Main Frickley Colliery band.

🇬🇧	CAPSTICK COMES HOME/SHEFFIELD GRINDER *(Jumped from 54-10 in one week)*	3	04 APR 81	DINGLES

CAPTAIN & TENNILLE

The Captain (Daryl Dragon) met his future wife (Toni) Tennille whilst on tour in The Beach Boys band. Their first release 'The Way I Want To Touch You' failed first time around, but their next single became the first of 14 US chart hits before Alabama born Toni went solo in 80 – so far without success.

🇬🇧	DO THAT TO ME ONE MORE TIME	7	15 MAR 80	CASABLANCA
🇺🇸	LOVE WILL KEEP US TOGETHER *(UK No. 32 – Comp. Neil Sedaka – Grammy Record of Year)*	1(4)	21 JUN 75	A&M
	THE WAY I WANT TO TOUCH YOU *(UK No. 28)*	4	29 NOV 75	A&M
	LONELY NIGHT (ANGEL FACE)	3	27 MAR 76	A&M
	SHOP AROUND *(Miracles 60 US hit)*	4	10 JUL 76	A&M
	MUSKRAT LOVE	4	20 NOV 76	A&M
	YOU NEVER DONE IT LIKE THAT *(UK No. 63)*	10	18 NOV 78	A&M
	DO THAT TO ME ONE MORE TIME	1(1)	16 FEB 80	CASABLANCA

CAPTAIN SENSIBLE

Member of Johnny Moped and Nick Kent's Subterraneans before becoming bassist with punk stars The Damned. Born Ray Burns in Croydon he had a smash with a song from South Pacific. He was also on Poker (78), Crass (81), Animus (86) and Deltic (88).

🇬🇧	HAPPY TALK *(Jumped from 33-1 – a UK record)*	1(2)	03 JUL 82	A&M
	GLAD IT'S ALL OVER/DAMNED ON 45	6	14 APR 84	A&M

Also see The Damned

IRENE CARA

New York born actress/singer/dancer/composer and musician who debuted on Broadway aged 8. She starred in Roots, Fame and The Cotton Club and has an enviable transatlantic track record. Oddly the film theme Fame did not sell in the UK until the TV series started. After legal battles she joined Elektra in 87.

🇬🇧	FAME *(Song originally called 'Let' – jumped from 51-4)*	1(3)	17 JUL 82	RSO
	FLASHDANCE....WHAT A FEELING *(From the film 'Flashdance' – Academy Award winner)*	2	09 JUL 83	CASABLANCA
🇺🇸	FAME	4	13 SEP 80	RSO
	FLASHDANCE....WHAT A FEELING	1(6)	28 MAY 83	CASABLANCA
	BREAKDANCE	8	09 JUN 84	GEFFEN

CARAVELLES

London based female duo Lois Lane (Wilkinson) and Andrea Simpson who were named after a French plane. They beat The Beatles to the US Top 10 in 64 (year of the British invasion) but unlike them they never returned. US follow up was another oldie 'Have You Ever Been Lonely'. They were later on Fontana, Polydor and Pye.

🇬🇧	YOU DON'T HAVE TO BE A BABY TO CRY *(Tennessee Ernie Ford 56 US hit)*	6	06 SEP 63	DECCA
🇺🇸	YOU DON'T HAVE TO BE A BABY TO CRY	3	21 DEC 63	SMASH

BELINDA CARLISLE

L.A. born ex member of the first really successful girl rock group The Go-Go's. Her initial solo project gave her instant fame in the US and 18 months later she had a transatlantic topper and a Top 10 trio of singles from her 'Heaven On Earth' LP.

🇬🇧	HEAVEN IS A PLACE ON EARTH *(On track were Thomas Dolby and Michelle Phillips)*	1(2)	16 JAN 88	VIRGIN
	I GET WEAK	10	26 MAR 88	VIRGIN
	CIRCLE IN THE SAND	4	04 JUN 88	VIRGIN
	LEAVE A LIGHT ON	4	28 OCT 89	VIRGIN
🇺🇸	MAD ABOUT YOU *(UK No. 67 in 88)*	3	09 AUG 86	IRS
	HEAVEN IS A PLACE ON EARTH	1(1)	05 DEC 87	MCA
	I GET WEAK	2	19 MAR 88	MCA
	CIRCLE IN THE SAND	7	18 JUN 88	MCA

Also see The Go-Go's

CARL CARLTON

First recorded at 12 as 'Little' Carl Carlton on local Detroit labels Lando and Golden World and first hit on Backbeat at 16 in 68. He has had 20 black music hits including this version of a Robert Knight hit, produced by Knight's producer Bobby Russell. He was later on Mercury, 20th Century, RCA and Casablanca.

🇺🇸	EVERLASTING LOVE	6	23 NOV 74	ABC

ERIC CARMEN

Cleveland (US) born singer/songwriter. First recorded for Epic in 70 then joined local group The Choir who became The Raspberries and had US hits up to Eric's departure in 75. He scored three US Top 20s before 78 and wrote big hits for Sean Cassidy and Reno & Wilson. He returned to the top in 88 thanks to Dirty Dancing.

🇺🇸	ALL BY MYSELF *(UK No. 12)* *(Based on Rachmaninov's Piano Concerto No. 2)*	2	06 MAR 76	ARISTA
	HUNGRY EYES *(From the film 'Dirty Dancing')*	4	13 FEB 88	RCA
	MAKE ME LOSE CONTROL	3	13 AUG 88	ARISTA

Also see The Raspberries

KIM CARNES

Hollywood born singer once worked in The New Christy Minstrels with Kenny Rogers (they later had hit duets together). This distinctive vocalist recorded on Amos in 71, A&M in 75 and Ariola in 79 before hitting on EMI. Apart from Kenny she has also had chart duets with Barbra Streisand, Gene Cotton and James Ingram.

🇬🇧	BETTE DAVIS EYES *(Originally by composer Jackie De Shannon)*	10	23 MAY 81	EMI AM.
🇺🇸	DON'T FALL IN LOVE WITH A DREAMER *(With KENNY ROGERS)*	4	24 MAY 80	UA
	MORE LOVE *(Miracles 67 US hit)*	10	16 AUG 80	EMI AM.
	BETTE DAVIS EYES *(Top US record 81 & Grammy winner Top Single year)*	1(9)	16 MAY 81	EMI AM.

CARPENTERS

This ultra-successful New Haven duo recorded on the Magic Lamp label and on RCA in 66 as The Richard Carpenter Trio. After a spell under the name Spectrum, Richard and his sister Karen signed to A&M and became the best loved pop/MOR duo of the 70s in both the US & UK selling millions of LPs and singles on the way. Karen died from a heart attack resulting from anorexia in 83.

	(THEY LONG TO BE) CLOSE TO YOU	6	10 OCT 70	A&M
	GOODBYE TO LOVE/I WON'T LAST A DAY			
	WITHOUT YOU	9	11 NOV 72	A&M
	YESTERDAY ONCE MORE	2	18 AUG 73	A&M
	TOP OF THE WORLD	5	10 NOV 73	A&M
	PLEASE MR POSTMAN (Marvelettes 61 US hit)	2	15 FEB 75	A&M
	ONLY YESTERDAY	7	17 MAY 75	A&M
	CALLING OCCUPANTS OF INTERPLANETARY CRAFT	9	12 NOV 77	A&M
	(US No. 32 – Klaatu 77 US hit)			
	(THEY LONG TO BE) CLOSE TO YOU	1(4)	25 JUL 70	A&M
	WE'VE ONLY JUST BEGUN (UK No. 28)	2	31 OCT 70	A&M
	(Song was an advert for Crocker Bank)			
	FOR ALL WE KNOW	3	13 MAR 71	A&M
	(Composed by Royer & Griffin of Bread)			
	RAINY DAYS AND MONDAYS	2	19 JUN 71	A&M
	SUPERSTAR (UK No. 18)	2	16 OCT 71	A&M
	HURTING EACH OTHER	2	26 FEB 72	A&M
	GOODBYE TO LOVE	7	26 AUG 72	A&M
	SING	3	21 APR 73	A&M
	YESTERDAY ONCE MORE	2	28 JUL 73	A&M
	TOP OF THE WORLD	1(2)	01 DEC 73	A&M
	PLEASE MR. POSTMAN	1(1)	25 JAN 75	A&M
	ONLY YESTERDAY	4	24 MAY 75	A&M

VIKKI CARR

Born Florencia Bisenta De Casillas Martinez Cardona in Texas she first sang with The Pepe Callahan Mexican-Irish band in L.A. She recorded the first version of 'He's A Rebel' and success first came in Australia and then in the UK. Her emotive style of singing gave her a few more minor US hits in the late 60s.

	IT MUST BE HIM	2	29 JUL 67	LIBERTY
	IT MUST BE HIM	3	04 NOV 67	LIBERTY

RAFFAELLA CARRA

Top Italian TV star scored a UK hit with an Italian 'B' side which had previously topped the French chart. Her UK follow up was 'California'.

	DO IT AGAIN	9	27 MAY 78	EPIC

PAUL CARRACK

Sheffield (UK) born Paul was in Warm Dust, sang on hits with Ace ('How Long') and Squeeze ('Tempted') and had been in Roxy Music and The Frankie Miller Band before getting his US Top 10 solo hit. After a few more US solo chart records he went to the top again as the singer on Mike & The Mechanics 89 hits. He also returned to the US Top 40 in 89 as a solo artist.

	DON'T SHED A TEAR (No. 60 UK in 89)	9	13 FEB 88	CHRYSALIS

Also see Ace/Mike & The Mechanics

RONNIE CARROLL

Belfast born ballad singer, who normally covered US hits, got his start as an impersonator in the show Hollywood Doubles and had the first of four UK-only Top 20s with 'Walk Hand In Hand' in 56.

	ROSES ARE RED	2	31 AUG 62	PHILIPS
	(Entered at No. 9 – Bobby Vinton 62 US hit)			
	SAY WONDERFUL THINGS	5	05 APR 63	PHILIPS
	(US No. 91 – UK's Eurovision entry)			

JASPER CARROTT

Birmingham (UK) comic and major UK TV star has sold a lot of LPs in the UK and had a one-off hit with a double sided comedy record (The 'B' side was banned).

	FUNKY MOPED/MAGIC ROUNDABOUT	5	20 SEP 75	DJM

CARS

Boston (US) band evolved from the group Cap'n Swing in 76. First LP 'Cars', recorded in the UK, launched their transatlantic chart career, which included as many awards for videos as records. Singers Ric Ocasek and Ben Orr, who had previously recorded in the folk trio Milkwood on Paramount in 72, have also had solo hits.

	MY BEST FRIEND'S GIRL (US No. 35)	3	25 NOV 78	ELEKTRA
	(Entered at No. 10 – was the first UK picture disc)			
	DRIVE	5	13 OCT 84	ELEKTRA
	DRIVE	4	31 AUG 85	ELEKTRA
	(Royalties from this re-issue went to 'Live Aid')			
	SHAKE IT UP	4	27 FEB 82	ELEKTRA
	YOU MIGHT THINK	7	28 APR 84	ELEKTRA
	(It won the first International Music Video Award)			
	DRIVE	3	29 SEP 84	ELEKTRA
	TONIGHT SHE COMES	7	11 JAN 86	ELEKTRA

CLARENCE CARTER

Blind soul/blues singer from Alabama first recorded in 61 as part of duo Clarence & Calvin (Scott). Duo also recorded as The C & C Boys and The Soul Brothers on Fairlane, Duke and Atco. His first solo hit was 'Tell Daddy' in 67 and he has had 22 black music hits since on Atlantic, Fame, ABC, Venture and in 89 on Ichiban.

	PATCHES	2	31 OCT 70	ATLANTIC
	(Originally by Chairmen of The Board)			
	SLIP AWAY	6	05 OCT 68	ATLANTIC
	PATCHES	4	19 SEP 70	ATLANTIC

MEL CARTER

Cincinnatti born black ballad singer who specialised in updating oldies. He recorded for Arwin, Mercury, Philips and Derby (Sam Cooke's own label) before getting the first of his three US-only Top 40s. He appeared less successfully on Peacock, Bell, Amos, Private Stock and Cream.

	HOLD ME THRILL ME KISS ME	8	28 AUG 65	IMPERIAL
	(Karen Chandler 53 US hit)			

CASCADES

San Diego quintet whose second release on Valiant, composed by their leader John Gummoe, was a Transatlantic Top 10 hit. They later recorded on RCA, Charter, Liberty, Arwin, Smash, ABC Probe, UNI, Canbase, London and Renee but never hit the heights again.

	RHYTHM OF THE RAIN	4	12 APR 63	WARNER
	RHYTHM OF THE RAIN	3	09 MAR 63	VALIANT

JOHNNY CASH

'The Man In Black' is the world's best known country singer. First recorded for Sun in 55 and has had a staggering 129 country and 50 US pop hits (6 in UK). He is a member of the Country Music Hall of Fame, has had a highway named after him, had a top rated TV series, travelled the world as an ambassador for country music, beaten drugs and fathered country star Rosanne Cash.

	A BOY NAMED SUE (original by Shel Silverstein)	4	04 OCT 69	CBS
	A THING CALLED LOVE (original by Jerry Reed)	4	13 MAY 72	CBS
	(With The Evangel Temple Choir)			
	A BOY NAMED SUE	2	23 AUG 69	COLUMBIA

CASINOS

Nine man act from Cincinnatti fronted by Gene Hughes. Debut single 'The Gallup' stalled but their next record gave them their only Top 40 hit. Gene went solo unsuccessfully and is now a well known music business personality in Nashville.

 THEN YOU CAN TELL ME GOODBYE   6   25 FEB 67   FRATERN.
(UK No. 28 – Original by Johnny Nash)

MAMA CASS

The heavyweight member of the million selling quartet The Mamas & The Papas was born Ellen Cohen in Baltimore. Her biggest US chart record was 'Dream A Little Dream of Me' (US 12/UK 11). She died prematurely in London in 74.

 IT'S GETTING BETTER *(US No. 30)*   8   04 OCT 69   STATESIDE

Also see Mamas & The Papas

DAVID CASSIDY

New York born singer/actor and star of The Partridge Family. He was the No. 1 transatlantic pin-up of his time with his career taking off in the UK as it was fading in the US. He later recorded for RCA in 75 and MCA in 79 and in 85 returned to the UK Top Ten. He also starred in the musical Time.

COULD IT BE FOREVER/CHERISH *(US No. 37)*	2	27 MAY 72	BELL
HOW CAN I BE SURE	1(2)	30 SEP 72	BELL
(US No. 25 – Young Rascals 67 US hit)			
I'M A CLOWN/SOME KIND OF A SUMMER	3	14 APR 73	BELL
DAYDREAMER/THE PUPPY SONG	1(3)	27 OCT 73	BELL
IF I DIDN'T CARE	9	01 JUN 74	BELL
(Ink Spots 39 hit – Entered at No. 8)			
THE LAST KISS	6	16 MAR 85	ARISTA
(Above three not charted in US)			
CHERISH *(Association 66 US hit)*	9	25 DEC 71	BELL

Also see The Partridge Family

SHAUN CASSIDY

David Cassidy's younger half-brother and son of The Partridge Family's Shirley Jones. Starring in the popular TV series The Hardy Boys helped start his equally successful US-only singing career. He joined the soap opera General Hospital in 87.

DA DOO RON RON *(Crystals 63 hit)*	1(1)	16 JUL 77	WARNER
THAT'S ROCK 'N' ROLL	3	22 OCT 77	WARNER
HEY DEANIE *(Last two composed Eric Carmen)*	7	14 JAN 78	WARNER

JIMMY CASTOR BUNCH

Jimmy replaced fellow New Yorker Frankie Lymon in The Teenagers in 57. He recorded on Jet Set, Smash, Compass, Decca and Capitol before getting the first of two US-only Top 20s with his group. Act has also been on Atlantic, Cotillion, Salsoul, Long Distance, Dream, Sleeping Bag, CFM, Catawba and CBS.

TROGLODYTE (CAVE MAN)	6	24 JUN 72	RCA

CASUALS

UK quartet fronted by Alan Taylor won UK TV talent show Opportunity Knocks three times and had some success in Italy before scoring in their homeland. They were voted most promising UK group of 68. They followed their UK hit with 'Toy'.

JESAMINE *(Act called British Casuals in US)*	2	19 OCT 68	DECCA

CERRONE

French born composer/musician/producer Jean-Marc Cerrone had a transatlantic Top 40 in 77 with 'Love In C Minor', from his million selling French LP of the same name. He followed it in 78 with his biggest single; vocalists on which included UK hit act Stephanie DeSykes and Blue Mink's Madeline Bell.

SUPERNATURE *(US No. 70)*	8	26 AUG 78	ATLANTIC

PETER CETERA

Chicago born, ex lead singer of the very popular group Chicago since their inception. Though he had recorded solo previously he did not leave the group until 85 and he then collected two US No. 1s by the end of 86.

GLORY OF LOVE *(From film 'Karate Kid 11')*	3	20 SEP 86	FULL MOON
GLORY OF LOVE	1(2)	02 AUG 86	FULL MOON
THE NEXT TIME I FALL *(And AMY GRANT)*	1(1)	06 DEC 86	FULL MOON
ONE GOOD WOMAN	4	01 OCT 88	FULL MOON
AFTER ALL *(With CHER)*	6	13 MAY 89	GEFFEN
(From the film 'Chances Are')			

Also see Chicago

CHAD & JEREMY

Between 64 & 66 the UK folk/rock duo Chad Stuart & Jeremy Clyde had 11 US hits yet never charted in their homeland. They broke up in 67 and Chad recorded on Sidewalk before going back into acting. In 89 Jeremy was seen in the UK TV series William Tell.

A SUMMER SONG	7	17 OCT 64	WORLD ARTIST

CHAIRMEN OF THE BOARD

Detroit quartet featuring the unmistakable voice of Norman 'General' Johnson , the ex leader of The Showman ('It Will Stand') and solo artist. They were equally popular on both sides of the Atlantic and helped establish Holland, Dozier & Holland's Invictus label. Norman also wrote the Clarence Carter hit 'Patches' (released as a 'B' side by them).

GIVE ME JUST A LITTLE MORE TIME	3	19 SEP 70	INVICTUS
YOU'VE GOT ME DANGLING ON A STRING	5	05 DEC 70	INVICTUS
(US No. 38)			
GIVE ME JUST A LITTLE MORE TIME	3	21 MAR 70	INVICTUS

CHAKACHAS

Belgian group led by Gaston Boogaerts had a one-off hit with this Disco novelty. They re-recorded it unsuccessfully as 'Jungle Fever 75' on Polydor.

JUNGLE FEVER *(UK No. 29)*	8	25 MAR 72	POLYDOR

RICHARD CHAMBERLAIN

TV's Dr. Kildare was equally popular in the US & UK in 62/63. He also had a transatlantic Top 20 with 'Love Me Tender' (UK 15/US 21) and he is still a top international TV actor.

THEME FROM DOCTOR KILDARE			
(THREE STARS WILL SHINE TONIGHT) *(UK No.11)*	10	04 AUG 62	MGM

CHAMPAIGN

Septet from Champaign, Illinois, had a Transatlantic Top 20 hit in 81 and returned to the US Top 40 two years later with 'Try Again' (23). Vocalist Paulie Carman recorded solo and had some black music chart entries in 86.

HOW 'BOUT US *(US No. 12)*	5	20 JUN 81	CBS

GENE CHANDLER

The biggest of the Chicago soul singer's 36 black music hits (over 24 years) was actually by The Dukays (Gene sang lead) but released under his name alone for contractual reasons. He finally made the UK Top 20 in 79 with 'Get Down' (UK 11/US 53).

 DUKE OF EARL (No. 29 UK)　　　　　1(3)　17 FEB 62　VEE JAY

BRUCE CHANNEL

Texan singer/songwriter who first recorded in the late 50s for King and Manco. He says his transatlantic Top 10 took 10 minutes to write and 13 to record. He returned to the UK Top 20 with 'Keep On' in 68 (12) and also recorded for Jamie in 73, Elektra in 80 and Le Cam in 85 and is now a top country writer.

 HEY! BABY　　　　　　　　　　　2　13 APR 62　MERCURY
(Also cut 'Come on Baby', 'Oh Baby' & 'No Other Baby')

HEY! BABY　　　　　　　　　　　1(3)　10 MAR 62　SMASH
(It was first released on Le Cam)

CHANTAYS

Teenage instrumental group from California led by Bob Spikard had a one-off transatlantic Top 10 hit (it was the first surf hit in the UK). Their unsuccessful follow up was 'Monsoon'.

 PIPELINE (UK No. 16)　　　　　　　4　04 MAY 63　DOT

HARRY CHAPIN

New York folk/rocker who started with his family's act The Chapins and first hit with 'Taxi' in 72. His only transatlantic Top 40 hit was 'W-O-L-D' (US 36/UK 34). He helped raise millions of dollars to help world hunger (long before Band Aid) and died in a car crash in 81.

CAT'S IN THE CRADLE　　　　　　1(1)　21 DEC 74　ELEKTRA

TRACY CHAPMAN

Unique black folk singer and ex-busker from Cleveland whose debut LP sold over 10 million worldwide, helped in part by her substituting for Stevie Wonder in the 88 UK Nelson Mandela concert. She has since won numerous awards including a Grammy and her second LP 'Crosssroads' was also a transatlantic Top 10 hit.

 FAST CAR　　　　　　　　　　　5　16 JUL 88　ELEKTRA
FAST CAR　　　　　　　　　　　6　27 AUG 88　ELEKTRA

CHARLENE

L.A. born Charlene Duncan joined Motown in 73 and was the first white act on that label to get a No. 1 – which she did with a re-release of a track that had peaked at 97 in the US five years earlier. She later had a small hit with 'Used To Be', a duet with Stevie Wonder. She also recorded for Ariola in 78.

I'VE NEVER BEEN TO ME　　　　　1(1)　26 JUN 82　MOTOWN
I'VE NEVER BEEN TO ME　　　　　3　22 MAY 82　MOTOWN

JIMMY CHARLES

When he was just 18 the New Jersey born singer had his sole US Top 40, which was composed by Phil Medley (of 'Twist & Shout' fame). Among his later recordings was the UK written Christmas standard 'I Saw Mommy Kissing Santa Claus'.

 A MILLION TO ONE (& The Revelletts)　5　26 SEP 60　PROMO

RAY CHARLES

Georgia born blind singer/musician and writer was the first pop act to be termed 'genius'. His first release in The Maxim Trio in 49 was a No. 2 R&B hit. Solo hits started in the mid 50's on Atlantic. In the 60s he was one of the top transatlantic black acts. He has notched up 74 US & 16 UK pop successes. He was in the USA For Africa group and now has regular country hits. He was featured on Quincy Jones Top 20 hit 'I'll be Good To You' in 90.

 HIT THE ROAD JACK (Comp. Percy Mayfield)　4　03 NOV 61　HMV
I CAN'T STOP LOVING YOU　　　　1(2)　11 JUL 62　HMV
(Don Gibson 58 US hit)
YOU DON'T KNOW ME (Eddy Arnold 56 US hit)　6　19 OCT 62　HMV
TAKE THESE CHAINS FROM MY HEART　4　21 JUN 63　HMV
(Hank Williams 53 Country hit)

WHAT'D I SAY (PT. 1) (His 22nd R&B hit)　6　16 AUG 59　ATLANTIC
GEORGIA ON MY MIND　　　　　1(1)　14 NOV 60　ABC-PARA
(UK No. 18 – Frankie Trumbauer 31 hit)
ONE MINT JULEP (Clovers 52 R&B hit)　8　01 MAY 61　IMPULSE
HIT THE ROAD JACK　　　　　　1(2)　09 OCT 61　ABC-PARA
UNCHAIN MY HEART　　　　　　9　13 JAN 62　ABC-PARA
I CAN'T STOP LOVING YOU　　　　1(5)　02 JUN 62　ABC-PARA
YOU DON'T KNOW ME　　　　　　2　08 SEP 62　ABC-PARA
YOU ARE MY SUNSHINE (Bing Crosby 41 hit)　7　29 DEC 62　ABC-PARA
TAKE THESE CHAINS FROM MY HEART　8　25 MAY 63　ABC-PARA
BUSTED　　　　　　　　　　　4　19 OCT 63　ABC-PARA
(UK No. 18 – Johnny Cash 63 Country hit)
CRYING TIME (UK No. 50 – Buck Owens song)　6　19 FEB 66　ABC-PARA

RAY CHARLES SINGERS

Conductor and arranger from Chicago who worked on TV shows like those of Perry Como and Glen Campbell. He scored one major US hit which he followed with another Italian song 'Al-Di-La'.

LOVE ME WITH ALL YOUR HEART　　3　13 JUN 64　COMMAND

TINA CHARLES

UK's pop disco queen of 76 had three UK-only Top 10s with producer/composer Biddu. She cut her first single at 16 (Elton John was on it) in 70, was a member of Wild Honey (73), sang on cover version LPs and sang lead vocal on 5,000 Volts first hit. She was also on Bell, Mam, Polydor and Sonet/Typhoon.

I LOVE TO LOVE (BUT MY BABY LOVES TO DANCE)　1(3)　06 MAR 76　CBS
DANCE LITTLE LADY DANCE　　　　6　02 OCT 76　CBS
DR. LOVE　　　　　　　　　　　4　22 JAN 77　CBS

CHAS & DAVE

Cockney duo of Chas Hodges (ex Heads, Hands & Feet and Cliff Bennett's Band) and Dave Peacock mix old music hall and pub sounds with rock, which they dub 'Rockney'. Always a popular club/pub act they have had a string of UK-only hits, not only as a duet but also with UK soccer and snooker stars.

RABBIT　　　　　　　　　　　8　17 JAN 81　ROCKNEY
AIN'T NO PLEASING YOU　　　　　2　17 APR 82　ROCKNEY
SNOOKER LOOPY (With The Matchroom Mob)　6　24 MAY 86　ROCKNEY

Also see Tottenham Hotspur

CHEAP TRICK

Illinois quartet fronted by Rick Nielsen and Robin Zander. Rick started in 61 in groups like The Phaetons, Boyz, Grim Reapers, Fuse (on Epic in 69) and Sick Man of Europe. This act formed in 74, first recorded for Epic in 77 and hit in Japan first. They had two hot spells one in the late 70s and one a decade later.

I WANT YOU TO WANT ME (UK No. 29)　7　21 JUL 79　EPIC
THE FLAME　　　　　　　　　　1(2)　09 JUL 88　EPIC
DON'T BE CRUEL (Elvis Presley 56 hit)　4　08 OCT 88　EPIC

CHUBBY CHECKER

Philadelphia born (real name Ernest Evans) singer first charted in 59 with 'The Class', a record of impersonations. After a couple of flops he revived Hank Ballard's 'The Twist' which became the first of a string of 35 US hits (many being dance songs), the latest being in 88. After Elvis, he was the first successful rock LP act and in one week had four LPs in the Top 12.

THE TWIST (Hank Ballard 59 R&B hit)	9	19 JAN 62	COLUMBIA
LET'S TWIST AGAIN	1(2)	21 FEB 62	COLUMBIA
(Hit a few times in UK on chart 44 weeks)			
LET'S TWIST AGAIN (Re-issue)	5	27 DEC 75	LONDON
THE TWIST (YO, TWIST) (With THE FAT BOYS)	2	02 JUL 88	POLY/URBAN
(US. No. 19)			
THE TWIST	1(1)	19 SEP 60	PARKWAY
PONY TIME (Goodtimers 60 US hit)	1(3)	27 FEB 61	PARKWAY
LET'S TWIST AGAIN	8	07 AUG 61	PARKWAY
THE FLY	7	13 NOV 61	PARKWAY
THE TWIST (Only record to top US chart twice)	1(2)	13 JAN 62	PARKWAY
SLOW TWISTIN' (With DEE DEE SHARPE – UK No.19)	3	14 APR 62	PARKWAY
POPEYE (THE HITCHHIKER)	10	10 NOV 62	PARKWAY
LIMBO ROCK (UK 29 – Champs 62 US hit)	2	22 DEC 62	PARKWAY

CHEECH & CHONG

L.A. based rock comedians Richard 'Cheech' Marin and Thomas Chong, (ex of Bobby Taylor & The Vancouvers). They had a handful of US-only hit singles & LPs (3 Top 5). They also made several movies and were later on Epic in 77, Warner in 78 and MCA in 85.

EARACHE MY EYE – (Featuring ALICE BOWIE)	9	05 OCT 74	ODE

CHELSEA F.C.

London soccer team had a one-off UK hit. They were the first non-International side to make the Top 10.

BLUE IS THE COLOUR	5	11 MAR 72	PENNY F.

CHER

Born Cherilyn LaPierre she has been a transatlantic superstar for over two decades. As a session singer she recorded under many names for Phil Spector before teaming with Sonny Bono. Her second solo 45 scored and she has had many hits and misses since then in the US & UK. She also found fame as a TV star and movie actress and returned to the charts in 89 as hot as ever before.

ALL I REALLY WANT TO DO (Bob Dylan song)	9	11 SEP 65	LIBERTY
BANG BANG (MY BABY SHOT ME DOWN)	3	07 MAY 66	LIBERTY
GYPSIES TRAMPS AND THIEVES	4	04 DEC 71	MCA
(Song originally 'Gypsies & White Trash')			
I FOUND SOMEONE	5	16 JAN 88	GEFFEN
(Written & produced by Michael Bolton)			
IF I COULD TURN BACK TIME	6	28 OCT 89	GEFFEN
(The female record span of UK Top 10 hits)			
BANG BANG (MY BABY SHOT ME DOWN)	2	23 APR 66	IMPERIAL
YOU BETTER SIT DOWN KIDS	9	23 DEC 67	IMPERIAL
GYPSYS TRAMPS & THIEVES	1(2)	06 NOV 71	KAPP
THE WAY OF LOVE	7	25 MAR 72	KAPP
HALF-BREED	1(2)	06 OCT 73	MCA
DARK LADY (UK No. 36)	1(1)	23 MAR 74	MCA
TAKE ME HOME	8	12 MAY 79	CASABLANCA
I FOUND SOMEONE	10	05 MAR 88	GEFFEN
AFTER ALL (And PETER CETERA)	6	13 MAY 89	GEFFEN
(From the film 'Chances Are')			
IF I COULD TURN BACK TIME	3	23 SEP 89	GEFFEN
JUST LIKE JESSE JAMES (UK No. 11)	8	23 DEC 89	GEFFEN

Also see Sonny & Cher

CHERRELLE

Born Cheryl Norton in L.A., the cousin of fellow chart star Pebbles. She has also had solo transatlantic single and LP success (produced by Jam & Lewis) and recorded the original version of Robert Palmer's hit 'I Didn't Mean To Turn You On'.

SATURDAY LOVE (And ALEXANDER O'NEAL)	6	18 JAN 86	TABU
(US No. 26 – entered UK Dance chart at No. 1)			

NENEH CHERRY

Daughter of US jazz man Don Cherry, worked in the UK with bands like The Slits, Rip Rig & Panic, Morgan McVey, The The and GMC. An old Morgan McVey 'B' side about the Buffalo design company, when remixed by Tim Simenon of Bomb The Bass, became her first hit. She was a double winner at the 90 BRITS awards.

BUFFALO STANCE	3	14 JAN 89	CIRCA
MANCHILD	5	03 JUN 89	CIRCA
BUFFALO STANCE	3	24 JUN 89	VIRGIN
KISSES ON THE WIND (UK No. 20)	8	30 SEP 89	VIRGIN

CHIC

New York group formed by Nile Rodgers and Bernard Edwards, both previously in The Big Apple Band, became one of the hottest and most influential dance acts of the 70's with smashes on both sides of the Atlantic. Nile and Bernard went on to become two of the top producers of the 80s. Top soul star Luther Vandross sang on their first three LPs.

DANCE DANCE DANCE (YOWSAH YOWSAH YOWSAH)	6	14 JAN 78	ATLANTIC
EVERYBODY DANCE (US No. 38)	9	13 MAY 78	ATLANTIC
LE FREAK	7	16 DEC 78	ATLANTIC
(A re-mix as 'Jack Le Freak' No. 19 UK in 87)			
I WANT YOUR LOVE	4	07 APR 79	ATLANTIC
GOOD TIMES (Song used in 'Rappers Delight')	5	21 JUL 79	ATLANTIC
DANCE,DANCE,DANCE (YOWSAH YOWSAH YOWSAH)	6	25 FEB 78	ATLANTIC
LE FREAK	1(6)	09 DEC 78	ATLANTIC
I WANT YOUR LOVE	7	05 MAY 79	ATLANTIC
GOOD TIMES (Top US Soul Record 79)	1(1)	18 AUG 79	ATLANTIC

CHICAGO

Chicago based act were the 70s most popular jazz/rock group and with some style changes became a top AOR act in the 80s. They started as Big Thing, changed to Chicago Transit Authority which they then shortened. They have had 18 Gold LPs with five making No.1 in the US and 44 US chart singles (7 in UK). Singer Peter Cetera has had a successful solo career.

I'M A MAN (Spencer Davis 67 hit)	8	07 FEB 70	CBS
25 OR 6 TO 4	7	29 AUG 70	CBS
IF YOU LEAVE ME NOW	1(3)	13 NOV 76	CBS
HARD TO SAY I'M SORRY	4	09 OCT 82	FULL MOON
(From the film 'Summer Lovers')			
HARD HABIT TO BREAK	8	24 NOV 84	FULL MOON
MAKE ME SMILE	9	06 JUN 70	COLUMBIA
25 OR 6 TO 4	4	12 SEP 70	COLUMBIA
DOES ANYBODY REALLY KNOW WHAT TIME	7	09 JAN 71	COLUMBIA
BEGINNINGS/COLOUR MY WORLD	7	14 AUG 71	COLUMBIA
SATURDAY IN THE PARK	3	23 SEP 72	COLUMBIA
FEELIN' STRONGER EVERY DAY	10	18 AUG 73	COLUMBIA
JUST YOU 'N' ME	4	08 DEC 73	COLUMBIA
(I'VE BEEN) SEARCHIN' SO LONG	9	11 MAY 74	COLUMBIA
CALL ON ME	6	10 AUG 74	COLUMBIA
OLD DAYS	5	07 JUN 75	COLUMBIA
IF YOU LEAVE ME NOW	1(2)	23 OCT 76	COLUMBIA
BABY WHAT A BIG SURPRISE (UK No. 41)	4	03 DEC 77	COLUMBIA
HARD TO SAY I'M SORRY	1(2)	11 SEP 82	FULL MOON
HARD HABIT TO BREAK	3	20 OCT 84	FULL MOON
YOU'RE THE INSPIRATION (UK No. 14)	3	19 JAN 85	FULL MOON
WILL YOU STILL LOVE ME	3	21 FEB 87	WARNER
I DON'T WANNA LIVE WITHOUT YOUR LOVE	3	30 AUG 88	REPRISE
LOOK AWAY (Top US single of 89)	1(2)	10 DEC 88	REPRISE
YOU'RE NOT ALONE	10	25 MAR 89	REPRISE

Also see Peter Cetera

CHICORY TIP

Kent (UK) pop quartet, led by Peter Hewson, recorded tracks like 'I Love Onions' in 71 before the biggest of their three UK Top 20s gave composer Giorgio Moroder his first UK & US chart record.

 **SON OF MY FATHER** (US No. 91)   1(3)   19 FEB 72   CBS
(Act called CHICORY in US – Orig. by Giorgio Moroder)

CHIFFONS

Female quartet from the Bronx led by Judy Craig. Recorded for Big Tree in 60, Reprise in 62, and Wildcat in 62, before having a handful of hits. Their biggest hit inspired George Harrison to write 'My Sweet Lord' (which they recorded in 75). They were later on Rust (as The 4 Pennies), B.T. Puppy, Buddah and Groove.

 **SWEET TALKIN' GUY** (US hit 6 years before)   4   22 APR 72   LONDON
HE'S SO FINE (No. 11 UK)   1(4)   30 MAR 63   LAURIE
ONE FINE DAY   5   13 JUL 63   LAURIE
(Originally written by Carole King for Little Eva)
SWEET TALKIN' GUY   10   25 JUN 66   LAURIE

CHILD

Photogenic teenage UK group with lead singer Graham Bilbrough and twins Tim and Keith Attack who achieved three UK-only chart records.

IT'S ONLY MAKE BELIEVE   10   02 SEP 78   ARIOLA HANS
(Conway Twitty 58 hit)

CHI-LITES

Chicago Soul quartet, who were first known as The Hi-Lites and Marshall & The Chi-Lites, recorded for Mercury, Revue, Daran, Biscayne, Ja-Wes and Blue Rock before getting real success. Act led by Marshall Thompson and Eugene Record was one of the top black acts of the early 70s and were especially popular in the UK.

HAVE YOU SEEN HER   3   19 FEB 71   MCA
HOMELY GIRL (US No. 54)   5   04 MAY 74   BRUNSWICK
TOO GOOD TO BE FORGOTTEN   10   30 NOV 74   BRUNSWICK
HAVE YOU SEEN HER/OH GIRL (Re-issue)   5   12 JUL 75   BRUNSWICK
IT'S TIME FOR LOVE (US No. 94)   5   18 OCT 75   BRUNSWICK
YOU DON'T HAVE TO GO   3   11 SEP 76   BRUNSWICK
HAVE YOU SEEN HER   3   11 DEC 71   BRUNSWICK
(They re-recorded it in 81 on 20th Century)
OH GIRL   1(1)   27 MAY 72   BRUNSWICK

CHINA CRISIS

Liverpool duo Gary Daly and Eddie Lundon first recorded for Inevitable in 82 and their second release 'Christian' was the first of four UK-only Top 20s. Their biggest LP to date 'Flaunt The Imperfection' was produced by Steely Dan's Walter Becker.

WISHFUL THINKING   9   28 JAN 84   VIRGIN

CHORDETTES

Female quartet from Wisconsin (US) started recording in 51, were regulars on The Arthur Godfrey show and became the first group on top TV show Bandstand. After a few flops they scored the first of their three Transatlantic Top 20s and had their last hit in 61. Member Janet later became Phil Everly's mother-in-law.

BORN TO BE WITH YOU   8   07 SEP 56   LONDON
LOLLIPOP (Original by Ronald & Ruby)   6   09 MAY 58   LONDON
MR. SANDMAN (UK No. 11)   1(7)   24 NOV 54   CADENCE
BORN TO BE WITH YOU   8   14 JUL 56   CADENCE
LOLLIPOP   2   31 MAR 58   CADENCE

CHRISTIANS

Garry, Russell and Roger Christian (now a soloist) teamed with singer/composer Henry Priestman and scored the first of their two UK-only Top 20s 'Ideal World' (14) in 87. In 89 they were part of the Liverpool group of stars who had a UK No. 1 with 'Ferry Cross The Mersey'.

HARVEST FOR THE WORLD (Isley Brothers 76 hit)   8   29 OCT 88   ISLAND

CHRISTIE

London based trio fronted by Jeff Christie had two UK Top 10s in a five month period with Jeff's song 'Yellow River' (subsequently used to advertise BT's Yellow Pages) topping charts around the world and selling three million. Despite this great start they quickly faded from the scene. Jeff went solo in 80.

YELLOW RIVER (US No. 23)   1(1)   06 JUN 70   CBS
SAN BERNADINO (US No. 100)   7   14 NOV 70   CBS

DAVID CHRISTIE

French based singer/songwriter had a one-off UK hit with this dance/novelty. He followed it with 'Our Time Has Come' and later recorded for Record Shack in 85 and Ocean in 88.

SADDLE UP   9   25 SEP 82   KR

LOU CHRISTIE

Born Lugee Sacco in Pennsylvania he first recorded in The Classics on Starr, then in Lugee & The Lions on Robee, before soloing on American Music Maker, World, HAC and C & C, where first hit 'The Gypsy Cried' was cut. He last charted in 74 but has recorded off and on since then, including duets with Lesley Gore and Pia Zadora and has recorded as Sacco on Lifesong.

I'M GONNA MAKE YOU MINE   2   01 NOV 69   BUDDAH
TWO FACES HAVE I   6   01 JUN 63   ROULETTE
(Written with mystic Twyla Herbert)
LIGHTNIN' STRIKES (UK No. 11)   1(1)   19 FEB 66   MGM
I'M GONNA MAKE YOU MINE   10   25 OCT 69   BUDDAH

TONY CHRISTIE

Born Tony Fitzgerald in Doncaster (UK) this cabaret artist scored five UK-only Top 40s in the early 70s. Amongst these was his version of Neil Sedaka's 'Is This The Way To Amarillo' (UK 18) which sold over a million worldwide. He recorded on A1 in 85.

I DID WHAT I DID FOR MARIA   2   12 JUN 71   MCA

GIGLIOLA CINQUETTI

Verona (Italy) born singer who had two UK-only Top 20s both thanks to the Eurovison song contest. In 64 she hit No. 17 with the contest winner 'Non Ho L'eta Per Amarti' and her biggest hit came with the 74 runner up song.

GO (BEFORE YOU BREAK MY HEART)   8   01 JUN 74   CBS

CITY BOY

Sextet from Birmingham (UK) featuring singer Lol Mason who were originally known as Back-In-The-Band. The group, who were produced by the acclaimed Robert 'Mutt' Lange, moved to the US after their hits there but split up shortly after.

5-7-0-5 (US No. 27)   8   19 AUG 78   VERTIGO

CLANNAD

Popular Irish folk group formed by the Bhraonain family in the early 70s (Clannad being Gaelic for family). The theme from a TV show gave them a UK hit and they returned to the UK Top 20 (with guest vocalist Bono (from U2) with 'In a Lifetime' (20 in 86 & 17 in 89). One time member Enya scored a solo UK No. 1 in 88.

THEME FROM HARRY'S GAME	5	20 NOV 82	RCA
(First Gaelic song in Top 10)			

JIMMY CLANTON

Fifties teen idol from Louisiana. His second release on New Orleans label Ace gave him the first of a trio of US Top 10s. He started as a member of The Rockets and in his career he made movies and also recorded on Drew-Blan (as Jimmy Dale), Vin, Philips, Mala, Imperial, Laurie, Spiral Staircase and Starfire.

JUST A DREAM *(Later cut 'Just a Moment')*	4	25 AUG 58	ACE
GO JIMMY GO	5	01 FEB 60	ACE
(Written as 'Go Bobby Go' for Bobby Rydell)			
VENUS IN BLUE JEANS	7	06 OCT 62	ACE
(Co-written by Neil Sedaka)			

ERIC CLAPTON

Best known UK rock guitarist. Played in The Roosters and Casey Jones & The Engineers, The Yardbirds, John Mayall's Bluesbreakers and the un-sung supergroup Powerhouse before launching the ultra-successful Cream, followed by the chart topping Blind Faith and another one-off act Derek & The Dominos. As a soloist he has been a regular transatlantic LP and single chart maker since 70.

I SHOT THE SHERIFF *(Originally by Bob Marley)*	9	17 AUG 74	RSO
I SHOT THE SHERIFF	1(1)	14 SEP 74	RSO
LAY DOWN SALLY	3	01 APR 78	RSO
(UK No. 39 and No. 26 Country chart)			
PROMISES *(UK No. 37)*	9	20 JAN 79	RSO
I CAN'T STAND IT	10	02 MAY 81	RSO

Also see Derek & The Dominos/Yardbirds/Cream

CLAUDINE CLARK

At 17 the Georgia soul singer cut her first 45 'Teenage Blues' with The Spinners on Herald. She was also on Gotham and as Joy Dawn on Swan, before her sole US hit. Follow up was 'Walk Me Home From The Party'. She was later on Jamie and TCF.

PARTY LIGHTS	5	01 SEP 62	CHANCELLOR

DAVE CLARK FIVE

Next to The Beatles, the UK's biggest act in the US in the early 60s (record for most appearances on Ed Sullivan Show). Dave had his first group in 58 and recorded on Piccadilly in 62. Their third single on Columbia was their only UK No. 1 and was the first of many transatlantic hit singles and LPs. Dave is now a successful dealer in rock videos and stage projects like Time.

GLAD ALL OVER	1(2)	18 JAN 64	COLUMBIA
BITS AND PIECES	2	14 MAR 64	COLUMBIA
CAN'T YOU SEE THAT SHE'S MINE	10	27 JUN 64	COLUMBIA
CATCH US IF YOU CAN *(From the film)*	5	14 AUG 65	COLUMBIA
EVERYBODY KNOWS	2	02 DEC 67	COLUMBIA
(US No. 43 – his second hit with the same title)			
RED BALLOON *(Original by Raymond Froggatt)*	7	12 OCT 68	COLUMBIA
GOOD OLD ROCK 'N' ROLL	7	24 JAN 70	COLUMBIA
(Cat Mother & The All Night Newsboys 69 US hit)			
EVERYBODY GET TOGETHER	8	28 MAR 70	COLUMBIA
(Youngbloods 67 US hit)			

GLAD ALL OVER	6	25 APR 64	EPIC
BITS AND PIECES	4	02 MAY 64	EPIC
CAN'T YOU SEE THAT SHE'S MINE	4	18 JUL 64	EPIC
BECAUSE	3	12 SEP 64	EPIC
I LIKE IT LIKE THAT *(Chris Kenner 61 US hit)*	7	07 AUG 65	EPIC
CATCH US IF YOU CAN	4	25 SEP 65	EPIC
OVER AND OVER)	1(1)	25 DEC 65	EPIC
(UK No. 45 – Bobby Day 58 US hit)			
YOU GOT WHAT IT TAKES	7	13 MAY 67	EPIC
(UK No. 28 – Marv Johnson 59 hit)			

DEE CLARK

Delecta Clark first recorded with Red Saunders Hambone Kids in 52 and then in The Goldentones, The Kool Gents, The Delegates and with The Upsetters (taking Little Richard's place). 'Nobody But You' his fourth solo was the first of 10 US hits. In the UK he debuted in the Top 20 in 75 with 'Ride A Wild Horse' (16).

RAINDROPS	2	26 JUN 61	VEE JAY
(He re-recorded it as 'Raindrops 73')			

PETULA CLARK

Surrey (UK) born singer/actress was a child protege, making her first film at 11 and first record at 16 in 49. She had a run of UK-only hits in the 50s and her work with Tony Hatch won her a Grammy and made her the top selling UK female act of the 60s in the US. She returned to the UK Top 10 in 88 giving her a UK Top 10 singles span of 34 years – a record for a UK act.

SUDDENLY THERE'S A VALLEY	7	06 JAN 56	PYE NIXA
(Gogi Grant 55 US hit)			
WITH ALL MY HEART *(Jody Sands 57 US hit)*	4	27 SEP 57	PYE NIXA
ALONE *(Shepherd Sisters 57 hit)*	8	13 DEC 57	PYE NIXA
SAILOR	2	03 FEB 61	PYE
(Entered at No. 6 – Lolita 61 US hit)			
ROMEO	4	18 AUG 61	PYE
DOWNTOWN	2	19 DEC 64	PYE
MY LOVE	4	05 MAR 66	PYE
I COULDN'T LIVE WITHOUT YOUR LOVE	6	30 JUL 66	PYE
THIS IS MY SONG	1(2)	16 FEB 67	PYE
(Written by Charlie Chaplin)			
DOWNTOWN '88 *(Re-mix of 64 hit)*	10	24 DEC 88	PRT

DOWNTOWN	1(2)	23 JAN 65	WARNER
I KNOW A PLACE *(UK No. 17)*	3	01 MAY 65	WARNER
MY LOVE	1(2)	12 FEB 66	WARNER
I COULDN'T LIVE WITHOUT YOUR LOVE	9	20 AUG 66	WARNER
THIS IS MY SONG	3	15 APR 67	WARNER
(From the film 'Countess of Hong Kong')			
DON'T SLEEP IN THE SUBWAY *(UK No. 12)*	5	08 JUL 67	WARNER

CLASH

Controversial and confrontational London based punk/new wave band which evolved out of The 101s and The London S.S. included Joe Strummer, Mick Jones and Topper Headon. Together with The Sex Pistols they helped change the face of UK music in the late 70s. Despite having 20 chart records in their homeland they never had a Top 10 UK single (they had three UK Top 10 LPs). Band broke up in 86.

ROCK THE CASBAH *(UK No. 30)*	8	22 JAN 83	EPIC

CLASSICS 1V

Quintet led by Detroit born Dennis Yost. They recorded for Capitol, Twist and Arlen before getting a string of US-only Top 40s. Members Dean Daugherty and J.R. Cobb left to form Atlanta Rhythm Section with the bands producer Buddy Buie. Dennis formed a new Classics 1V who appeared on Playback in 89.

SPOOKY *(UK No. 46 – Mike Sharpe 67 US hit)*	3	10 FEB 68	IMPERIAL
STORMY	5	28 DEC 68	IMPERIAL
TRACES	2	29 MAR 69	IMPERIAL

Also see Atlanta Rhythm Section

JUDY CLAY & WILLIAM BELL

Judy is a New York session singer who can be heard on many Atlantic hits. She was on Ember in 61 and Scepter in 64 before having two hit duets with Billy Vera. She had two more hit duets both with William Bell – the other being 'My Baby Specialises'.

 PRIVATE NUMBER (US No. 75)   8   25 JAN 69   STAX

TOM CLAY

US West Coast DJ, who recorded on Big Top in 60, had a one-off US hit with this moving medley of two pop standards interspersed with news snippets about the deaths of Martin Luther King and the Kennedys. He followed it with 'Baby I Need Your Loving'.

 WHAT THE WORLD NEED NOW IS LOVE/
ABRAHAM, MARTIN & JOHN (Vocal by Blackberries)   8   14 AUG 71   MOWEST

JIMMY CLIFF

Born Jimmy Chambers, he is probably the best known living reggae singer/ composer. He had a Jamaican No. 1 with 'Hurricane Hattie' in 61, sang with Byron Lee's Dragonaires and first joined Island in 65 . He is a Grammy winner and has starred in two top movies 'The Harder they Come' and 'Club Paradise'. He also wrote UK Top 20 hits for Desmond Dekker, UB40 and The Pioneers.

 WONDERFUL WORLD BEAUTIFUL PEOPLE
(US No. 25)   6   22 NOV 69   TROJAN
WILD WORLD (Cat Stevens song)   8   12 SEP 70   ISLAND

BUZZ CLIFFORD

Born Reese Clifford in Illinois. He had a one-off transatlantic Top 20 with his second 45, a novelty R'n'R song featuring the producer/composer's two children – Mike (age 4) & Lulu (age 2) Parker. Follow up was '3 Little Fishes' and he was later on Roulette (62), RCA (66), Capitol (67), A&M (67) and Dot (69).

BABY SITTIN' BOOGIE (UK No. 14)   6   13 MAR 61   COLUMBIA

CLIMAX

Five piece L.A. band featuring ex Outsiders Sonny Geraci and Walt Nims. Follow up to their sole Top 40 was 'Life and Breath'.

PRECIOUS AND FEW   3   26 FEB 72   CAROUSEL

CLIMAX BLUES BAND

Stafford (UK) quintet led by Peter Haycock and Colin Cooper were on Parlophone in 69, Harvest in 70 and Polydor in 74. They had a one-off UK LP and single hit but in the US they had nine chart LPs over 11 years and returned to the Top 20 with 'I Love You' (12) in 81 (which Pete revived in 90 as part of H Factor).

 COULDN'T GET IT RIGHT   10   20 NOV 76   BTM
COULDN'T GET IT RIGHT   3   21 MAY 77   SIRE

CLIMIE FISHER

UK duo are singer/writer Simon Climie (in 87 his 'I Knew You Were Waiting (For Me)' was a Transatlantic No. 1 for Aretha & George) and keyboard player Rob Fisher, who had been in Neon with Curt & Roland from Tears for Fears and in the US hit duo Naked Eyes. As a duo their fourth single started their run of mainly UK charters.

 RISE TO THE OCCASION   10   16 JAN 88   EMI
LOVE CHANGES (EVERYTHING) (REMIX) (US No. 23) 2   23 APR 88   EMI

Also see Naked Eyes

PATSY CLINE

Top country singer born Virginia Hensley in Virginia. Was on 4 Star in 54 and Coral in 55 before the first of her US-only hits in 57 'Walking After Midnight' (12). Her biggest sellers came between 61 and her plane crash death in 63 (25,000 attended her funeral). She was elected to the Country Hall of Fame in 73 and had her life story made into the movie Sweet Dreams in 85.

CRAZY (Willie Nelson song)   9   27 NOV 61   DECCA
(Voted No. 2 all time US Juke Box record)

CLOUT

The five girl and one boy group from South Africa were formed by Lee Tomlinson and Ingi Herbst. They recorded on their local label Sunshine, won many awards in their homeland, and followed their one-off hit with 'Let It Grow'. They were also on EMI.

SUBSTITUTE (US No. 67 – Orig. Righteous Bros.)   2   05 AUG 78   CARRERRE

CLUB NOUVEAU

Spin off group from The Timex Social Club, fronted by Jay King and including Denzil Foster and Thomas McElroy (later to form their own duo). They first hit on the black music chart with 'Jealousy' (an answer to 'Rumors'). They were top 'New Black Act of 87'.

LEAN ON ME (Bill Withers 72 hit)   3   18 APR 87   KING JAY
LEAN ON ME   1(2)   21 MAR 87   WARNER

COAST TO COAST

UK group's hit had lead vocals by Alan Mills, who quit the act before their hit. New singer Sandy Fontaine mimed on TV and sang on their other chart hit 'Let's Jump The Broomstick' (28). They re-appeared in 85 on Barry Collings Music.

(DO) THE HUCKLEBUCK   5   14 MAR 81   POLYDOR
(Paul Williams 49 R&B hit)

ODIA COATES – SEE PAUL ANKA FOR HIT DETAILS

EDDIE COCHRAN

Very influential L.A. R'n'R star started in The Cochran Brothers on Ekko in 54 and recorded for Crest and Capeheart before his cover of 'Sittin' In The Balcony' gave him a US hit (22). Died in a car crash whilst touring the UK (where he was most popular) in 60. He is a R'n'R legend and re-charted (UK) as late as 88 and can be heard on the 89 Jive Bunny hits.

C'MON EVERYBODY (US No. 35 – UK No.14 in 88)   6   17 APR 59   LONDON
THREE STEPS TO HEAVEN   2   24 JUN 60   LONDON
(Did not make US Top 100 – backed by Crickets)

JOE COCKER

Sheffield (UK) singer who has had many transatlantic single & LP hits. In 59 he joined The Cavaliers (who became Vance Arnold & The Avengers). His first single was 'I'll Cry Instead' on Decca in 64 and fame came with another Beatles song four years later. He was a star of Woodstock and his 'Mad Dogs & Englishmen' tour was a great success. He returned to the Top 20 in 83 and 89.

WITH A LITTLE FROM MY FRIENDS   1(1)   09 NOV 68   REGAL ZONO
(US No. 68)
(Friends on track inc. Jimmy Page & Steve Winwood)
DELTA LADY   10   08 NOV 69   REGAL ZONO
(US No. 69 – Leon Russell song about Rita Coolidge)
UP WHERE WE BELONG (And JENNIFER WARNES) 7   12 FEB 83   ISLAND
(From the film 'An Officer & a Gentleman')
THE LETTER (UK No. 39 – Box Tops 67 hit)   7   30 MAY 70   A&M
(With Leon Russell & The Shelter People)
YOU ARE SO BEAUTIFUL   5   29 MAR 75   A&M
UP WHERE WE BELONG (And JENNIFER WARNES) 1(3)   06 NOV 82   ISLAND

COCKNEY REBEL – SEE STEVE HARLEY FOR HIT DETAILS

COMMANDER CODY & HIS LOST PLANET AIRMEN

Cody (George Frayne) from Idaho and ex-member of The Fantastic Surfing Beavers (!) led this West Coast Rock/Western Swing band. They had several successful US-only LPs and singles which included many revivals of 40s and 50s songs. The group, who were also on Warner and Arista, broke up in 76.

HOT ROD LINCOLN (Charlie Ryan 60 US hit)	9	03 JUN 72	PARAMOUNT

DENNIS COFFEY & THE DETROIT GUITAR BAND

Top Detroit session man played on many hits for acts like The Jackson 5. After his hit he stayed on the star signs theme with singles like 'Taurus' and 'Capricorn's Thing'. He later had black music hits with his act C.J. & Co and was on Orpheus in 90.

SCORPIO	6	08 JAN 71	SUSSEX

COLDCUT

UK Club DJs Matt Black and Jonathan More are the master-minds behind this successful UK-only act. Their records first introduced the public to Yazz and Lisa Stansfield. They have also had chart hits re-mixing other acts records.

DOCTORIN' THE HOUSE (US Dance No. 3)	6	12 MAR 88	AHEAD OF OUR TIME

NAT 'KING' COLE

Velvet voiced Nat is one of the world's top all time MOR acts. He first recorded in 36 and formed his famous trio in 39; they were popular throughout the 40s and he went solo in 48. He had 58 US hits and 32 in the UK, but oddly no No. 1s. He topped the UK LP chart in 78 and had a Top 10 UK hit in 88 (23 years after his death) which gave him a UK Top 10 span of 35 years – the record.

A BLOSSOM FELL	3	18 MAR 55	CAPITOL
DREAMS CAN TELL A LIE	10	24 FEB 56	CAPITOL
TOO YOUNG TO GO STEADY	8	29 JUN 56	CAPITOL
WHEN I FALL IN LOVE (Doris Day 52 US hit) (Not US hit - his daughter hit with it in 88)	2	14 JUN 57	CAPITOL
LET THERE BE LOVE (With George Shearing)	10	10 AUG 62	CAPITOL
RAMBLIN' ROSE	4	26 OCT 62	CAPITOL
WHEN I FALL IN LOVE (Re-entry - he returned to Top 10 after 25 years)	4	02 JAN 88	CAPITOL
DARLING JE VOUS AIME BEAUCOUP	10	30 APR 55	CAPITOL
A BLOSSOM FELL	2	30 JUL 55	CAPITOL
SEND FOR ME/MY PERSONAL POSSESSION (UK No. 21)	6	29 JUL 57	CAPITOL
LOOKING BACK/DO I LIKE IT ('A' Co-written by Brook Benton)	5	26 MAY 58	CAPITOL
RAMBLIN' ROSE	2	22 SEP 62	CAPITOL
THOSE LAZY CRAZY DAYS OF SUMMER	6	29 JUN 63	CAPITOL

NATALIE COLE

Grammy winning L.A. born daughter of Nat 'King' Cole had a string of US-only Top 20s (inc. 5 black music No. 1s) mostly produced by her husband Marvin Yancey and Chuck Jackson (Jesse's brother). After a quiet spell, which included duets with Peabo Bryson and Ray Parker Jr. she scored two transatlantic Top 10s in the late 80s.

PINK CADILLAC	5	23 APR 88	MANHATTAN
MISS YOU LIKE CRAZY	2	03 JUN 89	EMI
THIS WILL BE (UK No. 32)	6	22 NOV 75	CAPITOL
I'VE GOT LOVE ON MY MIND	5	30 APR 77	CAPITOL
OUR LOVE	10	15 APR 78	CAPITOL
PINK CADILLAC (Bruce Springsteen song)	5	07 MAY 88	EMI MANHAT
MISS YOU LIKE CRAZY	7	08 JUL 89	EMI

DAVE & ANSIL COLLINS

Jamaican reggae duo had two UK Top 10s in just three months. Dave later had solos on Rhino and GTI Collins, and was in the group Cargo on Streetwave. Ansil was on Camel, Londisc and Oneness.

DOUBLE BARREL (US No. 22 – First UK No. 1 by a black duo)	1(2)	01 MAY 71	TECHNIQUE
MONKEY SPANNER	7	17 JUL 71	TECHNIQUE

JUDY COLLINS

Denver (US) born singer was one of the leading figures in the 60s folk boom. She signed to Elektra in 61 and had four US-only LP hits before her version of a Joni Mitchell song put her in the US Top 10 in 68 and in the UK Top 20 in 69. Though still recording her sales in the 80s have not matched up to the previous decades.

AMAZING GRACE (US No. 15 – spent record 67 weeks on UK chart)	5	13 FEB 71	ELEKTRA
SEND IN THE CLOWNS (US No. 36)	6	31 MAY 75	ELEKTRA
BOTH SIDES NOW (UK No. 14)	8	21 DEC 68	ELEKTRA

PHIL COLLINS

Very successful London born singer/ writer/producer/drummer and actor. He took over as Genesis' singer in 77 and has had two very lucrative trans-atlantic recording careers since – both in the group and as a soloist. Everything he touches turns to gold if not platinum. He had a record 25 Top 40 singles in the US in the 80s and has been involved in numerous charity projects and won countless awards, with no doubt many more to come.

IN THE AIR TONIGHT (US No. 19)	2	07 FEB 81	VIRGIN
YOU CAN'T HURRY LOVE (Supremes 66 hit)	1(2)	15 JAN 83	VIRGIN
AGAINST ALL ODDS (TAKE A LOOK AT ME NOW) (From the film)	2	28 APR 84	VIRGIN
EASY LOVER (With PHILIP BAILEY)	1(4)	23 MAR 85	CBS
ONE MORE NIGHT	4	27 APR 85	VIRGIN
SEPARATE LIVES (And MARILYN MARTIN) (From film 'White Nights' – comp. Stephen Bishop)	4	14 DEC 85	VIRGIN
IN THE AIR TONIGHT (Ben Leibrand Remix)	4	02 JUL 88	VIRGIN
GROOVY KIND OF LOVE (Originally by Patti Labelle – 2 weeks to No. 1)	1(2)	10 SEP 88	VIRGIN
TWO HEARTS (Composed with Lamont Dozier)	6	03 DEC 88	VIRGIN
ANOTHER DAY IN PARADISE	2	18 NOV 89	VIRGIN
YOU CAN'T HURRY LOVE	10	05 FEB 83	ATLANTIC
AGAINST ALL ODDS (TAKE A LOOK AT ME NOW) (When No. 1 it was one of 40 UK hits in US 100!)	1(3)	21 APR 84	ATLANTIC
EASY LOVER (With PHILIP BAILEY)	2	02 FEB 85	COLUMBIA
ONE MORE NIGHT	1(2)	30 MAR 85	ATLANTIC
SUSSUDIO	1(1)	06 JUL 85	ATLANTIC
DON'T LOSE MY NUMBER	4	28 SEP 85	ATLANTIC
SEPARATE LIVES (And MARILYN MARTIN)	1(1)	30 NOV 85	ATLANTIC
TAKE ME HOME (UK No. 19)	7	10 MAY 86	ATLANTIC
GROOVY KIND OF LOVE	1(2)	22 OCT 88	ATLANTIC
TWO HEARTS	1(2)	21 JAN 89	ATLANTIC
ANOTHER DAY IN PARADISE (3rd No. 1 in row-backing vocals inc. David Crosby)	1(4)	23 DEC 89	ATLANTIC

Also see Genesis

JESSI COLTER

Born Miriam Johnson in Phoenix (US) she debuted under that name on Jamie in 61 assisted by Duane Eddy, who she married in 62. She joined RCA in 69 and married top Country star Waylon Jennings the same year. She has had one US Top 40 and six country Top 20s, half of them duets with Waylon whom she still tours with.

I'M NOT LISA	4	21 JUN 75	CAPITOL

COMMODORES

Formed from two Alabama acts The Mighty Mystics and The Jays and fronted from 67-81 by Lionel Richie. They first recorded on Atlantic in 69 before joining Motown in 72 and became one of the top black acts of the 70s. After Lionel left their only major hit was 'Nightshift' written by member William Orange and sung by him and new vocalist from the UK J.D. Nicholas (ex Heatwave).

EASY (Also No. 15 UK in 88 when used in ad.)	9	13 AUG 77	MOTOWN
THREE TIMES A LADY (Jumped from 46-5)	1(5)	19 AUG 78	MOTOWN
SAIL ON	8	29 SEP 79	MOTOWN
STILL	4	24 NOV 79	MOTOWN
NIGHTSHIFT	3	09 MAR 85	MOTOWN
(Tribute to Marvin Gaye and Jackie Wilson)			
SWEET LOVE	5	24 APR 76	MOTOWN
JUST TO BE CLOSE TO YOU (UK No. 62)	7	27 NOV 76	MOTOWN
EASY	4	27 AUG 77	MOTOWN
BRICK HOUSE (UK No. 32)	5	05 NOV 77	MOTOWN
THREE TIMES A LADY	1(2)	12 AUG 78	MOTOWN
SAIL ON	4	13 OCT 79	MOTOWN
STILL	1(1)	17 NOV 79	MOTOWN
LADY YOU BRING ME UP (UK No. 56)	8	05 SEP 81	MOTOWN
OH NO (UK No. 44)	4	05 DEC 81	MOTOWN
NIGHTSHIFT	3	20 APR 85	MOTOWN

Also see Lionel Richie

COMMUNARDS

UK duo featured vocalist Jimmy Somervillle (ex Bronski Beat) and multi-instrumentalist Richard Coles. Their third release, with guest vocalist Sarah Jayne Morris, went on to be the biggest UK single of 86. They did a lot to help AIDS research and strongly supported all gay issues. Jimmy went solo in 89.

DON'T LEAVE ME THIS WAY	1(4)	13 SEP 86	LONDON
(US No. 40 – US Dance No. 1 – Thelma Houston 76 hit)			
SO COLD THE NIGHT	8	20 DEC 86	LONDON
NEVER CAN SAY GOODBYE	4	21 NOV 87	LONDON
(US No. 51 – US Dance No. 2 – Jackson Five 71 hit)			

Also see Jimmy Somerville

PERRY COMO

Ex barber from Pennsylvania has sung on a staggering 151 US chart records since saying hello in 40 with the Ted Weems Orchestra and 'Goody Goodbye'. In the UK he has had 27 hits since 52 with his transatlantic peak being the late 50s when his TV show was topping the ratings on both sides of the Atlantic. In 75 he became the oldest person to top the UK LP chart at age 63.

HOT DIGGITY	4	22 JUN 56	HMV
MORE	10	09 NOV 56	HMV
MAGIC MOMENTS	1(8)	28 FEB 58	RCA
(First Burt Bacharach song to go to No. 1)			
CATCH A FALLING STAR	9	21 MAR 58	RCA
KEWPIE DOLL (US No. 12)	9	30 MAY 58	RCA
LOVE MAKES THE WORLD GO ROUND (US No. 33)	6	09 JAN 59	RCA
TOMBOY (US No. 29)	10	03 APR 59	RCA
DELAWARE (US No. 22)	3	11 MAR 60	RCA
IT'S IMPOSSIBLE	4	27 FEB 71	RCA
AND I LOVE YOU SO	3	26 MAY 73	RCA
(US No. 29 – Don McLean song)			
FOR THE GOOD TIMES (Ray Price 70 US hit)	7	24 NOV 73	RCA
KO KO MO (I LOVE YOU SO)	4	19 FEB 55	RCA
(Gene & Eunice 55 R&B hit)			
TINA MARIE (UK No. 24)	5	15 OCT 55	RCA
HOT DIGGITY (DOG ZIGGITY BOOM)	2	28 APR 56	RCA
MORE	4	21 JUL 56	RCA
ROUND AND ROUND	1(1)	06 APR 57	RCA
CATCH A FALLING STAR/MAGIC MOMENTS	3	24 FEB 58	RCA
(First official RIAA Gold record)			
IT'S IMPOSSIBLE	10	23 JAN 71	RCA
(Last US Top 20 giving him a 31 year span)			

CONGREGATION

UK session group fronted by Brian Keith, previously with Plastic Penny. In the US name changed to The English Congregation to avoid confusion with Mike Curb's Congregation. Follow up was 'Jesahel'/'Sing Me a Love Song'. Brian joined Pye in 74.

SOFTLY WHISPERING I LOVE YOU (US No. 29)	4	08 JAN 72	COLUMBIA

ARTHUR CONLEY

Atlanta born soul singer was discovered by Otis Redding and recorded most of his hits in Muscle Shoals. He was on Jotis and Fame before having a transatlantic Top 10 with a song produced by Otis and based on Sam Cooke's 'Yeah Man'. He had six other US hits the next biggest being 'Funky Street' (US 14/UK 46).

SWEET SOUL MUSIC	7	17 JUN 67	ATLANTIC
(In 72 his record 'More Sweet Soul Music' failed)			
SWEET SOUL MUSIC	2	13 MAY 67	ATCO

RAY CONNIFF & THE SINGERS

Massachusetts born arranger/conductor. Was on Brunswick in 52, joined Columbia in 56 and before long the 'Ray Conniff Sound' (distinctive mix of instruments and multi-tracked voices) was known internationally. Although he had no UK hit singles over the next 18 years he charted over 50 LPs in the US and 12 in the UK.

SOMEWHERE, MY LOVE	9	13 AUG 66	COLUMBIA
(From the film 'Dr. Zhivago')			

BILLY CONNOLLY

Scottish comedian, TV personality and one time folk singer had a left field UK smash with his second single on Polydor – a parody of Tammy Wynette's country hit. His follow ups included 'No Chance (No Change)' and 'In The Brownies (In The Navy)'.

D.I.V.O.R.C.E.	1(1)	22 NOV 75	POLYDOR

BILL CONTI

Rhode Island (US) born conductor/composer. He worked in Italy for six years before moving back to the US to work on film scores like Harry & Tonto and the three Rocky films – the first of which included his sole US Top 40 single.

GONNA FLY NOW (Theme from Rocky)	1(1)	02 JUL 77	UA

CONTOURS

Detroit Soul sextet which included Billy Gordon had five years of US-only hits. Act who were formed in 58 once featured Temptation Dennis Edwards. Their biggest hit re-entered the US Top 20 in 88 (it was in Dirty Dancing film). In the UK there were 3 covers of their hit and Brian Poole & The Tremeloes version was a No. 1.

DO YOU LOVE ME (Returned to No. 11 in 88)	3	20 OCT 62	GORDY

SAM COOKE

One of the first members of the R'n'R Hall of Fame. Sam was a very popular singer/composer whose sixth solo record started his run of 43 US hits and 8 in the UK. His songs and records are still heard today and his influence can be heard in many black and white acts. His biggest UK hit came in 86, 22 years after his murder in 64. His daughter Linda is half of Womack and Womack.

CHAIN GANG	7	04 NOV 60	RCA
CUPID (US No. 17)	8	15 SEP 61	RCA
TWISTIN' THE NIGHT AWAY	4	06 APR 62	RCA
WONDERFUL WORLD (US No. 12 in 60)	2	05 APR 86	RCA

YOU SEND ME *(UK No. 29)*	1(2)	02 DEC 57	KEEN	
CHAIN GANG	2	02 OCT 60	RCA	
TWISTIN' THE NIGHT AWAY	9	24 MAR 62	RCA	
ANOTHER SATURDAY NIGHT *(UK No. 18)*	10	25 MAY 63	RCA	
THE SHAKE	7	27 FEB 65	RCA	

COOKIE CREW

First UK female rap stars are Londoners Susie Q (whose brother John Banfield is in The Pasadenas), Remedee (Debbie Price) and DJ Max (Maxine). They started in The Warm Milk and Cookie Crew in 83, had some success with 'Females' in 87. They first charted with The Beatmasters and have since had hits of their own.

ROK DA HOUSE *(With THE BEATMASTERS)*	5	06 FEB 88	RHYTHM KING

COOKIES

Top New York session trio in the 50s and 60s who first charted in 56 with 'In Paradise'. After many personnel and label changes (Atlantic, Josie, RCA) the new trio, still with Ethel 'Earl-Jean' McCrae, hit with 'Chains' (which was covered by The Beatles) before scoring their biggest US-only hit.

DON'T SAY NOTHIN' (BAD ABOUT MY BABY)	7	27 APR 63	DIMENSION

RITA COOLIDGE

Nashville born singer sang backing vocals for Delaney & Bonnie, appeared on the 'Mad Dogs & Englishmen' tour and worked with Eric Clapton. She had a small hit on Pepper in 69 and solo success really started in 72. The Joe Cocker hit 'Delta Lady' was written about her and she was married to Kris Kristofferson from 73-79.

WE'RE ALL ALONE *(Composed Boz Scaggs)*	6	08 AUG 77	A&M
(YOUR LOVE HAS LIFTED ME) HIGHER AND HIGHER *(UK No. 48)* *(Jackie Wilson 67 hit)*	2	10 SEP 77	A&M
WE'RE ALL ALONE	7	26 NOV 77	A&M

ALICE COOPER

Top 70s shock-rock star who returned to the Top 10 in 89. Detroit born Vincent Furnier formed The Spiders, who were on Santa Cruz, who evolved into Nazz and joined Frank Zappa's Straight label. Their first charter came in Canada with 'Eighteen' (US 21) in 71. Act had many hit transatlantic LPs and singles in the 70s. Alice was still popular on the H.M. circuit in 1990.

SCHOOL'S OUT	1(3)	12 AUG 72	WARNER
ELECTED *(US No. 26)*	4	28 OCT 72	WARNER
HELLO HURRAY *(US No. 35)*	6	17 MAR 73	WARNER
NO MORE MR. NICE GUY *(US No. 25)*	10	12 MAY 73	WARNER
POISON	2	28 AUG 89	EPIC
SCHOOL'S OUT	7	29 JUL 72	WARNER
YOU AND ME	9	13 AUG 77	WARNER
POISON	7	25 NOV 89	EPIC

CORNELIUS BROTHERS & SISTER ROSE

Family trio Edward, Carter & Rose Cornelius from Florida whose backing group were other members of their 17 strong family. They first recorded on Platinum and had four US-only Top 40's.

TREAT HER LIKE A LADY	3	03 JUL 71	UA
TOO LATE TO TURN BACK NOW	2	15 JUL 72	UA

DAVE 'BABY' CORTEZ

Dave Cortez Clowney from Detroit had worked with The Pearls, Valentines and The Jesters. He recorded solos on Ember, Okeh, Winley and Paris and his third on Clock was the first of two US-only Top 10s. He later recorded for Emit in 62, Argo in 64, Epic in 64, Roulette in 65, All Platinum and Tetragrammaton.

THE HAPPY ORGAN	1(1)	11 MAY 59	CLOCK
RINKY DINK *(Jimmy Castor played sax on it)*	10	15 SEP 62	CHESS

BILL COSBY

Top US comedian and TV personality for over 25 years. He has an enviable collection of Gold LPs and Grammy awards but to date has only had one US Top 40 single. He is a popular TV star in the UK too but has had no chart records as yet.

LITTLE OLE MAN (UPTIGHT-EVERYTHING'S ALRIGHT) *(Parody of Stevie Wonder 65 hit)*	4	14 OCT 67	WARNER

ELVIS COSTELLO

Born Declan McManus in London, he fronted Flip City before going solo, backed firstly by Huey Lewis' group Clover and later by The Attractions. His first singles stiffed but 'Watching The Detectives' went to 15 in UK. He is one of the most important acts to emerge from the UK new wave music scene, and is best known in the US for his LPs. However 'Veronica' (co-written with Paul McCartney) gave him his first US Top 20 in 89.

OLIVER'S ARMY	2	10 MAR 79	RADAR
I CAN'T STAND UP FOR FALLING DOWN	4	08 MAR 80	F. BEAT
A GOOD YEAR FOR THE ROSES *(George Jones 70 Country hit)*	6	07 NOV 81	F. BEAT

JOHN COUGAR – SEE JOHN COUGAR MELLANCAMP FOR HIT DETAILS

COUNT FIVE

Teenage quartet from California fronted by Kenn Ellner. This group who wore Dracula type cloaks scored a one-off US hit. Follow up was 'Peace of Mind'.

PSYCHOTIC REACTION	5	15 OCT 66	DOUBLE SHOT

JULIE COVINGTON

UK singer/actress who was on Columbia in 70, sang backing vocals for Steve Winwood and sold nearly a million in the UK with a song from Evita (a female record at that time). She had another UK – only Top 20 with Alice Cooper's 'Only Women Bleed' (12) and was in hit UK TV series Rock Follies which spawned a No. 1 LP.

DON'T CRY FOR ME ARGENTINA	1(1)	12 FEB 77	MCA

COWSILLS

Family act from Rhode Island (US) consisted of mother Barbara, six brothers and sister Susan. The act that inspired The Partridge Family were first on Johnny Nash's label Joda and then on Philips. For 18 months they were one of the top US groups. They were also on London (71) and Susan made solos on Warner (76).

THE RAIN, THE PARK & OTHER THINGS	2	02 DEC 67	MGM
INDIAN LAKE	10	13 JUL 68	MGM
HAIR *(Top 2 in US that week both from musical 'Hair')*	2	10 MAY 69	MGM

MICHAEL COX

Liverpool singer who was often on top UK Pop TV shows Oh Boy, Boy Meets Girls and Wham. He had two non-chart records on Decca before getting a one-off UK hit with a John D. Loudermilk song. He later recorded on HMV and Parlophone.

 ANGELA JONES *(Johnny Ferguson 60 US hit)* 8 22 JUL 60 TRIUMPH

FLOYD CRAMER

Louisiana born pianist is probably Nashville's best known session man, having played on scores of hits including many by Elvis and Jim Reeves. He was on Abbot in 53 and MGM in 55 before joining RCA in 58 and notched up three US Top 10s in just eight months.

ON THE REBOUND	3	12 MAY 61	RCA
LAST DATE	2	28 NOV 60	RCA
ON THE REBOUND	4	17 APR 61	RCA
SAN ANTONIO ROSE *(Bob Wills 39 hit)*	8	17 JUL 61	RCA

LES CRANE

TV personality from San Francisco had a one-off transatlantic Top 10 with a recital of a poem penned in 1906 by Max Ehrmann, who died 27 years before this hit. The poem had been used a year earlier by King Crimson in an advert. Follow up to this Grammy winner was 'Children Learn What They Live'.

DESIDERATA	7	01 APR 72	WARNER
DESIDERATA	8	04 DEC 71	WARNER

JOHNNY CRAWFORD

L.A. born singer/actor was an original 'Mouseketeer' and starred in the TV series The Rifleman. He had four US-only Top 40s in 62/63 and recorded for Sidewalk in 68.

CINDY'S BIRTHDAY 8 23 JUN 62 DEL-FI

MICHAEL CRAWFORD

UK actor/singer has been a top UK stage and TV star for 25 years. His sole UK hit came from the hit musical The Phantom Of The Opera which he played the lead in on Broadway and in London.

THE MUSIC OF THE NIGHT/WISHING YOU 7 14 DEC 87 POLYDOR
WERE SOMEHOW HERE AGAIN
(The 'B' side was by SARAH BRIGHTMAN)

RANDY CRAWFORD

Distinctive Georgia born singer has had more success in the UK than her homeland where none of her four UK Top 20s even made the charts. She recorded for Columbia in 73 and Warner in 77 before her first charter 'Street Life' with The Crusaders. Her biggest US hit was 'Knockin' On Heaven's Door' (black No.4) in 89.

ONE DAY I'LL FLY AWAY	2	20 SEP 80	WARNER
ALMAZ	4	07 FEB 87	WARNER

Also see The Crusaders

CREAM

Often called the first supergroup, the UK trio consisted of Eric Clapton, Jack Bruce and Ginger Baker. They were one of the first LP orientated acts and had two very successful years before splitting in 69. Their LP sales continued well after this and they are regarded as one of the most important and influential rock acts. Ginger re-united with Jack on his 89 tour.

 SUNSHINE OF YOUR LOVE *(UK No.25)* 5 31 AUG 68 ATCO
WHITE ROOM *(UK No.28)* 6 09 NOV 68 ATCO

Also see Eric Clapton

CREEDENCE CLEARWATER REVIVAL

One of the world's top acts of 69/70, this Californian quartet mixed original songs with the feel of 50s R'n'R. They were first called The Blue Velvets (on Orchestra) and then The Golliwogs (on Scorpio). First charter was 'Susie Q' (US No.11) and they had a long string of transatlantic hits. Brothers John & Tom Fogerty went solo and John topped the US LP chart in 85.

PROUD MARY	8	12 JUL 69	LIBERTY
BAD MOON RISING	1(3)	20 SEP 69	LIBERTY
TRAVELLIN' BAND	8	09 MAY 70	LIBERTY
UP AROUND THE BEND	3	18 JUL 70	LIBERTY
PROUD MARY	2	08 MAR 69	FANTASY
BAD MOON RISING	2	28 JUN 69	FANTASY
GREEN RIVER *(UK No.19)*	2	27 SEP 69	FANTASY
DOWN ON THE CORNER/FORTUNATE SON *(UK No.31)*	3	20 DEC 69	FANTASY
TRAVELIN' BAND/WHO'LL STOP THE RAIN	2	07 MAR 70	FANTASY
UP AROUND THE BEND	4	06 JUN 70	FANTASY
LOOKIN' OUT MY BACK DOOR	2	03 OCT 70	FANTASY
HAVE YOU EVER SEEN THE RAIN *(UK No.36)*	8	13 MAR 71	FANTASY
SWEET HITCH-HIKER *(UK No.36)*	6	28 AUG 71	FANTASY

Also see John Fogerty

KID CREOLE & THE COCONUTS

Act fronted by New York based August Darnell and Coati Mundi (Andy Hernandez), both ex Dr. Buzzard's Original Savannah Band. They were one of the top UK acts of 82 but their Latin-ish pop/dance music and their unique act failed to get them a hit in the US. The Coconuts changed their name to Boomerang but never came back.

I'M A WONDERFUL THING (BABY)	4	26 JUN 82	ZE
STOOL PIGEON	7	14 AUG 82	ZE
ANNIE I'M NOT YOUR DADDY	2	30 OCT 82	ZE

BERNARD CRIBBINS

UK actor and TV personality. He started recording on Parlophone in 60 and had three UK-only Top 40s with comedy material in 62.

HOLE IN THE GROUND 7 23 MAR 62 PARLOPHONE

CRICKETS

They only charted in the US when Buddy Holly sang lead but in the UK they had 8 other hits. They cut the original versions of 'More Than I Can Say', 'I Fought The Law', 'Someone, Someone' and 'When You Ask About Love' – all Top 10s for other acts. Act who were the second hit group in the 50s with that name are still working with original members Jerry Allison, Joe B.Mauldin and Sonny Curtis.

THAT'LL BE THE DAY *(Previously flopped as a solo by Buddy)*	1(3)	01 NOV 57	VOGUE CORAL
OH BOY *(US No. 11)*	3	31 JAN 58	CORAL
MAYBE BABY *(US No. 18)*	4	18 APR 58	CORAL
DON'T EVER CHANGE *(Vocalists include Glen Campbell)*	5	03 AUG 62	LIBERTY
THAT'LL BE THE DAY	1(1)	23 SEP 57	BRUNSWICK

JIM CROCE

Philadelphian singer/songwriter recorded unsuccessfully with his wife as Jim & Ingrid on Capitol in the late 60s. He had 10 US-only hits including two No. 1s. He died in a plane crash in 73. In 74 he simultaneously had three singles and three LPs in the US charts, the LPs at No's 1, 2 and 20.

YOU DON'T MESS AROUND WITH JIM	8	02 SEP 72	ABC
BAD, BAD LEROY BROWN	1(2)	21 JUL 73	ABC
I GOT A NAME *(From the film 'Last American Hero')*	10	17 NOV 73	ABC
TIME IN A BOTTLE *(Used in the TV play 'She Lives')*	1(2)	29 DEC 73	ABC
I'LL HAVE TO SAY I LOVE YOU IN A SONG	9	27 APR 74	ABC

BING CROSBY

The world's biggest selling and most charted singer with sales of over 300 million and having had 299 US Top 20 hits! He started in The Rhythm Boys in 26, with Paul Whiteman, and had his first solo charter in 31. He has won numerous awards for singing and acting and his 'White Christmas' is the world's top selling single. He died in 77 and has had two UK Top 10s since.

🇬🇧	TRUE LOVE (& Grace Kelly) (From the film 'High Society')	4	12 JAN 57	CAPITOL
	AROUND THE WORLD (US No. 25 – From the film)	5	21 JUN 57	BRUNSWICK
	WHITE CHRISTMAS (Charted in US 20 different times-UK Gold record)	5	24 DEC 77	MCA
	PEACE ON EARTH/LITTLE DRUMMER BOY (With DAVID BOWIE) (Biggest age gap between a chart duo – 40 years)	3	25 DEC 82	RCA
🇺🇸	TRUE LOVE (And GRACE KELLY)	4	12 JAN 57	CAPITOL

CROSBY, STILLS & NASH

Influential soft rock supergroup comprising David Crosby (ex Byrds), Stephen Stills (ex Buffalo Springfield) & Graham Nash (ex Hollies). They have had many hit transatlantic hit LPs & singles (especially in the US) both as a trio and with additional member Neil Young. The quartet returned to both US & UK charts in 89.

🇺🇸	JUST A SONG BEFORE I GO	7	27 AUG 77	ATLANTIC
	WASTED ON THE WAY	9	21 AUG 82	ATLANTIC

CHRISTOPHER CROSS

Texas singer/songwriter, and one time Doobie Brothers road manager, had a fantastic start to his career being 'Top New US Act of 80' and winning a record five Grammys in 81. Unfortunately he could not keep the pace up. He moved on to Reprise in 88.

🇬🇧	ARTHUR'S THEME (BEST THAT YOU CAN DO) (From the film 'Arthur')	7	06 FEB 82	WARNER
🇺🇸	RIDE LIKE THE WIND (UK No. 69 – Backing vocals by Michael McDonald)	2	26 APR 80	WARNER
	SAILING (UK No. 48)	1(1)	30 AUG 80	WARNER
	ARTHUR'S THEME (BEST THAT YOU CAN DO)	1(3)	17 OCT 81	WARNER
	THINK OF LAURA	9	04 FEB 84	WARNER

THE CROWD

One-off UK hit made to raise money for families of victims of the Bradford Football fire disaster where more than 50 people died at a game. Acts included Gerry (& The Pacemakers) Marsden, Joe Fagin, Jim Diamond, The Searchers, The Hollies and Lemmy.

🇬🇧	YOU'LL NEVER WALK ALONE (Gerry & Pacemakers 63 UK hit-sold 100,000 in 2 days)	1(2)	15 JUN 85	SPARTAN

CROWDED HOUSE

Australian group fronted by ex Split Enz member Neil Finn, who has won Australian awards for his writing. First release was a budget priced 12″ single (including 'Something So Strong') which flopped but since then they have had four US hits.

🇺🇸	DON'T DREAM IT'S OVER (UK No. 27)	2	25 APR 87	CAPITOL
	SOMETHING SO STRONG	7	25 JUL 87	CAPITOL

CROWN HEIGHTS AFFAIR

New York funk band led by Phil Thomas started as Neu Day Express. They were on RCA in 74 and joined De-Lite a year later. To date they have had more success in the UK. They signed to SBK in 89.

🇬🇧	YOU GAVE ME LOVE (US No. 102)	10	14 JUN 80	DE-LITE

CRUSADERS

Previously called The Nite Hawks, Swingsters, Modern Jazz Sextet and The Jazz Crusaders. This group which contains top session men Wilton Felder, 'Stix' Hooper, Joe Sample and Wayne Henderson has often appeared on LP and single charts over the last two decades.

🇬🇧	STREET LIFE (US No. 36)	5	15 SEP 79	MCA

CRYSTALS

Female Brooklyn quartet often fronted by La La Brooks. Their debut hit was 'There's No Other' in 61 which like all their hits were produced by Phil Spector and are great examples of his 'Wall of Sound'. They are considered one of the leading 'girl groups' of the 60s even though they did not sing on their biggest US hit.

🇬🇧	DA DOO RON RON (Returned UK No. 15 in 74) (Sonny & Cher on backing vocals)	4	26 JUL 63	LONDON
	THEN HE KISSED ME	2	11 OCT 63	LONDON
🇺🇸	HE'S A REBEL (No. 19 UK – comp. Gene Pitney) (Sang by The Blossoms – original by Vikki Carr)	1(2)	03 NOV 62	UA
	DA DOO RON RON (Same backing track as original Blossoms version)	3	08 JUN 63	PHILLES
	THEN HE KISSED ME	6	14 SEP 63	PHILLES

CUFF LINKS

On their first hit Ron Dante (of The Archies and Detergents) was a one man group and was multi-tracked 15 times. When he decided not to continue he was replaced by Rupert Holmes. Ron later recorded on Mercury, Scepter, Bell, Handshake, Musicor, Columbia and Dot and produced Barry Manilow's first hits.

🇬🇧	TRACY	4	10 JAN 70	MCA
	WHEN JULIE COMES AROUND (US No. 41)	10	02 MAY 70	MCA
🇺🇸	TRACY	9	25 OCT 69	DECCA

CULTURE CLUB

The most successful new group of 83/84 was fronted by the unmistakable Boy George (London born George O'Dowd). He started in Bow Wow Wow then formed In Praise Of Lemmings who became Sex Gang Children then Culture Club. Their first two singles failed but for the next four years they were transatlantic superstars. George who had many problems went solo in 87 but has yet to repeat the success he enjoyed with Culture Club.

🇬🇧	DO YOU REALLY WANT TO HURT ME	1(3)	23 OCT 82	VIRGIN
	TIME (CLOCK OF THE HEART)	3	18 DEC 82	VIRGIN
	CHURCH OF THE POISON MIND (Entered At No.9 – Vocal inc. Helen Terry)	2	16 APR 83	VIRGIN
	KARMA CHAMELEON (Entered at No. 3 – UK Gold record – Top record 83)	1(6)	24 SEP 83	VIRGIN
	VICTIMS	3	24 DEC 83	VIRGIN
	IT'S A MIRACLE (US No. 13)	4	31 MAR 84	VIRGIN
	THE WAR SONG (US No. 17 – Entered at No. 3)	2	13 OCT 84	VIRGIN
	MOVE AWAY (US No. 12)	7	22 MAR 86	VIRGIN
🇺🇸	DO YOU REALLY WANT TO HURT ME	2	26 MAR 83	EPIC
	TIME (CLOCK OF THE HEART)	2	18 JUN 83	EPIC
	I'LL TUMBLE 4 YA	9	27 AUG 83	EPIC
	CHURCH OF THE POISON MIND	10	03 DEC 83	EPIC
	KARMA CHAMELEON	1(3)	04 FEB 84	VIRGIN
	MISS ME BLIND	5	21 APR 84	VIRGIN

Also see Boy George

43

BURTON CUMMINGS

Canadian singer and keyboard player had five solo US-only hits after winding up the successful act Guess Who in 75. The biggest, his own composition, earned him a Gold record.

 STAND TALL — 10 — 08 JAN 77 — PORTRAIT

Also see Guess Who

CUPID'S INSPIRATION

UK quartet, previously known as Ends, were led by Terry Rice-Milton, who was once called 'The Face of 69'. Like many acts at the time they played at the 'Star Club' in Hamburg before getting their sole UK chart entry. Their follow up 'My World' reached No. 33 in UK. Terry later recorded for Pye.

 YESTERDAY HAS GONE — 4 — 13 JUL 68 — NEMS
(Originally by Little Anthony & The Imperials)

CURE

Sussex (UK) group first called The Easy Cure and fronted by charismatic Robert Smith. They signed to Ariola in 77 but never recorded. Their debut record was 'Killing An Arab' on Small Wonder. First UK hit was their fifth release 'A Forest'. Cult act finally had a US chart record in 89 with their 16th UK entry. They are now one of the most popular live acts in the UK.

THE LOVE CATS — 7 — 19 NOV 83 — FICTION
LULLABY *(Top UK video of 89 in BRITS awards)* — 5 — 29 APR 89 — FICTION
LOVE SONG — 2 — 21 OCT 89 — ELEKTRA

CURIOSITY KILLED THE CAT

London pop/rock quartet, featuring one time model Ben Volpeliere-Pierrot, were a top teen appeal act in the UK in the late 80s. Their second single was their biggest hit which they followed with a re-issue of their first 'Misfit'. After a break the group returned to the UK-only Top 20 in 89 with 'Name and Number' (14).

DOWN TO EARTH — 3 — 14 FEB 87 — MERCURY
MISFIT *(US No. 42)* — 7 — 04 JUL 87 — MERCURY
(Video was the last produced by Andy Warhol)

CURVED AIR

Much hyped band whose first album was the first picture LP included singer Sonja Kristina, Darryl Way and later Stewart Copeland (of Police). Before they split in 77 they had three Top 20 UK-only LPs and 1 single. They were also on Decca and BTM and in 84 the act re-appeared on the Pearl Key label. Sonja was in another group Escape on Chopper (80).

BACK STREET LUV — 4 — 18 SEP 71 — WARNER

CUTTING CREW

UK band fronted by singer/composer Nick Van Eede, who had been a solo act on Barn in 78. They gave Virgin Records their first US No. 1 but have not yet repeated the success of their debut hit.

(I JUST) DIED IN YOUR ARMS — 4 — 20 SEP 86 — SIREN
(I JUST) DIED IN YOUR ARMS — 1(2) — 02 MAY 87 — VIRGIN
I'VE BEEN IN LOVE BEFORE — 9 — 21 NOV 87 — VIRGIN

CYRKLE

Pennsylvania based quartet was the first US act handled by Beatles manager Brian Epstein. Led by Donald Dannemann they followed their biggest hit with another US-only Top 20 'Turn Down Day' (No. 16). Group broke up shortly after Epstein's death.

RED RUBBER BALL *(Paul Simon song)* — - — 2 — 09 JUL 66 — COLUMBIA

D

D. MOB

Act masterminded by ex A&R man and Club DJ Dancing Danny D (Danny Poku). First of their hits was tailor-made for the UK acid house craze and each hit has featured a different artist. Their two Top 10s missed the US pop chart but were No. 1 dance records there as was their first US Top 20 'C'mon And Get My Love' (UK 15) in 90.

 WE CALL IT ACIEED *(Featuring GARY HAISMAN)* — 3 — 22 OCT 88 — FFRR
IT IS TIME TO GET FUNKY *(Featuring LRS)* — 9 — 01 JUL 89 — LONDON

TERRY DACTYL & THE DINOSAURS

UK group fronted by singer/songwriter John Lewis who normally recorded as Brett Marvin & The Thunderbolts but had this one-off novelty hit under this name. Follow up was 'On A Saturday Night' (45 UK). John returned to the Top 10 later as Jona Lewie.

 SEASIDE SHUFFLE — 2 — 12 AUG 72 — UK
(Record was out year before on Sonet and flopped)

DADDY DEWDROP

Real name Richard Monda and he came from Cleveland (US). He had a one-off US hit which he followed with 'March Of The White Corpuscles'. He later recorded for Capitol and Inphasion.

CHICK-A-BOOM — 9 — 08 MAY 71 — SUNFLOWER

DALE & GRACE

Louisiana duo of Dale Houston and Grace Broussard, who had previously both been solo artists, had the first of their US-only Top 10s with a Don & Dewey oldie (a hit later by Donny & Marie Osmond). They later recorded for Guyden and Hanna-Barbera.

 I'M LEAVING IT UP TO YOU — 1(2) — 23 NOV 63 — MONTEL
STOP AND THINK IT OVER — 8 — 07 MAR 64 — MONTEL

ROGER DALTREY

London born singer with The Who also had several transatlantic solo chart records in the 70s and 80s. His biggest US solo hit was the No. 20 'Without Your Love'. He also had success as an actor and can be seen in TV ads for American Express cards.

 GIVING IT ALL AWAY   5   12 MAY 73   TRACK

Also see The Who

DAMIAN

UK singer/actor/cabaret performer whose version of the song from The Rocky Horror Show was first released on Sedition in 86. It charted in 87 (51) and in 88 (64) before an S.A.W. remix finally put it in the UK Top 10 in 89.

 THE TIME WARP *(SAW remix)*   7   16 SEP 89   JIVE

MICHAEL DAMIAN

US singer/actor who appeared in the soap opera The Young & The Restless. He had two LPs out on CBS Canada and first charted in 81 with 'She Did It' (on Leg) and eight years later hit the top (US only) with a song featured in the film Dream A Little Dream.

 ROCK ON *(David Essex 73 hit)*   1(1)   03 JUN 89   CYPRESS

DAMNED

UK group included Dave Vanian, Captain Sensible and Rat Scabies. In 76 they released the first UK punk LP and first single 'New Rose' (both produced by Nick Lowe) and in 77 they were the first UK punk band to play in the US. Their sixth single 'Love Song' charted in 79, then several personnel and label changes later they had the only Top 10 of their 15 UK-only hits.

 ELOISE *(Barry Ryan 68 hit)*   3   22 FEB 86   MCA

DANA

London born singer (real name Rosemary Brown) was 18 when the song with which she won the Eurovision song contest for Ireland topped the UK chart and went on to sell over two million worldwide. She had four more UK-only Top 20s in the next six years. She later recorded on Creole (81), Towerbell (82), Word (82) and Ritz (85).

 ALL KINDS OF EVERYTHING   1(2)   18 APR 70   REX
PLEASE TELL HIM I SAID HELLO   8   15 MAR 75   GTO
IT'S GONNA BE A COLD COLD CHRISTMAS   4   27 DEC 75   GTO

VIC DANA

New York born pop/MOR singer was on Atlas (with The Parakeets), Carlton and Lido before replacing Gary Troxel in The Fleetwoods. The first of his 15 US-only chart records was in 61. He was later on Columbia, MGM and Casino.

 RED ROSES FOR A BLUE LADY   10   03 APR 65   DOLTON
(Vaughn Monroe 49 hit)

CHARLIE DANIELS BAND

Fiddle player Daniels fronted The Jaguars and was on Hanover in 61 and Paula in 66 before becoming a Nashville session man and playing on records like Dylan's 'Nashville Skyline'. In 71 he formed his Grammy winning band and started his famous 'Volunteer Jams' in 74. He has had six US Top 40s and is still a country chart regular.

UNEASY RIDER   9   11 AUG 73   KAMA SUTRA
THE DEVIL WENT DOWN TO GEORGIA *(UK No. 14)*   3   15 SEP 79   EPIC

JOHNNY DANKWORTH

London born jazz sax playing husband of Cleo Laine fronts the most popular band of its kind in the UK. He even had two Top 10 singles, one of which charted in the US (in pre-Beatles days) and one which was covered there by the late Cannonball Adderley.

 EXPERIMENTS WITH MICE *(US No. 61)*   7   13 JUL 56   PARLOPHONE
AFRICAN WALTZ   10   12 MAY 61   COLUMBIA

DANNY WILSON

Dundee (UK) band previously called Spencer Tracy features brothers Kit & Gary Clark. Their hit was unsuccessfully released in the UK in Feb 87, six months later it scored in the US and on its third release eight months later it finally gave them the first hit in the UK. They broke up in 90.

MARY'S PRAYER *(US No. 23)*   3   30 APR 88   VIRGIN

TERENCE TRENT D'ARBY

Unpredictable New York singer/songwriter/performer fronted the group Touch while in the services in Germany. He moved to the UK and spent two years preparing his debut LP which topped charts worldwide (it was the first debut LP by a US act to enter the UK chart at No. 1). In 89 he released a 45 as E.G. O'Reilly but his long awaited second LP sold disappointingly.

IF YOU LET ME STAY *(US No. 68)*   7   11 APR 87   CBS
WISHING WELL   4   11 JUL 87   CBS
SIGN YOUR NAME   2   23 JAN 88   CBS

WISHING WELL   1(1)   07 MAY 88   COLUMBIA
SIGN YOUR NAME   4   13 AUG 88   COLUMBIA

BOBBY DARIN

Born Walden Cassotto in the Bronx, Darin had eight years of transatlantic hits which varied from R'n'R to MOR. His first record was 'Rock Island Line' in 56 and after eight more flops he charted in 58. Apart from singing he was also an actor and was later on Direction and Motown. He died in 73.

DREAM LOVER   1(4)   03 JUL 59   LONDON
MACK THE KNIFE *(Louis Armstrong 56 hit)*   1(2)   16 OCT 59   LONDON
BEYOND THE SEA (LA MER)   8   12 FEB 60   LONDON
CLEMENTINE *(US No. 21 – Bing Crosby 41 hit)*   10   15 APR 60   LONDON
LAZY RIVER   3   21 APR 61   LONDON
(US No. 14 – Hoagy Carmichael 32 hit)
YOU MUST HAVE BEEN A BEAUTIFUL BABY   10   27 OCT 61   LONDON
(Bing Crosby 31 hit)
MULTIPLICATION *(US No. 30)*   5   12 JAN 62   LONDON
THINGS   3   17 AUG 62   LONDON
IF I WERE A CARPENTER *(Tim Harden song)*   9   19 NOV 66   ATLANTIC

SPLISH SPLASH *(UK No. 18)*   4   21 JUL 58   ATCO
QUEEN OF THE HOP *(US No. 24)*   9   17 NOV 58   ATCO
DREAM LOVER   2   07 JUN 59   ATCO
MACK THE KNIFE   1(9)   05 OCT 59   ATCO
(Top US single 59 and Grammy winner)
BEYOND THE SEA (LA MER)   6   28 JAN 60   ATCO
YOU MUST HAVE BEEN A BEAUTIFUL BABY   5   16 OCT 61   ATCO
THINGS   3   25 AUG 62   ATCO
YOU'RE THE REASON I'M LIVING   3   16 MAR 63   CAPITOL
18 YELLOW ROSES *(US No. 37)*   10   15 JUN 63   CAPITOL
IF I WERE A CARPENTER   8   05 NOV 66   ATLANTIC

JAMES DARREN

Actor/singer, born James Ercolani in Philadelphia, first came to the public's attention in the film Gidget in 59. His first release was 'There's No Such Thing' in 59 and he scored three US-only Top 20s in the early 60s. He later recorded for Warner, Kirshner, Buddah, Private Stock (where he briefly re-charted in 77) and RCA.

GOODBYE CRUEL WORLD *(US No. 25)*   3   04 DEC 61   COLPIX
HER ROYAL MAJESTY *(Co-written Carole King)*   6   17 MAR 62   COLPIX

DARTS

London based doo-wop revival act evolved out of Rocky Sharpe & The Razors, and had four lead singers including Den Hegarty and Rita Ray. They had 12 UK-only hits between 77-80 including three successive No.2s. This entertaining act, often produced by Tommy Boyce, were later on Sunburst (82) and Choice Cuts (83).

DADDY COOL/ THE GIRL CAN'T HELP IT *(Rays 57 US hit/ Little Richard 57 hit)*	6	10 DEC 77	MAGNET
COME BACK MY LOVE *(Wrens/Cardinals oldie)*	2	04 MAR 78	MAGNET
BOY FROM NEW YORK CITY *(Ad-Libs 65 US hit)*	2	03 JUN 78	MAGNET
IT'S RAINING *(Originally by Irma Thomas)*	2	02 SEP 78	MAGNET
GET IT	10	03 MAR 79	MAGNET
DUKE OF EARL *(Produced by Roy Wood – Gene Chandler 62 hit)*	6	25 AUG 79	MAGNET

DAVID & JONATHAN

Duo were the very successful UK songwriters Roger Greenaway and Roger Cook. They had the US hit version of The Beatles' 'Michelle' (No. 18), with their second release under this name, but failed to chart there with their UK Top 10 track. Greenaway is now a top UK music industry figure and Cook is a top Nashville writer.

LOVERS OF THE WORLD UNITE	7	10 SEP 66	COLUMBIA

Also see Blue Mink/Pipkins

F.R. DAVID

Tunisia born singer/producer who lived in France, where in 72 he produced the big local hit 'Superman Superman'. He was later in Vangelis' band, Les Variations and Cafe De Paris. He followed his only transatlantic hit 'Words' naturally with 'Music'.

WORDS *(US No. 62)*	2	30 APR 83	CARRERE

PAUL DAVIDSON

Kingston studio engineer had a UK hit with a record that did little in his native Jamaica. His one-off was a reggae version, with strings, of the old Allman Brothers number.

MIDNIGHT RIDER *(Joe Cocker 72 hit)*	10	24 JAN 76	TROPICAL

DAVE DAVIES

Long time member of The Kinks (with brother Ray) had two UK-only Top 20s in the same year, the other being 'Susannah's Still Alive' (No. 20). He later recorded for RCA and Warner.

DEATH OF A CLOWN	3	05 AUG 67	PYE

Also see The Kinks

WINDSOR DAVIES & DON ESTELLE

UK actors both featured in the TV situation comedy It Ain't Half Hot Mum had a one-off UK hit with an old Ink Spots song. They followed it with the Mills Brothers 'Paper Doll'. Don was later on EMI, Christy, UA and Lofty (named after his TV character).

WHISPERING GRASS	1(3)	07 JUN 75	EMI

MAC DAVIS

Texan singer/songwriter recorded for Jamie in 62, Vee Jay in 63 and Capitol in 65. He had four US-only Top 20 hits in the 70s and continued having country hits in the 80s. He also wrote hits for Elvis (2), Kenny Rogers and Bobby Goldsboro, appeared in movies and had his own TV series.

BABY DON'T GET HOOKED ON ME *(UK No. 29)*	1(3)	23 SEP 72	COLUMBIA
STOP AND SMELL THE ROSES	9	26 OCT 74	COLUMBIA

PAUL DAVIS

Singer/writer from Mississippi had a successful pop career with eight US-only Top 40s to his credit. He went into the country music field in 86 and has since had two No.1s, one in a duet with Marie Osmond and one in a trio with Paul Overstreet and Tanya Tucker. He has also written many top country hits for other acts.

I GO CRAZY *(Took a record 28 weeks to get to the Top 10)*	7	18 MAR 78	BANG
'65 LOVE AFFAIR	6	22 MAY 82	ARISTA

SAMMY DAVIS JR

Without doubt one of the world's top all-round entertainers. He started recording in 54 and was the first vocalist to top the US LP charts in 55. In his long and successful career he also notched up a handful of transatlantic hit singles. He died in 90.

LOVE ME OR LEAVE ME *(US No. 20 – Ruth Etting 29 hit)*	8	23 SEP 55	BRUNSWICK
SOMETHING'S GOTTA GIVE	9	16 JUL 55	DECCA
THE CANDY MAN *(From 'Willy Wonka & The Chocolate Factory')*	1(3)	10 JUN 72	MGM

SKEETER DAVIS

Born Mary Penick in Kentucky, she teamed with her best friend Betty Jack Davis to form the Davis Sisters and recorded for Fortune in 52. Betty was killed in a car crash just before their first hit made No 1 in the country chart. Skeeter had 41 solo country hits and a transatlantic Top 20 single.

THE END OF THE WORLD *(UK No. 18 – she sang it with Betty Jack in mind)*	2	23 MAR 63	RCA
I CAN'T STAY MAD AT YOU	7	02 NOV 63	RCA

SPENCER DAVIS GROUP

Spencer Davis joined fellow Birmingham (UK) act the Muff-Woody Jazz Band to form the SDG in 63. Their first four singles were covers of US R&B singles and the fifth went to No. 1 and was the first of five successive UK Top 20s. Brothers Steve & Muff Winwood left in 67 and the SDG was never the same. Spencer re-appeared in 84, dueting with Dusty Springfield, while Steve enjoyed an illustrious career that continues to flourish.

KEEP ON RUNNIN' *(US No. 76 – Composed reggae star Jackie Edwards)*	1(1)	22 JAN 66	FONTANA
SOMEBODY HELP ME *(US No. 47)*	1(2)	16 APR 66	FONTANA
GIMME SOME LOVING	2	26 NOV 66	FONTANA
I'M A MAN	9	11 FEB 67	FONTANA
GIMME SOME LOVIN'	7	25 FEB 67	UA
I'M A MAN	10	06 MAY 67	UA

Also see Traffic/Steve Winwood

TYRONE DAVIS

Despite having over 40 black music and 15 US pop hits this Mississippi soul star has yet to make the UK chart. He first recorded as Tyrone The Wonder Boy in 65 and has been on ABC, Columbia, Highrise, Ocean Front and Future.

CAN I CHANGE MY MIND	5	22 FEB 69	DAKAR
TURN BACK THE HANDS OF TIME	3	23 MAY 70	DAKAR

DAWN – SEE TONY ORLANDO FOR HIT DETAILS

DORIS DAY

The No. 1 female singer/actress of the 50s was born Doris Kappelhoff in Cincinnati. Her first hit was as vocalist on Les Brown's No. 1 'Sentimental Journey' in 45. She had the first of her four solo US No. 1s in 48 and most of her hits before 55. She re-appeared in the UK charts in the late 80s.

	READY WILLING AND ABLE	8	15 APR 55	PHILIPS
	WHATEVER WILL BE WILL BE	1(6)	10 AUG 56	PHILIPS
	MOVE OVER DARLING (UK No. 45 in 87)	8	02 MAY 64	CBS
	WHATEVER WILL BE WILL BE	3	11 AUG 56	COLUMBIA

TAYLOR DAYNE

Long Island (US) singer born Leslie Wundermann fronted various rock bands before scoring in the dance music field with her rock styled vocals. She has had three Grammy nominations and was one of the top transatlantic female singers in the late 80s.

	TELL IT TO MY HEART	3	20 FEB 88	ARISTA
	PROVE YOUR LOVE	8	16 APR 88	ARISTA
	TELL IT TO MY HEART	7	23 JAN 88	ARISTA
	PROVE YOUR LOVE	7	07 MAY 88	ARISTA
	I'LL ALWAYS LOVE YOU (UK No. 41)	3	24 SEP 88	ARISTA
	DON'T RUSH ME	2	21 JAN 89	ARISTA
	WITH EVERY BEAT OF MY HEART	5	16 DEC 89	ARISTA

DAZZ BAND

Grammy-winning funk band from Ohio fronted by sax man Bobby Harris. Originally recorded, and charted, as Kinsman Dazz on 20th Century in 78. Biggest UK hit was 'Let It All Blow' (UK 12/US 84) in 84. Group have since charted on Geffen in 86 and RCA in 88.

	LET IT WHIP	5	17 JUL 82	MOTOWN

DEACON BLUE

Glasgow band fronted by singer/songwriter Ricky Ross, named after Steely Dan's 'Deacon Blues'. Their fourth UK-only chart record was their first Top 10. Their third LP 'When The World Knows Your Name' entered at No.1 in UK.

	REAL GONE KID (Their seventh single)	8	26 NOV 88	CBS

DEAD END KIDS

Five man Glasgow band, produced by hitmaker Barry Blue, were very popular in Ireland and had a UK one-off hit with an old Honeycombs song. They followed it with 'Breakaway' (also the title of their LP) and later revived 'Glad All Over'.

	HAVE I THE RIGHT?	6	30 APR 77	CBS

DEAD OR ALIVE

Singer Pete Burns was in Mystery Girls and Nightmares In Wax before forming this group. Act's two singles on Indie labels Inevitable and Black Eyes failed, as did their first few on Epic. Teaming with producers Stock, Aitken & Waterman gave them their first Top 10 placing. They have since had three more UK Top 20s, two US dance No.1s and a No.15 there with 'Brand New Lover' (UK 31).

	YOU SPIN ME ROUND (LIKE A RECORD)	1(2)	09 MAR 85	EPIC
	(US No. 11 – took 15 weeks to reach No. 1)			

HAZELL DEAN

Chelmsford (UK) singer had been in The Vandals, Union Express and a group with Trevor Horn. She also had six singles on Decca in 76 and was a regular on the TV show One More Time in 77. Most of her UK-only chart records have been made by the S.A.W. team, and she signed with their Lisson label in 89.

	SEARCHIN'	6	09 JUN 84	PROTO
	WHATEVER I DO (WHEREVER I GO)	4	18 AUG 84	PROTO
	WHO'S LEAVING WHO	4	30 APR 88	EMI
	(Anne Murray 86 country hit)			

JIMMY DEAN

Born Seth Ward in Texas, his first single 'Bumming Around' was a No. 5 country hit in 52 on 4 Star (where he also cut the original version of 'Release Me'). He was on Mercury in 55 and in 61 his 11th Columbia single was a Transatlantic Top 10. He had a hit TV series between 63-66 and in 76 his 'I.O.U.' was a gold single.

	BIG BAD JOHN	3	17 NOV 61	PHILIPS
	(Song inspired by his 6'5" friend John Mentoe)			
	BIG BAD JOHN	1(5)	06 NOV 61	COLUMBIA
	P.T. 109 (About President Kennedy)	8	26 MAY 62	COLUMBIA

DeBARGE

Family quartet from Michigan includes Eldra, James (who married Janet Jackson) and Bunny DeBarge. They had the first of eight black music Top 40s in 82 and the first of four US pop Top 20s 'All This Time' in 83. Eldra and Bunny have also had solo hits.

	RHYTHM OF THE NIGHT	4	18 MAY 85	GORDY
	RHYTHM OF THE NIGHT	3	27 APR 85	GORDY
	(From the film The Last Dragon)			
	WHO'S HOLDING DONNA NOW	6	10 AUG 85	GORDY

Also see El Debarge

EL DeBARGE

Leader of family group DeBarge has had four black music Top 10s, the others being 'You Wear it Well', 'Love Always' and 'Real Love'.

	WHO'S JOHNNY (From the film Short Circuit)	3	05 JUL 86	GORDY

Also see Debarge

CHRIS DE BURGH

Born Chris Davidson in Argentina, his first success was in Brazil with 'Flying' in 75. After many releases, he had his first UK chart entry in 81. Five years and a few minor transatlantic charters later, he had his biggest hit with his 24th single.

	THE LADY IN RED	1(3)	02 AUG 86	A&M
	MISSING YOU	3	26 NOV 88	A&M
	LADY IN RED (1 of 2 Irish hits in US Top 3)	3	23 MAY 87	A&M

LYNSEY DE PAUL

London based singer/songwriter and classically trained pianist Lynsey (Rubin) had five UK-only Top 20s between 72-77 and was voted top British female act of 72. She is a well known face on UK TV and recorded for Warner in 74, DJM in 77 and MCA in 81.

	SUGAR ME (Co-written with Barry Blue)	5	16 SEP 72	MAM
	NO HONESTLY	7	23 NOV 74	JET

STEPHANIE DE SYKES

Essex (UK) singer started on TV's Opportunity Knocks (as Stephanie Ryton) and became a top session singer. Her two UK-only Top 20s (the other was 'We'll Find Our Day') were both in the soap opera Crossroads. She married Mojos singer Stu James, also recorded as Debbie Stanford and was later on DJM, Ammo and Ariola.

 BORN WITH A SMILE ON MY FACE (with RAIN) | 2 | 03 AUG 74 | BRADLEY'S

DAVE DEE, DOZY, BEAKY, MICK & TITCH

Pop quintet from Salisbury (UK) previously known as Dave Dee (an ex policeman who was at the scene of Eddie Cochran's death) & The Bostons. Their first two releases flopped then they hit the UK Top 40 13 times without managing a US Top 40 entry. Dave went solo in 70 with little success then became a record executive. The group recorded as DBM&T and re-appeared on Earlobe in 81.

HOLD TIGHT	4	16 APR 66	FONTANA
HIDEAWAY	10	02 JUL 66	FONTANA
BEND IT	2	08 OCT 66	FONTANA
SAVE ME	3	31 DEC 66	FONTANA
OKAY!	4	01 JUL 67	FONTANA
ZABADAK (US No. 52)	3	04 NOV 67	FONTANA
LEGEND OF XANADU	1(1)	23 MAR 68	FONTANA
LAST NIGHT IN SOHO	8	03 AUG 68	FONTANA

JOEY DEE & THE STARLITERS

New Jersey born Joey Dinicola was on Scepter and Bonus in 60 and was leader of New York's Peppermint Lounge house band where the twist re-surfaced to sweep the world. It was Joey's first hit, and Chubby's old one that made it happen. Act had four US-only Top 20s and included at times Jimi Hendrix and three of The Rascals. Dee is now spokesman for 'oldies' acts in the US.

PEPPERMINT TWIST (PT. 1)	1(2)	13 JAN 62	ROULETTE
SHOUT (PT. 1) (Isley Brothers 59 US hit)	6	05 MAY 62	ROULETTE

KIKI DEE

Born Pauline Matthews in Yorkshire, her first release was on Fontana in 63 (as was Elton's in 65). After many small selling singles, she became the first UK act to sign to Motown in 70. Her biggest solo hit was 'I've Got The Music In Me' (UK 19/US 12). With Elton she later released 'Loving You Is Sweeter Than Ever'.

DON'T GO BREAKING MY HEART (With ELTON JOHN)	1(6)	24 JUL 76	ROCKET
DON'T GO BREAKING MY HEART (With ELTON JOHN)	1(4)	07 AUG 76	ROCKET

DEELE

Cincinnati group fronted by Darnell Bristol and Carlos Greene, also including the hottest US writing and production team of the late 80s, Antonio 'L.A.' Reid and Kenny 'Babyface' Edmunds. Group first hit the black music chart with 'Body Talk' in 83 (No. 3) and had their debut US-only Top 10 pop hit five years later.

 TWO OCCASIONS | 10 | 21 MAY 88 | SOLAR

Also see Babyface

DEEP PURPLE

UK hard rock band hit first in the US with a string of revivals in 68. They were one of the top live bands of 70s, selling millions of LPs and playing to SRO crowds everywhere. Group has had many members, best known being Ian Gillan, Ritchie Blackmore, John Lord, Roger Glover and Ian Paice who were all in the reformed group in 84.

BLACK NIGHT (US No. 66)		2	17 OCT 70	HARVEST
STRANGE KIND OF WOMAN		8	20 MAR 71	HARVEST
HUSH (UK No. 62 in 88) (Joe South Song – Billy Joe Royal 67 US hit)		4	21 SEP 68	TETRAGRAM
SMOKE ON THE WATER (UK No. 21)		4	28 JUL 73	WARNER

RICK DEES & HIS CAST OF IDIOTS

Memphis DJ had a one-off transatlantic Top 10 with a novelty that was first on his local Freetone label. He followed it with 'Dis-Gorilla'. He was sacked by his radio station but went on to be one of the very top US DJs and host of TV series Solid Gold.

DISCO DUCK		6	09 OCT 76	RSO
DISCO DUCK	1(1)		16 OCT 76	RSO

DEF LEPPARD

Sheffield (UK) quintet fronted by Joe Elliott have had a string of transatlantic hits. Their third LP 'Pyromania' sold seven million in the US alone whilst the LP 'Hysteria' sold over 12 million and spent a record 96 weeks in the US Top 40. It is the top selling LP ever by a UK group (including The Beatles and Stones) and it was also the first metal LP to sell a million CDs.

ANIMAL (US No.19) (Their ninth single)		6	22 AUG 87	BLUDGEON RIFF
HYSTERIA (UK No. 26)		10	26 MAR 88	MERCURY
POUR SOME SUGAR ON ME (UK No. 18)		2	23 JUL 88	MERCURY
LOVE BITES (UK No. 11)	1(1)		08 OCT 88	MERCURY
ARMAGEDDON IT (UK No. 20)		3	21 JAN 89	MERCURY

DeFRANCO FAMILY

Family quartet from Ontario fronted by 14 year old Tony DeFranco, sold two million with their first 45 and looked set to be the next teen sensation. However, they only managed one more US-only Top 20 with a revival of 'Save The Last Dance For Me' (No. 18).

HEARTBEAT – IT'S A LOVEBEAT	3	17 NOV 73	20TH CENTURY

DESMOND DEKKER & THE ACES

Jamaican born reggae artist first recorded for his local Yabba label in 63. He was the island's 'King of Bluebeat' (an annual award) five times between 63-69. His first UK chart hit was '007' (No.14) in 67. He was the first reggae/ska act to make the US Top 10 and the first to top the UK charts.

ISRAELITES	1(1)		19 APR 69	PYRAMID
YOU CAN GET IT IF YOU REALLY WANT (The Aces not credited – Jimmy Cliff song)		2	03 OCT 70	TROJAN
IT MEK		7	19 JUL 69	PYRAMID
THE ISRAELITES (Re-entry)		10	07 JUN 75	CACTUS
THE ISRAELITES		9	28 JUN 69	UNI

DELEGATES

A 'cut-up' hit (inc. bits of other records) put together by US DJ Bob DeCarlo. Follow up was 'Richard M. Nixon, Face The Issues'.

CONVENTION '72	8	18 NOV 72	MAINSTREAM

DELFONICS

Soul trio from Philadelphia who started life as a quartet, The Four Gents. They recorded on Moon Shoot, Cameo and Fling before their five year 16-hit run on Philly Groove. They were fronted by brothers William & Wilbert Hart and in 71 included Major Harris, who went on to solo success. They were on Arista in 78.

LA-LA MEANS I LOVE YOU (UK No. 19 in 71)	4	06 APR 68	PHILLY GROOVE
DIDN'T I (BLOW YOUR MIND THIS TIME) (UK No. 22 in 71)	10	21 MAR 70	PHILLY GROOVE

DELIVERANCE SOUNDTRACK – SEE ERIC WEISSBERG FOR HIT DETAILS

DELLS

Soulful Chicago quartet fronted by Johnny Funches have had black music hits for four decades. The group first recorded as The El Rays on Checker in 54 and first hit with 'Oh What A Nite' in 56, which they re-recorded, scoring a Top 10 in 69. Only UK hit was 'I Can Sing A Rainbow' (UK 15/US 22). They were also on Vee Jay, Argo, Mercury, ABC, MCA, Skylark, 20th Century, TMI and Private I.

	STAY IN MY CORNER	10	24 AUG 68	CADET
	(Re-recording of their 65 Vee Jay record)			
	OH WHAT A NITE	10	27 SEP 69	CADET
	(They also cut 'Oh What a Good Nite')			

JOHN DENVER

The 70s top selling folk/pop act was born Henry Deutchendorf in New Mexico. He joined the Chad Mitchell Trio in 65 and his first solo success came in 71 (his song 'Leaving On A Jet Plane' was a hit for Peter, Paul & Mary in 69). He had 10 Top 20 LPs in the US (8 in UK) and nine Top 20 US singles (1 in UK). He also made movies and TV specials. He was on Windstar in 88.

	ANNIE'S SONG	1(1)	12 OCT 74	RCA
	TAKE ME HOME, COUNTRY ROADS *(Feat. Fat City)*	2	28 AUG 71	RCA
	(The composers had never been to West Virginia)			
	ROCKY MOUNTAIN HIGH	9	03 MAR 73	RCA
	SUNSHINE ON MY SHOULDERS	1(1)	30 MAR 74	RCA
	ANNIE'S SONG *(Song about his wife Annie)*	1(2)	27 JUL 74	RCA
	BACK HOME AGAIN	5	09 NOV 74	RCA
	THANK GOD I'M A COUNTRY BOY	1(1)	07 JUN 75	RCA
	I'M SORRY	1(1)	27 SEP 75	RCA

KARL DENVER

Glasgow folk/country singer/yodeller who with his trio had five UK-only Top 20s in pre-Beatles days. He had previously worked in the country field in the US and had been on the Grand Ole Opry. He was on Mercury in 66 and had a UK indie hit in 89 on Factory with a revival of his 62 hit 'Wimowch'.

	MEXICALI ROSE *(Bing Crosby 38 hit)*	9	27 OCT 61	DECCA
	WIMOWEH	3	09 MAR 62	DECCA
	(Based on same tune as 'The Lion Sleeps Tonight')			
	NEVER GOODBYE	9	20 APR 62	DECCA

DEODATO

Brazilian born musician/producer worked with acts like Aretha and Frank Sinatra before having a transatlantic Top 10 with the Richard Strauss composed theme from the film 2001. His follow up was 'Rhapsody In Blue'. Later he successfully produced acts like Kool & The Gang and recorded on MCA in 74 and Warner in 78.

	ALSO SPRACH ZARATHUSTRA (2001)	7	26 MAY 73	CTI
	ALSO SPRACH ZARATHUSTRA (2001)	2	31 MAR 73	CTI

DEPECHE MODE

Essex (UK) based foursome fronted by Dave Gahan and originally including multi-talented Vince Clarke. They were on the Some Bizzare album in 80 before starting a run of 16 UK Top 20 singles (1 in US) and eight UK-only Top 10 albums. In the US they have had two Top 3 dance singles and now sell out stadium tours there.

	JUST CAN'T GET ENOUGH	8	17 OCT 81	MUTE
	SEE YOU	6	13 MAR 82	MUTE
	EVERYTHING COUNTS	6	20 AUG 83	MUTE
	(Live version issued in 89 as a single)			
	PEOPLE ARE PEOPLE *(US No 13 & German No. 1)*	4	07 APR 84	MUTE
	MASTER AND SERVANT *(US No. 87)*	9	22 SEP 84	MUTE

DEREK & THE DOMINOES

Short lived group put together by Eric Clapton included Duane Allman, Bobby Whitlock, Jim Gordon and Carl Radle. 'Layla', arguably Eric's best and certainly best known song, flopped when released in 70 in the UK but hit twice there later. Bobby and Carl later sued Eric over unpaid royalties.

	LAYLA	7	26 AUG 72	POLYDOR
	(Song about Mrs George Harrison, later Mrs Clapton)			
	LAYLA	4	03 APR 82	RSO
	LAYLA	10	05 AUG 72	ATCO

Also see Eric Clapton/Cream

TERI DeSARIO – SEE K.C. & THE SUNSHINE BAND FOR HIT DETAILS

JACKIE DeSHANNON

Born Sharon Myers in Kentucky she recorded in The Nomads and as Jackie Dee, Jackie Shannon and Sherry Lee Myers and was on Sage, Glenn, Fraternity, Dot, P.J., Sand, Gone and Edison Int. She first cut 'Needles & Pins' and wrote 'When You Walk In The Room' (both hits by The Searchers), 'Come And Stay With Me' (Marianne Faithfull) and 'Bette Davis Eyes' (Kim Carnes). She has never made the UK chart. She is married to singer Randy Edelman.

	WHAT THE WORLD NEEDS NOW IS LOVE	7	24 JUL 65	IMPERIAL
	PUT A LITTLE LOVE IN YOUR HEART	4	30 AUG 69	IMPERIAL

DESIRELESS

French chanteuse had a one-off UK charter with a track that had previously been a big European hit. She followed it with 'John'.

	VOYAGE VOYAGE (REMIX)	5	11 JUN 88	CBS

DETROIT EMERALDS

Arkansas soul trio led by Abe Tilmon originally hit in 68 with 'Show Time' on Ric Tic. They had five black music and four UK Top 20s but never made the US pop Top 20. Abe died in 83.

	FEEL THE NEED IN ME	4	17 MAR 73	JANUS
	(A re-recording in 77 reached 12 UK & 90 in US)			

WILLIAM DeVAUGHN

Washington soul singer had one major hit with a composition of his own, on which he was backed by MFSB. His follow up was 'Blood Is Thicker Than Water' (US 43). He recorded for HCRC in 82.

	BE THANKFUL FOR WHAT YOU GOT	4	20 JUN 74	ROXBURY
	(UK No. 31 and UK No. 44 in 80)			

BARRY DeVORZON & PERRY BOTKIN JR.

Top writers/arrangers and producers co-wrote their US hit in 71 as a film theme. Later it was used in the soap opera The Young & The Restless and in the 76 Olympics by Romanian gymnast Nadia Comaneci. Barry recorded R'n'R in the 50s, wrote 'Dreaming' (Johnny Burnette) and fronted Barry & The Tamerlanes.

	NADIA'S THEME (THE YOUNG & THE RESTLESS)	8	11 DEC 76	A&M

DEXY'S MIDNIGHT RUNNERS

Midlands (UK) band put together by Kevin Rowland, who first recorded with The Killjoys on Raw in 77. First release 'Dance Stance' charted and they scored eight UK Top 20s in the next six years. The act, who had many personnel changes, only scored in the US with their LP 'Too-Rye-Ay' (14) which their No. 1 hit came from. Kevin's solo work in the late 80s failed to chart.

 GENO 1(2) 03 MAY 80 LNF
(About US act Geno Washington who had no US hits)
THERE THERE MY DEAR 7 02 AUG 80 LNF
COME ON EILEEN 1(4) 07 AUG 82 MERCURY
(Feat. The Emerald Express – UK Gold-Top record 82)
JACKIE WILSON SAID (As Kevin Rowland &...) 5 09 OCT 82 MERCURY
(Van Morrison song about US Soul singer)
 COME ON EILEEN 1(1) 23 APR 83 MERCURY

DENNIS DeYOUNG

Chicago born lead singer of Styx had one solo US Top 40 and followed it with 'Don't Wait For Heroes'. In 89 he formed Damn Yankees with Ted Nugent and Tommy Shaw (ex-Styx) on Warner.

DESERT MOON 10 10 NOV 84 A&M

Also see Styx

JIM DIAMOND .

Glasgow born one-time vocalist with Alexis Korner recorded on Bradley's in 75 and Bandit in 77 and was in hit act PhD in 82. He had two UK-only Top 10s, the first co-written with Graham Lyle of Gallagher & Lyle. He was also featured on The Crowd's No. 1 and recorded on Tembo in 87 and WEA in 89.

I SHOULD HAVE KNOWN BETTER 1(1) 01 DEC 84 A&M
HI HO SILVER (TV theme) 5 22 MAR 86 A&M

Also see PhD

NEIL DIAMOND

Unmistakable singer/songwriter born Noah Kaminsky in New York. He recorded in the duo Neil & Jack on Duel in 60 and as a soloist on Columbia in 64. He first hit as writer of 'Sunday & Me' (Jay & The Americans) and his song 'I'm A Believer' scored for The Monkees as his solo career was taking off. To date, the man who broke the record for indoor concert attendance has had a staggering 37 Top 40 US hits (9 UK) and over two dozen Transatlantic Top 100 LPs.

CRACKLIN' ROSIE (20th US hit – first in UK) 3 05 DEC 70 UNI
SWEET CAROLINE 8 13 MAR 71 UNI
I AM... I SAID 4 12 JUN 71 UNI
YOU DON'T BRING ME FLOWERS 5 23 DEC 78 COLUMBIA
(Released as Barbra (Streisand) & Neil)
CHERRY CHERRY 6 15 OCT 66 BANG
GIRL, YOU'LL BE A WOMAN SOON 10 27 MAY 67 BANG
SWEET CAROLINE 4 16 AUG 69 UNI
HOLLY HOLY 6 27 DEC 69 UNI
CRACKLIN' ROSIE 1(1) 10 OCT 70 UNI
I AM... I SAID 4 08 MAY 71 UNI
SONG SUNG BLUE 1(1) 01 JUL 72 UNI
(UK No. 14 – US Top Easy Listening Single 72)
LONGFELLOW SERENADE 5 23 NOV 74 COLUMBIA
YOU DON'T BRING ME FLOWERS 1(2) 02 DEC 78 COLUMBIA
(Released as Barbra (Streisand) & Neil)
LOVE ON THE ROCKS (UK No. 17) 2 10 JAN 81 COLUMBIA
HELLO AGAIN (UK No. 51) 6 28 MAR 81 CAPITOL
AMERICA 8 13 JUN 81 CAPITOL
(Above 3 from film The Jazz Singer)
HEARTLIGHT (UK No. 47) 5 13 NOV 82 COLUMBIA

DICK & DEEDEE

Dick St. John started as a solo act and teamed with fellow L.A. resident Dee Dee Sperling in 61 and the duo scored three US-only Top 20s, starting with their biggest hit (originally released as the 'B' side on Lama). They were later on Warner and Dot while Dick had solo singles on Congress, Philips, Pom Pom and Rona.

 THE MOUNTAIN'S HIGH (UK No. 27) 2 02 OCT 61 LIBERTY

DICKIES

US punk parody group led by Leonard Graves Phillips and including drummer Billy Club, had six UK-only hits giving their special 100 MPH treatment to songs like 'Silent Night', 'Nights In White Satin' and the theme from the children's TV show Banana Splits.

 BANANA SPLITS (TRA LA LA SONG) 7 12 MAY 79 A&M

BARBARA DICKSON

UK pop/MOR artist started in folk clubs, was spotted whilst in the show John, Paul, George, Ringo & Bert, and her first hit was produced by Jr. Campbell. Her UK-only success has been mainly in the LP field although she has had four Top 20 singles. She has also recorded for Decca, Epic, Contour, Legacy, MCA and K-Tel.

 ANSWER ME (Frankie Laine 53 hit) 9 14 FEB 76 RSO
I KNOW HIM SO WELL (With ELAINE PAIGE) 1(1) 02 FEB 85 RCA
(From Chess-First White female duo No. 1 UK chart)

MARK DINNING

Oklahoma born, younger brother of 40s stars The Dinning Sisters (Patti Page used to baby sit for him). He had some flops before a song written by sister Jean became his only Top 40 and the first 'disaster record' to top a chart. He later recorded for Cameo, Hickory, UA and he sadly joined his 'Teen Angel' in 86.

TEEN ANGEL (UK No. 28) 1(2) 08 FEB 60 MGM

DINO

New York based singer had his first US-only chart entry with the dance hit 'Summer Girls', which took a year from release to chart in 88. He was on the sell-out New Kids On The Block 89 tour with his band Mod Squad and his debut LP went gold.

I LIKE IT (He also wrote and produced this) 7 12 AUG 89 4TH & B.

DION

The ex leader of The Belmonts has had two dozen US solo hits since debuting with 'Lonely Teenager' (No. 12 in 60). In 89 he returned to the transatlantic charts (on Arista) and his early work was sampled in Jive Bunny's No. 1 'That's What I Like'. He has also been on Warner, Big Tree, Spector, Strawberry and Lifeso. After dropping out due to alcohol and drugs he 'found God' and an attempted comeback in 1990 was moderately successful.

 RUNAROUND SUE (Backed by Del Satins) 10 17 NOV 61 TOP RANK
RUNAROUND SUE 1(2) 23 OCT 61 LAURIE
THE WANDERER (UK No. 12 in 62 & No. 16 in 76) 2 24 FEB 62 LAURIE
(His song was a Country No. 1 in 88)
LOVERS WHO WANDER 3 09 JUN 62 LAURIE
LITTLE DIANE 8 18 AUG 62 LAURIE
LOVE CAME TO ME 10 22 DEC 62 LAURIE
RUBY BABY (Drifters 56 R&B hit) 2 23 FEB 63 COLUMBIA
DONNA THE PRIMA DONNA 6 26 OCT 63 COLUMBIA
DRIP DROP 6 28 DEC 63 COLUMBIA
(First by The Drifters-above 3 with The Wanderers)
ABRAHAM, MARTIN AND JOHN 4 14 DEC 68 LAURIE

Also see Dion & The Belmonts

DION & THE BELMONTS

Influential New York trio led by Dion DiMucci originally recorded as Dion & The Timberlanes (on Jubilee and Mohawk). Their third release as the Belmonts 'I Wonder Why' (UK hit for Showaddywaddy in 78) was the first of their seven US Top 40s. Dion went solo in 60 and the group (with Carlo Mastrangelo as lead) had two more Top 40s and recorded on Sabrina, UA, Dot and Strawberry.

🇺🇸	A TEENAGER IN LOVE (Song first called 'Great To Be Young & In love')	5	19 MAY 59	LAURIE
	WHERE OR WHEN (Hal Kemp 37 hit)	3	08 FEB 60	LAURIE

Also see Dion

DIRE STRAITS

Top UK band fronted by Scots born guitar virtuoso Mark Knopfler. First single 'Sultans Of Swing' in 78 was unsuccessful in UK until it took off in the US. They pack stadiums across the world and to date have sold nearly 50 million LPs. In the UK their 'Brothers In Arms' is the all time top selling LP (over 3 million) and next to The Beatles they have spent more weeks on the UK LP chart than any UK group. They have had seven Top 5 LPs (UK) and five Top 20s (US). Knopfler has also recorded film soundtracks.

🇬🇧	SULTANS OF SWING (Back to UK No. 62 in 88)	8	07 APR 79	VERTIGO
	ROMEO AND JULIET	8	21 FEB 81	VERTIGO
	PRIVATE INVESTIGATIONS	2	18 SEP 82	VERTIGO
	MONEY FOR NOTHING (Comp. by Mark and Sting (who sings backing vocals)	4	10 AUG 85	VERTIGO
	WALK OF LIFE	2	25 JAN 86	VERTIGO
🇺🇸	SULTANS OF SWING	4	07 APR 79	WARNER
	MONEY FOR NOTHING	1(3)	21 SEP 85	WARNER
	WALK OF LIFE	7	25 JAN 86	WARNER

DIRT BAND – SEE NITTY GRITTY DIRT BAND FOR HIT DETAILS

DISCO TEX & THE SEX-O-LETTES

Brainchild of top producer/writer Bob Crewe this session group featured the vocals of Monti Rock III (Joe Montanez Jr.), owner of a chain of hairdressing shops and the actor who played the disco DJ in Saturday Night Fever. Group recorded until 77.

🇬🇧	GET DANCING	8	21 DEC 74	CHELSEA
	I WANNA DANCE WIT CHOO' (US No. 23)	6	17 MAY 75	CHELSEA
🇺🇸	GET DANCIN'	10	08 FEB 75	CHELSEA

SACHA DISTEL

French entertainer started recording in the late 50s and got his sole UK hit with a Burt Bacharach song that had been written, with Bob Dylan in mind, for the film Butch Cassidy And The Sundance Kid.

🇬🇧	RAINDROPS KEEP FALLIN' ON MY HEAD (B.J. Thomas 69 US hit)	10	14 MAR 70	WARNER

DIXIEBELLES

Female trio from Memphis comprised Shirley Thomas, Mary Hunt and Mildred Pratcher. They did much local session work and saw their two US-only chart records go into the Top 20 – the other being 'Southtown USA' (15).

🇺🇸	(DOWN AT) PAPA JOE'S	9	30 NOV 63	SS7

DIXIE CUPS

New Orleans trio, originally called the Mel-Tones, which included sisters Ann & Rosa Lee Hawkins. This popular 60s girl group also had two other US-only Top 20s 'People Say' (12) and 'Iko Iko' (US 20 & UK 23). They later recorded on ABC in 65.

🇺🇸	CHAPEL OF LOVE (UK No. 22) (First recorded, but not released, by The Ronettes)	1(3)	06 JUN 64	RED BIRD

ANITA DOBSON

UK actress/singer had a UK Top 10 with a vocal of the theme from EastEnders, the soap in which she starred. She also recorded with Queen's Brian May and was on Parlophone and Fanfare.

🇬🇧	ANYONE CAN FALL IN LOVE	4	16 AUG 86	BBC

DOCTOR & THE MEDICS

Failed 6' 5" UK doctor Clive Jackson fronted this Arthur Brown styled psychedelic group. They had some Indie success on Illegal in 85 and took Norman Greenbaum's (who once recorded as Dr. Norman Greenbaum) song to the top again. Follow up was 'Burn'.

🇬🇧	SPIRIT IN THE SKY (US No.69)	1(3)	07 JUN 86	IRS

DR. FEELGOOD

Essex (UK) pub-rock band led by Wilko Johnson were named after an earlier US R&B act. They were UK media favourites and a popular live act but never charted in the US. They had a No. 1 UK LP with 'Stupidity' and six chart 45s. Group were also on Liberty, Stiff and Chiswick and their many personnel changes led to their end.

🇬🇧	MILK AND ALCOHOL (Co-writer Nick Lowe)	9	17 FEB 79	UA

DR. HOOK

A popular 70s band fronted by Ray Sawyer (who had recorded on Sandy in 62) and Dennis Locorriere. Their 'tongue in cheek' style and fun live shows helped them achieve eight years of regular transatlantic hits. They broke up in the early 80s.

🇬🇧	SYLVIA'S MOTHER (Released as Dr. Hook & The Medicine Show')	2	29 JUL 72	CBS
	A LITTLE BIT MORE (US No.11 – in UK was at No. 2 five weeks)	2	24 JUL 76	CAPITOL
	IF NOT YOU (US No. 55)	5	20 NOV 76	CAPITOL
	WHEN YOU'RE IN LOVE WITH A BEAUTIFUL WOMAN	1(3)	17 NOV 79	CAPITOL
	BETTER LOVE NEXT TIME (US No. 12)	8	26 JAN 80	CAPITOL
	SEXY EYES	4	12 APR 80	CAPITOL
🇺🇸	SYLVIA'S MOTHER (first two as Dr. Hook & the Medicine Show)	5	03 JUN 72	COLUMBIA
	THE COVER OF 'ROLLING STONE' (In UK rel. as 'The Cover of the 'Radio Times')	6	17 MAR 73	COLUMBIA
	ONLY SIXTEEN (Sam Cooke 59 hit)	6	17 APR 76	CAPITOL
	SHARING THE NIGHT TOGETHER (UK No. 43)	6	06 JAN 79	CAPITOL
	WHEN YOU'RE IN LOVE WITH A BEAUTIFUL WOMAN	6	11 AUG 79	CAPITOL
	SEXY EYES	5	24 MAY 80	CAPITOL

DR. JOHN

Born Mac Rebennack in New Orleans he has played on hundreds of sessions over the last 30 years. As an artist he has been on Rex (59), Ace (61), A&M (65), Columbia (73), Sceptre (74), RCA (78), Horizon (79), Clean Cut (85), Maison De Soul (85) and Warner (89). He achieved his biggest hits on Atco between 68-73.

🇺🇸	RIGHT PLACE WRONG TIME	9	30 JUN 73	ATCO

KEN DODD

Popular Liverpool comedian/singer has had many UK-only hits since 60 with MOR ballads. He recorded as The Diddy Men in 65 and has also recorded on Images in 81, PRT in 84 and Ritz in 84. His tax evasion case in 89 – which he won – was front page news in the UK.

	LOVE IS LIKE A VIOLIN	9	02 SEP 60	DECCA
	TEARS (UK Gold record)	1(5)	02 OCT 65	COLUMBIA
	THE RIVER	3	24 DEC 65	COLUMBIA
	PROMISES	6	11 JUN 66	COLUMBIA

JOE DOLAN

The leader of the popular Irish showband The Drifters first recorded for Pye in 64. He had five UK-only hits and also sold well in Europe. He recorded for Ritz in 83.

	MAKE ME AN ISLAND (Co-writer Albert Hammond)	3	16 AUG 69	PYE

THOMAS DOLBY

UK based keyboard and computer wizard was born in Egypt and before his solo hits had played on multi-platinum LPs by Foreigner and Def Leppard. His third UK charter was a US Top 10 and his biggest UK hit was 'Hyperactive' (UK 17/US 62). He has since worked with George Clinton, David Bowie, Prefab Sprout and Belinda Carlisle.

	SHE BLINDED ME WITH SCIENCE (UK No. 49)	5	14 MAY 83	CAPITOL

JOE DOLCE

Ohio born performer who had a one-off No. 1, firstly in Australia and then in the UK, with this Italian styled novelty. Follow up was 'If You Want To Be Happy'.

	SHADDUP YOU FACE (US No. 53)	1(3)	21 FEB 81	EPIC

DOLLAR

Photogenic UK duo David Van Day and Thereza Bazaar (both ex-Guys'n'Dolls) were popular with UK teen buyers and charted 14 records there. Their only US entry was 'Shooting Star' (US 74/UK 14). They split in 83 and reformed in 86. David recorded solo on WEA in 83, Record Shack in 85, Union in 89 and Thereza was on MCA in 85.

	LOVE'S GOTTA HOLD ON ME	4	29 SEP 79	CARRERE
	I WANT TO HOLD YOUR HAND (Beatles 64 hit)	9	26 JAN 80	CARRERE
	MIRROR MIRROR (MON AMOUR)	4	16 JAN 82	WEA
	GIVE ME BACK MY HEART	4	24 APR 82	WEA
	OH L'AMOUR	7	06 FEB 88	LONDON
	(Originally a US Dance No. 3 by Erasure)			

FATS DOMINO

New Orleans' most famous son Antoine 'Fats' Domino first charted in 50 with 'The Fat Man' and was rockin' and rollin' before the term was coined. He may not have the 20 self written million sellers that are claimed but he has had over 50 US hits (20 in the UK) and he is one of the Kings of R'n'R.

	BLUEBERRY HILL (Glenn Miller 40 hit)	6	08 FEB 57	LONDON
	I'M IN LOVE AGAIN (UK No. 12)	4	23 JUN 56	IMPERIAL
	BLUEBERRY HILL	3	19 JAN 57	IMPERIAL
	BLUE MONDAY	9	02 FEB 57	IMPERIAL
	(UK No. 23 – Originally by Smiley Lewis)			
	I'M WALKIN' (UK No. 19)	5	06 APR 57	IMPERIAL
	VALLEY OF TEARS/IT'S YOU I LOVE (UK No. 25)	6	22 JUL 57	IMPERIAL
	WHOLE LOTTA LOVING	6	13 JAN 59	IMPERIAL
	I WANT TO WALK YOU HOME (UK No. 14)	8	13 SEP 59	IMPERIAL
	BE MY GUEST (UK No. 11 - Co-writ Tommy Boyce)	8	06 DEC 59	IMPERIAL
	WALKIN' TO NEW ORLEANS (UK No. 22)	6	15 AUG 60	IMPERIAL

DON & JUAN

New York duo whose real names were Roland Trone and Claude Johnson (both ex-Genies) had a one-off US Top 40 with a soul ballad that Claude wrote. They also recorded on Twirl and Mala. Follow up was 'Two Fools Are We'. They were playing 'oldies' shows in 87.

	WHAT'S YOUR NAME	7	17 MAR 62	BIG TOP

BO DONALDSON & THE HEYWOODS

Seven piece group from Ohio fronted by Bob Donaldson. They did a lot of live work in the 60s and released four singles on Family as The Heywoods. They were regulars on the TV show Action 73 before getting their first big hit. They had three US-only Top 40s and later recorded for Capitol and Playboy.

	BILLY, DON'T BE A HERO (Paper Lace 74 UK hit)	1(2)	15 JUN 74	ABC

LONNIE DONEGAN

Glasgow born Anthony Donegan was the 'King Of Skiffle'- the folk/R'n'R craze that swept the UK in the 50s. His first release was an EP in 55 and he was the first UK male singer to make the US Top 10 (and the first to do it twice). Until The Beatles he was the most successful ever UK chart act with 28 Top 30s in a row, many of them his unique versions of US folk and blues songs. He was a great influence on many UK acts who emerged in the early 60s, including John Lennon whose first 'group' was a skiffle band.

	ROCK ISLAND LINE (Ledbelly song)	8	03 FEB 56	DECCA
	LOST JOHN/STEWBALL (US No. 58)	2	06 JUL 56	PYE
	BRING A LITTLE WATER SYLVIE/DEAD OR ALIVE	7	28 SEP 56	PYE
	(Ledbelly song)			
	DON'T YOU ROCK ME DADDY-O (Vipers 57 UK hit)	4	22 FEB 57	PYE
	CUMBERLAND GAP	1(5)	12 APR 57	PYE
	GAMBLIN' MAN/PUTTING ON THE STYLE	1(2)	28 JUN 57	PYE
	(Woody Guthrie song)			
	MY DIXIE DARLING (Carter Family song)	10	08 NOV 57	PYE
	GRAND COOLIE DAM (Woody Guthrie song)	6	30 MAY 58	PYE
	TOM DOOLEY (Kingston Trio 58 hit)	3	05 DEC 58	PYE
	DOES YOUR CHEWING GUM LOSE ITS FLAVOUR	3	27 FEB 59	PYE
	(Hare & Jones 24 hit)			
	BATTLE OF NEW ORLEANS (Johnny Horton 59 hit)	2	24 JUL 59	PYE
	MY OLD MAN'S A DUSTMAN	1(3)	25 MAR 60	PYE
	(First UK record to enter UK chart at No. 1)			
	I WANNA GO HOME (Aka 'Sloop John B')	5	17 JUN 60	PYE
	HAVE A DRINK ON ME (Based on Ledbelly song)	7	16 JUN 61	PYE
	MICHAEL ROW THE BOAT (Highwaymen 61 hit)	6	15 SEP 61	PYE
	ROCK ISLAND LINE	8	21 MAY 56	IMPERIAL
	DOES YOUR CHEWING GUM LOSE ITS FLAVOUR	5	25 SEP 61	DOT
	(Released unsuccessfully in US in 59)			

RAL DONNER

Chicago born, Elvis styled singer, first recorded for Scottie in 58 and Tau. First of his four US Top 40s was a version of Elvis' 'Girl Of My Best Friend' (19th) in 61. He was later on Reprise, Fontana, Red Bird, Mid Eagle, Rising Sons, MJ, Sunlight, Chicago Fire, Starfire and Thunder. He recorded the soundtrack for 'This Is Elvis' and died age 41 in 84.

	YOU DON'T KNOW WHAT YOU GOT (UNTIL YOU LOSE IT) (UK No. 21)	4	04 SEP 61	GONE

DONOVAN

Glasgow born singer/songwriter started as the UK's answer to Dylan but established a style of his own which resulted in a string of transatlantic hits in the 60s. He has recorded often since the 70s but his twee flower child image worked against him and he never returned to chart heights.

🏴 CATCH THE WIND (US No. 23)		4	17 APR 65	PYE
(Entered UK chart same week as 1st Bob Dylan hit)				
COLOURS (US No. 61)		4	03 JUL 65	PYE
SUNSHINE SUPERMAN		2	31 DEC 66	PYE
MELLOW YELLOW		8	04 MAR 67	PYE
(Backing vocals include Paul McCartney)				
THERE IS A MOUNTAIN (US No. 11)		8	18 NOV 67	PYE
JENIFER JUNIPER (UK No. 26)		5	16 MAR 68	PYE
HURDY GURDY MAN		4	22 JUN 68	PYE
🇺🇸 SUNSHINE SUPERMAN		1(1)	03 SEP 66	EPIC
MELLOW YELLOW		2	10 DEC 66	EPIC
HURDY GURDY MAN		5	03 AUG 68	EPIC
ATLANTIS (UK No. 23)		7	24 MAY 69	EPIC

JASON DONOVAN

Photogenic Australian singer/actor who, like Kylie Minogue, his co-star in the top Aussie soap opera Neighbours, records with the S.A.W. team. To date he has hit the UK-only Top 5 with every release and sold 1.5 million in the UK alone of his debut LP, which was the UK's top seller of 89. He was the UK's No. 1 male teen appeal star of the late 80s.

🏴 NOTHING CAN DIVIDE US		5	24 SEP 88	PWL
ESPECIALLY FOR YOU (With Kylie Minogue)		1(3)	07 JAN 89	PWL
(Top selling UK single of 88 – Jumped from 9-1)				
TOO MANY BROKEN HEARTS (Entered at No. 2)		1(2)	11 MAR 89	PWL
SEALED WITH A KISS (Brian Hyland 62 hit)		1(2)	10 JUN 89	PWL
(First Australian track to enter UK chart at No.1)				
EVERY DAY (I LOVE YOU MORE) (Entered at No. 3)		2	16 SEP 89	PWL
UNTIL YOU COME BACK TO ME (Entered at No. 7)		2	16 DEC 89	PWL

DOOBIE BROTHERS

Californian band evolved from Pud and were originally fronted by Tom Johnson. Their second LP contained their debut hit 'Listen To The Music' (US 11/UK 29). Jeff 'Skunk' Baxter joined in 74 and Michael McDonald replaced Johnson in 75 and the act had 15 US (3 UK) Top 40s over the next decade . They split in 82, re-united (with Johnson) in 89 and returned to the US single and LP Top 20.

🇺🇸 LONG TRAIN RUNNING		8	30 JUN 73	WARNER
BLACK WATER (Was 'B' side of 'Another Park')		1	15 MAR 75	WARNER
Another Sunday' which was a No. 32 hit in 74)				
WHAT A FOOL BELIEVES		1(1)	14 APR 79	WARNER
(UK No. 31 in 79 & UK No. 57 in 87 – Grammy winner)				
REAL LOVE		5	25 OCT 80	WARNER
THE DOCTOR (UK No. 73)		9	15 JUL 89	CAPITOL

DOOLEYS

The largest UK family act to chart (seven of them at times) had seven UK-only Top 40s in the late 70s. They were previously on Alaska in 74 as The Dooley Family, and BBC in 75 and were on R'n'R in 83.

🏴 LOVE OF MY LIFE		9	17 DEC 77	GTO
WANTED		3	04 AUG 79	GTO
THE CHOSEN FEW		7	27 OCT 79	GTO

VAL DOONICAN

Irish pop/country singer was very popular in the UK in the 60s, with five UK Top 10 LPs and a dozen UK Top 40 singles. He also had a successful TV series and later recorded for RCA and Philips.

🏴 WALK TALL		3	19 DEC 64	DECCA
THE SPECIAL YEARS		7	13 FEB 65	DECCA
ELUSIVE BUTTERFLY (Bob Lind 66 hit)		5	23 APR 66	DECCA
WHAT WOULD I BE		2	17 DEC 66	DECCA
IF THE WHOLE WORLD STOPPED LOVING		3	02 DEC 67	PYE
(Roy Drusky 66 country hit)				

DOORS

L.A. based rock band fronted by controversial and confrontational singer/ writer Jim Morrison. Their first single 'Break On Through' failed but in the four years before Jim's death they had seven US (2 UK) Top 40 singles and seven Top 10 US-only LPs. Jim, who died mysteriously in Paris in 1971, is considered by many to be one of rock music's legendary figures and great writers, and interest in The Doors continues as a result of their strong influence on many new wave and indie bands. They sold more LPs in 1980, when a controversial biography of Morrison was published, than at the height of their popularity in the late sixties.

🇺🇸 LIGHT MY FIRE (UK No. 49)		1(3)	29 JUL 67	ELEKTRA
HELLO, I LOVE YOU		1(2)	10 AUG 68	ELEKTRA
TOUCH ME		3	15 FEB 69	ELEKTRA

LEE DORSEY

Ex boxer and garage mechanic from New Orleans. Started recording on Instant in 55 and later for Rex, Ace and ABC before getting his first hit. A popular soul act on both sides of the Atlantic in the 60s, he died in 86. He also recorded on Smash, Constellation, Spring, Sansu and Polydor.

🏴 WORKING IN THE COAL MINE		8	17 SEP 66	STATESIDE
HOLY COW (US No. 23)		6	19 NOV 66	STATESIDE
🇺🇸 YA YA		7	31 OCT 61	FURY
WORKING IN THE COAL MINE		8	03 SEP 66	AMY

DOUBLE

Swiss group fronted by Kurt Maloo and Felix Haug (ex-Yello) followed their one-off hit with 'Woman Of The World'.

🏴 THE CAPTAIN OF YOUR HEART (US No. 16)		8	15 FEB 86	POLYDOR

CARL DOUGLAS

Jamaican born singer/songwriter had been recording in the UK for a decade before having a Transatlantic No. 1 with a song recorded in 20 minutes at the end of a session. He had a minor hit with the follow up 'Dance The Kung Fu' and a UK-only Top 20 with 'Run Back' in 77. He later recorded on Blue Mountain and Landslide.

🏴 KUNG FU FIGHTING		1(3)	21 SEP 74	PYE
🇺🇸 KUNG FU FIGHTING		1(2)	07 DEC 74	20TH CENTURY
(First UK black act to top US black music chart)				

CRAIG DOUGLAS

Born Terry Perkins on the Isle of Wight (UK) he was a UK teenage pin-up in the early 60s. He first recorded for Decca in 58 and most of his nine UK-only Top 20s were covers of US hits. In 62 The Beatles supported him on tour. He later recorded on Fontana (64), Pye (69), Cube (71), Battersea (83) and Easy On The Ear (83).

🏴 ONLY SIXTEEN (Sam Cooke 59 hit)		1(4)	11 SEP 59	TOP RANK
PRETTY BLUE EYES (Steve Lawrence 59 US hit)		4	26 FEB 60	TOP RANK
A HUNDRED POUNDS OF CLAY		7	05 MAY 61	TOP RANK
(Gene McDaniels 61 US hit)				
TIME (Originally by Jerry Jackson)		8	18 AUG 61	TOP RANK
OUR FAVOURITE MELODIES (Gary Criss 62 US hit)		9	27 JUL 62	COLUMBIA

MIKE DOUGLAS

Top US TV show host and singer with Kay Kysers Band in the 40s. He followed his one-off US hit with 'Here's To My Jenny'.

🇺🇸 THE MEN IN MY LITTLE GIRL'S LIFE		6	05 FEB 66	EPIC

DOVELLS

Philadelphia quartet, previously called The Brooktones, were fronted by Len Barry. Their first release 'No No No' did not happen but the second was the biggest of their five US-only Top 40s. Len left for solo success in 63 and the group later recorded on Jamie, Swan, MGM, Event, Abcko, Verve and Paramount.

 BRISTOL STOMP *(Group also has hit with 'Bristol Twistin' Annie')* — 2 — 23 OCT 61 — PARKWAY
YOU CAN'T SIT DOWN *(Phil Upchurch 61 US hit)* — 3 — 15 JUN 63 — PARKWAY

Also see Len Barry

JOE DOWELL

Indiana born singer had the biggest of his three US-only chart records with a song from Elvis' army film G.I. Blues. Joe went into the army in 62 and later recorded for Monument and re-appeared in 85 on Journey.

WOODEN HEART *(Co-written by Bert Kaempfert)* — 1(1) — 28 AUG 61 — SMASH
(Ray Stevens played organ on the track)

CHARLIE DRAKE

Top UK comedian who had one of the UK's best R'n'R voices. In the 60s he concentrated on comedy material and is best known in the US for 'My Boomerang Won't Come Back' (US 21/UK 14).

SPLISH SPLASH *(Bobby Darin 58 hit)* — 7 — 12 SEP 58 — PARLOPHONE
MR. CUSTER *(Larry Verne 60 US hit)* — 10 — 11 NOV 60 — PARLOPHONE

DRAMATICS

Detroit soul quartet, fronted by Ron Banks, who came together in 64 and recorded on Wingate in 66 and Sport in 67. They have had 34 black music hits since then (no UK charters) and been on Cadet, Jupar, ABC, MCA, Stax, Mainstream, Capitol and Fantasy.

WHATCHA SEE IS WHATCHA GET — 9 — 25 SEP 71 — VOLT
IN THE RAIN — 5 — 22 APR 72 — VOLT

DREAM ACADEMY

UK trio fronted by Nick Laird-Clowes had a dream start with a Transatlantic Top 20 but so far they have been unable to repeat this success. Follow up was 'The Love Parade'.

LIFE IN A NORTHERN TOWN *(UK No. 15)* — 7 — 22 FEB 86 — WARNER

DREAMLOVERS

Philadelphia quartet whose big hit was a doo-wop ballad written by member Don Hogan. The group, who still do 'oldies' shows, were formed in 56 and have done a lot of session work – including Chubby Checker's No. 1 'The Twist'. They were later on End, Warner, Swan, Len, Casino, V-Tone, Cameo, Mercury and Columbia.

WHEN WE GET MARRIED — 10 — 18 SEP 61 — HERITAGE

DRIFTERS

Established in 53 by ex Domino Clyde McPhatter, the group have had numerous personnel changes, hits and writs since then. They still work solidly, but because of the many ex-members, there is likely to be more than one 'Drifters' appearing somewhere in the world at the same time. In the 50s they were a top R&B act, in the 60s they had a string of US pop hits and in the 70s a run of UK hits giving them a 26 year chart run. They were inducted in the R'n'R Hall of Fame at the same time as The Beatles.

SAVE THE LAST DANCE FOR ME — 2 — 25 NOV 60 — LONDON
(Singer Ben E.King revived it on Manhattan (87))
AT THE CLUB/SATURDAY NIGHT AT THE MOVIES — 3 — 03 JUN 72 — ATLANTIC
(US No. 43 & UK No. 35 in 65(A) US No. 18 in 64(B))
COME ON OVER TO MY PLACE *(US No. 60)* — 9 — 30 SEP 72 — ATLANTIC
(US No. 60 & UK No. 40 in 65)
LIKE SISTER AND BROTHER — 7 — 01 SEP 73 — BELL
KISSIN' IN THE BACK ROW OF THE MOVIES — 2 — 06 JUL 74 — BELL
DOWN ON THE BEACH TONIGHT — 7 — 09 NOV 74 — BELL
THERE GOES MY FIRST LOVE — 3 — 04 OCT 75 — BELL
CAN I TAKE YOU HOME LITTLE GIRL — 10 — 10 JAN 76 — BELL
YOU'RE MORE THAN A NUMBER IN MY LITTLE RED BOOK — 5 — 29 JAN 77 — ARISTA

THERE GOES MY BABY — 2 — 16 AUG 59 — ATLANTIC
SAVE THE LAST DANCE FOR ME — 1(3) — 17 OCT 60 — ATLANTIC
UP ON THE ROOF *(Co-written by Carole King)* — 5 — 09 FEB 63 — ATLANTIC
ON BROADWAY — 9 — 27 APR 63 — ATLANTIC
UNDER THE BOARDWALK *(UK No. 45)* — 4 — 22 AUG 64 — ATLANTIC

JULIE DRISCOLL, BRIAN AUGER & THE TRINITY

Julie, who was voted top UK female singer of 68, started recording in 63 on Columbia and was on Parlophone in 65. Brian also recorded on Columbia in 65 before they came together for their sole UK hit with a Bob Dylan song. The most photographed star of 68 joined Working Week as their singer in 89.

THIS WHEEL'S ON FIRE — 5 — 22 JUN 68 — MARMALADE

DRIVER 67

Unusual pop novelty record masterminded by Paul Phillips. He followed this one-off UK hit with 'Headlights/Tailights'.

CAR 67 — 7 — 03 FEB 79 — LOGO

DUBLINERS

Traditional Irish folk band, which included Ronnie Drew, had two UK-only Top 20s in 67 – the other being 'Black Velvet Band' (15). Always a popular live band, they recorded on many labels and returned to the charts 20 years later with The Pogues. They retired in 89 after 27 years together.

SEVEN DRUNKEN NIGHTS — 7 — 27 MAY 67 — MAJOR MINOR
THE IRISH ROVER *(With THE POGUES)* — 8 — 11 APR 87 — POGUE MAHONE

STEPHEN 'TIN TIN' DUFFY

UK singer's first release (as Tin Tin) 'Hold It' was a small hit (UK 55), his second missed and he made the UK-only Top 20 with the next two – the other being 'Icing On The Cake' (No. 14). He re-appeared in 89 with the five-man pop/folk group Lilac Time.

KISS ME — 4 — 09 MAR 85 — 10

GEORGE DUKE – SEE STANLEY CLARKE FOR HIT DETAILS

PATTY DUKE

New York actress/singer was the youngest person to win an Oscar when aged 14 in 62 for her role in The Miracle Worker. She had her own US TV series 63-66 and had four US-only hits in 8 months. She later headed the Screen Actors' Guild and her autobiography Call Me Annie (her real Christian name) was published in 87.

DON'T JUST STAND THERE — 8 — 14 AUG 65 — UA
(Originally by the Five Chords)

DAVID DUNDAS

Professional jingle writer and son of the Marquess of Zetland. This UK singer/songwriter/actor had a Transatlantic Top 20 with a song he wrote for a UK Brutus jeans commercial. He managed one further UK hit in 77 'Another Funny Honeymoon' (29) and later recordings included 'Fly Baby Fly' (nothing to do with jeans)!

JEANS ON (US No. 17)		3	07 AUG 76	AIR

CLIVE DUNN

UK TV actor known for his grandad type roles. He unsuccessfully released 'Too Old' in 62 and had his one-off UK hit nine years later. Follow up was the similar themed 'My Lady (Nana)'.

GRANDAD (US cover Walter Brennan – grandpa in 'Real McCoys')	1(3)	09 JAN 71	COLUMBIA

ROBBIE DUPREE

Born Robbie Dupuis in Brooklyn, he once played in a local band with Nile Rodgers (of Chic). He had two US-only Top 20s in 80 – the other being 'Hot Rod Hearts'(15). He later recorded on Fourth & Broadway in 87.

STEAL AWAY		6	12 JUL 80	ELEKTRA

SIMON DUPREE AND THE BIG SOUND

UK band joined Parlophone in 66 and their fourth release gave them the biggest of their two UK-only hits (in the US it was recorded by the Rooftop Singers). The follow up and only other chart record was 'For Whom The Bell Tolls' (43). Group evolved into Gentle Giant in the 70s.

KITES		9	06 JAN 68	PARLOPHONE

DUPREES

Joey Vann (Joe Canzano) fronted the Jersey City vocal group whose blend of 50s group harmonies and 40s big band sounds gave them four US-only Top 40s. They were originally known as The Parisians and also recorded on Regatta, Columbia, Heritage, Colossus and RCA.

YOU BELONG TO ME (Jo Stafford 52 hit)		7	22 SEP 62	COED

DURAN DURAN

Photogenic Birmingham (UK) based band fronted by former child actor Simon Le Bon were a major part of the UK 'New Romantic' movement of 81. Initially they were a UK-only sensation but their fifth UK hit broke them in the US and started a long run of transatlantic smashes – many with outstanding videos. Members have tried other recording projects, like Arcadia and Power Station, with less success. Now known as Duranduran.

GIRLS ON FILM		5	22 AUG 81	EMI
HUNGRY LIKE THE WOLF		5	26 JUN 82	EMI
SAVE A PRAYER (US No. 16)		2	11 SEP 82	EMI
RIO (US No. 14)		9	11 DEC 82	EMI
IS THERE SOMETHING I SHOULD KNOW (Entered chart at No. 1)	1(2)	26 MAR 83	EMI
UNION OF THE SNAKE (Entered at No. 4)	3	05 NOV 83	EMI
NEW MOON ON MONDAY	9	11 FEB 84	EMI
THE REFLEX (Entered at No. 5)	1(4)	05 MAY 84	EMI
THE WILD BOYS (Entered at No. 5)	2	17 NOV 84	PARLOPHONE
A VIEW TO KILL (Entered at No. 7)	2	25 MAY 85	PARLOPHONE
NOTORIOUS	7	08 NOV 86	EMI
ALL SHE WANTS IS (As Duranduran – US No. 22 & US No. 1 Dance)	9	14 JAN 89	EMI

HUNGRY LIKE THE WOLF		3	26 MAR 83	HARVEST
IS THERE SOMETHING I SHOULD KNOW	4	06 AUG 83	CAPITOL
UNION OF THE SNAKE	3	24 DEC 83	CAPITOL
NEW MOON ON MONDAY	10	17 MAR 84	CAPITOL
THE REFLEX (Mixed Nile Rodgers)	1(2)	23 JUN 84	CAPITOL
THE WILD BOYS	2	15 DEC 84	CAPITOL
A VIEW TO KILL (From the James Bond film)	1(2)	13 JUL 85	CAPITOL
NOTORIOUS	2	10 JAN 87	CAPITOL
I DON'T WANT YOUR LOVE (UK No. 14)	4	03 DEC 88	CAPITOL

Also see Power Station/Arcadia

IAN DURY & THE BLOCKHEADS

Inimitable Essex (UK) born singer/composer formed and fronted the popular live act Kilburn & The High Roads from 70-75. The Blockheads were formed in 77 and their second LP charted followed by three UK-only Top 10 singles in a row. The group didn't release a single for a year and by then interest in them was waning. Ian later recorded on Polydor (81), EMI (85) and WEA (89).

WHAT A WASTE		9	03 JUN 78	STIFF
HIT ME WITH YOUR RHYTHM STICK	1(1)	27 JAN 79	STIFF
REASONS TO BE CHEERFUL (PT. 3) (Jumped 46-5)	3	18 AUG 79	STIFF

BOB DYLAN

Arguably the most influential singer/songwriter of the rock age. Born Bob Zimmerman in Minnesota, he first recorded on a Harry Belafonte session in 61 and his first single in 62 'Mixed Up Confusion' flopped. He is the artist most responsible for the 60s folk/protest movement and over the last 26 years has had 22 LPs in the US (28 in UK) Top 20 and six singles in the US (10 in UK) Top 20. Always a greater live attraction than record seller, he has nevertheless seen over 50 covers of his songs in the US chart and 43 in the UK. A reviewer in early 62 said "Could have a big following when he finds his own style" – he did.

TIMES THEY ARE A-CHANGIN'		7	17 APR 65	CBS
SUBTERRANEAN HOMESICK BLUES (US No. 39)	9	22 MAY 65	CBS
LIKE A ROLLING STONE	4	18 SEP 65	CBS
POSITIVELY 4TH STREET	8	04 DEC 65	CBS
RAINY DAY WOMEN NOS. 12 & 35	7	04 JUN 66	CBS
LAY LADY LAY	5	11 OCT 69	CBS
LIKE A ROLLING STONE	2	11 SEP 65	COLUMBIA
POSITIVELY 4TH STREET	7	06 NOV 65	COLUMBIA
RAINY DAY WOMEN #12 & 35	2	21 MAY 66	COLUMBIA
LAY LADY LAY	7	06 SEP 69	COLUMBIA

RONNIE DYSON

Washington singer had a lead role in the Broadway show Hair. He scored a Top 10 with a song from another musical Salvation. He has had a further 12 black music entries and his biggest UK hit was 'When You Get Right Down To It' (34).

(IF YOU LET ME MAKE LOVE TO YOU THEN) WHY CAN'T I TOUCH YOU?	8	29 AUG 70	COLUMBIA

E

808 STATE

Manchester (UK) house music quartet includes Martin Price, Graham Massey and club DJs Darren and Andy. They met at Martin's record shop and were named after the Roland 808 drum machine. Their third LP 'Ninety' included their first UK pop hit.

PACIFIC		10	02 DEC 89	ZTT

SHEILA E

San Franciscan Sheila Escovedo played percussion in bands with her brothers and father before she was 16. She worked with Marvin Gaye, Lionel Richie, Herbie Hancock and Jeffrey Osborne before Prince helped her achieve fame. Her only UK chart record to date is 'The Belle Of St. Mark' (UK 18/US 11).

THE GLAMOROUS LIFE		7	06 OCT 84	WARNER

EAGLES

The top country rock act of the 70s was formed in Los Angeles by Glenn Frey and Don Henley in 71. They backed Linda Ronstadt on 'Silk Purse' and their debut record 'Take It Easy' (US 12) was the first of 13 US Top 20's (3 in UK). The Eagles also scored 5 US No.1 LPs (2 No. 2s UK). They split in 82 and four of the five members had subsequent solo hits.

HOTEL CALIFORNIA		8	14 MAY 77	ASYLUM
WITCHY WOMAN		9	18 NOV 72	ASYLUM
BEST OF MY LOVE		1(1)	01 MAR 75	ASYLUM
ONE OF THESE NIGHTS (UK No. 23)		1(1)	02 AUG 75	ASYLUM
LYIN' EYES (UK No. 23)		2	08 NOV 75	ASYLUM
TAKE IT TO THE LIMIT (UK No. 12)		4	13 MAR 76	ASYLUM
NEW KID IN TOWN (UK No. 20)		1(1)	26 FEB 77	ASYLUM
HOTEL CALIFORNIA		1(1)	07 MAY 77	ASYLUM
HEARTACHE TONIGHT (UK No. 40)		1(1)	10 NOV 79	ASYLUM
THE LONG RUN (UK No. 66)		8	02 FEB 80	ASYLUM
I CAN'T TELL YOU WHY		8	19 APR 80	ASYLUM

Also see Glenn Frey/Don Henley

EARTH, WIND & FIRE

L.A. R&B/funk band formed by ex Chess session man Maurice White, who recorded as Salty Peppers on Capitol before joining Warners in 71. Phillip Bailey joined in 72, replacing R&B veteran Wade Flemons. The Grammy winning act were one of the top sellers of the 70s, with 16 US Top 40 singles and 12 Top 40 LPs. They split in 84, re-united in 87 and in 90 when Bailey again sang with them.

SEPTEMBER		3	27 JAN 79	CBS
BOOGIE WONDERLAND (And THE EMOTIONS)		4	09 JUN 79	CBS
AFTER THE LOVE HAS GONE		4	18 AUG 79	CBS
LET'S GROOVE		3	28 NOV 81	CBS
SHINING STAR		1(1)	24 MAY 75	COLUMBIA
SING A SONG		5	07 FEB 76	COLUMBIA
GOT TO GET YOU INTO MY LIFE (UK No. 33) (Beatles 76 US hit)		9	16 SEP 78	COLUMBIA
SEPTEMBER		8	10 FEB 79	ARC
BOOGIE WONDERLAND (And THE EMOTIONS)		6	14 JUL 79	ARC
AFTER THE LOVE HAS GONE		2	15 SEP 79	ARC
LET'S GROOVE		3	19 DEC 81	ARC

EAST OF EDEN

Folky UK foursome which included violinist Dave Arbus. They had a one-off UK hit with a track they recorded as a joke, which only hit after they had left the label. Their follow up was 'Ramadhan'. They later recorded on Atlantic, Harvest and UA.

JIG A JIG		7	22 MAY 71	DERAM

SHEENA EASTON

Grammy winning Scottish singer leapt to instant UK fame after appearance on The Big Time – a documentary style TV talent programme. She later took the US by storm, becoming the only singer to have Top 10 hits on the pop, black music, country and dance charts. She now lives and works mainly in the US.

9 TO 5 (a.k.a. MORNING TRAIN)		3	16 AUG 80	EMI
MODERN GIRL (US No. 18)		8	20 SEP 80	EMI
(Both above singles were in Top 10 together)				
FOR YOUR EYES ONLY		8	08 AUG 81	EMI
MORNING TRAIN (a.k.a. 9 TO 5)		1(2)	02 MAY 81	EMI AM.
FOR YOUR EYES ONLY (From James Bond film)		4	17 OCT 81	LIBERTY
WE'VE GOT TONIGHT (With KENNY ROGERS) (UK No.28 – a Bob Seger song)		6	26 MAR 83	LIBERTY
TELEFONE (LONG DISTANCE LOVE AFFAIR)		9	29 OCT 83	EMI AM.
STRUT		7	24 NOV 84	EMI AM.
SUGAR WALLS (Prince song)		9	02 FEB 85	EMI AM.
THE LOVER IN ME (UK No. 15)		2	04 MAR 89	MCA

EASYBEATS

Australian based group included Harry Vanda and George Young and had five big Australian hits before their sole transatlantic Top 20. Their 'Hello How Are You' made No. 20 UK. Harry and George later hit as writers and producers with acts like AC/DC and John Paul Young and their own group Flash & The Pan.

FRIDAY ON MY MIND (US No. 16)		6	17 DEC 66	UA

Also see Flash & The Pan

ECHO & THE BUNNYMEN

Leader Ian McCulloch named his group after their drum machine. They first recorded on Zoo in 80 and had 13 UK-only hit singles and six Top 20 LPs, most of which peaked low on the US charts. Ian went solo in 89 and their new vocalist was Noel Burke, from St Vitus Dance.

THE CUTTER (Their 8th single)		8	05 FEB 83	KOROVA
THE KILLING MOON		9	04 FEB 84	KOROVA

EDDIE & THE HOTRODS – SEE 'THE RODS' FOR HIT DETAILS

DUANE EDDY

The inventor of the 'twangy' guitar sound was born in New York State and first recorded on Ford. First hit was 'Moovin' n' Groovin'' produced, as were all his hits, in Phoenix by his co-writer Lee Hazlewood. He was top selling instrumentalist of the 50s and is the only instrumentalist to hit in every decade since.

PETER GUNN THEME (US No. 27)		6	10 JUL 59	LONDON
SHAZAM (US No. 45)		6	13 MAY 60	LONDON
BECAUSE THEY'RE YOUNG (From the film)		2	02 SEP 60	LONDON
PEPE (US No.18) (From the film)		4	27 JAN 61	LONDON
THEME FROM DIXIE (US No. 39)		5	05 MAY 61	LONDON
BALLAD OF PALADIN (US No. 33)		10	31 AUG 62	RCA
DANCE WITH THE GUITAR MAN (US No. 12)		4	07 DEC 62	RCA
PLAY ME LIKE YOU PLAY YOUR GUITAR (Above two with The Rebelettes)		9	05 APR 75	GTO
PETER GUNN (with ART OF NOISE) (US No. 50) (His 59 hit – Both times in Top 10 with Cliff Richard's 'Living Doll')		8	12 APR 86	CHINA
REBEL-'ROUSER (UK No. 19)		6	28 JUL 58	JAMIE
FORTY MILES OF BAD ROAD (UK No. 11)		9	26 JUL 59	JAMIE
BECAUSE THEY'RE YOUNG		4	04 JUL 60	JAMIE

EDELWEISS

Martin Gletschermayer's group claimed to be the first to combine authentic Austrian folk music with rap, hip hop and house! They come from the same roster as Falco and feature the yodels of Maria Mathis. Follow up was 'I Can't Get No... (Edelweiss)'.

 BRING ME EDELWEISS   5   27 MAY 89   WEA

EDISON LIGHTHOUSE

UK group originally called Greenfield Hammer and fronted by session singer Tony Burrows (see White Plains, Flowerpot Men, First Class, Ivy League, Brotherhood of Man and The Pipkins) had a one-off Top 10 hit. They were also on Greenstone in 81.

 LOVE GROWS (WHERE MY ROSEMARY GOES)   1(5)   31 JAN 70   BELL
(2 Weeks to No. 1 – jumped from 11-1)

LOVE GROWS (WHERE MY ROSEMARY GOES)   5   04 APR 70   BELL

DAVE EDMUNDS

Welsh guitarist had his first success in Love Sculpture (previously called The Image and The Human Beans). As a solo act his back to basics R'n'R gave him a string of UK hits and some US chart entries. He was a member of Rockpile with Nick Lowe and he produced Shakin' Stevens, Dion, Everly Brothers, Fabulous Thunderbirds and gold records for The Stray Cats.

 I HEAR YOU KNOCKING *(Jumped from 16-1)*   1(6)   28 NOV 70   MAM
BABY I LOVE YOU *(Ronettes 64 hit)*   8   03 MAR 73   ROCKFIELD
BORN TO BE WITH YOU *(Chordettes 56 hit)*   5   14 JUL 73   ROCKFIELD
GIRLS TALK *(US No. 65)*   4   21 JUL 79   SWAN SONG
I HEAR YOU KNOCKING *(Smiley Lewis 55 US hit)*   4   13 FEB 71   MAM

Also see Love Sculpture

EDWARD BEAR

Canadian pop/rock trio fronted by Larry Evoy had two US-only Top 40 hits, the other being the follow up 'Close Your Eyes' (37th).

 LAST SONG   3   03 MAR 73   CAPITOL

JONATHAN EDWARDS

Raised in Virginia, he recorded in the mid 60s with bluegrass group Sugar Creek, previously called The Rivermen. After his sole US pop hit he was on Reprise in 76, Warner in 77 and debuted on the country charts on MCA in 88.

 SUNSHINE   4   15 JAN 72   CAPRICORN

RUPIE EDWARDS

Jamaican reggae singer started in The Virtues, ran two record shops, edited the local music magazine Record Retailer and produced acts like The Ethiopians. He was also on Big and Bullet and had 2 UK-only Top 40s; the other being 'Lego Skanga' (No.32).

 IRE FEELINGS (SKANGA) *(Banned on UK radio)*   9   14 DEC 74   CACTUS
(Skanga is Jamaican for the Ska guitar sound)

WALTER EGAN

New Yorker who first played in unsuccessful group The Malibooz. His first two solo LPs, which included his sole US Top 40 hit, were produced by Lindsey Buckingham and Stevie Nicks.

 MAGNET AND STEEL   8   26 AUG 78   COLUMBIA

EIGHTH WONDER

After a few flops the much publicised London group (previously called Spice) fronted by photogenic singer/actress Patsy Kensit and with the help of the S.A.W. production team, finally got the first of their two UK-only Top 20s to date.

 I'M NOT SCARED   7   16 APR 88   CBS

DONNIE ELBERT

Distinctive New York singer who first hit in 57 with 'What Can I Do' on Deluxe and returned 13 years later with a handful of transatlantic entries. He also recorded for Parkway, Rare Bullet, Jalynne, Gateway, VJ, All Platinum, Avco, Cub, Checker, Atco, Bradley's, Polydor and Deram. He died in 89.

 WHERE DID OUR LOVE GO   8   29 JAN 72   LONDON
(US No.15 – Supremes 64 hit)

ELECTRIC LIGHT ORCHESTRA

String section dominated band fronted by Birmingham's (UK) Jeff Lynne, that once included The Move's Roy Wood. They had many personnel changes and many transatlantic hits over the years. They became a trio in 86 and Jeff has recently concentrated on production and writing for acts like Tom Petty and The Traveling Wilburys (a group he was in). A re-mix of his 'The Eve Of The War' was a UK smash in 89. Lynne released first solo LP in 90.

10538 OVERTURE *(Roy Wood left after this)*   9   26 AUG 72   HARVEST
ROLL OVER BEETHOVEN   6   17 FEB 73   HARVEST
(US No.42 – Chuck Berry 56 US hit)
EVIL WOMAN   10   31 JAN 76   JET
LIVIN' THING *(US No. 13)*   4   18 DEC 76   JET
ROCKARIA   9   19 MAR 77   JET
TELEPHONE LINE   8   18 JUN 77   JET
MR. BLUE SKY *(US No. 35)*   6   25 FEB 78   JET
(First of 3 consecutive No. 6 hits)
WILD WEST HERO   6   05 AUG 78   JET
SWEET TALKIN' WOMAN *(US No. 17)*   6   21 OCT 78   JET
SHINE A LITTLE LOVE   6   09 JUN 79   JET
THE DIARY OF HORACE WIMP   8   11 AUG 79   JET
DON'T BRING ME DOWN   3   22 SEP 79   JET
CONFUSION/LAST TRAIN TO LONDON   8   01 DEC 79   JET
(US No. 37 &39)
XANADU *(With OLIVIA NEWTON-JOHN)*   1(2)   12 JUL 80   JET
(First No. 1 for both acts)
HOLD ON TIGHT   4   05 SEP 81   JET
CAN'T GET IT OUT OF MY HEAD   9   15 MAR 75   UA
EVIL WOMAN   10   14 FEB 76   UA
TELEPHONE LINE   7   24 SEP 77   UA
SHINE A LITTLE LOVE   8   21 JUL 79   JET
DON'T BRING ME DOWN   4   08 SEP 79   JET
XANADU *(With OLIVIA NEWTON-JOHN)*   8   11 OCT 80   MCA
HOLD ON TIGHT   10   03 OCT 81   JET

Also see Jeff Lynne/Roy Wood/Wizzard

ELGINS

Detroit quartet featuring Saundra Edwards. They recorded as The Emeralds on State and as The Downbeats on Duke and UA and as The Elgins for Flip (60), Miracle (61), Nite (62), Titan (62), Dot (63), Lummtone (63), Congress (64) and Valiant (65) before joining Motown (65). They were later on UK label Nightmare (89).

 HEAVEN MUST HAVE SENT YOU *(US No. 50 in 66)*   3   05 JUN 71   TAMLA MOTOWN

YVONNE ELLIMAN

Hawaiian born singer/actress who for four years played Mary Magdalene in Jesus Christ Superstar. She appeared with Eric Clapton on his 1974 comeback tour and sang on two of his LPs as well as scoring solo hits in the US and UK. She also recorded on Decca/MCA in 72, Purple in 73 and Warner in 80.

🇬🇧	LOVE ME *(US No. 14)*	6	18 DEC 76	RSO
	IF I CAN'T HAVE YOU	4	27 MAY 78	RSO
	(From 'Saturday Night Fever')			
🇺🇸	IF I CAN'T HAVE YOU	1(1)	13 MAY 78	RSO

SHIRLEY ELLIS

New Yorker who was a winner at the Apollo talent shows in the 50s. She was a member of The Metronomes and wrote for The Heartbreakers in the 50s before meeting her manager (and later her husband), the top R&B writer Lincoln Chase who penned her hits. She joined Karate in 66 and then Columbia.

🇬🇧	THE CLAPPING SONG *(Back to No. 59 in 78)*	6	26 JUN 65	LONDON
🇺🇸	THE NITTY GRITTY	8	11 JAN 64	CONGRESS
	(Follow up was (That's) What The Nitty Gritty Is)			
	THE NAME GAME	3	30 JAN 65	CONGRESS
	THE CLAPPING SONG	8	24 APR 65	CONGRESS

EMERSON LAKE & PALMER

Members of UK super trio were Keith Emerson (ex Nice, T-Bones and P.P. Arnold's band), Greg Lake (ex King Crimson) and Carl Palmer (ex Arthur Brown and Atomic Rooster). They sold millions of LPs in US & UK in the 70s. They split in 78 but a re-union in 87 did not work out.

🇬🇧	FANFARE FOR THE COMMON MAN	2	16 JUL 77	ATLANTIC

Also see Greg Lake

EMOTIONS

Three Chicago sisters Wanda, Jeanette and Sheila Hutchinson, who previously were called Three Ribbons And A Bow, formed the act in 68 and recorded on One-derful, Vee Jay and Twin Stacks before moving to Volt in 69. This distinctive trio has had 30 black hits and they have also been on Stax, Brainstorm and Red label.

🇬🇧	BEST OF MY LOVE	4	08 OCT 77	CBS
	BOOGIE WONDERLAND *(with EARTH, WIND & FIRE)*	4	09 JUN 79	CBS
🇺🇸	BEST OF MY LOVE	1(5)	20 AUG 77	COLUMBIA
	BOOGIE WONDERLAND *(With EARTH, WIND & FIRE)*	6	14 JUL 79	ARC

HARRY ENFIELD

UK alternative comic who had a one-off hit with a comic rap featuring one of the characters he portrays – a plasterer called Loadsamoney.

🇬🇧	LOADSAMONEY (DOIN' UP THE HOUSE)	4	14 MAY 88	MERCURY

ENGLAND DAN & JOHN FORD COLEY

This duo are Dan Seals (brother of Jimmy in Seals & Crofts), who got his name from touring England in his early days, and fellow Texan John Ford Coley. They recorded together in Southwest F.O.B. and had seven singles on A&M before getting the first of six US Top 40s and one in UK. Dan is now a top country singer.

🇺🇸	I'D REALLY LOVE TO SEE YOU TONIGHT			
	(UK No. 26)	2	25 SEP 76	BIG TREE
	NIGHTS ARE FOREVER WITHOUT YOU	10	11 DEC 76	BIG TREE
	WE'LL NEVER HAVE TO SAY GOODBYE AGAIN	9	15 APR 78	BIG TREE
	(Top US adult contemporary record of 78)			
	LOVE IS THE ANSWER *(UK No. 45)*	10	26 MAY 79	BIG TREE

ENGLAND WORLD CUP SQUAD

The English soccer team scored a UK No. 1 with their first release and with a completely new line up they returned to the Top 10 12 years later. Both hits were in World Cup years.

🇬🇧	BACK HOME	1(3)	16 MAY 70	PYE
	(First Soccer record to make the UK Top 20)			
	THIS TIME (WE'LL GET IT RIGHT) ENGLAND			
	WE'LL FLY THE FLAG	2	08 MAY 82	ENGLAND

ENYA

Eithne (Enya) Ni Bhraonain joined her family's successful group Clannad in 80 for two years. She released solo LP 'Enya' in 87 and her follow up 'Evening Falls' also made the UK Top 20.

🇬🇧	ORINOCO FLOW *(US No. 24)*	1(3)	29 OCT 88	WEA

Also see Clannad

EQUALS

Mixed North London group fronted by twins Derv & Lincoln Gordon and Eddie (Eddy) Grant, and scored three UK-only Top 10s in 18 months. Eddie went on to have transatlantic Top 10 hits in the 80s. They were on Mercury in 76, Ice in 78 and Moggie in 83.

🇬🇧	BABY COME BACK *(US No. 32)*	1(3)	06 JUL 68	PRESIDENT
	(Originally rel. in 66 and a hit first in Germany)			
	VIVA BOBBIE JOE	6	30 AUG 69	PRESIDENT
	BLACK SKIN BLUE EYED BOYS	9	30 JAN 71	PRESIDENT

Also see Eddy Grant

ERASURE

After scoring in Depeche Mode, Yazoo and Assembly, Vince Clarke formed this synth rock act with vocalist Andy Bell (ex The Void). It took five releases before they hit the UK Top 40 but they are now one of the most consistently successful UK singles and LP acts and are building a strong following in the US too.

🇬🇧	SOMETIMES	2	13 DEC 86	MUTE
	VICTIM OF LOVE *(U.S. Dance No. 1)*	7	06 JUN 87	MUTE
	THE CIRCUS	6	31 OCT 87	MUTE
	SHIP OF FOOLS	6	19 MAR 88	MUTE
	A LITTLE RESPECT *(US No. 14 & No. 2 Dance)*	4	22 OCT 88	MUTE
	CRACKERS INTERNATIONAL (E.P.)	2	07 JAN 89	MUTE
	(4 Track EP – their 8th consecutive Top 20)			
	DRAMA! *(Entered at No. 6)*	4	07 OCT 89	MUTE

Also see Yazoo/Depeche Mode/Assembly

ERUPTION

Six piece dance group who were on the roster of Frank Farian the top German producer. Vocalist Precious Wilson later went solo on Hansa in 79, Epic in 81, Jive in 85 and S&M in 90.

🇬🇧	I CAN'T STAND THE RAIN *(US No. 18)*	5	25 MAR 78	ATLANTIC
	(Anne Peebles 73 US hit)			
	ONE WAY TICKET	4	12 MAY 79	ATLANTIC/HAN
	(Old Neil Sedaka 'B'-lyric full of 50s hit titles)			

ESCAPE CLUB

UK trio fronted by Trevor Steel. They toured with acts like The Alarm and China Crisis and had various unsuccessful UK releases on Bright (83), EMI (85) and Parlophone (86) before scoring their first US-only hit. Follow up was 'Shake For The Sheik' (US 28).

🇺🇸	WILD WILD WEST	1(1)	12 NOV 88	ATLANTIC

ESSEX

Quintet formed by US Marines and featuring distinctive singer Anita Humes from Pennsylvania. They had another US-only Top 20 with 'A Walkin' Miracle' and both hits were recorded while the four men in the group were in service. They also recorded on Bang in 66 and Anita had solo releases on Roulette.

🇺🇸	**EASIER SAID THAN DONE** *(Originally 'B' – has rhythm of a teletype machine)*	1(2)	06 JUL 63	ROULETTE

DAVID ESSEX

London born (real name David Cook) singer/actor/composer was a top UK act for over a decade. He recorded unsuccessfully in the 60s on Fontana, UNI, Pye and Decca before starting his long winning streak in 73. Surprisingly this photogenic and talented star only had a real US hit with 'Rock On'.

🇬🇧	**ROCK ON** *(revived by Michael Damian 89)*	3	15 SEP 73	CBS
	LAMPLIGHT *(US No. 71)*	7	08 DEC 73	CBS
	GONNA MAKE YOU A STAR	1(3)	16 NOV 74	CBS
	STARDUST	7	18 JAN 75	CBS
	ROLLIN' STONE	5	26 JUL 75	CBS
	HOLD ME CLOSE *(Jumped from 48-9)*	1(3)	04 OCT 75	CBS
	OH WHAT A CIRCUS	3	23 SEP 78	MERCURY
	SILVER DREAM MACHINE (PT. 1)	4	03 MAY 80	MERCURY
	A WINTER'S TALE	2	15 JAN 83	MERCURY
	TAHITI *(From 'Mutiny On The Bounty')*	8	08 OCT 83	MERCURY
🇺🇸	**ROCK ON**	5	09 MAR 74	COLUMBIA

GLORIA ESTEFAN (& MIAMI SOUND MACHINE)

The Miami Sound Machine (originally Miami Latin Boys) were formed in 73 and Cuban born singer/songwriter Gloria joined in 74. They first recorded on Audio Latino in 75, joined Epic in 79 and sold well in the Latin market before their first hit (which was in the UK). Gloria, who is now the longest serving member, took front billing in 87 and they are now one of the world's top acts.

🇬🇧	**DR. BEAT** *(As Miami Sound Machine)*	6	22 SEP 84	EPIC
	ANYTHING FOR YOU	10	17 SEP 88	EPIC
	1-2-3	9	12 NOV 88	EPIC
	CAN'T STAY AWAY FROM YOU	7	18 MAR 89	EPIC
	(Above 3 as Gloria Estefan & Miami Sound Machine)			
	DON'T WANNA LOSE YOU	6	29 JUL 89	EPIC
🇺🇸	**CONGA** *(As Miami Sound Machine)*	10	08 FEB 86	EPIC
	BAD BOY *(UK No.16) (As Miami Sound Machine)*	8	10 MAY 86	EPIC
	WORDS GET IN THE WAY	5	20 SEP 86	EPIC
	RHYTHM IS GONNA GET YOU *(UK No. 16 in 89)*	5	01 AUG 87	EPIC
	CAN'T STAY AWAY FROM YOU	6	05 MAR 88	EPIC
	ANYTHING FOR YOU	1(2)	14 MAY 88	EPIC
	1-2-3	3	20 AUG 88	EPIC
	(Above 5 as Gloria Estefan & Miami Sound Machine)			
	DON'T WANNA LOSE YOU	1(1)	16 SEP 89	EPIC

DON ESTELLE – SEE WINDSOR DAVIES FOR HIT DETAILS

DEON ESTUS

Detroit born singer and bass player, started in Brainstorm, and has worked with acts like George Michael, Wham!, Marvin Gaye and Jellybean. He recorded in UK on Legacy in 84, Sedition in 85 and Geffen in 86, before signing to George's own Mika label where he scored with a track produced by George. Follow up was 'Spell'.

🇺🇸	**HEAVEN HELP ME** *(No. 41 UK)*	5	29 APR 89	MIKA/POLY

EUROPE

Swedish rock group fronted by singer/writer Joey Tempest. When known as The Force they represented Sweden in the 82 Eurovision Song Contest. They have had four transatlantic Top 40s to date.

🇬🇧	**THE FINAL COUNTDOWN** *(They were second Swedish group to top chart)*	1(2)	29 NOV 86	EPIC
🇺🇸	**THE FINAL COUNTDOWN**	8	28 MAR 87	EPIC
	CARRIE *(UK No. 22)*	3	10 OCT 87	EPIC

EURYTHMICS

Dave Stewart first recorded in Harrison & Stewart on Multicord, was in Longdancer on Rocket, and in The Catch with Annie Lennox which evolved into successful group The Tourists. Dave & Annie then formed The Eurythmics whose sixth single cracked the Top 40 and from then on they notched up a run of transatlantic hits which made them the most charted UK mixed duo of all time.

🇬🇧	**SWEET DREAMS (ARE MADE OF THIS)** *(Recorded on an eight track machine)*	2	19 MAR 83	RCA
	LOVE IS A STRANGER *(US No. 23)*	6	23 APR 83	RCA
	WHO'S THAT GIRL *(US No. 21)*	3	30 JUL 83	RCA
	RIGHT BY YOUR SIDE *(US No. 29)*	10	03 DEC 83	RCA
	HERE COMES THE RAIN AGAIN	8	04 FEB 84	RCA
	SEXCRIME (NINETEEN EIGHTY FOUR) *(US No. 81)* *(US No.81 and U.S. Dance No. 2)*	4	08 DEC 84	VIRGIN
	THERE MUST BE AN ANGEL (PLAYING WITH MY HEART) *(US No. 22)* *(Stevie Wonder was on Harmonica)*	1	27 JUL 85	RCA
	SISTERS ARE DOIN' IT FOR THEMSELVES *(And ARETHA FRANKLIN) (US No. 18)*	9	23 NOV 85	RCA
	THORN IN MY SIDE *(US No. 68)*	5	04 OCT 86	RCA
🇺🇸	**SWEET DREAMS (ARE MADE OF THIS)**	1(1)	03 SEP 83	RCA
	HERE COMES THE RAIN AGAIN	4	31 MAR 84	RCA
	WOULD I LIE TO YOU? *(UK No. 17)*	5	13 JUL 85	RCA

Also see Tourists

MAUREEN EVANS

Cardiff (Wales) singer was a local star in the late 50s and had a small hit with 'The Big Hurt' in 60. She took time off to start a family and returned with her only big hit, a song based on the classic 'Dance Of The Hours' (aka 'Hello Muddah Hello Faddah').

🇬🇧	**LIKE I DO** *(Originally by Nancy Sinatra)*	5	01 FEB 63	ORIOLE

PAUL EVANS

New York singer/writer had his transatlantic hits 20 years apart. He wrote hits 'When' – Kalin Twins, 'Roses Are Red' – Bobby Vinton, 'Let's Pretend' – Lulu and 'Johnny Will' – Pat Boone. Also recorded for RCA in 57, Decca in 58, Atco in 59, Carlton in 61, Kapp in 62, Epic in 64, Columbia in 68, Laurie in 71, Dot in 73, Mercury in 74, Big Tree in 75 and Musicor in 77.

🇬🇧	**HELLO THIS IS JOANNIE (THE TELEPHONE ANSWERING MACHINE SONG)** *(Oddly it did not chart in US)*	6	20 JAN 79	SPRING
🇺🇸	**SEVEN LITTLE GIRLS SITTING IN THE BACK SEAT** *(UK No. 25) (Feat. The CURLS – Sue Singleton & Sue Terry)*	9	08 NOV 59	GUARANTEED
	HAPPY-GO-LUCKY-ME	10	13 JUN 60	GUARANTEED

BETTY EVERETT

Mississippi soul singer recorded for Cobra in 57, C.J. in 61 and One-derful in 62 before joining Vee Jay in 63. She scored the first of ten US hits (two with Jerry Butler) with 'You're No Good' (later a hit for The Swinging Blue Jeans and Linda Ronstadt). She was later on ABC, Uni, Fantasy, SS7, UA and 20th Century.

🇺🇸	**SHOOP SHOOP SONG (IT'S IN HIS KISS)** *(UK No.34 in 68 – Original by Merry Clayton in 63)*	6	11 APR 64	VEE JAY
	LET IT BE ME *(With JERRY BUTLER)* *(Original by Jill Corey 57)*	5	07 NOV 64	VEE JAY

KENNY EVERETT

Zany UK D.J. and TV personality had a one-off UK hit with this rap based on his Sid Snot character in his TV series.

SNOT RAP	9	16 APR 83	RCA	

EVERLY BROTHERS

The most successful duo of the rock'n'roll years in the US and UK. Don & Phil started in The Everly Family and first recorded as a duo on Columbia in 56. They had 17 US Top 20's and 21 in UK. They broke up in 73 and had solo careers until they re-united 10 years later and re-charted in 84. They have won numerous awards and were the first non-solo act in the R'n'R Hall of Fame.

BYE BYE LOVE *(Song was turned down by 29 acts first inc. Elvis)*	6	30 AUG 57	LONDON
WAKE UP LITTLE SUSIE *(In 89 it was sampled on Jive Bunny's 'Swing The Mood')*	2	13 DEC 57	LONDON
BIRD DOG	2	27 JUN 58	LONDON
ALL I HAVE TO DO IS DREAM/CLAUDETTE *(Their biggest hit – it took 15 minutes to write)*	1(7)	14 NOV 58	LONDON
PROBLEMS	6	06 FEB 59	LONDON
('TIL) I KISSED YOU	2	23 OCT 59	LONDON
CATHY'S CLOWN *(Top UK record 60)*	1 9	27 APR 60	WARNER
WHEN WILL I BE LOVED	5	26 AUG 60	LONDON
SO SAD (TO WATCH GOOD LOVE GO BAD)	5	07 OCT 60	WARNER
WALK RIGHT BACK	1(4)	03 MAR 61	WARNER
TEMPTATION *(US No. 27 – Bing Crosby 34 hit)*	1(1)	12 JUL 61	WARNER
CRYIN' IN THE RAIN *(Carole King song)*	6	16 FEB 62	WARNER
NO ONE CAN MAKE MY SUNSHINE SMILE	10	30 NOV 62	WARNER
THE PRICE OF LOVE *(Not in US chart)*	2	19 JUN 65	WARNER
BYE BYE LOVE	2	17 JUN 57	CADENCE
WAKE UP LITTLE SUSIE	1(1)	14 OCT 57	CADENCE
BIRD DOG/DEVOTED TO YOU	2	10 FEB 58	CADENCE
ALL I HAVE TO DO IS DREAM	1(4)	12 MAY 58	CADENCE
PROBLEMS	2	14 DEC 58	CADENCE
('TIL) I KISSED YOU *(Backed by Crickets)*	4	20 SEP 59	CADENCE
LET IT BE ME *(U.K. No.18 – Originally by Jill Corey 57)*	7	22 FEB 60	CADENCE
CATHY'S CLOWN *(Written about Don's High School girlfriend)*	1(5)	23 MAY 60	WARNER
WHEN WILL I BE LOVED	8	18 JUL 60	CADENCE
SO SAD (TO WATCH GOOD LOVE GO BAD)	7	09 OCT 60	WARNER
EBONY EYES *(UK No. 17)*	8	20 MAR 61	WARNER
WALK RIGHT BACK	7	27 MAR 61	WARNER
CRYIN' IN THE RAIN	6	03 MAR 62	WARNER
THAT'S OLD FASHIONED (THAT'S THE WAY LOVE SHOULD BE)	9	23 JUN 62	WARNER

PHIL EVERLY & CLIFF RICHARD

A one-off hit featuring Everly Brother Phil and the UK's top all time male recording artist. It was Phil's first hit for 18 years.

SHE MEANS NOTHING TO ME	9	19 MAR 83	CAPITOL

Also see Everly Brothers/Cliff Richard

EVERY MOTHERS' SON

Brothers Larry & Dennis Larden had sung folk music in their hometown New York before forming this five man rock band. They had four US-only charters, the biggest being their first hit.

COME ON DOWN TO MY BOAT	6	08 JUL 67	MGM

EVERYTHING BUT THE GIRL

Tracey Thorn started in The Marine Girls and both her and duo partner Ben Watt had solo indie hits on Cherry Red before their first unsuccessful duet for that label. They first charted with 'Each And Everyone' in 84 and had the biggest of their UK-only hits with their 11th single – a revival of a Rod Stewart smash.

I DON'T WANT TO TALK ABOUT IT *(First recorded by Neil Young & Crazy Horse in 71)*	3	23 JUL 88	BLANCO

EXCITERS

Originally a quartet, later a duo, this New York act was put together by Herb Rooney (ex Beltones) and featured the vocals of his wife-to-be Brenda Reid. They had the original of 'Do-Wah-Diddy' and also recorded on Roulette, Bang, Shout, Today and RCA. Only UK hit 'Reaching For The Best'(31st) on 20th Century.

TELL HIM *(Song was later UK hit for Billie Davis and Hello)*	4	19 JAN 63	UA

EXILE

Kentucky band, originally called The Exiles, featured singer/ writer J.P. Pennington. They recorded on Wooden Nickle in 73 and first charted on Atco in 77. Teaming with top UK producers/ writers Chinn & Chapman, gave them their Top 10 hit. They have had 10 country No 1s since 83 and made personnel changes in 89.

KISS YOU ALL OVER	6	23 SEP 78	RAK
KISS YOU ALL OVER	1(4)	30 SEP 78	WARNER

EXPOSE

Trio of Ann Curless, Jeanette Jurado and Gioia Carmen are the foremost exponents of the 'Miami Sound' and the most successful girl group in the US since The Supremes. They first recorded 'Point of No Return' as X-Posed in 84 and it later became one of their fantastic string of 6 Top 10 US-only hits in a row.

COME GO WITH ME	5	04 APR 87	ARISTA
POINT OF NO RETURN	5	18 JUL 87	ARISTA
LET ME BE THE ONE	7	31 OCT 87	ARISTA
SEASONS CHANGE *(4th Top 10 of their debut LP – a record for groups)*	1(1)	20 FEB 88	ARISTA
WHAT YOU DON'T KNOW	8	15 JUL 89	ARISTA
WHEN I LOOKED AT HIM	10	21 OCT 89	ARISTA

F

SHELLEY FABARES

Californian singer/actress played Mary Stone in Donna Reed's US-only TV show. She first recorded in 60 and launched her big hit on Donna's show two years later. Her follow up was 'Johnny Loves Me' (No.21 US). She was later on Vee Jay and Dunhill and starred in a couple of Elvis movies and one with Herman's Hermits.

 JOHNNY ANGEL (UK No. 26)   1(2)   07 APR 62   COLPIX

BENT FABRIC

One of Denmark's best known music and TV personalities (real name Bent Fabricius-Bjerre) and head of one of their top record companies. He had a one-off US Top 40 with this piano instrumental which he composed. His follow up was 'Chicken Feed'.

 ALLEY CAT   7   29 SEP 62   ATCO

FABULOUS THUNDERBIRDS

Texan R&B influenced rock band fronted by Ken Wilson were formed in 77. Although they were a very popular live act they never really hit until the title track from their sixth LP gave them their sole US Top 10 to date.

 TUFF ENUFF   10   12 JUL 86   CBS ASSOC.

FACES

After Steve Marriott left The Small Faces, Rod Stewart and Ron Wood (ex Jeff Beck band) were brought in. Rod's solo career took off at the same time as the group hit, and as he became a star the group became known as Rod Stewart & The Faces. After many LP and single chart records, the members went their own ways in 75.

STAY WITH ME (US No. 17)   6   05 FEB 72   WARNER
CINDY INCIDENTALLY (US No. 48)   2   10 MAR 73   WARNER
POOL HALL RICHARD/I WISH IT WOULD RAIN 8   12 JAN 74   WARNER

Also see Rod Stewart/Small Faces

JOE FAGIN

UK actor/singer star had a one-off UK Top 40 hit with the theme from the TV series Auf Wiederseh'n Pet. His follow up, 'Breakin' Away', was also from the series.

THAT'S LIVING (ALRIGHT)   3   28 JAN 84   TOWERBELL

YVONNE FAIR

Virginia born soul singer recorded with the James Brown Band on King in 62. She recorded on Dade and Smash before joining Motown in 68 where she had a UK smash with an old Gladys Knight track. She also appeared in the film 'Lady Sings The Blues'.

IT SHOULD HAVE BEEN ME (US No. 85)   5   06 MAR 76   TAMLA MOTOWN

FAIRGROUND ATTRACTION

Winners of BRITS awards for Best Single and Album ('The First Of A Million Kisses') of 88 in the UK. They were fronted by Glasgow born singer Eddi (Sadenia) Reader and composer Mark E. Nevin. Sadly Eddi quit in 90.

PERFECT (US No. 80 and small country hit) 1(1)   14 MAY 88   RCA
FIND MY LOVE   7   20 AUG 88   RCA

FAIR WEATHER

After leaving Amen Corner singer Andy Fairweather-Low and three other members formed this short lived act and had a one-off UK hit.

 NATURAL SINNER   6   15 AUG 70   RCA

Also see Andy Fairweather-Low/Amen Corner

ANDY FAIRWEATHER-LOW

Welsh singer and ex leader of Amen Corner and Fair Weather had a couple of years out of the limelight before launching a solo career that started well but didn't prosper. In the US his only chart entry came with the solo 'Spider Jiving' (87). He later recorded on WEA in 80 and Stiff in 86.

REGGAE TUNE   10   19 OCT 74   A&M
WIDE EYED AND LEGLESS   6   10 JAN 76   A&M

Also see Amen Corner/Fair Weather

ADAM FAITH

Born Terry Nelhams in London, he was in The Worried Men skiffle group and the duo Terry & Freddy. As a soloist he had a few flops on HMV and Top Rank before starting a very long and successful UK career. In the US he had one Top 40 'It's Alright' in 63. He later went into management (Leo Sayer), production and acting.

WHAT DO YOU WANT   1(3)   04 DEC 59   PARLOPHONE
(At the time thought to be a Buddy Holly rip-off)
POOR ME   1(2)   04 MAR 60   PARLOPHONE
SOMEONE ELSE'S BABY   2   06 MAY 60   PARLOPHONE
MADE YOU/WHEN JOHNNY COMES MARCHING 5   15 JUL 60   PARLOPHONE
(Banned in US where Fabian covered it)
HOW ABOUT THAT   3   07 OCT 60   PARLOPHONE
LONELY PUP (IN A CHRISTMAS SHOP)   4   30 DEC 60   PARLOPHONE
(First UK act have first 6 hits in Top 5)
WHO AM I/THIS IS IT   7   24 FEB 61   PARLOPHONE
DON'T YOU KNOW IT   9   04 AUG 61   PARLOPHONE
THE TIME HAS COME   5   17 NOV 61   PARLOPHONE
AS YOU LIKE IT   5   25 MAY 62   PARLOPHONE
DON'T THAT BEAT ALL   9   21 SEP 62   PARLOPHONE
THE FIRST TIME   5   11 OCT 63   PARLOPHONE
(Feat. The Roulettes – Composed by Chris Andrews)

PERCY FAITH

Canadian born orchestra leader and arranger worked with many of Columbia's top acts in the early 50s and also scored 13 Top 40 pre-rock hits of his own, including 'Delicado' and 'Song From Moulin Rouge'. He died in 1976.

THEME FROM 'A SUMMER PLACE'   4   18 MAR 60   PHILIPS
THEME FROM 'A SUMMER PLACE'   1(9)   18 APR 60   COLUMBIA
(Top US record 60)

MARIANNE FAITHFULL

Austrian baroness' daughter, born in London, and probably best known as Mick Jagger's girlfriend in the sixties, has been beset by highly publicised personal problems over the years. She shared her manager with the Stones and has a transatlantic cult following. She resurfaced in 79 and in 89 (with help from Bono and Steve Winwood).

AS TEARS GO BY (US No. 22)   9   11 SEP 64   DECCA
(US No. 22 – composed by Jagger & Richards)
COME AND STAY WITH ME   4   27 MAR 65   DECCA
(US No.26 – Jackie De Shannon song)
THIS LITTLE BIRD   6   22 MAY 65   DECCA
(US No.32 – originally by John D. Loudermilk)
SUMMER NIGHTS (US No. 24)   10   14 AUG 65   DECCA

FALCO

Austria's most successful rock act. Born Johann Hoelzel in Vienna, he was the first Austrian to have a transatlantic No. 1. He also had the original hit with 'Der Kommissar' (After The Fire) and had another German No. 1 with the controversial 'Jeanny'.

🇬🇧 ROCK ME AMADEUS	1(1)	10 MAY 86	A&M
VIENNA CALLING (US No. 18)	10	14 JUN 86	A&M
🇺🇸 ROCK ME AMADEUS	1(3)	29 MAR 86	A&M

HAROLD FALTERMEYER

German born writer/musician/arranger and producer was a protege of Giorgio Moroder and appeared on many of his productions. He also worked on the music in the films Midnight Express, American Gigolo and Top Gun.

🇬🇧 AXEL F (From film 'Beverly Hills Cop')	2	06 JUL 85	MCA
🇺🇸 AXEL F	3	01 JUN 85	MCA

GEORGIE FAME

Singer/keyboard player from Lancashire (UK) had backed Gene Vincent, Eddie Cochran and Billy Fury before he was 18. He was handled by top UK manager Larry Parnes and made his debut record in 63. He was one of the earliest R&B performers on the UK club scene. In 65 he scored the first of his 13 UK chart records. In 89 he and his band backed Van Morrison on tour. He joined Food For Thought in 90.

🇬🇧 YEH YEH	1(2)	16 JAN 65	COLUMBIA
(US No. 21 – Mongo Santamaria 63 US hit)			
GET AWAY (US No. 70)	1(1)	23 JUL 66	COLUMBIA
(Both above records with The Blue Flames)			
BALLAD OF BONNIE & CLYDE	1(1)	27 JAN 68	CBS
🇺🇸 THE BALLAD OF BONNIE AND CLYDE	7	13 APR 68	EPIC

FAMILY

Formed in 66 in Leicester (UK) from two groups, The Roaring Sixties and The Farinas, and fronted by Roger Chapman. The band at times included John Wetton, Tony Ashton and Rick Grech. They were a popular live act in the UK with five UK Top 20 LPs and three Top 20 singles but no US Top 100 entries.

🇬🇧 IN MY OWN TIME	4	04 SEP 71	REPRISE

FAMILY DOGG

Mixed UK based group fronted by producer/singer/writer Steve Rowland which included Albert Hammond and featured Jimmy Page's guitar work. Steve previously recorded solo on Fontana in 67 and they first recorded a year before their one-off UK hit.

🇬🇧 WAY OF LIFE	6	19 JUL 69	BELL

FANTASTIC JOHNNY C – SEE UNDER 'C' FOR HIT DETAILS

FANTASTICS

New York vocal quartet fronted by Don Haywood (father of hit act Haywoode) who had originally recorded as The Troubadours on Baton in 54, and recorded one of the great doo-wop records 'Can I Come Over Tonight' as The Velours on Onyx in 57. They toured the UK as The Fabulous Temptations, changed their name yet again and had a one-off UK hit. The follow up was 'Something Wonderful'.

🇬🇧 SOMETHING OLD, SOMETHING NEW	9	24 APR 71	BELL

FAR CORPORATION

Master-minded by producer Fred Farian of Milli Vanilli and Boney M fame, this group of session musicians included Toto members David Paich and Bobby Kimball. Their one-off hit was the classic Led Zeppelin track which for many years was the most requested song on US FM radio. Follow up was 'You Are The Woman'.

🇬🇧 STAIRWAY TO HEAVEN (US No. 89)	8	16 NOV 85	ARISTA

DON FARDON

The ex lead singer of UK band The Sorrows went solo in 67 and first charted with a tribute to soccer star George Best called 'Belfast Boy'. His biggest UK hit flopped when first released in 67, became a US hit in 68, was finally a UK hit in 70 and the song went to No. 1 in the US in 71 when covered by The Raiders.

🇬🇧 INDIAN RESERVATION (US No. 20 in 68)	3	21 NOV 70	YOUNG BLOOD

DONNA FARGO

Born Yvonne Vaughn in North Carolina, she was on Ramco (67), Challenge (68) and Decca (72) before her first of two US-only Top 20s 'The Happiest Girl In The Whole USA'(11th). She was the Top Female Country act of 74, has had 37 country hits and was on Warner (76), MCA (82), RCA (82), Columbia (83) and Mercury (86).

🇺🇸 FUNNY FACE	5	06 JAN 73	DOT

CHRIS FARLOWE ·

Born John Deighton in London. He was one of the UK's first R&B singers, recording 'Air Travel' (first by Bob & Ray) on Decca in 62 and he was a popular club act in early 60s. His No 1 was written by Mick Jagger and Keith Richards. He later sang with Colosseum and Atomic Rooster and was featured on Jeff Beck's 88 LP. He was also on MGM, Polydor, Charly, Cat Brand New and Taurus. He now runs a shop in Islington which sells Nazi memorabilia.

🇬🇧 OUT OF TIME (7th single release)	1(1)	30 JUL 66	IMMEDIATE

JOHN FARNHAM

Veteran Australian singer/actor and TV star is one of their top acts of all time. His first release was the Aussie No. 1 'Sadie The Cleaning Lady' in 68. He was in the Little River Band for four years and finally charted in the UK in 87 and the US in 90.

🇬🇧 YOU'RE THE VOICE (In US Top 100 in 90)	6	04 JUL 87	WHEATLEY

FAT BOYS

New York rappers and actors consisted of Darren Robinson, Mark Morales and Damon Wimbley who first charted with 'Fat Boys' (under the name Disco 3) on Sutra in 84 and have since scored with both singles and LPs, not to mention their success in various movies.

🇬🇧 WIPEOUT (And The BEACH BOYS) (US No.12)	2	12 SEP 87	URBAN
THE TWIST (YO, TWIST) (US No. 16)	2	02 JUL 88	POLY/URBAN
(Feat. CHUBBY CHECKER – originally by Hank Ballard)			

FAT LARRY'S BAND

Philadelphia band led by Larry James. They were more popular in the UK (three charters) than in their homeland where 'Boogie Town' (black chart No. 43) as FLB was their biggest hit. Larry, who was also on Stax and Atlantic, died in 87 (age 38).

 ZOOM *(Released in US 82 & 86 without success)* | 2 | 09 OCT 82 | VIRGIN

FATBACK BAND

US funk band led by North Carolina drummer Bill Curtis have had nine UK hits and 31 records on the US black music chart but oddly have yet to make the US Pop Top 100. Their 'I Found Lovin' (which did not chart at all in the US) is an anthem in UK clubs.

 (DO THE) SPANISH HUSTLE | 10 | 13 MAR 76 | POLYDOR
I FOUND LOVIN' *(Got 49 UK in 84)* | 7 | 17 OCT 87 | MASTER MIX

PHIL FEARON

Singer/songwriter/producer and musician who was in hit acts Hi-Tension and Kandidate and had guested in Proton Plus. His nine UK-only hits were recorded in his own studio in North London and he is one of the most successful black UK acts of all time.

 DANCING TIGHT *(As GALAXY feat. Phil Fearon)* | 4 | 21 MAY 83 | ENSIGN
WHAT DO I DO | 5 | 31 MAR 84 | ENSIGN
EVERYBODY'S LAUGHING | 10 | 04 AUG 84 | ENSIGN
(Above 2 as Phil Fearon & Galaxy)
I CAN PROVE IT | 8 | 23 AUG 86 | ENSIGN

JOSE FELICIANO

Distinctive singer/writer/guitarist who was born blind in Puerto Rico. He moved to New York and was signed to RCA to record for the Latin market in 63. When he recorded for the pop market he was an instant star. He later recorded for Private Stock and Motown and he joined EMI in 89.

 LIGHT MY FIRE *(Only UK hit of song)* | 6 | 02 NOV 68 | RCA
LIGHT MY FIRE *(Doors 65 US hit)* | 3 | 31 AUG 68 | RCA

FREDDY FENDER

Tex/Mex singer born Baldemar Huerta in Texas. Recorded under his own name for Falcon in 56 and on Duncan, Argo, Talent Scout (as Scotty Wayne), Imperial, Norco, Instant, Arv, Starflite, Arvee, Checker, Pacemaker, Pa-Go-Go, GRT, Crazy Cajun, Goldband and ABC prior to the first of his seven US-only hits and 21 country charters.

BEFORE THE NEXT TEARDROP FALLS | 1(1) | 31 MAY 75 | ABC/DOT
(He previously released it on Crazy Cajun)
WASTED DAYS AND WASTED NIGHTS | 8 | 27 SEP 75 | ABC/DOT
(He originally recorded it on Duncan)

FENDERMEN

Named after the guitars they played, this Wisconsin (US) duo were Jim Sundquist and Phil Humphrey. Their follow up was another oldie – Huey Smith's 'Don't You Just Know It'.

MULE SKINNER BLUES *(UK No. 27)* | 5 | 11 JUL 60 | SOMA

JAY FERGUSON

Before going solo this Californian had been in two popular groups – Spirit and Jo Jo Gunne. He had another US-only hit with 'Shakedown Cruise' and joined Capitol in 80.

THUNDER ISLAND | 9 | 01 APR 78 | ASYLUM

Also see Jo Jo Gunne

FERRANTE & TEICHER

MOR pianists Arthur Ferrante and Louis Teicher had been playing together since they were six and recorded for Davis in 57 and covered Russ Conway's UK No. 1 'Side Saddle' on ABC in 59. Against the trend they had a string of US hits in the 60s.

 EXODUS *(From the film)* | 6 | 31 MAR 61 | LONDON
THEME FROM THE APARTMENT *(From the film)* | 10 | 05 SEP 60 | UA
EXODUS *(Top US record of 61)* | 2 | 23 JAN 61 | UA
TONIGHT *(From West Side Story)* | 8 | 11 DEC 61 | UA
MIDNIGHT COWBOY *(From the film)* | 10 | 17 JAN 70 | UA

FERRY AID

A charity record with money going to the Zeebrugge Ferry Disaster Appeal (it sunk killing over 200 people). Stars on the record included Boy George, Mark Knopfler, Mark King and Rick Astley.

LET IT BE *(Beatles 70 hit-entered No. 1)* | 3 | 04 APR 87 | THE SUN
(Gave producers S.A.W. 2nd No. 1 in a row)

BRYAN FERRY

Durham (UK) born singer has split his time since 71 between solo recordings and those of his group Roxy Music with equal success (18 Top 20 UK LPs between them). His sophisticated style has always kept him at the top in the UK and although he is a cult figure in the US his work has never cracked their Top 20.

A HARD RAIN'S GONNA FALL *(Bob Dylan song)* | 10 | 27 OCT 73 | ISLAND
LET'S STICK TOGETHER *(re-mix UK No. 12 in 88)* | 4 | 03 JUL 76 | ISLAND
(Originally by Wilburt Harrison)
EXTENDED PLAY (E.P.) | 7 | 04 SEP 76 | ISLAND
THIS IS TOMORROW | 9 | 12 MAR 77 | POLYDOR
SLAVE TO LOVE | 10 | 01 JUN 85 | EG

Also see Roxy Music

KAREL FIALKA

Bengal born, UK based Czechoslovakian immigrant singer/songwriter first recorded on his own Red Shift label and first charted on Blueprint with 'The Eyes Have It' in 80. He recorded on Carrere in 83 and scored another UK-only hit in 87, this time featuring his step-son Matthew. Follow up was 'Eat Drink Dance'.

HEY MATTHEW | 9 | 26 SEP 87 | IRS

FICTION FACTORY

Five piece Scottish group led by Kevin Patterson who with fellow members Eddie Jordan and Chic Medley had been in The RB's. They followed their UK hit with 'Ghosts of Love', which had been their first release, and they changed labels to Foundry in 85.

(FEELS LIKE) HEAVEN | 6 | 04 FEB 84 | CBS

FIDDLER'S DRAM

Mixed UK septet, featuring vocalist Cathy Le Surf, had a one off UK hit with a folkish novelty about a Welsh holiday resort. The group, who had previously recorded many folk records, followed up with 'Beercart Lane'.

DAY TRIP TO BANGOR (DIDN'T WE HAVE A LOVELY TIME) | 3 | 05 JAN 80 | DINGLES

FIFTH DIMENSION

West Coast group recorded as The Hi-Fi's until Harry Elston left to form Friends of Distinction. They then recorded on Bronco and Soul City as The Versatiles. They notched up 20 Top 40's in the US (2 in UK) and eight Top 40 US-only LPs. Marilyn McCoo and Bill Davis Jr. left and became a hit duo scoring with 'You Don't Have To Be A Star' in 77.

UP UP & AWAY		7	08 JUL 67	SOUL CITY
STONED SOUL PICNIC (Laura Nyro song)		3	27 JUL 68	SOUL CITY
AQUARIUS/LET THE SUNSHINE IN (UK No. 11)		1(6)	12 APR 69	SOUL CITY
WEDDING BELL BLUES		1(3)	08 NOV 69	SOUL CITY
(UK No. 16 – Another Laura Nyro song)				
ONE LESS BELL TO ANSWER		2	26 DEC 70	BELL
(LAST NIGHT) I DIDN'T GET TO SLEEP AT ALL		8	17 JUN 72	BELL
IF I COULD REACH YOU		10	25 NOV 72	BELL

Also see Marilyn McCoo & Billy Davis Jr.

FINE YOUNG CANNIBALS

Formed by ex Beat members David Steele and Andy Cox who brought in singer/actor Roland Gift from ska group The Akrylix. They were overnight stars in the UK and broke wide open in the States four years later to become one of the biggest selling pop acts in the world in 89.

JOHNNY COME HOME (US No. 76)		8	13 JUL 85	LONDON
SUSPICIOUS MINDS (Elvis Presley 69 hit)		8	01 FEB 86	LONDON
EVER FALLEN IN LOVE (Buzzcocks 78 UK hit)		9	18 APR 87	LONDON
SHE DRIVES ME CRAZY		5	21 JAN 89	LONDON
GOOD THING		7	29 APR 89	LONDON
SHE DRIVES ME CRAZY		1(4)	15 APR 89	IRS
GOOD THING (From the film Scandal)		1(1)	08 JUL 89	IRS

FIREBALLS

New Mexico based rock band who recorded for Top Rank in 59 and Hamilton and Jaro in 60. Jimmy Gilmer (ex Decca act in 59) joined as a pianist/singer in 60 and helped give them their biggest hit. They are best known in UK as the act who played rhythm tracks on Buddy Holly's demo tapes. Jimmy is now an executive of SBK records.

SUGAR SHACK (As Jimmy Gilmer & The Fireballs)		1(5)	12 OCT 63	DOT
(They later recorded 'Sugar In The Woods')				
BOTTLE OF WINE		9	02 MAR 68	ATCO

FIREFALL

Boulder (US) AOR quintet led by singer/composer Rick Roberts and including Mark Andes, ex of Heart and Spirit. They had a string of US-only hits including three Top 20s, the others being 'Just Remember I Love You' and 'Strange Way'.

YOU ARE THE WOMAN		9	11 DEC 76	ATLANTIC

FIRM

UK act includes John O'Connor and Graham Lister. They had the first of their two UK-only Top 20 novelty hits in 82 with 'Arthur Daley ('E's Alright)' based on a UK TV show, then hit No. 1 five years later with a track about the popular US TV show of the 60s.

STAR TREKKIN'		1(2)	20 JUN 87	BARK
(Took 3 weeks To No. 1 – jumped from 13-1)				

FIRST CHOICE

Philadelphia female trio featuring Rochelle Fleming. Initially known as The Debronettes, they first recorded for Sceptre and their debut transatlantic hit was 'Armed & Extremely Dangerous' (UK 16/US 28). They were later on Warner and Goldmind.

SMARTY PANTS (US No. 56)		9	25 AUG 73	BELL

FIRST CLASS

UK session group who fared better in the US with three charters. Their Beach Boys styled hit featured singers Tony Burrows, Chas Mills and John Carter amongst others. They were later on Private Stock in 76, CBS in 77, Epic in 78 and Sunny in 83.

BEACH BABY		4	05 OCT 74	UK
(UK No.13- they re-recorded it on Sunny in 83)				

FIRST EDITION – SEE KENNY ROGERS FOR HIT DETAILS

SCOTT FITZGERALD & YVONNE KEELY

Yvonne had recorded as a soloist on UA in 75 before teaming with session vocalist Scott for this one-off UK hit. Scott later appeared on UA in 78, Creole in 80, Young Blood in 84 and represented the UK in the 88 Eurovision song contest. Yvonne later teamed unsuccessfully with Steve Flanagan.

IF I HAD WORDS		3	18 FEB 78	PEPPER
(Featuring The Thomas More School Choir)				

FIVE AMERICANS

Dallas based pop quintet fronted by Michael Rabon. They recorded for ABC in 65 and had their first of six US-only hits with 'I See The Light' (26) on HBR. Their biggest hit was produced by old rock'n'roll star Dale Hawkins.

WESTERN UNION		5	22 APR 67	ABNAK

FIVE MAN ELECTRICAL BAND

Les Emmerson was the leader of the Canadian rock quintet who had been very popular in their homeland as The Staccatos (on Capitol) before going to the West Coast and getting a new name and label. They had five US-only hits, including the unusual 'Werewolf'.

SIGNS (A re-recording of a track on Capitol)		3	28 AUG 71	LIONEL

FIVE STAIRSTEPS

Discovered by Curtis Mayfield, they were one of the first family acts in the Soul field. The six-member Burke family, included Kenny (later a hit solo act) and the then four year old Cubie. They had 17 US-only hits in a five year period after first scoring with the Mayfield-produced 'You Waited Too Long' in 66.

O-O-O CHILD		8	18 JUL 70	BUDDAH

FIVE STAR

UK's top black family act are five members of the Essex based Pearson Family (fronted by Deniece) who are managed by their ex singer father Buster. First single was 'Problematic' in 83 and their fourth release 'All Fall Down' was the first of many hits for the award winning group. They joined Epic in 90.

SYSTEM ADDICT		3	15 FEB 86	TENT
CAN'T WAIT ANOTHER MINUTE (US No. 41)		7	03 MAY 86	TENT
FIND THE TIME		7	09 AUG 86	TENT
RAIN OR SHINE		2	04 OCT 86	TENT
STAY OUT OF MY LIFE		9	21 FEB 87	TENT
THE SLIGHTEST TOUCH		4	02 MAY 87	TENT

5000 VOLTS

UK session group, put together by producer/composer Tony Eyers. They got a lot of bad press when it was discovered that the singer on the record was not the girl miming on TV. The real singer was Tina Charles, later a star in her own right.

 I'M ON FIRE *(US No. 26)*		4	27 SEP 75	PHILIPS
DR. KISS KISS		8	14 AUG 76	PHILIPS

FIXX

Five man London based rock group fronted by Cy Curnin and originally called The Portraits. They have yet the crack the UK Top 40 even though they have had five US Top 40s to date.

ONE THING LEADS TO ANOTHER	4	05 NOV 83	MCA

ROBERTA FLACK

North Carolina born singer/pianist's debut record was on Columbia in 67. She joined Atlantic in 69 and first charted in a duet with school friend Donny Hathaway with 'You've Got A Friend' in 71 and a year later she had two LPs in the US Top 5. After a quiet period her 'Oasis' was a black music No. 1 in 89. 'Killing Me Softly With His Song' was written by Lori Lieberman about Don McLean and his song 'American Pie'.

KILLING ME SOFTLY WITH HIS SONG		6	24 MAR 73	ATLANTIC
TONIGHT I CELEBRATE MY LOVE *(With PEABO BRYSON (US No. 16)*		2	17 SEP 83	CAPITOL
THE CLOSER I GET TO YOU *(US No. 2)*		3	13 MAY 78	ATLANTIC
BACK TOGETHER AGAIN *(US No. 56)* *(And DONNY HATHAWAY for the above two singles)*		3	28 JUN 80	ATLANTIC
THE FIRST TIME EVER I SAW YOUR FACE *(UK No. 14 – Top US single of 72)*		6	15 APR 72	ATLANTIC
WHERE IS THE LOVE *(And DONNY HATHAWAY – UK No. 29)*		5	12 AUG 72	ATLANTIC
KILLING ME SOFTLY WITH HIS SONG		1(5)	24 FEB 73	ATLANTIC
FEEL LIKE MAKIN' LOVE *(UK No. 34 – Top US Soul single 74)*		1(1)	10 AUG 74	ATLANTIC

FLASH AND THE PAN

Off-shoot group from The Easybeats, this Australian pop quartet was led by singer/composer/producers George Young and Harry Vanda. Their first UK charter was 'And The Band Played On' No. 54 in 78, and their only US entry was 'Hey, St. Peter' No. 76 in 79.

WAITING FOR A TRAIN	7	25 JUN 83	EASYBEAT

Also see Easybeats

FLEETWOOD MAC

One of the most successful UK bands of all time whose 'Rumours' LP topped the US charts for a record 31 weeks. Their first chart records came at home and over the next two decades they scored many hits in the US & UK. They have had many styles and personnel changes, starting as a blues band led by the now reclusive Peter Green and ultimately becoming a top AOR band with the introduction of Americans Stevie Nicks and Lindsey Buckingham in 75.

ALBATROSS *(They were top UK act of 69)*		1(1)	01 FEB 69	BLUE HORIZON
MAN OF THE WORLD		2	31 MAY 69	IMMEDIATE
OH WELL *(US No. 55)*		2	08 NOV 69	REPRISE
THE GREEN MANALISHI		10	20 JUN 70	REPRISE
ALBATROSS *(Re-issue)*		2	23 JUN 73	CBS
TUSK		6	10 NOV 79	WARNER
OH DIANE		9	19 FEB 83	WARNER
BIG LOVE		9	16 MAY 87	WARNER
LITTLE LIES *(Their first transatlantic Top 5)*		5	31 OCT 87	WARNER
EVERYWHERE *(US No.14)*		4	23 APR 88	WARNER
GO YOUR OWN WAY *(UK No. 38)*		10	12 MAR 77	WARNER
DREAMS *(UK No. 24)*		1(1)	18 JUN 77	WARNER
DON'T STOP *(UK No. 32)*		3	24 SEP 77	WARNER
YOU MAKE LOVIN' FUN *(UK No. 45)*		9	17 DEC 77	WARNER
TUSK		8	03 NOV 79	WARNER
SARA *(UK No. 37)*		7	02 FEB 80	WARNER
HOLD ME		4	24 JUL 82	WARNER
BIG LOVE		5	30 MAY 87	WARNER
LITTLE LIES		4	07 NOV 87	WARNER

FLEETWOODS

High school trio from Washington who originally called themselves Two Girls & A Guy. Their first single, which they wrote themselves, gave the distinctive trio a transatlantic Top 10 hit and they followed it with a string of US-only hits. The group's popularity waned when singer Gary Troxel had to join the Navy.

COME SOFTLY TO ME		6	15 MAY 59	LONDON
COME SOFTLY TO ME *(The first R'n'R Accapella million seller)*		1(4)	13 APR 59	DOLPHIN
MR. BLUE *(Was written for The Platters)*		1(1)	16 NOV 59	DOLTON
TRAGEDY *(Thomas Wayne 59 US hit)*		10	29 MAY 61	DOLTON

BERNI FLINT

Winning TV show 'Opportunity Knocks' gave the UK singer/songwriter his sole UK Top 40 hit. Follow up 'Southern Comfort' reached 48. He re-appeared on Sumatra in 83.

I DON'T WANT TO PUT A HOLD ON YOU	3	23 APR 77	EMI

FLOATERS

Detroit soul quartet (discovered by The Detroit Emeralds) fronted by Ralph Mitchell and Charles Clark. They nearly had a transatlantic table topper with their second release on ABC, a one-off hit in which they told the world what star signs they all were.

FLOAT ON *(Group later recorded 'Whatever Your Sign')*		1(1)	27 AUG 77	ABC
FLOAT ON *(Top US Soul record 77)*		2	17 SEP 77	ABC

FLOCK OF SEAGULLS

Another Liverpool quartet that did well on both sides of the Atlantic. Featuring the voice and haircut of Mike Score, they first recorded on Cocteau in 81. They scored with a handful of transatlantic Top 40s and picked up a Grammy on the way. They recorded on Crescendo in 89.

WISHING (IF I HAD A PHOTOGRAPH OF YOU) *(US No. 26)*		10	11 DEC 82	JIVE
I RAN (SO FAR AWAY) *(UK No. 43)*		9	23 OCT 82	JIVE

FLOWERPOT MEN

UK session group had a one-off UK hit with a 'Flower Power' cash-in record. Group members included Tony Burrows (again), Neil Landon, both ex-Ivy League, and (briefly) Jon Lord. Follow up was 'A Walk In The Sky'.

LET'S GO TO SAN FRANCISCO *(Act called the Flower Pots in the US)*	4	23 SEP 67	DERAM

FLYING LIZARDS

UK act formed by David Cunningham and featuring the voice of Deborah Evans. Their first single was 'Summertime Blues' and they also cut another oldie 'Dizzy Miss Lizzy'. They appeared on Statik in 84 and David later worked with The Pop Group, Modettes, Electric Chairs and This Heat.

🇬🇧	MONEY *(Cost $14 to record)* *(US No. 50 – Barrett Strong 60 US hit)*	5	08 SEP 79	VIRGIN

FLYING MACHINE

UK session group put together by ace writer/producer Tony Macauley. Oddly they had no success at home but scored one big US hit. UK group Pinkerton's Assorted Colours toured the US as Flying Machine when the record was a hit there.

🇺🇸	SMILE A LITTLE SMILE FOR ME	5	22 NOV 69	JANUS

Also see Pinkerton's Assorted Colours

FLYING PICKETS

UK acappella group who recorded on AVM in 82 and specialised in revivals like their UK Xmas No. 1 in 83 (a recent Yazoo hit). The record was one of the biggest ever chart jumpers (60-9) and made the biggest drop from No. 1 (to No. 10). Their novelty appeal was limited to Europe. They were on Creole in 86.

🇬🇧	ONLY YOU *(First acapella No. 1 in UK)*	1(4)	10 DEC 83	10
	WHEN YOU'RE YOUNG AND IN LOVE *(Marvelettes 67 US hit)*	7	05 MAY 84	10

FOCUS

Highly regarded Dutch guitarist Jan Akkerman, formerly with Brainbox, and organist/flute player Thijs Van Leer were main men in this progressive rock group with classic overtones. They had some transatlantic single & LP hits before Jan left in 76. Replacement was Philip Catherine and P.J. Proby also recorded with them.

🇬🇧	SYLVIA *(US No. 89 – they had 2 in UK Top 20 at same time)*	4	24 APR 73	POLYDOR
🇺🇸	HOCUS POCUS *(UK No. 20 – recorded as a joke)*	9	02 JUN 73	SIRE

DAN FOGELBERG

Illinois born folk rocker's first LP in 72 'Home Free' did little but his second 'Souvenirs' was the first of 10 US-only Top 40 LPs for him. In 75 his 'Part Of The Plan' became the first of this singer/songwriter's 11 Top 40 US-only singles.

🇺🇸	LONGER *(UK No. 59)*	2	15 MAR 80	FULL MOON
	HARD TO SAY	7	31 JAN 81	FULL MOON
	SAME OLD LANG SYNE	9	21 FEB 81	FULL MOON
	LEADER OF THE BAND	9	06 MAR 82	FULL MOON

JOHN FOGERTY

Ex leader of the very successful Creedence Clearwater Revival. His first solo chart record had been under the name The Blue Ridge Rangers with 'Jambalaya'(No. 16 US) in 72 and he also wrote and recorded the rock anthem 'Rockin' All Over the World' in 75. After an eight year absence he returned with a US No. 1 LP 'Centrefield' (UK 48) which included his solo US Top 10.

🇺🇸	THE OLD MAN DOWN THE ROAD	10	02 MAR 85	WARNER

WAYNE FONTANA & THE MINDBENDERS

Manchester (UK) group evolved out of The Jets. Their first 45 was an unsuccessful version of Bo Diddley's 'Road Runner'. Their sixth single was the first of four (1 in US) Top 40s before group and singer split in 65. Wayne's (born Glyn Ellis) had two solo UK-only Top 20's 'Come On Home' (16) and 'Pamela Pamela' (11). Mindbender Eric Stewart joined 10cc and became a successful songwriter and producer.

🇬🇧	UM UM UM UM UM UM *(Major Lane 64 US hit)*	5	28 NOV 64	FONTANA
	GAME OF LOVE	2	27 FEB 65	FONTANA
🇺🇸	GAME OF LOVE	1(1)	24 APR 65	FONTANA

Also see The Mindbenders

FORCE M.D'S

Five man act from Staten Island who combined hip hop and doo-wop. Originally known as Dr. Rock & The MC's, they are fronted by Antoine Lundy and first charted with 'Let Me Love You' in 84.

🇺🇸	TENDER LOVE *(UK No. 23 – from film* *'Krush Groove)*	10	12 APR 8	WARNER

EMILE FORD & THE CHECKMATES

He was the first black UK male act to top the UK charts and he managed to string together five consecutive UK-only Top 20 hits, three of which were updated version of old songs. He later recorded for labels like Piccadilly, Decca, Sunflight, Unigram and Transdisc, and the group recorded on Decca and Parlophone.

🇬🇧	WHAT DO YOU WANT TO MAKE THOSE EYES AT ME FOR *(Cover of Johnny Otis version)*	1(6)	08 JAN 60	PYE
	ON A SLOW BOAT TO CHINA *(Kay Kyser 48 hit)*	4	04 MAR 60	PYE
	COUNTING TEARDROPS *(Cover of Barry Mann)*	7	13 JAN 61	PYE

LITA FORD

London born ex guitarist with The Runaways (alongside Joan Jett). As a soloist she was on Mercury in 83 and first charted with 'Kiss Me Deadly' (US 12/UK 75) before she and her metal duet partner Ozzy Osbourne both saw their names in a singles Top 10 for the first time.

🇺🇸	CLOSE MY EYES FOREVER *(And OZZY OSBOURNE – UK No. 47)*	8	17 JUN 89	RCA

FOREIGNER

Anglo-American group includes Londoner Mick Jones (ex Spooky Tooth and Leslie West Band) and New York vocalist Lou Gramm. Their singles and LPs were instant hits especially in the US where they have had 12 Top 20 singles and 6 Top 10 LPs. Lou has also had US solo chart records and Mick co-produced Van Halen's '5150' and Billy Joel's 'Storm Front'. A new LP is due in 90.

🇬🇧	WAITING FOR A GIRL LIKE YOU	8	23 JAN 82	ATLANTIC
	I WANT TO KNOW WHAT LOVE IS *(Backing vocals inc. Tom Bailey & Jennifer Holiday)*	1(3)	19 JAN 85	ATLANTIC
🇺🇸	FEELS LIKE THE FIRST TIME *(UK No. 39)*	4	18 JUN 77	ATLANTIC
	COLD AS ICE *(UK No. 24)*	6	22 OCT 77	ATLANTIC
	HOT BLOODED *(UK No. 42)*	3	09 SEP 78	ATLANTIC
	DOUBLE VISION	2	18 NOV 78	ATLANTIC
	URGENT *(UK No. 54 – with Jr. Walker on Sax)*	4	05 SEP 81	ATLANTIC
	WAITING FOR A GIRL LIKE YOU *(10 weeks at No.2-a record. Thomas Dolby on track)*	2	28 NOV 81	ATLANTIC
	I WANT TO KNOW WHAT LOVE IS *(Backing vocals The New Jersey Mass Choir)*	1(2)	02 FEB 85	ATLANTIC
	SAY YOU WILL *(UK No. 71)*	6	20 FEB 88	ATLANTIC
	I DON'T WANT TO LIVE WITHOUT YOU	5	28 MAY 88	ATLANTIC

FORREST

Texan Forrest M. Thomas Jr. had two UK-only Top 20s with state-of-the-art dance revivals of 'oldies' which he made in Holland. The other was the Detroit Emeralds' song 'Feel The Need in Me'.

 ROCK THE BOAT *(Hues Corporation 74 hit)*   4   12 MAR 83   CBS

LANCE FORTUNE

Born Chris Morris in Birkenhead (UK) he learned classical guitar and started in a local instrumental trio. He joined manager Larry Parnes' stable of acts when he was 19 and his follow up and only other chart entry was 'This Love I Have For You' (UK 26).

BE MINE   9   18 MAR 60   PYE

FORTUNES

Formed in the early 60s by Barry Pritchard, the act brought in vocalist Glen Dale and first recorded for Decca in 64. Their record 'Caroline' was used as the theme for the UK pirate radio station. They had five UK Top 20s (2 in US) over a seven year period.

YOU'VE GOT YOUR TROUBLES	2	21 AUG 65	DECCA
HERE IT COMES AGAIN *(US No. 27)*	4	13 NOV 65	DECCA
FREEDOM COME FREEDOM GO *(US No. 72)*	6	23 OCT 71	CAPITOL
STORM IN A TEACUP *(Co-writ. Lynsey De Paul)*	7	26 FEB 72	CAPITOL
YOU'VE GOT YOUR TROUBLES	7	09 OCT 65	PRESS

FOUNDATIONS

The first UK act to score on the US soul chart was this multi-racial group fronted by Clem Curtis, and later by Colin Young. Their hits were written and produced by Tony Macauley & John Mcleod. Clem cut with new Foundations on IDM (84) and Opium (87).

BABY, NOW THAT I FOUND YOU *(US No. 11)*	1(2)	11 NOV 67	PYE
(Re-recorded by Clem Curtis & Foundations in 87)			
BUILD ME UP BUTTERCUP	2	11 JAN 69	PYE
IN THE BAD BAD OLD DAYS *(US No. 51)*	8	12 APR 69	PYE
BUILD ME UP BUTTERCUP	3	22 FEB 69	UNI
(Co-written by Mike D'Abo of Manfred Mann)			

FOUR PENNIES

Blackburn (UK) quartet fronted by singer/composer Lionel Morton, who had been a solo act for five years, had four UK-only Top 20 hits in 18 months. Lionel went on to be a childrens TV presenter.

JULIET *(Re-recorded it as The Pennies in 76)*   1(1)   23 MAY 64   PHILIPS

FOUR SEASONS

Top US group of the early 60s whose No. 1s spanned 14 years. Fronted by distinctive Frankie Valli (born Frankie Castellucio) they were called The Variety Trio, The Variatones and The Romans before charting in 56 as the Four Lovers (they had many singles under this name). Their second 45 as the Four Seasons started their amazing run of hits. They are in the R'n'R Hall of Fame.

SHERRY	7	07 NOV 62	STATESIDE
RAG DOLL	2	25 SEP 64	PHILIPS
LET'S HANG ON!	4	22 JAN 66	PHILIPS
THE NIGHT *(As Frankie Valli & Four Seasons)*	7	10 MAY 75	MOWEST
WHO LOVES YOU	6	18 OCT 75	WARNER
DECEMBER '63 (OH WHAT A NIGHT)	1(2)	21 FEB 76	WARNER
SILVER STAR *(US No. 38)*	3	22 MAY 76	WARNER

SHERRY	1(5)	15 SEP 62	VEE JAY
(Jumped from 11-1 – song originally called 'Terry')			
BIG GIRLS DON'T CRY *(UK No. 14)*	1(5)	17 NOV 62	VEE JAY
WALK LIKE A MAN	1(3)	02 MAR 63	VEE JAY
(UK No.12 – 1st group to get 3 US No. 1s in a row)			
CANDY GIRL	3	24 AUG 63	VEE JAY
DAWN (GO AWAY)	3	22 FEB 64	PHILIPS
RONNIE	6	16 MAY 64	PHILIPS
RAG DOLL	1(2)	18 JUL 64	PHILIPS
SAVE IT FOR ME	10	26 SEP 64	PHILIPS
LET'S HANG ON!	3	11 DEC 65	PHILIPS
WORKING MY WAY BACK TO YOU *(UK No. 50)*	9	05 MAR 66	PHILIPS
I'VE GOT YOU UNDER MY SKIN	9	15 OCT 66	PHILIPS
(UK No.12 – Ray Noble 36 hit)			
TELL IT TO THE RAIN *(UK No. 37)*	10	21 JAN 67	PHILIPS
C'MON MARIANNE	9	15 JUL 67	PHILIPS
WHO LOVES YOU	3	15 NOV 75	WARNER
DECEMBER '63 (OH WHAT A NIGHT)	1(3)	13 MAR 76	WARNER

Also see Frankie Valli

FOUR TOPS

Quartet who started as The Four Aims, recorded for Chess, Columbia, Red Top and Riverside in the 50s before joining Motown where they first hit with 'Baby I Need Your Loving' (US 11). With Levi Stubbs as lead singer, The Tops can lay claim to being the longest surviving intact group in the world. They are in the R'n'R Hall of Fame.

REACH OUT I'LL BE THERE	1(3)	29 OCT 66	TAMLA MOTOWN
(A S.A.W. Re-mix reached No. 11 in UK in 88)			
STANDING IN THE SHADOWS OF LOVE	6	28 JAN 67	TAMLA MOTOWN
BERNADETTE	8	22 APR 67	TAMLA MOTOWN
WALK AWAY RENEE	3	13 JAN 68	TAMLA MOTOWN
(US No. 14 – Left Banke 66 US hit)			
IF I WERE A CARPENTER	7	06 APR 68	TAMLA MOTOWN
(US No.20-Bobby Darin 66 hit- comp. by Tim Hardin)			
I CAN'T HELP MYSELF *(Also UK No. 23 in 65)*	10	18 APR 70	TAMLA MOTOWN
IT'S ALL IN THE GAME	5	11 JUL 70	TAMLA MOTOWN
(US No. 24 – Tommy Edwards 53 & 58 hit)			
STILL WATER (LOVE) *(US No. 11)*	10	31 OCT 70	TAMLA MOTOWN
SIMPLE GAME *(US No. 90 – Moody Blues song)*	3	06 NOV 71	TAMLA MOTOWN
WHEN SHE WAS MY GIRL *(US No. 11)*	3	14 NOV 81	CASABLANCA
LOCO IN ACAPULCO *(From the film 'Buster')*	7	07 JAN 89	ARISTA
I CAN'T HELP MYSELF *(Top R&B single 65)*	1(2)	19 JUN 65	MOTOWN
IT'S THE SAME OLD SONG	5	28 AUG 65	MOTOWN
REACH OUT I'LL BE THERE	1(2)	15 OCT 66	MOTOWN
STANDING IN THE SHADOWS OF LOVE	6	21 JAN 67	MOTOWN
BERNADETTE	4	08 APR 67	MOTOWN
KEEPER OF THE CASTLE *(UK No. 18)*	10	13 JAN 73	DUNHILL
AIN'T NO WOMAN (LIKE THE ONE I'VE GOT)	4	07 APR 73	DUNHILL

FOURMOST

Liverpool act fronted by Brian O'Hara and Mike Millward who were known as The Four Jays and Four Mosts before Brian Epstein took over their management. They had six UK-only Top 40s in the early days of Merseybeat, the first two written by Lennon & McCartney. They last hit in 65 and Mike died a year later.

A LITTLE LOVING   6   30 MAY 64   PARLOPHONE

FOX

UK sextet formed by composer/producer/singer Kenny Young and featuring the distinctive voice of Noosha Fox, the only female member. They had three UK Top 20s before Noosha recorded solo on GTO, BBC and Earlobe.

ONLY YOU CAN *(US No. 53)*	3	22 MAR 75	GTO
S-S-S-SINGLE BED	4	15 MAY 76	GTO

SAMANTHA FOX

London singer and TV personality was the best known topless model in the UK in the 80's. She had been seen on a Spandau Ballet sleeve and a David Cassidy picture disc and had recorded on Lamborghini in 84, Genie in 86 and with Lemmy from Motorhead before starting her enviable string of transatlantic hits.

TOUCH ME (I WANT YOUR BODY)	3	05 APR 86	JIVE
DO YA DO YA (WANNA PLEASE ME) *(US No. 87)*	10	12 JUL 86	JIVE
NOTHING'S GONNA STOP ME NOW *(US No. 80)*	8	20 JUN 87	JIVE
TOUCH ME (I WANT YOUR BODY)	4	14 FEB 87	JIVE
NAUGHTY GIRLS (NEED LOVE TOO) *(UK No. 31)*	3	04 JUN 88	JIVE
I WANNA HAVE SOME FUN	8	11 FEB 89	JIVE
(UK No. 64 – US. Dance No.2)			

INEZ & CHARLIE FOXX

Brother and sister duo both born in North Carolina. Inez first recorded 'A Feeling' as a soloist for Brunswick in 62. As a duet they had eight Soul hits before Inez reverted to being a solo artist. They also recorded on Musicor, Dynamo and Volt.

MOCKINGBIRD *(UK No. 34 IN 69)*	7	07 SEP 63	SYMBOL

FOXY

Miami group led by Ish Ledesma first hit with 'Call Me Later' on Double Shot (70). Eight years later they had their biggest single. Ish is now well known on the US dance music scene.

GET OFF *(No. 1 in Holland)*	9	11 NOV 78	DASH

PETER FRAMPTON

Kent (UK) born pop/rocker was in The Herd who had three UK-only Top 20s in 67/68. 'The Face of 68' as he was then known formed Humble Pie and tasted transatlantic fame. He set up Frampton's Camel, went solo in 72 and in the late 70s was one of the US's top acts when his 'Frampton Comes Alive' LP became a best seller. Various comeback attempts have not really succeeded.

SHOW ME THE WAY	10	19 JUN 76	A&M
SHOW ME THE WAY	6	08 MAY 76	A&M
DO YOU FEEL LIKE WE DO *(UK No. 39)*	10	13 NOV 76	A&M
I'M IN YOU *(UK No. 41)*	2	30 JUL 77	A&M

Also see The Herd/Humble Pie

CONNIE FRANCIS

One of the world's biggest selling female singers of all time was born Concetta Franconero. Her first release was 'Freddie' in 55 and she had nine more flops before starting a run of 22 US Top 20s (18 in UK). She won countless awards and was also the first female to top the UK LP charts in 77. Interestingly she had her last Top 10 at age 23, which was younger than the other Italian-American pop queen, Madonna, was when she had her first.

WHO'S SORRY NOW *(Isham Jones 23 hit)*	1(6)	16 MAY 58	MGM
CAROLINA MOON/STUPID CUPID	1(6)	26 SEP 58	MGM
(Gene Austin 29 hit – 'B' US No.14)			
MY HAPPINESS *(Jon & Sandra Steele 48 hit)*	4	27 MAR 59	MGM
LIPSTICK ON YOUR COLLAR	3	21 AUG 59	MGM
MAMA	8	10 JUN 60	MGM
ROBOT MAN *(Not released in US)*	3	24 JUN 60	MGM
EVERYBODY'S SOMEBODY'S FOOL	7	02 SEP 60	MGM
MY HEART HAS A MIND OF ITS OWN	5	18 NOV 60	MGM
WHERE THE BOYS ARE *(From the film)*	8	21 APR 61	MGM
TOGETHER *(Paul Whiteman 28 hit)*	10	13 OCT 61	MGM

WHO'S SORRY NOW	5	24 MAR 58	MGM
MY HAPPINESS	2	18 JAN 59	MGM
LIPSTICK ON YOUR COLLAR	5	28 JUN 59	MGM
FRANKIE	9	05 JUL 59	MGM
AMONG MY SOUVENIRS *(UK No. 11)*	7	28 DEC 59	MGM
MAMA	8	11 APR 60	MGM
EVERYBODY'S SOMEBODY'S FOOL	1(2)	27 JUN 60	MGM
MY HEART HAS A MIND OF ITS OWN	1(2)	26 SEP 60	MGM
MANY TEARS AGO *(UK No. 12)*	7	26 DEC60	MGM
WHERE THE BOYS ARE	4	20 MAR 61	MGM
BREAKIN' IN A BRAND NEW BROKEN HEART *(UK No. 16)*	7	29 MAY 61	MGM
TOGETHER	6	07 AUG 61	MGM
WHEN THE BOY IN YOUR ARMS (IS THE BOY IN YOUR HEART) *(Cliff Richard 62 UK hit)*	10	13 JAN 62	MGM
DON'T BREAK THE HEART THAT LOVES YOU *(UK No. 30) (Song was Country No. 1 in 78)*	1(1)	31 MAR 62	MGM
SECOND HAND LOVE *(Prod Phil Spector)*	7	09 JUN 62	MGM
VACATION *(UK No. 13)*	9	01 SEP 62	MGM

FRANKE & THE KNOCKOUTS

New Jersey's Franke Previte (previously recorded with The Oxford Watch Band and Bull Angus) led this quintet who had three US-only Top 40's. Follow up was 'You're My Girl'. Franke later co-wrote hits 'The Time of My Life' and 'Hungry Eyes' from 'Dirty Dancing'.

SWEETHEART	10	06 JUN 81	MILLENNIUM

FRANKIE GOES TO HOLLYWOOD

Liverpool group fronted by Holly Johnson and originally named Hollycaust were the top UK act of 84. Despite being banned their first 45 hit the top and their second entered at No. 1. They broke many sales records (including first act to sell a million in UK with first two releases) and won many awards. Band broke up in 87 and after legal battles Holly started a solo career in 89.

RELAX	1(5)	28 JAN 84	ZTT
TWO TRIBES *(US No. 43)*	1(9)	16 JUN 84	ZTT
(Entered At No. 1 and act had Nos.1 & 2 on chart)			
THE POWER OF LOVE	1(1)	08 DEC 84	ZTT
(Equalled UK record when first 3 rels. hit No. 1)			
WELCOME TO THE PLEASURE DOME *(US No. 48)*	2	06 APR 85	ZTT
(Entered at No. 5)			
RAGE HARD	4	13 SEP 86	ZTT
(First act to have first five singles in UK Top 5)			
RELAX	10	16 MAR 85	ISLAND

ARETHA FRANKLIN

The 'Queen of Soul' started recording gospel in 56 and first charted in 61 with 'Won't Be Long' (Columbia). Her career really took off on joining Atlantic when she had a fantastic string of US hits. To date she's had 73 US hits (22 UK) and 87 records on the black music charts, making her the most successful female artist of the rock era in the US.

RESPECT	10	15 JUL 67	ATLANTIC
I SAY A LITTLE PRAYER	4	14 SEP 68	ATLANTIC
(Dionne Warwick 67 US hit)			
SISTERS ARE DOIN' IT FOR THEMSELVES	9	23 NOV 85	RCA
(With The EURYTHMICS) (US No. 18)			
I KNEW YOU WERE WAITING (FOR ME)	1(2)	07 FEB 87	EPIC
(And GEORGE MICHAEL – entered at No. 2 – first UK No. 1)			
I NEVER LOVED A MAN (THE WAY I LOVE YOU)	9	15 APR 67	ATLANTIC
RESPECT	1(2)	03 JUN 67	ATLANTIC
(Top R&B record 67 – Otis Redding 65 US hit)			
BABY I LOVE YOU *(UK No. 39)*	4	09 SEP 67	ATLANTIC
A NATURAL WOMAN (YOU MAKE ME FEEL LIKE)	8	04 NOV 67	ATLANTIC
CHAIN OF FOOLS *(UK No. 43 – Comp. Don Covay)*	2	20 JAN 68	ATLANTIC
(SWEET SWEET BABY) SINCE YOU'VE BEEN GONE *(UK No. 47)*	5	30 MAR 68	ATLANTIC
THINK *(UK No. 26)*	7	15 JUN 68	ATLANTIC
THE HOUSE THAT JACK BUILT	6	07 SEP 68	ATLANTIC
I SAY A LITTLE PRAYER	10	05 OCT 68	ATLANTIC
BRIDGE OVER TROUBLED WATER *(Simon & Garfunkel 70 hit)*	6	05 JUN 71	ATLANTIC

SPANISH HARLEM (UK No.1 – Ben E.King 60 hit)	2	11 SEP 71	ATLANTIC
ROCK STEADY	9	27 NOV 71	ATLANTIC
DAY DREAMING	5	06 MAY 72	ATLANTIC
UNTIL YOU COME BACK TO ME (THAT'S WHAT I'M GONNA DO) (UK No.26)	3	23 FEB 74	ATLANTIC
FREEWAY OF LOVE (UK No. 51)	3	31 AUG 85	ARISTA
WHO'S ZOOMIN' WHO (UK No. 11)	7	30 NOV 85	ARISTA
I KNEW YOU WERE WAITING (FOR ME) (And GEORGE MICHAEL)	1(2)	18 APR 87	ARISTA

RODNEY FRANKLIN

California jazz musician who plays piano, sax and organ. He has worked with acts like Freddie Hubbard, Marlena Shaw and Bill Summers. He started recording for Columbia in 78 and scored his only pop hit in the UK. Follow up was 'In The Centre'.

THE GROOVE	7	10 MAY 80	CBS

FRANTIQUE

Session trio featuring the voice of Vivienne Savoie. Their one-off hit was written and produced (in Philadelphia) by the successful French based team of Robinson and Bolden.

STRUT YOUR FUNKY STUFF	10	29 SEP 79	PHILLY INT.

JOHN FRED & HIS PLAYBOY BAND

John Fred (Gourrier) formed this Louisiana band, originally called The Playboys, in the 50s. They first scored with 'Shirley' (later a UK hit for Shakin' Stevens) on Montel. Their transatlantic Top 10 based on Beatles' 'Lucy In The Sky' (Jon thought they said 'Lucy In Disguise') was their seventh single on Paula.

JUDY IN DISGUISE (WITH GLASSES)	3	10 FEB 68	PYE INT.
JUDY IN DISGUISE (WITH GLASSES) (Originally called 'Beverly in Disguise')	1(2)	20 JAN 68	PAULA

FREDDIE & THE DREAMERS

Madcap Manchester (UK) group fronted by charismatic Freddie Garrity. Zany stage show quickly made them UK stars and they shot to fame in the US two years later. The gimmick wore thin and they broke up in 68. Freddie made solos, became a childrens TV host and subsequently re-formed the act.

IF YOU GOTTA MAKE A FOOL OF SOMEBODY (James Ray 61 US hit)	2	21 JUN 63	COLUMBIA
I'M TELLING YOU NOW	3	23 AUG 63	COLUMBIA
YOU WERE MADE FOR ME (US No. 21)	4	29 NOV 63	COLUMBIA
I UNDERSTAND (US No. 36 – G-Clefs 61 hit)	5	26 DEC 64	COLUMBIA
I'M TELLING YOU NOW (1st released in US 63)	1(2)	10 APR 65	TOWER

FREE

Ace guitarist Paul Kossoff (ex Black Cat Bones) enlisted singer Paul Rodgers (from Brown Sugar) to front a group who became one of the 70s top rock bands. They toured with Blind Faith in 69, saw their first LP and two singles go nowhere but the third became a rock classic. Personnel problems followed much LP and single success. Rodgers later formed Bad Company with drummer Simon Kirk and Kossoff died in 76.

ALL RIGHT NOW (Also got No. 15 in 73)	2	04 JUL 70	ISLAND
MY BROTHER JAKE	4	29 MAY 71	ISLAND
WISHING WELL	7	10 FEB 73	ISLAND
ALL RIGHT NOW	4	17 OCT 70	ISLAND

FREEEZ

Brit-Funk group first charted with 'Keep in Touch' on Calibre (originally on their own Pink Rhythm label). Act fronted by ex dance record salesman John Rocco have had seven US only chart entries. After group split John worked with Arthur Baker and had some US dance music charters. Group re-appeared on Siren in 87.

SOUTHERN FREEEZ (A remix went to No. 63 in 87) (Revived by John Rocca on Cobra 89)	8	07 MAR 81	BEGGARS
I.O.U. (A Re mix went to No. 23 in 87)	2	23 JUL 83	BEGGARS

BOBBY FREEMAN

San Franciscan singer/composer recorded with The Romancers on Dootone in 55 aged when only 14, and he was also in The Vocaleers. Between 58 and 64 he had nine US-only hits, many self-composed. He also recorded on Sound-O-Riffic, King, Loma, Gemini Star, Double Shot, Avco (as R.B. Freeman) and Touch.

DO YOU WANT TO DANCE (His composition became a R'n'R standard)	6	09 JUN 58	JOSIE
C'MON AND SWIM	5	29 AUG 64	AUTUMN

FREE MOVEMENT

L.A. vocal group which included the Jefferson brothers Claude & Adrian and Godoy Colbert, a one time member of top gospel act the Pilgrim Travellers. They had two US-only hits before vanishing.

I'VE FOUND SOMEONE OF MY OWN	5	13 NOV 71	DECCA

FRESH 4

Bristol (UK) DJ team Judge, Krust, Suv D, rapper Flynn and guest vocalist Lizz E. chalked up a UK hit at the very end of the 80s with a clever treatment of the old Rose Royce hit.

WISHING ON A STAR	10	21 OCT 89	10

DOUG E. FRESH & THE GET FRESH CREW

Doug E. together with Barry Bee and Chill Will had a one-off UK pop hit with their first US black music chart record, one of the cleverest rap records of its time. The follow up was 'All The Way To Heaven'.

THE SHOW	7	30 NOV 85	COOLTEMPO

GLENN FREY

Detroit singer/songwriter who started in The Longbranch Pennywhistle (with J.D. Souther). He also played in Linda Ronstadt's group before helping form the ultra-successful Eagles. Since going solo, he has had 7 US Top 40s (2 in UK) so far.

THE HEAT IS ON (Co-Writ. Harold Faltermeyer) (UK No. 12 – from the film 'Beverly Hills Cop')	2	16 MAR 85	MCA
YOU BELONG TO THE CITY (From the soundtrack of TVs 'Miami Vice')	2	16 NOV 85	MCA

DEAN FRIEDMAN

New Jersey singer/songwriter, who had his first song deal aged nine in 64. He had three UK chart records compared to only one in his homeland ('Ariel' No. 26). He joined Lifesong in 77 and later had records on UK labels Epic in 82 and Hi Rise in 85.

LUCKY STARS	3	21 OCT 78	LIFESONG

69

FRIEND AND LOVER

Mixed duo consisted of the then married couple James and Kathy Post. James had previously sung in The Rum Rangers and this duo originally recorded on ABC in 67. They followed their US hit with 'If Love Is In Your Heart'. They also appeared on Chess and Jim has recorded solo since on Fantasy and Flying Fish.

	REACH OUT OF THE DARKNESS (Prod. by Joe South with Ray Stevens on piano)	10	22 JUN 68	VERVE

FRIENDS OF DISTINCTION

M.O.R.-ish black group had three US-only Top 20s within a year. They included Harry Elston (once in The Hi-Fi's with a few of 5th Dimension) and Jessica Cleaves, a noted session singer and member of Earth, Wind & Fire, Raw Silk and other studio groups.

	GRAZIN' IN THE GRASS (Vocal version of Hugh Masekela 68 US hit)	6	14 JUN 69	RCA
	LOVE OR LET ME BE LONELY	6	02 MAY 70	RCA

FRIJID PINK

Detroit group had one Transatlantic Top Ten with their heavy rock version of the old Animals hit. Act led by Tom Beaudry were also on Lionel and Fantasy but never repeated the success of their third release on Parrot. Follow up was 'Sing A Song For Freedom'.

	HOUSE OF THE RISING SUN	4	16 MAY 70	DERAM
	HOUSE OF THE RISING SUN	7	04 APR 70	PARROT

FULL FORCE

Family group from Brooklyn includes Bow Legged Lou (Lucien) and Paul Anthony. They were originally called The Amplifiers and have also produced and written hits for Lisa Lisa, James Brown and Samantha Fox. To date their only solo pop success has been in the UK but they have had 11 black music hits so far in the US.

	ALICE I WANT YOU JUST FOR ME	9	25 JAN 86	CBS

BOBBY FULLER FOUR

El Paso based band included Bobby and his brother Randy. They recorded unsuccessfully on Yucca, Todd, Donna, Exeter and Liberty before getting their first and biggest hit with their fifth record on Mustang. Unfortunately Bobby died in his parked car in suspicious circumstances shortly after the hit.

	I FOUGHT THE LAW (UK No. 33 – originally by The Crickets)	9	12 MAR 66	MUSTANG

FUN BOY THREE

Splinter group from the very popular UK band The Specials. Members were Terry Hall, Neville Staples and Lynval Golding. They scored six Top UK-only Top 20s in just 18 months and introduced the world to Bananarama before splitting up.

	IT AIN'T WHAT YOU DO IT'S THE WAY THAT YOU DO IT (And BANANARAMA) (Jimmy Lunceford 39 hit)	4	13 MAR 82	CHRYSALIS
	REALLY SAYING SOMETHING (With BANANARAMA)	5	01 MAY 82	DERAM
	THE TUNNEL OF LOVE	10	05 MAR 83	CHRYSALIS
	OUR LIPS ARE SEALED	7	21 MAY 83	CHRYSALIS

FARLEY 'JACKMASTER' FUNK

The first 'House' record to go pop came from Chicago club DJ Farley, who was one of the Hot Mix 5 on station WBMX (later the Jackmaster 5 on WGCI). This one-off hit featured the 6½ octave voice of Darryl Pandy who later appeared on labels like Nightmare. He was on Full House in 90.

	LOVE CAN'T TURN AROUND (Top UK Dance record of 86)	10	27 SEP 86	D.J. INTERNAT

FUNKADELIC

Multi-talented trend setting George Clinton formed doo-wop group The Parliaments in 55. They recorded for ABC, New, Motown and Golden World before hitting with '(I Wanna) Testify' (US 20) in 67. The vocal group continued as Parliament and in 69 together with their backing musicians they also became Funkadelic. George went solo in 81 and now records on Prince's Paisley Park label.

	ONE NATION UNDER A GROOVE (PT. 1) (US No. 28)	9	20 JAN 79	WARNER

FUNK MASTERS

UK group put together by London based radio DJ Tony Williams who co-produced and wrote their one-off UK hit. Act which included rapper Bo Kool, had other releases like the earlier 'Invaders' & the ideal Xmas A & B sides 'Merry Christmas'/'Happy New Year'.

	IT'S OVER (Vocal by Julie Roberts)	8	16 JUL 83	MASTER FUNK

BILLY FURY

UK R'n'R superstar, born Ron Wycherley in Liverpool. He was one of Larry Parnes' stable of acts and first hit with his own song 'Maybe Tomorrow' in 59 (UK 18). Next to Cliff Richard, he was the top UK teen idol of the early 60s chalking up 10 UK-only Top 10s. He was later on Parlophone, Warner, Bus Stop, Fury, Magnum and Polydor (re-charting in 83). He died in 83.

	HALFWAY TO PARADISE (Tony Orlando 61 US hit - co-written Carole King)	5	14 JUL 61	DECCA
	JEALOUSY (Frankie Laine 51 hit)	4	06 OCT 61	DECCA
	I'LL NEVER FIND ANOTHER YOU (Originally by Tony Orlando)	3	19 JAN 62	DECCA
	LAST NIGHT WAS MADE FOR LOVE	6	01 MAY 62	DECCA
	ONCE UPON A DREAM	7	24 AUG 62	DECCA
	LIKE I'VE NEVER BEEN GONE	3	15 MAR 63	DECCA
	WHEN WILL YOU SAY I LOVE YOU	5	07 JUN 63	DECCA
	IN SUMMER	4	23 AUG 63	DECCA
	IT'S ONLY MAKE BELIEVE (Conway Twitty 58 hit)	10	15 AUG 64	DECCA
	IN THOUGHTS OF YOU	9	14 AUG 65	DECCA

G

KENNY G

Seattle born saxophonist Kenny Gorelick was in Barry White's Love Unlimited Orchestra while still a teenager and later worked with Jeff Lorber before going solo in 82. In 84 he had his first successes in the black music field and in the UK. He finally broke through in the US with a new age style instrumental which he followed with two Top 10 LPs there – 'Duo Tones' and 'Silhouette'.

SONGBIRD (UK No. 22)		4	11 JUL 87	ARISTA
(He was Top US Contemporary Jazz act of 87)				

PETER GABRIEL

London born singer left Genesis in 75 but did not release the first of his four eponymous LPs until 77. He has had many transatlantic hits since, including six UK Top 10 LPs and has won many awards for his videos.

GAMES WITHOUT FRONTIERS		4	15 MAR 80	CHARISMA
(US No.48 – Backing vocalists include Kate Bush)				
SLEDGEHAMMER		4	24 MAY 86	VIRGIN
(Won award most outstanding Pop promo video 86)				
DON'T GIVE UP (And KATE BUSH) (US No. 72)		9	15 NOV 86	VIRGIN
SLEDGEHAMMER		1(1)	26 JUL 86	GEFFEN
(Record replaced his old act Genesis at No. 1)				
BIG TIME (UK No. 13)		8	07 MAR 87	GEFFEN

Also see Genesis

GALAXY – SEE PHIL FEARON FOR HIT DETAILS

GALLAGHER & LYLE

Scottish singer/composers Benny Gallagher & Graham Lyle first recorded together in 67 and first hit as members of McGuinness Flint in 70. As a duo they notched up four UK-only Top 40s in a year. Since they broke up in 80 Graham has written hits for acts like Jim Diamond and Tina Turner, including her Grammy winner 'What's Love Got To Do With It' and 'I Don't Wanna Lose You'.

I WANNA STAY WITH YOU (UK No. 49)		6	03 APR 76	A&M
HEART ON MY SLEEVE (US No. 67)		6	19 JUN 76	A&M

Also see McGuinness Flint

PATSY GALLANT

Canadian singer had a one-off UK hit with a disco song about the US, which she co-produced. This track and follow up 'Are You Ready For Love' were on her 'Sugar Daddy' LP. She was on Miracle in 89.

FROM NEW YORK TO L.A.		6	08 OCT 77	EMI

GALLERY

Successful producer/musician Dennis Coffey put together this Detroit quintet featuring vocalist Jim Gold who had three US-only Top 40's. Their follow up was 'I Believe In Music'.

NICE TO BE WITH YOU		4	24 JUN 72	SUSSEX

JAMES GALWAY

Respected UK classical flautist had a left field UK hit single with his version of a John Denver song.

ANNIE'S SONG (With The National Philharmonic)		3	01 JUL 78	RCA RED SEAL

GAP BAND

Oklahoma family trio Ronnie, Charles & Robert Wilson named their band after three streets in Tulsa – Greenwood, Archer and Pine. They recorded on Shelter, MCA, A&M and Tattoo before getting the first of 29 black music hits, including the last No. 1 of the 80s 'All Of My Love' on Capitol. They have not had a US pop Top 20 yet.

OOPS UPSIDE YOUR HEAD (US No. 102)		6	16 AUG 80	MERCURY
BIG FUN		4	17 JAN 87	TOTAL EXP.

BORIS GARDINER

Jamaican reggae artist has played bass and sung with acts like The Upsetters, Carl Malcolm's Band and The Souvenirs. He first charted in 70 with 'Elizabethan Reggae' on Duke (UK 14) and 16 years later had two more UK-only Top 20s – the other being 'You're Everything To Me' (11th).

I WANT TO WAKE UP WITH YOU		1(3)	23 AUG 86	REVUE
(Originally by Mac Davis)				

ART GARFUNKEL

New York born singer/actor who started recording as Arty Garr on Octavia and Warwick and was later half of the record breaking Simon & Garfunkel duo. After they broke up he concentrated on acting and appeared in several top movies. On the record front he has fared better in the UK where he has had two No. 1s.

I ONLY HAVE EYES FOR YOU (US No. 18)		1(2)	25 OCT 75	CBS
(Based on The Flamingos 59 US hit version)				
BRIGHT EYES		1(6)	14 APR 79	CBS
(U.K. Gold – comp. Mike Batt – top UK record 79)				
ALL I KNOW (As GARFUNKEL)		9	10 NOV 73	COLUMBIA

Also see Simon & Garfunkel

GALE GARNETT

New Zealand born actress/singer/writer who moved to the US as a child. She appeared in many TV shows including Bonanza and 77 Sunset Strip and was in the group Gentle Reign before getting a US Top 40 hit and a Grammy for Best Folk Recording. Gale returned to acting when the records stopped selling.

WE'LL SING IN THE SUNSHINE		4	17 OCT 64	RCA

LEIF GARRETT

Hollywood born actor/singer made his movie debut at age five and appeared in the 'Walking Tall' films and many TV shows including Gunsmoke. He also notched up three US Top 20s as a teenager.

I WAS MADE FOR DANCIN'		4	17 FEB 79	SCOTTI BROS
I WAS MADE FOR DANCIN'		10	17 FEB 79	SCOTTI BROS

SEIDAH GARRETT – SEE MICHAEL JACKSON FOR HIT DETAILS

GARY'S GANG

New York disco group was the brainchild of producer/guitarist Eric Matthew and drummer Gary Turnier. Their biggest hit was recorded in Gary's garage. Follow up was 'Let's Lovedance Tonight' and another similar release was 'Do Ya Wanna Go Dancin'.

	KEEP ON DANCIN' *(US No. 41)*	8	24 MAR 79	CBS

BARBARA GASKIN – SEE DAVE STEWART FOR HIT DETAILS

MARVIN GAYE

One of the world's best known soul singers and composers was born in Washington and first recorded on Okeh in 57 with The Marquees, who became a reformed version of 50s stars The Moonglows. His fourth Tamla single in 62 'Stubborn Kind of Fellow' was the first of 56 US hits; the 30th of which gave him the first of his 21 UK charters. He was shot and killed by his father in 84.

	I HEARD IT THROUGH THE GRAPEVINE	1(3)	26 MAR 69	TAMLA MOTOWN
	(Song first recorded by The Miracles)			
	TOO BUSY THINKING ABOUT MY BABY	5	13 SEP 69	TAMLA MOTOWN
	ABRAHAM MARTIN & JOHN *(Dion 68 US hit)*	9	27 JUN 70	TAMLA MOTOWN
	YOU ARE EVERYTHING *(With DIANA ROSS)*	5	20 APR 74	TAMLA MOTOWN
	GOT TO GIVE IT UP	7	04 JUN 77	MOTOWN
	(SEXUAL) HEALING	4	20 NOV 82	CBS
	(Brackets in title in UK only)			
	I HEARD IT THROUGH THE GRAPEVINE	8	10 MAY 86	TAMLA MOTOWN
	(Re-issued due to use in TV ad.)			
	PRIDE AND JOY	10	20 JUL 63	TAMLA
	HOW SWEET IT IS TO BE LOVED BY YOU	6	30 JAN 65	TAMLA
	(UK No. 49)			
	I'LL BE DOGGONE	8	15 MAY 65	TAMLA
	AIN'T THAT PECULIAR	8	20 NOV 65	
	I HEARD IT THROUGH THE GRAPEVINE	1(7)	14 DEC 68	TAMLA
	TOO BUSY THINKING ABOUT MY BABY	4	28 JUN 69	TAMLA
	(Top R&B Single of 69)			
	THAT'S THE WAY LOVE IS	7	18 OCT 69	TAMLA
	WHAT'S GOING ON	2	10 APR 71	TAMLA
	MERCY MERCY ME (THE ECOLOGY)	4	21 AUG 71	TAMLA
	INNER CITY BLUES (MAKES ME WANNA HOLLER)	9	06 NOV 71	TAMLA
	TROUBLE MAN	7	03 FEB 73	TAMLA
	LET'S GET IT ON	1(2)	08 SEP 73	TAMLA
	(UK No. 31 – Top Soul Single of 73)			
	GOT TO GIVE IT UP (PT.1)	1(1)	25 JUN 77	TAMLA
	SEXUAL HEALING	3	29 JAN 83	COLUMBIA
	(Double Grammy winner and Top black chart 10 weeks)			

Also see Marvin Gaye & Tammi Terrell

MARVIN GAYE & TAMMI TERRELL

Born Tammy Montgomery in Philadelphia, she first worked with Little Joe (Cook) of The Thrillers and recorded on Wand, Checker Scepter and Try Me (James Brown's own label) under that name before moving to Motown. She had solo hits but her biggest ones were duets with Marvin. She died of a brain tumour in 70 after collapsing on stage into the arms of Marvin Gaye.

	ONION SONG *(US No. 50)*	9	13 DEC 69	TAMLA MOTOWN
	YOUR PRECIOUS LOVE	5	04 NOV 67	TAMLA
	IF I COULD BUILD MY WHOLE WORLD AROUND YOU	10	20 JAN 68	TAMLA
	(UK No. 41)			
	AIN'T NOTHING LIKE THE REAL THING *(UK No. 34)*	8	25 MAY 68	TAMLA
	YOU'RE ALL I NEED TO GET BY *(UK No. 19)*	7	14 SEP 68	TAMLA
	(Above two composed by Ashford & Simpson)			

Also see Marvin Gaye

CRYSTAL GAYLE

Kentucky coal miner's daughter, who like her elder sister Loretta Lynn is one of the most successful females of all time in country music with 51 hits so far including 18 No. 1s. She started with Decca in 70 and has had two transatlantic Top 20's – the other being 'Talking in Your Sleep' (US 18/ UK 11).

	DON'T IT MAKE MY BROWN EYES BLUE	5	14 JAN 78	UA
	DON'T IT MAKE MY BROWN EYES BLUE	2	26 NOV 77	UA
	YOU AND I *(With EDDIE RABBITT)*	7	12 FEB 83	ELEKTRA

GLORIA GAYNOR

New Jersey star was one of the first disco divas. She first recorded on Johnny Nash's Jocida label in 65 and was in Soul Satisfied and The Soul Messengers prior to her first club hit 'Honey Bee' (on both Columbia and MGM in 74). Over the next decade she had many transatlantic hits including 4 UK Top 20s.

	NEVER CAN SAY GOODBYE	2	25 JAN 75	MGM
	I WILL SURVIVE	1(4)	17 MAR 79	POLYDOR
	NEVER CAN SAY GOODBYE *(Jackson Five 71 hit)*	9	25 JAN 75	MGM
	I WILL SURVIVE	1(3)	10 MAR 79	POLYDOR

G-CLEFS

Massachusetts quintet included the Scott brothers Teddy, Chris, Timmy and Arnold. They first charted in 56 with 'Ka-Ding-Dong' (US 24) on Pilgrim (Freddy Cannon played on the session) which was covered by The Diamonds. Follow up was 'A Girl Has To Know'. They also recorded on Paris, Loma, Regina, Ditto and Veep.

	I UNDERSTAND (JUST HOW YOU FEEL) *(UK No. 16)*	9	04 DEC 61	TERRACE
	(Four Tunes 54 R&B hit with added 'Auld Lang Syne')			

DAVID GEDDES

Michigan singer/drummer recorded in the group Rock Garden on Capitol and as a soloist on Buddah without success before achieving two US-only Top 20s – the other being his follow up 'The Last Game Of The Season'(18). He was on H&L in 77.

	RUN JOEY RUN	4	04 OCT 75	BIG TREE

J. GEILS BAND

In the late 60s Jerome Geils formed the J. Geils Blues Band with vocalist Peter Wolf (ex The Hallucinations). They first hit in 71 with the Valentinos song 'Lookin' For A Love'. They had 10 US (2 UK) Top 40s in 11 years. Wolf left in 83 and had a solo US Top 20 in 84 with 'Lights Out' (12) and was on MCA in 90.

	CENTREFOLD	3	27 FEB 82	EMI AM.
	CENTERFOLD	1(6)	06 FEB 82	EMI AM.
	FREEZE-FRAME *(UK No. 27)*	4	10 APR 82	EMI AM.

GENESIS

Multi-talented UK trio who record together and individually. Act started as Garden Wall and were discovered by Jonathan King. Their first single was 'The Silent Sun' on Decca in 68. In 70 Phil Collins joined original members Mike Rutherford and Tony Banks and took over vocals when Peter Gabriel left in 75. Group were one of the top acts of the 80s and have had numerous transatlantic single & LP hits, including 12 UK Top 10 LPs.

	FOLLOW YOU FOLLOW ME *(US No. 23)*	7	15 APR 78	CHARISMA
	TURN IT ON AGAIN *(US No. 58)*	8	05 APR 80	CHARISMA
	ABACAB *(US No. 26)*	9	05 SEP 81	CHARISMA
	(US No. 26 – Title is the chord sequence of song)			
	3 X 3 (E.P.)	10	12 JUN 82	CHARISMA
	('Paperplate' from the E.P. was US No.33)			
	MAMA *(US No. 73)*	4	17 SEP 83	CHARISMA

THAT'S ALL *(UK No. 16)*		6	11 FEB 84	ATLANTIC
INVISIBLE TOUCH *(UK No. 15)*		1(1)	19 JUL 86	ATLANTIC
THROWING IT ALL AWAY *(UK No. 27)*		4	11 OCT 86	ATLANTIC
LAND OF CONFUSION *(UK No. 14)*		4	31 JAN 87	ATLANTIC
TONIGHT TONIGHT TONIGHT *(UK No. 18)*		3	04 APR 87	ATLANTIC
IN TOO DEEP *(UK No. 19 – from 'Mona Lisa')*		3	27 JUN 87	ATLANTIC

Also see Phil Collins/Mike & The Mechanics/Peter Gabriel

BOBBIE GENTRY

Singer/songwriter, born Bobbie Lee Streeter in Mississippi, was on Titan in 63 with Jody ('Endless Sleep') Reynolds before chalking up her four transatlantic Top 40s. She married singer Jim Stafford in 78 and is still popular on the club circuit.

I'LL NEVER FALL IN LOVE AGAIN *(Dionne Warwick 69 US hit)*		1(1)	18 OCT 69	CAPITOL
ALL I HAVE TO DO IS DREAM *(And GLEN CAMPBELL)* *(US No. 27 – Everly Brothers 58 hit)*		3	17 JAN 70	CAPITOL
ODE TO BILLIE JOE *(UK No. 13)* *(Re-charted in 76 when song made into a film)*		1(4)	26 AUG 67	CAPITOL

GENTRYS

Band fronted by Larry Raspberry was formed in 63 and had a local Memphis hit with 'Sometimes' on Youngstown in 65 and followed it with their sole US Top 40. They reformed in 70 on Sun with James Hart singing and had three small chart records and were then on Capitol in 71 and Stax in 74.

KEEP ON DANCING *(Original by The Aventis)*		4	30 OCT 65	MGM

GEORDIE

Now best remembered as the group that AC/DC's Brian Johnson started in. The Slade-like foursome which also included guitarist Tom Hill, were one of top UK bands in 73 with four Top 40s in that year. They were later on Red Bus in 82 and Neat in 83.

ALL BECAUSE OF YOU		6	28 APR 73	EMI

BARBARA GEORGE

New Orleans soul singer and writer scored a US Top 40 hit with one of her own compositions, which she followed with 'You Talk About Love'. She later recorded for Sue and Seven B.

I KNOW (YOU DON'T LOVE ME NO MORE)		3	27 JAN 62	AFO

SOPHIA GEORGE

Reggae singer from Kingston, Jamaica, was a teacher for deaf children before her one-off UK hit with her first release when she was just 19. She followed it unsuccessfully with 'Lazy Body'.

GIRLIE GIRLIE *(Jamaican No. 1)*		7	11 JAN 86	WINNER

GEORGIA SATELLITES

Atlanta rock quartet, built around Dan Baird and Rick Richards. They had a Top 5 US LP with 'Georgia Satellites' and have had three transatlantic chart records, the most recent in 89 was their version of 'Hippy Hippy Shake' from the film Cocktail.

KEEP YOUR HANDS TO YOURSELF *(UK No. 69)*		2	21 FEB 87	ELEKTRA

GERRY & THE PACEMAKERS

The first act in the UK to see their initial three releases all go to No. 1 and one of the most popular UK groups in the US in the early 60s. Led by Gerry Marsden (who had been in the Mars Bars) they were the second group to be managed by Brian Epstein and like The Beatles they had many transatlantic hits. Two of their 60s hits also topped the UK chart in the 80s with Gerry singing.

HOW DO YOU DO IT? *(Written for Adam Faith and rejected by Beatles)*		1(3)	03 APR 63	COLUMBIA
I LIKE IT *(US No. 17 – Entered at No. 9 – 1st cut by Dave Clark 5)*		1(4)	12 JUN 63	COLUMBIA
YOU'LL NEVER WALK ALONE *(US No. 48 – Entered at No. 7 – from show 'Carousel')*		1(3)	01 NOV 63	COLUMBIA
I'M THE ONE *(US No. 82)*		2	08 FEB 64	COLUMBIA
DON'T LET THE SUN CATCH YOU CRYING		6	09 MAY 64	COLUMBIA
FERRY ACROSS THE MERSEY *(Act re-recorded it on Deb in 83)*		8	23 JAN 65	COLUMBIA
DON'T LET THE SUN CATCH YOU CRYING		4	04 JUL 64	LAURIE
HOW DO YOU DO IT?		9	05 SEP 64	LAURIE
FERRY ACROSS THE MERSEY *(From the film)*		6	20 MAR 65	LAURIE

Also see The Crowd/Marsden, McCartney, Johnson, Christians

STAN GETZ/ASTRUD GILBERTO

The poll winning jazz saxophonist from Philadelphia who had played with such notables as Woody Herman, Stan Kenton, Benny Goodman and Jimmy Dorsey, teamed with the wife of Brazilian star Joao Gilberto for this one-off hit which won them a Grammy. He was still a regular jazz chart entrant in 90.

THE GIRL FROM IPANEMA *(UK No. 29)*		5	18 JUL 64	VERVE

ANDY GIBB

Youngest of the talented Gibb family saw his first three singles all top the US chart and also had six more US Top 40s and sold 15 million records before he was 21. His much publicised drug problems resulted in his losing TV and stage work in the early 80s. He filed for bankruptcy in 87 and sadly died aged 30 in 88.

AN EVERLASTING LOVE *(Only UK Top 20)*		10	09 SEP 78	RSO
I JUST WANT TO BE YOUR EVERYTHING *(UK No. 26)*		1(4)	30 JUL 77	RSO
(LOVE IS) THICKER THAN WATER		1(2)	04 MAR 78	RSO
SHADOW DANCING *(UK No. 42 – The Top US Single of 78)*		1(7)	17 JUN 78	RSO
AN EVERLASTING LOVE		5	23 SEP 78	RSO
(OUR LOVE) DON'T THROW IT ALL AWAY *(UK No. 32)*		9	16 DEC 78	RSO
DESIRE		4	08 MAR 80	RSO

ROBIN GIBB

The first of the Manchester (UK) born Gibb brothers to have a solo hit was Maurice's twin brother. In the US his biggest hit was 'Oh Darlin' (15) from the 'Sgt. Pepper' film.

SAVED BY THE BELL		2	16 AUG 69	POLYDOR

Also see The Bee Gees

DEBBIE GIBSON

The most successful teenage female singer/songwriter/producer of all time. She was also the first teenage girl to ever top the US LP and single chart simultaneously and was the first to get five Top 5 singles and two Top 10 LPs since Brenda Lee in 61. She is likely to continue her string of transatlantic hits into the 90s.

🇬🇧	SHAKE YOUR LOVE	7	13 FEB 88	ATLANTIC
	FOOLISH BEAT	9	23 JUL 88	ATLANTIC
🇺🇸	ONLY IN MY DREAMS *(She wrote it age 13)* *(UK No. 11 in 88 – Top selling US 12" of 87)*	4	05 SEP 87	ATLANTIC
	SHAKE YOUR LOVE	4	19 DEC 87	ATLANTIC
	OUT OF THE BLUE *(UK No. 19)*	3	09 APR 88	ATLANTIC
	FOOLISH BEAT *(1st No. 1 written, sung & prod. solely by a female)*	1(1)	25 JUN 88	ATLANTIC
	LOST IN YOUR EYES *(UK 34 – Written about her ex boyfriend Brian Bloom)*	1(3)	04 MAR 89	ATLANTIC

GIBSON BROTHERS

Martinique trio based in Paris and consisting of brothers Chris, Alex and Patrick Gibson. First success came in Europe and they topped the Dutch chart with 'Non Stop Dance' in 77. They had four UK-only Top 40s with their Euro disco style and in the US their only charter was 'Cuba' (US 81/UK 12). They were on Stiff in 83.

🇬🇧	OOH! WHAT A LIFE	10	01 SEP 79	ISLAND
	QUE SERA MI VIDA (1F YOU SHOULD GO)	5	08 DEC 79	ISLAND

ASTRUD GILBERTO – SEE STAN GETZ FOR HIT DETAILS

NICK GILDER

Born in London and raised in Canada he joined the group Sweeney Todd who had a North American hit in 76 with 'Roxy Roller' (Canada No. 1/US 90). His sole US Top 40 came from his second LP 'City Nights'. He followed it with 'Here Comes the Night'. He was also on Casablanca in 80, UK label Speed in 82 and RCA in 85.

🇺🇸	HOT CHILD IN THE CITY	1(1)	28 OCT 78	CHRYSALIS

JIM GILSTRAP

Texan singer was in the MOR act the Doodletown Pipers and the groups Side Effect and The Reason Why. He is one of the top US session singers, recording on many hits with acts like Stevie Wonder and Quincy Jones. As a solist he was on Bell in 74 and followed his only transatlantic hit with 'House of Strangers'.

🇬🇧	SWING YOUR DADDY *(US No. 55 – Composed by Kenny Nolan)*	4	19 APR 75	CHELSEA

GIRLSCHOOL – SEE HEADGIRL FOR HIT DETAILS

GLASS TIGER

Five man Canadian group featuring Scottish born singer/songwriter Alan Frew, spent some years working the local club circuit before scoring four US (1 UK) Top 40s and winning some Canadian awards.

🇺🇸	DON'T FORGET ME (WHEN I'M GONE) *(UK No. 29)*	2	11 OCT 86	MANHATTAN
	SOMEDAY *(UK No. 66)*	7	24 JAN 87	MANHATTAN

GARY GLITTER

One of the UK's best known acts of the 70s who had only one major US hit. Started recording at 15 in 60 for Decca then Parlophone as Paul Raven (real name Paul Gadd). He was a 'warm up man' for TV show 'Ready Steady Go' and joined MCA in 68. He recorded as Paul Monday and as Rubber Bucket before getting the first of his hits. The over the top king of glitter rock retired in 75 and has made many comebacks and many records (on many labels) since then. He is still popular on the live circuit and his antics are avidly covered in the tabloid press.

🇬🇧	ROCK & ROLL PART 2 *(His eighth single)* *(He re-recorded part of this on the Timelords No. 1)*	2	08 JUL 72	BELL
	I DIDN'T KNOW I LOVED YOU (TILL I SAW YOU ROCK AND ROLL) *(US No. 35)*	4	14 OCT 72	BELL
	DO YOU WANNA TOUCH ME (OH YEAH) *(Later a US hit for Joan Jett)*	2	03 FEB 73	BELL
	HELLO HELLO I'M BACK AGAIN	2	21 APR 73	BELL
	I'M THE LEADER OF THE GANG (I AM) *(In at No. 2 – he re-recorded it with Girl School)*	1(4)	28 JUL 73	BELL
	I LOVE YOU LOVE ME LOVE *(Entered at No. 1 – UK Gold – US cover Tommy James)*	1(4)	17 NOV 73	BELL
	REMEMBER ME THIS WAY *(Entered at No. 8)*	3	13 APR 74	BELL
	ALWAYS YOURS *(Entered at No. 5)*	1(1)	22 JUN 74	BELL
	OH YES! YOU'RE BEAUTIFUL	2	14 DEC 74	BELL
	LOVE LIKE YOU AND ME	10	17 MAY 75	BELL
	DOING ALRIGHT WITH THE BOYS	6	12 JUL 75	BELL
	ANOTHER ROCK AND ROLL CHRISTMAS *(First Top 10 for 9 years)*	7	22 DEC 84	ARISTA
🇺🇸	ROCK AND ROLL PART 2	7	09 SEP 72	BELL

Also see Glitter Band

GLITTER BAND

The nucleus of the band backed Gary Glitter in the 60's as Boston International and rejoined him when his first hit took off. The two-drummer group who included John Rossall and John Springate (both soloists later) soon had seven UK-only Top 20s of their own. In the US they only charted with 'Makes You Blind' (91).

🇬🇧	ANGEL FACE	4	20 APR 74	BELL
	JUST FOR YOU	10	20 AUG 74	BELL
	LET'S GET TOGETHER AGAIN	8	09 NOV 74	BELL
	GOODBYE MY LOVE	2	08 FEB 75	BELL
	THE TEARS I CRIED	8	03 MAY 75	BELL
	PEOPLE LIKE YOU AND PEOPLE LIKE ME	5	27 MAR 76	BELL

Also see Gary Glitter

GO WEST

UK duo of Peter Cox and Richard Drummie had four successive UK Top 20 hits and three US chart entries. They were voted Best Newcomers in the 86 BRITS awards.

🇬🇧	WE CLOSE OUR EYES *(US No. 41)*	5	13 APR 85	CHRYSALIS

GO-GO'S

The first successful girl vocal and instrumental group included current solo stars Belinda Carlisle and Jane Wieldin. The L.A. act was formed in 78 and got experience playing clubs on both sides of the Atlantic. They had 5 US-only Top 40s and 3 US Top 10 LPs including the No. 1 'Beauty & The Beat' before splitting in 85.

🇺🇸	WE GOT THE BEAT	2	10 APR 82	IRS
	VACATION *(They were Top US Act of 82)*	8	21 AUG 82	IRS

GODLEY & CREME

Manchester (UK) duo Kevin Godley and Lol Creme started in the Sabres and recorded as Frabjoy & Runcible Spoon on Marmalade. Their first hit was as half of Hotlegs, who evolved into 10CC and had many transatlantic triumphs. They split it in 76 and achieved three UK Top 20s as a duo. Their highest US charter was 'Cry' (US 16/UK 19). They are best known now as award winning video directors.

🏴󠁧󠁢󠁥󠁮󠁧󠁿	UNDER YOUR THUMB	3	17 OCT 81	POLYDOR
	WEDDING BELLS	7	26 DEC 81	POLYDOR

Also see Hotlegs/10CC

ANDREW GOLD

California born singer/writer/musician and much used session man is the son of film score writer Ernest Gold ('Exodus' etc). Formed own group Bryndle (which included Karla Bonoff) in the 60s and joined Linda Ronstadt's band in the early 70s. He had three UK Top 20s and later teamed with Graham Gouldman in hitmakers Wax.

🏴󠁧󠁢󠁥󠁮󠁧󠁿	NEVER LET HER SLIP AWAY *(US No. 67)*	5	06 MAY 78	ASYLUM
🇺🇸	LONELY BOY *(UK No. 11)*	7	11 JUN 77	ASYLUM

Also see Wax

GOLDEN EARRING

Holland's most successful rock band fronted by Barry Hay and featuring guitarist George Kooymans. First of many Dutch hits came in 64 and debut UK release was on Major Minor in 69. They moved to the UK and had a Transatlantic Top 20 hit in 74 and returned to the US Top 10 nine years later. Act were on 21 in 86.

🏴󠁧󠁢󠁥󠁮󠁧󠁿	RADAR LOVE *(US No. 13)* *(A Re-recording got 44 in UK in 77)*	7	19 JAN 74	TRACK
🇺🇸	TWILIGHT ZONE	10	26 MAR 83	21

GOLDIE

UK group hit with a song written by Black and McDonald and produced by Tab Martin. Their followed up 'To Be Alone' and other releases like 'We Make The Same Mistake Again' and 'How Many Times' failed.

🏴󠁧󠁢󠁥󠁮󠁧󠁿	MAKING UP AGAIN	7	24 JUN 78	BRONZE

BOBBY GOLDSBORO

Florida born singer/songwriter worked in Roy Orbison's backing group in the early 60s before scoring his first US solo hit with 'Molly' – his second release on Laurie in 62. He had 26 US chart records and had four visits to the UK Top 20. He was later on Vista in 74 and Epic in 77.

🏴󠁧󠁢󠁥󠁮󠁧󠁿	HONEY *(Original by Bob Shane)*	2	01 JUN 68	UA
	SUMMER (THE FIRST TIME) *(US No. 21)*	9	01 SEP 73	UA
	HONEY *(Back in chart and reached No. 2 again)*	2	26 APR 75	UA
🇺🇸	SEE THE FUNNY LITTLE CLOWN	9	14 MAR 64	UA
	HONEY	1(5)	13 APR 68	UA

GOODIES

UK comedy trio had their own highly acclaimed UK TV show. Member Bill Oddie recorded on Parlophone in 65 and Decca in 69. The trio were on Columbia and Decca (including 'Stuff That Gibbon') before their run of five UK-only Top 40 hits. They went to EMI in 78.

🏴󠁧󠁢󠁥󠁮󠁧󠁿	THE IN BETWEENIES/FATHER CHRISTMAS			
	DO NOT TOUCH ME	7	04 JAN 75	BRADLEY'S
	FUNKY GIBBON/SICK MAN BLUES *(US No. 79)*	4	12 APR 75	BRADLEY'S

DICKIE GOODMAN

The King of 'break-ins' or 'cut-ups' i.e. where bits of other records are included to humorous effect. With Bill Buchanan he hit in 56 with 'Flying Saucer' and afterwards made many similar tracks, with 12 of them (on 8 different labels!) charting. Due to legal reasons he had no UK releases. Sadly he died in 89.

🇺🇸	MR. JAWS	4	11 OCT 75	CASH

GOOMBAY DANCE BAND

Mixed group from Montserrat included husband and wife Oliver & Alicia Bendt. Recorded their sole UK Top 40 in Germany where it hit first. Their UK follow up 'Sun of Jamaica' had been their first UK single in 80. Act later appeared on Starblend and WEA.

🏴󠁧󠁢󠁥󠁮󠁧󠁿	SEVEN TEARS	1(3)	27 MAR 82	EPIC

GOONS

Innovative comedians Peter Sellers, Spike Milligan and Harry Seccombe were the UKs favourite funny men in the 50s and had two hits based on their radio show 'The Goons'. Oddly one of these was a UK hit in 73, and in 83 they also had an Australian No. 1.

🏴󠁧󠁢󠁥󠁮󠁧󠁿	I'M WALKING BACKWARDS FOR CHRISTMAS	4	13 JUL 56	DECCA
	BLOODNOK'S ROCK 'N' ROLL CALL/			
	YING TONG SONG	3	28 SEP 56	DECCA
	YING TONG SONG	9	11 OCT 73	DECCA

LESLEY GORE

New Yorker recorded with Quincy Jones while only 16 and her first record topped the US chart with the next three all making the Top 5. In all she had eight US (2 UK) Top 20s. She later made films and was on Crewe, Motown, A&M and Manhattan and co-wrote the Fame soundtrack. She was doing 'oldies' shows in 89.

🏴󠁧󠁢󠁥󠁮󠁧󠁿	IT'S MY PARTY	9	26 JUL 63	MERCURY
🇺🇸	IT'S MY PARTY	1(2)	08 JUN 63	MERCURY
	(Previously recorded by Shirelles and Crystals)			
	JUDY'S TURN TO CRY	5	17 AUG 63	MERCURY
	SHE'S A FOOL	5	07 DEC 63	MERCURY
	YOU DON'T OWN ME	2	15 FEB 64	MERCURY

EYDIE GORME

New York songstress who was on Coral in 53, ABC in 55 and UA in 61 and was a regular on Steve Allen's Tonight show in the mid 50's. She was a popular Vegas act both as a soloist and with husband Steve Lawrence. She had 17 US hits and three in the UK.

🏴󠁧󠁢󠁥󠁮󠁧󠁿	I WANT TO STAY HERE *(With STEVE LAWRENCE)*	3	20 SEP 63	CBS
🇺🇸	BLAME IT ON THE BOSSA NOVA *(UK No. 32)*	7	02 MAR 63	COLUMBIA
	(UK No. 32 – Co-written by Barry Mann)			

JAKI GRAHAM

Wolverhampton (UK) singer was in the Medium Wave Band and can be heard on many records, including UB40's hit 'Many Rivers To Cross'. Her second solo 45 hit and she became the UK's top black female act of the mid 80s with six UK-only Top 20s, four as a soloist and two with David Grant. She has also had four US black music charters returning to that chart in 90 on Orpheus.

🏴󠁧󠁢󠁥󠁮󠁧󠁿	COULD IT BE I'M FALLING IN LOVE			
	(With DAVID GRANT) (Spinners 72 US hit)	5	27 APR 85	CHRYSALIS
	ROUND AND ROUND	9	27 JUL 85	EMI
	SET ME FREE	7	14 JUN 86	EMI

75

LARRY GRAHAM

Larry was the bass player with Sly & The Family Stone from 67 to 72, then he formed Graham Central Station who had 14 black music hits including the No. 1 'Your Love'. He went solo in 80 and had another black No. 1 with the track that gave him a US Top 10 and started his run of ballad hits in the early 80s.

 ONE IN A MILLION YOU   9   20 SEP 80   WARNER

LOU GRAMM

New Yorker was in the group Black Sheep before joining the multi-platinum selling group Foreigner as vocalist. His debut solo LP in 87 'Ready or Not' (US 27) included his first US Top 10.

 MIDNIGHT BLUE   5   18 APR 87   ATLANTIC

Also see Foreigner

GRAND FUNK (RAILROAD)

Michigan group featuring Mark Farner and Don Brewer, both ex Terry Knight & The Pack. Though loathed by critics, they were most successful hard rock band in the US in the early 70s with 10 consecutive platinum LPs and sell out stadium tours. They had nine US Top 40 hits but their only UK chart record was a No. 40 single. Re-formed briefly in 81 on Full Moon.

 WE'RE AN AMERICAN BAND   1(1)   29 SEP 73   CAPITOL
THE LOCO-MOTION   1(2)   04 MAY 74   CAPITOL
(Little Eva 62 hit – co-written by Carole King)
SOME KIND OF WONDERFUL   3   22 FEB 75   CAPITOL
(Originally by the Soul Brothers 6)
BAD TIME   4   07 JUN 75   CAPITOL

GRANDMASTER FLASH, MELLE MEL & THE FURIOUS FIVE

DJ Grandmaster (Joseph Saddler), who had previously worked with Kurtis Blow, and rapper Melle Mel (Melvin Glover) were the premier DJ-rap team of the early 80s and the first to score with important messages in their raps. They first recorded on Enjoy and debuted on the black music chart with 'Freedom' in 80. Their fifth entry was the first of three UK-only Top 10s.

 THE MESSAGE *(US No. 62)*   8   18 SEP 82   SUGAR HILL
WHITE LINES *(Not with Furious Five)*   7   28 JUL 84   SUGAR HILL
(Took a record 23 weeks to make Top 10)
STEP OFF (PT. 1)   8   19 JAN 85   SUGAR HILL
(Act just Melle Mel & Furious Five)

GRANGE HILL CAST

Spearheading the UK 'Just Say No – To Drugs' campaign was this one-off hit by the young cast of UK TV series about Grange Hill school. They followed it with 'You Know The Teacher'.

 JUST SAY NO   5   26 APR 86   BBC

AMY GRANT – SEE PETER CETERA FOR HIT DETAILS

DAVID GRANT

London based singer/writer whose first hits came as front man for the popular duo Linx. He went solo in 83 and to date has chalked up five UK-only Top 20s, the last two with Jaki Graham. He joined Polydor in 87 and Fourth & Broadway in 89.

 WATCHING YOU WATCHING ME   10   03 SEP 83   CHRYSALIS
COULD IT BE I'M FALLING IN LOVE   5   27 APR 85   CHRYSALIS
(And JAKI GRAHAM – Spinners 72 hit)

EDDY GRANT

London based singer/writer born in Guyana formed the popular group The Equals in 66. Left the band in 72 and formed own label Ice and his first solo LP included the much covered title track 'Walkin' On Sunshine' and the first of his 6 UK (1 US) Top 20s 'Living On The Front Line' (UK 11). He joined Parlophone in 89.

 DO YOU FEEL MY LOVE   8   13 DEC 80   ENSIGN
I DON'T WANNA DANCE *(US No. 53)*   1(3)   13 NOV 82   ICE
ELECTRIC AVENUE   2   22 JAN 83   ICE
GIMME HOPE JO'ANNA   7   12 MAR 88   ICE
ELECTRIC AVENUE   2   02 JUL 83   PORTRAIT

GRASS ROOTS

Writers P.F. Sloan and Steve Barri sang on the Grass Roots first two records and when act hit in 66 they enlisted California group 13th Floor to take over from them. Group featured Rob Grill and Warren Etner and had 14 US-only Top 40s. They were later on Haven and MCA and Rob made a solo LP with some of Fleetwood Mac.

LET'S LIVE FOR TODAY   8   01 JUL 67   DUNHILL
MIDNIGHT CONFESSIONS   5   02 NOV 68   DUNHILL
SOONER OR LATER   9   31 JUL 71   DUNHILL

GRATEFUL DEAD

San Franciscan act, which includes Jerry Garcia and Bob Weir, started as The Warlocks and first recorded on MGM. They were one of the leading 60s psychedelic groups and they still sell millions of LPs and pack stadiums. To date they have had 26 US (6 UK) chart LPs with their biggest hits coming in the late 80s.

TOUCH OF GREY   9   26 SEP 87   ARISTA

DOBIE GRAY

Texan born Leonard Ainsworth Jr, was on Stripe in 60 and first charted on Cordak in 63. The only trans-atlantic hit for this unique folk/soul/country singer was 'The 'In' Crowd' on Charger in 65 (US 13/UK 25). He was also on Capitol, Anthem, White Whale, Infinity, Arista, Capricorn and Thunderbird. His big hit, also covered by Rod Stewart, was written by Mentor Williams.

DRIFT AWAY   5   12 MAY 73   DECCA

GREAT WHITE

L.A. based rock foursome, fronted by Jack Russell, first released an EP 'Out Of The Night' in 83. They made the US LP chart with their debut on EMI which they followed with an LP on Telegraph. Their fourth chart single was their biggest hit to date.

ONCE BITTEN TWICE SHY *(Ian Hunter 75 UK hit)*   5   12 AUG 89   CAPITOL

R.B. GREAVES

R.B. (Ronald Bertram) is half Seminole Indian, was born in Guyana and is a nephew of Sam Cooke. He toured the UK in 63 as Sonny Childe (recording on Polydor) and had two US-only Top 40s. He was also on Midsong Int, Bareback MGM, 20th Century and Sunflower.

TAKE A LETTER MARIA   2   22 NOV 69   ATCO

AL GREEN

Arkansas born soul singer/writer was one of the 70s top selling acts. He first charted on Hot Line Music Journal in 67 but it took four years before he had the first of his 10 US (3 UK) Top 20s & six US (1 UK) Top 20 LPs. From 79 he recorded gospel only (which he won Grammys for) and he later became a church minister.

🇬🇧	TIRED OF BEING ALONE (US No. 11)	4	06 NOV 71	LONDON
	LET'S STAY TOGETHER	7	12 FEB 72	LONDON
🇺🇸	LET'S STAY TOGETHER (Top US soul single 72)	1(1)	12 FEB 72	HI
	LOOK WHAT YOU DONE FOR ME (UK No. 44)	4	27 MAY 72	HI
	I'M STILL IN LOVE WITH YOU (UK No. 35)	3	02 SEP 72	HI
	YOU OUGHT TO BE WITH ME	3	23 DEC 72	HI
	CALL ME (COME BACK HOME)	10	14 APR 73	HI
	HERE I AM (COME AND TAKE ME)	10	08 SEP 73	HI
	SHA-LA-LA (MAKE ME HAPPY) (UK No. 20)	7	21 DEC 74	HI
	PUT A LITTLE LOVE IN YOUR HEART (With ANNIE LENNOX) (UK No. 28)	9	14 JAN 89	A&M

NORMAN GREENBAUM

Folk singer/songwriter from Massachusetts formed West Coast group Dr. West's Medicine Show and Junk Band, who charted with 'The Eggplant That Ate Chicago' on Go Go in 66. He recorded on Gregar and his first solo on Reprise was as Dr. Norman Greenbaum. His fourth single on that label gave him his only Top 40 hit.

🇬🇧	SPIRIT IN THE SKY	1(2)	02 MAY 70	REPRISE
🇺🇸	SPIRIT IN THE SKY	3	18 APR 70	REPRISE

LORNE GREENE

Canadian born TV actor who found world fame in Bonanza. He first recorded ('My Sons, My Sons') in 61 and had a one-off hit in 64 (the year of The Beatles) with a song about another Ringo.

🇺🇸	RINGO (UK No. 22)	1(1)	05 DEC 64	RCA

GREYHOUND

Jamaican reggae group, who also recorded as The Uniques, were fronted by Glenroy Oakley. They had three UK-only Top 20s in less than a year. The others being 'Moon River' (No. 12) and 'I Am What I Am' (No. 20)

🇬🇧	BLACK AND WHITE (Originally by UK Spinners)	6	17 JUL 71	TROJAN

LARRY GROCE

Texan born folk/pop singer and writer who originally recorded for MGM in 73 and Vista in 74 where he cut songs like 'Winnie The Pooh For President'. He notched up a US one-off hit with a fun song about junk food and followed it with 'Bumper Sticker Song'.

🇺🇸	JUNK FOOD JUNKIE	9	20 MAR 76	WARNER

HENRY GROSS

Brooklyn born, he started as guitarist with Sha-Na-Na and first recorded solo on ABC and A&M. He had two US Top 40s, the other was the follow up to his Beach Boys-ish hit, 'Springtime Mama'.

🇺🇸	SHANNON (UK No. 32- Song about an Irish setter not a girl)	6	05 JUN 76	LIFESONG

GUESS WHO

Canada's top group of the 70s evolved out of Chad Allen & The Expressions. First hit was a cover of Johnny Kidd's 'Shakin' All Over'(US 22) in 65. They were on Scepter, Amy, Fontana and Dial and in 69 the act who included Randy Bachman and Burton Cummings had the first of eight US Top 20s (1 in UK). Randy left in 70 and Burton wound the act up in 75 but both had more chart records.

🇺🇸	THESE EYES	6	31 MAY 69	RCA
	LAUGHING	10	23 AUG 69	RCA
	NO TIME	5	28 FEB 70	RCA
	AMERICAN WOMAN (UK No.19)	1(3)	09 MAY 70	RCA
	SHARE THE LAND	10	05 DEC 70	RCA
	CLAP FOR THE WOLFMAN	6	05 OCT 74	RCA

Also see Bachman Turner Overdrive/Burton Cummings

GUN

UK group which included brothers Adrian & Paul Gurvitz and Louis Farrell. They had several more releases but did not chart again. The brothers left to join Ginger Baker in Three Man Army and Adrian, who penned their hit, had solo success later.

🇬🇧	RACE WITH THE DEVIL	8	21 DEC 68	CBS

Also see Adrian Gurvitz

GUNS N' ROSES

Formed from ex members of L.A. Guns and Hollywood Rose in 85 and featuring W. Axl Rose (real name Bill Bailey). First release was an E.P. 'Live... Like A Suicide', which was included on their second LP 'G'N'R Lies'. Their first LP 'Appetite For Destruction' sold over eight million and they were first act for 15 years to have two LPs in the US Top 5 together. They also had four US Top 10s in nine months and were the Top New Artists in the US in 88.

🇬🇧	PARADISE CITY	6	01 APR 89	GEFFEN
	SWEET CHILD O' MINE (REMIX) (Winner MTV award Best Heavy Metal video 89)	6	17 JUN 89	GEFFEN
	PATIENCE	10	08 JUL 89	GEFFEN
🇺🇸	SWEET CHILD O' MINE (5' 55" 7" single) (Written by Axl about Erin Everly (Don's daughter)	1(2)	10 SEP 88	GEFFEN
	WELCOME TO THE JUNGLE (UK No. 24)	7	24 DEC 88	GEFFEN
	PARADISE CITY (At 6'46" one of longest ever Top 10s)	5	11 MAR 89	GEFFEN
	PATIENCE	4	03 JUN 89	GEFFEN

ADRIAN GURVITZ

UK singer/guitarist had previously played in Gun, Three Man Army (the Gurvitz brothers), Baker-Gurvitz Army with Ginger Baker and who had a UK chart LP in 75 in Graham Edge's (Ex Moody Blues) Band. Follow up to his sole UK Top 40 was 'Your Dream'.

🇬🇧	CLASSIC	8	27 MAR 82	RAK

ALSO SEE GUN

GWEN GUTHRIE

New Jersey singer was in group East Coast with Cameo's Larry Blackmon and recorded backing vocals for acts like Madonna, Billy Joel, Stevie Wonder and Quincy Jones. She also sang lead on The Limit's 85 UK hit 'Say Yeah' (17) and her first solo charter was 'It Should Have Been You' on Island in 82. She joined Warner in 88.

🇬🇧	AIN'T NOTHING GOIN' ON BUT THE RENT (US No.42 – Top US Club Play record of 86)	5	16 AUG 86	BOILING P.

GUYS & DOLLS

Mixed pop sextet included Julie Forsythe (daughter of Top UK entertainer Bruce) plus Dominic, Martine and Paul. They had five UK-only hits and a Dutch No. 1 with 'You're My World'. Group members Thereza and David later formed the sucessful duo Dollar.

🇬🇧	THERE'S A WHOLE LOT OF LOVING	2	29 MAR 75	MAGNET
	YOU DON'T HAVE TO SAY YOU LOVE ME (Dusty Springfield 66 hit)	5	20 MAR 76	MAGNET

HAIRCUT 100

Kent (UK) based act fronted by photogenic Nick Heyward saw their first four singles all make the UK Top 10. The group split in 83 and Nick put his first three solo records in UK Top 20. Without him the group failed to hit the heights again.

🏴󠁧󠁢󠁥󠁮󠁧󠁿	FAVOURITE SHIRTS (BOY MEETS GIRL)	4	21 NOV 81	ARISTA
	LOVE PLUS ONE (US No. 37)	3	13 MAR 82	ARISTA
	FANTASTIC DAY	9	01 MAY 82	ARISTA
	NOBODY'S FOOL	9	04 SEP 82	ARISTA

BILL HALEY

The 'Father of Rock 'n' Roll'. Haley didn't invent it but he had the first R'n'R No. 1 (his 16th single) with the biggest ever selling rock single and he was the one who first popularised it worldwide. In the 40s he was in The Down Homers, The 4 Aces Of Western Swing and The Saddlemen. He first charted in 53 and had many transatlantic hits between 55-57. He was on over 20 labels and packed houses around the world right up to his death in 81. His music featured strongly in the Jive Bunny hits of 89.

🏴󠁧󠁢󠁥󠁮󠁧󠁿	SHAKE RATTLE & ROLL (Joe Turner 54 R&B hit)	4	21 JAN 55	BRUNSWICK
	ROCK AROUND THE CLOCK (Re-entry)	1(5)	25 NOV 55	BRUNSWICK
	(In UK Top 30 six times-first UK only gold record)			
	ROCK-A-BEATIN' BOOGIE (US No. 17)	4	13 JAN 56	BRUNSWICK
	SEE YOU LATER, ALLIGATOR	7	16 MAR 56	BRUNSWICK
	(Originally by Bobby Charles)			
	THE SAINTS ROCK 'N' ROLL (US No. 18)	5	06 JUL 56	BRUNSWICK
	ROCKIN' THROUGH THE RYE (US No. 78)	3	21 SEP 56	BRUNSWICK
	(One of 5 of his records in UK Top 20 in same week)			
	ROCK AROUND THE CLOCK	5	02 NOV 56	BRUNSWICK
	(Originally by Sonny Dae in 52)			
	RIP IT UP (US No. 25 – Little Richard 56 hit)	4	07 DEC 56	BRUNSWICK
	DON'T KNOCK THE ROCK (From the film)	7	15 FEB 57	BRUNSWICK
🇺🇸	SHAKE RATTLE & ROLL	7	13 NOV 54	DECCA
	ROCK AROUND THE CLOCK	1(8)	09 JUL 55	DECCA
	(Spent 38 weeks on US Chart and 57 on UK)			
	SEE YOU LATER, ALLIGATOR	6	11 FEB 56	DECCA

DARYL HALL

His biggest solo hit was from his second LP 'Three Hearts In The Happy Ending Machine' and was produced by Eurythmic Dave Stewart. He had previously recorded solo on Amy in 69 and Parallax.

🇺🇸	DREAMTIME (UK No. 28)	5	04 OCT 86	RCA

Also see Hall & Oates

DARYL HALL & JOHN OATES

The most successful of all duos in the US (far fewer hits in the UK) with 16 Top 10 singles and 7 Top 20 LPs. Both of these Philadelphians were in 60s groups – Daryl in The Temptones and The Romeos and John in The Masters. John also recorded in rock group Gulliver, who had an LP on Elektra in 69. As a duo they joined Atlantic in 72 and their first hit came from their second LP together. They split for a while but got together again in 88.

🏴󠁧󠁢󠁥󠁮󠁧󠁿	I CAN'T GO FOR THAT (NO CAN DO)	8	27 FEB 82	RCA
	MANEATER	6	20 NOV 82	RCA
🇺🇸	SARA SMILE	4	26 JUN 76	RCA
	(Song about Sara Sandy Allen their lyricist)			
	SHE'S GONE (UK No. 42 – was US No. 60 in 74)	7	30 OCT 76	ATLANTIC
	RICH GIRL	1(2)	26 MAR 77	RCA
	KISS ON MY LIST (UK No. 33)	1(3)	11 APR 81	RCA
	YOU MAKE MY DREAMS	5	04 JUL 81	RCA
	PRIVATE EYES (UK No. 32)	1(2)	07 NOV 81	RCA
	I CAN'T GO FOR THAT (NO CAN DO)	1(1)	30 JAN 82	RCA
	(Fourth successive No. 1 – a record for Duos)			
	DID IT IN A MINUTE	9	22 MAY 82	RCA
	MANEATER	1(4)	18 DEC 82	RCA

ONE ON ONE (UK No. 63)	7	09 APR 83	RCA
FAMILY MAN (UK No. 15)	6	25 JUN 83	RCA
SAY IT ISN'T SO (UK No. 69)	2	17 DEC 83	RCA
ADULT EDUCATION (UK No. 63)	8	07 APR 84	RCA
OUT OF TOUCH (UK No. 62)	1(2)	08 DEC 84	RCA
METHOD OF MODERN LOVE (UK No. 21)	5	16 FEB 85	RCA
EVERYTHING YOUR HEART DESIRES	3	11 JUN 88	ARISTA

Also see Daryl Hall

HAMILTON, JOE FRANK & REYNOLDS

Dan Hamilton, Joe Frank Carollo and Tommy Reynolds had all been in the 60s hit act The T-Bones. When that group broke up these experienced session men formed this trio and had eight US hits between 71-76. Tommy was replaced by Alan Dennison in 72.

🇺🇸	DON'T PULL YOUR LOVE	4	24 JUL 71	DUNHILL
	FALLIN' IN LOVE (UK No. 33)	1(1)	23 AUG 75	PLAYBOY

LYNNE HAMILTON

Chorley (UK) born singer was in the duo The Caravelles (after their hits) before emigrating to Australia. She had a No.2 there in 79 with the theme to the Aussie TV series Prisoner – Cell Block H. In 80 Patti Page had some success with the song in the US and it was released by public demand in the UK in 89.

🏴󠁧󠁢󠁥󠁮󠁧󠁿	ON THE INSIDE (Theme 'Prisoner-Cell Block H')	3	03 JUN 89	AI

MARVIN HAMLISCH

New York pianist/composer/conductor first scored as the writer of two Lesley Gore hits. He won an Oscar and a Grammy for his song 'The Way We Were' (hit for both Barbra Streisand and Gladys Knight) and had a one-off hit as an artist with his arrangement of the Scott Joplin song used in the film The Sting.

🇺🇸	THE ENTERTAINER (UK No. 25)	3	18 MAY 74	MCA

JAN HAMMER

Czechoslovak born jazz/rock keyboard wizard played in the Mahavishnu Orchestra before releasing the first of his many solo LPs in 74. He was on Nemporer, Epic (had two hit LPs with Jeff Beck), ECM, Asylum and CBS. He had pop hits around the world with his music from the TV series Miami Vice.

🏴󠁧󠁢󠁥󠁮󠁧󠁿	MIAMI VICE THEME	5	26 OCT 85	MCA
	CROCKETT'S THEME	2	24 OCT 87	MCA
🇺🇸	MIAMI VICE THEME	1(1)	09 NOV 85	MCA

ALBERT HAMMOND

London born singer/songwriter was in The Diamond Boys, Albert & Richard, Los Cuico Ricardos and Hammond/(Mike) Hazlewood in the 60s. With Mike he wrote hits for Leapy Lee, Blue Mink, Joe Dolan and The Pipkins and sang in hit acts Family Dogg and The Magic Lanterns. He had nine US hits but his only UK hit was 'Free Electric Band' (UK 19/US 48). He is still a top writer with big hits for acts like Whitney Houston, Starship, Leo Sayer and Tina Turner.

🇺🇸	IT NEVER RAINS IN SOUTHERN CALIFORNIA	5	16 DEC 72	MUMS
	(Written in Fulham in Western London)			

HERBIE HANCOCK

Noted Chicago jazz keyboard player played with Hank Mobley, Lee Morgan and Donald Byrd, and between 63-68 with Miles Davis. He combined jazz/funk and electronics and had Top 20 US LPs in 74 with 'Head Hunters'and 'Thrust' and had the first of four UK-only Top 40s in 78 with 'I Thought It Was You'. In the 80s his video award winning 'Rockit' gave him his only Top 10 record.

 ROCKIT (US No. 71)   8   20 AUG 83   CBS

HAPPENINGS

New Jersey quartet who first recorded as the Four Graduates on Rust. This act, whose lead vocalist was Bob Miranda, saw their second release under their new name become the biggest of their four US-only Top 20s – all of which were revivals of 'oldies'.

 SEE YOU IN SEPTEMBER (Tempos 59 US hit)   3   27 AUG 66   B.T.PUPPY
I GOT RHYTHM (UK No. 28 – Red Nichols 31 hit)   3   27 MAY 67   B.T.PUPPY

PAUL HARDCASTLE

London born keyboard player (ex-Direct Drive) had four small UK hits and a No. 5 US black music hit ('Rain Forest') prior to his world-wide smash '19'. He became a most in-demand re-mixer in the UK and followed his multi-million seller with three UK-only Top 20s.

 19 (US No. 15)   1(5) 11 MAY 85   CHRYSALIS
(Mike Oldfield credited as part composer)
DON'T WASTE MY TIME (Vocal Carol Kenyon)   8   01 MAR 86   CHRYSALIS

STEVE HARLEY (& COCKNEY REBEL)

Londoner Steve formed the group in 73 and scored with their third single. He put a new group together in 75 and took lead billing. A year later he went solo, moved to the US and tried unsuccessfully to get a hit there. Ten years after he returned to the Top 10 in a duet with Sarah Brightman.

 JUDY TEEN   5   22 JUN 74   EMI
MR. SOFT (First two rel. as Cockney Rebel)   8   31 AUG 74   EMI
MAKE ME SMILE (COME UP AND SEE ME)
(US No. 96)   1(2) 22 FEB 75   EMI
(Rel. as Steve Harley & Cockney Rebel-jumped 9-1)
HERE COMES THE SUN   10   21 AUG 76   EMI
(Released as Steve Harley – Beatles song)
THE PHANTOM OF THE OPERA   7   08 FEB 86   POLYDOR
(Released as Steve Harley With
SARAH BRIGHTMAN)

JIMMY HARNEN WITH SYNCH

Sextet from Pennsylvania first charted with their 89 US Top 10 hit in 86 when it reached No. 77 – it was then credited solely to Synch. It equalled the slowest ever climb to the Top Ten of 28 weeks. After the belated success Jimmy recorded new material and tried to launch his career again.

 WHERE ARE YOU NOW   10   10 JUN 89   WTG

ANITA HARRIS

Somerset (UK) born singer, TV personality and one time skating star. She was in the Cliff Adams Singers and first recorded solo in 61 on Parlophone. She was on Vocalion, Pye and Decca before the first of her three UK-only Top 40s. She joined Columbia in 72.

 JUST LOVING YOU (Composed Tom Springfield)   6   26 AUG 67   CBS

JET HARRIS & TONY MEEHAN

Bassist Jet and drummer Tony were ex members of Britain's very successful group The Shadows. Jet had two solo UK-only Top 40s before they teamed up in 63. The duo found instant fame and their three releases all made the UK Top 10. In 63, after a bad car crash, Jet seemed to lose interest and smashed all his guitars. Tony then recorded alone and had a small UK hit. Jet recorded on Fontana in 67 and re-recorded all his hits in 88. In the interim much publicity ensued when it was discovered he was working as a bus conductor.

 DIAMONDS   1(4) 23 JAN 63   DECCA
(First instrumental duo to top UK chart)
SCARLETT O'HARA   2   17 MAY 63   DECCA
APPLEJACK   6   27 SEP 63   DECCA

Also see The Shadows

KEITH HARRIS & ORVILLE

UK ventriloquist and his duck dummy had three UK chart records. Their un-charted follow up was 'Will You Still Love Me'.

 ORVILLE'S SONG   4   15 JAN 83   BBC

MAJOR HARRIS

Virginia born soul singer sang in The Jarmels (not on their hits) and The Impacts in the early 60s. He recorded solo for Okeh in 68 and with the Nat Turner Rebellion in 69. He replaced Randy Cain in The Delfonics in 71 and he (& his Boogie Blues band) signed to Atlantic in 75 . He later recorded for WMOT and Pop Art.

 LOVE WON'T LET ME WAIT (UK No. 37)   5   21 JUN 75   ATLANTIC

MAX HARRIS

UK pianist/arranger had been in the bands of Ambrose, Ronnie Munro, Maurice Winnick, George Chisholm and Jack Parnell. He had a one-off hit with the theme from Anthony Newley's unusual UK TV series Gurney Slade. He was later on Parlophone and Pye.

GURNEY SLADE (Covered in US by Ray Anthony)   10   09 DEC 60   FONTANA

RICHARD HARRIS

Top Irish actor had a transatlantic Top 10 with a seven minute song about a park in L.A. The track was from his 'A Tramp Shining' LP which was produced by Jim Webb, writer of the hit.

MACARTHUR PARK (Also UK No. 38 in 72)   4   27 JUL 68   RCA
MACARTHUR PARK (Record recorded in 1 take)   2   22 JUN 68   DUNHILL

ROLF HARRIS

Australian born singer/writer/painter and 'wobble board' player moved to the UK in the 50s and regularly appeared on TV there since then. He played on a Kate Bush LP and has had five UK and three US hits. He was the first Australian soloist to top the UK chart.

TIE ME KANGAROO DOWN SPORT   7   19 AUG 60   COLUMBIA
(Covered in the US by Pat Boone)
SUN ARISE (US No. 61)   2   21 DEC 62   COLUMBIA
TWO LITTLE BOYS   1(5) 20 DEC 69   COLUMBIA
TIE ME KANGAROO DOWN SPORT   3   13 JUL 63   EPIC

GEORGE HARRISON

The first Beatle to have a solo No.1 single and LP and the first to tour. Before joining the 'Fab Four' he was in local Liverpool group The Rebels. He organised the Bangla-Desh concert in 71, formed his own label Dark Horse in 74 and launched his successful Handmade Films company in 79. He has had numerous transatlantic hits, the latest as part of the Traveling Wilburys.

🇬🇧	MY SWEET LORD *(Entered at No. 7)* *(Top record of 71 – song first cut by Billy Preston)*	1(5)	30 JAN 71	APPLE
	BANGLA DESH *(US No. 23)*	10	28 AUG 71	APPLE
	GIVE ME LOVE (GIVE ME PEACE ON EARTH)	8	30 JUN 73	APPLE
	GOT MY MIND SET ON YOU *(Orig. by James Ray – his first Top 10 for 14 years)*	2	14 NOV 87	DARK HORSE
🇺🇸	MY SWEET LORD *(Backing vocals by producer Phil Spector)*	1(4)	26 DEC 70	APPLE
	WHAT IS LIFE	10	27 MAR 71	APPLE
	GIVE ME LOVE (GIVE ME PEACE ON EARTH)	1(1)	30 JUN 73	APPLE
	ALL THOSE YEARS AGO *(UK No. 13 – Paul & Ringo also on track)*	2	04 JUL 81	DARK HORSE
	GOT MY MIND SET ON YOU	1(1)	16 JAN 88	DARK HORSE

Also see The Beatles

NOEL HARRISON

Actor/singer son of famous UK actor Rex Harrison had his sole UK hit with the Thomas Crown Affair theme. In the US he had two small hits earlier, the biggest being 'A Young Girl' (51) in 65.

🇬🇧	WINDMILLS OF YOUR MIND	8	03 MAY 69	REPRISE

HARRY J. & THE ALL STARS

Jamaican instrumental reggae quintet led by keyboard player Harry Johnson. They charted twice in the UK (11 years apart) with a track that Lee Perry & The Upsetters had arranged and played the rhythm on. They were also on Harry J, Green Door and Blue Mountain.

🇬🇧	LIQUIDATOR *(Also UK No. 42 in 80)*	9	29 NOV 69	TROJAN

DEBBIE HARRY

Blondie's singer first recorded solo in 81 and her debut LP 'Koo Koo' and singles (produced by Rodgers & Edwards) fared less well than expected. She got involved in film making and then her second LP 'Rockbird' in 86 met with a similar fate. However her 89 come-back on Sire looks more encouraging, especially in the UK.

🇬🇧	FRENCH KISSIN' IN THE USA *(US No. 57)*	8	06 DEC 86	CHRYSALIS

Also see Blondie

COREY HART

Canadian rock singer/songwriter and keyboard player who grew up in Spain and Mexico, had eight US-only Top 40s between 84-87.

🇺🇸	SUNGLASSES AT NIGHT	7	01 SEP 84	EMI AM.
	NEVER SURRENDER	3	17 AUG 85	EMI AM.

RICHARD HARTLEY/MICHAEL REED ORCHESTRA

UK synth player had a one-off UK hit with the music used by top dance-skating duo Torvill & Dean. The other side of the EP was by the UK based orchestra. The lead track was Ravel's 'Bolero'.

🇬🇧	THE MUSIC OF TORVILL & DEAN EP	9	07 APR 84	SAFARI

DAN HARTMAN

Multi-instrumentalist from Pennsylvania who was in Edgar Winter's band from 71 to 75. As an artist he has had 3 UK Top 20s (1 in US) and as a writer/producer he had hits with James Brown, .38 Special, 3 Degrees, Living In A Box and Tavares. In 89 he wrote the UK No. 1 by Black Box and produced two Top 20s by Tina Turner.

🇬🇧	INSTANT REPLAY *(US No. 29)*	8	18 NOV 78	SKY
🇺🇸	I CAN DREAM ABOUT YOU *(UK No. 12 from the film 'Streets of Fire')*	6	18 AUG 84	MCA

SENSATIONAL ALEX HARVEY BAND

Glasgow singer started in 50s skiffle groups, formed his own band in 59 and first recorded in 65 on Fontana. In 72 he formed this group from members of Teargas. Their rock theatrics made them a popular live act and they had three UK-only Top 40s before his death from a heart attack in 82 at the end of a hectic European tour.

🇬🇧	DELILAH *(Tom Jones 68 hit)*	7	16 AUG 75	VERTIGO

DONNY HATHAWAY

Chicago born singer/writer/keyboard player first recorded as duo June (Conquest) & Donnie (charted 45 R&B in 69) on Buddah. Then he worked for Chess, Stax, UNI and Kapp. He had 15 black music hits – the biggest and only transatlantic pop Top 40s, with old school friend Roberta Flack. Supposedly committed suicide in 79.

🇬🇧	BACK TOGETHER AGAIN *(With ROBERTA FLACK)* *(US No. 56)*	3	28 JUN 80	ATLANTIC
🇺🇸	WHERE IS THE LOVE *(With ROBERTA FLACK)* *(UK No. 29)*	5	12 AUG 72	ATLANTIC
	THE CLOSER I GET TO YOU *(With ROBERTA FLACK)* *(UK No. 42)*	2	13 MAY 78	ATLANTIC

EDWIN HAWKINS SINGERS

Originally named the Northern California State Youth Choir, they were a 40 plus church choir led by Oakland born Edwin. They recorded an album (on a two track machine) which was picked up by Buddah and included their Top 10 smash. In the US they returned to the charts with Melanie. They were on Lecton in 90.

🇬🇧	OH HAPPY DAY *(Biggest ever gospel record)*	2	21 JUN 69	BUDDAH
🇺🇸	OH HAPPY DAY *(Vocal Dorothy Morrison)*	4	31 MAY 69	PAVILION
	LAY DOWN (CANDLES IN THE RAIN) *(With MELANIE)*	6	11 JUL 70	BUDDAH

HAWKWIND

Originally known as Group X then Hawkwind Zoo, the group have had numerous personnel changes. Members have included Dave Brock, Nik Turner, the late Robert Calvert, Ian 'Lemmy' Kilminster and Ginger Baker. They had 19 UK LP chart records between 71-88 and had two Top 20 singles. In the US they scored three small LP hits.

🇬🇧	SILVER MACHINE *(Returned to No. 34 in 78 and to No.67 in 83)*	3	19 AUG 72	UA

ISAAC HAYES

Singer/songwriter was in The Teen Tones, Swing Cats and Sir Isaac & The Doo Dads. He recorded on Brunswick and in 64 joined Stax and played on, produced and wrote hits for many acts. His innovative second LP 'Hot Buttered Soul' took soul to a new plateau. His music and Black Moses image earned him Grammys and transatlantic hits. By 76 sales slowed and he was bankrupt. Later records on Polydor and Columbia sold reasonably well for the 70s 'King of Rap'.

🇬🇧	THEME FROM 'SHAFT' *(From the film)*	4	18 DEC 71	STAX
	DISCO CONNECTION *(As Isaac Hayes Movement)*	10	01 MAY 76	ABC
🇺🇸	THEME FROM 'SHAFT'	1(2)	20 NOV 71	ENTERPRISE

JUSTIN HAYWARD

Swindon (UK) singer was on Pye and Parlophone before joining the Moody Blues in 66. His only solo hit came from the 'War Of The Worlds' LP as did the Top 5 hit 'The Eve Of The War' by Jeff Wayne on which he sang. With Moody Blues bassist John Lodge he made an LP 'Blue Jays' during the group's five year sabbatical and their second single from it was a Top 10 hit.

	BLUE GUITAR (And JOHN LODGE) (US No. 94)	8	15 NOV 75	THRESHOLD
	FOREVER AUTUMN (US No. 47)	5	26 AUG 78	CBS

Also see The Moody Blues

LEE HAZLEWOOD – SEE NANCY SINATRA FOR HIT DETAILS

MURRAY HEAD

UK singer/actor who recorded on Columbia in 65 and first charted in 70 with the hit version of 'Superstar' (from Jesus Christ Superstar) (US 14/UK 47). He was on Island in 75, Music Lovers in 81 and Virgin in 84 and his only Transatlantic Top 20 came in 85 with another Tim Rice show song, this time from Chess.

	ONE NIGHT IN BANGKOK (UK No. 12)	3	18 MAY 85	RCA

ROY HEAD (& THE TRAITS)

Texan rock/country singer had seven US chart entries (1 UK) including five with The Traits. The much recorded act has been on Ascot, TNT, Lori, Backbeat, Renner, Pacemaker, Mega, Shannon, Churchill, NSD, Avion, Texas Crude, Scepter, Mercury, Dunhill, Shannon, Dot, ABC, Elektra and TMI. Roy has also had two dozen country hits since debuting on that chart in 74.

	TREAT HER RIGHT (UK No. 30)	2	16 OCT 65	BACK BEAT

HEADGIRL

Act is a combination of UK metal groups Motorhead and female foursome Girlschool. Fronting the girl group, who were formed in 78, were Kim McAuliffe and Enid Williams, both ex Painted Lady. They had four UK chart singles and a Top 5 LP 'Hit'n'Run' (US 182). Group later had personnel changes and continued recording.

	ST. VALENTINE'S DAY MASSACRE E.P.	5	28 FEB 81	BRONZE

Also see Motorhead

JEFF HEALEY BAND

Blind singer from Toronto whose 'lap' guitar style won him many fans in the US and awards in his homeland Canada. His second single from his debut LP 'See The Light' gave him his first Top 20 hit. He and his trio are in the film Road House.

	ANGEL EYES	5	02 SEP 89	ARISTA

HEART

Seattle (US) band initially known as The Army and then White Heart. Since 74 act fronted by the Wilson sisters – singer Ann and guitarist Nancy. Their first LP 'Dreamboat Annie' in 76 sold over two million and they have since had eight US Top 20 LPs and 11 US Top 20 singles. They finally broke through in the UK in the mid 80s when several of their older 45s hit for the first time.

	ALONE	3	08 AUG 87	CAPITOL
	NEVER/THESE DREAMS	8	26 MAR 88	CAPITOL
	MAGIC MAN	9	06 NOV 76	MUSHROOM
	TELL IT LIKE IT IS	8	10 JAN 81	EPIC
	WHAT ABOUT LOVE? (UK No. 14 in 88)	10	24 AUG 85	CAPITOL
	NEVER	4	07 DEC 85	CAPITOL

	THESE DREAMS (Vocal Nancy Wilson)	1(1)	22 MAR 86	CAPITOL
	NOTHIN' AT ALL (UK No. 38 in 88)	10	21 JUN 86	CAPITOL
	ALONE	1(3)	11 JUL 87	CAPITOL
	WHO WILL YOU RUN TO (UK No. 30)	7	03 OCT 87	CAPITOL

Also see Mike Reno & Ann Wilson

HEATWAVE

Ohio brothers Keith & Johnny Wilder fronted this multi-national and inter-racial group that also included the UK's most successful black music writer Rod Temperton (hits for Michael Jackson, Aretha, George Benson etc). The group, who had six UK Top 20s and three in the US, faded from the scene in the early 80s.

	BOOGIE NIGHTS (Produced Barry Blue)	2	05 MAR 77	GTO
	ALWAYS AND FOREVER/MIND BLOWING DECISIONS (US No. 18)	9	09 DEC 78	GTO
	BOOGIE NIGHTS	2	12 NOV 77	EPIC
	THE GROOVE LINE (UK No. 12)	7	15 JUL 78	EPIC

HEAVEN 17

Trio, named after A Clockwork Orange group, are ex Human League synth men Martin Ware and Ian Marsh with singer Glenn Gregory. Act had five UK-only Top 40s and three Top 20 LPs. Martin and Ian produced Tina Turner's comeback 'Let's Stay Together', Martin co-produced Terence Trent D'Arby's No.1 LP and Glenn was in Band Aid.

	TEMPTATION (Vocal Glenn and Carol Kenyon)	2	21 MAY 83	VIRGIN
	COME LIVE WITH ME	5	30 JUL 83	VIRGIN

BOBBY HEBB

Black Nashville born singer/songwriter appeared on the Grand Ole Opry when only 12. He dueted with Sylvia ('Pillow Talk') Robinson in the early 60s and recorded as Bobby & Sylvia. He wrote his big hit in 63 after the violent deaths of his brother Hal (who was in 50s group The Marigolds) and President Kennedy. He also wrote the Grammy winning 'A Natural Man' for Lou Rawls.

	SUNNY (UK No. 12) (Also cut 'My Pretty Sunshine' and 'Sunny 76')	2	20 AUG 66	PHILIPS

HEDGEHOPPERS ANONYMOUS

Quartet formed by RAF ground staff at Leighton Buzzard (UK), which included Leslie Dash, and who were originally called The Trendsetters. They had a one-off hit with a Jonathan King production but the follow up 'Please Don't Hurt Your Heart For Me' and their numerous other records failed to chart.

	IT'S GOOD NEWS WEEK (US No. 48)	5	06 NOV 65	DECCA

HEINZ

Heinz Burt, the bass player on the Transatlantic No. 1 'Telstar' by The Tornados, went solo in 63. His second release, a tribute to Eddie Cochran written and produced by Joe Meek, was the first of four UK Top 40s. He re-appeared on Cargo records in 81.

	JUST LIKE EDDIE	8	06 SEP 63	DECCA

HELLO

Photogenic London teeny bop quartet who included singer Bob Bradbury and Keith Marshall. They were proteges of hit writer Russ Ballard who penned their first unsuccessful releases and the last of their two UK hits (A US hit later when covered by Ace Frehley). Keith later had a UK solo No.12 with 'Only Crying'.

	TELL HIM (Exciters 62 US hit)	6	07 DEC 74	BELL
	NEW YORK GROOVE	9	15 NOV 75	BELL

JIMMY HELMS

Florida born singer recorded on Scottie in 59 and later on Symbol, Decca, Date, Capitol and his own label Oracle. He was a regular on the Merv Griffin Show in 68 and appeared in the musical Hair. He moved to the UK and had a UK hit. He was on Pye in 75.

 GONNA MAKE YOU AN OFFER YOU CAN'T REFUSE 8 17 MAR 73 CUBE

JOE HENDERSON

Born in Mississippi, he had two R&B entries 'Baby Don't Leave Me' and this US Top 40 hit. He had a style similar to Brook Benton and later recorded for Kapp in 64 and Ric in 65, and died in 66.

 SNAP YOUR FINGERS 8 07 JUL 62 TODD

JIMI HENDRIX EXPERIENCE

Seattle born singer/writer and guitarist was one of the most in-fluential artists of the rock era. He started playing with acts like Little Richard and The Isley Brothers and his first group was billed Jimmy James & The Blue Flames. He moved to the UK to get the break he needed and in total had 10 US and 11 UK Top 20 LPs. Jimi was a master showman who starred at the Monterey, Wood-stock and Isle of Wight festivals and tragically died in 70.

HEY JOE	6	04 FEB 67	POLYDOR
PURPLE HAZE (US No. 65)	3	06 MAY 67	TRACK
THE WIND CRIES MARY	6	03 JUN 67	TRACK
ALL ALONG THE WATCHTOWER (Bob Dylan song)	5	30 NOV 68	TRACK
(US No. 20 – Oddly only US Top 40 single)			
VOODOO CHILE	1(1)	21 NOV 70	TRACK

DON HENLEY

Texas born drummer, vocalist and composer had his own group Shiloh before joining Linda Ronstadt's backing group in 71 and then forming the multi-platinum group The Eagles. He went solo in 81 and has had a string of mainly US hits since then.

LEATHER & LACE (With STEVIE NICKS)	6	23 JAN 82	MODERN
DIRTY LAUNDRY (UK No. 59)	3	08 JAN 83	ASYLUM
THE BOYS OF SUMMER (UK No. 12)	5	09 FEB 85	GEFFEN
ALL SHE WANTS TO DO IS DANCE	9	04 MAY 85	GEFFEN
THE END OF THE INNOCENCE (UK No. 48)	6	26 AUG 89	GEFFEN

CLARENCE 'FROGMAN' HENRY

R&B singer and pianist was born in Louisiana and was in Bobby Mitchell's New Orleans band in 55. He got his nickname from his frog impression on his first hit 'Ain't Got No Home' (US 20 in 56). He was also on Parrot, Dial, Roulette, and UK label Rockney in 83 and he still regularly performs.

BUT I DO	3	16 JUN 61	PYE INT
YOU ALWAYS HURT THE ONE YOU LOVE	6	28 JUL 61	PYE INT.
(US No. 12 – Mills Brothers 44 hit)			
BUT I DO	4	24 APR 61	ARGO

HERD

UK group started as a vehicle for Ken Howard and Alan Blaikley's (of Honeycombs and Dave Dee fame) songs and became one of the UK's top teeny bop acts of the time. Quartet included Peter Frampton, who joined at 16, and Andy Bown. Peter – 'The Face of 68' – left in 69 and went on to even more acclaim in the 70s.

FROM THE UNDERWORLD	6	04 NOV 67	FONTANA
I DON'T WANT OUR LOVING TO DIE	5	11 MAY 68	FONTANA

Also see Peter Frampton/Humble Pie

HERMAN'S HERMITS

Manchester group fronted by Peter Noone (ex-Heartbeats) are one of the all time most popular UK acts in the US. The group had 14 US Top 20 singles and 17 in the UK (often with different tracks) and six Top 20 US LPs and two in the UK. They sold over 40 million records, made several films, then split in 71. They have played many revival shows and Peter, who has since made many solo records, hosted the US TV show My Generation in 89.

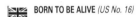

I'M INTO SOMETHING GOOD (US No. 13)	1(2)	25 SEP 64	COLUMBIA
(Earl-Jean 64 US hit – Peter re-did it in 89 on Cypress)			
SILHOUETTES (Rays 57 US hit)	3	13 MAR 65	COLUMBIA
WONDERFUL WORLD (Sam Cooke 60 hit)	7	22 MAY 65	COLUMBIA
A MUST TO AVOID (From the film 'Hold On')	6	29 JAN 66	COLUMBIA
NO MILK TODAY (US No. 35)	7	05 NOV 66	COLUMBIA
THERE'S A KIND OF HUSH	7	18 MAR 67	COLUMBIA
SUNSHINE GIRL	8	17 AUG 68	COLUMBIA
SOMETHING'S HAPPENING	6	18 JAN 69	COLUMBIA
MY SENTIMENTAL FRIEND	2	17 MAY 69	COLUMBIA
YEARS MAY COME, YEARS MAY GO	8	07 MAR 70	COLUMBIA

CAN'T YOU HEAR MY HEARTBEAT	2	27 MAR 65	MGM
MRS. BROWN YOU'VE GOT A LOVELY DAUGHTER	1(3)	01 MAY 65	MGM
(Orig.Tom Courtenay – This not released in UK – Entered US chart No. 12 & No. 1 in 3 weeks – recd. in 10 mins)			
SILHOUETTES	5	15 MAY 65	MGM
WONDERFUL WORLD (Act had 3 in Top 20 at time)	4	10 JUL 65	MGM
I'M HENRY VIII I AM	1(1)	07 AUG 65	MGM
(Old UK music hall song – this not released in UK)			
JUST A LITTLE BIT BETTER (UK No. 15)	7	16 OCT 65	MGM
A MUST TO AVOID	8	22 JAN 66	MGM
LISTEN PEOPLE	3	12 MAR 66	MGM
LEANING ON THE LAMP POST	9	07 MAY 66	MGM
(Orig. George Formby – from the film 'Hold On')			
DANDY	5	05 NOV 66	MGM
THERE'S A KIND OF HUSH	4	25 MAR 67	MGM

PATRICK HERNANDEZ

French singer, whose backing vocalists once included Madonna, was in many rock groups before making this disco classic with his own com-position. He also recorded on Recorded Delivery in 81.

BORN TO BE ALIVE (US No. 16) 10 11 AUG 79 GEM

HI TENSION

London based octet fronted by David Joseph. They were forerunners of the Brit funk movement and scored two UK-only Top 20s, the first being another of their songs 'Hi Tension' (13). Act were later on EMI and Streetwave and David had two solo UK Top 40 hits.

BRITISH HUSTLE/PEACE ON EARTH 8 16 SEP 78 ISLAND

BERTIE HIGGINS

Singer/songwriter and drummer from Florida who worked with Tommy Roe's group The Roemans between 64-66. His big US-only hit was inspired by the Humphrey Bogart film of the same name. He was on CBS in 85 and made the country charts in 88 on Southern Tracks.

KEY LARGO (UK No. 60) 8 17 APR 82 KAT FAMILY

HIGHWAYMEN

Folk quintet, who sang in four languages, were led by Dave Fisher and were formed at the Wesleyan University in Connecticut. They had five US hits including 'Cottonfields' (No. 13). Act decided to concentrate on their studies rather than stay in music.

 MICHAEL 1(1) 06 OCT 61 HMV
(Old slave song – they revived it again in 65)

 MICHAEL 1(2) 04 SEP 61 UA
(Voted top record of 61 by US DJs)

BENNY HILL

A top UK TV star since the 50's, and a well known British funny man in the US. He has made films and has had four UK-only Top 40s.

 ERNIE (THE FASTEST MILK MAN IN THE WEST)   1(4)   11 DEC 71   COLUMBIA

CHRIS HILL

Top UK club DJ and record company executive. He was the first UK act to 'do a Dickie Goodman' i.e. using segments of other records linked together by a story and like Goodman he used an Xmas theme.

 RENTA SANTA   10   27 DEC 75   PHILIPS
BIONIC SANTA   10   25 DEC 76   PHILIPS

DAN HILL

Singer/songwriter from Toronto first charted in 76 with 'Growin' Up' (US 67) and had two US Top 10's a decade apart.

 SOMETIMES WHEN WE TOUCH   3   04 MAR 78   20TH CENTURY
(UK No. 46 – co-written with Barry Mann)
CAN'T WE TRY (Duet with VONDA SHEPPARD)   6   12 SEP 87   COLUMBIA

VINCE HILL

UK MOR singer was a member of The Raindrops in the 50s and did countless radio sessions before first charting in 62. He has had a further 10 chart entries including three UK-only Top 20s; the others being 'Roses of Picardy' (13) and 'Look Around' (12). He was also on Piccadilly, Ember, Celebrity and Multi Media. He is still a popular cabaret performer.

 EDELWEISS (From 'The Sound of Music')   2   25 MAR 67   COLUMBIA

AL HIRT

Top selling New Orleans trumpeter who played in a lot of big bands like Tommy & Jimmy Dorsey's in the late 40s. He recorded for Audio Fidelity in the mid 50s and joined RCA in 60. In the 60's he notched up 18 US-only chart LPs including nine Top 40s.

 JAVA (Song named after a racehorse)   4   29 FEB 64   RCA

RON HOLDEN

Singer/song writer from Seattle, played with The Thunderbirds who backed him on his one-off US-only hit and the follow up 'Gee But I'm Lonesome'. He also recorded on Rampart, Challenge, Baronet, Eldo and Now. He still works oldies shows on the West Coast.

 LOVE YOU SO   7   13 JUN 60   DONNA

MICHAEL HOLLIDAY

Dublin born singer who had a style similar to Bing Crosby, made his stage debut at Radio City in New York. The first of his UK-only hits was 'Nothin' To Do' (20) in 56. Most of his 11 charters were covers of US hits. He committed suicide in 63.

 THE STORY OF MY LIFE   1(2)   14 FEB 58   COLUMBIA
STAIRWAY OF LOVE   3   13 JUN 58   COLUMBIA
(Above two both Marty Robbins US hits)
STARRY EYED (Gary Stites 59 US hit)   1(1)   29 JAN 60   COLUMBIA

HOLLIES

Manchester group, known for their distinctive harmonies, were one of the most successful and influential acts of the 60s. Formed by Allen Clarke and Graham Nash who both started in the Two Teens, The Fourtones and The Deltas. US hits came after they stopped releasing cover versions. Graham left in 68 to form Crosby, Stills & Nash and Allen left in 71 and rejoined in 73. The original group returned briefly in 83 and had a UK No. 1 in 88.

STAY (Maurice Williams 61 hit)   8   01 FEB 64   PARLOPHONE
JUST ONE LOOK (US No. 98 – Doris Troy 63 US hit)   2   28 MAR 64   PARLOPHONE
HERE I GO AGAIN   4   20 JUN 64   PARLOPHONE
WE'RE THROUGH   7   31 OCT 64   PARLOPHONE
YES I WILL   9   20 MAR 65   PARLOPHONE
I'M ALIVE   1(3)   26 JUN 65   PARLOPHONE
LOOK THROUGH ANY WINDOW (US No. 32)   4   02 OCT 65   PARLOPHONE
I CAN'T LET GO (US No. 42)   2   19 MAR 66   PARLOPHONE
BUS STOP   5   16 JUL 66   PARLOPHONE
STOP STOP STOP   2   05 NOV 66   PARLOPHONE
ON A CAROUSEL (US No. 11)   4   18 MAR 67   PARLOPHONE
CARRIE-ANNE   3   24 JUN 67   PARLOPHONE
JENNIFER ECCLES (US No. 40)   7   20 APR 68   PARLOPHONE
SORRY SUZANNE (US No. 56)   3   05 APR 69   PARLOPHONE
HE AIN'T HEAVY, HE'S MY BROTHER   3   01 NOV 69   PARLOPHONE
(Previously recorded by Kelly Gordon and Joe Cocker)
I CAN'T TELL THE BOTTOM FROM THE TOP   7   16 MAY 70   PARLOPHONE
(US No. 82 – Elton John on keyboards)
THE AIR THAT I BREATHE   2   23 MAR 74   POLYDOR
HE AIN'T HEAVY, HE'S MY BROTHER   1(1)   24 SEP 88   EMI
(Their span of No. 1's covers 23 years – a record)

BUS STOP   5   17 SEP 66   IMPERIAL
STOP STOP STOP   7   10 DEC 66   IMPERIAL
CARRIE-ANN   9   12 AUG 67   EPIC
HE AIN'T HEAVY, HE'S MY BROTHER   7   21 MAR 70   EPIC
(Piano on track played by Elton John)
LONG COOL WOMAN (IN A BLACK DRESS)   2   02 SEP 72   EPIC
(UK No. 32)
THE AIR THAT I BREATHE   6   03 AUG 74   EPIC
(Written by Albert Hammond)

BUDDY HOLLY

Born Charles Holley in Lubbock Texas, he is one of the greats of rock music and one of its best respected singer/songwriters. Oddly, this R'n'R Hall of Fame member had less US chart success than you might think and each of his singles (solo and with The Crickets) peaked lower than the last on the UK & US charts until his untimely death in 59. This unique artist has influenced many acts and his songs and records are still heard worldwide.

PEGGY SUE (Originally called 'Cindy Lou')   6   17 JAN 58   CORAL
RAVE ON (US No.41 – Original by Sonny West)   5   01 AUG 58   CORAL
IT DOESN'T MATTER ANYMORE   1(3)   24 APR 59   CORAL
(US No. 13 – written by Paul Anka)
BROWN EYED HANDSOME MAN   3   19 APR 63   CORAL
(Chuck Berry 56 R&B hit)
BO DIDDLEY (Bo Diddley 55 R&B hit)   8   05 JUL 63   CORAL
PEGGY SUE   3   30 DEC 57   CORAL

Also see The Crickets

HOLLYWOOD ARGYLES

Act had a one-off US-only smash, masterminded and sung by Gary Paxton. He had previously hit as Flip of Skip & Flip, and also recorded on London, Liberty, Garpax, Brent, Rori, Capitol, MGM, Time, California, Felsted, Rev, RCA and Private Stock. The group whose follow up was 'Gun Tottin' Critter Called Jack' also recorded on Felsted, Paxley, Chattahoochie, Bakersfield Centennial, Kammy and Finer Arts.

 ALLEZ-OOP   1(1)   11 JUL 60   LUTE
(Gary later cut 'Allez-Oop was a Two Dab Man')

83

HOLLYWOOD BEYOND

Birmingham (UK) group fronted by Mark Rogers mixed funk/rock/jazz and pop. They had two UK-only hits, the other being the follow up 'No More Tears' (47). They recorded on Warriors Dance in 89 and Mark re-appeared in 90 on the US label Freetown.

 WHAT'S THE COLOUR OF MONEY?   7   02 AUG 86   WEA
(Backing vocalists include Mica Paris)

EDDIE HOLMAN

Soul singer from Virginia who had an unmistakable falsetto style. He recorded on Leopard in 62 and Ascot in 63 and first charted with 'This Can't Be True' on Parkway in 66. He joined Bell in 67 and later recorded on Silver Blue in 74 and Salsoul in 76.

 HEY THERE LONELY GIRL   4   16 NOV 74   ABC
(Hit US 4 years prior- Orig. Ruby & The Romantics)

HEY THERE LONELY GIRL   2   21 FEB 70   ABC

CLINT HOLMES

Born in Bournemouth (UK) this singer grew up in New York and was a one time protege of Dionne Warwick. His one-off US-only hit, which featured his producer Paul Vance's son Philip, took a year to chart. He later recorded on Atlantic and Private Stock.

 PLAYGROUND IN MY MIND   2   16 JUN 73   EPIC

RUPERT HOLMES

Cheshire (UK) born singer/writer/producer/arranger has worked with acts like Barbra Streisand, Gene Pitney, Drifters, Sparks, Strawbs and Sailor and his songs have been recorded by numerous top acts. He was in hit act the Cufflinks and was on Epic in 73 and had the first of six US chart records on Private Stock in 78.

ESCAPE (THE PINA COLADA SONG) *(UK No. 23)*   1(2)   22 DEC 79   INFINITY
HIM *(UK No. 31)*   6   29 MAR 80   MCA

JOHN HOLT

Jamaican reggae singer and composer who wrote hits like 'The Tide Is High' (Blondie) which was first recorded by his group The Paragons and 'O.K. Fred' (Erroll Dunkley). He has also recorded on over two dozen labels including Greensleeves, Jackpot, Ackee, Hoss, Natty Congo, Black Joy, Arts & Crafts and Basket.

 HELP ME MAKE IT THROUGH THE NIGHT   6   25 JAN 75   TROJAN
(Kris Kristofferson song – Sammi Smith 71 US hit)

HONDELLS

Group fronted by Richie Burns were named after a TV advert for Honda which they sang. They had two more US-only chart records including the follow up 'My Buddy Seat' and were on Amos in 69.

 LITTLE HONDA *(Written by Brian Wilson)*   9   31 OCT 64   MERCURY

HONEYBUS

UK foursome were a vehicle for singer Pete Dello (Blumson) who wrote their one-off UK hit which was their third release on Deram. The follow up was 'Girl Of Independent Means'. Pete quickly quit and the group folded but re-appeared on Warner in 73. The song is well known in the UK as the Nimble bread jingle.

 I CAN'T LET MAGGIE GO   8   27 APR 68   DERAM

HONEYCOMBS

UK quintet were originally called the Sherabons and were re-named after their female drummer Ann 'Honey' Lantree. Lead vocalist was Londoner Dennis D'Ell (Dalziel). They had two UK Top 20s, the other being 'That's The Way' (12). Dennis went solo in 67.

 HAVE I THE RIGHT?   1(2)   29 AUG 64   PYE

HAVE I THE RIGHT?   5   14 NOV 64   INTERPHON

HONEY CONE

Edna Wright (aka Sandy Wynns), Shellie Clark (ex-Ikettes) and Carolyn Willis (ex-Bob B. Soxx & The Blue Jeans) all had a lot of experience before singing together for Holland, Dozier & Holland's label Hot Wax and chalking up four US-only Top 40s.

 WANT ADS *(First cut by Glasshouse)*   1(1)   12 JUN 71   HOT WAX
(Co-written Norman Johnson (Chairmen of the Board)

HONEYDRIPPERS

Supergroup comprised Robert Plant, Jeff Beck, Nile Rodgers and Jimmy Page who came together for one LP project performing old rock'n'roll songs. The LP hit No.4 in the US and 56 in the UK.

SEA OF LOVE *(UK No. 56 – Phil Phillips 59 Hit)*   3   05 JAN 85   ES PARANZA

MARY HOPKIN

Welsh folk singer, who first recorded in Welsh on Cambrian, was spotted by Twiggy on UK TV show Opportunity Knocks and with help from Paul McCartney she had five UK (2 US) Top 20s. She later recorded as Hobby Horse (Bell) and in Sundance (Bronze) and Oasis (WEA) as well as on Regal Zonophone, Good Earth, RCA and in 89 Trax.

THOSE WERE THE DAYS   1(6)   28 SEP 68   APPLE
(Entered at No.7 – original Russian folk song)
GOODBYE *(US No. 13)*   2   19 APR 69   APPLE
TEMMA HARBOUR *(US No. 39)*   6   21 FEB 70   APPLE
KNOCK KNOCK WHO'S THERE   2   04 APR 70   APPLE
(US No. 92 – Eurovision entry – entered at No. 7)

THOSE WERE THE DAYS   2   02 NOV 68   APPLE
(First English lyric version by The Limeliters)

BRUCE HORNSBY & THE RANGE

Virginia born singer/writer's quartet had their first Top 20 in the UK but were soon more popular in their homeland. Their LP 'The Way It Is' peaked at No. 3 in the US (26 UK) and their second 'Scenes From The Southside' peaked at 5 in the US (18 UK).

THE WAY IT IS *(UK No.15)*   1(1)   13 DEC 86   RCA
MANDOLIN RAIN *(UK No. 70)*   4   21 MAR 87   RCA
(They were Top Adult Contemporary act of 87 in US)
THE VALLEY ROAD *(UK No. 44)*   5   02 JUL 88   RCA

JOHNNY HORTON

Texan country singer recorded for Cormac and Abbott in 51, Mercury in 52 and Dot, before having his first of 12 country hits. He was a regular on the Louisiana Hayride from 51-58. He died in a car crash in 60 – as did his wife's first husband Hank Williams when returning from the same Texas night club in 53.

THE BATTLE OF NEW ORLEANS   1(2)   01 JUN 59   COLUMBIA
(UK No. 16 – originally by Jimmy Driftwood)
SINK THE BISMARCK   3   25 APR 60   COLUMBIA
NORTH TO ALASKA *(UK No. 21 – from the film)*   4   19 DEC 60   COLUMBIA

HOT

The L.A. based mixed race duo Sugar & Spice (Gwen Owens and Cathy Carson) plus Juanita Curiel, became Hot in 76. The trio followed their sole US-only Top 40 with 'Just Cause I'm Guilty'.

 ANGEL IN YOUR ARMS   6   16 JUL 77   BIG TREE

HOT BUTTER

Moog player Stan Free, who had also played with The Boston Pops, starred on this hit which was masterminded by producers Steve & Bill Jerome and Danny Jordan (ex-Detergents). They later revived 'Percolator' – the Billie Joe Hunter track which it resembled.

POPCORN   5   19 AUG 72   PYE INT.
POPCORN   9   21 OCT 72   MUSICOR

HOT CHOCOLATE

Formed in Brixton (UK) in 69 they first recorded as the Hot Chocolate Band on Apple. Members Errol Brown and Tony Wilson wrote not only their hits but also hits for Mary Hopkin and Herman's Hermits. They had a staggering string of UK successes with 32 hits in a 17 year period. They split in 87, the year their 'Greatest Hits' LP was a UK No.1, and Erroll went solo.

LOVE IS LIFE   6   19 SEP 70   RAK
I BELIEVE (IN LOVE)   8   18 SEP 71   RAK
BROTHER LOUIE *(Covered by The Stories in US)*   7   12 MAY 73   RAK
EMMA   3   06 APR 74   RAK
A CHILD'S PRAYER   7   13 SEP 75   RAK
YOU SEXY THING   2   29 NOV 75   RAK
SO YOU WIN AGAIN *(US No. 31)*   1(3)   02 JUL 77   RAK
PUT YOUR LOVE IN ME   10   24 DEC 77   RAK
NO DOUBT ABOUT IT   2   24 MAY 80   RAK
GIRL CRAZY   7   22 MAY 82   RAK
IT STARTED WITH A KISS   5   07 AUG 82   RAK
WHAT KINDA BOY YOU LOOKING FOR (GIRL)   10   28 MAY 83   RAK
YOU SEXY THING *(REMIX)*   10   14 FEB 87   EMI

 EMMA   8   26 APR 75   BIG TREE
YOU SEXY THING   3   07 FEB 76   BIG TREE
EVERY I'S A WINNER *(UK No. 12)*   6   10 FEB 79   INFINITY

HOT GOSSIP – SEE SARAH BRIGHTMAN FOR HIT DETAILS

HOTLEGS

Ex Mindbender Eric Stewart with Kevin Godley and Lol Creme formed this short lived act (3 singles and 1 LP) whose African sounding debut sold over two million. Shortly after they started 10cc.

NEANDERTHAL MAN *(US No. 22)*   2   15 AUG 70   FONTANA

HOTSHOTS

UK reggae group had a one-off UK charter with a revival of the Royal Guardsmen's old transatlantic hit.

SNOOPY VS. THE RED BARON   4   14 JUL 73   MOONCREST

HOUSEMARTINS

Billed as 'The fourth best band in Hull' this quartet included Paul Heaton and Norman Cook. Their first single 'Flag Day' in 85 failed but they were voted 'Best Newcomers of 87' and managed eight UK-only chart records before splitting in 88. Paul then formed Beautiful South with recent Housemartin Dave Hemmingway and Norman had a UK No. 1 in 90 as producer of Beats International.

 HAPPY HOUR   3   28 JUN 86   GO! DISCS
CARAVAN OF LOVE   1(1)   20 DEC 86   GO! DISCS
(Isley, Jasper & Isley 85 US hit)

HOUSE MASTER BOYZ & THE RUDE BOY OF HOUSE

A one-off UK-only hit with a complex story behind it. Track is a Chicago house number covered by Farley 'Jackmaster' Funk (who once recorded as Rude Boy Farley Keith). The track was then altered a lot by UK duo the House Engineers before its release. To top it all, an unconnected UK trio appeared to promote the record.

 HOUSE NATION   8   03 OCT 87   MAGNETIC DAN

THELMA HOUSTON

Singer and actress from Mississippi recorded on Capitol in 67 and had her first hit 'Save The Country' on Dunhill in 70. She joined Tamla in 76 and was later on RCA and MCA.

DON'T LEAVE ME THIS WAY *(UK No. 13)*   1(1)   23 APR 77   TAMLA

WHITNEY HOUSTON

Record breaking, award winning daughter of soul singer Cissy Houston and cousin of Dionne Warwick. She started in a gospel group at 11 and was singing on records by Chaka Khan and Lou Rawls by 15. She had a record seven US No. 1s in a row and sold a total of over 25 million of her first two LPs. She is the only woman to enter the US LP chart at No. 1 (with 'Whitney') and the only US female to sell a million of her first two LPs in the UK.

SAVING ALL MY LOVE FOR YOU   1(2)   14 DEC 85   ARISTA
(Originally by Marilyn McCoo & Billy Davis Jr.)
HOW WILL I KNOW *(Written for Janet Jackson)*   5   22 FEB 86   ARISTA
GREATEST LOVE OF ALL *(Orig. George Benson)*   8   17 MAY 86   ARISTA
(Was 'B' side of 'Someone For Me' her first single)
I WANNA DANCE WITH SOMEBODY
(WHO LOVES ME)   1(2)   06 JUN 87   ARISTA
SO EMOTIONAL   5   28 NOV 87   ARISTA
LOVE WILL SAVE THE DAY   10   04 JUN 88   ARISTA
ONE MOMENT IN TIME   1(2)   15 OCT 88   ARISTA
(Co-written by Albert Hammond – The US Olympic theme)

YOU GIVE GOOD LOVE   3   27 JUL 85   ARISTA
('B' side was 'Greatest Love of All')
SAVING ALL MY LOVE FOR YOU   1(1)   26 OCT 85   ARISTA
HOW WILL I KNOW   1(2)   15 FEB 86   ARISTA
(It replaced her cousin Dionne at top of chart)
GREATEST LOVE OF ALL   1(3)   17 MAY 86   ARISTA
(Composer Linda Creed died as record climbed chart)
I WANNA DANCE WITH SOMEBODY
(WHO LOVES ME)   1(2)   27 JUN 87   ARISTA
(Composed by the duo Boy Meets Girl)
DIDN'T WE ALMOST HAVE IT ALL *(UK No. 14)*   1(2)   26 SEP 87   ARISTA
SO EMOTIONAL   1(1)   09 JAN 88   ARISTA
(Producer Narada M. Walden's 4th No. 1 in 9 months)
WHERE DO BROKEN HEARTS GO   1(2)   23 APR 88   ARISTA
(UK No. 14 - Her 7th successive No. 1 in US)
LOVE WILL SAVE THE DAY   9   27 AUG 88   ARISTA
ONE MOMENT IN TIME   5   12 NOV 88   ARISTA

BILLY HOWARD

UK comic had a one-off UK-only hit with his self produced parody of Roger Miller's 'King Of The Road', which included his impressions of various TV cops. Follow up was 'The Disco Cops'.

KING OF THE COPS   6   24 JAN 76   PENNY F.

ROBERT HOWARD & KYM MAZELLE

Dr. Robert of the Blow Monkeys originally recorded this track with Sam Brown but the version that was released featured Kym Mazelle. Kym, a one-time neighbour of the Jacksons in Gary, Indiana, recorded as a soloist on Republic and EMI's Syncopate label.

WAIT   7   11 FEB 89   RCA

Also see Blow Monkeys

HUDSON-FORD

Richard Hudson and John Ford started together in the Velvet Opera before joining The Strawbs in 69. They wrote that group's big hit 'Part Of The Union' and left in 73. They had four UK-only Top 40s as a duo, one being under the name The Monks.

 PICK UP THE PIECES   8   15 SEP 73   A&M

Also see The Monks/The Strawbs

HUE & CRY

Brothers Pat and Greg Kane from Glasgow were on Stampede in 86 and their first single was 'Here Comes Everybody'. They have had two UK-only Top 20s – the other being 'Looking For Linda' (15).

 LABOUR OF LOVE   6   08 AUG 87   CIRCA

HUES CORPORATION

Mixed trio named after millionaire recluse Howard Hughes' corporation were forced to change their spelling after their first releases on Liberty in 70. Tommy Brown (ex-Just Us) sang lead on their big hit and left to go solo shortly after, being replaced by Karl Russell. They were later on Warner/Curb and Polydor.

 ROCK THE BOAT   6   17 AUG 74   RCA
ROCK THE BOAT   1(1)   06 JUL 74   RCA

HUMAN BEINZ

Cleveland rock band who specialised in reviving R&B oldies and had two US-only hits, the other being a version of Bobby Bland's 'Turn On Your Love Light'.

NOBODY BUT ME *(Originally by Isley Brothers)*   8   03 FEB 68   CAPITOL

HUMAN LEAGUE

Sheffield (UK) group formed in 77 by synth players Martin Ware and Ian Marsh (ex-Dead Daughters and The Future). They debuted with 'Being Boiled' on Fast products in 78. They were the first of the UK synth bands to score in the US. Martin and Ian left to form B.E.F., which became Heaven 17, and singer Phil Oakey and the group later recorded their last big hits with producers Jam & Lewis.

LOVE ACTION (I BELIEVE IN LOVE)	3	22 AUG 81	VIRGIN
OPEN YOUR HEART	6	17 OCT 81	VIRGIN
DON'T YOU WANT ME *(UK Million seller)*	1(4)	12 DEC 81	VIRGIN
BEIN' BOILED *(Re-recording of 1st single)*	6	30 JAN 82	VIRGIN
MIRROR MAN *(US No. 30 – Entered at No. 9)*	2	04 DEC 82	VIRGIN
(KEEP FEELING) FASCINATION	2	14 MAY 83	VIRGIN
HUMAN	8	06 SEP 86	VIRGIN
DON'T YOU WANT ME	1(3)	19 JUN 82	A&M
(KEEP FEELING) FASCINATION	8	20 AUG 83	A&M
HUMAN *(Jam & Lewis' 6th Top 10 of the year)*	1(1)	22 NOV 86	A&M

Also see Heaven 17

HUMBLE PIE

Fronted by leaders of two of the UKs top bands, Peter Frampton (ex Herd) and Steve Marriot (ex Small Faces), their sales in the UK were disappointing. However, in the US where the singers were unknown, the group were more successful and had 9 chart LPs. Peter left in 71 and the group broke up in 75, re-uniting briefly in 80.

 NATURAL BORN BUGIE   4   13 SEP 69   IMMEDIATE

Also see Peter Frampton/Herd/Small Faces

ENGELBERT HUMPERDINCK

Born Gerry Dorsey in Madras, India, he recorded under his own name on Decca in 58 and Pye in 64. Like Tom Jones, with whom he shared a manager, he scored on both sides of the Atlantic with country-orientated MOR songs, had his own TV series, was big in Vegas and recorded for the country market when his pop sales slowed down. He is currently (90) a very big LP seller in Germany. His first UK hit prevented The Beatles' 'Penny Lane/Strawberry Fields Forever' from becoming their 13th consecutive No. 1.

RELEASE ME (AND LET ME LOVE AGAIN) *(UK Gold – He had the 3 top records in the UK in 67)*	1(6)	04 MAR 67	DECCA
THERE GOES MY EVERYTHING *(US No. 20)* *(US No. 20 – Jack Greene 66 country hit)*	2	17 JUN 67	DECCA
THE LAST WALTZ *(US No. 25 – UK Gold)*	1(5)	09 SEP 67	DECCA
AM I THAT EASY TO FORGET *(US No. 18)* *(Carl Belew 59 country hit)*	3	27 JAN 68	DECCA
A MAN WITHOUT LOVE *(US No. 19)*	2	18 MAY 68	DECCA
LES BICYCLETTES DE BELSIZE *(US No. 31)*	5	26 OCT 68	DECCA
THE WAY IT USED TO BE *(US No. 42)*	3	15 MAR 69	DECCA
WINTER WORLD OF LOVE *(US No. 16)*	7	13 DEC 69	DECCA
RELEASE ME (AND LET ME LOVE AGAIN) *(Ray Price 54 country hit)*	4	27 MAY 67	PARROT
AFTER THE LOVIN' *(No. 40 country hit)*	8	22 JAN 77	EPIC

STEVE 'SILK' HURLEY

Influential Chicago House music star refused to promote the first house No. 1 as he claimed he would receive no money for it as he was now in the RCA act J.M. Silk. Oddly this UK smash never hit in his homeland. The 12" was 26 minutes long which should have disqualified it from the UK singles chart!

 JACK YOUR BODY   1(2)   24 JAN 87   DJ INT.
(Was first out April 86 – 12" has four mixes)

BRIAN HYLAND

Singer from Queens, New York, had his own group The Delphis when he was only 12 and topped the US chart with his second release (the first 'Rosemary' flopped) before he was 17. In all he had 22 US chart entries and seven in the UK over a period of 15 years.

ITSY BITSY TEENIE WEENIE YELLOW POLKA DOT BIKINI *(About two year old Paula Vance)*	10	05 AUG 60	LONDON
GINNY COME LATELY *(US No. 21)*	5	08 JUN 62	HMV
SEALED WITH A KISS	5	07 SEP 62	HMV
SEALED WITH A KISS *(Returned to Top 10)*	7	02 AUG 75	ABC
ITSY BITSY TEENIE WEENIE YELLOW POLKA DOT BIKINI	1(1)	08 AUG 60	LEADER
SEALED WITH A KISS	3	28 JUL 62	ABC PAR.
GYPSY WOMAN *(UK No. 42)* *(Produced by Del Shannon – Impressions 61 US hit)*	3	05 DEC 70	UNI

JANIS IAN

Born Janis Fink in New York, this singer/songwriter started with Elektra and first charted on Verve with 'Society's Child' (14 US) in 67, which was released a year before when she was only 15. She has had eight US-only chart LPs including the No. 1 'Between The Lines' but never made the UK Top 40. She was also on Capitol in 71 and Polydor where she re-recorded 'Society's Child' in 75.

AT SEVENTEEN		3	13 SEP 75	COLUMBIA
(Grammy winner as 'Best Female Vocal of 75')				

ICEHOUSE

Four-man Australian rock group fronted by Iva Davies. The group who were originally called Flowers first charted in the US in 81 and scored two US Top 20s – the first being 'Crazy' (14) in 88. Their biggest UK hit was in 83 with 'Hey Little Girl' (UK 17).

ELECTRIC BLUE *(UK No. 53)*		7	21 MAY 88	CHRYSALIS

IDES OF MARCH

Seven-man group from Chicago were fronted by singer/songwriter James Peterik. Their first single 'You Wouldn't Listen' on Parrot made No. 42 in the US in 66 and their eighth single gave them their biggest hit. After a failed comeback in the 70s Jim formed Survivor, who scored a string of hits in the 80s.

VEHICLE *(UK No. 31)*		2	23 MAY 70	WARNER

Also see Survivor

BILLY IDOL

Born William Broad in Middlesex (UK) he formed one of the pioneer punk bands Chelsea, which evolved into the UK hit act Generation X. In 81 after seven singles the band broke up and he relocated to New York. He has been a regular transatlantic chart entrant since then, quite often with updates of his older recordings.

WHITE WEDDING		6	10 AUG 85	CHRYSALIS
(US No. 36 – He originally released this song in 82)				
REBEL YELL *(US No. 46)*		6	12 OCT 85	CHRYSALIS
(US No. 46 – he originally released the song in 84)				
MONY MONY		7	31 OCT 87	CHRYSALIS
(He originally released the song in 81)				
EYES WITHOUT A FACE *(UK No. 18)*		4	14 JUL 84	CHRYSALIS
TO BE A LOVER *(UK No. 22 – Orig. Willam Bell)*		6	20 DEC 86	CHRYSALIS
MONY MONY *(Tommy James & Shondells 68 hit)*		1(1)	21 NOV 87	CHRYSALIS

FRANK IFIELD

Coventry (UK) born singer emigrated to Australia, where at 15 he had his own radio and TV show. He joined UK Columbia in 59 and had a few flops and small hits before striking transatlantic gold and scoring three successive UK No.1s with his yodelling 'oldies' formula. He had 14 UK Top 40s before 67 and was later on Decca in 69, MAM in 72, Spark in 75, Warner in 79 and PRT in 82.

I REMEMBER YOU *(UK Gold record)*		1 8	18 JUL 62	COLUMBIA
LOVESICK BLUES *(US No. 44)*		1(5)	09 NOV 62	COLUMBIA
(Entered at No 8 – UK Gold – Hank Williams 49 hit)				
WAYWARD WIND *(Gogi Grant 56 hit)*		1(1)	20 FEB 63	COLUMBIA
NOBODY'S DARLIN' BUT MINE		4	26 APR 63	COLUMBIA
(Johnny Sea 60 country hit)				
CONFESSIN'		1(3)	12 JUL 63	COLUMBIA
(US No. 58 – Entered at No. 10 – Guy Lombardo 30 hit)				
DON'T BLAME ME *(Ethel Waters 33 hit)*		8	15 FEB 64	COLUMBIA
I REMEMBER YOU *(Jimmy Dorsey 42 hit)*		5	13 OCT 62	VEE JAY

JULIO IGLESIAS

Madrid born singer, who had his first UK release in 70, was the first solo Spanish artist to top the UK chart. He sings in five languages, plays to packed houses everywhere and has sold over 100 million records worldwide.

BEGIN THE BEGUINE (VOLVER A EMPEZAR)		1(1)	05 DEC 81	CBS
QUIEREME MUCHO (YOURS)		3	27 MAR 82	CBS
MY LOVE *(Featuring STEVIE WONDER)*		5	03 SEP 88	CBS
(US No. 80 – was first rel. May 88 with no success)				
TO ALL THE GIRLS I'VE LOVED BEFORE *(UK No. 17)*		5	19 MAY 84	COLUMBIA
(And WILLIE NELSON – Willie's first UK hit)				

IMAGINATION

Soulful UK trio, fronted by the charismatic singer/writer Leee John, chalked up nine UK-only Top 40s in three years thanks in part to their original and slightly risque stage shows. They later recorded for RCA and their 'Instinctual' was a US dance No. 1 in 88. They had a UK Top 5 LP in 89 with a 'Greatest Hits' package.

BODY TALK		4	18 JUL 81	R&B
JUST AN ILLUSION		2	03 APR 82	R&B
MUSIC AND LIGHTS		5	03 JUL 82	R&B

IMPRESSIONS

Formed in Chicago in 57 as The Roosters, the quartet included Jerry Butler and Curtis Mayfield. Jerry left in 58 and Curtis led them in the 60s when they had an impressive 15 US Top 40s. Curtis left in 70 and the group kept charting until the late 80s by which time they'd had 50 R&B hits. In the UK they only had one hit ever 'First Impressions' which did not chart in the US.

IT'S ALL RIGHT		4	09 NOV 63	ABC-PARAMOUNT
KEEP ON PUSHING		10	18 JUL 64	ABC-PARAMOUNT
AMEN *(all these hits were written by Curtis)*		7	09 JAN 65	ABC-PARAMOUNT

Also see Curtis Mayfield

LOS INDIOS TABAJARAS

The only Brazilian Indians to chart were Lima brothers Natalicio and Antenor, who had been born in the jungle town of Ceara. They started off playing tribal folk songs and scored a one-off Transatlantic Top 10. Follow up was 'Always In My Heart'.

MARIA ELENA		7	13 DEC 63	RCA
MARIA ELENA		6	16 NOV 63	RCA

INFORMATION SOCIETY

Techno-rock foursome whose first release was 'Running' on the Minneapolis label Wide Angle in 86. The group includes songwriter and programmer Paul Robb and singer/sampler Kurt Valaquen. Their US-only charter started in New York and Miami's Latin clubs.

WHAT'S ON YOUR MIND (PURE ENERGY)		3	22 OCT 88	TOMMY BOY
WALKING AWAY		9	18 FEB 89	TOMMY BOY

JORGEN INGMANN

Jorgen Ingmann-Pederson is the most successful Danish instrumentalist of all time. The Copenhagen born guitarist just missed the US No. 1 spot with his cover of the Shadows UK chart topper. He followed it with 'Anna' (US 54).

APACHE *(Originally recorded by Bert Weedon)*		2	03 APR 61	ATCO

JAMES INGRAM

Soulful singer from Ohio has had six US Top 20 hits but oddly none of them have been solo records. James, who was in the group Revelation Funk, has scored in duets (& even once in a trio) with Quincy Jones (which won him a Grammy), Kenny Rogers, Kim Carnes, Michael McDonald, plus of course Linda Ronstadt and Patti Austin.

🇬🇧	SOMEWHERE OUT THERE *(With LINDA RONSTADT)*	8	22 AUG 87	MCA
🇺🇸	BABY COME TO ME *(With PATTI AUSTIN)* *(UK No. 11)*	1(2)	19 FEB 83	QWEST
	SOMEWHERE OUT THERE *(With LINDA RONSTADT)* *(From the film 'An American Tail')*	2	14 MAR 87	MCA

LUTHER INGRAM

Singer/composer from Tennessee recorded in the mid 60s on Decca, Smash, Hib and Atlantic before starting a run of 20 black music hits from 69 on Koko. His 12th single on that label gave him his biggest hit and it was later covered by Rod Stewart.

🇺🇸	IF LOVING YOU IS WRONG (I DON'T WANT TO BE RIGHT) *(His song was a country No. 1 in 79)*	3	05 AUG 72	KOKO

INNER CITY

US group masterminded by Detroit's Kevin Saunderson with vocals by Paris Gray, who had previously recorded solo and with House Master Baldwin on Future Sounds. They were one of the most popular acts in the UK in the late 80s, while in the US their main success has been in the clubs where they have notched up four dance No. 1s and were the most played act in 89.

🇬🇧	BIG FUN	8	24 SEP 88	10
	GOOD LIFE *(No. 73 US)*	4	07 JAN 89	10
	AIN'T NOBODY BETTER	10	29 APR 89	10
	(All these records topped the US dance chart)			

INTRUDERS

Philadelphia soul quartet which includes Sam 'Little Sonny' Brown. They recorded on Gowan in 61 and Excel in 65 before becoming the first act signed to producers Gamble & Huff's label which gave them their first million seller. They had 24 R&B hits. In the UK their biggest record was 'She's A Winner' (UK 14) – a US pop flop.

🇺🇸	COWBOYS TO GIRLS	6	18 MAY 68	GAMBLE

INXS

Formed in Sydney, Australia, in 77 and known as the Farriss Brothers until 79. They started on Deluxe, joined RCA in 81, WEA in 82 and Atlantic in 83 and had a lot of local success. The act, who are fronted by Michael Hutchence, really came to the US & UK public's attention when they appeared on 'Live Aid' in 85. Since then they have had an enviable transatlantic track record.

🇬🇧	NEED YOU TONIGHT *(7th UK chart entry – hit 10 months after US hit)*	2	26 NOV 88	MERCURY
🇺🇸	WHAT YOU NEED *(UK No. 51)*	5	12 APR 86	ATLANTIC
	NEED YOU TONIGHT	1(1)	30 JAN 88	ATLANTIC
	DEVIL INSIDE *(UK No. 47)*	2	16 APR 88	ATLANTIC
	NEW SENSATION *(UK No. 25)*	3	23 JUL 88	ATLANTIC
	NEVER TEAR US APART *(UK No. 25)* *(They won five MTV awards in 88)*	7	05 NOV 88	ATLANTIC

IRISH ROVERS

Irish born folk quintet who moved to Canada in the early 60's. The group, which includes the Millar brothers Will, George & Joe, had their own CBS TV series for six years and had two US-only Top 40's – the other being 'Wasn't That a Party' as The Rovers in 81.

🇺🇸	THE UNICORN	7	25 MAY 68	DECCA

IRON MAIDEN

Top UK heavy metal band formed in 76, with Steve Harris being the only original member left. First release was an EP on their Rock Hard label and they joined EMI in 79. In the UK group have had seven Top 5 LPs and 18 Top 40 singles. In the US they have had no single hits but the LP '7th Son Of A 7th Son' hit No. 12 in 88. Lead singer Bruce Dickinson replaced Paul Di'Anno in 81.

🇬🇧	RUN TO THE HILLS *(Seventh UK chart record)*	7	13 MAR 82	EMI
	CAN I PLAY WITH MADNESS *(Entered at No.4 – their 17th chart record)*	3	02 APR 88	EMI
	THE EVIL THAT MEN DO	5	20 AUG 88	EMI
	THE CLAIRVOYANT	6	26 NOV 88	EMI
	INFINITE DREAMS	6	25 NOV 89	EMI

BIG DEE IRWIN

Born Defosca Ervin, he fronted The Pastels, who hit with 'So Far Away' in the 50s. He recorded solo on Hull, 20th Century, Roulette, Wild Deuce, Rotate, Amy, Imperial, Phil L.A. of Soul, Cub, Fairmount and Signpost. He followed his one-off hit with 'Soul Waltzin''. He is now a top music business executive.

🇬🇧	SWINGING ON A STAR *(Featuring LITTLE EVA)* *(US No. 38 – Bing Crosby 44 hit)*	7	18 JAN 64	COLPIX

ISLEY BROTHERS

Cincinnati born trio consisted of Rudolph, Ronald and the late O'Kelly. First recorded for Teenage in 57 then on Mark X, Gone and Cindy before hitting with 'Shout' in 59 on RCA. In the early 60s they were on Atlantic, Wand, UA and T-Neck before joining Tamla. Brothers Ernie & Marvin plus Chris Jasper joined the act from 69-84. They are still adding to their 59 black music hits.

🇬🇧	THIS OLD HEART OF MINE *(US No. 12)* *(Was No. 47 (66)) – Ronald & Rod Stewart re-did (89))*	3	23 NOV 68	TAMLA MOTOWN
	BEHIND A PAINTED SMILE	5	24 MAY 69	TAMLA MOTOWN
	HARVEST FOR THE WORLD *(US No. 63)*	10	07 AUG 76	EPIC
🇺🇸	IT'S YOUR THING *(UK No. 30)* *(Grammy winner)*	2	03 MAY 69	T-NECK
	THAT LADY *(UK No. 14)* *(Orig. recorded as 'Whose That Lady'on UA in 64)*	6	06 OCT 73	T-NECK
	FIGHT THE POWER PT. 1 *(Top soul record 75)*	4	27 SEP 75	T-NECK

IT BITES

Cumbrian (UK) rock quartet fronted by Francis Dunnery first recorded in 86. Since then they have played in many parts of the world including the US, Russia and Japan and toured with Robert Plant and Jethro Tull. Their follow up was 'Whole New World'.

🇬🇧	CALLING ALL THE HEROES	6	23 AUG 86	VIRGIN

BURL IVES

Well known and well loved folk singer/actor. Born in Illinois, he started on Broadway in the 30s and had his own radio show in 44. He has written half a dozen books, won an Academy Award for his part in The Big Country, starred in the TV series The Bold Ones and has had 10 Top 40 US hits spanning from 48-62.

🇬🇧	A LITTLE BITTY TEAR	7	16 FEB 62	BRUNSWICK
🇺🇸	A LITTLE BITTY TEAR	9	10 FEB 62	DECCA
	FUNNY WAY OF LAUGHIN' *(UK No. 29)*	10	19 MAY 62	DECCA

IVY LEAGUE

Trio of UK session singers: John Carter (Shakespeare), Ken Lewis (Hawker), who had hit as Carter-Lewis, and Perry Ford (Bryan Pugh). Top session man Tony Burrows replaced John in 66 and Neil Landon replaced Ken and act evolved into the Flowerpot Men.

🇬🇧 FUNNY HOW LOVE CAN BE		8	06 MAR 65	PICCADILLY
TOSSING AND TURNING *(US No. 83)*		3	24 JUL 65	PICCADILLY

Also see The Flowerpot Men

IVY THREE

Charles Koppelman, who is one of today's very top record company executives, started out as part of this one-hit wonder act formed in Long Island in 59. They later recorded the similar 'Bagoo'.

🇺🇸 YOGI *(Based on the cartoon Yogi Bear)*	8	19 SEP 60	SHELL

J

L.L. COOL J

New York rap star first charted with 'I Can't Live Without My Radio' in 85. He has had two Top 10 US LPs 'Bigger & Deffer' and 'Walking With A Panther' and two US Top 20 singles. The other was 'I'm That Type Of Guy' (15) in 89.

🇬🇧 I NEED LOVE *(US No. 14)*		8	17 OCT 87	CBS

JACK 'N' CHILL

The UK's first instrumental house hit came from Ed Stratton, Vlad Naslas and front man Rodney, an ex dancer and model. The former two had previous success as re-mixers and as hip-hop jingle writers and performers. Their follow up was 'Beating The Heat'.

🇬🇧 THE JACK THAT HOUSE BUILT *(Was 48th in 87)*		6	13 FEB 88	OVAL

TERRY JACKS

Winnipeg born singer started in The Chessmen and had his first charter with his wife Susan in the duo The Poppy Family. He went solo in 72 and his third release, originally on the Goldfish label, sold six million copies. He was on Private Stock in 75.

🇬🇧 SEASONS IN THE SUN *(Written by Jacques Brel in 61)*		1(4)	06 APR 74	BELL
IF YOU GO AWAY *(US No. 68)*		8	20 JUL 74	BELL
🇺🇸 SEASONS IN THE SUN *(Recorded Prev. by Kingston Trio and Beach Boys)*		1(3)	02 MAR 74	BELL

Also see The Poppy Family

DEE D. JACKSON

Born Deidre Cozier in Oxford (UK) she had her first success in Germany with 'Man Of A Man' in 77. Dee D, who toured with a robot, followed up her one-off hit with 'Meteor Man'.

🇬🇧 AUTOMATIC LOVER *(Baltimora sang backing vocals on the track)*		4	13 MAY 78	MERCURY

JANET JACKSON

Singer/writer/actress is the youngest of the nine Jackson children. She first appeared on stage with her brothers at age seven and by 10 was on TV in Good Times. She was also in top rated shows Different Strokes and Fame and joined A&M in 82. Her first big hit came with her third LP 'Control', since when she has had much success and won many awards in the US & UK.

🇬🇧 WHAT HAVE YOU DONE FOR ME LATELY		3	03 MAY 86	A&M
WHEN I THINK OF YOU		10	06 AUG 86	A&M
LET'S WAIT AWHILE		3	04 APR 87	BREAKOUT
🇺🇸 WHAT HAVE YOU DONE FOR ME LATELY		4	17 MAY 86	A&M
NASTY *(UK No. 19)*		3	19 JUL 86	A&M
WHEN I THINK OF YOU *(US Top 3 then all by females for the first time)*		1(2)	11 OCT 86	A&M
CONTROL *(UK No. 42)*		5	24 JAN 87	A&M
LET'S WAIT AWHILE		2	21 MAR 87	A&M
MISS YOU MUCH *(UK No. 22)*		1(4)	07 OCT 89	A&M
RHYTHM NATION *(UK No. 23)* *(UK No. 23 – record had Grammy winning video)*		2	06 JAN 90	A&M

JERMAINE JACKSON

With his brothers Tito and Jackie he started performing at the age of nine in 63. He married Berry Gordy's daughter Hazel and stayed with Motown after leaving the Jackson 5 in 75. His first solo hit was in 72 and the hits continued when he joined Arista in 84. He also had a European No.1 in a duet with Pia Zadora in 85.

🇬🇧 LET'S GET SERIOUS		8	14 JUN 80	MOTOWN
DO WHAT YOU DO *(US No. 13)*		6	30 MAR 85	ARISTA
🇺🇸 DADDY'S HOME *(Shep & Limelites 61 US hit)*		9	17 MAR 73	MOTOWN
LET'S GET SERIOUS *(Top black music hit 80)*		9	12 JUL 80	MOTOWN

Also see The Jacksons

JOE JACKSON

Midlands (UK) born singer/songwriter and pianist has experimented in many areas of music including reggae, big band jazz, salsa, jump blues and swing in his career which started with groups Arms & Legs and Edward Bear in the early 70s. This unique performer, who dislikes making videos, has a big UK & US cult following.

🇬🇧 IT'S DIFFERENT FOR GIRLS		5	02 FEB 80	A&M
STEPPIN' OUT		6	29 JAN 83	A&M
🇺🇸 STEPPIN' OUT		6	11 DEC 82	A&M

MICHAEL JACKSON

His LP 'Thriller' is the best selling record (over 40 million) of all time. He was the first entertainer to earn over $100 million in a year. He has won countless awards, including a record seven Grammys in the same year. He was the first act to enter the US & UK LP chart at No. 1 and he has two of the UK's three top selling LPs of all time. He has the world's top selling music video and topped a record five different US music charts in the same week. He has earned millions from sponsorship and has given millions to charity. He bought The Beatles publishing company and has been presented with an award for selling over 100 million records in the 80s.

🇬🇧 GOT TO BE THERE		5	04 MAR 72	TAMLA MOTOWN
ROCKIN' ROBIN *(Bobby Day 58 hit)*		3	24 JUN 72	TAMLA MOTOWN
AIN'T NO SUNSHINE *(Bill Withers 71 US hit)*		8	16 SEP 72	TAMLA MOTOWN
BEN *(From the film)*		7	09 DEC 72	TAMLA MOTOWN
DON'T STOP TILL YOU GET ENOUGH		3	20 OCT 79	EPIC
OFF THE WALL		7	15 DEC 79	EPIC
ROCK WITH YOU		7	01 MAR 80	EPIC

SHE'S OUT OF MY LIFE	3	24 MAY 80	EPIC
ONE DAY IN YOUR LIFE *(US No. 55)*	1(2)	27 JUN 81	MOTOWN
THE GIRL IS MINE *(With PAUL McCARTNEY)*	8	20 NOV 82	EPIC
BILLIE JEAN	1(1)	05 MAR 83	EPIC
BEAT IT *(Had most expensive video at time)*	3	23 APR 83	EPIC
WANNA BE STARTIN' SOMETHING	8	25 JUN 83	EPIC
SAY SAY SAY *(With PAUL McCARTNEY)* *(In US Paul McCartney's name was listed first)*	2	19 NOV 83	PARLOPHONE
THRILLER	10	26 NOV 83	EPIC
FAREWELL MY SUMMER LOVE *(US No. 38)*	7	30 JUN 84	MOTOWN
I JUST CAN'T STOP LOVING YOU *(Duet with SEIDAH GARRETT)*	1(2)	15 AUG 87	EPIC
BAD *(Entered at No. 5)*	3	03 OCT 87	EPIC
THE WAY YOU MAKE ME FEEL	3	09 JAN 88	EPIC
DIRTY DIANA	4	23 JUL 88	EPIC
SMOOTH CRIMINAL *(Seventh Top 10 single from 'Bad' – a UK LP record)*	8	03 DEC 88	EPIC
LEAVE ME ALONE *(Entered at No. 4)*	2	04 MAR 89	EPIC
GOT TO BE THERE	4	11 DEC 71	MOTOWN
ROCKIN' ROBIN	2	29 APR 72	MOTOWN
BEN	1(1)	14 OCT 72	MOTOWN
DON'T STOP TILL YOU GET ENOUGH	1(1)	13 OCT 79	MOTOWN
ROCK WITH YOU	1(4)	19 JAN 80	EPIC
OFF THE WALL	10	12 APR 80	EPIC
SHE'S OUT OF MY LIFE	10	21 JUN 80	EPIC
THE GIRL IS MINE *(And PAUL McCARTNEY)*	2	08 JAN 83	EPIC
BILLIE JEAN	1(7)	05 MAR 83	EPIC
BEAT IT *(Guitar Eddie Van Halen)*	1(3)	30 APR 83	EPIC
WANNA BE STARTIN' SOMETHING	5	16 JUL 83	EPIC
HUMAN NATURE *(Comp. Steve Porcaro of Toto)*	7	17 SEP 83	EPIC
P.Y.T. (PRETTY YOUNG THING) *(UK No. 11)* *(UK No. 11 – composed by James Ingram)*	10	26 NOV 83	EPIC
SAY SAY SAY *(With PAUL McCARTNEY)* *(Entered at No. 26 – highest US entry for 12 years)*	1(6)	10 DEC 83	COLUMBIA
THRILLER *(Entered at No. 20 – highest US entry since 60s)*	4	03 MAR 84	EPIC
I JUST CAN'T STOP LOVING YOU *(Duet with SEIDAH GARRETT)*	1(1)	19 SEP 87	EPIC
BAD	1(2)	24 OCT 87	EPIC
THE WAY YOU MAKE ME FEEL	1(1)	23 JAN 88	EPIC
THE MAN IN THE MIRROR *(UK No. 21)*	1(2)	26 MAR 88	EPIC
DIRTY DIANA	1(1)	02 JUL 88	EPIC
SMOOTH CRIMINAL	7	14 JAN 89	EPIC

Also see Jackson Five

JACKSON FIVE

The world's most successful family act have had 31 US hit singles (27 UK) and 20 US chart LPs (12 UK) selling over 100 million records. They won a talent show at the Apollo theatre in 66, were recommended to Motown by Gladys Knight in 67 and recorded two flops on Steeltown in 68. Their 'Victory' tour in 84 made millions but record sales since have slowed down. Jermaine has had solo hits and Michael has not done 'Bad'.

I WANT YOU BACK	2	07 MAR 70	TAMLA MOTOWN
ABC	8	06 JUN 70	TAMLA MOTOWN
THE LOVE YOU SAVE	7	22 AUG 70	TAMLA MOTOWN
I'LL BE THERE	4	23 JAN 71	TAMLA MOTOWN
LOOKIN' THROUGH THE WINDOWS *(US No. 16)*	9	02 DEC 72	TAMLA MOTOWN
DOCTOR MY EYES *(Jackson Browne 72 US hit)*	9	10 MAR 73	TAMLA MOTOWN
SHOW YOU THE WAY TO GO *(US No. 28)* *(All tracks from now were released as The Jacksons)*	1(1)	25 JUN 77	EPIC
BLAME IT ON THE BOOGIE *(US No. 54 – Mick Jackson 78 hit (no relation))*	8	04 NOV 78	EPIC
SHAKE YOUR BODY (DOWN TO THE GROUND)	4	21 APR 79	EPIC
CAN YOU FEEL IT *(US No. 77)*	6	02 MAY 81	EPIC
WALK RIGHT NOW *(US No. 73)*	7	08 AUG 81	EPIC
I WANT YOU BACK '88 *(REMIX)* *(Released as Michael Jackson & Jackson Five)*	8	07 MAY 88	EPIC
I WANT YOU BACK	1(1)	31 JAN 70	MOTOWN
ABC	1(2)	25 APR 70	MOTOWN
THE LOVE YOU SAVE	1(2)	27 JUN 70	MOTOWN
I'LL BE THERE *(Top soul single 70)*	1(5)	17 OCT 70	MOTOWN
MAMA'S PEARL *(UK No. 25)*	2	27 FEB 71	MOTOWN
NEVER CAN SAY GOODBYE *(UK No. 33)*	2	08 MAY 71	MOTOWN
SUGAR DADDY	10	22 JAN 72	MOTOWN
DANCING MACHINE	2	18 MAY 74	MOTOWN
ENJOY YOURSELF *(UK No. 42)* *(All tracks from now were released as The Jacksons)*	6	19 FEB 77	EPIC
SHAKE YOUR BODY (DOWN TO THE GROUND)	7	19 MAY 79	EPIC
STATE OF SHOCK *(UK No. 14)* *(UK No. 14 – Vocal Michael & Mick Jagger)*	3	04 AUG 84	EPIC

Also see Michael Jackson, Jermaine Jackson

JACKY

One time singer in the UK MOR group The Raindrops, Jackie Lee had two UK-only Top 20 hits with themes from children's TV shows; the other being 'Rupert' (14) released under her full name in 71.

WHITE HORSES	10	18 MAY 68	PHILIPS

MICK JAGGER

The inimitable Rolling Stones front man and the Thin White Duke joined together on one single in aid of Ethiopian relief. It topped the UK chart in its first week – a feat neither act had achieved before. In the UK label name credits were reversed.

DANCING IN THE STREET *(And DAVID BOWIE)* *(Martha & The Vandellas 64 hit)*	1(4)	07 SEP 85	EMI AM.
DANCING IN THE STREET *(And DAVID BOWIE)*	7	12 OCT 85	EMI AM.

Also see Rolling Stones/Jackson Five

JAGGERZ

Pittsburgh rock sextet which included Donnie Iris (Domenic Ierace), first recorded on Gamble & Huff's Gamble label in 68. They followed their one-off US Top 40 hit with 'I Call My Baby Candy' and were on Wooden Nickel in 75. Donnie toured with Wild Cherry and had three solo US-only Top 40s in the early 80s.

THE RAPPER	2	21 MAR 70	KAMA SUTRA

JAM

One of the UK's top all time acts who oddly never had a US single chart entry. Formed in 75 and fronted by Paul Weller they had a mid 60s 'Who' image and sound. Everything they released charted and by the time they split in 82 they'd had six Top 20 LPs and 13 Top 20 singles including four No.1s. They won numerous UK polls and when all their singles were re-released in 83 they had a record 15 hits in the Top 100. Paul later formed Style Council.

THE ETON RIFLES	3	24 NOV 79	POLYDOR
GOING UNDERGROUND *(Entered at No. 1)*	1(3)	22 MAR 80	POLYDOR
START *(Entered at No. 3)*	1(1)	06 SEP 80	POLYDOR
FUNERAL PYRE *(Entered at No. 4)*	4	06 JUN 81	POLYDOR
ABSOLUTE BEGINNERS *(Entered at No. 1)*	4	31 OCT 81	POLYDOR
TOWN CALLED MALICE/PRECIOUS *(Entered at No.1)*	1(3)	13 FEB 82	POLYDOR
JUST WHO IS THE FIVE O'CLOCK HERO	8	10 JUL 82	POLYDOR
THE BITTEREST PILL (I EVER HAD TO SWALLOW) *(Entered at No. 5)*	2	25 SEP 82	POLYDOR
BEAT SURRENDER *(Their last record and third one to enter at No. 1)*	1(2)	04 DEC 82	POLYDOR

Also see Style Council

JIMMY JAMES & THE VAGABONDS

British based soul band fronted by Jimmy and showcasing Count Prince Miller were a popular 60s UK club act. They recorded on Columbia in 65, Piccadilly in 66, and first charted in 68 with 'Come To Me Softly' (US 76). In the UK they had three Top 40s, the last two in 76 when under the guidance of producer Biddu.

NOW IS THE TIME	5	14 AUG 76	PYE

TOMMY JAMES

Born Tommy Jackson in Ohio, his first 45 was 'Long Pony Tail' in 62 and then he had his long run of hits with The Shondells. After leaving them in 70 he had 13 US-only chart entries.

DRAGGIN' THE LINE	4	14 AUG 71	ROULETTE

Also see Tommy James & The Shondells

TOMMY JAMES & THE SHONDELLS

They released their first hit in 64 on Snap and 18 months later a DJ in Pittsburgh started playing it and it became a US No. 1. After this fairy tale start the group scored a further 18 US (2 UK) hits including nine Top 10s before Tommy went solo. Tiffany, Billy Idol and Joan Jett have all had hit covers of the group's hits. They were still doing 'oldies' shows in 89.

 MONY MONY	1(3)	03 AUG 68	MAJOR MINOR
HANKY PANKY	1(2)	16 JUL 66	ROULETTE
(US No. 38 – Originally by The Raindrops in 63)			
I THINK WE'RE ALONE NOW	4	22 APR 67	ROULETTE
MIRAGE	10	17 JUN 67	ROULETTE
MONY MONY	3	15 JUN 68	ROULETTE
CRIMSON & CLOVER	1(2)	01 FEB 69	ROULETTE
SWEET CHERRY WINE	7	03 MAY 69	ROULETTE
CRYSTAL BLUE PERSUASION	2	26 JUL 69	ROULETTE

Also see Tommy James

JAN & DEAN

L.A.'s Jan Berry & Dean Torrence's first group was called The Barons and their first hit was under the name Jan & Arnie. They had the first surf music No. 1 which Beach Boy Brian Wilson wrote and sang on. After two dozen US hits Jan was very badly injured in a car crash and was out of the business until the late 70s. There was a TV movie of their lives called Dead Man's Curve.

JENNIE LEE *(Recorded in Jan's garage)*	8	30 JUN 58	ARWIN
(Released as JAN & ARNIE (Arnie Ginsburg))			
BABY TALK	10	31 AUG 59	DORE
(They later cut 'She's Still Talking Baby Talk')			
SURF CITY *(UK No. 26) (1st surfing No. 1)*	1(2)	20 JUL 63	LIBERTY
(They later cut 'Folk City' and 'Sun City')			
DRAG CITY	10	18 JAN 64	LIBERTY
DEAD MAN'S CURVE	8	09 MAY 64	LIBERTY
THE LITTLE OLD LADY (FROM PASADENA)	3	01 AUG 64	LIBERTY

HORST JANKOWSKI

Berlin born multi-instrumentalist started out playing piano for Caterina Valente when he was only 16 and later worked with acts like Ella Fitzgerald and Miles Davis. His follow up was 'Simpel Gimpel' and his 'Genius of Jankowski' LP went gold in the US.

A WALK IN THE BLACK FOREST *(US No. 12)*	3	28 AUG 65	MERCURY
(He later recorded 'Black Forest Holiday')			

JAPAN

London group included brothers David (later David Sylvian) and Steve Batt and Mick Karn. They recorded six unsuccessful singles for Hansa in the late 70s before the New Romantic movement helped start them on a run of a 12 UK-only hits (including five Hansa re-issues). Sylvian returned to the Top 20 as a soloist and with Ryvichi Sakamoto, and the group who split in 82 re-formed in 90.

GHOSTS	5	10 APR 82	VIRGIN
I SECOND THAT EMOTION	9	31 JUL 82	HANSA
(Smokey Robinson & The Miracles 67 hit)			

JEAN-MICHEL JARRE

Son of noted French composer Maurice Jarre was a child prodigy who made his first LP in 69. He has had nine UK-only Top 20 LPs and was the first Western musician to play in China. He is best known for his spectacular outdoor mega-concerts which he has held in Paris, Houston and London.

 OXYGENE PART 1V *(US No. 65)*	4	10 SEP 77	POLYDOR
(A new version reached No. 65 in UK in 89)			

AL JARREAU

Milwaukee's Grammy winning singer was previously in a trio with George Duke and made his first LP 'We Got By' in 75. In the US his biggest single to date is 'We're In This Love Together' (US 15/UK 55) in 81 and he has had three Top 40 LPs.

MOONLIGHTING ('THEME') *(US No. 23)*	8	21 MAR 87	WEA

JAY & THE AMERICANS

Originally known as the Harbor-Lites on Malo and Jaro, the group's first singer was John 'Jay' Traynor (ex-Mystics). He was replaced in 62 by David 'Jay' Black. They had 18 US-only hits between 62-70. Jay Black still performs and member Kenny Vance is now a successful producer.

SHE CRIED	5	19 MAY 62	UA
COME A LITTLE BIT CLOSER	3	21 NOV 64	UA
(Composed by Tommy Boyce & Bobby Hart)			
CARA MIA *(David Whitfield 54 hit)*	4	31 JUL 65	UA
THIS MAGIC MOMENT *(Drifters 60 US hit)*	6	08 MAR 69	UA

JAY & THE TECHNIQUES

Seven-man mixed raced act from Pennsylvania was fronted by Jay Proctor, who had been in groups since the late 50s. They had two US-only Top 20s, the other being 'Keep The Ball Rollin'' (14). They were later on Gordy, Silver Blue and Event.

APPLES PEACHES PUMPKIN PIE	6	23 SEP 67	SMASH

JAYNETTS

Bronx based female quartet including Mary Sue Wells, followed their hypnotic one-off US hit with 'Dear Abby'. Johnnie Louise Richardson of 50s hit act Johnnie & Joe joined the group later.

SALLY, GO 'ROUND THE ROSES	2	28 SEP 63	TUFF
(Buddy Miles played drums on the track)			

JEFFERSON AIRPLANE/JEFFERSON STARSHIP

Act signed to RCA in 65 but never charted until joined by Grace Slick (ex-Great Society) in 67, who wrote and sang their biggest hits. After personnel changes, they changed named to Jefferson Starship in 71. Mickey Thomas joined them in 79 and they became simply Starship in 85. In all have had nine Top 20 US singles and 15 US Top 20 LPs yet only had their first UK Top 20 in 85. There have been countless personnel changes, off-shoots and solo projects. The original group re-united in 89 but sales of the LP were disappointing.

SOMEBODY TO LOVE *(Their 5th single on RCA)*	5	17 JUN 67	RCA
(Starship's Mickey Thomas revived it in 77 on MCA)			
WHITE RABBIT	8	29 JUL 67	RCA
MIRACLES	3	18 OCT 75	GRUNT
COUNT ON ME	8	13 MAY 78	GRUNT
(Last two hits as JEFFERSON STARSHIP)			

Also see Starship

JELLY BEANS

Mixed Jersey City (US) quintet included sisters Elyse & Maxine Herbert. They followed their one US Top 40 with 'Baby Be Mine'.

I WANNA LOVE HIM SO BAD	9	08 AUG 64	RED BIRD

JELLYBEAN

New York club DJ turned producer, re-mixer and eventually artist John 'Jellybean' Benitez had four UK Top 20s in 87/88. His first hit was the Madonna song 'Sidewalk Talk' in 85 (US 18/UK 47).

 WHO FOUND WHO   10   19 DEC 87   CHRYSALIS
(Featuring ELISA FIORILLO – US No. 16)

JESUS AND MARY CHAIN

Notorious Scottish group featuring the Reid brothers Jim & William. Their first release was an indie chart topper 'Upside Down' on Creation in 84. Loved by the music press and often banned on both sides of the Atlantic, they have scored nine UK-only chart singles and have built a cult following in the US.

 APRIL SKIES   8   09 MAY 87   BLANCO

JETHRO TULL

Eccentric singer/writer and flautist from Edinburgh, Ian Anderson fronts the group whose music has varied from progressive rock to olde English folk. Their first release in 68 on MGM failed but since then they have had 15 Top 20 LPs in the UK and 13 in the US. Though less successful in the 80s they surprisingly won a first Grammy award for hard rock/heavy metal in 89.

LIVING IN THE PAST *(US No. 11)*	3	28 JUN 69	ISLAND
SWEET DREAM	7	22 NOV 69	CHRYSALIS
THE WITCH'S PROMISE/TEACHER	4	14 FEB 70	CHRYSALIS

JETS

Minneapolis family (originally from Tonga) group are Leroy, Eddie, Eugene, Haini, Rudy, Kathi, Elizabeth & Moana Wolfgramm. These talented multi-instrumentalists were aged between 14-23 when they first hit the Top 10.

CRUSH ON YOU	5	07 MAR 87	MCA
(Produced by Ollie Brown of Ollie & Jerry)			
CRUSH ON YOU	3	21 JUN 86	MCA
YOU GOT IT ALL	3	07 MAR 87	MCA
CROSS MY BROKEN HEART	7	01 AUG 87	MCA
ROCKET 2 U *(UK No. 69)*	6	02 APR 88	MCA
MAKE IT REAL	4	25 JUN 88	MCA

JOAN JETT & THE BLACKHEARTS

Philadelphian singer/guitarist joined The Runaways when just 15 and recorded three LPs with them before leaving in 78. She tried to make it as a soloist in Europe and was on Ariola in 80. Her first hit came in 82 when she and The Blackhearts were the Top US group. She has had five US Top 40s (1 UK) and a No. 2 US LP.

I LOVE ROCK 'N' ROLL	4	08 MAY 82	EPIC
(Originally by The Arrows)			
I LOVE ROCK 'N' ROLL	1(7)	20 MAR 82	BOARDWALK
CRIMSON AND CLOVER	7	19 JUN 82	BOARDWALK
(UK No.60 – Tommy James & the Shondells 68 US hit)			
I HATE MYSELF FOR LOVING YOU *(UK No. 46)*	8	01 OCT 88	BLACKHEART

JIGSAW

Pop quartet fronted by Des Dyer were from Brisbane, Australia. They recorded on Philips in 71 and have often re-recorded their hit, which was written by Des and fellow member Clive Scott.

SKY HIGH *(From film 'The Dragon Flies')*	9	29 NOV 75	SPLASH
(Their latest version was on Libido Urge in 89)			
SKY HIGH	3	06 DEC 75	CHELSEA

JILTED JOHN

Singer/drama student Graham Fellows from Sheffield had a one-off UK hit with a novelty track that inspired answer records from Gordon the Moron and Julie & Gordon. The hit, first released on Rabid, was followed up by 'True Love Stories'.

 JILTED JOHN   4   23 SEP 78   EMI INT.

JIVE BUNNY & MASTERMIXERS

Club DJ Les Hemstock and Andy Pickles from Yorkshire scored an unprecedented three No. 1 UK hits in less than five months with dance tracks full of samples from hit records of the 50s, 60s & 70s. The much maligned records and their LP also topped charts right around the world, selling millions of copies.

SWING THE MOOD *(US No. 11)*	1(5)	05 AUG 89	MUSIC FACTORY
THAT'S WHAT I LIKE	1(3)	21 OCT 89	MUSIC FACTORY
(Entered at No. 4 – In US 100 in 90)			
LET'S PARTY *(Entered at No. 1)*	1(1)	16 DEC 89	MUSIC FACTORY

JIVE FIVE

New York group formed by Eugene Pitt after he left chart group The Genies (who included Don & Juan). They were one of the last doo-wop styled acts to hit and their first release was their biggest. They later recorded on Sketch, UA, Musicor, Ambient Sound, Decca, Avco and Brut – the last two as the Jyve Fyve.

MY TRUE STORY   3   11 SEP 61   BELTONE

JOBOXERS

The UK group evolved out of the respected punk group Subway Sect, whose main man Vic Goddard brought in US vocalist Dig Wayne to front the new five piece band. They clocked up three UK Top 40s in 83 but faded from the scene shortly after.

 BOXER BEAT   3   09 APR 83   RCA
JUST GOT LUCKY *(US No. 36)*   7   04 JUN 83   RCA

BILLY JOEL

The ultra-successful Long Island singer/songwriter was in The Echoes, The Emeralds, The Lost Souls, The Hassles (two LPs on UA) and in the hard rock duo Attila (one LP on Epic). He then recorded solo on Family/Philips in 71 and as Bill Martin he played piano in a bar until Columbia found him. To date he has had 7 US (5 UK) Top 10 LPs (including four that have sold over five million in the US alone) and 21 US (7 UK) Top 20 singles.

TELL HER ABOUT IT	4	14 JAN 84	CBS
AN INNOCENT MAN	8	03 MAR 84	CBS
WE DIDN'T START THE FIRE	7	21 OCT 89	CBS
(Co-produced with Mick Jones of Foreigner)			
JUST THE WAY YOU ARE *(UK No. 19)*	3	18 FEB 78	COLUMBIA
(About his one time wife and manager Elizabeth)			
MY LIFE *(UK No. 12)*	3	06 JAN 79	COLUMBIA
YOU MAY BE RIGHT	7	03 MAY 80	COLUMBIA
IT'S STILL ROCK AND ROLL TO ME *(UK No. 14)*	1(2)	19 JUL 80	COLUMBIA
TELL HER ABOUT IT	1(1)	24 SEP 83	COLUMBIA
(Was prod. Phil Ramone's 2nd US No. 1 in a row)			
UPTOWN GIRL	3	12 NOV 83	COLUMBIA
(About his future wife Christie Brinkley)			
AN INNOCENT MAN	10	25 FEB 84	COLUMBIA
YOU'RE ONLY HUMAN (SECOND WIND)	9	31 AUG 85	COLUMBIA
MODERN WOMAN *(From 'Ruthless People')*	10	26 JUL 86	EPIC
A MATTER OF TRUST *(UK No. 52)*	10	18 OCT 86	COLUMBIA
WE DIDN'T START THE FIRE	1(2)	09 DEC 89	COLUMBIA

ELTON JOHN

The UKs biggest selling solo artist started life as Reg Dwight in Middlesex. The award winning singer/song-writer/pianist first recorded in 65 in Bluesology and his first solo singles on Philips failed. He did various session work including singing on 'cover version' LPs. This outrageous showman has an unbelievable track record with 22 UK Top 20 LPs (19 in US) and 27 UK Top 20 singles (30 in US). He has 24 US Gold LPs and was the first act to enter the US LP chart at No. 1 (which he did twice) and he still packs stadiums all around the world.

🇬🇧 YOUR SONG	7	13 FEB 71	DJM
ROCKET MAN	2	03 JUN 72	DJM
CROCODILE ROCK	5	25 NOV 72	DJM
DANIEL	4	17 FEB 73	DJM
SATURDAY NIGHT'S ALRIGHT FOR FIGHTING (US No. 12)	7	21 JUL 73	DJM
GOODBYE YELLOW BRICK ROAD	6	27 OCT 73	DJM
LUCY IN THE SKY WITH DIAMONDS (Beatles song)	10	14 DEC 74	DJM
PINBALL WIZARD (From 'Tommy')	7	03 APR 76	DJM
DON'T GO BREAKING MY HEART (And KIKI DEE) (Jumped from 49-9 - His only UK No. 1)	1(6)	24 JUL 76	ROCKET
SONG FOR GUY	4	13 JAN 79	ROCKET
BLUE EYES (US No. 12)	8	24 APR 82	ROCKET
I GUESS THAT'S WHY THEY CALL IT THE BLUES	5	02 JUL 83	ROCKET
I'M STILL STANDING (US No. 12)	4	27 AUG 83	ROCKET
SAD SONGS (SAY SO MUCH)	7	23 JUN 84	ROCKET
PASSENGERS	5	08 SEP 84	ROCKET
NIKITA	3	09 NOV 85	ROCKET
CANDLE IN THE WIND (Live recording of his old hit)	5	13 FEB 88	ROCKET
🇺🇸 YOUR SONG	8	23 JAN 71	UNI
ROCKET MAN	6	15 JUL 72	UNI
HONKY CAT (UK No. 31)	8	23 SEP 72	UNI
CROCODILE ROCK	1(2)	03 FEB 73	MCA
DANIEL	2	02 JUN 73	MCA
GOODBYE YELLOW BRICK ROAD	2	08 DEC 73	MCA
BENNIE AND THE JETS (Not UK hit)	1(1)	13 APR 74	MCA
DON'T LET THE SUN GO DOWN ON ME (UK No.16 - backing vocals inc. Captain & Tennille)	2—	27 JUL 74	MCA
THE BITCH IS BACK (UK No. 15)	4	02 NOV 74	MCA
LUCY IN THE SKY WITH DIAMONDS	1(2)	04 JAN 75	MCA
PHILADELPHIA FREEDOM (UK No. 12)	1(2)	12 APR 75	MCA
SOMEONE SAVED MY LIFE TONIGHT (UK No. 22 - Elton's least favourite track)	4	16 AUG 75	MCA
ISLAND GIRL (UK No. 14)	1(3)	01 NOV 75	MCA
DON'T GO BREAKING MY HEART (and KIKI DEE) (They also rel. 'Loving You Is Sweeter Than Ever')	1(4)	07 AUG 76	ROCKET
SORRY SEEMS TO BE THE HARDEST WORD (UK No.11)	6	25 DEC 76	MCA/ROCKET
MAMA CAN'T BUY YOU LOVE (He was top US singles and LP act of the 70s)	9	25 AUG 79	MCA
LITTLE JEANNIE (UK No. 33)	3	26 JUL 80	MCA
I GUESS THAT'S WHY THEY CALL IT THE BLUES (Stevie Wonder on Harmonica)	4	28 JAN 84	GEFFEN
SAD SONGS (SAY SO MUCH)	5	11 AUG 84	GEFFEN
NIKITA	7	22 MAR 86	GEFFEN
CANDLE IN THE WIND (LIVE)	6	23 JAN 88	MCA
I DON'T WANNA GO ON LIKE THAT (UK No. 30)	2	30 AUG 88	MCA

ROBERT JOHN

Brooklyn born falsetto styled singer had his first hit at age 12 in 58 as Bobby Pedrick with 'White Bucks And Saddle Shoes' (US 74). He was later lead singer of Bobby & The Consoles on Diamond and in 68 had the second of his 9 US (2 UK) hits.

🇺🇸 THE LION SLEEPS TONIGHT (Produced by The Tokens who had first hit version)	3	11 MAR 72	ATLANTIC
SAD EYES (UK No. 31) (It took 21 weeks on US chart to hit No. 1)	1(1)	06 OCT 79	EMI AM.

JOHNNY & THE HURRICANES

Toledo (US) based instrumental group fronted by Johnny Paris (Pocisk). He was in Mack Vickery's band in 57 before forming the group (first called The Orbits) who first recorded on Twirl in 59. Their distinctive Hammond organ sound gave them 6 UK (2 US) Top 20s. They were later on Jeff, Mala and their own Atila label.

🇬🇧 RED RIVER ROCK (revival of 'Red River Valley')	3	13 NOV 59	LONDON
BEATNIK FLY (US No. 15 – based on 'Blue Tailed Fly')	8	08 APR 60	LONDON
DOWN YONDER (US No. 48 – Hare & Jones 21 hit)	10	24 JUN 60	LONDON
ROCKING GOOSE (US No. 60)	4	25 NOV 60	LONDON
🇺🇸 RED RIVER ROCK (They revived it as 'Red River Rock '67')	5	06 SEP 59	WARWICK

JOHNNY HATES JAZZ

Vocalist Clark Datchler, whose father had been in hit 50s act The Stargazers, had two solo singles on RAK before joining with Calvin Hayes, son of label boss Mickie Most, to form this group whose first release failed. Before Clark left to be replaced by Phil Thornally, they were a top teen attraction and had four UK Top 20s.

🇬🇧 SHATTERED DREAMS	5	23 MAY 87	VIRGIN
🇺🇸 SHATTERED DREAMS	2	14 MAY 88	VIRGIN

SAMMY JOHNS

Singer/songwriter from North Carolina first recorded as part of The Devilles on Dixie. Followed his sole Top 40 with 'Rag Doll'. He also recorded on Warner in 76, MCA and Southern Tracks in 86.

🇺🇸 CHEVY VAN (He had a country hit with a re-recording in 86)	5	03 MAY 75	GRC

DON JOHNSON

Actor/singer from Missouri is best known for his role in TVs Miami Vice and as a friend of Barbra Streisand with whom he had the hit duet 'Till I Loved You (UK 16/US 25) in 88.

🇺🇸 HEARTBEAT (UK No. 46)	5	18 OCT 86	EPIC

HOLLY JOHNSON

William 'Holly' Johnson was born in the Sudan and was raised in Liverpool. He had been in Big In Japan and made unsuccessful solo singles before forming Hollycaust who became hit act Frankie Goes To Hollywood. After a long legal battle he had his first solo releases in 89 and he chalked up four UK chart entries that year.

🇬🇧 LOVE TRAIN (US No. 65)	4	11 FEB 89	MCA
AMERICANOS	4	22 APR 89	MCA

JOHNNY JOHNSON & THE BANDWAGON

This US soul band had six UK hits and yet only managed one small soul chart entry in the US. The group, which also included Terry Lewis, Artie Fullilove and Billy Bradley, were also on EMI in 73.

🇬🇧 BREAKIN' DOWN THE WALLS OF HEARTACHE (Act simply called BANDWAGON)	4	23 NOV 68	DIRECTION
SWEET INSPIRATION	10	05 SEP 70	BELL
BLAME IT ON THE PONY EXPRESS	7	09 JAN 71	BELL

LAURIE JOHNSON

UK orchestra leader/composer who was on Polygon in 53 had the biggest hit with this much recorded TV theme. He later wrote the music for TV shows such as The Avengers and The Professionals.

🇬🇧 SUCU-SUCU (Four versions made UK chart)	4	27 OCT 61	PYE

MARV JOHNSON

Detroit soul singer first sang in The Serenaders in the mid 50s and first recorded on Kudo in 58. His 'Come To Me' (US 30) was the first release on Berry Gordy's Tamla label in 59. After his hits he returned to Motown to work in promotion and recorded for the UK label Nightmare in 89.

YOU GOT WHAT IT TAKES	5	18 MAR 60	LONDON
I'LL PICK A ROSE FOR MY ROSE	10	01 MAR 69	TAMLA MOTOWN
YOU GOT WHAT IT TAKES	10	08 FEB 60	UA
I LOVE THE WAY YOU LOVE (UK No. 28)	9	11 APR 60	UA

JO JO GUNNE

L.A. quartet formed in 71 by ex-Spirit members Jay Ferguson and Mark Andes and named after a Chuck Berry track. The group broke up in 75. Jay went solo with some success and Mark re-formed Spirit in 76 and then had more chart hits in Firefall and Heart.

RUN RUN RUN (US No. 27)	6	06 MAY 72	ASYLUM

Also see Jay Ferguson

JON & VANGELIS

Lancashire born Jon Anderson started with The Warriors on Decca and Parlophone before becoming a Yes man in 68. He had several solo successes as well as the hits with Greek superstar Vangelis.

I HEAR YOU NOW (US No. 58)	8	16 FEB 80	POLYDOR
I'LL FIND MY WAY HOME (US No. 51)	6	23 JAN 82	POLYDOR

Also see Vangelis/Yes

ALED JONES

Welsh choirboy Aled had six Top 40 UK-only LPs before retiring in 87 when he was 16 to concentrate on his school exams. He also had records on RCA, Sain/Priority and 10/Virgin.

WALKING IN THE AIR (From 'The Snowman')	5	28 DEC 85	HMV

HOWARD JONES

Buckinghamshire (UK) synth wizard and singer/composer only started recording at 28 and has had nine UK Top 20s (5 US). His first LP 'Humans Lib' entered the UK chart at No. 1. He appeared in Live Aid, opened a vegetarian restaurant in New York, and in 90 appeared on Eastwest.

NEW SONG (US No. 27)	3	22 OCT 83	WEA
WHAT IS LOVE (US No. 33)	2	14 JAN 84	WEA
PEARL IN THE SHELL	7	16 JUN 84	WEA
LIKE TO GET TO KNOW YOU WELL (US No. 49)	4	25 AUG 84	WEA
THINGS CAN ONLY GET BETTER	6	23 FEB 85	WEA
LOOK MAMA	10	27 APR 85	WEA
THINGS CAN ONLY GET BETTER	5	15 JUN 85	ELEKTRA
NO ONE IS TO BLAME (UK No. 16)	4	05 JUL 86	ELEKTRA
(Prod. Phil Collins-re-recording of an 85 LP track)			

JIMMY JONES

Falsetto voiced soul singer from Birmingham (US) sang in the Sparks Of Rhythm in 55 and formed The Savoys in 56 who evolved into the hit doo-wop act The Pretenders. He had two transatlantic Top 3 hits in five months and later recorded on Roulette, Vee Jay, Capitol, Parkway, Bell, Taylor and Epic.

HANDY MAN	3	25 MAY 60	MGM
(Was cut as a song demo – backing vocals The Cues)			
GOOD TIMIN'	1(3)	01 JUL 60	MGM
(First US black solo rock/R&B act to top chart)			
HANDY MAN	2	28 FEB 60	CUB
GOOD TIMIN'	3	23 MAY 60	CUB
(He often re-recorded the above two hits)			

JOE JONES

New Orleans singer/writer recorded on Capitol in 54, Herald in 57 and Roulette in 58 before getting his sole Top 40 hit on Ric (picked up by Roulette). He later had hits as a producer of Alvin Robinson and the Dixie Cups records.

YOU TALK TOO MUCH	3	14 NOV 60	ROULETTE
(Third time record was released)			

ORAN 'JUICE' JONES

Houston born and New York based soul singer who first charted under the single name Juice with 'You Can't Hide From Love'. The follow up, under his full name, gave him his sole transatlantic Top Ten hit to date. He joined Def Jam's OBR label in 89.

THE RAIN	4	13 DEC 86	DEF JAM
THE RAIN	9	15 NOV 86	DEF JAM

PAUL JONES

Born Paul Pond in Portsmouth, he was in the Mann-Hugg Blues Brothers (later Manfred Mann) from 62-66. He had instant solo success and was later on Philips, Private Stock, RCA and RSO. He formed The Blues Band in 79, which split in 82, appeared in Cats and other musicals and has worked as a DJ.

HIGH TIME	4	12 NOV 66	HMV
I'VE BEEN A BAD BAD BOY	5	11 FEB 67	HMV

Also see Manfred Mann

RICKIE LEE JONES

Singer/songwriter who comes from Chicago won a Grammy as Best New Act of 79. She has had two US Top 5 LPs but has not returned to the singles Top 20 since her debut. She joined Geffen in 89.

CHUCK E.'S IN LOVE	4	07 JUL 79	WARNER
(UK No. 18 – song about musician Chuck E. Weiss)			

SHIRLEY JONES – SEE 'THE PARTRIDGE FAMILY' FOR HIT DETAILS

TAMMY JONES

UK singer tipped as a 'Face of 69' by a UK pop paper. As a TV talent show winner, she had a one-off UK hit and followed it up with 'While We're Still Young'. She also recorded on Monarch in 80 and Blue Waters in 85.

LET ME TRY AGAIN	5	17 MAY 75	EPIC

TOM JONES

South Wales born Tom Woodward started singing as Tommy Scott (& The Senators, & The Playboys) and even Tiger Tom before recording for EMI in 63 and then Decca where his second 45 gave him the first of 21 UK Top 20 singles (11 US) and 16 UK Top 20 LPs (7 US). He has had a top TV rated TV series, has been a long-time Las Vegas star and has had 16 country hits too – a record for a UK act. He made a UK chart come back in 87 and joined Jive Records in 89.

IT'S NOT UNUSUAL	1(1)	13 MAR 65	DECCA
(Lead guitar Jimmy Page – written for Sandie Shaw)			
GREEN GREEN GRASS OF HOME (US No. 11)	1(6)	03 DEC 66	DECCA
(UK Gold record – Originally by Johnny Darrell 65)			
DETROIT CITY	8	18 MAR 67	DECCA
(US No. 27 – Bobby Bare 63 hit)			
FUNNY FAMILIAR FORGOTTEN FEELING	7	20 MAY 67	DECCA
(US No. 49 – Don Gibson 66 country hit)			
I'LL NEVER FALL IN LOVE AGAIN	2	26 AUG 67	DECCA
(Originally by composer Lonnie Donegan)			
I'M COMIN' HOME (US No. 57)	2	23 DEC 67	DECCA
DELILAH (US No. 15) (Third No. 2 in a row)	2	30 MAR 68	DECCA

HELP YOURSELF *(US No. 35)*	3	07 SEP 68	DECCA
LOVE ME TONIGHT *(US No. 13)*	9	31 MAY 69	DECCA
WITHOUT LOVE *(Clyde McPhatter 57 US hit)*	10	03 JAN 70	DECCA
DAUGHTER OF DARKNESS *(US No. 13)*	5	09 MAY 70	DECCA
TILL *(US No. 41 – Roger Williams 57 US hit)*	2	20 NOV 71	DECCA
THE YOUNG NEW MEXICAN PUPPETEER *(US No. 80)*	6	29 APR 72	DECCA
A BOY FROM NOWHERE *(from 'Matador')*	2	23 MAY 87	EPIC
KISS *(with ART OF NOISE) (US No. 31)*	5	05 NOV 88	CHINA
🇺🇸 IT'S NOT UNUSUAL	10	29 MAY 65	PARROT
WHAT'S NEW PUSSYCAT? *(UK No. 11 – From film)*	3	31 JUL 65	PARROT
I'LL NEVER FALL IN LOVE AGAIN *(Was 49 in 67)*	6	13 SEP 69	PARROT
WITHOUT LOVE (THERE IS NOTHING)	5	31 JAN 70	PARROT
SHE'S A LADY *(UK No. 13 – Comp. Paul Anka)*	2	20 MAR 71	PARROT

JANIS JOPLIN

Texas born blues singer was in The Waller Creek Boys before joining Big Brother & The Holding Company in 66. She left the group in 68, and had her biggest hits after her death in 70. Oddly, she never made the UK singles chart.

🇺🇸 ME AND BOBBY MCGEE *(Roger Miller 69 US hit)*	1(2)	20 MAR 71	COLUMBIA

JOURNEY

San Francisco group formed in 73 by ex members of numerous top groups including Neal Schon (ex-Santana). Their name was changed from The Golden Gate Rhythm Section and big hits came when singer Steve Perry joined in 77. They had 18 US-only Top 40 singles and 6 US (1 UK) Top 20 LPs. They broke up in 87 and Neal and fellow member Jonathan Cain formed Bad English.

🇺🇸 WHO'S CRYING NOW *(UK No. 46)*	4	03 OCT 81	COLUMBIA
DON'T STOP BELIEVING *(UK No. 62)*	9	19 DEC 81	COLUMBIA
OPEN ARMS	2	27 FEB 82	COLUMBIA
SEPARATE WAYS (WORLDS APART)	8	19 MAR 83	COLUMBIA
ONLY THE YOUNG *(From film 'Vision Quest')*	9	23 MAR 85	GEFFEN
BE GOOD TO YOURSELF	9	31 MAY 86	COLUMBIA

Also see Steve Perry/Bad English

JUDGE DREAD

Singer/comedian Alex Hughes borrowed the name 'Judge Dread' from a track recorded by reggae star Prince Buster. Alex's rude reggae hits 'Big 6', 'Big 7' and 'Big 8' were inspired by 'Big 5' another Prince Buster record. In all he had nine UK-only Top 40s, all of which were banned on radio. He was also on EMI, Trojan and Rhino.

🇬🇧 BIG SEVEN *(He re-recorded it as 'Big Seven 85' on Creole)*	8	13 JAN 73	BIG SHOT
JE T'AIME (MOI NON PLUS) *(Jane Birkin & Serge Gainsbourg 69 hit)*	9	26 JUL 75	CACTUS

JUNIOR

Norman 'Junior' Giscombe is a London based singer/composer who recorded for labels like Arrawak in the early 80s. He charted first in the US and was the Top New Black Artist of 82 there. He has since had five black music Top 40s and seven UK chart entries.

🇬🇧 MAMA USED TO SAY *(US No. 30) (First released in Sep 81 with no success)*	7	05 JUN 82	MERCURY
ANOTHER STEP (CLOSER TO YOU) *(With KIM WILDE)*	6	16 MAY 87	MCA

JIMMY JUSTICE

UK pop singer called 'the British Ben E. King' had two flop singles before his three Tony Hatch produced UK-only Top 20s in 62. He and his group The Excheckers toured with the Larry Parnes stage shows. He was later on Decca and B & C.

🇬🇧 WHEN MY LITTLE GIRL IS SMILING *(Co-Written by Carole King – Drifters 62 hit)*	3	20 APR 62	PYE

K

BERT KAEMPFERT

The late German bandleader/composer and producer started in the Hans Busch orchestra and had 4 US (1 UK) Top 40 hits. He wrote many hits including No. 1s for himself, Frank Sinatra ('Strangers In The Night'), Elvis and Joe Dowell (the latter two with 'Wooden Heart') and was The Beatles' first producer back in 61.

🇺🇸 WONDERLAND BY NIGHT *(Last song to have 3 versions together in Top 20)*	1(3)	09 JAN 61	DECCA

KAJAGOOGOO

Group were formed when UK band Handstands joined with vocalist Limahl (Chris Hamill). With help from Duran Duran's Nick Rhodes they became the UK's most talked about new act of 83. Limahl went solo in 83 and the band, who later shortened their name to Kaja, had some US dance success but never returned to the top.

🇬🇧 TOO SHY *(Co-Produced by Nick Rhodes)*	1(2)	19 FEB 83	EMI
OOH TO BE AH	7	09 APR 83	EMI
BIG APPLE	8	24 OCT 83	EMI
🇺🇸 TOO SHY	5	09 JUL 83	EMI AM.

NICK KAMEN

Singer/model/actor and songwriter from Essex (UK) became a household face (and body!) in the UK after appearing in a Levis Jeans ad and strung together four UK-only Top 40s.

🇬🇧 EACH TIME YOU BREAK MY HEART *(Co-written and produced by Madonna)*	5	06 DEC 86	WEA

EDEN KANE

The first of three Sarstedt brothers to have UK-only Top 10s, was born Richard Sarstedt in Delhi, India, and his first release was 'Hot Chocolate Baby' on Pye in 60. He was one of the UK's top teen idols before The Beatles and his five hits all made the Top 10.

🇬🇧 WELL I ASK YOU *(Had 4 US cover versions including Bobby Vinton)*	1(2)	21 JUL 61	DECCA
GET LOST	8	29 SEP 61	DECCA
FORGET ME NOT	3	02 FEB 62	DECCA
I DON'T KNOW WHY *(Wayne King 31 hit)*	7	01 JUN 62	DECCA
BOYS CRY *(And THE DOWNBEATS)*	8	21 MAR 64	FONTANA

KANSAS

Six man Kansas rock band fronted by Steve Walsh had their first release in 74 and their chart debut in 76 with 'Carry On Wayward Son' (US 11/UK 51). They have had four US-only Top 20 LPs and 45s. Steve left in 81 but he returned in 86 when they reformed.

DUST IN THE WIND		6	15 APR 78	KIRSHNER

KAOMA

Europe's biggest dance craze of 89 came from this French group formed by Jean-Claude Bonaventura from members of Toure Kunda. Vocals were by Loalwa Braz, a Brazilian based in Paris. Their follow up 'Dancardo Lambada' was also a European hit and their 'World Beat' LP was a US Top 20 CD in 90.

LAMBADA *(US Top 100 in 90 – based on Bolivian folk song)*		4	09 DEC 89	CBS

KATRINA & THE WAVES

UK based act includes songwriter Kimberley Rew (ex-Soft Boys) and US vocalist Katrina Leskanich. The group's debut release was in 83 and their first and biggest hit came two years later. They returned to the US Top 20 in 89 with 'That's The Way'(16) on SBK.

WALKING ON SUNSHINE		8	08 JUN 85	CAPITOL
WALKING ON SUNSHINE		9	22 JUN 85	CAPITOL

JANET KAY

UK born reggae singer and actress starred in an all black UK TV comedy series and had many reggae charters on labels like Ballistic, Body Music, Local, All Tone, Matumbi, Arrawak, Tom Tom, Soho, Sarge, Liberty, Sarge, Arista and Solid Groove.

SILLY GAMES		2	14 JUL 79	SCOPE

KAYE SISTERS

Un-related UK female trio Carol, Sheila and Shan, who first charted as The Three Kayes in 56, worked a lot with UK star Frankie Vaughan. Named after their organiser Carmen Kaye, they recorded many cover versions of US hits. Shan Palmer has since appeared as a regular in a couple of UK soap operas.

GOTTA HAVE SOMETHING IN THE BANK FRANK *(Originally by Bob Jaxon)*		8	15 NOV 57	PHILIPS
COME SOFTLY TO ME *(Fleetwoods 59 hit)*		9	22 MAY 59	PHILIPS
(Above two hit with FRANKIE VAUGHAN)				
PAPER ROSES *(Anita Bryant 60 US hit)*		10	09 SEP 60	PHILIPS

KC & THE SUNSHINE BAND

Top selling disco act were formed by singer/writer/producers Harry Casey (KC) and Richard Finch. They wrote and produced many hits on TK Records including George McCrae's 'Rock You Baby' and all their 10 UK (9 US) Top 40s, which included an amazing five No. 1s. The group, who first hit in the UK, broke up when TK went bankrupt in 83. KC went to Epic where he had his only UK No. 1.

QUEEN OF CLUBS *(US No. 66)*		7	28 SEP 74	JAYBOY
THAT'S THE WAY (I LIKE IT)		4	06 SEP 75	JAYBOY
PLEASE DON'T GO		3	19 JAN 80	TK
GIVE IT UP *(US No. 18)*		1(3)	13 AUG 83	EPIC
GET DOWN TONIGHT *(UK No. 21)*		1(1)	30 AUG 75	TK
THAT'S THE WAY (I LIKE IT)		1(2)	22 NOV 75	TK
(SHAKE, SHAKE, SHAKE) SHAKE YOUR BOOTY		1(1)	11 SEP 76	TK
I'M YOUR BOOGIE MAN *(UK No. 41)*		1(1)	11 JUN 77	TK
KEEP IT COMIN' LOVE *(UK No. 31)*		2	01 OCT 77	TK
PLEASE DON'T GO		1(1)	05 JAN 80	TK
YES, I'M READY *(With TERI DeSARIO) (As KC)*		2	01 MAR 80	CASABLANCA

ERNIE K-DOE

Born Ernie Kador in New Orleans, he recorded with The Blue Diamonds (who included Huey 'Piano' Smith) in 54 on Savoy, and his first solo came in 55. He also recorded on Ember in 60, Instant in 63, Duke in 67, Janus in 71 and Island in 75 but never returned to the Top 40.

MOTHER-IN-LAW *(No. 22 UK)*		1(1)	22 MAY 61	MINIT
(Later had 'My Mother in Law (Is In My Hair Again)')				

Yvonne Keely – See Scott Fitzgerald

KEITH

Philadelphian James 'Keith' Keefer first recorded on Columbia as Keith & The Admirations in 65 and had three US Top 40s in six months before being drafted into the military. He was later on RCA and Discreet.

98.6 *(UK No. 24) (Backed by The Tokens)*		7	11 FEB 67	MERCURY

GRACE KELLY – SEE BING CROSBY FOR HIT DETAILS

JOHNNY KEMP

Born in the Bahamas, he moved to New York in the late 70s and hit the black Top 20 in 86 with 'Just Another Lover'. He has had two US-only Top 40s, the latest being 'Birthday Suit'(36) in 89.

JUST GOT PAID *(UK No. 68)*		10	13 AUG 88	COLUMBIA

EDDIE KENDRICKS

Alabama born singer formed The Primes who were renamed The Temptations and had a staggering run of hits, often with his lead vocal. He went solo in 71 and has since had over two dozen black music hits and six US Top 40s (2 UK). He re-united briefly with The Temptations in 82 and recorded as a duo with David Ruffin, another ex-member, in 87. He joined A&B in 90. His lead tenor or high harmony vocal was heard on more than 20 soul and pop hits between 63 and 71.

KEEP ON TRUCKIN' (PT 1) *(UK No. 18)*		1(2)	10 NOV 73	TAMLA
BOOGIE DOWN *(UK No. 39)*		2	09 MAR 74	TAMLA

Also see The Temptations

CHRIS KENNER

Late R&B singer/songwriter from New Orleans first recorded on Baton in 56. He wrote and first released the R&B/soul classics 'Land Of A Thousand Dances', 'Sick & Tired' and 'Something You Got'. He also was on Imperial, Pontchartrain, Ron and Uptown.

I LIKE IT LIKE THAT (PT.1)		2	31 JUL 61	INSTANT

KENNY

UK pop quintet who included Andy Walton and Jan Style, joined the Bill Martin & Phil Coulter writing and production team when The Bay City Rollers left. All of their four chart records hit the UK-only Top 20.

THE BUMP		3	18 JAN 75	RAK
FANCY PANTS		4	05 APR 75	RAK
JULIE ANN		10	13 SEP 75	RAK

NIK KERSHAW

Singer/songwriter and multi-instrumentalist from Ipswich (UK) started in the group Half Pint Hog. He first recorded in Fusion on Telephone in 80, when he cut an early version of 'Human Racing' which was later one of his 11 UK (1 US) chart entries.

🇬🇧	WOULDN'T IT BE GOOD (US No. 46)	4	03 MAR 84	MCA
	I WON'T LET THE SUN GO DOWN ON ME (Re-issue)	2	30 JUN 84	MCA
	(Originally was a No. 47 hit in 83)			
	THE RIDDLE	3	08 DEC 84	MCA
	(His fifth Top 20 hit in 84 – a record)			
	WIDE BOY	9	06 APR 85	MCA
	DON QUIXOTE	10	17 AUG 85	MCA

CHAKA KHAN

Born Yvette Stevens in Illinois, her first professional bands were Lyfe and The Babysitters before helping to form hit act Rufus. She also recorded solos after 78 which have had more success in the UK where she has scored five Top 20s. She returned to the US Top 20 in 89 as guest singer with Quincy Jones.

🇬🇧	I FEEL FOR YOU (A re-mix got No. 45 in 89)	1(3)	10 NOV 84	WARNER
	(Stevie Wonder on harmonica and rap by Melle Mel)			
	I'M EVERY WOMAN (REMIX)	8	13 MAY 89	WARNER
	(Comp. Ashford & Simpson – Was UK No. 11 in 78)			
🇺🇸	I FEEL FOR YOU (Prince song)	3	23 NOV 84	WARNER

Also see Rufus

JOHNNY KIDD & THE PIRATES

Born Fred Heath in London, he was one of the few UK rock performers who wrote good rock songs before The Beatles. Johnny, who performed with an eye-patch, is respected by rock critics even though he recorded many cover versions too. He died in a car crash in 66.

🇬🇧	SHAKIN' ALL OVER	3	22 JUL 60	HMV
	(Johnny's song which Guess Who hit with in the US)			
	I'LL NEVER GET OVER YOU	5	06 SEP 63	HMV

KIDS FROM 'FAME'

The US TV series Fame was a smash hit in the UK and spawned three Top 20 singles and four Top 20 LPs, the first of which was No. 1 for 12 weeks. In the US their biggest hit was a lowly No. 98 LP with a live album recorded in the UK.

🇬🇧	HI-FIDELITY (Featuring Valerie Land)	5	04 SEP 82	RCA
	STARMAKER	3	23 OCT 82	RCA

GREG KIHN BAND

California singer/songwriter signed with Beserkley in 74 and had his first LP in 76. He was a US cult favourite for some years before his run of three Top 40 LPs cleverly titled 'Rockhinroll', 'Khintinued' and 'Kihnspiracy', with his sole Top 20 hit coming from the last one. He joined EMI in 84.

🇺🇸	JEOPARDY (UK No. 63)	2	07 MAY 83	BESERKLEY

ANDY KIM

Born Andy Joachim in Montreal, he started as a writer and co- wrote 'Sugar Sugar' the Transatlantic No. 1 for the Archies. He first recorded on Red Bird in 65 and had five US-only Top 40s in the 60s. He also recorded in Canada as Baron Longfellow. His first release on his own Ice label in Canada became his biggest hit.

🇬🇧	ROCK ME GENTLY	2	12 OCT 74	CAPITOL
🇺🇸	BABY I LOVE YOU (Ronettes 63 hit)	9	26 JUL 69	STEED
	ROCK ME GENTLY	1(1)	28 SEP 74	CAPITOL

KING FLOYD

New Orleans soul singer first recorded on the L.A. labels Original Sound and Uptown in 65. He has had 10 black music hits but never returned to the US Top 100. He was also on Pulsar, VIP and Dial.

🇺🇸	GROOVE ME	6	30 JAN 71	CHIMNEYVILLE

KING

Even though they had been dropped by WEA this group led by Coventry's (UK) charismatic Paul King (ex-Reluctant Stereotypes) were thought to be one of 85s brightest prospects. The group, who had a sponsorship deal with footware company Dr. Martens, scored five UK-only Top 40s and split in 86.

🇬🇧	LOVE & PRIDE (US No. 55) (Was UK No. 84 in 84)	2	09 FEB 85	CBS
	ALONE WITHOUT YOU	8	07 SEP 85	CBS

BEN E. KING

Born Ben E. Nelson in North Carolina. In the late 50s he sang with the Four B's, Moonglows and Five Crowns who became The Drifters in 59. He sang lead on their two biggest US hits before going solo in 60. He has had two US Top 10 come-backs and finally hit the UK Top 20 26 years after going solo.

🇬🇧	STAND BY ME (Re-issue)	1(3)	21 FEB 87	ATLANTIC
	(Used in a TV jeans Ad. – Jumped from 19-1)			
🇺🇸	SPANISH HARLEM	10	13 MAR 61	ATCO
	STAND BY ME	4	12 JUN 61	ATCO
	(He co-wrote this pop/soul/country standard)			
	SUPERNATURAL THING PART 1	5	26 APR 75	ATLANTIC
	STAND BY ME (Re-issue) (From the film)	9	20 DEC 86	ATLANTIC

CAROLE KING

The most successful female song writer of all time was born Carol Klein in Brooklyn. When just 14 she was in The Cosines and she recorded solo for ABC, RCA and Alpine in the 50s. As a writer she has had literally dozens of big hits (often with her ex husband Gerry Goffin). As a singer she had eight consecutive Gold LPs in the 70s including the 15 million seller 'Tapestry', which spent 302 weeks on the US chart. She was still playing to SRO crowds in 89.

🇬🇧	IT MIGHT AS WELL RAIN UNTIL SEPTEMBER	3	19 OCT 62	LONDON
	(US No. 22 – she wrote it for Bobby Vee)			
	IT'S TOO LATE (Grammy winning song)	6	18 SEP 71	A&M
🇺🇸	IT'S TOO LATE (Top Easy Listening song of 71)	1(5)	19 JUN 71	ODE
	SWEET SEASONS	9	04 MAR 72	ODE
	JAZZMAN	2	09 NOV 74	ODE
	NIGHTINGALE	9	01 MAR 75	ODE

CLAUDE KING

Louisiana singer recorded for Specialty and Gotham in 52. He has since had 30 country hits and one Top 40 pop hit. He also recorded on Cinnamon and True in the 70s.

🇺🇸	WOLVERTON MOUNTAIN	6	21 JUL 62	COLUMBIA

EVELYN 'CHAMPAGNE' KING

The story goes that this Bronx born singer was discovered at top producers Gamble & Huff's studio whilst helping her mother clean it. True or not she has since had 14 Top 20 black music hits, many of which hit the transatlantic pop charts too.

🇬🇧	LOVE COME DOWN (US No. 17 – her 5th UK hit)	7	02 OCT 82	EMI
🇺🇸	SHAME (UK No. 39)	9	07 SEP 78	RCA
	(The top selling transatlantic 12" at the time)			

JONATHAN KING

London born pop svengali discovered such acts as Genesis, Bay City Rollers and 10 CC. He also had seven UK Top 40s under his own name and big UK-only hits as The Weathermen, 100 Ton & A Feather, Sakkarin and Shag. Not to mention producing hits for Hedgehoppers Anonymous, The Piglets and St. Cecilia and running his own successful UK label. He now writes for a tabloid and hosts a TV show Entertainment USA featuring US hit videos. Throughout his career he has always been a controversial figure, often at odds with popular opinion.

EVERYONE'S GONE TO THE MOON *(US No. 17)*		4	28 AUG 65	DECCA
UNA PALOMA BLANCA		5	11 OCT 75	UK

Also see 100 Ton & A Feather/Shag

SOLOMON KING

Big voiced US MOR singer won a Sacred Special Merit Award in 65 when on RCA. He then moved to the UK and recorded on UA in 66. He later had two UK Top 40s, the other being the follow up 'When We're Young'. He was also on Decca in 73 and Pinnacle in 76.

 SHE WEARS MY RING		3	24 FEB 68	COLUMBIA

KING BROTHERS

UK pop/MOR family trio started by winning a TV talent competition while in their early teens in the 50s. They chalked up 10 UK-only Top 40s with covers of US hits. They joined Pye in 63 and Dennis King went on to be one of the UK's top TV music writers.

A WHITE SPORT COAT *(Marty Robbins 57 US hit)*		6	19 JUL 57	PARLOPHONE
STANDING ON THE CORNER *(Four Lads 56 US hit)*		6	06 MAY 60	PARLOPHONE

KINGSMEN

This quartet from Oregon (US) were fronted by Jack Ely and started playing together in 57. Jack left after their first hit and formed The Courtmen who recorded 'Louie Louie 66' and 'Louie Go Home' in 66. The group with new leader Lynn Easton had another seven US-only hits, most of them revivals, and joined Capitol in 73.

LOUIE LOUIE *(UK No. 26) (US No. 97 in 66)* *(Originally by Richard Berry & The Pharaohs in 56)*		2	14 DEC 63	WAND
THE JOLLY GREEN GIANT *(Cut as a Joke-they later did 'Little Green Thing')*		4	06 MAR 65	WAND

KINGSTON TRIO

Bob Shane, Nick Reynolds and Dave Guard were the biggest selling folk act between 58-63 notching up 14 US-only Top 10 LPs and selling over 20 million records. They won countless awards at the time and helped pave the way for the 60s folk boom.

TOM DOOLEY *(Their 3rd single – based on life of Tom Dula)*		5	02 JAN 59	CAPITOL
TOM DOOLEY *(Grammy winning record – prev. by Tarriers in 57)*		1(1)	17 NOV 58	CAPITOL
REVEREND MR. BLACK		8	15 MAY 63	CAPITOL

KINKS

London foursome are already members of the R'n'R Hall of Fame thanks to their scores of transatlantic hits over the past 25 years. Their mainman is singer/songwriter Ray Davies whose commercial tunes and pictorial lyrics have made him one of rock's premier composers. The group have had many problems over the years but regularly bounce back into the charts.

 YOU REALLY GOT ME *(Their third single and first chart record)*	1(2)	11 SEP 64	PYE
ALL DAY AND ALL OF THE NIGHT	2	21 NOV 64	PYE
TIRED OF WAITING FOR YOU	1(1)	20 FEB 65	PYE
SET ME FREE *(US No. 23)*	9	26 JUN 65	PYE
SEE MY FRIEND	10	04 SEP 65	PYE
TILL THE END OF THE DAY *(US No. 50)*	8	15 JAN 66	PYE
DEDICATED FOLLOWER OF FASHION *(US No. 36)*	4	02 APR 66	PYE
SUNNY AFTERNOON *(US No. 14)*	1(2)	09 JUL 66	PYE
DEAD END STREET *(US No. 73)*	5	24 DEC 66	PYE
WATERLOO SUNSET *(Originally called 'Liverpool Sunset')*	2	27 MAY 67	PYE
AUTUMN ALMANAC	3	18 NOV 67	PYE
LOLA	2	08 AUG 70	PYE
APE MAN *(US No. 45)*	5	23 JAN 71	PYE
YOU REALLY GOT ME	7	28 NOV 64	REPRISE
ALL DAY AND ALL OF THE NIGHT	7	06 FEB 65	REPRISE
TIRED OF WAITING FOR YOU	6	24 APR 65	REPRISE
LOLA	9	24 OCT 70	REPRISE
COME DANCING *(UK No. 12)*	6	16 JUL 83	ARISTA

FERN KINNEY

Mississippi Miss whose UK No. 1 never charted in her homeland. She started with The Poppies, as had her successful Malaco label mate Dorothy Moore. Her biggest US hit was 'Groove Me' (54).

TOGETHER WE ARE BEAUTIFUL *(Originally by Ken Leray the writer in 77)*		1(1)	15 MAR 80	WEA

KATHY KIRBY

Blonde bombshell who first came to the public's attention on tours with Duane Eddy and Cliff Richard. She joined Decca in 62 and had two other UK-only Top 20's 'Dance On' (11) and 'You're The One' (17). Her only US entry was 'The Way Of Love' (88) in 65.

SECRET LOVE *(Doris Day 54 hit)*		3	13 DEC 63	DECCA
LET ME GO LOVER *(Joan Weber 54 hit)*		10	14 MAR 64	DECCA

KISS

Kiss have evolved from a critically slammed but enormously successful glitter/hard rock group to a well respected metal band and have picked up 17 gold albums en route. In the 70s their outrageous stage show and make-up attracted a 'Kiss Army' who lapped up the comic books and TV shows about the faceless New York foursome Peter, Ace, Gene and Paul. They never made the UK Top 20 until they shed their make up in 83.

CRAZY CRAZY NIGHTS *(US No. 71)*		4	24 OCT 87	VERTIGO
BETH *(Written for Peter Criss' wife Lydia)* *(Only Top 10 hit of their 20 US chart singles)*		7	04 DEC 76	CASABLANCA

MAC & KATIE KISSOON

UK based brother and sister from Trinidad. They had five UK chart entries and had the US hit of 'Chirpy Chirpy Cheep Cheep' (US 20/UK 41). They were also on Young Blood, Crazy Viking and Scoop. Katie also made solo singles in the 80s for Jive.

 SUGAR CANDY KISSES		3	08 FEB 75	POLYDOR
DON'T DO IT BABY		9	24 MAY 75	STATE

KLYMAXX

All girl octet from L.A. had three US-only Top 20s and seven other black music chart entries. The group who started on Solar in 81 included Joyce 'Fenderella' Irby, who has since gone solo on Motown, and Bernadette Cooper who formed Madame X in 87 both of whom have had black music Top 10 hits since leaving.

| I MISS YOU | 5 | 28 DEC 85 | MCA/CONSTELLA |

KNACK

Detroit foursome led by Doug Feiger sold five million of their debut LP and had the biggest US single of 79. However there was a backlash against their pop new wave sound and the group quickly dropped out of fashion and folded in 82. Doug, who had started in Sky who recorded on RCA in 71, later formed Taking Chances.

| MY SHARONA | 6 | 28 JUL 79 | CAPITOL |
| MY SHARONA | 1(6) | 25 AUG 79 | CAPITOL |

GLADYS KNIGHT & THE PIPS

The veteran singer was a winner on 'Ted Macks Amateur Hour' in 51 when just 6. She was in The Magnificents in the 50s and made her first record with her family group The Pips in 57 on Brunswick. She has won numerous awards in her 30 year spell at the top and chalked up 16 US Top 20 (9 UK) singles and 59 black music hits.

THE WAY WE WERE/TRY TO REMEMBER (MEDLEY)	4	31 MAY 75	BUDDAH
(US No. 11 – Barbra Streisand 73 US hit)			
THE BEST THING THAT EVER HAPPENED	7	30 AUG 75	BUDDAH
MIDNIGHT TRAIN TO GEORGIA	10	05 JUN 76	BUDDAH
BABY DON'T CHANGE YOUR MIND (US No. 52)	4	09 JUL 77	BUDDAH
LICENCE TO KILL	6	08 JUL 89	MCA
(Without The Pips – James Bond film theme)			
EVERY BEAT OF MY HEART (as THE PIPS)	6	10 JUL 61	VEE JAY
I HEARD IT THROUGH THE GRAPEVINE (UK No. 47)	2	16 DEC 67	SOUL
IF I WERE YOUR WOMAN	9	13 FEB 71	SOUL
NEITHER ONE OF US (WANTS TO BE THE FIRST TO SAY GOODBYE) (UK No. 31)	2	07 APR 73	SOUL
MIDNIGHT TRAIN TO GEORGIA	1(2)	27 OCT 73	BUDDAH
I'VE GOT TO USE MY IMAGINATION	4	19 JAN 74	BUDDAH
BEST THING THAT EVER HAPPENED TO ME	3	27 APR 74	BUDDAH
ON AND ON (From the film 'Claudine')	5	13 JUL 74	BUDDAH

JEAN KNIGHT

New Orleans soul singer recorded for Tribe in 64 and Jetsteam in 66. She followed her one US Top 40 with 'You Think You're Hot Stuff'. She later was on Chelsea, Cotillion, Dial and Soulin.

| MR. BIG STUFF (Top US Soul Single /1) | 2 | 14 AUG 71 | STAX |

ROBERT KNIGHT

Tennessee soul singer first recorded on Dot in 60 with his group The Paramounts. His biggest US hit 'Everlasting Love' (13/UK 19 – seven years after in 84) was a UK No. 1 for Love Affair who also covered his 'Rainbow Road'. He joined Private Stock in 75.

| LOVE ON A MOUNTAIN TOP | 10 | 26 JAN 74 | MONUMENT |
| (Old US 'B' side – became UK northern soul hit) | | | |

KOKOMO

Nom-de-plume for the well known pianist and arranger Jimmy 'Wiz' Wisner. He also recorded for labels like Chancellor and Columbia.

| ASIA MINOR (Adpt. from Grieg Piano Concerto) | 8 | 17 APR 61 | FELSTED |

KON KAN

Project put together by Canadians Barry Harris and Kevin Wayne. Their Transatlantic Top 20 hit contained samples from Lynn Anderson's 70 hit 'Rose Garden'. Follow up was 'Puss n'Boots'.

| I BEG YOUR PARDON (US No. 15) | 5 | 15 APR 89 | ATLANTIC |

JOHN KONGOS

Johannesburg born singer, songwriter and multi-instrumentalist whose records had a unique mix of African music and rock. With help from producer Gus Dudgeon he had two Top 5 UK hits. In the 60s he had been on RCA, Piccadilly and Dawn. He has also done much session work including playing on Def Leppard's 'Pyromania'.

| HE'S GONNA STEP ON YOU AGAIN (US No. 70) | 4 | 03 JUL 71 | FLY |
| TOKOLOSHE MAN | 4 | 11 DEC 71 | FLY |

KOOL & THE GANG

Bass player Robert 'Kool' Bell formed the group in 64 originally as The Jazziacs. Their first US hit came in 73, when they were a mainly instrumental act, but it took six years and the commercial influence of producer Deodata to give them a UK hit. They have now had 32 US hits and 22 in the UK. The group were on the first Band Aid record. In 88 singer James 'J.T.' Taylor left.

LADIES NIGHT	9	24 NOV 79	MERCURY
CELEBRATION	7	29 NOV 80	DE-LITE
GET DOWN ON IT	3	16 JAN 82	DE-LITE
OOH LA LA LA (LET'S GO DANCING) (US No. 30)	6	13 NOV 82	DE-LITE
JOANNA/TONIGHT	2	10 MAR 84	DE-LITE
(WHEN YOU SAY YOU LOVE SOMEBODY) IN THE HEART	7	28 APR 84	DE-LITE
CHERISH	4	06 JUL 85	DE-LITE
JUNGLE BOOGIE (Their 10th R&B hit)	4	09 MAR 74	DE-LITE
HOLLYWOOD SWINGING	6	06 JUL 74	DE-LITE
LADIES NIGHT	8	12 JAN 80	DE-LITE
TOO HOT (UK No. 23)	5	05 APR 80	DE-LITE
CELEBRATION	1(2)	07 FEB 81	DE-LITE
GET DOWN ON IT	10	22 MAY 82	DE-LITE
JOANNA	2	11 FEB 84	DE-LITE
MISLED (UK No. 28)	10	09 MAR 85	DE-LITE
FRESH (UK No. 11)	9	08 JUN 85	DE-LITE
CHERISH	2	21 SEP 85	DE-LITE
VICTORY (UK No. 30)	10	24 JAN 87	MERCURY
(Their 7th Top 20 in a row with a 1 word title)			
STONE LOVE (UK No. 45)	10	02 MAY 87	MERCURY

KORGIS

Ex-Stackridge members James Warren and Andy Davis from Bath (UK) were backed by the Short Wave Band on both their self-composed UK Top 20 singles. The other one was their previous release 'If I Had You' (13). They were later on London, Marvellous and Sonet.

| EVERYBODY'S GOT TO LEARN SOMETIME (US No.18) | 5 | 28 JUN 80 | RIALTO |

KRAFTWERK

This German group who were formed in 70 greatly influenced the rock and dance music scenes of the 70s & 80s with their all electronic machine-like riffs and music. The two founder members Ralf Hutter and Florian Schneider first recorded as Organization. Act's biggest US single was 'Autobahn' (US 25/UK 11) in 75.

| THE MODEL/COMPUTER LOVE | 1(1) | 06 FEB 82 | EMI |
| (First German record to top UK chart) | | | |

BILLY J. KRAMER & THE DAKOTAS

Born Billy Ashton in Liverpool he started with local band The Coasters before joining Manchester's Dakotas. They were managed by Brian Epstein and shot to instant fame having a successful but brief spell at the top. They broke up in 68 and he has made many records since and played numerous revival shows.

DO YOU WANT TO KNOW A SECRET	1(2)	31 MAY 63	PARLOPHONE
(Was a US hit for the writers The Beatles)			
BAD TO ME	1(2)	23 AUG 63	PARLOPHONE
I'LL KEEP YOU SATISFIED (US No. 30)	5	22 NOV 63	PARLOPHONE
(Above three written by Lennon & McCartney)			
LITTLE CHILDREN	1(2)	21 MAR 64	PARLOPHONE
FROM A WINDOW (US No. 23)	10	22 AUG 64	PARLOPHONE
(Another Lennon & McCartney song)			
LITTLE CHILDREN	7	13 JUN 64	IMPERIAL
BAD TO ME	9	27 JUN 64	IMPERIAL

KRUSH

Mixed House Music trio from Nottingham (UK) co-wrote their only UK chart hit to date. Singer Ruth Joy also made solos in 89.

HOUSE ARREST	3	16 JAN 88	CLUB

L

L.A. MIX

Recording project put together by UK Club DJ and re-mixer Les Adams. This dance act first charted with 'Don't Stop (Jammin')' in 87 and have had three more UK-only chart entries since.

CHECK THIS OUT	6	04 JUN 88	BREAKOUT

LABELLE

Philadelphia born Patti Labelle (Patti Holt) started in The Ordettes with Cindy Birdsong. They later formed The Bluebelles with Nona Hendrix and Sarah Dash and charted in 62 on Newtown. In 70 they became Labelle and had two unsuccessful LPs on Warner before getting their only Top 40 with a song first cut by 11th Hour.

LADY MARMALADE (VOULEZ-VOUS COUCHER AVEC MOI CE SOIR?) (UK No.17)			
(Co-Writ. Kenny Nolan had 2 No. 1s in row)	1(1)	29 MAR 75	EPIC

Also see Patti Labelle

PATTI LABELLE

When Labelle broke up in 77 strong-voiced Patti went solo and has had regular black music hits since including 11 Top 20s. She also scored two US Top 20 pop singles (the other being 'New Attitude' No. 17 in 85) and a No. 1 US pop LP 'Winner In You' in 86. Patti, who has hits in four decades, was produced by Prince in 89.

ON MY OWN (And MICHAEL MCDONALD)	2	17 MAY 86	MCA
(They recorded voices and made video separately)			
ON MY OWN (And MICHAEL MCDONALD)	1(3)	14 JUN 86	MCA
(Top black music record 86)			

Also see Labelle

CLEO LAINE

UK singer born Clementina Campbell, wife of jazz band leader Johnny Dankworth, has recorded in many styles from jazz to MOR to classics. She started in 52 and is a popular live act in both the UK and US where she has had six small LP chart hits.

YOU'LL ANSWER TO ME (Patti Page 61 US hit)	3	13 OCT 61	FONTANA

FRANKIE LAINE

Big voiced MOR vocalist was born Frankie Lo Vecchio in Chicago. He replaced Perry Como in Freddy Carlone's band in 37 and first recorded with black group Johnny Moore's Three Blazers in 45 on Exclusive. He joined Mercury in 47 and has had 70 US chart entries with sales close to 100 million. In 53 he spent a record 27 weeks at No. 1 in the UK. He is still a big crowd puller.

SIXTEEN TONS (Merle Travis song)	10	27 JAN 56	PHILIPS
COOL WATER (Sons of the Pioneers 41 hit)	2	05 AUG 55	PHILIPS
STRANGE LADY IN TOWN	6	12 AUG 55	PHILIPS
HAWKEYE	7	30 DEC 55	PHILIPS
A WOMAN IN LOVE (US No. 19)	1(4)	19 OCT 56	PHILIPS
RAWHIDE (From the TV series)	6	06 JAN 60	PHILIPS
MOONLIGHT GAMBLER (UK No. 13)	5	26 JAN 57	COLUMBIA

GREG LAKE

Bournemouth (UK) born bass player and singer started in The Gods and joined King Crimson in 69 – leaving in 70 to form Emerson, Lake & Palmer. His one UK hit has become a British Xmas standard. He signed with Chrysalis in 80, later joined Asia on their Asian tour and in 85 re-formed ELP as Emerson, Lake & (Cozy) Powell.

I BELIEVE IN FATHER CHRISTMAS (US No. 95)	2	27 DEC 75	MANTICORE

Also see Emerson, Lake & Palmer

LAMBRETTAS

One of the leading bands in the short-lived 60s mod music revival of the late 70s. The foursome who included Jez Bird and Doug Sanders managed another UK-only Top 20 with 'D-a-a-ance' (12).

POISON IVY (Coasters 59 hit)	7	05 APR 80	ROCKET

MAJOR LANCE

Chicago singer, whose hits were produced and written by Curtis Mayfield, helped introduce 'The Chicago Soul Sound' of the 60s. He started on Mercury in 59 and had 6 US (1 UK) Top 40s. He was later on Dakar, Curtom, Volt, Soul, Osiris, Playboy, Pye, Kat Family and Columbia. He was jailed on drug charges in 78.

THE MONKEY TIME	8	07 SEP 63	OKEH
UM, UM, UM, UM, UM, UM	5	08 FEB 64	OKEH
(UK – No. 40 – He re-recorded it in 75 on Playboy)			

LANDSCAPE

UK futurist/technopop quintet, included Richard James Burgess, released their first LP in 79 and scored their first of two UK-only Top 40s in 81. They tried to return as Landscape III in 83 and then Richard went into production, hitting with Spandau Ballet, Adam Ant, King, 5 Star, Living In a Box and Colonel Abrams.

 EINSTEIN A GO-GO   5   11 APR 81   RCA

LARKS

L.A. based 50s group Don Julian & The Meadowlarks, first recorded in 54 on RPM and cut the doo-wop classic 'Heaven & Paradise' on Dooto in 55. Act had its biggest hit as The Larks with a dance craze song that Don had written. Follow up was 'Soul Jerk'.

 THE JERK   7   16 JAN 65   MONEY

NICOLETTE LARSON

Kansas City born singer sang backing vocals for Hoyt Axton and Commander Cody before doing session work with acts like Linda Ronstadt, Neil Young, Van Halen, Christopher Cross and The Doobie Brothers. She has had 4 US-only chart singles and LPs.

 LOTTA LOVE   8   17 FEB 79   WARNER
(Comp. Neil Young-she sang with him on his version)

DENISE LA SALLE

Born Denis Craig in Mississippi, this raunchy soul singer and writer first recorded on Tarpen/Chess in 67. She has had 16 black music hits and has also recorded on Westbound, ABC, MCA and Malaco.

 MY TOOT TOOT (Banned by some stations)   6   20 JUL 85   EPIC
(Original by Rockin' Sydney)

STACY LATTISAW

Child protege from Washington made her first LP (with Van McCoy) when she was 12 and sang at the White House a year later. Her second LP, produced by Narada Michael Walden, contained her biggest US hit 'Let Me Be Your Angel' (21). She has also recorded hit duets with New Editions Johnny Gill (including a No. 1 black music hit in 90) and has had 22 black music hits to date.

 JUMP TO THE BEAT   3   12 JUL 80   ATLANTIC

CYNDI LAUPER

Quirky New York singer/songwriter won the Grammy for Best New Act of 84, sold over 4 million of her debut solo LP and also won numerous video awards. Fame did not come overnight though as she had been in Doc West in 74, spent three years in Flyer and cut a flop LP with Blue Angel on Polydor. Though she initially ran neck and neck with Madonna, recent sales have been disappointing.

GIRLS JUST WANT TO HAVE FUN	2	04 FEB 84	PORTRAIT
TIME AFTER TIME	3	14 JUL 84	PORTRAIT
I DROVE ALL NIGHT	7	24 JUN 89	EPIC
GIRLS JUST WANT TO HAVE FUN	2	10 MAR 84	PORTRAIT
TIME AFTER TIME	1(2)	09 JUN 84	PORTRAIT
SHE BOP (UK No. 46)	3	01 SEP 84	PORTRAIT
ALL THROUGH THE NIGHT (UK No. 64)	5	08 DEC 84	PORTRAIT
THE GOONIES 'R' GOOD ENOUGH	10	13 JUL 85	PORTRAIT
TRUE COLORS (UK No. 12)	1(2)	25 OCT 86	PORTRAIT
CHANGE OF HEART (UK No. 67)	3	14 FEB 87	PORTRAIT
I DROVE ALL NIGHT	6	08 JUL 89	EPIC

LAUREL & HARDY

Stan Laurel (born Arthur Jefferson) from Ulverston (UK) and Norvell (Oliver) Hardy from Georgia had fairly successful solo careers before joining together in the 20s and making a string of hit movies including Way Out West which their rather belated debut hit came from. Unfortunately neither lived to see their 38 year old track hit No. 2. Follow up was 'Another Fine Mess'.

 THE TRAIL OF THE LONESOME PINE   2   20 DEC 75   UA
(Featuring the AVALON BOYS Inc. Chill Wills)

STEVE LAWRENCE

Born Sam Leibowitz in New York. He appeared on Arthur Godfrey's Talent Show in 52 and became a regular on Steve Allen's Tonight show in 54, where he met his wife and sometimes duet partner Eydie Gorme. He first hit in the 50s with cover versions on King and Coral before scoring with original material in the early 60s.

FOOTSTEPS (Co-written by Barry Mann)	7	03 JUN 60	HMV
I WANT TO STAY HERE (And EYDIE GORME) (US No. 28 – Composed Carole King)	3	20 SEP 63	CBS
PRETTY BLUE EYES	9	04 JAN 60	ABC PARA.
FOOTSTEPS	7	04 APR 60	ABC PARA.
PORTRAIT OF MY LOVE (Matt Monro 60 UK hit)	9	08 MAY 61	UA
GO AWAY LITTLE GIRL (Co-writ. Carole King)	1(2)	12 JAN 63	COLUMBIA

VICKI LAWRENCE

Singer/actress from California who played Carol Burnett's sister in Carol's TV series. As a vocalist, she started in folk groups, became a member of the Young Americans in 64 and first recorded on Elf and UA. She married songwriter Bobby Russell ('Honey', 'Little Green Apples') who penned her only US Top 40 hit.

THE NIGHT THE LIGHTS WENT OUT IN GEORGIA   1(2)   07 APR 73   BELL
(Song rejected by Cher)

VICKY LEANDROS

Greek born, German raised singer who has had three UK-only chart entries and who twice represented Luxemburg in the Eurovision song contest. In 67 she came fourth with 'Love Is Blue' (the song was later a US No. 1) and in 72 she won with 'Apres Toi'. She returned briefly to the UK Top 40 with 'The Love In Your Eyes' (73).

COME WHAT MAY (APRES TOI)   2   13 MAY 72   PHILIPS

LED ZEPPELIN

The most successful and influential rock/heavy metal pioneers included ex-Yardbird guitarist Jimmy Page, ex CBS solo singer Robert Plant, former session man John Paul Jones on bass and John Bonham on drums. Zeppelin started life as the New Yardbirds, won numerous awards, broke Beatles' attendance records and had eight UK No. 1 LPs (6 US). They never released a single in the UK and stopped recording after Bonham's death in 80. They came together for 'Live Aid' with Phil Collins on drums and rumours of a reformation with Bonham's son Jason on drums are perpetually rife.

WHOLE LOTTA LOVE   4   31 JAN 70   ATLANTIC

BRENDA LEE

Child protege born Brenda Tarpley in Georgia appeared on the Perry Como and Ed Sullivan shows before she was 13. 'Little Miss Dynamite's third 45 'One Step At A Time' was the first of 52 US (22 UK) hits. She won numerous polls and awards and set many records for teenage singers. Since her decade of pop Top 40 hits ended in 67 she has notched up 33 country hits.

SWEET NOTHIN'S		4	03 JUN 60	BRUNSWICK
I'M SORRY		10	19 AUG 60	BRUNSWICK
(Recorded in 5 mins – Piano by Floyd Cramer)				
SPEAK TO ME PRETTY		5	04 MAY 62	BRUNSWICK
HERE COMES THAT FEELING *(US No. 89)*		7	06 JUL 62	BRUNSWICK
ROCKIN' AROUND THE CHRISTMAS TREE		6	28 DEC 62	BRUNSWICK
(US No. 14 – first released in 58)				
AS USUAL *(US No. 12)*		5	08 FEB 64	BRUNSWICK
(US No. 12 – She had 210 weeks on UK chart & no No. 1)				
SWEET NOTHIN'S *(Her 11th single)*		4	18 APR 60	DECCA
THAT'S ALL YOU GOTTA DO *(Comp. Jerry Reed)*		6	05 JUL 60	DECCA
I'M SORRY		1(3)	18 JUL 60	DECCA
I WANT TO BE WANTED *(UK No. 31)*		1(1)	24 OCT 60	DECCA
EMOTIONS *(UK No. 29)*		7	13 FEB 61	DECCA
YOU CAN DEPEND ON ME		6	08 MAY 61	DECCA
DUM DUM *(UK No. 22 – Comp. Jackie De Shannon)*		4	31 JUL 61	DECCA
FOOL #1		3	13 NOV 61	DECCA
(UK No. 38 – First recorded by Loretta Lynn)				
BREAK IT TO ME GENTLY *(UK No. 46)*		4	03 MAR 62	DECCA
EVERYBODY LOVES ME BUT YOU		6	26 MAY 62	DECCA
ALL ALONE AM I *(UK No. 11)*		3	10 NOV 62	DECCA
LOSING YOU *(UK No. 12)*		6	25 MAY 63	DECCA

CURTIS LEE

Both of this Arizona singer's US-only hits were Top 5 UK hits for Showaddywaddy in the late 70s – the other one being their No. 1 hit 'Under The Moon of Love'. Curtis had been discovered by singer Ray Peterson and had debuted on Ray's Dunes label with 'Pledge of Love'. He was later on Fabor in 64 and Mira and Rojac in 67.

PRETTY LITTLE ANGEL EYES *(Comp. Boyce & Hart)*		7	07 AUG 61	DUNES
(Prod Phil Spector – backing vocals The Halos)				

DEE C. LEE

UK artist came to the public's attention as a backing singer for Wham! and then Style Council. Her first solo was 'Selina Wow Wow' in 84 and then she had her sole UK Top 40 hit with a song she had written two years before. In 89 she formed Slam/Slam. She is married to Paul Weller.

SEE THE DAY		3	07 DEC 85	CBS

DICKEY LEE

Memphis singer recorded with The Collegiates on Sun Records in 57 and in the 60s had three US-only Top 20s – the others being 'I Saw Linda Yesterday' (14) and the eerie 'Laurie' (14). He wrote the 'She Thinks I Still Care' (country No. 1 twice) and had 29 country hits as a singer between 71-82 and many more as a writer.

PATCHES		6	06 OCT 62	SMASH

JOHNNY LEE

Texas country singer born Johnny Lee Ham. The one time regular at (Mickey) Gilley's Club near Houston first hit the country charts on ABC in 75 and has since had 30 more entries including five No. 1s. His only pop Top 40 hit came from the film 'Urban Cowboy'. He also recorded on GRT, Asylum, Warner and Curb.

LOOKIN' FOR LOVE		5	20 SEP 80	FULL MOON

LEAPY LEE

Actor/singer born Lee Graham in Eastbourne (UK). He appeared in several London West End shows in the late 50s. He was on Pye in 65 and his big hit sold 3 million world-wide. He made one more appearance in the Top 40 with 'Good Morning' (UK 29) in 70.

LITTLE ARROWS *(US No. 16 pop & No. 11 country)*		2	12 OCT 68	MCA
(Co-writ. Albert Hammond-voted Worst Record of 68)				

LEEDS UNITED F.C.

Yorkshire soccer club were among the UK's most successful sides at the time of their one-off hit. They are currently making a comeback.

LEEDS UNITED		10	27 MAY 72	CHAPTER ONE

LEFT BANKE

New York baroque rock group led by Michael Brown with vocals from Steve Martin. They had two US-only Top 20s – the other being 'Pretty Ballerina' (15). Brown left in 67 and later recorded with Montage on Laurie, The Stories on Kama Sutra and The Beckies on Sire. The group without Brown had an LP in 78 on Camerica.

WALK AWAY RENEE		5	29 OCT 66	SMASH
(Song written about Renee Fladen)				

LEMON PIPERS

Cincinnati quintet originally called Ivan & The Sabres were fronted by singer Ivan Browne and included Bill Bartlett. The bubblegum act, whose first single failed, followed their one transatlantic Top 20 with 'Rice Is Nice'. Group broke up in 69 and Bartlett later formed hit act Ram Jam.

GREEN TAMBOURINE		7	16 MAR 68	PYE INT.
GREEN TAMBOURINE		1	03 FEB 68	BUDDAH

JOHN LENNON

The ex Beatle was one of the century's greatest singers and songwriters. After scores of hits with the group he went solo in 69 and had a further 12 US (11 UK) Top 20 singles and 9 US (10 UK) Top 20 LPs. He retired in 75 and was murdered in New York in December 80 after completing his chart topping come-back LP.

GIVE PEACE A CHANCE		2	26 JUL 69	APPLE
(As PLASTIC ONO BAND – recd. in Montreal hotel)				
INSTANT KARMA *(Co-writ & prod Phil Spector)*		5	28 FEB 70	APPLE
(As LENNON/ONO & PLASTIC ONO BAND – Entered at No. 7)				
POWER TO THE PEOPLE		7	03 APR 71	APPLE
(And THE PLASTIC ONO BAND – US No. 11)				
HAPPY XMAS (WAR IS OVER)		4	23 DEC 72	APPLE
(As JOHN & YOKO & PLASTIC ONO BAND)				
IMAGINE		6	15 NOV 75	APPLE
(JUST LIKE)STARTING OVER *(Jumped from 21-1)*		1(1)	20 DEC 80	GEFFEN
(Had peaked at 8 & dropped to 21 before his death)				
HAPPY XMAS (WAR IS OVER) *(Re-entry)*		2	10 JAN 81	APPLE
(Feat. HARLEM COMMUNITY CHOIR – jumped from 45-4)				
IMAGINE *(Re-entry at No. 9 – UK Gold)*		1(4)	10 JAN 81	APPLE
(He had No. 1 & 2 on UK chart)				
WOMAN *(Entered at No. 3)*		1(2)	07 FEB 81	GEFFEN
(Last of a record three No.1's in two months)				
NOBODY TOLD ME		6	28 JAN 84	ONO MUSIC
INSTANT KARMA (WE ALL SHINE ON)		3	28 MAR 70	APPLE
(As JOHN ONO LENNON)				
IMAGINE *(Entered at No. 20)*		3	13 NOV 71	APPLE
WHATEVER GETS YOU THRU THE NIGHT		1(1)	16 NOV 74	APPLE
(UK No. 36)				
(As JOHN LENNON & THE PLASTIC ONO NUCLEAR BAND)				
#9 DREAM *(UK No. 23)*		9	22 FEB 75	APPLE
(JUST LIKE) STARTING OVER		1(5)	27 DEC 80	GEFFEN
WOMAN		2	21 MAR 81	GEFFEN
WATCHING THE WHEELS *(UK No. 30)*		10	23 MAY 81	GEFFEN
NOBODY TOLD ME		5	03 MAR 84	POLYDOR

JULIAN LENNON

The first Beatle child was born John Charles Julian Lennon in 63, shortly after the group had their first No. 1. He has so far had three US (2 UK) Top 40's and a Transatlantic Top 20 LP 'Valotte'.

 TOO LATE FOR GOODBYES	6	03 NOV 84	CHARISMA
VALOTTE (UK No. 55)	9	12 JAN 85	ATLANTIC
TOO LATE FOR GOODBYES	5	23 MAR 85	ATLANTIC

ANNIE LENNOX & AL GREEN

The Eurythmics singer got together with the top 70s soul man on a one-off single which returned him to the US Top 10 after 15 years.

PUT A LITTLE LOVE IN YOUR HEART	9	14 JAN 89	A&M
(UK No. 28 – Jackie De Shannon 69 US hit)			

Also see Eurythmics/Al Green

KETTY LESTER

Singer/TV actress born Revoyda Frierson in Arkansas was helped in her early days by 30s star Cab Calloway whom she toured with. She followed her sole Transatlantic Top 40 with another oldie 'But Not For Me'. She was also on Everest in 63, RCA in 64 and Tower in 65.

LOVE LETTERS (Dick Haymes 45 hit)	4	18 MAY 62	LONDON
LOVE LETTERS	5	14 APR 62	ERA

LETTERMEN

MOR/pop vocal trio of Tony Butala (was solo on Topic), Jim Pike (was solo on Warner) and Bob Engemann. They had a decade of US-only hits including six Top 20 singles and 32 chart LPs (9 were gold). They later had success with TV jingles and joined Applause in 82.

WHEN I FALL IN LOVE (Doris Day 52 US hit)	7	27 JAN 62	CAPITOL
GOIN' OUT OF MY HEAD/CAN'T TAKE MY EYES OFF YOU (MEDLEY) (Little Anthony/ Andy Williams hits)	7	10 FEB 68	CAPITOL

LEVEL 42

Formed as a jazz/funk instrumental group in London in 80 and fronted by noted bass player/singer Mark King. They started on Elite and had a big UK specialist following before recording more commercial material and getting a string of hits. Boon and Phil Gould left this popular live group in 87.

THE SUN GOES DOWN (LIVING IT UP)	10	10 SEP 83	POLYDOR
(Their ninth chart record)			
SOMETHING ABOUT YOU	6	09 NOV 85	POLYDOR
LESSONS IN LOVE (US No. 12)	3	10 MAY 86	POLYDOR
RUNNING IN THE FAMILY (US No. 83)	6	07 MAR 87	POLYDOR
TO BE WITH YOU AGAIN	10	09 MAY 87	POLYDOR
IT'S OVER	10	26 SEP 87	POLYDOR
SOMETHING ABOUT YOU	7	31 MAY 86	POLYDOR

LEVERT

Trio from Ohio are one of the top new acts on the US black music scene. The members are Gerald & Sean Levert, the sons of O'Jays member Eddie, and Marc Gordon. Their first release on Tempre in 85 failed but they have since had eight black music Top 5s and are writing and producing hits for others too, including The O'Jays.

CASANOVA	9	19 SEP 87	ATLANTIC
CASANOVA	5	31 OCT 87	ATLANTIC

JONA LEWIE

Singer and unusual songwriter John Lewis previously fronted Brett Marvin & The Thunderbolts and their hit alter-ego Terry Dactyl & The Dinosaurs. As a soloist he had first recorded on Sonet and later had two UK-only Top 20s, the first being his third Stiff single 'You'll Always Find Me In The Kitchen At Parties' (16).

STOP THE CAVALRY (Jumped from 69-15)	3	13 DEC 80	STIFF
(Sold three million and was Top 10 in 11 Countries)			

BARBARA LEWIS

Detroit soul singer/composer first recorded on Atlantic in 62 and had five US-only Top 40s. Records of hers have also been covered by UK acts The Searchers and Peter & Gordon and given them Top 20 hits. She was also on Enterprise in 70 and Reprise in 72.

HELLO STRANGER (Featuring THE DELLS)	3	22 JUN 63	ATLANTIC

BOBBY LEWIS

This orphan from Indianapolis had the Top US Single of 61 which was also the Top R&B single of the decade. He once sang with Duke Ellington and recorded in the 50s on Chess, Parrot, Spotlight, Mercury (including 'Yay Yay I Feel So Gay') and Roulette. He had four US-only hits and was still doing 'oldies' shows in 87.

TOSSIN' AND TURNIN'	17	10 JUL 61	BELTONE
(Co-written by Ritchie Adams of The Fireflies)			
ONE TRACK MIND	9	18 SEP 61	BELTONE

GARY LEWIS & THE PLAYBOYS

Comic Jerry (Levitch) Lewis' son Gary's pop quintet had a record seven US Top 20s with their first seven singles. He was drafted in 67 and group never hit the Top 20 again despite several come-back attempts. His sole UK hit was 'My Heart's Symphony' in 75 (UK 36/US 13 in 66) which had become a 'Northern soul' favourite.

THIS DIAMOND RING	1(2)	20 FEB 65	LIBERTY
(Written by Al Kooper & Leon Russell for Bobby Vee)			
COUNT ME IN (Comp. Glen D.Hardin of Crickets)	2	08 MAY 65	LIBERTY
SAVE YOUR HEART FOR ME	2	21 AUG 65	LIBERTY
EVERYBODY LOVES A CLOWN	4	06 NOV 65	LIBERTY
SHE'S JUST MY STYLE	3	08 JAN 66	LIBERTY
SURE GONNA MISS HER	9	09 APR 66	LIBERTY
GREEN GRASS	8	18 JUN 66	LIBERTY
(All above hits arranged by Leon Russell)			

HUEY LEWIS & THE NEWS

New York born singer/songwriter Hugh Cregg III fronted Clover from 76-79, the group who backed Elvis Costello on his first LP. They had four 45s and two LPs all of which failed. He returned to the US and formed The News in 80. Their first LP was also unsuccessful but then they started an enviable run of 13 US (3 UK) Top 20s. The UK were late discovering them but they won 'Top International Act' at the 86 BRITS awards. They joined EMI in 90.

THE POWER OF LOVE (Re-entry)	9	15 MAR 86	CHRYSALIS
(Was No.11 in 85 – Re-entry part due to BRITS award)			
DO YOU BELIEVE IN LOVE	7	17 APR 82	CHRYSALIS
(Was on B-side of their only UK Top 10)			
HEART AND SOUL (UK No. 61)	8	26 NOV 83	CHRYSALIS
I WANT A NEW DRUG	6	24 MAR 84	CHRYSALIS
THE HEART OF ROCK 'N' ROLL (UK No. 49)	6	09 JUN 84	CHRYSALIS
IF THIS IS IT	6	08 SEP 84	CHRYSALIS
THE POWER OF LOVE (From 'Back To The Future')	1(2)	24 AUG 85	CHRYSALIS
STUCK WITH YOU (UK No. 12)	1(3)	20 SEP 86	CHRYSALIS
HIP TO BE SQUARE (UK No. 41)	3	06 DEC 86	CHRYSALIS
JACOB'S LADDER	1(1)	14 MAR 87	CHRYSALIS
I KNOW WHAT I LIKE	9	30 MAY 87	CHRYSALIS
DOING IT ALL FOR MY BABY	6	19 SEP 87	CHRYSALIS
PERFECT WORLD (UK No. 48)	3	10 SEP 88	CHRYSALIS

JERRY LEE LEWIS

The 'Killer' from Louisiana has topped the pop, country and R&B charts and is in the 'R'n'R Hall of Fame. He first recorded in 56 and had three Transatlantic Top 10s before trouble over his 13 year old wife slowed his career down. In 68 he turned to country music where he has since had 55 chart entries. He has appeared in films and his bio-pic 'Great Balls of Fire' came out in 89. His live act is legendary and he is still rockin' his life away.

WHOLE LOTTA SHAKIN' GOIN' ON *(Originally by Roy Hall)*	8	01 NOV 57	LONDON
GREAT BALLS OF FIRE	1(2)	10 FEB 58	LONDON
BREATHLESS	8	02 MAY 58	LONDON
WHAT'D I SAY *(US No. 30 – Ray Charles 59 US hit)*	9	02 JUN 61	LONDON
WHOLE LOTTA SHAKIN' GOIN' ON	3	18 SEP 57	SUN
GREAT BALLS OF FIRE	2	06 JAN 58	SUN
BREATHLESS	9	07 APR 58	SUN

LINDA LEWIS

Distinctive London singer/songwriter was with Herbie Goins & The Nightimers before joining White Rabbit in 67 and then Ferris Wheel for two years. She went solo on Warner in 70 and has had four UK-only Top 40s. She was also on Epic (83) and Electricity (85) and recorded with sisters Dee & Shirley as the Lewis Sisters.

IT'S IN HIS KISS *(Betty Everett 64 US hit)*	6	09 AUG 75	ARISTA

RAMSEY LEWIS TRIO

Ex members of The Clefs – Ramsey, Eldee Young and Isaac Holt formed this instrumental pop/jazz trio in 56 and they had three US-only Top 20s. Eldee and Isaac left to form chart act Young-Holt Unlimited and their later replacements included Maurice White (of Earth, Wind & Fire). Ramsey has had 30 US LP entries to date.

THE "IN" CROWD *(Grammy Top Jazz Instrumental 65-Dobie Gray 65 hit)*	5	09 OCT 65	ARGO

JOHN LEYTON

UK singer/actor's first records were unsuccessful but when he played a pop singer in TV's 'Harpers West One' the song he featured shot to No. 1. He followed it with six more UK-only Top 40s and was a top teen attraction in the early 60s. He also appeared in top films like 'The Great Escape'.

JOHNNY REMEMBER ME	1(4)	25 AUG 61	TOP RANK
WILD WIND *(All his hits were produced by Joe Meek)*	2	13 OCT 61	TOP RANK

LIEUTENANT PIGEON

Unusual looking novelty instrumental group featuring Mrs. Fletcher at the piano and her son Nigel (ex Stavely Makepeace). They had two UK-only Top 20s, the other being 'Desperate Dan' (17). Their last Decca 45 was appropriately called 'Goodbye'.

MOULDY OLD DOUGH	1(4)	14 OCT 72	DECCA

GORDON LIGHTFOOT

Canada's best known male folk singer/songwriter. He first recorded on Chateau in 60, was on ABC and UK labels Decca in 62 and Fontana in 63. He joined UA in 65 where he released five LPs but fame as a singer only came when he joined Reprise in 70. He has had seven US-only Top 40 LPs and his songs like 'For Loving Me' and 'Early Morning Rain' have become folk/country standards.

IF YOU COULD READ MY MIND *(UK No. 30)*	5	20 FEB 71	REPRISE
SUNDOWN *(UK No. 33)*	1(1)	29 JUN 74	REPRISE
CAREFREE HIGHWAY	10	09 NOV 74	REPRISE
THE WRECK OF THE EDMUND FITZGERALD *(UK No. 40)*	2	20 NOV 76	REPRISE

LIL LOUIS

Chicago club DJ Louis Jordan had records like 'War Games', 'Video Clash' and 'Seven Days' before having a European smash which also topped the US dance chart. He followed it with 'Black Out' and returned to the UK Top 20 with 'I Called U' (16) in 90.

FRENCH KISS *(US No. 51 – Top 5 in France)*	2	19 AUG 89	FFRR/LONDON

LIMAHL

Chris Hamill's (Limahl is an anagram) advert for a backing group led to the formation of Kajagoogoo, which he left to go solo in 83. He had two UK Top 20s, the other being his solo debut 'Only For You' (16) and he was popular on the US dance scene.

NEVER ENDING STORY *(US No. 17)* *(Prod. & Comp. Giorgio Moroder – From the film)*	4	24 NOV 84	EMI

Also see Kajagoogoo

LIMMIE & THE FAMILY COOKING

Ohio family trio led by Limmie Snell were a lot more popular in the UK than in their homeland. They had three UK-only Top 40s and the act, with personnel changes, still tours Britain.

YOU CAN DO MAGIC *(US No. 84)*	3	01 SEP 73	AVCO
A WALKIN' MIRACLE *(Essex 63 US hit)*	6	04 MAY 74	AVCO

BOB LIND

Baltimore born folk/rock singer/songwriter was first on Verve Folkways and followed his sole transatlantic Top 40 hit with 'Remember The Rain' (US 64/UK 46). He semi-retired in the late 60s, recorded on Capitol in 72 and does the occasional show.

ELUSIVE BUTTERFLY	5	02 APR 66	FONTANA
ELUSIVE BUTTERFLY	5	12 MAR 66	WORLD PACIFIC

LINDISFARNE

Newcastle (UK) folk/rock quintet evolved from the group Brethren (previously Downtown Faction) and included singer Alan Hull and Rod Clements. Act had five UK-only Top 40 LPs including their No. 1 'Fog On The Tyne'. Rod left in 73 and Alan made solo LPs in 73 and 75. They broke up in 75 and re-united in 78 on Atlantic. They were later on Mercury in 79, LMP in 83 and Lindisfarne in 85.

MEET ME ON THE CORNER	5	25 MAR 72	CHARISMA
LADY ELEANOR *(US No. 82)*	3	10 JUN 72	CHARISMA
RUN FOR HOME *(US No. 33)*	10	29 JUL 78	MERCURY

MARK LINDSAY

Idaho born singer was the lead vocalist with the US hit band Paul Revere & The Raiders. He had eight US-only solo chart records.

ARIZONA *(Originally by Family Dogg)*	10	14 FEB 70	COLUMBIA

Also see Paul Revere & The Raiders

LAURIE LINGO & THE DIPSTICKS

Nom-de-plume for top UK radio DJs Dave Lee Travis and Paul Burnett. In 85 they returned to the UK chart as the Pee Bee Squad.

CONVOY GB *(Parody of C.W. McCall's 'Convoy')*	4	08 MAY 76	STATE

LINX

London based group fronted by David Grant and Stix were one of the first UK acts to make the US black music charts. They had three UK-only Top 20s, the others being 'You're Lying' and 'So This is Romance' (both 15). David successfully went solo in 83.

 INTUITION   7   11 APR 81   CHRYSALIS
(Revived in 88 by David Grant on Fresher)

Also see David Grant

LIPPS INC.

Project put together by Minneapolis producer/writer Steven Greenberg with vocals by Cynthia Johnson. He had been in Atlas & Greenberg for six years and Cynthia had sung in Flyte Tyme (later Prince's group Time). The follow up 'Rock it' had previously been an instrumental by Steven. Act re-appeared on Wide Angle in 85.

FUNKYTOWN   2   28 JUN 80   CASABLANCA
FUNKYTOWN   1(4)   31 MAY 80   CASABLANCA

LIQUID GOLD

London mixed quartet fronted by Ellie Hope, who had been in the trio Ellie with her sisters on Phonogram in 74. Their first hit was 'Anyway You Do It' (UK 41) in 78 and their biggest US record was 'My Baby's Baby' (45) in 79. Ellie later recorded solos and did a lot of session work. The group appeared on Ecstasy in 84.

DANCE YOURSELF DIZZY   2   05 APR 80   POLO
(Produced & Composed by Adrian Baker)
SUBSTITUTE   8   28 JUN 80   POLO

LISA LISA & CULT JAM

Lisa Velez fronts this New York trio whose eight Top 10 black music hits were all produced by Full Force. They first charted in the UK with their only UK Top 40 hit 'I Wonder If I Take You Home' (UK 12/US 34) which was also the Top US Dance Single of 85.

ALL CRIED OUT (And FULL FORCE)   8   25 OCT 86   COLUMBIA
(Featuring Paul Anthony & Bow Legged Lou)
HEAD TO TOE   1(1)   20 JUN 87   COLUMBIA
LOST IN EMOTION *(UK No. 58)*   1(1)   17 OCT 87   COLUMBIA

LITTLE ANTHONY & THE IMPERIALS

Anthony (Gourdine) recorded with The Duponts in 55 on Winley, Savoy and Royal Roost and then with The Chesters (who became The Imperials) in 57 on Apollo. The New York act had 19 US hits over 16 years and their only UK hit was a US flop 'Better Use Your Head' (UK 15) in 76. They were also on Veep, UA, Avco and Janus.

TEARS ON MY PILLOW   5   13 OCT 58   END
(UK No. 1 for Kylie Minogue in 90)
GOIN' OUT OF MY HEAD   6   26 DEC 64   DCP
HURT SO BAD   10   13 MAR 65   DCP

LITTLE CAESAR & THE ROMANS

L.A. quintet, previously called the Up-Fronts, had one of the last Doo-Wop hits with a nostalgic song about the 50s group scene which the act's members including Caesar (Carl Burnett) had all been part of. The follow up was 'Hully Gully Again'.

THOSE OLDIES BUT GOODIES
(REMIND ME OF YOU)   9   26 JUN 61   DEL-FI
(Also cut 'Memories Of Those Oldies But Goodies')

LITTLE DIPPERS

Quartet of Nashville session singers had a one-off hit. Act, who included later country star Darrell McCall, were on Dot in 64.

FOREVER   9   28 MAR 60   UNIVERSITY

LITTLE EVA

Carole King's one-time baby sitter Eva (Boyd) from North Carolina had two Transatlantic Top 20s. The first, about a non-existent dance, had been written for Dee Dee Sharp. The second was 'Let's Turkey Trot' (US 20/UK 14). Singer who had first charted with Big Dee Irwin was also on Verve, Spring, Amy and Bell.

THE LOCO-MOTION *(Also UK No. 11 in 72)*   2   19 OCT 62   LONDON
(Inspired record 'Little Eva' by The Locomotions)
THE LOCO-MOTION *(backed by The Cookies)*   1(1)   25 AUG 62   DIMENSION
(Co-writ. Carole King – Eva re-cut it on Bell in 72)

Also see Big Dee Irwin

LITTLE RIVER BAND

Australian pop/rock sextet evolved from the group Mississippi in 75. Vocalist was UK born Glenn Shorrock who had been in 60s act The Twilights. They logged 13 US-only Top 40 hits, with Aussie superstar John Farnham taking over vocals on the last two. They became LRB in 85, Glenn returned in 87 and they were on MCA in 90.

REMINISCING   3   28 OCT 78   HARVEST
LADY   10   07 APR 79   HARVEST
LONESOME LOSER   6   29 SEP 79   CAPITOL
COOL CHANGE   10   19 JAN 80   CAPITOL
THE NIGHT OWLS   6   07 NOV 81   CAPITOL
TAKE IT EASY ON ME   10   06 MAR 82   CAPITOL

Also see John Farnham

LIVERPOOL F.C.

UK's most successful soccer team both on the field and in the studio with four hits in 11 years including this clever rap track.

ANFIELD RAP (RED MACHINE IN FULL EFFECT)   3   21 MAY 88   VIRGIN

LIVING IN A BOX

Manchester's Richard Darbyshire fronts this trio which also includes Marcus Vere and San Franciscan Anthony Critchlow. They won the coveted Gold Prize at the 89 Tokyo Music Festival. Bobby Womack sang on their UK Top 40 hit 'So The Story Goes' (34).

LIVING IN A BOX *(US No. 17)*   5   16 MAY 87   CHRYSALIS
BLOW THE HOUSE DOWN   10   11 MAR 89   CHRYSALIS
ROOM IN YOUR HEART   5   04 NOV 89   CHRYSALIS

LOBO

Singer/songwriter born Roland Kent Lavoie in Tallahassee. He was in The Rumors, The Sugar Beats, Me & The Other Guys and The Legends which included Jim Stafford (Lobo later produced Jim's 'Spiders & Snakes') and Gram Parsons. He was on Laurie in 69 and chalked up 16 US (2 UK) hits. In the 80s he has had regular country charters as a writer and an artist on Evergreen and Lobo.

ME AND YOU AND A DOG NAMED BOO   4   24 JUL 71   PHILIPS
(Also recorded 'Gus The Dancing Dog')
I'D LOVE YOU TO WANT ME   5   13 JUL 74   UK
(UK hit two years after US)
ME AND YOU AND A DOG NAMED BOO   5   15 MAY 71   BIG TREE
I'D LOVE YOU TO WANT ME   2   18 NOV 72   BIG TREE
DON'T EXPECT ME TO BE YOUR FRIEND   8   17 FEB 73   BIG TREE

LOBO

West Indian styled vocalist based in Holland whose real name was Imrich Lobo. He had a one-off UK hit with a Euro dance track. The Rotterdam resident's popular live act included the Fame Girls.

 THE CARIBBEAN DISCO SHOW   8   29 AUG 81   POLYDOR

LOS LOBOS

L.A. based Mexican-American quintet which includes Cesar Rosas and David Hidalgo made their debut LP in 78. An EP recorded on Slash in 83 won them their first Grammy. Their big break came when they were seen in the film La Bamba which gave them a No. 1 LP and single.

 LA BAMBA *(200 year old song)*   1(2)   01 AUG 87   SLASH
LA BAMBA *(Ritchie Valens 59 US hit)*   1(3)   29 AUG 87   SLASH

HANK LOCKLIN

Country artist started performing in 42, was a regular on the 'Louisiana Hayride' in the late 40s and first hit the country chart in 49 on Four Star. He has had 33 country hits including eight Top 10s. He was Major of McLellan, Florida in the 60s.

PLEASE HELP ME, I'M FALLING   8   01 AUG 60   RCA
(UK 13 – it was the country No. 1 for 14 weeks)

JOHN LODGE – SEE JUSTIN HAYWARD/MOODY BLUES FOR HIT DETAILS

JOHNNY LOGAN

Irish based Australian singer, born Sean Sherrard, is the only act to win the Eurovision Song Contest twice. The two winners (the second his own song) gave him his two UK-only smash hits. He also had releases on Piccadilly in 80 and Plaza in 88.

 WHAT'S ANOTHER YEAR   1(2)   17 MAY 80   EPIC
HOLD ME NOW   2   13 JUN 87   EPIC

LOGGINS & MESSINA

Kenny Loggins signed to Columbia in 71 as a solo act and was to be produced by ex-Buffalo Springfield and Poco man Jim Messina but instead they became a duo and they notched up six US-only Top 40 LPs and three US-only Top 20 singles before splitting in 76. Jim was later on Warner and was in the re-united Poco in 89. Their big hit was also a hit for HM/glam rockers Poison in 89.

 YOUR MAMA DON'T DANCE   4   27 JAN 73   COLUMBIA

DAVE LOGGINS

Tennessee singer/songwriter (who is a distant cousin of Kenny) first recorded for Vanguard in 71 and his song 'Pieces of April' was a hit for Three Dog Night. He had one US Top 40 single and is now a top country writer and had a duet No. 1 with Anne Murray.

 PLEASE COME TO BOSTON   5   10 AUG 74   EPIC

KENNY LOGGINS

Washington singer/songwriter had been in Mercury act Gator Creek, Second Helping and even toured in the Electric Prunes before starting the successful Loggins & Messina partnership. As a solo act he has had 12 US (1 UK) singles and five US-only Top 40 LPs.

FOOTLOOSE   6   19 MAY 84   CBS
WHENEVER I CALL YOU 'FRIEND'   5   28 OCT 78   COLUMBIA
(Co-writer Melissa Manchester)
I'M ALRIGHT *(From the film 'Caddyshack')*   7   11 OCT 80   COLUMBIA
FOOTLOOSE *(From the film)*   1(3)   31 MAR 84   COLUMBIA
DANGER ZONE   2   26 JUL 86   COLUMBIA
(UK No. 45 – From the film 'Top Gun')
NOBODY'S FOOL *(From the film 'Caddyshack 11')*   8   17 SEP 88   COLUMBIA

LOLITA

The first Austrian female to hit the US Top 10 was Vienna's Lolita Ditta who was a TV and film star in Germany. Her follow up was 'Goodbye Jimmy Joe' (94). She was later on Four Corners.

SAILOR (YOUR HOME IS THE SEA)   5   19 DEC 60   KAPP
(Sung In German – In the UK Petula Clark had the hit)

LONDON BOYS

Singing and dancing duo Dennis and Edem from London relocated to Hamburg, Germany, where they first hit with 'Dance Dance Dance'. In 89 they achieved three UK-only Top 20s with their hi-nrg pop dance tracks, the other being 'Harlem Desire' (17).

REQUIEM *(Was UK No. 59 in 88)*   4   13 MAY 89   WEA
LONDON NIGHTS   2   22 JUL 89   TELDEC/WEA

LONDON SYMPHONY ORCHESTRA – SEE JOHN WILLIAMS FOR HIT DETAILS

SHORTY LONG

Alabama soul singer Frederick 'Shorty' Long spent two years in the Ink Spots in the 50s. He recorded for Tri-Phi in 62 and cut the original of 'Devil With A Blue Dress'. His first hit was 'Function At The Junction'. He unfortunately drowned in 69.

HERE COMES THE JUDGE *(UK No. 30)*   8   06 JUL 68   SOUL

LOOK

Four-man UK band which included singer Johnny Fontaine and guitarist Mick Buss. They followed their one-off UK Top 40 with 'Three Steps Away'. They were on Towerbell in 83.

I AM THE BEAT   6   24 JAN 81   MCA

LOOKING GLASS

New Jersey foursome were fronted by Elliott Lurie. They had two US-only Top 40s – the other being 'Jimmy Loves Mary-Anne' a year later. Shortly after they split and Elliott tried a solo career.

BRANDY (YOU'RE A FINE GIRL)   1(1)   26 AUG 72   EPIC

TRINI LOPEZ

Latin American singer Trinidad Lopez from Dallas recorded for King in 59. His LP 'Trini Lopez at PJs', recorded during his 18 month residency at the Hollywood club, was a US No. 2 (UK 7). He had 7 Top 40 US (2 UK) LPs and 4 US Top 40 (3 UK) singles. He was later on Capitol in 72, Private Stock in 75 and Roulette in 77.

IF I HAD A HAMMER *(Pete Seeger song)*   4   04 OCT 63   REPRISE
IF I HAD A HAMMER   3   07 SEP 63   REPRISE
(Peter, Paul & Mary 62 US hit)

GLORIA LORING & CARL ANDERSON

Soul singer Carl, who played Judas in 'Jesus Christ Superstar', had previous black music hits before getting a one-off smash with soap opera star Gloria. They both dueted unsuccessfully later, Carl with Angela Bofill and Gloria with Bobby Caldwell. She also recorded solo on Evolution and Atlantic and he was solo on Epic.

 FRIENDS AND LOVERS   2   27 SEP 86   USA CARRERE

LOVE AFFAIR

London pop quintet fronted by Steve Ellis recorded on Decca in 67. They had five successive UK-only Top 20s and were one of the top teeny bop acts of the time. The group, who admitted they did not play on their debut hit, changed their name to L.A. in 70. Steve left and was on Parlophone in 72 and Ariola in 78. They were later on Parlophone, Pye, Creole and re-appeared in 88 on Hit The Deck.

 EVERLASTING LOVE (Robert Knight 67 US hit)   1(2)   02 FEB 68   CBS
RAINBOW VALLEY (Original by Robert Knight)   5   08 JUN 68   CBS
A DAY WITHOUT LOVE   6   26 OCT 68   CBS
BRINGING ON BACK THE GOOD TIMES   9   16 AUG 69   CBS

LOVE AND ROCKETS

Northampton band formed by ex-Bauhaus members Daniel Ash, Kevin Haskins (who had both been in Tones On Tail on Situation Two in 83) and David J. They have had a US cult following since 85 and hit the US Top 20 LPs and singles for the first time in 89.

 SO ALIVE (Top Modern Rock track of 89 in US)   3   05 AUG 89   RCA

LOVE SCULPTURE

Welsh rock trio led by Dave Edmunds originally recorded as The Image on Parlophone. Their third release as Love Sculpture was their only hit, which they followed with 'Farandole'. Act split in 69 and Dave had a successful career as a soloist and a producer.

 SABRE DANCE   6   04 JAN 69   PARLOPHONE

Also see Dave Edmunds

LOVE UNLIMITED ORCHESTRA

A group of session musicians put together as a vehicle for singer/composer and conductor Barry White's orchestral ideas. Act had five US-only chart LPs and one Transatlantic Top 20 single.

 LOVE'S THEME   10   23 FEB 74   PYE
LOVE'S THEME   11   09 FEB 74   20TH CENTURY

Also see Barry White

LOVERBOY

Canadian rock group features singer Mike Reno and guitarist Paul Dean. They have had no UK chart records but have strung together nine US Top 40 singles and three US Top 20 LPs. Mike, who started in Moxy, also had a hit duet with Heart's Ann Wilson.

 LOVIN' EVERY MINUTE OF IT   9   02 NOV 85   COLUMBIA
THIS COULD BE THE NIGHT   10   29 MAR 86   COLUMBIA

Also see Mike Reno & Ann Wilson

LENE LOVICH

Distinctive Detroit born singer/songwriter moved to the UK when 13. In 75 she joined The Diversions, who had five unsuccessful singles. Her first solo was a version of 'I Think We're Alone Now'. She has had two UK-only Top 20s, the other being the follow up 'Say When' (19). She was on the US Pathfinder label in 89.

 LUCKY NUMBER   3   24 MAR 79   STIFF

LOVIN' SPOONFUL

Singer John Sebastian, ex member of the Even Dozen Jug Band, formed the New York group with Zal Yanovsky, ex-member of the Halifax Three. The pair had also played together in The Mugwumps with Mama Cass and Denny of The Mamas & The Papas. The group's Good Time folk/rock music gave them many transatlantic hits before Zal and John left. John later had solo success too.

 DAYDREAM   2   07 MAY 66   PYE INT.
SUMMER IN THE CITY   8   20 AUG 66   KAMA SUTRA
DO YOU BELIEVE IN MAGIC   9   16 OCT 65   KAMA SUTRA
YOU DIDN'T HAVE TO BE SO NICE   10   22 JAN 66   KAMA SUTRA
DAYDREAM   2   09 APR 66   KAMA SUTRA
DID YOU EVER HAVE TO MAKE UP YOUR MIND?   2   11 JUN 66   KAMA SUTRA
SUMMER IN THE CITY   1(3)   13 AUG 66   KAMA SUTRA
RAIN ON THE ROOF   10   19 NOV 66   KAMA SUTRA
NASHVILLE CATS (UK No. 26)   8   28 JAN 67   KAMA SUTRA
(Seventh Top 10 with first seven singles – a record)

NICK LOWE

UK singer/writer started in Kippington Lodge who evolved into Brinsley Schwarz. He recorded on Stiff in 75, Radar in 77 and F-Beat in 82 and has produced acts like Elvis Costello, The Damned, Dr. Feelgood and The Pretenders. His biggest US hit was "Cruel To Be Kind' a transatlantic No. 12 in 79. He was on Reprise in 90.

I LOVE THE SOUND OF BREAKING GLASS   7   01 APR 78   RADAR

L.T.D.

L.T.D. (Love, Togetherness & Devotion) were a 10 piece soul band from North Carolina featuring the voice of Jeffrey Osborne. Jeffrey went solo in 80 and the group, who have had 10 black music Top 20s, replaced him with Andre Ray and Leslie Wilson.

BACK IN LOVE AGAIN   4   24 DEC 77   A&M

LULU

Born Marie Lawrie in Glasgow, she joined the six man Luvvers (previously The Gleneagles) when just 14. They hit with their first single and split in 66 when she joined Columbia. She has since had 11 UK (4 US – all different!) Top 40s, has won many awards, appeared in films and is still often seen on UK TV. She was also on Atco, Polydor, Chelsea, Alfa, Rocket, Lifestyle and joined Mercury in 90.

SHOUT (US No. 94 – Isley Brothers 59 US hit)   7   20 JUN 64   DECCA
LEAVE A LITTLE LOVE   8   17 JUL 65   DECCA
(Above two as Lulu & The Luvvers)
THE BOAT THAT I ROW (Neil Diamond song)   6   13 MAY 67   COLUMBIA
(In UK 'To Sir With love' was the B-side)
ME THE PEACEFUL HEART (US No. 53)   9   23 MAR 68   COLUMBIA
I'M A TIGER (Composed Marty Wilde)   9   07 DEC 68   COLUMBIA
BOOM BANG-A-BANG   2   12 APR 69   COLUMBIA
(Eurovision Song Contest winning song)
THE MAN WHO SOLD THE WORLD   3   16 FEB 74   POLYDOR
(David Bowie song)
SHOUT   8   16 AUG 86   JIVE/DECCA
(Sales of re-issue and new version were combined)
TO SIR WITH LOVE (Top US Single of 64)   1(5)   21 OCT 67   EPIC

BOB LUMAN

Texan singer/songwriter was a well respected rockabilly artist in the 50s and was in the film 'Carnival Rock' in 57. He has also been on Imperial, Capitol, Hickory, Epic and Polydor and had 39 country hits including seven Top 20s. He had a one-off Transatlantic Top 40 about living, but died in 78 aged 41.

🇬🇧 LET'S THINK ABOUT LIVING	6	28 OCT 60	WARNER
🇺🇸 LET'S THINK ABOUT LIVING	7	24 OCT 60	WARNER

VICTOR LUNDBERG

Michigan born ex soldier and radio newsman had a controversial one-off hit encouraging young men to fight in Vietnam. It encouraged many young men to make answer records saying "No", including Every Father's Teenage Son with 'A Letter To Dad'.

🇺🇸 AN OPEN LETTER TO MY TEENAGE SON	10	02 DEC 67	LIBERTY

ARTHUR LYMAN

Multi-instrumentalist from Hawaii who had worked with the Martin Denny Trio. He had a gold album in 58 with 'Taboo' and three US-only chart singles with his vibraphone-led exotic MOR music.

🇺🇸 YELLOW BIRD	4	24 JUL 61	HI FI

BARBARA LYNN

Texan R&B singer/songwriter and guitarist born Barbara Lynn Ozen had nine US-only hits, only one of which made the Top 40. The Rolling Stones recorded her 'Oh! Baby (We Got a Good Thing Goin')' and she later recorded on Tribe, Atlantic and Jetstream.

🇺🇸 YOU'LL LOSE A GOOD THING *(Her composition was a No. 1 country hit in 76)*	8	11 AUG 62	JAMIE

TAMI LYNN

L.A. based soul singer, who had no US success, twice hit the UK Top 40 with the same Jerry Wexler produced song. She later recorded an underrated concept album for UK label Contempo.

🇬🇧 I'M GONNA RUN AWAY FROM YOU *(UK No. 36 in 75)*	4	26 JUN 71	MOJO

PHIL LYNOTT

Dublin born singer/songwriter and bass player in Thin Lizzy charted with his first solo 45 'Dear Miss Lonely Hearts' (32) in 80. He had a further five UK-only entries including the 'Top Of The Pops' TV theme 'Yellow Pearl' (14). He launched his new group Grand Slam in 84 and sadly died in 86.

🇬🇧 OUT IN THE FIELDS *(With GARY MOORE)*	5	08 JUN 85	VIRGIN/10

Also see Thin Lizzy

LYNYRD SKYNYRD

Top Southern rock band evolved out of My Backyard formed in 65 by Ronnie Van Zant, Allen Collins and Gary Rossington. Named after a gym teacher Leonard Skinner, they have had eight US (three UK) Top 40 LPs and three US-only Top 20s including 'Freebird' their sole UK hit (charting in 76, 79 and 82!). Ronnie was amongst the members killed in a plane crash in 77. The surviving members of the group then became the Rossington-Collins band. Collins died in 1990.

🇺🇸 SWEET HOME ALABAMA	8	26 OCT 74	MCA

M

M

UK musician Robin Scott recorded under this name and had a Transatlantic Top 10. He followed it with 'Moonlight & Musak' (UK). A remix reached No.15 in the UK in 89.

🇬🇧 POP MUZIK	2	12 MAY 79	MCA
🇺🇸 POP MUZIK	1(1)	03 NOV 79	SIRE

M.C. MIKER 'G' & DEEJAY SVEN

Dutch duo were 18 year old Dutch club DJ Sven, and rapper Miker 'G'. Their one-off UK hit included bits of Madonna's 'Holiday' and Cliff Richard's 'Summer Holiday'. Follow up was 'Celebration Rap'. In 87 they were on Nine O Nine and Mike was on A1 in 90.

🇬🇧 HOLIDAY RAP	6	13 SEP 86	DEBUT

MAC BAND featuring THE McCAMPBELL BROTHERS

Eight-piece band from Michigan featuring Charles, Kelvin, Ray & Derrick McCampbell missed the US pop chart but topped the black music chart with the first of their two UK Top 40s – the other being 'Stalemate'. MAC supposedly stands for Men After Christ.

🇬🇧 ROSES ARE RED *(Written for the Whispers)*	8	23 JUL 88	

KIRSTY MacCOLL

Daughter of the well known folk singer/songwriter Ewan MacColl. She married top producer Steve Lillywhite. She has had four UK-only Top 20s; the others being 'There's A Guy Works Down The Chipshop Swears He's Elvis' (14) in 81 and 'Days' (12) in 89. Her song 'They Don't Know' was a hit for Tracy Ullman in 83. She appears regularly on the French and Saunders TV comedy show.

🇬🇧 A NEW ENGLAND *(Billy Bragg song)*	7	23 FEB 85	STIFF
🇬🇧 FAIRYTALE OF NEW YORK *(With THE POGUES)*	2	26 DEC 87	POGUE MAHONE

BYRON MACGREGOR

Canadian news reader who worked in Detroit had a one-off US hit with a patriotic recitation that had been written by another Canadian. His follow ups included 'Thank You America'.

🇺🇸 AMERICANS *(Originally by Gordon Sinclair)*	4	09 FEB 74	WESTBOUND

MARY MACGREGOR

Minnesota singer whose first release was a version of 'I've Never Been To Me' in 77. She had six US chart entries, two of which were written by Peter Yarrow of Peter, Paul & Mary, namely her transatlantic hit and 'The Wedding Song'. She was on RSO in 79.

🇬🇧 TORN BETWEEN TWO LOVERS *(She says this record contributed to her divorce)*	4	12 MAR 77	ARIOLA AM.
🇺🇸 TORN BETWEEN TWO LOVERS	1(2)	05 FEB 77	ARIOLA AM.

LONNIE MACK

Lonnie McIntosh from Indiana got his big break when his group's singer did not turn up and they had to become an instrumental act with guitarist Lonnie in front. He had four US hits in the 60s and made his UK chart debut (47) in 79 with a re-issue of his big hit. He was on Roulette in 75, Capitol in 77 and Epic in 88.

MEMPHIS (UK No. 47 – Orig. by Chuck Berry)	5	20 JUL 63	FRATERN.

MADNESS

One of the UKs most successful groups had 21 Top 20 singles and seven Top 20 LPs. The 'Nutty' boys started as The North London Invaders in 76 before naming themselves after a Prince Buster song. They brought in singer Graham 'Suggs' McPherson in 78 and charted with their first single on 2-Tone before joining Stiff. Despite their amazing UK popularity they only achieved one US Top 20 single. They started their own label Zarjazz in 84, split up in 86 and re-formed as four piece The Madness in 88.

ONE STEP BEYOND	7	01 DEC 79	STIFF
MY GIRL	3	26 JAN 80	STIFF
WORK REST & PLAY (E.P.) (Included 'Night Boat To Cairo')	6	12 APR 80	STIFF
BAGGY TROUSERS	3	11 OCT 80	STIFF
EMBARRASSMENT	4	06 DEC 80	STIFF
RETURN OF THE LOS PALMAS SEVEN	7	21 FEB 81	STIFF
GREY DAY	4	16 MAY 81	STIFF
SHUT UP	7	10 OCT 81	STIFF
IT MUST BE LOVE (US No. 33 – Labi Siffre 72 UK hit)	4	09 JAN 82	STIFF
HOUSE OF FUN (Took just 2 weeks to No. 1)	1(2)	29 MAY 82	STIFF
DRIVING MY CAR (Entered at No. 6)	4	31 JUL 82	STIFF
OUR HOUSE	5	18 DEC 82	STIFF
TOMORROW'S (JUST ANOTHER DAY)/ MADNESS (IS ALL IN THE MIND)	8	05 MAR 83	STIFF
WINGS OF A DOVE	2	10 SEP 83	STIFF
THE SUN AND THE RAIN (US No. 72)	5	19 NOV 83	STIFF
OUR HOUSE	7	23 JUL 83	GEFFEN

MADONNA

New York's Madonna Ciccone holds most of the records for female singers in the rock era. Prior to her endless run of gold singles and platinum albums she was in acts like The Millionaires, Modern Dance, Emmemon, Emmy, The Breakfast Club and the Patrick Hernandez Review. Her first two solo singles flopped but since then she has a track record only surpassed by Elvis and The Beatles. She has had world sales of over 75 million albums and most of her singles have passed the million sales mark.

HOLIDAY (US No. 16 – Written by Jellybean)	6	18 FEB 84	SIRE
LIKE A VIRGIN	3	12 JAN 85	SIRE
MATERIAL GIRL	3	16 MAR 85	SIRE
CRAZY FOR YOU (From film 'Vision Quest') (One of three different 45s together in UK Top 20)	2	29 JUN 85	GEFFEN
INTO THE GROOVE (Top US dance chart) (Entered at No. 4 – 7" single not released in US)	1(3)	03 AUG 85	SIRE
HOLIDAY (Re-issue) (She was No. 1 & 2 on UK chart – a female record)	2	17 AUG 85	SIRE
ANGEL (Entered at No. 10)	5	28 SEP 85	SIRE
GAMBLER	4	26 OCT 85	GEFFEN
DRESS YOU UP (A record eighth UK Top 10 in 85)	5	14 DEC 85	SIRE
BORDERLINE (Was UK No. 56 in 84)	2	15 FEB 86	SIRE

LIVE TO TELL (Entered at No. 10) (Her ninth UK Top 5 in just 18 months)	2	10 MAY 86	SIRE
PAPA DON'T PREACH	1(3)	12 JUL 86	SIRE
TRUE BLUE (Entered at No. 3)	1(1)	11 OCT 86	SIRE
OPEN YOUR HEART (Entered at No. 8)	4	20 DEC 86	SIRE
LA ISLA BONITA	1(2)	25 APR 87	SIRE
WHO'S THAT GIRL (Entered at No. 3)	1(1)	25 JUL 87	SIRE
CAUSING A COMMOTION (Entered at No. 7)	4	26 SEP 87	SIRE
THE LOOK OF LOVE	9	19 DEC 87	SIRE
LIKE A PRAYER (Entered at No. 2) (Her sixth UK No. 1 – the female record)	1(3)	25 MAR 89	SIRE
EXPRESS YOURSELF (Entered at No. 10)	5	10 JUN 89	SIRE
CHERISH	3	23 SEP 89	SIRE
DEAR JESSIE (Entered at No. 9) (Her 20th UK Top 5 – a female record)	5	30 DEC 89	SIRE
VOGUE	1	12 APR 90	SIRE
BORDERLINE	10	16 JUN 84	SIRE
LUCKY STAR	4	20 OCT 84	SIRE
LIKE A VIRGIN	1(6)	22 DEC 84	SIRE
MATERIAL GIRL	2	23 MAR 85	SIRE
CRAZY FOR YOU	1(1)	11 MAY 85	GEFFEN
ANGEL	5	29 JUN 85	SIRE
DRESS YOU UP	5	05 OCT 85	SIRE
LIVE TO TELL (From film 'At Close Range')	1(1)	07 JUN 86	SIRE
PAPA DON'T PREACH	1(2)	16 AUG 86	SIRE
TRUE BLUE	3	15 NOV 86	SIRE
OPEN YOUR HEART (Her 11th Top 10 in a row – a new female record)	1(1)	07 FEB 87	SIRE
LA ISLA BONITA	4	02 MAY 87	SIRE
WHO'S THAT GIRL (Her sixth solo No. 1 – a female record at the time)	1(1)	22 AUG 87	SIRE
CAUSING A COMMOTION	2	24 OCT 87	SIRE
LIKE A PRAYER	1(4)	15 APR 89	SIRE
EXPRESS YOURSELF (Voted Best video of 89)	2	15 JUL 89	SIRE
CHERISH (Her 16th Top 5 in a row – the female record)	2	07 OCT 89	SIRE

MAI TAI

Female trio from Guyana, Jettie, Carolien & Mildred who recorded in Holland. Their biggest US record was 'Female Intuition' (US 71/UK 54). They were also on Mercury, Injection and Electricity.

HISTORY (US dance No. 3)	8	29 JUN 85	VIRGIN
BODY AND SOUL	9	21 SEP 85	VIRGIN

MAIN INGREDIENT

Soul trio who had recorded as The Poets on Red Bird and as The Insiders on RCA, were originally fronted by Don McPherson. They had a couple of small hits before Don's untimely death in 71. His replacement Cuba Gooding helped them get the biggest of their 11 US (1 UK) hits. The act has split and re-united often and added an 11th black music Top 20 in 89 on Polydor. Cuba also cut solos.

EVERYBODY PLAYS THE FOOL	3	14 OCT 72	RCA
JUST DON'T WANT TO BE LONELY (UK No. 27)	10	04 MAY 74	RCA

MAISONETTES

Birmingham (UK) based 60s styled quintet fronted by Lol Mason (ex-City Boy). Group got a lot of press when the two attractive ex shop assistants Elaine Williams & Denise Ward left the group as they released the follow up to their one-off hit, 'Where I Stand'.

HEARTACHE AVENUE	7	22 JAN 83	READY STEADY

CARL MALCOLM

Jamaican reggae singer, whose group had included Boris Gardiner, had been on Trojan and Black Wax before getting a one-off UK hit on Jonathan King's label. At the time an identikit cover version of the catchy tune by UK act The Diversions reached No. 34.

FATTIE BUM-BUM (The first promo copies showed act as Max Romeo)	8	11 OCT 75	UK

MAMAS & THE PAPAS

New York foursome John & Michelle Phillips, Denny Doherty & Cass Elliot were all group veterans having between them been in The Halifax Three, Big Three, Mugwumps and (New) Journeymen. They had 7 US (4 UK) Top 20s, mostly written by John who also penned the flower power anthem 'San Francisco'. They split in 68 with Mama Cass becoming a solo star (until her death in 74) and Michelle a film star. Denny and John reformed the group without them in 82.

	MONDAY MONDAY	3	18 JUN 66	RCA
	DEDICATED TO THE ONE I LOVE	2	20 MAY 67	RCA
	CREEQUE ALLEY	9	26 AUG 67	RCA
	CALIFORNIA DREAMIN' (UK No. 23)	4	12 MAR 66	DUNHILL
	MONDAY MONDAY	1(3)	07 MAY 66	DUNHILL
	I SAW HER AGAIN (UK No. 11)	5	30 JUL 66	DUNHILL
	WORDS OF LOVE (UK No. 47)	5	21 JAN 67	DUNHILL
	DEDICATED TO THE ONE I LOVE (Originally by The Five Royales)	2	25 MAR 67	DUNHILL
	CREEQUE ALLEY	5	03 JUN 67	DUNHILL

MAN 2 MAN MEET MAN PARISH

New York dance group including ex stripper Paul and Miki Zone (ex-The Fasts). They were joined on their one-off hit by Man Parish who had a US dance hit 'Hip Hop Be Bop'. Sadly Mike and fellow member Michael Rudetski have died. They were also on Nightmare.

	MALE STRIPPER (Third entry – got 64 in 86) (Video banned by th BBC – remix on XYZ in 89)	4	28 FEB 87	BOLTS

MANCHESTER UNITED FOOTBALL CLUB

The best supported UK soccer side have had two UK-only Top 20s, the other being 'Glory Glory Man. United' in 83.

	WE ALL FOLLOW MAN. UNITED	10	25 MAY 85	COLUMBIA

MELISSA MANCHESTER

New York AOR singer/songwriter was with MB records in 67, played a singer in the soap opera Search For Tomorrow and worked in Bette Midler's group The Harlettes in 71. Her first solo LP in 73 charted and since then she has had four Top 20 US-only LPs and seven US-only Top 40 singles. She joined MCA in 85.

	MIDNIGHT BLUE (Co-Writ. Carole Bayer Sager)	6	09 AUG 75	ARISTA
	DON'T CRY OUT LOUD	10	31 MAR 79	ARISTA
	YOU SHOULD HEAR HOW SHE TALKS ABOUT YOU	5	18 SEP 82	ARISTA

HENRY MANCINI & HIS ORCHESTRA

Cleveland born composer/orchestra leader and arranger has won more Grammys (he has had 70 nominations!) and Oscars than any one else. He was first noted for his arrangements in the film The Glenn Miller Story in 54. He has written numerous TV and film themes including 'Peter Gunn', 'Moon River', 'Mr. Lucky', 'Days of Wine and Roses' and 'Pink Panther Theme'.

	HOW SOON	10	24 OCT 64	RCA
	LOVE THEME FROM ROMEO & JULIET (From the film)	1(2)	28 JUN 69	RCA

MANFRED MANN

Formed in 62 as The Mann-Hugg Blues Brothers the group included Mike Hugg and singer Paul (Pond) Jones. Their third single was the first of 22 UK (12 US) chart entries for Manfred (Michael Lubowitz) over two decades. Like The Byrds in America, they specialised in covering Bob Dylan songs. Jones went solo in 66 and was replaced by Mike D'Abo. In 69 group evolved into Manfred Mann Chapter Three and then in 72 into Manfred Mann's Earth Band.

	5-4-3-2-1	5	15 FEB 64	HMV
	DO WAH DIDDY DIDDY (Exciters 64 US hit)	1(2)	15 AUG 64	HMV
	SHA LA LA (US No. 12 – Shirelles 64 US hit)	3	14 NOV 64	HMV
	COME TOMORROW (US No. 50 – Orig. Marie Knight)	4	06 FEB 65	HMV
	IF YOU GOTTA GO GO NOW (Bob Dylan song)	2	09 OCT 65	HMV
	PRETTY FLAMINGO (US No. 29)	1(3)	07 MAY 66	HMV
	JUST LIKE A WOMAN (Bob Dylan song)	10	17 SEP 66	FONTANA
	SEMI-DETACHED SUBURBAN MR.JAMES	2	19 NOV 66	FONTANA
	HA HA SAID THE CLOWN	4	22 APR 67	FONTANA
	MIGHTY QUINN (Bob Dylan song)	1(2)	17 FEB 68	FONTANA
	MY NAME IS JACK (Original by John Simon)	8	13 JUL 68	FONTANA
	FOX ON THE RUN (US No. 97)	5	01 FEB 69	FONTANA
	RAGAMUFFIN MAN	8	31 MAY 69	FONTANA
	JOYBRINGER (As Manfred Mann's Earth Band)	9	06 OCT 73	VERTIGO
	BLINDED BY THE LIGHT (Vocal Chris Thompson – Original Bruce Springsteen)	6	25 SEP 76	BRONZE
	DAVY'S ON THE ROAD AGAIN (Last two as MANFRED MANN'S EARTH BAND)	6	17 JUN 78	BRONZE
	DO WAH DIDDY DIDDY	1(2)	17 OCT 64	ASCOT
	MIGHTY QUINN	10	13 APR 68	MERCURY
	BLINDED BY THE LIGHT	1(1)	19 FEB 77	WARNER

Also see Paul Jones

CHUCK MANGIONE

Jazz/pop flugelhorn playing composer and many time Grammy winner was in the Jazz Brothers on Riverside in 60, with his brother Gap. He also played with jazz greats Maynard Ferguson, Kai Winding and Art Blakey. He has had two US-only Top 20s, the other being 'Give It All You Got' (18) in 80.

	FEELS SO GOOD	4	10 JUN 78	A&M

MANHATTAN TRANSFER

Versatile and nostalgic vocal harmony group formed by Tim Hauser, who was in The Viscounts, The Criterions, and had played with Jim Croce in 69 on Capitol. With a new line up they first charted in 75 and have since chalked up 4 US (8 UK) Top 40s.

	CHANSON D'AMOUR (Art & Dotty Todd 58 US hit-did not make US 100)	1(3)	12 MAR 77	ATLANTIC
	THE BOY FROM NEW YORK CITY (Ad-Libs 65 US hit-Grammy winner Best Group Record)	7	08 AUG 81	ATLANTIC

MANHATTANS

New Jersey soul group evolved from The Dulcets and were on Piney and Avanti before charting in 65 on Carnival. Singer George Smith sadly died in 70 and was replaced by Gerald Alston (later solo on Motown). They have had 43 black music hits including 20 Top 20s .

	KISS AND SAY GOODBYE	4	31 JUL 76	CBS
	HURT (US No. 97 – Roy Hamilton 54 R&B hit)	4	06 NOV 76	CBS
	KISS AND SAY GOODBYE	1(2)	24 JUL 76	COLUMBIA
	SHINING STAR (UK No. 45)	5	19 JUL 80	COLUMBIA

BARRY MANILOW

Brooklyn born singer/songwriter is one of the world's most popular solo performers. He started writing and singing jingles in the late 60s and was Bette Midler's producer and arranger before going solo. He has had nine Top 20 LPs in both the US & UK and once had five different LPs together on the US chart. He has sold over 50 million LPs but his sales dropped off in the late 80s.

	I WANNA DO IT WITH YOU (Only Top 10 of 16 UK chart entries)	8	06 NOV 82	ARISTA

MANDY *(UK No. 11 – Scott English 71 UK hit)* *(Most of his hits produced by Ron Dante)*	1(1)	18 JAN 75	BELL
COULD IT BE MAGIC *(UK No. 25 – was a re-issue)*	6	20 SEP 75	ARISTA
I WRITE THE SONGS *(Written by Bruce Johnson)* *(Written about Brian Wilson by fellow Beach Boy)*	1(1)	17 JAN 76	ARISTA
TRYIN' TO GET THE FEELING AGAIN	10	22 MAY 76	ARISTA
WEEKEND IN NEW ENGLAND *(Comp. Randy Edelman)*	10	26 FEB 77	ARISTA
LOOKS LIKE WE MADE IT	1(1)	23 JUL 77	ARISTA
CAN'T SMILE WITHOUT YOU *(UK No. 43)*	3	22 APR 78	ARISTA
COPACABANA (AT THE COPA) *(UK No. 42 as 'B')*	8	12 AUG 78	ARISTA
SOMEWHERE IN THE NIGHT *(UK No. 42)* *(Above two tracks were A & B-sides in UK)*	9	17 FEB 79	ARISTA
SHIPS *(Originally by Ian Hunter)*	9	01 DEC 79	ARISTA
I MADE IT THROUGH THE RAIN *(UK No. 37)*	10	31 JAN 81	ARISTA

BARRY MANN

As a singer Brooklyn born Barry Iberman only scored a one-off Top 40 hit with a novelty. He is however one of the most successful writers, often with Cynthia Weil, of the rock era with hits spanning 30 years. He was also on JDS, Colpix, Red Bird, Capitol, Scepter, RCA, Arista, UA, Warner, Casablanca and New Design.

WHO PUT THE BOMP (IN THE BOMP, BOMP, BOMP, BOMP) *(Featuring The Halos)*	7	25 SEP 61	ABC

JOHNNY MANN SINGERS

Mixed choir headed by the musical director of the 'Joey Bishop Show' were on Swan in 59 and had three US Top 100 chart LPs. Only 45 charter was in the UK with a cover of a Fifth Dimension hit.

UP UP AND AWAY *(US No. 91)*	6	19 AUG 67	LIBERTY

MANUEL & HIS MUSIC OF THE MOUNTAINS

A pseudonym for UK orchestra leader and arranger Geoff Love. Under this name he had four UK-only Top 40s between 59-76.

RODRIGO'S GUITAR CONCERTO DE ARANJUEZ	3	28 FEB 76	EMI

MARBLES

UK duo of Graham Bonnet and Trevor Gordon. They had two UK-only Top 10s, both penned and produced by Graham's cousins The Bee Gees. They were voted second Most Promising Group of 68 but split in 70. Graham later had hits as a soloist and with Rainbow.

ONLY ONE WOMAN	5	02 NOV 68	POLYDOR

Also see Graham Bonnet/Rainbow

MARCELS

Inter-racial Pittsburgh vocal quintet fronted by Cornelius Harp were one of the last of the 50s style vocal groups and they specialised in giving standards the doo-wop treatment. The group, who had personnel changes, also recorded on 888, Queen Bee, Monogram, Owl, St. Clair, Baron and Chartbound and still sometimes perform.

BLUE MOON *(Glen Gray 35 hit)* *(Recorded in 8 minutes at end of a session)*	1(2)	05 MAY 61	PYE INT
BLUE MOON *(Treatment based on 'Zoom Zoom Zoom' by Collegians)*	1(3)	03 APR 61	COLPIX
HEARTACHES *(Guy Lombardo 31 hit)*	7	27 NOV 61	COLPIX

LITTLE PEGGY MARCH

Child prodigy born Margaret Battavio in Philadelphia. She is the youngest female to top the US chart, which she did at 15 with her second single. She had three US-only Top 40s before she was 16. She was later popular in Germany and was back on RCA in 86.

I WILL FOLLOW HIM *(Composed Paul Mauriat)*	1(3)	27 APR 63	RCA

ERNIE MARESCA

New York songwriter wrote Dion's biggest hits 'Runaround Sue' and 'The Wanderer'. As a singer he joined Seville in 60 and had a one-off hit which he followed with 'Something To Shout About'. He later recorded on Providence in 65 and Dion's label Laurie in 66.

SHOUT! SHOUT! (KNOCK YOURSELF OUT) *(Feat. The Del Satins-track on Jive Bunny hit 90)*	6	19 MAY 62	SEVILLE

KELLY MARIE

As Keli Brown this Scottish singer was a four times winner of 'Opportunity Knocks' in 74. She joined Pye in 76 and had hits overseas before charting in her homeland. She had three UK-only Top 40s and she was backed on stage and TV by the Ebony Brothers.

FEELS LIKE I'M IN LOVE *(Orig. rel Feb. 79)* *(Composed by Ray Dorset, leader of Mungo Jerry)*	1(2)	13 SEP 80	CALIBRE

TEENA MARIE

Singer, producer and multi-instrumentalist, born Mary Christine Brockert in California. She is the most popular white female singer in the black music field with 20 chart entries to date.

BEHIND THE GROOVE	6	28 JUN 80	MOTOWN
LOVERGIRL	4	30 MAR 85	EPIC

MARILLION

Formed in Buckinghamshire (UK) as Silmarillion in 78, they added singer Fish (Derek Dick) in 81 and signed to EMI in 83. Before Fish went solo in 88 (replaced by Steve Hogarth) the popular live act had scored 11 UK-only Top 40s and six UK-only Top 10 LPs.

KAYLEIGH	2	15 JUN 85	EMI
LAVENDER	5	21 SEP 85	EMI
INCOMMUNICADO *(Entered at No. 6)*	6	23 MAY 87	EMI

MARILYN

London based transvestite protege of Boy George, who was born Peter Robinson, attracted a lot of UK media attention and managed to achieve three UK-only Top 40s. An image change – replacing his long blonde locks with short cropped hair in 85 – failed to help him cut another hit.

CALLING YOUR NAME	4	03 DEC 83	MERCURY

MARKETTS

L.A. instrumental session group who had the first surf hit with 'Surfers Stomp' in 62 and had two TV inspired US-only Top 20s, the other being 'Batman' (17) in 66. Members at times included Leon Russell and Glen Campbell. Act were later on World Pacific in 67, UNI in 69, Mercury in 73 and Farr in 76 (as the New Marketts).

OUT OF LIMITS *(Originally called 'Outer Limits')*	3	01 FEB 64	WARNER

MAR-KEYS

Instrumental group formed in Memphis in 58 became the house band at Satellite (re-named Stax) Records and gave the label its first big hit. Members Steve Cropper and Duck Dunn left to form Booker T. & The MGs. Follow up was the similar 'Morning After'.

LAST NIGHT	3	31 JUL 61	SATELLITE

BOB MARLEY & THE WAILERS

The best known reggae artist of all time first recorded in his native Jamaica in 61. The group, who were formed in 64, had local success and songs of Bob's became hits for Johnny Nash in 67 and Eric Clapton in 74. He had his first UK charter in 75 (it's said with his 60th single) and made the US Top 10 LPs in 76. In all he had 12 UK-only Top 40 singles and 7 Top 20 UK (2 US) Top 20 LPs. After his death in 81 he was given a state funeral in Jamaica, featured on postage stamps and a Marley Museum was built.

🇬🇧	JAMMING/PUNKY REGGAE PARTY	9	04 FEB 78	ISLAND
	IS THIS LOVE	9	01 APR 78	ISLAND
	COULD YOU BE LOVED	5	19 JUL 80	ISLAND
	NO WOMAN NO CRY (Was No. 22 in 75)	8	18 JUL 81	ISLAND
	BUFFALO SOLDIER	4	11 JUN 83	ISLAND
	ONE LOVE/PEOPLE GET READY	5	19 MAY 84	ISLAND

MARMALADE

Glasgow band formed in 61 as Dean Ford & The Gaylords. After four singles on Columbia they changed their name and label, then their fourth for CBS was the first of their 11 UK (1 US) Top 40s. Singer Junior Campbell left for solo success in 71. The band, which has had many personnel changes, continued to work the clubs.

🇬🇧	LOVIN' THINGS	6	06 JUL 68	CBS
	OB-LA-DI OB-LA-DA (Beatles song) (The first Scottish act to top the chart)	1(3)	04 JAN 69	CBS
	BABY MAKE IT SOON	9	19 JUL 69	CBS
	REFLECTIONS OF MY LIFE	3	24 JAN 70	DECCA
	RAINBOW (US No. 51)	3	22 AUG 70	DECCA
	COUSIN NORMAN	6	02 OCT 71	DECCA
	RADANCER	6	13 MAY 72	DECCA
	FALLING APART AT THE SEAMS (US No. 49)	9	27 MAR 76	TARGET
🇺🇸	REFLECTIONS OF MY LIFE	10	09 MAY 70	LONDON

M/A/R/R/S

A one-off amalgam of two indie rock acts A R Kane and Colourbox was named after the first name initials of the members. The influential scratch/ sample track topped charts around the world and was the first 45 to top the UK pop, dance and indie charts.

🇬🇧	PUMP UP THE VOLUME (US No.13 – The US Top Pop and Dance single of 88)	1(2)	03 OCT 87	4AD

MARSDEN/McCARTNEY/JOHNSON/CHRISTIANS

Liverpool artists Gerry Marsden (of the Pacemakers), Paul McCartney, Holly Johnson (of Frankie Goes To Hollywood) and The Christians collaborated to raise money for the fund set up when 95 Liverpool football fans died before an FA Cup semi-final match at Sheffield.

🇬🇧	FERRY 'CROSS THE MERSEY (Entered at No. 1) (Gerry (Marsden) & The Pacemakers 64 hit)	1(3)	20 MAY 89	PWL

MARSHALL HAIN

UK sextet fronted by keyboard player/songwriter Julian Marshall and singer Kit Hain. Their follow up 'Coming Home' was their only other charter (UK 39). Kit recorded on Harvest in 79, Decca in 81 and Mercury in 83. Julian teamed with US singer Deborah Berg and formed Eye to Eye who had two US chart singles.

🇬🇧	DANCING IN THE CITY (US No. 43)	3	15 JUL 78	HARVEST

LENA MARTELL

MOR/cabaret singer from Glasgow had been recording for 18 years before joining the one-hit wonders. Her follow up was another Kris Kristofferson song 'Why Me'. She was on Country House in 84.

🇬🇧	ONE DAY AT A TIME (Marilyn Sellars 74 country hit)	1(3)	27 OCT 79	PYE

MARTHA & THE MUFFINS

Mixed Canadian group included two Marthas; Martha Ladley who went solo in 81 and Martha Johnson their main singer. They were on RCA in 83

and as M&M they had US dance success with 'Black Stations/ White Stations' in 84. They were on UK label Radical in 89.

🇬🇧	ECHO BEACH	10	29 MAR 80	DINDISC

MARTHA & THE VANDELLAS

Alabama born Martha Reeves with Annette Sterling & Rosalind Ashford first recorded as The Del-Phis on Checkmate. They got a deal with Motown after backing Marvin Gaye on some of his early hits. The trio had 12 US (7 UK) Top 40s before Martha went solo in 72. A re-formed group were on the UK label Nightmare in 89.

🇬🇧	DANCING IN THE STREET (Was UK No. 29 in 64)	4	08 FEB 69	TAMLA MOTOWN
🇺🇸	HEAT WAVE	4	21 SEP 63	GORDY
	QUICKSAND	8	04 JAN 64	GORDY
	DANCING IN THE STREET	2	17 OCT 64	GORDY
	NOWHERE TO RUN (UK No. 26 in 69)	8	10 APR 65	GORDY
	I'M READY FOR LOVE (UK No. 29)	9	10 DEC 66	GORDY
	JIMMY MACK (UK No. 21)	10	15 APR 67	GORDY

MARTIKA

Californian singer/songwriter of Cuban descent. Before she was a teenager she was in the film 'Annie' and she was a star of the US TV show 'Kids Incorporated' (being on four albums of the show). She first hit in the dance field and has had a very impressive start to her recording career.

🇬🇧	TOY SOLDIERS	5	19 AUG 89	CBS
	I FEEL THE EARTH MOVE (US No. 25 – Composed by Carole King)	7	11 NOV 89	CBS
🇺🇸	TOY SOLDIERS	1(2)	22 JUL 89	COLUMBIA

DEAN MARTIN

Very popular singer/actor/entertainer born Dino Crocetti in Ohio. He started in Sam Watkins Band and teamed up very successfully with comedian Jerry Lewis between 46-56. A top MOR/cabaret performer and part of Frank Sinatra's Rat Pack, he has had a string of film and record hits.

🇬🇧	NAUGHTY LADY OF SHADY LANE (Ames Brothers 55 US hit)	5	04 MAR 55	CAPITOL
	LET ME GO LOVER (Joan Weber 55 hit)	3	25 MAR 55	CAPITOL
	UNDER THE BRIDGES OF PARIS	6	15 APR 55	CAPITOL
	MEMORIES ARE MADE OF THIS	1(4)	17 FEB 56	CAPITOL
	RETURN TO ME	2	05 SEP 58	CAPITOL
	VOLARE (US No. 12 – Domenico Modugno 58 hit)	2	26 SEP 58	CAPITOL
	GENTLE ON MY MIND (Glen Campbell 67 US hit)	2	05 APR 69	REPRISE
🇺🇸	MEMORIES ARE MADE OF THIS	1(5)	07 JAN 56	CAPITOL
	RETURN TO ME	4	09 JUN 58	CAPITOL
	EVERYBODY LOVES SOMEBODY (UK No. 11)	1(1)	15 AUG 64	REPRISE
	THE DOOR IS STILL OPEN TO MY HEART (UK No. 42 – Cardinals 55 R&B hit)	6	14 NOV 64	REPRISE
	I WILL (Vic Dana 62 US hit)	10	11 DEC 65	REPRISE

JUAN MARTIN

Before getting his one-off pop hit, the Spanish born classical guitarist had albums on Argo, Decca, EMI and Polydor and had often been seen guesting on various UK TV variety shows.

🇬🇧	LOVE THEME FROM 'THE THORN BIRDS' (From the TV mini-series)	10	18 FEB 84	WEA

MARILYN MARTIN – SEE PHIL COLLINS FOR HIT DETAILS

WINK MARTINDALE

Top US TV games show host was born Winston Conrad in Tennessee. He was a DJ in 50, recorded on OJ in 57 and hosted the TV show Teenage Dance Party in 59. His sole transatlantic Top 10 hit charted in three different years in the UK spending 41 weeks in the chart. Later 45s included 'Lincoln's Gettysburg Address'.

	DECK OF CARDS	5	28 JUN 63	LONDON
	(Was No. 18 in 59 and No. 22 in 73)			
	DECK OF CARDS *(T. Texas Tyler 48 country hit)*	7	01 NOV 59	DOT

AL MARTINO

Philadelphia born singer/actor Al Cini topped the very first UK chart in 52 with his debut hit 'Here in My Heart' (US 1). He was one of the most successful MOR singers in the US in the 60s and in total has had 38 US (10) UK chart entries.

	SPANISH EYES *(Co-written Bert Kaempfert)*	5	18 AUG 73	CAPITOL
	(US No. 15 in 65 and was UK No. 49 in 70)			
	I LOVE YOU BECAUSE *(UK No. 48)*	3	01 JUN 63	CAPITOL
	(Leon Payne 50 country hit)			
	I LOVE YOU MORE AND MORE EVERY DAY	9	21 MAR 64	CAPITOL

HANK MARVIN – SEE CLIFF RICHARD – FOR HIT DETAILS

LEE MARVIN

New York born film actor had a surprise one-off UK and Australian chart topper with a song from his film Paint Your Wagon.

	WAND'RIN' STAR	1(3)	07 MAR 70	PARAMOUNT
	(Sold two million worldwide but did not chart in US)			

RICHARD MARX

Chicago born singer/songwriter started doing jingles, then backing vocals with Lionel Richie before writing his first hit 'What About Me' (Kenny Rogers). He was one of the top acts of the late 80s and was the first soloist to put his first seven hits in the US Top 5. He is married to Cynthia Rhodes from Animotion.

	RIGHT HERE WAITING	2	23 SEP 89	EMI
	DON'T MEAN NOTHING	3	29 AUG 87	MANHATTAN
	SHOULD'VE KNOWN BETTER *(UK No. 50)*	3	12 DEC 87	EMI MANHAT.
	ENDLESS SUMMER NIGHTS *(UK No. 50)*	2	26 MAR 88	EMI MANHAT.
	HOLD ON TO THE NIGHTS	1(1)	23 JUL 88	EMI MANHAT.
	SATISFIED *(UK No. 52)*	1(1)	24 JUN 89	EMI
	RIGHT HERE WAITING *(Third No. 1 in a row)*	1(3)	12 AUG 89	EMI
	ANGELIA *(UK No. 45)*	4	02 DEC 89	EMI

MARY JANE GIRLS

Female funk foursome formed by Rick James included Candi Ghant and Jo Jo McDuffie. Risque act, who started off backing Rick, had one-off Top 20 hits in both the US & UK. In the UK it was 'All Night Long' (UK 13/US 101). Act was revamped in 89 as Breathless.

	IN MY HOUSE *(Prod. & Comp. Rick James)*	7	08 JUN 85	GORDY

HUGH MASEKELA

South African trumpeter who studied music in London and New York where he formed his own band in 64. He recorded on MGM in 67 and had his sole US Top 40 with a jazzy instrumental. He was also on Blue Thumb, Chisa, Casablanca, Horizon, Warner and Jive.

	GRAZING IN THE GRASS	1(2)	20 JUL 68	UNI

MASH

A group of uncredited sessions singers recorded this theme song to the film (and later TV show) M.A.S.H. in 70 and it made them UK one-hit wonders a decade later. It did not chart in the US.

	THEME FROM M*A*S*H (SUICIDE IS PAINLESS)	1(3)	31 MAY 80	CBS

BARBARA MASON

Philadelphian soul singer/songwriter who first recorded for the local Crusader label in 64, has had 18 black music hits since. She was also on Atlantic, Buddah (where she was produced by Curtis Mayfield), National General, Prelude, WMOT and West End.

	YES, I'M READY	5	31 JUL 65	ARTIC
	(She recorded it again as 'Yes I'm Ready '80')			

MATCHBOX

UK rockabilly quintet first called Matchbox and The Hellraisers were fronted by Graham Fenton. The group, who had Gene Vincent leanings, had four UK-only Top 20s – the others being 'Rockabilly Rebel', 'Midnite Dynamos' and 'Over The Rainbow – You Belong To Me'.

	WHEN YOU ASK ABOUT LOVE *(Orig. by Crickets)*	4	01 NOV 80	MAGNET

MATCHROOM MOB WITH CHAS & DAVE

The cream of the UK's snooker players teamed with 'Rockney' specialists Chas & Dave for a novelty one-off hit.

	SNOOKER LOOPY	6	24 MAY 86	ROCKNEY

JOHNNY MATHIS

Frank Sinatra and Elvis are the only males to have had more US LP success than this San Franciscan singer. Since he first charted in 57 he has had 64 US (24 UK) chart LPs including 18 US (9 UK) Top 10s and he has scored nine US & UK Top 20 singles. His 'Greatest Hits' LP spent nearly 10 years on the US chart – a record for a soloist.

	A CERTAIN SMILE *(US No. 14)*	4	21 NOV 58	FONTANA
	SOMEONE *(US No. 35)*	6	11 SEP 59	FONTANA
	(Josea Belvin 59 R&B hit)			
	MY LOVE FOR YOU *(US No. 47)*	10	18 NOV 60	FONTANA
	I'M STONE IN LOVE WITH YOU	10	15 MAR 75	CBS
	(Stylistics 72 US hit)			
	WHEN A CHILD IS BORN (SOLEADO) *(Not US hit)*	1(2)	25 DEC 76	CBS
	TOO MUCH, TOO LITTLE, TOO LATE	3	13 MAY 78	CBS
	(And DENIECE WILLIAMS)			
	IT'S NOT FOR ME TO SAY *(From film 'Lizzie')*	6	08 JUL 57	COLUMBIA
	CHANCES ARE/THE TWELFTH OF NEVER	4	28 OCT 57	COLUMBIA
	GINA	6	17 NOV 62	COLUMBIA
	WHAT WILL MY MARY SAY *(UK No. 49)*	9	09 MAR 63	COLUMBIA
	TOO MUCH, TOO LITTLE, TOO LATE	1(1)	03 JUN 78	COLUMBIA
	(And DENIECE WILLIAMS)			

MATTHEWS SOUTHERN COMFORT

Formed in 69 by ex-Fairport Convention and Pyramid singer Ian Matthews from Lincolnshire (UK). He left shortly after they hit (with their third 45) and group continued as Southern Comfort. Ian recorded in Plainsong and as a soloist had a US No. 13 in 78 with 'Shake It'. In 87 he joined new age label Windham Hill.

	WOODSTOCK *(US No. 23 – Joni Mitchell song)*	1(3)	31 OCT 70	UNI
	(Crosby, Stills, Nash & Young 70 US hit)			

SUSAN MAUGHAN

Whilst this UK pop singer was with the Ray Ellington Quartet she also made solo singles; the fourth of which was her solo UK Top 40 hit. Her follow up was 'Hand A Handkerchief To Helen'. She recorded on Ember in 74.

 BOBBY'S GIRL (*Marcia Blaine 62 US hit*)   4   30 NOV 62   PHILIPS

PAUL MAURIAT

French orchestra leader/composer co-wrote the big hit 'I Will Follow Him' (Little Peggy March/Petula Clark). He also played harpsichord on his sole transatlantic hit which came from his fourth US released LP. He remained a top act in his homeland.

 LOVE IS BLUE   1(5)   10 FEB 68   PHILIPS
(*UK No.12-song was fourth in Eurovision song contest*)

SIMON MAY

London based singer/composer/arranger has had a lot of UK success with TV related songs. He has written many TV themes including EastEnders and Howards Way and wrote hits for Kate Robbins, Stephanie DeSykes, Nick Berry and Anita Dobson. As an artist he was on Philips in 75 and had two UK-only charters.

 SUMMER OF MY LIFE   7   23 OCT 76   PYE

CURTIS MAYFIELD

Chicago born ex leader of The Impressions. He wrote most of their hits and many for Major Lance and Gene Chandler and also wrote film scores for movies like Superfly and Let's Do It Again (which included the US No. 1 by the Staple Singers). He started his own label Curtom in 68 and in 70 went solo. In the 70s he had 15 US (1 UK) chart LPs and 4 US (1 UK) Top 40s. In 87 he had a small UK hit singing with the Blow Monkeys.

 FREDDIE'S DEAD   4   04 NOV 72   CURTOM
        SUPERFLY (*First two from 'Superfly'*)   8   13 JAN 73   CURTOM

Also see The Impressions

C.W. McCALL

Iowa advertising man William Fries created the character of truck driver C.W. McCall for a bread commercial. In this disguise he had nine Top 40 country hits, the third of which gave him his sole transatlantic hit and made US CB radio lingo famous world-wide.

 CONVOY (*Jumped 41-7*)   2   29 MAR 76   MGM
 CONVOY (*Top US country hit 76*)   1(1)   10 JAN 76   MGM

PETER McCANN

Singer/songwriter from Connecticut had just the one US chart single as a vocalist but has since written many country hits. He has also recorded on Epic and Columbia.

        DO YOU WANNA MAKE LOVE   5   06 AUG 77   20TH CENTURY

PAUL McCARTNEY/WINGS

The world's most successful songwriter who as a singer has had 111 US (70 UK) hits with tracks he was on. The ex Beatle's LP track record is 53 US (42 UK) chart entries. He is the owner of the only Rhodium record presented by Guinness for his amazing achievements which also include being the only writer to have two songs on the US black music and country charts in the same week. His sales started declining, especially in the US, in the late 80s so he embarked on his first major tour for 13 years in 89.

Title	Pos	Date	Label
ANOTHER DAY (*All records until 80 credited to WINGS*)	2	13 MAR 71	APPLE
MARY HAD A LITTLE LAMB (*US No. 28*)	9	24 JUN 72	APPLE
HI HI HI/C MOON	5	13 JAN 73	APPLE
MY LOVE (*As PAUL McCARTNEY & WINGS*)	9	28 APR 73	APPLE
LIVE AND LET DIE	9	30 JUN 73	APPLE
JET	7	23 MAR 74	APPLE
BAND ON THE RUN (*Above two as PAUL McCARTNEY & WINGS*)	3	03 AUG 74	APPLE
LISTEN TO WHAT THE MAN SAID	6	21 JUN 75	CAPITOL
SILLY LOVE SONGS	2	12 JUN 76	PARLOPHONE
LET 'EM IN	2	14 AUG 76	PARLOPHONE
MULL OF KINTYRE (*Not US hit – 'B' was US No. 33*) (*UK Gold-was top all time seller at the time*)	1(9)	03 DEC 77	CAPITOL
WITH A LITTLE LUCK	5	22 APR 78	PARLOPHONE
GOODNIGHT TONIGHT	5	05 MAY 79	PARLOPHONE
WONDERFUL CHRISTMASTIME	6	05 JAN 80	PARLOPHONE
COMING UP (*Jumped 55 places in 1 week*)	2	03 MAY 80	PARLOPHONE
WATERFALLS	9	19 JUL 80	PARLOPHONE
EBONY AND IVORY (*And STEVIE WONDER*) (*First black & white duo to top the UK chart*)	1(3)	24 APR 82	PARLOPHONE
THE GIRL IS MINE (*With MICHAEL JACKSON*) (*Artists listed other way round in US*)	8	20 NOV 82	EPIC
SAY SAY SAY (*And MICHAEL JACKSON*)	2	19 NOV 83	PARLOPHONE
PIPES OF PEACE (*Last of two UK No. 1s, neither made the US chart*)	1(2)	14 JAN 84	PARLOPHONE
NO MORE LONELY NIGHTS (*BALLAD*)	2	27 OCT 84	PARLOPHONE
WE ALL STAND TOGETHER (*feat. FROG CHORUS*)	3	22 DEC 84	PARLOPHONE
ONCE UPON A LONG AGO	10	12 DEC 87	PARLOPHONE
ANOTHER DAY (*all as Wings until 80*)	5	17 APR 71	APPLE
UNCLE ALBERT/ADMIRAL HALSEY (*As PAUL & LINDA McCARTNEY*)	1(1)	04 SEP 71	APPLE
HI, HI, HI	10	03 FEB 73	APPLE
MY LOVE (*As PAUL McCARTNEY & WINGS*)	1(4)	02 JUN 73	APPLE
LIVE AND LET DIE (*From the film*)	2	11 AUG 73	APPLE
HELEN WHEELS (*UK No. 12*)	10	12 JAN 74	APPLE
JET	7	30 MAR 74	APPLE
BAND ON THE RUN	1(1)	08 JUN 74	APPLE
JUNIOR'S FARM/SALLY G (*UK No. 16*) (*Above four as PAUL McCARTNEY & WINGS*)	3	11 JAN 75	APPLE
LISTEN TO WHAT THE MAN SAID	1(1)	19 JUL 75	CAPITOL
SILLY LOVE SONGS (*Top US single of 76*)	1(5)	22 MAY 76	CAPITOL
LET 'EM IN	3	14 AUG 76	CAPITOL
MAYBE I'M AMAZED (*UK No. 28*)	10	02 APR 77	CAPITOL
WITH A LITTLE LUCK	1(2)	20 MAY 78	CAPITOL
GOODNIGHT TONIGHT	5	19 MAY 79	COLUMBIA
COMING UP (*LIVE AT GLASGOW*) (*As PAUL McCartney & WINGS – in UK 'B' was hit side*)	1(3)	28 JUN 80	COLUMBIA
EBONY AND IVORY (*And STEVIE WONDER*)	1 7	15 MAY 82	COLUMBIA
TAKE IT AWAY (*UK No. 15*)	10	21 AUG 82	COLUMBIA
THE GIRL IS MINE (*And MICHAEL JACKSON*)	2	13 NOV 82	EPIC
SAY SAY SAY (*And MICHAEL JACKSON*) (*Entered at 26 (highest US chart entry since 71)*)	1(6)	10 DEC 83	COLUMBIA
NO MORE LONELY NIGHTS (*From 'Give My Regards To Broad Street'*)	6	08 DEC 84	COLUMBIA
SPIES LIKE US (*UK No. 16 – From the film*)	7	08 FEB 86	COLUMBIA

Also see The Beatles

DELBERT McCLINTON

Texan rock singer was harmonica player on Bruce Channel's smash 'Hey Baby' and taught John Lennon how to play it. He first recorded in 60 and was on UK Decca in 62. He charted in 65 in the Ron-Dels and in 72 as half of Delbert & Glen and had a one-off Top 40 in 81. He was also on Paramount, ABC, MCA, Capricorn and joined Curb in 89.

 GIVING IT UP FOR YOUR LOVE   8   21 FEB 81   CAPITOL

MARILYN McCOO & BILLY DAVIS, JR.

Husband and wife duo who were both in the hit act Fifth Dimension for ten years and left in 76. They had two US Top 20s, the other one being their follow up 'Your Love' (15). The duo also did the original version of 'Saving All My Love For You' (Whitney Houston). Marilyn later hosted the top US TV show 'Solid Gold'.

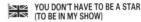 YOU DON'T HAVE TO BE A STAR (TO BE IN MY SHOW)   7   30 APR 77   ABC

        YOU DON'T HAVE TO BE A STAR (TO BE IN MY SHOW)   1(1)   08 JAN 77   ABC

Also see Fifth Dimension

VAN McCOY

Late producer/musician/composer from Washington, recorded in The Starliters on End in 59 and had hits in the 60s with acts like Aretha Franklin, Shirelles, Drifters, Gladys Knight and Peaches & Herb. As an artist he was also on Rockin', Liberty, Columbia, Epic, Share, Buddah, Silver Blue and MCA and had four UK & US hits.

🇬🇧	THE HUSTLE	3	05 JUL 75	AVCO
	THE SHUFFLE	4	21 MAY 77	H & L
🇺🇸	THE HUSTLE	1(1)	26 JUL 75	AVCO
	(Featuring the Soul City Symphony)			

McCOYS

Indiana pop/rock quartet formed in 62 by the Zehringer brothers Rick & Randy whose first record came out as by the Rick Z Combo. They had three US (1 UK) Top 40s, joined Mercury in 68 and in the early 70s recorded as backing group for Johnny Winter and his brother Edgar (Rick produced them). Rick later had solo hits.

🇬🇧	HANG ON SLOOPY	5	16 OCT 65	IMMEDIATE
	(Same back track as Strangeloves earlier recording)			
🇺🇸	HANG ON SLOOPY *(Vibrations 64 US hit)*	1(1)	02 OCT 65	BANG
	(Rick re-recorded it as a solo in 75 on Blue Sky)			
	FEVER *(Little Willie John 56 R&B hit)*	7	25 DEC 65	BANG

GEORGE McCRAE

Florida born soul singer, who had been in The Jiving Jets and Atsugi Express, recorded in a duo with his wife Gwen on Alston in 69 and was on UA in 71. He has had 10 black music chart hits – the first and biggest being one of the 70s great disco records.

🇬🇧	ROCK YOUR BABY	1(2)	27 JUL 74	JAYBOY
	I CAN'T LEAVE YOU ALONE *(US No. 50)*	9	26 OCT 74	JAYBOY
	IT'S BEEN SO LONG	4	30 AUG 75	JAYBOY
	(All co-written by K.C. of The Sunshine Band)			
🇺🇸	ROCK YOUR BABY	1(2)	13 JUL 74	TK

GWEN McCRAE

She started by dueting with her husband George McCrae in 69 and recorded on Columbia in 72. Her sole US hit was her fifth single on Florida label Cat. Her only UK charter came with a re-issue of 'All This Love That I'm Giving' (63) in 88

🇺🇸	ROCKIN' CHAIR *(Backing vocal George McCrae)*	9	02 AUG 75	CAT

GENE McDANIELS

Kansas born artist sang gospel music professionally when just 13. He joined Liberty in 59 and scored six US-only Top 40s, two of which were Top 10s in the UK by local acts. He later wrote hits for Roberta Flack and Joe Simon and was later on Columbia and Ode.

🇺🇸	A HUNDRED POUNDS OF CLAY	3	08 MAY 61	LIBERTY
	(Banned in the UK on religious grounds)			
	TOWER OF STRENGTH	5	13 NOV 61	LIBERTY
	(Feat. The Johnny Mann singers)			
	CHIP CHIP	10	03 MAR 62	LIBERTY

MICHAEL McDONALD

St. Louis singer/songwriter formed Mike & The Majestics in the mid 60s and recorded solo on RCA in 70 and Bell in 72 before briefly joining Steely Dan in 74 and then the Doobie Brothers where he had many hits between 75-82. He has had 5 US (3 UK) Top 40s since, including duets with James Ingram and Patti Labelle.

🇬🇧	ON MY OWN *(With PATTI LABELLE)*	2	17 MAY 86	MCA
	(The first Top 10 solos in the UK for both acts)			
🇺🇸	I KEEP FORGETTIN' (EVERYTIME YOU'RE NEAR)	4	23 OCT 82	WARNER
	(UK No. 43-based on Chuck Jacksons 62 US hit)			
	ON MY OWN *(With PATTI LABELLE)*	1(3)	14 JUN 86	MCA
	(They recorded vocals and the video separately)			
	SWEET FREEDOM *(UK No. 12)*	7	30 AUG 86	MCA
	(From the film 'Running Scared')			

Also see The Doobie Brothers

McFADDEN AND WHITEHEAD

Singer/songwriter/producers Gene McFadden & John Whitehead were in the Stax group The Epsilons (aka Talk Of The Town). They were later part of the Gamble & Huff team, writing hits for The O'Jays, Harold Melvin & The Blue Notes and The Intruders as well as their own one-off Transatlantic Top 20 hit. They were also on Gamble in 72, Capitol in 82 and John was on Mercury in 88.

🇬🇧🇺🇸	AIN'T NO STOPPIN' US NOW *(US No. 13)*	5	16 JUN 79	PHILLY INT.

BOBBY McFERRIN

Jazzy singer/musician who had won five Grammys prior to getting more for his Transatlantic Top 10 hit. He had previously been on Elektra. He followed his hit with 'Thinking About Your Body'.

🇬🇧	DON'T WORRY BE HAPPY *(from film 'Cocktail')*	2	22 OCT 88	MANHATTAN
🇺🇸	DON'T WORRY BE HAPPY	1(2)	24 SEP 88	EMI MANHAT.

MAUREEN McGOVERN

Ohio act started as a folk singer and four of her six US-only hits were theme songs. In the UK her one charter was the old Oscar winning song 'The Continental' (UK 12). Her big hit was also an Oscar winner and did not even chart until after the awards. She was also on RCA, Epic, Warner, and appeared on CBS in 88.

🇺🇸	THE MORNING AFTER	1(2)	04 AUG 73	20TH CENTURY
	(From the film The Poseidon Adventure)			

FREDDIE McGREGOR

Jamaican reggae star made the first of his many records when only seven in 64. He has worked with Bob Marley and has had two UK-only chart records. He was also been on Greensleeves, Music Works, Cha Cha, Hitbound, Intense, Hawkeye, Polydor, Tads, Big Ship, Ras, Spiderman, Thompson Sound, Yashemabata, White and Penthouse!

🇬🇧	JUST DON'T WANT TO BE LONELY	9	01 AUG 87	GERMAIN
	(Main Ingredient 74 US hit)			

McGUINNESS FLINT

Tom McGuinness, who had been in The Roosters with Eric Clapton, teamed with another former Manfred Mann man Hughie Flint to front the band who also included Benny Gallagher and Graham Lyle (later a successful duo). They were voted the Best New Group of 70 in a UK Poll. They broke up in 75 and Tom later formed The Blues Band.

🇬🇧	WHEN I'M DEAD AND GONE *(US No. 47)*	2	12 DEC 70	CAPITOL
	MALT AND BARLEY BLUES	5	29 MAY 71	CAPITOL

Also see Manfred Mann

BARRY McGUIRE

Oklahoma folk/pop singer was on Mosaic in 61 and sang on the New Christy Minstrels biggest hit 'Green Green' in 63. His big hit featured a guide vocal which was not meant for release. He was also on Era, Mira and Ode and later went into acting and sang in the spiritual group Agape Force. In the 70s he became a born again Christian and recorded religious albums.

🇬🇧	EVE OF DESTRUCTION	3	30 OCT 65	RCA
🇺🇸	EVE OF DESTRUCTION *(Banned by many stations)*	1(1)	25 SEP 65	DUNHILL

SCOTT McKENZIE

Singer from Virginia was in The Smoothies and The Journeymen with John Philips (Mamas & The Papas) who wrote and co-produced his sole Transatlantic Top 10. He had previously recorded solo on Capitol in 65. His follow up was 'Like An Old Time Movie'.

 SAN FRANCISCO (BE SURE TO WEAR FLOWERS IN YOUR HAIR) *(Became the anthem of 'Flower Power')* — 1(4) 12 AUG 67 CBS

SAN FRANCISCO (BE SURE TO WEAR FLOWERS IN YOUR HAIR) — 4 01 JUL 67 ODE

MALCOLM McLAREN

Manager/entrepreneur and artist who helped change the face of pop music with his group The Sex Pistols. He also handled The New York Dolls, Adam Ant and Bow Wow Wow before launching the first of his own string of hits. He had three UK-only Top 20s, the other being the unusual offering 'Madam Butterfly' (UK 13) in 84. He had a US No. 1 dance track in 89 with 'Deep in Vogue'.

 BUFFALO GALS *(The first scratch hit)* — 9 15 JAN 83 CHARISMA
DOUBLE DUTCH — 3 06 AUG 83 CHARISMA

DON McLEAN

Singer/songwriter started performing folk music around his home town New York in 68. His first of 6 US (5 UK) Top 40s is regarded as one of the classic records of all time. He also wrote 'And I Love You So', the Perry Como hit, and 'Killing Me Softly With His Song' was written about him. He had the first of three small country hits in 87 and joined Capitol in 88.

 AMERICAN PIE — 2 04 MAR 72 UA
VINCENT *(US No. 12 – about Van Gogh)* — 1(2) 17 JUN 72 UA
CRYING *(Roy Orbison 61 hit)* — 1(3) 21 JUN 80 EMI

AMERICAN PIE (PTS 1 & 2) *(Top US single 72)* *(8½ mins long – starts in mono & ends stereo)* — 1(4) 15 JAN 72 UA
CRYING — 5 21 MAR 81 MILLENNIUM

CLYDE McPHATTER

Distinctive and influential North Carolina singer fronted two hit acts in the 50s, Billy Ward & Dominoes and The Drifters. He went solo in 55 and in the next decade had 15 R&B Top 20s, with his only transatlantic hit was 'Treasure of Love' (US 16/UK 27). He was also on MGM, Amy, Deram and Decca, and died in 72.

A LOVER'S QUESTION *(Co-written Brook Benton)* — 6 18 JAN 59 ATLANTIC
LOVER PLEASE — 7 21 APR 62 MERCURY

RALPH McTELL

Well known UK folk singer from Kent had two UK-only Top 40 LPs before a version of his best known composition, with added strings and female chorus, gave him a surprise pop smash.

 STREETS OF LONDON — 2 11 JAN 75 REPRISE

CHRISTINE McVIE

Before marrying John McVie the Birmingham (UK) singer was known as Christine Perfect, and as part of Chicken Shack she had a UK Top 20 hit with 'I'd Rather Go Blind' (14) in 69. She was voted Top Female Vocalist of 69 in a UK poll and joined her husband's group Fleetwood Mac in 70 and recorded her solo hit whilst with them.

 GOT A HOLD ON ME — 10 24 MAR 84 WARNER

ABIGAIL MEAD & NIGEL GOULDING

She was the daughter of top film director Stanley Kubrick and he was an extra in the film from which their one-off UK hit came.

 FULL METAL JACKET (I WANNA BE YOUR DRILL INSTRUCTOR) *(US flop – from the film)* — 2 10 OCT 87 WARNER

SISTER JANET MEAD

The second singing nun to have a US hit came from Australia where she hosted rock masses. She had a one-off left field chart record with her version of the well known prayer.

THE LORD'S PRAYER — 4 13 APR 74 A&M

MEAT LOAF

Singer/actor born Marvin Lee Aday in Dallas. He fronted L.A. band Meat Loaf Soul in 67 and in 70 charted on Rare Earth in the duo Stoney & Meatloaf. He teamed with producer/writer Jim Steinman and the result was the LP 'Bat Out Of Hell' that spent a record 395 weeks on the UK LP chart. He has had five UK-only Top 10 LPs and his biggest US 45 was 'Two Out of Three Ain't Bad' (US 11/UK 32).

 DEAD RINGER FOR LOVE *(Cher did backing vocals)* — 5 06 FEB 82 EPIC

MECO

Multi talented Pennsylvania born Meco Monardo arranged Tommy James smash 'Crimson And Clover'. He also produced big hits for Gloria Gaynor and Carol Douglas before scoring the first of 5 US (1 UK) Top 40s – all disco versions of film orientated songs.

 STAR WARS THEME/CANTINA BAND — 7 22 OCT 77 RCA
STAR WARS THEME/CANTINA BAND — 1(2) 01 OCT 77 MILLENNIUM

GLENN MEDEIROS

This 16 year old singer had the biggest ever hit made in his home state of Hawaii. The record hit in spring 87 in the US, was a smash in France and most of Europe months later and finally gave him a UK No. 1 in the summer of 88. His follow up was 'Watching Over You'. In 89 he was produced by another hot young act Bobby Brown.

 NOTHING'S GONNA CHANGE MY LOVE FOR YOU *(US No. 12 – jumped from 11-1 – orig. George Benson)* — 1(4) 09 JUL 88 LONDON

MEDICINE HEAD

Midlands (UK) based rock act featured John Fiddler and Peter Hope Evans and had four UK-only Top 40s. They were produced at times by Keith Relf (ex-Yardbirds) and Tony Ashton (Gardner & Dyke) and were also on Dandelion, WWA and Harvest.

ONE AND ONE IS ONE — 3 09 JUN 73 POLYDOR

BILL MEDLEY

The California born ex-Righteous Brother had his first solo single on Reprise in 65. Before his one-off duet hit in 87 he had five small US-only pop hits on MGM, Liberty (including a version of Linda Ronstadt's hit 'Don't Know Much') and Planet and six solo country hits on UA and RCA in the 80s.

 (I'VE HAD) THE TIME OF MY LIFE *(And JENNIFER WARNES) (From film 'Dirty Dancing')* — 6 21 NOV 87 RCA
(I'VE HAD) THE TIME OF MY LIFE *(And JENNIFER WARNES) (Co-writ. Franke (& Knockouts) Previte)* — 1(1) 28 NOV 87 RCA

Also see Righteous Brothers

TONY MEEHAN – SEE JET HARRIS FOR HIT DETAILS

MELLE MEL – SEE GRANDMASTER FLASH FOR HIT DETAILS

MEL (SMITH) & KIM (WILDE) – SEE KIM WILDE FOR HIT DETAILS

MEL & KIM

Sisters Mel & Kim Appleby had four UK Top 10s with S.A.W. productions. Despite little US pop success they were a top dance music act there. They were also part of Ferry Aid whose hit replaced their 'Respectable' at the top of the UK chart. At their peak Mel got cancer and died in 90.

SHOWING OUT *(US No. 78 and Top US Club Play record 87)*		3	22 NOV 86	SUPREME
RESPECTABLE *(US dance No. 1)* *(First No. 1 written by S.A.W. team)*		1(1)	28 MAR 87	SUPREME
F.L.M.		7	18 JUL 87	SUPREME
THAT'S THE WAY IT IS		10	12 MAR 88	SUPREME

MEL & TIM

St. Louis based Mel Harden and Tim McPherson had two US-only Top 20s – the other being 'Starting All Over Again' on Stax in 72. Mel had sung with The Individuals and Tim had been in The Vandels before they teamed up on Gene Chandler's Bamboo label.

BACKFIELD IN MOTION *(Co-writ Gene Chandler)*		10	13 DEC 69	BAMBOO

MELANIE

Unmistakable New York folk singer/songwriter Melanie Safka had two unsuccessful 45s on Columbia in 67. Her appearance at Woodstock inspired the first of her six US (4 UK Top 40s) 'Lay Down'. One of the last hippy stars, she was also on Atlantic, RCA, Midsong, Portrait, World United, Amherst and Tomato.

RUBY TUESDAY *(US No. 52 – Rolling Stones song)*		9	07 NOV 70	BUDDAH
BRAND NEW KEY *(Was voted Worlds Top Female singer in 72 UK poll)*		4	22 JAN 72	BUDDAH
LAY DOWN (CANDLES IN THE RAIN) *(And The EDWIN HAWKINS SINGERS)*		6	11 JUL 70	BUDDAH
BRAND NEW KEY		1(3)	25 DEC 71	NEIGHBORHOOD

JOHN COUGAR MELLENCAMP

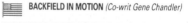

Rural rocker from Indiana who was in Trash in 71, first recorded on MCA in 76 (as Johnny Cougar) and in 78 he was launched in the UK on Riva without success. He was one of the most consistent US hitmakers in the 80s scoring 18 US-only Top 20s. He also does a lot of charity work and helped organise 'Farm Aid'.

HURTS SO GOOD		2	07 AUG 82	RIVA
JACK & DIANE *(UK No. 25)*		1(4)	18 SEP 82	RIVA
CRUMBLIN' DOWN		9	26 NOV 83	RIVA
PINK HOUSES		8	11 FEB 84	RIVA
LONELY OL' NIGHT		6	12 OCT 85	RIVA
SMALL TOWN *(UK No. 53)*		6	28 DEC 85	RIVA
R.O.C.K IN THE U.S.A. *(A SALUTE TO 60S ROCK)* *(UK No. 67)*		2	05 APR 86	RIVA
PAPER IN FIRE		9	03 OCT 87	MERCURY
CHERRY BOMB		8	09 JAN 88	MERCURY

HAROLD MELVIN & THE BLUE NOTES

Philadelphia soul group first recorded in 56 on Josie and first charted in 60 on Val-ue. In 70 Teddy Pendergrass took over vocals from John Atkins and the act had 4 US (5 UK) Top 40s before he left in 76. They were also on Brooke, Landa, Dot, Port, ABC, Source, Arctic, Phil L.A. of Soul, MCA and Philly World.

IF YOU DON'T KNOW ME BY NOW		9	27 JAN 73	CBS
DON'T LEAVE ME THIS WAY		5	26 FEB 77	PHILLY INT.
IF YOU DON'T KNOW ME BY NOW		3	09 DEC 72	PHILLY INT
THE LOVE I LOST (PT. 1) *(UK No. 21)*		7	08 DEC 73	PHILLY INT.

MEN AT WORK

Australian rock quintet fronted by Scotsman Colin Hay. Their first single was a US No. 1 as was their debut LP 'Business As Usual' (No. 1 for 15 weeks a record for a debut LP). They were Best New Group at the 83 Grammys and their second LP was also a Top 5 hit. Group had personnel problems and Hay went solo in 87.

DOWN UNDER		1(3)	29 JAN 83	EPIC
WHO CAN IT BE NOW? *(UK No. 45)*		1(1)	30 OCT 82	COLUMBIA
DOWN UNDER		1(4)	15 JAN 83	COLUMBIA
OVERKILL *(UK No. 21)*		3	04 JUN 83	COLUMBIA
IT'S A MISTAKE *(UK No. 33)*		6	20 AUG 83	COLUMBIA

MEN WITHOUT HATS

Montreal rock group fronted by singer/songwriter Ivan Doroschuk had a transatlantic Top 10 with a quirky electro pop track. They returned to No. 20 in the US in 88 with 'Pop Goes The World'.

THE SAFETY DANCE		6	05 NOV 83	STATIK
THE SAFETY DANCE		3	10 SEP 83	BACKSTREET

SERGIO MENDES

Brazilian MOR/jazz musician's first group was called Bossa Rio in the bossa nova days. He moved to the US with his group Brasil '65 and recorded on Atlantic. Act became Brasil '66 and had five US-only Top 40 LPs in the 60s. In the 70s they became Brasil '77.

THE LOOK OF LOVE *(From Casino Royale)*		4	06 JUL 68	A&M
THE FOOL ON THE HILL *(Beatles song)* *(Above two as Sergio Mendes & Brasil '66)*		6	28 SEP 68	A&M
NEVER GONNA LET YOU GO *(UK No. 45)* *(Vocals by Joe Pizzulo & Leza Miller)*		4	09 JUL 83	A&M

MENTAL AS ANYTHING

Australian group formed in 76 have had many local hits including 'The Nips Are Getting Bigger' (about drinks), since charting in 79. The follow up to their UK hit was 'You're So Strong'.

LIVE IT UP *(From Crocodile Dundee)* *(They first recorded this song in 84)*		3	07 MAR 87	EPIC

FREDDIE MERCURY

Charismatic leader of supergroup Queen was born Freddie Bulsara in Zanzibar. He first recorded in 73 as Larry Lurex and apart from his numerous hits with Queen he had had four UK-only Top 40s – the other being 'I Was Born To Love You' (11).

LOVE KILLS *(US No. 69 – from 'Metropolis')*		10	06 OCT 84	CBS
THE GREAT PRETENDER *(Platters 55 hit)*		4	14 MAR 87	PARLOPHONE
BARCELONA *(And MONTSERRAT CABALLE)*		8	14 NOV 87	POLYDOR

Also see Queen

MERCY

Florida group formed at high school by Jack Sigler Jr. who also wrote their big US hit. Their follow up was 'Forever' on Warner.

LOVE (CAN MAKE YOU HAPPY)		2	31 MAY 69	SUNDI

MERSEYBEATS

Liverpool foursome achieved six UK only Top 10s between 63-66. Act, who were fronted by Tony Crane, broke up in 66 with Tony and fellow member Billy Kinsley continuing as The Merseys.

I THINK OF YOU *(Composed by Daniel Boone)*		5	07 MAR 64	FONTANA
SORROW *(Originally by The McCoys)* *(Released as The MERSEYS)*		4	04 JUN 66	FONTANA

JIM MESSINA – SEE LOGGINS & MESSINA FOR HIT DETAILS

MFSB

Large studio band, put together by Gamble and Huff with arranger Thom Bell, who evolved out of their earlier session band The Music Makers. Mother, Father, Sister, Brother (MFSB) followed their transatlantic hit with 'Love Is The Message'.

	TSOP (THE SOUND OF PHILADELPHIA) *(UK No. 22)*	1(2)	20 APR 74	PHILLY INT.
	(Feat. the THREE DEGREES – 'Soul Train' TV Theme)			

MIAMI SOUND MACHINE – SEE GLORIA ESTEFAN FOR HIT DETAILS

GEORGE MICHAEL

Ex Wham! singer was the top transatlantic male artist of the late 80s. His self produced/arranged/written/played and sung album 'Faith' was the first by a male to sell a million CDs, the first by a UK male to top the US chart for 11 weeks, and the first by a white act to top the black music chart. He was also the youngest person to win the UK Songwriter Of The Year award. He has packed stadiums around the world and he also took part in Band Aid and Live Aid and was in the Nelson Mandela birthday show.

	CARELESS WHISPER *(UK Gold)*	1(3)	18 AUG 84	EPIC
	A DIFFERENT CORNER *(Jumped 77-1 on 12" chart)*	1(3)	12 APR 86	EPIC
	I KNEW YOU WERE WAITING (FOR ME)	1(2)	07 FEB 87	ARISTA
	(With ARETHA FRANKLIN – Entered at No. 2)			
	I WANT YOUR SEX *(Banned on many stations)*	3	20 JUN 87	EPIC
	(Entered at No. 4 – from 'Beverly Hills Cop 11')			
	FAITH *(Entered at No. 10)*	2	31 OCT 87	EPIC
	ONE MORE TRY	8	30 APR 88	EPIC
	CARELESS WHISPER	1(3)	16 FEB 85	COLUMBIA
	(US label said by WHAM! – Top US single of 85)			
	A DIFFERENT CORNER	7	14 JUN 86	COLUMBIA
	I KNEW YOU WERE WAITING (FOR ME)	1(2)	18 APR 87	ARISTA
	(With ARETHA FRANKLIN) (2nd Narada prod. No. 1 in row)			
	I WANT YOUR SEX	2	08 AUG 87	COLUMBIA
	FAITH *(Top US single of 88)*	1(3)	12 DEC 87	COLUMBIA
	FATHER FIGURE *(UK No. 11)*	1(2)	27 FEB 88	COLUMBIA
	ONE MORE TRY *(Was black music No. 1 too)*	1(3)	28 MAY 88	COLUMBIA
	MONKEY *(UK No. 13)*	1(2)	27 AUG 88	COLUMBIA
	KISSING A FOOL	5	26 NOV 88	COLUMBIA
	(UK No. 18 – he was top act in US in 88)			

Also see Wham!

LEE MICHAELS

Multi instrumentalist was known for his hard rock keyboard style. He was in the band The Sentinels in 65 and then Joel Scott Hill group before forming his own band. He joined A&M in 68 and his first of two US-only Top 40s came from his third chart LP for them. He later recorded on Columbia, ABC and his own Squish label.

	DO YOU KNOW WHAT I MEAN	6	09 OCT 71	A&M

KEITH MICHELL

Australian actor/singer, perhaps best known for his role as TV's 'Henry VII', had three UK-only chart entries – the biggest being a double sided children's novelty record.

	CAPTAIN BEAKY/WILFRED THE WEASEL	5	16 FEB 80	POLYDOR

MIDDLE OF THE ROAD

Glasgow MOR/pop quartet, previously named Part Four and Los Caracos, were fronted by only female member Sally Carr. They moved to Italy where their five UK-only Top 40s were recorded. Their first hit (originally by Lally Scott) was a big Euro hit before charting in the UK. They were on OK in 80 and Pulsar in 82.

	CHIRPY CHIRPY CHEEP CHEEP *(Jumped from 16-1)*	1(5)	19 JUN 71	RCA
	(They claim it sold nearly 10 million world-wide)			
	TWEEDLE DEE TWEEDLE DUM	2	16 OCT 71	RCA
	SOLEY SOLEY	5	08 JAN 72	RCA

BETTE MIDLER

New Jersey born singer/entertainer/actress appeared in various musicals in the 60s and recorded her first LP in 72 with her producer/pianist Barry Manilow. She won her first Grammy for Best New Act of 73. In 79 she starred in the first of a string of hit films The Rose. Her first UK chart entry only came in 89.

	WIND BENEATH MY WINGS	5	22 JUL 89	ATLANTIC
	(Gary Morris 83 country hit – Grammy Record of year)			
	BOOGIE WOOGIE BUGLE BOY	8	21 JUL 73	ATLANTIC
	(Andrews Sisters 41 hit)			
	THE ROSE *(From the film 'The Rose')*	3	28 JUN 80	ATLANTIC
	(Grammy winner Top Female performance of 80)			
	WIND BENEATH MY WINGS	1(1)	10 JUN 89	ATLANTIC
	(Co-Written by Larry Henley of The Newbeats)			

MIDNIGHT OIL

Politically committed Australian hard rock band fronted by Peter Garrett had their first US release in 84 and had built a large cult following there before their LP 'Diesel And Dust' and Top 20 single broke them internationally. Follow up 45 was 'The Dead Heart'.

	BEDS ARE BURNING	6	13 MAY 89	CBS/SPRINT
	(US No. 17 – Was UK No. 48 in 88)			

MIDNIGHT STAR

Kentucky soul group formed in 76 by the Calloway brothers Reginald & Vincent and featuring singer Belinda Lipscomb. They had two UK Top 20s, the other being 'Headlines' (UK 16/US 69) and hit the US Top 20 with 'Operator' (US 18/UK 66). In 89 the brothers formed Calloway who also hit the black music Top 20.

	MIDAS TOUCH *(US No. 42)*	8	01 NOV 86	SOLAR

MIGIL FIVE

London based white bluebeat band named after members Mike Felix (MI) and Gil Lucas (GIL). They hit with their second release and also had a UK-only charter with its follow up 'Near You' (31) – another oldie. They were on Columbia in 67 and Joy in 69.

	MOCKINGBIRD HILL *(Patti Page 51 hit)*	10	02 MAY 64	PYE

MIKE + THE MECHANICS

Genesis guitarist Mike Rutherford's band that has also featured Paul Young (from Sad Cafe) and Paul Carrack. Mike had previously recorded as a soloist in 80 on Charisma. He was the only person to have two US No 1s in the 80s with two different groups.

	THE LIVING YEARS *(Vocal Paul Carrack)*	2	28 JAN 89	WEA
	(Co-written B.A. Robertson)			
	SILENT RUNNING	6	08 MAR 86	ATLANTIC
	(UK No. 21 – From film 'On Dangerous Ground')			
	ALL I NEED IS A MIRACLE	5	07 JUN 86	ATLANTIC
	THE LIVING YEARS	1(1)	25 MAR 89	ATLANTIC

Also see Genesis

JOHN MILES

Singer/songwriter/musician from Jarrow (UK) recorded on Decca in 71 and on Orange in 73. He had three UK Top 20s, the other being his first hit 'Highfly' (UK 17/US 68). He was on Harvest in 81, EMI in 83, Valentino in 85 and had a song in the UK heat of Eurovision Song Contest in 90.

	MUSIC *(US No. 88 – produced by Alan Parsons)*	3	10 APR 76	DECCA
	SLOW DOWN *(US No. 34)*	10	23 JUL 77	DECCA

PAUL MILES-KINGSTON – SEE SARAH BRIGHTMAN FOR HIT DETAILS

MILK & HONEY

Israel's second successive Eurovision song contest winner featured female vocalist Gali Atari with three male singers. The group, who were put together for the contest, were also on Bellaphon in 80. The song, performed by another act, had been an unplaced entrant in the previous years contest in Israel.

🇬🇧	HALLELUJAH	5	21 APR 79	POLYDOR

FRANKIE MILLER

Scottish singer/songwriter was in the Stoics and Jude (with Robin Trower) before recording solo for Chrysalis. His live band has included Henry McCullough (later in Wings) and Robbie McIntosh (later in AWB) and Paul Carrack (Mike & Mechanics etc.). A critics' favourite but has never had the success expected of him.

🇬🇧	DARLIN'	6	11 NOV 78	CHRYSALIS

NED MILLER

Utah born country singer/songwriter recorded his sole Top 40 Transatlantic hit in 57. He had 11 country hits and also recorded on Dot in 57, Radio in 58, Jackpot in 60, Capitol in 61 and again in 65 and Republic in 70. His follow up was 'One Among The Many'.

🇬🇧	FROM A JACK TO A KING	2	12 APR 63	LONDON
🇺🇸	FROM A JACK TO A KING	6	16 FEB 63	FABOR

ROGER MILLER

Grammy winning Texan country singer/songwriter recorded on Mercury in 57 and on Decca and Starday in 58. He played drums in Faron Young's band in 62 and became one of the top country stars of the 60s with 12 US (4 UK) Top 40s and a total of 31 country Top 40s. He also wrote the top Broadway show 'Big River' in 85, and his songs have been recorded by Andy Williams and Del Shannon. Following his big hit he opened a hotel in Nashville called Roger Millers 'King Of The Road' Motor Inn.

🇬🇧	KING OF THE ROAD	1(1)	15 MAY 65	PHILIPS
🇺🇸	DANG ME	7	02 AUG 64	SMASH
	CHUG-A-LUG	9	07 NOV 64	SMASH
	KING OF THE ROAD	4	20 MAR 65	SMASH
	ENGINE ENGINE # 9 (US No. 33)	7	12 JUN 65	SMASH
	ENGLAND SWINGS (US No. 13)	8	18 DEC 65	SMASH

STEVE MILLER BAND

San Francisco based rock/blues singer/guitarist formed his first band The Marksmen Combo at 12. This act included Boz Scaggs as did his later groups The Ardells (aka The Fabulous Night Trains). As The Steve Miller Blues Band he played the 67 Monterey Pop Festival. They had the first of 10 US (three UK) Top 40 LPs in 68.

🇬🇧	ABRACADABRA	2	10 JUL 82	MERCURY
🇺🇸	THE JOKER	1(1)	12 JAN 74	CAPITOL
	ROCK'N ME (UK No. 11)	1(1)	06 NOV 76	CAPITOL
	FLY LIKE AN EAGLE	2	12 MAR 77	CAPITOL
	JET AIRLINER	8	09 JUL 77	CAPITOL
	ABRACADABRA	1(2)	04 SEP 82	CAPITOL

MILLI VANILLI

The hottest new duo of 89 were German based Rob Pilatus, who had been in Dupont on MCA, and Guadeloupe born Fabrice Morvan, both sons of American servicemen. The duo, who had been in the 87 Eurovision Song contest, were named after a New York club and were produced by ultra-successful Fred Farian in Germany. Their debut LP, which contained a record three No. 1s, sold over six million in the US alone and they had four gold singles in 89.

🇬🇧	GIRL YOU KNOW IT'S TRUE (Orig. by Numarx)	3	05 NOV 88	COOLTEMPO
	GIRL I'M GONNA MISS YOU	2	28 OCT 89	COOLTEMPO
🇺🇸	GIRL YOU KNOW IT'S TRUE	2	01 APR 89	ARISTA
	BABY DON'T FORGET MY NUMBER	1(16)	01 JUL 89	ARISTA
	GIRL I'M GONNA MISS YOU	1(2)	23 SEP 89	ARISTA
	BLAME IT ON THE RAIN (UK No. 53)	1(2)	25 NOV 89	ARISTA
	(UK No. 53 – Duo won Grammy as Best New Act of 89)			

MILLIE (SMALL)

Jamaican blue beat (forerunner of reggae) singer Millie Small (she used her full name in the US) had two transatlantic Top 40s before she was 18 – the other being her follow up 'Sweet William' (US 40/UK 30). She later unsuccessfully revived other 50s hits like 'See You Later Alligator' and 'Bloodshot Eyes'.

🇬🇧	MY BOY LOLLIPOP	2	23 MAY 64	FONTANA
	(First hit for Island records – also UK No.46 in 87)			
🇺🇸	MY BOY LOLLIPOP (Orig. Barbie Gaye in 56)	2	04 JUL 64	SMASH

FRANK MILLS

Canadian musician/composer first charted in 72 on Sunflower with 'Love Me, Love Me Love' (US 46) and had his second and biggest US-only hit with this piano instrumental seven years later.

🇺🇸	MUSIC BOX DANCER	3	05 MAY 79	POLYDOR

GARRY MILLS

Kent (UK) singer had recorded a string of cover versions of US hits before scoring with this Tony Hatch song. Ironically his biggest hit was covered heavily in the US where four versions charted including one by similarly named Garry Miles (Buzz Cason).

🇬🇧	LOOK FOR A STAR	5	22 JUL 60	TOP RANK
	(US No. 26 – From the film 'Circus of Horrors')			

HAYLEY MILLS

London born film star daughter of actor Sir John Mills was one of few UK acts to have a transatlantic Top 20 before The Beatles.

🇺🇸	LET'S GET TOGETHER	8	24 OCT 61	VISTA
	(UK No. 17 – from the film The Parent Trap)			

STEPHANIE MILLS

New York born singer/actress appeared on Broadway when only seven, played the Apollo at 10 and at 15 played the lead in The Wiz on Broadway (for four years). She recorded on ABC in 74 and Motown in 75 and has also charted on 20th Century, Casablanca and MCA. To date she has had 18 black music Top 20s, including five No.1s, and also has had five Gold LPs to date.

🇬🇧	NEVER KNEW LOVE LIKE THIS BEFORE	4	29 NOV 80	20TH CENTURY
🇺🇸	NEVER KNEW LOVE LIKE THIS BEFORE	6	15 NOV 80	20TH CENTURY

119

RONNIE MILSAP

Blind singer/pianist from North Carolina. He played in the J.J. Cale Band, cut soul records on Scepter and was on Warner, Boblo, Pacemaker, Festival and Chips before becoming one of the all time top country acts. To date he has had 55 country hits including an amazing 35 No. 1s, not to mention six US-only Top 40 pop hits.

(THERE'S) NO GETTIN' OVER ME		5	05 SEP 81	RCA

GARNET MIMMS & THE ENCHANTERS

West Virginia singer recorded in gospel groups The Evening Stars and The Norfolk Four (both on Savoy). He formed The Gainors in 59 who were on Cameo, Mercury and Red Top. Formed in 61 this soul quartet had four US-only Top 40s. The Enchanters were later on Warner and Loma and he appeared on Veep, Verve, GSF and Arista.

CRY BABY		4	12 OCT 63	UA

MINDBENDERS

After Wayne Fontana left in 66 this Manchester act had two more UK Top 20s – the other being 'Ashes To Ashes' (UK 14/US 55). In 70 the group's Eric Stewart joined Hotlegs who evolved into 10CC.

A GROOVY KIND OF LOVE (Originally by Patti LaBelle & Bluebelles)		2	12 MAR 66	FONTANA
A GROOVY KIND OF LOVE (Co-written by Carole Bayer Sager)		2	28 MAY 66	FONTANA

Also see Wayne Fontana & Mindbenders/10CC/Hotlegs

MARCELLO MINEREBI

Italian orchestra leader had a one-off UK hit with the dance song from Zorba The Greek film. Herb Alpert had the US hit with it.

ZORBA'S DANCE		6	04 SEP 65	DURIUM

LIZA MINNELLI

Daughter of top star Judy Garland. She first recorded in 63 and had seven US (2 UK) chart LPs in the 60s and 70s, with the only single success coming in 89 in the UK when she teamed with The Pet Shop Boys.

LOSING MY MIND (From 'Follies' – Prod. and Comp. Pet Shop Boys)		6	19 AUG 89	EPIC

KYLIE MINOGUE

Australian singer/actress was the top female in the UK in the late 80s. A star of the soap opera Neighbours she recorded with the S.A.W. team and saw her first seven 45s all make the Top 4 – a record achievement. She was the youngest female to top the LP charts, had the biggest selling ever debut LP (1.9 million) and the biggest selling female LP of all time in the UK. She also sold a record 350,000 of her first video.

I SHOULD BE SO LUCKY (Us No. 28) (First record by Australian female to be No. 1)	1(5)	20 FEB 88	PWL
GOT TO BE CERTAIN	2	28 MAY 88	PWL
THE LOCO-MOTION (Little Eva 62 hit) (Entered at No. 2 – the UK female record)	2	06 AUG 88	PWL
JE NE SAIS PAS POURQUOI	2	12 NOV 88	PWL
ESPECIALLY FOR YOU (And JASON DONOVAN) (Entered at No. 2 – UK Gold)	1(3)	07 JAN 89	PWL
HAND ON YOUR HEART (Entered at No. 2)	1(1)	13 MAY 89	PWL
WOULDN'T CHANGE A THING (Her fourth single to enter at No. 2)	2	05 AUG 89	PWL
NEVER TOO LATE	4	11 NOV 89	PWL
THE LOCO-MOTION (Co-written by Carole King) (She topped Aussie chart with earlier mix in 87)	3	12 NOV 88	GEFFEN

SUGAR MINOTT

Reggae star from Kingston, Jamaica, who was originally in The African Brothers before going solo in 77. He formed his own Black Roots label in 78 and since then has appeared on over 50 other labels in the UK! His follow up was 'Never My Love' (UK 52).

GOOD THING GOING (WE'VE GOT A GOOD THING GOING) (Originally by The Jackson Five)	4	25 APR 81	RCA

MIRACLES

Detroit soul group formed in 57 as The Matadors featured one of the great singer/songwriters – William 'Smokey' Robinson. They recorded on End in 58 and Chess in 59 and gave Motown their first No. 1 (R&B) in 61. They had an enviable string of 27 US Top 40s (5 UK) before Smokey left in 72. He was replaced by Billy Griffin who sang on their last US No. 1 which was also their last hit.

THE TRACKS OF MY TEARS (US No 16 in 65)	9	14 JUN 69	TAMLA MOTOWN
TEARS OF A CLOWN	1(1)	12 SEP 70	TAMLA MOTOWN
(Above two as SMOKEY ROBINSON & THE MIRACLES)			
LOVE MACHINE	3	07 FEB 76	TAMLA MOTOWN
SHOP AROUND	2	20 FEB 61	TAMLA
YOU'VE REALLY GOT A HOLD ON ME	8	09 FEB 63	TAMLA
MICKEY'S MONKEY	8	21 SEP 63	TAMLA
I SECOND THAT EMOTION (UK No. 27)	4	16 DEC 67	TAMLA
BABY, BABY DON'T YOU CRY	8	01 MAR 69	TAMLA
THE TEARS OF A CLOWN	1(2)	12 DEC 70	TAMLA
(Above three as SMOKEY ROBINSON & THE MIRACLES)			
LOVE MACHINE	1(1)	06 MAR 76	TAMLA

Also see Smokey Robinson

MIRAGE

Recording group including Liverpool singer Kiki Billy were masterminded by producer Nigel Wright of Shakatak and Yell fame. They specialised in medleys of hits and to date have had six UK-only chart entries. Apart from the Jack discs they scored with a George Benson medley featuring Roy Gayle.

JACK MIX 11 (Medley of current dance hits)	4	06 JUN 87	DEBUT
JACK MIX 1V (Medley of current dance hits)	8	21 NOV 87	DEBUT

DANNY MIRROR

Top Dutch producer Eddy Ouwens (who produced Teach-In amongst others) had the UK and Dutch Elvis tribute hit under this name. In 81 he released an Elvis medley called 'Suspicion' on Albion.

I REMEMBER ELVIS PRESLEY (THE KING IS DEAD)	4	15 OCT 77	SONET

MR. BIG

UK rock quartet featuring two drummers and fronted by Dicken. They had several releases before getting the first of two UK-only Top 40s, the other being the follow up 'Feels Like Calling Home' (35).

ROMEO	4	05 MAR 77	EMI

MR. BLOE

UK session group featuring pianist Zack Lawrence had a one-off UK hit with a cover version of Cool Heat's 70 US hit.

GROOVIN' WITH MR. BLOE	2	27 JUN 70	DJM

MR MISTER

Phoenix born songwriters and session musicians Richard Page and Steve George were in The Pages on Epic before forming this AOR quartet in 81. Their second LP 'Welcome To The Real World' topped the US chart, as did the first two singles from it.

BROKEN WINGS		4	25 JAN 86	RCA
BROKEN WINGS		1(2)	07 DEC 85	RCA
KYRIE (UK No. 11)		1(2)	01 MAR 86	RCA
IS IT LOVE		8	31 MAY 86	RCA

GUY MITCHELL

One of the top sellers of the early 50s was born Al Cernick in Detroit. He sang with Carmen Cavallaro's Orchestra in the 40s, recorded country material under his real name and joined Columbia in 50. He appeared in several films and had 14 US (13 UK) Top 20s. He was later on Joy, Reprise, and Starday.

SINGING THE BLUES (Marty Robbins 57 US hit)		1(1)	04 JAN 57	PHILIPS
KNEE DEEP IN THE BLUES		3	08 MAR 57	PHILIPS
(US No. 21 – Marty Robbins 57 country hit)				
ROCK-A-BILLY		1(1)	17 MAY 57	PHILIPS
HEARTACHES BY THE NUMBER		5	05 FEB 60	PHILIPS
(Ray Price 59 country hit)				
SINGING THE BLUES		1(9)	08 DEC 56	COLUMBIA
(Whistling on record by Ray Conniff)				
ROCK-A-BILLY		10	06 MAY 57	COLUMBIA
HEARTACHES BY THE NUMBER		1(2)	14 DEC 59	COLUMBIA
(He re-recorded it in 69 on Starday)				

JONI MITCHELL

Distinctive folk singer/songwriter born Roberta Anderson in Alberta, Canada, whose best known songs are 'Both Sides Now' and 'Woodstock'. She has had 12 US (10 UK) Top 40 LPs since 68 and has experimented with her music, working with people like Thomas Dolby, Charlie Mingus, Willie Nelson, Peter Gabriel and Billy Idol. Her only UK hit 45 was 'Big Yellow Taxi' (UK 11/US 24).

HELP ME		7	08 JUN 74	ASYLUM

MIXMASTER

Italian House track created by Daniele 'D.J. Lelewel' Davoli the man behind Black Box and Starlight. It's a piano led track with samples from acts like Joe Tex, KAOS and Loleatta Holloway.

GRAND PIANO		9	10 NOV 09	DCM

MIXTURES

Australian quartet led by Mick Flinn. First hit down under with 'Fancy Meeting You Here' and a cover of 'In The Summertime'. Group had a one-off transatlantic hit with a Mungo Jerry styled song. They followed it with 'Henry Ford', an automobile song. They were on UA in 73.

THE PUSHBIKE SONG (US No. 44)		2	06 FEB 71	POLYDOR
(Written in 66 by ex member Idris Jones)				

HANK MIZELL

Recorded on Eko in 57 this basic R'n'R track became a UK and Dutch smash hit 19 years later for its composer and producer from Florida. He followed it with a new recording 'Kangaroo Rock'.

JUNGLE ROCK		3	01 MAY 76	CHARLY

MOBILES

Anna Marie led this Brighton (UK) based band who got the sack from their day jobs for appearing on Top Of The Pops to promote their sole Top 40 hit. Their follow up was 'Amour Amour'. They joined MCA in 84.

DROWNING IN BERLIN		9	06 FEB 82	RIALTO

MOCEDADES

Spanish folk sextet, featuring the Amezaga sisters Amaya & Izaskum, had a one-off US hit. Follow up was 'Dime Senor'.

ERES TU (TOUCH THE WIND)		9	23 MAR 74	TARA
(Spanish entry for 73 Eurovision song contest)				

MODERN ROMANCE

London based good time pop sextet that included David Jaymes and John Du Prez, evolved out of The Leyton Buzzards. They started as a salsa styled band and had their first of seven UK-only Top 20s with 'Everybody Salsa' (12). They were on RCA and Carrere in 85.

AY AY AY AY MOOSEY		10	05 DEC 81	WEA
BEST YEARS OF OUR LIVES		4	08 JAN 83	WEA
HIGH LIFE		8	19 MAR 83	WEA
WALKING IN THE RAIN		7	24 SEP 83	WEA

MODERN TALKING

Top German duo claimed to have sold over 30 million records in Europe and collected 140 gold and 40 platinum records! Their biggest hit was the five million seller 'You're My Heart, You're My Soul'. Follow up to their big UK hit was 'Atlantis is Calling'.

BROTHER LOUIE		4	30 AUG 86	RCA

MOJOS

Liverpool quintet, formed in 62 as The Nomads, released their first single 'Forever' in 63 and had three UK-only Top 40s in 64. Singer Stu James (Stuart Slater) later married Stephanie De Sykes and went on to be a leading music publishing executive.

EVERYTHING'S ALRIGHT		9	02 MAY 64	DECCA

MOMENTS

New Jersey soul trio of William Brown (ex Broadways and Uniques), Al Goodman (ex Covettes and Vipers) and Harry Ray (ex Establishment) who joined them after their US Top 10. They had 28 R&B hits starting in 68 and became Ray, Goodman & Brown in 78. Mark Greene, the group's original lead singer, left to go solo after the group's first hit.

GIRLS (And THE WHATNAUTS)		3	29 MAR 75	ALL PLAT.
DOLLY MY LOVE		10	23 AUG 75	ALL PLAT.
JACK IN THE BOX		7	26 FEB 77	ALL PLAT.
(None of their UK hits made the US pop chart)				
LOVE ON A TWO-WAY STREET		3	30 MAY 70	STANG

Also see Ray, Goodman & Brown

EDDIE MONEY

Hard rocker ex New York policeman Eddie Mahoney moved to the West coast and formed a group called The Rockets. He had his first solo LP in 77 and has since had four US Top 40 LPs and nine US Top 40 singles but no UK chart entries yet.

TAKE ME HOME TONIGHT		4	15 NOV 86	COLUMBIA
(Featuring Ronnie Spector singing 'Be My Baby')				
WALK ON WATER		9	24 DEC 88	COLUMBIA

MONKEES

Formed for a TV series in 66, they were the world's top act in 67 selling millions of records. In less than two years Davy, Peter, Mike & Mickey, who did not play on many of their biggest hits, chalked up 11 US (8 UK) Top 40 singles and 4 UK and 5 US Top 5 LPs (including a record four US No. 1s in a year). They broke up in 69 and re-united (minus Mike) in 86 when they returned to the US Top 20 singles and put seven LPs in the US chart simultaneously.

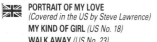

I'M A BELIEVER *(Jumped from 42-4)*	1(4)	21 JAN 67	RCA
A LITTLE BIT ME, A LITTLE BIT YOU	3	22 APR 67	RCA
(Above two composed Neil Diamond)			
ALTERNATE TITLE	2	22 JUL 67	RCA
(Not rel US. – orig. title 'Randy Scouse Git')			
DAYDREAM BELIEVER *(Composed John Stewart)*	5	13 JAN 68	RCA
LAST TRAIN TO CLARKSVILLE	1(1)	05 NOV 66	COLGEMS
(UK No. 23 – composed Boyce & Hart)			
I'M A BELIEVER *(Composed Neil Diamond)*	1 7	31 DEC 66	COLGEMS
A LITTLE BIT ME, A LITTLE BIT YOU	2	29 APR 67	COLGEMS
(Davy Jones was only Monkee on the record)			
PLEASANT VALLEY SUNDAY	3	19 AUG 67	COLGEMS
(UK No. 11 – co-written Carole King)			
DAYDREAM BELIEVER *(Top US in three weeks)*	1(4)	02 DEC 67	COLGEMS
(Was also US No. 79 in 86)			
VALLERI *(UK No. 12 – Comp. Boyce & Hart)*	3	30 MAR 68	COLGEMS

MATT MONRO

Born Terry Parsons, this ex-London bus driver with a Sinatra type voice sang with the BBC show band and recorded on Decca in 56 and Fontana in 58. Voted Top International Act in a US DJ poll in 61, the original version of Elvis' hit 'Softly As I Leave You' was among his 11 UK (2 US) Top 40s. His biggest LP was 'Heart-breakers' (UK No. 5) in 80. He died in 84.

PORTRAIT OF MY LOVE	3	27 JAN 61	PARLOPHONE
(Covered in the US by Steve Lawrence)			
MY KIND OF GIRL *(US No. 18)*	5	24 MAR 61	PARLOPHONE
WALK AWAY *(US No. 23)*	4	07 NOV 64	PARLOPHONE
YESTERDAY *(The UK hit of the Beatles song)*	8	06 NOV 65	PARLOPHONE

GERRY MONROE

South Shields (UK) singer scored a record number of votes on TVs Opportunity Knocks. He hit with his first release at age 37 and had five more UK-only Top 40s in the early 70s with MOR versions of old standards. His only other Top 20 hit was Fats Waller's 36 hit 'It's A Sin To Tell A Lie' (13).

SALLY *(Gracie Fields 30s UK success)*	4	04 JUL 70	CHAPTER ONE
MY PRAYER *(Inkspots 39 hit)*	9	19 DEC 70	CHAPTER ONE

LOU MONTE

Italian American comic/vocalist from New Jersey had been singing since before the war and had seven US-only chart hits between 53 and 63 – the first being 'At The Darktown Strutters Ball' (7). He was also on RCA, Roulette, Musicor, GRP, and on Laurie in 76.

PEPINO THE ITALIAN MOUSE	5	12 JAN 63	REPRISE
(Also recorded 'Pepino's Friend Pasqual')			

HUGO MONTENEGRO & HIS ORCHESTRA

The late New York conductor/composer first recorded in 55 and was Harry Belafonte's arranger in the 50s. He wrote several film scores and first charted with the soundtrack LP from the TV show The Man From U.N.C.L.E. in 66. He had one Transatlantic Top 40.

THE GOOD, THE BAD AND THE UGLY	1(4)	16 NOV 68	RCA
(From the film)			
THE GOOD, THE BAD AND THE UGLY	2	01 JUN 68	RCA

CHRIS MONTEZ

L.A. born Chris Montanez recorded for Guaranteed in 61 and his second single on Monogram became a dance classic, especially in the UK where it charted three times over a 17 year period. Influenced by Ritchie Valens, he later had four US (2 UK) Top 40s produced by Herb Alpert on his A&M label.

LET'S DANCE	2	14 NOV 62	LONDON
THE MORE I SEE YOU	3	13 AUG 66	PYE INT
(US No. 16 – Dick Haymes 45 hit)			
LET'S DANCE *(Re-issue-also UK No. 47 in 79)*	9	18 NOV 72	LONDON
LET'S DANCE	4	06 OCT 62	MONOGRAM
(He re-recorded it on Jamie in 73)			

MOODY BLUES

Midlands (UK) based classic rock quintet formed in 64, was shelved between 72-78, and were still charting in the late 80s with total sales of over 50 million. Their second 45 was their only No. 1 and was the first of 12 US (9 UK) Top 40s. The group has included Denny Laine, Graham Edge, Justin Hayward and John Lodge, all of whom also have had success outside the band. LP-wise they have had an enviable 14 US (13 UK) Top 40s.

GO NOW! *(Originally by Bessie Banks)*	1(1)	30 JAN 65	DECCA
QUESTION *(US No. 21)*	2	30 MAY 70	THRESHOLD
NIGHTS IN WHITE SATIN *(Re-entry)*	9	06 JAN 73	DERAM
(Also UK No. 19 in 67 and UK No. 14 in 79)			
GO NOW!	10	17 APR 65	LONDON
NIGHTS IN WHITE SATIN	2	04 NOV 72	DERAM
YOUR WILDEST DREAMS	9	12 JUL 86	THRESHOLD

Also see Justin Hayward

BOB MOORE & HIS ORCHESTRA

Top Nashville session bass player who had worked with Elvis, Pat Boone, Connie Francis, Roy Orbison and Brenda Lee, followed his one-off instrumental hit with 'Ooh La La'.

MEXICO	7	02 OCT 61	MONUMENT

DOROTHY MOORE

Mississippi born singer was the leader of The Poppies (they also included Fern Kinney) and has done much session work. She went solo on Avco in 72, first charted on GSF in 73 and has chalked up 13 black music chart entries and two UK Top 20s – the other being 'I Believe In You' (UK 20/ US 27). She was on Handshake in 82.

MISTY BLUE *(Wilma Burgess 66 country hit)*	5	07 AUG 76	CONTEMPO
MISTY BLUE	3	12 JUN 76	MALACO

GARY MOORE

Ex-guitarist with Skid Row (where he first played with Phil Lynott) and ex-member of Thin Lizzy and Jon Hiseman's Colosseum. He has had 10 UK-only hits, the biggest two being with Phil Lynott. He returned to the UK chart in 90 with top blues man Albert King.

PARISIENNE WALKWAYS	8	19 MAY 79	MCA
(Featuring vocals by Phil Lynott)			
OUT IN THE FIELDS *(And PHIL LYNOTT)*	5	08 JUN 85	10

MELBA MOORE

New York singer/actress who starred in Broadway productions like Hair and Purlie. She recorded on Musicor in 66 and got the first of her 30 black music hits in 75 and the biggest of them in the late 80s. Surprisingly she has yet to hit the US pop Top 40. She has also been on UA, Mercury, Epic, Capitol and EMI America.

THIS IS IT *(US No. 91)*	9	12 JUN 76	BUDDAH

GIORGIO MORODER & PHIL OAKEY

Amazingly successful Italian born producer/composer/musician who first recorded in the late 60s, first hit with his song 'Son Of My Father' in 72 and produced Donna Summer's string of hits from 75. He also produced and wrote numerous other big hits and his teaming with Human League's singer produced two UK-only charters.

TOGETHER IN ELECTRIC DREAMS	3	27 OCT 84	VIRGIN

ENNIO MORRICONE

The Italian composer of many film themes including the Top 10 hit 'The Good, The Bad And The Ugly' had been recording since the early 60s. He had his only hit with a UK TV theme that had flopped when released three years earlier on Private Stock.

CHI MAI THEME (FROM THE TV SERIES THE LIFE AND TIMES OF DAVID LLOYD GEORGE)	2	02 MAY 81	BBC

MORRIS MINOR & THE MAJORS

Comic UK act followed their one-off rap parody hit with 'This Is The Chorus'. They were on Pacific Minor in 89.

STUTTER RAP (NO SLEEP 'TIL BEDTIME)	4	16 JAN 88	10/VIRGIN

VAN MORRISON

Highly respected Belfast born singer/songwriter who played in Deanie Sands & The Javelins and The Monarchs before forming the hit R&B band Them. He went solo in 67 and has since had 12 UK (6 US) Top 40 LPs. He has had 11 US Top 40 singles, yet oddly it took him until 89 to get a UK Top 40 (a duet with Cliff Richard).

BROWN EYED GIRL	10	30 SEP 67	BANG
DOMINO	9	02 JAN 71	WARNER

Also see Them

MORRISSEY

Unmistakable singer/songwriter leader of The Smiths. Born Stephen Morrissey, he wrote the book James Dean Isn't Dead and ran the New York Dolls fan club before forming the very influential group. His first solo LP 'Viva Hate' entered the UK chart at No. 1 and his five singles since then have all made the UK-only Top 20. In total he has charted 21 times in just six years – a UK record.

SUEDEHEAD	5	05 MAR 88	HMV
(Entered at 6 – higher than any Smiths single got)			
EVERYDAY IS LIKE SUNDAY	9	18 JUN 88	HMV
LAST OF THE FAMOUS INTERNATIONAL PLAYBOYS	6	11 FEB 89	HMV
(Entered the 12", cassette & CD single charts at No. 1)			
INTERESTING DRUG	9	29 APR 89	HMV
(Backing vocalists include Kirsty McColl)			

Also see The Smiths

MOTELS

L.A. rock quintet fronted by Martha Davis evolved out of The Warfield Foxes and first recorded on Capitol in 79. They had two small UK hits before getting the first of their four US Top 40s. Martha later recorded solo and also dueted with Sly Stone.

ONLY THE LONELY	9	17 JUL 82	CAPITOL
SUDDENLY LAST SUMMER	9	19 NOV 83	CAPITOL

MOTLEY CRUE

Top L.A. heavy rock group includes singer Vince Neil (ex-Rock Candy) and bass player/composer Frank Ferrano better known as Nikki Sixx. Their first LP was on their own Leather label in 82 and since then they have picked up five Gold LPs and three US-only Top 20 singles. In the UK they have had three Top 40 LPs to date.

DR. FEELGOOD	6	28 OCT 89	ELEKTRA

MOTORHEAD

Influential and loud UK heavy metal trio featuring Lemmy (Ian Kilminster) who had been in groups like The Motown Sect and Opal Butterfly before joining Hawkwind in 71. Act was formed in 75 and recorded for UA, Stiff and Chiswick in the late 70s. They have had 13 UK chart 45s and 12 UK hit LPs including the No. 1 'No Sleep Till Hammersmith'. In the US they have not hit the Top 100. They have had many personnel changes and joined GWR in 86.

THE GOLDEN YEARS (E.P.)	8	10 MAY 80	BRONZE
MOTORHEAD LIVE	6	18 JUL 81	BRONZE

Also see Headgirl

MOTORS

UK rock group quartet who ended up as a duo containing the singer/songwriters Nick Garvey and Andy McMaster (both ex Ducks Deluxe). Act had two UK Top 20s – the other being 'Forget About You' (13). Only US charter was 'Love And Loneliness' (78) in 80.

AIRPORT	4	08 JUL 78	VIRGIN

MOTT THE HOOPLE

Hereford (UK) rock band previously called Silence, were fronted by Ian Hunter and first recorded in 69. Group were a top live act but real sales only came when David Bowie produced them. They had five UK-only Top 20s and Ian left in 74 and had a solo hit in 75 with 'Once Bitten Twice Shy' (US hit for Great White in 89).

ALL THE YOUNG DUDES (US No. 37)	3	09 SEP 72	CBS
(Composed and produced by David Bowie)			
ALL THE WAY FROM MEMPHIS	10	29 SEP 73	CBS
ROLL AWAY THE STONE	8	08 DEC 73	CBS

NANA MOUSKOURI

This popular European MOR singer was born in Athens and first recorded in 59. She had a gold record in 61 with 'The White Rose Of Athens' and first charted (LP) in the UK in 69, which was the year she recorded 'The First Time Ever I Saw Your Face'. She has had nine UK-only Top 40 LPs but only a one-off single hit.

ONLY LOVE	2	01 FEB 86	PHILIPS
(She recorded it (in France) twice on two labels)			

MOUTH & MCNEAL

Dutch duo Willem Duyn and Maggie McNeil (Sjoukje Van't Spijker) had both recorded solo before getting together in 71. Oddly neither their US or UK Top 10 hits charted in the other country.

I SEE A STAR *(In Eurovision Song Contest)*	8	08 JUN 74	DECCA
HOW DO YOU DO?	8	22 JUL 72	PHILIPS

MOVE

Birmingham (UK) based group evolved out of Carl Wayne & The Vikings (on Pye in 64) and also included singer/songwriter Roy Wood. Carl left in 70 to be replaced by Jeff Lynne and after an enviable nine UK-only Top 20s the act evolved into the Electric Light Orchestra just as they got their only US entry 'Do Ya' (93).

NIGHT OF FEAR *(Based on '1812 Overture')*	2	28 JAN 67	DERAM
I CAN HEAR THE GRASS GROW	5	06 MAY 67	DERAM
FLOWERS IN THE RAIN	2	07 OCT 67	REGAL ZONO.
(Was the first record played on BBC Radio 1 (UK))			
FIRE BRIGADE	3	16 MAR 68	REGAL ZONO.
BLACKBERRY WAY	1(1)	08 FEB 69	REGAL ZONO.
BRONTOSAURUS	7	23 MAY 70	REGAL ZONO.
CALIFORNIA MAN	7	17 JUN 72	HARVEST

Also see Wizzard/Roy Wood/Electric Light Orchestra

ALISON MOYET

Essex (UK) born singer was with The Vicars and The Screaming Abdabs before joining Vince Clarke in the successful duo Yazoo (Yazz in the US). 'Alf' as she was known hit the Top two of the UK LP chart with her first two solo albums, won the BRITS award for Top UK Female of 84 and has notched up eight hit singles. Her biggest US success was 'Invisible' (US 31/UK 21).

LOVE RESURRECTION (US No. 82)	10	28 JUL 84	CBS
ALL CRIED OUT	8	27 OCT 84	CBS
THAT OLE DEVIL CALLED LOVE	2	23 MAR 85	CBS
(Originally by Billie Holiday)			
IS THIS LOVE (Co-writer Dave Stewart)	3	10 JAN 87	CBS
WEAK IN THE PRESENCE OF BEAUTY	6	28 MAR 87	CBS
LOVE LETTERS (Ketty Lester 62 hit)	4	19 DEC 87	CBS

Also see Yazoo

MUD

Pop/R'n'R good time foursome, fronted by Les Gray, were one of the Top UK bands of the 70s. They recorded for CBS in 67 (first record 'Flower Power') and Philips in 69. Their first of 14 UK-only Top 20s was 'Crazy' (12) in 73 but the hits stopped when they joined RCA. Les went solo on Warner in 77 and Runaway in 82.

DYNA-MITE (Was No. 1 in Holland)	4	10 NOV 73	RAK
TIGER FEET	1(4)	26 JAN 74	RAK
(Top UK record of 74 – Jumped from 10-1)			
THE CAT CREPT IN	2	20 APR 74	RAK
ROCKET	6	10 AUG 74	RAK
LONELY THIS CHRISTMAS (Also UK 61 in 85)	1(4)	21 DEC 74	RAK
THE SECRETS THAT YOU KEEP	3	08 MAR 75	RAK
(The first of their seven UK hits in 75)			
OH BOY (Crickets 58 hit)	1(2)	03 MAY 75	RAK
(Entered at No. 6 was top in two weeks)			
MOONSHINE SALLY	10	05 JUL 75	RAK
L-L-LUCY	10	18 OCT 75	PRIVATE STOCK
SHOW ME YOU'RE A WOMAN	8	13 DEC 75	PRIVATE STOCK
LEAN ON ME (Bill Withers 72 hit)	7	18 DEC 76	PRIVATE STOCK

MARIA MULDAUR

Born Maria Grazia Rosa Domenica d'Amato in New York, she was in high school groups The Cameos and The Cashmeres. In the mid 60s she was in the Even Dozen Jug Band (with John Sebastian) and the Jim Kweskin Jug Band. She recorded two LPs with her husband Geoff before going solo. She had a Top 5 US LP and two US Top 20 45s, the other being 'I'm A Woman' (12). She joined Warner in 78.

MIDNIGHT AT THE OASIS (UK No. 21)	6	01 JUN 74	REPRISE

MUNGO JERRY

UK good time jug band led by singer/songwriter Ray Dorset sold seven million of their first hit. The group, originally called Good Earth, had another seven UK-only Top 40s. Ray recorded solo in 75 and they were also on Polydor in 75, Stagecoach in 81, Scratch in 82 and Orbit in 85. Ray later wrote Kelly Marie's No. 1.

IN THE SUMMERTIME (First 3 track No. 1 UK)	17	13 JUN 70	DAWN
(Top UK single of 70 – jumped from 13-1)			
BABY JUMP	1(2)	06 MAR 71	DAWN
LADY ROSE	5	26 JUN 71	DAWN
ALRIGHT ALRIGHT ALRIGHT	3	04 AUG 73	DAWN
(Jacques Dutronc French hit)			
IN THE SUMMERTIME	3	12 SEP 70	JANUS
(They re-recorded it on Illegal in 87)			

MUPPETS

The world famous children's TV series created by Jim Henson managed to get two UK-only Top 20 LPs (one a No. 1) and singles. The other 45 hit was 'The Muppet Show Music Hall EP' (19).

HALFWAY DOWN THE STAIRS	7	18 JUN 77	PYE
(Vocals by Jerry Nelson who played Robin)			

MURMAIDS

College girl trio were the Fischer sisters Carol & Terry, with Sally Gordon. They followed their one-off hit with 'Heartbreak Ahead'. They also recorded on Liberty in 68.

POPSICLES AND ICICLES	3	11 JAN 64	CHATTAHOOCHEE
(Composed by David Gates – later with Bread)			

MICHAEL MURPHEY

Dallas born singer/songwriter started in The Texas Twosome and first charted in the Lewis & Clarke Expedition in 67. This one time 'cosmic cowboy' has had six US-only pop hits and since 76 has notched up 26 country chart entries, including 16 Top 20s.

WILDFIRE	3	21 JUN 75	EPIC

EDDIE MURPHY

Enormously successful internationally known film star and comedian from New York has had four US chart LPs with a mix of humorous material and songs plus this US Top 20 single.

PARTY ALL THE TIME (Prod. & comp. Rick James)	2	28 DEC 85	COLUMBIA

WALTER MURPHY & THE BIG APPLE BAND

New York multi-instrumentalist and one time arranger for The Tonight Show orchestra followed his one-off transatlantic hit with 'Flight 76' (based on 'Flight of the Bumble Bee').

A FIFTH OF BEETHOVEN (UK No. 28)	1(1)	09 OCT 76	PRIVATE STOCK
(Disco version of Beethoven's Fifth Symphony)			

ANNE MURRAY

Canada's most successful female singer is this Nova Scotia born country/folk/MOR artist. She first recorded on her local Arc label in 69 and she became one of the top US country stars chalking up 51 chart hits to date which includes 10 No. 1s. She also has scored eight US-only Top 20 pop hits.

SNOWBIRD (UK No. 23)	8	26 SEP 70	CAPITOL
DANNY'S SONG	7	14 APR 73	CAPITOL
(Written by Kenny Loggins about singer brother Dan)			
YOU WON'T SEE ME (Beatles song)	8	13 JUL 74	CAPITOL
YOU NEEDED ME (UK No. 22)	1(1)	04 NOV 78	CAPITOL

MUSIC EXPLOSION

Ohio pop/rock band who featured singer Jamie Lyons gave producers Jerry Kasenetz and Jeff Katz (the men behind bubblegum music) their first smash with their one-off Top 40 hit. They followed it with 'Sunshine Games' and Jamie later went solo on Laurie.

LITTLE BIT O' SOUL	2	08 JUL 67	LAURIE

MUSICAL YOUTH

Five Birmingham (UK) schoolboys led by Dennis Seaton and featuring 11 year old guitarist Kelvin Grant were overnight sensations. They had 7 UK (1 US) Top 40s (one with Donna Summer) in 16 months before fading from the scene.

PASS THE DUTCHIE	1(3)	02 OCT 82	MCA
(Jumped from 26-1 – based on a Mighty Diamonds song)			
NEVER GONNA GIVE YOU UP	6	05 MAR 83	MCA
PASS THE DUTCHIE	10	26 FEB 83	MCA

N

JIMMY NAIL

UK singer/TV actor, best known for his portrayal of Geordie Oz in Auf Wiederseh'n Pet had a one-off hit produced by Queens' Roger Taylor.

 LOVE DON'T LIVE HERE ANYMORE   3   25 MAY 85   VIRGIN
(Rose Royce 78 hit)

NAKED EYES

Bath (UK) based duo were singer Pete Byrne and keyboard wizard Rob Fisher. Both had been in Neon with Curt Smith and Roland Orzabal, later of Tears For Fears. The duo's synth led pop was more popular in the US and they achieved four US-only Top 40s before splitting in 84. Rob later formed hit act Climie Fisher.

 ALWAYS SOMETHING THERE TO REMIND ME   8   11 JUN 83   EMI AM.
(UK No. 59 – Lou Johnson 64 US hit)

Also see Climie Fisher

NAPOLEON XIV

One of the oddest transatlantic hits of all time came from songwriter Jerry Samuels. His tale of madness inspired answer records like 'Down On The Funny Farm (Oh Vey)' by Josephine X111. His follow up was 'I'm In Love With My Little Red Tricycle'. Jerry, who had written a Sammy Davis hit, was on Silver Blue in 74.

 THEY'RE COMING TO TAKE ME AWAY HA-HAAA!   4   27 AUG 66   WARNER
THEY'RE COMING TO TAKE ME AWAY HA-HAAA!   3   13 AUG 66   WARNER
(Re-charted US No. 87 in 73-cost $15 to record!)

NARADA (MICHAEL WALDEN)

Michigan producer/writer/singer started playing with acts like Ted Nugent and Bob Seger before joining The Mahavishnu Orchestra from 72-76. One of the 80s top producers/composers, he has had numerous hits including ones by Aretha Franklin and Starship and one week produced the US No. 1 and 2. He has had 40 black music hits but has yet to get a US pop Top 40.

 I SHOULDA LOVED YA *(US No. 66)*   8   17 MAY 80   ATLANTIC
(As Narada Michael Walden)
DIVINE EMOTIONS *(as Narada)*   8   21 MAY 88   REPRISE

JOHNNY NASH

Texan singer/actor/composer first recorded and charted in 57 and has sung in many styles in his career. In the 60s he settled in the UK and had a string of reggae styled hits (giving Bob Marley his first hit as a a writer). He has also recorded on ABC, Warner, Groove, Argo, Joda, Atlantic, MGM, Jad and UK label Sierra in 85.

HOLD ME TIGHT   5   14 SEP 68   REGAL ZONO.
YOU GOT SOUL   6   08 FEB 69   MAJOR MINOR
(US No. 58 – originally recorded by Bill Johnson)
CUPID *(US No. 39 – Sam Cooke 61 hit)*   6   03 MAY 69   MAJOR MINOR
I CAN SEE CLEARLY NOW   5   22 JUL 72   CBS
(Re-mix made UK No. 54 in 89)
THERE ARE MORE QUESTIONS THAN ANSWERS   9   28 OCT 72   CBS
TEARS ON MY PILLOW   1(1)   12 JUL 75   CBS

HOLD ME TIGHT   5   09 NOV 68   JAD
I CAN SEE CLEARLY NOW   1(4)   04 NOV 72   EPIC

NASHVILLE TEENS

Arthur Sharp and Ray Phillips fronted this Surrey (UK) pop act whose biggest hits were written by Nashville songwriter John D. Loudermilk. This Mickie Most produced act were also on Major Minor, UA, Parlophone and Enterprise. In 89 Ray was in the revival group The British Invasion All Stars.

 TOBACCO ROAD *(US No. 14)*   6   08 AUG 64   DECCA
GOOGLE EYE *(Both comp. John D. Loudermilk)*   10   14 NOV 04   DECCA

NATASHA

Ex-member of The Flirts, Natasha England went solo in 80 and had the first of two UK-only hits with an old Dixie Cups song on her husband's label. Her follow up was 'The Boom Boom Room' (UK 44).

 IKO IKO   10   17 JUL 82   TOWERBELL

DAVID NAUGHTON

Singer/actor/dancer from Connecticut who starred in the US TV show 'Makin' It' and the film An American Werewolf In London. He had a one-off hit with a song from the film Meatballs.

MAKIN' IT *(US No. 44)*   5   21 JUL 79   RSO

NAZARETH

Scottish hard rock group led by Dan McCafferty who specialised in heavy versions of folk songs. They evolved from The Shadettes and first recorded in 71. Their third LP 'Razamanaz' was the first of their 13 US (7 UK) chart albums and they have also chalked up five UK (1 US) Top 20 singles.

BROKEN DOWN ANGEL   9   02 JUN 73   MOONCREST
BAD BAD BOY   10   11 AUG 73   MOONCREST
LOVE HURTS *(Originally by Roy Orbison)*   8   13 MAR 76   A&M

neil

Popular UK actor Nigel Planer had earlier written with Julian Marshall (of Marshall Hain) and had been David Essex's understudy in Evita. He had a one-off novelty hit in the guise of neil, the hippy he played in the UK TV and MTV comedy series The Young Ones.

 HOLE IN MY SHOE *(Traffic 67 hit)*   2   21 JUL 84   WEA
(Entered at No. 5 – a record for a new act)

Also see The Young Ones

PHYLLIS NELSON

Singer/songwriter from Indiana was the first black female to top the UK chart with own composition. Her first success came in 80 with the dance hit 'Don't Stop The Train'. The follow up to her UK-only smash 'I Like You' was the Top Dance 12″ of 86 in the US.

MOVE CLOSER   1(1)   04 MAY 85   CARRERE
(First rel. Apr 84 – Only No. 1 of year with no video)

RICK(Y) NELSON

One of the top three US teen idols of the 50s was the New Jersey born singer/actor who had played himself on his parents US-only TV show The Adventures Of Ozzie & Harriet since 49. He notched up 52 US (18 UK) chart entries and 10 Top 40 US-only LPs. His sales waned with the British Invasion of 64 and he later leaned more towards country/rock. He died in a plane crash in 85.

🇬🇧	POOR LITTLE FOOL	8	12 SEP 58	LONDON
	SOMEDAY (Mills Brothers 49 hit)	9	12 DEC 58	LONDON
	IT'S LATE	3	22 MAY 59	LONDON
	HELLO MARY LOU/TRAVELLIN' MAN	3	07 JUL 61	LONDON
	(A-side originally by the writer Gene Pitney)			
🇺🇸	A TEENAGERS ROMANCE/I'M WALKIN'	2	10 JUN 57	VERVE
	(B-side Fats Domino 57 US hit)			
	BE-BOP BABY/HAVE I TOLD YOU LATELY THAT			
	I LOVE YOU (B-side Bing Crosby 50 hit)	3	28 OCT 57	IMPERIAL
	STOOD UP/WAITIN' IN SCHOOL (UK No. 27)	2	13 JAN 58	IMPERIAL
	(B-side composed by Johnny Burnette)			
	BELIEVE WHAT YOU SAY/MY BUCKET'S GOT			
	A HOLE IN IT (A-side co-written by Johnny Burnette)	4	21 APR 58	IMPERIAL
	POOR LITTLE FOOL (Entered at No. 18)	1(2)	04 AUG 58	IMPERIAL
	I GOT A FEELING (UK No. 27)	10	09 NOV 58	IMPERIAL
	LONESOME TOWN	7	30 NOV 58	IMPERIAL
	IT'S LATE	9	05 APR 59	IMPERIAL
	NEVER BE ANYONE ELSE BUT YOU (UK No. 14)	6	05 APR 59	IMPERIAL
	SWEETER THAN YOU (UK No. 19)	9	02 AUG 59	IMPERIAL
	JUST A LITTLE TOO MUCH (UK No. 11)	9	16 AUG 59	IMPERIAL
	(Composed by Johnny Burnette)			
	HELLO MARY LOU	9	22 MAY 61	IMPERIAL
	TRAVELIN' MAN (Written for Sam Cooke)	1(2)	29 MAY 61	IMPERIAL
	YOUNG WORLD (UK No. 21 – hits to end as Rick)	5	21 APR 62	IMPERIAL
	TEENAGE IDOL (UK No. 39)	5	22 SEP 62	IMPERIAL
	IT'S UP TO YOU (UK No. 25)	6	02 FEB 63	IMPERIAL
	FOR YOU (UK No. 14)	6	15 FEB 64	DECCA
	GARDEN PARTY (UK No. 41)	6	04 NOV 72	DECCA
	(Featuring The Stone Canyon Band)			

SANDY NELSON

The best known drummer of the early 60s started in a California high school group with Jan & Dean and Beach Boy Bruce Johnson before recording with Kip Tyler & The Flips (on Challenge and Ebb). He played on many West Coast hits, recorded numerous solo projects and as an artist he had 3 US (4 UK) Top 40s.

🇬🇧	TEEN BEAT	9	11 DEC 59	TOP RANK
	LET THERE BE DRUMS (Entered at No. 8)	3	12 JAN 62	LONDON
	(Later did 'Let There Be Drums '66')			
🇺🇸	TEEN BEAT (His 'Teen Beat 65' was US No. 44)	4	18 OCT 59	ORIGINAL S.
	LET THERE BE DRUMS	7	18 DEC 61	IMPERIAL
	(In 69 did 'Let There Be Drums & Bass')			

WILLIE NELSON

Top country act has had 106 country hits including 20 No. 1s (and had six (1 UK) Top 40 pop hits) since first charting in 62. The ultra-successful Texan singer/songwriter has won countless awards including several Grammys. He was one of the original 'Outlaws', has charted with 20 different duet partners, runs the 4th Of July Picnics and is president of 'Farm Aid'.

🇺🇸	ALWAYS ON MY MIND	5	12 JUN 82	COLUMBIA
	(UK No. 49 – Top country single of 82)			
	TO ALL THE GIRLS I'VE LOVED BEFORE	5	19 MAY 84	COLUMBIA
	(With JULIO IGLESIAS – Top country single of 84)			

NENA

German rock quintet fronted by Gabriele (Nena) Kerner who had previously been in Stripes. Her first German No. 1 'Just A Dream' was the UK follow up to her sole Trans-atlantic Top 10 hit. She went solo in Germany in 89. Oddly enough, it was the German language version of '99 Red Balloons' which was a hit in the US (and Australia).

🇬🇧	99 RED BALLOONS (English language version)	1(3)	03 MAR 84	EPIC
🇺🇸	99 LUFTBALLONS (German language version)	2	03 MAR 84	EPIC

ROBBIE NEVIL

Singer/songwriter had been writing for acts like El Debarge, The Pointer Sisters and Vanity since 83. He was the first act signed to the Manhattan label in 84. So far he has not repeated the success of his first LP and the singles from it.

🇬🇧	C'EST LA VIE	3	31 JAN 87	MANHATTAN
	(Song first recorded by Beau Williams in 84)			
🇺🇸	C'EST LA VIE	2	17 JAN 87	MANHATTAN/EMI
	WOT'S IT TO YA (UK No. 43)	10	01 AUG 87	MANHATTAN

AARON NEVILLE

New Orleans singer was in The Avalons in 55 and The Hawkettes in 58 before his first solo hit on Minit in 60. He had a record 23 year gap between US Top 10 hits and in that period he was in the Neville Brothers. He has also been on Instant, Safari, Mercury, Bell, Polydor and Airecords. His son Ivan hit the US Top 40 in 88.

🇬🇧	DON'T KNOW MUCH (With LINDA RONSTADT)	2	02 DEC 89	ELEKTRA
	(Combined ages of singers was 91)			
🇺🇸	TELL IT LIKE IT IS	2	28 JAN 67	PAR-LO
	DON'T KNOW MUCH (With LINDA RONSTADT)	2	23 DEC 89	ELEKTRA
	(Co-writter Barry Mann – Bette Midler 77 hit)			

NEW EDITION

Boston quintet, featuring Bobby Brown, started in 83 aged between 13-15. Initially hotter in the UK, they had legal problems with their mentor Maurice Starr and left his Streetwise label in 84. Bobby successfully went solo in 86 and was replaced by Johnny Gill. Act have had 14 Top 40 black hits and six US (2 UK) Top 40 pop hits. In 90 three of the group formed Bell Bev Devoe.

🇬🇧	CANDY GIRL (US No. 46)	1(1)	28 MAY 83	LONDON
🇺🇸	COOL IT NOW	4	05 JAN 85	MCA
	IF IT ISN'T LOVE	7	17 SEP 88	MCA

NEW KIDS ON THE BLOCK

Boston quintet, including Joe McIntye (aged 13 when the group started) and the Knight brothers Jordan & Jon, were formed by Maurice Starr as a white New Edition in 84. They first hit on the black music chart in 86 with 'Be My Girl'. They were the top US act of 89 selling seven million 'Hangin' Tough' LPs there and earning four gold 45s from it. They were the first teenage group to simultaneously have the No. 1 LP and single and the first act to sell one million of a video in the US (20 times platinum!).

🇬🇧	YOU GOT IT (THE RIGHT STUFF)	1(3)	25 NOV 89	CBS
🇺🇸	PLEASE DON'T GO GIRL	10	08 OCT 88	COLUMBIA
	YOU GOT IT (THE RIGHT STUFF)	3	11 MAR 89	COLUMBIA
	I'LL BE LOVING YOU (FOREVER) (UK Top 10 in 90)	1	17 JUN 89	COLUMBIA
	(First teenage group to be No. 1 since Jackson 5)			
	HANGIN' TOUGH (UK No. 1 in 90)	1(1)	09 SEP 89	COLUMBIA
	(B-side 'Didn't I' was also a US Top 10 hit)			
	COVER GIRL	2	04 NOV 89	COLUMBIA
	DIDN'T I (BLOW YOUR MIND) (Delfonics 70 hit)	8	18 NOV 89	COLUMBIA
	THIS ONE'S FOR THE CHILDREN	7	06 JAN 90	COLUMBIA

NEW ORDER

Quartet fronted by Barney Sumner (aka Bernard Dicken/Albrecht) evolved out of Joy Division after Ian Curtis' death in 80. They have had six UK Top 20s and four UK Top 10 LPs. In the US their biggest successes have been in the dance field with four Top 3 hits. 'Blue Monday' spent over 200 weeks in the UK Top 200. In 90 they recorded England's World Cup (soccer) anthem.

🇬🇧	BLUE MONDAY (Was also No. 12 in Mar 83)	9	15 OCT 83	FACTORY
	(Took record 30 weeks to make Top 10 – UKs Top selling 12")			
	TRUE FAITH (US No. 32 and US dance No. 3)	4	15 AUG 87	FACTORY
	(BRITS award Best Music Video of year)			
	BLUE MONDAY 1988 (US dance No. 1)	3	14 MAY 88	FACTORY
	(No. 68 US – new mix supervised by Quincy Jones)			

NEW SEEKERS

Formed in 69 by ex-Seeker Keith Potger and including Lyn Paul, Eve Graham (ex Cyril Stapleton Band) and German born Marty Kristian. Their first 45 stiffed but world-wide they sold over 25 million records and had 12 UK (3 US) Top 40s. They broke up in 74 and Lyn later re-corded on Polydor, Pye and Crash. A reformed group were on CBS in 76, EMI in 80 and Tom Cat in 85.

🇬🇧	NEVER ENDING SONG OF LOVE (Delaney & Bonnie 71 US hit)	2	07 AUG 71	PHILIPS
	I'D LIKE TO TEACH THE WORLD TO SING (Coke ad. – UK Gold and top single of the year)	1(4)	08 JAN 72	POLYDOR
	BEG STEAL OR BORROW (US No. 81 – UK's Eurovision Entry)	2	25 MAR 72	POLYDOR
	CIRCLES (US No. 87)	4	22 JUL 72	POLYDOR
	YOU WON'T FIND ANOTHER FOOL LIKE ME	1(1)	19 JAN 74	POLYDOR
	I GET A LITTLE SENTIMENTAL OVER YOU	5	30 MAR 74	POLYDOR
🇺🇸	I'D LIKE TO TEACH THE WORLD TO SING (Song originally called 'True Love & Apple Pie')	7	15 JAN 72	ELEKTRA

NEW VAUDEVILLE BAND

Grammy winner for Best Contemporary R'n'R record of 67 was a 20s styled novelty played by UK session men and sung by producer/ composer Geoff Stephens (who had discovered Donovan and had written many UK hits). On the road, the seven man group was fronted by Alan Klein. They were also on Decca, SRT and Dansan.

🇬🇧	WINCHESTER CATHEDRAL (Was the top selling UK record in US that year)	4	15 OCT 66	FONTANA
	PEEK-A-BOO (US No. 72)	7	25 FEB 67	FONTANA
🇺🇸	WINCHESTER CATHEDRAL (Geoff's song has been recorded over 400 times)	1(3)	03 DEC 66	FONTANA

NEW WORLD

Australian pop trio fronted by John 'Fuzz' Lee won a UK TV talent show and strung together four UK-only Top 20s in 15 months – the others being 'Kara Kara' and a cover of 'Rose Garden'.

🇬🇧	TOM-TOM TURNAROUND	6	31 JUL 71	RAK
	SISTER JANE (Both hits comp. Chinn & Chapman)	9	10 JUN 72	RAK

NEWBEATS

Nashville based trio led by Larry Henley and including the Mathis brothers Dean and Marc. Using their Christian names the brothers had a hit with 'Tell Him No' in 59 on Bullseye and also recorded on Argo, Checker and Check Mate. Larry, who had five solos on Hickory before the group was formed, was also on Capricorn, Atco, Viking and Epic and co-wrote the 90 Grammy winning song 'The Wind Beneath My Wings'. The trio were later on Playboy and Buddah.

🇬🇧	RUN, BABY RUN (BACK INTO MY ARMS) (US No. 12 six years earlier)	10	04 DEC 71	LONDON
🇺🇸	BREAD AND BUTTER (UK No. 15)	2	19 SEP 64	HICKORY

BOOKER NEWBERRY III

Ohio soul singer had two UK-only charters – the other being his follow up 'Teddy Bear' (44). He had previously sung in The Mystic Nights in 71 and with Sweet Thunder. He was on Omni in 86.

🇬🇧	LOVE TOWN	6	11 JUN 83	POLYDOR

ANTHONY NEWLEY

London singer/actor/composer first appeared in films in the late 40s and started singing in the 59 film Idle On Parade. He co-wrote the hit musical Stop The World I Want To Get Off. He moved to the US with his wife Joan Collins after notching up nine UK-only Top 20s. He became a top Las Vegas cabaret act and later recorded on RCA, MCA, MGM, Columbia (UK), Verve and UA.

🇬🇧	I'VE WAITED SO LONG (from 'Idle on Parade')	3	05 JUN 59	DECCA
	PERSONALITY (Lloyd Price 59 hit)	6	03 JUL 59	DECCA
	WHY (Frankie Avalon 59 hit)	1(5)	05 FEB 60	DECCA
	DO YOU MIND (US No. 91 – covered there by Andy Williams)	1(1)	22 APR 60	DECCA
	IF SHE SHOULD COME TO YOU (US No. 67)	6	02 SEP 60	DECCA
	STRAWBERRY FAIR (Traditional song)	3	02 DEC 60	DECCA
	AND THE HEAVENS CRIED (Ronnie Savoy 61 US hit)	8	07 APR 61	DECCA

RANDY NEWMAN

Much respected composer/singer first recorded on Dot in 62 (produced by Pat Boone). He has written big hits for Gene Pitney, Cilla Black and Alan Price as well as Three Dog Night's No. 1 'Mama Told Me'. Oddly he has only had one Top 40 hit as a singer.

🇺🇸	SHORT PEOPLE (Answer record 'Tall People' by The Short People)	2	28 JAN 78	WARNER

JUICE NEWTON

Award winning pop/country singer born Judy Cohen in Virginia, formed Dixie Peach in 71 and Silver Spur in 72. With the latter she recorded on RCA in 75 and Capitol in 77. Act split in 78 and she has since had seven US-only Top 40s and four country No. 1s.

🇺🇸	ANGEL OF THE MORNING (UK No. 43 – Originally by Evie Sands)	4	02 MAY 81	CAPITOL
	QUEEN OF HEARTS (Produced by Dave Edmunds)	2	19 SEP 81	CAPITOL
	THE SWEETEST THING (I'VE EVER KNOWN) (She had recorded this unsuccessfully on RCA in 75)	7	13 FEB 82	CAPITOL
	LOVE'S BEEN A LITTLE BIT HARD ON ME	7	10 JUL 82	CAPITOL

WAYNE NEWTON

One of the biggest earning cabaret stars recorded with his brothers on Capitol in 59 and on George in 61. He has had 17 US-only charters and was regularly on the Jackie Gleason TV show in the early 60s. In 89 he dueted with Tammy Wynette and debuted on the country charts.

🇺🇸	DADDY DON'T YOU WALK SO FAST (Daniel Boone 71 UK hit)	4	05 AUG 72	CHELSEA

OLIVIA NEWTON-JOHN

Top female singer in the US in the 70s was born in Cambridge (UK) and grew up in Australia. She was in girl quartet The Sol Four and the duo Pat (Carroll) & Olivia. Her first 45 was on UK Decca in 66 and she was in Don Kirshner's short lived Toomorrow in 70. She notched up a run of 20 US (14 UK) Top 20 singles and 10 US (3 UK) Top 20 LPs. She also starred in several films but her sales waned in the 80s.

🇬🇧	IF NOT FOR YOU (US No. 25 – Bob Dylan song)	7	24 APR 71	PYE INT.
	BANKS OF THE OHIO (US No. 94 – Trad song)	6	20 NOV 71	PYE INT.
	SAM (US No. 20)	6	09 JUL 77	EMI
	YOU'RE THE ONE THAT I WANT (With JOHN TRAVOLTA) (UK Gold) (The UKs third top seller of all time)	1(1)	10 JUN 78	RSO
	SUMMER NIGHTS (With JOHN TRAVOLTA) (UK Gold – jumped from 11-1)	1(7)	30 SEP 78	RSO
	HOPELESSLY DEVOTED TO YOU (Above three all from 'Grease')	2	18 NOV 78	RSO
	A LITTLE MORE LOVE	4	27 JAN 79	EMI
	XANADU (And ELO) (From the film)	1(2)	12 JUL 80	JET
	PHYSICAL (Her 11th Gold and 2nd Platinum single)	7	21 NOV 81	EMI

🇺🇸 LET ME BE THERE *(Also the first of 10 country Top 20s)*	6	09 FEB 74	MCA	
IF YOU LOVE ME (LET ME KNOW)	5	29 JUN 74	MCA	
I HONESTLY LOVE YOU *(Grammy 'Record of Year')* *(Only one of her first five US hits to chart in UK)*	1(2)	05 OCT 74	MCA	
HAVE YOU NEVER BEEN MELLOW	1(1)	08 MAR 75	MCA	
PLEASE MR. PLEASE *(She was the Top Female Country Act of 75)*	3	09 AUG 75	MCA	
SUMMER NIGHTS *(With JOHN TRAVOLTA)*	5	30 OCT 78	RSO	
HOPELESSLY DEVOTED TO YOU	3	30 OCT 78	RSO	
A LITTLE MORE LOVE	3	17 FEB 79	MCA	
MAGIC *(UK No. 32)*	1(4)	02 AUG 80	MCA	
XANADU *(Above two from the film 'Xanadu')*	8	11 OCT 80	MCA	
PHYSICAL *(Top US single of 82)* *(Equal most weeks at top of US chart in rock era)*	1(10)	21 NOV 81	MCA	
MAKE A MOVE ON ME *(UK No. 43)*	5	03 APR 82	MCA	
HEART ATTACK *(UK No. 46)*	3	06 NOV 82	MCA	
TWIST OF FATE *(UK No. 57)* *(12th US Top 5 a female record at the time)*	5	07 JAN 84	MCA	

PAUL NICHOLAS

London singer/actor and son of a top music business lawyer was in Screaming Lord Sutch's Savages in 64. He was in the musicals Hair, Grease and Jesus Christ Superstar and was on Polydor and Epic prior to scoring four UK Top 40s. He also starred in the Tommy and Stardust films and was a top UK TV star in the 80s.

🇬🇧 DANCING WITH THE CAPTAIN	8	06 NOV 76	RSO	
GRANDMA'S PARTY	9	08 JAN 77	RSO	
🇺🇸 HEAVEN ON THE 7TH FLOOR *(UK No. 40)*	6	26 NOV 77	RSO	

STEVIE NICKS

Singer/composer from Phoenix was in Fritz with Lindsey Buckingham. Together they formed the duo Buckingham-Nicks in 73 and then joined Fleetwood Mac in 75. As a soloist she has had 6 US (1 UK) Top 20s. The UK hit was 'Rooms On Fire' (UK 16/US 16) in 89.

🇺🇸 STOP DRAGGIN' MY HEART AROUND *(And TOM PETTY & THE HEARTBREAKERS – UK No. 50)*	3	05 SEP 81	MODERN	
LEATHER AND LACE *(And DON HENLEY)*	6	23 JAN 82	MODERN	
STAND BACK	5	20 AUG 83	MODERN	
TALK TO ME *(UK No. 68)*	4	25 JAN 86	MODERN	

Also see Fleetwood Mac

NICOLE

German singer/songwriter Nicole Hohloch won the Eurovision song contest at 17 with her second German hit, which was to be her sole UK Top 40 entry. Her follow up was 'Give Me More Time'.

🇬🇧 A LITTLE PEACE *(Jumped from 8-1)* *(Entered at No. 8 – a record at time for new act)*	1(2)	15 MAY 82	CBS	

MAXINE NIGHTINGALE

Middlesex (UK) born singer first recorded with Cyril Stapleton on Pye in 68 and was in the musicals Hair, Godspell and Jesus Christ Superstar in the early 70s. She was also on Windsong in 79.

🇬🇧 RIGHT BACK WHERE WE STARTED FROM	8	29 NOV 75	UA	
🇺🇸 RIGHT BACK WHERE WE STARTED FROM	2	01 MAY 76	UA	
LEAD ME ON	5	15 SEP 79	WINDSONG	

NIGHT RANGER

California rock quintet, including Brad Gillis and Jack Blades both ex-members of Rubicon (who had a Top 40 hit in 78) and Stereo. Their first LP 'Dawn Patrol' on Boardwalk made the US Top 40 in 82 and they have since had five US-only Top 20 singles. In 90 Jack joined supergroup Damn Yankees on Warner.

🇺🇸 SISTER CHRISTIAN	5	09 JUN 84	MCA	
SENTIMENTAL STREET	8	27 JUL 85	MCA/CAMEL	

NILSSON

Grammy winning New York singer/songwriter recorded unsuccessfully on Tower and Mercury in the mid 60s. Songs of his have charted for acts like Three Dog Night, Sandie Shaw and David Cassidy. His 'Pussy Cats' LP was produced by his friend John Lennon. (Harry) Nilsson has had eight US (2 UK) Top 40s and he was also on Spector (duetting with Cher) and Musicor.

🇬🇧 WITHOUT YOU *(Comps. Pete Ham & Tom Evans of Badfinger)*	1(5)	11 MAR 72	RCA	
🇺🇸 EVERYBODY'S TALKIN' *(UK No. 23)* *(From 'Midnight Cowboy' – Original by Fred Neil)*	6	11 OCT 69	RCA	
WITHOUT YOU *(Composers (see above) both committed suicide)*	1(4)	19 FEB 72	RCA	
COCONUT *(UK No. 42)*	8	26 AUG 72	RCA	

NINA & FREDERICK

The first major Scandinavian act in the UK were Baron Frederick Van Pallandt and his wife the Baroness Nina from Copenhagen. This Danish duo, who had a UK TV series in 61, achieved three UK-only Top 40s. Nina recorded solo on Pye in the 70s.

🇬🇧 LITTLE DONKEY	5	16 DEC 60	COLUMBIA	

1910 FRUITGUM CO

The first and most successful bubblegum stars were a session group with lead vocals by Joey Levine (also the voice of the Ohio Express and Reunion). Under the Kasenetz-Katz production team they had five US (1 UK) Top 40 hits before the bubble (gum) burst in 70.

🇬🇧 SIMON SAYS	2	04 MAY 68	PYE INT.	
🇺🇸 SIMON SAYS	4	09 MAR 68	BUDDAH	
1 2 3 RED LIGHT	5	14 SEP 68	BUDDAH	
INDIAN GIVER	5	22 MAR 69	BUDDAH	

NITTY GRITTY DIRT BAND

Known in 66 as the Illegitimate Jug Band (when Jackson Browne was a member) this Californian country/rock band has had many personnel changes but often included Jeff Hanna and John McEuen. After some US-only pop success in the 70s they concentrated on the country field in the 80s and had 14 successive Top 10s.

🇺🇸 MR. BOJANGLES *(Jerry Jeff Walker song)*	9	20 FEB 71	LIBERTY	

CLIFF NOBLES & CO.

Alabama soul group were on Atlantic in 66 and had their sole Top 40 hit with the B-side of their second release on Phil L.A. of Soul. Their later releases included 'Horse Fever', 'The Camel', 'Pony The Horse'. Cliff later recorded on Roulette and Moonshot.

🇺🇸 THE HORSE *(Instrumental featuring Philly session men)*	2	13 JUL 68	PHIL L.A.	

KENNY NOLAN

L.A. songwriter/singer wrote hits 'Lady Marmalade' and 'My Eyes Adored You' (two consecutive US No. 1s) and 'Get Dancin''. He was on Dot in 68, MGM in 70, Lion in 71 and fronted Eleventh Hour in 74. He had two US-only Top 20s – the other being 'Love's Grown Deep' (20). He was later on Polydor in 78 and Casablanca in 79.

🇺🇸 I LIKE DREAMIN'	3	12 MAR 77	20TH CENTURY	

NOLANS

Irish female MOR/pop family group originally billed as the Nolan Sisters, had seven UK Top 20 singles and four UK Top 20 LP's. They had been on EMI in 74 and Target in 75 and first charted with the TV advertised LP '20 Giant Hits' (No. 3) in 78. Sisters Anne and Denise left, and act were on Spartan in 85 and Towerbell in 86.

🇬🇧	I'M IN THE MOOD FOR DANCING	3	09 FEB 80	EPIC
	GOTTA PULL MYSELF TOGETHER	9	25 OCT 80	EPIC
	ATTENTION TO ME	9	09 MAY 81	EPIC

CHRIS NORMAN – SEE SUZI QUATRO/SMOKIE FOR HIT DETAILS

NU SHOOZ

Oregon (US) duo were songwriter/guitarist John Smith and his wife, singer Valerie Day. Their follow up 'Point Of No Return' was also a Transatlantic charter (US 28/UK 48).

🇬🇧	I CAN'T WAIT	2	28 JUN 86	ATLANTIC
🇺🇸	I CAN'T WAIT	3	14 JUN 86	ATLANTIC

GARY NUMAN

Electronic rocker born Gary Webb in London, sang in Meanstreet before forming Tubeway Army in 77. Their fourth single 'Are Friends Electric' was a UK No. 1 but after that all his releases were under his name alone. He has achieved 32 UK (1 US) charters including hits with Bill Sharpe, Dramatis and Radio Heart. He formed Numa records in 84 and in 88 joined Illegal.

🇬🇧	CARS (A re-mix was UK No. 16 in 87)	1(1)	22 SEP 79	BEGGARS BANQU
	COMPLEX	6	01 DEC 79	BEGGARS BANQU
	WE ARE GLASS (Entered at No. 10)	5	31 MAY 80	BEGGARS BANQU
	I DIE: YOU DIE (Entered at No. 8)	6	06 SEP 80	BEGGARS BANQU
	SHE'S GOT CLAWS	6	05 SEP 81	BEGGARS BANQU
	WE TAKE MYSTERY (TO BED) (Entered at No. 9)	9	19 JUN 82	BEGGARS BANQU
🇺🇸	CARS	9	07 JUN 80	ATCO

Also see Tubeway Army

O

OAK RIDGE BOYS

Formed as a gospel quartet in Oak Ridge, Tennessee, during World War II. Many personnel changes later, when they included Duane Allen and Joe Bonsall, they became one of the top all time country groups notching up 32 Top 10 hits including 16 No. 1s. They had another US-only pop Top 20 with 'Bobbie Sue' (12).

🇺🇸	ELVIRA (Dallas Frazier 66 US hit)	5	25 JUL 81	MCA

PHIL OAKEY   SEE GIORGIO MORODER/HUMAN LEAGUE FOR HIT DETAILS

OCEAN

Canadian pop quintet, fronted by the only female member Janice Morgan, followed their one-off US Top 40 with 'Deep Enough For Me'.

🇺🇸	PUT YOUR HAND IN THE HAND	2	31 MAY 71	KAMA SUTRA

BILLY OCEAN

Trinidad's most successful soul singer/songwriter was born Leslie Charles. He moved to the UK and sang in groups like The Go and Dry Ice and first recorded as Scorched Earth in 74. In the 70s he had four UK-only Top 20s and after a quiet spell he returned to win a Grammy and to collect nine US Top 20s and another six in the UK.

🇬🇧	LOVE REALLY HURTS WITHOUT YOU (US No. 22)	2	27 MAR 76	GTO
	RED LIGHT SPELLS DANGER	2	23 APR 77	GTO
	CARIBBEAN QUEEN (NO MORE LOVE ON THE RUN) (Released first unsuccessfully as 'European Queen')	6	17 NOV 84	JIVE
	SUDDENLY	4	15 JUN 85	JIVE
	WHEN THE GOING GETS TOUGH, THE TOUGH GET GOING (From film 'The Jewel of the Nile')	1(4)	08 FEB 86	JIVE
	GET OUTTA MY DREAMS GET INTO MY CAR	3	27 FEB 88	JIVE
🇺🇸	CARIBBEAN QUEEN (NO MORE LOVE ON THE RUN)	1(2)	03 NOV 84	JIVE
	LOVERBOY (UK No. 15)	2	23 FEB 85	JIVE
	SUDDENLY	4	08 JUN 85	JIVE
	WHEN THE GOING GETS TOUGH, THE TOUGH GET GOING	2	15 FEB 86	JIVE
	THERE'LL BE SAD SONGS (TO MAKE YOU CRY) (UK No. 12)	1(1)	05 JUL 86	JIVE
	LOVE ZONE (UK No. 49)	10	27 SEP 86	JIVE
	GET OUTTA MY DREAMS GET INTO MY CAR	1(2)	09 APR 88	JIVE

DES O'CONNOR

Veteran UK MOR singer/comedian and TV personality first recorded in 57 on Columbia and has had eight UK-only Top 40s – the last two coming 16 years apart. He joined Ariola in 87.

🇬🇧	CARELESS HANDS (Mel Torme 49 hit)	6	09 DEC 67	COLUMBIA
	I PRETEND	1(1)	27 JUL 68	COLUMBIA
	ONE TWO THREE O'LEARY	4	14 DEC 68	COLUMBIA
	THE SKYE BOAT SONG (With ROGER WHITTAKER)	10	06 DEC 86	TEMBO

HAZEL O'CONNOR

Singer/songwriter/model/actress from Coventry (UK) joined Albion Records in 78 and shot to fame in the punk film Breaking Glass in 80. She later recorded unsuccessfully for RCA in 84, Greenpeace in 85, Red Bus and BBC in 86 and First Night in 87.

🇬🇧	EIGHTH DAY (From Breaking Glass)	5	06 SEP 80	A&M
	D-DAYS	10	11 APR 81	ALBION
	WILL YOU (From Breaking Glass)	8	20 JUN 81	A&M

ALAN O'DAY

Hollywood singer/songwriter wrote the No. 1 hit 'Angie Baby' for Helen Reddy. He recorded on Viva in 73 and followed his one-off No. 1 with 'Started Out Dancing, Ended Up Making Love'. He now writes the music for various TV shows including The Muppet Babies.

🇺🇸	UNDERCOVER ANGEL	1(1)	09 JUL 77	PACIFIC

ODYSSEY

New York based dance music trio were sisters Lillian and Louise Lopez from the Virgin Islands and Tony Reynolds from Manila. They had five UK Top 10s but oddly only scored one US Top 40.

🇬🇧	NATIVE NEW YORKER (US No. 21)	5	28 JAN 78	RCA
	USE IT UP AND WEAR IT OUT	1(2)	26 JUL 80	RCA
	IF YOU'RE LOOKIN' FOR A WAY OUT	6	18 OCT 80	RCA
	GOING BACK TO MY ROOTS (Originally by Lamont Dozier in 77)	4	04 JUL 81	RCA
	INSIDE OUT (Last four never made US Top 100)	3	03 JUL 82	RCA

ESTHER & ABI OFARIM

The first act from Israel to have a UK No. 1 were the husband and wife team born Esther Zaled and Abi Reichstadt. She recorded solo in 64 and their smash was their second release as a duo. They had another UK-only Top 20 with the follow up 'One More Dance' (13). She recorded as a soloist again on Columbia in 72.

CINDERELLA ROCKAFELLA	1(3)	02 MAR 68	PHILIPS
(US No. 68 – originally by Nancy Ames)			

OHIO EXPRESS

Ohio quintet first released their debut hit 'Beg, Borrow Or Steal' (US 29 on Cameo) as by the Rare Breed on Attack. They joined the top bubble gum label Buddah and had four US (1 UK) Top 40s all produced by Kasenetz-Katz and all with vocals by Joey Levine (also the voice of The 1910 Fruitgum Co and Reunion).

YUMMY YUMMY YUMMY	5	20 JUL 68	PYE INT.
YUMMY YUMMY YUMMY	4	15 JUN 68	BUDDAH

OHIO PLAYERS

Originally formed as the Ohio Untouchables in 59, the Ohio group which included Leroy 'Sugarfoot' Bonner, recorded in the 60s on Thelma, Lupine, TRC, Compass and Capitol without success. They were one of the top soul groups of the 70s, scoring eight US-only Top 40s and five US-only Top 40 LPs. They later recorded on Arista, Boardwalk, Air City and Track with limited success.

FIRE	1(1)	08 FEB 75	MERCURY
LOVE ROLLERCOASTER	1(1)	31 JAN 76	MERCURY

O'JAYS

Top Ohio R&B group, which includes Eddie Levert, have had 49 black music hits since 63 (inc. nine No.1s) and nine US (8 UK) Pop Top 40s. Previously known as The Triumphs and The Mascots they have also been on Wayco, King, Apollo, Minit, SS7, Little Star, Imperial, Bell, Neptune, Saru, Astroscope, All Platinum, TSOP and EMI.

LOVE TRAIN	9	07 APR 73	CBS
BACK STABBERS *(UK No. 14)*	3	07 OCT 72	PHILLY INT.
(UK No. 14 – co-written by McFadden & Whitehead)			
LOVE TRAIN	1(1)	24 MAR 73	PHILLY INT.
PUT YOUR HANDS TOGETHER	10	02 MAR 74	PHILLY INT.
FOR THE LOVE OF MONEY	9	15 JUN 74	PHILLY INT.
I LOVE MUSIC (PT. 1) *(UK No. 13)*	5	24 JAN 76	PHILLY INT.
USE TA BE MY GIRL	4	08 JUL 78	PHILLY INT.

O'KAYSIONS

Originally called The Kays this Carolina blue-eyed soul group, led by Donny Weaver, followed their one-off Top 40 hit with 'Love Machine'. They re-recorded their hit on 1 – Catcher in 85.

GIRL WATCHER	5	05 OCT 68	ABC

DANNY O'KEEFE

Washington singer/songwriter who was on Jerden, Piccadilly and Cotillion before getting his sole hit (from his second LP). He later recorded on Warner in 77 and re-appeared on Chameleon in 89.

GOODTIME CHARLIE'S GOT THE BLUES	9	04 NOV 72	SIGNPOST

MIKE OLDFIELD

Classical rock multi-instrumentalist/composer from Reading (UK). First recorded (with sister Sally) as Sallyangie in 68. His main US success was the ten million selling 'Tubular Bells' LP and its single. In the UK he had nine Top 20 LPs and six top 40 singles.

IN DOLCE JUBILO/ON HORSEBACK	4	17 JAN 76	VIRGIN
PORTSMOUTH	3	08 JAN 77	VIRGIN
MOONLIGHT SHADOW *(Vocal by Maggie Reilly)*	4	02 JUL 83	VIRGIN
(A tribute to John Lennon and Houdini)			
TUBULAR BELLS *(UK No. 31)*	7	11 MAY 74	VIRGIN
(Grammy winning theme from 'The Exorcist')			

OLIVER

Born William Swofford in North Carolina, he was in The Virginians and The Good Earth before going solo and achieving 3 US (1 UK) Top 40s. He was later on UA in 71, Paramount in 73 and MCA in 82.

GOOD MORNING STARSHINE	6	04 OCT 69	CBS
(Same backing track as earlier Eddie Rambeau cut)			
GOOD MORNING STARSHINE *(From Hair)*	3	12 JUL 69	JUBILEE
JEAN *(From The Prime Of Miss Jean Brodie)*	2	04 OCT 69	CREWE

OLLIE & JERRY

Producers/writers/session men and ex-members of hit act Raydio Ollie Brown (who had played on Rolling Stones and Stevie Wonder records) and Jerry Knight had this one Transatlantic Top 10.

BREAKIN'...THERE'S NO STOPPING US	5	07 JUL 84	POLYDOR
(From the film 'Breakin')			
BREAKIN'...THERE'S NO STOPPING US	9	04 AUG 84	POLYDOR

100 PROOF AGED IN SOUL

Detroit soul trio Clyde Wilson (also recorded as Steve Mancha), Eddie Anderson and Levi Stubbs' (of Four Tops) brother Joe who had been in The Contours and Falcons. They had four US-only charters.

SOMEBODY'S BEEN SLEEPING	8	14 NOV 70	HOT WAX

ONE HUNDRED TON AND A FEATHER

Pseudonym used by top UK producer Jonathan King on this one-off hit and then again on Pye in 77.

IT ONLY TAKES A MINUTE *(Tavares 75 US hit)*	9	24 JUL 76	UK

ALEXANDER O'NEAL

Minneapolis singer had the band Alexander in the late 70s and was in Flyte Tyme with Jam & Lewis (who later produced his records) before going solo in 80. He was one of the most popular soul singers in the late 80s, especially in the UK where he packed Wembley for eight days. To date he has had four UK-only Top 20s.

SATURDAY LOVE *(With CHERRELLE) (US No. 26)*	6	18 JAN 86	TABU
(Entered UK Dance chart No. 1 – remix UK No. 55 in 90)			
CRITICIZE *(US No. 74)*	4	05 DEC 87	TABU

OPUS

Veteran Austrian pop group led by Herwig Rudisser. They had been hitting in their homeland for a decade before getting their one-off Transatlantic Top 40. Their follow up was 'Flyin' Head'.

LIVE IS LIFE *(US No. 32)*	6	06 AUG 85	POLYDOR

ORANGE JUICE

Glasgow pop/rock foursome led by Edwyn Collins (previously in The Nu Sonics) had nine UK-only charters. Formed in 77, they were on Postcard in 81 and by 84 they were reduced to a duo who split in 85. Edwyn went solo on WEA and Elevation in 87 and Demon in 89.

RIP IT UP		8	02 APR 83	POLYDOR

ROY ORBISON

Distinctive Texan singer/songwriter, who started with The Wink Westerners and The Teen Kings, was one of the 60s top solo acts. He has had 31 US (30 UK) chart entries between 56 (debut hit 'Ooby Dooby') and 89. The 'Big O' was also on Jewel, Sun, RCA, MGM, Mercury, Asylum, Warner and ZTT and his songs have been hits for many acts. He died in 88 as he was enjoying his biggest ever US hit LP in the Grammy winning supergroup The Traveling Wilburys with Bob Dylan, George Harrison, Tom Petty and Jeff Lynn.

ONLY THE LONELY *(His composition was a No. 1 country hit in 69)*	1(3)	14 OCT 60	LONDON
BLUE ANGEL	10	13 JAN 61	LONDON
RUNNING SCARED	9	14 JUL 61	LONDON
DREAM BABY	3	06 APR 62	LONDON
IN DREAMS	5	31 MAY 63	LONDON
FALLING *(US No. 22)*	9	21 JUN 63	LONDON
BLUE BAYOU *(US No. 29)*	5	25 OCT 63	LONDON
IT'S OVER	1(2)	27 JUN 64	LONDON
OH PRETTY WOMAN	1(2)	10 OCT 64	LONDON
PRETTY PAPER *(US No.15 – was released before 'Only The Lonely')*	6	19 DEC 64	LONDON
TOO SOON TO KNOW *(US No. 68)*	3	24 SEP 66	LONDON
YOU GOT IT *(23 year gap between UK Top 10 hits – a record)*	3	04 FEB 89	VIRGIN
ONLY THE LONELY *(His 10th single)* *(He wrote the song for Elvis Presley)*	2	25 JUL 60	MONUMENT
BLUE ANGEL	9	07 NOV 60	MONUMENT
RUNNING SCARED	1(1)	05 JUN 61	MONUMENT
CRYIN' *(UK No. 25)*	2	09 OCT 61	MONUMENT
DREAM BABY	4	07 APR 62	MONUMENT
IN DREAMS	7	30 MAR 63	MONUMENT
MEAN WOMAN BLUES *(UK No. 14)* *(UK No. 14 – Originally by Elvis Presley)*	5	02 NOV 63	MONUMENT
IT'S OVER	9	23 MAY 64	MONUMENT
OH PRETTY WOMAN	1(3)	26 SEP 64	MONUMENT
YOU GOT IT	9	15 APR 89	VIRGIN

ORCHESTRAL MANOEUVRES IN THE DARK

The mainstays of this Liverpool act are Andy McCluskey and Paul Humphreys who were originally in The Id. Their first release was 'Electricity' on Factory in 79. In the UK they have had 21 UK chart 45s and seven UK Top 40 LPs. In the late 80s they were hotter in the US with three Top 20 singles.

ENOLA GAY	8	01 NOV 80	DINDISC
SOUVENIR	3	19 SEP 81	DINDISC
JOAN OF ARC	5	14 NOV 81	DINDISC
MAID OF ORLEANS (THE WALTZ JOAN OF ARC)	4	20 FEB 82	DINDISC
LOCOMOTION	5	12 MAY 84	VIRGIN
IF YOU LEAVE *(UK No. 48)* *(UK No. 48 – from the film 'Pretty in Pink')*	4	31 MAY 86	A&M

TONY ORLANDO/DAWN

New York born Michael Cassavitis was in The Five Gents and also recorded solo on Milo in the 50s and had three US (1 UK) hits in 61 when he was 17. In the 60s he recorded under various names on UA, Diamond, Harbor, Atco, Cameo, Life and A&M. In the 70s he formed the trio Dawn who had a run of 14 US (6 UK) Top 40s. The act split in 77 and he went solo on Casablanca.

BLESS YOU *(US No. 15 – Co-writ. Barry Mann)* *(All hits below as DAWN were produced by The Tokens)*	8	27 OCT 61	FONTANA
CANDIDA *(Orig. vocal by Frankie Paris)*	9	27 FEB 71	BELL
KNOCK THREE TIMES *(Above two as Dawn)*	1(5)	15 MAY 71	BELL
WHAT ARE YOU DOING SUNDAY *(US No. 39)*	3	28 AUG 71	BELL
TIE A YELLOW RIBBON ROUND THE OLD OLE OAK TREE *(Top record of 73)* *(Above two as Dawn feat. Tony Orlando)*	1(4)	21 APR 73	BELL
CANDIDA	3	03 OCT 70	BELL
KNOCK THREE TIMES	1(3)	23 JAN 71	BELL
TIE A YELLOW RIBBON ROUND THE OLD OLE OAK TREE *(Top record of 73)* *(True story of a Florida convict)*	1(4)	21 APR 73	BELL
SAY, HAS ANYBODY SEEN MY SWEET GYPSY ROSE *(UK No. 12)*	3	15 SEP 73	BELL
STEPPIN' OUT (GONNA BOOGIE TONIGHT) *(Last two as Tony Orlando & Dawn)*	7	26 OCT 74	BELL
HE DON'T LOVE YOU (LIKE I LOVE YOU) *(Jerry Butler 60 US hit)*	1(3)	03 MAY 75	ELEKTRA

ORLEANS

New York based rock quintet featured the voice and songs of John Hall. They recorded on ABC in 73 and scored three US only Top 20s. John left in 77 to go solo on Elektra and the group recorded on Infinity in 79 and MCA in 86.

DANCE WITH ME	6	18 OCT 75	ASYLUM
STILL THE ONE	5	23 OCT 76	ASYLUM

ORLONS

Pop/soul quartet from Philadelphia included Shirley Brickley and Rosetta Hightower. They achieved five US-only Top 20s in just 15 months. Group were on Planet and Calla in 66 and ABC in 67 and broke up in 68. Rosetta moved to the UK and Shirley died in 77.

THE WAH-WATUSI	2	21 JUL 62	CAMEO
DON'T HANG UP	4	08 DEC 62	CAMEO
SOUTH STREET	3	30 MAR 63	CAMEO

ORVILLE THE DUCK – SEE KEITH HARRIS FOR HIT DETAILS

OZZY OSBOURNE – SEE LITA FORD/BLACK SABBATH FOR HIT DETAILS

DONNY OSMOND

The focal point of the successful Osmonds group had eight solo US (7 UK) Top 20s in the 70s and was one of the top teen appeal acts of that decade. He also teamed with sister Marie for some hits. Against all odds he returned to the top end of the US Top 20 in 89.

PUPPY LOVE *(Paul Anka 60 hit)* *(His first three US Top 10 solos were UK flops)*	1(5)	08 JUL 72	MGM
TOO YOUNG *(US No. 13 – Nat 'King' Cole 51 hit)*	5	30 SEP 72	MGM
WHY *(US No. 13 – Frankie Avalon 59 hit)*	3	02 DEC 72	MGM
THE TWELFTH OF NEVER *(Johnny Mathis 57 US hit – based on old folk song)*	1(1)	31 MAR 73	MGM
YOUNG LOVE *(US No. 23)* *(Jumped from 16-1 – originally by Ric Cartey in 56)*	1(4)	25 AUG 73	MGM
WHEN I FALL IN LOVE *(US No. 14 – Doris Day 52 US hit)*	4	01 DEC 73	MGM

SWEET AND INNOCENT (Original by Roy Orbison)	7	05 JUN 71	MGM
GO AWAY LITTLE GIRL (Steve Lawrence 62 hit)	1(3)	11 SEP 71	MGM
HEY GIRL/I KNEW YOU WHEN	9	15 JAN 72	MGM
('A' Freddie Scott 63 US hit/'B' Billy Joe Royal 65 US hit)			
PUPPY LOVE	3	01 APR 72	MGM
THE TWELFTH OF NEVER	8	28 APR 73	MGM
SOLDIER OF LOVE (UK No. 29 in 88)	2	03 JUN 89	CAPITOL

Also see Osmonds/Donny & Marie Osmond

DONNY & MARIE OSMOND

Brother and sister duo, from the most successful all time recording family, had six US (4 UK) Top 40s. They had their own successful US TV series from 76-78 and both had many solo hits.

I'M LEAVING IT (ALL) UP TO YOU	2	07 SEP 74	MGM
(Originally by Don & Dewey)			
MORNING SIDE OF THE MOUNTAIN	5	01 FEB 75	MGM
(Tommy Edwards 51 & 59 US hit)			
I'M LEAVING IT (ALL) UP TO YOU	4	14 SEP 74	MGM
MORNING SIDE OF THE MOUNTAIN	8	25 JAN 75	MGM

Also see Donny Osmond/Marie Osmond/Osmonds

LITTLE JIMMY OSMOND

The 'baby' of the million selling Mormon family was the youngest artist ever to top the UK chart which he did at age just nine! Surprisingly he was the first Osmond to record solo which he did in 70. He had a third UK-only Top 20 with the Isley Brothers song 'I'm Gonna Knock On Your Door'. He is now a rock impresario.

LONG HAIRED LOVER FROM LIVERPOOL	1(4)	23 DEC 72	MGM
(US No. 38 – Top UK record of 72)			
TWEEDLE DEE (US No. 59 – Lavern Baker 55 hit)	4	21 APR 73	MGM

MARIE OSMOND

The only female in the Osmond team started singing at 14 and has had three solo US (1 UK) Top 40s as well as her hits with brother Donny. She has also had 22 country hits including seven Top 20s.

PAPER ROSES (Anita Bryant 60 hit)	2	08 DEC 73	MGM
PAPER ROSES (Was a country No. 1)	5	03 NOV 73	MGM

Also see Donny & Marie Osmond

OSMONDS

Top 70s teeny bopper act were formed in the late 50s. The Utah based family group were Alan, Wayne, Merrill, Jay, and Donny who joined in 63 at age 6. They were on Andy Williams TV show from 62-67, then they joined Jerry Lewis' TV show. As a MOR/pop act they recorded on MGM, Barnaby and UNI before changing to a Jackson Five styled group and getting seven US (6 UK) Top 20s. In the 80s after Donny had gone solo the group notched up 11 country hits. In 90 some of Alan's sons recorded as The Osmond Boys.

CRAZY HORSES (US No. 14)	2	25 NOV 72	MGM
(The acts first three US Top 20s flopped in the UK)			
GOING HOME (US No. 36)	4	04 AUG 73	MGM
LET ME IN (US No. 36)	2	10 NOV 73	MGM
(One of 13 UK hits by the Osmond family in 73)			
LOVE ME FOR A REASON	1(3)	31 AUG 74	MGM
(Jumped from 19-1 – Composed by Johnny Bristol)			
THE PROUD ONE	5	21 JUN 75	MGM
(US No. 22 – Frankie Valli 66 US hit)			
ONE BAD APPLE	1(5)	13 FEB 71	MGM
YO-YO (Composed by Joe South)	3	16 OCT 71	MGM
DOWN BY THE LAZY RIVER (UK No. 40)	4	04 MAR 72	MGM
LOVE ME FOR A REASON	10	19 OCT 74	MGM

Also see Donny Osmond/Donny & Marie Osmond

GILBERT O'SULLIVAN

After being in The Doodles and Rick's Blues the unmistakable Irish singer/songwriter and pianist had singles as Gilbert on CBS and Major Minor. The first 45 'What's In A Kiss' was a UK Top 20 when re-issued in 80. He then joined Gordon Mills, the manager of Tom Jones and Engelbert and strung together 13 UK (4 US) Top 20 singles and 5 UK (1 US) Top 20 LPs. He returned to the UK chart in 90 on Chrysalis.

NOTHING RHYMED	8	19 DEC 70	MAM
NO MATTER HOW I TRY	5	18 NOV 71	MAM
ALONE AGAIN (NATURALLY)	3	01 APR 72	MAM
OOH-WAKKA-DOO-WAKKA-DAY	8	08 JUL 72	MAM
CLAIR	1(2)	11 NOV 72	MAM
GET DOWN	1(2)	17 APR 73	MAM
WHY OH WHY OH WHY	6	01 DEC 73	MAM
ALONE AGAIN (NATURALLY)	1(6)	29 JUL 72	MAM
(The No. 2 single of the year in US)			
CLAIR	2	30 DEC 72	MAM
GET DOWN	7	18 AUG 73	MAM

OTTAWAN

Pam and Pat, a duo from Guadaloupe, were based in France and had four UK-only charters. Their catchy Euro dance tracks were put together by the same team behind the Gibson Brothers hits.

D.I.S.C.O.	2	11 OCT 80	CARRERE
HANDS UP (GIVE ME YOUR HEART)	3	26 SEP 81	CARRERE

OUR KID

Teenage quartet from Liverpool including Kevin Rown (then 12) were winners on UK TV talent show 'New Faces'. The well choreographed act had trouble with educational authorities and were banned from TV and live work. They followed their one-off UK hit with 'I'm In Love With You'.

YOU JUST MIGHT SEE ME CRY	2	03 JUL 76	POLYDOR

OUTFIELD

UK pop/rock trio Tony Lewis, Alan Jackman and John Spinks joined Columbia in 85. They had two US-only Top 20s in 86 – the other one being 'All The Love In The World' (19).

YOUR LOVE	6	10 MAY 86	COLUMBIA

OUTSIDERS

Cleveland based rock foursome, who were originally known as The Starfires, had four US-only Top 40s in 66. They were on Bell and Kapp in 70 and broke up shortly after. Lead singer Sonny Geraci returned to the US Top 10 in 72 in the group Climax.

TIME WON'T LET ME	5	16 APR 66	CAPITOL

Also see Climax

OVERLANDERS

Started in 63 as a UK answer to The Kingston Trio. The group, which included Paul Arnold and Pete Bartholomew, became a quintet, had a small US hit with 'Yesterdays Gone' (75) in 64 and followed their one-off UK smash with 'My Life'.

MICHELLE (Beatles song – jumped from 11-1)	1(3)	29 JAN 66	PYE

OZARK MOUNTAIN DAREDEVILS

Country/rockers from Missouri had previously called themselves Buffalo Chips & Burlap Socks and Cosmic Corncob & His Amazing Mountain Daredevils. They had two US-only Top 40 singles and LPs and last charted on Columbia in 80. The group re-formed in 89 and included original members Steve Cash and John Dillon.

JACKIE BLUE	3	17 MAY 75	A&M

P

PABLO CRUISE

Ultra smooth San Francisco rock quartet featured ex Stoneground singer Dave Jenkins. They had the first of six US hit LPs in 75 and in 77 started a string of five US-only Top 40 singles.

☆	WHATCHA GONNA DO	6	20 AUG 77	A&M
	LOVE WILL FIND A WAY	6	26 AUG 78	A&M

· PATTI PAGE

'The Singing Rage' was born Clara Fowler in Muskogee, Oklahoma. She was one of the top selling artists and best known TV faces in the US in the 50s and has chalked up over 80 US (1 UK) chart entries since debuting in 48. Her hits were among the first to use multi-tracked vocals.

☆	ALLEGHENY MOON	5	24 AUG 56	MERCURY
	OLD CAPE COD	8	22 JUL 57	MERCURY
	HUSH, HUSH SWEET CHARLOTTE *(From the film)*	8	26 JUN 65	COLUMBIA

ELAINE PAIGE

MOR/pop singer/actress was on EMI in 76 and had the title role in Evita in 78. She is basically an LP act and has had four UK-only Top 20 LPs to date. She later had releases on Avatar, Inspiration, WEA, Siren and joined First Night in 89.

☆	MEMORY *(From the musical 'Cats')* *(Biggest hit of the 600 versions of this song)*	6	04 JUL 81	POLYDOR
	I KNOW HIM SO WELL *(With BARBARA DICKSON)* *(From 'Chess' – UK's top selling female duo record)*	1(1)	02 FEB 85	RCA

ROBERT PALMER

Yorkshire born singer was in Mandrake Paddle Steamer, The Alan Bown Set, Dada and Vinegar Joe before going solo in 74. He has been a transatlantic chart regular since 76, having had six US (4 UK) Top 20 singles. This Grammy winner was in the supergroup Power Station in 85 and he had his hottest spell after that, thanks partly to his videos with the striking all girl backing group.

☆	ADDICTED TO LOVE *(His first UK Top 10 after eight years of chart hits)*	5	14 JUN 86	ISLAND
	I DIDN'T MEAN TO TURN YOU ON *(Cherrelle 84 US hit)*	9	02 AUG 86	ISLAND
	SHE MAKES MY DAY	6	12 NOV 88	EMI
☆	ADDICTED TO LOVE *(His 18th solo single)*	1(1)	03 MAY 86	ISLAND
	I DIDN'T MEAN TO TURN YOU ON	2	08 NOV 86	ISLAND
	SIMPLY IRRESISTIBLE *(UK No. 44)*	2	10 SEP 88	EMI MANHAT.

PAPER LACE

Singing drummer Phil Wright led this Nottingham pop quintet who won on TVs Opportunity Knocks in 74 and had three UK Top 20s. In the US their first UK hit went to No. 1 when covered by Bo Donaldson & The Heywoods. They were later on Concord and EMI.

☆	BILLY, DON'T BE A HERO *(US No. 96 – Jumped from 8-1)*	1(3)	16 MAR 74	BUS STOP
	THE NIGHT CHICAGO DIED	3	01 JUN 74	BUS STOP
☆	THE NIGHT CHICAGO DIED	1(1)	17 AUG 74	MERCURY

VANESSA PARADIS

Teenage singer from France followed her one-off French language UK hit with 'Marilyn & John'. The hit was released over a year later in the US to good reviews but failed to chart.

☆	JOE LE TAXI	3	19 MAR 88	FA PRODS

PARIS SISTERS

Californian sisters Priscilla, Albeth & Sherrell started singing at ages 9, 13 and 11. They recorded 'Old Enough To Cry' in 57 on Imperial and had five US-only hits in the early 60s. They were later on MGM, Mercury, Decca, Cavalier, Reprise, Capitol and GNP.

☆	I LOVE HOW YOU LOVE ME *(Co-written by Barry Mann and prod. Phil Spector)*	5	31 OCT 61	GREGMARK

MICA PARIS

Critically acclaimed London based singer, with a gospel music background, was born Michelle Wallen. She got three UK-only Top 40s in 88 from her Top 10 UK debut LP 'So Good' and a duet with US soul act Will Downing of 'Where Is The Love' also made the UK Top 20 in 89. In the US she has had three black music hits.

☆	MY ONE TEMPTATION *(US No. 97)*	7	11 JUN 88	4TH & BROAD

RYAN PARIS

Italian singer/songwriter who had been performing around Rome for a decade had one of Europe's top summer hits of 83 with his first release. He followed his sole UK chart entry with 'Fall In Love'.

☆	DOLCE VITA	5	17 SEP 83	CARRERE

SIMON PARK ORCHESTRA

Keyboard player from Market Harborough (UK) saw his one-off UK hit peak at 41 in 72 – then a year later watched it leap to No.1 in just three weeks. His follow up was 'High Fi'. The instrumental smash was the theme for the UK TV series 'Van Der Valk'.

☆	EYE LEVEL *(Jumped from 14-1)* *(Was a Gold record in France-where it was recorded)*	1(4)	29 SEP 73	COLUMBIA

RAY PARKER JR.

Detroit born singer/writer was a top session guitarist with Motown and Invictus and later worked with acts like Stevie Wonder and Barry White. He formed Raydio (which included Jerry Knight of Ollie & Jerry) in 77 and went solo in 82. He was one of the most successful black music crossover acts of the 70s and 80s with 12 US (4 UK) Top 40s, not to mention 14 black music Top 20s.

☆	GHOSTBUSTERS *(Sold almost a million in UK alone)*	2	22 SEP 84	ARISTA
	GHOSTBUSTERS *(Returned to UK Top 10 when the film was released)*	6	05 JAN 85	ARISTA
☆	JACK AND JILL *(UK No. 11)*	8	15 APR 78	ARISTA
	YOU CAN'T CHANGE THAT *(Above two as RAYDIO)*	9	18 AUG 79	ARISTA
	A WOMAN NEEDS LOVE (JUST LIKE YOU DO) *(Released as RAY PARKER JR. & RAYDIO)*	4	20 JUN 81	ARISTA
	THE OTHER WOMAN	4	12 JUN 82	ARISTA
	GHOSTBUSTERS *(Huey Lewis sued him over the songs likeness to 'I Want A New Drug')*	1(3)	11 AUG 84	ARISTA

ROBERT PARKER

New Orleans singer/sax player recorded on Ron in 49 and played on many hits from the Crescent City in the 50s. He was also on Ace, Imperial, Minit, Silver Fox, SS Int. and Island and had other foot songs like 'Happy Feet' and 'Tip Toe' but no other Top 40s. He was still playing around New Orleans in 90.

☆	BAREFOOTIN' *(UK No. 24)*	7	18 JUN 66	NOLA

JOHN PARR

One time Nottingham brick layer had his first hit in the US in 84 with 'Naughty Naughty' (23). He followed his sole Transatlantic Top 10 with 'Love Grammar'. He has also produced and written for Roger Daltrey and Meat Loaf.

🇬🇧 ST. ELMO'S FIRE (MAN IN MOTION) *(From the film 'Man in Motion')*		6	19 OCT 85	LONDON
🇺🇸 ST. ELMO'S FIRE (MAN IN MOTION)		1(2)	07 SEP 85	ATLANTIC

ALAN PARSONS PROJECT

UK project, which often uses guest singers, is built around the works of Alan, who engineered The Beatles 'Abbey Road' and Pink Floyd's 'Dark Side of The Moon', and Eric Woolfson. They started on 20th Century in 76 and have scored five US-only Top 20 LPs and eight US-only Top 40 singles with their often mystical recordings. Alan has also produced Pilot, Cockney Rebel and John Miles.

🇺🇸 EYE IN THE SKY	3	10 OCT 82	ARISTA

DAVID PARTON

Stoke (UK) based singer/songwriter worked with Tony Hatch and wrote Sweet Sensation's two UK hits (including 'Sad Sweet Dreamer' their Transatlantic Top 20). He had a one-off vocal hit with his version of a Stevie Wonder song. His follow up was 'In Everything You Do' and he later did a Stevie Wonder medley on DJM.

🇬🇧 ISN'T SHE LOVELY	4	29 JAN 77	PYE

DOLLY PARTON

Country music's No. 1 female singer/songwriter first recorded on Goldband in 59 when just 13. She was on Mercury in 62 and first charted with her sixth single 'Dumb Blonde' on Monument in 67. She has since notched up a staggering 88 country hits including 23 No. 1s. Pop-wise she has had seven US (2 UK) Top 40s. She has also had hit films, a TV series and is a transatlantic household name.

🇬🇧 JOLENE *(US No. 60)*		7	19 JUN 76	RCA
ISLANDS IN THE STREAM *(With KENNY ROGERS)*		7	07 JAN 84	RCA
🇺🇸 HERE YOU COME AGAIN *(UK No. 75)* *(Co-written by Barry Mann)*		3	14 JAN 78	RCA
9 TO 5 *(UK No. 47) (From the film)*		1(2)	21 FEB 81	RCA
ISLANDS IN THE STREAM *(With KENNY ROGERS)*		1(2)	29 OCT 83	RCA

PARTRIDGE FAMILY

Fictitious TV family whose members Shirley Jones and her real life step-son David Cassidy were the only ones to appear on the group's records. The show and the hits ran from 70-73 (a few months behind in UK) and teeny bop idol David also recorded solo hits from 72. In all, they chalked up seven US (5 UK) Top 40s.

🇬🇧 BREAKING UP IS HARD TO DO *(US No. 28 – Neil Sedaka 62 UK hit)*		3	12 AUG 72	BELL
LOOKIN' THROUGH THE EYES OF LOVE *(US No. 39 – Gene Pitney 65 UK hit)*		9	24 FEB 73	BELL
WALKING IN THE RAIN *(Ronettes 64 hit)*		10	09 JUN 73	BELL
🇺🇸 I THINK I LOVE YOU *(UK No. 18)*		1(3)	21 NOV 70	BELL
DOESN'T SOMEBODY WANT TO BE WANTED		6	27 MAR 71	BELL
I'LL MEET YOU HALFWAY		9	12 JUN 71	BELL

Also see David Cassidy

DON PARTRIDGE

Bournemouth born London busker had three UK-only Top 40s with his one-man band style of pop. In 69 after a couple of flops, he quit recording and returned to entertaining people in the streets.

🇬🇧 ROSIE *(He claims it cost £5 to record)*		4	16 MAR 68	COLUMBIA
BLUE EYES		3	22 JUN 68	COLUMBIA

PASADENAS

UK quintet includes Rockin' Jeff and John Andrew Banfield (brother of Susie Q from the Cookie Crew). The group, who have a good image and are well choreographed, have had three UK Top 40s to date, including their biggest hit which tells the story of soul music.

🇬🇧 TRIBUTE (RIGHT ON) *(US No. 52 – written and prod. by Pete Wingfield)*		5	02 JUL 88	CBS

PAT & MICK

Two London based radio DJs (from Capital Radio) Pat Sharp and Mick Brown had two UK-only Top 20s, both in aid of the charity 'Help A London Child'. The other hit (as Mick & Pat) was another revival – the Michael Zager Band's 'Let's All Chant'(11).

🇬🇧 I HAVEN'T STOPPED DANCING YET *(Gonzales 79 hit)*		9	08 APR 89	PWL

BILLY PAUL

Jazzy singer born Paul Williams in Philadelphia had sung in The Flamingos, Blue Notes and his own Billy Paul Trio. His first 45 was 'Why Am I' on Jubilee in 52. He was on Gamble & Huff's (who wrote & produced most of his hits) earlier Neptune and Gamble labels. He had six UK (2 US) Top 40s and joined Ichiban in 89. His first appearance on US radio as a singer was in 46 – at the age of 12.

🇺🇸 ME AND MRS. JONES *(UK No. 12)*	1(3)	16 DEC 72	PHILLY INT.

OWEN PAUL

Glasgow singer who was previously in The Venigmas. His third single gave him a one-off hit which he followed with 'Pleased To Meet You'. He was on NBR in 87.

🇬🇧 MY FAVOURITE WASTE OF TIME *(Originally by Marshall Crenshaw)*		3	12 JUL 86	EPIC

PAUL & PAULA

This duo were Texan student Ray Hildebrand and Jill Jackson. Their first and biggest hit was first released as by Jill & Ray on Lecam. They had three US (2 UK) Top 40s and recorded other songs like 'Dear Paula', 'It's All Over Paula' and 'Dear Paul'. Ray recorded solo on Le Cam, Josie, Charay, Metromedia, Dot and Tower and Jill was on Reprise. Ray had some country success in the 80s.

🇺🇸 HEY PAULA *(UK No. 11)* *(Duo re-recorded it on Le Cam (twice!) and Vicman)*		1(3)	09 FEB 63	PHILIPS
YOUNG LOVERS *(UK No. 12)*		6	20 APR 63	PHILIPS

FREDA PAYNE

Detroit born singer worked in the jazz field in the 60s with Duke Ellington, Pearl Bailey and Quincy Jones. She was on ABC in 62, Impulse in 65 and MGM in 66. Her second single on Holland, Dozier & Holland's label gave her the first of 3 US (2 UK) Top 40s. She was later on ABC, Capitol and Sutra.

🇬🇧 BAND OF GOLD *(The first ever UK No. 1 by a black solo female singer)*		1(6)	19 SEP 70	INVICTUS
🇺🇸 BAND OF GOLD *(In 86 dueted with Belinda Carlise on her version)*		3	25 JUL 70	INVICTUS

PEACHES & HERB

The original Peaches was Francine Barker (ex Sweet Things) and the B-side of her first 45 with Washington born Herb Fame (Herb Feemster). 'Let's Fall In Love' was the first of their five US only Top 40s in the 60s. Herb returned in the 70s with a new Peaches, Linda Greene, and the duo scored their first transatlantic hits.

🇬🇧	REUNITED	4	02 JUN 79	CBS
🇺🇸	CLOSE YOUR EYES *(Five Keys 55 R&B hit)*	8	06 MAY 67	DATE
	SHAKE YOUR GROOVE THING *(UK No. 26)*	5	17 MAR 79	POLYDOR
	REUNITED	1(4)	05 MAY 79	POLYDOR

PEARLS

London based session duo were Lyn Cornell, an ex member of The Vernons Girls and solo act on Decca since 60, and Ann Simmons. They had four UK-only hits and were on Private Stock in 76.

🇬🇧	GUILTY	10	06 JUL 74	BELL
	(Prod & co-writ. record trivia expert Phil Swern)			

JOHNNY PEARSON ORCHESTRA

London pianist/composer played in jazz group The Rhythm Makers while in his teens and was a founder member of the Malcolm Mitchell Trio in the early 50s. He was on Parlophone in 62, Columbia in 66 and was Cilla Black's musical director in the mid 60s. He had a transatlantic hit as Sounds Orchestral, wrote a lot of TV music and led the Top Of The Pops orchestra.

🇬🇧	SLEEPY SHORES *(from TV soap opera Owen MD)*	8	08 JAN 72	PENNY F.

Also see Sounds Orchestral

PEBBLES

Born Perri McKissack in California. She worked with hit act Con Funk Shun in the early 80s. She is married to top producer L.A. Reid who, with Babyface, has produced and written three top three black music hits for her. She is the cousin of soul star Cherrelle.

🇬🇧	GIRLFRIEND	8	23 APR 88	MCA
🇺🇸	GIRLFRIEND	5	23 APR 88	MCA
	MERCEDES BOY *(UK No. 42)*	2	09 JUL 88	MCA

DONALD PEERS

The late UK MOR singer who was best known for his 44 hit 'In A Shady Nook (By A Babbling Brook)' made a comeback to the charts late in life scoring two UK-only Top 40s. The other was 'Give Me One More Chance' (36) in 72.

🇬🇧	PLEASE DON'T GO	3	08 MAR 69	COLUMBIA

PEPPERS

French session duo consisted of synth player Mat Camison and drummer Pierre Dahan. They had a one-off instrumental hit with their European smash. They also had three black music entries.

🇬🇧	PEPPER BOX *(US No. 76)*	6	23 NOV 74	SPARK

PEPSI & SHIRLIE

Ex backing singers for Wham! Pepsi DeMacque and Shirlie Holliman had a great 87 with four UK charters, a lot of UK media coverage and even their own clothing line. They have not re-charted since.

🇬🇧	HEARTACHE *(US No. 78 & US Dance No. 2)*	2	07 FEB 87	POLYDOR
	GOODBYE STRANGER	9	13 JUN 87	POLYDOR

EMILIO PERICOLI

Italian singer/actor had a sole US hit with a San Remo song contest winner that was also heard in the films Rome Adventure and Lovers Must Learn. Follow up was 'Romantico Amore'.

🇺🇸	AL DI LA *(UK No. 23)*	6	07 JUL 62	WARNER

STEVE PERRY

Californian singer who was in Tim Bogert's band Alien Project before fronting hit act Journey in 77. A duet with Kenny Loggins 'Don't Fight It' was a US No. 17 in 82. He had four US-only solo Top 20s in 84 and starred in the USA for Africa project.

🇺🇸	OH, SHERRIE	3	09 JUN 84	COLUMBIA

Also see Journey

PET SHOP BOYS

Award winning UK duo are singer Neil Tennant (ex Dust), one time assistant editor of pop magazine Smash Hits, and keyboard player Chris Lowe (ex One Under The Eight). To date they have notched up 12 UK (6 US) Top 20s including four UK No. 1s equalling the duo record held by Wham! and The Everly Brothers. They have also helped bring back Dusty Springfield and Liza Minnelli to the charts.

🇬🇧	WEST END GIRLS *(Re-recording)* *(Flop when originally recorded for Epic in 84)*	1(2)	11 JAN 86	PARLOPHONE
	SUBURBIA *(US No. 70)*	8	18 OCT 86	PARLOPHONE
	IT'S A SIN *(Entered at No. 5)*	1(3)	04 JUL 87	PARLOPHONE
	WHAT HAVE I DONE TO DESERVE THIS *(And DUSTY SPRINGFIELD – entered at No. 10)*	2	29 AUG 87	PARLOPHONE
	RENT	8	31 OCT 87	PARLOPHONE
	ALWAYS ON MY MIND *(Entered at No. 4 – Brenda Lee 72 Country hit)*	1(3)	19 DEC 87	PARLOPHONE
	HEART *(Entered at No. 7)*	1(3)	09 APR 88	PARLOPHONE
	DOMINO DANCING *(US No. 18)*	7	01 OCT 88	PARLOPHONE
	LEFT TO MY OWN DEVICES *(US No. 84)*	4	03 DEC 88	PARLOPHONE
	IT'S ALRIGHT *(Entered at No. 5 – Original by Sterling Void)*	5	08 JUL 89	PARLOPHONE
🇺🇸	WEST END GIRLS	1(1)	10 MAY 86	EMI AM.
	OPPORTUNITIES (LET'S MAKE LOTS OF MONEY) *(UK No. 11 – was released in UK before first hit)*	10	02 AUG 86	EMI AM.
	IT'S A SIN	9	14 NOV 87	EMI MANHAT.
	ALWAYS ON MY MIND	4	21 MAY 88	EMI MANHAT.
	WHAT HAVE I DONE TO DESERVE THIS *(And DUSTY SPRINGFIELD – they wrote the song in 84)*	2	20 FEB 88	EMI MANHAT.

PETER & GORDON

UK duo Peter Asher and Gordon Waller had a Transatlantic No. 1 with their first 45 (written by Peter's sister's boyfriend Paul McCartney). Before splitting in 68 they had seven UK (10 US) Top 40s. Peter became a Grammy winning producer working with Linda Ronstadt and James Taylor. Gordon recorded several unsuccessful solos.

🇬🇧	A WORLD WITHOUT LOVE	1(2)	25 APR 64	COLUMBIA
	NOBODY I KNOW *(US No. 12 – Above two written by Lennon & McCartney)*	10	04 JUL 64	COLUMBIA
	TRUE LOVE WAYS *(US No. 14 – Buddy Holly 60 UK hit)*	2	22 MAY 65	COLUMBIA
	TO KNOW YOU IS TO LOVE YOU *(US No. 24 – Teddy Bears 58 hit)*	5	10 JUL 65	COLUMBIA
🇺🇸	A WORLD WITHOUT LOVE *(Covered unsuccessfully in US by Bobby Rydell)*	1(1)	27 JUN 64	CAPITOL
	I GO TO PIECES *(Composed by Del Shannon)*	9	20 FEB 65	CAPITOL
	LADY GODIVA *(UK No. 16)*	6	10 DEC 66	CAPITOL

PETER, PAUL & MARY

Top folk music trio Peter Yarrow, Paul Stookey and Mary Travers were formed in New York in 61. They had a string of 12 US (3 UK) Top 40s in the 60s, not to mention 10 US (3 UK) Top 20 LPs. They had the first 'protest song' hits of the 60s and gave Bob Dylan his first hit as a writer. This popular live act broke up in 70 and they have all recorded solo since. They have also re-united occasionally, including a European tour in 83.

🇬🇧	LEAVIN' ON A JET PLANE	2	14 FEB 70	WARNER
🇺🇸	IF I HAD A HAMMER (Pete Seeger song)	10	13 OCT 62	WARNER
	PUFF THE MAGIC DRAGON	2	11 MAY 63	WARNER
	BLOWIN' IN THE WIND (UK No. 13)	2	17 AUG 63	WARNER
	DON'T THINK TWICE IT'S ALL RIGHT (Above two Bob Dylan songs)	9	26 OCT 63	WARNER
	I DIG ROCK AND ROLL MUSIC	9	23 SEP 67	WARNER
	LEAVING ON A JET PLANE (John Denver song – orig. called 'Babe I Have To Go')	1(2)	20 DEC 69	WARNER

PETERS & LEE

Rolling Stone Charlie Watts' uncle Lennie Peters, who has been blind since he was 16, recorded solo on Pye in 66 and joined with Di Lee in 70. This MOR/cabaret duo were Oppportunity Knocks winners and had four UK-only Top 20s and four UK-only Top 10 LPs. They also recorded on Pye and Celebrity in 80, AI in 86 and President in 89 and he was on EMI in 81, Lifestyle in 82 and Relax in 85.

🇬🇧	WELCOME HOME	1(1)	21 JUL 73	PHILIPS
	DON'T STAY AWAY TOO LONG	3	18 MAY 74	PHILIPS

PAUL PETERSON

Californian singer/actor was an original 'Mousketeer' when he was nine and when he was 13 he played Jeff Stone in US TV's Donna Reed Show. He had two US-only Top 20s, the other one being his debut hit 'She Can't Find Her Keys' (19) in 62. He was on Motown in 67 and he now writes books with over a dozen published to date.

🇺🇸	MY DAD (Co-written by Barry Mann) (Sung in Donna Reed's show to his dad (Carl Betz))	6	26 JAN 63	COLPIX

RAY PETERSON

Texan singer with a 4½ octave range (who was a victim of polio at an early age) had four US (1 UK) Top 40s starting with the original version of Elvis' 'The Wonder Of You' in 59. He later recorded on MGM, Reprise, Decca, UNI, Rose and Cloud 9.

🇺🇸	TELL LAURA I LOVE HER (Banned in the UK) (He re-recorded it on UNI in 71)	7	01 AUG 60	RCA
	CORINNA, CORINNA (Joe Turner 56 US hit)	9	09 JAN 61	DUNES

TOM PETTY & THE HEARTBREAKERS

Florida rocker was in The Epics and Mudcrutch who evolved into The Heartbreakers and recorded on Shelter in 76. They first hit in the UK but have since had big US-only success with four Top 10 LPs and nine Top 20 singles. He has recorded with Bob Dylan and Stevie Nicks and is in the Traveling Wilburys. He appeared in 'Live Aid' and played 'Farm Aid' and Amnesty International shows.

🇺🇸	DON'T DO ME LIKE THAT	10	02 FEB 80	BACKSTREET
	STOP DRAGGIN' MY HEART AROUND (With STEVIE NICKS – UK No. 50)	3	05 SEP 81	MODERN

PhD

UK duo consisted of singer Jim Diamond and synth player Tony Hymas. Their debut single broke in Germany first and then gave them their only UK charter. Follow up was 'Little Suzie's On The Up'. Jim later returned to the top as a soloist.

🇬🇧	I WON'T LET YOU DOWN	3	08 MAY 82	WEA

Also see Jim Diamond

ESTHER PHILLIPS

Born Esther Jones in Texas she was the youngest female to top the R&B charts (age 14) and had scored seven R&B Top 10s before she was 17 in 52. She had ten further R&B hits between 62 and her untimely death in 84. She also recorded on Savoy, RPM, Federal, Warwick, Atlantic, Roulette, Mercury and Winning.

🇬🇧	WHAT A DIFF'RENCE A DAY MAKES (US No. 20 – Dorsey Brothers 34 hit)	6	08 NOV 75	KUDU
🇺🇸	RELEASE ME (As Little Esther Phillips) (Ray Price 54 country hit)	8	22 DEC 62	LENOX

BOBBY 'BORIS' PICKETT & THE CRYPT KICKERS

Singer/actor from Massachusetts who sang in The Cordials and used his Boris Karloff impression to get his sole Transatlantic (& Transylvanian) Top 10 hit. Bobby was a New York taxi driver and in a folk duo when it was a monster hit for a second time (first time in UK) 11 years later. His other releases included 'Monster Swim', 'Monsters' Holiday', 'Monster Man Jam' and 'Monster Concert'.

🇬🇧	MONSTER MASH	3	06 OCT 73	LONDON
🇺🇸	MONSTER MASH (Was revived by Vincent Price in 77)	1(2)	20 OCT 62	GARPAX
	MONSTER MASH (On US chart 37 weeks)	10	11 AUG 73	PARROT

WILSON PICKETT

The 'Wicked Pickett' was one of the 60s top soul singers. He sang lead on the classic 'I Found A Love' by The Falcons in 62 and recorded solo for Cub, Correctone and Double L before joining Atlantic. He has had 49 soul chart entries including 33 Top 20s. His biggest UK hit was 'In The Midnight Hour' (UK 12/US 21). He later recorded on RCA, Wicked, Big Tree, EMI and Motown.

🇺🇸	LAND OF 1,000 DANCES (UK No. 22 – Chris Kenner 63 R&B hit)	6	10 SEP 66	ATLANTIC
	FUNKY BROADWAY (UK No. 43 – Dyke & The Blazers 67 R&B hit)	8	30 SEP 67	ATLANTIC

PICKETTYWITCH

UK group fronted by Polly Brown and including Chris Warren had two UK-only Top 20s – the other being 'Sad Old Kinda Movie'. Both were written by Tony Macauley and John McLeod (who produced them). Polly had a US No. 16 with a solo 45 'Up In A Puff Of Smoke' in 75.

🇬🇧	THAT SAME OLD FEELING (US No. 67)	5	21 MAR 70	PYE

PIGBAG

West Country (UK) instrumental sextet which included Simon Underwood (ex Pop Group) and singer Angela Jaegar. Their first 45 became their third and biggest chart single when it finally charted a year after its release. Act's only other Top 40 was 'The Big Bean'. They disbanded in 83.

🇬🇧	PAPA'S GOT A BRAND NEW PIGBAG	3	01 MAY 82	Y

PIGLETS

Session singer Barbara Kay sang on this one-off hit project from top UK producer Jonathan King. The 'group' also released 'This Is Reggae' and later re-surfaced on King's own UK label.

🇬🇧	JOHNNY REGGAE	3	20 NOV 71	BELL

PILOT

Scottish pop foursome including Dave Paton and Billy Lyall got a US gold disc for their first hit 'Magic' and topped the UK chart with a song of Dave & Bill's. They were voted Top Tip For 75 (above Queen) in a UK paper but faded quickly. Billy went solo in 76 and Paton later recorded with Kate Bush and Alan Parsons.

 JANUARY *(US No. 87 – Jumped from 9-1)* — 1(3) — 01 FEB 75 — EMI

MAGIC *(UK No. 11 – both prod. Alan Parsons)* — 5 — 12 JUL 75 — EMI

PILTDOWN MEN

Team of L.A. session men including Lincoln Mayorga and Ed Cobb (ex 4 Preps) had three UK Top 20s but only managed one small US hit 'Brontosaurus Stomp' (75). In fact in the end they made records just for the UK, stopping after their second flop. In 63 UK act Sons of The Piltdown Men briefly recorded.

 MACDONALD'S CAVE *(Based on 'Old McDonald')* — 8 — 11 NOV 60 — CAPITOL

PINK FLOYD

Top progressive rock band, which included Roger Waters and Dave Gilmour, started out playing R&B in 65. They were one of the first psychedelic bands and have specialised in live performances with superb sound and extravagant lighting effects. Original singer/songwriter Syd Barrett left in 68. They have had 13 UK (6 US) Top 10 LPs including the epic 'Dark Side Of The Moon' which spent over 700 weeks (14 years) on the US chart selling 11 million! Waters left after a row in 83 but Floyd's 88 World tour was still seen by 10 million people in 15 countries. That year Forbes magazine reported that their gross for the year was $57 million.

 SEE EMILY PLAY *(Orig. called 'Games For May')* — 6 — 29 JUL 67 — COLUMBIA
ANOTHER BRICK IN THE WALL (PT. 2) — 1(4) — 15 DEC 79 — HARVEST
(UK Gold – record was banned in South Africa)

ANOTHER BRICK IN THE WALL — 1(4) — 22 MAR 80 — COLUMBIA

PINKEES

UK pop group who were the subject of a Scotland Yard chart hype probe after their one-off UK hit unexpectedly jumped from 27-8 to drop to 12 the next week. The follow up was 'I'll Be There'. The group's sound was astonishingly like The Beatles.

DANGER GAMES — 8 — 23 OCT 82 — CREOLE

PINKERTON'S ASSORTED COLOURS

UK pop quintet fronted by Samuel 'Pinkerton' Kemp and including the writer of their sole Top 40 hit Tony Newman. Their follow up was 'Don't Stop Lovin' Me Baby'. Later on Pye they recorded as Pinkerton's Colours and Pinkertons. The group also toured the US as Flying Machine when that session group hit over there in 69.

 MIRROR MIRROR — 9 — 12 FEB 66 — DECCA
(They later recorded 'Behind The Mirror')

PIONEERS

Jamaican reggae trio who started as session singers included George Agard. They first hit with 'Long Shot Kick De Bucket' in 69 (it returned to the chart in 80 during the Two-Tone craze). They followed their biggest hit with another UK-only hit 'Give And Take'(35). They were also on Ice in 78 and Creole in 85.

 LET YOUR YEAH BE YEAH *(Jimmy Cliff song)* — 5 — 11 SEP 71 — TROJAN
(Covered in US by Brownsville Station)

PIPKINS

On record the duo were top UK songwriter Roger Greenaway and top session singer Tony Burrows, but live they were Davey Sands (ex Essex) and ballroom DJ Len Marshall. They followed their one-off Transatlantic Top 10 with 'Yakety Yak'.

 GIMME DAT DING *(Co-written Albert Hammond)* — 6 — 18 APR 70 — COLUMBIA
GIMME DAT DING — 9 — 18 JUL 70 — CAPITOL

PIPS – SEE GLADYS KNIGHT FOR HIT DETAILS

PIRANHAS

Brighton (UK) rock sextet which included 'Boring' Bob Grover. They had two UK-only Top 20s with fun remakes of 50s instrumental hits with additional words – the other one being 'Zambesi'. They also recorded on Attrix in 78, Virgin in 79 and Dakota in 81.

TOM HARK — 6 — 30 AUG 80 — SIRE
(Elias & His Zig Zag Jive Flutes 58 UK hit)

GENE PITNEY

Distinctive singer/songwriter from Connecticut. He recorded on Decca (in Jamie & Jane) in 59, on Blaze (as Billy Bryan) and on Festival before charting in 61. He wrote big hits like 'He's A Rebel', 'Rubber Ball' and 'Hello Mary Lou'. In the 60s he strung together 16 US (20 UK) Top 40s. Always a popular live act in the UK he got his first No. 1 there 28 years after his chart debut!

TWENTY FOUR HOURS FROM TULSA *(US No. 17)* — 5 — 04 JAN 64 — UA
THAT GIRL BELONGS TO YESTERDAY *(US No. 49)* — 8 — 28 MAR 64 — UA
(Written for him by Jagger and Richards)
I'M GONNA BE STRONG *(Co-written Barry Mann)* — 2 — 05 DEC 64 — STATESIDE
I MUST BE SEEING THINGS *(US No. 31)* — 6 — 06 MAR 65 — STATESIDE
LOOKIN THROUGH THE EYES OF LOVE *(US No. 28)* — 3 — 10 JUL 65 — STATESIDE
PRINCESS IN RAGS *(US No. 37)* — 9 — 04 DEC 65 — STATESIDE
BACKSTAGE *(US No. 25)* — 4 — 12 MAR 66 — STATESIDE
NOBODY NEEDS YOUR LOVE — 2 — 16 JUL 66 — STATESIDE
JUST ONE SMILE *(US No. 64)* — 8 — 10 DEC 66 — STATESIDE
(Above two composed by Randy Newman)
SOMETHING'S GOTTEN HOLD OF MY HEART — 5 — 09 DEC 67 — STATESIDE
SOMETHING'S GOTTEN HOLD OF MY HEART — 1(4) — 28 JAN 89 — PARLOPHONE
(With MARC ALMOND- Gene's first No. 1)

(THE MAN WHO SHOT) LIBERTY VALENCE — 4 — 16 JUN 62 — MUSICOR
ONLY LOVE CAN BREAK A HEART — 2 — 03 NOV 62 — MUSICOR
(First two not in UK chart)
IT HURTS TO BE IN LOVE *(US No. 36)* — 7 — 03 OCT 64 — MUSICOR
I'M GONNA BE STRONG — 9 — 12 DEC 64 — MUSICOR

PLASTIC BERTRAND

The first Belgian act in the UK Top 10 for 15 years was this ex member of punk bands Stalag 6 and Hubble Bubble. He followed his international hit with 'Sha La La La Lee'. He was also on Vertigo.

CA PLANE POUR MOI *(US No. 47)* — 8 — 24 JUN 78 — SIRE

PLASTIC ONO BAND – SEE JOHN LENNON FOR HIT DETAILS

PLASTIC PENNY

UK group led by strong voiced Brian Keith and featuring drummer Nigel Olsson had a one-off UK hit. Brian left in 69 and later hit again as the singer in (English) Congregation and Nigel joined Spencer Davis and then Elton John's bands and had solo hits.

EVERYTHING I AM *(Box Tops B-side)* — 6 — 03 FEB 68 — PAGE ONE

Also see Congregation

PLATTERS

The top 50s vocal group were fronted by Tony Williams. They were formed in 53 and had some unsuccessful 45s on Federal (inc. a version of 'Only You'). They were in many R'n'R films and had 22 US Top 40s (the last in 67) and eight in the UK. They also scored five US Top 20 LPs and had their first UK one in 78. Tony went solo in 61 and the group (with numerous changes) still performs.

THE GREAT PRETENDER/ONLY YOU	5	21 SEP 56	MERCURY
(First UK release coupled two earlier US hits)			
MY PRAYER	4	09 NOV 56	MERCURY
TWILIGHT TIME (Three Suns 44 hit)	3	11 JUN 58	MERCURY
SMOKE GETS IN YOUR EYES	1(1)	20 MAR 59	MERCURY
(Paul Whiteman 34 hit)			
ONLY YOU	5	05 NOV 55	MERCURY
THE GREAT PRETENDER (No. 1 R&B for 10 weeks)	2	18 FEB 56	MERCURY
(YOU'VE GOT) THE MAGIC TOUCH	5	05 MAY 56	MERCURY
MY PRAYER	1(2)	04 AUG 56	MERCURY
(No. 3 US single of 56 – 'Great Pretender' was No. 2)			
TWILIGHT TIME (No. 1 in just 3 weeks)	1(1)	21 APR 58	MERCURY
SMOKE GETS IN YOUR EYES	1(3)	19 JAN 59	MERCURY
HARBOR LIGHTS	8	28 MAR 60	MERCURY
(UK No. 11 – Frances Langford 37 hit)			

PLAYER

L.A. based pop quintet included Liverpool born Peter Beckett and Texan J.C. Crowley. They first recorded on Haven and had 3 US (1 UK) Top 40s. They were also on Casablanca and RCA. J.C., who co-wrote their biggest hit, had solo country success in the late 80s.

BABY COME BACK (UK No. 32)	1(3)	14 JAN 78	RSO
THIS TIME I'M IN IT FOR LOVE	10	03 JUN 78	RSO

PLAYERS ASSOCIATION

New York session funk group put together by multi-instrumentalist/ composer Chris Hills and producer Danny Weiss (both ex Everything Is Everything) and including blind synth wizard Mike Mandel had three UK-only charters.

TURN THE MUSIC UP	8	31 MAR 79	VANGUARD

POGUES

Formed in London by the so called 'ugliest man in rock' Shane McGowan (ex Nipple Erectors) and first called Pogue Mahone (Gaelic for 'Kiss My Arse'). Their third 45 was the first of their 11 UK-only chart entries for this unique punk-Celtic band.

THE IRISH ROVER (And The Dubliners)	8	11 APR 87	STIFF
FAIRYTALE OF NEW YORK (Feat. Kirsty MacColl)	2	26 DEC 87	POGUE MAHONE

POINTER SISTERS

Sisters Ruth, Bonnie and Anita (later joined by June) did much session work before recording on Atlantic in 71. 'Yes We Can Can' (US No.11) in 73 on Blue Thumb was the first of 16 US (8 US) Top 40s. Bonnie went solo in 78 and Anita and June have also recorded alone. This soulful act who were originally likened to the Andrews Sisters, won a Grammy for 'Fairytale' as 'Best Country Single' of 74!

SLOW HAND	10	26 SEP 81	PLANET
AUTOMATIC	2	19 MAY 84	PLANET
JUMP (FOR MY LOVE)	6	30 JUN 84	PLANET
FIRE (UK No. 34 – Bruce Springsteen song)	2	24 FEB 79	PLANET
(Previously recorded by Robert Gordon)			
HE'S SO SHY	3	25 OCT 80	PLANET
SLOW HAND	2	29 AUG 81	PLANET
AUTOMATIC (Top US dance record of 84)	5	14 APR 84	PLANET
JUMP (FOR MY LOVE)	3	07 JUL 84	PLANET
I'M SO EXCITED	9	27 OCT 84	PLANET
(UK No. 11 – different version was US No. 30 in 82)			
NEUTRON DANCE	6	16 FEB 85	PLANET
(UK No. 31 – from the film 'Beverly Hills Cop')			

POISON

L.A. glam heavy metal band fronted by Bret Michaels and including C.C. Deville and Rikki Rocket were one of the hottest new bands in the US in the late 80s with six Top 20 singles and a Transatlantic Top 20 LP 'Open Up And Say... Ahh' (2 US/18 UK).

TALK DIRTY TO ME (UK No. 67)	9	16 MAY 87	ENIGMA
NOTHIN' BUT A GOOD TIME (UK No. 35)	6	09 JUL 88	ENIGMA
EVERY ROSE HAS ITS THORNS (UK No. 13)	1(3)	24 DEC 88	ENIGMA
YOUR MAMA DON'T DANCE	10	15 APR 89	ENIGMA
(UK No. 13 – Loggins & Messina 72 US hit)			

POLICE

Gordon 'Sting' Sumner (ex Last Exit), Andy Summers (ex New Animals and Soft Machine) and Stewart Copeland (ex Curved Air) formed this ultra successful trio in 77. Their first release was 'Fall Out' on Illegal in 78. The award winning trio, who packed stadiums around the world, chalked up 15 UK (8 US) Top 20 singles and six UK Top 10 LPs (inc. five successive No. 1s) and four US Top 10s. They broke up when they were at the very top. Singer/songwriter Sting has since made several films.

CAN'T STAND LOSING YOU	2	04 AUG 79	A&M
(Re-issue – Was UK No. 42 in 78)			
MESSAGE IN A BOTTLE	1(3)	29 SEP 79	A&M
(Entered at No. 8 – US No. 74)			
WALKING ON THE MOON (Entered at No. 5)	1(1)	08 DEC 79	A&M
SO LONELY (Re-issue)	6	15 MAR 80	A&M
DON'T STAND SO CLOSE TO ME	1(4)	27 SEP 80	A&M
(Entered at No. 1 – Top UK record of 80)			
DE DO DO DO, DE DA DA DA (Entered at No. 9)	5	20 DEC 80	A&M
INVISIBLE SUN (Entered at No. 9)	2	03 OCT 81	A&M
EVERY LITTLE THING SHE DOES IS MAGIC	1(1)	14 NOV 81	A&M
EVERY BREATH YOU TAKE (Entered at No. 7)	1(4)	04 JUN 83	A&M
WRAPPED AROUND YOUR FINGER	7	06 AUG 83	A&M
DE DO DO DO, DE DA DA DA	10	17 JAN 81	A&M
DON'T STAND SO CLOSE TO ME (Grammy winner)	10	11 APR 81	A&M
EVERY LITTLE THING SHE DOES IS MAGIC	3	05 DEC 81	A&M
EVERY BREATH YOU TAKE (Top US song of 83)	1(8)	09 JUL 83	A&M
(When No. 1 half of US Top 30 were by UK acts)			
KING OF PAIN (UK No. 17)	3	08 OCT 83	A&M
WRAPPED AROUND YOUR FINGER	8	03 MAR 84	A&M

Also see Sting

SU POLLARD

UK comic actress and TV personality had her sole UK Top 40 hit with a song used in a TV documentary series about a couple marrying. She followed it with 'You've Lost That Lovin' Feeling'.

STARTING TOGETHER	2	22 FEB 86	RAINBOW

BRIAN POOLE & THE TREMELOES

Essex (UK) group formed in 59 and debuted on Decca in 62. Their third 45 was the first of their eight UK-only Top 40s (six of them cover versions of US records). Brian unsuccessfully went solo in 66 and has since re-appeared occasionally and was in The Travelin' Wrinklies in 89. The Tremeloes went on to even greater fame.

TWIST AND SHOUT	4	02 AUG 63	DECCA
(Song first released by Carla Thomas)			
DO YOU LOVE ME (Contours 62 US hit)	1(4)	04 OCT 63	DECCA
(Brian re-recorded it on Outlook in 83)			
CANDY MAN (Originally by Roy Orbison)	6	07 MAR 64	DECCA
SOMEONE SOMEONE (US No. 97 – Orig. Crickets)	2	04 JUL 64	DECCA
(Brian re-recorded it on Sumatra in 83)			

Also see The Tremeloes

IGGY POP

Born James Jewel Osterburg in Michigan, he was in The Iguanas, The Prime Movers and the Psychedelic Stooges who evolved into The Stooges and recorded on Elektra in 69. This wild and charismatic personality had a solo LP on RCA in 77 produced by his friend David Bowie but had to wait another decade for his only real hit.

REAL WILD CHILD (WILD ONE) *(Originally by Johnny O'Keefe)*		10	24 JAN 87	A&M

POPPY FAMILY

Canadian pop quartet featured husband and wife team Terry and Susan (nee Peklevits) Jacks. They had five US (1 UK) charters before they broke up in 73 when Terry and Susan separated and started solo careers. Susan was on Mercury and Terry had hits on Bell.

WHICH WAY YOU GOIN' BILLY	7	26 SEP 70	DECCA
WHICH WAY YOU GOIN' BILLY	2	06 JUN 70	LONDON

Also see Terry Jacks

MIKE POST

Top composer/conductor had success in the 60s as Kenny Rogers and Mason Williams' producer. He was on Reprise in 65 and on Warner in 69 as the Mike Post Coalition. He composed the themes to many top TV shows and has seen three of them make the US Top 40. He also produced Dolly Parton's US No. 1 '9 to 5'.

THE ROCKFORD FILES	10	09 AUG 75	MGM
THE THEME FROM HILL STREET BLUES *(UK No. 25)*	10	14 NOV 81	ELEKTRA
(Featuring LARRY CARLTON)			

COZY POWELL

Top UK drummer has appeared in many top acts including Jeff Beck's group, Emerson, Lake & Powell, Michael Schenker Group, and Rainbow. He was also the UK's most successful drummer in the 70s with three UK-only Top 20s – the other being 'The Man In Black' (18). He was later on Ariola in 79 and Polydor in 81.

DANCE WITH THE DEVIL *(US No. 49 – covered in US by Sandy Nelson)*	–	4	19 JAN 74	RAK
NA NA NA		10	14 SEP 74	RAK

POWER STATION

Supergroup contained Duran Duran's John and Andy Taylor, Chic's Tony Thompson and singer Robert Palmer. They made one eponymous LP which their three Transatlantic hits came from.

SOME LIKE IT HOT *(UK No. 14)*	6	11 MAY 85	CAPITOL
GET IT ON (BANG A GONG)	9	03 AUG 85	CAPITOL
(UK No. 22 – T-Rex 72 hit)			

Also see Duran Duran/Chic/Robert Palmer

JOEY POWERS

Born in the same town as Perry Como – Cannonsburg, Pennsylvania. This one-time wrestling coach at Ohio State University was on RCA in 62 and followed his sole hit with 'Jenny Won't You Wake Up'.

MIDNIGHT MARY	10	04 JAN 64	AMY

PRATT & McCLAIN

Californian Jerry McClain was in The American Scene with Michael Omartian (later a top producer) before first working with Texan Truett Pratt in session group Brotherlove. The duo followed their only big hit with 'Devil With The Blue Dress On'.

HAPPY DAYS	5	05 JUN 76	REPRISE
(UK No. 31 – From the TV series)			

PREFAB SPROUT

Newcastle (UK) trio who feature singer/songwriter Paddy McAloon. They first recorded on their own Candle label in 82 and had the first of their seven US-only chart entries in 84. Thomas Dolby co-produced their biggest selling LP 'From Langley Park To Memphis' which also featured Stevie Wonder and Pete Townshend.

THE KING OF ROCK 'N' ROLL	7	28 MAY 88	KITCHENWARE

ELVIS PRESLEY

The most important, influential, best documented and biggest selling solo artist of the 20th Century. His first three 45s did not chart and the next two were only country hits but thereafter he had a staggering 62 US (77 UK) Top 20 singles and 38 US (51 UK) Top 20 LPs. The King has also topped the R&B, Country, Pop & MOR charts. He has sold over 500 million records, had scores of hit films, broken endless attendance records and has won every music award going. He sold 20 million records in the 24 hours after his death in 77 and soon after had nine 45s on the UK chart and an amazing 27 LPs in the UK Top 100.

BLUE SUEDE SHOES *(US No. 20 – Carl Perkins 56 hit)*	9	15 JUN 56	HMV
HEARTBREAK HOTEL	2	22 JUN 56	HMV
HOUND DOG *(Willie Mae Thornton 53 R&B No. 1)*	2	26 OCT 56	HMV
BLUE MOON *(US No. 55 – Glen Gray 35 hit)*	9	23 NOV 56	HMV
TOO MUCH *(Original by Bernard Hardison)*	6	31 MAY 57	HMV
ALL SHOOK UP	1(7)	12 JUL 57	HMV
TEDDY BEAR *(One of five 45s in UK Top 20)*	3	02 AUG 57	HMV
PARALYSED *(US No. 59)*	8	13 SEP 57	HMV
PARTY *(From the film 'Loving You')*	2	25 OCT 57	RCA
SANTA BRING MY BABY BACK TO ME	7	13 DEC 57	RCA
JAILHOUSE ROCK *(First ever record to enter UK chart at No. 1)*	1(3)	24 JAN 58	RCA
DON'T	2	28 MAR 58	RCA
WEAR MY RING AROUND YOUR NECK	3	23 MAY 58	RCA
HARD HEADED WOMAN	2	08 AUG 58	RCA
KING CREOLE *(From the film)*	2	17 OCT 58	RCA
ONE NIGHT/I GOT STUNG *('A' Smiley Lewis 56 R&B hit)*	1(3)	30 JAN 59	RCA
A FOOL SUCH AS I/I NEED YOUR LOVE TONIGHT *('A' Hank Snow 52 country hit)*	1(5)	15 MAY 59	RCA
BIG HUNK O' LOVE	4	07 AUG 59	RCA
STUCK ON YOU *(Entered at No. 3)*	2	15 APR 60	RCA
A MESS OF BLUES *(US No. 32)*	3	12 AUG 60	RCA
GIRL OF MY BEST FRIEND *(Not rel. as 45 in US)*	6	09 SEP 60	RCA
IT'S NOW OR NEVER *(Entered at No. 1)* *(UK's fastest million seller at the time 6.5 weeks)*	1(9)	04 NOV 60	RCA
ARE YOU LONESOME TONIGHT? *(Entered at No. 2 – Vaughn Deleath 27 hit)*	1(4)	27 JAN 61	RCA
WOODEN HEART *(Co-written by Bert Kaempfert)* *(Entered at No. 5 – Not released as 45 in US)*	1(3)	24 MAR 61	RCA
SURRENDER *(Entered at No. 1)*	1(5)	26 MAY 61	RCA
WILD IN THE COUNTRY *(US No. 26 – Entered at No. 3 from the film)*	1(1)	22 SEP 61	RCA
HIS LATEST FLAME *(Entered at No. 2)*	1(3)	10 NOV 61	RCA
ROCK-A-HULA-BABY *(US No. 23 – entered at No. 4)*	2	09 FEB 62	RCA
CAN'T HELP FALLING IN LOVE *(Above two from the film 'Blue Hawaii')*	3	23 MAR 62	RCA
GOOD LUCK CHARM *(Entered at No. 3)*	1(5)	18 MAY 62	RCA
SHE'S NOT YOU	1(3)	14 SEP 62	RCA
RETURN TO SENDER *(Entered at No. 5)*	1(2)	14 DEC 62	RCA
ONE BROKEN HEART FOR SALE *(US No. 11)* *(From the film 'It Happened At The World's Fair')*	8	08 MAR 63	RCA
DEVIL IN DISGUISE	2	19 JUL 63	RCA
KISSIN' COUSINS *(US No. 12 – from the film)*	10	11 JUL 64	RCA
CRYING IN THE CHAPEL *(Darrell Glenn 53 country hit)*	1(1)	19 JUN 65	RCA
LOVE LETTERS *(US No. 19 – same arrangement as Ketty Lester 62 hit)*	6	06 AUG 66	RCA
IF EVERY DAY WAS LIKE CHRISTMAS	9	31 DEC 66	RCA
IN THE GHETTO *(Composed Mac Davis)*	2	25 JUL 69	RCA
SUSPICIOUS MINDS *(Original by Mark James)*	2	17 JAN 70	RCA
DON'T CRY DADDY *(Composed by Mac Davis)*	8	21 MAR 70	RCA
THE WONDER OF YOU *(Top UK single of 70)*	1(6)	01 AUG 70	RCA
I'VE LOST YOU *(US No. 32)*	9	28 NOV 70	RCA
YOU DON'T HAVE TO SAY YOU LOVE ME *(US No. 11 – Dusty Springfield 66 hit)*	9	23 JAN 71	RCA
THERE GOES MY EVERYTHING *(US No. 21 – Jack Greene 66 country hit)*	6	10 APR 71	RCA
RAGS TO RICHES *(US No. 33 – Tony Bennett 53 hit)*	9	05 JUN 71	RCA

HEARTBREAK HOTEL/HOUND DOG (Re-issue)	10	21 AUG 71	RCA
I JUST CAN'T HELP BELIEVING	6	22 JAN 72	RCA
(Co-written Barry Mann – B.J. Thomas 70 US hit)			
UNTIL IT'S TIME FOR YOU TO GO	5	22 APR 72	RCA
(US No. 48 – Originally by Buffy Sainte Marie)			
AN AMERICAN TRILOGY (US No. 66)	8	01 JUL 72	RCA
(US No. 66 – Mickey Newbury 71 US hit)			
BURNING LOVE	7	21 OCT 72	RCA
ALWAYS ON MY MIND	9	20 JAN 73	RCA
(Brenda Lee 72 country hit – this was 'B' in US)			
MY BOY (US No. 20 – Richard Harris 72 US hit)	5	04 JAN 75	RCA
PROMISED LAND (US No.14 – Chuck Berry 65 hit)	9	01 FEB 75	RCA
GIRL OF MY BEST FRIEND	9	16 OCT 76	RCA
SUSPICION	9	12 FEB 77	RCA
(Not rel. as 45 in US – Terry Stafford 64 US hit)			
MOODY BLUE (US No. 31 – orig. Mark James)	6	02 APR 77	RCA
WAY DOWN (US No. 18 – jumped from 42-4)	1(5)	03 SEP 77	RCA
MY WAY (US No. 22 – Frank Sinatra 69 hit)	9	07 JAN 78	RCA
IT'S ONLY LOVE/BEYOND THE REEF	3	20 SEP 80	RCA

HEARTBREAK HOTEL	1 8	21 APR 56	RCA
(His 6th RCA release – his 5 Sun 45s were first)			
I WANT YOU, I NEED YOU, I LOVE YOU (UK No. 25)	1(1)	28 JUL 56	RCA
(He was No. 1 in US for a record 24 weeks in 56)			
HOUND DOG/DON'T BE CRUEL	1(11)	18 AUG 56	RCA
(Top for 11 weeks a record in the rock era)			
LOVE ME TENDER (UK No. 11 – Entered US at No. 12)	1(5)	03 NOV 56	RCA
(The first single with a million advance orders)			
LOVE ME (Original by Willie & Ruth)	7	05 JAN 57	RCA
(One of his ten simultaneous Top 100 entries!)			
TOO MUCH	1(3)	09 FEB 57	RCA
ALL SHOOK UP (Took just 3 weeks to hit No. 1)	1(8)	13 APR 57	RCA
TEDDY BEAR (From film 'Loving You')	1(7)	08 JUL 57	RCA
JAILHOUSE ROCK (From the film)	1(7)	21 OCT 57	RCA
DON'T/I BEG OF YOU	1(5)	10 FEB 58	RCA
WEAR MY RING AROUND YOUR NECK	2	28 APR 58	RCA
(Entered at No. 7 – the record at the time)			
HARD HEADED WOMAN (From film 'King Creole')	1(2)	21 JUL 58	RCA
I GOT STUNG	8	23 NOV 58	RCA
ONE NIGHT	4	28 DEC 58	RCA
I NEED YOUR LOVE TONIGHT	4	19 APR 59	RCA
A FOOL SUCH AS I	2	26 APR 59	RCA
BIG HUNK O' LOVE	1(2)	10 AUG 59	RCA
STUCK ON YOU	1(4)	16 MAY 60	RCA
IT'S NOW OR NEVER (Based on 'O Sole Mio')	1(5)	15 AUG 60	RCA
ARE YOU LONESOME TONIGHT?	1(6)	28 NOV 60	RCA
SURRENDER (based on 'Come Back To Sorrento')	1(2)	20 MAR 61	RCA
I FEEL SO BAD (Chuck Willis 54 R&B hit)	5	05 JUN 61	RCA
(MARIE'S THE NAME) HIS LATEST FLAME	4	18 SEP 61	RCA
LITTLE SISTER	5	02 OCT 61	RCA
CAN'T HELP FALLING IN LOVE	2	03 FEB 62	RCA
GOOD LUCK CHARM	1(2)	21 APR 62	RCA
SHE'S NOT YOU	5	08 SEP 62	RCA
RETURN TO SENDER	2	17 NOV 62	RCA
(from the film 'Girls! Girls! Girls!')			
(YOU'RE THE) DEVIL IN DISGUISE	3	10 AUG 63	RCA
BOSSA NOVA BABY (UK No. 12)	8	16 NOV 63	RCA
(UK No. 12 – from the film 'Fun In Acapulco')			
CRYING IN THE CHAPEL	3	12 JUN 65	RCA
IN THE GHETTO	3	14 JUN 69	RCA
SUSPICIOUS MINDS	1(1)	01 NOV 69	RCA
(Backing vocalists include Ronnie Milsap)			
DON'T CRY DADDY	6	31 JAN 70	RCA
THE WONDER OF YOU/MAMA LIKED THE ROSES	3	27 JUN 70	RCA
(Ray Peterson 59 US hit)			
BURNING LOVE (Original by Arthur Alexander)	2	28 OCT 72	RCA

BILLY PRESTON

Texan singer/organist has worked with acts like The Beatles (co-billed on 'Get Back'), Little Richard, Rolling Stones, Sam Cooke, Sly & The Family Stone and Ray Charles. His biggest UK solo hit was 'That's The Way God Planned It' (UK 11/US 62). He was also on Derby, Vee Jay, Capitol, MGM, Apple and ERC (UK).

	WITH YOU I'M BORN AGAIN (and SYREETA)	2	19 JAN 80	MOTOWN
	OUTA-SPACE (UK No. 72 – Grammy winner)	2	08 JUL 72	A&M
	WILL IT GO ROUND IN CIRCLES	1(2)	07 JUL 73	A&M
	SPACE RACE	4	24 NOV 73	A&M
	NOTHING FROM NOTHING	1(1)	19 OCT 74	A&M
	WITH YOU I'M BORN AGAIN	4	19 APR 80	MOTOWN

Also see The Beatles

JOHNNY PRESTON

Born Johnny Courville in Texas he was in The Shades, was helped by the Big Bopper (J.P. Richardson), and had three US & UK Top 20s – the other being the Shirley & Lee's song 'Feel So Fine' (US 14/UK 18). He was later on Imperial, TCF Hall, ABC and Hallway.

	RUNNING BEAR (Written by Big Bopper)	1(1)	18 MAR 60	MERCURY
	(He re-recorded it as 'Running Bear 65')			
	CRADLE OF LOVE	2	27 MAY 60	MERCURY
	RUNNING BEAR	1(3)	18 JAN 60	MERCURY
	(Backing vocalists were George Jones & Big Bopper)			
	CRADLE OF LOVE	7	02 MAY 60	MERCURY

PRETENDERS

Ohio singer/songwriter Chrissie Hynde played in many groups and wrote for the UK pop paper New Musical Express before forming this group in London in 78. Their debut LP entered in the UK at No. 1 and despite many personnel problems and changes they have had eight UK (4 US) Top 20s and five UK (3 US) Top 20 LPs. Act played Live Aid and the Nelson Mandela concert. She also sang on UB40's UK No. 1 'I Got You Babe'.

	BRASS IN POCKETT (US No. 14)	1(2)	19 JAN 80	REAL
	TALK OF THE TOWN	8	19 APR 80	REAL
	I GO TO SLEEP (Ray Davies [Kinks] song)	7	05 DEC 81	REAL
	DON'T GET ME WRONG	10	01 NOV 86	REAL
	HYMN TO HER	8	17 JAN 87	REAL
	BACK ON THE CHAIN GANG (UK No. 17)	5	19 MAR 83	SIRE
	DON'T GET ME WRONG	10	27 DEC 86	SIRE

PRETTY POISON

New Jersey dance music quintet includes singer Jade Starling and Whey Cooler. They first hit in 84 (black music) with 'Nightime' which, when re-mixed, was the follow up to their big pop hit.

	CATCH ME I'M FALLING (from film 'Hiding Out')	8	19 DEC 87	VIRGIN

PRETTY THINGS

The group with the longest hair in the early 60s included singer Phil May and Dick Taylor. After seven UK-only hits they joined EMI in 67, Columbia in 68, Harvest in 70, Warner in 72 and Swansong in 74. In the 70s they had two small US LP hits and two of their old songs were recorded by Bowie. In 76 Phil, the only original left, quit.

	DON'T BRING ME DOWN	10	21 NOV 64	FONTANA

ALAN PRICE

Keyboard playing singer formed the Jarrow (UK) based Alan Price Combo in 58 that grew into the successful Animals, which he left in 65. After five UK only solo Top 20s he teamed with Georgie Fame briefly for a TV series and records. He was also on Deram in 69, Polydor in 75, Jet in 78, Safari in 84, Trojan in 86 and Ariola in 88 and has had film success as a score writer and actor.

🇬🇧	I PUT A SPELL ON YOU (US No. 80 – Originally by Screaming Jay Hawkins)	9	23 APR 66	DECCA
	SIMON SMITH & HIS AMAZING DANCING BEAR (Composed by Randy Newman)	4	01 APR 67	DECCA
	THE HOUSE THAT JACK BUILT (First three hits as the Alan Price Set)	4	02 SEP 67	DECCA
	JARROW SONG (He re-recorded it on Mooncrest in 86)	6	22 JUN 74	WARNER

Also see The Animals

MAXI PRIEST

London reggae singer of Jamaican parentage has had eight UK hits including another Top 20 with a revival of The Persuaders song 'Some Guys Have All The Luck' (12). His biggest hit was produced by Sly & Robbie in Jamaica. He joined Charisma in 90.

🇬🇧	WILD WORLD (US No. 25 – Cat Stevens 71 US hit)	5	25 JUN 88	10

PRIMITIVES

Coventry based (UK) mixed group fronted by Australian Tracy Tracy. They started recording on their own Lazy label in 86 and after a couple of indie hits they signed the label to RCA and have since had five UK-only chart 45s and a Top 10 LP 'Lovely'.

🇬🇧	CRASH	5	19 MAR 88	LAZY

PRINCE

One of the top acts of all time was born Prince Rogers Nelson in Minneapolis. This multi talented singer/songwriter/musician/actor/producer and performer was in Grand Central (who became Champagne) in 72 and recorded with 94 East before his first solo release in 78. He has won countless awards and notched up 17 US (13 UK) Top 20 singles and seven US (4 UK) Top 10 LPs. His LP 'Purple Rain' was No. 1 in the US for a record 24 weeks, sold 1.3 million in its first day and a total of over 9 million in the US alone. The controversial artist packs stadiums world-wide, has written and produced many big hits for other acts (often under pseudonyms) and owns his own successful label and studio.

🇬🇧	WHEN DOVES CRY	4	28 JUL 84	WARNER
	PURPLE RAIN	8	06 OCT 84	WARNER
	1999/LITTLE RED CORVETTE (A-side US No. 12) (A-side was UK No. 25 in 83,'B-side UK No.34 in 83)	2	26 JAN 85	WARNER
	LET'S GO CRAZY/TAKE ME WITH YOU	7	09 MAR 85	WARNER
	KISS (All above as Prince & The Revolution)	6	22 MAR 86	PAISLEY
	SIGN O' THE TIMES	10	28 MAR 87	PAISLEY
	ALPHABET STREET	9	14 MAY 88	PAISLEY
	BATDANCE (Entered at No. 3)	2	01 JUL 89	WARNER
🇺🇸	LITTLE RED CORVETTE	6	21 MAY 83	WARNER
	DELIRIOUS	8	26 NOV 83	WARNER
	WHEN DOVES CRY (Top US Pop & Black single of 84)	1(5)	07 JUL 84	WARNER
	LET'S GO CRAZY (In Top 10 same week as 'Let's Go Crazy')	1(2)	29 SEP 84	WARNER
	PURPLE RAIN	2	17 NOV 84	WARNER
	I WOULD DIE 4 U (UK No. 58) (Above four from film 'Purple Rain')	8	02 FEB 85	WARNER
	RASPBERRY BERET (UK No. 25)	2	20 JUL 85	PAISLEY
	POP LIFE (UK No. 60) (In 85 had record 10 nominations in US music awards)	7	21 SEP 85	PAISLEY
	KISS (Last six as Prince & The Revolution) (His third to Top US pop, black and dance charts)	1(2)	19 APR 86	PAISLEY
	SIGN O' THE TIMES	3	25 APR 87	PAISLEY
	U GOT THE LOOK (UK No. 11 – other vocalist SHEENA EASTON)	2	17 OCT 87	PAISLEY

	I COULD NEVER TAKE THE PLACE OF YOU (UK No. 29)	10	06 FEB 88	PAISLEY
	ALPHABET STREET	8	25 JUN 88	PAISLEY
	BATDANCE (From the film 'Batman')	1(1)	05 AUG 89	WARNER

PRINCESS

Ex London shop assistant Desiree Heslop sang on sessions for acts like Mai Tai and Osibisa before scoring four UK-only Top 40s. She was on Polydor in 87 and Touch Tone in 89.

🇬🇧	SAY I'M YOUR NO. 1	7	31 AUG 85	SUPREME

P.J. PROBY

Before becoming a 60s star in the UK the Texan singer, who was born James Smith, recorded as Jett Powers and Orville Wood and sang in The Moondogs. Sporting an 18th century image complete with pony tail, he scored 11 UK-only Top 40s between 64-68 and made headlines when his trousers split on stage. He was later on Columbia, Ember, Seven Sun, Rooster, and Savoy in 85 but successive comeback attempts have failed.

🇬🇧	HOLD ME (US No. 70 – Art Hickman 20 hit)	3	11 JUL 64	DECCA
	TOGETHER (Paul Whiteman 28 hit)	8	10 OCT 64	DECCA
	SOMEWHERE (US No. 91)	6	16 JAN 65	LIBERTY
	MARIA (Above two from West Side Story)	8	18 DEC 65	LIBERTY

PROCLAIMERS

Unmistakably Scottish folk/pop duo Charlie and Craig Reid have so far notched up two UK-only Top 20s – the other being 'I'm Gonna Be' (11) in 88. Their 'Sunshine on Leith' LP was also a small US hit.

🇬🇧	LETTER FROM AMERICA (Prod. Gerry Rafferty)	3	05 DEC 87	CHRYSALIS

PROCOL HARUM

Gary Booker, Matthew Fisher and Robin Trower were members of this Southend (UK) based classical rock band who evolved from The Paramounts in 66. Over the next decade they had many chart singles and LPs, the biggest being their six million selling debut single with its surreal lyrics based around a classical chord progression. Matthew left in 69, Robin started his solo career in 71 and when the group split in 77 Gary also recorded solo.

🇬🇧	A WHITER SHADE OF PALE (Based on Bachs Suite No. 3 in D Major)	1(6)	10 JUN 67	DERAM
	HOMBURG (US No. 34)	6	21 OCT 67	REGAL ZONO.
🇺🇸	A WHITER SHADE OF PALE	5	29 JUL 67	DERAM

PSEUDO ECHO

One of Australia's top groups of the 80s first charted in the US with 'Living In A Dream' in 87. The rock quartet fronted by Bruce Canham followed their sole transatlantic charter with 'Listening' (a track they had first released in 84 in their homeland).

🇬🇧	FUNKY TOWN (Lipps Inc 80 hit)	8	29 JUL 87	RCA
🇺🇸	FUNKY TOWN	6	18 JUL 87	RCA

P.I.L. (PUBLIC IMAGE LTD.)

Group formed by Johnny (Rotten) Lydon after the demise of The Sex Pistols. The influential anti-rock'n'roll act, who originally called themselves The Carnivorous Buttock Flies, have had their share of controversy and UK hits with four Top 20 singles and three Top 20 LPs. In the US the group have a big cult following.

🇬🇧	PUBLIC IMAGE	9	04 NOV 78	VIRGIN
	THIS IS NOT A LOVE SONG	5	08 OCT 83	VIRGIN

Also see Sex Pistols

GARY PUCKETT & THE UNION GAP

Pop quintet from San Diego who wore Civil War uniforms and were called The Outcasts before naming themselves after the Washington town. In 68 they were the top group in the US and the top US group in the UK. Before splitting in 71 they scored six US (2 UK) Top 20s. Gary and fellow member Kerry Chater later recorded solo. Chater also wrote songs for Bobby Darin, Cass Elliot and Charlie Rich.

🇬🇧	YOUNG GIRL	1(4)	25 MAY 68	CBS
	LADY WILLPOWER	5	12 OCT 68	CBS
	YOUNG GIRL (Re-entry)	6	20 JUL 74	CBS
🇺🇸	WOMAN, WOMAN (Original by Jimmy Payne)	4	13 JAN 68	COLUMBIA
	YOUNG GIRL	2	06 APR 68	COLUMBIA
	LADY WILLPOWER	2	20 JUL 68	COLUMBIA
	OVER YOU	7	26 OCT 68	COLUMBIA
	THIS GIRL IS A WOMAN NOW	9	11 OCT 69	COLUMBIA

PURE PRAIRIE LEAGUE

Cincinnati country rock band with an ever changing personnel were on RCA from 71 and over the next decade scored four US-only Top 40 LPs and singles. Drummer Billy Hinds was the longest serving member and one-time singer Vince Gill is now a country star.

🇺🇸	LET ME LOVE YOU TONIGHT	10	12 JUL 80	CASABLANCA

JAMES & BOBBY PURIFY

Cousins James Purify and Bobby Dickey from Florida (ex members of The Sextets) had four US Top 40s. Bobby was replaced by Ben Moore in 74 when they joined Casablanca. They cut their big hit twice with different producers – the first version was never released.

🇺🇸	I'M YOUR PUPPET (Original by Dan Penn) (UK No. 12 in 76 a decade after the US hit)	6	26 NOV 66	BELL

BILL PURSELL

Californian pianist and music teacher in Nashville had a one-off US hit with an instrumental arranged by Bill Justis (of 'Raunchy' fame). Follow up was 'Loved'. He re-appeared on Alston in 77.

🇺🇸	OUR WINTER LOVE (Orig. released in Canada as 'Long Island Sound')	9	30 MAR 63	COLUMBIA

PUSSYCAT

Mixed Dutch septet's European smash was the first of two UK-only Top 40s – the other being the follow up 'Smile' (24). They also topped the Dutch chart with 'My Broken Souvenirs' and later had releases on Logo in 80 and EMI in 81.

🇬🇧	MISSISSIPPI	1(4)	16 OCT 76	SONET

PYTHON LEE JACKSON

Australian rock group led by David Bentley hired little known Rod Stewart to do guide vocals on this track in 70. They kept his rough vocal on and it became a transatlantic charter in 72.

🇬🇧	IN A BROKEN DREAM (US No. 56)	3	28 OCT 72	YOUNGBLOOD

Q

STACEY Q

L.A. dance music singer was born Stacey Swain. She had two US-only Top 40s – the other being the follow up 'We Connect'.

🇺🇸	TWO OF HEARTS	3	11 OCT 86	ATLANTIC

QUANTUM JUMP

UK quartet, who featured vocalist Rupert Hine and his co-writers John Parry & Trevor Morais, recorded on Decca in 77. They followed their sole UK hit with 'No American Starship'.

🇬🇧	THE LONE RANGER	5	30 JUN 79	ELECTRIC

QUARTERFLASH

Husband and wife Marv and Rindy Ross previously recorded their biggest hit as members of the Portland (US) based Seafood Mama in 80. They joined with members of Pilot (not the UK group) to form this sextet, re-recorded it and it became the first of their three US-only Top 40s. The eponymous LP also hit the US Top 10.

🇺🇸	HARDEN MY HEART (UK No. 49)	3	13 FEB 82	GEFFEN

SUZI QUATRO

Pioneer female rocker from Detroit started in Suzi Soul & The Pleasure Seekers (later called Cradle) in 65. She moved to the UK in 72 and her second release was the first of her 11 UK Top 40s. Her pop/hard rock was much less successful in her homeland. She was later on RSO, Dreamland, Polydor, PRT and First Night. She is now a UK TV personality and in 89 toured Russia and joined WEA. In recent years she has appeared in the UK TV fifties sit-com Happy Days, and in the UK series Minder.

🇬🇧	CAN THE CAN (US No. 56)	1(1)	16 JUN 73	RAK
	48 CRASH	3	18 AUG 73	RAK
	DEVIL GATE DRIVE (US cover by Tommy James) (Writers Chinn & Chapman's second No.1 in a row)	1(2)	23 FEB 74	RAK
	THE WILD ONE	7	30 NOV 74	RAK
	IF YOU CAN'T GIVE ME LOVE (US No. 45)	4	15 APR 78	RAK
🇬🇧	STUMBLIN' IN (And CHRIS NORMAN) (UK No. 41)	4	12 MAY 79	RSO

QUEEN

One of the most popular acts of the rock era. Led by Freddie Mercury (who had recorded as Larry Lurex) and including Brian May (who had recorded in The Others and Smile) their first 45 missed but they have since had 26 UK (9 US) Top 20 singles and 15 UK (5 US) Top 10 LPs. This multi-award winning pomp rock band with their unmistakable harmonies have the UK's top selling 'Hits' LP by a UK act (1.9 million) and have smashed attendance records around the world. Freddie has also had much solo success.

🇬🇧	SEVEN SEAS OF RHYE	10	13 APR 74	EMI
	KILLER QUEEN (US No. 12)	2	16 NOV 74	EMI
	BOHEMIAN RHAPSODY (UK gold) (Joint longest running No. 1 in UK in rock era)	1(9)	29 NOV 75	EMI
	YOU'RE MY BEST FRIEND (US No. 16)	7	17 JUL 76	EMI
	SOMEBODY TO LOVE (US No.13 – entered at No. 4)	2	11 DEC 76	EMI
	WE ARE THE CHAMPIONS	2	03 DEC 77	EMI
	DON'T STOP ME NOW (US No. 86)	9	31 MAR 79	EMI
	CRAZY LITTLE THING CALLED LOVE	2	24 NOV 79	EMI
	ANOTHER ONE BITES THE DUST	7	27 SEP 80	EMI
	FLASH (US No. 42 – from the film)	10	10 JAN 81	EMI
	UNDER PRESSURE (And DAVID BOWIE) (US No. 29 – entered at No. 8)	1(2)	21 NOV 81	EMI
	RADIO GA GA (US No. 16) (Entered at No. 4 – was top in 17 countries)	2	11 FEB 84	EMI
	I WANT TO BREAK FREE (US No. 45 – First No. 1 on UK video Jukebox chart)	3	28 APR 84	EMI
	IT'S A HARD LIFE (US No. 72)	6	04 AUG 84	EMI
	ONE VISION (US No. 61 – entered at No. 9)	7	23 NOV 85	EMI
	A KIND OF MAGIC (US No. 42)	3	26 APR 86	EMI
	I WANT IT ALL (US No. 50 – entered at No. 3)	3	13 MAY 89	PARLOPHONE
	BREAKTHRU'	7	08 JUL 89	PARLOPHONE
🇺🇸	BOHEMIAN RHAPSODY (180 vocal overdubs in places!)	9	24 APR 76	ELEKTRA
	WE ARE THE CHAMPIONS	4	04 FEB 78	ELEKTRA
	CRAZY LITTLE THING CALLED LOVE	1(4)	23 FEB 80	ELEKTRA
	ANOTHER ONE BITES THE DUST	1(3)	04 OCT 80	ELEKTRA

Also see Freddie Mercury

? (QUESTION MARK) & THE MYSTERIANS

Tex/Mex garage band led by the mysterious Rudy Martinez recorded their No. 1 hit in a front room (the studio (!) of Pa Go Go Records in Texas . They followed their Farfisa organ fronted 60s punk classic with their only other Top 40 'I Need Somebody' (US 22). They were later on Capitol, Tangerine, Chicory and Super K.

🇺🇸	96 TEARS (UK No. 37) (First called 'Too Many Teardrops' then '69 Tears')	1(1)	29 OCT 66	CAMEO

QUIET RIOT

L.A. heavy rock foursome fronted by Kevin Dubrow were formed in 75 and included the late Randy Rhoads (later with Ozzy Osbourne). They had two LPs out in Japan but broke up in the late 70s. Kevin reformed them in 83 and for a year they were a top selling act and their LP 'Metal Health' sold over four million in the US.

🇺🇸	CUM ON FEEL THE NOIZE (B-side of UK No. 45 – Slade 73 hit)	5	19 NOV 83	PASHA

R

EDDIE RABBITT

New Yorker Eddie Thomas, recorded on 20th Century in 64, moved to Nashville in 68 and in 71 Elvis hit with his song 'Kentucky Rain'. He first charted as a singer in 74 and has since had 35 country Top 20s including 16 No. 1s. Pop-wise he has had eight US-only Top 40s. He was later on Warner, RCA and Universal.

🇺🇸	DRIVIN' MY LIFE AWAY	5	04 OCT 80	ELEKTRA
	I LOVE A RAINY NIGHT (UK No. 53)	1(2)	28 FEB 81	ELEKTRA
	STEP BY STEP	5	17 OCT 81	ELEKTRA
	YOU AND I (And CRYSTAL GAYLE)	7	12 FEB 83	ELEKTRA

RACEY

UK teenybop group fronted by Richard Gower were part of the 70s hit stable of writer/producers Chinn & Chapman. The group who were formed in 74 hit with their second 45 and had four UK-only Top 40s.

🇬🇧	LAY YOUR LOVE ON ME	3	06 JAN 79	RAK
	SOME GIRLS	2	21 APR 79	RAK

GERRY RAFFERTY

Scottish singer was in the Humblebums (with comic Billy Connolly) in the late 60s. He recorded solo on Transatlantic in 71 and led hit group Stealers Wheel from 72-75. He has since had 3 UK (5 US) Top 40s as a soloist and his 'City to City' LP was a US No.1.

🇬🇧	BAKER STREET (A Re-mix was UK No. 53 in 90)	3	01 APR 78	UA
	NIGHT OWL	5	07 JUL 79	UA
🇺🇸	BAKER STREET (Gerry wrote the song in London's Baker Street)	2	24 JUN 78	UA

Also see Stealers Wheel

RAH BAND

Multi instrumentalist/composer/arranger and producer Richard Hewson with his vocalist wife Liz make up this studio band. He has produced or arranged hits for The Beatles, Cliff Richard, James Taylor, Shakin' Stevens, Wings and Mary Hopkin. The band have also been on Ebony, DJM, Sound, TMT, KR, Supreme and Creole.

🇬🇧	THE CRUNCH (Re-recorded it as 'Crunch '85')	6	20 AUG 77	GOOD EARTH
	CLOUDS ACROSS THE MOON	6	27 APR 85	RCA

RAIDERS – SEE PAUL REVERE & THE RAIDERS FOR HIT DETAILS

RAINBOW

Hard rock band evolved from Elf and were led by guitarist Ritchie Blackmore after he left Deep Purple in 75. Other members included Cozy Powell and singer Ronnie James Dio. In 79 Graham Bonnet took over vocals and Roger Glover (ex Deep Purple) joined. Act had many personnel changes and had seven UK (1 US) Top 40s and 10 UK (4 US) Top 40 LPs before Ritchie & Roger re-joined Deep Purple in 84.

 SINCE YOU'VE BEEN GONE (US No. 57)   6   13 OCT 79   POLYDOR
ALL NIGHT LONG   5   15 MAR 80   POLYDOR
I SURRENDER   3   28 FEB 81   POLYDOR
(First and third hit composed by Russ Ballard)

Also see Cozy Powell

RAM JAM

Rock quartet formed by ex Lemon Piper Bill Bartlett included Howie Blauvelt, who had played with Billy Joel. They followed their one-off Transatlantic Top 20, which was produced by Kasenetz-Katz, with 'Keep Your Hands On The Wheel' (released in UK as by The American Ram Jam Band).

 BLACK BETTY (US No. 18 – Old Leadbelly song)   7   29 OCT 77   EPIC
(Returned to UK Top 20 in 90 when remixed)

RAMONES

Top punk rock quartet from New York fronted by Joey Ramone (Jeffrey Hyman) formed in 74 and started recording in 76. This influential act were more popular in the UK scoring four UK-only Top 40s. Their producers included Phil Spector and 10cc's Graham Gouldman. This popular live act joined Beggars Banquet in 85.

 BABY I LOVE YOU   8   23 FEB 80   SIRE
(Produced by Phil Spector – Ronettes 63 hit)

RAMRODS

Connecticut instrumental quartet included girl drummer Claire, brother Richard and featured guitarist Vincent E. Lee (Bell). They hit with her arrangement of Vaughn Monroe's 49 smash complete with cows. The follow up was 'Loch Lomond Rock'. Vinny later made solo records and did sessions.

RIDERS IN THE SKY (US No. 30)   7   10 MAR 61   LONDON
(They later had 'Take Me Back To My Boots & Saddles')

RANDY & THE RAINBOWS

50s styled New York vocal quintet, first called the Dialtones on Goldisc, were fronted by Dom 'Randy' Safuto. In 78 their hit was recorded by Blondie as 'Denis' and they re-did it as 'Debbie' in 82 on Ambient Sound. Their follow up was 'Why Do Kids Grow Up'. They were also on Mike, B.T. Puppy and Crystal Ball.

DENISE (Produced by The Tokens)   10   24 AUG 63   RUST

RARE EARTH

Motown's most successful white act started in Detroit as The Sunliners. Group who included Rob Richards and Gil Bridges first recorded on Verve. Motown re-named a label for them and they had six US-only Top 40 singles and four US-only Top 40 LPs. They moved to Prodigal in 77 and RCA in 82.

GET READY (Temptations 66 hit)   4   13 JUN 70   RARE EARTH
(I KNOW) I'M LOSING YOU (Temptations 66 hit)   7   03 OCT 70   RARE EARTH
I JUST WANT TO CELEBRATE   7   11 SEP 71   RARE EARTH

RASCALS

New York quartet were Felix Cavaliere, Eddie Brigati and Gene Cornish (all ex-Joey Dee & Starlighters) and session drummer Dino Danelli. They had 13 US (2 UK) Top 40s and six US-only Top 20 LPs. Gene and Dino left in 71 to form Bulldog and later Fotomaker. The group disbanded in 72 and re-united (without Eddie) briefly in 88 for a 'Groovin' 88' tour.

GROOVIN' (As The Young Rascals)   8   01 JUL 67   ATLANTIC
GOOD LOVIN' (Olympics 65 US hit)   1   30 APR 66   ATLANTIC
GROOVIN'   1(4) 20 MAY 67   ATLANTIC
A GIRL LIKE YOU (UK No. 37)   10   12 AUG 67   ATLANTIC
HOW CAN I BE SURE   4   21 OCT 67   ATLANTIC
(Above records as The Young Rascals)
A BEAUTIFUL MORNING   3   25 MAY 68   ATLANTIC
PEOPLE GOT TO BE FREE   1(5) 17 AUG 68   ATLANTIC

RASPBERRIES

Cleveland pop rock quartet evolved out of chart band The Choir. They brought in singer/songwriter Eric Carmen who had recorded on Epic as a soloist and in Cyrus Eric and The Quick (also on Mercury). Act had four US-only Top 40s with Eric's songs before he went solo successfully in 75.

GO ALL THE WAY   5   07 OCT 72   CAPITOL

Also see Eric Carmen

RATTLES

Top German rock quartet fronted by Achim Reishel who had played in their home town Hamburg with The Beatles in 62 were the first German group in the UK or US chart. Their follow up was 'You Can't Have Sunshine Everyday'.

THE WITCH   8   07 NOV 70   DECCA
(US No. 79 – a re-recording of their 68 German hit)

LOU RAWLS

Chicago singer was in The Flamingos and Pilgrim Travellers before recording solo in 59 on Herb Alpert's label Shardee. He was on Candix in 60 and Capitol in 61 where he had the first of six US (1 UK) Top 40s in 66. He won Grammys for 'Dead End Street' in 67 and 'A Natural Man' in 71. He also recorded on MGM, Arista, Epic, Gamble & Huff and joined Blue Note in 89.

YOU'LL NEVER FIND ANOTHER LOVE LIKE MINE   10   11 SEP 76   PHILLY INT.
YOU'LL NEVER FIND ANOTHER LOVE LIKE MINE   2   04 SEP 76   PHILLY INT.

RAY, GOODMAN & BROWN

Harry Ray, Al Goodman and Billy Brown who previously had a lot of success as The Moments chalked up a further 10 black music hits when the New Jersey trio left All Platinum and had to change their name. Harry Ray had a brief solo career and re-joined the act who were later on Panoramic and EMI.

SPECIAL LADY   5   19 APR 80   POLYDOR

Also see The Moments

RAYDIO – SEE RAY PARKER JR. FOR HIT DETAILS

CHRIS REA

Middlesbrough singer/songwriter and ex member of Magdelene had his first solo record 'So Much Love' in 74. His first big hit was 'Fool (If You Think It's Over)' (US 12/UK 30) in 78. He was a top European star long before he finally debuted in the UK Top 10 with his 18th chart entry in 89.

THE ROAD TO HELL (PT. 2)   10   04 NOV 89   WEA

READY FOR THE WORLD

Funk sextet from Michigan fronted by Melvin Riley Jr. Their first chart record was 'Tonight' (black music No. 6) which was originally on their own Blue Lake label. They have since had six Top 10 black hits.

OH SHEILA (UK No. 50)	1(1)	12 OCT 85	MCA
LOVE YOU DOWN (UK No. 60)	9	21 FEB 87	MCA

REAL THING

Liverpool soul quartet includes Chris & Eddie Amoo. Their first release was on EMI in 73 and they were UK's top black act of the late 70s with nine UK-only Top 40s. They were on Calibre in 81, EMI in 82 and in 86 re-mixes of three of their 70s hits returned to the UK chart. They have since been on Jive in 87 and RCA in 89. Chris has recorded solo on Precision and EMI.

YOU TO ME ARE EVERYTHING (US No. 74)	1(3)	26 JUN 76	PYE INT.
CAN'T GET BY WITHOUT YOU	2	25 SEP 76	PYE
CAN YOU FEEL THE FORCE	5	10 MAR 79	PYE
(Jumped from 60-18 – a remix was UK No. 24 in 86)			
YOU TO ME ARE EVERYTHING (The decade remix)	5	05 APR 86	PRT
CAN'T GET BY WITHOUT YOU	6	14 JUN 86	PRT
(The second decade remix)			

REBEL MC/DOUBLE TROUBLE

Londoner Rebel MC (Mike West) and Double Trouble recorded on B-Ware before getting two UK-only Top 20s together – the first of their rap/reggae fusion hits being 'Just Keep Rockin' (11). They went their separate ways in 90.

STREET TUFF (The top selling UK rap single)	3	28 OCT 89	DESIRE

REBELS

Instrumental group's sole Top 40 hit featured twins Mickey & Jim Kipler. Follow ups including the similar 'Another Wild Weekend' and 'Monday Morning' released by The Rockin' Rebels who were supposedly a different group (possibly The Hot Toddy's of 'Rockin' Crickets' fame).

WILD WEEKEND	8	09 MAR 63	SWAN

REDBONE

Swamp rock foursome formed by American Indians in L.A. in 68 and fronted by ex recording duo Pat (who had also recorded solo on Unity in 62) & Lolly (who had been on Mercury in 65) Vegas. The quartet who had a Dutch No. 1 in 73 with 'We Were All Wounded At Wounded Knee' also recorded on RCA in 77.

WITCH QUEEN OF NEW ORLEANS (US No. 21)	2	23 OCT 71	EPIC
COME AND GET YOUR LOVE	5	20 APR 74	EPIC

RED BOX

Pop singer/songwriting duo Julian Close from Bristol and Simon Toulson Clarke from Yorkshire. They first worked together in 78 and had one indie hit 'Chenko' on Cherry Red before their two UK-only Top 10 hits. They moved to the East West label in 90.

LEAN ON ME (AH-LI-AYO)	3	12 OCT 85	SIRE
FOR AMERICA	10	22 NOV 86	SIRE

OTIS REDDING

Best known 60s soul singer started as a Little Richard sound alike in 59 and then recorded solo and with The Shooters, Pinetoppers and Johnny Jenkins Combo on Finer Arts, Confederate, Alshire, Gerald, Transworld and Bethlehem. His first hit 'These Arms Of Mine' in 63 was a soul milestone and in 65 he had his first Pop Top 40. In 67 he played the Monterey Festival and was voted Top Male Singer in a UK magazine (Elvis had won it since 56). Soon afterwards he died in a plane crash.

(SITTIN' ON) THE DOCK OF THE BAY	3	30 MAR 68	STAX
(Grammy winner he wrote it on a San Francisco house boat)			
(SITTIN' ON) THE DOCK OF THE BAY	1(4)	16 MAR 68	VOL1
(He died three days after recording it)			

HELEN REDDY

Top Australian singer had her own TV series down under before migrating to New York in 66. She recorded on Fontana in 68 and her first of 11 US (1 UK) Top 20s and 7 US (2 UK) Top 20 LPs came in 71. She had her own US TV series, hosted The Midnight Special and starred in the film Pete's Dragon.

ANGIE BABY (Composed Alan O'Day)	5	15 FEB 75	CAPITOL
I AM WOMAN (First Australian to have No. 1)	1(1)	09 DEC 72	CAPITOL
(Her own song became theme for women's liberation)			
DELTA DAWN (Tanya Tucker 72 country hit)	1(1)	15 SEP 73	CAPITOL
LEAVE ME ALONE (RUBY RED DRESS)	3	29 DEC 73	CAPITOL
YOU AND ME AGAINST THE WORLD	9	07 SEP 74	CAPITOL
ANGIE BABY	1(1)	28 DEC 74	CAPITOL
AIN'T NO WAY TO TREAT A LADY	8	11 OCT 75	CAPITOL
(Original by Harriot Schock)			

JERRY REED

Singer/songwriter/actor born Jerry Hubbard in Atlanta. He was on Capitol in 55, NRC in 59 and then Columbia. The first of his 56 country hits (inc. 26 Top 20s) was his 28th single 'Guitar Man' (later a hit for Elvis) in 67. He has been in many films, had his own TV series and returned to Capitol in 85.

WHEN YOU'RE HOT, YOU'RE HOT	9	26 JUN 71	RCA
AMOS MOSES	8	27 FEB 71	RCA

LOU REED

Influential and unpredictable New York singer/songwriter born Lou Firbank first recorded age 14 in The Shades ('So Blue'). He was a founder member of The Velvet Underground and first recorded solo, in the UK, in 72. Oddly, he has had only one transatlantic hit but has a large cult following.

WALK ON THE WILD SIDE (US No. 16)	10	02 JUN 73	RCA
(US No. 16 – Co-Produced by David Bowie)			

JIM REEVES

Velvet voiced Texan is one of country music's best known acts. The ex DJ recorded on Macy's in 50, then Abott and Fabor and had the first of 73 country hits (including 11 No. 1s) in 53. Pop-wise he had four US Top 40s and an amazing 21 in the UK; 14 were after his death in a plane crash in 64. He also had 20 UK Top 20 LPs (including a record eight together in the Top 20 in 64).

WELCOME TO MY WORLD	7	12 JUL 63	RCA
I LOVE YOU BECAUSE	5	18 APR 64	RCA
(Leon Payne 50 country hit)			
I WON'T FORGET YOU (US No. 93)	3	04 SEP 64	RCA
(Above two 45s were No. 1 & 2 Top UK singles of 64)			
THERE'S A HEARTACHE FOLLOWING ME	6	12 DEC 64	RCA
(He was UK's top record act of 64 – beating Beatles)			
IT HURTS SO MUCH	8	27 FEB 65	RCA
DISTANT DRUMS (US No.45 – Top UK record of 66)	1(5)	24 SEP 66	RCA
(First No. 1 comp. solely by a female (Cindy Walker))			
HE'LL HAVE TO GO (UK No. 11)	2	07 MAR 60	RCA

REFLECTIONS

Detroit pop quintet were formed from two doo-wop groups The Del Prados and The Parisians and were led by New Yorker Tony Micale. They started on Kayko and followed their one-off Top 40 with 'Like Columbus Did'. Tony went solo and they later recorded on ABC, Flax, Tigre, Wand and Mad Dog.

 (JUST LIKE) ROMEO & JULIET   6   30 MAY 64   GOLDEN WORLD

REGINA

New York based dance music singer Regina Richards has not managed to chart again since getting her debut transatlantic hit with a Madonna sound-a-like track co-written and co-produced by Steve Bray who often works with Madonna.

 BABY LOVE *(UK No. 50 – sax by David Sanborn)*   10   13 SEP 86   ATLANTIC
(Was on West 78th Street records)

MIKE REID

UK comic/actor had a one-off hit with a Cockney version of the fairy story which he followed with 'The King's New Clothes'. He is now a star of the top TV soap opera EastEnders. He was also on Satril in 78 and Pel in 80.

 THE UGLY DUCKLING   10   19 APR 75   PYE

NEIL REID

Winning TVs Opportunity Knocks helped 11 year old Neil have a Top 40 single and LP (he is the youngest person to top the UK LP chart). His follow up 45 was 'That's What I Want To Be'. He recorded on Philips in 74.

 MOTHER OF MINE   2   15 JAN 72   DECCA

R.E.M.

Georgia quartet led by Michael Stipe were formed in 80. Their first release was 'Radio Free Europe' on Hib-Tone. They joined IRS in 82 and were instant favourites with rock critics and soon became regular transatlantic Top 40 LP chart entrants. They joined Warner for a huge advance in 88 after Rolling Stone magazine had dubbed them 'America's Greatest Rock Band'.

 THE ONE I LOVE *(UK No. 51)*   9   05 DEC 87   IRS
STAND *(UK No. 48)*   6   08 APR 89   WARNER

RENAISSANCE

Eclectic LP orientated UK band, who fused folk/jazz/classics and rock. Act originally and briefly included ex-Yardbirds Keith Relf and Jim McCarty. Annie Haslam fronted the group who were on Island in 69, Capitol in 72, Sire in 74 and IRS in 81. They had eight US (3 UK) LP charters.

 NORTHERN LIGHTS   10   19 AUG 78   WARNER

DIANE RENAY

Pop singer born Renee Diane Kushner in Philadelphia hit with a song written by vocalist Eddie Rambeau and produced by Bob Crewe. Her follow up 'Kiss Me Sailor' (US 29) was her only other Top 40 hit. She was on New Voice in 65.

 NAVY BLUE   6   14 MAR 64   20TH CENTURY

RENEE AND RENATO

Anglo-Italian MOR duo Hilary Lester and Renato Pagliari followed their one-off UK Top 40 with 'Just One More Kiss'. He recorded solo on Lifestyle in 83.

 SAVE YOUR LOVE   1(3)   18 DEC 82   HOLLYWOOD

MIKE RENO & ANN WILSON

The lead singers of hit acts Loverboy and Heart had a one-off hit with a track from the film Footloose which was written by Eric Carmen.

 ALMOST PARADISE...LOVE THEME FROM FOOTLOOSE   7   14 JUL 84   COLUMBIA

Also see Loverboy/Heart

REO SPEEDWAGON

Illinois rock quintet were formed in 68 and added singer Kevin Cronin in 72. They first hit with their third LP in 74 and their ninth chart LP 'Hi Infidelity' was a US No.1 for 15 weeks selling seven million. They have had nine US (3 UK) Top 20 singles and were one of the top US acts of the 80s.

 KEEP ON LOVING YOU   7   16 MAY 81   EPIC
 KEEP ON LOVING YOU   1(1)   21 MAR 81   EPIC
TAKE IT ON THE RUN *(UK No. 19)*   5   30 MAY 81   EPIC
KEEP THE FIRE BURNIN'   7   14 AUG 82   EPIC
CAN'T FIGHT THIS FEELING *(UK No. 16)*   1(3)   09 MAR 85   EPIC

REUNION

One of three Top 10 acts that Joey Levine sang lead with (the others being Ohio Express and The 1910 Fruitgum Company). They followed their one-off transatlantic charter with the similarly themed 'Disco Tekin'.

 LIFE IS A ROCK (BUT THE RADIO ROLLED ME)   8   16 NOV 74   RCA
(UK No. 33 – song inc. names of acts & hit titles)

PAUL REVERE & THE RAIDERS

One of the top 60s US acts who oddly never charted in the UK. First called The Downbeats in 59 and fronted by Paul and singer Mark Lindsay. They first charted in 61 on Gardenia and were also on Jerden and Sande before their run of 14 Top 40s. Regulars on TVs Where The Action Is this top teeny bop act, who sported revolutionary war outfits, had many members including Joe Frank and Freddie Weller who both had hits after leaving. Paul and the group were later on 20th Century and Drive and played a lot of 'oldies' shows.

 KICKS *(Their 17th single)*   4   14 MAY 66   COLUMBIA
HUNGRY *(First two co-written by Barry Mann)*   6   30 JUL 66   COLUMBIA
GOOD THING   4   14 JAN 67   COLUMBIA
HIM OR ME – WHAT'S IT GONNA BE   5   10 JUN 67   COLUMBIA
INDIAN RESERVATION (THE LAMENT OF THE CHEROKEE RESERVATION INDIAN) *(As The Raiders – vocal Freddy Weller)*   1(1)   24 JUL 71   COLUMBIA

Also see Mark Lindsay

REVOLUTION – SEE PRINCE FOR HIT DETAILS

REYNOLDS GIRLS

UK female duo Linda and Aisling had a one-off hit with a S.A.W. production and song which they followed with 'Get Real' on Renotone.

 I'D RATHER JACK   8   01 APR 89   PWL

RHYTHM HERITAGE

L.A. instrumental session group included Ray Parker, Tom Scott and well known producer Jay Graydon and was put together by other top producers Steve Barri and Michael Omartian. They had a second US-only Top 20 with 'Barretta's Theme'.

THEME FROM S.W.A.T. (From the TV series)	1(1)	28 FEB 76	ABC
(Composed by Barry DeVorzon)			

CHARLIE RICH

'The Silver Fox' was born in Arkansas and was in jazz act The Velvetones before recording on Sun in 58. He charted on Philips in 60 and Smash in 65 and in the 70s had 6 US (3 UK) Top 40s. This singer/songwriter was a top country act in the 70s and has scored 45 country hits including nine No 1s. He also recorded on Groove, RCA, Hi, Mercury, UA and Elektra.

THE MOST BEAUTIFUL GIRL	2	30 MAR 74	CBS
(Originally by Norro Wilson as 'Hey Mister' in 68)			
THE MOST BEAUTIFUL GIRL	1(2)	15 DEC 73	EPIC
(Top Country record of 74)			

CLIFF RICHARD

The UK's most successful all time artist was born Harry Webb in India. He was in The Quintones and Dick Teague Skiffle Group before forming Harry Webb & The Drifters who evolved into his group The Shadows. He has won endless awards and sold over 75 million records around the world. He has had a record 59 UK Top 10s and 29 Top 10 LPs. He was given an OBE by the Queen, made several hit films, had his own TV series and holds the record for Top Of The Pops appearances (over 80). He was voted Best New Singer in 58 and in the 80s was the only act to have nine Top 10 LPs in the UK. In the US, where he is virtually unknown compared to the UK, he has had four Top 20 singles and has yet to make the Top 40 LPs.

MOVE IT	2	24 OCT 58	COLUMBIA
(Was intended to be B-side of 'Schoolboy Crush')			
HIGH CLASS BABY	7	12 DEC 58	COLUMBIA
MEAN STREAK (first three hits with Drifters)	10	22 MAY 59	COLUMBIA
LIVING DOLL (US No. 30 – first million seller)	1(6)	31 JUL 59	COLUMBIA
TRAVELLIN' LIGHT	1(5)	30 OCT 59	COLUMBIA
VOICE IN THE WILDERNESS	2	03 FEB 60	COLUMBIA
(From the film 'Expresso Bongo')			
FALL IN LOVE WITH YOU	2	08 APR 60	COLUMBIA
PLEASE DON'T TEASE	1(4)	22 JUL 60	COLUMBIA
NINE TIMES OUT OF TEN (Entered at No. 7)	2	30 SEP 60	COLUMBIA
I LOVE YOU (Entered at No. 8)	2	13 JAN 61	COLUMBIA
THEME FOR A DREAM	2	17 MAR 61	COLUMBIA
GEE WHIZ IT'S YOU	6	28 APR 61	COLUMBIA
A GIRL LIKE YOU (Entered at No. 10)	4	10 JUN 61	COLUMBIA
WHEN THE GIRL IN YOUR ARMS IS THE GIRL IN YOUR HEART (Entered at No. 4 – not with Shadows)	2	25 OCT 61	COLUMBIA
THE YOUNG ONES (His first Gold record) (Entered at No.1 – above two from film 'The Young Ones')	1(6)	12 JAN 62	COLUMBIA
I'M LOOKING OUT THE WINDOW (Orig. Peggy Lee) (Entered at No. 6 – not with The Shadows)	2	18 MAY 62	COLUMBIA
DO YOU WANNA DANCE (Bobby Freeman 58 US hit)	10	08 JUN 62	COLUMBIA
IT'LL BE ME (Entered at No. 9 – original by Jerry Lee Lewis)	2	21 SEP 62	COLUMBIA
THE NEXT TIME (Entered at No. 10)	1(1)	28 DEC 62	COLUMBIA
BACHELOR BOY (US No. 99)	3	25 JAN 63	COLUMBIA
SUMMER HOLIDAY (Entered at No. 9) (Above three from the film 'Summer Holiday')	1(3)	08 MAR 63	COLUMBIA
LUCKY LIPS (US No.62 – entered at No.10 – Ruth Brown 57 US hit)	4	17 MAY 63	COLUMBIA
IT'S ALL IN THE GAME (US No. 25 – entered at No. 6 – Tommy Edwards 58 hit)	2	20 SEP 63	COLUMBIA
DON'T TALK TO HIM	2	29 NOV 63	COLUMBIA
I'M THE LONELY ONE (US No. 92)	8	22 FEB 64	COLUMBIA
CONSTANTLY (Not with The Shadows)	4	06 JUN 64	COLUMBIA
ON THE BEACH (From film 'Wonderful Life')	7	08 AUG 64	COLUMBIA
THE TWELFTH OF NEVER (Not with The Shadows – Johnny Mathis 57 US hit)	8	31 OCT 64	COLUMBIA
I COULD EASILY FALL	6	02 JAN 65	COLUMBIA
THE MINUTE YOU'RE GONE (Sonny James 63 country hit)	1(1)	17 APR 65	COLUMBIA
WIND ME UP (LET ME GO)	2	25 DEC 65	COLUMBIA
(Above two recorded in Nashville with Billy Sherrill)			
VISIONS (Above three not with The Shadows)	7	20 AUG 66	COLUMBIA
TIME DRAGS BY (From film 'Finders Keepers')	10	05 NOV 66	COLUMBIA
IN THE COUNTRY (From the show 'Cinderella') (All hits above with The Shadows unless stated)	6	21 JAN 67	COLUMBIA
IT'S ALL OVER (Only by Everly Brothers)	9	15 APR 67	COLUMBIA
THE DAY I MET MARIE	10	30 SEP 67	COLUMBIA
ALL MY LOVE	6	30 DEC 67	COLUMBIA
CONGRATULATIONS (US No. 99 – second in Eurovision song contest)	1(2)	13 APR 68	COLUMBIA
BIG SHIP	8	21 JUN 69	COLUMBIA
THROW DOWN A LINE (Released as CLIFF & HANK (B. Marvin of The Shadows)	7	04 OCT 69	COLUMBIA
GOODBYE SAM HELLO SAMANTHA	6	04 JUL 70	COLUMBIA
POWER TO ALL OUR FRIENDS (Eurovision entry)	4	24 MAR 73	EMI
DEVIL WOMAN	9	05 JUN 76	EMI
WE DON'T TALK ANYMORE	1(4)	25 AUG 79	EMI
CARRIE (US No. 34)	4	01 MAR 80	EMI
DREAMING	8	13 SEP 80	EMI
WIRED FOR SOUND (US No. 71)	4	12 SEP 81	EMI
DADDY'S HOME (US No. 23 – Shep & The Limelites 61 US hit)	2	12 DEC 81	EMI
THE ONLY WAY OUT (US No. 64)	10	07 AUG 82	EMI
SHE MEANS NOTHING TO ME (With PHIL EVERLY) (His 50th UK Top 10 entry)	9	19 MAR 83	CAPITOL
TRUE LOVE WAYS (Originally by Buddy Holly) (With L.S.O. – Prod. Richard Hewson of Rah Band)	8	30 APR 83	EMI
PLEASE DON'T FALL IN LOVE	7	17 DEC 83	EMI
LIVING DOLL (with THE YOUNG ONES) (Re-make) (Entered at No. 4 – for Comic Relief charity)	1(3)	29 MAR 86	WEA
ALL I ASK OF YOU (and SARAH BRIGHTMAN)	3	25 OCT 86	POLYDOR
MY PRETTY ONE (Originally by Jackie Rae)	6	11 JUL 87	EMI
SOME PEOPLE	3	26 SEP 87	EMI
MISTLETOE AND WINE (Made his span of UK No. 1s a record 29 years)	1(4)	10 DEC 88	EMI
THE BEST OF ME (Written by Richard Marx) (Entered at No. 2 – originally by David Foster)	2	10 JUN 89	EMI
I JUST DON'T HAVE THE HEART (Prod. S.A.W.) (His 100th solo UK release – entered at No. 10)	3	02 SEP 89	EMI
DEVIL WOMAN (His 66th UK chart entry)	6	25 SEP 76	ROCKET
WE DON'T TALK ANYMORE	7	19 JAN 80	EMI AM.
DREAMING (Co-written by Leo Sayer)	10	22 NOV 80	EMI AM.

LIONEL RICHIE

Alabama singer/songwriter left top act The Commodores in 82 after writing and producing Kenny Rogers No. 1 'Lady' in 80 and dueting with Diana Ross on another No. 1. His three solo LPs have all been transatlantic Top 10 hits and he had 13 successive US Top 10 singles and nine UK Top 20s. He has won many awards for records and videos including a Grammy for the 10 million selling LP 'Can't Slow Down'. He co-wrote and sang the 80s top single 'We Are The World' and only Irving Berlin has written more No. 1s.

ENDLESS LOVE (With DIANA ROSS) (Top black music record of 81)	7	26 SEP 81	MOTOWN
TRULY	6	04 DEC 82	MOTOWN
ALL NIGHT LONG (ALL NIGHT) (He closed the L.A. Olympic games with this song)	2	29 OCT 83	MOTOWN
RUNNING WITH THE NIGHT	9	21 JAN 84	MOTOWN
HELLO (Motown's second biggest seller in UK)	1(6)	24 MAR 84	MOTOWN
SAY YOU, SAY ME (From film 'White Nights')	8	14 DEC 85	MOTOWN
DANCING ON THE CEILING	7	23 AUG 86	MOTOWN
ENDLESS LOVE (With DIANA ROSS) (At this time he produced the No.1 pop, soul and country 45s)	1(9)	15 AUG 81	MOTOWN
TRULY	1(2)	27 NOV 82	MOTOWN
YOU ARE (UK No. 43)	4	26 MAR 83	MOTOWN
MY LOVE (UK No. 70)	5	11 JUN 83	MOTOWN
ALL NIGHT LONG (ALL NIGHT) (Motown's top selling single of all time)	1(4)	12 NOV 83	MOTOWN
RUNNING WITH THE NIGHT	7	04 FEB 84	MOTOWN
HELLO (Backing vocals include Richard Marx)	1(2)	12 MAY 84	MOTOWN
STUCK ON YOU (UK No. 12)	3	25 AUG 84	MOTOWN
PENNY LOVER (UK No. 18)	8	01 DEC 84	MOTOWN
SAY YOU, SAY ME (He is only writer to have No. 1s for eight years in a row)	1(4)	21 DEC 85	MOTOWN
DANCING ON THE CEILING	2	13 SEP 86	MOTOWN
LOVE WILL CONQUER ALL (UK No. 45)	9	29 NOV 86	MOTOWN
BALLERINA GIRL (UK No. 17)	7	21 FEB 87	MOTOWN

Also see The Commodores

JONATHAN RICHMAN & THE MODERN LOVERS

Quirky Boston singer/songwriter formed his first group in 71, joined Warner in 72 and Beserkley in 75. They had two UK-only Top 20s in 77 – the other being 'Roadrunner' (11), which was recorded in 75. The group have had many personnel changes and later recorded on Sire and Rounder.

 EGYPTIAN REGGAE   5   17 DEC 77   BESERKLEY

STAN RIDGWAY

L.A. based Stanard was the leader of electronic rock group Wall Of Voodoo before chalking up his sole chart solo. His follow up was 'Big Heat'.

 CAMOUFLAGE   4   09 AUG 86   IRS

RIGHTEOUS BROTHERS

Blue eyed soul duo Bill Medley and Bobby Hatfield (ex-Variatones) had recorded in The Paramours on Smash and Moonglow, the label they first dueted on in 63. Their debut for Phil Spector's label is a rock classic and was the biggest of their 10 US (5 UK) Top 40s. Bill went solo in 67, they reformed briefly in 74 then Bill again went solo successfully in the 80s.

YOU'VE LOST THAT LOVIN' FEELIN' *(In UK Top 200 for over 100 weeks – a record)*	1(2)	06 FEB 65	LONDON
YOU'VE LOST THAT LOVIN' FEELIN' *(Co-writ. Barry Mann – duo and Bill re-recorded it)*	10	22 MAR 69	LONDON
YOU'VE LOST THAT LOVIN' FEELIN' *(Also B – side of Berlin's No.1 'Take My Breath Away')*	1(2)	06 FEB 65	PHILLES
JUST ONCE IN MY LIFE *(Co-writ. Carole King)*	9	15 MAY 65	PHILLES
UNCHAINED MELODY *(UK No. 14 – Al Hibbler 55 hit)*	4	28 AUG 65	PHILLES
EBB TIDE *(UK No.48 – Frank Chacksfield 53 hit)*	5	08 JAN 66	PHILLES
(YOU'RE MY) SOUL AND INSPIRATION *(UK No. 15 – Co-written by Barry Mann)*	1(3)	09 APR 66	VERVE
ROCK AND ROLL HEAVEN *(Written by Alan O'Day)*	3	20 JUL 74	HAVEN

Also see Bill Medley

JEANNIE C. RILEY

Born Jeannie C. Stephenson in Texas, she started as a demo singing secretary in Nashville. Her first hit shot to the top in the US selling over five million worldwide and winning a Grammy. She later recorded on MGM, Mercury and Warner and had 23 country hits between 68-76.

 HARPER VALLEY P.T.A. *(First recd. Alice Joy)*   1(1)   21 SEP 68   PLANTATION
(UK No. 12 – written by country star Tom T. Hall)

WALDO DE LOS RIOS

Late Argentinian conductor and composer who lived in Spain. He had previous releases on Vault in 69 and UA in 71 and had one transatlantic charter with a Mozart update that had first been a European smash.

 MOZART SYMPHONY No. 40 IN G MINOR *(US No. 67)*   5   01 MAY 71   A&M

RIP CHORDS

L.A. session group included Beach Boy Bruce Johnson and Doris Day's son Terry Melcher (who also charted as Bruce & Terry). Act started on Abco and had five US-only charters. Bruce & Terry were not in the group who toured.

 HEY LITTLE COBRA   4   08 FEB 64   COLUMBIA

MINNIE RIPERTON

Chicago singer with a five octave range recorded as Andrea Davis and in The Gems on Chess before fronting black psychedelic group Rotary Connection on four LPs. She soloed in 70 on Janus, joined Stevie Wonder's Wonderlove, had one smash hit, joined Capitol in 78 and died of cancer in 79 age 31.

 LOVIN' YOU *(Produced by Stevie Wonder)*   2   03 MAY 75   EPIC
LOVIN' YOU   1(1)   05 APR 75   EPIC

RITCHIE FAMILY

Philadelphia disco session group featured a vocal trio including Cassandra Ann Wooten and were formed by producer/arranger Ritchie Rome. They had two US Top 20s – the other being' Brazil' (US 11/UK 41) on 20th Century.

 THE BEST DISCO IN TOWN *(US No. 17)*   10   16 OCT 76   POLYDOR

JOHNNY RIVERS

One of the top acts in the US in the 60s was this New York rocker born Johnny Ramistella. He recorded with The Spades on Suede in 56 and had solos on Dee Dee, Cub, Guyden, Gone, Era, Capitol, Chancellor and Coral before the first of his 13 US Top 20 singles and eight US Top 40 LPs. He launched his own Soul City label in 66 hitting with acts like The Fifth Dimension. Johnny, who failed to chart in the UK, retired in the 80s.

MEMPHIS *(Chuck Berry 63 UK hit)*	2	11 JUL 64	IMPERIAL
MOUNTAIN OF LOVE *(Harold Dorman 60 US hit)*	9	05 DEC 64	IMPERIAL
SEVENTH SON *(Original by Muddy Waters)*	7	03 JUL 65	IMPERIAL
SECRET AGENT MAN *(The US TV theme to UK show called 'Danger Man')*	3	23 APR 66	IMPERIAL
POOR SIDE OF TOWN	1(1)	12 NOV 66	IMPERIAL
BABY I NEED YOUR LOVIN' *(Four Tops 64 hit)*	3	11 MAR 67	IMPERIAL
THE TRACKS OF MY TEARS *(Miracles 69 hit – written by Smokey Robinson)*	10	08 JUL 67	IMPERIAL
ROCKIN' PNEUMONIA & THE BOOGIE WOOGIE FLU *(Huey 'Piano' Smith 57 US hit)*	6	20 JAN 73	UA
SWAYIN' TO THE MUSIC (SLOW DANCIN') *(Original by Jack Tempchin & The Funky Kings)*	10	22 OCT 77	BIG TREE

RIVIERAS

Six man Indiana pop group fronted by Bill Dobslaw had a one-off US Top 40 with an old Joe Jones song. Their follow up was 'Little Donna'.

 CALIFORNIA SUN   5   29 FEB 64   RIVIERA

ROACHFORD

With help from Terence Trent D'Arby, black pop rocker Andrew Roachford and his four man band got a deal with CBS and his first LP came out in Spring 88. It took almost a year before he really broke through and scored his biggest hit to date and collected a gold disc for his debut LP.

 CUDDLY TOY *(US No. 25 – was UK No. 61 in 88)*   4   04 FEB 89   CBS

KATE ROBBINS

Singer/comedian/impressionist and second cousin of Paul McCartney was in Prima Donna (UK's Eurovision song contest act) in 80. She followed her one- off hit with 'I Want You Back'. She was on Bright in 84 and is regularly seen on UK TV where she and her brother have had their own series.

 MORE THAN IN LOVE   2   13 JUN 81   RCA
(Featured in UK TV soap opera 'Crossroads')

MARTY ROBBINS

Legendary country singer/songwriter was born Marty Robinson in Arizona. He first charted with his third release in 52 and has since had 89 country hits including 62 Top 20s. Pop-wise the master of Tex-Mex music had 13 US (3 UK) Top 40s. A member of the Country Hall of Fame, he died in 82.

🇬🇧	DEVIL WOMAN (US No. 16)	6	30 NOV 62	CBS
🇺🇸	A WHITE SPORTS COAT (AND A PINK CARNATION)	2	03 JUN 57	COLUMBIA
	EL PASO (UK No. 19)	1(2)	04 JAN 60	COLUMBIA
	(In 76 he had a country No. 1 with 'El Paso City')			
	DON'T WORRY (First hit to use a fuzz guitar)	3	20 MAR 61	COLUMBIA

AUSTIN ROBERTS

Virginian singer who was on Philips in 68 and ABC in 71 had two US-only Top 20s – the other being 'Something's Wrong With Me' No. 11 in 72 on Chelsea. He also recorded on Arista in 78.

🇺🇸	ROCKY (UK No. 22)	9	11 OCT 75	PRIVATE STOCK

MALCOLM ROBERTS

Big voiced UK MOR singer first charted on RCA in 67 and had two UK-only Top 20s – the other being 'Love Is All' No. 12 in 69. He later recorded on Columbia in 71, EMI in 73, UA in 77, Cheapskate in 81 and Dakota in 83.

🇬🇧	MAY I HAVE THE NEXT DREAM WITH YOU	8	07 DEC 68	MAJOR MINOR

B.A. ROBERTSON

Scottish singer/songwriter who had four solo UK-only Top 20s in less than a year and a Top 20 duet with Maggie Bell – 'Hold Me' (11) in 81 on Swansong. He also recorded for Epic and After Hours in 83 and BBC in 86 and co-wrote the big 89 transatlantic hit 'The Living Years' by Mike + The Mechanics.

🇬🇧	BANG BANG	2	08 SEP 79	ASYLUM
	KNOCKED IT OFF	8	24 NOV 79	ASYLUM
	TO BE OR NOT TO BE	9	05 JUL 80	ASYLUM

SMOKEY ROBINSON

'The greatest living poet in America' Bob Dylan called this very successful Detroit singer/songwriter who left left top group The Miracles in 72 (after 17 years) to go solo. He is an executive of Motown records, composer of dozens of hits, a member of the 'R'n'R Hall of Fame' and has scored 38 black music hits and eight US (2 UK) Pop Top 40s.

🇬🇧	BEING WITH YOU	1(2)	13 JUN 81	MOTOWN
🇺🇸	CRUISIN'	4	02 FEB 80	TAMLA
	BEING WITH YOU	2	23 MAY 81	TAMLA
	JUST TO SEE HER (UK No. 52)	8	03 JUL 87	TAMLA
	(UK No. 52 – Grammy winner top male R&B record)			
	ONE HEARTBEAT	10	03 OCT 87	TAMLA

Also see The Miracles

TOM ROBINSON

Cambridge (UK) born rocker was in folky group Cafe Society on The Kinks' Konk label in 75 and formed the Tom Robinson Band in 77. In 79 he set up Sector 27 and he recorded solo from 82. He had five UK-only Top 40s and is probably best known for the gay anthem 'Glad To Be Gay'. He has also been on Deviant, Statik, IDS, Castaway and was on RCA in 87.

🇬🇧	2-4-6-8 MOTORWAY	5	12 DEC 77	EMI
	(As Tom Robinson Band)			
	WAR BABY	6	09 JUL 83	PANIC

VICKI SUE ROBINSON

Disco diva from Philadelphia was in the Broadway productions of Jesus Christ Superstar and Hair. She followed her sole Top 40 with 'Daylight'.

🇺🇸	TURN THE BEAT AROUND	10	14 AUG 76	RCA

ROCK FOLLIES

Group of singing actresses including Julie Covington and Rula Lenska were formed for a TV series about a rock group. They had a one-off chart 45 and their eponymous LP topped the UK chart. Julie later had a solo No. 1 single.

🇬🇧	O.K.	10	04 JUN 77	POLYDOR

Also see Julie Covington

ROCKER'S REVENGE

New York dance music group put together by top producer Arthur Baker and featuring singer Donnie Calvin. They had two UK-only Top 40s, the other being Jimmy Cliff's song 'The Harder They Come' (30). They were on Rar in 88.

🇬🇧	WALKING ON SUNSHINE (Orig. by Eddy Grant)	4	18 SEP 82	LONDON

ROCKIN' BERRIES

Birmingham (UK) pop quintet featured singer Geoff Turton and the comic activities of Clive Lea. They started on Decca in 63 and strung together seven UK-only charters (often with cover versions). They later went into cabaret and also recorded on Epic (as The Berries), Satril and DJM.

🇬🇧	HE'S IN TOWN	3	21 NOV 64	PICCADILLY
	(Tokens 64 US hit – co-written by Carole King)			
	POOR MAN'S SON (Reflections 65 US hit)	5	05 JUN 65	PICCADILLY

ROCKSTEADY CREW

New York singing/break-dancing quintet included Crazy Legs, Baby Love and Prince Ken Swift. They performed in a Malcolm McLaren video and the film Flash Dance. They followed their one-off UK Top 40 hit with 'Uprock'.

🇬🇧	(HEY YOU) THE ROCKSTEADY CREW	6	22 OCT 83	VIRGIN

ROCKWELL

Born Kennedy Gordy in Detroit, he is the son of Motown owner Berry, and first sang in the high school band Essence. He followed his sole transatlantic Top 10 with 'Obscene Phone Caller'.

🇬🇧	SOMEBODY'S WATCHING ME	6	03 MAR 84	MOTOWN
	(Backing vocals by Michael Jackson)			
🇺🇸	SOMEBODY'S WATCHING ME	2	24 MAR 84	MOTOWN

CLODAGH RODGERS

London based Northern Ireland born singer debuted with Michael Holliday in 57. She first recorded as Cloda Rodgers for Decca in 62 and was on Columbia in 65. Her ninth single was the first of five UK-only Top 40s at the end of the 60s. She later recorded on Polydor in 76 and Precision in 80.

🇬🇧	COME BACK AND SHAKE ME	3	10 MAY 69	RCA
	GOODNIGHT MIDNIGHT	4	09 AUG 69	RCA
	JACK IN THE BOX (Eurovision song)	4	10 APR 71	RCA

JIMMIE RODGERS

Washington born pop/folk singer was one of the top MOR acts of the late 50s. He was a winner on Arthur Godfrey's Talent Scout TV show and later notched up 14 US (5 UK) Top 40s. He later recorded on Dot, A&M, Epic and Scrimshaw (where he had some country success in the late 70s).

KISSES SWEETER THAN WINE (Weavers 51 hit)	7	17 JAN 58	COLUMBIA
ENGLISH COUNTRY GARDEN	8	13 JUL 62	COLUMBIA
(Trad. folk song was the B-side in US) US			
HONEYCOMB (UK No.30 – banned on UK radio)	1(2)	23 SEP 57	ROULETTE
KISSES SWEETER THAN WINE	8	22 DEC 57	ROULETTE
SECRETLY (He re-recorded it in 78)	3	23 JUN 58	ROULETTE
ARE YOU REALLY MINE	10	01 SEP 58	ROULETTE

RODS (EDDIE & THE HOT RODS)

Southend (UK) punk styled rock band Eddie & The Hot Rods featured vocalist Barrie Masters and scored five UK-only charters in the late 70s. Barrie left to join The Inmates and in the 80s bassist Paul Gray (who had also been in The Damned) formed a new group with the same name on Waterfront.

DO ANYTHING YOU WANNA DO (As THE RODS)	9	24 SEP 77	ISLAND

TOMMY ROE

Atlanta pop/rock singer/songwriter had records with The Satins on Mark IV, Trumpet and Judd. His second 45 on Judd was the Buddy Holly influenced 'Sheila', which he re-recorded and hit with two years later. His 11 US (6 UK) Top 40s spanned 62-71 and he had some country hits in the 80s. He was also on MGM, Monument, Warner, MCA and Mercury.

SHEILA	2	12 OCT 62	HMV
THE FOLK SINGER (US No. 84)	7	26 APR 63	HMV
DIZZY	1(1)	07 JUN 69	STATESIDE
(Co-writ. Freddy Weller (of Paul Revere & Raiders))			
SHEILA	1(2)	01 SEP 62	ABC PAR.
EVERYBODY (UK No.13 – re-recorded it in 76))	3	07 DEC 63	ABC PAR.
SWEET PEA	8	30 JUL 66	ABC PAR.
HOORAY FOR HAZEL	6	05 NOV 66	ABC
DIZZY	1(3)	15 MAR 69	ABC
JAM UP JELLY TIGHT	8	17 JAN 70	ABC

ROGER

Ohio's Roger Troutman is the leader of hit family group Zapp. He has also worked with George Clinton and Sly Stone. He has had two black music No.1s, the first being in 81 with a revival of 'I Heard It Through The Grapevine'.

I WANT TO BE YOUR MAN (UK No. 61)	3	13 FEB 88	REPRISE

JULIE ROGERS

MOR/cabaret singer born Julie Rolls in London sang in Teddy Foster's Band. She had three UK Top 40s and followed her multi million selling hit with 'Hawaiian Wedding Song'. She was later on Ember and Pye.

THE WEDDING (Originally by Anita Bryant)	3	31 OCT 64	MERCURY
THE WEDDING	10	02 JAN 65	MERCURY

KENNY ROGERS (& THE FIRST EDITION)

Top MOR/country/pop singer and actor first recorded in Houston group The Scholars in 55 on Cue and Imperial. He then recorded solo on Carlton, Kenlee and Mercury. He was in The Bobby Doyle Trio, The Lively Ones and The New Christy Minstrels before forming The First Edition whose second single was the first of his 26 US (8 UK) Top 40 singles. This Grammy winner also had 20 Gold LPs and 16 US (5 UK) Top 40 LPs. He joined RCA in 83 (for a record $20 million) where his biggest hits were in country music. He rejoined Reprise in 90.

RUBY, DON'T TAKE YOUR LOVE TO TOWN	2	13 DEC 69	REPRISE
(Six weeks at No. 2 – original by Johnny Darrell)			
SOMETHING'S BURNING	8	04 APR 70	REPRISE
(US No. 11 – Composed Mac Davis)			
LUCILLE	1(1)	18 JUN 77	UA
COWARD OF THE COUNTY	1(2)	16 FEB 80	UA
ISLANDS IN THE STREAM (And DOLLY PARTON)	7	07 JAN 84	RCA
JUST DROPPED IN (TO SEE WHAT CONDITION MY CONDITION WAS IN) (Mickey Newbury song)	5	16 MAR 68	REPRISE
RUBY, DON'T TAKE YOUR LOVE TO TOWN	6	02 AUG 69	REPRISE
LUCILLE (First of 16 Country No. 1s)	5	18 JUN 77	UA
SHE BELIEVES IN ME (UK No. 42)	5	07 JUL 79	UA
YOU DECORATED MY LIFE	7	17 NOV 79	UA
COWARD OF THE COUNTY	3	26 JAN 80	UA
DON'T FALL IN LOVE WITH A DREAMER (And KIM CARNES)	4	24 MAY 80	UA
LADY (UK No. 12 – Prod. & Comp. Lionel Richie)	1(6)	15 NOV 80	LIBERTY
I DON'T NEED YOU	3	15 AUG 81	LIBERTY
WE'VE GOT TONIGHT	6	26 MAR 83	LIBERTY
(And SHEENA EASTON – UK No.28 – Bob Seger 78 US hit)			
ISLANDS IN THE STREAM (And DOLLY PARTON)	1(2)	29 OCT 83	RCA

ROLLING STONES

'The world's greatest rock band' was formed by UK R&B fans and their act in 62 was 100% covers of US songs. Their first UK tour in 63 was only half full as was the first US tour. However Mick Jagger's mid-Atlantic accent, his James Brown styled stage act and the group's anti-establishment image soon made them top stars. Their debut 45 was a Chuck Berry song 'Come On' (it was nearly Bo Diddley's 'Diddley Daddy'). After two years Mick and Keith Richards starting writing and became one of the best and most successful songwriting teams ever. They have now scored an amazing 29 US (25 UK) Top 20 singles and a record 31 US Top 10 LPs and 27 in the UK and collected 33 gold and 15 platinum LPs. Astoundingly in 89 they had 15 of the top 20 grossing shows in the US and their tour took over $100 million.

NOT FADE AWAY (US No. 48 – Orig. by Crickets)	3	28 MAR 64	DECCA
IT'S ALL OVER NOW (US No. 26)	1(1)	18 JUL 64	DECCA
(US No. 26 – Valentinos 64 US hit)			
LITTLE RED ROOSTER	1(1)	05 DEC 64	DECCA
(Not rel. in UK on 45 – original by Howlin' Wolf)			
THE LAST TIME	1(3)	20 MAR 65	DECCA
(Based on Staple Singers 'Maybe The Last Time')			
(I CAN'T GET NO) SATISFACTION	1(2)	11 SEP 65	DECCA
GET OFF OF MY CLOUD	1(3)	06 NOV 65	DECCA
(Jumped from 17-1 – Last of five successive No. 1s)			
19TH NERVOUS BREAKDOWN	2	19 FEB 66	DECCA
PAINT IT BLACK (Entered at No. 5)	1(1)	28 MAY 66	DECCA
HAVE YOU SEEN YOUR MOTHER, BABY, STANDING IN THE SHADOW?	5	15 OCT 66	DECCA
LET'S SPEND THE NIGHT TOGETHER/ RUBY TUESDAY	3	11 FEB 67	DECCA
(A-side US No. 55 (Banned on many stations there))			
WE LOVE YOU/DANDELION	8	09 SEP 67	DECCA
(A-side US No. 50 & B-side US No. 14)			
JUMPING JACK FLASH	1(2)	22 JUN 68	DECCA
HONKY TONK WOMEN (Entered at No. 9)	1(5)	26 JUL 69	DECCA
BROWN SUGAR	2	15 MAY 71	R. STONE
(Song inspired by singer Claudia Linnear)			
TUMBLING DICE	5	13 MAY 72	R. STONE
ANGIE (Inspired by David Bowie's wife)	5	15 SEP 73	R. STONE
IT'S ONLY ROCK 'N ROLL (BUT I LIKE IT)	10	17 AUG 74	R. STONE
(US No. 16)			
FOOL TO CRY	6	05 JUN 76	R. STONE
MISS YOU	3	17 JUN 78	R. STONE
EMOTIONAL RESCUE	9	26 JUL 80	R. STONE
START ME UP	7	12 SEP 81	R. STONE

TIME IS ON MY SIDE *(Not released in UK on 45 – Original by Irma Thomas)*	6	05 DEC 64	LONDON
THE LAST TIME	9	01 MAY 65	LONDON
(I CAN'T GET NO) SATISFACTION	1(4)	10 JUL 65	LONDON
GET OFF OF MY CLOUD	1(2)	06 NOV 65	LONDON
AS TEARS GO BY *(Not released on 45 in UK)*	6	29 JAN 66	LONDON
19TH NERVOUS BREAKDOWN	2	19 MAR 66	LONDON
PAINT IT BLACK	1(2)	11 JUN 66	LONDON
MOTHERS LITTLE HELPER *(Not rel on 45 in UK)*	8	13 AUG 66	LONDON
HAVE YOU SEEN YOUR MOTHER BABY STANDING IN THE SHADOW?	9	29 OCT 66	LONDON
RUBY TUESDAY	1(1)	04 MAR 67	LONDON
JUMPIN' JACK FLASH	3	06 JUL 68	LONDON
HONKY TONK WOMEN *(First hit after Brian Jones death)*	1(4)	23 AUG 69	LONDON
BROWN SUGAR	1(2)	29 MAY 71	R. STONE
TUMBLING DICE	7	27 MAY 72	R. STONE
ANGIE	1(1)	20 OCT 73	R. STONE
FOOL TO CRY	10	05 JUN 76	R. STONE
MISS YOU	1(1)	05 AUG 78	R. STONE
BEAST OF BURDEN	8	11 NOV 78	R. STONE
EMOTIONAL RESCUE	3	06 SEP 80	R. STONE
START ME UP	2	31 OCT 81	R. STONE
UNDERCOVER OF THE NIGHT *(UK No. 11 where the video was banned)*	9	24 DEC 83	R. STONE
HARLEM SHUFFLE *(UK No. 13 – Bob & Earl 63 hit)*	5	03 MAY 86	R. STONE
MIXED EMOTIONS *(UK No. 36)*	5	14 OCT 89	COLUMBIA

Also see Mick Jagger

ROMANTICS

Wally Palmar was the leader of this Detroit rock foursome. They were formed in 77, first recorded in 79 and have four US-only charters. They are remembered as the first rock band to appear on US TV's Soul Train.

TALKING IN YOUR SLEEP	3	28 JAN 84	NEMPEROR

MAX ROMEO

Kingston (Jamaica) based reggae singer had several hits there in his teens including 'Blowin' in The Wind'. He had a one-off UK hit with a UK recording which was banned by the BBC. He also recorded on Camel, Pama, GG, Bullet, Highnote, Dynamic, Soundtrac, Island, King Kong and Mango.

WET DREAM	10	16 AUG 69	UNITY

RONETTES

Sisters Ronnie and Estelle Bennett and cousin Nedra Talley were initially called The Dolly Sisters and first recorded as Ronnie & The Relatives on May in 61. They joined Phil Spector's label in 63 and had 5 US (3 UK) Top 40s and became the epitome of the 60s girl groups. They won a Grammy, toured with The Beatles and broke up in 66. Ronnie married Phil and recorded on A&M, Apple, Buddah, Tom Cat, Alston, Epic, Polish and joined CBS in 87. She has sung with Bruce Springsteen and on Eddie Money's 86 hit.

BE MY BABY *(Backing vocals include Cher)*	4	08 NOV 63	LONDON
BE MY BABY	2	12 OCT 63	PHILLES

RONNY & THE DAYTONAS

Nashville based hot rod music group were led by singer/songwriter John 'Bucky' Wilkin, the son of top country writer Marijon Wilkin ('One Day At A Time' and 'Waterloo'etc). Act had five US-only hits and he was also in the early Allman Brothers group The Allman Joys and recorded as a soloist.

G.T.O.	4	26 SEP 64	MALA

LINDA RONSTADT

Grammy winning Arizona singer formed pop folk trio The Stone Poneys in 64 (who had a US No. 13 with 'Different Drum' in 67) and recorded solo in 69. She formed a backing group in 71 who evolved into The Eagles. Most of her 14 US (2 UK) Top 20s were revivals. She has had 17 gold LPs with eight of them making the US-only Top 10.

SOMEWHERE OUT THERE *(And JAMES INGRAM)* *(She got her first UK Top 20 with her 12th US one)*	8	22 AUG 87	MCA
DON'T KNOW MUCH *(Feat. AARON NEVILLE)* *(Bette Midler 77 US Hit)*	2	02 DEC 89	ELEKTRA
YOU'RE NO GOOD *(Betty Everett 63 US hit)*	1(1)	15 FEB 75	CAPITOL
WHEN WILL I BE LOVED *(Everly Bros. 60 hit)*	2	21 JUN 75	CAPITOL
HEAT WAVE/LOVE IS A ROSE *(Martha & The Vandellas 63 US hit)*	5	15 NOV 75	ASYLUM
IT'S SO EASY *(Original by The Crickets)*	5	10 DEC 77	ASYLUM
BLUE BAYOU *(UK No. 35 – Roy Orbison 63 hit)* *(Above two tracks were in the US Top 5 together)*	3	17 DEC 77	ASYLUM
OOH BABY BABY *(Miracles 65 US hit)*	7	20 JAN 79	ASYLUM
HOW DO I MAKE YOU	10	22 MAR 80	ASYLUM
HURT SO BAD *(Little Anthony 65 US hit)*	8	24 MAY 80	ASYLUM
SOMEWHERE OUT THERE *(And JAMES INGRAM)* *(From the film 'An American Tail')*	2	14 MAR 87	MCA
DON'T KNOW MUCH *(Featuring AARON NEVILLE)* *(Co-written by Barry Mann)*	2	23 DEC 89	ELEKTRA

ROOFTOP SINGERS

Folk trio formed by Erik Darling, who had been in the hit 50s groups The Tarriers and The Weavers and had co-written the big hit 'The Banana Boat Song'. Trio also featured Lynne Taylor (she died in 82) who had sung with Benny Goodman. The follow up 'Tom Cat' was their only other US Top 20 hit.

WALK RIGHT IN *(UK No. 11) (Orig by Gus Cannon)*	1(2)	26 JAN 63	VANGUARD

ROSE ROYCE

Eight man funk band started as Total Concept Unlimited and backed Edwin Starr, Undisputed Truth and The Temptations. They brought in singer Gwen Dickey and scored 4 US (7 UK) Top 40s before Gwen left (to be replaced by Richee Benson) in 80. They later recorded on Epic, C&R, Omni and Montage.

CAR WASH *(Also UK No. 20 in 88)*	9	12 FEB 77	MCA
WISHING ON A STAR *(Gwen Dickey revived it in 89 on Swanyard)*	3	04 MAR 78	WARNER
LOVE DON'T LIVE HERE ANYMORE *(US No. 32)*	2	07 OCT 78	WHITFIELD
CAR WASH *(Gwen Dickey revived it in 89)*	1(1)	29 JAN 77	MCA
I WANNA GET NEXT TO YOU *(UK No. 14 – above two from the film 'Car Wash')*	10	07 MAY 77	MCA

DAVID ROSE & HIS ORCHESTRA

London born composer/arranger and conductor who was once married to Judy Garland. He worked on many film and TV scores including Bonanza and Little House On The Prairie. He had two Top 40s during the war and had to wait 18 years for another with a track he recorded four years before it hit.

THE STRIPPER *(Originally was the B-side)*	1(1)	07 JUL 62	MGM

ROSIE & THE ORIGINALS

San Diego based group featured the distinctive voice of 15 year old Rosie Hamlin. They had a one-off hit (with a favourite track of John Lennon's) and she then went solo on Brunswick. She has recorded since without success.

ANGEL BABY *(Entered US Top 100 at 40)* *(Used in the late 80s film Colors)*	5	23 JAN 61	HIGHLAND

DIANA ROSS

The most charted female singer in the rock era was born Diane Earle in Detroit and left the ultra successful Supremes in 70 after 31 US chart hits. She has become one of the World's top solo entertainers and has notched up 20 US (19 UK) solo Top 20s plus 26 US LP hits and a female record of 28 UK chart LPs. She has also starred in hit films The Lady Sings The Blues, Mahogany and The Wiz and had her own top rated TV specials. She re-joined Motown in 89 as an artist and major share holder.

	AIN'T NO MOUNTAIN HIGH ENOUGH *(Written and Produced by Ashford & Simpson)*	6	17 OCT 70	TAMLA MOTOWN
	REMEMBER ME *(US No. 16)*	7	08 MAY 71	TAMLA MOTOWN
	I'M STILL WAITING *(US No. 63)* *(Her first UK No.1 for 15 years – an apt title!)*	1(4)	21 AUG 71	TAMLA MOTOWN
	SURRENDER *(US No. 38)*	10	27 NOV 71	TAMLA MOTOWN
	TOUCH ME IN THE MORNING	9	04 AUG 73	TAMLA MOTOWN
	ALL OF MY LIFE	9	09 FEB 74	TAMLA MOTOWN
	YOU ARE EVERYTHING *(And MARVIN GAYE)* *(Stylistics 71 US hit)*	5	20 APR 74	TAMLA MOTOWN
	THEME FROM MAHOGANY (DO YOU KNOW WHERE YOU'RE GOING TO) *(From the film)*	5	24 APR 76	TAMLA MOTOWN
	LOVE HANGOVER	10	29 MAY 76	TAMLA MOTOWN
	UPSIDE DOWN	2	09 AUG 80	MOTOWN
	MY OLD PIANO	5	11 OCT 80	MOTOWN
	ENDLESS LOVE *(And LIONEL RICHIE)*	7	26 SEP 81	MOTOWN
	WHY DO FOOLS FALL IN LOVE *(Frankie Lymon & The Teenagers 56 hit)*	4	12 DEC 81	CAPITOL
	WORK THAT BODY *(US No. 44)*	7	03 JUL 82	CAPITOL
	CHAIN REACTION *(US No. 66 – Comp. Bee Gees)* *(Made her the oldest female soloist to hit No. 1)*	1(3)	08 MAR 86	CAPITOL
	AIN'T NO MOUNTAIN HIGH ENOUGH *(Marvin Gaye & Tami Terrell 67 hit)*	1(3)	19 SEP 70	MOTOWN
	TOUCH ME IN THE MORNING	1(1)	18 AUG 73	MOTOWN
	THEME FROM MAHOGANY (DO YOU KNOW WHERE YOU'RE GOING TO)	1(1)	24 JAN 76	MOTOWN
	LOVE HANGOVER	1(2)	29 MAY 76	MOTOWN
	UPSIDE DOWN *(Written & produced by Rodgers & Edwards)*	1(4)	06 SEP 80	MOTOWN
	I'M COMIN' OUT *(UK No. 13)*	5	15 NOV 80	MOTOWN
	IT'S MY TURN *(UK No. 16 – From the film)* *(Co-written by Carole Bayer Sager)*	9	24 JAN 81	RCA
	ENDLESS LOVE *(And LIONEL RICHIE)*	1(9)	15 AUG 81	MOTOWN
	WHY DO FOOLS FALL IN LOVE	7	16 DEC 81	RCA
	MIRROR MIRROR *(UK No. 36 – Composed by Michael Sembello)*	8	06 MAR 82	RCA
	MUSCLES *(UK No. 15 – Produced & written by Michael Jackson)*	10	13 NOV 82	RCA
	MISSING YOU *(Tribute to Marvin Gaye – comp. & prod. Lionel Richie)*	10	13 APR 85	RCA

Also see The Supremes

NINI ROSSO

Italian trumpet star born Celeste Rosso in Turin was awarded the first European Common Market gold disc for this international five million seller. He also wrote and recorded the UK Top 10 hit 'Legions Last Patrol'.

	IL SILENZIO *(Based on 'The Last Post')* *(Covered in the US by Al Hirt)*	8	16 OCT 65	DURIUM

DAVID LEE ROTH

Flamboyant and extrovert rocker from Indiana was in the Red Ball Jets in 73 and fronted hit act Van Halen from 75-85. He has clocked up four US-only Top 20 singles – the others being 'Just A Gigolo/I Ain't Got Nobody' (12) and 'Yankee Rose' (16).

	CALIFORNIA GIRLS *(UK No. 68 – Beach Boys 65 hit)*	3	02 MAR 85	WARNER
	JUST LIKE PARADISE *(UK No. 27)*	6	12 MAR 88	WARNER

Also see Van Halen

DEMIS ROUSSOS

Greek MOR singer and entertainer was born in Egypt. He was in the top European trio Aphrodite's Child in the early 60s (they had a UK Top 40 with 'Rain And Tears' in 68). This multi instrumentalist has had six UK-only Top 40 LPs and 45s and is one of a few acts to top the singles chart with an EP.

	HAPPY TO BE ON AN ISLAND IN THE SUN	5	20 DEC 75	PHILIPS
	THE ROUSSOS PHENOMENON E.P. *(The first EP (four track 45) to top UK chart)*	1(1)	17 JUL 76	PHILIPS
	WHEN FOREVER HAS GONE	2	23 OCT 76	PHILIPS

JOHN ROWLES

New Zealand born MOR singer had two UK-only Top 20s – the other being his follow up 'Hush Not A Word To Mary' (12). In 71 he had a small US hit with 'Cheryl Moana Marie' (64). He also recorded for Columbia in 74.

	IF I ONLY HAD TIME	3	20 APR 68	MCA

ROXETTE

The first Swedish act to score more than one US No.1 were not Abba but singer/songwriter Per Gessle and vocalist Marie Fredricksson. Both members of the duo were previously in groups and their debut LP together 'Pearls Of Passion' went platinum in Sweden. They put three 45s from their second LP in the US Top 20 in 89 and look set to have a bright future.

	THE LOOK	7	27 MAY 89	EMI
	THE LOOK *(Top exactly 12 years after last Swedish No.1)*	1(1)	08 APR 89	EMI
	LISTEN TO YOUR HEART *(No. 62 UK)* *(First US Top 10 hit available only on cassette)*	1(1)	04 NOV 89	EMI

ROXY MUSIC

The key members of the critically acclaimed understated art rock group are the ever fashionable singer Bryan Ferry from Washington (UK), guitarist Phil Manzanera and sax player Andy Mackay. The group have had 13 UK-only Top 20s and 9 UK-only Top 10 LPs. Other notable ex-members include Eno, Eddie Jobson, Paul Carrack and John Wetton. Bryan has also had a string of mainly UK successes as a soloist and Andy also had success as a writer and producer.

	VIRGINIA PLAIN *(Also UK No. 11 in 77)*	4	16 SEP 72	ISLAND
	PYJAMARAMA	10	14 APR 73	ISLAND
	STREET LIFE	9	15 DEC 73	ISLAND
	LOVE IS A DRUG *(US No. 30)*	2	08 NOV 75	ISLAND
	DANCE AWAY *(US No. 44)*	2	26 MAY 79	POLYDOR
	ANGEL EYES	4	01 SEP 79	POLYDOR
	OVER YOU *(US No. 80)*	5	14 JUN 80	POLYDOR
	OH YEAH (ON THE RADIO)	5	16 AUG 80	POLYDOR
	JEALOUS GUY *(John Lennon song)*	1(2)	14 MAR 81	EG
	MORE THAN THIS	6	10 APR 82	EG

Also see Bryan Ferry

ROY 'C'

New Yorker Roy Charles Hammond sang with The Genies until 65 when he recorded his two time UK-only pop hit. He later recorded on Alaga, Shout, Mercury and joined Evejim/Ichiban in 89. He has had six black music hits.

	SHOTGUN WEDDING *(He also recorded 'The Wedding Is Over')*	6	21 MAY 66	ISLAND
	SHOTGUN WEDDING *(re-issue)* *(It was re-released again in the UK in 81)*	8	06 JAN 73	UK

ROYAL GUARDSMEN

Florida pop sextet included singer Barry 'Snoopy' Winslow and Chris Nunley. They also charted in the US with 'The Return Of The Red Baron' (15) and 'Snoopy For President' (85). They broke up in 68.

🇬🇧	SNOOPY VS. THE RED BARON *(They also recorded 'Snoopy Vs. The Black Knight')*	8	25 FEB 67	STATESIDE
🇺🇸	SNOOPY VS. THE RED BARON *(They also recorded 'Snoopy's Christmas')*	2	31 DEC 66	LAURIE

ROYAL PHILHARMONIC ORCHESTRA

Louis Clark, who had arranged for acts like ELO, scored three hit LPs with well known classics performed over a non-stop dance groove. They also had one similar Top 40 transatlantic 45. They later did 'Hooked On Amadeus', 'Hooked On Christmas', 'Hooked On Can Can', 'Hooked On Rodgers & Hammerstein', 'Hooked On America' and even 'Hooked On Scotland The Brave'.

🇬🇧	HOOKED ON CLASSICS	2	15 AUG 81	RCA
🇺🇸	HOOKED ON CLASSICS	10	30 JAN 82	RCA

ROYAL SCOTS DRAGOON GUARDS

Scottish army pipe and drum band led by Tony Crease amazingly had three UK Top 40 singles including a No. 13 hit with 'Little Drummer Boy'.

🇬🇧	AMAZING GRACE *(US No. 11)* *(Top UK record of 72-First large band to top chart)*	1(5)	15 APR 72	RCA

BILLY JOE ROYAL

Pop/country singer from Georgia started with The Corvetts and in 61 first recorded on Fairlane. He was on Tollie, All Wood and Players and had 4 US (1 UK) Top 40s in the 60s. He was later on Scepter, Private Stock, MGM, Atlantic, Mercury, Kat Family, Southern Tracks. In 86 he got the first of eight Top 20 country hits so far and he collected his first gold LP in 89.

🇺🇸	DOWN IN THE BOONDOCKS *(UK No. 38 – Composed by Joe South)*	9	28 AUG 65	COLUMBIA

RUBETTES

Successful 70s act from London included singer Alan Williams and had previously backed hit act Barry Blue. They chalked up nine UK (1 US) Top 40s with their 70s brand of r'n'r. Their transatlantic hit also featured the voice of Paul DaVinci who went solo straight after.

🇬🇧	SUGAR BABY LOVE *(US No. 37 – UK No. 1 in just three weeks)*	1(4)	18 MAY 74	POLYDOR
	JUKE BOX JIVE	3	07 DEC 74	POLYDOR
	I CAN DO IT	7	05 APR 75	STATE
	BABY I KNOW	10	19 MAR 77	STATE

RUBY & THE ROMANTICS

Group were formed when Ohio's Ruby Nash joined the all male group The Supremes. They also had the original version of the hits 'Hey There Lonely Boy' (Girl) and 'When You're Young And In Love' and 'Hurting Each Other'. They had eight US (1 UK) chart records and became an all female trio in 68.

🇺🇸	OUR DAY WILL COME *(UK No. 26)*	1(1)	23 MAR 63	KAPP

BRUCE RUFFIN

Born Bernard Downer in Kingston (Jamaica) this reggae singer recorded with Winston Riley's group before getting his first local solo hits in 68 (one being the Dawn song 'Candida'). He moved to London and had two UK Top 20s – the other being 'Rain' (19). He was also on RCA, Slick, WEA and Trojan.

🇬🇧	MAD ABOUT YOU	9	29 JUL 72	RHINO

DAVID RUFFIN

Mississippi singer recorded solo on Anna and Checkmate in 61 and was The Temptations main lead singer between 63-68. He had eight black music solo charters and re-joined The Temptations in 82. He also hit the Top 20 with Hall & Oates in 85 and had chart duets with Eddie Kendricks in the late 80s.

🇬🇧	WALK AWAY FROM LOVE	10	14 FEB 76	TAMLA
🇺🇸	MY WHOLE WORLD ENDED (THE MOMENT YOU LEFT ME)	9	29 MAR 69	MOTOWN
	WALK AWAY FROM LOVE	9	24 JAN 76	MOTOWN

JIMMY RUFFIN

Brother of David Ruffin was on Miracle in 61 and was a Motown session singer before getting the first of 4 US (8 UK) Top 40s. In the UK three of his hits later re-entered the Top 40. He has also been on Atco, Epic, ERC, EMI and joined Polydor in 87 and was in the one-off chart act Council Collective.

🇬🇧	WHAT BECOMES OF THE BROKENHEARTED	8	31 DEC 66	TAMLA MOTOWN
	FAREWELL IS A LONELY SOUND *(Also UK No. 30 in 74)*	8	02 MAY 70	TAMLA MOTOWN
	I'LL SAY FOREVER MY LOVE *(US No. 77)*	7	08 JUL 70	TAMLA MOTOWN
	IT'S WONDERFUL	6	21 NOV 70	TAMLA MOTOWN
	WHAT BECOMES OF THE BROKENHEARTED *(Re-issue)*	4	24 AUG 74	TAMLA MOTOWN
	HOLD ON TO MY LOVE *(Comp. & Prod. Robin Gibb)*	7	17 MAY 80	RSO
🇺🇸	WHAT BECOMES OF THE BROKENHEARTED	7	29 OCT 66	SOUL
	HOLD ON TO MY LOVE	10	03 MAY 80	RSO

RUFUS

Chicago act evolved from hit act American Breed and were previously called Ask Rufus. Group have included David Wolinski and of course Chaka Khan (who replaced Paulette McWilliams). They have had 10 US (1 UK) Top 40 singles and six Top 20 US-only LPs. Chaka has also had much solo success since 78.

🇬🇧	AIN'T NOBODY *(And CHAKA KHAN)* *(US No. 22 – song originally called 'I'm So Happy')*	8	21 APR 84	WARNER
🇺🇸	TELL ME SOMETHING GOOD *(Stevie Wonder song)*	3	24 AUG 74	ABC
	ONCE YOU GET STARTED	10	12 APR 75	ABC
	SWEET THING *(Last two as Rufus featuring Chaka Khan)*	5	03 APR 76	ABC

Also see Chaka Khan/American Breed

RUN D.M.C.

Top rap stars from New York are Joseph Simmons (Run), Darryl McDaniels (DMC) and DJ Jason Mizell (Jam Master Jay). Trio have had 10 black music hits and were the first rap act to have both gold and platinum LPs. The act, who have had riots at their live shows, were in the film Krush Groove and starred in their own film Tougher Than Leather.

🇬🇧	WALK THIS WAY *(Aerosmith 76 US hit)*	8	27 SEP 86	LONDON
🇺🇸	WALK THIS WAY *(Features Aerosmith's Steve Tyler & Joe Perry)*	4	27 SEP 86	PROFILE

TODD RUNDGREN

Singer/songwriter/producer/musician and video pioneer from Pennsylvania was in Money, Woody's Truckstop and charted in Nazz on SGC in 68 and as Runt on Ampex and Bearsville in 70. He had four US (1 UK) Top 40s and has produced Grand Funk Railroad, Meat Loaf, Hall & Oates, Cheap Trick and Badfinger. He was also was the main man in hit act Utopia who recorded from 82-86.

🇺🇸	HELLO IT'S ME *(Was US No.66 in 69 by his group Nazz)*	5	22 DEC 73	BEARSVILLE

JENNIFER RUSH

The first single by a female soloist to sell a million in the UK came from this New York born, German based singer. Her third German hit took four months on the UK chart to climb to No. 1. She also hit the UK-only Top 20 with her follow up 'Ring Of Ice' (14). Her biggest success in her homeland was a duet with Elton John 'Flames of Paradise' (36) in 87.

 POWER OF LOVE   1(5)   12 OCT 85   CBS
(US No. 57 – 6 mins. long – Top single of 85 in UK)

MERRILEE RUSH (& THE TURNABOUTS)

Seattle singer who was helped to get a deal by Paul Revere And The Raiders. Her fourth single was her sole US Top 40 hit which she followed with 'That Kind Of Woman'. She was on Sceptre in 72 and on UA in 76.

ANGEL OF THE MORNING *(Original Evie Sands)*   7   29 JUN 68   BELL

PATRICE RUSHEN

Well respected L.A. jazz/soul singer/songwriter was a child prodigy giving piano recitals when she was only six. She has done a lot of session work with top jazz acts and has scored 15 black music hits to date.

 FORGET ME NOTS *(US No. 23)*   8   29 MAY 82   ELEKTRA

BRENDA RUSSELL

Singer/songwriter was born Brenda Gordon in New York, moved to Canada where she joined The Tiaras and recorded with her husband as Brian & Brenda in 78. She has also done session work with acts like Barbra Streisand, Elton John, Robert Palmer, Neil Sedaka, Donna Summer and Bette Midler. Her only other transatlantic hit was 'So Good So Right' in 79 (US 30/UK 51).

 PIANO IN THE DARK *(UK No. 26)*   6   04 JUN 88   A&M
(And JOE ESPOSITO from group Brooklyn Dreams)

RUTS

Reggae influenced London punk group fronted by Malcolm Owen started on People Unite. They had four UK-only hits before Malcolm's untimely death in 80. Group later recorded with less success on Bohemian, Link and Dojo.

BABYLON'S BURNING   7   14 JUL 79   VIRGIN

BARRY RYAN

Born Barry Sapherson in Leeds (UK) he was a son of 50s UK star Marion Ryan. With his twin brother Paul he had a string of eight UK-only hits between 65-67. His first solo hit (written by Paul) was a European smash selling over three million. He also had another five UK-only charters and was later on Polydor in 71 and Dawn in 75. His big hit was covered by punks The Damned in 86, and he is still writing and recording.

ELOISE *(US No. 86)*   2   23 NOV 68   MGM

BOBBY RYDELL

Philadelphian born Bobby Ridarelli was drummer in Rocco & The Saints in 57 and had solos on Veko and Venise in 58. His third 45 on Cameo gave him the first of his 19 US (4 UK) Top 40s. This early 60s teenagers' pin-up later recorded on Capitol, Reprise, RCA, Perception and Pickwick.

WE GOT LOVE	6	06 DEC 59	CAMEO
WILD ONE *(UK No. 12)*		28 MAR 60	CAMEO
SWINGIN' SCHOOL	5	20 JUN 60	CAMEO
(From the film 'Because They're Young')			
VOLARE *(UK No. 18 – Domenico Modugno 58 Hit)*	4	05 SEP 60	CAMEO
THE CHA CHA CHA	10	17 NOV 62	CAMEO
FORGET HIM *(UK No. 15)*	4	18 JAN 64	CAMEO

MITCH RYDER & THE DETROIT WHEELS

Detroit rocker born William Levise Jr. was on groups Tempest and The Preps and first recorded in Billy Lee & The Rivieras on Carrie and Hyland. The act known for their two song medleys had 5 US (1 UK) Top 40s. He went solo in 67 and in 70 formed the group Detroit. He had some success in Germany and recorded on Riva in 83, produced by John Cougar Mellencamp.

JENNY TAKE A RIDE! *(He re-recorded it in 71)*	10	29 JAN 66	NEW VOICE
(US No. 33 – Medley Little Richard & Chuck Willis songs)			
DEVIL WITH A BLUE DRESS ON & GOOD GOLLY MISS MOLLY *(Medley of Shorty Long/Little Richard songs)*	4	26 NOV 66	NEW VOICE
SOCK IT TO ME-BABY!	6	25 MAR 67	NEW VOICE

S

S'EXPRESS

Dance project masterminded by London club DJ Mark Moore combines the feel of 70s disco music with the dance sounds of the 80s. They were one of the UK's top acts of the late 80s with three Top 10s in less than a year.

THEME FROM S'EXPRESS	1(2)	30 APR 88	RHYTHM KING
(US No. 91 – US Dance No. 1)			
SUPERFLY GUY *(US Dance No. 2)*	5	13 AUG 88	RHYTHM KING
HEY MUSIC LOVER	6	04 MAR 89	RHYTHM KING
(A homage to Sly Stone – vocal by Billie Ray Martin)			

SABRINA

Bouncy Italian pop singer Sabrina Salerno had a one-off UK Top 40 with her big European hit. She has also had releases on Videogram, RCA and PWL.

BOYS (SUMMERTIME LOVE)   3   25 JUN 88   CBS
(Single had peaked UK No. 60 in Feb 88)

SAD CAFE

Manchester (UK) group, formed from members of Gyro and Mandala, were fronted by Paul Young (not the solo singer) and had two UK-only Top 20s – the other being 'My Oh My' (14). Their biggest US hit was 'Run Home Girl' (71). They were also on Swan Song, Polydor, Legacy and Atlantic and Paul was later in Mike + The Mechanics. Their hits were produced by Eric Stewart of 10CC, and they were a popular live band, especially in their home town.

EVERY DAY HURTS   3   03 NOV 79   RCA
(Produced by Eric Stewart of 10cc)

SADE

Photogenic smooth jazz-orientated pop singer/songwriter Helen Folasade Adu was born in Nigeria and based in the UK. She was in Arriva and Pride who evolved into Sade. Act were an instant hit, their first LP selling over six million world-wide. The award winning group's second LP was a transatlantic topper. Single-wise they have had five UK (4 US) Top 40s to date.

YOUR LOVE IS KING (US No. 54)	6	31 MAR 84	EPIC
SMOOTH OPERATOR (UK No. 19)	5	18 MAY 85	PORTRAIT
THE SWEETEST TABOO (UK No. 31)	5	01 MAR 86	PORTRAIT

STAFF SGT. BARRY SADLER

New Mexican born ex member of the Green Berets (US Army special forces) had a controversial No. 1 single and LP with patriotic songs about the Vietnam war. His only other charter was the follow up 'The 'A' Team' (US 28). He later tried to make it in Nashville as a country act, where he was involved in the shooting death of a fellow songwriter. He died in 89 aged 49.

THE BALLAD OF THE GREEN BERETS (UK No. 24)	1(1)	05 MAR 66	RCA
(Single and LP were two of RCA's fastest sellers ever)			

SAFARIS

L.A. vocal quartet fronted by Jim Stephens followed their sole Top 40 hit with 'The Girl With The Story In Her Eyes'. They were on Valiant in 63.

IMAGE OF A GIRL (Feat. The Phantom's Band)	6	01 AUG 60	ELDO

CAROLE BAYER SAGER

Successful song writer was born in New York and co-wrote No. 1 hits 'Groovy Kind Of Love' and 'When I Need You'. She also recorded on Metromedia in 72 and Epic and Boardwalk in 81. She married top composer Burt Bacharach in 82 and has since written many hits with him.

YOU'RE MOVING OUT TODAY (US No. 69)	6	18 JUN 77	ELEKTRA
(US No. 69 – She co-wrote with Bette Midler)			

SAILOR

Distinctive pop quartet included Norwegian born singer George Kajanus (Hultgren), an ex member of Eclection, and German born Phil Pickett. Formed in 74 they had three UK-only Top 40s. Act split in the late 70s and re-formed in 81 on Chameleon. Phil later joined Culture Club and co-wrote 'Karma Chameleon'.

GLASS OF CHAMPAGNE	2	17 JAN 76	EPIC
GIRLS GIRLS GIRLS	7	24 APR 76	EPIC
(Both hits produced by Rupert Holmes)			

ST. WINIFRED'S SCHOOL

Well known UK school choir had the UK's 80 Christmas hit after failing to chart the Xmas before with 'Bread & Fishes'. The first choir to get a No. 1 had also sung on Brian & Michael's unusual UK No. 1 hit in 78.

THERE'S NO ONE QUITE LIKE GRANDMA	1(1)	27 DEC 80	MFP

Also see Brian & Michael

CRISPIAN ST. PETERS

Pop singer/guitarist born Peter Smith in Kent had the first of his three UK and US charters with his fourth single.

YOU WERE ON MY MIND	2	12 FEB 66	DECCA
(US No. 36 in 67 – We Five 65 US hit)			
PIED PIPER (Changin' Times 65 US hit)	5	14 MAY 66	DECCA
THE PIED PIPER	4	30 JUL 66	JAMIE

KYU SAKAMOTO

Japanese romantic comedian and film star is their most successful world-wide recording artist. He had been a top act there since 59. He followed his sole transatlantic hit with 'China Nights' (Shrina No Yoru)'. He died in the 85 Japanese Airlines disaster.

SUKIYAKI (Orig. title 'Ue O Muite Aruko')	8	02 AUG 63	HMV
(Title means 'Don't look down when you're walking')			
SUKIYAKI (Biggest Japanese hit in US & UK)	1(3)	15 JUN 63	CAPITOL

SALT'N'PEPA

Top female rap team are New Yorker Cheryl 'Salt' James, Sandy 'Pepa' Denton from Jamaica and DJ Spinderella (Latoya). They have had eight black music chart entries but despite good US sales little pop chart success. In the UK they hit thanks in part to being on the first 'Nelson Mandela' show.

PUSH IT/TRAMP (US No. 19 and Gold record)	2	16 JUL 88	CHAMPION
(B-side Lowell Fulson 67 R&B hit)			
TWIST AND SHOUT (Originally by Carla Thomas)	4	26 NOV 88	FFRR

SAM & DAVE

Top 60s soul duo were Sam Moore from Miami and Dave Prater from Georgia. They recorded on Roulette in 62 and had their first of 13 US (4 UK) chart entries in 66. They split and re-united often in the 70s and called it a day in 81. Dave teamed with a new Sam (Sam Daniels) in 82, recorded a Sam & Dave medley for Stars On 45 in 85, and was killed in a car crash in 88.

SOUL MAN (U.K. No. 24 – R&B Grammy winner)	2	04 NOV 67	STAX
(Was revived by Sam Moore & Lou Reed in 86)			
I THANK YOU (UK No. 34)	9	23 MAR 68	STAX
(Both hits co-produced and co written Isaac Hayes)			

SAM THE SHAM & THE PHARAOHS

Turban clad Texan novelty rock group led by Domingo 'Sam' Samudio. Before notching up their six US (1 UK) Top 40s they had recorded on Tupelo, Dingo and XL. Group split in late 60s and Sam recorded solo on Atlantic.

WOOLY BULLY (UK No. 11 – originally on XL)	2	05 JUN 65	MGM
LIL' RED RIDING HOOD (UK No. 46)	2	06 AUG 66	MGM

SANDPIPERS

L.A. based MOR trio Jim Brady, Richard Schoff and Michael Piano met in the Mitchell Boys Choir. They were first called The Grads and recorded on Valiant, MGM and Mercury. Their debut 45 under their new name became their first of two US Top 20s the other being 'Come Saturday Morning' (17).

GUANTANAMERA	7	15 OCT 66	PYE INT
GUANTANAMERA	9	17 SEP 66	A&M

SANFORD/TOWNSEND BAND

L.A. based Ed Sanford and John Townsend's rock band followed their sole charter with 'Does It Have To Be You'.

SMOKE FROM A DISTANT FIRE	9	17 SEP 77	WARNER

SAMANTHA SANG

Australian child prodigy (first radio show at age eight) was born Cheryl Gray. She had her first release aged 16 in 68 and had records on Parlophone and Atco in 69 and Polydor in 71. She followed her sole transatlantic hit with 'You Keep Me Dancing' and in 79 joined UA/Liberty.

EMOTION (UK No.11 – comp. Barry & Robin Gibb)	3	18 MAR 78	PRIVATE STOCK

MONGO SANTAMARIA

Cuban Latin/jazz bandleader and percussionist who had played in Perez Prado and Ray Charles' bands. He previously recorded on Riverside and Fantasy. He made the original version of Georgie Fame's 'Yeh Yeh' and had nine US-only LP entries. He later recorded on Columbia and Atlantic.

 WATERMELON MAN   10   27 APR 63   BATTLE
(He re-recorded this on Columbia in 69)

SANTANA

Formed by Mexican Carlos Santana as The Santana Blues Band in 66, their distinctive Latin rock was heard at Woodstock in 69 when they had the first of 14 US & UK Top 40 LPs (inc. 11 gold discs). They have also scored 10 US (2 UK) Top 40 singles the biggest UK 45 being 'She's Not There' (UK 11/US 27). Carlos often records outside the group, who despite many changes of personnel, still maintain their popularity and the respect of critics.

 EVIL WAYS *(Was also a Carlos solo 45 in 72)*   9   21 MAR 70   COLUMBIA
BLACK MAGIC WOMAN *(Fleetwood Mac 68 UK hit)*   4   09 JAN 71   COLUMBIA

MIKE SARNE

The first mixed duo to top the UK chart were London singer/actor Mike (Scheuer), who had previously been in 10 films as Mike Shaw, and 18 year old Yorkshire born actress Wendy Richard. Within a year he scored another three US-only Top 40s. He recorded with The LeRoys in 64 and then turned to film directing. Wendy recorded a duet with actress Diana Berry in 63 and is now one of the stars of UK TV soap opera EastEnders.

 COME OUTSIDE *(And WENDY RICHARD)*   1(2) 22 JUN 62   PARLOPHONE
(Revived in 86 by Wendy Richard & Mike Berry on WEA)

PETER SARSTEDT •

Singer/songwriter was one of the three hit making brothers – the others being Robin and Eden Kane. He started recording in 63 as Wes Sands on Columbia. He had just the two UK hits and recorded in the Sarstedt Brothers in 73 on Regal Zonophone. He was later on Warner in 75 (whilst living in the US), Ariola/Hansa in 78, Songwriters Workshop in 80, Steiner in 81, Peach River in 82, Audiotrax in 84 and Filmtrax in 86.

 WHERE DO YOU GO TO MY LOVELY *(US No. 70)*   1(4) 01 MAR 69   UA
(Ivor Novello Award as 'Song of the Year')
FROZEN ORANGE JUICE   10   05 JUL 69   UA

ROBIN SARSTEDT

The last of the Sarstedt brothers to hit the UK Top 10 did so with a 30s style arrangement of an old Hoagy Carmichael song (produced by Ray Singer as were his brother Peter's hits) which he followed with another standard 'Let's Fall In Love'. He had recorded on RCA in 70 (as Clive Sarstedt) and was later on Piccadilly, Rak and Spectra.

 MY RESISTANCE IS LOW   3   05 JUN 76   DECCA
(Recorded in 75 after he met Hoagy Carmichael)

TELLY SAVALAS

Top TV and film actor had a UK-only smash with a Bread song. He followed it with 'You've Lost That Lovin' Feelin' (UK 47). His other releases included 'Who Loves Ya Baby' inspired by his role in TVs Kojak. He also had releases in the UK on Jam in 74 and Satril in 80.

 IF   1(2) 08 MAR 75   MCA

LEO SAYER

Sussex (UK) singer/songwriter led Terraplane Blues and recorded in Patches before joining manager Adam Faith (ex UK pop star) in 72. He wrote most of Roger Daltrey's 'Daltrey' LP. His second solo single was the first of 14 UK (8 US) Top 40 singles and 10 UK (4 US) Top 40 LPs. This unique artist was a chart regular for a decade but little was heard from him in the late 80s.

THE SHOW MUST GO ON   2   19 JAN 74   CHRYSALIS
(US No. 4 when covered by Three Dog Night)
ONE MAN BAND *(US No. 96)*   6   29 JUN 74   CHRYSALIS
LONG TALL GLASSES   4   05 OCT 74   CHRYSALIS
(Originally called 'I Can Dance')
MOONLIGHTING   2   20 SEP 75   CHRYSALIS
YOU MAKE ME FEEL LIKE DANCING   2   20 NOV 76   CHRYSALIS
WHEN I NEED YOU   1(3) 19 FEB 77   CHRYSALIS
(Written by Carole Bayer Sager & Albert Hammond)
HOW MUCH LOVE *(US No. 17)*   10   07 MAY 77   CHRYSALIS
I CAN'T STOP LOVIN' YOU (THOUGH I TRY)   6   14 OCT 78   CHRYSALIS
MORE THAN I CAN SAY   2   02 AUG 80   CHRYSALIS
(Song was originally a Crickets B-side)
HAVE YOU EVER BEEN IN LOVE   10   10 APR 82   CHRYSALIS

LONG TALL GLASSES (I CAN DANCE)   9   03 MAY 75   WARNER
YOU MAKE ME FEEL LIKE DANCING   1(1) 15 JAN 77   WARNER
(Grammy winner Top R&B song)
WHEN I NEED YOU   1(1) 14 MAY 77   WARNER
MORE THAN I CAN SAY   2   06 DEC 80   WARNER

SCAFFOLD

Liverpool based fun folk/pop trio led by Paul McCartney's brother Mike McGear had five UK-only Top 40s. Formed in 62 they started recording in 66 and were later on WEA and Bronze. Mike later also recorded solo.

THANK U VERY MUCH *(US No. 69)*   4   06 JAN 68   PARLOPHONE
LILLY THE PINK   1(2) 14 DEC 68   PARLOPHONE
(Based on folk song 'Lydia Pinkham')
LIVERPOOL LOU   7   22 JUN 74   WARNER

BOZ SCAGGS

Ohio singer/songwriter was with Steve Miller in The Marksmen and The Ardells (later Fabulous Night Train) in the early 60s. He formed the short lived Wigs then joined Steve's band. As a soloist he was on Atlantic in 69 and first charted in 71. He had the first of seven US (4 UK) Top 40s in 76 and had another transatlantic Top 20 with 'Lido Shuffle' (US 11/UK 13). He had four US(1 UK) Top 40 LPs and is best known for the five million selling 'Silk Degrees'. He retired in 83 and returned to the US Top 40 in 88.

WHAT CAN I SAY *(US No. 42)*   10   05 MAR 77   CBS
LOWDOWN *(US No. 28 – R&B Grammy winner)*   3   09 OCT 76   COLUMBIA
(Co-written by Steve Porcaro of Toto)

SCANDAL FEATURING PATTY SMYTH

New York rock band led by Zack Smith and fronted by Patty. They first recorded in 82 and had five US-only chart 45s and two US Top 40 LPs. Zack left in 84 and Patty continued to record with the band and as a soloist.

THE WARRIOR *(Co-written by Nick Gilder)*   7   22 SEP 84   COLUMBIA

JOEY SCARBURY •

Canadian singer recorded on Dunhill in 69, Bell in 71, and had his first chart single in 71 with 'Mixed Up Guy' on Lionel. He was also a session singer for people like Mike Post and Loretta Lynn. He was on Big Tree in 73, Playboy in 74 and Columbia in 77, and had his second and biggest hit in 81. He joined RCA in 84 and co-wrote a country No. 1 in 90.

THEME FROM 'GREATEST AMERICAN HERO'   2   15 AUG 81   ELEKTRA
(From the TV series)

SCOTLAND WORLD CUP SQUAD

The Scottish soccer team have had two UK-only Top 20s – the other being 'Easy Easy' (20th) in 74. Amazingly they also had a No. 3 LP.

🇬🇧	WE HAVE A DREAM (In the UK Top 10 same time as the England team)	5	15 MAY 82	WEA

FREDDIE SCOTT

Soul singer/songwriter from Rhode Island was on Arrow, Joy and Enrica before having nine black music hits including the No. 1 'Are You Lonely For Me Baby' in 66 on Shout. He also recorded on Columbia, Elephant 1V, PIP, Mainstream, Vanguard and Probe.

🇺🇸	HEY GIRL (Co-written by Carole King)	10	07 SEP 63	COLPIX

JACK SCOTT

Canadian rock/country singer/songwriter born Jack Scafone Jr. He led the country band The Southern Drifters before first recording on ABC Paramount in 57. He chalked up nine US (4 UK) Top 40s and was also on Capitol, Groove, Guaranteed, RCA, Jubilee, GRT, Dot and Ponie. He still does a lot of club work in the US and UK.

🇬🇧	MY TRUE LOVE (Featuring The Chantones)	9	14 NOV 58	LONDON
	WHAT IN THE WORLD'S COME OVER YOU	6	18 MAR 60	TOP RANK
🇺🇸	MY TRUE LOVE/LEROY (B-side about his friend Bill (Leroy) Johnson)	7	01 SEP 58	CARLTON
	GOODBYE BABY	8	16 FEB 59	CARLTON
	WHAT IN THE WORLD'S COME OVER YOU	5	22 FEB 60	TOP RANK
	BURNING BRIDGES	3	13 JUN 60	TOP RANK

LINDA SCOTT

New York singer born Linda Sampson had her biggest hit when only 15 and in high school. She notched up three US (1 UK) Top 40s before she was 17 but despite releases on Congress, Kapp and RCA she never hit the heights again.

🇬🇧	I'VE TOLD EVERY LITTLE STAR (Jack Denny 33 hit)	8	16 JUN 61	COLUMBIA
🇺🇸	I'VE TOLD EVERY LITTLE STAR	3	01 MAY 61	CANADIAN AM.
	DON'T BET MONEY HONEY	0	20 AUG 61	CANADIAN AM.

SCRITTI POLITTI

Group's name is Italian for 'political writing' and they are fronted by Welshman Green Strohmeyer-Gartside. They were on St. Pancras in 78 and Rough Trade in 79 and first charted in 81 with 'The Sweetest Girl'. They have had 10 more UK chart entries since and in the US their only Top 40 was 'Perfect Way' (US 11/UK 48) in 85. Green has also had his songs cut by Madness, Chaka Khan and Al Jarreau.

🇬🇧	WOOD BEEZ (PRAY LIKE ARETHA FRANKLIN) (US No. 91-prod. by Aretha's producer Arif Mardin)	10	21 APR 84	VIRGIN
	THE WORD GIRL (Feat. Ranking Ann)	6	22 JUN 85	VIRGIN

SEALS & CROFTS

Texan singer/songwriting multi-instrumentalists Jim Seals and Dash Crofts played and recorded (on Edmoral and Atlantic) with Dean Beard's Crew Cats in 57 and joined hit act The Champs in the late 50s. Jim also recorded solo on Carlton in 58 and Challenge in 62. They played together again in The Dawnbreakers in 66 and first recorded as a duo in 70 on Talent Associates. They had no UK hits but chalked up six US Top 40 LPs and eight Top 40 singles before quitting music in the late 70s for religious reasons.

🇺🇸	SUMMER BREEZE	6	25 NOV 72	WARNER
	DIAMOND GIRL	6	28 JUL 73	WARNER
	GET CLOSER (Feat. Carolyn Willis of Honeycone)	6	24 JUL 76	WARNER

SEARCHERS

Liverpool pop group famed for their harmonies had a UK No. 1 with their first single and a further 11 UK (7 US) Top 40s in the next three years. Act, who did numerous cover versions, were fronted by Mike Pender and Tony Jackson (who went solo in 64). They later were on Liberty, World Pacific, RCA and Sire with little success. Mike left in 85 to form a new group.

🇬🇧	SWEETS FOR MY SWEET (Drifters 61 US hit)	1(3)	02 AUG 63	PYE
	SUGAR AND SPICE (US No. 44)	3	08 NOV 63	PYE
	NEEDLES AND PINS (Co-written Sonny Bono) (US No. 13 – Jackie DeShannon 63 US hit)	1(3)	01 FEB 64	PYE
	DON'T THROW YOUR LOVE AWAY (US No. 16) (US No. 16 – originally by The Orlons)	1(2)	09 MAY 64	PYE
	WHEN YOU WALK IN THE ROOM (US No. 35) (Composed and originally by Jackie DeShannon)	3	24 OCT 64	PYE
	GOODBYE MY LOVE (US No. 52 – originally by Jimmy Hughes)	4	03 APR 65	PYE
🇺🇸	LOVE POTION NUMBER NINE (Not released as 45 in UK – Clovers 59 US hit)	3	16 JAN 65	KAPP

JOHN SEBASTIAN

New York born leader of the top 60s group Lovin' Spoonful first recorded solo on Kama Sutra in 68, had his one US Top 20 US LP on MGM in 70 and a sole Top 40 single in 76. He became a well known US radio DJ in 90.

🇺🇸	WELCOME BACK (From the US TV series 'Welcome Back Kotter')	1(1)	08 MAY 76	REPRISE

Also see Lovin' Spoonful

HARRY SECOMBE

Welsh comedian/singer and TV personality has been a top UK star since the early 50s. He first recorded in 52 and has had three UK-only Top 20 singles and five Top 20 LPs. He was also part of the hit comedy act The Goons.

🇬🇧	THIS IS MY SONG (Composed by Charlie Chaplin)	2	01 APR 67	PHILIPS

Also see The Goons

NEIL SEDAKA

Top New York singer/songwriter started recording in The Tokens on Melba in 56. He had solo 45s on Decca, Legion and Guyden before stringing together 13 US (9 UK) Top 40s before 64. He has also written Top 10s for Connie Francis, Captain & Tennille and Andy Williams. He was on SGC in 68 and Kirshner in 72 when he moved to the UK. In the 70s he had another eight UK (7 UK) Top 40s. He was also on Elektra, MGM, MCA/Curb and PRT (UK).

🇬🇧	I GO APE (US No. 42)	9	12 JUN 59	RCA
	OH! CAROL (also UK No. 19 in 72) (Inspired by Carole King who later made 'Oh Neil')	3	18 DEC 59	RCA
	CALENDAR GIRL	8	03 MAR 61	RCA
	LITTLE DEVIL (US No. 11)	9	09 JUN 61	RCA
	HAPPY BIRTHDAY, SWEET SIXTEEN	3	26 JAN 62	RCA
	BREAKING UP IS HARD TO DO (Backing vocals The Cookies)	7	31 AUG 62	RCA
🇺🇸	OH! CAROL	9	06 DEC 59	RCA
	STAIRWAY TO HEAVEN (UK No. 12)	9	09 MAY 60	RCA
	CALENDAR GIRL	4	13 FEB 61	RCA
	HAPPY BIRTHDAY, SWEET SIXTEEN	6	07 JAN 62	RCA
	BREAKING UP IS HARD TO DO (Loosely based on 'It Will Stand' by The Showmen)	1(2)	11 AUG 62	RCA
	NEXT DOOR TO AN ANGEL (UK No. 29)	5	17 NOV 62	RCA
	LAUGHTER IN THE RAIN (UK No. 15 a year before)	1(1)	01 FEB 75	ROCKET
	BAD BLOOD (His biggest US hit – Elton John on backing vocals)	1(3)	11 OCT 75	ROCKET
	BREAKING UP IS HARD TO DO (Slow version) (Only song to have two versions in US Top 10 by same act)	8	21 FEB 76	ROCKET

SEEKERS

The first Australian act to top the UK chart were this folk/pop quartet fronted by Judith Durham. They moved to the UK and had eight UK (3 US) Top 20s before Judith went solo in 67. Member Bruce Woodley co-wrote Cyrkle's big hit and Keith Potger formed the popular New Seekers in 70.

🇬🇧	I'LL NEVER FIND ANOTHER YOU *(Top record and Top Act in UK in 65)*	1(2)	27 FEB 65	COLUMBIA
	A WORLD OF OUR OWN *(US No. 19)*	3	15 MAY 65	COLUMBIA
	THE CARNIVAL IS OVER *(UK Gold record)*	1(3)	27 NOV 65	COLUMBIA
	WALK WITH ME *(All above comp. Tom Springfield, ex Springfields)*	10	01 OCT 66	COLUMBIA
	MORNINGTOWN RIDE *(US No. 44)*	2	24 DEC 66	COLUMBIA
	GEORGY GIRL *(Co-writ. Tom Springfield & singer/actor Jim Dale)*	3	25 MAR 67	COLUMBIA
🇺🇸	I'LL NEVER FIND ANOTHER YOU *(The song was a country No. 1 in 67)*	4	15 MAY 65	CAPITOL
	GEORGY GIRL *(From the film)*	2	04 FEB 67	CAPITOL

BOB SEGER

The Decibels, Town Criers, Doug Brown & The Omens (aka The Beach Bums on Are You Kidding Me label!) were acts this Michigan rocker was in before he recorded with his backing group The Last Heard on Hideout (& Cameo). He first charted with his eighth 45 'Ramblin' Gamblin Man' (US No.17) in 68. He recorded on his own Palladium label in 71 and rejoined Capitol in 75 and then had six consecutive US-only Top 10 LPs and 16 US-only Top 40 singles.

🇺🇸	NIGHT MOVES *(Bob's favourite song)*	4	12 MAR 77	CAPITOL
	STILL THE SAME *(Feat. Silver Bullet Band)*	4	22 JUL 78	CAPITOL
	FIRE LAKE	6	03 MAY 80	CAPITOL
	AGAINST THE WIND	5	14 JUN 80	CAPITOL
	TRYIN' TO LIVE MY LIFE WITHOUT YOU	5	07 NOV 81	CAPITOL
	SHAME ON THE MOON *(Feat. Silver Bullet band – Comp. Rodney Crowell)*	2	26 FEB 83	CAPITOL
	SHAKEDOWN *(Song written for Glen Frey) (From the film Beverly Hills Cop II)*	1(1)	01 AUG 87	MCA

SELECTER

Mixed UK 2 Tone group from Coventry were fronted by Pauline Black and included composer Noel Davies. They had four UK-only Top 40s including 'Three Minute Hero' (16). Act went to Chrysalis in 80. Pauline left in 81 and in 84 joined Sunday Best with Lynval Golding and Neville Staples (ex Fun Boy Three).

🇬🇧	ON MY RADIO	8	17 NOV 79	2 TONE

PETER SELLERS & SOPHIA LOREN

UK comedian teamed with fellow film star on two UK-only Top 40s. The ex-Goon who first recorded in 54 had three solo UK-only Top 40s. Sophia had recorded on RCA in 56 and Columbia in 58 and was later on Warner.

🇬🇧	GOODNESS GRACIOUS ME	3	25 NOV 60	PARLOPHONE

Also see The Goons

MICHAEL SEMBELLO

Philadelphian singer/songwriter is also a top session guitarist working with Donna Summer, Diana Ross (he wrote her 'Mirror, Mirror'), The Jacksons and Stevie Wonder whom he toured with for eight years. His sole Top 40 was written about a mass murderer and only came to be in the film Flash Dance by mistake. He was also on Warner in 83 and A&M in 85.

🇺🇸	MANIAC *(UK No. 43)*	1(2)	10 SEP 83	CASABLANCA

SENSATIONS

Yvonne Baker led this Philadelphia R&B group who started life as The Cavaliers in 54. They hit the R&B charts twice in 56 before Yvonne left to start a family. They reformed in 61 and they had three more chart records. Yvonne later recorded solo on Modern, Jamie and Parkway.

🇺🇸	LET ME IN	4	17 MAR 62	ARGO

SERENDIPITY SINGERS

Nine piece pop/folk group who included Bryan Sennett and Lynne Weintraub were formed at the University of Colorado and had two US-only Top 40s. They were also on UA in 67.

🇺🇸	DON'T LET THE RAIN COME DOWN (CROOKED LITTLE MAN)	6	09 MAY 64	PHILIPS

TAJA SEVELLE

Female singer/songwriter and one time DJ was a part of the late 80s booming music scene in Minneapolis. She scored a UK Top 40 with one of her own songs which she followed with 'Wouldn't You Love To Love Me' (UK 59).

🇬🇧	LOVE IS CONTAGIOUS *(US No. 62)*	7	19 MAR 88	PAISLEY

SEVERINE

Paris born female singer won the European song contest, when it was held in Ireland, for Monaco with her one-off UK hit when she was 21.

🇬🇧	UN BANC, UN ARBRE, UNE RUE	9	29 MAY 71	PHILIPS

SEX PISTOLS

Extremely controversial London group that included Johnny Rotten (Lydon) and Sid Vicious (John Beverly). Assembled by manager Malcolm McLaren, they were the leaders of the UK punk movement and one of the most influential acts on the rock era. They broke taboos, were banned from numerous places and sacked by two record labels. They scored 10 UK-only Top 40 singles and four UK-only Top 40 LPs. Act never made the US Top 100 and split whilst on tour there. Johnny then formed P.I.L. and Sid died while awaiting trial for murder in 79.

🇬🇧	GOD SAVE THE QUEEN	2	11 JUN 77	VIRGIN
	PRETTY VACANT *(Jumped from 45-7)*	6	30 JUL 77	VIRGIN
	HOLIDAYS IN THE SUN	8	29 OCT 77	VIRGIN
	NO ONE IS INNOCENT/MY WAY *(B-side Frank Sinatra 69 hit)*	7	15 JUL 78	VIRGIN
	SOMETHING ELSE/FRIGGIN' IN THE RIGGIN' *(A-side Eddie Cochran 59 hit)*	3	31 MAR 79	VIRGIN
	SILLY THING/WHO KILLED BAMBI *(B-side was by Ten Pole Tudor)*	6	21 APR 79	VIRGIN
	C'MON EVERYBODY *(Eddie Cochran 58 hit)*	3	14 JUL 79	VIRGIN

Also see P.I.L.

SHADOWS

The UK's most successful instrumental act have scored 24 Top 20 singles and 16 Top 20 LPs spanning a record 30 years (not to mention dozens of hits with Cliff Richard) but have never entered the US charts. Mainstays of the group Hank Marvin and Bruce Welch were in The Railroaders and first recorded in 58 in The Five Chesternuts. Their first three 45s (two as The Drifters) flopped but they became the top selling and most imitated group in the UK before The Beatles. Members Jet Harris and Tony Meehan left in 68 before contentrating on separate projects. They re-united in 75 continuing their amazing string of hits.

🇬🇧	APACHE *(First recorded by Bert Weedon) (Cover by Jorgen Ingmann was US No. 2)*	1(6)	19 AUG 60	COLUMBIA
	MAN OF MYSTERY *(From the film series)*	6	02 DEC 60	COLUMBIA
	F.B.I. *(Entered at No. 10)*	4	17 FEB 61	COLUMBIA
	FRIGHTENED CITY *(Entered at No. 9)*	3	02 JUN 61	COLUMBIA

158

KON-TIKI (Entered at No. 6) (They then had Top Single, LP & EP – a UK first)		3(1)	15 SEP 61	COLUMBIA
THE SAVAGE (Covered in US by The Ventures)		9	24 NOV 61	COLUMBIA
WONDERFUL LAND		1(9)	14 MAR 62	COLUMBIA
GUITAR TANGO (Entered at No. 8)		4	10 AUG 62	COLUMBIA
DANCE ON (Composed by The Avons)		1(3)	04 JAN 63	COLUMBIA
FOOT TAPPER (From film 'Summer Holiday')		1(1)	29 MAR 63	COLUMBIA
ATLANTIS		2	28 JUN 63	COLUMBIA
SHINDIG		6	04 OCT 63	COLUMBIA
THE RISE & FALL OF FLINGEL BUNT		5	06 JUN 64	COLUMBIA
DON'T MAKE MY BABY BLUE		10	28 AUG 65	COLUMBIA
(Frankie Laine 63 US hit – first vocal Top 10)				
DON'T CRY FOR ME ARGENTINA		5	10 FEB 79	EMI
THEME FROM THE DEER HUNTER (CAVATINA)		9	02 JUN 79	EMI

Also see Cliff Richard/Jet Harris & Tony Meehan

SHADOWS OF KNIGHT

Garage band from Chicago fronted by Sim Sohns had two US-only Top 40s in 66 – the other being the follow up 'Oh Yeah' (39). They re-appeared briefly in 68 as a Kasenetz-Katz bubblegum rock group on Team and Super K. They also re-recorded their big hit as 'Gloria 69' on Atco.

 GLORIA (Originally by Them) 10 07 MAY 66 DUNWICH

SHAG

Jonathan King revived the famous children's nursery rhyme (a hit by Johnny Thunder and Frankie Vaughan in 62) under this pseudonym.

 LOOP DI LOVE 4 18 NOV 72 UK

SHAKATAK

UK jazz/funk group, who started as Shack Attack, are fronted by keyboard playing composer Bill Sharpe. Their first chart hits were instrumentals but they had the biggest of their 14 UK-only charters with 45s featuring singer Jill Saward. They have sold millions of LPs in Japan and Bill has also had hits in a duo with Gary Numan.

 NIGHT BIRDS 9 24 APR 82 POLYDOR
DOWN ON THE STREET 9 04 AUG 84 POLYDOR

SHAKESPEARS SISTER

Female rock duo, named after a Smiths track, features Dave Stewart's wife Siobhan (nee Fahey) ex Bananarama member and Marcella Detroit. They first charted with their second single which they followed with 'Run Silent'.

 YOU'RE HISTORY 7 19 AUG 89 FFRR/LONDON

Also see Bananarama

SHALAMAR

Act's first hit 'Uptown Festival' in 77 was sung by session singers. In 79 the group were two dancers from US TV's Soul Train Jeffrey Daniel and Jody Watley plus Howard Hewett. They became transatlantic fashion and trend setters with Jeffrey taking the limelight (he helped introduce body popping to the UK). They had 11 UK (4 US) Top 40s before Jody and Jeffrey left in 84. They all recorded solo and both Howard (who left in 86) and to a greater extent Jody became stars in their own right.

I CAN MAKE YOU FEEL GOOD		7	01 MAY 82	SOLAR
A NIGHT TO REMEMBER (US No. 44)		5	17 JUL 82	SOLAR
THERE IT IS		5	02 OCT 82	SOLAR
DEAD GIVEAWAY (US No. 22)		8	02 JUL 83	SOLAR
THE SECOND TIME AROUND (UK No. 45)		8	22 MAR 80	SOLAR

Also see Jody Watley

SHAM 69

Punk rockers formed by socially conscious songwriter Jimmy Pursey. The quintet had five UK-only Top 20s in just 15 months. The group have also had releases later on Step Forward and Legacy and Jimmy went solo in 80 with little success.

IF THE KIDS ARE UNITED	9	12 AUG 78	POLYDOR
HURRY UP HARRY	10	04 NOV 78	POLYDOR
HERSHAM BOYS	6	18 AUG 79	POLYDOR
(Group got name from graffiti saying 'Hersham 68')				

SHANGRI-LAS

The most successful white girl group of the mid 50s was made up of two sets of New York sisters Betty & Mary Weiss and twins Mary & Marge Ganser. They chalked up six US (2 UK) Top 40s with their distinctive records. Marge later died of a drug overdose and the girls continued as a trio.

LEADER OF THE PACK	3	18 NOV 72	KAMA SUTRA
(Record had three separate chart runs in UK)				
LEADER OF THE PACK (was on two labels)	7	03 JUL 76	CHARLY/ CONTEMPO
(Originally reached UK No. 11 in 65)				
REMEMBER (WALKIN' IN THE SAND) (UK No. 14)	5	26 SEP 64	RED BIRD
LEADER OF THE PACK	1(1)	28 NOV 64	RED BIRD
(15 year old Billy Joel was on Piano)				
I CAN NEVER GO HOME ANYMORE	6	11 DEC 65	RED BIRD

SHANNON

Dance music singer born Brenda Shannon Greene in Washington had three UK (1 US) Top 40s. She followed her classic hit with 'Give Me Tonight'. Act who was the Top US Dance Artist of 84 joined Atlantic in 87.

LET THE MUSIC PLAY (UK No. 14) 8 25 FEB 84 MIRAGE

DEL SHANNON

Michigan singer/songwriter was born Charles Westover. His first 45 was a UK & US No. 1 and in all he scored 14 UK (8 US) Top 40s. He was the first act to chart in the US with a Beatles song ('From Me To You' in 77). He wrote Peter & Gordon's hit 'I Go To Pieces' and produced Top 10s for Brian Hyland and Smith. He was also on Berlee in 63, Amy in 64, Liberty in 66, Dunhill in 69, UA in 73, Island in 75 and last hit the US Top 40 in 82 on Network (produced by Tom Petty). He had a sole country hit in 85 on Warner and committed suicide in 90.

RUNAWAY	1(1)	19 MAY 61	LONDON
HATS OFF TO LARRY	8	13 OCT 61	LONDON
SO LONG BABY (US No. 28)	10	05 JAN 62	LONDON
HEY LITTLE GIRL (US No. 38)	4	11 MAY 62	LONDON
SWISS MAID (US No. 64 – comp. Roger Miller)	3	16 NOV 62	LONDON
LITTLE TOWN FLIRT (US No. 12)	4	08 FEB 63	LONDON
TWO KINDS OF TEARDROPS (US No. 50)	6	24 MAY 63	LONDON
KEEP SEARCHIN' (WE'LL FOLLOW THE SUN)	3	13 FEB 65	STATESIDE
RUNAWAY	1(4)	24 APR 61	BIG TOP
HATS OFF TO LARRY	5	31 JUL 61	BIG TOP
KEEP SEARCHIN'(WE'LL FOLLOW THE SUN)	9	30 JAN 65	AMY

HELEN SHAPIRO

The UK's first big female star of the 60s debuted on the charts when just a 14 year old schoolgirl. The deep voiced poll winning act was in the films 'It's Trad Dad' and 'Play It Cool'. She had 10 UK-only Top 40s and last hit when she was 17. On tour she was supported by The Beatles who wrote 'Misery' for her and she recorded 'It's My Party' before Lesley Gore. She was later was Pye, Phoenix, DJM, Magnet, Arista, Oval and in 89 on Calligraph.

DON'T TREAT ME LIKE A CHILD	5	12 MAY 61	COLUMBIA
YOU DON'T KNOW (Sold million world-wide)	1(3)	04 AUG 61	COLUMBIA
WALKIN' BACK TO HAPPINESS (US No. 100)	1(4)	13 OCT 61	COLUMBIA
(Sold million worldwide – she re-recorded in 89)				
TELL ME WHAT HE SAID	2	23 MAR 62	COLUMBIA
LITTLE MISS LONELY	8	10 AUG 62	COLUMBIA

FEARGAL SHARKEY

Londonderry (Ireland) based singer was the leader of the popular UK act The Undertones from 75-83. He was in the one-off act Assembly who had a UK Top 10. He has had four UK-only Top 40s – the first being on Zarjazz.

 A GOOD HEART (US No. 74 – Prod Dave Stewart) · 1(2) · 16 NOV 85 · VIRGIN
(Composed by Maria McKee about Benmont Tench)
YOU LITTLE THIEF · 5 · 18 JAN 86 · VIRGIN
(Composed by Benmont Tench about Maria McKee)

Also see Assembly/Undertones

DEE DEE SHARP

Born Dione LaRue in Philadelphia she started as a session singer in 61 and was featured on Chubby Checker's 'Slow Twistin'. As a soloist she had four US-only Top 10s in 12 months. She later recorded on Atco, Fairmount, Gamble, TSOP and Philly Int, where she married the boss Kenny Gamble.

MASHED POTATO TIME	2	05 MAY 62	CAMEO
GRAVY (FOR MY MASHED POTATOES)	9	14 JUL 62	CAMEO
RIDE	5	08 DEC 62	CAMEO
DO THE BIRD	10	13 APR 63	CAMEO

SANDIE SHAW

Top 60s UK pop singer was born Sandra Goodrich in Essex. Discovered by UK star Adam Faith, her second 45 was the first of 16 UK-only Top 40s (the last coming in 84 with an indie Chart No.1 recorded with The Smiths). In 67 the barefoot singer became the first UK act to win the Eurovision song contest. She joined CBS in 77, Palace in 83, Polydor in 86 and Rough Trade in 88.

 (THERE'S) ALWAYS SOMETHING THERE TO REMIND ME (US No. 52) · 1(3) · 24 OCT 64 · PYE
(Lou Johnson 64 US hit – jumped 11-1)
GIRL DON'T COME (US No. 42) · 3 · 23 JAN 65 · PYE
I'LL STOP AT NOTHING · 4 · 13 MAR 65 · PYE
LONG LIVE LOVE (US No. 97 – jumped from 8-1) · 1(3) · 29 MAY 65 · PYE
MESSAGE UNDERSTOOD · 6 · 23 OCT 65 · PYE
TOMORROW · 9 · 19 FEB 66 · PYE
(Above five hits written by Chris Andrews)
PUPPET ON A STRING · 1(3) · 29 APR 67 · PYE
(Eurovision winner – sold four million world-wide)
MONSIEUR DUPONT · 6 · 05 APR 69 · PYE

GARY SHEARSTON

Australian pop singer had a one-off UK hit with a clever arrangement of the Cole Porter standard. He made a couple of LPs in the UK and in 88 was on the Australian Larrikin label.

 I GET A KICK OUT OF YOU · 7 · 26 OCT 74 · CHARISMA

SHEER ELEGANCE

Black London based pop trio Dennis Robinson, Bev Gordon (known as Little Henry – the ex-leader of Earthquake) and songwriter Herbie Watkins. Their first release 'Going Downtown' missed but they managed to get two UK-only top 20s – the other being their second 45 Herbie's song 'Milky Way' (18).

 LIFE IS TOO SHORT GIRL · 9 · 08 MAY 76 · PYE INT.

PETER SHELLEY

UK songwriter/producer and reluctant singer. He was the singer on Alvin Stardust first smash 'My Coo-Ca-Choo', had two hits under his own name and returned to writing and producing in 77 after some lengthy legal problems.

 GEE BABY (US No. 81) · 4 · 19 OCT 74 · MAGNET
LOVE ME LOVE MY DOG · 3 · 19 APR 75 · MAGNET

ANNE SHELTON

One of the UK's top female singers in the pre rock years. She first became popular during World War II when she worked with Ambrose, Glenn Miller and Bing Crosby. She had the first English version of 'Lilli Marlene' and had a couple of US Top 40s in 49. She also managed a further four UK-only Top 20s between 55-61.

 LAY DOWN YOUR ARMS (US No. 59) · 1(4) · 21 SEP 56 · PHILIPS
(Covered in US by The Chordettes)
SAILOR · 8 · 10 FEB 61 · PHILIPS

SHEP & THE LIMELITES

One of the best 50s group singers James 'Shep' Sheppard fronted this New York based doo-wop trio who had six US-only charters. Their biggest hit was a sequel record to Shep's earlier group The Heartbeats records 'A Thousand Miles Away' and '500 Miles To Go'. Shep was found dead in his car in 70.

 DADDY'S HOME · 2 · 29 MAY 61 · HULL
(They later recorded 'What Did Daddy Do')

SHERBET

Australian pop rock quintet fronted by Daryl Braithwaite had 12 gold LPs in their homeland and a one-off transatlantic hit. They shortened their name to The Sherbs and had a small US hit with 'I Have The Skill' (No.61) in 81.

 HOWZAT (US No. 61) · 4 · 16 OCT 76 · EPIC

SHERIFF

Freddy Curci led this Canadian group whose small 83 hit became a US No. 1 in 89 (five years after they had broken up). It contained the longest note (25½ seconds) ever in a US Top 40 hit and was also the oldest recording to ever top the US chart.

WHEN I'M WITH YOU · 1(1) · 04 FEB 89 · CAPITOL

ALLAN SHERMAN

Comic script writer (for acts like Jackie Gleason and Joe E. Lewis) from Chicago had three successive No. 1 US LPs in the early 60s – a record for comedy and from the last one he had his sole transatlantic hit. Allan who also invented and produced the TV show I've Got A Secret died in 73.

HELLO MUDDUH, HELLO FADDUH (UK No. 17) · 2 · 24 AUG 63 · WARNER
(He reached US No. 59 with an updated version in 64)

BOBBY SHERMAN

Teen idol from California was a regular on US TVs Shindig and Here Comes The Bride. He recorded on Starcrest, Dot, Cameo, Condor, Decca, Parkway and Epic before getting his five US-only Top 20s. This singer/actor and multi-instrumentalist was later on Janus and now works in TV production.

LITTLE WOMAN	3	04 OCT 69	METROMEDIA
LA LA LA (IF I HAD YOU)	9	10 JAN 70	METROMEDIA
EASY COME, EASY GO	9	11 APR 70	METROMEDIA
JULIE, DO YA LOVE ME (UK No. 28)	5	19 SEP 70	METROMEDIA

PLUTO SHERVINGTON

Jamaican reggae singer/songwriter had two UK Top 20s – his other hit being 'Your Honour' (19) on KR in 82. This multi-instrumentalist had many West Indian No. 1's and also produced Paul Davidson's Top 10 UK hit.

DAT (West Indian hit in 74) · 6 · 06 MAR 76 · OPAL

SHIRELLES

New Jersey R&B quartet, originally called The Poquellos, fronted by Shirley Alston were one of the 60s most successful girl groups. They first recorded and charted on Tiara/Decca in 58 and in the 60s had 12 US (3 UK) Top 40s. The Beatles covered their 'Baby It's You' and 'Boys' and Manfred Mann took 'Sha La La'. They were later on Mercury, Bell, Black Rock, UA and RCA. Shirley went solo in 75 recording on Prodigal and then Strawberry.

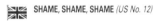	WILL YOU LOVE ME TOMORROW (Co-written by Carole King)	3	03 MAR 61	TOP RANK
	WILL YOU LOVE ME TOMORROW (Their fifth single on Scepter)	1(2)	30 JAN 61	SCEPTER
	DEDICATED TO THE ONE I LOVE (first rel. 58) (They re-recorded it in 71 – Orig. Five Royales)	3	27 MAR 61	SCEPTER
	MAMA SAID	4	29 MAY 61	SCEPTER
	BABY IT'S YOU	8	03 FEB 62	SCEPTER
	SOLDIER BOY (UK No. 30) (Song written in five minutes at the session)	1(3)	05 MAY 62	SCEPTER
	FOOLISH LITTLE GIRL	4	25 MAY 63	SCEPTER

SHIRLEY AND COMPANY

Shirley Goodman (nee Pixley) had been half of the top R&B duo Shirley & Lee who had five US-only charters in the mid 50s. Her unmistakable quavery soprano voice hit again two decades later backed by session singers (including Kenny Jeremiah ex singer of the Soul Survivors) on a Transatlantic Top 20, which she followed with the similar 'Cry Cry Cry'.

	SHAME, SHAME, SHAME (US No. 12)	6	01 MAR 75	ALL PLAT.

SHOCKING BLUE

Dutch group fronted by Mariska Veres and formed by Robby Van Leeuwen (ex Motions) led the short lived Dutch invasion in 70. The group who were together from 67-74 followed their one Top 40 with another No. 1 hit in Holland 'Mighty Joe'. They were later on Buddah, MGM and Polydor.

	VENUS	8	28 FEB 70	PENNY F.
	VENUS	1(1)	07 FEB 70	COLOSSUS

TROY SHONDELL

Indiana pop singer and multi instrumentalist's big hit was first released on his own Gold Crest label. He later moved to Nashville and had some country success on Star-Fox in 79, TeleSonic in 80 and AVM in 88. He also recorded on Everest, Decca, Ric, TRX and Bright Star.

	THIS TIME (UK No. 17 – Orig. Thomas Wayne)	6	24 OCT 61	LIBERTY

SHOWADDYWADDY

R'n'R revival act from Leicester (UK) who included Dave Bartram and Buddy Gask had a remarkable run of 23 UK-only Top 40s. The fun band's hits were nearly all revivals of US R'n'R hits of the previous two decades. Their early hits were produced by Mike Hurst (ex-Springfields).

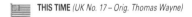	HEY ROCK AND ROLL	2	15 JUN 74	BELL
	THREE STEPS TO HEAVEN (Jumped from 50-13 – Eddie Cochran 60 UK hit)	2	14 JUN 75	BELL
	HEARTBEAT (Buddy Holly 58 hit)	7	20 SEP 75	BELL
	UNDER THE MOON OF LOVE (Curtis Lee 61 US hit)	1(3)	04 DEC 76	BELL
	WHEN (Kalin Twins 58 hit)	3	09 APR 77	ARISTA
	YOU GOT WHAT IT TAKES (Marv Johnson 59 hit)	2	20 AUG 77	ARISTA
	DANCIN' PARTY (Chubby Checker 62 US Hit)	4	26 NOV 77	ARISTA
	I WONDER WHY (Dion & Belmonts 58 US hit)	2	15 APR 78	ARISTA
	A LITTLE BIT OF SOAP (Jarmels 61 US hit)	5	22 JUL 78	ARISTA
	PRETTY LITTLE ANGEL EYES (Curtis Lee 61 US hit – Composed Boyce & Hart)	5	25 NOV 78	ARISTA

LABI SIFFRE

London born singer/songwriter/guitarist first charted with his fourth Pye International release 'It Must Be Love' (later covered by Madness) (14) in 71. He had another two UK-only Top 40s in the 70s and had his biggest hit 15 years later. He also recorded on EMI in 74 and Chrysalis in 87.

	(SOMETHING INSIDE) SO STRONG	4	16 MAY 87	CHINA

SIGUE SIGUE SPUTNIK

Much hyped London band more concerned with appearance than music included Tony James (ex-Chelsea and Generation X) and Martin Degville never achieved the success they anticipated and in all had three UK-only Top 40s. Tony joined Sisters of Mercy in 90.

	LOVE MISSILE F1-11 (Entered at No. 7)	3	08 MAR 86	PARLOPHONE

SILKIE

Folk/pop foursome based in Hull (UK), who featured the voice of Silvia Tatler, had the hit version of The Beatles song from the film 'Help'. The Beatles also helped produce the track and played on it. It was their second single and their only chart record.

	YOU'VE GOT TO HIDE YOUR LOVE AWAY (UK No. 28)	10	27 NOV 65	FONTANA

SILVER CONVENTION

German based Grammy winning female disco trio who included Penny Mclean (who later had solo disco success). They first charted in the UK with 'Save Me' and had four UK (2 US) Top 40s.

	GET UP AND BOOGIE (THAT'S RIGHT)	7	08 MAY 76	MAGNET
	FLY ROBIN FLY (UK No. 28) (Song originally called 'Run Rabbit Run')	1(3)	29 NOV 75	MIDLAND INT.
	GET UP AND BOOGIE 2	2	12 JUN 76	MIDLAND INT.

SIMON & GARFUNKEL

Top folk rock duo Paul Simon and Art Garfunkel first charted as Tom & Jerry in 57 with 'Hey, Schoolgirl' (US 49). Tom & Jerry also appeared on Hunt, Bell, Ember, ABC and Mercury. They have scored 15 US (7 UK) Top 40 singles and six US & UK Top 10 LPs. They have also spent more time on the UK LP chart than any one but The Beatles and at one time in 68 they had three of the Top 5 US LPs. They split at their peak in 70 and have occasionally worked together since. Songwriter Paul has had many solo hits and Art has charted too and acted in films.

	HOMEWARD BOUND (Written on Wigan (UK) railway station)	9	14 MAY 66	CBS
	MRS. ROBINSON	4	10 AUG 68	CBS
	MRS. ROBINSON (E.P.)	9	08 FEB 69	CBS
	THE BOXER	6	07 JUN 69	CBS
	BRIDGE OVER TROUBLED WATER (BRITS award as Top International 45 between 52-77)	1(3)	28 MAR 70	CBS
	THE SOUNDS OF SILENCE (Drums & guitar were added without duos knowledge)	1(2)	01 JAN 66	COLUMBIA
	HOMEWARD BOUND	5	26 APR 66	COLUMBIA
	I AM A ROCK (UK No. 17 – originally a Paul Simon solo in 64)	3	11 JUN 66	COLUMBIA
	MRS. ROBINSON (Double Grammy winning record)	1(3)	01 JUN 68	COLUMBIA
	THE BOXER	7	17 MAY 69	COLUMBIA
	BRIDGE OVER TROUBLED WATER (Multi Grammy winner and Top US Single of 70)	1(6)	28 FEB 70	COLUMBIA
	CECILIA	4	30 MAY 70	COLUMBIA
	MY LITTLE TOWN	9	13 DEC 75	COLUMBIA

Also see Paul Simon/Art Garfunkel

CARLY SIMON

New York singer/songwriter first charted in 64 with sister Lucy in The Simon Sisters. Grammy winner in 72 as Best New Artist, she has notched up 10 US (5 UK) Top 20 singles and 5 US (2 UK) Top 20 LPs to date.

🇬🇧 YOU'RE SO VAIN (Inc. vocals from Mick Jagger)	4	20 JAN 73	ELEKTRA
NOBODY DOES IT BETTER	7	17 SEP 77	ELEKTRA
(From the film 'The Spy Who Loves Me')			
WHY (US No. 74 – also UK No. 56 in 89)	10	02 OCT 82	WEA
COMING ROUND AGAIN (US No. 18)	10	28 FEB 87	ARISTA
(From film 'Heartburn' – she has UK Top 10 every 5 years)			
🇺🇸 THAT'S THE WAY I'VE ALWAYS HEARD IT SHOULD BE	10	10 JUL 71	ELEKTRA
YOU'RE SO VAIN	1(3)	06 JAN 73	ELEKTRA
MOCKINGBIRD (And JAMES TAYLOR – her ex-husband)	5	23 MAR 74	ELEKTRA
(UK No. 34 – Inez Foxx 63 US hit)			
NOBODY DOES IT BETTER	2	22 OCT 77	ELEKTRA
(Co-written by Carole Bayer Sager)			
YOU BELONG TO ME (Co-writ. Michael McDonald)	6	24 JUN 78	ELEKTRA

JOE SIMON

Louisiana singer was in The Golden Tones and first recorded for Hush in 60. He had the first of 49 black music hits (including 28 Top 20s) on Vee Jay in 65. He has also had 31 US pop hits with his sole UK entry being 'Step By Step' (UK 14/US 37) in 73. He has also been on Gee-Bee, Dot, Irall, Sound Stage 7, Compleat and Posse.

🇺🇸 GET DOWN, GET DOWN (GET ON THE FLOOR)	8	21 JUN 75	SPRING

PAUL SIMON

Top New Jersey singer/songwriter recorded demos with Carole King as The Cosines and recorded as a soloist under the names True Taylor on Big, Paul Kane on Tribute, Jerry Landis on Warwick, Canadian American and Amy and Tico & The Triumphs on Amy (he had small US hits under the last two names). After his many hits in Simon & Garfunkel he has notched up seven US (4 UK) Top 20s and six US & UK Top 20 LPs including the Grammy winners 'Still Crazy After All These Years' and 'Graceland'.

🇬🇧 MOTHER & CHILD REUNION (Recorded in Jamaica)	5	18 MAR 72	CBS
TAKE ME TO THE MARDI GRAS	7	14 JUL 73	CBS
YOU CAN CALL ME AL (US No. 23)	4	18 OCT 86	WARNER
🇺🇸 MOTHER AND CHILD REUNION	4	01 APR 72	COLUMBIA
KODACHROME	2	07 JUL 73	COLUMBIA
LOVES ME LIKE A ROCK (UK No. 39)	2	06 OCT 73	COLUMBIA
(Feat. The Dixie Hummingbirds)			
50 WAYS TO LEAVE YOUR LOVER (UK No. 23)	1(3)	07 FEB 76	COLUMBIA
SLIP SLIDIN' AWAY	5	28 JAN 78	COLUMBIA
(UK No. 36 – Backing vocals The Oak Ridge Boys)			
LATE IN THE EVENING (UK No. 58)	6	27 SEP 80	WARNER

Also see Simon & Garfunkel

NINA SIMONE

Jazz influenced singer/pianist known as 'The High Priestess Of Soul' was born Eunice Waymon in South Carolina. Her biggest US hit was her chart debut in 59 'I Loves You Porgy' (18). She was active in the Black Power movement in the 60s. She had a UK comeback in 87 with a 28 year old track.

🇬🇧 AIN'T GOT NO – I GOT LIFE/DO WHAT YOU GOTTA DO (US No. 94) (A-side from the musical 'Hair')	2	21 DEC 68	RCA
TO LOVE SOMEBODY (Bee Gees 67 hit)	5	08 FEB 69	RCA
MY BABY JUST CARES FOR ME	5	21 NOV 87	CHARLY
(Was UK Indie Top 10 in 85 – used in TV perfume ad.)			

SIMPLE MINDS

Top Scottish rock group fronted by Jim Kerr evolved out of punk band Johnny & The Self Abusers (on Chiswick). They first charted in 79 on Zoom and have since had 14 UK (4 US) Top 20s and four UK No.1 LPs and are one of the top stadium rock acts of late 80s. They starred in Live Aid and the first Nelson Mandela show and have toured for Amnesty International.

🇬🇧 DON'T YOU (FORGET ABOUT ME)	7	04 MAY 85	VIRGIN
(Their 15th single – was also UK No. 62 in 86)			
ALIVE AND KICKING	7	26 OCT 85	VIRGIN
SANCTIFY YOURSELF (US No. 14)	10	08 FEB 86	VIRGIN
ALL THE THINGS SHE SAID (US No. 28)	9	19 APR 86	VIRGIN
BELFAST CHILD (Entered at No.2 – an EP record)	1(2)	25 FEB 89	VIRGIN
(Second longest No. 1 6' 39")			
🇺🇸 DON'T YOU (FORGET ABOUT ME)	1(1)	18 MAY 85	A&M
(From the film Breakfast Club)			
ALIVE & KICKING	3	28 DEC 85	A&M

SIMPLY RED

Manchester group fronted by the unmistakable singer/songwriter Mick Hucknall whose previous group The Frantic Elevators had recorded on Eric's, Crackin' Up, No Waiting and TJM between 79-83. They have had 7 UK (2 US) Top 20s and they had UK's top selling LP of 89 with 'A New Flame' (over 1.2 million in UK and 5 million world-wide). They moved to East West in 90.

🇬🇧 HOLDING BACK THE YEARS	2	24 MAY 86	WEA
(Originally peaked in UK at No. 51 in 85)			
IF YOU DON'T KNOW ME BY NOW	2	15 APR 89	ELEKTRA
(Harold Melvin & The Blue Notes 72 hit)			
🇺🇸 HOLDING BACK THE YEARS	1(1)	12 JUL 86	ELEKTRA
(Orig. rel. on No Waiting by The Frantic Elevators)			
IF YOU DON'T KNOW ME BY NOW	1(1)	15 JUL 89	ELEKTRA

JOYCE SIMS

New York black dance music singer/songwriter/pianist and producer had the first of her five UK-only Top 40s with 'All And All' (16) in 86.

🇬🇧 COME INTO MY LIFE	7	30 JAN 88	LONDON

FRANK SINATRA

One of the century's most acclaimed and influential pop stylists. Born in New Jersey he started in the Hoboken Four and first recorded with the Harry James Band in 39. In 40 he joined the Tommy Dorsey Orchestra, sang on many of their hits and went solo in 42. This first real 'teen idol' has had over 160 solo US chart singles and 36 in the UK. He has also scored 63 US (50 UK) chart LPs including 31 US Top 10s (a record for solo artists). He has won every award possible and had his own successful label Reprise. This pop music legend has also had string of hit movies and has packed theatres around the world for half a century.

🇬🇧 LEARNIN' THE BLUES	2	26 AUG 55	CAPITOL
LOVE AND MARRIAGE (From TV prod. Our Town)	3	20 JAN 56	CAPITOL
THE TENDER TRAP (From the film)	2	10 FEB 57	CAPITOL
ALL THE WAY (From film The Joker Is Wild)	3	17 JAN 58	CAPITOL
HIGH HOPES	6	06 NOV 59	CAPITOL
(US No. 30 – from the film A Hole In The Head)			
OL' MACDONALD (US No. 25 – entered at No. 9)	9	25 NOV 60	CAPITOL
STRANGERS IN THE NIGHT	1(4)	04 JUN 66	REPRISE
(Co-written Bert Kaempfert)			
SOMETHIN' STUPID (With NANCY SINATRA)	1(2)	15 APR 67	REPRISE
MY WAY (US No. 27 – Top UK record of 69)	5	31 MAY 69	REPRISE
(Also UK No. 18 in 70, UK No. 22 in 71 & No. 50 in 72)			
LOVE'S BEEN GOOD TO ME (US No. 75)	8	08 NOV 69	REPRISE
THEME FROM NEW YORK NEW YORK	4	15 MAR 86	REPRISE
(From the film)			
(US No. 32 in 80 and UK No. 59 in 80)			
🇺🇸 LEARNIN' THE BLUES	2	23 JUL 55	CAPITOL
LOVE AND MARRIAGE	6	14 JAN 56	CAPITOL
HEY! JEALOUS LOVER	8	08 DEC 56	CAPITOL
STRANGERS IN THE NIGHT	1(1)	02 JUL 66	REPRISE
(From the film A Man Could Get Killed)			
THAT'S LIFE (UK No. 46 – Orig. O.C. Smith)	4	24 DEC 66	REPRISE
SOMETHIN' STUPID (With NANCY SINATRA)	1(4)	15 APR 67	REPRISE

NANCY SINATRA

New Jersey born oldest child of Frank Sinatra. She appeared in the 60 Frank Sinatra/Elvis Presley TV special and first recorded on her dad's Reprise label in 61. She had the original of 'Like I Do' (Maureen Evans UK hit) in 62 and has had 10 US (7 UK) Top 40s. She has also starred in several films and later recorded on Private Stock, RCA and Elektra.

🇬🇧	THESE BOOTS ARE MADE FOR WALKIN' *(Her 14th single release and first chart entry)*	1(3)	19 FEB 66	REPRISE
	SUGAR TOWN	8	18 FEB 67	REPRISE
	SOMETHIN' STUPID *(And FRANK SINATRA)* *(Follow up duet 'Feelin' Kinda Sunday' was a miss)*	1(2)	15 APR 67	REPRISE
	DID YOU EVER *(And LEE HAZLEWOOD)* *(Charlie Louvin & Melba Montgomery 71 country hit)*	2	25 SEP 71	REPRISE
🇺🇸	THESE BOOTS ARE MADE FOR WALKIN'	1(1)	26 FEB 66	REPRISE
	HOW DOES THAT GRAB YOU DARLIN' *(UK No. 19)* *(She re-recorded above two on RCA in 73)*	7	14 MAY 66	REPRISE
	SUGAR TOWN *(Above three hits all composed by Lee Hazlewood)*	5	31 DEC 66	REPRISE
	SOMETHIN' STUPID *(And FRANK SINATRA)*	1(4)	15 APR 67	REPRISE

SINGING NUN

Grammy winning Belgian nun Sister Luc-Gabrielle (Jeanine Deckers) who recorded as Souer Sourire ('Sister Smile') was the first female (and the first white act) to simultaneously top the US single and LP charts. Follow up to her sole hit 45 was 'Tous Les Chemins'. She committed suicide in 85 aged 52.

🇬🇧	DOMINIQUE	7	20 DEC 63	PHILIPS
🇺🇸	DOMINIQUE	1(4)	07 DEC 63	PHILIPS

SINITTA

Seattle born and UK based daughter of disco diva Miquel Brown. She had appeared in films and in musicals before recording on Midas in 83. To date she has scored six UK-only Top 20s with her hi-nrg dance tracks.

🇬🇧	SO MACHO/CRUISING	2	09 AUG 86	FANFARE
	TOY BOY	4	22 AUG 87	FANFARE
	CROSS MY BROKEN HEART	6	02 APR 88	FANFARE
	RIGHT BACK WHERE WE STARTED FROM *(US No. 84 – Maxine Nightingale 76 hit)*	4	17 JUN 89	FANFARE

SIOUXSIE & THE BANSHEES

Susan Ballion fronts this long running successful punk act. Group also includes drummer 'Budgie', who records with Siouxsie as The Creatures, and Steve 'Severin' Bailey who recorded in The Glove with one time Banshee Robert Smith (The Cure). They have had 15 UK-only Top 40s and nine UK-only Top 20 LPs. Their 'Peek-A-Boo' was the Top Modern Rock track in the US in 88.

🇬🇧	HONG KONG GARDEN	7	16 SEP 78	POLYDOR
	DEAR PRUDENCE *(Beatles song written about Mia Farrow's sister)*	3	15 OCT 83	WONDERLAND

SISTER SLEDGE

Kathy, Debbie, Joni and Kim Sledge from Philadelphia did backing vocals for Gamble & Huff and recorded as Sister Sledge on Money in 71. They first charted on Atco in 74 and most of their hits were written and produced by Nile Rodgers and Bernard Edwards. Act were more popular in the UK where they had seven Top 20s (2 in US). Kathy went solo in 89.

🇬🇧	HE'S THE GREATEST DANCER	6	14 APR 79	ATLANTIC/COT
	WE ARE FAMILY *(A remix was UK No. 33 in 84)*	8	16 JUN 79	ATLANTIC
	LOST IN MUSIC *(REMIX)* *(Original mix was UK No. 17 in 79)*	4	29 SEP 84	COTILLION/ATL
	FRANKIE *(US No. 75)* *(Written by a Swiss housewife about Sinatra)*	1(4)	29 JUN 85	ATLANTIC
🇺🇸	HE'S THE GREATEST DANCER	9	12 MAY 79	COTILLION
	WE ARE FAMILY	2	16 JUN 79	COTILLION

SISTERS OF MERCY

Leeds based Gothic rock group led by Andrew Eldritch had their first 45 in 80, appeared on CNT in 82 and first charted in 84. Group's Wayne Hussey (ex Dead or Alive) and Craig Adams left to form The Mission in 85. After recording as Sisterhood Andrew added Patricia Morrison (ex Gun Club) and the group had the biggest of its six UK-only hits. Patricia left in 90 and was replaced by Tony James (ex-Sigue Sigue Sputnik etc). They moved to East West in 90.

🇬🇧	THIS CORROSION	7	10 OCT 87	MERCIFUL RELE

PETER SKELLERN

Lancashire singer/songwriter first recorded in March Hare (aka Harlan County). He had two UK-only Top 20s the other being 'Hold On To Love' (14) in 75. In 84 he was in Oasis with Mary Hopkin on WEA. He was later on Island, Mercury, Safari, Sierra, BBC, Sonet and Alligator.

🇬🇧	YOU'RE A LADY *(US No. 50)*	3	14 OCT 72	DECCA

SKID ROW

New Jersey metal group fronted by controversial Sebastian Bach (Bierk). Their old friends Bon Jovi helped get them a deal and had them on their US tour. One of the most talked about new metal bands they have not suffered from Seb's problems with obscenity laws whilst on stage.

🇺🇸	18 AND LIFE *(UK No. 12)*	4	23 SEP 89	ATLANTIC

SKIDS

Innovative Scottish new wave band formed in 77 included Stuart Adamson and fellow songwriter and singer Richard Jobson. They had 10 UK-only charters before Stuart left to form Big Country and Richard became a poet/journalist/magazine columnist.

🇬🇧	INTO THE VALLEY	10	24 MAR 79	VIRGIN

SKY

UK classical/pop instrumental group included top musicians John Williams, Herbie Flowers (who composed Clive Dunn's UK No.1 'Grandad') and Kevin Peek. Album orientated act had six UK-only Top 20 LPs and a transatlantic single hit. This critically acclaimed group also performed sell out concerts around the world before John left in 83.

🇬🇧	TOCCATA *(US No. 83)*	5	03 MAY 80	ARIOLA

SKYLARK

Canadian group formed by pianist David Foster and featuring vocalist Donny Gerrard had their sole hit with their second 45. David went on to become a top writer/producer and Donny had six small black music hits.

🇺🇸	WILDFLOWER	9	26 MAY 73	CAPITOL

SLADE

The most popular UK group of the early 70s included singer Noddy Holder who had first recorded on EMI in 65 in Steve Brett & The Mavericks. The group were called The N'Betweens (on Columbia in 66) and Ambrose Slade (on Fontana in 69). Their fourth 45 as Slade was the first of 33 UK hits (the majority written by Noddy and bass player Jimmy Lea) including six No. 1s. They also had six UK-only Top 20 LPs including three No. 1s. In the US their only Top 20 came in 84. They were also featured on a Jive Bunny UK No. 1 in 89. Noddy is now a Manchester based DJ.

🇬🇧	COZ I LUV YOU	1(4)	13 NOV 71	POLYDOR
	LOOK WOT YOU DUN	4	19 FEB 72	POLYDOR
	TAKE ME BAK 'OME *(US No. 97)*	1(1)	01 JUL 72	POLYDOR
	MAMA WEER ALL CRAZEE NOW *(US No. 76)*	1(3)	09 SEP 72	POLYDOR
	GUDBUY T'JANE *(US No. 68)*	2	16 DEC 72	POLYDOR

CUM ON FEEL THE NOIZE *(US No. 98)* *(First of a record three 45s to enter at No. 1)*	1(4)	03 MAR 73	POLYDOR
SKWEEZE ME PLEEZE ME *(Entered at No. 1)*	1(3)	30 JUN 73	POLYDOR
MY FRIEND STAN	2	13 OCT 73	POLYDOR
MERRY XMAS EVERYBODY *(Entered at No. 1)* *(UK Gold – also charted in 81, 82, 83, 84, 85 & 86)*	1(4)	15 DEC 73	POLYDOR
EVERYDAY	3	20 APR 74	POLYDOR
BANGIN' MAN *(Entered at No. 4)*	3	13 JUL 74	POLYDOR
FAR FAR AWAY *(Entered at No. 3)*	2	26 OCT 74	POLYDOR
THANKS FOR THE MEMORY (WHAM BAM THANK YOU MAM)	7	31 MAY 75	POLYDOR
WE'LL BRING THE HOUSE DOWN	10	21 FEB 81	CHEAPSKATE
MY OH MY *(US No. 37)*	2	24 DEC 83	RCA
RUN RUNAWAY *(US No. 20 – biggest US hit)*	7	10 MAR 84	RCA

PERCY SLEDGE

Alabama singer had been in his cousin soul star Jimmy Hughes' group The Singing Clouds before joining the Esquires Combo whose members included Calvin Lewis and Andrew Wright who wrote his biggest hit. He had four US (1 UK) Top 20s in the 60s and a Dutch No. 1 in 69. In 87, thanks to its use in a Levis ad, his classic southern soul hit returned to the UK Top 10.

WHEN A MAN LOVES A WOMAN	4	25 JUN 66	ATLANTIC
WHEN A MAN LOVES A WOMAN *(21 year old 45)* *(Was No. 2 when 26 year old Ben E. King's 45 was top!)*	2	28 FEB 87	ATLANTIC
WHEN A MAN LOVES A WOMAN	1(2)	28 MAY 66	ATLANTIC

SLIK

Scottish pop band first called Salvation. Their debut 45 failed but they then had two UK-only Top 20s written and produced by the hit Martin & Coulter team. Band included James 'Midge' Ure who later scored in The Rich Kids, Visage, Ultravox, Band Aid (which he helped organise) and as a soloist.

FOREVER & EVER	1(1)	14 FEB 76	BELL

Also see Midge Ure

SLY & THE FAMILY STONE

Influential West Coast funk rock band led by Texan Sylvester 'Sly' Stewart. He had recorded as a soloist, in a duet the Stewart Brothers and in groups The Cogic Singers (with Billy Preston), The Viscaynes and The Stoners. He had also produced hits for The Beau Brummels and Bobby Freeman. In 67 the group debuted on Loadstone. They had 10 US (5 UK) Top 40s and five US-only Top 20 LPs. They were one of the top live acts of the late 60s, starred at 'Woodstock' and helped shape 70s funk. Sly's drug problems hurt his career and he was bankrupt by 76. He has had several unsuccessful comebacks.

DANCE TO THE MUSIC	7	17 AUG 68	DIRECTION
DANCE TO THE MUSIC	8	20 APR 68	EPIC
EVERYDAY PEOPLE *(UK No. 36)*	1(4)	15 FEB 69	EPIC
HOT FUN IN THE SUMMERTIME	2	18 OCT 69	EPIC
THANK YOU (FALETTINME BE MICE ELF AGIN)	1(2)	14 FEB 70	EPIC
FAMILY AFFAIR *(UK No. 15)*	1(3)	04 DEC 71	EPIC

SLY FOX

Duo Gary 'Mudbone' Cooper (ex P-Funk) and Michael Camacho followed their funky Beatle-esque one-off Top 10 with 'If Push Comes To Shove'.

LET'S GO ALL THE WAY	3	19 JUL 86	CAPITOL
LET'S GO ALL THE WAY	7	12 APR 86	CAPITOL

SMALL FACES

Mod R&B/rock quartet included singer Steve Marriott (who had recorded solo on Decca in 63 when aged 16), Ian McLagan, Ronnie Lane and Kenny Jones. They were an instant success and had 12 UK (1 US) Top 40s, mostly written by Steve and Ronnie. They split in 69 when Steve formed Humble Pie and the others plus Rod Stewart became The Faces. In 76 two of their hits re-charted and the group briefly reformed. Jones later joined and left The Who, McLagan is a session player in L.A., Marriott leads a band on the London pub circuit and Ronnie lives in the USA where his MS inspired the all star benefit concerts in 1983.

SHA LA LA LA LEE	3	19 MAR 66	DECCA
HEY GIRL	10	28 MAY 66	DECCA
ALL OR NOTHING *(Steve Marriott made new version on Trax in 89)*	1(1)	17 SEP 66	DECCA
MY MIND'S EYE	4	10 DEC 66	DECCA
ITCHYCOO PARK *(US No. 16)*	3	23 SEP 67	IMMEDIATE
TIN SOLDIER *(US No. 73)*	9	27 JAN 68	IMMEDIATE
LAZY SUNDAY *(Also UK No. 39 in 76)*	2	11 MAY 68	IMMEDIATE
ITCHYCOO PARK *(Re-issue)*	9	17 JAN 76	IMMEDIATE

Also see Humble Pie/Faces

MILLIE SMALL – SEE MILLIE FOR HIT DETAILS

SMITH

Short lived L.A. based rock group fronted by Gayle McCormick from St. Louis. They followed their sole Top 40 with 'Take A Look Around'. Gayle later had some solo success on Dunhill and was also on Shady Brook.

BABY IT'S YOU *(Produced by Del Shannon)*	5	01 NOV 69	DUNHILL

HURRICANE SMITH

Singer/musician Norman Smith was an EMI Records engineer and producer, and worked with The Beatles, Pink Floyd and Little Richard. He had three UK (1 US) Top 40s as an artist, recorded on Pye in 76 and returned to producing.

DON'T LET IT DIE	2	03 JUL 71	COLUMBIA
OH BABE WHAT WOULD YOU SAY?	4	03 JUN 72	COLUMBIA
OH BABE WHAT WOULD YOU SAY?	3	17 FEB 73	CAPITOL

MEL SMITH – SEE KIM WILDE FOR HIT DETAILS

O.C. SMITH

Jazz/MOR/pop singer born Ocie Smith in Louisiana. He was in Sy Oliver's Band before recording on Cadence in 56 and was with Count Basie's band in the early 60s. In all he had 10 US (2 UK) charters. He also recorded on MGM, Broadway, Big Top, Caribou, Shady Brook, Family, Motown and Rendezvous.

SON OF HICKORY HOLLERS TRAMP *(US No. 40)* *(Johnny Darrell 68 country hit)*	2	06 JUL 68	CBS
LITTLE GREEN APPLES *(Roger Miller 68 country hit)*	2	26 OCT 68	COLUMBIA

PATTI SMITH GROUP

Critically acclaimed Chicago poetess and new wave/punk singer. She first recorded in 74 on Mer/Sire. She has had one Top 40 single and two US (1 UK) Top 20 LPs. In 79 she quit music to return in 88 with the LP 'Dream of Life'.

BECAUSE THE NIGHT *(US No. 13 – Written Bruce Springsteen)*	5	27 MAY 78	ARISTA

REX SMITH

Singer/actor from Florida first recorded in the hard rock band Rex. In 79 he played a rock star in the TV-movie Sooner Or Later which the biggest of his two hits came from – the other being a duet with Rachel Sweet in 81. He later starred on Broadway in Grease and The Pirates Of Penzance.

 YOU TAKE MY BREATH AWAY   10   23 JUN 79   COLUMBIA

SAMMI SMITH

Californian born singer has had 37 country hits to date with one crossover pop Top 40 hit. She has also recorded on Columbia, Elektra, Zodiac, Cyclone, Sound Factory, Step One and joined Playback in 90.

 HELP ME MAKE IT THROUGH THE NIGHT   8   27 MAR 71   MEGA
(Original hit of the Kris Kristofferson song)

WHISTLING JACK SMITH

Liverpool's Billy Moeller (who previously recorded as Coby Wells) fronted this one-off Transatlantic Top 20, although the whistling was by the Mike Sammes Singers. The follow up was 'I Was Bizet's Carmen'.

 I WAS KAISER BILL'S BATMAN *(US No. 20)*   5   01 APR 67   DERAM

SMITHS

Innovative and influential Manchester group included the distinctive vocalist Morrissey and his co-writer Johnny Marr. They had numerous indie No. 1s and at one time in 84 they had the Indie top three. Their first 45 'Hand In Glove' (later a hit for Sandie Shaw) missed the pop chart but then they chalked up 15 UK-only Top 40s and seven UK-only Top 10 LPs. The act, who have a big cult following in the US, split in 87. Morrissey continued his run of hits and Johnny became a much in demand guitarist.

HEAVEN KNOWS I'M MISERABLE NOW   10   09 JUN 84   ROUGH TRADE
(B-side about The Moors Murders was banned)
SHEILA TAKE A BOW   10   02 MAY 87   ROUGH TRADE
(Was recorded as a radio session for DJ John Peel)

Also see Morrissey

SMOKIE

UK pop quartet led by Chris Norman were once called Kindness and first recorded as Smokey (changed to avoid problems with Mr. Robinson). Many of their 11 UK only Top 20s were written by the hit Chinn & Chapman duo. Chris later had a US Top 10 with Suzi Quatro and is now a top German star. They recorded on Mean in 82 and Priority in 87 and made the UK Top 100 in 90.

 IF YOU THINK YOU KNOW HOW TO LOVE ME   3   06 AUG 75   RAK
(US No. 96)
DON'T PLAY YOUR ROCK 'N' ROLL TO ME   8   25 OCT 75   RAK
(First two hits as SMOKEY)
LIVING NEXT DOOR TO ALICE *(US No. 25)*   5   08 JAN 77   RAK
IT'S YOUR LIFE   5   20 AUG 77   RAK
NEEDLES AND PINS   10   12 NOV 77   RAK
(US No. 68 – Jackie DeShannon 63 US hit)
OH CAROL   5   17 JUN 78   RAK

Also see Suzi Quatro

(FATHER ABRAHAM &) THE SMURFS

Dutch novelty act first hit in Holland in the early 70s and had three UK-only Top 20s based on the children's story characters The Smurfs. Other hits were 'Dippety Day' (13) and 'Christmas Day In Smurfland' (19). They later appeared on Dureco and Creole.

 THE SMURF SONG *(Was No. 2 for six weeks)*   2   24 JUN 78   DECCA

PHOEBE SNOW

Well regarded jazz/folk/pop singer/songwriter born Phoebe Laub in New York had two US Top 40s – the other one with Paul Simon. Her only UK hit was 'Every Night' (37) in 79. She later recorded on Columbia and Mirage.

POETRY MAN   5   12 APR 75   SHELTER

SOFT CELL

Electro rock duo formed in Leeds (UK) in 79 by singer Marc Almond and his co-writer/synth player David Ball. First release was an EP on their own Big Frock label, then they were on the influential 'Some Bizarre' album. Their second single was the first of nine UK (1 US) Top 40s. They also had four UK-only Top 20 LPs before going their separate ways in 84. Marc had further hits as a soloist.

 TAINTED LOVE *(Also No. 43 in 82 & 43 in 85)*   1(2)   05 SEP 81   SOME BIZZARE
(Top UK single of 81 – originally by Gloria Jones)
BEDSITTER   4   05 DEC 81   SOME BIZZARE
SAY HELLO WAVE GOODBYE   3   20 FEB 82   SOME BIZZARE
TORCH *(They were UK's top act of 82)*   2   19 JUN 82   SOME BIZZARE
WHAT *(Originally by Judy Street)*   3   28 AUG 82   SOME BIZZARE
TAINTED LOVE *(Took 23 weeks to make Top 10)*   8   17 JUL 82   SIRE
(On US Top 100 for a record 43 weeks)

Also see Marc Almond

JOANIE SOMMERS

New York singer, who did the Pepsi Cola jingles in the early 60s, first charted in 60 with 'One Boy' and followed her biggest hit with 'When The Boys Get Together'. She was on Columbia in 66 and re-appeared on ABC in 78.

JOHNNY GET ANGRY *(UK No. 27)*   7   21 JUL 62   WARNER

SONIA

The youngest female to top the UK chart since Mary Hopkin in 68 was this bouncy 17 year old pop singer and actress from Liverpool. She was another of the hit acts from the S.A.W. stable and in 89 she had two UK-only Top 20s – the other being 'Can't Forget You' (17).

 YOU'LL NEVER STOP ME FROM LOVING YOU   1(2)   22 JUL 89   CHRYSALIS

SONNY

Singer/songwriter who started as an A&R man at Specialty Records. He recorded as Don Christy, Sonny Christie and Ronny Sommers on Specialty, Fidelity, Go, Name, Sawmi, Rush and Highland. He co-wrote 'Needles & Pins' and many of Sonny & Cher's hits. He had some acting success after the duo split and in 88 he was elected Mayor of Palm Springs.

LAUGH AT ME *(Re-release)*   9   18 SEP 65   ATLANTIC
(Was first released before first Sonny & Cher hit)
LAUGH AT ME   10   25 SEP 65   ATCO

SONNY & CHER

Detroit's Salvatore 'Sonny' Bono and Californian Cher (Cherilyn LaPier) were one of the 60s top transatlantic acts, not to mention the most successful man and wife duo of all time. They met as session singers for Phil Spector and were married in 63, when they first recorded together on Vault (as Caesar and Cleo). The hippy dressed duo scored eight US (6 UK) Top 20s and had their own TV series from 71 to 74, when they were divorced.

I GOT YOU BABE   1(2)   28 AUG 65   ATLANTIC
(First US mixed duo to top the UK chart)
LITTLE MAN *(US No. 21 – also top in Holland)*   4   01 OCT 66   ATLANTIC
ALL I EVER NEED IS YOU   8   19 FEB 72   MCA
(Ray Sanders 71 country hit)

🇺🇸 I GOT YOU BABE *(Was recorded as B-side)*	1(3)	14 AUG 65	ATCO
BABY DON'T GO	8	09 OCT 65	REPRISE
(UK No. 11 – first released as by Caesar & Cleo)			
THE BEAT GOES ON *(UK No. 29)*	6	25 FEB 67	ATCO
ALL I EVER NEED IS YOU	7	25 DEC 71	KAPP
A COWBOY'S WORK IS NEVER DONE	8	29 APR 72	KAPP

Also see Sonny/Cher

S.O.S. BAND

Atlanta funk band featured singer Mary Davis until 87 when Pennye Ford (ex soloist and in Reach) took over. The 'Sounds of Success' band have had 18 black music hits, many produced and written by Jam and Lewis (group gave the top duo their first hit). Their biggest of eight UK hits was 'Just Be Good To Me' (13) – a No. 1 in 90 by Beats International. Mary was on Tabu in 90.

🇺🇸 TAKE YOUR TIME (DO IT RIGHT) (PT. 1) *(UK No. 51)*	3	16 AUG 80	TABU

SOUL II SOUL

Double Grammy winning London based soul/dance group masterminded by Jazzie B (Beresford Romeo) and Nellee Hooper (who was in Wild Bunch on Fourth & Broadway). They spent 10 years perfecting the sound which made them the most successful and influential UK based black group of all time. They were the first black act ever to top the UK single and LP chart simultaneously and the first UK act to win awards from the US TV show Soul Train. Sometime singer Caron Wheeler recorded solo in 90 on EMI.

🇬🇧 KEEP ON MOVIN' *(US No. 11)*	5	25 MAR 89	10
(Feat. Reggae Philharmonic Orchestra)			
BACK TO LIFE (HOWEVER DO YOU WANT ME)	1(4)	24 JUN 89	10
(Above two feat. CARON WHEELER)			
GET A LIFE *(Entered at No. 5)*	3	16 DEC 89	10
(Inc. US cousin Marcy Lewis & other family members)			
🇺🇸 BACK TO LIFE *(Featuring CARON WHEELER)*	4	16 DEC 89	VIRGIN
(They had the Top 2 12" singles in US in 89)			

SOUL SURVIVORS

East Coast (US) blue eyed soul band formed by brothers Richard and Charles Ingui and singer Kenny Jeremiah (previously the trio The Dedications). They followed their sole Top 20 with 'Explosion In Your Soul'. Act were also on Dot, Decca, Atco and a re-formed group were on Gamble & Huff's Philly Int. and TSOP labels in the mid 70s. Kenny was later in hit act Shirley & Co.

🇺🇸 EXPRESSWAY TO YOUR HEART	4	04 NOV 67	CRIMSON
(Written & produced by Gamble & Huff)			

DAVID SOUL

Actor/singer born David Solberg in Chicago first found transatlantic fame as Ken Hutchinson in TV's Starsky & Hutch. In the late 60s he had often sung on US TVs Merv Griffin Show (as 'the covered man'- wearing a hood!). He had recorded on MGM and Paramount before having 5 UK (1 US) Top 20s.

🇬🇧 DON'T GIVE UP ON US	1(4)	15 JAN 77	PRIVATE STOCK
(UK Gold – Top UK record of 77 and top singles act)			
GOING IN WITH MY EYES OPEN	2	02 APR 77	PRIVATE STOCK
(Entered at No. 5 – US No. 54)			
SILVER LADY *(US No. 52)*	1(3)	08 OCT 77	PRIVATE STOCK
LET'S HAVE A QUIET NIGHT IN	8	14 JAN 78	PRIVATE STOCK
🇺🇸 DON'T GIVE UP ON US	1(1)	16 APR 77	PRIVATE STOCK

JIMMY SOUL

Born Jimmy McCleese in New York, he sang in gospel group The Nightingales and was originally known as 'The Wonder Boy'. He had two US-only charters the other being 'Twistin' Matilda' (22) in 62.

🇺🇸 IF YOU WANNA BE HAPPY	1(3)	18 MAY 63	SPQR

SOUNDS ORCHESTRAL

Session orchestra put together by top UK arranger/conductor and pianist Johnny Pearson who had previously worked with acts like Connie Francis and Shirley Bassey. The follow up to their sole Top 10 was 'Canadian Sunset'.

🇬🇧 CAST YOUR FATE TO THE WIND	5	23 JAN 65	PICCADILLY
🇺🇸 CAST YOUR FATE TO THE WIND	10	08 MAY 65	PARKWAY
(Vince Guaraldi Trio 62 US hit)			

Also see Johnny Pearson

JOE SOUTH

Atlanta all-rounder wrote 'Rose Garden', 'Down In The Boondocks' and 'Hush', produced Billie Joe Royal and played guitar with Bob Dylan, Aretha Franklin and Simon & Garfunkel. As a singer he charted on NRC in 58 and Fairlane in 61. He was on MGM in 63, Apt in 64 and Columbia in 66 and had two US (1 UK) Top 20s in the late 60s. He later had LPs on Island.

🇬🇧 GAMES PEOPLE PLAY *(US No. 12)*	6	29 MAR 69	CAPITOL
(Grammy winner for Best Song)			

J.D. SOUTHER

Detroit singer/songwriter was in Longbranch Pennywhistle with Glen Frey, had written for Linda Ronstadt and Bonnie Raitt and been in the short lived Souther-Hillman-Furay Band. He first recorded solo in 72 and had one other US hit – a duet with James Taylor 'Her Town Too' (11) in 81. He was also on Warner, Asylum, Blue Moon and joined EMI America in 86.

🇺🇸 YOU'RE ONLY LONELY	7	15 DEC 79	COLUMBIA

RED SOVINE

Woodrow Wilson Sovine was a country singer/songwriter from West Virginia. He started performing in 35, had his own band in 47 and got the first of 29 country hits (spanning 25 years) in 55. He was also on Decca and Gusto. He died in 80 and his sole US pop Top 40 record was a UK smash a year later.

🇬🇧 TEDDY BEAR *(US No. 40 in 76)*	4	20 JUN 81	STARDAY

BOB B. SOXX & THE BLUE JEANS

Session group put together by Phil Spector – on their big hit they were Fanita James and Darlene Love (both ex Blossoms) and Bobby Sheen. The trio had two other US-only hits and the girls were replaced by other noted session singers Gloria Jones and Carolyn Willis. Bobby also recorded as a soloist on Liberty, Dimension, Capitol, UA, Warner and Chelsea.

🇺🇸 ZIP-A-DEE DOO-DAH	8	12 JAN 63	PHILLES
(Johnny Mercer 47 hit)			

SPACE

French electro-disco session act produced by Jean Philippe Iliesco and including Didier Marovani and Roland Romanelli and singer Madeline Bell (ex Blue Mink). They had one US charter too – 'My Love Is Music' (60) in 79.

🇬🇧 MAGIC FLY	2	10 SEP 77	PYE INT

SPAGNA

Italian female Euro dance act from Verona had two UK-only Top 40s in 87 – the other being 'Every Girl And Boy' (23).

🇬🇧 CALL ME *(European Gold record)*	2	22 AUG 87	CBS

SPANDAU BALLET

The first new romantic act to chart evolved from London group The Makers, who were formed in 76. Group, who include Gary & Martin Kemp and singer Tony Hadley, charted from the start (on their own label) and created a lot of media interest. They have had 15 UK (1 US) Top 20 singles and six UK (1 US) Top 20 LPs. They were in Live Aid and on Band Aid and are big crowd pullers. They joined CBS in 86 after lengthy legal problems with Chrysalis. The Kemp brothers also star in a film about London crooks the Kray twins.

🇬🇧	TO CUT A LONG STORY SHORT	5	06 DEC 80	REFORMATION
	MUSCLEBOUND/GLOW	10	09 MAY 81	REFORMATION
	CHANT No. 1 (I DON'T NEED THIS PRESSURE ON) (feat. Beggar & Co (UK funk band))	3	01 AUG 81	REFORMATION
	INSTINCTION (Remixed by Trevor Horn)	10	15 MAY 82	CHRYSALIS
	LIFELINE	7	23 OCT 82	CHRYSALIS
	TRUE (Entered at No. 10)	1(4)	30 APR 83	REFORMATION
	GOLD (US No. 29)	2	20 AUG 83	REFORMATION
	ONLY WHEN YOU LEAVE (US No. 34 – Entered at No. 5)	3	16 JUN 84	REFORMATION
	I'LL FLY FOR YOU	9	08 SEP 84	REFORMATION
	THROUGH THE BARRICADES	6	22 NOV 86	REFORMATION
🇺🇸	TRUE	4	22 AUG 83	CHRYSALIS

SPANKY & OUR GANG

Chicago folk pop act, fronted by sole female member Elaine 'Spanky' McFarlane (ex New Wine Singers), had five US-only Top 40s in the late 60s. They re-formed unsuccessfully on Epic in 75 and then Spanky took over as lead singer with hit act The Mamas & The Papas.

🇺🇸	SUNDAY WILL NEVER BE THE SAME (Was written for and rejected by Mamas & Papas)	9	24 JUN 67	MERCURY

SPARKS

Quirky rock band, fronted by the unmistakable Mael brothers Ron & Russell, evolved from the L.A. group Halfnelson. Their first two US recorded LPs did little so they moved to the UK and formed a new line-up. In the 70s they had eight UK Top 40s and three Top 20 LPs, were voted Best Newcomers of 74 but had no US hits. In the 80s they were on Why Fi, Echo, Atlantic, MCA/Curb, Fine Art/Rhino and Carrere and scored two small US-only charters.

	THIS TOWN AIN'T BIG ENOUGH FOR THE BOTH OF US	2	01 JUN 74	ISLAND
	AMATEUR HOUR	7	10 AUG 74	ISLAND
	BEAT THE CLOCK	10	04 AUG 79	VIRGIN

BILLIE JO SPEARS

Texan country singer first recorded on Abbot in 53 (when aged 16) and had the first of 34 country hits in 68 on Capitol. In the UK she was one of the most successful country acts ever with three Top 40 singles and two Top 20 LPs. In her homeland she had little crossover pop sales. She was also on UA, Ritz, Premier and joined GBS in 88.

🇬🇧	BLANKET ON THE GROUND (US No. 78)	6	30 AUG 75	UA
	WHAT I'VE GOT IN MIND	4	04 SEP 76	UA

SPECIALS

Influential Coventry band were the leading 2 Tone act. They grew out of The Coventry Automatics and included Jerry Dammers (Gerald Dankin), Lynval Golding, Neville Staples, and singer Terry Hall. Elvis Costello produced their first LP and they had eight UK-only Top 10 singles and two Top 10 LPs on their own 2 Tone label. In 81 Terry, Lynval and Neville formed Fun Boy Three and Jerry re-named group Special AKA. Jerry is spokesman for Artists Against Apartheid and helped organise the first Nelson Mandela concert.

🇬🇧	GANGSTERS (As Specials A.K.A.)	6	01 SEP 79	2 TONE
	A MESSAGE TO YOU RUDY/NITE KLUB (As Specials Featuring Rico +)	10	17 NOV 79	2 TONE
	TOO MUCH TOO YOUNG E.P. (SPECIAL A.K.A. LIVE) (Jumped from 15-1 – the second EP to top UK chart)	1(2)	02 FEB 80	2 TONE
	RAT RACE/RUDE BUOYS OUTA JAIL	5	07 JUN 80	2 TONE
	STEREOTYPE/INTERNATIONAL JET SET	6	11 OCT 80	2 TONE
	DO NOTHING/MAGGIE'S FARM (B-side Bob Dylan song)	4	17 JAN 81	2 TONE
	GHOST TOWN	1(3)	11 JUL 81	2 TONE
	NELSON MANDELA (As SPECIAL AKA)	9	14 APR 84	2 TONE

Also see Fun Boy Three

SPINNERS

Detroit group (called The Detroit Spinners in UK), which included Phillipe Wynne, were originally called The Domingoes and first charted in 61 on Tri-Phi with Harvey Fuqua (ex-Moonglows) singing lead. They were then on Time and RCA and joined Motown in the mid 60s. After a quiet spell they notched up 15 US (9 UK) Top 40 singles and eight US (1 UK) Top 40 LPs. Phillipe went solo in 77 and died on stage in 84. Group joined Volt in 89.

🇬🇧	GHETTO CHILD (US No. 29)	7	03 NOV 73	ATLANTIC
	WORKING MY WAY BACK TO YOU/ FORGIVE ME, GIRL (Four Seasons 66 hit)	1(2)	12 APR 80	ATLANTIC
	CUPID-I'VE LOVED YOU FOR A LONG TIME (Sam Cooke 61 hit – last two prod. Michael Zager)	4	19 JUL 80	ATLANTIC
🇺🇸	I'LL BE AROUND (Was originally the B-side)	3	18 NOV 72	ATLANTIC
	COULD IT BE I'M FALLING IN LOVE (UK No. 32)	4	03 MAR 73	ATLANTIC
	THEN CAME YOU (With DIONNE WARWICKE) (They dueted again in 90 on Arista)	1(1)	26 OCT 74	ATLANTIC
	THEY JUST CAN'T STOP IT THE (GAMES PEOPLE PLAY)	5	25 OCT 75	ATLANTIC
	THE RUBBERBAND MAN (UK No. 16)	2	04 DEC 76	ATLANTIC
	WORKING MY WAY BACK TO YOU/ FORGIVE ME, GIRL	2	29 MAR 80	ATLANTIC
	CUPID-I'VE LOVED YOU FOR A LONG TIME (Lead singer on last two was John Edwards)	4	19 JUL 80	ATLANTIC

SPITTING IMAGE

UK novelty hit from the topical comedy puppet TV show of the same name. They had previously recorded on Elektra in 84, and also hit with the follow up 'Santa Claus Is On The Dole' (UK 22).

🇬🇧	THE CHICKEN SONG (Was No. 1 in just two weeks jumping from 11-1)	1(3)	17 MAY 86	VIRGIN

SPLODGENESSABOUNDS

Fun rock band who included Max Splodge, Baby Greensleeves, Pat Thetic, Miles Flat and Wiffy Arsher!. They also hit the UK Top 40 with their unusual version of Rolf Harris' No. 1 'Two Little Boys'.

🇬🇧	SIMON TEMPLAR/TWO PINTS OF LAGER AND A PACKET OF CRISPS PLEASE	7	28 JUN 80	DERAM

DUSTY SPRINGFIELD

Born Mary O'Brien in London she recorded in The Lana Sisters in the late 50s before forming the successful Springfields in 60. This critically hailed singer went solo in 63 and has had 16 UK (6 US) Top 20s and six UK-only Top 40 LPs. She moved to the US in 72 and recorded on Dunhill, UA, 20th Century and Casablanca. She later recorded with Spencer Davis and Richard Carpenter and sang solo on Hippodrome. She returned to the transatlantic charts in the company of her fans The Pet Shop Boys in 87.

🇬🇧	I ONLY WANT TO BE WITH YOU (US No. 12) (Was the first record on UK TVs 'Top of The Pops')	4	11 JAN 64	PHILIPS
	I JUST DON'T KNOW WHAT TO DO WITH MYSELF (Originally by Tommy Hunt)	3	25 JUL 64	PHILIPS
	LOSING YOU (US No. 91 – Co-written by Tom Springfield)	9	05 DEC 64	PHILIPS
	IN THE MIDDLE OF NOWHERE	8	31 JUL 65	PHILIPS
	SOME OF YOUR LOVIN' (Co-writer Carole King) (Backing singers inc. Madeleine Bell & Doris Troy)	8	23 OCT 65	PHILIPS
	YOU DON'T HAVE TO SAY YOU LOVE ME (65 Italian San Remo song festival winning song)	1(1)	30 APR 66	PHILIPS
	GOIN' BACK (Co-writer Carole King)	10	30 JUL 66	PHILIPS
	ALL I SEE IS YOU (US No. 20)	9	08 OCT 66	PHILIPS
	I CLOSE MY EYES AND COUNT TO TEN	4	10 AUG 68	PHILIPS
	SON-OF-A PREACHER MAN	9	04 JAN 69	PHILIPS
	WHAT HAVE I DONE TO DESERVE THIS (With PET SHOP BOYS – song written in 84)	2	29 AUG 87	PARLOPHONE

WISHIN' AND HOPIN' (UK hit for Merseybeats)	6	01 AUG 64	PHILIPS
YOU DON'T HAVE TO SAY YOU LOVE ME	4	16 JUL 66	PHILIPS
SON-OF-A PREACHER MAN	10	18 JAN 69	ATLANTIC
WHAT HAVE I DONE TO DESERVE THIS	2	20 FEB 88	EMI MANHAT.
(With PET SHOP BOYS – her biggest US hit)			

Also see The Springfields

RICK SPRINGFIELD

Australian singer/songwriting actor was in Rock House, Wackedy Wak and the top Aussie teeny bop group Zoot before going solo and hitting the US Top 20 with 'Speak To The Sky' (14) in 72. In the late 70s he became a well known US TV actor appearing in soap operas The Young & The Restless and General Hospital. He had his other 16 US (1 UK) Top 40s and five US-only Top 40 LPs in the 80s. He was also on Capitol, Columbia, Chelsea and Mercury.

JESSIE'S GIRL (UK No. 23)	1(2)	01 AUG 81	RCA
(Grammy winner as Best Male Rock Record of 81)			
I'VE DONE EVERYTHING FOR YOU	4	28 NOV 81	RCA
(Was his first on RCA – originally by Sammy Hager)			
DON'T TALK TO STRANGERS	2	22 MAY 82	RCA
AFFAIR OF THE NIGHT	9	18 JUN 83	RCA
LOVE SOMEBODY (From the film 'Hard To Hold')	5	05 MAY 84	RCA

SPRINGFIELDS

Formed in 60 by brother & sister Dusty & Tom Springfield (Mary and Dion O'Brien) and Tim Field (replaced by Mike Hurst). The UK's top pop folk act had five UK Top 40s before splitting in 63. They were the first UK vocal group to hit the US Top 20 and the first UK act to make the country Top 20 – the record being 'Silver Threads & Golden Needles'. They all recorded solo and Dusty became a star, Tom a top writer and Mike a hit producer.

ISLAND OF DREAMS	7	15 FEB 63	PHILIPS
SAY I WON'T BE THERE	5	19 APR 63	PHILIPS

Also see Dusty Springfield

BRUCE SPRINGSTEEN

'The Boss' is rock's most energetic performer and packs stadiums worldwide. Before his first release in 73 he had been in The Castiles, Earth, Child, Steel Mill and Dr. Zoom & The Sonic Boom. In 74 Rolling Stone critic Jon Landau (now Bruce's manager) wrote "I saw rock and roll future – and its name is Bruce Springsteen" and in 75 he was the first rocker to be on the front page of Time and Newsweek. His two 73 LPs finally charted in 75 and they were followed by seven US (5 UK) Top 5 LPs including the 12 million selling 'Born In The USA' and a live five LP box set that entered the US chart at No. 1 (a very rare feat). He had the first of 12 US (9 UK) Top 20s in 80. His songs have given big hits to Manfred Mann, Pointer Sisters, Patti Smith and Natalie Cole. He was in USA for Africa, Artists Against Apartheid and worked for Amnesty Int.

DANCING IN THE DARK	4	16 FEB 85	CBS
(Also UK No. 28 in 84 – B-side was 'Pink Cadillac')			
I'M ON FIRE/BORN IN THE U.S.A.	5	13 JUL 85	CBS
SANTA CLAUS IS COMIN' TO TOWN	9	21 DEC 85	EPIC
(George Hall 34 hit)			
HUNGRY HEART (UK No. 44)	5	03 JAN 81	COLUMBIA
DANCING IN THE DARK	2	30 JUN 84	COLUMBIA
COVER ME (UK No. 38)	7	20 OCT 84	COLUMBIA
BORN IN THE U.S.A.	9	19 JAN 85	COLUMBIA
(From the third biggest selling LP ever in the US)			
I'M ON FIRE	6	13 APR 85	COLUMBIA
GLORY DAYS (UK No. 17)	5	03 AUG 85	COLUMBIA
I'M GOIN' DOWN	9	26 OCT 85	COLUMBIA
MY HOMETOWN	6	25 JAN 86	COLUMBIA
WAR (UK No. 18 – Edwin Starr 70 hit)	8	27 DEC 86	COLUMBIA
BRILLIANT DISGUISE (UK No. 20)	5	21 NOV 87	COLUMBIA
TUNNEL OF LOVE (UK No. 45)	9	06 FEB 88	COLUMBIA

SPRINGWATER

UK instrumentalist Phil Cordell had a one-off hit under this pseudonym. He also recorded an LP 'Born Again' on the Motown group label Prodigal in the late 70s and was on Fabulous in 80 and Flying in 82.

I WILL RETURN (He re-recorded it in 80)	5	20 NOV 71	POLYDOR

SQUEEZE

London new wave band includes singer/songwriters Chris Difford and Glenn Tilbrook and keyboard player 'Jools' Holland. In 77 they first recorded on Deptford Fun City and they notched up five UK-only Top 20s before splitting in 82. Chris and Glenn became a duo and 'Jools' a popular TV personality. They reunited in 85 and had a transatlantic Top 20 in 87 with 'Hourglass' (US 15/UK 16). They returned to Deptford Fun City in 90.

COOL FOR CATS	2	14 APR 79	A&M
UP THE JUNCTION	2	07 JUL 79	A&M
LABELLED WITH LOVE	4	07 NOV 81	A&M
(Singer Paul Carrack left as this was released)			

JIM STAFFORD

Pop/country singer/songwriter and TV host from Florida started in The Legends with Gram Parsons and Lobo (Kent Lavoie). He married singer Bobbie Gentry and had another Transatlantic Top 20 with 'My Girl Bill' (US 12/UK 20). He was also on Polydor and Warner in 76, Elektra in 81, Town House in 82 and Columbia in 84.

SPIDERS & SNAKES (UK No. 14)	3	02 MAR 74	MGM
(Written by David Bellamy of the Bellamy Brothers)			
WILDWOOD WEED (Both 45s produced by Lobo)	7	24 AUG 74	MGM

TERRY STAFFORD

Oklahoma singer, was in the Eugene Nelson band, The Lively Ones and The Surfmen and first recorded solo on A&M in 63. After his only Top 20 he recorded on Mercury, Sidewalk, Warner, MGM, Melodyland, Player Int. and in the 70s had a few country hits on Atlantic and Casino.

SUSPICION (UK No. 31 – orig. Elvis Presley)	3	11 APR 64	CRUSADER

FRANK STALLONE

Philadelphian singer/songwriting brother of top actor Sylvester. He first recorded in Valentine and debuted on the chart in 80 on Scotti Brothers. He was in the films Rocky and Staying Alive which his big hit came from.

FAR FROM OVER (UK No. 68)	10	01 OCT 83	RSO

STAMPEDERS

Canadian rock/pop trio fronted by singer/songwriter Rich Dodson. They had two big Canadian hits 'Carry Me' and 'Morning Magic' before scoring the first and biggest of their three US-only charters. Follow up was 'Devil You'.

SWEET CITY WOMAN	8	23 OCT 71	BELL

LISA STANSFIELD

The first white UK female to top the black chart was from Rochdale. She had previously recorded on Devil and Polydor in 82 and been a children's TV presenter (Razzmatazz). She sang in Blue Zone (on Rockin' Horse and Arista) who had a US hit 'Jackie' (54) in 88. So far she has notched up two UK Top 20s – the other being 'This is The Right Time' (13). She won BRITS award as Best Newcomer in 89 and is a very bright prospect for the 90s.

ALL AROUND THE WORLD (US No. 3 in 90)	1(2)	11 APR 89	ARISTA
(Written by her co-members in Blue Zone)			

STAPLE SINGERS

Originally formed by Roebuck 'Pop' Staples in 51 as a family gospel act. They recorded on United, Vee Jay, Riverside and had the first of their 15 US (2 UK) hits in 67 on Epic. Unmistakable singer Mavis Staples also recorded solo from 70 and in 89 she was produced by Prince. They were in the films Wattstax, Soul To Soul and The Last Waltz. They later recorded on 20th Century, Warner and Private I.

I'LL TAKE YOU THERE (UK No. 30)		1(1)	03 JUN 72	STAX
IF YOU'RE READY COME GO WITH ME (UK No. 34)	9		22 DEC 73	STAX
LET'S DO IT AGAIN (From the film)		1(1)	27 DEC 75	CURTOM

STARBUCK

Seven man rock group from Atlanta followed their sole Top 40 with 'I Got To Know' and were on UA in 78. Leader singer/songwriter Bruce Blackman had hit in 68 in Eternity's Children on Tower and scored in 80 as Korona on UA.

MOONLIGHT FEELS RIGHT	3	31 JUL 76	PRIVATE STOCK

ALVIN STARDUST

Born Bernard Jewry in London, his UK-only hits span 24 years. He had two charters in the early 60s as Shane Fenton (& The Fentones) and 11 years later returned with his new name and image (owing a little to Gene Vincent and Dave Berry) to front the hit record 'My Coo Ca Choo' (which he did not sing on). He then recorded an impressive eight more UK-only Top 20s. He was later on RCA, Fury and Honeybee and is now a children's TV personality.

MY COO-CA-CHOO (Vocal by Peter Shelley)	2	01 DEC 73	MAGNET
JEALOUS MIND	1(1)	09 MAR 74	MAGNET
RED DRESS	7	25 MAY 74	MAGNET
YOU YOU YOU	6	28 SEP 74	MAGNET
PRETEND (Using Carl Mann's 59 arrangement)	4	03 OCT 81	STIFF
I FEEL LIKE BUDDY HOLLY (Comp. Mike Batt)	7	02 JUN 84	STIFF
I WON'T RUN AWAY	7	08 DEC 84	CHRYSALIS

STARLAND VOCAL BAND

MOR/pop quartet included husband and wife Bill & Kathy 'Taffy' Danoff. They had been in Fat City, the group who worked with John Denver, and they wrote his hit 'Take Me Home, Country Roads'. They followed their sole Top 40 with 'California Day'.

AFTERNOON DELIGHT (UK No. 18)	1(2)	10 JUL 76	WINDSONG

STARLIGHT

One of three UK-only Top 10 projects in late 89 that were masterminded by Italian Daniele 'D.J. Lelewel' Davoli. His other hits came from Black Box and Mixmaster. It was originally on the Italian Discomagic label.

NUMERO UNO	9	09 SEP 89	CITY BEAT

EDWIN STARR

Strong voiced soul singer was born Charles Hatcher in Nashville. He was in Bill Doggett's band in the early 60s and then in The Future Tones and in the mid 60s chart group The Holidays. He has had four US (7 UK) solo Top 40s and has also recorded on Ric Tic, Granite, Montage, and whilst in the UK on Bradley's, Hippodrome, Avatar and UK.

WAR	3	14 NOV 70	TAMLA MOTOWN
CONTACT (US No. 65)	6	17 FEB 79	20TH CENTURY
H.A.P.P.Y. RADIO (US No. 79)	9	30 JUN 79	RCA
TWENTY FIVE MILES (UK No. 36)	6	26 APR 69	GORDY
(He re-recorded it in 80 – composed by Johnny Bristol)			
WAR	1(3)	29 AUG 70	GORDY

FREDDIE STARR

Popular UK comedian/TV personality and hamster fancier started in Freddie Starr and The Midnighters and first recorded on Decca in 63 ('Peter Gunn Locomotion'). He has also recorded on Towerbell, Savoir Faire, WEA, GL, Thunderbird, Kamera and PVK and debuted in the Top 20 LPs in 89.

IT'S YOU	9	16 MAR 74	TIFFANY

RINGO STARR

The Beatles' drummer was born Richard Starkey in Liverpool. He started in Ed Clayton's skiffle group and was in Rory Storme's Hurricanes before replacing Pete Best in the Fab Four just in time for their first EMI recording session. He first recorded solo in 70 (before the group split) and has had 10 US (5 UK) Top 40s and is the only ex-Beatle to have two consecutive US No. 1s. He has starred in many films, been a children's TV narrator and was the first Beatle to become a grandfather. In 89 he successfully toured the US with his All Star Band.

IT DON'T COME EASY	4	08 MAY 71	APPLE
(Guitarists George Harrison & Stephen Stills)			
BACK OFF BOOGALOO	2	29 APR 72	APPLE
(Above two produced by George Harrison)			
PHOTOGRAPH (Co-written George Harrison)	8	17 NOV 73	APPLE
YOU'RE SIXTEEN	4	06 APR 74	APPLE
(Originally by Jerry Naylor as 'You're 13')			
IT DON'T COME EASY	4	05 JUN 71	APPLE
BACK OFF BOOGALOO (He re-recorded it in 81)	9	13 MAY 72	APPLE
PHOTOGRAPH	1(1)	24 NOV 73	APPLE
YOU'RE SIXTEEN	1(1)	26 JAN 74	APPLE
(Nilsson and Paul McCartney also on the record)			
OH MY MY	5	27 APR 74	APPLE
ONLY YOU (UK No. 28 – Platters 56 hit)	6	11 JAN 75	APPLE
NO NO SONG	3	05 APR 75	APPLE

Also see The Beatles

STARS ON 45/STARSOUND

Session group from Holland masterminded by producer Jaap Eggermont (one time member of Golden Earring) based on the bootleg 'Bits and Pieces' 12" records. Their hits started a world-wide medley craze. In the UK group had four Top 20s and were known as Starsound.

STARS ON 45 (Included many Beatles songs)	2	09 MAY 81	CBS
STARS ON 45 (VOL. 2)	2	18 JUL 81	CBS
(US No. 67 – Included many Abba songs)			
STARS ON 45 (MEDLEY)	1(1)	20 JUN 81	RADIO

Starsound – See Stars on 45

STARSHIP

Top rock act evolved from Jefferson Airplane and Jefferson Starship in 85 and were fronted by Mickey Thomas and Grace Slick. They scored three US No. 1s in 18 months. Grace left in 89 to join the reformed Jefferson Airplane.

NOTHING'S GONNA STOP US NOW	1(4)	09 MAY 87	RCA
(UK's No. 2 single of 87 – Grace was 47 at the time)			
WE BUILT THIS CITY (UK No. 12)	1(2)	16 NOV 85	GRUNT
SARA (UK No. 66)	1(1)	15 MAR 86	GRUNT
NOTHING'S GONNA STOP US NOW (Prod. Narada)	1(2)	04 APR 87	GRUNT
(Co-written Albert Hammond – from film 'Mannequin')			
IT'S NOT OVER ('TIL IT'S OVER)	9	29 AUG 87	GRUNT

Also see Jefferson Airplane/Jefferson Starship

STATLER BROTHERS

All time top country group were formed in 55 as The Kingsmen. This harmony quartet from Virginia which includes brothers Don & Harold Reid toured with Johnny Cash for eight years from 63. Their third 45 was their only pop Top 40 hit and was the first of 65 country chart entries including 46 Top 20s.

FLOWERS ON THE WALL *(UK No. 38)*	4	08 JAN 66	COLUMBIA

CANDI STATON

Alabama born soul singer who was in the Jewel Gospel trio aged only 10. She had the first of 10 US (6 UK) chart records in 69 on Fame. The one time Mrs. Clarence Carter also recorded on Minaret, L.A., Source, Sugarhill and has now returned to the gospel music field.

YOUNG HEARTS RUN FREE *(US No. 20)*	2	10 JUL 76	WARNER
NIGHTS ON BROADWAY *(Bee Gees 75 US hit)*	6	03 SEP 77	WARNER

STATUS QUO

No other group has had as many UK hit 45s as this London hard rock boogie band led by Francis Rossi and Rick Parfitt. They have had 39 hit singles including 21 Top 10s and 19 Top 20 LPs – yet they have never cracked the US Top 10. This influential band started with three flop singles as the The Spectres and one as Traffic Jam. They have been a top UK live act for over 20 years and opened the Live Aid show.

PICTURES OF MATCHSTICK MEN *(US No. 12)*	7	24 FEB 68	PYE
ICE IN THE SUN *(US No. 70 – Comp. Marty Wilde)*	8	12 OCT 68	PYE
PAPER PLANE	8	10 FEB 73	VERTIGO
CAROLINE	5	27 OCT 73	VERTIGO
BREAK THE RULES	8	25 MAY 74	VERTIGO
DOWN DOWN	1(1)	18 JAN 75	VERTIGO
ROLL OVER LAY DOWN	9	07 JUN 75	VERTIGO
RAIN	7	06 MAR 76	VERTIGO
WILD SIDE OF LIFE *(Hank Thompson 52 country hit)*	9	22 JAN 77	VERTIGO
ROCKIN' ALL OVER THE WORLD *(Orig. John Fogerty UK No. 17 in 88 as 'Running...')*	3	19 NOV 77	VERTIGO
WHATEVER YOU WANT	4	06 OCT 79	VERTIGO
WHAT YOU'RE PROPOSING	2	01 NOV 80	VERTIGO
SOMETHING 'BOUT YOU BABY	9	07 MAR 81	VERTIGO
ROCK 'N' ROLL	8	26 DEC 81	VERTIGO
DEAR JOHN	10	17 APR 82	VERTIGO
OL' RAG BLUES	9	24 SEP 83	VERTIGO
MARGUERITA TIME	3	14 JAN 84	VERTIGO
THE WANDERER *(Dion 61 hit)*	7	03 NOV 84	VERTIGO
ROLLING HOME *(Produced by Dave Edmunds)*	9	24 MAY 86	VERTIGO
IN THE ARMY NOW *(Originally by Bolland)*	2	01 NOV 86	VERTIGO
BURNING BRIDGES (ON AND OFF AND ON AGAIN)	5	31 DEC 88	VERTIGO

STEALERS WHEEL

Critically hailed London rock quartet fronted by Gerry Rafferty (ex Humblebums with Billy Connolly) managed to score three UK (2 US) Top 40s before personality problems broke them up. Gerry later hit as a solo act.

STUCK IN THE MIDDLE WITH YOU	8	16 JUN 73	A&M
STUCK IN THE MIDDLE WITH YOU *(Produced by Leiber and Stoller)*	6	12 MAY 73	A&M

Also see Gerry Rafferty

STEAM

New York based studio group put together by producer Paul Leka. Their big hit featured the voice of Garrett Scott who went solo on Mercury after the single. They followed their sole Top 40 with 'I've Gotta Make You Love Me'.

NA NA HEY HEY KISS HIM GOODBYE *(Was recorded as a B-side)*	9	21 MAR 70	FONTANA
NA NA HEY HEY KISS HIM GOODBYE	1(2)	06 DEC 69	FONTANA

TOMMY STEELE

UK's first R'n'R star had been in C&W band Jack Fallon & The Sons Of The Saddle and was the first act managed by Larry Parnes. The London born Tommy Hicks' debut single 'Rock With The Caveman' was one of his 13 UK-only Top 20s. He starred in several films including one of his life-story (filmed just a few months after his first hit!). He later became a top stage and film star and all round entertainer.

SINGING THE BLUES *(Marty Robbins 56 US hit)*	1(1)	11 JAN 57	DECCA
BUTTERFINGERS	8	19 JUL 57	DECCA
WATER WATER/HANDFUL OF SONGS *(From the film The Tommy Steele Story)*	5	13 SEP 57	DECCA
NAIROBI *(Original by Bob Merrill)*	3	04 APR 58	DECCA
COME ON LET'S GO *(Ritchie Valens 58 US hit)*	10	26 DEC 58	DECCA
LITTLE WHITE BULL *(From the film Tommy The Toreador)*	6	08 JAN 60	DECCA
WHAT A MOUTH *(Old music hall song)*	4	08 JUL 60	DECCA

STEELEYE SPAN

Formed in 69, this electric folk act included Maddy Prior (who had previously recorded with fellow member Tom Hart) and Ashley Hutchings (ex Fairport Convention). Ashley left in 71 before the group scored their two UK-only Top 20s – the other being the acappella 'Gaudette' (14) in 73. Maddy also recorded solo and the group first broke up in 78 to re-surface in the 80s.

ALL AROUND MY HAT *(Prod. Mike Batt)*	5	06 DEC 75	CHRYSALIS

STEELY DAN

Critically acclaimed jazzy pop group featured Walter Becker and Donald Fagen who were previously in Jay & The Americans' backing group. Members Michael McDonald and Jeff Baxter left to join The Doobie Brothers. After 10 US (2 UK) Top 40 singles and eight US (6 UK) Top 40 LPs they disbanded in 81. Their biggest UK success 'Haitian Divorce' (17) was not a 45 in the US. Donald later scored as a soloist and Walter had some success as a producer.

DO IT AGAIN *(UK No. 39 – vocal by David Palmer)*	6	10 FEB 73	ABC
RIKKI DON'T LOSE THAT NUMBER *(UK No. 58)*	4	03 AUG 74	ABC
HEY NINETEEN	10	14 FEB 81	MCA

STEPPENWOLF

L.A. based hard rockers evolved from the Canadian group Sparrow who were on Columbia. Act included East German John Kay (Joachim Krauledat) and Mars Bonfire (Dennis Edmonton) who composed the biggest of their seven US (1 UK) Top 40s. Group who also had eight US (1 UK) Top 40 LPs first broke up in 72 and reformed on Mums in 74 and Epic in 75. John has recorded solo on Columbia, Dunhill and Mercury. John and a re-formed group were still recording in 88.

BORN TO BE WILD *(Used in film Easy Rider)* *(UK No. 30 – their sixth single)*	2	24 AUG 68	DUNHILL
MAGIC CARPET RIDE	3	30 NOV 68	DUNHILL
ROCK ME	10	19 APR 69	DUNHILL

CAT STEVENS

Top 70s singer/songwriter now known as Yusef Islam was born Steven Georgiou in London. Discovered by Mike Hurst (ex-Springfields) he was the first act on Deram. He had the first of his 11 US Top 40s five years after the first of his nine UK ones. He also had six UK (7 US) Top 10 LPs. He has written big hits for The Tremeloes, P.P. Arnold, Jimmy Cliff and Maxi Priest. He was also a top live act until he retired in 79 having become a Muslim. A hits LP put him back in UK Top 10 LPs in 90.

MATTHEW AND SON	2	04 FEB 67	DERAM
I'M GONNA GET ME A GUN *(He was voted Most Promising UK Singer of 67)*	6	29 APR 67	DERAM
LADY D'ARBANVILLE *(Flute by Peter Gabriel)* *(Inspired by his girlfriend Patti D'Arbanville)*	8	08 AUG 70	ISLAND
MORNING HAS BROKEN *(Children's hymn – features Rick Wakeman on piano)*	9	29 JAN 72	ISLAND

🇺🇸 PEACE TRAIN	7	06 NOV 71	A&M	
MORNING HAS BROKEN	6	27 MAY 72	A&M	
OH VERY YOUNG	10	01 JUN 74	A&M	
ANOTHER SATURDAY NIGHT *(UK No. 19)*	6	05 OCT 74	A&M	
(UK No. 19 – Sam Cooke 63 hit)				

CONNIE STEVENS

Brooklyn actress/singer born Concetta Ingolia was in TV's Hawaiian Eye and '77 Sunset Strip' and recorded on Faro in 59 before having two transatlantic Top 20s. She later starred in many films and TV shows and married singer Eddie Fisher. She also recorded on MGM in 68 and Bell in 70.

🇺🇸 KOOKIE KOOKIE (LEND ME YOUR COMB)	4	01 MAY 59	WARNER	
(UK No. 22) (With Edd 'Kookie' Byrnes)				
SIXTEEN REASONS *(UK No. 11)*	3	02 MAY 60	WARNER	

RAY STEVENS

Humorous pop country singer/songwriter was born Ray Ragsdale in Georgia. Before getting the first of his 27 US (7 UK) hits in 61 he had been on Prep, Trumpet, NRC and Capitol. Since 69 he has had 30 country hits and he earned his first gold LP in the late 80s. He has also been on Warner, RCA and MCA.

🇬🇧 EVERYTHING IS BEAUTIFUL	6	06 JUN 70	CBS	
(First UK hit – 12 years after first UK release)				
BRIDGET THE MIDGET (THE QUEEN OF THE BLUES)	2	03 APR 71	CBS	
(US No. 50)				
THE STREAK	1(1)	15 JUN 74	JANUS	
MISTY *(US No. 14)*	2	12 JUL 75	JANUS	
🇺🇸 AHAB, THE ARAB	5	04 AUG 62	MERCURY	
GITARZAN	8	31 MAY 69	MONUMENT	
EVERYTHING IS BEAUTIFUL	1(2)	30 MAY 70	BARNABY	
THE STREAK	1(3)	18 MAY 74	BARNABY	

SHAKIN' STEVENS

Welsh born Michael Barratt was an 80s UK phenomenon. This R'n'R revival star started with The Sunsets in 68 and they first recorded on EMI in 70. They then had records on CBS, Polydor, Dureco, Pink Elephant and Dynamo (last three Dutch labels) Mooncrest and Track. His fourth solo 45 'Hot Dog' (UK 24) for Epic in 80 was his debut hit and he has since scored 22 UK-only Top 20s (a record for a UK soloist in the 80s) and 10 UK-only chart LPs.

🇬🇧 THIS OLE HOUSE *(Stuart Hamblen 54 US hit)*	1(3)	28 MAR 81	EPIC	
(Backed by Matchbox – song about a dying man's hut)				
YOU DRIVE ME CRAZY *(Jumped from 39-5)*	2	16 MAY 81	EPIC	
GREEN DOOR *(Jim Lowe 56 hit-jump from 22-1)*	1(4)	01 AUG 81	EPIC	
IT'S RAINING *(Original by Irma Thomas)*	10	24 OCT 81	EPIC	
OH JULIE *(Covered in US by Barry Manilow)*	1(1)	30 JAN 82	EPIC	
SHIRLEY *(John Fred 59 US hit)*	6	01 APR 82	EPIC	
I'LL BE SATISFIED *(Jackie Wilson 59 US hit)*	10	06 NOV 82	EPIC	
THE SHAKIN' STEVENS E.P.	2	25 DEC 82	EPIC	
(Includes Elvis Presley song 'Blue Christmas')				
CRY JUST A LITTLE BIT *(US No. 67)*	3	19 NOV 83	EPIC	
A LOVE WORTH WAITING FOR	2	07 APR 84	EPIC	
(Produced by Richard Hewson of Kah Band)				
A ROCKIN' GOOD WAY *(And Bonnie Tyler)*				
(as Shaky & Bonnie) (Jumped 57-13)				
(Original by Priscilla Bowman)	5	21 JAN 84	CBS	
A LETTER TO YOU	10	29 SEP 84	EPIC	
(A country No. 1 in 89 by Eddy Raven)				
TEARDROPS	5	08 DEC 84	EPIC	
MERRY CHRISTMAS EVERYONE	1(2)	28 DEC 85	EPIC	
(Was also UK No. 58 in 86)				
WHAT DO YOU WANT TO MAKE THOSE EYES				
AT ME FOR	5	12 DEC 87	EPIC	
(Based on the Johnny Otis 59 version of 1917 song)				

B.W. STEVENSON

Texan pop singer had no success with his first two RCA LPs but the title song from his third gave him his sole Top 40 hit. His follow up was 'The River Of Love'. He was also on Warner in 76 and Private Stock in 79 and had the original version of the Three Dog Night hit 'Shambala'.

🇺🇸 MY MARIA	9	29 SEP 73	RCA	

AL STEWART

Glasgow born folk rock singer/songwriter first recorded on Decca in 66 and had four albums on Columbia, one of which made the UK Top 40. His first US chart LP came in 74 and in all he has scored four US (3 UK) Top 40 LPs and four US (1 UK) Top 40 singles. He was on RCA in the early 80s and re-appeared on Enigma in 88.

🇺🇸 YEAR OF THE CAT *(UK No. 31)*	8	05 MAR 77	JANUS	
TIME PASSAGES *(Both produced by Alan Parsons)*	7	09 DEC 78	ARISTA	
(Top US adult contemporary song of 78)				

AMII STEWART

Washington born singer/actress and dancer scored with disco revivals of 60s hit songs. Based at times in the UK and Italy, she also had a UK Top 20 with 'Friends' (12) in 84 on RCA. She was on Handshake in 81, and in both 80 and 86 she twice charted with 'My Guy'/'My Girl' with two different partners, Johnny Bristol and Deon Estus, on Atlantic and Sedition respectively.

🇬🇧 KNOCK ON WOOD *(Eddie Floyd 66 hit)*	6	19 MAY 79	ATLANTIC/HAN	
LIGHT MY FIRE/137 DISCO HEAVEN (MEDLEY)	5	14 JUL 79	ATLANTIC	
(US No. 69 – Doors 67 US hit)				
KNOCK ON WOOD/LIGHT MY FIRE (REMIX)	7	21 SEP 85	SEDITION	
(First dance re-mix of a 70s hit to chart in UK)				
🇺🇸 KNOCK ON WOOD	1(1)	21 APR 79	ARIOLA	

ANDY STEWART

Popular Scottish MOR entertainer had a surprise smash (an indie No. 1) with a novelty song he had made a small UK and US hit 28 years before in 61!

🇬🇧 DONALD WHERE'S YOUR TROOSERS	4	30 DEC 89	STONE	
(US No. 77 in 61)				

BILLY STEWART

Distinctive Washington born soul singer/songwriter known as 'Fat Boy' sang in The Rainbows, who had two 45s on Pilgrim in 55, and with help from Bo Diddley's band recorded for Argo in 56. He was on Okeh in 57 and UA in 61 and had 12 US (1 UK) charters. He was sadly killed in a car crash in 70.

🇺🇸 SUMMERTIME *(UK No. 39)*	10	27 AUG 66	CHESS	

DAVE STEWART & BARBARA GASKIN

Kent keyboardist (not the one in The Eurythmics) had been in groups like Uriel, Khan, Egg and Hatfield & The North (Barbara also sang in the last two). He had two UK-only Top 20s in 81 the other being another revival – 'What Becomes Of The Broken Hearted' (13) with singer Colin Blunstone.

🇬🇧 IT'S MY PARTY *(Lesley Gore 63 hit)*	1(4)	17 OCT 81	BROKEN	

JERMAINE STEWART

Singer from Ohio had been a Soul Train dancer in the 70s. He had also recorded backing vocals for acts like Boy George and Shalamar before chalking up the first of his four US (5 UK) hits to date.

🇬🇧 WE DON'T HAVE TO... *(Title shortened in UK)*	2	20 SEP 86	10	
SAY IT AGAIN *(US No. 27)*	7	27 FEB 88	10	
🇺🇸 WE DON'T HAVE TO TAKE OUR CLOTHES OFF	5	09 AUG 86	ARISTA	

JOHN STEWART

San Diego pop folk singer/songwriter first recorded in rock band The Furies in 59. He then formed folk trio The Cumberland Three and replaced Dave Guard in The Kingston Trio from 61-67. He wrote The Monkees smash 'Daydream Believer' and first charted as a soloist in 69 on Capitol. His biggest success came a decade later when produced by Lindsey Buckingham.

GOLD (Backing vocals Inc. Lindsey Buckingham & Stevie Nicks)		5	04 AUG 79	RSO

ROD STEWART

The gravel voiced singer was born in London of Scottish parents and is one of rock's legends. He started in The Five Demensions on Pye in 63 and before success came in 71 (as a soloist and in The Faces) he had been in Long John Baldry's group, The Soul Agents, Steampacket, Shotgun Express, The Jeff Beck Group and made solos on Decca, Columbia and Immediate. To date he has scored 23 UK (16 US) Top 20 singles and 17 UK (12 US) Top 20 LPs. He has won many awards, packed stadiums around the world and has earned 14 gold LPs. He has also had a record seven UK No. 1 albums and his fondness for long legged blondes has led to a much publicised private life.

MAGGIE MAY (Also UK No. 31 in 76)	1(5)	09 OCT 71	MERCURY
YOU WEAR IT WELL (US No. 13)	1(1)	02 SEP 72	MERCURY
ANGEL/WHAT MADE MILWAUKEE FAMOUS (US No. 40) (B-side Jerry Lee Lewis 68 country hit)	4	09 DEC 72	MERCURY
OH NO NOT MY BABY (US No. 59 – Maxine Brown 64 US hit)	6	22 SEP 73	MERCURY
FAREWELL/BRING IT ON HOME TO ME/ YOU SEND ME (Last two songs previous Sam Cooke hits)	7	19 OCT 74	MERCURY
SAILING (Also UK No. 41 in 87 – US No. 58)	1(4)	06 SEP 75	WARNER
THIS OLD HEART OF MINE (Isley Bros. 66 hit) (US No. 83 – US Top 20 in 90 (re-recd. with Ron Isley)	4	06 DEC 75	RIVA
TONIGHT'S THE NIGHT (GONNA BE ALRIGHT)	5	26 JUN 76	RIVA
THE KILLING OF GEORGIE (US No. 30)	2	18 SEP 76	RIVA
SAILING (Re-entry – comp. Gavin Sutherland)	3	16 OCT 76	WARNER
I DON'T WANT TO TALK ABOUT IT/ FIRST CUT IS THE DEEPEST ('B' comp. Cat Stevens – US No. 46/US No. 21)	1(4)	21 MAY 77	RIVA
YOU'RE IN MY HEART (Entered at No. 7)	3	29 OCT 77	RIVA
HOTLEGS/I WAS ONLY JOKING (US Nos. 28/22)	5	18 FEB 78	RIVA
OLE OLA (MUHLER BRASILEIRA) (Feat. Scotland World Cup Football Squad)	4	10 JUN 78	RIVA
DA YA THINK I'M SEXY	1(1)	02 DEC 78	RIVA
TONIGHT I'M YOURS (DON'T HURT ME) (US No. 20)	8	21 NOV 81	RIVA
BABY JANE (US No. 14)	1(3)	02 JUL 83	WARNER
WHAT AM I GONNA DO (US No. 35)	3	10 SEP 83	WARNER
EVERY BEAT OF MY HEART (US No. 83)	2	19 JUL 86	WARNER

MAGGIE MAY	1(5)	02 OCT 71	MERCURY
TONIGHT'S THE NIGHT (GONNA BE ALRIGHT) (Top US single in 77 survey)	1(8)	13 NOV 76	WARNER
YOU'RE IN MY HEART	4	14 JAN 78	WARNER
DA YA THINK I'M SEXY	1(4)	10 FEB 79	WARNER
PASSION (UK No. 17)	5	07 FEB 81	WARNER
YOUNG TURKS (UK No. 11)	5	19 DEC 81	WARNER
INFATUATION (UK No. 27)	6	28 JUL 84	WARNER
SOME GUYS HAVE ALL THE LUCK (UK No. 15) (Persuaders 73 US hit)	10	27 OCT 84	WARNER
LOVE TOUCH (From the film 'Legal Eagles' – UK No. 27)	6	09 AUG 86	WARNER
MY HEART CAN'T TELL YOU NO (UK No. 49 – Co-written by Simon Climie)	4	01 APR 89	WARNER

Also see Faces/Python Lee Jackson

STING

The lead singer and bass player of ultra-successful group The Police was born Gordon Sumner in Newcastle (UK). He started in various local jazz rock bands and recorded with The Newcastle Big Band and Last Exit before joining The Police in 77. As a soloist he has won Grammy and BRITS awards and had six US (2 UK) Top 20 singles and two US (3 UK) Top 20 LPs. He has also recorded with Phil Collins, Dire Straits, Miles Davis and as part of Band Aid. He took part in Live Aid, Nelson Mandela's birthday show and Amnesty Int and A.A.A. tours and is very committed to conserving tropical rain forests.

IF YOU LOVE SOMEBODY SET THEM FREE (UK No. 26)	3	03 AUG 85	A&M
FORTRESS AROUND YOUR HEART (UK No. 49)	8	26 OCT 85	A&M
WE'LL BE TOGETHER (UK No. 41)	7	05 DEC 87	A&M

Also see The Police

STONE ROSES

Critically acclaimed guitar rock group from Manchester. The act fronted by Ian Brown won most of the UK music magazine polls in 89 and look set to be a top act in the early 90s. Their first release was 'So Young' on Thin Sliced in 85 and they were also on Black in 87. They had the first of their two UK-only charters in 89 with 'She Bangs The Drum'.

FOOL'S GOLD/WHAT THE WORLD IS WAITING FOR	8	02 DEC 89	SILVERTONE

R & J STONE

Russell (who had previously recorded on Major Minor and Decca as a soloist) and his wife Joanne, who was the New Jersey born cousin of Madeline Bell, first met whilst both session singers in James Last's choir. They followed their one-off hit with 'No Other Way'. Joanne died prematurely in 79.

WE DO IT	5	07 FEB 76	RCA

STORIES

New York rock foursome which included singer Ian Lloyd (Buonconciglio), who had recorded as Lloyd London, and Michael Brown (ex Left Banke) had one Top 40 single before splitting. Ian went solo on Polydor in 76 and Scotti Brothers in 79 and Michael helped formed The Beckies.

BROTHER LOUIE (Hot Chocolate 73 UK hit)	1(2)	25 AUG 73	KAMA SUTRA

Also see Left Banke

STRANGLERS

Leading UK New Wave act were formed in 74 as The Guildford Stranglers. To date they have put 29 singles in the UK singles chart (at least one a year since 77) and 12 LPs into the UK Top 20. Lead singer Hugh Cornwall has also recorded solo on Portrait in 85 and on Virgin in 88. One of their hits in 86 was 'Big In America' – oddly something the group have never been.

PEACHES/GO BUDDY GO (A-side banned by BBC)	8	09 JUL 77	UA
SOMETHING BETTER CHANGE/STRAIGHTEN OUT	9	20 AUG 77	UA
NO MORE HEROES	8	22 OCT 77	UA
GOLDEN BROWN	2	13 FEB 82	LIBERTY
STRANGE LITTLE GIRL	7	21 AUG 82	LIBERTY
EUROPEAN FEMALE	9	22 JAN 83	EPIC
ALL DAY AND ALL OF THE NIGHT (Kinks 64 hit)	7	16 JAN 88	EPIC

STRAWBERRY ALARM CLOCK

Psychedelic group from L.A., who were originally called Thee Sixpence, were fronted by Ed King and Lee Freeman. They had two US-only Top 40s – the other being the follow up ' Tomorrow' (23). Ed later played for a while in Lynyrd Skynyrd and co-wrote their hit 'Free Bird'.

INCENSE AND PEPPERMINTS (Recorded as B-side) (Singer on track was just a friend of the group!)	1(1)	25 NOV 67	UNI

STRAWBERRY SWITCHBLADE

Scottish female punk duo, who were named after an Orange Juice song, consisted of Rose McDowell and Jill Bryson. They previously recorded on 92 Happy Customers in 83 and followed their only Top 40 with 'Let Her Go'.

 SINCE YESTERDAY · 5 · 26 JAN 85 · KOROVA

STRAWBS

Leicester (UK) based folk rock group were originally called The Strawberry Hill Boys in 67. Formed by Dave Cousins they included Richard Hudson and John Ford (who left to become Hudson-Ford in 73), Rick Wakeman (who left in 71) and Blue Weaver. In 75 the group relocated to the US where they had seven small chart LPs before they split in the late 70s and Dave went solo.

 PART OF THE UNION · 2 · 17 FEB 73 · A&M.
(Composed by Hudson & Ford)

Also see Hudson-Ford

STRAY CATS

The most successful of the rockabilly revival acts were the New York trio of Brian Setzer (ex Bloodless Pharoahs), Lee Rocker (Lee Drucher) and Slim Jim Phantom (Jim McDonell). They launched their career from the UK and had four UK & US Top 40 singles and a two million selling LP 'Built For Speed'. They split in 84 and Brian recorded solo and Lee and Jim formed Phantom, Rocker & Slick with Earl Slick. They re-united on EMI Manhattan in 89.

 RUNAWAY BOYS · 9 · 20 DEC 80 · ARISTA
ROCK THIS TOWN *(Returned to UK chart in 89)* · 9 · 21 FEB 81 · ARISTA
(Both hits produced by Dave Edmunds)

 ROCK THIS TOWN · 9 · 11 DEC 82 · EMI AM.
STRAY CAT STRUT *(UK No. 11)* · 3 · 26 FEB 83 · EMI AM.
(SHE'S) SEXY + 17 *(UK No. 29)* · 5 · 01 OCT 83 · EMI AM.

BARBRA STREISAND

The world's most successful singer/actress was born in New York and first appeared on Broadway in 62. The album orientated MOR pop superstar first charted in 63 and has since had a record 31 US (9 UK) Top 20 LPs and has picked up 34 US gold LPs. The multi-award winner has also had 12 US (6 UK) Top 20 singles. She has also appeared in numerous hit films, some of which she has produced and directed too.

 EVERGREEN (LOVE THEME FROM A STAR IS BORN) · 3 · 28 MAY 77 · CBS
YOU DON'T BRING ME FLOWERS · 5 · 23 DEC 78 · COLUMBIA
(As BARBRA & NEIL (And NEIL DIAMOND))
NO MORE TEARS (ENOUGH IS ENOUGH) · 3 · 01 DEC 79 · COLUMBIA/ CASABLANCA
(And DONNA SUMMER – released on two labels)
WOMAN IN LOVE *(Jumped from 9-1)* · 1(3) · 25 OCT 80 · CBS
(Gibb brothers (Bee Gees) song and production)

 PEOPLE *(From the musical 'Funny Girl')* · 5 · 27 JUN 64 · COLUMBIA
STONEY END *(UK No. 2 – comp. Laura Nyro)* · 6 · 23 JAN 71 · COLUMBIA
THE WAY WE WERE *(Grammy Song of the Year)* · 1(3) · 02 FEB 74 · COLUMBIA
(From the film – UK No. 31 – Top US single of 74)
EVERGREEN (LOVE THEME FROM "A STAR IS BORN") · 1(3) · 05 MAR 77 · COLUMBIA
(Grammy winning female pop vocal performance of 77)
MY HEART BELONGS TO ME · 4 · 30 JUL 77 · COLUMBIA
YOU DON'T BRING ME FLOWERS · 1(2) · 02 DEC 78 · COLUMBIA
(As BARBRA & NEIL)
(They both originally released the song as solos)
THE MAIN EVENT/FIGHT *(From the film)* · 3 · 11 AUG 79 · COLUMBIA
NO MORE TEARS (ENOUGH IS ENOUGH) · 1(2) · 24 NOV 79 · COLUMBIA
(And DONNA SUMMER)
WOMAN IN LOVE · 1(3) · 25 OCT 80 · COLUMBIA
GUILTY *(And BARRY GIBB – UK No. 34)* · 3 · 10 JAN 81 · COLUMBIA
WHAT KIND OF FOOL *(And BARRY GIBB)* · 10 · 21 MAR 81 · COLUMBIA

STRING-A-LONGS

New Mexican instrumental quintet featured guitarist/composer Jimmy Torres were produced by Norman Petty (as was Buddy Holly). The A & B-side titles of their only big hit got mixed up and their composition 'Tell The World' accidentally hit as 'Wheels'! They were also on Dot, Atco & Ohn-J.

 WHEELS · 3 · 06 MAR 61 · WARWICK
(UK No. 11 – They later recorded 'Spinnin' My Wheels')

STYLE COUNCIL

Paul Weller ex-leader of the very successful UK band The Jam set up this soul/jazz orientated act with Mick Talbot (ex-Merton Parkas and The Bureau). This politically committed act helped UK miners during their strike and took part in Band Aid, Live Aid and the Red Wedge tours. Like The Jam, their hits were limited to the UK where they had 12 Top 20 singles and five Top 10 LPs before splitting in 90.

 SPEAK LIKE A CHILD *(Entered at No. 6)* · 4 · 26 MAR 83 · POLYDOR
LONG HOT SUMMER *(Entered at No. 8)* · 3 · 20 AUG 83 · POLYDOR
(A remix was UK. No. 48 in 89)
MY EVER CHANGING MOOD *(Entered at No. 8)* · 5 · 25 FEB 84 · POLYDOR
GROOVIN' (YOU'RE THE BEST THING)/
BIG BOSS GROOVE *(Maxi-single)* · 5 · 02 JUN 84 · POLYDOR
SHOUT TO THE TOP · 7 · 20 OCT 84 · POLYDOR
WALLS COME TUMBLING DOWN! · 6 · 18 MAY 85 · POLYDOR
IT DIDN'T MATTER · 9 · 24 JAN 87 · POLYDOR

Also see The Jam

STYLISTICS

Smooth Philadelphia soul vocal team were formed from The Monarchs and the Percussions and featured Russell Thompkins Jr. Their first of 17 US (16 UK) hits came in 71 (with a re-issue of their first 45 from 69 on Sebring). In the UK the big hits continued after they did in the US and their 'Best of' LP was the Top LP of 75 and the biggest seller ever by a black act there.

 I'M STONE IN LOVE WITH YOU · 9 · 25 NOV 72 · AVCO
ROCKIN' ROLL BABY *(US No. 14)* · 6 · 09 FEB 74 · AVCO
YOU MAKE ME FEEL BRAND NEW · 2 · 24 AUG 74 · AVCO
LET'S PUT IT ALL TOGETHER *(US No. 18)* · 9 · 16 NOV 74 · AVCO
SING BABY SING · 4 · 31 MAY 75 · AVCO
CAN'T GIVE YOU ANYTHING (BUT MY LOVE) · 1(3) · 16 AUG 75 · AVCO
(US No. 51)
NA NA IS THE SADDEST WORD · 5 · 13 DEC 75 · AVCO
FUNKY WEEKEND *(US No. 76)* · 10 · 06 MAR 76 · AVCO
CAN'T HELP FALLING IN LOVE · 4 · 22 MAY 76 · AVCO
(Elvis Presley 61 hit)
16 BARS · 7 · 11 SEP 76 · H & L

 YOU ARE EVERYTHING · 9 · 22 JAN 72 · AVCO
BETCHA BY GOLLY, WOW *(UK No. 13)* · 3 · 06 MAY 72 · AVCO
I'M STONE IN LOVE WITH YOU · 10 · 09 DEC 72 · AVCO
BREAK UP TO MAKE UP *(UK No. 34)* · 5 · 07 APR 73 · AVCO
YOU MAKE ME FEEL BRAND NEW · 2 · 15 JUN 74 · AVCO

STYX

Top Chicago pomp rock quintet which featured Dennis DeYoung & Tommy Shaw evolved from The Tradewinds and TW4. They first charted in 72 on Wooden Nickel and afterwards they notched up 14 US (1 UK) Top 40 singles and six US (1 UK) Top 20 LPs. In 84 Dennis and Tommy 'rested' the group and both had solo successes. In 90 they both joined supergroup Damn Yankees on Warner.

 BABE · 6 · 26 JAN 80 · A&M
 LADY · 6 · 08 MAR 75 · WOODEN NICKEL
COME SAIL AWAY · 8 · 28 JAN 78 · A&M
BABE · 1 · 08 DEC 79 · A&M
THE BEST OF TIMES *(UK No. 42)* · 3 · 21 MAR 81 · A&M
TOO MUCH TIME ON MY HANDS · 9 · 23 MAY 81 · A&M
MR. ROBOTO · 3 · 16 APR 83 · A&M
DON'T LET IT END *(UK No. 56)* · 6 · 02 JUL 83 · A&M

Also see Dennis DeYoung

SUGARHILL GANG

The first rap hit (it was also No. 1 in Canada and Holland) came from this New York trio – Wonder Mike, Master Gee and Big Bank Hank. They never managed to crack the Top 40 again but rap, which they introduced to the world, became the biggest new music form of the 80s.

RAPPER'S DELIGHT *(US No. 36)* *(Based on Chic's 'Good Times' – remix in* *UK 75 in 89)*		3	15 DEC 79	SUGARHILL

SUGARLOAF

Jerry Corbetta led this Denver based pop rock quartet whose biggest hits came five years apart. They also recorded on UA and Brut.

GREEN EYED LADY		3	17 OCT 70	LIBERTY
DON'T CALL US WE'LL CALL YOU *(As Sugarloaf feat. Jerry Corbetta)*		9	29 MAR 75	CLARIDGE

DONNA SUMMER

The queen of disco music was born LaDonna Gaines in Boston (US) and sang in Crow before relocating to Germany where she teamed with Giorgio Moroder. She had European hits with 'Hostage' and 'Lady Of The Night' before getting the first of 14 US (18 UK) Top 20s and eight US (6 UK) Top 20 LPs. She was the first female singer to have three consecutive US No. 1 LPs and was the first act signed to Geffen. After a quiet spell she returned to the Top 10 in 89.

LOVE TO LOVE YOU BABY		4	07 FEB 76	GTO
I FEEL LOVE		1(4)	23 JUL 77	GTO
DEEP DOWN INSIDE *(from the film 'Deep End')*		5	10 SEP 77	CASABLANCA
LOVE'S UNKIND		3	14 JAN 78	GTO
I LOVE YOU		10	14 JAN 78	CASABLANCA
MACARTHUR PARK *(Richard Harris 68 hit)*		5	28 OCT 78	CASABLANCA
NO MORE TEARS (ENOUGH IS ENOUGH) *(And Barbra Streisand – record on two labels)*		3	01 DEC 79	CASABLANCA/ CBS
THIS TIME I KNOW IT'S FOR REAL		3	25 MAR 89	WARNER
I DON'T WANNA GET HURT *(Above two produced and written by S.A.W.)*		7	03 JUN 89	WARNER

LOVE TO LOVE YOU BABY		2	07 FEB 76	OASIS
I FEEL LOVE		6	12 NOV 77	CASABLANCA
LAST DANCE *(Oscar & Grammy winner)* *(UK No. 51 – From the film 'Thank God It's Friday')*		3	12 AUG 78	CASABLANCA
MACARTHUR PARK		1(3)	11 NOV 78	CASABLANCA
HEAVEN KNOWS *(Feat. BROOKLYN DREAMS –* *UK No.34)*		4	10 MAR 79	CASABLANCA
HOT STUFF *(UK No. 11 – Grammy winner)*		1(3)	02 JUN 79	CASABLANCA
BAD GIRLS *(UK No. 14)*		1(5)	14 JUL 79	CASABLANCA
DIM ALL THE LIGHTS *(UK No. 29)*		2	10 NOV 79	CASABLANCA
NO MORE TEARS *(And Barbra Streisand)*		1(2)	24 NOV 79	CASABLANCA/ COLUMBIA
ON THE RADIO *(UK No. 32)*		5	15 MAR 80	CASABLANCA
THE WANDERER *(UK No. 48)*		3	15 NOV 80	GEFFEN
LOVE IS IN CONTROL (FINGER ON THE TRIGGER) *(UK No. 18)* *(Prod. & co-writ. Quincy Jones)*		10	25 SEP 82	WARNER
SHE WORKS HARD FOR THE MONEY *(UK No. 25)*		3	06 AUG 83	MERCURY
THIS TIME I KNOW IT'S FOR REAL		7	24 JUN 89	ATLANTIC

SUNNY

Top UK session singer Sunny Leslie, who had recorded in the duo Sue & Sunny on Columbia in 65 and Deram in 70, followed her one-off hit with 'A Warm And Tender Romance'. She also recorded solo on DJM in 79.

DOCTOR'S ORDERS *(Prod.& Comp. Roger* *Greenaway)*		7	04 MAY 74	CBS

SUPERTRAMP

Top progressive rock quintet from London were led by Richard Davies and Roger Hodgson. 'Dreamer' (UK 13/US 15 in 80) was the first of five UK (9 US) Top 40 singles. Their first two LPs failed but they then had eight UK (6 US) Top 40s including the No. 1 'Breakfast In America'. Roger went solo in 83.

THE LOGICAL SONG		7	28 APR 79	A&M
BREAKFAST IN AMERICA *(US No. 62)*		9	04 AUG 79	A&M

THE LOGICAL SONG		6	16 JUN 79	A&M
TAKE THE LONG WAY HOME		10	15 DEC 79	A&M

SUPREMES

The most successful girl group of all time were Detroit's Diana Ross, Mary Wilson and Florence Ballard, who first recorded on Lupine in 69 as The Primettes. Their chart debut came in 62 and in all they had 45 US (29 UK) chart singles (including 12 US No. 1s) and 35 US (15 UK) chart LPs. Florence left the pop/soul trio in 67 (and died in poverty in 76), Diana left for further success in 70 and the new trio folded after Mary left in 76.

WHERE DID OUR LOVE GO *(Song was written for The Marvelettes)*		3	03 OCT 64	STATESIDE
BABY LOVE *(Also UK No. 12 in 74)* *(First record by a girl group to top chart)*		1(2)	21 NOV 64	STATESIDE
STOP! IN THE NAME OF LOVE *(Also UK No. 62 in 89)*		6	17 APR 65	TAMLA MOTOWN
YOU CAN'T HURRY LOVE		3	01 OCT 66	TAMLA MOTOWN
YOU KEEP ME HANGIN' ON		8	24 NOV 66	TAMLA MOTOWN
THE HAPPENING *(From the film)*		6	10 JUN 67	TAMLA MOTOWN
REFLECTIONS *(As Diana Ross & The Supremes)*		5	30 SEP 67	TAMLA MOTOWN
I'M GONNA MAKE YOU LOVE ME *(As Diana Ross &* *The Supremes & Temptations)* *(Dee Dee Warwick 66 US hit)*		3	22 FEB 69	TAMLA MOTOWN
UP THE LADDER TO THE ROOF		6	30 MAY 70	TAMLA MOTOWN
STONED LOVE		3	06 FEB 71	TAMLA MOTOWN
NATHAN JONES *(US No. 16)*		5	18 SEP 71	TAMLA MOTOWN
FLOY JOY		9	01 APR 72	TAMLA MOTOWN
(US No. 16 – written & produced Smokey Robinson)				
AUTOMATICALLY SUNSHINE *(US No. 37)*		10	05 AUG 72	TAMLA MOTOWN

WHERE DID OUR LOVE GO *(Their 10th single)*		1(2)	22 AUG 64	MOTOWN
BABY LOVE		1(4)	21 NOV 64	MOTOWN
COME SEE ABOUT ME *(UK No. 27)*		1(2)	19 DEC 64	MOTOWN
STOP!IN THE NAME OF LOVE		1(2)	27 MAR 65	MOTOWN
BACK IN MY ARMS AGAIN *(UK No. 40)*		1	12 JUN 65	MOTOWN
I HEAR A SYMPHONY *(UK No. 39)*		1(2)	20 NOV 65	MOTOWN
MY WORLD IS EMPTY WITHOUT YOU		5	19 FEB 66	MOTOWN
LOVE IS LIKE AN ITCHING IN MY HEART		9	28 MAY 66	MOTOWN
YOU CAN'T HURRY LOVE		1(2)	10 SEP 66	MOTOWN
YOU KEEP ME HANGIN' ON		1(2)	19 NOV 66	MOTOWN
LOVE IS HERE AND NOW YOU'RE GONE *(UK No.17)*		1(1)	11 MAR 67	MOTOWN
THE HAPPENING		1(1)	13 MAY 67	MOTOWN
REFLECTIONS *(End of a run of four No. 1s – record No. was 1111!)*		2	09 SEP 67	MOTOWN
IN AND OUT OF LOVE *(UK No. 13)*		9	09 NOV 67	MOTOWN
LOVE CHILD *(UK No. 15 – co-written by R.Dean Taylor)*		1(2)	30 NOV 68	MOTOWN
I'M GONNA MAKE YOU LOVE ME *(As Diana Ross & The Supremes & The Temptations)*		2	11 JAN 69	MOTOWN
I'M LIVIN' IN SHAME *(UK No. 14)*		10	22 FEB 69	MOTOWN
SOMEDAY WE'LL BE TOGETHER *(UK No. 13)* *(Orig. by Johnny (Bristol – who produced it)* *and Jackey)* *(Above six as Diana Ross & The Supremes)*		1(1)	27 DEC 69	MOTOWN
UP THE LADDER TO THE ROOF		10	18 APR 70	MOTOWN
STONED LOVE		7	19 DEC 70	MOTOWN

Also see Diana Ross

AL B. SURE!

Boston born singer/songwriter/producer and multi-instrumentalist saw the first of his five black hits to date go to No. 1. He also guested on Quincy Jones' all star 89 LP 'Back On The Block'. He had a lot of press in US when sued for rape which he was later cleared of (with little press!).

NITE AND DAY		7	16 JUL 88	WARNER

SURFACE

Singer/songwriting/producers Bernard Jackson, David Townsend and Dave Conley are one of the top new black music groups. They first hit in 83 on Salsoul and have had six black Top 10s (inc. three No. 1s and three US-only pop Top 20s) since 87. They have also produced and written hits for others.

SHOWER ME WITH YOUR LOVE	•	5	16 SEP 89	COLUMBIA

SURFARIS

Californian surf quintet's sole Top 40 hit which was first out on Princess features drummer Ron Wilson. They were later on Decca, Del-Fi, Felsted (where they made 'Psyche Out'). Ron Wilson & The Surfaris were still working in 87 when their hit came back to the chart by the Fat Boys and Beach Boys.

	WIPEOUT (Was recorded as the B-side)	8	23 AUG 63	LONDON
	WIPE OUT (Laugh by manager Dave Smallins) (Also US No. 16 in 66 – was to be called 'Stiletto')	2	10 AUG 63	DOT

SURVIVOR

Formed by Jim Peterik (ex leader of hit act The Ides of March) and Frank Sullivan (ex Mariah) in 78. They wrote hits for .38 Special and Don Felder before getting their first Transatlantic Top 10 with a track from their third LP. Many of their eight US (2 UK) Top 40s feature singer Jimi Jamison.

	EYE OF THE TIGER (From the film 'Rocky III') (First US rock band top in UK for six years)	1(4)	04 SEP 82	SCOTTI BROTHE
	BURNING HEART	5	01 MAR 86	SCOTTI BROTHE
	EYE OF THE TIGER (Lead vocal Dave Bickler)	1(6)	24 JUL 82	SCOTTI BROTHE
	HIGH ON YOU	8	23 MAR 85	SCOTTI BROTHE
	THE SEARCH IS OVER	4	13 JUL 85	SCOTTI BROTHE
	BURNING HEART (From the film 'Rocky 1V')	2	01 FEB 86	SCOTTI BROTHE
	IS THIS LOVE	9	17 JAN 87	SCOTTI BROTHE

Also see The Ides of March

SUTHERLAND BROTHERS AND QUIVER

Both folk rock duo Ian & Gavin Sutherland and the group Quiver had made two LPs (on Island/Warner) before merging and charting in the US in 73 with 'You Got Me Anyway'(48) on Island. In 75 Rod Stewart hit with Gavin's song 'Sailing' and in 76 they had two UK only Top 40s. Quiver left soon after and the brothers continued recording as a duo on CBS and RCA.

	ARMS OF MARY (US No. 81)	5	22 MAY 76	CBS

BILLY SWAN

Missouri born singer wrote Clyde McPhatter's Top 10 hit 'Lover Please' for his own band Mirt Mitley & the Rhythm Steppers when just 16. He had just one Top 40 hit and 16 country entries between 74-87. He produced Tony Joe White's first three LPs and has played in the bands of Kris Kristofferson and Willie Nelson. He was also on Rising Sons, Elf, Columbia, MGM, A&M, Epic and Mercury and in 86 formed Black Tie with Randy Meisner (ex Eagles).

	I CAN HELP	6	18 JAN 75	MONUMENT
	I CAN HELP	1(2)	23 NOV 74	MONUMENT

PATRICK SWAYZE Feat. WENDY FRASER

The acting duo had a one-off hit with a song from their box office smash film Dirty Dancing. It was the third US Top 5 single from the movie.

	SHE'S LIKE THE WIND (UK No. 17)	3	27 FEB 88	RCA

KEITH SWEAT

The top new black act of 88 in the US was born in New York. His first 45 was 'My Mind Is Made Up' on Stadium in 86. He joined Elektra in 87 and in 88 had three Top 3 black music hits including a duet with Jacci McGhee. In 90 he returned to the charts with the group Entouch.

	I WANT HER (UK No. 26 – Top Black Music Single of 88)	5	02 APR 88	VINTERTAINMEN

SWEET

Top 70s glam rock group fronted by Brian Connolly evolved from Wainwright's Gentlemen (also included Ian Gillan – later of Deep Purple) and Sweetshop (who recorded on Fontana and Parlophone). Their first Chinn & Chapman song 'Funny Funny' (UK 13) in 71 was their first of 13 UK (5 US) Top 20s. Brian went solo in 79 and later formed a completely new Sweet.

	CO-CO (US No. 99)	2	10 JUL 71	RCA
	LITTLE WILLIE	4	01 JUL 72	RCA
	WIG WAM BAM	4	07 OCT 72	RCA
	BLOCKBUSTER (US No. 73)	1(5)	27 JAN 73	RCA
	HELL RAISER (Entered at No. 4)	2	12 MAY 73	RCA
	BALLROOM BLITZ (Entered at No. 2)	2	22 SEP 73	RCA
	TEENAGE RAMPAGE (Entered at No. 6) (Covered in US by Bo Donaldson & Heywoods)	2	26 JAN 74	RCA
	THE SIX TEENS (All above written by Chinn & Chapman)	9	27 JUL 74	RCA
	FOX ON THE RUN (Their fifth No. 2 hit)	2	12 APR 75	RCA
	LOVE IS LIKE OXYGEN	9	15 FEB 78	POLYDOR
	LITTLE WILLY	3	05 MAY 73	BELL
	BALLROOM BLITZ	5	18 OCT 75	CAPITOL
	FOX ON THE RUN	5	17 JAN 76	CAPITOL
	LOVE IS LIKE OXYGEN	8	24 JUN 78	CAPITOL

SWEET DREAMS

UK session duo who consisted of Tony Jackson and Polly Brown had a one-off hit. Tony has also recorded under several names, sang in Paul Young's group and did the sound-a-like voices (of Marvin Gaye and Sam Cooke) for the UK Levi Jeans ads. Polly (who blacked her face to promote this 45) fronted hit act Pickettywitch and had a US Top 20 as a soloist.

	HONEY HONEY (US No. 68)	10	31 AUG 74	BRADLEY'S

Also see Pickettywitch

SWEET PEOPLE

French group led by 31 year old composer/pianist Alain Morisod followed their sole hit with 'Lake Como'. Alain had previously had 23 LPs released in his home country.

	ET LES OISEAUX CHANTAIENT (AND THE BIRDS WERE SINGING) (Also UK No. 73 in 87)	4	18 OCT 80	POLYDOR

SWEET SENSATION

Manchester soul group led by 16 year old Marcel King were winners on TV's 'New Faces'. Their second 45 was a transatlantic Top 20 which they followed with 'Purely By Coincidence' (UK 11) both written and co-produced by David Parton. Marcel left in 76 and recorded for Wanted, A&M, Factory and Debut.

	SAD SWEET DREAMER (US No. 14)	1(1)	19 OCT 74	PYE

SWING OUT SISTER

Pop jazz act formed by Martin Jackson (ex-Magazine) and Andy Connell (ex-A Certain Ratio) and fronted by photogenic Corrine Drewery (ex Working Week). Their first 45 missed but their first LP was a UK No. 1 and they had a Grammy nomination. Act had no releases in 88 and Jackson left in 89 before the release of their second LP 'Kaleidoscope World'. By 90 their fortunes appeared to be on the wane.

	BREAKOUT	4	22 NOV 86	MERCURY
	SURRENDER	7	24 JAN 87	MERCURY
	BREAKOUT	6	14 NOV 87	MERCURY

SWINGING BLUE JEANS

Liverpool rock foursome originally called The Bluegenes included singer Ray Ennis. They had three UK-only Top 20s with Mersey styled revivals of US hits – the other being Little Richard's 'Good Golly Miss Molly' (UK 11/US 43). Ray has often re-formed them to record and work the oldies circuit.

HIPPY HIPPY SHAKE *(US No. 43)* *(Original by Chan Romero – Also UK No. 101 in 89)*	2	25 JAN 64	HMV
YOU'RE NO GOOD *(US No. 97)* *(US No. 97 – Betty Everett 63 US hit)*	3	04 JUL 64	HMV

SYLVERS

Family group from Memphis included Leon, Edmund and Foster Sylvers. They had eight US-only charters – the first on Pride in 72. They also recorded on MGM, Casablanca and Geffen. Leon became a top producer and writer, Edmund had a solo hit and Foster, who had a solo Top 40 in 73 when he was only 11, signed with A&M in 90 with his group Hy Tech.

BOOGIE FEVER	1(1)	15 MAY 76	CAPITOL
HOT LINE	5	29 JAN 77	CAPITOL

SYLVESTER

One of the best disco music singers was born Sylvester James in L.A. He sang with the group The Cockettes and was backed by Two Tons o'Fun (a.k.a. The Weather Girls). His biggest US hit was 'Dance (Disco Heat)' (US 19/UK 29). He was also on Megatone and Warner. He died in 88.

YOU MAKE ME FEEL (MIGHTY REAL) *(US No. 36)*	8	07 OCT 78	FANTASY

SYLVIA

Swedish singer Sylvia Vrethammar had the UK hit with the smash European song (a hit for Samantha in Belgium and Holland's Imca Marina in Germany). This holiday makers 'Spanish national anthem' was written by two Belgians and an Englishman. Her only other hit was 'Hasta La Vista' (UK 38).

Y VIVA ESPANA	4	14 SEP 74	SONET

SYLVIA

One of the first and most successful female producers and record label owners (Sugarhill and All Platinum). As Little Sylvia (Vanderpool) she recorded on Columbia in 50, Savoy in 51, Jubilee in 52 and Cat in 54. She charted in Mickey (Baker) & Sylvia on Groove, Vik and Willow between 56-61. She recorded as Sylvia Robbins on Sue and Jubilee in 64 and started recording under the one name in 68. She has produced hits for acts like The Moments, Shirley & Co and Grandmaster Flash. She had a further 11 black music charters after her sole Top 40 pop hit and was on Bon Ami in 87.

PILLOW TALK *(UK No. 14 – she had written it for Al Green)*	3	09 JUN 73	VIBRATION

SYNDICATE OF SOUND

Don Baskin was the singer of this San Jose garage rock band who followed their sole Top 40 hit with 'Rumors'. They had previously been on Del-Fi in 65 and were later on Capitol in 69 and Buddah in 70.

LITTLE GIRL *(This record was previously on Scarlet and Hush)*	8	09 JUL 66	BELL

SYREETA – FOR HIT DETAILS SEE BILLY PRESTON

SYSTEM

Singer Mic Murphy, who was in Mic & The Soul Shakers, and Ohio born synth player David Frank are this inter-racial techno-funk New York based duo who have had eight black music charters to date, including 'You Are In My System' which was a UK hit for Robert Palmer in 83.

DON'T DISTURB THE GROOVE	4	18 JUL 87	ATLANTIC

T

T. REX

Very successful and influential UK act was fronted by London born ex-male model and child actor Marc Bolan (Feld). He had three solo 45s (on Decca and EMI) and three in mod band John's Children (on Track) before forming Tyrannosaurus Rex with Steve Peregrine Took (replaced in 69 by Mickey Finn). Big hits came when they changed labels, shortened the name and enlarged and electrified the act in 70. 'T-Rextasy' swept the UK and they had 15 UK (1 US) Top 20s and 10 UK (1 US) Top 20 LPs. Sales slowed, the group folded in 75 and Marc died in a car crash in 77. Loyal fans have kept his name in the UK charts since including an Indie No. 1 in 85 with 'Megarex'.

RIDE A WHITE SWAN *(US No. 76)*	2	23 JAN 71	FLY
HOT LOVE *(US No. 72)*	1(6)	20 MAR 71	FLY
GET IT ON	1(4)	24 JUL 71	FLY
(Flo & Eddie from The Turtles are on above two 45s)			
JEEPSTER	2	27 NOV 71	FLY
TELEGRAM SAM *(Entered at No. 3 – US No. 67)*	1(2)	05 FEB 72	T. REX
DEBORA/ONE INCH ROCK *(As Tyrannosaurus Rex)*	7	29 APR 72	MAGNI FLY
(Re-issue – 'A' was UK No. 34 & 'B' UK No. 28 in 68)			
METAL GURU *(Entered at No. 9)*	1(4)	20 MAY 72	EMI
CHILDREN OF THE REVOLUTION	2	23 SEP 72	EMI
SOLID GOLD EASY ACTION *(Entered at No. 8)*	2	06 JAN 73	EMI
20TH CENTURY BOY *(Entered at No. 3)*	3	10 MAR 73	EMI
THE GROOVER *(Entered at No. 6)*	4	23 APR 73	EMI
BANG A GONG (GET IT ON)	10	04 MAR 72	FLY
(Title changed to save confusion with Chase hit)			

TACO

German based Taco Ockerse was born in Indonesia of Dutch parents. This singer/actor formed the group Taco's Bizz in 80. His sole hit came from an LP of standards he recorded, as did the follow up 'Cheek To Cheek'

PUTTIN' ON THE RITZ *(Harry Richman 30 hit)* *(Irving Berlin's last hit song before his death)*	4	03 SEP 83	RCA

TAFFY

Italian based female singer followed her sole Top 40 with 'Step By Step'. Her hit, co-written and produced by Claudio Cecchetto, broke out of the Continental dance club scene and was one of many hi-nrg hits of the period.

I LOVE MY RADIO	6	14 FEB 87	TRANSGLOBAL

TALKING HEADS

Top New York new wave group includes Scottish born David Byrne (ex-Bizadi), Tina Weymouth and husband Chris Frantz (both ex-The Artistics). They first recorded in 76 and have had 3 US (3 UK – all different) Top 40s and 7 US (8 UK) Top 40 LPs. David has also recorded solo and with Eno and produced other acts. Tina & Chris have hit in their spin-off group Tom Tom Club. In 90 act announced it would tour as The Shrunken Heads but without the eccentric David.

ROAD TO NOWHERE *(Their 17th UK single)*	6	30 NOV 85	EMI
BURNING DOWN THE HOUSE	9	26 NOV 83	SIRE

Also see Tom Tom Club

TAMS

Atlanta soul vocal group which includes the Pope brothers Joseph and Charles. They recorded on Swan in 60 and first charted in 62 on Arlen. They had three UK (1 US) Top 40s and in the 80s were still a top beach music act in the south (US). They returned to the UK Top 40 in 87 with a shag single (a dance craze!) on Virgin (banned in UK and Australia). They were also on Heritage, General American, Apt, MGM South, 123, Capitol and Dunhill.

HEY GIRL DON'T BOTHER ME *(US No. 41 in 64)*	1(3)	18 SEP 71	PROBE
WHAT KIND OF FOOL (DO YOU THINK I AM)	9	22 FEB 64	ABC

TASTE OF HONEY

L.A. soul/dance act fronted by Janice Marie Johnson and Hazel Payne. Formed in 72, they were the first black act to win the Grammy for Best New Artist (79). They became a duo in 80 and had their second and last Top 40 in 81. They split in 84 and Janice's solo LP was called 'One Taste Of Honey'.

BOOGIE OOGIE OOGIE *(Remix was UK No. 59 in 85)*	3	12 AUG 78	CAPITOL
BOOGIE OOGIE OOGIE	1(3)	09 SEP 78	CAPITOL
SUKIYAKI *(Kyu Sakamoto 63 hit)*	3	13 JUN 81	CAPITOL

TAVARES

Massachusetts family soul group included Antone, Ralph and Feliciano Tavares. Between 64-69 they were called Chubby & The Turnpikes and recorded on Capitol in 67. They first hit in 73 and in the next decade had 14 US (9 UK) charters. They joined RCA in 82.

HEAVEN MUST BE MISSING AN ANGEL *(US No. 15 – Remix was UK No. 12 in 86)*	4	14 AUG 76	CAPITOL
DON'T TAKE AWAY THE MUSIC *(US No. 34)*	4	13 NOV 76	CAPITOL
WHODUNIT *(US No. 22)*	5	07 MAY 77	CAPITOL
MORE THAN A WOMAN *(US No. 32 – From the film Saturday Night Fever)*	7	27 MAY 78	CAPITOL
IT ONLY TAKES A MINUTE *(UK No. 46 in 86)*	10	25 OCT 75	CAPITOL

JAMES TAYLOR

Successful and influential singer/songwriter from Boston (US) was in The Fabulous Corsairs and recorded in The Flying Machine (not the hit act) before joining Apple in 68. The LP orientated singer has had nine US (2 UK) Top 20 LPs plus nine US (1 UK) Top 20 singles, all produced by Peter Asher (ex-Peter & Gordon). He married Carly Simon in 72, has taken part in numerous benefits and was involved in the 'No Nukes' campaign.

YOU'VE GOT A FRIEND *(Composed Carole King)* *(Grammy winner – Best Male Vocal Performance)*	4	16 OCT 71	WARNER
FIRE AND RAIN *(UK No. 42)*	3	31 OCT 70	WARNER
YOU'VE GOT A FRIEND	1(1)	31 JUL 71	WARNER
MOCKINGBIRD *(With CARLY SIMON)* *(Inez Foxx 63 hit)*	5	23 MAR 74	WARNER
HOW SWEET IT IS (TO BE LOVED BY YOU) *(Marvin Gaye 65 hit)*	5	30 AUG 75	WARNER
HANDY MAN *(Jimmy Jones 60 hit)* *(Grammy Winner Male Vocal Performance)*	4	10 SEP 77	COLUMBIA

JOHNNIE TAYLOR

Arkansas R&B singer recorded in the Five Echoes on Sabre in 54 and then replaced Sam Cooke in top gospel group The Soul Stirrers. He first soloed on Sam Cooke's own Sar label in 61 and had the first of his 21 US (1 UK) hits on Derby in 63. He was still getting black music hits in 90 on Malaco.

WHO'S MAKING LOVE *(One of his 15 black music Top 10s)*	5	07 DEC 68	STAX
DISCO LADY *(UK No. 25)* *(Top US Soul Single of 76 and he was Top Soul Act)*	1(4)	03 APR 76	COLUMBIA

R. DEAN TAYLOR

Canadian singer/songwriter/producer was on Mala in 62 and joined VIP in 65 (one of the few white acts on a Motown owned label). He had four UK (1 US) Top 40s and co-wrote The Supremes 'Love Child'. In 73 he was on his own label Jane and was then on Polydor in 74, Farr in 76 and 20th Century in 81.

INDIANA WANTS ME	2	05 JUN 71	TAMLA MOTOWN
THERE'S A GHOST IN MY HOUSE *(A 66 US flop that became a UK northern soul hit)*	3	15 JUN 74	TAMLA MOTOWN
INDIANA WANTS ME	5	07 NOV 70	RARE EARTH

T-BONES

Instrumental studio group put together by producer Joe Saraceno which included Dan Hamilton, Joe Frank Carollo & Tommy Reynolds later to have their own hits as a trio. Follow up was 'Sippin' & Chippin' – another TV ad.

NO MATTER WHAT SHAPE (YOUR STOMACH'S IN) *(A US Alka Seltzer jingle)*	3	05 FEB 66	LIBERTY

Also see Hamilton, Joe Frank & Reynolds

TEARDROP EXPLODES

Liverpool based group were a vehicle for the critically acclaimed Welsh singer/songwriter Julian Cope who had been in The Crucial Three with Ian McCulloch (Echo..) and Pete Wylie (Wah!). They first recorded on Zoo in 79 and their fourth 45 was the first of seven UK-only chart entries. Julian went solo in 83 and has since had eight UK (1 US) charters. Their third LP which had been recorded in 82 was first released in 90.

REWARD	6	21 MAR 81	VERTIGO

TEARS FOR FEARS

Pop rock duo from Bath Curt Smith and Roland Orzabal first recorded in Graduate on Precision in 80 and were in Neon (which included Rob Fisher from Climie Fisher) in 81. Their third single was the first of nine UK (4 US) Top 20s. There was a four year gap between their platinum albums 'Songs From The Big Chair' in 85 and the Beatles-esque 'The Seeds Of Love'.

MAD WORLD	3	06 NOV 82	MERCURY
CHANGE *(US No. 73)*	4	19 FEB 83	MERCURY
PALE SHELTER *(Remix of their second 45 – was UK No. 73 in 85)*	5	07 MAY 83	MERCURY
SHOUT	4	26 JAN 85	MERCURY
EVERYBODY WANTS TO RULE THE WORLD *(BRITS winner Top Single Of The Year)*	2	20 APR 85	MERCURY
EVERYBODY WANTS TO RUN THE WORLD *(Amended lyric of above hit – for 'Race Against Time')*	5	05 JUN 86	MERCURY
SOWING THE SEEDS OF LOVE *(Entered at No. 9)*	5	16 SEP 89	FONTANA
EVERYBODY WANTS TO RULE THE WORLD	1(2)	08 JUN 85	MERCURY
SHOUT *(Eighth non US record in a row at No. 1 – a record)*	1(3)	03 AUG 85	MERCURY
HEAD OVER HEELS *(UK No. 12 – They were second Top Group in US in 85)*	3	09 NOV 85	MERCURY
SOWING THE SEEDS OF LOVE *(Had award winning video)*	2	28 OCT 89	FONTANA

TECHNOTRONIC

Belgium's most successful act is this dance music project put together by Jo Bogaert, MC Eric, The Hi Tek 3 and Ya Kid K (Zaire born Barbara Kamosi Maoso Duogi) who co-wrote and sang their first big hit, although credit was given to Felly who had been in the group Glamour previously. Act kept the transatlantic hits coming in 90 when they joined Madonna on her world tour.

🇬🇧	PUMP UP THE JAM (Featuring FELLY)	2	07 OCT 89	SWANYARD
🇺🇸	PUMP UP THE JAM (Featuring FELLY)	2	27 JAN 90	SBK

TEE SET

Top Dutch act led by singer/songwriter Peter Tetteroo followed their only US Top 40 with 'If You Do Believe In Love'. Peter also had solo Dutch hits.

🇺🇸	MA BELLE AMIE	5	14 MAR 70	COLOSSUS

TEMPERANCE SEVEN

Nine(!) man novelty act played late 20s jazz under the musical direction of Captain Cephas Howard and featured the megaphone vocals of Mr. Paul MacDowell (a soloist on Fontana in 62). They had four UK-only hits in 61.

🇬🇧	YOU'RE DRIVING ME CRAZY (Guy Lombardo 30 hit)	1(1)	26 APR 61	PARLOPHONE
	PASADENA (Entered at No. 6) (Murray & Smalle 24 hit – both prod. George Martin)	3	20 JUN 61	PARLOPHONE

NINO TEMPO & APRIL STEVENS

New York singer/saxophonist Nino LoTempio worked with Glenn Miller and Benny Goodman's bands, played on Phil Spector sessions and has recorded on RCA, UA, Tower and A&M. His sister April had three US-only Top 40s in 51 (when 15) on RCA and was later on King, Imperial, Contract, Society, MGM, Verve and A&M. Together they had four US (2 UK) Top 40s and have also been on White Whale, Bell, Marina, ABC, A&M, Chelsea and Epic.

🇺🇸	DEEP PURPLE (UK No. 20 – Larry Clinton 39 hit) (Was recorded in just 15 minutes as the B-side)	1(1)	16 NOV 63	ATCO

TEMPTATIONS

Detroit vocal group, which has included Eddie Kendricks, David Ruffin, Dennis Edwards (ex Contours) and Paul Williams, are the most successful soul group ever, having spent over 25 years as top stars. Formed from members of two groups The Primes (on Lupine) and The Distants (on Northern/Warwick) they were first called The Elgins and joined Miracle in 61. Their third single was the first of 52 US (26 UK) hits and 41 US (12 UK) chart LPs. David left in 68, Eddie and Paul (who unfortunately died in 73) left in 71. In 82 the former two briefly rejoined. The group were still charting in 89.

🇬🇧	I'M GONNA MAKE YOU LOVE ME (With SUPREMES) (Their 18th UK single – Dee Dee Warwick 66 US hit)	3	22 FEB 69	TAMLA M
	GET READY (US No. 29 in 66 – Produced by Smokey Robinson)	10	29 MAR 69	TAMLA M
	BALL OF CONFUSION	7	07 NOV 70	TAMLA MOTOWN
	JUST MY IMAGINATION (RUNNIN' AWAY WITH ME)	8	10 JUL 71	TAMLA MOTOWN
🇺🇸	MY GIRL (UK No.45 – Composed and produced by Smokey Robinson)	1(1)	06 MAR 65	GORDY
	BEAUTY IS ONLY SKIN DEEP (UK No. 18)	3	01 OCT 66	GORDY
	(I KNOW) I'M LOSING YOU (UK No. 19)	8	31 DEC 66	GORDY
	ALL I NEED	8	17 JUN 67	GORDY
	YOU'RE MY EVERYTHING (UK No. 26)	6	16 SEP 67	GORDY
	I WISH IT WOULD RAIN (UK No. 45)	4	17 FEB 68	GORDY
	I'M GONNA MAKE YOU LOVE ME (With SUPREMES)	2	28 DEC 68	MOTOWN
	CLOUD NINE (Motown's first Grammy winner) (UK No.15 – they had two 45s together in US Top 6)	6	11 JAN 69	GORDY
	RUN AWAY CHILD, RUNNING WILD	6	29 MAR 69	GORDY
	I CAN'T GET NEXT TO YOU (UK No. 13)	1(2)	18 OCT 69	GORDY
	PSYCHEDELIC SHACK (UK No. 33)	7	28 FEB 70	GORDY
	BALL OF CONFUSION (THAT'S WHAT THE WORLD IS TODAY)	3	27 JUN 70	GORDY
	JUST MY IMAGINATION (RUNNING AWAY WITH ME)	1(2)	03 APR 71	GORDY
	PAPA WAS A ROLLIN' STONE (UK No. 14) (Instrumental side was a Grammy winner)	1(1)	02 DEC 72	GORDY
	MASTERPIECE (Grammy winner)	7	28 APR 73	GORDY

Also see Eddie Kendricks/David Ruffin

10CC

Multi talented art pop quartet. Act included Graham Gouldman who had written big hits for The Yardbirds, Herman's Hermits and The Hollies and had recorded in The Whirlwinds (HMV in 64), The Mockingbirds (Columbia), hit act Ohio Express (Buddah) and as a soloist on Decca, RCA, CBS and Mercury. Member Eric Stewart had been in hit act The Mindbenders and Lol Creme and Kevin Godley had recorded on Marmalade. Together they had their first of 13 UK (2 US) Top 20s as Hotlegs. Godley & Creme left in 76 and had much success recording and as video producers and Graham scored as half of RCA duo Wax.

🇬🇧	DONNA	2	21 OCT 72	UK
	RUBBER BULLETS (US No. 73)	1(1)	23 JUN 73	UK
	THE DEAN AND I	10	15 SEP 73	U.K.
	WALL STREET SHUFFLE	10	13 JUL 74	UK
	LIFE IS A MINESTONE	7	03 MAY 75	MERCURY
	I'M NOT IN LOVE (Jumped from 41-8) (In UK often voted Best Pop Record Of All Time)	1(2)	28 JUN 75	MERCURY
	ART FOR ART'S SAKE (US No. 83)	5	17 JAN 76	MERCURY
	I'M MANDY FLY ME (US No. 60)	6	10 APR 76	MERCURY
	THINGS WE DO FOR LOVE	6	15 JAN 77	MERCURY
	GOOD MORNING JUDGE (US No. 69)	5	28 MAY 77	MERCURY
	DREADLOCK HOLIDAY (US No. 44) (Only one of their next 12 singles charted)	1(1)	23 SEP 78	MERCURY
🇺🇸	I'M NOT IN LOVE	2	26 JUL 75	MERCURY
	THE THINGS WE DO FOR LOVE	5	16 APR 77	MERCURY

Also see Mindbenders/Hotlegs/Godley & Creme

TEN CITY

Innovative deep house trio led by Bryon Stingily and including Herb Lawson and Byron Burke, all of whom had been in other Chicago acts. Their first record was 'Devotion' in 87. They are tipped for big success in the 90s.

🇬🇧	THAT'S THE WAY LOVE IS	8	04 FEB 89	ATLANTIC

TEN POLE TUDOR

Raucous Scottish pub-styled sing-along punk quintet led by Eddie Tenpole. Follow up 'Wonderbar' (16) was their other UK-only Top 20. Eddie later returned to acting and was in 'Sid And Nancy' and 'Absolute Beginners'. He also appeared in The Sex Pistols' movie The Great Rock 'n' Roll Swindle, and sang on the Pistols' 'Who Killed Bambi'.

🇬🇧	SWORDS OF A THOUSAND MEN	6	23 MAY 81	STIFF

Also see Sex Pistols

TEN YEARS AFTER

Album orientated blues based progressive rock band which evolved from the Nottingham based Jaybirds and featured the speedy guitar playing of Alvin Lee. These stars of Woodstock had just the one UK single success but had eight UK (5 US) Top 40 LPs before they wound up in 74. Alvin later formed Alvin Lee & Co. and Ten Years Later and the group re-united in 89 on Chrysalis.

🇬🇧	LOVE LIKE A MAN (US No. 98)	10	08 AUG 70	DERAM

TAMMI TERRELL – SEE MARVIN GAYE & TAMMI TERRELL FOR HIT DETAILS

JOE TEX

Texan singer/songwriter born Joe Arlington was known as 'Soul Brother No. 2'. He first recorded for King in 55 and before charting was also on Ace, Anna, Parrot, Checker and Jalynne. This unmistakable singer/rapper (monologues) had 27 US (1 UK) charters. He later became a Muslim (Yusef Hazziez), joined Polydor in 80, Handshake in 81 and died in 82.

🇬🇧	AIN'T GONNA BUMP NO MORE (WITH NO BIG FAT WOMAN) (US No. 12)	2	28 MAY 77	EPIC
🇺🇸	HOLD WHAT YOU'VE GOT *(His 29th single and first hit!)*	5	30 JAN 65	DIAL
	SKINNY LEGS AND ALL	10	30 DEC 67	DIAL
	I GOTCHA	2	06 MAY 72	DIAL

TEXAS

Glasgow country/blues/rock quartet includes singer Sharleen Spiteri and guitarist Ally McErlaine. They followed their first hit with 'Thrill Is Gone'. Their LP 'Southside' was a No. 3 UK hit.

🇬🇧	I DON'T WANT A LOVER *(US No. 77)*	8	04 MAR 89	MERCURY

THEM

Singer/songwriter Van Morrison fronted this Irish R&B group whose second 45, which was the first of their two hits, was coupled with Van's song 'Gloria' (US 71) which became a rock music standard. Van left in 66 and went on to solo fame. They continued for a while without success.

🇬🇧	BABY PLEASE DON'T GO *(Originally by Big Joe Williams)*	10	13 FEB 65	DECCA
	HERE COMES THE NIGHT *(US No. 24 – Lulu 64 UK hit)*	2	24 APR 65	DECCA

Also see Van Morrison

THIN LIZZY

Irish hard rock trio featured Phil Lynott (ex Skid Row, Sugar Shack and Orphanage) and has included Gary Moore, Snowy White and Midge Ure. Their first four UK LPs failed but still they notched up nine UK (1 US) Top 20 singles and eight UK (1 US) Top 20 LPs. They split in 83 and Phil continued as a soloist (he had his first solo hit in 80) until his death in 86

🇬🇧	WHISKY IN THE JAR	6	24 FEB 73	DECCA
	THE BOYS ARE BACK IN TOWN *(US No. 12)*	8	03 JUL 76	VERTIGO
	WAITING FOR AN ALIBI	9	24 MAR 79	VERTIGO
	KILLER ON THE LOOSE	10	11 OCT 80	VERTIGO

Also see Gary Moore/Snowy White

THIRD WORLD

Highly regarded Jamaican group who fuse soul/reggae and African music. They were formed in 73 and feature singer William 'Bunny Rugs' Clarke who replaced Milton Hamilton in 76. The have had three UK Top 20s to date – the other being 'Cool Meditation' (17) in 79. They joined Mercury in 89.

🇬🇧🇺🇸	NOW THAT WE'VE FOUND LOVE *(US No. 47)* *(Re-mix was UK No. 22 in 85 – Orig. by The O'Jays)*	10	14 OCT 78	ISLAND
	DANCING ON THE FLOOR (HOOKED ON LOVE)	10	25 JUL 81	CBS

.38 SPECIAL

Florida based southern rock sextet who evolved from Sweet Rooster in 75 and include Donnie Van Zant (whose brother Ronnie was in Lynyrd Skynyrd) and Don Barnes. To date they have achieved eight US Top 40 singles and four Top 40 LPs with no UK success yet. In 89 they lengthened their name.

🇺🇸	CAUGHT UP IN YOU	10	03 JUL 82	A&M
	SECOND CHANCE *(as Thirty Eight Special)* *(Top Adult Contemporary Single of 89 in US)*	6	06 MAY 89	A&M

B.J. THOMAS

Oklahoma born MOR/pop/country singer first recorded with The Triumphs in 64 on Hickory and went solo in 66. He had 26 US (1 UK) pop chart entries between 66-77. A born again Christian, he was the Top Inspirational Act in the US in 81 and has won Grammys for his gospel recordings.

🇺🇸	I'M SO LONESOME I COULD CRY *(Feat. Triumphs)* *(First rel. on Pacemaker – Original Hank Williams)*	8	09 APR 66	SCEPTER
	HOOKED ON A FEELING	5	28 DEC 68	SCEPTER
	RAINDROPS KEEP FALLIN' ON MY HEAD *(UK No. 38)* *(From the film 'Butch Cassidy & Sundance Kid')*	1(4)	03 JAN 70	SCEPTER
	I JUST CAN'T HELP BELIEVING *(Co-written by Barry Mann)*	9	22 AUG 70	SCEPTER
	(HEY WON'T YOU PLAY) ANOTHER SOMEBODY DONE SOMEBODY WRONG SONG *(One of seven country Top 20s)*	1(1)	26 APR 75	ABC

CARLA THOMAS

Memphis born singer/songwriting daughter of Rufus Thomas started in the Teentown Singers in 53. She had two US-only Top 20s – the other being Isaac Hayes' song 'B-A-B-Y' (14) in 66. She also had a Transatlantic Top 40 duet with Otis Redding on Lowell Fulson's song 'Tramp' (US 26/UK 18).

🇺🇸	GEE WHIZ (LOOK AT HIS EYES) *(Originally released on Satellite (later Stax))*	10	27 MAR 61	ATLANTIC

EVELYN THOMAS

Chicago soul/dance singer had sung with the Mood Makers and Electric Funk before hitting with her solo release 'Weak Spot' (UK 26) on 20th Century in 76. All her four UK charters were written and produced by ex-UK club DJ Ian Levine. She was also on Nightmare and Seabright in 86 and Megatone in 89.

🇬🇧	HIGH ENERGY *(US No. 85 – Also Top in Germany)*	5	16 JUN 84	RECORD SHACK

NICKY THOMAS

Jamaican reggae singer, who had previously worked in a record shop, had his first hit with his fifth West Indian release – a revival of a Waylon Jennings 67 country hit. The sweetening strings were added in the UK by Johnny Arthey.

🇬🇧	LOVE OF THE COMMON PEOPLE	9	11 JUL 70	TROJAN

RUFUS THOMAS

Memphis based singer/songwriter and one time radio DJ first recorded in 50 on Talent. He was on Chess in 52, first charted on Sun in 53 and joined Meteor in 56. He had 11 US hits, the majority connected with dance crazes. His only UK entry was 'Do The Funky Chicken' (UK 18/US 28). He was later on Artists of America, AVI, Gusto and Hi. His daughter Carla was also a hit act.

🇺🇸	WALKING THE DOG	10	07 DEC 63	ABC

TIMMY THOMAS

Soul singer/songwriter and organist from Indiana recorded on Goldwax in 67. He followed his sole Transatlantic Top 40 with a further 12 black music hits. He was also on TM, Marlin and Gold Mountain.

🇺🇸	WHY CAN'T WE LIVE TOGETHER *(UK No. 12)*	3	10 FEB 73	GLADES

THOMPSON TWINS

Formed by Yorkshireman Tom Bailey in 77, the group had releases on Dirty Discs, Latent (an Indie hit) and Tee. In 81 Alannah Currie and Joe Leeway joined the group and in 82 they became a trio and scored the first of 10 UK (7 US) Top 40s and three UK (2 US) Top 20 LPs. They appeared at Live Aid (being joined on stage by Madonna). Joe left in 86 and the duo took a year off and then joined Warners. Their main success since has been in the US where they have had two Top 40s and two Top 3 dance singles.

🇬🇧	LOVE ON YOUR SIDE (US No. 45)	9	05 MAR 83	ARISTA
	WE ARE DETECTIVE	7	07 MAY 83	ARISTA
	HOLD ME NOW	4	10 DEC 83	ARISTA
	DOCTOR DOCTOR (US No. 11)	3	18 FEB 84	ARISTA
	YOU TAKE ME UP (US No. 44)	2	21 APR 84	ARISTA
🇺🇸	HOLD ME NOW	3	05 MAY 84	ARISTA
	LAY YOUR HANDS ON ME (UK No. 13)	6	23 NOV 85	ARISTA
	(Part of royalties went to Oxfam's Ethiopian Fund)			
	KING FOR A DAY (UK No. 22)	8	22 MAR 86	ARISTA

SUE THOMPSON

Missouri born Eva Sue McKee joined Mercury in 53 and after many 45s the distinctive singer went to Decca and Columbia. In the 60s she scored her five US-only Top 40s and she had 12 small country hits between 72-76.

🇺🇸	SAD MOVIES (MAKE ME CRY)	5	24 OCT 61	HICKORY
	NORMAN (Both hits comp. John D. Loudermilk)	3	24 FEB 62	HICKORY

KEN THORNE & HIS ORCHESTRA

Keyboard player from Norwich left the Vic Lewis orchestra in 50 to play the organ in Ely Cathedral. He had his sole hit at age 39 with a rush-released version (out 5 days after the recording) of Nini Rosso's Italian war film theme. His follow up was 'The Long March'.

🇬🇧	THEME FROM 'THE LEGION'S LAST PATROL'	9	16 AUG 63	HMV

THREE DEGREES

Philadelphia based pop/soul trio, which has included Fayette Pinkney and Sheila Ferguson (previously a soloist on Landa and Swan), first recorded and hit on Swan in 65. They were also on Warner, Metromedia, Neptune and Roulette before becoming top stars in the UK (they played at Prince Charles' 30th birthday party). In all they have had 11 UK (3 US) Top 40s and five UK (1 US) Top 40 LPs. They were also on Epic, Ichiban and Supreme where they became the first 'name act' to be produced by Stock, Aitken & Waterman.

🇬🇧	WHEN WILL I SEE YOU AGAIN	1(2)	17 AUG 74	PHILLY INT.
	TAKE GOOD CARE OF YOURSELF	9	03 MAY 75	PHILLY INT.
	WOMEN IN LOVE	3	03 FEB 79	ARIOLA
	THE RUNNER	10	14 APR 79	ARIOLA
	MY SIMPLE HEART	9	22 DEC 79	ARIOLA
🇺🇸	TSOP (THE SOUND OF PHILADELPHIA)	1(2)	20 APR 74	PHILLY INT.
	(With MFSB – UK No. 22 – Theme to TV's 'Soul Train')			
	WHEN WILL I SEE YOU AGAIN	2	14 DEC 74	PHILLY INT.

THREE DOG NIGHT

Very successful L.A. based pop rock group included Irish born Danny Hutton (ex-producer and soloist on HBR, MGM and Almo), Cory Wells (ex-The Enemies on MGM and Valiant) and Chuck Negron (who had recorded on Columbia). They achieved a remarkable 18 US (1 UK) Top 20s and 11 US-only Top 20 LPs. They split in 76 and reformed in 81 and again in 89 for a revival tour.

🇬🇧	MAMA TOLD ME (NOT TO COME)	3	05 SEP 70	STATESIDE
	(Composed Randy Newman – Original by Eric Burdon)			
🇺🇸	ONE (Composed Nilsson)	5	28 JUN 69	DUNHILL
	EASY TO BE HARD (From the musical Hair)	4	27 SEP 69	DUNHILL
	ELI'S COMING (Composed Laura Nyro)	10	29 NOV 69	DUNHILL
	MAMA TOLD ME (NOT TO COME)	1(2)	11 JUL 70	DUNHILL
	JOY TO THE WORLD (UK No. 22)	1(6)	17 APR 71	DUNHILL
	(UK No. 22 – Top US single of 71)			
	LIAR (Originally by Argent)	7	28 AUG 71	DUNHILL
	AN OLD FASHIONED LOVE SONG	4	18 DEC 71	DUNHILL
	NEVER BEEN TO SPAIN	5	12 FEB 72	DUNHILL
	BLACK & WHITE (Greyhound 71 UK hit)	1(1)	16 SEP 72	DUNHILL
	(An early civil rights song written in 55)			
	SHAMBALA (B.W. Stevenson 73 US hit)	3	28 JUL 73	DUNHILL
	THE SHOW MUST GO ON (Leo Sayer 73 UK hit)	4	25 MAY 74	DUNHILL

JOHNNY THUNDER

R&B singer from Florida whose sole Top 40 was an update of a nursery rhyme. He had sung briefly in The Drifters and had 45s (under real name Gil Hamilton) on Fury, Capitol (including the first version of The Exciters/ Hello hit 'Tell Him') and Vee Jay. He was later on Calla, UA and Arista.

🇺🇸	LOOP DE LOOP (Backing vocals The Bobbettes)	4	09 FEB 63	DIAMOND

THUNDERCLAP NEWMAN

Group assembled by The Who's Pete Townshend included eccentric pianist and former postman Andy Newman, diminutive guitarist Jimmy McCulloch, drummer/songwriter John 'Speedy' Keen and Pete himself on bass. The group went separate ways in 70 with Andy and John recording solos and Jimmy joining Wings before his untimely death in 79.

🇬🇧	SOMETHING IN THE AIR	1(3)	05 JUL 69	TRACK
	(US No. 37 – Jumped From 7-1)			

BOBBY THURSTON

Soulful dance music vocalist and percussion player, who had his own group Spectrum Ltd and had been on Avco in 76. He followed his sole hit with 'You Got What It Takes' which had been his previous single in the US.

🇬🇧	CHECK OUT THE GROOVE	10	03 MAY 80	EPIC

TIFFANY

Tiffany Darwish from California topped the US chart with her second 45 when she was only 16, helped in part by a US shopping mall P.A. tour. Her debut LP sold over four million and she also scored 5 US & UK Top 40s. Legal problems with her mother and manager/producer slowed her career down.

🇬🇧	I THINK WE'RE ALONE NOW	1(3)	30 JAN 88	MCA
	(The youngest US female to top the UK chart)			
	COULD'VE BEEN	4	02 APR 88	MCA
	I SAW HIM STANDING THERE (Beatles 64 hit)	8	11 JUN 88	MCA
🇺🇸	I THINK WE'RE ALONE NOW	1(2)	07 NOV 87	MCA
	(Tommy James & The Shondells 67 US hit)			
	COULD'VE BEEN	1(2)	06 FEB 88	MCA
	I SAW HIM STANDING THERE	7	23 APR 88	MCA
	ALL THIS TIME (UK No. 47)	6	11 FEB 89	MCA

TIGHT FIT

UK session group fronted by photogenic Steve Grant, Denise Gyngell and Julie Harris chalked up five UK (1 US) charters before the girls were replaced in 82. Steve recorded solo on Record Shack in 84.

🇬🇧	BACK TO THE SIXTIES	4	15 AUG 81	JIVE
	(US No. 89 – a medley of 60s hits)			
	THE LION SLEEPS TONIGHT (Tokens 61 hit)	1(3)	06 MAR 82	JIVE
	FANTASY ISLAND	5	29 MAY 83	JIVE

TANITA TIKARAM

Distinctive singer/songwriter was born in Germany and is based in Basingstoke (UK). Whilst still in her teens she hit No. 3 in the UK with her debut LP 'Ancient Heart' and so far has had four UK-only chart 45s. She moved to East West Records in 90.

 GOOD TRADITION (Co-produced by Rod Argent)   10   27 AUG 88   WEA

'TIL TUESDAY

Aimee Mann fronts this Boston (US) pop rock quartet who have had five US chart singles and three US chart LPs but no UK hits as yet.

VOICES CARRY   8   13 JUL 85   EPIC

JOHNNY TILLOTSON

Florida born pop/country singer/songwriter first charted in 58 and his sixth single was the first of his 13 US (4 UK) Top 40s in the early 60s. He was later on Amos, UA, Buddah, Columbia, Reward (where he made the country chart in 84) and joined Atlantic in 90.

	POETRY IN MOTION	1(3)	06 JAN 61	LONDON
	POETRY IN MOTION	2	14 NOV 60	CADENCE
	WITHOUT YOU	7	18 SEP 61	CADENCE
	IT KEEPS RIGHT ON A-HURTIN'	3	16 JUN 62	CADENCE
	TALK BACK TREMBLING LIPS	7	04 JAN 64	MGM
	(Ernie Ashworth 63 country No. 1)			

TIMELORDS

One-off project from members of the top indie band The Justified Ancients of MuMu (JAMMS) who included the multi-talented Bill Drummond (ex Big In Japan) and fellow Scotsman Jimmy Cauty. Act, who also had input from synth wizard Nick Coler and Ian Richardson, purposely never recorded a follow up.

DOCTORIN' THE TARDIS (US No. 66)   1(1)   18 JUN 88   KLF
(Includes 'Dr. Who Theme' and 'Rock & Roll')

TIMEX SOCIAL CLUB

Californian rap group fronted by Michael Marshall. Their producer Jay King quickly formed Club Nouveau and answered TSC's hit with 'Jealousy' when he and the group fell out. Act became simply Social Club after having problems with the watch company later in 86.

 RUMORS (UK No. 13)   8   16 AUG 86   JAY

TITANIC

Instrumental group which included Norwegians Janny Loseth and Kjell Asperud had a one-off UK hit. They made several LPs and were later on Egg and Souplet.

 SULTANA   5   30 OCT 71   CBS

TOKENS

New York group started as The Linc-Tones (which included Neil Sedaka) on Melba, then became Darrell & The Oxfords on Roulette. With the line up of Hank Medress, Jay Siegel and the Margo brothers Mitch & Phil they had the first of four US (1 UK) Top 40s on Warwick in 61. They also recorded (often with pseudonyms) on Music Makers, BT Puppy, Swing, Laurie, Warner, Buddah, Bell, Atco, Kirshner, Columbia, Rust and Crystal Ball. Members have also produced big hits with The Chiffons, The Happenings, Dawn and Robert John.

 THE LION SLEEPS TONIGHT (Their seventh 45)   1(3)   07 JAN 62   RCA
(UK No. 13 – they re-recorded it on Downtown in 88)

TOM TOM CLUB

Spin-off recording act from Talking Heads features drummer Chris Franz and his bass playing wife Tina Weymouth. Act who were named after the club they first rehearsed in and to date have had three UK (1 US) charters.

 WORDY RAPPINGHOOD   7   18 JUL 81   ISLAND

Also see Talking Heads

TOMMY TUTONE

Tommy Heath leads this Californian rock quintet that features guitarist Jim Keller. Act had three US-only chart LPs and two chart singles.

 867-5309/JENNY   4   22 MAY 82   COLUMBIA

TONE LOC

West Coast rapper called after his street gang name Tony Loco. His first release 'On Fire' in 88 did little but in 89 a track he had recorded on an eight track tape machine became the biggest selling single in the US since USA for Africa. He is also the first black rapper to have a No. 1 LP.

WILD THING   2   18 FEB 89   DELICIOUS VIN
(UK No. 21 – Sold two million in US)
FUNKY COLD MEDINA   3   29 APR 89   DELICIOUS VIN
(UK No. 13 – Both hits co-written by Young MC)

TOPOL

Well known film and stage actor had a one-off hit with the hit number from the musical Fiddler On The Roof in which he played the lead role in the UK.

 IF I WERE A RICH MAN   9   15 JUL 67   CBS

MEL TORME

Critically hailed jazz singer/songwriter/actor and musician known as 'The Velvet Fog' was born Mel Howard in Chicago. In the 40s he played drums with Chico Marx, formed The Mel-Tones and co-wrote the Christmas standard 'The Christmas Song'. He has had two UK hits and had eight US Top 20s between 45-52 including a No. 1 with 'Careless Hands' in 49.

MOUNTAIN GREENERY   4   17 AUG 56   VOGUE-CORAL
COMING HOME BABY (US No. 36)   8   18 JAN 63   LONDON

TORNADOS

London based instrumentalists including Alan Caddy, Clem Cattini (both ex-Johnny Kidd's Pirates) and Heinz Burt, were the first UK group to top the US charts. They were eccentric producer Joe Meek's house band and also worked with John Leyton and Billy Fury. Their second 45, written by Meek, sold five million world-wide and they had three more UK-only Top 20s. Heinz went solo in 63, the group split in 66 and Alan and Clem became session men playing on scores of hits.

 TELSTAR   1(5)   05 OCT 62   DECCA
(Also made 'Early Bird' named after another satellite)
GLOBETROTTER   2   01 FEB 63   DECCA
(One of three instrumentals in the UK Top 5)
TELSTAR   1(3)   22 DEC 62   LONDON
(They re-recorded it on Spark in 75)

Also see Heinz

TOTO

L.A. based pop rock band made up of top session musicians including David Paich, the Porcaro brothers Steve, Jeff & Mike, with singer Bobby Kimball (until 84). Before recording their 11 US (4 UK) Top 40s they backed acts like Boz Scaggs, Barbra Streisand and Aretha Franklin. In 83 they won a record five Grammys and in 84 Bobby left (he later hit in Far Corporation). The band who played in USA for Africa also had four US (2 UK) Top 40 LPs.

AFRICA (Jumped from 89-39)	3	26 FEB 83	CBS
HOLD THE LINE (UK No. 14)	5	13 JAN 79	COLUMBIA
ROSANNA (Grammy winning Song Of The Year) (UK No. 12 – Inspired by actress Rosanna Arquette)	2	03 JUL 83	COLUMBIA
AFRICA	1(1)	05 FEB 83	COLUMBIA
I WON'T HOLD YOU BACK (UK No. 37)	10	07 MAY 83	COLUMBIA

TOTO COELO

UK female group who included Laura James and Rebecca Louise Field (both ex Eurovision group Belle & The Devotions) had two UK charters – the other being the follow up 'Dracula's Tango' (54). In the US their hit was banned by some stations. They appeared on Debut in 85.

I EAT CANNIBALS PT. 1 (Produced Barry Blue) (US No. 66 as Total Coelo – so no clash with Toto)	8	04 SEP 82	RADIALCHOICE

TOTTENHAM HOTSPUR F.A. CUP FINAL SQUAD

London based 11 man team scored three UK-only Top 20s – the others being 'Tottenham Tottenham' and 'Hot Shot Tottenham'. Group have had many personnel changes over the years but usually include the duo Chas and Dave.

OSSIE'S DREAM (SPURS ARE ON THEIR WAY TO WEMBLEY) (Jumped 45-8) (Featuring Ossie Ardiles)	5	23 MAY 81	ROCKNEY

TOURISTS

UK quintet which starred Dave Stewart (ex Longdancer) and Annie Lennox evolved from The Catch, who recorded in 77. They had four UK-only Top 40s and made three LPs before Dave & Annie became Eurythmics in 80.

I ONLY WANT TO BE WITH YOU (US No. 83 – Dusty Springfield 64 hit)	4	15 DEC 79	LOGO
SO GOOD TO BE BACK HOME AGAIN	8	01 MAR 80	LOGO

Also see The Eurythmics

PETE TOWNSHEND

London born guitarist and principal songwriter for the ultra-successful group The Who first recorded solo in 72. He has since had two US (1 UK) Top 40 singles and four US (3 UK) Top 40 LPs.

LET MY LOVE OPEN THE DOOR (UK No. 46)	9	16 AUG 80	ATCO

Also see The Who

TOY DOLLS

Sunderland fun rock trio Olga, Flip and Happy Bob formed in 80 and were on GRC in 81 and Zonophone in 82. They first recorded their one-off pop hit in 82 (an Indie Top 10 then). Their other 45s include 'James Bond Lives Down Our Street' and 'We Are Mad'. They were on Neat in 87.

NELLIE THE ELEPHANT	4	29 DEC 84	VOLUME

TOYAH

Birmingham (UK) born actress Toyah Willcox who starred in the films Jubilee and Quadrophenia was a top UK new wave punk singer and had eight UK-only Top 40s in the early 80s. This distinctive vocalist was also on Portrait in 85 and E.G. in 87 (with her guitarist husband Robert Fripp). She is still a top TV and stage actress in the UK.

FOUR FROM TOYAH E.P. (Inc. 'It's a Mystery')	4	28 MAR 81	SAFARI
I WANT TO BE FREE	8	06 JUN 81	SAFARI
THUNDER IN MOUNTAINS	4	24 OCT 81	SAFARI

TOYS

New York female R&B pop trio Barbara Harris, Barbara Parritt and June Montiero were voted the most promising girl group of 66 in the US. They had two US Top 20s – the other being 'Attack' (US 18/UK 36). They later recorded on Philips and Musicor.

A LOVERS CONCERTO (They later made 'My Love Sonata')	5	04 DEC 65	STATESIDE
A LOVERS CONCERTO (Based on Bach's 'Minuet in G')	2	30 OCT 65	DYNOVOICE

T'PAU

Shrewsbury based pop rock sextet formed by singer Carol Decker and guitarist Ronnie Rogers which evolved from their group The Lazers. They first charted in the US (their only hit there) and then had six successive UK Top 40s and a UK million selling debut LP 'Bridge Of Spies'.

HEART AND SOUL (Originally flopped when released in Jan. 87)	4	19 SEP 87	SIREN
CHINA IN YOUR HAND (The 600th UK No. 1)	1(5)	14 NOV 87	SIREN
VALENTINE	9	20 FEB 88	SIREN
HEART AND SOUL	4	08 AUG 87	VIRGIN

TRACIE

Derby born singer Tracie Young was a protege of Jam/Style Council vocalist Paul Weller and had five UK-only charters on his Respond label.

THE HOUSE THAT JACK BUILT	9	23 APR 83	RESPOND

TRAFFIC

Multi faceted progressive rock group formed by Steve Winwood on leaving The Spencer Davis Group. Other original members included Dave Mason and Jim Capaldi (both ex Hellions). Between 67-74 they had many musical and personnel changes (including Ric Grech from Blind Faith, and several Muscle Shoals session musicians) and scored five UK (8 US) Top 40 LPs. Steve, Dave and Jim all had solo recording success later.

PAPER SUN (US No. 94)	5	01 JUL 67	ISLAND
HOLE IN MY SHOE (Written and sung by Dave Mason)	2	21 OCT 67	ISLAND
HERE WE GO ROUND THE MULBERRY BUSH (From the film)	8	16 DEC 67	ISLAND

Also see Steve Winwood/Jim Capaldi/Spencer Davis

TRAMMPS

Philadelphia soul/disco group, which included top session man Earl Young and Jimmy Ellis. Members had come from groups like The Exceptions (on Pro and Parkway), The Cordels, The Volcanos (who charted on Artic in 65) and The Whirlwinds. They had the first of 14 black hits in 72 and in 77 had their only transatlantic Top 20 hit 'Disco Inferno' (US 11/UK 16). They were also on Golden Fleece and Atlantic.

HOLD BACK THE NIGHT (US No. 35)	5	08 NOV 75	BUDDAH

TRANSVISION VAMP

Photogenic London based singer/songwriter Wendy James fronts this pop rock group who scored four UK-only Top 20s and two UK only Top 5 LPs in the last 18 months of the 80s and look set to be a top UK act of the early 90s.

I WANT YOUR LOVE	5	23 JUL 88	MCA
BABY I DON'T CARE	3	22 APR 89	MCA

TRANS-X

Pascal Languirand led this Canadian synth dominated hi-nrg trio which featured singer Laurie Gill. Their sole hit had originally been a European smash. They were on Atlantic in 86.

 LIVING ON VIDEO *(US No. 61)* 9 03 AUG 85 BOILING P.

TRASHMEN

Unmistakable Minneapolis/St. Paul surf rock group which included Tony Andreason and Steve Wahrer. Both their US-only charters (the other being 'Bird Dance Beat') were based on R&B hits by The Rivingstons. They also recorded on Argo, Tribe and Bear. Drummer Steve died of cancer in 89.

 SURFIN' BIRD *(They later made 'Bird '65')* 4 25 JAN 63 GARRETT

JOHN TRAVOLTA

New Jersey actor/singer starred in top TV series Welcome Back Kotter and had three US-only Top 40s before his appearance in Saturday Night Fever made him an international star. In 78 he chalked up four UK (2 US) Top 20s and he picked up two UK million sellers and successive No. 1s (a very rare event). He starred in many films including Grease and Urban Cowboy. Oddly a duet 'Take A Chance' by John and Olivia failed to chart in 84.

YOU'RE THE ONE THAT I WANT *(UK Gold record)* 1(9) 17 JUN 78 RSO
(Ties for the most weeks at No. 1 in the rock era)
SUMMER NIGHTS *(UK Gold record)* 1(7) 30 SEP 78 RSO
(First two - And OLIVIA NEWTON-JOHN -
Jumped 56-11-1)
SANDY *(At one time he had the UK No. 1 & 2)* 2 04 NOV 78 POLYDOR
(All above from the film 'Grease')
LET HER IN 10 24 JUL 76 MIDLAND INT.
YOU'RE THE ONE THAT I WANT 1(1) 10 JUN 78 RSO
SUMMER NIGHTS 5 30 OCT 78 RSO
(Last two - And OLIVIA NEWTON-JOHN)

TREMELOES

Essex pop group which included Len 'Chip' Hawkes and Alan Blakely backed Brian Poole on 63-65 UK hits and had even more success on their own. After two chart misses they scored 13 UK (3 US) Top 40s and had hits all around the World. They were later on DJM, AMI and Meteor

HERE COMES MY BABY 4 04 MAR 67 CBS
(US No. 13 - Cat Stevens song)
SILENCE IS GOLDEN *(US No. 11)* 1(3) 20 MAY 67 CBS
(They re-recorded in 84 - original by Four Seasons)
EVEN THE BAD TIMES ARE GOOD *(US No. 36)* 4 26 AUG 67 CBS
SUDDENLY YOU LOVE ME *(US No. 44)* 6 10 FEB 68 CBS
MY LITTLE LADY 6 12 OCT 68 CBS
(CALL ME) NUMBER ONE *(No. 2 despite title!)* 2 22 NOV 69 CBS
ME AND MY LIFE 4 17 OCT 70 CBS

Also see Brian Poole & The Tremeloes

JACKIE TRENT

Stoke born act had three UK-only Top 40s as a solo singer and a string of top hits as a co-writer (including many for Petula Clark) with her husband Tony Hatch. She also recorded on Piccadilly and UK Columbia.

WHERE ARE YOU NOW (MY LOVE) 1(1) 22 MAY 65 PYE

TRIO

German trio which included the songwriting team of Remmler & Kralle were produced by Klaus Voorman (ex Manfred Mann). They followed their hypnotic and repetitive one-off hit with 'Anna- Let Me In Let Me Out'. Their hit song was later used in a UK washing machine advert.

 DA DA DA 2 24 JUL 82 MOBILE SUIT

TROGGS

Reg Presley (Ball) was the singer of this Hampshire pop rock quartet whose five million selling second single gave them the first of eight UK (3 US) Top 40s in less than two years. The group who had a raw punk-like quality were also on Penny Farthing, Raw, Pye, Private Stock, Stagecoach and 10 and Reg was in the novelty pop act the Travelin' Wrinklies in 89.

WILD THING 2 28 MAY 66 FONTANA
(Originally by Jordan Christopher & The Wild Ones)
WITH A GIRL LIKE YOU *(US No. 29)* 1(2) 06 AUG 66 FONTANA
I CAN'T CONTROL MYSELF *(US No. 43)* 2 29 OCT 66 PAGE ONE
ANY WAY THAT YOU WANT ME 8 14 JAN 67 PAGE ONE
LOVE IS ALL AROUND 5 25 NOV 67 PAGE ONE
WILD THING 1(2) 30 JUL 66 FONTANA/ATCO
(Due to dispute was on two labels)
LOVE IS ALL AROUND 7 18 MAY 68 FONTANA

DORIS TROY

Born Doris Payne in New York this singer/songwriter was in gospel group The Halos and Jay & Dee and first recorded solo on Everest in 60. She moved to the UK in the late 60s and became a most in demand session singer. Her sole UK charter was 'Whatcha Gonna Do About It' (37 in 64). She also recorded on Calla, Capitol, Major Minor, Apple, Polydor and Midland Int.

JUST ONE LOOK 10 27 JUL 63 ATLANTIC
(Composed with Gregory Carroll of The 4 Buddies)

ANDREA TRUE CONNECTION

Nashville born disco singer, TV commercial writer, clothes designer and one time X-rated movie actress had two US & UK Top 40s in the late 70s. The follow up to her transatlantic hit was 'Party Line' (US 80).

MORE, MORE, MORE *(Produced by Michael Zager)* 5 15 MAY 76 BUDDAH
MORE, MORE, MORE 4 17 JUL 76 BUDDAH

TUBES

Notorious, innovative and sometimes outrageous theatrical rock group from Arizona featured Fee Waybill. The popular live act had just 2 US & UK Top 40s the first being 'White Punks On Dope' (UK 28) in 77 on A&M.

SHE'S A BEAUTY 10 02 JUL 83 CAPITOL

TUBEWAY ARMY

Noted electronic band were the vehicle for Gary Numan's first hit. Group also included Gary's uncle Jess Lidyard and bass player Paul Gardiner.

ARE 'FRIENDS' ELECTRIC *(Their third release)* 1(4) 30 JUN 79 BEGGARS BANQU

Also see Gary Numan

IKE & TINA TURNER

Mississippi born Ike was one of the great R&B figures of the 50s. He played on, produced or wrote many important records including ones by B.B. King, Howlin' Wolf and Johnny Ace and the very early R'n'R hit 'Rocket 88' by Jackie Brenston (member of Ike's group) in 51. Tina joined the band in 56 and in 60 they had the first of 20 US (4 UK) hits. They were also on Sue, Sonja, Kent, Warner, Loma, Modern, Innis, Pompeii, Philles, Blue Thumb, Tangerine and Minit. They broke up in 75 and Tina went on to even greater fame. Ike was jailed in 88 on drug related charges.

RIVER DEEP MOUNTAIN HIGH 3 09 JUL 66 LONDON
(US No. 88 - Also UK No.33 in 69)
NUTBUSH CITY LIMITS *(US No. 22)* 4 13 OCT 73 UA
PROUD MARY 4 27 MAR 71 LIBERTY
(Creedence Clearwater Revival 69 hit)

Also see Tina Turner

TINA TURNER

Unmistakable raw soulful singer was born Annie Mae Bullock in Tennessee. She was an R&B star in 60, left Ike Turner in 75 and in the 80s finally became recognised as one of the world's top singers and performers. To date she has had 13 US (9 UK) solo Top 40 singles and four UK (2 US) Top 10 LPs (including the 15 million selling 'Private Dancer'). She was part of USA For Africa, appeared in Live Aid and has broken box office records around the World (180,000 saw her in one show in Rio!). She is also the oldest female to top the US singles and the UK LP chart.

🇬🇧	LET'S STAY TOGETHER (Al Green 72 hit) (US No. 26 – Produced Marsh & Ware (Heaven 17))	6	10 DEC 83	CAPITOL
	WHAT'S LOVE GOT TO DO WITH IT (Triple Grammy winning record)	3	11 AUG 84	CAPITOL
	WE DON'T NEED ANOTHER HERO (THUNDERDOME) (Above two co-writ. Graham Lyle (Gallagher & Lyle))	3	03 AUG 85	CAPITOL
	THE BEST (US No. 15 – Produced Dan Hartman)	5	23 SEP 89	CAPITOL
	I DON'T WANNA LOSE YOU (Composed by Graham Lyle and Albert Hammond)	8	16 DEC 89	CAPITOL
🇺🇸	WHAT'S LOVE GOT TO DO WITH IT (First US No. 1 – record 24 years after debut hit)	1(3)	01 SEP 84	CAPITOL
	BETTER BE GOOD TO ME (UK No. 45)	5	24 NOV 84	CAPITOL
	PRIVATE DANCER (UK No. 26 – composed Mark Knopfler (Dire Straits))	7	23 FEB 85	CAPITOL
	WE DON'T NEED ANOTHER HERO (THUNDERDOME) (From her film 'Mad Max Beyond Thunderdome')	2	14 SEP 85	CAPITOL
	TYPICAL MALE (UK No. 33- co-written Graham Lyle)	2	18 OCT 86	CAPITOL

Also see Ike & Tina Turner

TURTLES

L.A. based pop rock group who included Mark Volman & Howard Kaylan (Kaplin) were known previously as The Nightriders, The Crosswind Singers and recorded as The Crossfires in 63 on Capco and Lucky Token. They had 17 US (3 UK) charters and disbanded in 70. Mark & Eddie joined Frank Zappa's group and then became Flo & Eddie recording on Reprise, Columbia and Epiphany. The group re-united and toured in 82, 85 and 89. In 90 Flo & Eddie had become top rated US radio DJs.

🇬🇧	SHE'D RATHER BE WITH ME	4	08 JUL 67	LONDON
	ELENORE (They re-recorded it as Flo & Eddie)	7	23 NOV 68	LONDON
🇺🇸	IT AIN'T ME BABE (Bob Dylan song)	8	18 SEP 65	WHITE WHALE
	HAPPY TOGETHER (UK No. 12)	1(3)	25 MAR 67	WHITE WHALE
	SHE'D RATHER BE WITH ME	3	17 JUN 67	WHITE WHALE
	ELENORE	6	02 NOV 68	WHITE WHALE
	YOU SHOWED ME (Original by The Byrds) (They sued De La Soul for sampling bits of this)	6	01 MAR 69	WHITE WHALE

TWEETS

A group of British session singers had the UK hit with this much recorded European song. First released in 73 as 'Tchip Tchip' it was a huge Dutch hit in 80 by The Electronicas and had been a smash in France, Germany and Belgium under various titles before it landed in the UK. The act also released classics like 'Tweets On 45' (on RCA) and 'Plump Song' (on Crash).

🇬🇧	THE BIRDIE SONG (BIRDIE DANCE)	2	10 OCT 81	PRT

TWINKLE

London based singer born Lynn Ripley had two UK-only Top 40s. Her debut hit was the UK's first home grown 'death disc' and she also hit with the follow up 'City Lights' (21). Later she sang of other boys 'Tommy' and 'Poor Old Johnny' with less success.

🇬🇧	TERRY (She re-recorded it on Galaxy in 78)	4	09 JAN 65	DECCA

CONWAY TWITTY

No one has had more country No. 1s than this Mississippi singer/song-writer. He was in the Phillips County Ramblers, Arkansas Cotton Choppers, The Cimmarons, and as Harold Jenkins (his real name) & The Rockhousers he recorded for Sun. He first charted on Mercury in 57 and in the late 50s he was a top transatlantic r'n'r star. In 66 he notched up the first of his 90 country hits of which a remarkable 40 have hit No. 1. He has also had nine US (4 UK) pop Top 40s. He owns a leisure complex called 'Twitty City'.

🇬🇧	IT'S ONLY MAKE BELIEVE (He co-wrote this often charted song)	1(5)	19 DEC 58	MGM
	MONA LISA (US No. 29 – Nat 'King' Cole 50 hit)	5	25 SEP 59	MGM
🇺🇸	IT'S ONLY MAKE BELIEVE	1(2)	10 NOV 58	MGM
	DANNY BOY (Traditional Irish song) (Re-recorded as 'Rosalena' in the UK)	10	06 DEC 59	MGM
	LONELY BLUE BOY (Song originally made by Elvis Presley as 'Danny')	6	08 FEB 60	MGM

BONNIE TYLER

Born Gaynor Hopkins this raspy voiced pop rock singer started in the group Mumbles and had the first of seven UK (3 US) Top 40s with her debut single. In the 70s she hit with country orientated material, then in the 80s with a harder sound and image she became the first Welsh act to get a US No. 1.

🇬🇧	LOST IN FRANCE	9	27 NOV 76	RCA
	IT'S A HEARTACHE (US country No. 10)	4	14 JAN 78	RCA
	TOTAL ECLIPSE OF THE HEART (Male vocal on track by Rory Dodd)	1(2)	12 MAR 83	CBS
	A ROCKIN' GOOD WAY (With SHAKIN' STEVENS) (Released as by SHAKY & BONNIE)	5	21 JAN 84	CBS
	HOLDING OUT FOR A HERO (US No. 34) (From 'Footloose' – flopped when out in March 84)	2	14 SEP 85	CBS
🇺🇸	IT'S A HEARTACHE	3	24 JUN 78	RCA
	TOTAL ECLIPSE OF THE HEART (Produced by Jim Steinman)	1(4)	01 OCT 83	COLUMBIA

TYMES

Philadelphian sweet soul group formed in the late 50s as The Latineers were fronted by George Williams. They had four US & UK Top 40s including a US No. 1 in the 60s and a UK No. 1 in the 70s. They were also on Winchester, MGM, Columbia and Capitol. George later re-located to London.

🇬🇧	MS GRACE (US No. 91 – comp. John & Johanna Hall of Orleans)	1(1)	25 JAN 75	RCA
🇺🇸	SO MUCH IN LOVE (UK No. 17 – they re-recorded it on RCA in 74)	1(1)	03 AUG 63	PARKWAY
	WONDERFUL! WONDERFUL! (Johnny Mathis 57 US hit)	7	28 SEP 63	PARKWAY

TYPICALLY TROPICAL

Session duo were record producer Jeff Calvert with Max West. They had their only hit with their own song inspired by a holiday Jeff had in the West Indies. They later recorded on Pye in 77, Hobo in 79 and Whisper in 81.

🇬🇧	BARBADOS	1(1)	09 AUG 75	GULL

U2

One of the top rock acts of the 80s, this Dublin quartet features singer Paul 'Bono' Hewson and guitarist David 'The Edge' Evans. First known as Feedback, then The Hype, their debut record was on CBS (Ireland) in 78 and they first hit with their fourth UK single 'Fire' in 81. They have had 11 UK (5 US) Top 20 singles and seven UK (4 US) Top 20 LPs including the UK's top selling Live LP 'Under A Blood Red Sky' and the multi platinum 'Joshua Tree' (first million selling CD) and 'Rattle And Hum'. These Grammy and BRITS winners pack stadiums world-wide and have been involved in numerous charity events including Live Aid, Band Aid and shows for Amnesty International.

🇬🇧	NEW YEAR'S DAY (US No. 53)	10	05 FEB 83	ISLAND
	PRIDE (IN THE NAME OF LOVE) (US No. 33)	3	29 SEP 84	ISLAND
	(Dedicated to Martin Luther King – entered at No. 8)			
	THE UNFORGETTABLE FIRE (Entered at No. 8)	6	11 MAY 85	ISLAND
	WITH OR WITHOUT YOU (Entered at No. 4)	4	28 MAR 87	ISLAND
	I STILL HAVEN'T FOUND WHAT I'M LOOKING FOR	6	13 JUN 87	ISLAND
	WHERE THE STREETS HAVE NO NAME (US No. 13)	4	12 SEP 87	ISLAND
	(Entered at No.4)			
	DESIRE (Entered at No. 2)	1(1)	08 OCT 88	ISLAND
	ANGEL OF HARLEM (US No. 14)	9	24 DEC 88	ISLAND
	WHEN LOVE COMES TO TOWN (And B.B. KING)	6	22 APR 89	ISLAND
	(US No. 68 – B.B.'s first UK hit in 40 years recording)			
	ALL I WANT IS YOU (Entered at No. 5)	4	01 JUL 89	ISLAND
🇺🇸	WITH OR WITHOUT YOU	1(3)	16 MAY 87	ISLAND
	(Made them first Irish group to top US chart)			
	I STILL HAVEN'T FOUND WHAT I'M LOOKING FOR	1(2)	08 AUG 87	ISLAND
	DESIRE	3	26 NOV 88	ISLAND

UB40

Birmingham (UK) based multi-racial reggae group which includes the Campbell brothers Ali & Rob (sons of folk singer/left wing campaigner Ian Campbell) and Earl Falconer. They were one of the top acts of the 80s in the UK having scored 17 Top 20 singles and 10 Top 20 LPs. In the US they have a loyal following but only one Top 20 45 & LP.

🇬🇧	KING/FOOD FOR THOUGHT	4	19 APR 80	GRADUATE
	(A-side dedicated to Martin Luther King)			
	MY WAY OF THINKING/I THINK IT'S GOING TO				
	RAIN TODAY (B-side comp. Randy Newman)	6	19 JUL 80	GRADUATE
	THE EARTH DIES SCREAMING/DREAM A LIE	10	29 NOV 80	GRADUATE
	ONE IN TEN	7	05 SEP 81	DEP INT.
	(Concerning the UK's unemployment figures)			
	RED RED WINE (Neil Diamond 68 US hit)	1(3)	03 SEP 83	DEP INT.
	(Their previous four 45s missed the Top 20)			
	PLEASE DON'T MAKE ME CRY	10	05 NOV 83	DEP INT.
	IF IT HAPPENS AGAIN	9	06 OCT 84	DEP INT.
	I GOT YOU BABE (Feat. CHRISSIE HYNDE)	1(1)	31 AUG 85	DEP INT.
	(US No. 28 – exactly 20 years after Sonny & Cher hit)			
	DON'T BREAK MY HEART	3	23 NOV 85	DEP INT.
	SING OUR OWN SONG	5	26 JUL 86	DEP INT.
	BREAKFAST IN BED (Feat. CHRISSIE HYNDE)	6	02 JUL 88	DEP INT.
	(Originally by Jeanette 'Baby' Washington)			
	HOMELY GIRL (Chi Lites 74 hit)	6	02 DEC 89	DEP INT.
🇺🇸	RED RED WINE (A hit five years after UK)	1(1)	15 OCT 88	A&M
	(Took record 25 weeks to No. 1 – was US			
	No. 34 in 84)			

TRACEY ULLMAN

Comedienne, actress and singer from Buckinghamshire was a successful UK TV star prior to stringing together five UK (1 US) Top 40s in 16 months. Her video for 'My Guy' (UK 23 in 84) featured Labour Party leader Neil Kinnock. She later re-located to the US and had a successful TV series there.

🇬🇧	BREAKAWAY	4	16 APR 83	STIFF
	(US No. 70 – originally by Irma Thomas)			
	THEY DON'T KNOW (Orig. by Kirsty MacColl)	2	15 OCT 83	STIFF
	(Paul McCartney appeared in the video)			
	MOVE OVER DARLING (Doris Day 64 UK hit)	8	10 DEC 83	STIFF
🇺🇸	THEY DON'T KNOW	8	28 APR 84	MCA

ULTRAVOX

Influential UK electro rock band included synth player/songwriter Billie Currie and was formed in 73. Previously known as Tiger Lilly, The Zips, Fire of London and London Soundtrack they first recorded in 75 on Gull. They were on Island from 76-79 when singer John Foxx left and had some solo success. They first hit after new vocalist Midge Ure joined and they scored 16 UK-only Top 40 singles and seven UK-only Top 10 LPs before 87.

🇬🇧	VIENNA	2	14 FEB 81	CHRYSALIS
	ALL STOOD STILL	8	27 JUN 81	CHRYSALIS
	DANCING WITH TEARS IN MY EYES	3	09 JUN 84	CHRYSALIS

Also see Midge Ure

PIERO UMILIANI

Italian orchestra conductor/arranger first hit with this novelty track in the US in 69 when it was in the soundtrack of the film Sweden Heaven & Hell. It is also known as the chase music in the Benny Hill TV series.

🇬🇧	MAH NA MAH NA (US No. 55 in 69)	8	28 MAY 77	EMI INT.
	(Its third UK release – feat. in Muppets TV series)			

UNDERTONES

Irish pop rock quintet which featured singer Feargal Sharkey were formed in 75. Their debut 45 'Teenage Kicks' was first released on Good Vibration and it charted on Sire in 78. They formed own Ardeck label in 80 and broke up in 83. Feargal went on to greater success while some of the remaining members formed That Petrol Emotion.

🇬🇧	MY PERFECT COUSIN (Their sixth single)	9	17 MAY 80	SIRE

Also see Feargal Sharkey

UNDISPUTED TRUTH

When they had their only Top 40 pop hit (they have had 15 black music entries) act was the trio of Billie Calvin, Brenda Evans and Joe Harris. After 73 only Joe remained and later members included Chaka Khan's sister Taka Boom. They were the first artists to record The Temptations hit 'Papa Was A Rolling Stone'.

🇺🇸	SMILING FACES SOMETIME	3	04 SEP 71	GORDY

UNION GAP – SEE GARY PUCKETT FOR HIT DETAILS

UNIT 4 PLUS 2

Hertfordshire (UK) pop band were the quartet Unit Four plus two new members. Peter Moules was the singer and they included Tom Moeller and Lem Lubin (Russ Ballard was briefly with them later). They had two UK-only Top 20s – the other being the follow up 'You've Never Been In Love Like This Before' (14). They were on Fontana in 67.

🇬🇧	CONCRETE AND CLAY (US No. 28)	1(1)	10 APR 65	DECCA

UPSETTERS

Jamaican group which was led by musician/composer/arranger Lee Perry and included Jackie Robinson and Glenroy Adams. They have played on numerous reggae hits, including Harry J's UK Top 10. They have also recorded on Down Town, Lord Koos, Summit, Randys, Dynamic, Grape, Duke and Jackpot.

 THE RETURN OF DJANGO   5   08 NOV 69   UPSETTER
(Features sax player Val Bennett)

MIDGE URE

Before recording solo James 'Midge' Ure had been in hit acts Slik (previously Salvation), Ultravox and Visage. In 84 together with Bob Geldof he masterminded the Band Aid project and co-wrote their No. 1. He also helped organise the Live Aid and Nelson Mandela 70th Birthday shows. He is the only person to be in the UK charts in five different acts all of which oddly failed to make the US Top 40.

 NO REGRETS   9   10 JUL 82   CHRYSALIS
      IF I WAS   1(1)   05 OCT 85   CHRYSALIS
(One of 32 UK charters in the 80s he has been on!)

Also see Slik/Ultravox/Visage/Band Aid

USA FOR AFRICA

The top selling 45 of the 80s (over four million) was conceived by Harry Belafonte and based on the UK Band Aid project. It featured stars like Lionel Richie, Stevie Wonder, Paul Simon, Kenny Rogers, Tina Turner, Billy Joel, Michael Jackson, Diana Ross, Dionne Warwick, Willie Nelson, Bruce Springsteen, Daryl Hall, Huey Lewis, Cyndi Lauper, Bob Dylan and Ray Charles. Sales of the 45 and LP raised over $50 million for Ethiopia. The song was performed by many of the artists on the record as the climax to the Live Aid concert in Philadelphia in 85.

 WE ARE THE WORLD *(Entered at No. 7)*   1(2)   20 APR 85   CBS
(Composed by Lionel Richie & Michael Jackson)

      WE ARE THE WORLD *(Entered at No. 21)*   1(4)   13 APR 85   COLUMBIA
(Produced by Quincy Jones)

V

RICKY VALANCE

London based pop singer and ex-male model was born David Spencer in Ynysddu in South Wales. He had been in the R.A.F. and sang in Sid Phillips Band before scoring his sole UK hit with a cover of Ray Peterson's hit US 'death disc' (Ray's label at first refused to release his version giving Ricky a clear field). He was on Decca in 65 and Revolver in 81.

 TELL LAURA I LOVE HER *(Re-recorded it in 81)*   1(2)   30 SEP 60   COLUMBIA

FRANKIE VALLI

New Jersey born Frankie Castellucio started as a soloist in 53 on Corona (as Frankie Valley). From 66-77 he recorded as a soloist and as lead of the top 60s group The Four Seasons (they re-united in the mid 80s). His voice has helped sell over 75 million records and he has had 14 US (5 UK) solo hits. His distinctive voice is probably the best known falsetto in pop.

 MY EYES ADORED YOU   5   08 MAR 75   PRIVATE STOCK
(Co-writ. Kenny Nolan – orig. recorded for Motown)
      GREASE *(Composed by Barry Gibb)*   3   30 SEP 78   RSO

   CAN'T TAKE MY EYES OFF YOU   2   29 JUL 67   PHILIPS
      MY EYES ADORED YOU   1(1)   22 MAR 75   PRIVATE STOCK
      SWEARIN' TO GOD *(UK No. 31)*   6   26 JUL 75   PRIVATE STOCK
      GREASE *(From the film)*   1(2)   26 AUG 78   RSO

Also see Four Seasons

LEROY VAN DYKE

Missouri born country/MOR entertainer first charted in 57 with 'The Auctioneer' (a job he used to hold). Over the next 20 years he had a further 18 country hits and two transatlantic pop Top 40s. He also recorded on Dot, Warner, Kapp, Decca, ABC, Plantation and Sun.

 WALK ON BY   5   09 FEB 62   MERCURY
   WALK ON BY   5   11 DEC 61   MERCURY

VAN HALEN

Top selling, crowd pulling Californian hard rockers who included the Dutch born Van Halen brothers Eddie & Alex and flamboyant singer David Lee Roth (this trio first played together in Mammoth). Their eponymous debut LP sold two million and they have now had seven US-only Top 10 LPs and eight US (2 UK) Top 20 singles. In 83 they earned a record $1.5 million for one Californian show. In 85 David went solo and was replaced by Sammy Hagar (who continued recording as a soloist) with all parties continuing to hit.

JUMP   7   17 MAR 84   WARNER
(Record was involved in a UK chart hype scandal)
      WHY CAN'T THIS BE LOVE   8   24 MAY 86   WARNER

   JUMP   1(5)   25 FEB 84   WARNER
      WHY CAN'T THIS BE LOVE   3   17 MAY 86   WARNER
(Their first 45 featuring Sammy Hagar)
      WHEN IT'S LOVE *(UK No. 28)*   5   10 SEP 88   WARNER

Also see David Lee Roth

VANGELIS

Greek born keyboard player/composer Evangelos Papathanassoiu had been in Formynx and top French based trio Aphrodites Child (with Demis Roussos). He hit the UK LP chart in 76 and then in 80 teamed with Jon Anderson of Yes (whom he nearly joined in 74). He had a sole transatlantic Top 10 single with the title track from his No. 1 US LP containing music from the film.

   CHARIOTS OF FIRE *(UK No. 12 in 81)*   1(1)   08 MAY 82   POLYDOR
(From the film – 21 weeks on chart before No. 1)

Also see Jon & Vangelis

VANILLA FUDGE

Influential New York psychedelic group originally called The Pigeons were fronted by Mark Stein (who had been on Cameo in 59) and included Tim Bogert and Carmine Appice. They had five US (1 UK) Top 40 LPs and two US (1 UK) Top 40 singles before splitting in 70. Tim & Carmine had success in Cactus and with Jeff Beck and Mark joined Boomerang but did not come back to the chart. They re-formed and recorded on Atlantic without success in the 80s.

   (YOU KEEP ME) HANGIN' ON *(UK No. 18 in 67)*   6   31 AUG 68   ATCO
(Extended version of The Supremes 66 hit)

VANITY FARE

Pop quartet from Kent led by Trevor Brice first hit with 'I Live For The Sun' (UK 20) in 68 and had two Transatlantic Top 20s the following year. They were also on Philips in 72, 20th Century in 73 and Polydor in 76.

🇬🇧	EARLY IN THE MORNING (US No. 12)	8	16 AUG 69	PAGE ONE
🇺🇸	HITCHIN' A RIDE (UK No. 16)	5	27 JUN 70	PAGE ONE

GINO VANNELLI

Blue-eyed soul styled rock singer/songwriter from Montreal, Canada, who scored 10 US-only chart singles and two Top 20 LPs between 74-87.

🇺🇸	I JUST WANNA STOP	4	09 DEC 78	A&M
	LIVING INSIDE MYSELF	6	30 MAY 81	ARISTA

RANDY VANWARMER

Denver born pop country singer/songwriter who spent some of his teenage years working in a fish and chip shop in Cornwall (UK)! He had a one-off Top 40 hit and in the 80s had some country chart success on 16th Avenue and wrote Top 10 country hits for The Oak Ridge Boys and Michael Johnson.

🇬🇧	JUST WHEN I NEEDED YOU MOST (Was the original B-side – he re-recorded it in 89)	8	15 SEP 79	BEARSVILLE
🇺🇸	JUST WHEN I NEEDED YOU MOST	4	16 JUN 79	BEARSVILLE

VAPORS

Sussex quartet led by singer/songwriter Dave Fenton were discovered by Bruce Foxton of The Jam and first recorded in 79. They split up after three UK (1 US) chart entries in 81.

🇬🇧	TURNING JAPANESE (US No. 36)	3	29 MAR 80	UA

FRANKIE VAUGHAN

Born Frankie Abelson in Liverpool, he was a top of the bill UK MOR/pop singer/entertainer/film star (who once co-starred with Marilyn Monroe) in the 50s and 60s. He was on Decca in 50 and had the first of his 20 UK-only Top 20s (many covers of US hits) in 54 on HMV. He made many releases for the US market but only charted there once – 'Judy' (100 in 58). He was later on Columbia in 67, Pye in 75, SRT in 79, TER in 83, PRT in 84 and Spartan in 87. He has done much charity work and received an OBE from the Queen in 65.

🇬🇧	GREEN DOOR (Jim Lowe 56 hit)	2	07 DEC 56	PHILIPS
	GARDEN OF EDEN (Joe Valino 56 hit)	1(4)	25 JAN 57	PHILIPS
	MAN ON FIRE/WANDERIN' EYES ('A' orig. Bing Crosby – 'B' Charlie Gracie 57 hit)	6	01 NOV 57	PHILIPS
	GOTTA HAVE SOMETHING IN THE BANK FRANK (And The KAYE SISTERS) (Original by Bob Jaxon)	8	15 NOV 57	PHILIPS
	KISSES SWEETER THAN WINE (Weavers 51 hit)	8	17 JAN 58	PHILIPS
	KEWPIE DOLL (Perry Como 58 hit)	10	06 JUN 58	PHILIPS
	COME SOFTLY TO ME (and the KAYE SISTERS) (Fleetwoods 59 hit)	9	22 MAY 59	PHILIPS
	THE HEART OF A MAN	5	04 SEP 59	PHILIPS
	TOWER OF STRENGTH (Gene McDaniels 61 US hit)	1(4)	29 NOV 61	PHILIPS
	LOOP DE LOOP (Johnny Thunder 62 US hit)	5	15 FEB 63	PHILIPS
	THERE MUST BE A WAY (Joni James 59 US hit)	7	14 OCT 67	COLUMBIA

BOBBY VEE

Top early 60s pop idol was born Robert Velline in North Dakota and got his first break substituting for Buddy Holly on a show after his death. His first 45 on Soma/Liberty in 59 charted and in all he had 38 US (10 UK) hits. This Holly-influenced teenager, who also recorded with The Crickets, at one time had Bob Dylan in his band (The Shadows). He has also had seven UK (1 US) Top 20 LPs, the last being in 80. He now often works the 'oldies' circuit.

🇬🇧	RUBBER BALL (His sixth single)	3	10 FEB 61	LONDON
	MORE THAN I CAN SAY (US No. 61 – Original by The Crickets)	4	19 MAY 61	LONDON
	HOW MANY TEARS (US No. 63)	10	08 SEP 61	LONDON
	TAKE GOOD CARE OF MY BABY (Above two co-written Carole King)	1(1)	01 DEC 61	LONDON
	RUN TO HIM	8	19 JAN 62	LIBERTY
	THE NIGHT HAS A THOUSAND EYES (From the film Just For Fun)	3	01 MAR 63	LIBERTY
🇺🇸	DEVIL OR ANGEL (Clovers 56 R&B hit)	6	16 OCT 60	LIBERTY
	RUBBER BALL (Co-written by Gene Pitney)	6	09 JAN 61	LIBERTY
	TAKE GOOD CARE OF MY BABY (He re-recorded it in 73 – Orig. recorded by Dion)	1(3)	18 SEP 61	LIBERTY
	RUN TO HIM	2	25 DEC 61	LIBERTY
	THE NIGHT HAS A THOUSAND EYES	3	02 FEB 63	LIBERTY
	COME BACK WHEN YOU GROW UP (And The STRANGERS)	3	09 SEP 67	LIBERTY

SUZANNE VEGA

Critically acclaimed New York folk singer/songwriter first hit in the UK in 86. She has had three UK (1 US) Top 40s and followed her big US hit with 'Gypsy'. He second LP 'Solitude Standing' made the Transatlantic Top 20.

🇺🇸	LUKA (UK No. 23)	3	22 AUG 87	A&M

VENTURES

The most successful and influential US instrumental group are this Washington quartet which includes guitarists Nokie Edwards, Don Wilson & Bob Bogle. Earlier known as The Marksmen and The Versatones they first recorded on their own Blue Horizon label in 59. The LP orientated act's track record is six US (2 UK) Top 40 singles and 37 US-only chart LPs (only two groups have more!) many of which were also big hits in Japan.

🇬🇧	WALK-DON'T RUN	9	30 SEP 60	TOP RANK
	PERFIDIA (US No. 15 – Xavier Cugat 41 hit)	5	13 JAN 61	LONDON
🇺🇸	WALK-DON'T RUN (Originally on Blue Horizon)	2	29 AUG 60	DOLTON
	WALK-DON'T RUN '64 (They also did 'Walk-Don't Run '77' on UA)	8	22 AUG 64	DOLTON
	HAWAII FIVE-O (From the TV series)	4	10 MAY 69	LIBERTY

BILLY VERA & BEATERS

California pop singer/songwriter born Billy McCord Jr. He was on Rust in 62 with The Contrasts (aka Knight-Riders) and on Cameo in 66 in Blue Eyed Soul. He first charted in 67 dueting with Judy Clay (Whitney Houston's cousin) on Atlantic. The biggest of his three US-only Top 40s came with a five year old live recording. He has also been on Alfa, Midland Int, RCA, and Capitol.

🇺🇸	AT THIS MOMENT (Was US No. 79 in 81) (Play on TV's 'Family Ties' made it re-chart)	1(2)	24 JAN 87	RHINO

LARRY VERNE

Minneapolis performer followed his No. 1 novelty with his only other charter 'Mr. Livingstone'(75). His other records included 'The Coward That Won The West', 'I'm a Brave Little Soldier' and 'Return of Mr. Custer'.

🇺🇸	MR. CUSTER	1(1)	10 OCT 60	ERA

VILLAGE PEOPLE

Outrageous 'macho' disco sextet of gay stereotypes were briefly top worldwide stars (selling around 15 million 45s & LPs). The camp and witty New Yorkers, who started as a session group, included Victor Willis and Randy Jones and had three US (4 UK) Top 40s and four US (2 UK) Top 40 LPs. They were later on RCA and Mega.

🇬🇧	Y.M.C.A. (UK Gold record)	1(3)	06 JAN 79	MERCURY
	IN THE NAVY	2	31 MAR 79	MERCURY
🇺🇸	Y.M.C.A.	2	03 FEB 79	CASABLANCA
	IN THE NAVY	3	19 MAY 79	CASABLANCA

VILLAGE STOMPERS

Greenwich village trad jazz octet, which included Frank Hubbell and Joe Muranyi, had a one-off Top 10 US single and LP.

 WASHINGTON SQUARE   2   23 NOV 63   EPIC

BOBBY VINTON

Top US pop balladeer in the early 60s was born in Pennsylvania and led the band that backed Dick Clark's shows in 60. He was on Alpine (in 59) and Melody before getting his first hit with his fourth Epic 45. He had 44 US (2 UK) chart singles including 29 Top 40s and 24 US-only chart LPs. He was later on Elektra, Bobby, Memory Lane and in the 80s and had some country success on Tapestry, Larc and Curb.

ROSES ARE RED (MY LOVE) *(UK No. 13)*   1(4)   14 JUL 62   EPIC
(Composed by Paul Evans – orig. Darrell & Oxfords)
BLUE ON BLUE   3   06 JUL 63   EPIC
BLUE VELVET *(Tony Bennett 51 hit)*   1(3)   21 SEP 63   EPIC
THERE I'VE SAID IT AGAIN   1(4)   04 JAN 64   EPIC
(UK No. 34 – Vaughn Monroe 45 hit)
MY HEART BELONGS ONLY TO YOU   9   28 MAR 64   EPIC
MR. LONELY *(Recorded in 62)*   1(1)   12 DEC 64   EPIC
PLEASE LOVE ME FOREVER   6   18 NOV 67   EPIC
(Originally by Tommy Edwards)
I LOVE HOW YOU LOVE ME   9   14 DEC 68   EPIC
(Co-written Barry Mann – Paris Sisters 61 US hit)
MY MELODY OF LOVE   3   16 NOV 74   ABC

VISAGE

Steve Strange (born Steve Harrington in Wales), who was in Moors Murderers with Chrissie Hynde in 77, fronted this new romantic dance group which at times included Rusty Egan and Midge Ure. They were on Radar in 79 and had five UK-only Top 40s. Steve returned unsuccessfully in Strange Cruise in 86.

FADE TO GREY   8   07 FEB 81   POLYDOR
(Composed Midge Ure & Billy Currie of Ultravox)

Also see Midge Ure/Ultravox

VOGUES

Pennsylvanian pop/MOR vocal group first known as The Val-Aires were fronted by William Burkette. These revival specialists had 14 US-only hits in the late 60s. They were also on MGM, Bell, 20th Century, ABC and Mainstream.

YOU'RE THE ONE   4   06 NOV 65   CO & CE
(Petula Clark 65 UK hit – first on Blue Star label)
FIVE O'CLOCK WORLD   4   15 JAN 66   CO & CE
TURN AROUND LOOK AT ME   7   17 AUG 68   REPRISE
(Glen Campbell 61 US hit)
MY SPECIAL ANGEL *(Bobby Helms 57 hit)*   7   12 OCT 68   REPRISE

W

ADAM WADE

Smooth black balladeer in the Johnny Mathis mould charted with his first single 'Tell Her For Me' in 60 and had 11 other UK-only chart entries. He was later on Epic, Warner, Remember, Perception, Kirshner and Dalya. He hosted TV's 'Musical Chairs' in 76 and had a TV talk show in the 80s.

 TAKE GOOD CARE OF HER   7   01 MAY 61   COED
(The song topped the country chart in 66)
THE WRITING ON THE WALL   5   05 JUL 61   COED
AS IF I DIDN'T KNOW   10   10 SEP 61   COED

WADSWORTH MANSION

Singer/songwriter Steve Jabecki fronted this soft rock group who followed their one-off hit with another of his songs 'Michigan Harry Slaughter'.

 SWEET MARY   7   27 FEB 71   SUSSEX

JACK WAGNER

Missouri born singer/actor who found fame playing Frisco Jones in TV's General Hospital followed his sole Top 40 with 'Lady Of My Heart'.

ALL I NEED   2   12 JAN 85   QWEST

WAH!

Liverpool act which was a vehicle for charismatic singer/songwriter Pete Wylie (ex Crucial Three with Ian McCulloch and Julian Cope). Group has also been known as Wah! Heat, Say Wha!, JF Wah!, Shambako! and had their other UK-only Top 20 'Come Back' as The Mighty Wah! on Beggars Banquet in 84.

 THE STORY OF THE BLUES   3   22 JAN 83   ETERNAL
(Originally written as 'The Story Of The Booze')

JOHN WAITE

Lancashire (UK) born singer/bassist was leader of the successful pop rock group The Babys (three US-only Top 40s) until they broke up in 81. His second solo LP included the only Transatlantic Top 20 of his career. In 89 he fronted the hit group Bad English.

MISSING YOU   9   27 NOV 84   EMI
(Took four minutes to write)

MISSING YOU   1(1)   22 SEP 84   EMI AM.

Also see Bad English

JOHNNY WAKELIN

Brighton (UK) based singer/songwriter had two novelty pop/reggae hits about Muhammad Ali. His unsuccessful later 45s included 'Tennessee Hero' about Elvis in 75 and 'Bruno' about UK boxer Frank Bruno in 85.

BLACK SUPERMAN(MUHAMMAD ALI) *(US No. 21)*   7   15 FEB 75   PYE
(And THE KINSHASHA BAND)
IN ZAIRE   4   21 AUG 76   PYE

NARADA MICHAEL WALDEN – SEE NARADA FOR HIT DETAILS

WALKER BROTHERS

US trio who were top UK teen favourites in the late 60s. They were fronted by Scott Engel and the other members were ex-child actor John Maus and Gary Leeds who had played drums for Johnny Rivers and P.J. Proby and was in The Standells. They had four UK-only Top 10 LPs and seven UK (2 US) Top 20 singles. They broke up in 67 and all three recorded solo, with Scott having the greatest success. They re-united and re-charted briefly in the mid 70s.

MAKE IT EASY ON YOURSELF   1(1)   25 SEP 65   PHILIPS
(US No. 16 – Jerry Butler 62 US hit)
MY SHIP IS COMING IN   3   22 JAN 66   PHILIPS
(US No. 63 – originally by Jimmy Radcliffe)
THE SUN AIN'T GONNA SHINE (ANYMORE)   1(4)   19 MAR 66   PHILIPS
(US No. 13 – Jumped from 10-1 – Orig. Frankie Valli)
NO REGRETS *(Originally by Tom Rush)*   7   14 FEB 76   GTO

Also see Scott Walker

JR. WALKER & THE ALL STARS

Unmistakable tenor sax star born Autry DeWalt II in Indiana. He originally played in The Jumping Jacks and first recorded with the All Stars on Harvey in 62. His third single was the first of 21 US (6 UK) chart entries. He had four UK Top 20s, the biggest being '(I'm A) Road Runner' (UK 12/US20).

	SHOTGUN	4	03 APR 65	SOUL
	WHAT DOES IT TAKE TO WIN YOUR LOVE	4	09 AUG 69	SOUL
	(UK No. 13 – Top US Soul record of 69)			

SCOTT WALKER

Ohio singer born Noel Scott Engel recorded on Orbit in 58, Arvee in 59, Liberty in 61 and Challenge in 63. He was in The Routers who hit with 'Let's Go' (US 19) on Warner in 62 and in The Dalton Boys with John Maus, before they formed the Walker Brothers. This influential pop ballad singer had four UK Top 10 solo LPs and three Top 20 singles but no US solo success.

	JOANNA	7	08 JUN 68	PHILIPS

Also see Walker Brothers

STEVE WALSH

Top UK club DJ had a one-off Top 40 hit with his distinctive version of the Fatback Band dance classic complete with crowd participation. He died in 88 after an accident incurred whilst he was filming a video in Europe.

	I FOUND LOVIN'	9	17 OCT 87	A1

TREVOR WALTERS

London based top reggae star who started in the band Santic had two UK-only Top 40s – the first being 'Love Me Tonight' (27 in 81). He has also been on Magnet, Bare, Must Dance, Diamond C, Whale, Jah Bunny, Starlight, Priority, Ital, Champion, Polydor, I&S, Time, Adelphi and Beta.

	STUCK ON YOU	9	25 AUG 84	SANITY

WANG CHUNG

Pop rock trio from Kent fronted by Jack Hues recorded as Huang Chung on Rewind in 80 and Arista in 82 before changing the spelling on joining Epic in 83. Their biggest UK hit was 'Dance Hall Days' (UK 21/US 16) in 84.

	EVERYBODY HAVE FUN TONIGHT	2	27 DEC 86	GEFFEN
	LET'S GO	9	11 APR 87	GEFFEN

WAR

Californian Latin jazz funk band evolved from Night Shift (previously The Creators). In 70 and 71 they charted as Eric Burdon's (ex-Animals) backing group. Act who included Lonnie Jordan, Lee Oskar and Howard Scott then had 12 US (4 UK) Top 40s and had seven US-only Top 20 LPs. They were also on MCA in 78, Lax in 81, RCA in 82, Coco Plum in 85 and Priority in 87.

	SPILL THE WINE (With ERIC BURDON)	3	22 AUG 70	MGM
	THE WORLD IS A GHETTO	7	10 FEB 73	UA
	THE CISCO KID	2	28 APR 73	UA
	GYPSY MAN	8	15 SEP 73	UA
	WHY CAN'T WE BE FRIENDS?	6	23 AUG 75	UA
	LOW RIDER *(UK No. 12) (Re-recorded it in 87)*	7	29 NOV 75	UA
	SUMMER	7	25 SEP 76	UA

ANITA WARD

Memphis born pop soul singer, who first recorded in 71, had a one-off transatlantic No. 1 with a song written (originally for 11 year old Stacy Lattisaw) and produced by singer Frederick Knight. Her follow up was 'Don't Drop My Love'. The ex-teacher re-appeared on Parallax in 89.

	RING MY BELL	1(2)	16 JUN 79	TK
	(Frederick Knight played all instruments on it)			
	RING MY BELL	1(2)	30 JUN 79	JUANA

CLIFFORD T. WARD

Well regarded singer/songwriter and ex-Worcestershire schoolteacher. He started as Cliff Ward & The Cruisers, was in The Secrets and recorded the first of many soft pop LPs on Dandelion in 72. He had two UK-only Top 40s and was also on Philips, Polydor, Mercury, Luv, WEA and joined Tembo in 86.

	GAYE	8	28 JUL 73	CHARISMA

JENNIFER WARNES

Noted pop/MOR singer from Seattle worked with The Smothers Brothers in 67 as Jennifer Warren. She has had nine US (3 UK) charters. She was on Parrott in 68, Warner in 69, Arista in 75 and joined Cypress in 87.

	UP WHERE WE BELONG *(With JOE COCKER)*	7	12 FEB 83	ISLAND
	(Oscar winner song)			
	I'VE HAD THE TIME OF MY LIFE			
	(With BILL MEDLEY) (From the film 'Dirty Dancing')	6	21 NOV 87	RCA
	RIGHT TIME OF THE NIGHT	6	07 MAY 77	ARISTA
	UP WHERE WE BELONG *(With JOE COCKER)*	1(3)	06 NOV 82	ISLAND
	(From the film 'An Officer And A Gentleman')			
	I'VE HAD THE TIME OF MY LIFE *(With BILL MEDLEY)*	1(1)	28 NOV 87	RCA

WARRANT

L.A. heavy rock quintet includes singer/songwriter Jani Lane and guitarist Erik Turner. The first two 45s from their two million selling debut LP 'Dirty Rotten Filthy Stinking Rich' were both US-only Top 40s. Act, who have been sued by The Bay City Rollers over plagiarism, should have a bright future.

	HEAVEN	2	23 SEP 89	COLUMBIA
	(BCR said song similar to 'The Way I Feel Tonight')			

DIONNE WARWICK

Top MOR/soul singer for a quarter of a century. Born in New Jersey she sang in the Drinkard Singers (with her aunt Cissy Houston – Whitney's mother) and session group The Gospelaires. In 63 she scored the first of 55 US (14 UK) charters (with 30 of her US Top 40 hits being co-written by Burt Bacharach) and 32 US (10 UK) chart LPs. She took part in USA For Africa and to date has helped raise over $1 million for AIDS research.

	WALK ON BY	9	09 MAY 64	PYE INT.
	DO YOU KNOW THE WAY TO SAN JOSE	8	08 JUN 68	PYE INT.
	HEARTBREAKER	2	13 NOV 82	ARISTA
	(Fiftieth UK hit composed by the Gibb brothers)			
	ALL THE LOVE IN THE WORLD	10	08 JAN 83	ARISTA
	(Above two prod. Barry Gibb & comp. Bee Gees)			
	ANYONE WHO HAD A HEART *(UK No. 42)*	8	15 FEB 64	SCEPTER
	WALK ON BY	6	13 JUN 64	SCEPTER
	MESSAGE TO MICHAEL *(Original by Lou Johnson)*	8	14 MAY 66	SCEPTER
	I SAY A LITTLE PRAYER	4	09 DEC 67	SCEPTER
	(THEME FROM) VALLEY OF THE DOLLS *(UK No. 28)*	2	24 FEB 68	SCEPTER
	(From the film – Co-written by Andre Previn)			
	DO YOU KNOW THE WAY TO SAN JOSE	10	18 MAY 68	SCEPTER
	(Grammy winner)			
	THIS GIRL'S IN LOVE WITH YOU	7	08 MAR 69	SCEPTER
	(Herb Alpert 68 hit)			
	I'LL NEVER FALL IN LOVE AGAIN	6	14 FEB 70	SCEPTER
	(Grammy winner – Bobbie Gentry 69 UK hit)			
	THEN CAME YOU *(UK No. 29)*	1(1)	26 OCT 74	WARNER
	(And THE SPINNERS – They dueted again in 90)			
	I'LL NEVER LOVE THIS WAY AGAIN	5	20 OCT 79	ARISTA
	(Grammy Winner)			
	(UK No. 62 in 83 – produced by Barry Manilow)			
	HEARTBREAKER	10	15 JAN 83	ARISTA
	THAT'S WHAT FRIENDS ARE FOR	1(4)	18 JAN 86	ARISTA
	(As DIONNE & FRIENDS – UK No. 16)			
	(Monies earned went to AIDS research)			
	(Top US 45 of 86 – Grammy winner –			
	Orig. Rod Stewart)			

WAS (NOT WAS)

Acclaimed Detroit funk rock group formed by Don Fagenson and David Weiss first recorded in 80 and charted (black music) in 82 on Ze. Their second LP was on Geffen and their first pop hit came in the UK. They have also produced for other acts including Bonnie Raitt and the B-52's (producing the group's biggest hits in 89/90).

| | WALK THE DINOSAUR | 10 | 07 NOV 87 | FONTANA |
| | WALK THE DINOSAUR | 7 | 01 APR 89 | CHRYSALIS |

DINAH WASHINGTON

Unmistakable jazz/R&B/blues singer born Ruth Jones in Alabama sang on four black music hits with Lionel Hampton's band between 43-46. The first of her 37 black music and 8 US (1 UK) pop Top 40 solo hits came in 48 for the seven times married 'Queen Of The Harlem Blues'. She died in 63.

	WHAT A DIFF'RENCE A DAY MAKES	8	11 AUG 59	MERCURY
	(Dorsey Brothers 34 hit)			
	BABY (YOU GOT WHAT IT TAKES)	5	21 MAR 60	MERCURY
	(And BROOK BENTON)			
	A ROCKIN' GOOD WAY (And BROOK BENTON)	7	27 JUN 60	MERCURY
	(Brook's song first recorded by Priscilla Bowman)			

GROVER WASHINGTON JR.

One of jazz's top sellers is this Philadelphia based tenor sax player. At 16 he formed his own band The Four Clefs and he had the first of 14 black music hits in 72 on Kudu. He has also recorded on Motown and Columbia and has had nine US (1 UK) Top 40 LPs and one crossover pop Top 40 single.

| | JUST THE TWO OF US | 2 | 02 MAY 81 | ELEKTRA |
| | (UK No. 34 – And BILL WITHERS) | | | |

WATERFRONT

Welsh pop rock duo first known as Official Secrets are singer Chris Duffy and guitarist/co-writer Phil Cilia. Their big hit only scored in the UK after its US success – it had flopped when first released in Sept. 88.

| | CRY (UK No. 17) | 10 | 17 JUN 89 | POLYDOR |

DENNIS WATERMAN

Top UK actor/singer/songwriter hit with the theme song from his popular TV series Minder. He followed this sole Top 20 entry with 'Wasn't Love Strong Enough'. He had previously recorded on DJM and was later on C&D.

| | I COULD BE SO GOOD FOR YOU | 3 | 29 NOV 80 | EMI |

JODY WATLEY

Chicago born singer started as a dancer on TV's Soul Train and became a member of the hit pop soul act Shalamar from 78-83. She appeared on the Band Aid record in 84 and in 87 her eponymous LP went gold. To date she has had five US (1 UK) Top 20 singles making her one of the most successful new female singers of the late 80s.

	LOOKING FOR A NEW LOVE	2	02 MAY 87	MCA
	(UK No. 13 – spent four weeks at No. 2)			
	DON'T YOU WANT ME (UK No. 55)	6	19 DEC 87	MCA
	SOME KIND OF LOVER	10	16 APR 88	MCA
	REAL LOVE (UK No. 31)	2	20 MAY 89	MCA
	FRIENDS (With ERIK B & RAKIM)	9	26 AUG 89	MCA

Also see Shalamar

JEFF WAYNE

US producer/musician/songwriter produced David Essex's first hits including 'Rock On'. He was also the creator/writer and producer of the all star LP 'War Of The Worlds' (UK 5/US 98) in 78, the year that the original version of his 89 hit reached UK No. 36. He has released little in the 80s.

| | EVE OF THE WAR | 3 | 09 DEC 89 | CBS |
| | (Vocal Justin Hayward – Ben Liebrand remix) | | | |

WE FIVE

Folk pop quintet from California, who evolved from The Ridge Runners, were led by Mike Stewart (the brother of John) and included vocalist Beverly Bivens. They followed their hit with their only other charter 'Let's Get Together' (US 31). They were later on Vault in 70 and Verve and MGM in 73.

| | YOU WERE ON MY MIND | 3 | 25 SEP 65 | A&M |

WEATHER GIRLS

Heavyweight hi-nrg/R&B duo were San Francisco based Martha Wash and Izora Armstead (a mother of 11!). They were previously known as Two Tons O'Fun and backed Sylvester. They followed their one-off hit with 'Success'. The hilarious video for 'Raining' featured men falling out of the sky!

| | IT'S RAINING MEN | 2 | 31 MAR 84 | CBS |
| | (US No. 46 in Jan 83 – Also UK No. 73 in Aug 83) | | | |

MARTI WEBB

UK MOR/pop vocalist/actress whose six UK-only charters in the 80s included 'Always There' (13) on BBC in 86. Her biggest success to date was as the star of Andrew Lloyd Webber's musical Tell Me On A Sunday (UK 2 LP) in 80.

	TAKE THAT LOOK OFF YOUR FACE	3	08 MAR 80	POLYDOR
	(From the musical Tell Me On A Sunday)			
	BEN (Michael Jackson 72 hit)	5	06 JUL 85	STARBLEND
	(Proceeds went to fund children's transplants)			

FRED WEDLOCK

Well known folk singer from Bristol (UK) followed his novelty one-off hit with 'Jobsworth' on the Megafunk label. He also had releases on Village Thing and EMI.

| | OLDEST SWINGER IN TOWN | 6 | 21 FEB 81 | ROCKET |

WEE PAPA GIRL RAPPERS

Leading UK female rap duo Ty Tim and Total S (Samantha and Sandra Lawrence) got their name from the patois phrase 'oui papa'. They previously worked with DJ MC JC and the Rap Attack Sound System. They had five UK-only charters in the last two years of the 80s.

| | WEE RULE | 6 | 22 OCT 88 | JIVE |

ERIC WEISSBERG & STEVE MANDELL

Two top New York session musicians who had a one-off transatlantic Top 20 with a bluegrass instrumental (based on Arthur Smith's 'Feuding Banjos') from the film Deliverance. They then toured as the group Deliverance.

| | DUELING BANJOS (UK No. 17 – Grammy winner) | 2 | 24 FEB 73 | WARNER |
| | (Eric re-recorded it as a solo in 79 on Automatic) | | | |

BOB WELCH

L.A. guitarist and singer was the first non-Englishman in Fleetwood Mac. He left them after three years in 74 and formed short lived rock trio Paris in 76. In the US in the late 70s he had four Top 40 singles and two Top 20 LPs.

SENTIMENTAL LADY *(Produced by Lindsey Buckingham & Christine McVie)*		8	07 JAN 78	CAPITOL

Also see Fleetwood Mac

LENNY WELCH

Asbury Park born black MOR/balladeer recorded for Decca in 59 and had nine US-only chart entries between 60-72. He also had records on Kapp in 65, Mercury in 68, Commonwealth United in 69, Roulette in 70, Atco in 72, Mainstream in 75 and Big Tree in 78.

SINCE I FELL FOR YOU *(He re-recorded it in 66 – Paul Gayten 47 hit)*		4	28 DEC 63	CADENCE

LAWRENCE WELK

North Dakota born accordionist and bandleader is an American institution. The 'King Of Champagne Music' has been a top TV and MOR record star for over 50 years. His mix of Polka and 'sweet music' has given him over 40 US-only chart LPs and he also owns a top music publishing company.

CALCUTTA *(Written in 58 as 'Tivoli Melody')*		1(2)	13 FEB 61	DOT

MARY WELLS

Detroit singer/songwriter had the first US hit on Motown and notched up 12 US (1 UK) Top 40s in just four years (11 on Motown) and was voted most promising US female singer of 62. She was also on 20th Century in 64, Atco in 66, Jubilee in 68, Reprise in 71, On Epic in 82 and Nightmare in 87.

MY GUY *(Also UK No. 14 in 72)* *(First hit from the Tamla-Motown labels in UK)*		5	20 JUN 64	STATESIDE
THE ONE WHO REALLY LOVES YOU		8	09 JUN 62	MOTOWN
YOU BEAT ME TO THE PUNCH		9	22 SEP 62	MOTOWN
TWO LOVERS *(She later recorded 'Two Lovers History')*		7	19 JAN 63	MOTOWN
MY GUY *(Co-written Smokey Robinson)* *(She had re-recorded version on Allegiance in 84)*		1(2)	16 MAY 64	MOTOWN

KEITH WEST

UK singer was in The In Crowd on Parlophone and whilst in Tomorrow, which also included Steve Howe later of Yes, he recorded his hit with producer/songwriter Mark Wirtz (it was meant to be released as by Keith Tomorrow). The follow up 'Sam' (UK 38) also came from the never finished 'Teenage Opera'. Tomorrow folded in 68 and he recorded on Deram in 72 and EMI in 74.

EXCERPT FROM A TEENAGE OPERA		2	09 SEP 67	PARLOPHONE

WET WET WET

Top UK teen appeal group in the late 80s started in 82 as The Vortex Motion and featured singer Marti Pellow (Mark McLoughlin). The Scottish blue eyed soul band won a BRITS Best Newcomers award and some UK music paper polls. They have also had six UK-only Top 20 singles and three Top 3 LPs.

WISHING I WAS LUCKY *(US No. 58)*		6	06 JUN 87	PRECIOUS
SWEET LITTLE MYSTERY *(Inc. words from Van Morrison's 'Sense Of Wonder')*		5	05 SEP 87	PRECIOUS
ANGEL EYES (HOME AND AWAY) *(Inc. words from Squeeze's 'Heartbreaking World')*		5	09 JAN 88	PRECIOUS
SWEET SURRENDER		6	07 OCT 89	PRECIOUS
WITH A LITTLE HELP FROM MY FRIENDS/ SHE'S LEAVING HOME *('B' by BILLY BRAGG)* *(Money went to a Child helpline)*		1(3)	21 MAY 88	CHILDLINE

WET WILLIE

Alabama based boogie-rock septet, first known as Fox, included brothers James & Jack Hall. They had the first of two flop LPs in 71 and then had eight small US LP hits and three US-only Top 40s. They disbanded in 80.

KEEP ON SMILIN'		10	24 AUG 74	CAPRICORN

WHAM!

London singer/songwriter George Michael (Georgios Panayiotou) and Andrew Ridgeley were both in The Executive before forming one of the most successful duos of all time. In just three years they sold nearly 40 million records, had three platinum LPs, 10 UK (6 US) Top 20 singles and equalled the Everly Brothers record for duos of four UK No. 1s. These award and poll winners were the first pop group to play in China and their farewell show in 86 at Wembley drew a capacity 72,000 fans. George went on to even greater stardom and after some time away Andrew recorded in 90.

YOUNG GUNS (GO FOR IT)		3	04 DEC 82	INNERVISION
WHAM RAP *(Re-issue of their first 45)*		8	19 FEB 83	INNERVISION
BAD BOYS *(US No. 60)*		2	04 JUN 83	INNERVISION
CLUB TROPICANA *(Song was on their 81 demo tape)*		4	20 AUG 83	INNERVISION
WAKE ME UP BEFORE YOU GO GO *(Entered at No. 4)*		1(2)	02 JUN 84	EPIC
FREEDOM *(Entered at No. 3)*		1(3)	20 OCT 84	EPIC
LAST CHRISTMAS/EVERYTHING SHE WANTS *(UK Gold)* *(Entered at No. 2 – Band Aid (with George on) at No. 1)*		2	15 DEC 84	EPIC
I'M YOUR MAN *(Entered at No. 2)*		1(2)	30 NOV 85	EPIC
LAST CHRISTMAS *(Re-issue & UK No. 45 in 86)*		6	28 DEC 85	EPIC
THE EDGE OF HEAVEN/WHERE DID YOUR HEART GO *(B-side US No. 50 – first double single top in UK)*		1(2)	28 JUN 86	EPIC
WAKE ME UP BEFORE YOU GO-GO		1(3)	17 NOV 84	COLUMBIA
EVERYTHING SHE WANTS		1(2)	25 MAY 85	COLUMBIA
FREEDOM *(They were top selling group in US in 85)*		3	28 SEP 85	COLUMBIA
I'M YOUR MAN		3	01 FEB 86	COLUMBIA
THE EDGE OF HEAVEN *(Elton John on piano)*		10	16 AUG 86	COLUMBIA

Also see George Michael

WHATNAUTS – SEE THE MOMENTS FOR HIT DETAILS

WHISPERS

L.A. soul group, which includes twins Walter and Wallace Scott, started on Dore in 64, first charted on Soul Clock in 70 and all their four UK (3 US) Top 40s came in the 80s on Solar. They have also recorded for Whip, Roker, Janus and Soul Train and have notched up 38 black music chart entries.

AND THE BEAT GOES ON *(US No. 19)*		2	23 FEB 80	SOLAR
IT'S A LOVE THING *(US No. 28)*		9	11 APR 81	SOLAR
ROCK STEADY *(UK No. 30 – first hit for producers L.A. & Babyface)*		7	29 AUG 87	SOLAR

WHISTLE

K.D. and Jazz together with Jamaican cutmaster Silver Spinner make up this Brooklyn based rap/hip hop trio who followed their novelty UK hit (the first of their seven black music charters) with 'Please Love Me'.

(NOTHIN' SERIOUS) JUST BUGGIN'		7	15 MAR 86	CHAMPION

IAN WHITCOMB

Singer/songwriter from Surrey formed Bluesville in Ireland and signed to US label Jerden. After his brief spell of stardom with his brand of wild R'n'R he successfully turned to writing books on the history of music. He also produced Mae West and Goldie Horn and recorded on UA, First American, Argo, Great Northwest, Audiophile, Sierra Brier, Stomp Off and Warner.

YOU TURN ME ON		8	17 JUL 65	TOWER

WHITE LION

New York based rock band features Danish born singer Mike Tramp and his co-writer guitarist Vito Bratta. In 84 they joined Elektra who kept them under contract but released no records (some of these tracks were on Grand Slamm later). So far they have had five US-only hits and two US-only Top 20 LPs.

WAIT		8	21 MAY 88	ATLANTIC
WHEN THE CHILDREN CRY		3	04 FEB 89	ATLANTIC

BARRY WHITE

L.A. based heavyweight singer/songwriter/producer was one of the top 70s soul/disco stars. He was in The Upfronts on Lummtone in 60 and worked with Bob & Earl and The Five Du-Tones. He was A&R man for Mustang/Bronco in the late 60s and formed Love Unlimited (including his future wife Glodean) in 69. As a soloist this distinctive act scored 10 US (14 UK) Top 20s and had seven US & UK Top 40 LPs. He also hit with his Love Unlimited Orchestra. He returned to the charts on A&M in 87 and was on a Quincy Jones black music No. 1 in 90.

CAN'T GET ENOUGH OF YOUR LOVE, BABE	8	21 SEP 74	PYE INT.
YOU'RE THE FIRST, THE LAST, MY EVERYTHING	1(2)	07 DEC 74	20TH CENTURY
WHAT AM I GONNA DO WITH YOU	5	22 MAR 75	20TH CENTURY
LET THE MUSIC PLAY (US No. 32)	9	17 JAN 76	20TH CENTURY
YOU SEE THE TROUBLE WITH ME	2	03 APR 76	20TH CENTURY
(Co-writer Ray Parker Jr.)			
I'M GONNA LOVE YOU JUST A LITTLE MORE BABY	3	23 JUN 73	20TH CENTURY
(UK No. 23)			
NEVER, NEVER GONNA GIVE YA UP (UK No. 14)	7	12 JAN 74	20TH CENTURY
CAN'T GET ENOUGH OF YOUR LOVE, BABE	1(1)	21 SEP 74	20TH CENTURY
YOU'RE THE FIRST, THE LAST, MY EVERYTHING	2	04 JAN 75	20TH CENTURY
WHAT AM I GONNA DO WITH YOU	8	19 APR 75	20TH CENTURY
IT'S ECSTASY WHEN YOU LAY DOWN NEXT TO ME	4	12 NOV 77	20TH CENTURY
(UK No. 40)			

Also see Love Unlimited Orchestra

KARYN WHITE

L.A. singer was fired by the group Legacy in 85 for being 'uncommercial'. She became a top session singer working with acts like Richard Marx, Ray Parker Jr. and The Commodores. She first charted as the vocalist on Jeff Lorber's 'Facts of Love' in 86. As a soloist she works with L.A. & Babyface who helped make her the top new singer in black music in 89.

THE WAY YOU LOVE ME	7	04 FEB 89	WARNER
(Had topped black music chart three months before)			
SUPERWOMAN (UK No. 11 – Top Black 45 of 89)	8	15 APR 89	WARNER
SECRET RENDEZVOUS	6	26 AUG 89	WARNER
(UK 52 – Top US club play record of 89)			

SNOWY WHITE

Guitarist/singer from the Isle of Wight had played with acts like Pink Floyd, Cliff Richard, Al Stewart and Steve Harley before joining Thin Lizzy between 80-82. He had a sole solo Top 40 and later recorded on Legend.

BIRD OF PARADISE	6	21 JAN 84	TOWERBELL

Also see Thin Lizzy

TONY JOE WHITE

Swamp rock singer/songwriter from Louisiana. He started with Tony & The Mojos and Tony & The Twilights. Oddly he only had one US & UK Top 40 – in the UK it was 'Groupie Girl' (22) in 70. He was on Warner in 71, 20th Century in 76, Arista in 78 and had some country hits on Casablanca and Columbia in the early 80s. He also wrote the Brook Benton/Randy Crawford hit 'Rainy Night In Georgia' and Tina Turner's 90 hit 'Steamy Windows'.

POLK SALAD ANNIE (Produced by Billy Swann)	8	23 AUG 69	MONUMENT

WHITE PLAINS

UK session act formed by Greenaway & Cook featured the often heard voice of Tony Burrows. They became a working quintet with lead singer Peter Nelson after they hit. They had five UK (1 US) Top 40s and were on Bradley's in 76 and PVK in 78.

MY BABY LOVES LOVIN' (US No. 13)	9	28 FEB 70	DERAM
JULIE, DO YA LOVE ME	8	05 DEC 70	DERAM
(Bobby Sherman 70 US hit)			

WHITESNAKE

Top heavy metal act was formed by ex Deep Purple singer David Coverdale (who had previously been in Beautiful Losers with Chris Rea) in 78 and has included musicians like Jon Lord, Ian Paice (also ex-Deep Purple) and Cozy Powell. The first of their six UK (2 US) Top 20s and seven UK (2 US) Top 10 LPs came in 80. These stars of many rock festivals really scored in the US in 87 and their eponymous LP went on to sell over eight million.

IS THIS LOVE (Their 13th UK charter)	9	04 JUL 87	EMI
HERE I GO AGAIN	9	28 NOV 87	EMI
(Remix of their UK No. 34 in 82)			
HERE I GO AGAIN	1(1)	10 OCT 87	GEFFEN
IS THIS LOVE	2	19 DEC 87	GEFFEN

ROGER WHITTAKER

Popular Kenya born UK based MOR singer/whistler and entertainer recorded on Fontana in 62 as Rog Whittaker and on Columbia in 65. He has had six UK (1 US) Top 40s in the 70s and has also had seven UK (1 US) Top 40 LPs.

I DON'T BELIEVE IN IF ANYMORE	8	23 MAY 70	COLUMBIA
(Covered in the US by Johnny Tillotson)			
THE LAST FAREWELL (US No. 19)	2	13 SEP 75	EMI
THE SKYE BOAT SONG (And DES O'CONNOR)	10	06 DEC 86	TEMBO
(Roger had first released it as a solo 45 in 68)			

WHO

One of the all time great rock bands featured songwriter/guitarist Pete Townshend, singer Roger Daltrey, bassist John Entwistle and drummer and 'Wild Man Of Rock' Keith Moon. They evolved from West London group The Detours and recorded on Fontana in 64 as The High Numbers. The premiere mod band known at first for 'Maximum R&B' and for smashing their instruments, they have had 17 (8 US) Top 20s and 16 UK (11 US) Top 20 LPs. Making their reputation as live performers, they starred at The Monterey Pop Festival in 67 and Woodstock in 69, the year they launched the rock opera 'Tommy'. Drummer Keith died in 78. These R'n'R Hall of Famers split in 83, re-formed for Live Aid and their comeback US tour with an expanded line-up in 89 earned them $30 million.

I CAN'T EXPLAIN (US No. 93)	8	17 APR 65	BRUNSWICK
(Also on record Jimmy Page and The Ivy League)			
ANYWAY ANYHOW ANYWHERE	10	03 JUL 65	BRUNSWICK
(Used as theme on TVs 'Ready, Steady Go')			
MY GENERATION (US No. 74)	2	27 NOV 65	BRUNSWICK
SUBSTITUTE	5	16 APR 66	REACTION
I'M A BOY	2	01 OCT 66	REACTION
HAPPY JACK (US No. 24)	3	21 JAN 67	REACTION
PICTURES OF LILY (US No. 51)	4	20 MAY 67	TRACK
I CAN SEE FOR MILES	10	18 NOV 67	TRACK
PINBALL WIZARD (US No. 19 – from 'Tommy')	4	26 APR 69	TRACK
WON'T GET FOOLED AGAIN (US No. 15)	9	14 AUG 71	TRACK
JOIN TOGETHER	9	22 JUL 72	TRACK
SQUEEZE BOX	10	28 JAN 76	POLYDOR
SUBSTITUTE (Re-issue)	7	20 NOV 76	POLYDOR
YOU BETTER YOU BET (US No. 18)	9	21 MAR 81	POLYDOR
(They spent 243 weeks on UK chart with no No. 1s)			
I CAN SEE FOR MILES (Their eighth US 45)	9	25 NOV 67	DECCA

Also see Pete Townshend & Roger Daltrey

JANE WIEDLIN

Wisconsin singer/guitarist charted in 83 with The Sparks on 'Cool Places' (US 49), whilst still with the top female group The Go-Go's. As a soloist she first hit in 85 and three years later had her sole Top 40 to date.

 RUSH HOUR (UK No. 12)		9	30 JUL 88	EMI MAN.

Also see The Go-Go's

WIGAN'S CHOSEN FEW

The instrumental B-side of a 68 flop by a Canadian surf group became a UK smash when the speed was altered and the sounds of a steam hammer and Sheffield Wednesday (soccer team) fans were added. The word Wigan was added to the act's name for legal reasons and as a tribute to the UK town where the record was first played. The act never knew of their belated success and no follow ups were released. They also were on Canadian American.

FOOTSEE		9	22 FEB 75	DISCO DEMAND

WILD CHERRY

Ohio based white funk band featured singer/songwriter/producer Bob Parissi and Mark Avsec. Act, who also were on Brown Bag, UA and A&M, had a sole Top 40 hit. Mark later had success as a producer and Bob was a radio DJ in 90.

PLAY THAT FUNKY MUSIC		7	13 NOV 76	EPIC
PLAY THAT FUNKY MUSIC (Also No. 1 soul hit)		1(3)	18 SEP 76	EPIC

KIM WILDE

London born Kim Smith is the daughter of 50s/60s UK star Marty Wilde. Her debut single was a transatlantic Top 40 and she has since had 11 UK (1 US) Top 20s, many written and produced by her father and brother, ex-teenage singer Ricky. This BRITS winner was also part of No. 1 act Ferry Aid and supported Michael Jackson on his 88 European tour.

KIDS IN AMERICA (US No. 25) (At one stage taken off the UK chart for hyping)		2	20 MAR 81	RAK
CHEQUERED LOVE		4	23 MAY 81	RAK
YOU KEEP ME HANGIN' ON (Supremes 66 hit)		2	15 NOV 86	MCA
ANOTHER STEP (CLOSER TO YOU) (And JUNIOR)		6	16 MAY 87	MCA
ROCKIN' AROUND THE CHRISTMAS TREE (With MEL SMITH) (Brenda Lee 60 hit–proceeds to Comic Aid)		3	26 DEC 87	10
YOU CAME (US No. 41)		3	13 AUG 88	MCA
NEVER TRUST A STRANGER		7	22 OCT 88	MCA
FOUR LETTER WORD		6	14 JAN 89	MCA
YOU KEEP ME HANGIN' ON		1(1)	06 JUN 87	MCA

MARTY WILDE

Top 50s/60s UK R'n'R star was born Reg Smith in London. He sang in The Hound Dogs and as Reg Patterson and has had eight UK-only Top 20s. He was on Columbia in 63, Decca 64 (as the Wilde Three, which included Justin Hayward), US Heritage in 69 (he charted there as Shannon), Magnet in 73 and Kaleidoscope in 82. He covered many US songs and in later years became a top songwriter himself, with hits by Lulu and many by his daughter Kim.

ENDLESS SLEEP (Jody Reynolds 58 US hit)		4	29 AUG 58	PHILIPS
DONNA (Ritchie Valens 59 hit)		3	15 MAY 59	PHILIPS
A TEENAGER IN LOVE (Dion & the Belmonts 59 hit)		2	10 JUL 59	PHILIPS
SEA OF LOVE (Phil Phillps 59 US hit)		3	30 OCT 59	PHILIPS
BAD BOY (US No. 45) (First original hit – covered in US by Robin Luke)		7	08 JAN 60	PHILIPS
RUBBER BALL (Bobby Vee 61 hit – written by Gene Pitney)		7	10 FEB 61	PHILIPS

MATTHEW WILDER

Singer/songwriter and keyboard player from New York did session work for acts like Bette Midler and Rickie Lee Jones. He had recorded on Arista in 82 and followed his sole Top 20 hit with 'The Kids American' (US 33).

BREAK MY STRIDE		4	11 FEB 84	EPIC
BREAK MY STRIDE		5	21 JAN 84	PRIVATE I

WILL TO POWER

Miami group features singer/writer/producer Bob Rosenberg, Suzi Carr and sax man Doctor J. They first charted in the US in 87 with 'Dreamin'' (50) and they followed up their one big hit to date with 'Fading Away'.

BABY I LOVE YOUR WAY/FREEBIRD (MEDLEY) (Bigger UK hit than either of the original versions)		6	21 JAN 89	EPIC
BABY I LOVE YOUR WAY/FREEBIRD (MEDLEY) (Peter Frampton 76 hit and Lynyrd Skynyrd 74 hit)		1(1)	03 DEC 88	EPIC

ALYSON WILLIAMS

Harlem born soul singer sang backups for Whodini and Kurtis Blow in 82. She was briefly on Profile in 86, sang lead with Orange Krush and dueted with Def Jam acts Oran 'Juice' Jones, Tashan and Chuck Stanley before soloing on that label. To date the photogenic lady has had three UK-only charters.

I NEED YOUR LOVIN'		8	16 SEP 89	DEF JAM

ANDY WILLIAMS

One of the top all time MOR singers was born in Iowa and started singing in The Williams Brothers with his three brothers (they backed Bing Crosby on a No. 1 hit in 44, when Andy was 7). He was on Steve Allen's 'Tonight' Show as a soloist from 52-55 and recorded on MGM in 51 and X-Vik in 54. He had 44 US (21 UK) charters and 33 US (24 UK) chart LPs between 56-84. He also had a top transatlantic TV series in the 60s.

BUTTERFLY (Charlie Gracie 57 hit)		1(2)	24 MAY 57	LONDON
CAN'T GET USED TO LOSING YOU		3	17 MAY 63	CBS
ALMOST THERE (US No. 67 – from the film 'I'd Rather Be Rich')		2	16 OCT 65	CBS
CAN'T TAKE MY EYES OFF YOU (Frankie Valli 67 US hit)		5	04 MAY 68	CBS
CAN'T HELP FALLING IN LOVE (US No. 88 – Elvis Presley 61 hit)		3	28 MAR 70	CBS
HOME LOVIN' MAN (Greenaway & Cook song)		7	12 DEC 70	CBS
(WHERE DO I BEGIN) LOVE STORY (From the film)		4	24 APR 71	CBS
SOLITAIRE (Neil Sedaka song)		4	09 MAR 74	CBS
CANADIAN SUNSET (Eddie Heywood 56 hit)		10	15 SEP 56	CADENCE
BUTTERFLY		4	30 MAR 57	CADENCE
I LIKE YOUR KIND OF LOVE (UK No. 16)		10	19 OCT 57	CADENCE
LONELY STREET		5	08 NOV 59	CADENCE
THE VILLAGE OF ST. BERNADETTE (Anne Shelton 59 UK hit)		7	25 JAN 60	CADENCE
CAN'T GET USED TO LOSING YOU		2	13 APR 63	COLUMBIA
(WHERE DO I BEGIN) LOVE STORY		9	03 APR 71	COLUMBIA

DANNY WILLIAMS

South African born Johnny Mathis styled MOR singer was based in the UK and appeared on many pop TV shows there in the late 50s. He had three UK Top 20s in the early 60s and one of his UK misses became his only big US hit. He was later on Deram, Philips, Piccadilly, Columbia and returned briefly to the UK Top 40 in 77 with 'Dancin' Easy' on Ensign (30).

MOON RIVER (Henry Mancini 61 US hit)		1(1)	27 DEC 61	HMV
WONDERFUL WORLD OF THE YOUNG		9	04 MAY 62	HMV
WHITE ON WHITE		9	17 MAY 64	UA

DENIECE WILLIAMS

Soul singer/songwriter born Deniece Chandler in Iowa, first recorded on Toddlin' Town in 67. From 71-74 she was part of Stevie Wonder's backing group Wonderlove. As a soloist she has had five UK (4 US) Top 40s. In the late 80s she became a top gospel star on Word whilst still hitting the black music chart on MCA.

FREE *(US No. 25 – Produced Maurice White)*	1(2)	07 MAY 77	CBS
THAT'S WHAT FRIENDS ARE FOR	8	27 AUG 77	CBS
TOO MUCH TOO LITTLE TOO LATE *(With JOHNNY MATHIS)*	3	13 MAY 78	CBS
LET'S HEAR IT FOR THE BOY *(From the film 'Footloose')*	2	02 JUN 84	CBS
TOO MUCH TOO LITTLE TOO LATE *(With JOHNNY MATHIS – his first No. 1 hit)*	1(1)	03 JUN 78	COLUMBIA
IT'S GONNA TAKE A MIRACLE *(Royalettes 65 US hit)*	10	12 JUN 82	ARC/COLUMBIA
LET'S HEAR IT FOR THE BOY *(Composed by Boy Meets Girl)*	1(2)	26 MAY 84	COLUMBIA

JOHN WILLIAMS

The noted New York born composer and conductor has also written and had hit 45s from many other top film scores including Jaws (US 32), Close Encounters Of The Third Kind (US 13), Superman (US 81) and E.T. (UK 17).

STAR WARS (MAIN TITLE) *(And The LONDON SYMPHONY ORCHESTRA)*	10	17 SEP 77	20TH CENTURY

MASON WILLIAMS

Guitarist/songwriter from Texas who worked with The Smothers Brothers in the 60s, first recorded on Mercury in 66 and wrote the UK No. 1 'Cinderella Rockafella'. He had a one-off transatlantic Top 10 with an unusual classics meets rock instrumental. Today he successfully writes books.

CLASSICAL GAS *(Produced by Mike Post)*	9	12 OCT 68	WARNER
CLASSICAL GAS	2	03 AUG 68	WARNER

MAURICE WILLIAMS & THE ZODIACS

South Carolina R&B group started as The Royal Charms in 55 and first hit with Maurice's song 'Little Darlin' as The Gladiolas in 57 (song was a million seller for The Diamonds). In 58 they became The Excellos and as The Zodiacs they were on Cole and Selwyn in 59 and Soma in 60. They followed their only Top 40 hit with 'I Remember'. They were later on Veep, Atlantic, Scepter, Sphere Sound, Vee Jay, Sea-Horn, 440/Plus, R&M and Candi.

STAY *(Later released live version on Deesu)*	10	27 JAN 61	TOP RANK
STAY *(Falsetto by Henry Gaston)* *(The shortest million selling single at 1½ mins)*	1(1)	21 NOV 60	HERALD

ROGER WILLIAMS

Top US MOR pianist was born Louis Weertz in Omaha. He was a winner on Arthur Godfrey Talent Scouts and had seven US-only Top 40s and a remarkable 38 US-only chart LPs, all on Kapp.

AUTUMN LEAVES	1(4)	29 OCT 55	KAPP
BORN FREE *(From the film)*	7	17 DEC 66	KAPP

VANESSA WILLIAMS

New York born singer/actress sprang to fame as the first black woman to win the 'Miss America' title, which was taken away shortly after due to a porn magazine scandal. She has had three black music Top 10s including 'Darlin' I' the follow up to her biggest hit.

DREAMIN' *(UK No. 74)*	8	08 APR 89	WING

BRUCE WILLIS

Popular transatlantic TV and film actor also had record success with his 'The Return of Bruno' LP and a couple of R&B revivals included on it.

RESPECT YOURSELF *(Staple Singers 71 US hit – Co-writ. Luther Ingram)*	7	28 MAR 87	MOTOWN
UNDER THE BOARDWALK *(backed by TEMPTATIONS)* *(US No. 59 – The Drifters 64 US hit)*	2	11 JUL 87	MOTOWN
RESPECT YOURSELF	5	07 MAR 87	MOTOWN

VIOLA WILLS

Soul singer from L.A. has worked with producer Barry White at Bronco in 66 and toured with Joe Cocker in his 'Mad Dogs And Englishmen' tour. The hi-nrg/dance star has three sons who record as The Iveys. She has also appeared on Charly in 80, Touch in 84, Sedition in 86, Nightmare in 86, Wide Angle in 87, Island 87, Rhythm King in 88 and Light House in 89.

GONNA GET ALONG WITHOUT YOU NOW *(Patience & Prudence 56 hit)*	8	10 NOV 79	ARIOLA/HAN.

AL WILSON

Mississippi soul singer was in The Jewels, The Rollers (who had a small hit in 61) and The Souls. In 68 he had the first of four US Top 40s with 'The Snake', which was his only UK charter in 75 (41). He has also been on Soul City in 68, Bell in 70, Carousel in 72, Playboy in 76 and Roadshow in 79.

SHOW AND TELL	1(1)	19 JAN 74	ROCKY ROAD

ANN WILSON – SEE HEART/MIKE RENO FOR HIT DETAILS

J. FRANK WILSON & THE CAVALIERS

Texan pop quintet had a one-off US smash with a death disc originally recorded in 62 by Wayne Cochran. Their follow up was 'Hey Little One'.

LAST KISS *(Also US No. 92 in 73 on Virgo)* *(Record originally released on Tamara)*	2	07 NOV 64	JOSIE

JACKIE WILSON

One of the all time top black acts. This distinctive Detroit singer recorded solo on Dee Gee in 51 and first hit as vocalist with Billy Ward & The Dominoes in 53. He went solo again in 57 and had 54 US (6 UK) charters which included 11 US Top 20s between 58-61. One of the great stage performers, he died in 84 having spent the last eight years of his life in a semi-comatose state after a very bad heart attack. Sadly he never lived to see his biggest UK hits including his first pop No. 1.

REET PETITE *(US No. 62 – first hit written by Berry Gordy)*	6	03 JAN 58	CORAL
I GET THE SWEETEST FEELING *(US No. 34 in 68)* *(Also UK No. 25 in 75 – his 49th US hit)*	9	16 SEP 72	MCA
REET PETITE *(re-release)* *(Took over 29 years from UK release to get to No. 1!)*	1(4)	27 DEC 86	SMP
I GET THE SWEETEST FEELING *(Re-release)*	3	14 MAR 87	SMP
(YOUR LOVE KEEPS LIFTING ME) HIGHER AND HIGHER *(Also UK No. 11 in 69 & UK No. 25 in 75)*	9	25 JUL 87	SMP
LONELY TEARDROPS *(Last song he sang before his heart attack in 75)*	7	08 FEB 59	BRUNSWICK
NIGHT *(Not rel. in UK at time due to copyright reasons)*	4	09 MAY 60	BRUNSWICK
ALONE AT LAST	8	28 NOV 60	BRUNSWICK
MY EMPTY ARMS *(Above three hits based on classical works)*	9	06 FEB 61	BRUNSWICK
BABY WORKOUT	5	13 APR 63	BRUNSWICK
(YOUR LOVE KEEPS LIFTING ME) HIGHER AND HIGHER	6	07 OCT 67	BRUNSWICK

MARI WILSON

Scottish born (Mairrhii Wilson) London based singer was known for her tall beehive hair-do and her 60s type sound. She had six UK-only charters backed by the Wilsations (first called The Imaginations and once included Julia Fordham). When the hits stopped she moved into jazzier circles.

 JUST WHAT I ALWAYS WANTED   8   09 OCT 82   COMPACT

MERI WILSON

Born in Japan, Dallas based night-club singer/songwriter. She did jingles and session work before getting her sole hit with her first single. She followed it with 'Rub A Dub Dub' in the UK and 'Midnight In Memphis' in the US. Later comebacks included another risque 45 – 'Peter The Meter Reader' in 81 on WMOT.

 TELEPHONE MAN *(US No. 18)*   6   24 SEP 77   PYE INT.
(11 labels rejected it before she got a deal)

KAI WINDING

Danish born jazz trombonist who had played in the duo J&K with J.J. Johnson and played with Stan Kenton. He recorded solo on Columbia in 59 and had his only hit with the much recorded film theme. He died aged 60 in 83.

 MORE *(From the film Mondo Cane)*   8   24 AUG 63   VERVE

PETE WINGFIELD

London singer/songwriter/pianist/producer had a one-off hit with a clever doo-wop styled novelty. He has played on countless sessions and backed many top acts on stage. He has also produced hits for The Pasadenas, Dexy's Midnight Runners and The Kane Gang and was in chart act The Olympic Runners.

 EIGHTEEN WITH A BULLET *(US No. 15)*   7   19 JUL 75   ISLAND
(Was No. 18 with a bullet on US chart 22.11.75)

WINGS – SEE PAUL McCARTNEY FOR HIT DETAILS

WINSTONS

Richard Spencer fronted this Washington septet made up of ex-members of Otis Redding's and The Impressions' backing bands. Richard wrote their sole Top 40 which they followed with 'Love Of The Common People' (US 54).

 COLOR HIM FATHER   7   19 JUL 69   METROMEDIA
(Grammy winner Best R&B song of 69)

EDGAR WINTER GROUP

Texas born keyboard player was in Black Plague with his brother Johnny whose group he was in from 68 until he recorded solo in 70. He formed his own group White Trash in 71 and hard rock quartet EWG in 72. EWG included Dan Hartman (ex-Legends), Rick Derringer (ex-McCoys) and Ronnie Montrose (ex-Sawbuck). He had eight US-only chart LPs and seven US (1UK) chart 45s. He was later on Blue Sky and in the 80s concentrated on session work.

 FRANKENSTEIN *(UK No. 18)*   1(1)   26 MAY 73   EPIC
(Originally the B-side – produced Rick Derringer)

RUBY WINTERS

Soul singer based in Cincinnati first charted in the the US in 67 on Diamond. Ten years later she had two UK-only Top 20s – the other being 'Come To Me' (11). She also was on Polydor, Playboy and Millennium.

 I WILL *(Soul hit in 73 – Vic Dana 62 US hit)*   4   17 DEC 77   CREOLE

STEVE WINWOOD

Singer/songwriter and keyboard player from Birmingham (UK) first found success in The Spencer Davis Group, Traffic and Blind Faith. The critically hailed award winner scored the first of his five UK (6 US) solo Top 40 LPs in 77 and he has also had two UK (9 US) Top 40 singles to date.

WHILE YOU SEE A CHANCE *(UK No. 45)*	7	18 APR 81	ISLAND
HIGHER LOVE *(Grammy winner)*	1(1)	30 AUG 86	ISLAND
(UK No. 13 – Backing vocals inc. Chaka Khan)			
THE FINER THINGS	8	25 APR 87	ISLAND
VALERIE *(UK No. 51 in 82 & UK No. 19 in 87)*	9	19 DEC 87	ISLAND
ROLL WITH IT *(UK No. 53)*	1(4)	30 JUL 88	VIRGIN
DON'T YOU KNOW WHAT THE NIGHT CAN DO	6	29 OCT 88	VIRGIN
(He was Top Adult Contemporary act in US in 88)			

Also see Spencer Davis/Traffic

BILL WITHERS

Distinctive folk styled soul singer/songwriter from West Virginia was 32 before he first recorded in 70. He was instantly successful and has since had six US (4 UK) Top 40s and his songs have given Top 10s hits to Michael Jackson and Club Nouveau. His biggest UK hit came with a re-mix in 88.

LOVELY DAY *(US No. 30)*	7	04 FEB 78	CBS
LOVELY DAY *(Remix)*	4	24 SEP 88	CBS
AIN'T NO SUNSHINE	3	18 SEP 71	SUSSEX
(Grammy Winner – Stephen Stills plays lead guitar)			
LEAN ON ME	1(3)	08 JUL 72	SUSSEX
(UK No. 18 – Grammy winning song in 88)			
USE ME	2	14 OCT 72	SUSSEX
JUST THE TWO OF US *(With GROVER WASHINGTON JR.)*	2	02 MAY 81	ELEKTRA
(Grammy winner)			

WIZZARD

Birmingham (UK) singer/songwriter Roy Wood, the colourful front man from hit UK act The Move, formed this group in 72 after a brief spell in ELO. They were a top UK-only act until they split in 75. During this period the talented Roy also had solo successes. Later he produced acts like The Darts and a new version of Wizzard's Xmas hit was used on a Jive Bunny 89 No. 1.

BALL PARK INCIDENT	6	13 JAN 73	HARVEST
SEE MY BABY JIVE	1(4)	19 MAY 73	HARVEST
ANGEL FINGERS	1(1)	22 SEP 73	HARVEST
I WISH IT COULD BE CHRISTMAS EVERY DAY	4	22 DEC 73	HARVEST
(Was UK 41 in 81 and UK No. 23 in 84)			
ROCK 'N ROLL WINTER	6	11 MAY 74	WARNER
ARE YOU READY TO ROCK	8	25 JAN 75	WARNER

Also see Move/ELO/Roy Wood

WOMACK & WOMACK

Soulful West Virginia duo Cecil Womack and his second wife Linda (the first was singer Mary Wells). He had been in The Womack Brothers and The Valentinos with his brothers (including Bobby) and Linda was Sam Cooke's daughter. To date they have had eight children and three UK-only Top 20s.

 TEARDROPS   3   17 SEP 88   4TH & B.

BOBBY WOMACK

Critically acclaimed singer/songwriter and one time member of The Womack Brothers, The Valentinos (they had the original of the Stones 'It's All Over Now' which Bobby wrote) and The Lovers. He recorded solo on Him (in 65), Checker and Atlantic before getting the first of his 11 black music hits and four US-only Top 40 pop hits in 68. He has also been on Columbia in 76, Arista in 79, Beverly Glen in 81, Motown in 84, MCA in 85 and Solar in 89.

 LOOKIN' FOR A LOVE   10   27 APR 74   UA
(Valentinos (he was a member) 62 US hit)

WOMBLES

Fictitious group formed by singer/composer Mike Batt to portray the litter conscious animals in a top UK children's TV series. Within their two year lifespan they scored eight UK Top 40s and three Top 20 LPs. In the US a specially recorded 45 'Wombling Summer Party' was their only hit (55).

🇬🇧	THE WOMBLING SONG *(They were top UK singles recording act of 74!)*	4	23 FEB 74	CBS
	REMEMBER YOU'RE A WOMBLE	3	11 MAY 74	CBS
	BANANA ROCK	9	20 JUL 74	CBS
	WOMBLING MERRY CHRISTMAS	2	04 JAN 75	CBS

Also see Mike Batt

STEVIE WONDER

The No. 1 black artist of the rock era and the top male singer in the US between 60 and 90 was born Steveland Judkins in Michigan. This very talented singer/songwriter joined Motown in 60 and as Little Stevie Wonder in 63 (when aged 13) became the first act to simultaneously top the US singles and LP chart (it was his second LP). He has won every conceivable award since then and has notched up 59 US (49 UK) hits and 23 US (14 UK) Chart LPs. The multi-Grammy winning act has packed stadiums world-wide and has also written and played on hits for many other acts. He was involved in USA For Africa, Dionne & Friends, the first Nelson Mandela show and was a leading campaigner to make Martin Luther King's birthday a US holiday.

🇬🇧	I WAS MADE TO LOVE HER *(His 11th UK 45)*	5	19 AUG 67	TAMLA MOTOWN
	FOR ONCE IN MY LIFE *(Tony Bennett 67 US hit)*	3	25 JAN 69	TAMLA MOTOWN
	MY CHERIE AMOUR *(Was the B-side)*	4	23 AUG 69	TAMLA MOTOWN
	YESTER-ME, YESTER-YOU, YESTERDAY	2	06 DEC 69	TAMLA MOTOWN
	NEVER HAD A DREAM COME TRUE *(US No. 26)*	6	02 MAY 70	TAMLA MOTOWN
	YOU ARE THE SUNSHINE OF MY LIFE *(Grammy for Top Pop Vocal Performance of 73)*	7	02 JUN 73	TAMLA MOTOWN
	HE'S MISSTRA KNOW IT ALL *(US B-side)*	10	11 MAY 74	TAMLA MOTOWN
	I WISH	5	22 JAN 77	TAMLA MOTOWN
	SIR DUKE *(Tribute to Duke Ellington)*	2	07 MAY 77	MOTOWN
	MASTER BLASTER (JAMMIN')	2	04 OCT 80	MOTOWN
	I AIN'T GONNA STAND FOR IT *(US No. 11)*	10	31 JAN 81	MOTOWN
	LATELY *(US No. 64)*	3	11 APR 81	MOTOWN
	HAPPY BIRTHDAY *(Martin Luther King tribute)* *(Entered at No. 9 – not released on 45 in US)*	2	08 AUG 81	MOTOWN
	EBONY AND IVORY *(With PAUL McCARTNEY)* *(First 45 by a black and white duo to hit No. 1)*	1(3)	24 APR 82	PARLOPHONE
	DO I DO *(US No. 13)*	10	26 JUN 82	MOTOWN
	I JUST CALLED TO SAY I LOVE YOU *(UK Gold)* *(Entered at No.3 – his first No. 1 & Motown's top UK 45)*	1(6)	08 SEP 84	MOTOWN
	PART TIME LOVER	3	21 SEP 85	MOTOWN
	MY LOVE *(With JULIO IGLESIAS)* *(Was flop when first released four months earlier)*	5	03 SEP 88	CBS
🇺🇸	FINGERTIPS (PT. 2) *(as Little Stevie Wonder)* *(His fourth 45 – the first live single at No. 1)*	1(3)	10 AUG 63	TAMLA
	UPTIGHT (EVERYTHING'S ALRIGHT) *(UK No. 14)*	3	12 FEB 66	TAMLA
	BLOWIN' IN THE WIND *(UK No. 36 – Bob Dylan song)*	9	03 SEP 66	TAMLA
	A PLACE IN THE SUN *(UK No. 20)*	9	24 DEC 66	TAMLA
	I WAS MADE TO LOVE HER	2	29 JUL 67	TAMLA

SHOO-BE-DOO-BE-DOO-DA-DAY *(UK No. 46)*	9	25 MAY 68	TAMLA
FOR ONCE IN MY LIFE	2	28 DEC 68	TAMLA
MY CHERIE AMOUR *(Original title 'Oh My Marcia' about a girlfriend)*	4	26 JUL 69	TAMLA
YESTER-ME, YESTER-YOU, YESTERDAY *(Produced and co-written by Johnny Bristol)*	7	13 DEC 69	TAMLA
SIGNED SEALED DELIVERED I'M YOURS *(UK No. 15)*	3	08 AUG 70	TAMLA
HEAVEN HELP US ALL *(UK No. 29)*	9	28 NOV 70	TAMLA
IF YOU REALLY LOVE ME *(UK No. 20)*	8	16 OCT 71	TAMLA
SUPERSTITION *(He wrote it for Jeff Beck)* *(UK No. 11 – Grammy for Best R&B song & performance)*	1(1)	27 JAN 73	TAMLA
YOU ARE THE SUNSHINE OF MY LIFE	1(1)	19 MAY 73	TAMLA
HIGHER GROUND *(UK No. 29)*	4	13 OCT 73	TAMLA
LIVING FOR THE CITY *(UK No. 15 – Grammy winner for Best R&B Song)*	8	12 JAN 74	TAMLA
YOU HAVEN'T DONE NOTHIN *(UK No. 30 – backing vocals by The Jackson Five)*	1(1)	02 NOV 74	TAMLA
BOOGIE ON REGGAE WOMAN *(UK No. 12 – Grammy Best R&B Performance)*	3	01 FEB 75	TAMLA
I WISH *(First hit after signing a record $13 million deal)*	1(1)	22 JAN 77	TAMLA
SIR DUKE	1(3)	21 MAY 77	TAMLA
SEND ONE YOUR LOVE *(UK No. 52)*	4	22 DEC 79	TAMLA
MASTER BLASTER (JAMMIN')	5	06 DEC 80	TAMLA
THAT GIRL *(UK No. 39)*	4	20 MAR 82	TAMLA
EBONY AND IVORY *(With PAUL McCARTNEY)*	1(7)	15 MAY 82	COLUMBIA
I JUST CALLED TO SAY I LOVE YOU *(Oscar winner from film 'The Woman In Red')*	1(3)	13 OCT 84	MOTOWN
PART TIME LOVER *(First 45 to top pop, black, dance and A/C charts)*	1(1)	01 NOV 85	TAMLA
GO HOME *(UK No. 67)*	10	01 FEB 86	TAMLA

BRENTON WOOD

Louisiana pop soul singer was born Alfred Smith and first recorded in Little Freddy & The Rockets in 58. He was later in The Quotations and recorded solo on Brent in 66. He had 3 US (1 UK) Top 40s in 67 and later recorded on Whiz (as Shirley & Alfred with Shirley Goodman of Shirley & Co.), Warner, Cream and Prophecy.

🇬🇧	GIMME LITTLE SIGN	8	10 FEB 68	LIBERTY
🇺🇸	GIMME LITTLE SIGN	9	14 OCT 67	DOUBLE SHOT

ROY WOOD

Charismatic and unmistakable (multi-coloured long hair) lead singer of The Move and Wizzard. He had started in groups like The Falcons, The Lawmen, Gerry Levine & The Avengers and Mike Sheridan & The Nightriders. The multi-instrumentalist and producer had four UK-only solo Top 20s between 73-75. He later formed Wizzo (on Warner) and The Helicopters with little success. Birmingham born Wood was also a founder member of Electric Light Orchestra but he left after their first LP.

🇬🇧	FOREVER	8	26 JAN 74	HARVEST

Also see Move/ELO/Wizzard

BETTY WRIGHT

Miami singer recorded on Deep City in 66 (when aged 13) and has been a black music chart regular since 68 with 33 entries to date. The biggest of her four UK hits was the Grammy winning 'Where Is The Love' (UK 25/US 96) in 75. She has also sung on hits by KC & The Sunshine Band and has also had releases on Epic, Jamaica, First String, Ms. B. and RCA.

🇺🇸	CLEAN UP WOMAN	6	29 JAN 72	ALSTON

GARY WRIGHT

Keyboard playing singer/songwriter/producer and ex-child actor was a mainstay of UK based hard rock band Spooky Tooth until they split in 74. His first and biggest solo success came with the 75 LP 'The Dream Weaver' (US 7) and his two US-only Top 10s from it. He returned on Cypress in 88.

DREAM WEAVER		2	27 MAR 76	WARNER
LOVE IS ALIVE		2	31 JUL 76	WARNER

WURZELS

West Country (UK) comedy folk pop group who first charted in 67 with their original lead singer Adge Cutler (who died in a car crash in 74). The trio Tommy Banner, Tony Baylis and Pete Budd's 'country yokel' parodies gave them three UK-only Top 40s. They were also on CBS, Dingles, JM, Far End, Goldliner and Fire.

COMBINE HARVESTER (BRAND NEW KEY)		1(2)	12 JUN 76	EMI
(Parody of Melanie hit)				
I AM A CIDER DRINKER (PALOMA BLANCA)		3	25 SEP 76	EMI
(Parody of George Baker Selection hit)				

TAMMY WYNETTE

'The First Lady Of Country Music' was born Virginia Pugh in Mississippi. She had the first of 65 country hits (including 20 No. 1s) in 66. She was married to top country star George Jones from 68-75 and they had many hit duets. In 81 a TV movie of her life 'Stand By Your Man' was made. Pop-wise she had 1 US (3 UK) Top 40s and three UK-only Top 40 LPs.

STAND BY YOUR MAN *(US No. 19 in 68)*		1(3)	17 MAY 75	EPIC
(Re-issue – first female country act to top UK chart)				

MARK WYNTER

London based clean cut pop singer had four UK-only Top 20s in the early 60s with versions of US hit songs. He later successfully went into acting and became a children's TV presenter.

VENUS IN BLUE JEANS *(Jimmy Clanton 62 US hit)*		5	26 OCT 62	PYE
GO AWAY LITTLE GIRL		10	11 JAN 63	PYE
(Steve Lawrence 62 US hit -co-written Carole King)				

X

XTC

Wiltshire based art pop band evolved from The Helium Kidz and featured singer/songwriter Andy Partridge. Their first release '3 D' came out in 77. They had the first of their nine UK-only hit 45s with their fifth release. They have had nine UK (2 US) chart LPs. They have also recorded recently as The Dukes of Stratosphear.

SENSES WORKING OVERTIME		10	20 FEB 82	VIRGIN

Y

YARBROUGH & PEOPLES

Dallas soul duo Calvin Yarbrough (ex Grand Theft) and Alisa Peoples who had sung in church together formed their own act in 77. The Gap Band helped them get a deal and they have now had seven black music Top 20s and a transatlantic Top 10. They joined Total Experience in 82.

DON'T STOP THE MUSIC *(US No. 19)*		7	31 JAN 81	MERCURY

YARDBIRDS

Successful and influential 60s UK R&B psychedelic pop band evolved from The Metropolitan Blues Quartet and included singer Keith Relf and Jim McCarty and for a time guitarists Eric Clapton, Jeff Beck and Jimmy Page. After seven UK (9 US) charters they split in 68. Keith formed Renaissance and unfortunately died in 76. McCarty formed Box Of Frogs in 83 and was in the British Invasion All Stars in 89. Jimmy formed the New Yardbirds which became Led Zeppelin and Jeff and Eric went on to become solo superstars.

FOR YOUR LOVE		2	17 APR 65	COLUMBIA
HEART FULL OF SOUL		2	10 JUL 65	COLUMBIA
EVIL HEARTED YOU/STILL I'M SAD		3	06 NOV 65	COLUMBIA
(A-side and above two hits comp. Graham Gouldman)				
THE SHAPE OF THINGS *(US No. 11)*		3	26 MAR 66	COLUMBIA
(Keith did a solo 'Shapes In My Mind' that year)				
OVER UNDER SIDEWAYS DOWN *(US No. 13)*		10	18 JUN 66	COLUMBIA
FOR YOUR LOVE		6	03 JUL 65	EPIC
HEART FULL OF SOUL		9	25 SEP 65	EPIC

Also see Eric Clapton/Led Zeppelin

YAZOO

Keyboard/synth wizard and songwriter Vince Clarke formed this duo with Alison 'Alf' Moyet (ex-The Vicars and The Screaming Abdabs) after he left Depeche Mode. In their 18 months together they scored four UK-only Top 20s and both their LPs made the Top 2 UK chart spots. Alison became a top UK solo artist and Vince scored in Assembly and the very successful Erasure.

ONLY YOU *(US No. 67 – were called Yaz there)*		2	22 MAY 82	MUTE
(B-side 'Situation' was US No. 73)				
DON'T GO		3	31 JUL 82	MUTE
NOBODY'S DIARY		3	11 JUN 83	MUTE

Also see Alison Moyet/Assembly/Depeche Mode/Erasure

YAZZ

London based singer, model and dancer Yasmin Evans first scored when fronting Coldcut's biggest hit. She was voted most promising new singer of 88 in the UK. In just 14 months she chalked up five UK-only Top 20s – her biggest being a revival of an Otis Clay soul song.

DOCTORIN' THE HOUSE *(With COLDCUT)*		6	12 MAR 88	AHEAD OF OUR TIME
(Feat. The Plastic Population – US Dance No. 3)				
THE ONLY WAY IS UP *(US No. 96 & US dance No. 2)*		1(5)	06 AUG 88	BIG LIFE
(Feat. The Plastic Population – jumped from 10-1)				
STAND UP FOR YOUR LOVE RIGHTS		2	19 NOV 88	BIG LIFE
FINE TIME		9	18 FEB 89	BIG LIFE

YELLO

Switzerland's top group are Dieter Meiler, Boris Blank and Carlos Peron. The unpredictable trio had their first release in 79 and the first of their eight UK (1 US) charters in 83 with 'I Love You' (the world's first 3D picture disc). They have also been on Do It, Stiff and Elektra.

	THE RACE (Their 12th UK single)	7	24 SEP 88	MERCURY

YELLOW DOG

UK based group evolved from the hit act Fox and featured US singer/songwriter Kenny Young (who had written many hits and had been on MGM in 63) and Herbie Armstrong. They followed their sole Top 40 hit with 'Wait Until Midnight'. They recorded three LPs and were on Escape in 81.

	JUST ONE MORE NIGHT	8	04 MAR 78	VIRGIN

YES

A top progressive UK rock band for two decades. Yes men have included Jon Anderson (previously recorded solo and in The Warriors on Decca), Steve Howe (ex-Tomorrow), Rick Wakeman (ex-Strawbs) and Trevor Horn (ex-Buggles). The LP orientated act who have had many personnel and direction changes have scored 11 UK & US Top 20 LPs with 4 UK (5 US) Top 40 singles. Many members of this stadium-filling group have also recorded successfully outside of Yes. In 89 two sets of ex-members had legal battles over the name resulting in the re-naming of one to Anderson, Bruford, Wakeman & Howe.

	WONDROUS STORIES	7	08 OCT 77	ATLANTIC
	OWNER OF A LONELY HEART (UK No. 28 – Produced by Trevor Horn)	1(2)	21 JAN 84	ATCO

Also see Asia/Jon & Vangelis/Strawbs/Buggles

DENNIS YOST – SEE CLASSICS IV FOR HIT DETAILS

YOUNG M.C.

UK born and New York raised rapper with a degree in economics, co-wrote Tone-Loc's first two smash hits. This respected rap Grammy winner who started recording solo in 88 signed a lucrative deal to promote Pepsi in 90.

	BUST A MOVE (UK No. 73 – No. 1 in Canada) (This track first released in US in June 89)	7	14 OCT 89	DELICIOUS VIN

YOUNG ONES – SEE CLIFF RICHARD FOR HIT DETAILS

YOUNG RASCALS – SEE RASCALS FOR HIT DETAILS

FARON YOUNG

Very successful Louisiana country singer who first recorded on Gotham in 51 and has since had 88 country hits including 53 Top 20s. He appeared in many country films and started the top magazine Music City News. Pop-wise 'The Young Sheriff' has had just one Top 40 in the UK and US ('Hello Walls' US 12 in 61). He has also recorded on Capitol, MCA and Step One.

	IT'S FOUR IN THE MORNING (US No. 92)	3	16 SEP 72	MERCURY

JOHN PAUL YOUNG

Glasgow born, Liverpool (the one in Australia) based pop singer had his first local hit with 'Pasadena' and charted in the US with 'Yesterday's Hero' on Ariola America in 75. Eight 45s and 3 LPs later he had his sole Transatlantic Top 40 which he followed in the US with 'Lost In Your Love'.

	LOVE IS IN THE AIR (Produced & composed by Vanda & Young (Easybeats)	5	03 JUN 78	ARIOLA
	LOVE IS IN THE AIR	7	14 OCT 78	SCOTTI BROS

KAREN YOUNG

Sheffield based MOR/cabaret singer was discovered by The Bachelors in 62. She recorded on Pye in 65 and Philips in 67. Her sixth single was her only chart record and she followed it with 'Allentown Jail'.

	NOBODY'S CHILD	6	18 OCT 69	MAJOR MINOR

KATHY YOUNG WITH THE INNOCENTS

Californian pop star had her biggest of two US-only Top 40s when she was just 15. She was backed by a trio, featuring Jim West, who had previously recorded as The Echoes on Andex in 59. She later recorded on Monogram (inc. a duet with Chris Montez) and Starfire and they went to Decca in 63.

	A THOUSAND STARS (Original by The Rivileers)	3	12 DEC 60	INDIGO

NEIL YOUNG

Critically acclaimed Canadian singer/songwriter recorded in The Mynah Birds (with Rick James) in 65 before moving to California and forming the influential Buffalo Springfield with Steve Stills in 66. In 69 he joined the ultra-successful Crosby, Stills, Nash and Young and also made his first solo records. On his own (and often with his group Crazy Horse) he has recorded in many musical styles and has had 15 US (9 UK) Top 40 LPs. The holder of 11 gold LPs, he was sued by his label Geffen in 83 for $3 million for not making commercial enough records. While many of his peers have lacked direction, Young retains an ability to surprise.

	HEART OF GOLD	10	15 APR 72	REPRISE
	HEART OF GOLD	1(1)	18 MAR 72	REPRISE

PAUL YOUNG

Luton (UK) born singer/songwriter first recorded and charted in Street-band on Logo in 78. From 79-82 he fronted the Chrysalis group The Q-Tips. His third solo 45 was the first of seven UK (2 US) Top 20s and three UK (1 US) Top 20 LP including the seven million selling 'No Parlez'. He won BRITS awards two years running, appeared in 'Live Aid' and the first Nelson Mandela show. In 90 he was back in the charts with 'Softly Whispering I Love You' and 'Oh Girl'.

	WHEREVER I LAY MY HAT (THAT'S MY HOME) (US No. 70 – Original by Marvin Gaye)	1(3)	23 JUL 83	CBS
	COME BACK AND STAY (US No. 22) (Composed by Jack Lee of The Nerves)	4	24 SEP 83	CBS
	LOVE OF THE COMMON PEOPLE (US No. 45) (Re-issue of his second 45 – Orig. Waylon Jennings)	2	03 DEC 83	CBS
	I'M GONNA TEAR YOUR PLAYHOUSE DOWN (US No. 13 – Ann Peebles 73 R&B hit)	9	20 OCT 84	CBS
	EVERYTHING MUST CHANGE (US No. 56)	9	22 DEC 84	CBS
	EVERYTIME YOU GO AWAY (Originally by Hall & Oates)	4	23 MAR 85	CBS
	EVERYTIME YOU GO AWAY	1(1)	27 JUL 85	COLUMBIA

YOUNG-HOLT UNLIMITED

Jazzy soul instrumental group formed by bass player Eldee Young and drummer Isaac 'Red' Holt who had both spent 10 years in the hit Ramsey Lewis Trio. They had their first of two US-only Top 40s in 66 with 'Wack Wack'. In 74 Isaac left and formed Red Holt Unlimited on Paula.

	SOULFUL STRUT	3	18 JAN 69	BRUNSWICK

Also see Ramsey Lewis Trio

SYDNEY YOUNGBLOOD

Seventies styled soul singer/songwriter and multi-instrumentlist Sydney Ford was in the US forces stationed in Germany before coming to the UK and first recording on Circa in 88. To date he has had two UK-only Top 20s – the other being 'Sit and Wait'(16). He works with the NT Gang (Youngblood Posse, Souly M and Serious Genius).

 IF ONLY I COULD   3   07 OCT 89   CIRCA

YOUNGBLOODS

New Yorker Jesse Colin Young (Perry Miller) who led this Californian based folk rock group originally recorded solo on Capitol in 64 and Mercury (the label the group were on first). They were later on Racoon, had a handful of small US hits and disbanded in 72. Jesse had eight solo US-only LP chart entries over the next six years on Warner and Elektra.

 GET TOGETHER *(Was also US No. 62 in 67)*   5   06 SEP 69   RCA

YOUNG IDEA

UK duo Tony Cox and Douglas MacCrae-Brown first recorded on Columbia in 65 and their sole charter came with their fourth 45 – a cover of a Beatles LP track that was a bigger hit for Joe Cocker a year later. Their follow up was 'Mister Lovin' Luggage Man'.

 WITH A LITTLE HELP FROM MY FRIENDS   10   22 JUL 67   COLUMBIA

TIMI YURO

Soulful white female singer from Chicago first recorded for Liberty in 59. She had 11 US-only charters including the 'What's A Matter Baby' (12) in 62. She was also on Mercury in 64 and Playboy in 75 and when 'Hurt' returned and topped the Dutch chart in 81 she returned too and signed to Polydor.

 HURT *(Roy Hamilton 54 R&B hit)*   4   11 SEP 61   LIBERTY

Z

HELMUT ZACHARIAS ORCHESTRA

Noted German orchestra leader and violinist had his sole US hit in 56 with 'When The Lilacs Bloom Again' (19). His only UK hit came with an instrumental Olympic games theme. In the Olympic vein he later had 'Mexico Melody', 'Munich Melody' and 'Moscow Melody'.

 TOKYO MELODY   9   21 NOV 64   POLYDOR

ZAGER & EVANS

Nebraska pop rock duo Denny Zager and Rick Evans had both been in The Eccentrics in 62 and Denny was also in The Devilles in 65. Together they had just the one hit, recorded at ex-Cricket Tommy Allsup's studio, which sold over four million world-wide. Follow up was 'Mister Turn Key'. They joined Vanguard in 71 and Rick later recorded solo on his own label.

 IN THE YEAR 2525 (EXORDIUM & TERMINUS)   1(3)   30 AUG 69   RCA
(Written by Rick Evans in 04)

IN THE YEAR 2525 (EXORDIUM & TERMINUS)   1(6)   12 JUL 69   RCA
(Originally released on their own Truth label)

MICHAEL ZAGER BAND

New Jersey composer/arranger/pianist was in Genya Ravan's Ten Wheel Drive from 68-73. He then worked with acts like Peabo Bryson, The Spinners, Andrea True and Cissy Houston. With session musicians he formed his own disco band and he followed his one transatlantic hit with 'Freak'/'Soul to Soul'. The band were also on Bang and Capitol, Columbia and EMI.

 LET'S ALL CHANT *(US No. 36)*   8   13 MAY 78   PRIVATE STOCK

GEORGHE ZAMFIR

Top Romanian pan-pipe player had a surprise UK one-off hit with an instrumental version of a traditional Eastern funeral piece.

 (LIGHT OF EXPERIENCE) DOINA DE JALE   4   18 SEP 76   EPIC
(Used in the BBC TV series 'Light of Experience')

LENA ZAVARONI

Whilst still only 10 this Scottish MOR pop singer had two UK-only Top 40s and a Top 10 LP thanks to her appearances on TV's Opportunity Knocks. In the US her hit was the last record Stax really pushed before they went out of business. She has often been seen on TV since, works in cabaret and has since recorded on BBC, Galaxy and President.

 MA HE'S MAKING EYES AT ME *(US No. 91)*   10   02 MAR 74   PHILIPS
(Dick Robertson 40 hit)

ZOMBIES

Pop rock quintet formed in Hertfordshire included singer Colin Blunstone and keyboard player Rod Argent. Their first 45 was the biggest of their five US (2 UK) charters. They joined CBS in 67 and broke up later that year. In 69, when an old track became a US smash, they briefly recorded again. Colin later had solo UK hits and Rod scored in Argent and as a producer.

 SHE'S NOT THERE *(UK No. 12)*   2   12 DEC 64   PARROT
(Colin re-recorded it as Neil MacArthur in 70)

TELL HER NO *(UK No. 42)*   6   27 FEB 65   PARROT

TIME OF THE SEASON   3   29 MAR 69   DATE

Also see Argent

ZZ TOP

Inimitable boogie rock band from Texas are Billy Gibbons (ex Moving Sidewalks), Dusty Hill & Frank Beard who both recorded in The Warlocks (on Paradise and Ara) a.k.a. American Blues. The trio first recorded in 69 on Scat and first hit in 72 on London. They have had six US (2 UK) Top 20 LPs and seven US (5 UK) Top 40 singles. Known for their 'car' videos, long beards and record breaking tours they only really hit in the UK in 83 a decade after the US.

GIMME ALL YOUR LOVIN' *(US No. 37)*   10   17 NOV 84   WARNER
(Was UK No. 61 in 83 – had award winning video)

LEGS *(UK No. 16)*   8   21 JUL 84   WARNER

SLEEPING BAG *(UK No. 27)*   8   14 DEC 85   WARNER

TOP ARTISTS

The top artists are calculated by giving 20 points to a single that reaches No. 1, 19 to a record that peaks at No. 2 down to 11 points for a record whose peak position is No. 10. A bonus 2 points are also given to singles that peak between 6–10 and a bonus three points for a record that peaks between 1–5 and finally the number of weeks a record may spend at No. 1 are added to the total. In cases where two (or more) acts share the same total points, the one with the most Top 10s is listed first, if both have the same number of Top 10 hits then the one with the most Top 20s is listed first.

The combined UK and US chart is not meant to reflect total sales as obviously American hits sell in larger quantities. It is solely meant to give a picture of the most popular transatlantic acts of the period involved.

NB If points from the 1950s were included then Elvis Presley would top the UK, US and combined total points charts covering the 50–90 period.

TOP ARTISTS IN THE UK IN THE 60s

NAME OF ACT	POINTS
1. CLIFF RICHARD	692
2. BEATLES	567
3. ELVIS PRESLEY	472
4. ROLLING STONES	300
5. HOLLIES	295
6. SHADOWS	295
7. MANFRED MANN	262
8. KINKS	220
9. ROY ORBISON	214
10. ADAM FAITH	208
11. BEACH BOYS	195
12. CILLA BLACK	192
13. TOM JONES	185
14. GENE PITNEY	184
15. BILLY FURY	180
16. ENGELBERT HUMPERDINCK	178
17. EVERLY BROTHERS	173
18. DUSTY SPRINGFIELD	170
19. SANDIE SHAW	167
20. HERMAN'S HERMITS	165
21. WHO	165
22. DAVE DEE, DOZY, BEAKY, MICK & TITCH	156
23. BACHELORS	153
24. DEL SHANNON	151
25. ANIMALS	147
26. FRANK IFIELD	144
27. SEARCHERS	139
28. SUPREMES	135
29. SMALL FACES	135
30. GERRY & THE PACEMAKERS	133
31. DONOVAN	131
32. SEEKERS	128
33. PETULA CLARK	126
34. TREMELOES	122
35. BEE GEES	119
36. DAVE CLARK FIVE	117
37. BOBBY DARIN	116
38. JIM REEVES	116
39. BOBBY VEE	114
40. SHIRLEY BASSEY	113

TOP FEMALE SOLO ARTISTS IN THE US IN THE 60s

NAME OF ACT	POINTS
1. BRENDA LEE	236
2. CONNIE FRANCIS	201
3. ARETHA FRANKLIN	161
4. PETULA CLARK	125
5. DIONNE WARWICK	118
6. NANCY SINATRA	86
7. LESLEY GORE	85
8. MARY WELLS	70
9. DEE DEE SHARP	68
10. TAMMI TERRELL	63

TOP MALE SOLO ARTISTS IN THE UK IN THE 60s

NAME OF ACT	POINTS
1. CLIFF RICHARD	692
2. ELVIS PRESLEY	472
3. ROY ORBISON	214
4. ADAM FAITH	208
5. TOM JONES	185
6. GENE PITNEY	184
7. BILLY FURY	180
8. ENGELBERT HUMPERDINCK	178
9. DEL SHANNON	151
10. FRANK IFIELD	144
11. DONOVAN	131
12. BOBBY DARIN	116
13. JIM REEVES	116
14. BOBBY VEE	114
15. DUANE EDDY	111
16. ANTHONY NEWLEY	105
17. BOB DYLAN	100
18. FRANK SINATRA	100
19. VAL DOONICAN	99
20. EDEN KANE	92

TOP MALE SOLO ARTISTS IN THE US IN THE 60s

NAME OF ACT	POINTS
1. ELVIS PRESLEY	357
2. RAY CHARLES	196
3. MARVIN GAYE	189
4. ROY ORBISON	177
5. DION	172
6. BOBBY VINTON	170
7. STEVIE WONDER	169
8. CHUBBY CHECKER	162
9. JOHNNY RIVERS	131
10. BOBBY VEE	124
11. BOBBY DARIN	106
12. TOMMY ROE	104
13. JAMES BROWN	97
14. NEIL SEDAKA	95
15. BOBBY RYDELL	94
16. BROOK BENTON	94
17. GARY U.S BONDS	89
18. JACKIE WILSON	85
19. ROGER MILLER	81
20. DONOVAN	81

TOP ARTISTS IN THE US IN THE 60s

NAME OF ACT	POINTS
1. BEATLES	679
2. SUPREMES	401
3. ELVIS PRESLEY	357
4. BEACH BOYS	257
5. FOUR SEASONS	255
6. ROLLING STONES	248
7. BRENDA LEE	236
8. HERMAN'S HERMITS	216
9. TEMPTATIONS	215
10. CONNIE FRANCIS	201
11. RAY CHARLES	196
12. MARVIN GAYE	189
13. ROY ORBISON	177
14. DION	172
15. BOBBY VINTON	170
16. STEVIE WONDER	169
17. CHUBBY CHECKER	162
18. ARETHA FRANKLIN	161
19. DAVE CLARK FIVE	154
20. MONKEES	145
21. TOMMY JAMES & THE SHONDELLS	140
22. GARY LEWIS & THE PLAYBOYS	139
23. EVERLY BROTHERS	137
24. JOHNNY RIVERS	131
25. SHIRELLES	127
26. PETULA CLARK	125
27. LOVIN' SPOONFUL	125
28. MAMAS & THE PAPAS	125
29. BOBBY VEE	124
30. DIONNE WARWICK	118
31. PETER, PAUL & MARY	110
32. SIMON & GARFUNKEL	107
33. BOBBY DARIN	106
34. FOUR TOPS	106
35. TOMMY ROE	104
36. RIGHTEOUS BROTHERS	104
37. ASSOCIATION	104
38. MARTHA & THE VANDELLAS	99
39. JAMES BROWN	97
40. TURTLES	96

TOP FEMALE SOLO ARTISTS IN THE UK IN THE 60s

NAME OF ACT	POINTS
1. CILLA BLACK	192
2. DUSTY SPRINGFIELD	170
3. SANDIE SHAW	167
4. PETULA CLARK	126
5. SHIRLEY BASSEY	113
6. HELEN SHAPIRO	109
7. BRENDA LEE	104
8. CONNIE FRANCIS	99
9. LULU	98
10. NANCY SINATRA	66

TOP GROUPS IN THE UK IN THE 60s

NAME OF ACT	POINTS
1. BEATLES	567
2. ROLLING STONES	300
3. HOLLIES	295
4. SHADOWS	295
5. MANFRED MANN	262
6. KINKS	220
7. BEACH BOYS	195
8. EVERLY BROTHERS	173
9. HERMAN'S HERMITS	165
10. WHO	165
11. DAVE DEE, DOZY, BEAKY, MICK &TITCH	156
12. BACHELORS	153
13. ANIMALS	147
14. SEARCHERS	139
15. SUPREMES	135
16. SMALL FACES	135
17. GERRY & THE PACEMAKERS	133
18. SEEKERS	128
19. TREMELOES	122
20. BEE GEES	119

TOP GROUPS IN THE US IN THE 60s

NAME OF ACT	POINTS
1. BEATLES	679
2. SUPREMES	379
3. BEACH BOYS	257
4. FOUR SEASONS	255
5. ROLLING STONES	248
6. HERMAN'S HERMITS	216
7. TEMPTATIONS	193
8. DAVE CLARK FIVE	154
9. MONKEES	145
10. TOMMY JAMES & THE SHONDELLS	140
11. GARY LEWIS & THE PLAYBOYS	139
12. EVERLY BROTHERS	137
13. SHIRELLES	127
14. LOVIN' SPOONFUL	125
15. MAMAS & THE PAPAS	125
16. PETER, PAUL & MARY	110
17. SIMON & GARFUNKEL	107
18. FOUR TOPS	106
19. RIGHTEOUS BROTHERS	104
20. ASSOCIATION	104

TOP GROUP IN THE UK & US COMBINED IN THE 60s

NAME OF ACT	POINTS
1. BEATLES	1,246
2. ROLLING STONES	548
3. SUPREMES	535
4. BEACH BOYS	452
5. HERMAN'S HERMITS	381
6. HOLLIES	344
7. FOUR SEASONS	313
8. EVERLY BROTHERS	310
9. MANFRED MANN	300
10. SHADOWS	295
11. DAVE CLARK FIVE	271
12. KINKS	269
13. MONKEES	234
14. TEMPTATIONS	227
15. FOUR TOPS	201
16. GERRY & THE PACEMAKERS	184
17. MAMAS & THE PAPAS	182
18. WHO	179
19. ANIMALS	173
20. SIMON & GARFUNKEL	172

TOP ARTISTS IN THE US & UK COMBINED IN THE 60s

NAME OF ACT	POINTS
1. BEATLES	1,246
2. ELVIS PRESLEY	829
3. CLIFF RICHARD	692
4. ROLLING STONES	548
5. SUPREMES	535
6. BEACH BOYS	452
7. ROY ORBISON	391
8. HERMAN'S HERMITS	381
9. HOLLIES	344
10. BRENDA LEE	340
11. FOUR SEASONS	313
12. EVERLY BROTHERS	310
13. CONNIE FRANCIS	300
14. MANFRED MANN	300
15. SHADOWS	295
16. RAY CHARLES	278
17. DAVE CLARK FIVE	271
18. KINKS	269
19. GENE PITNEY	256
20. PETULA CLARK	251
21. STEVIE WONDER	251
22. MARVIN GAYE	248
23. BOBBY VEE	238
24. TOM JONES	236
25. MONKEES	234
26. TEMPTATIONS	227
27. BOBBY DARIN	222
28. DUSTY SPRINGFIELD	220
29. DONOVAN	212
30. DEL SHANNON	211
31. ADAM FAITH	208
32. FOUR TOPS	201
33. CHUBBY CHECKER	201
34. ENGELBERT HUMPERDINCK	198
35. ARETHA FRANKLIN	194
36. CILLA BLACK	192
37. DION	185
38. GERRY & THE PACEMAKERS	184
39. MAMAS & THE PAPAS	182
40. BILLY FURY	180

TOP MALE SOLO ARTIST IN US & UK COMBINED IN THE 60s

NAME OF ACT	POINTS
1. ELVIS PRESLEY	829
2. CLIFF RICHARD	692
3. ROY ORBISON	391
4. RAY CHARLES	278
5. GENE PITNEY	256
6. STEVIE WONDER	251
7. MARVIN GAYE	248
8. BOBBY VEE	238
9. TOM JONES	236
10. BOBBY DARIN	222
11. DONOVAN	212
12. DEL SHANNON	211
13. ADAM FAITH	208
14. CHUBBY CHECKER	201
15. ENGELBERT HUMPERDINCK	198
16. DION	185
17. BILLY FURY	180
18. BOB DYLAN	176
19. FRANK SINATRA	171

TOP FEMALE SOLO ARTISTS IN THE UK & US COMBINED IN THE 60s

NAME OF ACT	POINTS
1. BRENDA LEE	340
2. CONNIE FRANCIS	300
3. PETULA CLARK	251
4. DUSTY SPRINGFIELD	220
5. ARETHA FRANKLIN	194
6. CILLA BLACK	192
7. SANDIE SHAW	167
8. NANCY SINATRA	152
9. DIONNE WARWICK	147
10. SHIRLEY BASSEY	113

TOP ARTISTS IN THE UK IN THE 70s

NAME OF ACT	POINTS
1. ABBA	349
2. ELVIS PRESLEY	339
3. ROD STEWART	325
4. SLADE	301
5. PAUL McCARTNEY	251
6. T. REX	237
7. GARY GLITTER	237
8. DAVID BOWIE	224
9. MUD	216
10. ELECTRIC LIGHT ORCHESTRA	212
11. BAY CITY ROLLERS	210
12. 10CC	209
13. SHOWADDYWADDY	209
14. SWEET	206
15. ELTON JOHN	188
16. BONEY M	185
17. STYLISTICS	182
18. DIANA ROSS	171
19. BEE GEES	164
20. QUEEN	163
21. LEO SAYER	159
22. STATUS QUO	158
23. OLIVIA NEWTON-JOHN	154
24. HOT CHOCOLATE	146
25. DAVID ESSEX	145
26. DRIFTERS	142
27. DONNA SUMMER	140
28. DONNY OSMOND	138
29. GILBERT O'SULLIVAN	137
30. NEW SEEKERS	134
31. SEX PISTOLS	129
32. BLONDIE	129
33. CARPENTERS	124
34. WIZZARD	120
35. DARTS	113
36. CHI-LITES	112
37. ROXY MUSIC	111
38. ROLLING STONES	111
39. OSMONDS	109
40. MICHAEL JACKSON	108

TOP FEMALE SOLO ARTISTS IN THE UK IN THE 70s

NAME OF ACT	POINTS
1. DIANA ROSS	171
2. OLIVIA NEWTON-JOHN	154
3. DONNA SUMMER	140
4. SUZI QUATRO	106
5. TINA CHARLES	63
6. BARBRA STREISAND	61
7. DENIECE WILLIAMS	61
8. DANA	60
9. KATE BUSH	57
10. GLORIA GAYNOR	49

TOP MALE SOLO ARTISTS IN THE UK IN THE 70s

NAME OF ACT	POINTS
1. ELVIS PRESLEY	339
2. ROD STEWART	325
3. PAUL McCARTNEY	251
4. GARY GLITTER	237
5. DAVID BOWIE	224
6. ELTON JOHN	188
7. LEO SAYER	159
8. DAVID ESSEX	145
9. DONNY OSMOND	139
10. GILBERT O'SULLIVAN	137
11. MICHAEL JACKSON	108
12. DAVID CASSIDY	108
13. BARRY WHITE	95
14. DAVID SOUL	90
16. STEVIE WONDER	87
17. RAY STEVENS	85
18. JOHN TRAVOLTA	84
19. DAVE EDMUNDS	83
20. GLEN CAMPBELL	81

TOP GROUPS IN THE UK IN THE 70s

NAME OF ACT	POINTS
1. ABBA	349
2. SLADE	301
3. T. REX	237
4. MUD	216
5. ELECTRIC LIGHT ORCHESTRA	212
6. BAY CITY ROLLERS	210
7. 10CC	209
8. SHOWADDYWADDY	209
9. SWEET	206
10. BONEY M	185
11. STYLISTICS	182
12. BEE GEES	164
13. QUEEN	163
14. STATUS QUO	158
15. HOT CHOCOLATE	146
16. DRIFTERS	142
17. NEW SEEKERS	134
18. SEX PISTOLS	129
19. BLONDIE	129
20. CARPENTERS	124

TOP MALE SOLO ARTISTS IN THE US IN THE 70s

NAME OF ACT	POINTS
1. ELTON JOHN	336
2. PAUL McCARTNEY	309
3. STEVIE WONDER	248
4. BARRY MANILOW	179
5. JOHN DENVER	152
6. RINGO STARR	139
7. AL GREEN	128
8. MARVIN GAYE	121
9. BARRY WHITE	118
10. ANDY GIBB	115
11. NEIL DIAMOND	112
12. PAUL SIMON	109
13. ROD STEWART	106
14. JAMES TAYLOR	103
15. DONNY OSMOND	92
16. JIM CROCE	92
17. BILLY PRESTON	91
18. MICHAEL JACKSON	90
19. JOHN LENNON	80
20. GORDON LIGHTFOOT	78

TOP GROUPS IN THE US IN THE 70s

NAME OF ACT	POINTS
1. BEE GEES	292
2. CARPENTERS	264
3. CHICAGO	215
4. JACKSON FIVE	181
5. EAGLES	176
6. THREE DOG NIGHT	174
7. COMMODORES	143
8. WAR	123
9. CAPTAIN & TENNILLE	121
10. GLADYS KNIGHT & THE PIPS	121
11. KC & THE SUNSHINE BAND	119
12. AMERICA	118
13. ROLLING STONES	117
14. BREAD	111
15. EARTH, WIND & FIRE	111
16. O'JAYS	111
17. SPINNERS	106
18. TEMPTATIONS	102
19. CREEDENCE CLEARWATER REVIVAL	96
20. TONY ORLANDO & DAWN	95

TOP ARTISTS IN THE US IN THE 70s

NAME OF ACT	POINTS
1. ELTON JOHN	336
2. PAUL McCARTNEY	309
3. BEE GEES	292
4. CARPENTERS	264
5. STEVIE WONDER	248
6. CHICAGO	215
7. DONNA SUMMER	207
8. OLIVIA NEWTON-JOHN	191
9. JACKSON FIVE	181
10. BARRY MANILOW	179
11. EAGLES	176
12. THREE DOG NIGHT	174
13. BARBRA STREISAND	160
14. JOHN DENVER	152
15. COMMODORES	143
16. RINGO STARR	139
17. AL GREEN	128
18. WAR	123
19. HELEN REDDY	122
20. ROBERTA FLACK	122
21. CAPTAIN & TENNILLE	121
22. GLADYS KNIGHT & THE PIPS	121
23. MARVIN GAYE	121
24. LINDA RONSTADT	121
25. KC & THE SUNSHINE BAND	119
26. AMERICA	118
27. BARRY WHITE	118
28. ROLLING STONES	117
29. ANDY GIBB	115
30. NEIL DIAMOND	112
31. BREAD	111
32. EARTH, WIND & FIRE	111
33. O'JAYS	111
34. PAUL SIMON	109
35. SPINNERS	106
36. ROD STEWART	106
37. CHER	105
38. JAMES TAYLOR	103
39. TEMPTATIONS	102
40. DIANA ROSS	99

TOP FEMALE SOLO ARTISTS IN THE US IN THE 70s

NAME OF ACT	POINTS
1. DONNA SUMMER	207
2. OLIVIA NEWTON-JOHN	191
3. BARBRA STREISAND	160
4. HELEN REDDY	122
5. ROBERTA FLACK	122
6. LINDA RONSTADT	121
7. CHER	105
8. DIANA ROSS	99
9. CARLY SIMON	97
10. ARETHA FRANKLIN	93

TOP ARTISTS IN THE US & UK COMBINED IN THE 70s

NAME OF ACT	POINTS
1. PAUL McCARTNEY	560
2. ELTON JOHN	524
3. BEE GEES	456
4. ROD STEWART	434
5. ABBA	411
6. ELVIS PRESLEY	399
7. CARPENTERS	388
8. DONNA SUMMER	347
9. OLIVIA NEWTON-JOHN	345
10. STEVIE WONDER	335
11. SLADE	301
12. ELECTRIC LIGHT ORCHESTRA	290
13. JACKSON FIVE	282
14. SWEET	280
15. CHICAGO	272
16. DIANA ROSS	270
17. DAVID BOWIE	262
18. BAY CITY ROLLERS	261
19. GARY GLITTER	253
20. T. REX	250
21. STYLISTICS	239
22. DONNY OSMOND	231
23. ROLLING STONES	228
24. LEO SAYER	221
25. BARBRA STREISAND	221
26. COMMODORES	220
27. MUD	216
28. RINGO STARR	216
29. BARRY WHITE	213
30. SHOWADDYWADDY	209
31. GILBERT O'SULLIVAN	204
32. HOT CHOCOLATE	199
33. MICHAEL JACKSON	198
34. QUEEN	197
35. THREE DOG NIGHT	195
36. EAGLES	191
37. OSMONDS	191
38. GLADYS KNIGHT & THE PIPS	190
39. NEIL DIAMOND	187
40. TONY ORLANDO & DAWN	185

TOP SOLO FEMALE ARTISTS IN US & UK COMBINED IN THE 70s

NAME OF ACT	POINTS
1. DONNA SUMMER	347
2. OLIVIA NEWTON-JOHN	345
3. DIANA ROSS	270
4. BARBRA STREISAND	221
5. HELEN REDDY	141
6. ROBERTA FLACK	139
7. CARLY SIMON	133
8. SUZI QUATRO	126
9. CHER	125
10. LINDA RONSTADT	121

TOP MALE SOLO ARTISTS IN THE US & UK COMBINED IN THE 70s

NAME OF ACT	POINTS
1. PAUL McCARTNEY	560
2. ELTON JOHN	524
3. ROD STEWART	434
4. ELVIS PRESLEY	399
5. STEVIE WONDER	335
6. DAVID BOWIE	262
7. DONNY OSMOND	231
8. LEO SAYER	221
9. RINGO STARR	216
10. BARRY WHITE	213
11. GILBERT O'SULLIVAN	204
12. MICHAEL JACKSON	198
13. NEIL DIAMOND	187
14. BARRY MANILOW	179
15. JOHN DENVER	176
16. MARVIN GAYE	170
17. AL GREEN	164
18. DAVID ESSEX	164
19. JOHN LENNON	152
20. PAUL SIMON	144

TOP GROUPS IN THE US & UK COMBINED IN THE 70s

NAME OF ACT	POINTS
1. BEE GEES	456
2. ABBA	411
3. CARPENTERS	388
4. SLADE	301
5. ELECTRIC LIGHT ORCHESTRA	290
6. JACKSON FIVE	282
7. SWEET	280
8. CHICAGO	272
9. BAY CITY ROLLERS	261
10. T. REX	250
11. STYLISTICS	239
12. ROLLING STONES	228
13. COMMODORES	220
14. MUD	216
15. SHOWADDYWADDY	209
16. HOT CHOCOLATE	199
17. QUEEN	197
18. THREE DOG NIGHT	195
19. EAGLES	191
20. OSMONDS	191

TOP FEMALE SOLO ARTISTS IN THE UK IN THE 80s

NAME OF ACT	POINTS
1. MADONNA	469
2. KYLIE MINOGUE	186
3. KIM WILDE	156
4. WHITNEY HOUSTON	141
5. DIANA ROSS	119
6. ALISON MOYET	108
7. TINA TURNER	93
8. YAZZ	81
9. SINITTA	79
10. BELINDA CARLISLE	78

TOP ARTISTS IN THE UK IN THE 80s

NAME OF ACT	POINTS
1. MADONNA	469
2. MICHAEL JACKSON	334
3. CLIFF RICHARD	290
4. SHAKIN' STEVENS	283
5. MADNESS	271
6. DURAN DURAN	235
7. DAVID BOWIE	226
8. PHIL COLLINS	220
9. WHAM!	218
10. UB40	217
11. PET SHOP BOYS	210
12. PAUL McCARTNEY	197
13. BANANARAMA	190
14. QUEEN	188
15. STEVIE WONDER	186
16. KYLIE MINOGUE	186
17. SPANDAU BALLET	183
18. JAM	178
19. CULTURE CLUB	177
20. STATUS QUO	170
21. U2	166
22. EURYTHMICS	165
23. KIM WILDE	156
24. ADAM & THE ANTS	154
25. A—HA	153
26. POLICE	152
27. BROS	147
28. HUMAN LEAGUE	141
29. WHITNEY HOUSTON	141
30. TEARS FOR FEARS	140
31. PRINCE	139
32. JASON DONOVAN	139
33. RICK ASTLEY	138
34. GEORGE MICHAEL	135
35. ERASURE	134
36. BUCKS FIZZ	131
37. LIONEL RICHIE	129
38. ELTON JOHN	129
39. STYLE COUNCIL	126
40. FRANKIE GOES TO HOLLYWOOD	126

TOP GROUPS IN THE UK IN THE 80s

NAME OF ACT	POINTS
1. MADNESS	271
2. DURAN DURAN	235
3. WHAM!	218
4. UB40	217
5. PET SHOP BOYS	210
6. BANANARAMA	190
7. QUEEN	188
8. SPANDAU BALLET	183
9. JAM	178
10. CULTURE CLUB	177
11. STATUS QUO	170
12. U2	166
13. EURYTHMICS	165
14. ADAM & THE ANTS	154
15. A—HA	153
16. POLICE	152
17. BROS	147
18. HUMAN LEAGUE	141
19. TEARS FOR FEARS	140
20. ERASURE	134

TOP MALE SOLO ARTISTS IN THE UK IN THE 80s

NAME OF ACT	POINTS
1. MICHAEL JACKSON	334
2. CLIFF RICHARD	290
3. SHAKIN' STEVENS	283
4. DAVID BOWIE	226
5. PHIL COLLINS	220
6. PAUL McCARTNEY	197
7. STEVIE WONDER	186
8. PRINCE	139
9. JASON DONOVAN	139
10. RICK ASTLEY	138
11. GEORGE MICHAEL	135
12. LIONEL RICHIE	129
13. ELTON JOHN	129
14. PAUL YOUNG	116
15. JOHN LENNON	115
16. HOWARD JONES	109
17. NIK KERSHAW	90
18. BILLY OCEAN	85
19. ROD STEWART	84
20. BILLY JOEL	79

TOP ARTISTS IN THE US IN THE 80s

NAME OF ACT	POINTS
1. MADONNA	377
2. MICHAEL JACKSON	366
3. PRINCE	280
4. LIONEL RICHIE	279
5. DARYL HALL & JOHN OATES	251
6. PHIL COLLINS	244
7. HUEY LEWIS & THE NEWS	230
8. WHITNEY HOUSTON	228
9. GEORGE MICHAEL	210
10. DURAN DURAN	189
11. BRUCE SPRINGSTEEN	186
12. KOOL & THE GANG	169
13. AIR SUPPLY	165
14. BILLY JOEL	164
15. CYNDI LAUPER	163
16. RICHARD MARX	158
17. JANET JACKSON	154
18. GLORIA ESTEFAN	153
19. PAUL McCARTNEY	153
20. BILLY OCEAN	151
21. BON JOVI	151
22. DIANA ROSS	149
23. CHICAGO	147
24. JOHN COUGAR MELLENCAMP	141
25. OLIVIA NEWTON—JOHN	134
26. KENNY ROGERS	133
27. NEW KIDS ON THE BLOCK	132
28. STEVIE WONDER	132
29. SHEENA EASTON	128
30. HEART	127
31. GENESIS	123
32. CULTURE CLUB	116
33. ELTON JOHN	115
34. POINTER SISTERS	114
35. POLICE	114
36. BANGLES	114
37. STEVE WINWOOD	113
38. DEBBIE GIBSON	111
39. EXPOSE	106
40. WHAM!	106

TOP SOLO MALE ARTISTS IN THE US IN THE 80s

NAME OF ACT	POINTS
1. MICHAEL JACKSON	366
2. PRINCE	280
3. LIONEL RICHIE	279
4. PHIL COLLINS	244
5. GEORGE MICHAEL	210
6. BRUCE SPRINGSTEEN	186
7. BILLY JOEL	164
8. RICHARD MARX	158
9. PAUL McCARTNEY	153
10. BILLY OCEAN	151
11. JOHN COUGAR MELLENCAMP	141
12. KENNY ROGERS	133
13. STEVIE WONDER	132
13. ELTON JOHN	115
14. STEVE WINWOOD	113
15. ROD STEWART	105
16. RICK SPRINGFIELD	100
17. BOBBY BROWN	97
18. CHRISTOPHER CROSS	86
19. PETER CETERA	86
20. JOHN LENNON	82

TOP GROUPS IN THE US IN THE 80s

NAME OF ACT	POINTS
1. DARYL HALL & JOHN OATES	251
2. HUEY LEWIS & THE NEWS	230
3. DURAN DURAN	189
4. KOOL & THE GANG	169
5. AIR SUPPLY	165
6. BON JOVI	151
7. CHICAGO	147
8. NEW KIDS ON THE BLOCK	132
9. HEART	127
10. GENESIS	123
11. CULTURE CLUB	116
12. POINTER SISTERS	114
13. POLICE	114
14. BANGLES	114
15. EXPOSE	106
16. WHAM!	106
17. FOREIGNER	103
18. INXS	102
19. SURVIVOR	100
20. JOURNEY	99

TOP FEMALE SOLO ARTISTS IN THE US IN THE 80s

NAME OF ACT	POINTS
1. MADONNA	377
2. WHITNEY HOUSTON	228
3. CYNDI LAUPER	163
4. JANET JACKSON	154
5. GLORIA ESTEFAN	153
6. DIANA ROSS	149
7. OLIVIA NEWTON-JOHN	134
8. SHEENA EASTON	128
9. DEBBIE GIBSON	111
10. TINA TURNER	105
11. PAULA ABDUL	96
12. TAYLOR DAYNE	94
13. DONNA SUMMER	90
14. JODY WATLEY	88
15. BELINDA CARLISLE	83
16. TIFFANY	83
17. STEVIE NICKS	77
18. JUICE NEWTON	74
19. LINDA RONSTADT	72
20. CHER	66

TOP ARTISTS IN THE US & UK COMBINED IN THE 80s

NAME OF ACT	POINTS
1. MADONNA	846
2. MICHAEL JACKSON	700
3. PHIL COLLINS	464
4. DURAN DURAN	424
5. PRINCE	419
6. LIONEL RICHIE	408
7. WHITNEY HOUSTON	369
8. PAUL McCARTNEY	350
9. GEORGE MICHAEL	345
10. WHAM!	324
11. CLIFF RICHARD	319
12. STEVIE WONDER	318
13. PET SHOP BOYS	303
14. DAVID BOWIE	294
15. CULTURE CLUB	293
16. MADNESS	287
17. DARYL HALL & JOHN OATES	283
18. SHAKIN' STEVENS	283
19. KOOL & THE GANG	281
20. DIANA ROSS	268
21. POLICE	266
22. BANANARAMA	248
23. ELTON JOHN	244
24. HUEY LEWIS & THE NEWS	244
25. BILLY JOEL	243
26. UB40	241
27. QUEEN	241
28. BRUCE SPRINGSTEEN	239
29. U2	238
30. BILLY OCEAN	236
31. TEARS FOR FEARS	234
32. EURYTHMICS	228
33. CYNDI LAUPER	222
34. RICK ASTLEY	217
35. JANET JACKSON	209
36. KYLIE MINOGUE	207
37. HUMAN LEAGUE	206
38. TINA TURNER	198
39. JOHN LENNON	197
40. ROD STEWART	189

TOP MALE SOLO ARTISTS IN UK & US COMBINED IN THE 80s

NAME OF ACT	POINTS
1. MICHAEL JACKSON	700
2. PHIL COLLINS	464
3. PRINCE	419
4. LIONEL RICHIE	408
5. PAUL McCARTNEY	350
6. GEORGE MICHAEL	345
7. CLIFF RICHARD	319
8. STEVIE WONDER	318
9. DAVID BOWIE	294
10. SHAKIN' STEVENS	283
11. ELTON JOHN	244
12. BILLY JOEL	243
13. BRUCE SPRINGSTEEN	239
14. BILLY OCEAN	236
15. RICK ASTLEY	217
16. JOHN LENNON	197
17. ROD STEWART	189
18. RICHARD MARX	180
19. KENNY ROGERS	174
20. BOBBY BROWN	151

TOP FEMALE SOLO ARTISTS IN THE US & UK COMBINED IN THE 80s

NAME OF ACT	POINTS
1. MADONNA	846
2. WHITNEY HOUSTON	369
3. DIANA ROSS	268
4. CYNDI LAUPER	222
5. JANET JACKSON	209
6. KYLIE MINOGUE	207
7. TINA TURNER	198
8. GLORIA ESTEFAN	187
9. KIM WILDE	180
10. SHEENA EASTON	179
11. OLIVIA NEWTON-JOHN	175
12. BELINDA CARLISLE	161
13. TIFFANY	144
14. DEBBIE GIBSON	141
15. TAYLOR DAYNE	130
16. DONNA SUMMER	127
17. PAULA ABDUL	117
18. IRENE CARA	112
19. LINDA RONSTADT	109
20. ALISON MOYET	108

TOP GROUPS IN THE US & UK COMBINED IN THE 80s

NAME OF ACT	POINTS
1. DURAN DURAN	424
2. WHAM!	324
3. PET SHOP BOYS	303
4. CULTURE CLUB	293
5. MADNESS	287
6. DARYL HALL & JOHN OATES	283
7. KOOL & THE GANG	281
8. POLICE	266
9. BANANARAMA	248
10. HUEY LEWIS & THE NEWS	244
11. UB40	241
12. QUEEN	241
13. U2	238
14. TEARS FOR FEARS	234
15. EURYTHMICS	228
16. HUMAN LEAGUE	206
17. SPANDAU BALLET	203
18. GENESIS	185
19. BANGLES	184
20. CHICAGO	182

TOP ARTISTS IN THE UK BETWEEN 60–90

NAME OF ACT	POINTS
1. CLIFF RICHARD	1,060
2. ELVIS PRESLEY	832
3. BEATLES	637
4. DAVID BOWIE	469
5. MADONNA	469
6. PAUL McCARTNEY	448
7. MICHAEL JACKSON	442
8. ROLLING STONES	441
9. ABBA	437
10. ROD STEWART	409
11. STATUS QUO	359
12. HOLLIES	357
13. STEVIE WONDER	355
14. SLADE	352
15. QUEEN	351
16. SHADOWS	328
17. ELTON JOHN	317
18. TOM JONES	316
19. BEE GEES	310
20. DIANA ROSS	290
21. MADNESS	287
22. SHAKIN' STEVENS	283
23. MANFRED MANN	262
24. KINKS	261
25. ELECTRIC LIGHT ORCHESTRA	257
26. BEACH BOYS	253
27. GARY GLITTER	253
28. SUPREMES	240
29. T. REX	237
30. WHO	236
31. ROY ORBISON	235
32. DURAN DURAN	235
33. HOT CHOCOLATE	229
34. POLICE	224
35. BLONDIE	222
36. PHIL COLLINS	220
37. WHAM!	218
38. UB40	217
39. MUD	216
40. CILLA BLACK	213
41. GENE PITNEY	211
42. PET SHOP BOYS	210
43. BAY CITY ROLLERS	210
44. 10CC	209
45. SHOWADDYWADDY	209
46. JOHN LENNON	209
47. ADAM FAITH	208
48. SWEET	206
49. DAVID ESSEX	202
50. JAM	199
51. FOUR TOPS	198
52. OLIVIA NEWTON-JOHN	195
53. LEO SAYER	194
54. DUSTY SPRINGFIELD	192
55. ROXY MUSIC	191
56. BANANARAMA	190
57. FLEETWOOD MAC	187
58. KYLIE MINOGUE	186
59. BONEY M	185
60. U2	183
61. SPANDAU BALLET	183
62. STYLISTICS	182
63. HERMAN'S HERMITS	180
64. BILLY FURY	180
65. ENGELBERT HUMPERDINCK	178
66. DONNA SUMMER	177
67. CULTURE CLUB	177
68. EVERLY BROTHERS	173
69. SANDIE SHAW	167
70. EURYTHMICS	165
71. DRIFTERS	164
72. KIM WILDE	156
73. DAVE DEE, DOZY, BEAKY, MICK & TITCH	156
74. ADAM & THE ANTS	154
75. A-HA	153
76. BACHELORS	153
77. DEL SHANNON	151
78. SHIRLEY BASSEY	150
79. SMALL FACES	149
80. DAVE CLARK FIVE	148
81. MARMALADE	147
82. BROS	147
83. FRANK IFIELD	144
84. MARVIN GAYE	143
85. TREMELOES	142
86. HUMAN LEAGUE	141
87. WHITNEY HOUSTON	141
88. DUANE EDDY	140
89. TEARS FOR FEARS	140
90. MOVE	140
91. PRINCE	139
92. PETULA CLARK	139
93. ANDY WILLIAMS	139
94. SEARCHERS	139
95. DONNY OSMOND	139
96. JASON DONOVAN	139
97. RICK ASTLEY	138
98. GILBERT O'SULLIVAN	137
99. SPECIALS	137
100. GEORGE MICHAEL	135

TOP MALE SOLO ARTISTS IN THE UK BETWEEN 60–90

NAME OF ACT	POINTS
1. CLIFF RICHARD	1,060
2. ELVIS PRESLEY	832
3. DAVID BOWIE	469
4. PAUL McCARTNEY	448
5. MICHAEL JACKSON	442
6. ROD STEWART	409
7. STEVIE WONDER	355
8. ELTON JOHN	317
9. TOM JONES	316
10. SHAKIN' STEVENS	283
11. GARY GLITTER	253
12. ROY ORBISON	235
13. PHIL COLLINS	220
14. GENE PITNEY	211
15. JOHN LENNON	209
16. ADAM FAITH	208
17. DAVID ESSEX	202
18. LEO SAYER	194
19. BILLY FURY	180
20. ENGELBERT HUMPERDINCK	178
21. DEL SHANNON	151
22. FRANK IFIELD	144
23. MARVIN GAYE	143
24. DUANE EDDY	140
25. PRINCE	139
26. ANDY WILLIAMS	139
27. DONNY OSMOND	139
28. JASON DONOVAN	139
29. RICK ASTLEY	138
30. GILBERT O'SULLIVAN	137
31. GEORGE MICHAEL	135
32. ALVIN STARDUST	131
33. DONOVAN	131
34. LIONEL RICHIE	129
35. DAVID CASSIDY	125
36. FRANK SINATRA	120
37. BOBBY DARIN	116
38. JIM REEVES	116
39. PAUL YOUNG	116
40. BOBBY VEE	114

TOP GROUPS IN THE UK BETWEEN 60–90

NAME OF ACT	POINTS
1. BEATLES	637
2. ROLLING STONES	441
3. ABBA	437
4. STATUS QUO	359
5. HOLLIES	357
6. SLADE	352
7. QUEEN	351
8. SHADOWS	328
9. BEE GEES	310
10. MADNESS	287
11. MANFRED MANN	262
12. KINKS	261
13. ELECTRIC LIGHT ORCHESTRA	257
14. BEACH BOYS	253
15. SUPREMES	240
16. T. REX	237
17. WHO	236
18. DURAN DURAN	235
19. HOT CHOCOLATE	229
20. POLICE	224
21. BLONDIE	222
22. WHAM!	218
23. UB40	217
24. MUD	216
25. PET SHOP BOYS	210
26. BAY CITY ROLLERS	210
27. 10CC	209
28. SHOWADDYWADDY	209
29. SWEET	206
30. JAM	199
31. FOUR TOPS	198
32. ROXY MUSIC	191
33. BANANARAMA	190
34. FLEETWOOD MAC	187
35. BONEY M	185
36. U2	183
37. SPANDAU BALLET	183
38. STYLISTICS	182
39. HERMAN'S HERMITS	180
40. CULTURE CLUB	177

TOP FEMALE SOLO ARTISTS IN THE UK BETWEEN 60–90

NAME OF ACT	POINTS
1. MADONNA	469
2. DIANA ROSS	290
3. CILLA BLACK	213
4. OLIVIA NEWTON-JOHN	195
5. DUSTY SPRINGFIELD	192
6. KYLIE MINOGUE	186
7. DONNA SUMMER	177
8. SANDIE SHAW	167
9. KIM WILDE	156
10. SHIRLEY BASSEY	150
11. WHITNEY HOUSTON	141
12. PETULA CLARK	139
13. LULU	134
14. KATE BUSH	111
15. HELEN SHAPIRO	109
16. ALISON MOYET	108
17. SUZI QUATRO	106
18. BRENDA LEE	104
19. BONNIE TYLER	100
20. CONNIE FRANCIS	99
21. TINA TURNER	93
22. CHER	91
23. SARAH BRIGHTMAN	91
24. MARY HOPKIN	90
25. NANCY SINATRA	88
26. BARBRA STREISAND	87
27. DENIECE WILLIAMS	83
28. YAZZ	81
29. SINITTA	79
30. BELINDA CARLISLE	78

TOP ARTISTS IN THE US BETWEEN 60–90

NAME OF ACT	POINTS
1. BEATLES	745
2. STEVIE WONDER	549
3. PAUL McCARTNEY	462
4. ROLLING STONES	460
5. MICHAEL JACKSON	456
6. ELTON JOHN	451
7. ELVIS PRESLEY	417
8. SUPREMES	408
9. MADONNA	377
10. CHICAGO	362
11. BEE GEES	340
12. MARVIN GAYE	331
13. OLIVIA NEWTON-JOHN	325
14. ARETHA FRANKLIN	316
15. DARYL HALL & JOHN OATES	312
16. FOUR SEASONS	302
17. BEACH BOYS	301
18. DONNA SUMMER	297
19. TEMPTATIONS	295
20. PRINCE	280
21. LIONEL RICHIE	279
22. CARPENTERS	264
23. NEIL DIAMOND	252
24. DIANA ROSS	248
25. PHIL COLLINS	244
26. BARBRA STREISAND	239
27. BRENDA LEE	236
28. HUEY LEWIS & THE NEWS	230
29. WHITNEY HOUSTON	228
30. THREE DOG NIGHT	226
31. KENNY ROGERS	223
32. DIONNE WARWICK	218
33. HERMAN'S HERMITS	216
34. ROD STEWART	211
35. GEORGE MICHAEL	210
36. CHER	207
37. KOOL & THE GANG	206
38. BILLY JOEL	206
39. EAGLES	206
40. CONNIE FRANCIS	201
41. COMMODORES	199
42. RAY CHARLES	196
43. LINDA RONSTADT	193
44. BARRY MANILOW	192
45. ROY ORBISON	191
46. BOBBY VINTON	191
47. DURAN DURAN	189
48. BRUCE SPRINGSTEEN	186
49. FOREIGNER	183
50. CREEDENCE CLEARWATER REVIVAL	183
51. JACKSON FIVE	181
52. DION	172
53. SIMON & GARFUNKEL	170
54. AIR SUPPLY	165
55. KC & THE SUNSHINE BAND	165
56. CYNDI LAUPER	163
57. FLEETWOOD MAC	162
58. CHUBBY CHECKER	162
59. JOHN LENNON	162
60. JOHNNY RIVERS	161
61. NEIL SEDAKA	160
62. TOMMY JAMES & THE SHONDELLS	160
63. GLADYS KNIGHT & THE PIPS	160
64. RICHARD MARX	158
65. DAVE CLARK FIVE	154
66. JANET JACKSON	154
67. GLORIA ESTEFAN	153
68. JOHN DENVER	152
69. BILLY OCEAN	151
70. BON JOVI	151
71. SPINNERS	148
72. CAPTAIN & TENNILLE	145
73. MONKEES	145
74. FIFTH DIMENSION	142
75. AL GREEN	142
76. JOHN COUGAR MELLENCAMP	141
77. HEART	141
78. FOUR TOPS	139
79. GARY LEWIS & THE PLAYBOYS	139
80. RINGO STARR	139
81. EVERLY BROTHERS	137
82. POINTER SISTERS	136
83. MIRACLES	136
84. ANDY GIBB	135
85. AMERICA	133
86. EARTH, WIND & FIRE	132
87. NEW KIDS ON THE BLOCK	132
88. SHEENA EASTON	128
89. STYX	128
90. SHIRELLES	127
91. PAUL SIMON	126
92. LOVIN' SPOONFUL	125
93. PETULA CLARK	125
94. RIGHTEOUS BROTHERS	125
95. MAMAS & THE PAPAS	125
96. BOBBY VEE	124
97. PAUL ANKA	123
98. WAR	123
99. GENESIS	123
100. HELEN REDDY	122

TOP MALE SOLO ARTISTS IN THE US BETWEEN 60–90

NAME OF ACT	POINTS
1. STEVIE WONDER	549
2. PAUL McCARTNEY	462
3. MICHAEL JACKSON	456
4. ELTON JOHN	451
5. ELVIS PRESLEY	417
6. MARVIN GAYE	331
7. PRINCE	280
8. LIONEL RICHIE	279
9. NEIL DIAMOND	252
10. PHIL COLLINS	244
11. KENNY ROGERS	223
12. ROD STEWART	211
13. GEORGE MICHAEL	210
14. BILLY JOEL	206
15. RAY CHARLES	196
16. BARRY MANILOW	192
17. ROY ORBISON	191
18. BOBBY VINTON	191
19. BRUCE SPRINGSTEEN	186
20. DION	172
21. CHUBBY CHECKER	162
22. JOHN LENNON	162
23. JOHNNY RIVERS	161
24. NEIL SEDAKA	160
25. RICHARD MARX	158
26. JOHN DENVER	152
27. BILLY OCEAN	151
28. AL GREEN	142
29. JOHN COUGAR MELLENCAMP	141
30. RINGO STARR	139
31. ANDY GIBB	135
32. PAUL SIMON	126
33. BOBBY VEE	124
34. PAUL ANKA	123
35. BOB SEGER	119
36. TOMMY ROE	119
37. BARRY WHITE	118
38. JAMES BROWN	117
39. BROOK BENTON	114
40. DONNY OSMOND	114

TOP GROUPS IN THE US BETWEEN 60–90

NAME OF ACT	POINTS
1. BEATLES	745
2. ROLLING STONES	460
3. SUPREMES	408
4. CHICAGO	362
5. BEE GEES	340
6. DARYL HALL & JOHN OATES	312
7. FOUR SEASONS	302
8. BEACH BOYS	301
9. TEMPTATIONS	295
10. CARPENTERS	264
11. HUEY LEWIS & THE NEWS	230
12. THREE DOG NIGHT	226
13. HERMAN'S HERMITS	216
14. KOOL & THE GANG	206
15. EAGLES	206
16. COMMODORES	199
17. DURAN DURAN	189
18. FOREIGNER	183
19. CREEDENCE CLEARWATER REVIVAL	183
20. JACKSON FIVE	181
21. SIMON & GARFUNKEL	170
22. AIR SUPPLY	165
23. KC & THE SUNSHINE BAND	165
24. FLEETWOOD MAC	162
25. TOMMY JAMES & THE SHONDELLS	160
26. GLADYS KNIGHT & THE PIPS	160
27. DAVE CLARK FIVE	154
28. BON JOVI	151
29. SPINNERS	148
30. CAPTAIN & TENNILLE	145
31. MONKEES	145
32. FIFTH DIMENSION	142
33. HEART	141
34. FOUR TOPS	139
35. GARY LEWIS & THE PLAYBOYS	139
36. EVERLY BROTHERS	137
37. POINTER SISTERS	136
38. MIRACLES	136
39. AMERICA	133
40. EARTH, WIND & FIRE	132
40. NEW KIDS ON THE BLOCK	132

TOP FEMALE SOLO ARTISTS IN THE US BETWEEN 60–90

NAME OF ACT	POINTS
1. MADONNA	377
2. OLIVIA NEWTON–JOHN	325
3. ARETHA FRANKLIN	316
4. DONNA SUMMER	297
5. DIANA ROSS	248
6. BARBRA STREISAND	239
7. BRENDA LEE	236
8. WHITNEY HOUSTON	228
9. DIONNE WARWICK	218
10. CHER	207
11. CONNIE FRANCIS	201
12. LINDA RONSTADT	193
13. CYNDI LAUPER	163
14. JANET JACKSON	154
15. GLORIA ESTEFAN	153
16. SHEENA EASTON	128
17. PETULA CLARK	125
18. HELEN REDDY	122
19. ROBERTA FLACK	122
20. DEBBIE GIBSON	111
21. TINA TURNER	105
22. CARLY SIMON	97
23. PAULA ABDUL	96
24. TAYLOR DAYNE	94
25. JODY WATLEY	88
26. NANCY SINATRA	86
27. LESLEY GORE	85
28. NATALIE COLE	84
29. BELINDA CARLISLE	83
30. TIFFANY	83

TOP ARTISTS IN THE US & UK COMBINED BETWEEN 60–90

NAME OF ACT	POINTS	NATIONALITY (UK,US & SWEDEN)
1. BEATLES	1,382	UK
2. ELVIS PRESLEY	1,249	US
3. CLIFF RICHARD	1,106	UK
4. PAUL McCARTNEY	910	UK
5. STEVIE WONDER	904	US
6. ROLLING STONES	901	UK
7. MICHAEL JACKSON	898	US
8. MADONNA	846	US
9. ELTON JOHN	768	UK
10. BEE GEES	650	UK
11. SUPREMES	648	US
12. ROD STEWART	620	UK
13. DAVID BOWIE	575	UK
14. BEACH BOYS	554	US
15. DIANA ROSS	538	US
16. OLIVIA NEWTON-JOHN	520	UK
17. ABBA	514	SW
18. MARVIN GAYE	474	US
19. DONNA SUMMER	474	US
20. PHIL COLLINS	464	UK
21. HOLLIES	461	UK
22. CHICAGO	454	US
23. QUEEN	438	UK
24. ROY ORBISON	426	US
25. DURAN DURAN	424	UK
26. FOUR SEASONS	423	US
27. PRINCE	419	US
28. TOM JONES	408	UK
29. LIONEL RICHIE	408	US
30. HERMAN'S HERMITS	396	UK
31. ARETHA FRANKLIN	388	US
32. CARPENTERS	388	US
33. JOHN LENNON	371	UK
34. WHITNEY HOUSTON	369	US
35. TEMPTATIONS	360	US
36. STATUS QUO	359	UK
37. SLADE	352	UK
38. ELECTRIC LIGHT ORCHESTRA	350	UK
39. FLEETWOOD MAC	349	UK
40. GEORGE MICHAEL	345	UK
41. DARYL HALL & JOHN OATES	344	US
42. KINKS	341	UK
43. BRENDA LEE	340	US
44. POLICE	338	UK
45. FOUR TOPS	337	US
46. KOOL & THE GANG	332	US
47. SHADOWS	328	UK
48. NEIL DIAMOND	327	US
49. BARBRA STREISAND	326	US
50. KENNY ROGERS	326	US
51. WHAM!	324	UK
52. BLONDIE	324	US
53. JACKSON FIVE	312	US
54. EVERLY BROTHERS	310	US
55. MADNESS	303	UK
56. PET SHOP BOYS	303	UK
57. DAVE CLARK FIVE	302	UK
58. MANFRED MANN	300	UK
59. CONNIE FRANCIS	300	US
60. CHER	298	US
61. COMMODORES	297	US
62. CULTURE CLUB	293	UK
63. BILLY JOEL	285	US
64. GENE PITNEY	283	US
65. SHAKIN' STEVENS	283	UK
66. DIONNE WARWICK	282	US
67. HOT CHOCOLATE	282	UK
68. SWEET	280	UK
69. BILLY OCEAN	280	UK
70. RAY CHARLES	278	US
71. LEO SAYER	278	UK
72. GARY GLITTER	269	UK
73. DUSTY SPRINGFIELD	264	UK
74. PETULA CLARK	264	UK
75. SIMON & GARFUNKEL	261	US
76. BAY CITY ROLLERS	261	UK
77. CREEDENCE CLEARWATER REVIVAL	260	US
78. DONNY OSMOND	253	US
79. WHO	250	UK
80. T. REX	250	UK
81. BANANARAMA	248	UK
82. KC & THE SUNSHINE BAND	248	US
83. THREE DOG NIGHT	247	US
84. HUEY LEWIS & THE NEWS	244	US
85. DRIFTERS	243	US
86. CHUBBY CHECKER	242	US
87. UB40	241	UK
88. STYLISTICS	240	US
89. BRUCE SPRINGSTEEN	239	US
90. BOBBY VEE	238	US
91. U2	238	UK
92. TEARS FOR FEARS	234	UK
93. MONKEES	234	US
94. LINDA RONSTADT	230	US
95. DR. HOOK	230	US
96. GLADYS KNIGHT & THE PIPS	229	US
97. EURYTHMICS	228	UK
98. NEIL SEDAKA	226	US
99. FOREIGNER	224	UKUS
100. BOBBY DARIN	222	US

TOP GROUPS IN THE US & UK COMBINED BETWEEN 60–90

NAME OF ACT	POINTS
1. BEATLES	1,382
2. ROLLING STONES	901
3. BEE GEES	650
4. SUPREMES	648
5. BEACH BOYS	554
6. ABBA	514
7. HOLLIES	461
8. CHICAGO	454
9. QUEEN	438
10. DURAN DURAN	424
11. FOUR SEASONS	423
12. HERMAN'S HERMITS	396
13. CARPENTERS	388
14. TEMPTATIONS	360
15. STATUS QUO	359
16. SLADE	352
17. ELECTRIC LIGHT ORCHESTRA	350
18. FLEETWOOD MAC	349
19. DARYL HALL & JOHN OATES	344
20. KINKS	341
21. POLICE	338
22. FOUR TOPS	337
23. KOOL & THE GANG	332
24. SHADOWS	328
25. WHAM!	324
26. BLONDIE	324
27. JACKSON FIVE	312
28. EVERLY BROTHERS	310
29. MADNESS	303
30. PET SHOP BOYS	303
31. DAVE CLARK FIVE	302
32. MANFRED MANN	300
33. COMMODORES	297
34. CULTURE CLUB	293
35. HOT CHOCOLATE	282
36. SWEET	280
37. SIMON & GARFUNKEL	261
38. BAY CITY ROLLERS	261
39. CREEDENCE CLEARWATER REVIVAL	260
40. WHO	250
40. T. REX	250

TOP MALE SOLO ARTISTS IN THE US & UK COMBINED BETWEEN 60–90

NAME OF ACT	POINTS
1. ELVIS PRESLEY	1,249
2. CLIFF RICHARD	1,106
3. PAUL McCARTNEY	910
4. STEVIE WONDER	904
5. MICHAEL JACKSON	898
6. ELTON JOHN	768
7. ROD STEWART	620
8. DAVID BOWIE	575
9. MARVIN GAYE	474
10. PHIL COLLINS	464
11. ROY ORBISON	426
12. PRINCE	419
13. TOM JONES	408
14. LIONEL RICHIE	408
15. JOHN LENNON	371
16. GEORGE MICHAEL	345
17. NEIL DIAMOND	327
18. KENNY ROGERS	325
19. BILLY JOEL	285
20. GENE PITNEY	283
21. SHAKIN' STEVENS	283
22. BILLY OCEAN	280
23. RAY CHARLES	278
24. LEO SAYER	278
25. GARY GLITTER	269
26. DONNY OSMOND	253
27. CHUBBY CHECKER	242
28. BRUCE SPRINGSTEEN	239
29. BOBBY VEE	238
30. NEIL SEDAKA	226
31. BOBBY DARIN	222
32. DAVID ESSEX	221
33. RICK ASTLEY	217
34. RINGO STARR	216
35. BARRY WHITE	213
36. ENGELBERT HUMPERDINCK	213
37. DONOVAN	212
38. DEL SHANNON	211
39. ADAM FAITH	208
40. BARRY MANILOW	207

TOP FEMALE SOLO ARTISTS IN THE US & UK COMBINED BETWEEN 60–90

NAME OF ACT	POINTS
1. MADONNA	846
2. DIANA ROSS	538
3. OLIVIA NEWTON–JOHN	520
4. DONNA SUMMER	474
5. ARETHA FRANKLIN	388
6. WHITNEY HOUSTON	369
7. BRENDA LEE	340
8. BARBRA STREISAND	326
9. CONNIE FRANCIS	300
10. CHER	298
11. DIONNE WARWICK	282
12. DUSTY SPRINGFIELD	264
13. PETULA CLARK	264
14. LINDA RONSTADT	230
15. CYNDI LAUPER	222
16. CILLA BLACK	213
17. JANET JACKSON	209
18. KYLIE MINOGUE	207
19. TINA TURNER	198
20. GLORIA ESTEFAN	187
21. ROBERTA FLACK	182
22. KIM WILDE	180
23. SHEENA EASTON	179
24. SANDIE SHAW	167
25. SHIRLEY BASSEY	165
26. LULU	162
27. BELINDA CARLISLE	161
28. CARLY SIMON	159
29. NANCY SINATRA	152
30. BONNIE TYLER	148

BEG STEAL OR BORROW   New Seekers
BEGIN THE BEGUINE (VOLVER A EMPEZAR)
Julio Iglesias
BEGINNINGS   Chicago
BEHIND A PAINTED SMILE   Isley Brothers
BEHIND THE GROOVE   Teena Marie
BEIN' BOILED   Human League
BEING WITH YOU   Smokey Robinson
BELFAST   Boney M
BELFAST CHILD   Simple Minds
BELIEVE WHAT YOU SAY   Ricky Nelson
BEN   Marti Webb
BEN   Michael Jackson
BEND IT   Dave Dee, Dozy, Beaky, Mick & Titch
BEND ME SHAPE ME   Amen Corner
BEND ME, SHAPE ME   American Breed
BENNIE AND THE JETS   Elton John
BERNADETTE   Four Tops
THE BEST DISCO IN TOWN   Ritchie Family
THE BEST OF ME   Cliff Richard
BEST OF MY LOVE   Eagles
BEST OF MY LOVE   Emotions
THE BEST OF TIMES   Styx
THE BEST   Tina Turner
BEST THING THAT EVER HAPPENED TO ME
Gladys Knight & The Pips
BEST YEARS OF OUR LIVES   Modern Romance
BETCHA BY GOLLY, WOW   Stylistics
BETH   Kiss
BETTE DAVIS EYES   Kim Carnes
BETTER BE GOOD TO ME   Tina Turner
BETTER LOVE NEXT TIME   Dr. Hook
BEYOND THE REEF   Elvis Presley
BEYOND THE SEA (LA MER)   Bobby Darin
BIG APPLE   Kajagoogoo
BIG BAD JOHN   Jimmy Dean
BIG BOSS GROOVE   Style Council
BIG FUN   Inner City
BIG FUN   Gap Band
BIG GIRLS DONT CRY   Four Seasons
BIG HUNK O' LOVE   Elvis Presley
BIG IN JAPAN   Alphaville
BIG LOVE   Fleetwood Mac
BIG SEVEN   Judge Dread
BIG SHIP   Cliff Richard
BIG TIME   Peter Gabriel
BIGGEST PART OF ME   Ambrosia
BILLIE JEAN   Michael Jackson
BILLY, DON'T BE A HERO   Paper Lace
BILLY, DON'T BE A HERO
Bo Donaldson & The Heywoods
BIONIC SANTA   Chris Hill
BIRD DOG   Everly Brothers
BIRD OF PARADISE   Snowy White
THE BIRDIE SONG (BIRDIE DANCE)   Tweets
THE BIRDS AND THE BEES   Jewel Akens
THE BITCH IS BACK   Elton John
BITS AND PIECES   Dave Clark Five
THE BITTEREST PILL (I EVER HAD TO SWALLOW)
Jam
BLACK & WHITE   Three Dog Night
BLACK AND WHITE   Greyhound
BLACK BETTY   Ram Jam
BLACK IS BLACK   Los Bravos
BLACK IS BLACK   La Belle Epoque
BLACK MAGIC WOMAN   Santana
BLACK NIGHT   Deep Purple
BLACK SKIN BLUE EYED BOYS   Equals
BLACK SUPERMAN (MUHAMMAD ALI)
Johnny Wakelin & The Kinshasa Band
BLACK WATER   Doobie Brothers
BLACKBERRY WAY   Move
BLAME IT ON THE BOOGIE   Big Fun
BLAME IT ON THE BOOGIE   Jacksons
BLAME IT ON THE BOSSA NOVA   Eydie Gorme
BLAME IT ON THE PONY EXPRESS
Johnny Johnson & The Bandwagon
BLAME IT ON THE RAIN   Milli Vanilli
BLANKET ON THE GROUND   Billie Jo Spears
BLESS YOU   Tony Orlando
BLIND VISION   Blancmange
BLINDED BY THE LIGHT   Manfred Mann's Earth Band
BLOCKBUSTER   Sweet
BLOODNOK'S ROCK 'N' ROLL CALL   Goons
A BLOSSOM FELL   Nat 'King' Cole
BLOW THE HOUSE DOWN   Living In A Box
BLOWIN' IN THE WIND   Stevie Wonder
BLOWIN' IN THE WIND   Peter, Paul & Mary
BLUE ANGEL   Roy Orbison
BLUE BAYOU   Linda Ronstadt
BLUE BAYOU   Roy Orbison
BLUE EYES   Elton John
BLUE EYES   Don Partridge
BLUE GUITAR   Justin Hayward & John Lodge
BLUE IS THE COLOUR   Chelsea F.C.
BLUE JEAN   David Bowie
BLUE MONDAY   New Order
BLUE MONDAY   Fats Domino
BLUE MONDAY 1988 (No. 68 US)   New Order

BLUE MOON   Marcels
BLUE MOON   Elvis Presley
BLUE ON BLUE   Bobby Vinton
BLUE SUEDE SHOES   Elvis Presley
BLUE VELVET   Bobby Vinton
BLUEBERRY HILL   Fats Domino
BLUEBOTTLE BLUES   Goons
DO DIDDLEY   Buddy Holly
THE BOAT THAT I ROW   Lulu
BOBBY'S GIRL   Susan Maughan
BOBBY'S GIRL   Marcie Blane
BODY AND SOUL   Mai Tai
BODY TALK   Imagination
BOHEMIAN RHAPSODY   Queen
THE BOLL WEEVIL SONG   Brook Benton
BOOGALOO DOWN BROADWAY
Fantastic Johnny C
BOOGIE DOWN   Eddie Kendricks
BOOGIE FEVER   Sylvers
BOOGIE NIGHTS   Heatwave
BOOGIE ON REGGAE WOMAN   Stevie Wonder
BOOGIE OOGIE OOGIE   Taste of Honey
BOOGIE WONDERLAND
Earth, Wind & Fire with The Emotions
BOOGIE WOOGIE BUGLE BOY   Bette Midler
BOOM BANG-A-BANG   Lulu
BORDERLINE   Madonna
BORN FREE   Roger Williams
BORN IN THE U.S.A.   Bruce Springsteen
BORN TO BE ALIVE   Patrick Hernandez
BORN TO BE MY BABY   Bon Jovi
BORN TO BE WILD   Steppenwolf
BORN TO BE WITH YOU   Chordettes
BORN TO BE WITH YOU   Dave Edmunds
BORN WITH A SMILE ON MY FACE
Stephanie De Sykes
BOSSA NOVA BABY   Elvis Presley
BOTH SIDES NOW   Judy Collins
BOTTLE OF WINE   Fireballs
BOXER BEAT   Joboxers
THE BOXER   Simon & Garfunkel
BOY FROM NEW YORK CITY   Darts
THE BOY FROM NEW YORK CITY   Ad Libs
THE BOY FROM NEW YORK CITY   Manhattan Transfer
A BOY FROM NOWHERE   Tom Jones
A BOY NAMED SUE   Johnny Cash
BOYS (SUMMERTIME LOVE)   Sabrina
THE BOYS ARE BACK IN TOWN   Thin Lizzy
BOYS CRY   Eden Kane
BOYS KEEP SWINGIN'   David Bowie
THE BOYS OF SUMMER   Don Henley
BRAND NEW KEY   Melanie
BRANDY (YOU'RE A FINE GIRL)   Looking Glass
BRASS IN POCKET   Pretenders
BREAD AND BUTTER   Newbeats
BREAK AWAY   Beach Boys
BREAK DANCE PARTY   Break Machine
BREAK IT TO ME GENTLY   Brenda Lee
BREAK MY STRIDE   Matthew Wilder
BREAK THE RULES   Status Quo
BREAK UP TO MAKE UP   Stylistics
BREAKAWAY   Tracey Ullman
BREAKDANCE   Irene Cara
BREAKFAST IN AMERICA   Supertramp
BREAKFAST IN BED   UB40
BREAKIN' DOWN THE WALLS OF HEARTACHE
Johnny Johnson & The Bandwagon
BREAKIN' IN A BRAND NEW BROKEN HEART
Connie Francis
BREAKIN'...THERE'S NO STOPPING US   Ollie & Jerry
BREAKING UP IS HARD TO DO   Partridge Family
BREAKING UP IS HARD TO DO   Neil Sedaka
BREAKOUT   Swing Out Sister
BREAKTHRU'   Queen
BREATHLESS   Jerry Lee Lewis
BRICK HOUSE   Commodores
BRIDGE OVER TROUBLED WATER
Aretha Franklin
BRIDGE OVER TROUBLED WATER
Simon & Garfunkel
BRIDGET THE MIDGET (THE QUEEN OF THE BLUES)
Ray Stevens
BRIGHT EYES   Art Garfunkel
BRILLIANT DISGUISE   Bruce Springsteen
BRING A LITTLE WATER SYLVIE
Lonnie Donegan
BRING IT ON HOME TO ME   Animals
BRING IT ON HOME TO ME   Rod Stewart
BRING ME EDELWEISS   Edelweiss
BRINGING ON BACK THE GOOD TIMES
Love Affair
BRISTOL STOMP   Dovells
BRITISH HUSTLE   Hi Tension
BROKEN DOWN ANGEL   Nazareth
BROKEN WINGS   Mr Mister
BRONTOSAURUS   Move
BROTHER LOUIE   Modern Talking
BROTHER LOUIE   Stories
BROTHER LOUIE   Hot Chocolate

BROWN EYED GIRL   Van Morrison
BROWN EYED HANDSOME MAN   Buddy Holly
BROWN GIRL IN THE RING   Boney M
BROWN SUGAR   Rolling Stones
BUFFALO GALS   Malcolm McLaren
BUFFALO SOLDIER   Bob Marley & Wailers
BUFFALO STANCE   Neneh Cherry
BUILD ME UP BUTTERCUP   Foundations
THE BUMP   Kenny
BUONA SERA   Acker Bilk
BURNING BRIDGES   Jack Scott
BURNING BRIDGES (ON AND OFF AND ON AGAIN)
Status Quo
BURNING DOWN THE HOUSE   Talking Heads
BURNING HEART   Survivor
BURNING LOVE   Elvis Presley
BUS STOP   Hollies
BUST A MOVE   Young M.C.
BUSTED   Ray Charles
BUT I DO   Clarence 'Frogman' Henry
BUTTERFINGERS   Tommy Steele
BUTTERFLY   Andy Williams
BYE BYE BABY   Bay City Rollers
BYE BYE LOVE   Everly Brothers
C'EST LA VIE   Robbie Nevil
C'MON AND SWIM   Bobby Freeman
C'MON EVERYBODY   Sex Pistols
C'MON EVERYBODY   Eddie Cochran
C'MON MARIANNE   Four Seasons
CA PLANE POUR MOI   Plastic Bertrand
CALCUTTA   Lawrence Welk
CALENDAR GIRL   Neil Sedaka
CALIFORNIA DREAMIN'   Mamas & The Papas
CALIFORNIA GIRLS   David Lee Roth
CALIFORNIA GIRLS   Beach Boys
CALIFORNIA MAN   Move
CALIFORNIA SUN   Rivieras
CALL ME   Blondie
CALL ME   Spagna
CALL ME (COME BACK HOME)   Al Green
(CALL ME) NUMBER ONE   Tremeloes
CALL ON ME   Chicago
CALL UP THE GROUPS   Barron Knights
CALLING ALL THE HEROES   It Bites
CALLING OCCUPANTS OF INTERPLANETARY CRAFT
Carpenters
CALLING YOUR NAME   Marilyn
CAMOUFLAGE   Stan Ridgway
CAN CAN   Bad Manners
CAN I CHANGE MY MIND   Tyrone Davis
CAN I PLAY WITH MADNESS   Iron Maiden
CAN I TAKE YOU HOME LITTLE GIRL   Drifters
CAN THE CAN   Suzi Quatro
CAN YOU FEEL IT   Jacksons
CAN YOU FEEL THE FORCE   Real Thing
CAN'T BE WITHOUT YOU TONIGHT
Judy Boucher
CAN'T BUY ME LOVE   Beatles
CAN'T FIGHT THIS FEELING   Reo Speedwagon
CAN'T GET BY WITHOUT YOU   Real Thing
CAN'T GET ENOUGH   Bad Company
CAN'T GET ENOUGH OF YOUR LOVE, BABE
Barry White
CAN'T GET IT OUT OF MY HEAD
Electric Light Orchestra
CAN'T GET USED TO LOSING YOU
Andy Williams
CAN'T GET USED TO LOSING YOU   Beat
CAN'T GIVE YOU ANYTHING (BUT MY LOVE)
Stylistics
CAN'T HELP FALLING IN LOVE   Stylistics
CAN'T HELP FALLING IN LOVE   Elvis Presley
CAN'T HELP FALLING IN LOVE   Andy Williams
CAN'T SHAKE THE FEELING   Big Fun
CAN'T SMILE WITHOUT YOU   Barry Manilow
CAN'T STAND LOSING YOU   Police
CAN'T STAY AWAY FROM YOU
Gloria Estefan & Miami Sound Machine
CAN'T TAKE MY EYES OFF YOU   Boystown Gang
CAN'T TAKE MY EYES OFF YOU   Andy Williams
CAN'T TAKE MY EYES OFF YOU   Frankie Valli
CAN'T WAIT ANOTHER MINUTE   Five Star
CAN'T WE TRY   Dan Hill (Duet Vonda Shepard)
CAN'T YOU HEAR MY HEARTBEAT
Herman's Hermits
CAN'T YOU SEE THAT SHE'S MINE   Dave Clark Five
CANADIAN SUNSET   Andy Williams
CANDIDA   Dawn
CANDLE IN THE WIND   Elton John
CANDY GIRL   Four Seasons
CANDY GIRL   New Edition
CANDY MAN   Brian Poole & The Tremeloes
THE CANDY MAN   Sammy Davis Jr.
CAPSTICK COMES HOME   Tony Capstick
CAPTAIN BEAKY   Keith Michel
THE CAPTAIN OF YOUR HEART   Double
CAR 67   Driver 67
CAR WASH   Rose Royce
CARA MIA   Jay & The Americans

CARAVAN OF LOVE   Housemartins
CAREFREE HIGHWAY   Gordon Lightfoot
CARELESS HANDS   Des O'Connor
CARELESS WHISPER   George Michael
CARIBBEAN DISCO   Lobo
CARIBBEAN QUEEN (NO MORE LOVE ON THE RUN)
Billy Ocean
THE CARNIVAL IS OVER   Seekers
CAROLINA MOON   Connie Francis
CAROLINE   Status Quo
CARRIE   Cliff Richard
CARRIE   Europe
CARRIE-ANNE   Hollies
CARS   Gary Numan
CASANOVA   Levert
CAST YOUR FATE TO THE WIND   Sounds Orchestral
CAT AMONG THE PIGEONS   Bros
THE CAT CREPT IN   Mud
CAT'S IN THE CRADLE   Harry Chapin
CATCH A FALLING STAR   Perry Como
CATCH ME I'M FALLING   Pretty Poison
CATCH THE WIND   Donovan
CATCH US IF YOU CAN   Dave Clark Five
CATHY'S CLOWN   Everly Brothers
CAUGHT UP IN YOU   38 Special
CAUSING A COMMOTION   Madonna
CECILIA   Simon & Garfunkel
CELEBRATION   Kool & The Gang
CENTERFOLD   J. Geils Band
A CERTAIN SMILE   Johnny Mathis
THE CHA CHA CHA   Bobby Rydell
CHAIN GANG   Sam Cooke
CHAIN OF FOOLS   Aretha Franklin
CHAIN REACTION   Diana Ross
CHAINS OF LOVE   Pat Boone
CHANCE   Big Country
CHANCES ARE   Johnny Mathis
CHANGE   Tears For Fears
CHANGE OF HEART   Cyndi Lauper
CHANSON D'AMOUR   Manhattan Transfer
CHANT NO. 1 (I DON'T NEED THIS PRESSURE ON)
Spandau Ballet
CHAPEL OF LOVE   Dixie Cups
CHARIOTS OF FIRE   Vangelis
CHARMAINE   Bachelors
CHECK OUT THE GROOVE   Bobby Thurston
CHECK THIS OUT   L.A. Mix
CHEQUERED LOVE   Kim Wilde
CHERIE I LOVE YOU   Pat Boone
CHERISH   Madonna
CHERISH   David Cassidy
CHERISH   Kool & The Gang
CHERISH   Association
CHERRY BOMB   John Cougar Mellencamp
CHERRY CHERRY   Neil Diamond
CHEVY VAN   Sammy Johns
CHI MAI THEME   Ennio Morricone
CHICK-A-BOOM   Daddy Dewdrop
THE CHICKEN SONG   Spitting Image
A CHILD'S PRAYER   Hot Chocolate
CHILDREN OF THE REVOLUTION   T. Rex
CHINA GIRL   David Bowie
CHINA IN YOUR HAND   T'Pau
CHIP CHIP   Gene McDaniels
CHIQUITITA   Abba
CHIRPY CHIRPY CHEEP CHEEP   Middle of The Road
CHOCOLATE BOX   Bros
THE CHOSEN FEW   Dooleys
CHUCK E.'S IN LOVE   Rickie Lee Jones
CHUG-A-LUG   Roger Miller
CHURCH OF THE POISON MIND   Culture Club
CINDERELLA ROCKAFELLA   Esther & Abi Ofarim
CINDY INCIDENTALLY   Faces
CINDY'S BIRTHDAY   Johnny Crawford
CIRCLE IN THE SAND   Belinda Carlisle
CIRCLES   New Seekers
THE CIRCUS   Erasure
THE CISCO KID   War
CLAIR   Gilbert O'Sullivan
THE CLAIRVOYANT   Iron Maiden
CLAP FOR THE WOLFMAN   Guess Who
THE CLAPPING SONG   Shirley Ellis
CLASSIC   Adrian Gurvitz
CLASSICAL GAS   Mason Williams
CLEAN UP WOMAN   Betty Wright
CLEMENTINE   Bobby Darin
CLIMB EV'RY MOUNTAIN   Shirley Bassey
CLOSE (TO THE EDIT)   Art of Noise
CLOSE MY EYES FOREVER
Lita Ford (& Ozzy Osbourne)
CLOSE YOUR EYES   Peaches & Herb
THE CLOSER I GET TO YOU
Roberta Flack & Donny Hathaway
CLOUD NINE   Temptations
CLOUDS ACROSS THE MOON   Rah Band
CLUB TROPICANA   Wham!
C MOON   Paul McCartney
CO-CO   Sweet
COCONUT   Nilsson

COLD AS ICE   Foreigner
COLD HEARTED   Paula Abdul
COLD SWEAT (PART 1)   James Brown
COLOR HIM FATHER   Winstons
COLOUR MY WORLD   Chicago
COLOURS   Donovan
COMBINE HARVESTER (BRAND NEW KEY)
Wurzels
COME A LITTLE BIT CLOSER   Jay & The Americans
COME AND GET IT   Badfinger
COME AND GET YOUR LOVE   Redbone
COME AND STAY WITH ME   Marianne Faithfull
COME BACK AND SHAKE ME   Clodagh Rodgers
COME BACK AND STAY   Paul Young
COME BACK MY LOVE   Darts
COME BACK WHEN YOU GROW UP   Bobby Vee
COME DANCING   Kinks
COME GO WITH ME   Expose
COME INTO MY LIFE   Joyce Sims
COME LIVE WITH ME   Heaven 17
COME ON DOWN TO MY BOAT
Every Mothers' Son
COME ON EILEEN   Dexy's Midnight Runners
COME ON LET'S GO   Tommy Steele
COME ON OVER TO MY PLACE   Drifters
COME OUTSIDE   Mike Sarne and Wendy Richard
COME SAIL AWAY   Styx
COME SEE ABOUT ME   Supremes
COME SOFTLY TO ME   Fleetwoods
COME SOFTLY TO ME
Frankie Vaughan & The Kaye Sisters
COME TOGETHER   Beatles
COME TOMORROW   Manfred Mann
COME WHAT MAY   Vicky Leandros
COMING HOME BABY   Mel Torme
COMING ROUND AGAIN   Carly Simon
COMING UP   Paul McCartney
COMPLEX   Gary Numan
COMPUTER LOVE   Kraftwerk
CONCRETE AND CLAY   Unit 4 Plus 2
CONFESSIN'   Frank Ifield
CONFUSION   Electric Light Orchestra
CONGA   Miami Sound Machine
CONGRATULATIONS   Cliff Richard
CONSTANTLY   Cliff Richard
CONTACT   Edwin Starr
CONTROL   Janet Jackson
CONVENTION '72   Delegates
CONVERSATIONS   Cilla Black
CONVOY   C.W. McCall
CONVOY GB   Laurie Lingo & The Dipsticks
COOL CHANGE   Little River Band
COOL FOR CATS   Squeeze
COOL IT NOW   New Edition
COOL JERK   Capitols
COOL WATER   Frankie Laine
COPACABANA (AT THE COPA)   Barry Manilow
CORINNA, CORINNA   Ray Peterson
COTTONFIELDS   Beach Boys
COULD IT BE FOREVER   David Cassidy
COULD IT BE I'M FALLING IN LOVE
David Grant & Jaki Graham
COULD IT BE I'M FALLING IN LOVE   Spinners
COULD IT BE MAGIC   Barry Manilow
COULD YOU BE LOVED   Bob Marley & The Wailers
COULD'VE BEEN   Tiffany
COULDN'T GET IT RIGHT   Climax Blues Band
COUNT ME IN   Gary Lewis & The Playboys
COUNT ON ME   Jefferson Starship
COUNTING TEARDROPS   Emile Ford
COUSIN NORMAN   Marmalade
COVER GIRL   New Kids On The Block
COVER ME   Bruce Springsteen
THE COVER OF 'ROLLING STONE'   Dr. Hook
COWARD OF THE COUNTY   Kenny Rogers
A COWBOY'S WORK IS NEVER DONE
Sonny & Cher
COWBOYS TO GIRLS   Intruders
COZ I LUV YOU   Slade
CRACKERS INTERNATIONAL (E.P.)   Erasure
CRACKLIN' ROSIE   Neil Diamond
CRADLE OF LOVE   Johnny Preston
CRASH   Primitives
CRAZY   Patsy Cline
CRAZY CRAZY NIGHTS   Kiss
CRAZY FOR YOU   Madonna
CRAZY HORSES   Osmonds
CRAZY LITTLE THING CALLED LOVE   Queen
CREEQUE ALLEY   Mamas & The Papas
CRIMSON & CLOVER
Tommy James & The Shondells
CRIMSON AND CLOVER   Joan Jett & The Blackhearts
CRITICIZE   Alexander O'Neal
CROCKETT'S THEME   Jan Hammer
CROCODILE ROCK   Elton John
CROSS MY BROKEN HEART   Jets
CROSS MY BROKEN HEART   Sinitta
THE CROWN   Gaey Vyes & GB Experience
CRUEL SUMMER   Bananarama

CRUISIN'   Smokey Robinson
CRUISING   Sinitta
CRUMBLIN' DOWN   John Cougar Mellencamp
THE CRUNCH   Rah Band
CRUSH ON YOU   Jets
CRY   Waterfront
CRY BABY   Garnet Mimms & The Enchanters
CRY JUST A LITTLE BIT   Shakin' Stevens
CRY LIKE A BABY   Box Tops
CRY WOLF   A–Ha
CRYIN'   Roy Orbison
CRYIN' IN THE RAIN   Everly Brothers
CRYING   Don Mclean
THE CRYING GAME   Dave Berry
CRYING IN THE CHAPEL   Elvis Presley
CRYING TIME   Ray Charles
CRYSTAL BLUE PERSUASION
Tommy James & The Shondells
CUDDLY TOY   Roachford
CUM ON FEEL THE NOIZE   Slade
CUM ON FEEL THE NOIZE   Quiet Riot
CUMBERLAND GAP   Lonnie Donegan
CUPID   Johnny Nash
CUPID   Sam Cooke
CUPID–I'VE LOVED YOU FOR A LONG TIME (ME)
Spinners
CUT THE CAKE   Average White Band
THE CUTTER   Echo & The Bunnymen
D–DAYS   Hazel O'Connor
D.I.S.C.O.   Ottawan
D.I.V.O.R.C.E.   Billy Connolly
DA DA DA   Trio
DA DOO RON RON   Shaun Cassidy
DA DOO RON RON   Crystals
DA YA THINK I'M SEXY   Rod Stewart
DADDY COOL   Boney M
DADDY COOL   Darts
DADDY DON'T YOU WALK SO FAST   Wayne Newton
DADDY'S HOME   Cliff Richard
DADDY'S HOME   Jermaine Jackson
DADDY'S HOME   Shep & The Limelites
DAMNED ON 45   Captain Sensible
DANCE AWAY   Roxy Music
DANCE DANCE DANCE (YOWSAH YOWSAH
YOWSAH)   Chic
DANCE LITTLE LADY DANCE   Tina Charles
DANCE ON   Shadows
DANCE ON LITTLE GIRL   Paul Anka
DANCE TO THE MUSIC   Sly & The Family Stone
DANCE WITH ME   Orleans
DANCE WITH ME   Peter Brown
DANCE WITH THE DEVIL   Cozy Powell
DANCE WITH THE GUITAR MAN   Duane Eddy
DANCE YOURSELF DIZZY   Liquid Gold
DANCE, DANCE, DANCE   Beach Boys
DANCIN' PARTY   Showaddywaddy
DANCING IN THE CITY   Marshall Hain
DANCING IN THE DARK   Bruce Springsteen
DANCING IN THE STREET
David Bowie & Mick Jagger
DANCING IN THE STREET   Martha & The Vandellas
DANCING MACHINE   Jackson Five
(DANCING) ON A SATURDY NIGHT   Barry Blue
DANCING ON THE CEILING   Lionel Richie
DANCING ON THE FLOOR (HOOKED ON LOVE)
Third World
DANCING QUEEN   Abba
DANCING TIGHT   Galaxy Feat. Phil Fearon
DANCING WITH TEARS IN MY EYES   Ultravox
DANCING WITH THE CAPTAIN   Paul Nicholas
DANDELION   Rolling Stones
DANDY   Herman's Hermits
DANG ME   Roger Miller
DANGER GAMES   Pinkees
DANGER ZONE   Kenny Loggins
DANIEL   Elton John
DANNY BOY   Conway Twitty
DANNY'S SONG   Anne Murray
DARK LADY   Cher
DARLIN'   Frankie Miller
DARLING JE VOUS AIME BEAUCOUP
Nat 'King' Cole
DAT   Pluto Shervington
DAUGHTER OF DARKNESS   Tom Jones
DAVY'S ON THE ROAD AGAIN
Manfred Mann's Earth Band
DAWN (GO AWAY)   Four Seasons
DAY AFTER DAY   Badfinger
DAY DREAMING   Aretha Franklin
THE DAY I MET MARIE   Cliff Richard
DAY TRIP TO BANGOR   Fiddler's Dram
DAY TRIPPER   Beatles
A DAY WITHOUT LOVE   Love Affair
DAYDREAM   Lovin' Spoonful
DAYDREAM BELIEVER   Monkees
DAYDREAMER   David Cassidy
DAZZ   Brick
DE DO DO DO, DE DA DA DA   Police
DEAD END STREET   Kinks

DEAD GIVEAWAY   Shalamar
DEAD MAN'S CURVE   Jan & Dean
DEAD OR ALIVE   Lonnie Donegan
DEAD RINGER FOR LOVE   Meat Loaf
THE DEAN AND I   10CC
DEAR JESSIE   Madonna
DEAR JOHN   Status Quo
DEAR LADY TWIST   Gary U.S. Bonds
DEAR PRUDENCE   Siouxsie & The Banshees
DEATH OF A CLOWN   Dave Davies
DEBORA   Tyrannosaurus Rex
DECEMBER '63 (OH WHAT A NIGHT)   Four Seasons
DECK OF CARDS   Wink Martindale
DEDICATED FOLLOWER OF FASHION   Kinks
DEDICATED TO THE ONE I LOVE   Shirelles
DEDICATED TO THE ONE I LOVE
Mamas & The Papas
DEEP DOWN INSIDE   Donna Summer
DEEP PURPLE   Nino Tempo & April Stevens
DELAWARE   Perry Como
DELILAH   Tom Jones
DELILAH   Sensational Alex Harvey Band
DELIRIOUS   Prince & The Revolution
DELTA DAWN   Helen Reddy
DELTA LADY   Joe Cocker
DENIS   Blondie
DENISE   Randy & The Rainbows
DER KOMMISSAR   After The Fire
DESERT MOON   Dennis DeYoung
DESIDERATA   Les Crane
DESIRE   U2
DESIRE   Andy Gibb
DETROIT CITY   Tom Jones
DEVIL GATE DRIVE   Suzi Quatro
DEVIL IN DISGUISE   Elvis Presley
DEVIL INSIDE   INXS
DEVIL OR ANGEL   Bobby Vee
THE DEVIL WENT DOWN TO GEORGIA
Charlie Daniels Band
DEVIL WITH A BLUE DRESS ON & GOOD GOLLY
MISS MOLLY   Mitch Ryder & The Detroit Wheels
DEVIL WOMAN   Cliff Richard
DEVIL WOMAN   Marty Robbins
DEVIL'S ANSWER   Atomic Rooster
DEVOTED TO YOU   Everly Brothers
DIAMOND GIRL   Seals & Crofts
DIAMONDS   Herb Alpert
DIAMONDS   Jet Harris & Tony Meehan
DIANA   Paul Anka
DIANE   Bachelors
THE DIARY OF HORACE WIMP   Electric Light Orchestra
DID IT IN A MINUTE   Daryl Hall & John Oates
DID YOU EVER   Nancy Sinatra & Lee Hazlewood
DID YOU EVER HAVE TO MAKE UP YOUR MIND
Lovin' Spoonful
DIDN'T I (BLOW YOUR MIND THIS TIME)   Delfonics
DIDN'T I (BLOW YOUR MIND)
New Kids On The Block
DIDN'T WE ALMOST HAVE IT ALL   Whitney Houston
A DIFFERENT CORNER   George Michael
DIM ALL THE LIGHTS   Donna Summer
DIRTY DIANA   Michael Jackson
DIRTY LAUNDRY   Don Henley
DISCO CONNECTION   Isaac Hayes
DISCO DUCK   Rick Dees & His Cast Of Idiots
DISCO DUO   Johnnie Taylor
DISCO STOMP   Hamilton Bohannon
DISTANT DRUMS   Jim Reeves
DIVINE EMOTIONS   Narada
DIZZY   Tommy Roe
DO ANYTHING YOU WANNA DO   Rods
DO I DO   Stevie Wonder
DO I LIKE IT   Nat 'King' Cole
DO IT (TIL YOU'RE SATISFIED)   B.T. Express
DO IT AGAIN   Steely Dan
DO IT AGAIN   Beach Boys
DO IT AGAIN   Raffaella Carra
DO NOTHING   Specials
DO THAT TO ME ONE MORE TIME
Captain & Tennille
DO THE BIRD   Dee Dee Sharp
DO THE CONGA   Black Lace
DO THEY KNOW IT'S CHRISTMAS   Band Aid
DO THEY KNOW IT'S CHRISTMAS?   Band Aid 11
DO WAH DIDDY DIDDY   Manfred Mann
DO WHAT YOU DO   Jermaine Jackson
DO YA DO YA (WANNA PLEASE ME)   Samantha Fox
DO YOU BELIEVE IN LOVE   Huey Lewis & The News
DO YOU BELIEVE IN MAGIC   Lovin' Spoonful
DO YOU FEEL LIKE WE DO   Peter Frampton
DO YOU FEEL MY LOVE   Eddy Grant
DO YOU KNOW THE WAY TO SAN JOSE
Dionne Warwick
DO YOU KNOW WHAT I MEAN   Lee Michaels
DO YOU LOVE ME   Brian Poole & The Tremeloes
DO YOU LOVE ME   Contours
DO YOU MIND   Anthony Newley
DO YOU REALLY WANT TO HURT ME   Culture Club
DO YOU WANNA DANCE   Cliff Richard

DO YOU WANNA DANCE   Barry Blue
DO YOU WANNA MAKE LOVE   Peter McCann
DO YOU WANNA TOUCH ME (OH YEAH)
Gary Glitter
DO YOU WANT TO DANCE   Bobby Freeman
DO YOU WANT TO KNOW A SECRET   Beatles
DO YOU WANT TO KNOW A SECRET
Billy J. Kramer & The Dakotas
DOCTOR DOCTOR   Thompson Twins
DOCTOR MY EYES   Jackson Browne
DOCTOR MY EYES   Jackson Five
THE DOCTOR   Doobie Brothers
DOCTOR'S ORDERS   Sunny
DOCTORIN' THE HOUSE   Coldcut/Yazz
DOCTORIN' THE TARDIS   Timelords
DOES ANYBODY REALLY KNOW WHAT TIME IT IS
Chicago
DOES YOUR CHEWING GUM LOSE ITS FLAVOUR
Lonnie Donegan
DOES YOUR MOTHER KNOW   Abba
DOESN'T SOMEBODY WANT TO BE WANTED
Partridge Family
DOG EAT DOG   Adam & The Ants
DOING ALRIGHT WITH THE BOYS   Gary Glitter
DOING IT ALL FOR MY BABY
Huey Lewis & The News
DOLCE VITA   Ryan Paris
DOLLY MY LOVE   Moments
DOMINIQUE   Singing Nun
DOMINO   Van Morrison
DOMINO DANCING   Pet Shop Boys
DON QUIXOTE   Nik Kershaw
DON'T   Elvis Presley
DON'T ANSWER ME   Cilla Black
DON'T BE CRUEL   Bobby Brown
DON'T BE CRUEL   Cheap Trick
DON'T BE CRUEL   Elvis Presley
DON'T BET MONEY HONEY   Linda Scott
DON'T BLAME ME   Frank Ifield
DON'T BREAK MY HEART   UB40
DON'T BREAK THE HEART THAT LOVES YOU
Connie Francis
DON'T BRING ME DOWN   Animals
DON'T BRING ME DOWN   Pretty Things
DON'T BRING ME DOWN   Electric Light Orchestra
DON'T CALL US WE'LL CALL YOU
Sugarloaf/Jerry Corbetta
DON'T CRY   Asia
DON'T CRY DADDY   Elvis Presley
DON'T CRY FOR ME ARGENTINA   Julie Covington
DON'T CRY FOR ME ARGENTINA   Shadows
DON'T CRY OUT LOUD   Melissa Manchester
DON'T DISTURB THE GROOVE   System
DON'T DO IT BABY   Mac & Katie Kissoon
DON'T DO ME LIKE THAT
Tom Petty & The Heartbreakers
DON'T DREAM IT'S OVER   Crowded House
DON'T EVER CHANGE   Crickets
DON'T EXPECT ME TO BE YOUR FRIEND   Lobo
DON'T FALL IN LOVE WITH A DREAMER
Kenny Rogers & Kim Carnes
DON'T FORBID ME   Pat Boone
DON'T FORGET ME (WHEN I'M GONE)   Glass Tiger
DON'T FORGET TO REMEMBER   Bee Gees
DON'T GET ME WRONG   Pretenders
DON'T GIVE UP   Peter Gabriel & Kate Bush
DON'T GIVE UP ON US   David Soul
DON'T GO   Yazoo
DON'T GO BREAKING MY HEART
Elton John & Kiki Dee
DON'T HANG UP   Orlons
DON'T IT MAKE MY BROWN EYES BLUE
Crystal Gayle
DON'T JUST STAND THERE   Patty Duke
DON'T KNOCK THE ROCK   Bill Haley
DON'T KNOW MUCH
Linda Ronstadt (Feat. Aaron Neville)
DON'T LEAVE ME THIS WAY   Thelma Houston
DON'T LEAVE ME THIS WAY
Harold Melvin & The Blue Notes
DON'T LEAVE ME THIS WAY   Communards
DON'T LET IT DIE   Hurricane Smith
DON'T LET IT END   Styx
DON'T LET ME BE MISUNDERSTOOD   Animals
DON'T LET THE RAIN COME DOWN
Serendipity Singers
DON'T LET THE SUN CATCH YOU CRYING
Gerry & The Pacemakers
DON'T LET THE SUN GO DOWN ON ME
Elton John
DON'T LOOK BACK   Boston
DON'T LOSE MY NUMBER   Phil Collins
DON'T MAKE ME WAIT   Bomb The Bass
DON'T MAKE MY BABY BLUE   Shadows
DON'T MEAN NOTHING   Richard Marx
DON'T MESS WITH BILL   Marvelettes
DON'T PLAY YOUR ROCK 'N' ROLL TO ME   Smokey
DON'T PULL YOUR LOVE
Hamilton, Joe Frank & Reynolds

210

DON'T RUSH ME Taylor Dayne
DON'T SAY NOTHIN'(BAD ABOUT MY BABY) Cookies
DON'T SHED A TEAR Paul Carrack
DON'T SLEEP IN THE SUBWAY Petula Clark
DON'T STAND SO CLOSE TO ME Police
DON'T STAY AWAY TOO LONG Peters & Lee
DON'T STOP Fleetwood Mac
DON'T STOP BELIEVING Journey
DON'T STOP ME NOW Queen
DON'T STOP THE MUSIC Yarbrough & Peoples
DON'T STOP TILL YOU GET ENOUGH
Michael Jackson
DON'T TAKE AWAY THE MUSIC Tavares
DON'T TALK TO HIM Cliff Richard
DON'T TALK TO ME ABOUT LOVE Altered Images
DON'T TALK TO STRANGERS Rick Springfield
DON'T TELL ME Blancmange
DON'T TELL ME LIES Breathe
DON'T THAT BEAT ALL Adam Faith
DON'T THINK TWICE IT'S ALL RIGHT
Peter, Paul & Mary
DON'T THROW YOUR LOVE AWAY Searchers
DON'T TREAT ME LIKE A CHILD Helen Shapiro
DON'T TURN AROUND Aswad
DON'T WANNA LOSE YOU Gloria Estefan
DON'T WASTE MY TIME Paul Hardcastle
DON'T WORRY Marty Robbins
DON'T WORRY BE HAPPY Bobby McFerrin
DON'T YOU CARE Buckinghams
DON'T YOU KNOW IT Adam Faith
DON'T YOU KNOW WHAT THE NIGHT CAN DO
Steve Winwood
DON'T YOU ROCK ME DADDY-O
Lonnie Donegan
DON'T YOU THINK IT'S TIME Mike Berry
DON'T YOU WANT ME Jody Watley
DON'T YOU WANT ME Human League
DON'T YOU(FORGET ABOUT ME) Simple Minds
DON'T Elvis Presley
DONALD WHERE'S YOUR TROOSERS
Andy Stewart
DONNA 10CC
DONNA Marty Wilde
DONNA THE PRIMA DONNA Dion
THE DOOR IS STILL OPEN TO MY HEART
Dean Martin
(DO THE) SPANISH HUSTLE Fatback Band
(DO) THE HUCKLEBUCK Coast To Coast
DOUBLE BARREL Dave & Ansil Collins
DOUBLE DUTCH Malcolm McLaren
DOUBLE VISION Foreigner
DO WHAT YOU GOTTA DO Nina Simone
(DOWN AT) PAPA JOE'S Dixie Belles
DOWN BY THE LAZY RIVER Osmonds
DOWN DOWN Status Quo
DOWN IN THE BOONDOCKS Billy Joe Royal
DOWN ON THE BEACH TONIGHT Drifters
DOWN ON THE CORNER
Creedence Clearwater Revival
DOWN ON THE STREET Shakatak
DOWN TO EARTH Curiosity Killed The Cat
DOWN UNDER Men At Work
DOWN YONDER Johnny & The Hurricanes
DOWNTOWN Petula Clark
DR. BEAT Miami Sound Machine
DR. FEELGOOD Motley Crue
DR. KISS KISS 5000 Volts
DR. LOVE Tina Charles
DRAG CITY Jan & Dean
DRAGGIN' THE LINE Tommy James
DRAMA! Erasure
DREADLOCK HOLIDAY 10CC
DREAM A LIE UB40
DREAM BABY Roy Orbison
DREAM LOVER Bobby Darin
DREAM ON Aerosmith
DREAM WEAVER Gary Wright
DREAMIN' Johnny Burnette
DREAMIN' Vanessa Williams
DREAMING Cliff Richard
DREAMING Blondie
DREAMS Fleetwood Mac
DREAMS CAN TELL A LIE Nat 'King' Cole
DREAMTIME Daryl Hall
DRESS YOU UP Madonna
DRIFT AWAY Dobie Gray
DRIP DROP Dion
DRIVE Cars
DRIVE-IN SATURDAY David Bowie
DRIVIN' MY LIFE AWAY Eddie Rabbitt
DRIVING MY CAR Madness
DROP THE BOY Bros
DROWNING IN BERLIN Mobiles
DUELING BANJOS
Eric Weissberg & Steve Mandell
DUKE OF EARL Darts
DUKE OF EARL Gene Chandler
DUM DUM Brenda Lee
DUST IN THE WIND Kansas

DYNA-MITE Mud
DYNAMITE Bazuka
EACH TIME YOU BREAK MY HEART Nick Kamen
EARACHE MY EYE – FEAT. ALICE BOWIE
Cheech & Chong
EARLY IN THE MORNING Vanity Fare
THE EARTH DIES SCREAMING UB40
EASIER SAID THAN DONE Essex
EASY Commodores
EASY COME, EASY GO Bobby Sherman
EASY LOVER Philip Bailey & Phil Collins
EASY TO BE HARD Three Dog Night
EBB TIDE Righteous Brothers
EBONY AND IVORY
Paul McCartney & Stevie Wonder
EBONY EYES Everly Brothers
ECHO BEACH Martha & The Muffins
EDELWEISS Vince Hill
THE EDGE OF HEAVEN Wham!
EGYPTIAN REGGAE Jonathan Richman
EIGHT DAYS A WEEK Beatles
867-5309/JENNY Tommy Tutone
18 AND LIFE Skid Row
EIGHTEEN WITH A BULLET Pete Wingfield
18 YELLOW ROSES Bobby Darin
EIGHTH DAY Hazel O'Connor
EINSTEIN A GO GO Landscape
EL PASO Marty Robbins
ELEANOR RIGBY Beatles
ELECTED Alice Cooper
ELECTION DAY Arcadia
ELECTRIC AVENUE Eddy Grant
ELECTRIC BLUE Icehouse
ELENORE Turtles
ELI'S COMING Three Dog Night
ELOISE Barry Ryan
ELOISE Damned
ELUSIVE BUTTERFLY Val Doonican
ELUSIVE BUTTERFLY Bob Lind
ELVIRA Oak Ridge Boys
EMBARRASSMENT Madness
EMMA Hot Chocolate
EMOTION Samantha Sang
EMOTIONAL RESCUE Rolling Stones
EMOTIONS Brenda Lee
THE END OF THE INNOCENCE Don Henley
THE END OF THE WORLD Skeeter Davis
ENDLESS LOVE Diana Ross & Lionel Richie
ENDLESS SLEEP Marty Wilde
ENDLESS SUMMER NIGHTS Richard Marx
ENGINE ENGINE # 9 Roger Miller
ENGLAND SWINGS Roger Miller
ENGLISH COUNTRY GARDEN Jimmie Rodgers
ENJOY YOURSELF Jacksons
ENOLA GAY Orchestral Manoeuvres In The Dark
THE ENTERTAINER Marvin Hamlisch
ERES TU (TOUCH THE WIND) Mocedades
ERNIE (THE FASTEST MILK MAN IN THE WEST)
Benny Hill
ESCAPE (THE PINA COLADA SONG)
Rupert Holmes
ESPECIALLY FOR YOU
Kylie Minogue & Jason Donavan
ET LES OISEAUX CHANTAIENT Sweet People
ETERNAL FLAME Bangles
THE ETON RIFLES Jam
EUROPEAN FEMALE Stranglers
EVE OF DESTRUCTION Barry McGuire
EVE OF THE WAR Jeff Wayne
EVEN THE BAD TIMES ARE GOOD Tremeloes
EVEN THE NIGHTS ARE BETTER Air Supply
EVER FALLEN IN LOVE Fine Young Cannibals
EVERGREEN (LOVE THEME FROM A STAR IS BORN)
Barbra Streisand
(AN) EVERLASTING LOVE Andy Gibb
EVERLASTING LOVE Carl Carlton
EVERLASTING LOVE Love Affair
EVERY BEAT OF MY HEART Rod Stewart
EVERY BEAT OF MY HEART
Gladys Knight & The Pips
EVERY BREATH YOU TAKE Police
EVERY DAY (I LOVE YOU MORE) Jason Donovan
EVERY DAY HURTS Sad Cafe
EVERY I'S A WINNER Hot Chocolate
EVERY LITTLE STEP Bobby Brown
EVERY LITTLE THING SHE DOES IS MAGIC Police
EVERY LOSER WINS Nick Berry
EVERY ROSE HAS ITS THORN Poison
EVERY WOMAN IN THE WORLD Air Supply
EVERYBODY Tommy Roe
EVERYBODY DANCE Chic
EVERYBODY GET TOGETHER Dave Clark Five
EVERYBODY HAVE FUN TONIGHT Wang Chung
EVERYBODY KNOWS Dave Clark Five
EVERYBODY LOVES A CLOWN
Gary Lewis & The Playboys
EVERYBODY LOVES ME BUT YOU Brenda Lee
EVERYBODY LOVES SOMEBODY Dean Martin
EVERYBODY PLAYS THE FOOL Main Ingredient

EVERYBODY WANTS TO RULE THE WORLD
Tears For Fears
EVERYBODY WANTS TO RUN THE WORLD
Tears For Fears
EVERYBODY'S GOT TO LEARN SOMETIME Korgis
EVERYBODY'S LAUGHING Phil Fearon & Galaxy
EVERYBODY'S SOMEBODY'S FOOL
Connie Francis
EVERYBODY'S TALKIN' Nilsson
EVERYDAY Slade
EVERYDAY IS LIKE SUNDAY Morrissey
EVERYDAY PEOPLE Sly & The Family Stone
EVERYONE'S GONE TO THE MOON
Jonathan King
EVERYTHING COUNTS Depeche Mode
EVERYTHING I AM Plastic Penny
EVERYTHING I OWN Bread
EVERYTHING I OWN Boy George
EVERYTHING I OWN Ken Boothe
EVERYTHING IS BEAUTIFUL Ray Stevens
EVERYTHING MUST CHANGE Paul Young
EVERYTHING SHE WANTS Wham!
EVERYTHING THAT TOUCHES YOU Association
EVERYTHING YOUR HEART DESIRES
Daryl Hall & John Oates
EVERYTHING'S ALRIGHT Mojos
EVERYTIME YOU GO AWAY Paul Young
EVERYWHERE Fleetwood Mac
EVIL HEARTED YOU Yardbirds
THE EVIL THAT MEN DO Iron Maiden
EVIL WAYS Santana
EVIL WOMAN Electric Light Orchestra
EXCERPT FROM A TEENAGE OPERA Keith West
EXODUS Ferrante & Teicher
EXPERIMENTS WITH MICE Johnny Dankworth
EXPRESS B.T. Express
EXPRESS YOURSELF Madonna
EXPRESSWAY TO YOUR HEART Soul Survivors
EXTENDED PLAY (E.P.) Bryan Ferry
EYE IN THE SKY Alan Parsons Project
EYE LEVEL Simon Park Orchestra
EYE OF THE TIGER Survivor
EYES WITHOUT A FACE Billy Idol
F.B.I. Shadows
F.L.M. Mel & Kim
FADE TO GREY Visage
FAIRY TALE OF NEW YORK Pogues/Kirsty McColl
FAITH George Michael
FALL IN LOVE WITH YOU Cliff Richard
FALLIN' IN LOVE Hamilton, Joe Frank & Reynolds
FALLING Roy Orbison
FALLING APART AT THE SEAMS Marmalade
FAME Irene Cara
FAME David Bowie
FAMILY AFFAIR Sly & The Family Stone
FAMILY MAN Daryl Hall & John Oates
FANCY PANTS Kenny
FANFARE FOR THE COMMON MAN
Emerson Lake & Palmer
FANTASTIC DAY Haircut 100
FANTASY ISLAND Tight Fit
FAR FAR AWAY Slade
FAR FROM OVER Frank Stallone
FAREWELL IS A LONELY SOUND Jimmy Ruffin
FAREWELL MY SUMMER LOVE Michael Jackson
FAREWELL Rod Stewart
FASHION David Bowie
FAST CAR Tracy Chapman
FATHER CHRISTMAS DO NOT TOUCH ME Goodies
FATHER FIGURE George Michael
FATTIE BUM-BUM Carl Malcolm
FAVOURITE SHIRTS (BOY MEETS GIRL) Haircut 100
FEEL LIKE MAKIN' LOVE Bad Company
FEEL LIKE MAKIN' LOVE Roberta Flack
FEEL SO REAL Steve Arrington
FEEL THE NEED IN ME Detroit Emeralds
FEELIN' STRONGER EVERY DAY Chicago
FEELINGS Morris Albert
(FEELS LIKE) HEAVEN Fiction Factory
FEELS LIKE I'M IN LOVE Kelly Marie
FEELS LIKE THE FIRST TIME Foreigner
FEELS SO GOOD Chuck Mangione
FERNANDO Abba
FERRY 'CROSS THE MERSEY
Marsden/McCartney/Johnson/Christians
FERRY ACROSS THE MERSEY
Gerry & The Pacemakers
FEVER Peggy Lee
FEVER McCoys
FIELDS OF FIRE (400 MILES) Big Country
A FIFTH OF BEETHOVEN Walter Murphy
50 WAYS TO LEAVE YOUR LOVER Paul Simon
FIGARO Brotherhood of Man
FIGHT Barbra Streisand
FIGHT THE POWER PT. 1 Isley Brothers
THE FINAL COUNTDOWN Europe
FIND MY LOVE Fairground Attraction
FIND THE TIME Five Star
FINE TIME Yazz

THE FINER THINGS Steve Winwood
FINGER POPPIN' TIME Hank Ballard & The Midnighters
FINGERTIPS (PT. 2) Stevie Wonder
FINGS AIN'T WHAT THEY USED T'BE Max Bygraves
FIRE Pointer Sisters
FIRE Ohio Players
FIRE Crazy World Of Arthur Brown
FIRE AND RAIN James Taylor
FIRE BRIGADE Move
FIRE LAKE Bob Seger & The Silver Bullet Band
FIRST CUT IS THE DEEPEST Rod Stewart
FIRST OF MAY Bee Gees
THE FIRST TIME EVER I SAW YOUR FACE
Roberta Flack
THE FIRST TIME Robin Beck
THE FIRST TIME Adam Faith
500 MILES AWAY FROM HOME Bobby Bare
5-4-3-2-1 Manfred Mann
FIVE O'CLOCK WORLD Vogues
5-7-0-5 City Boy
THE FLAME Cheap Trick
FLASH Queen
FLASHDANCE....WHAT A FEELING Irene Cara
FLOAT ON Floaters
THE FLORAL DANCE
Brighouse and Rastrick Brass Band
FLOWERS IN THE RAIN Move
FLOWERS ON THE WALL Statler Brothers
FLOY JOY Supremes
FLY LIKE AN EAGLE Steve Miller Band
FLY ROBIN FLY Silver Convention
THE FLY Chubby Checker
THE FOLK SINGER Tommy Roe
FOLLOW YOU FOLLOW ME Genesis
FOOD FOR THOUGHT UB40
FOOL # 1 Brenda Lee
THE FOOL ON THE HILL Sergio Mendes & Brasil '66
A FOOL SUCH AS I Elvis Presley
FOOL TO CRY Rolling Stones
FOOL'S GOLD Stone Roses
FOOLED AROUND AND FELL IN LOVE Elvin Bishop
FOOLISH BEAT Debbie Gibson
FOOLISH LITTLE GIRL Shirelles
FOOT TAPPER Shadows
FOOTLOOSE Kenny Loggins
FOOTSEE Wigan's Chosen Few
FOOTSTEPS Steve Lawrence
FOR ALL WE KNOW Shirley Bassey
FOR ALL WE KNOW Carpenters
FOR AMERICA Red Box
FOR ONCE IN MY LIFE Stevie Wonder
FOR THE GOOD TIMES Perry Como
FOR THE LOVE OF MONEY O'Jays
FOR WHAT IT'S WORTH Buffalo Springfield
FOR YOU Rick Nelson
FOR YOUR EYES ONLY Sheena Easton
FOR YOUR LOVE Yardbirds
FOREVER Roy Wood
FOREVER Little Dippers
FOREVER & EVER Slik
FOREVER AUTUMN Justin Hayward
FOREVER YOUR GIRL Paula Abdul
FORGET HIM Bobby Rydell
FORGET ME NOT Eden Kane
FORGET ME NOTS Patrice Rushen
FORTRESS AROUND YOUR HEART Sting
FORTUNATE SON Creedence Clearwater Revival
48 CRASH Suzi Quatro
FORTY MILES OF BAD ROAD Duane Eddy
FOUR FROM TOYAH E.P. Toyah
FOUR LETTER WORD Kim Wilde
FOX ON THE RUN Manfred Mann
FOX ON THE RUN Sweet
FRANKENSTEIN Edgar Winter Group
FRANKIE Sister Sledge
FRANKIE Connie Francis
FREDDIE'S DEAD Curtis Mayfield
FREE Deniece Williams
FREEDOM Wham!
FREEDOM COME FREEDOM GO Fortunes
FREEWAY OF LOVE Aretha Franklin
FREEZE-FRAME J. Geils Band
FRENCH KISS Lil Louis
FRENCH KISSIN' IN THE USA Debbie Harry
FRESH Kool & The Gang
FRIDAY ON MY MIND Easybeats
FRIEND OR FOE Adam Ant
FRIENDLY PERSUASION Pat Boone
FRIENDS Arrival
FRIENDS Jody Watley With Erik B & Rakim
FRIENDS AND LOVERS
Gloria Loring & Carl Anderson
FRIGGIN' IN THE RIGGIN' Sex Pistols
FRIGHTENED CITY Shadows
FROM A JACK TO A KING Ned Miller
FROM A WINDOW Billy J. Kramer & The Dakotas
FROM ME TO YOU Beatles
FROM NEW YORK TO L.A. Patsy Gallant
FROM THE UNDERWORLD Herd

FROZEN ORANGE JUICE   Peter Sarstedt
FULL METAL JACKET
Abigail Mead & Nigel Goulding
FUN, FUN, FUN   Beach Boys
FUNERAL PYRE   Jam
FUNKIN' FOR JAMAICA (N.Y.)   Tom Browne
FUNKY BROADWAY   Wilson Pickett
FUNKY COLD MEDINA   Tone Loc
FUNKY GIBBON   Goodies
FUNKY MOPED   Jasper Carrott
FUNKY TOWN   Pseudo Echo
FUNKY WEEKEND   Stylistics
FUNKYTOWN   Lipps Inc.
FUNNY FACE   Donna Fargo
FUNNY FAMILIAR FORGOTTEN FEELING
Tom Jones
FUNNY HOW LOVE CAN BE   Ivy League
FUNNY WAY OF LAUGHIN'   Burl Ives
G.T.O.   Ronny & The Daytonas
GALVESTON   Glen Campbell
GAMBLER   Madonna
GAMBLIN' MAN   Lonnie Donegan
GAME OF LOVE
Wayne Fontana & The Mindbenders
GAMES PEOPLE PLAY   Joe South
GAMES WITHOUT FRONTIERS   Peter Gabriel
GANGSTERS   Specials
GARDEN OF EDEN   Frankie Vaughan
GARDEN PARTY   Rick Nelson
GAYE   Clifford T. Ward
GEE BABY   Peter Shelley
GEE WHIZ (LOOK AT HIS EYES)   Carla Thomas
GEE WHIZ IT'S YOU   Cliff Richard
GENO   Dexy's Midnight Runners
GENTLE ON MY MIND   Dean Martin
GEORGIA ON MY MIND   Ray Charles
GEORGY GIRL   Seekers
GET A LIFE   Soul II Soul
GET AWAY   Georgie Fame
GET BACK   Beatles
GET CLOSER   Seals & Crofts
GET DANCING   Disco Tex & The Sex-O-Lettes
GET DOWN   Gilbert O'Sullivan
GET DOWN ON IT   Kool & The Gang
GET DOWN TONIGHT   KC & The Sunshine Band
GET DOWN, GET DOWN (GET ON THE FLOOR)
Joe Simon
GET IT   Darts
GET IT ON   T. Rex
GET IT ON (BANG A GONG)   Power Station
GET LOST   Eden Kane
GET OFF   Foxy
GET OFF OF MY CLOUD   Rolling Stones
GET OUTTA MY DREAMS GET INTO MY CAR
Billy Ocean
GET READY   Rare Earth
GET READY   Temptations
GET TOGETHER   Youngbloods
GET UP AND BOOGIE   Silver Convention
GHETTO CHILD   Detroit Spinners
GHOST TOWN   Specials
GHOSTBUSTERS   Ray Parker Jr.
GHOSTS   Japan
GIGI   Billy Eckstine
GIMME ALL YOUR LOVIN'   ZZ Top
GIMME DAT DING   Pipkins
GIMME GIMME GIMME (A MAN AFTER MIDNIGHT)
Abba
GIMME HOPE JO'ANNA   Eddy Grant
GIMME LITTLE SIGN   Brenton Wood
GIMME SOME LOVING   Spencer Davis Group
GINA   Johnny Mathis
GINNY COME LATELY   Brian Hyland
THE GIRL CAN'T HELP IT   Darts
GIRL CRAZY   Hot Chocolate
GIRL DON'T COME   Sandie Shaw
THE GIRL FROM IPANEMA   Stan Getz/Astrud Gilberto
GIRL I'M GONNA MISS YOU   Milli Vanilli
THE GIRL IS MINE (WITH MICHAEL JACKSON)
Paul McCartney/Michael Jackson
A GIRL LIKE YOU   Cliff Richard
A GIRL LIKE YOU   Young Rascals
GIRL OF MY BEST FRIEND   Elvis Presley
GIRL WATCHER   O'Kaysions
GIRL YOU KNOW IT'S TRUE   Milli Vanilli
GIRL, YOU'LL BE A WOMAN SOON   Neil Diamond
GIRLFRIEND   Pebbles
GIRLIE GIRLIE   Sophia George
GIRLS   Moments and Whatnauts
GIRLS GIRLS GIRLS   Sailor
GIRLS JUST WANT TO HAVE FUN   Cyndi Lauper
GIRLS ON FILM   Duran Duran
GIRLS TALK   Dave Edmunds
GITARZAN   Ray Stevens
GIVE A LITTLE LOVE   Bay City Rollers
GIVE IT UP   KC & The Sunshine Band
GIVE ME BACK MY HEART   Dollar
GIVE ME JUST A LITTLE MORE TIME
Chairman Of The Board

GIVE ME LOVE (GIVE ME PEACE ON EARTH)
George Harrison
GIVE ME THE NIGHT   George Benson
GIVE PEACE A CHANCE   John Lennon
GIVING IT ALL AWAY   Roger Daltrey
GIVING IT UP FOR YOUR LOVE   Delbert McClinton
GIVING YOU THE BEST THAT I GOT   Anita Baker
GLAD ALL OVER   Dave Clark Five
GLAD IT'S ALL OVER   Captain Sensible
THE GLAMOROUS LIFE   Sheila E
GLASS OF CHAMPAGNE   Sailor
GLOBETROTTER   Tornados
GLORIA   Shadows of Knight
GLORIA   Laura Branigan
GLORY DAYS   Bruce Springsteen
GLORY OF LOVE   Peter Cetera
GO ALL THE WAY   Raspberries
GO AWAY LITTLE GIRL   Mark Wynter
GO AWAY LITTLE GIRL   Donny Osmond
GO AWAY LITTLE GIRL   Steve Lawrence
GO BUDDY GO   Stranglers
GO HOME   Stevie Wonder
GO JIMMY GO   Jimmy Clanton
GO NOW!   Moody Blues
GO WILD IN THE COUNTRY   Bow Wow Wow
GO YOUR OWN WAY   Fleetwood Mac
GO (BEFORE YOU BREAK MY HEART)
Gigliola Cinquetti
GOD ONLY KNOWS   Beach Boys
GOD SAVE THE QUEEN   Sex Pistols
GOIN' BACK   Dusty Springfield
GOIN' OUT OF MY HEAD
Little Anthony & The Imperials
GOIN' OUT OF MY HEAD/CAN'T TAKE MY EYES OFF
YOU   Lettermen
GOING BACK TO MY ROOTS   Odyssey
GOING HOME   Osmonds
GOING IN WITH MY EYES OPEN   David Soul
GOING UNDERGROUND   Jam
GOLD   John Stewart
GOLD   Spandau Ballet
GOLDEN BROWN   Stranglers
GOLDEN YEARS   David Bowie
THE GOLDEN YEARS (E.P.)   Motorhead
GOLDFINGER   Shirley Bassey
GONNA FLY NOW   Bill Conti
GONNA GET ALONG WITHOUT YOU NOW
Viola Wills
GONNA MAKE YOU A STAR   David Essex
GONNA MAKE YOU AN OFFER YOU CAN'T REFUSE
Jimmy Helms
GOODBYE MY LOVE   Searchers
A GOOD HEART   Feargal Sharkey
GOOD LIFE   Inner City
GOOD LOVIN'   Young Rascals
GOOD LUCK CHARM   Elvis Presley
GOOD MORNING FREEDOM   Blue Mink
GOOD MORNING JUDGE   10CC
GOOD MORNING STARSHINE   Oliver
GOOD OLD ROCK 'N' ROLL   Dave Clark Five
GOOD THING   Paul Revere & The Raiders
GOOD THING   Fine Young Cannibals
GOOD THING GOING   Sugar Minott
GOOD TIMES   Chic
GOOD TIMIN'   Jimmy Jones
GOOD TRADITION   Tanita Tikaram
GOOD VIBRATIONS   Beach Boys
A GOOD YEAR FOR THE ROSES   Elvis Costello
THE GOOD, THE BAD & THE UGLY
Hugo Montenegro & His Orchestra
GOODBYE   Mary Hopkin
GOODBYE BABY   Jack Scott
GOODBYE CRUEL WORLD   James Darren
GOODBYE MY LOVE   Glitter Band
GOODBYE SAM HELLO SAMANTHA   Cliff Richard
GOODBYE STRANGER   Pepsi & Shirlie
GOODBYE TO LOVE   Carpenters
GOODBYE YELLOW BRICK ROAD   Elton John
GOODNESS GRACIOUS ME
Peter Sellers & Sophia Loren
GOODNIGHT MIDNIGHT   Clodagh Rodgers
GOODNIGHT TONIGHT   Paul McCartney
GOODTIME CHARLIE'S GOT THE BLUES
Danny O'Keefe
GOODY TWO SHOES   Adam Ant
GOOGLE EYE   Nashville Teens
THE GOONIES 'R' GOOD ENOUGH   Cyndi Lauper
GOT A HOLD ON ME   Christine McVie
GOT MY MIND SET ON YOU   George Harrison
GOT TO BE CERTAIN   Kylie Minogue
GOT TO BE THERE   Michael Jackson
GOT TO GET YOU INTO MY LIFE
Cliff Bennett & The Rebel Rousers
GOT TO GET YOU INTO MY LIFE
Earth, Wind & Fire
GOT TO GET YOU INTO MY LIFE   Beatles
GOT TO GIVE IT UP   Marvin Gaye
GOTTA HAVE SOMETHING IN THE BANK FRANK
Frankie Vaughan & The Kaye Sisters

GOTTA PULL MYSELF TOGETHER   Nolans
GRAND COOLIE DAM   Lonnie Donegan
GRAND PIANO   Mixmaster
GRANDAD   Clive Dunn
GRANDMA'S PARTY   Paul Nicholas
GRAVY (FOR MY MASHED POTATOES)
Dee Dee Sharp
GRAZIN' IN THE GRASS   Friends Of Distinction
GRAZING IN THE GRASS   Hugh Masekela
GREASE   Frankie Valli
GREAT BALLS OF FIRE   Jerry Lee Lewis
THE GREAT PRETENDER   Freddie Mercury
THE GREAT PRETENDER   Platters
GREATEST LOVE OF ALL   Whitney Houston
GREEN DOOR   Shakin' Stevens
GREEN DOOR   Frankie Vaughan
GREEN EYED LADY   Sugarloaf
GREEN GRASS   Gary Lewis & The Playboys
GREEN GREEN GRASS OF HOME   Tom Jones
THE GREEN LEAVES OF SUMMER   Kenny Ball
THE GREEN MANALISHI   Fleetwood Mac
GREEN ONIONS   Booker T. & The M.G.'s
GREEN RIVER   Creedence Clearwater Revival
GREEN TAMBOURINE   Lemon Pipers
GREENFIELDS   Brothers Four
GREY DAY   Madness
THE GROOVE LINE   Heatwave
GROOVE ME   King Floyd
THE GROOVE   Rodney Franklin
THE GROOVER   T. Rex
GROOVIN'   Young Rascals
GROOVIN' WITH MR. BLOE   Mr. Bloe
GROOVIN'(YOU'RE THE BEST THING   Style Council
A GROOVY KIND OF LOVE   Phil Collins
A GROOVY KIND OF LOVE   Mindbenders
GUANTANAMERA   Sandpipers
GUDBUY T'JANE   Slade
GUILTY   Pearls
GUILTY   Barbra Streisand & Barry Gibb
GUITAR TANGO   Shadows
GURNEY SLADE   Max Harris
GYPSIES TRAMPS AND THIEVES   Cher
GYPSY MAN   War
GYPSY WOMAN   Brian Hyland
GYPSYS TRAMPS & THIEVES   Cher
H.A.P.P.Y. RADIO   Edwin Starr
HA HA SAID THE CLOWN   Manfred Mann
HAIR   Cowsills
HALF-BREED   Cher
HALFWAY DOWN THE STAIRS   Muppets
HALFWAY TO PARADISE   Billy Fury
HALLELUJAH   Milk & Honey
HALLELUJAH FREEDOM   Junior Campbell
HAND ON YOUR HEART   Kylie Minogue
HANDFUL OF SONGS   Tommy Steele
HANDS OFF—SHE'S MINE   Beat
HANDS TO HEAVEN   Breathe
HANDS UP (GIVE ME YOUR HEART)   Ottawan
HANDY MAN   Jimmy Jones
HANDY MAN   James Taylor
HANG 'EM HIGH   Booker T. & The M.G.'s
HANG ON IN THERE BABY   Johnny Bristol
HANG ON SLOOPY   McCoys
HANGIN' TOUGH   New Kids On The Block
HANGING ON THE TELEPHONE   Blondie
HANKY PANKY   Tommy James & The Shondells
THE HAPPENING   Supremes
HAPPY BIRTHDAY   Stevie Wonder
HAPPY BIRTHDAY   Altered Images
HAPPY BIRTHDAY, SWEET SIXTEEN   Neil Sedaka
HAPPY DAYS   Pratt & McClain
HAPPY HOUR   Housemartins
HAPPY JACK   Who
HAPPY TALK   Captain Sensible
HAPPY TO BE ON AN ISLAND IN THE SUN
Demis Roussos
HAPPY TOGETHER   Turtles
HAPPY XMAS (WAR IS OVER)   John Lennon
HAPPY-GO-LUCKY-ME   Paul Evans
HARBOR LIGHTS   Platters
A HARD DAY'S NIGHT   Beatles
HARD HABIT TO BREAK   Chicago
HARD HEADED WOMAN   Elvis Presley
A HARD RAIN'S GONNA FALL   Bryan Ferry
HARD TO SAY   Dan Fogelberg
HARD TO SAY I'M SORRY   Chicago
HARDEN MY HEART   Quarterflash
THE HARDER I TRY   Brother Beyond
HARLEM SHUFFLE   Bob & Earl
HARLEM SHUFFLE   Rolling Stones
HARPER VALLEY P.T.A.   Jeannie C. Riley
HARVEST FOR THE WORLD   Isley Brothers
HARVEST FOR THE WORLD   Christians
HATS OFF TO LARRY   Del Shannon
HAVE A DRINK ON ME   Lonnie Donegan
HAVE I THE RIGHT?   Dead End Kids
HAVE I THE RIGHT?   Honeycombs
HAVE I TOLD YOU LATELY THAT I LOVE YOU
Ricky Nelson

HAVE YOU EVER BEEN IN LOVE   Leo Sayer
HAVE YOU EVER SEEN THE RAIN
Creedence Clearwater Revival
HAVE YOU NEVER BEEN MELLOW
Olivia Newton-John
HAVE YOU SEEN HER   Chi-Lites
HAVE YOU SEEN YOUR MOTHER BABY STANDING IN
THE SHADOWS   Rolling Stones
HAWAII FIVE-O   Ventures
HAWKEYE   Frankie Laine
HAZY SHADE OF WINTER   Bangles
HE AIN'T HEAVY, HE'S MY BROTHER   Hollies
HE AIN'T NO COMPETITION   Brother Beyond
HE DON'T LOVE YOU (LIKE I LOVE YOU)
Tony Orlando & Dawn
HE WILL BREAK YOUR HEART   Jerry Butler
HE'LL HAVE TO GO   Jim Reeves
HE'LL HAVE TO STAY   Jeanne Black
HE'S A REBEL   Crystals
HE'S GONNA STEP ON YOU AGAIN   John Kongos
HE'S IN TOWN   Rockin' Berries
HE'S MISSTRA KNOW IT ALL   Stevie Wonder
HE'S SO FINE   Chiffons
HE'S SO SHY   Pointer Sisters
HE'S THE GREATEST DANCER   Sister Sledge
HEAD OVER HEELS   Tears For Fears
HEAD TO TOE   Lisa Lisa & Cult Jam
HEART   Pet Shop Boys
HEART AND SOUL   Huey Lewis & The News
HEART AND SOUL   T'Pau
HEART ATTACK   Olivia Newton-John
HEART FULL OF SOUL   Yardbirds
THE HEART OF A MAN   Frankie Vaughan
HEART OF GLASS   Blondie
HEART OF GOLD   Neil Young
THE HEART OF ROCK 'N' ROLL
Huey Lewis & The News
HEART ON MY SLEEVE   Gallagher & Lyle
HEARTACHE   Pepsi & Shirlie
HEARTACHE AVENUE   Maisonettes
HEARTACHE TONIGHT   Eagles
HEARTACHES   Marcels
HEARTACHES BY THE NUMBER   Guy Mitchell
HEARTBEAT   Don Johnson
HEARTBEAT   Showaddywaddy
HEARTBEAT – IT'S A LOVEBEAT   DeFranco Family
HEARTBREAK HOTEL   Elvis Presley
HEARTBREAKER   Dionne Warwick
HEARTLIGHT   Neil Diamond
HEARTS   Marty Balin
THE HEAT IS ON   Glenn Frey
HEAT OF THE MOMENT   Asia
HEAT WAVE   Martha & The Vandellas
HEAT WAVE   Linda Ronstadt
HEAVEN   Warrant
HEAVEN   Bryan Adams
HEAVEN HELP ME   Deon Estus
HEAVEN HELP US ALL   Stevie Wonder
HEAVEN IS A PLACE ON EARTH   Belinda Carlisle
HEAVEN KNOWS   Donna Summer
HEAVEN KNOWS I'M MISERABLE NOW   Smiths
HEAVEN MUST BE MISSING AN ANGEL   Tavares
HEAVEN MUST HAVE SENT YOU   Elgins
HEAVEN ON THE 7TH FLOOR   Paul Nicholas
HELEN WHEELS   Paul McCartney
HELL RAISER   Sweet
HELLO   Lionel Richie
HELLO AGAIN   Neil Diamond
HELLO GOODBYE   Beatles
HELLO HELLO I'M BACK AGAIN   Gary Glitter
HELLO HURRAY   Alice Cooper
HELLO IT'S ME   Todd Rundgren
HELLO MARY LOU   Ricky Nelson
HELLO MUDDUH, HELLO FADDUH   Allan Sherman
HELLO STRANGER   Barbara Lewis
HELLO SUSIE   Amen Corner
HELLO THIS IS JOANNIE   Paul Evans
HELLO, DOLLY!   Louis Armstrong
HELLO, I LOVE YOU   Doors
HELP   Bananarama
HELP ME   Joni Mitchell
HELP ME MAKE IT THROUGH THE NIGHT
Sammi Smith
HELP ME MAKE IT THROUGH THE NIGHT
John Holt
HELP ME, RHONDA   Beach Boys
HELP YOURSELF   Tom Jones
HELP!   Beatles
HER ROYAL MAJESTY   James Darren
HERE COMES MY BABY   Tremeloes
HERE COMES THAT FEELING   Brenda Lee
HERE COMES THE JUDGE   Shorty Long
HERE COMES THE NIGHT   Them
HERE COMES THE RAIN AGAIN   Eurythmics
HERE COMES THE SUN   Steve Harley
HERE I AM (COME AND TAKE ME)   Al Green
HERE I AM (JUST WHEN YOU THOUGHT I WAS
OVER YOU)   Air Supply
HERE I GO AGAIN   Hollies

HERE I GO AGAIN Whitesnake
HERE IT COMES AGAIN Fortunes
HERE WE GO ROUND THE MULBERRY BUSH
Traffic
HERE YOU COME AGAIN Dolly Parton
HEROES AND VILLAINS Beach Boys
HERSHAM BOYS Sham 69
HEY D.J. I CAN'T DANCE TO Beatmasters
HEY! BABY Bruce Channel
HEY DEANIE Shaun Cassidy
HEY GIRL Small Faces
HEY GIRL Freddie Scott
HEY GIRL Donny Osmond
HEY GIRL DON'T BOTHER ME Tams
HEY!JEALOUS LOVER Frank Sinatra
HEY JOE Jimi Hendrix Experience
HEY JUDE Beatles
HEY LITTLE COBRA Rip Chords
HEY LITTLE GIRL Del Shannon
HEY MATTHEW Karel Fialka
HEY MUSIC LOVER S'Express
HEY NINETEEN Steely Dan
HEY PAULA Paul & Paula
HEY ROCK AND ROLL Showaddywaddy
HEY THERE LONELY GIRL Eddie Holman
(HEY WON'T YOU PLAY) ANOTHER SOMEBODY
DONE SOMEBODY WRONG SONG B.J. Thomas
(HEY YOU) THE ROCKSTEADY CREW
Rocksteady Crew
HI HI HI Paul McCartney
HI HO SILVER Jim Diamond
HI-FIDELITY (Featuring Valerie Landsberg)
Kids From 'Fame'
HIDEAWAY Dave Dee, Dozy, Beaky, Mick & Titch
HIGH CLASS BABY Cliff Richard
HIGH ENERGY Evelyn Thomas
HIGH HOPES Frank Sinatra
HIGH IN THE SKY Amen Corner
HIGH LIFE Modern Romance
HIGH ON YOU Survivor
HIGH TIME Paul Jones
HIGHER AND HIGHER Jackie Wilson
HIGHER GROUND Stevie Wonder
HIGHER LOVE Steve Winwood
HIM Rupert Holmes
HIM OR ME – WHAT'S IT GONNA BE
Paul Revere & The Raiders
HIP TO BE SQUARE Huey Lewis & The News
HIPPY HIPPY SHAKE Swinging Blue Jeans
HIS LATEST FLAME Elvis Presley
HISTORY Mai Tai
HIT ME WITH YOUR BEST SHOT Pat Benatar
HIT ME WITH YOUR RHYTHM STICK
Ian Dury & Blockheads
HIT THAT PERFECT BEAT Bronski Beat
HIT THE ROAD JACK Ray Charles
HITCHIN' A RIDE Vanity Fare
HOCUS POCUS Focus
HOLD BACK THE NIGHT Trammps
HOLD ME Fleetwood Mac
HOLD ME P.J. Proby
HOLD ME CLOSE David Essex
HOLD ME IN YOUR ARMS Rick Astley
HOLD ME NOW Johnny Logan
HOLD ME NOW Thompson Twins
HOLD ME THRILL ME KISS ME Mel Carter
HOLD ME TIGHT Johnny Nash
HOLD ON TIGHT Electric Light Orchestra
HOLD ON TIGHT ELO
HOLD ON TO MY LOVE Jimmy Ruffin
HOLD ON TO THE NIGHTS Richard Marx
HOLD THE LINE Toto
HOLD TIGHT Dave Dee, Dozy, Beaky, Mick & Titch
HOLD WHAT YOU'VE GOT Joe Tex
HOLD YOUR HEAD UP Argent
HOLDING BACK THE YEARS Simply Red
HOLDING OUT FOR A HERO Bonnie Tyler
HOLE IN MY SHOE Traffic
HOLE IN MY SHOE Neil
HOLE IN THE GROUND Bernard Cribbins
HOLIDAY Madonna
HOLIDAY RAP M.C. Miker'G' & Deejay
HOLIDAYS IN THE SUN Sex Pistols
HOLLY HOLY Neil Diamond
HOLLYWOOD SWINGING Kool & The Gang
HOLY COW Lee Dorsey
HOMBURG Procol Harum
HOME LOVIN' MAN Andy Williams
HOMELY GIRL UB40
HOMELY GIRL Chi-Lites
HOMEWARD BOUND Simon & Garfunkel
HONEY Bobby Goldsboro
HONEY COME BACK Glen Campbell
HONEY HONEY Sweet Dreams
HONEYCOMB Jimmie Rodgers
HONG KONG GARDEN Siouxsie & The Banshees
HONKY CAT Elton John
HONKY TONK WOMEN Rolling Stones
HOOKED ON A FEELING B.J. Thomas

HOOKED ON A FEELING Blue Suede
HOOKED ON CLASSICS
Royal Philharmonic Orchestra
HOORAY FOR HAZEL Tommy Roe
HOORAY HOORAY IT'S A HOLI-HOLIDAY
Boney M
HOPELESSLY DEVOTED TO YOU
Olivia Newton-John
THE HORSE Cliff Nobles & Co.
HORSE WITH NO NAME America
HOT BLOODED Foreigner
HOT CHILD IN THE CITY Nick Gilder
HOT DIGGITY Perry Como
HOT FUN IN THE SUMMERTIME
Sly & The Family Stone
HOT LINE Sylvers
HOT LOVE T. Rex
HOT ROD LINCOLN Commander Cody
HOT STUFF Donna Summer
HOTEL CALIFORNIA Eagles
HOTEL HAPPINESS Brook Benton
HOTLEGS Rod Stewart
HOUND DOG Elvis Presley
HOUSE ARREST Krush
HOUSE NATION House Master Boyz
HOUSE OF FUN Madness
HOUSE OF THE RISING SUN Frijid Pink
HOUSE OF THE RISING SUN Animals
THE HOUSE THAT JACK BUILT Aretha Franklin
THE HOUSE THAT JACK BUILT Alan Price Set
THE HOUSE THAT JACK BUILT Tracie
HOW 'BOUT US Champaign
HOW ABOUT THAT Adam Faith
HOW CAN I BE SURE Young Rascals
HOW CAN I BE SURE David Cassidy
HOW CAN I FALL Breathe
HOW CAN YOU MEND A BROKEN HEART
Bee Gees
HOW DEEP IS YOUR LOVE Bee Gees
HOW DO I MAKE YOU Linda Ronstadt
HOW DO YOU DO Mouth & McNeal
HOW DO YOU DO IT? Gerry & The Pacemakers
HOW DOES THAT GRAB YOU DARLIN'
Nancy Sinatra
HOW LONG Ace
HOW MANY TEARS Bobby Vee
HOW MUCH I FEEL Ambrosia
HOW MUCH LOVE Leo Sayer
HOW SOON Henry Mancini & His Orchestra
HOW SWEET IT IS (TO BE LOVED BY YOU)
James Taylor
HOW SWEET IT IS TO BE LOVED BY YOU
Marvin Gaye
HOW WILL I KNOW Whitney Houston
HOWZAT Sherbet
HUMAN Human League
HUMAN NATURE Michael Jackson
A HUNDRED POUNDS OF CLAY Craig Douglas
A HUNDRED POUNDS OF CLAY Gene McDaniels
HUNGRY Paul Revere & The Raiders
HUNGRY EYES Eric Carmen
HUNGRY HEART Bruce Springsteen
HUNGRY LIKE THE WOLF Duran Duran
HUNTING HIGH AND LOW A-Ha
HURDY GURDY MAN Donovan
HURRY UP HARRY Sham 69
HURT Timi Yuro
HURT Manhattans
HURT SO BAD Linda Ronstadt
HURT SO BAD Little Anthony & The Imperials
HURT SO GOOD Susan Cadogan
HURTING EACH OTHER Carpenters
HURTS SO GOOD John Cougar Mellencamp
HUSH Deep Purple
HUSH, HUSH SWEET CHARLOTTE Patti Page
THE HUSTLE Van McCoy
HYMN TO HER Pretenders
HYSTERIA Def Leppard
I AIN'T GONNA STAND FOR IT Stevie Wonder
I ALMOST LOST MY MIND Pat Boone
I AM ...I SAID Neil Diamond
I AM A CIDER DRINKER (PALOMA BLANCA)
Wurzels
I AM A ROCK Simon & Garfunkel
I AM THE BEAT Look
I AM WOMAN Helen Reddy
I AM...I SAID Neil Diamond
I BEG OF YOU Elvis Presley
I BEG YOUR PARDON Kon Kan
I BELIEVE Bachelors
I BELIEVE (IN LOVE) Hot Chocolate
I BELIEVE IN FATHER CHRISTMAS Greg Lake
I CAN DO IT Rubettes
I CAN DREAM ABOUT YOU Dan Hartmann
I CAN HEAR MUSIC Beach Boys
I CAN HEAR THE GRASS GROW Move
I CAN HELP Billy Swan
I CAN MAKE YOU FEEL GOOD Shalamar
I CAN NEVER GO HOME ANYMORE Shangri-Las

I CAN PROVE IT Phil Fearon
I CAN SEE CLEARLY NOW Johnny Nash
I CAN SEE FOR MILES Who
I CAN'T CONTROL MYSELF Troggs
I CAN'T EXPLAIN Who
(I CAN'T GET NO) SATISFACTION Rolling Stones
I CAN'T GO FOR THAT (NO CAN DO)
Daryl Hall & John Oates
I CAN'T HELP MYSELF Four Tops
I CAN'T LEAVE YOU ALONE George McCrae
I CAN'T LET GO Hollies
I CAN'T LET MAGGIE GO Honeybus
I CAN'T STAND IT Eric Clapton
I CAN'T STAND THE RAIN Eruption
I CAN'T STAND UP FOR FALLING DOWN
Elvis Costello
I CAN'T STAY MAD AT YOU Skeeter Davis
I CAN'T STOP DANCING Archie Bell & The Drells
I CAN'T STOP LOVIN' YOU (THOUGH I TRY)
Leo Sayer
I CAN'T STOP LOVING YOU Ray Charles
I CAN'T TELL THE BOTTOM FROM THE TOP
Hollies
I CAN'T TELL YOU WHY Eagles
I CAN'T WAIT Nu Shooz
I CLOSE MY EYES AND COUNT TO TEN
Dusty Springfield
I COULD BE HAPPY Altered Images
I COULD BE SO GOOD FOR YOU
Dennis Waterman
I COULD EASILY FALL Cliff Richard
I COULD NEVER TAKE THE PLACE OF YOUR MAN
Prince
I COULDN'T LIVE WITHOUT YOUR LOVE
Petula Clark
I DID WHAT I DID FOR MARIA Tony Christie
I DIDN'T KNOW I LOVED YOU
(TILL I SAW YOU ROCK 'N' ROLL) Gary Glitter
I DIDN'T MEAN TO TURN YOU ON Robert Palmer
I DIE:YOU DIE Gary Numan
I DIG ROCK AND ROLL MUSIC Peter, Paul & Mary
I DON'T BELIEVE IN IF ANYMORE
Roger Whittaker
I DON'T BLAME YOU AT ALL
Smokey Robinson & The Miracles
I DON'T KNOW WHY Eden Kane
I DON'T LIKE MONDAYS Boomtown Rats
I DON'T LIKE TO SLEEP ALONE Paul Anka
I DON'T NEED YOU Kenny Rogers
I DON'T WANNA DANCE Eddy Grant
I DON'T WANNA GET HURT Donna Summer
I DON'T WANNA GO ON LIKE THAT Elton John
I DON'T WANNA LIVE WITHOUT YOUR LOVE
Chicago
I DON'T WANNA LOSE YOU Tina Turner
I DON'T WANT A LOVER Texas
I DON'T WANT OUR LOVING TO DIE Hero
I DON'T WANT TO LIVE WITHOUT YOU Foreigner
I DON'T WANT TO PUT A HOLD ON YOU
Berni Flint
I DON'T WANT TO TALK ABOUT IT
Everything But The Girl
I DON'T WANT TO TALK ABOUT IT Rod Stewart
I DON'T WANT YOUR LOVE Duran Duran
I DROVE ALL NIGHT Cyndi Lauper
I EAT CANNIBALS PT. 1 Toto Coelo
I FEEL FINE Beatles
I FEEL FOR YOU Chaka Khan
I FEEL LIKE BUDDY HOLLY Alvin Stardust
I FEEL LOVE Bronski Beat & Marc Almond
I FEEL LOVE Donna Summer
I FEEL SO BAD Elvis Presley
I FEEL THE EARTH MOVE Martika
I FOUGHT THE LAW Bobby Fuller Four
I FOUND LOVIN' Steve Walsh
I FOUND LOVIN' Fatback Band
I FOUND SOMEONE Cher
I GET A KICK OUT OF YOU Gary Shearston
I GET A LITTLE SENTIMENTAL OVER YOU
New Seekers
I GET AROUND Beach Boys
I GET THE SWEETEST FEELING Jackie Wilson
I GET WEAK Belinda Carlisle
I GO APE Neil Sedaka
I GO CRAZY Paul Davis
I GO TO PIECES Peter & Gordon
I GO TO SLEEP Pretenders
I GOT A FEELING Ricky Nelson
I GOT A NAME Jim Croce
I GOT RHYTHM Happenings
I GOT STUNG Elvis Presley
I GOT THE FEELIN' James Brown
I GOT YOU (I FEEL GOOD) James Brown
I GOT YOU BABE UB40
I GOT YOU BABE Sonny & Cher
GOTCHA Joe Tex
I GUESS THAT'S WHY THEY CALL IT THE BLUES
Elton John

I HATE MYSELF FOR LOVING YOU
Joan Jett & The Blackhearts
I HAVE A DREAM Abba
I HAVEN'T STOPPED DANCING YET Pat & Mick
I HEAR A SYMPHONY Supremes
I HEAR YOU KNOCKING Dave Edmunds
I HEAR YOU NOW Jon & Vangelis
I HEARD A RUMOUR Bananarama
I HEARD IT THROUGH THE GRAPEVINE
Gladys Knight & The Pips
I HEARD IT THROUGH THE GRAPEVINE Marvin Gaye
I HONESTLY LOVE YOU Olivia Newton-John
I JUST CALLED TO SAY I LOVE YOU Stevie Wonder
I JUST CAN'T HELP BELIEVING Elvis Presley
I JUST CAN'T HELP BELIEVING B.J. Thomas
I JUST CAN'T STOP LOVING YOU
Michael Jackson/Seidah Garrett
(I JUST) DIED IN YOUR ARMS Cutting Crew
I JUST DON'T HAVE THE HEART Cliff Richard
I JUST DON'T KNOW WHAT TO DO WITH MYSELF
Dusty Springfield
I JUST WANNA STOP Gino Vannelli
I JUST WANT TO BE YOUR EVERYTHING
Andy Gibb
I JUST WANT TO CELEBRATE Rare Earth
I KEEP FORGETTIN'(EVERYTIME YOU'RE NEAR)
Michael McDonald
I KNEW YOU WERE WAITING (FOR ME)
Aretha Franklin & George Michael
I KNEW YOU WHEN Donny Osmond
(I KNOW) I'M LOSING YOU Rare Earth
(I KNOW) I'M LOSING YOU Temptations
I KNOW (YOU DON'T LOVE ME NO MORE)
Barbara George
I KNOW A PLACE Petula Clark
I KNOW HIM SO WELL
Elaine Page & Barbara Dickson
I KNOW WHAT I LIKE Huey Lewis & The News
I LIKE DREAMIN' Kenny Nolan
I LIKE IT Gerry & The Pacemakers
I LIKE IT Dino
I LIKE IT LIKE THAT Dave Clark Five
I LIKE IT LIKE THAT (PT.1) Chris Kenner
I LIKE YOUR KIND OF LOVE Andy Williams
I LOST MY HEART TO A STARSHIP TROOPER
Sarah Brightman
I LOVE A RAINY NIGHT Eddie Rabbitt
I LOVE HOW YOU LOVE ME Paris Sisters
I LOVE HOW YOU LOVE ME Bobby Vinton
I LOVE MUSIC (PT. 1) O'Jays
I LOVE MY RADIO Taffy
I LOVE ROCK 'N' ROLL Joan Jett & The Blackhearts
I LOVE THE NIGHT LIFE (DISCO 'ROUND)
Alicia Bridges
I LOVE THE SOUND OF BREAKING GLASS
Nick Lowe & His Cowboy Outfit
I LOVE THE WAY YOU LOVE Marv Johnson
I LOVE TO LOVE (BUT MY BABY LOVES TO DANCE)
Tina Charles
I LOVE YOU Cliff Richard
I LOVE YOU Donna Summer
I LOVE YOU BABY Paul Anka
I LOVE YOU BECAUSE Al Martino
I LOVE YOU BECAUSE Jim Reeves
I LOVE YOU LOVE ME LOVE Gary Glitter
I LOVE YOU MORE AND MORE EVERY DAY
Al Martino
I MADE IT THROUGH THE RAIN Barry Manilow
I MISS YOU Klymaxx
I MUST BE SEEING THINGS Gene Pitney
I NEED LOVE L.L. Cool J
I NEED YOU America
I NEED YOU B.V.S.M.P.
I NEED YOUR LOVE TONIGHT Elvis Presley
I NEED YOUR LOVIN' Alyson Williams
I NEVER LOVED A MAN (THE WAY I LOVE YOU)
Aretha Franklin
I ONLY HAVE EYES FOR YOU Art Garfunkel
I ONLY WANNA BE WITH YOU Bay City Rollers
I ONLY WANT TO BE WITH YOU Tourists
I ONLY WANT TO BE WITH YOU Dusty Springfield
I OWE YOU NOTHING Bros
I PRETEND Des O'Connor
I PUT A SPELL ON YOU Alan Price Set
I QUIT Bros
I RAN (SO FAR AWAY) Flock Of Seagulls
I REMEMBER ELVIS PRESLEY (THE KING IS DEAD)
Danny Mirror
I REMEMBER HOLDING YOU Boys Club
I REMEMBER YOU Frank Ifield
I SAW HER AGAIN Mamas & The Papas
I SAW HIM STANDING THERE Tiffany
I SAY A LITTLE PRAYER Aretha Franklin
I SAY A LITTLE PRAYER Dionne Warwick
I SECOND THAT EMOTION
Smokey Robinson & The Miracles
I SECOND THAT EMOTION Japan
I SEE A STAR Mouth & McNeal
I SHOT THE SHERIFF Eric Clapton

213

I SHOULD BE SO LUCKY   Kylie Minogue
I SHOULD HAVE KNOWN BETTER   Jim Diamond
I SHOULDA LOVED YA   Narada Michael Walden
I STARTED A JOKE   Bee Gees
I STILL HAVEN'T FOUND WHAT I'M LOOKING FOR
U2
I SURRENDER   Rainbow
I THANK YOU   Sam & Dave
I THINK I LOVE YOU   Partridge Family
I THINK IT'S GONNA RAIN   UB40
I THINK OF YOU   Merseybeats
I THINK WE'RE ALONE NOW
Tommy James & The Shondells
I THINK WE'RE ALONE NOW   Tiffany
I UNDERSTAND   Freddie & The Dreamers
I UNDERSTAND (JUST HOW YOU FEEL)   G-Clefs
I WANNA DANCE WIT CHOO'
Disco Tex & The Sex-O-Lettes
I WANNA DANCE WITH SOMEBODY
(WHO LOVES ME)   Whitney Houston
I WANNA DO IT WITH YOU   Barry Manilow
I WANNA GET NEXT TO YOU   Rose Royce
I WANNA GO HOME   Lonnie Donegan
I WANNA HAVE SOME FUN   Samantha Fox
I WANNA LOVE HIM SO BAD   Jelly Beans
I WANNA STAY WITH YOU   Gallagher & Lyle
I WANT A NEW DRUG   Huey Lewis & The News
I WANT CANDY   Bow Wow Wow
I WANT HER   Keith Sweat
I WANT IT ALL   Queen
I WANT TO BE FREE   Toyah
I WANT TO BE WANTED   Brenda Lee
I WANT TO BE YOUR MAN   Roger
I WANT TO BREAK FREE   Queen
I WANT TO HOLD YOUR HAND   Beatles
I WANT TO HOLD YOUR HAND   Dollar
I WANT TO KNOW WHAT LOVE IS   Foreigner
I WANT TO STAY HERE
Steve Lawrence & Eydie Gorme
I WANT TO WAKE UP WITH YOU   Boris Gardiner
I WANT TO WALK YOU HOME   Fats Domino
I WANT YOU BACK   Bananarama
I WANT YOU BACK   Jackson Five
I WANT YOU TO WANT ME   Cheap Trick
I WANT YOU, I NEED YOU, I LOVE YOU
Elvis Presley
I WANT YOUR LOVE   Transvision Vamp
I WANT YOUR LOVE   Chic
I WANT YOUR SEX   George Michael
I WAS KAISER BILL'S BATMAN
Whistling Jack Smith
I WAS MADE FOR DANCIN'   Leif Garrett
I WAS MADE TO LOVE HER   Stevie Wonder
I WAS ONLY JOKING   Rod Stewart
I WILL   Ruby Winters
I WILL   Dean Martin
I WILL FOLLOW HIM   Little Peggy March
I WILL RETURN   Springwater
I WILL SURVIVE   Gloria Gaynor
I WISH   Stevie Wonder
I WISH IT COULD BE CHRISTMAS EVERY DAY   Wizzard
I WISH IT WOULD RAIN   Faces
I WISH IT WOULD RAIN   Temptations
I WON'T FORGET YOU   Jim Reeves
I WON'T HOLD YOU BACK   Toto
I WON'T LAST A DAY WITHOUT YOU   Carpenters
I WON'T LET THE SUN GO DOWN ON ME
Nik Kershaw
I WON'T LET YOU DOWN   PHD
I WON'T RUN AWAY   Alvin Stardust
I WONDER WHAT SHE'S DOING TONIGHT
Tommy Boyce & Bobby Hart
I WONDER WHY   Showaddywaddy
I WOULD DIE 4 U   Prince & The Revolution
I WOULDN'T TRADE YOU FOR THE WORLD
Bachelors
I WRITE THE SONGS   Barry Manilow
I'D LIKE TO TEACH THE WORLD TO SING
New Seekers
I'D LOVE YOU TO WANT ME   Lobo
I'D RATHER JACK   Reynolds Girls
I'D REALLY LOVE TO SEE YOU TONIGHT
England Dan & John Ford Coley
I'LL ALWAYS LOVE YOU   Taylor Dayne
I'LL BE AROUND   Spinners
I'LL BE DOGGONE   Marvin Gaye
I'LL BE GOOD TO YOU   Brothers Johnson
I'LL BE HOME   Pat Boone
I'LL BE LOVING YOU (FOREVER)
New Kids On The Block
I'LL BE SATISFIED   Shakin' Stevens
I'LL BE THERE   Jackson Five
I'LL BE THERE FOR YOU   Bon Jovi
I'LL FIND MY WAY HOME   Jon & Vangelis
I'LL FLY FOR YOU   Spandau Ballet
I'LL GET BY   Shirley Bassey
I'LL HAVE TO SAY I LOVE YOU IN A SONG   Jim Croce
I'LL KEEP YOU SATISFIED
Billy J. Kramer & The Dakotas

I'LL MEET YOU HALFWAY   Partridge Family
I'LL NEVER FALL IN LOVE AGAIN
Dionne Warwick
I'LL NEVER FALL IN LOVE AGAIN   Tom Jones
I'LL NEVER FALL IN LOVE AGAIN   Bobbie Gentry
I'LL NEVER FIND ANOTHER YOU   Seekers
I'LL NEVER FIND ANOTHER YOU   Billy Fury
I'LL NEVER GET OVER YOU
Johnny Kidd & The Pirates
I'LL NEVER LOVE THIS WAY AGAIN
Dionne Warwick
I'LL PICK A ROSE FOR MY ROSE   Marv Johnson
I'LL SAY FOREVER MY LOVE   Jimmy Ruffin
I'LL STOP AT NOTHING   Sandie Shaw
I'LL TAKE YOU THERE   Staple Singers
I'LL TUMBLE 4 YA   Culture Club
I'M A BELIEVER   Monkees
I'M A BOY   Who
I'M A CLOWN   David Cassidy
I'M A MAN   Spencer Davis Group
I'M A MAN   Chicago
I'M A TIGER   Lulu
I'M A WONDERFUL THING (BABY)
Kid Creole & The Coconuts
I'M ALIVE   Hollies
I'M ALRIGHT   Kenny Loggins
(I'M ALWAYS TOUCHED BY YOUR) PRESENCE DEAR
Blondie
I'M COMIN' HOME   Tom Jones
I'M COMIN' OUT   Diana Ross
I'M CRYING   Animals
I'M EVERY WOMAN   Chaka Khan
I'M GOIN' DOWN   Bruce Springsteen
I'M GONNA BE STRONG   Gene Pitney
I'M GONNA GET ME A GUN   Cat Stevens
I'M GONNA LOVE YOU JUST A LITTLE MORE BABY
Barry White
I'M GONNA MAKE YOU LOVE ME
Diana Ross, Supremes & Temptations
I'M GONNA MAKE YOU MINE   Lou Christie
I'M GONNA RUN AWAY FROM YOU   Tami Lynn
I'M GONNA TEAR YOUR PLAYHOUSE DOWN
Paul Young
I'M HENRY V111 I AM   Herman's Hermits
I'M IN LOVE AGAIN   Fats Domino
I'M IN THE MOOD FOR DANCING   Nolans
I'M IN YOU   Peter Frampton
I'M INTO SOMETHING GOOD   Herman's Hermits
I'M LEAVING IT (ALL) UP TO YOU
Donny & Marie Osmond
I'M LEAVING IT UP TO YOU   Dale & Grace
I'M LIVIN' IN SHAME   Diana Ross & The Supremes
I'M LOOKING OUT THE WINDOW   Cliff Richard
I'M MANDY FLY ME   10CC
I'M NOT IN LOVE   10CC
I'M NOT LISA   Jessi Colter
I'M NOT SCARED   Eighth Wonder
I'M ON FIRE   5000 Volts
I'M ON FIRE   Bruce Springsteen
I'M READY FOR LOVE   Martha & The Vandellas
I'M SO EXCITED   Pointer Sisters
I'M SO LONESOME I COULD CRY   B.J. Thomas
I'M SORRY   John Denver
I'M SORRY   Brenda Lee
I'M STILL IN LOVE WITH YOU   Al Green
I'M STILL STANDING   Elton John
I'M STILL WAITING   Diana Ross
I'M STONE IN LOVE WITH YOU   Stylistics
I'M STONE IN LOVE WITH YOU   Johnny Mathis
I'M TELLING YOU NOW   Freddie & The Dreamers
I'M THE LEADER OF THE GANG (I AM)
Gary Glitter
I'M THE LONELY ONE   Cliff Richard
I'M THE ONE   Gerry & The Pacemakers
I'M THE URBAN SPACEMAN
Bonzo Dog Doo-Dah Band
I'M WALKIN'   Fats Domino
I'M WALKIN'   Ricky Nelson
I'M WALKING BACKWARDS FOR CHRISTMAS
Goons
I'M YOUR BOOGIE MAN   KC & The Sunshine Band
I'M YOUR MAN   Wham!
I'M YOUR PUPPET   James & Bobby Purify
I'VE BEEN A BAD BAD BOY   Paul Jones
I'VE BEEN IN LOVE BEFORE   Cutting Crew
I'VE BEEN LOSING YOU   A-Ha
I'VE DONE EVERYTHING FOR YOU
Rick Springfield
I'VE FOUND SOMEONE OF MY OWN
Free Movement
I'VE GOT LOVE ON MY MIND   Natalie Cole
I'VE GOT TO USE MY IMAGINATION
Gladys Knight & The Pips
I'VE GOT YOU UNDER MY SKIN   Four Seasons
I'VE GOTTA GET A MESSAGE TO YOU   Bee Gees
(I'VE HAD) THE TIME OF MY LIFE
Bill Medley/Jennifer Warnes
I'VE LOST YOU   Elvis Presley
I'VE NEVER BEEN TO ME   Charlene

I'VE TOLD EVERY LITTLE STAR   Linda Scott
I'VE WAITED SO LONG   Anthony Newley
I (WHO HAVE NOTHING)   Shirley Bassey
I-2-3   Len Barry
I.O.U.   Freeze
ICE IN THE SUN   Status Quo
IF   Bread
IF   Telly Savalas
IF EVER YOU'RE IN MY ARMS AGAIN
Peabo Bryson
IF EVERY DAY WAS LIKE CHRISTMAS
Elvis Presley
IF I CAN'T HAVE YOU   Yvonne Elliman
IF I COULD BUILD MY WHOLE WORLD AROUND YOU
Marvin Gaye & Tammi Terrell
IF I COULD REACH YOU   Fifth Dimension
IF I COULD TURN BACK TIME   Cher
IF I DIDN'T CARE   David Cassidy
IF I HAD A HAMMER   Trini Lopez
IF I HAD A HAMMER   Peter, Paul & Mary
IF I HAD WORDS   Scott Fitzgerald & Yvonne Keely
IF I ONLY HAD TIME   John Rowles
IF I SAID YOU HAD A BEAUTIFUL BODY
Bellamy Brothers
IF I WAS   Midge Ure
IF I WERE A CARPENTER   Four Tops
IF I WERE A CARPENTER   Bobby Darin
IF I WERE A RICH MAN   Topol
IF I WERE YOUR WOMAN
Gladys Knight & The Pips
IF IT HAPPENS AGAIN   UB40
IF IT ISN'T LOVE   New Edition
IF LOVING YOU IS WRONG (I DON'T WANNA DO
RIGHT)   Luther Ingram
IF NOT FOR YOU   Olivia Newton-John
IF NOT YOU   Dr. Hook
IF ONLY I COULD   Sydney Youngblood
(IF PARADISE IS) TWICE AS NICE   Amen Corner
IF SHE SHOULD COME TO YOU   Anthony Newley
IF THE KIDS ARE UNITED   Sham 69
IF THE WHOLE WORLD STOPPED LOVING
Val Doonican
IF THIS IS IT   Huey Lewis & The News
IF YOU CAN'T GIVE ME LOVE   Suzi Quatro
IF YOU CAN'T STAND THE HEAT   Bucks Fizz
IF YOU COULD READ MY MIND   Gordon Lightfoot
IF YOU DON'T KNOW ME BY NOW
Harold Melvin & The Blue Notes
IF YOU DON'T KNOW ME BY NOW   Simply Red
IF YOU GO AWAY   Terry Jacks
IF YOU GOTTA GO GO NOW   Manfred Mann
IF YOU GOTTA MAKE A FOOL OF SOMEBODY
Freddie & The Dreamers
IF YOU LEAVE   Orchestral Manoeuvres In The Dark
IF YOU LEAVE ME NOW   Chicago
(IF YOU LET ME MAKE LOVE TO YOU THEN)
WHY CAN'T I TOUCH YOU   Ronnie Dyson
IF YOU LET ME STAY   Terence Trent D'Arby
IF YOU LOVE ME (LET ME KNOW)
Olivia Newton-John
IF YOU LOVE SOMEBODY SET THEM FREE   Sting
IF YOU REALLY LOVE ME   Stevie Wonder
IF YOU THINK YOU KNOW HOW TO LOVE ME
Smokey
IF YOU WANNA BE HAPPY   Jimmy Soul
IF YOU'RE LOOKIN' FOR A WAY OUT   Odyssey
IF YOU'RE READY COME GO WITH ME
Staple Singers
IKO IKO   Natasha
IL SILENZIO   Nina Rosso
IMAGE OF A GIRL   Safaris
IMAGINARY LOVER   Atlanta Rhythm Section
IMAGINE   John Lennon
IN A BROKEN DREAM   Python Lee Jackson
IN AND OUT OF LOVE   Diana Ross & The Supremes
THE IN BETWEENIES   Goodies
IN DOLCE JUBILO   Mike Oldfield
IN DREAMS   Roy Orbison
IN MY HOUSE   Mary Jane Girls
IN MY LITTLE CORNER OF THE WORLD
Anita Bryant
IN MY OWN TIME   Family
IN SUMMER   Billy Fury
IN THE AIR TONIGHT   Phil Collins
IN THE ARMY NOW   Status Quo
IN THE BAD BAD OLD DAYS   Foundations
IN THE COUNTRY   Cliff Richard
IN THE GHETTO   Elvis Presley
IN THE MIDDLE OF NOWHERE   Dusty Springfield
IN THE NAVY   Village People
IN THE RAIN   Dramatics
IN THE SUMMERTIME   Mungo Jerry
IN THE YEAR 2525 (EXORDIUM & TERMINUS)
Zager & Evans
IN THOUGHTS OF YOU   Billy Fury
IN TOO DEEP   Genesis
IN YOUR EYES   George Benson
IN YOUR ROOM   Bangles
IN ZAIRE   Johnny Wakelin

INCENSE AND PEPPERMINTS
Strawberry Alarm Clock
INCOMMUNICADO   Marillion
INDIAN GIVER   1910 Fruitgum Co
INDIAN LAKE   Cowsills
INDIAN RESERVATION   Don Fardon
INDIAN RESERVATION   Raiders
INDIANA WANTS ME   R. Dean Taylor
INFATUATION   Rod Stewart
INFINITE DREAMS   Iron Maiden
INNER CITY BLUES (MAKES ME WANNA HOLLER)
Marvin Gaye
AN INNOCENT MAN   Billy Joel
INSIDE OUT   Odyssey
INSTANT KARMA (WE ALL SHINE ON)
John Lennon
INSTANT REPLAY   Dan Hartman
INSTINCTION   Spandau Ballet
INTERESTING DRUG   Morrissey
INTERNATIONAL JET SET   Specials
INTO THE GROOVE   Madonna
INTO THE VALLEY   Skids
INTUITION   Linx
INVINCIBLE   Pat Benatar
INVISIBLE SUN   Police
INVISIBLE TOUCH   Genesis
IRE FEELINGS (SKANGA)   Rupie Edwards
THE IRISH ROVER   Pogues & The Dubliners
IS IT LOVE   Mr. Mister
IS THERE SOMETHING I SHOULD KNOW
Duran Duran
IS THIS LOVE   Survivor
IS THIS LOVE   Alison Moyet
IS THIS LOVE   Whitesnake
IS THIS LOVE   Bob Marley & The Wailers
ISLAND GIRL   Elton John
ISLAND OF DREAMS   Springfields
ISLANDS IN THE STREAM
Kenny Rogers & Dolly Parton
ISN'T SHE LOVELY   David Parton
THE ISRAELITES   Desmond Bekker & The Aces
IT AIN'T ME BABE   Turtles
IT AIN'T WHAT YOU DO IT'S THE WAY THAT
YOU DO IT   Fun Boy Three & Bananarama
IT DIDN'T MATTER   Style Council
IT DOESN'T HAVE TO BE THAT WAY
Blow Monkeys
IT DOESN'T MATTER ANYMORE   Buddy Holly
IT DON'T COME EASY   Ringo Starr
IT DON'T MATTER TO ME   Bread
IT HURTS SO MUCH   Jim Reeves
IT HURTS TO BE IN LOVE   Gene Pitney
IT IS TIME TO GET FUNKY   D. Mob
IT KEEPS RIGHT ON A-HURTIN'   Johnny Tillotson
IT MEK   Desmond Dekker & The Aces
IT MIGHT AS WELL RAIN UNTIL SEPTEMBER
Carole King
IT MUST BE HIM   Vikki Carr
IT MUST BE LOVE   Madness
IT NEVER RAINS IN SOUTHERN CALIFORNIA
Albert Hammond
IT ONLY TAKES A MINUTE   Tavares
IT ONLY TAKES A MINUTE
One Hundred Tons & A Feather
IT ONLY TOOK A MINUTE
Joe Brown & The Bruvvers
IT SHOULD HAVE BEEN ME   Yvonne Fair
IT STARTED WITH A KISS   Hot Chocolate
IT WOULD TAKE A STRONG MAN   Rick Astley
IT'LL BE ME   Cliff Richard
IT'S A HARD LIFE   Queen
IT'S A HEARTACHE   Bonnie Tyler
IT'S A LOVE THING   Whispers
IT'S A MAN'S MAN'S MAN'S WORLD
James Brown
IT'S A MIRACLE   Culture Club
IT'S A MISTAKE   Men At Work
IT'S A SIN   Pet Shop Boys
IT'S ALL IN THE GAME   Cliff Richard
IT'S ALL IN THE GAME   Four Tops
IT'S ALL OVER   Cliff Richard
IT'S ALL OVER NOW   Rolling Stones
IT'S ALL RIGHT   Impressions
IT'S ALRIGHT   Pet Shop Boys
IT'S BEEN SO LONG   George McCrae
IT'S DIFFERENT FOR GIRLS   Joe Jackson
IT'S ECSTASY WHEN YOU LAY DOWN NEXT TO ME
Barry White
IT'S FOR YOU   Cilla Black
IT'S FOUR IN THE MORNING   Faron Young
IT'S GETTING BETTER   Mama Cass
IT'S GONNA BE A COLD COLD CHRISTMAS   Dana
IT'S GONNA TAKE A MIRACLE   Deniece Williams
IT'S GOOD NEWS WEEK
Hedgehoppers Anonymous
IT'S IMPOSSIBLE   Perry Como
IT'S IN HIS KISS   Linda Lewis
IT'S JUST A MATTER OF TIME   Brook Benton
(IT'S JUST) THE WAY YOU LOVE ME   Paula Abdul

214

IT'S LATE Ricky Nelson
IT'S MY LIFE Animals
IT'S MY PARTY Dave Stewart & Barbara Gaskin
IT'S MY PARTY Lesley Gore
IT'S MY TURN Diana Ross
IT'S NO CRIME Babyface
IT'S NOT FOR ME TO SAY Johnny Mathis
IT'S NOT OVER (TIL IT'S OVER) Starship
IT'S NOT UNUSUAL Tom Jones
IT'S NOW OR NEVER Elvis Presley
IT'S ONLY LOVE Elvis Presley
IT'S ONLY MAKE BELIEVE Child
IT'S ONLY MAKE BELIEVE Billy Fury
IT'S ONLY MAKE BELIEVE Conway Twitty
IT'S ONLY MAKE BELIEVE Glen Campbell
IT'S ONLY ROCK 'N ROLL (BUT I LIKE IT)
Rolling Stones
IT'S OVER Roy Orbison
IT'S OVER Funk Masters
IT'S OVER Level 42
IT'S RAINING Shakin' Stevens
IT'S RAINING Darts
IT'S RAINING MEN Weather Girls
IT'S SO EASY Linda Ronstadt
IT'S STILL ROCK AND ROLL TO ME Billy Joel
IT'S THE SAME OLD SONG Four Tops
IT'S TIME FOR LOVE Chi Lites
IT'S TIME TO CRY Paul Anka
IT'S TOO LATE Carole King
IT'S TOO SOON TO KNOW Pat Boone
IT'S UP TO YOU Rick Nelson
IT'S WONDERFUL Jimmy Ruffin
IT'S YOU Freddie Starr
IT'S YOU I LOVE Fats Domino
IT'S YOUR LIFE Smokie
IT'S YOUR THING Isley Brothers
ITCHYCOO PARK Small Faces
ITSY BITSY TEENIE WEENIE YELLOW POLKA DOT
BIKINI Brian Hyland
JACK & DIANE John Cougar Mellencamp
JACK AND JILL Raydio
JACK IN THE BOX Moments
JACK IN THE BOX Clodagh Rodgers
JACK MIX 11 Mirage
JACK MIX 1V Mirage
THE JACK THAT HOUSE BUILT Jack 'n' Chill
JACK YOUR BODY Steve 'Silk' Hurley
JACKIE BLUE Ozark Mountain Daredevils
JACKIE WILSON SAID Dexy's Midnight Runners
JACKSON Nancy Sinatra
JACOB'S LADDER Huey Lewis & The News
JAILHOUSE ROCK Elvis Presley
JAM UP JELLY TIGHT Tommy Roe
JAMMING Bob Marley & Wailers
JANUARY Pilot
JAPANESE BOY Aneka
JARROW SONG Alan Price
JAVA Al Hirt
JAZZMAN Carole King
JE NE SAIS PAS POURQUOI Kylie Minogue
JE T'AIME (MOI NON PLUS) Judge Dread
JE T'AIME...MOI NON PLUS
Jane Birkin & Serge Gainsbourg
JEALOUS GUY Roxy Music
JEALOUS MIND Alvin Stardust
JEALOUSY Billy Fury
JEAN Oliver
THE JEAN GENIE David Bowie
JEANS ON David Dundas
JEEPSTER T. Rex
JENNIE LEE Jan & Arnie
JENNIFER ECCLES Hollies
JENIFER JUNIPER Donovan
JENNY TAKE A RIDE!
Mitch Ryder & The Detroit Wheels
JEOPARDY Greg Kihn Band
THE JERK Larks
JESAMINE Casuals
JESSIE'S GIRL Rick Springfield
JET Paul McCartney
JET AIRLINER Steve Miller Band
JIG A JIG East of Eden
JILTED JOHN Jilted John
JIMMY MACK Martha & The Vandellas
JINGLE BELL ROCK Max Bygraves
JINGLE JANGLE Archies
JIVE TALKIN' Bee Gees
JIVE TALKIN' Boogie Box High
JOAN OF ARC Orchestral Manoeuvres In The Dark
JOANNA Scott Walker
JOANNA Kool & The Gang
JOE LE TAXI Vanessa Paradis
JOHNNY ANGEL Shelley Fabares
JOHNNY B. GOODE Chuck Berry
JOHNNY COME HOME Fine Young Cannibals
JOHNNY GET ANGRY Joanie Sommers
JOHNNY REGGAE Piglets
JOHNNY REMEMBER ME John Leyton
JOHNNY WILL Pat Boone

JOIN TOGETHER Who
THE JOKER Steve Miller Band
JOLENE Dolly Parton
THE JOLLY GREEN GIANT Kingsmen
JOY Apollo 100
JOY AND PAIN Donna Allen
JOY TO THE WORLD Three Dog Night
JOYBRINGER Manfred Mann's Earth Band
JUDY IN DISGUISE (WITH GLASSES)
John Fred & His Playboy Band
JUDY TEEN Cockney Rebel
JUDY'S TURN TO CRY Lesley Gore
JUKE BOX JIVE Rubettes
JULIE ANN Kenny
JULIE, DO YA LOVE ME Bobby Sherman
JULIE, DO YA LOVE ME White Plains
JULIET Four Pennies
JUMP Van Halen
JUMP (FOR MY LOVE) Pointer Sisters
JUMP TO THE BEAT Stacy Lattisaw
JUMPING JACK FLASH Rolling Stones
JUNGLE BOOGIE Kool & The Gang
JUNGLE FEVER Chakachas
JUNGLE ROCK Hank Mizell
JUNIOR'S FARM Paul McCartney
JUNK FOOD JUNKIE Larry Groce
JUST A DREAM Jimmy Clanton
JUST A LITTLE Beau Brummels
JUST A LITTLE BIT BETTER Herman's Hermits
JUST A LITTLE TOO MUCH Ricky Nelson
JUST A SONG BEFORE I GO Crosby, Stills & Nash
JUST AN ILLUSION Imagination
JUST CAN'T GET ENOUGH Depeche Mode
JUST DON'T WANT TO BE LONELY
Freddie McGregor
JUST DON'T WANT TO BE LONELY
Main Ingredient
JUST DROPPED IN (TO SEE WHAT CONDITION MY
CONDITION IS IN) First Edition
JUST FOR YOU Glitter Band
JUST GOT LUCKY Joboxers
JUST GOT PAID Johnny Kemp
JUST LIKE A WOMAN Manfred Mann
JUST LIKE EDDIE Heinz
JUST LIKE JESSE JAMES Cher
JUST LIKE PARADISE David Lee Roth
(JUST LIKE) ROMEO & JULIET Reflections
(JUST LIKE) STARTING OVER John Lennon
JUST LOVING YOU Anita Harris
JUST MY IMAGINATION (RUNNIN' AWAY WITH ME)
Temptations
JUST ONCE IN MY LIFE Righteous Brothers
JUST ONE LOOK Hollies
JUST ONE LOOK Doris Troy
JUST ONE MORE NIGHT Yellow Dog
JUST ONE SMILE Gene Pitney
JUST SAY NO Grange Hill Cast
JUST THE TWO OF US Grover Washington Jr.
JUST THE WAY YOU ARE Billy Joel
JUST TO BE CLOSE TO YOU Commodores
JUST TO SEE HER Smokey Robinson
JUST WHAT I ALWAYS WANTED Mari Wilson
JUST WHEN I NEEDED YOU MOST
Randy Vanwarmer
JUST WHO IS THE FIVE O'CLOCK HERO Jam
JUST YOU 'N' ME Chicago
KARMA CHAMELEON Culture Club
KATE BUSH ON STAGE E.P. Kate Bush
KAYLEIGH Marillion
(KEEP FEELING) FASCINATION Human League
KEEP IT COMIN' LOVE KC & The Sunshine Band
KEEP ON DANCIN' Gary's Gang
KEEP ON DANCING Gentrys
KEEP ON DANCING Bay City Rollers
KEEP ON LOVING YOU Reo Speedwagon
KEEP ON MOVIN'
Soul 11 Soul Feat. Caron Wheeler
KEEP ON PUSHING Impressions
KEEP ON RUNNIN' Spencer Davis Group
KEEP ON SMILIN' Wet Willie
KEEP ON TRUCKIN'(PT 1) Eddie Kendricks
KEEP SEARCHIN'(WE'LL FOLLOW THE SUN)
Del Shannon
KEEP THE FIRE BURNIN' Reo Speedwagon
KEEP YOUR HANDS TO YOURSELF
Georgia Satellites
KEEPER OF THE CASTLE Four Tops
KEWPIE DOLL Frankie Vaughan
KEWPIE DOLL Perry Como
KEY LARGO Bertie Higgins
KICKS Paul Revere & The Raiders
KIDDIO Brook Benton
KIDS IN AMERICA Kim Wilde
KILLER ON THE LOOSE Thin Lizzy
KILLER QUEEN Queen
KILLING ME SOFTLY WITH HIS SONG
Roberta Flack
THE KILLING MOON Echo & The Bunnymen
THE KILLING OF GEORGIE Rod Stewart

KIND OF A DRAG Buckinghams
A KIND OF MAGIC Queen
KING CREOLE Elvis Presley
KING FOR A DAY Thompson Twins
KING OF PAIN Police
THE KING OF ROCK 'N' ROLL Prefab Sprout
KING OF THE COPS Billy Howard
KING OF THE ROAD Roger Miller
KING UB40
KINGS OF THE WILD FRONTIER Adam & The Ants
KISS Prince & The Revolution
KISS Art of Noise & Tom Jones
KISS ME Manhattans
KISS ME Stephen 'Tin Tin' Duffy
KISS ME HONEY HONEY KISS ME Shirley Bassey
KISS ON MY LIST Daryl Hall & John Oates
KISS YOU ALL OVER Exile
KISSES ON THE WIND Neneh Cherry
KISSES SWEETER THAN WINE Frankie Vaughan
KISSES SWEETER THAN WINE Jimmie Rodgers
KISSIN' COUSINS Elvis Presley
KISSIN' IN THE BACK ROW OF THE MOVIES
Drifters
KISSING A FOOL George Michael
KITES Simon Dupree And The Big Sound
KNEE DEEP IN THE BLUES Guy Mitchell
KNOCK KNOCK WHO'S THERE Mary Hopkin
KNOCK ON WOOD David Bowie
KNOCK ON WOOD Amii Stewart
KNOCK THREE TIMES Dawn
KNOCKED IT OFF B.A. Robertson
KNOWING ME KNOWING YOU Abba
KO KO MO (I LOVE YOU SO) Perry Como
KODACHROME Paul Simon
KOKOMO Beach Boys
KON-TIKI Shadows
KUNG FU FIGHTING Carl Douglas
KYRIE Mr. Mister
L-L-LUCY Mud
LA BAMBA Los Lobos
LA ISLA BONITA Madonna
LA LA LA (IF I HAD YOU) Bobby Sherman
LA-LA MEANS I LOVE YOU Delfonics
LABELLED WITH LOVE Squeeze
LABOUR OF LOVE Hue & Cry
LADIES NIGHT Kool & The Gang
LADY Styx
LADY Kenny Rogers
LADY Little River Band
LADY D'ARBANVILLE Cat Stevens
LADY ELEANOR Lindisfarne
LADY GODIVA Peter & Gordon
THE LADY IN RED Chris De Burgh
LADY LYNDA Beach Boys
LADY MADONNA Beatles
LADY MARMALADE Labelle
LADY ROSE Mungo Jerry
LADY WILLPOWER Gary Puckett & The Union Gap
LADY YOU BRING ME UP Commodores
LAMBADA Kaoma
LAMPLIGHT David Essex
LAND OF 1,000 DANCES Wilson Pickett
LAND OF CONFUSION Genesis
LAND OF MAKE BELIEVE Bucks Fizz
LAST CHRISTMAS Wham!
LAST DANCE Donna Summer
LAST DATE Floyd Cramer
THE LAST FAREWELL Roger Whittaker
LAST KISS J. Frank Wilson & The Cavaliers
THE LAST KISS David Cassidy
LAST NIGHT Mar-Keys
(LAST NIGHT) I DIDN'T GET TO SLEEP AT ALL
Fifth Dimension
LAST NIGHT IN SOHO
Dave Dee, Dozy, Beaky, Mick & Titch
LAST NIGHT WAS MADE FOR LOVE Billy Fury
LAST OF THE FAMOUS INTERNATIONAL
PLAYBOYS Morrissey
LAST SONG Edward Bear
THE LAST TIME Rolling Stones
LAST TRAIN TO CLARKSVILLE Monkees
LAST TRAIN TO LONDON Electric Light Orchestra
THE LAST WALTZ Engelbert Humperdinck
LATE IN THE EVENING Paul Simon
LATELY Stevie Wonder
LAUGH AT ME Sonny
LAUGHING Guess Who
THE LAUGHING GNOME David Bowie
LAUGHTER IN THE RAIN Neil Sedaka
LAVENDER Marillion
LAY ALL YOUR LOVE ON ME Abba
LAY DOWN (CANDLES IN THE RAIN)
Melanie/Edwin Hawkins Singers
LAY DOWN SALLY Eric Clapton
LAY DOWN YOUR ARMS Anne Shelton
LAY LADY LAY Bob Dylan
LAY YOUR HANDS ON ME Thompson Twins
LAY YOUR HANDS ON ME Bon Jovi
LAY YOUR LOVE ON ME Racey

LAYLA Derek & The Dominoes
LAZY RIVER Bobby Darin
LAZY SUNDAY Small Faces
LE FREAK Chic
LEAD ME ON Maxine Nightingale
LEADER OF THE BAND Dan Fogelberg
LEADER OF THE PACK Shangri-Las
LEAN ON ME Bill Withers
LEAN ON ME Club Nouveau
LEAN ON ME Mud
LEAN ON ME (AH-LI-AYO) Red Box
LEANING ON A LAMP POST Herman's Hermits
LEARNIN' THE BLUES Frank Sinatra
LEATHER AND LACE Stevie Nicks
LEAVE A LIGHT ON Belinda Carlisle
LEAVE A LITTLE LOVE Lulu
LEAVE ME ALONE Michael Jackson
LEAVE ME ALONE (RUBY RED DRESS)
Helen Reddy
LEAVING ON A JET PLANE Peter, Paul & Mary
LEEDS UNITED Leeds United F.C.
LEFT TO MY OWN DEVICES Pet Shop Boys
LEGEND OF XANADU
Dave Dee, Dozy, Beaky, Mick & Titch
LEGS ZZ Top
LEROY Jack Scott
LES BICYCLETTES DE BELSIZE
Engelbert Humperdinck
LESSONS IN LOVE Level 42
LET 'EM IN Paul McCartney
LET HER IN John Travolta
LET IT BE Ferry Aid
LET IT BE Beatles
LET IT BE ME Everly Brothers
LET IT BE ME Jerry Butler & Betty Everett
LET IT WHIP Dazz Band
LET ME BE THE ONE Expose
LET ME BE THERE Olivia Newton-John
LET ME GO LOVER Kathy Kirby
LET ME GO LOVER Dean Martin
LET ME IN Osmonds
LET ME IN Sensations
LET ME LOVE YOU TONIGHT
Pure Prairie League
LET ME TRY AGAIN Tammy Jones
LET MY LOVE OPEN THE DOOR Pete Townshend
LET THE HEARTACHES BEGIN Long John Baldry
LET THE LITTLE GIRL DANCE Billy Bland
LET THE MUSIC PLAY Barry White
LET THE MUSIC PLAY Shannon
LET THERE BE DRUMS Sandy Nelson
LET THERE BE LOVE Nat 'King' Cole
LET YOUR LOVE FLOW Bellamy Brothers
LET YOUR YEAH BE YEAH Pioneers
LET'S ALL CHANT Michael Zager Band
LET'S DANCE Chris Montez
LET'S DANCE David Bowie
LET'S DO IT AGAIN Staple Singers
LET'S GET IT ON Marvin Gaye
LET'S GET SERIOUS Jermaine Jackson
LET'S GET TOGETHER Hayley Mills
LET'S GET TOGETHER AGAIN Glitter Band
LET'S GO Wang Chung
LET'S GO ALL THE WAY Sly Fox
LET'S GO CRAZY Prince & The Revolution
LET'S GO TO SAN FRANCISCO Flowerpot Men
LET'S GROOVE Earth, Wind & Fire
LET'S HANG ON! Four Seasons
LET'S HAVE A QUIET NIGHT IN David Soul
LET'S HEAR IT FOR THE BOY Deniece Williams
LET'S LIVE FOR TODAY Grass Roots
LET'S PARTY Jive Bunny & The Mastermixers
LET'S PUT IT ALL TOGETHER Stylistics
LET'S SPEND THE NIGHT TOGETHER
Rolling Stones
LET'S STAY TOGETHER Tina Turner
LET'S STAY TOGETHER Al Green
LET'S STICK TOGETHER Bryan Ferry
LET'S THINK ABOUT LIVING Bob Luman
LET'S TWIST AGAIN Chubby Checker
LET'S WAIT AWHILE Janet Jackson
LET'S WORK TOGETHER Canned Heat
LETS GO, LET'S GO, LET'S GO
Hank Ballard & The Midnighters
LETTER FROM AMERICA Proclaimers
THE LETTER Box Tops
THE LETTER Joe Cocker
A LETTER TO YOU Shakin' Stevens
LIAR Three Dog Night
LICENCE TO KILL Gladys Knight
LIFE IN A NORTHERN TOWN Dream Academy
LIFE IS A MINESTONE 10CC
LIFE IS A ROCK (BUT THE RADIO ROLLED ME)
Reunion
LIFE IS TOO SHORT GIRL Sheer Elegance
LIFE ON MARS David Bowie
LIFELINE Spandau Ballet
LIGHT MY FIRE Jose Feliciano
LIGHT MY FIRE Doors

LIGHT MY FIRE/137 DISCO HEAVEN (MEDLEY)
Amii Stewart
LIGHTNIN' STRIKES Lou Christie
(LIGHT OF EXPERIENCE) DOINA DE JALE
Georghe Zamfir
LIKE A BABY Len Barry
LIKE A PRAYER Madonna
LIKE A ROLLING STONE Bob Dylan
LIKE A VIRGIN Madonna
LIKE CLOCKWORK Boomtown Rats
LIKE I DO Maureen Evans
LIKE I'VE NEVER BEEN GONE Billy Fury
LIKE SISTER AND BROTHER Drifters
LIKE TO GET TO KNOW YOU WELL Howard Jones
LIL' RED RIDING HOOD
Sam The Sham & The Pharaohs
LILLY THE PINK Scaffold
LIMBO ROCK Chubby Checker
THE LION SLEEPS TONIGHT Tight Fit
THE LION SLEEPS TONIGHT Robert John
THE LION SLEEPS TONIGHT Tokens
LIPSTICK ON YOUR COLLAR Connie Francis
LIQUIDATOR Harry J. & The All Stars
LISTEN PEOPLE Herman's Hermits
LISTEN TO WHAT THE MAN SAID Paul McCartney
LISTEN TO YOUR HEART Roxette
LITTLE ARROWS Leapy Lee
A LITTLE BIT ME, A LITTLE BIT YOU Monkees
A LITTLE BIT MORE Dr. Hook
LITTLE BIT O' SOUL Music Explosion
A LITTLE BIT OF SOAP Showaddywaddy
A LITTLE BITTY TEAR Burl Ives
LITTLE CHILDREN Billy J. Kramer & The Dakotas
LITTLE DEVIL Neil Sedaka
LITTLE DIANE Dion
LITTLE DONKEY Nina & Frederick
LITTLE DRUMMER BOY David Bowie/Bing Crosby
LITTLE GIRL Syndicate Of Sound
LITTLE GREEN APPLES O.C. Smith
LITTLE HONDA Hondells
LITTLE JEANNIE Elton John
LITTLE LIES Fleetwood Mac
A LITTLE LOVE AND UNDERSTANDING
Gilbert Becaud
A LITTLE LOVING Fourmost
LITTLE MAN Sonny & Cher
LITTLE MISS LONELY Helen Shapiro
A LITTLE MORE LOVE Olivia Newton-John
THE LITTLE OLD LADY (FROM PASADENA)
Jan & Dean
LITTLE OLE MAN (UPTIGHT–EVERYTHING'S ALRIGHT)
Bill Cosby
A LITTLE PEACE Nicole
LITTLE RED CORVETTE Prince & The Revolution
LITTLE RED ROOSTER Rolling Stones
A LITTLE RESPECT Erasure
LITTLE SISTER Elvis Presley
LITTLE THINGS Dave Berry
LITTLE TOWN FLIRT Del Shannon
LITTLE WHITE BULL Tommy Steele
LITTLE WILLY Sweet
LITTLE WOMAN Bobby Sherman
LIVE AND LET DIE Paul McCartney
LIVE IN TROUBLE Barron Knights
LIVE IS LIFE Opus
LIVE IT UP Mental As Anything
LIVE TO TELL Madonna
LIVERPOOL LOU Scaffold
LIVIN' ON A PRAYER Bon Jovi
LIVIN' THING Electric Light Orchestra
THE LIVING DAYLIGHTS A–Ha
LIVING DOLL Cliff Richard
LIVING DOLL Cliff Richard/Young Ones
LIVING FOR THE CITY Stevie Wonder
LIVING IN A BOX Living In A Box
LIVING IN AMERICA James Brown
LIVING IN SIN Bon Jovi
LIVING INSIDE MYSELF Gino Vannelli
LIVING NEXT DOOR TO ALICE Smokie
LIVING ON THE CEILING Blancmange
LIVING ON VIDEO Trans–X
THE LIVING YEARS Mike + The Mechanics
LOADSAMONEY (DOIN' UP THE HOUSE)
Harry Enfield
LOCO IN ACAPULCO Four Tops
THE LOCO–MOTION Kylie Minogue
THE LOCO–MOTION Little Eva
THE LOCO–MOTION Grand Funk
LOCOMOTION Orchestral Manoeuvres In The Dark
THE LOGICAL SONG Supertramp
LOLA Kinks
LOLLIPOP Chordettes
LONDON NIGHTS London Boys
THE LONE RANGER Quantum Jump
LONELY BLUE BOY Conway Twitty
LONELY BOY Paul Anka
LONELY BOY Andrew Gold
THE LONELY BULL Herb Alpert
LONELY DAYS Bee Gees

LONELY NIGHT (ANGEL FACE) Captain & Tennille
LONELY OL' NIGHT John Cougar Mellencamp
LONELY PEOPLE America
LONELY PUP (IN A CHRISTMAS SHOP)
Adam Faith
LONELY STREET Andy Williams
LONELY TEARDROPS Jackie Wilson
LONELY THIS CHRISTMAS Mud
LONESOME LOSER Little River Band
LONESOME TOWN Ricky Nelson
THE LONG AND WINDING ROAD Beatles
LONG COOL WOMAN(IN A BLACK DRESS)
Hollies
LONG HAIRED LOVER FROM LIVERPOOL
Little Jimmy Osmond
LONG HOT SUMMER Style Council
LONG LIVE LOVE Sandie Shaw
THE LONG RUN Eagles
LONG TALL GLASSES (I CAN DANCE) Leo Sayer
LONG TRAIN RUNNING Doobie Brothers
LONGER Dan Fogelberg
LONGFELLOW SERENADE Neil Diamond
LOOK AWAY Chicago
LOOK AWAY Big Country
LOOK FOR A STAR Garry Mills
LOOK MAMA Howard Jones
THE LOOK OF LOVE (PART 1) ABC
THE LOOK OF LOVE Madonna
THE LOOK OF LOVE Sergio Mendes & Brasil '66
THE LOOK Roxette
LOOK THROUGH ANY WINDOW Hollies
LOOK WHAT YOU DONE FOR ME Al Green
LOOK WOT YOU DUN Slade
LOOKIN' FOR A LOVE Bobby Womack
LOOKIN' FOR LOVE Johnny Lee
LOOKIN' OUT MY BACK DOOR
Creedence Clearwater Revival
LOOKIN' THROUGH THE EYES OF LOVE
Partridge Family
LOOKIN' THROUGH THE WINDOWS Jackson Five
LOOKING BACK Nat 'King' Cole
LOOKING FOR A NEW LOVE Jody Watley
LOOKS LIKE WE MADE IT Barry Manilow
LOOP DE LOOP Frankie Vaughan
LOOP DE LOOP Johnny Thunder
LOOP DI LOVE Shag
THE LORD'S PRAYER Sister Janet Mead
LOSING MY MIND Liza Minelli
LOSING YOU Dusty Springfield
LOSING YOU Brenda Lee
LOST IN EMOTION Lisa Lisa & Cult Jam
LOST IN FRANCE Bonnie Tyler
LOST IN LOVE Air Supply
LOST IN MUSIC Sister Sledge
LOST IN YOUR EYES Debbie Gibson
LOST JOHN Lonnie Donegan
LOST WITHOUT YOUR LOVE Bread
LOTTA LOVE Nicolette Larson
LOUIE LOUIE Kingsmen
LOVE & PRIDE King
LOVE (CAN MAKE YOU HAPPY) Mercy
LOVE ACTION (I BELIEVE IN LOVE)
Human League
LOVE AND AFFECTION Joan Armatrading
LOVE AND MARRIAGE Frank Sinatra
LOVE BITES Def Leppard
LOVE CAME TO ME Dion
LOVE CAN'T TURN AROUND
Farley 'Jackmaster' Funk
THE LOVE CATS Cure
LOVE CHANGES (EVERYTHING) Climie Fisher
LOVE CHANGES EVERYTHING Michael Ball
LOVE CHILD Diana Ross & The Supremes
LOVE COME DOWN Evelyn 'Champagne' King
LOVE DON'T LIVE HERE ANYMORE Jimmy Nail
LOVE DON'T LIVE HERE ANYMORE Rose Royce
LOVE GROWS (WHERE MY ROSEMARY GOES)
Edison Lighthouse
LOVE HANGOVER Diana Ross
LOVE HURTS Jim Capaldi
LOVE HURTS Nazareth
THE LOVE I LOST (PT. 1)
Harold Melvin & The Blue Notes
LOVE IN AN ELEVATOR Aerosmith
LOVE IN THE FIRST DEGREE Bananarama
LOVE IS A BATTLEFIELD Pat Benatar
LOVE IS A ROSE Linda Ronstadt
LOVE IS A STRANGER Eurythmics
LOVE IS ALIVE Gary Wright
LOVE IS ALL AROUND Troggs
LOVE IS BLUE Paul Mauriat
LOVE IS CONTAGIOUS Taja Sevelle
LOVE IS HERE AND NOW YOU'RE GONE
Supremes
LOVE IS IN CONTROL (FINGER ON THE TRIGGER)
Donna Summer
LOVE IS IN THE AIR John Paul Young

LOVE IS LIFE Hot Chocolate
LOVE IS LIKE A VIOLIN Ken Dodd
LOVE IS LIKE AN ITCHING IN MY HEART
Supremes
LOVE IS LIKE OXYGEN Sweet
LOVE IS THE ANSWER
England Dan & John Ford Coley
LOVE IS THE DRUG Roxy Music
(LOVE IS) THICKER THAN WATER Andy Gibb
LOVE KILLS Freddie Mercury
LOVE LETTERS Elvis Presley
LOVE LETTERS Ketty Lester
LOVE LETTERS Alison Moyet
LOVE LETTERS IN THE SAND Pat Boone
LOVE LIKE A MAN Ten Years After
LOVE LIKE YOU AND ME Gary Glitter
LOVE MACHINE Miracles
LOVE MAKES THE WORLD GO ROUND
Perry Como
LOVE ME Yvonne Elliman
LOVE ME Elvis Presley
LOVE ME DO Beatles
LOVE ME FOR A REASON Osmonds
LOVE ME LIKE I LOVE YOU Bay City Rollers
LOVE ME LOVE MY DOG Peter Shelley
LOVE ME OR LEAVE ME Sammy Davis Jr
LOVE ME TENDER Elvis Presley
LOVE ME TONIGHT Tom Jones
LOVE ME WITH ALL YOUR HEART
Ray Charles Singers
LOVE MISSILE F1–11 Sigue Sigue Sputnik
LOVE OF MY LIFE Dooleys
LOVE OF THE COMMON PEOPLE Nicky Thomas
LOVE OF THE COMMON PEOPLE Paul Young
LOVE ON A MOUNTAIN TOP Robert Knight
LOVE ON A TWO–WAY STREET Moments
LOVE ON THE ROCKS Neil Diamond
LOVE ON YOUR SIDE Thompson Twins
LOVE OR LET ME BE LONELY
Friends Of Distinction
LOVE PLUS ONE Haircut 100
LOVE POTION NUMBER NINE Searchers
LOVE REALLY HURTS WITHOUT YOU Billy Ocean
LOVE RESURRECTION Alison Moyet
LOVE ROLLERCOASTER Ohio Players
LOVE SHACK B–52'S
LOVE SO RIGHT Bee Gees
LOVE SOMEBODY Rick Springfield
LOVE SONG Cure
LOVE THEME FROM 'THE THORN BIRDS'
Juan Martin
LOVE THEME FROM 'ROMEO & JULIET'
Henry Mancini & His Orchestra
LOVE TO LOVE YOU BABY Donna Summer
LOVE TOUCH Rod Stewart
LOVE TOWN Booker Newberry 111
LOVE TRAIN O'Jays
LOVE TRAIN Holly Johnson
LOVE WILL CONQUER ALL Lionel Richie
LOVE WILL FIND A WAY Pablo Cruise
LOVE WILL KEEP US TOGETHER
Captain & Tennille
LOVE WILL SAVE THE DAY Whitney Houston
LOVE WON'T LET ME WAIT Major Harris
A LOVE WORTH WAITING FOR Shakin' Stevens
LOVE X LOVE George Benson
LOVE YOU DOWN Ready For The World
LOVE YOU INSIDE OUT Bee Gees
THE LOVE YOU SAVE Jackson Five
LOVE YOU SO Ron Holden
LOVE ZONE Billy Ocean
LOVE'S BEEN A LITTLE BIT HARD ON ME
Juice Newton
LOVE'S BEEN GOOD TO ME Frank Sinatra
LOVE'S GOTTA HOLD ON ME Dollar
LOVE'S JUST A BROKEN HEART Cilla Black
LOVE'S THEME Love Unlimited Orchestra
LOVE'S UNKIND Donna Summer
LOVELY DAY Bill Withers
THE LOVER IN ME Sheena Easton
LOVER PLEASE Clyde McPhatter
A LOVER'S QUESTION Clyde McPhatter
LOVERBOY Billy Ocean
LOVERGIRL Teena Marie
A LOVERS CONCERTO Toys
LOVERS OF THE WORLD UNITE
David & Jonathan
LOVERS WHO WANDER Dion
LOVES ME LIKE A ROCK Paul Simon
LOVESICK BLUES Frank Ifield
LOVIN' EVERY MINUTE OF IT Loverboy
LOVIN' THINGS Marmalade
LOVING YOU Minnie Riperton
LOW RIDER War
LOWDOWN Boz Scaggs
LUCILLE Kenny Rogers
LUCKY LIPS Cliff Richard
LUCKY NUMBER Lene Lovich
LUCKY STAR Madonna

LUCKY STARS Dean Friedman
LUCY IN THE SKY WITH DIAMONDS Elton John
LUKA Suzanne Vega
LULLABY Cure
LYIN' EYES Eagles
MA BAKER Boney M
MA BELLE AMIE Tee Set
MA HE'S MAKING EYES AT ME Lena Zavaroni
MACARTHUR PARK Richard Harris
MACARTHUR PARK Donna Summer
MACDONALD'S CAVE Piltdown Men
MACK THE KNIFE Bobby Darin
MAD ABOUT YOU Bruce Ruffin
MAD ABOUT YOU Belinda Carlisle
MAD WORLD Tears For Fears
MADE YOU Adam Faith
MADNESS (IS ALL IN THE MIND) Madness
MAGGIE MAY Rod Stewart
MAGGIE'S FARM Specials
MAGIC Olivia Newton-John
MAGIC CARPET RIDE Steppenwolf
MAGIC FLY Space
MAGIC MAN Heart
MAGIC MOMENTS Perry Como
MAGICAL MYSTERY TOUR (DOUBLE E.P.)
Beatles
MAGIC ROUNDABOUT Jasper Carrott
MAGNET AND STEEL Walter Egan
MAH NA MAH NA Piero Umiliani
MAID OF ORLEANS (THE WALTZ JOAN OF ARC)
Orchestral Manoeuvres In The Dark
THE MAIN EVENT Barbra Streisand
MAKE A MOVE ON ME Olivia Newton-John
MAKE IT EASY ON YOURSELF Walker Brothers
MAKE IT REAL Jets
MAKE IT WITH YOU Bread
MAKE ME AN ISLAND Joe Dolan
MAKE ME LOSE CONTROL Eric Carmen
MAKE ME SMILE Chicago
MAKE ME SMILE(COME UP AND SEE ME)
Steve Harley & Cockney Rebel
MAKE THE WORLD GO AWAY Eddy Arnold
MAKIN' IT David Naughton
MAKING LOVE OUT OF NOTHING AT ALL
Air Supply
MAKING UP AGAIN Goldie
MAKING YOUR MIND UP Bucks Fizz
MALE STRIPPER Man 2 Man Meet Man Parrish
MALT AND BARLEY BLUES McGuinness Flint
MAMA Genesis
MAMA Connie Francis
MAMA Dave Berry
MAMA CAN'T BUY YOU LOVE Elton John
MAMA LIKED THE ROSES Elvis Presley
MAMA SAID Shirelles
MAMA TOLD ME (NOT TO COME)
Three Dog Night
MAMA USED TO SAY Junior
MAMA WEER ALL CRAZEE NOW Slade
MAMA'S PEARL Jackson Five
MAMMA MIA Abba
THE MAN IN THE MIRROR Michael Jackson
MAN OF MYSTERY Shadows
MAN OF THE WORLD Fleetwood Mac
MAN ON FIRE Frankie Vaughan
(THE MAN WHO SHOT) LIBERTY VALENCE
Gene Pitney
THE MAN WHO SOLD THE WORLD Lulu
MAN WITH THE CHILD IN HIS EYES Kate Bush
A MAN WITHOUT LOVE Engelbert Humperdinck
MANCHILD Neneh Cherry
MANDOLIN RAIN Bruce Hornsby & The Range
MANDY Barry Manilow
MANEATER Daryl Hall & John Oates
MANIAC Michael Sembello
MANIC MONDAY Bangles
MANY TEARS AGO Connie Francis
MARCH OF THE SIAMESE CHILDREN Kenny Ball
MARGARITAVILLE Jimmy Buffett
MARGUERITA TIME Status Quo
MARIA P.J. Proby
MARIA ELENA Los Indios Tabajaras
MARIE Bachelors
(MARIE'S THE NAME) HIS LATEST FLAME
Elvis Presley
MARTHA'S HARBOUR All About Eve
MARY HAD A LITTLE LAMB Paul McCartney
MARY'S BOY CHILD – OH MY LORD Boney M
MARY'S PRAYER Danny Wilson
MASHED POTATO TIME Dee Dee Sharp
MASSACHUSETTS Bee Gees
MASTER AND SERVANT Depeche Mode
MASTER BLASTER (JAMMIN') Stevie Wonder
MASTERPIECE Temptations
MATCHSTALK MEN AND MATCHSTALK CATS
Brian & Michael
MATERIAL GIRL Madonna
A MATTER OF TRUST Billy Joel
MATTHEW AND SON Cat Stevens

MAY I HAVE THE NEXT DREAM WITH YOU
Malcolm Roberts
MAYBE BABY Crickets
MAYBE I'M AMAZED Paul McCartney
MAYBELLENE Chuck Berry
ME AND BOBBY MCGEE Janis Joplin
ME AND MRS. JONES Billy Paul
ME AND MY LIFE Tremeloes
ME AND YOU AND A DOG NAMED BOO Lobo
ME THE PEACEFUL HEART Lulu
MEAN STREAK Cliff Richard
MEAN WOMAN BLUES Roy Orbison
MEET ME ON THE CORNER Lindisfarne
MEET ME ON THE CORNER Max Bygraves
MEGABLAST Bomb The Bass
MELLOW YELLOW Donovan
MELTING POT Blue Mink
MEMORIES ARE MADE OF THIS Dean Martin
MEMORY Elaine Paige
MEMPHIS Johnny Rivers
MEMPHIS Lonnie Mack
MEMPHIS TENNESSEE Chuck Berry
THE MEN IN MY LITTLE GIRL'S LIFE Mike Douglas
MERCEDES BOY Pebbles
MERCY MERCY ME (THE ECOLOGY) Marvin Gaye
MERCY, MERCY, MERCY Buckinghams
MERRIE GENTLE POPS Barron Knights
MERRY CHRISTMAS EVERYONE Shakin' Stevens
MERRY XMAS EVERYBODY Slade
A MESS OF BLUES Elvis Presley
MESSAGE IN A BOTTLE Police
THE MESSAGE Grandmaster Flash/Melle Mell
MESSAGE TO MICHAEL Dionne Warwick
A MESSAGE TO YOU RUDY Specials
MESSAGE UNDERSTOOD Sandie Shaw
METAL GURU T. Rex
METHOD OF MODERN LOVE
Daryl Hall & John Oates
MEXICALI ROSE Karl Denver
MEXICO Bob Moore & His Orch
MIAMI VICE THEME Jan Hammer
MICHAEL Highwaymen
MICHAEL ROW THE BOAT Lonnie Donegan
MICHELLE Overlanders
MICKEY Toni Basil
MICKEY'S MONKEY Miracles
MIDAS TOUCH Midnight Star
MIDNIGHT AT THE OASIS Maria Muldaur
MIDNIGHT BLUE Melissa Manchester
MIDNIGHT BLUE Lou Gramm
MIDNIGHT CONFESSIONS Grass Roots
MIDNIGHT COWBOY Ferrante & Teicher
MIDNIGHT IN MOSCOW Kenny Ball
MIDNIGHT MARY Joey Powers
MIDNIGHT RIDER Paul Davidson
MIDNIGHT TRAIN TO GEORGIA
Gladys Knight & The Pips
MIGHTY QUINN Manfred Mann
MILK AND ALCOHOL Dr. Feelgood
A MILLION TO ONE Jimmy Charles
MIND BLOWING DECISIONS Heatwave
THE MINUTE YOU'RE GONE Cliff Richard
MIRACLES Jefferson Starship
MIRAGE Tommy James & The Shondells
MIRROR IN THE BATHROOM Beat
MIRROR MAN Human League
MIRROR MIRROR Pinkerton's Assorted Colours
MIRROR MIRROR Diana Ross
MIRROR MIRROR (MON AMOUR) Dollar
MISFIT Curiosity Killed The Cat
MISLED Kool & The Gang
MISS ME BLIND Culture Club
MISS YOU Rolling Stones
MISS YOU LIKE CRAZY Natalie Cole
MISS YOU MUCH Janet Jackson
MISSING YOU Diana Ross
MISSING YOU Chris De Burgh
MISSING YOU John Waite
MISSION BELL Donnie Brooks
MISSISSIPPI Pussycat
MISTLETOE AND WINE Cliff Richard
MISTY Ray Stevens
MISTY BLUE Dorothy Moore
MIXED EMOTIONS Rolling Stones
MOCKINGBIRD Carly Simon & James Taylor
MOCKINGBIRD Inez Foxx
MOCKINGBIRD HILL Migil Five
THE MODEL Kraftwerk
MODERN GIRL Sheena Easton
MODERN LOVE David Bowie
MODERN WOMAN Billy Joel
MONA LISA Conway Twitty
MONDAY MONDAY Mamas & The Papas
MONEY Flying Lizards
MONEY FOR NOTHING Dire Straits
MONEY HONEY Bay City Rollers
MONEY MONEY MONEY Abba
MONKEY George Michael
MONKEY SPANNER Dave & Ansil Collins

THE MONKEY TIME Major Lance
MONSIEUR DUPONT Sandie Shaw
MONSTER MASH Bobby 'Boris' Pickett
MONTEGO BAY Bobby Bloom
MONY MONY Tommy James & The Shondells
MONY MONY Billy Idol
MOODY BLUE Elvis Presley
MOODY RIVER Pat Boone
MOON RIVER Danny Williams
MOONLIGHT FEELS RIGHT Starbuck
MOONLIGHT GAMBLER Frankie Laine
MOONLIGHT SHADOW Mike Oldfield
MOONLIGHTING Leo Sayer
MOONLIGHTING ('THEME') Al Jarreau
MOONSHINE SALLY Mud
MORE Kai Winding
MORE Perry Como
THE MORE I SEE YOU Chris Montez
MORE LOVE Kim Carnes
MORE THAN A FEELING Boston
MORE THAN A WOMAN Tavares
MORE THAN I CAN SAY Leo Sayer
MORE THAN I CAN SAY Bobby Vee
MORE THAN IN LOVE Kate Robbins
MORE THAN THIS Roxy Music
MORE, MORE, MORE Andrea True Connection
THE MORNING AFTER Maureen McGovern
MORNING HAS BROKEN Cat Stevens
MORNING SIDE OF THE MOUNTAIN
Donny & Marie Osmond
MORNING TRAIN (A.K.A. 9 TO 5) Sheena Easton
MORNINGTOWN RIDE Seekers
THE MOST BEAUTIFUL GIRL Charlie Rich
MOTHER AND CHILD REUNION Paul Simon
MOTHER OF MINE Neil Reid
MOTHER-IN-LAW Ernie K-Doe
MOTHERS LITTLE HELPER Rolling Stones
MOTORHEAD LIVE Motorhead
MOULDY OLD DOUGH Lieutenant Pigeon
MOUNTAIN OF LOVE Johnny Rivers
THE MOUNTAIN'S HIGH Dick & Deedee
MOVE AWAY Culture Club
MOVE CLOSER Phyllis Nelson
MOVE IT Cliff Richard
MOVE OVER DARLING Doris Day
MOVE OVER DARLING Tracey Ullman
MOZART SYMPHONY NO. 40 IN G MINOR
Waldo De Los Rios
MR. BIG STUFF Jean Knight
MR. BLUE Fleetwoods
MR. BLUE SKY Electric Light Orchestra
MR. BOJANGLES Nitty Gritty Dirt Band
MR. CUSTER Larry Verne
MR. CUSTER Charlie Drake
MR. JAWS Dickie Goodman
MR. LONELY Bobby Vinton
MR. ROBOTO Styx
MR. SLEAZE Bananarama
MR. SOFT Cockney Rebel
MR. TAMBOURINE MAN Byrds
MRS. BROWN YOU'VE GOT A LOVELY DAUGHTER
Herman's Hermits
MRS. ROBINSON Simon & Garfunkel
MS GRACE Tymes
MULE SKINNER BLUES Fendermen
MULL OF KINTYRE Paul McCartney
MULTIPLICATION Bobby Darin
MUSCLEBOUND Spandau Ballet
MUSCLES Diana Ross
MUSIC John Miles
MUSIC AND LIGHTS Imagination
MUSIC BOX DANCER Frank Mills
THE MUSIC OF THE NIGHT Michael Crawford
THE MUSIC OF TORVILL & DEAN EP
Richard Hartley/Michael Reed O
A MUST TO AVOID Herman's Hermits
MY ARMS KEEP MISSING YOU Rick Astley
MY BABY JUST CARES FOR ME Nina Simone
MY BABY LOVES LOVIN' White Plains
MY BEST FRIEND'S GIRL Cars
MY BOY Elvis Presley
MY BOY LOLLIPOP Millie
MY BOYFRIEND'S BACK Angels
MY BROTHER JAKE Free
MY BUCKET'S GOT A HOLE IN IT Ricky Nelson
MY CAMERA NEVER LIES Bucks Fizz
MY CHERIE AMOUR Stevie Wonder
MY COO-CA-CHOO Alvin Stardust
MY CUP RUNNETH OVER Ed Ames
MY DAD Paul Peterson
MY DING-A-LING Chuck Berry
MY DIXIE DARLING Lonnie Donegan
MY EMPTY ARMS Jackie Wilson
MY EVER CHANGING MOOD Style Council
MY EYES ADORED YOU Frankie Valli
MY FAVOURITE WASTE OF TIME Owen Paul
MY FRIEND STAN Slade
MY GENERATION Who

MY GIRL Madness
MY GIRL Temptations
MY GIRL LOLLIPOP (MY BOY LOLLIPOP)
Bad Manners
MY GUY Mary Wells
MY HAPPINESS Connie Francis
MY HEART BELONGS TO ME Barbra Streisand
MY HEART BELONGS TO ONLY YOU
Bobby Vinton
MY HEART CAN'T TELL YOU NO Rod Stewart
MY HEART HAS A MIND OF ITS OWN
Connie Francis
MY HOME TOWN Paul Anka
MY HOMETOWN Bruce Springsteen
MY KIND OF GIRL Matt Monro
MY LIFE Billy Joel
MY LITTLE LADY Tremeloes
MY LITTLE TOWN Simon & Garfunkel
MY LOVE Lionel Richie
MY LOVE Petula Clark
MY LOVE Paul McCartney
MY LOVE Julio Iglesias/Stevie Wonder
MY LOVE FOR YOU Johnny Mathis
MY MARIA B.W. Stevenson
MY MELODY OF LOVE Bobby Vinton
MY MIND'S EYE Small Faces
MY NAME IS JACK Manfred Mann
MY OH MY Slade
MY OLD MAN'S A DUSTMAN Lonnie Donegan
MY OLD PIANO Diana Ross
MY ONE TEMPTATION Mica Paris
MY PERFECT COUSIN Undertones
MY PERSONAL POSSESSION Nat 'King' Cole
MY PRAYER Platters
MY PRAYER Gerry Monroe
MY PREROGATIVE Bobby Brown
MY PRETTY ONE Cliff Richard
MY RESISTANCE IS LOW Robin Sarstedt
MY SENTIMENTAL FRIEND Herman's Hermits
MY SHARONA Knack
MY SHIP IS COMING IN Walker Brothers
MY SIMPLE HEART Three Degrees
MY SPECIAL ANGEL Vogues
MY SWEET LORD George Harrison
MY TOOT TOOT Denise La Salle
MY TRUE LOVE Jack Scott
MY TRUE STORY Jive Five
MY WAY Frank Sinatra
MY WAY Elvis Presley
MY WAY Sex Pistols
MY WAY OF THINKING UB40
MY WHOLE WORLD ENDED David Ruffin
MY WORLD IS EMPTY WITHOUT YOU Supremes
NA NA HEY HEY KISS HIM GOODBYE
Bananarama
NA NA HEY HEY KISS HIM GOODBYE Steam
NA NA IS THE SADDEST WORD Stylistics
NA NA NA Cozy Powell
NADIA'S THEME (THE YOUNG & THE RESTLESS)
Barry DeVorzon & Perry Botkin
NAIROBI Tommy Steele
THE NAME GAME Shirley Ellis
THE NAME OF THE GAME Abba
NASHVILLE CATS Lovin' Spoonful
NASTY Janet Jackson
NATHAN JONES Supremes
NATIVE NEW YORKER Odyssey
NATURAL BORN BUGIE Humble Pie
NATURAL HIGH Bloodstone
NATURAL SINNER Fair Weather
A NATURAL WOMAN (YOU MAKE ME FEEL LIKE)
Aretha Franklin
NAUGHTY GIRLS(NEED LOVE TOO)
Samantha Fox
NAUGHTY LADY OF SHADY LANE Dean Martin
NAVY BLUE Diane Renay
NEANDERTHAL MAN Hotlegs
NEED YOU TONIGHT INXS
NEEDLES AND PINS Smokie
NEEDLES AND PINS Searchers
NEITHER ONE OF US Gladys Knight & The Pips
NELLIE THE ELEPHANT Toy Dolls
NELSON MANDELA Special Aka
NEUTRON DANCE Pointer Sisters
NEVER Heart
NEVER BE ANYONE ELSE BUT YOU
Ricky Nelson
NEVER BEEN TO SPAIN Three Dog Night
NEVER CAN SAY GOODBYE Communards
NEVER CAN SAY GOODBYE Jackson Five
NEVER CAN SAY GOODBYE Gloria Gaynor
NEVER ENDING SONG OF LOVE New Seekers
NEVER ENDING STORY Limahl
NEVER GONNA GIVE YOU UP Rick Astley
NEVER GONNA GIVE YOU UP Musical Youth
NEVER GONNA LET YOU GO Sergio Mendes
NEVER GOODBYE Karl Denver
NEVER HAD A DREAM COME TRUE
Stevie Wonder

NEVER KNEW LOVE LIKE THIS BEFORE
Stephanie Mills
NEVER LET HER SLIP AWAY Andrew Gold
NEVER MY LOVE Blue Suede
NEVER MY LOVE Association
NEVER NEVER Assembly
NEVER SURRENDER Corey Hart
NEVER TEAR US APART INXS
NEVER TOO LATE Kylie Minogue
NEVER TRUST A STRANGER Kim Wilde
NEVER, NEVER GONNA GIVE YA UP Barry White
NEVER Heart
NEW BEGINNING (MAMBA SAYRA) Bucks Fizz
A NEW ENGLAND Kirsty MacColl
NEW KID IN TOWN Eagles
NEW MOON ON MONDAY Duran Duran
NEW ORLEANS Gary U.S. Bonds
NEW SENSATION INXS
NEW SONG Howard Jones
NEW YEAR'S DAY U2
NEW YORK GROOVE Hello
NEXT DOOR TO AN ANGEL Neil Sedaka
THE NEXT TIME I FALL Peter Cetera & Amy Grant
THE NEXT TIME Cliff Richard
NICE TO BE WITH YOU Gallery
NIGHT Jackie Wilson
NIGHT BIRDS Shakatak
THE NIGHT CHICAGO DIED Paper Lace
NIGHT FEVER Bee Gees
NIGHT GAMES Graham Bonnett
THE NIGHT HAS A THOUSAND EYES Bobby Vee
NIGHT KLUB Specials
NIGHT MOVES
Bob Seger & The Silver Bullet Band
NIGHT OF FEAR Move
NIGHT OWL Gerry Rafferty
THE NIGHT OWLS Little River Band
THE NIGHT Frankie Valli & Four Seasons
THE NIGHT THE LIGHTS WENT OUT IN GEORGIA
Vicki Lawrence
THE NIGHT THEY DROVE OLD DIXIE DOWN
Joan Baez
A NIGHT TO REMEMBER Shalamar
NIGHTINGALE Carole King
NIGHTS ARE FOREVER WITHOUT YOU
England Dan & John Ford Coley
NIGHTS IN WHITE SATIN Moody Blues
NIGHTS ON BROADWAY Bee Gees
NIGHTS ON BROADWAY Candi Staton
NIGHTSHIFT Commodores
NIKITA Elton John
19 Paul Hardcastle
1999 Prince & The Revolution
19TH NERVOUS BREAKDOWN Rolling Stones
NINE TIMES OUT OF TEN Cliff Richard
9 TO 5 Dolly Parton
9 TO 5 (Aka MORNING TRAIN) Sheena Easton
98.6 Keith
99 LUFTBALLONS (99 RED BALLOONS) Nena
96 TEARS ? & The Mysterians
NITE AND DAY Al B. Sure!
THE NITTY GRITTY Shirley Ellis
NO ARMS COULD EVER HOLD YOU Bachelors
NO CHARGE J.J. Barrie
NO DOUBT ABOUT IT Hot Chocolate
NO HONESTLY Lynsey De Paul
NO MATTER HOW I TRY Gilbert O'Sullivan
NO MATTER WHAT Badfinger
NO MATTER WHAT SHAPE (YOUR STOMACH'S IN)
T-Bones
NO MILK TODAY Herman's Hermits
NO MORE HEROES Stranglers
NO MORE LONELY NIGHTS Paul McCartney
NO MORE MR. NICE GUY Alice Cooper
NO MORE TEARS (ENOUGH IS ENOUGH)
Barbra Streisand & Donna Summer
NO MORE THE FOOL Elkie Brooks
NO NO SONG Ringo Starr
NO ONE CAN MAKE MY SUNSHINE SMILE
Everly Brothers
NO ONE IS INNOCENT Sex Pistols
NO ONE IS TO BLAME Howard Jones
NO PARTICULAR PLACE TO GO Chuck Berry
NO REGRETS Midge Ure
NO REGRETS Walker Brothers
NO TIME Guess Who
NO WOMAN NO CRY Bob Marley & The Wailers
NOBODY BUT ME Human Beinz
NOBODY DOES IT BETTER Carly Simon
NOBODY I KNOW Peter & Gordon
NOBODY NEEDS YOUR LOVE Gene Pitney
NOBODY TOLD ME John Lennon
NOBODY'S CHILD Karen Young
NOBODY'S DARLIN' BUT MINE Frank Ifield
NOBODY'S DIARY Yazoo
NOBODY'S FOOL Haircut 100
NOBODY'S FOOL Kenny Loggins
NORMAN Sue Thompson
NORTH TO ALASKA Johnny Horton

NORTHERN LIGHTS Renaissance
NOT FADE AWAY Rolling Stones
NOTHIN' AT ALL Heart
NOTHIN' BUT A GOOD TIME Poison
NOTHING CAN DIVIDE US Jason Donovan
NOTHING FROM NOTHING Billy Preston
NOTHING RHYMED Gilbert O'Sullivan
NOTHING'S GONNA CHANGE MY LOVE FOR YOU
Glenn Medeiros
NOTHING'S GONNA STOP ME NOW
Samantha Fox
NOTHING'S GONNA STOP US NOW Starship
(NOTHIN' SERIOUS) JUST BUGGIN' Whistle
NOTORIOUS Duran Duran
NOW IS THE TIME
Jimmy James & The Vagabonds
NOW THAT WE'VE FOUND LOVE Third World
NOW THOSE DAYS ARE GONE Bucks Fizz
NOWHERE MAN Beatles
NOWHERE TO RUN Martha & The Vandellas
9 DREAM John Lennon
NUMERO UNO Starlight
NUT ROCKER B.Bumble & The Stingers
NUTBUSH CITY LIMITS Ike & Tina Turner
O DIO MIO Annette
O SUPERMAN Laurie Anderson
O-O-O CHILD Five Stairsteps
O.K. Rock Follies
OB—LA-DI OB—LA-DA Marmalade
ODE TO BILLIE JOE Bobbie Gentry
OFF THE WALL Michael Jackson
OH BABE WHAT WOULD YOU SAY?
Hurricane Smith
OH BOY Mud
OH BOY Brotherhood Of Man
OH BOY Crickets
OH CAROL Smokie
OH DIANE Fleetwood Mac
OH GIRL Chi—Lites
OH HAPPY DAY Edwin Hawkins Singers
OH JULIE Shakin' Stevens
OH L'AMOUR Dollar
OH LORI Alessi
OH MY MY Ringo Starr
OH NO Commodores
OH NO NOT MY BABY Rod Stewart
OH PRETTY WOMAN Roy Orbison
OH SHEILA Ready For The World
OH VERY YOUNG Cat Stevens
OH WELL Fleetwood Mac
OH WHAT A CIRCUS David Essex
OH WHAT A NITE Dells
OH YEAH (ON THE RADIO) Roxy Music
OH YES! YOU'RE BEAUTIFUL Gary Glitter
OH! CAROL Neil Sedaka
OH, SHERRIE Steve Perry
OKAY! Dave Dee, Dozy, Beaky, Mick & Titch
OL' MACDONALD Frank Sinatra
OL' RAG BLUES Status Quo
OLD CAPE COD Patti Page
OLD DAYS Chicago
AN OLD FASHIONED LOVE SONG
Three Dog Night
THE OLD LAMPLIGHTER Browns
THE OLD MAN DOWN THE ROAD John Fogerty
OLD RIVERS Walter Brennan
OLDEST SWINGER IN TOWN Fred Wedlock
OLE OLA (MULHER BRASILEIRA) Rod Stewart
OLIVER'S ARMY Elvis Costello
ON A CAROUSEL Hollies
ON A SLOW BOAT TO CHINA Emile Ford
ON AND ON Gladys Knight & The Pips
ON BROADWAY Drifters
ON BROADWAY George Benson
ON HORSEBACK Mike Oldfield
ON MY OWN Patti Labelle & Michael McDonald
ON MY RADIO Selecter
ON OUR OWN Bobby Brown
ON THE BEACH Cliff Richard
ON THE DARK SIDE
John Cafferty & The Beaver Brown Band
ON THE INSIDE Lynne Hamilton
ON THE RADIO Donna Summer
ON THE REBOUND Floyd Cramer
ON THE ROAD AGAIN Canned Heat
ONCE BITTEN TWICE SHY Great White
ONCE UPON A DREAM Billy Fury
ONCE UPON A LONG AGO Paul McCartney
ONCE YOU GET STARTED Rufus
ONE Three Dog Night
ONE Bee Gees
ONE AND ONE IS ONE Medicine Head
ONE BAD APPLE Osmonds
ONE BROKEN HEART FOR SALE Elvis Presley
ONE DAY AT A TIME Lena Martell
ONE DAY I'LL FLY AWAY Randy Crawford
ONE DAY IN YOUR LIFE Michael Jackson
ONE FINE DAY Chiffons

ONE GOOD WOMAN Peter Cetera
ONE HEARTBEAT Smokey Robinson
THE ONE I LOVE R.E.M.
ONE IN A MILLION YOU Larry Graham
ONE INCH ROCK Tyrannosaurus Rex
ONE IN TEN UB40
ONE LESS BELL TO ANSWER Fifth Dimension
ONE LOVE Bob Marley & The Wailers
ONE MAN BAND Leo Sayer
ONE MAN WOMAN/ONE WOMAN MAN
Paul Anka
ONE MINT JULEP Ray Charles
ONE MOMENT IN TIME Whitney Houston
ONE MORE NIGHT Phil Collins
ONE MORE TRY George Michael
ONE NATION UNDER A GROOVE (PT. 1)
Funkadelic
ONE NIGHT Elvis Presley
ONE NIGHT IN BANGKOK Murray Head
ONE OF THESE NIGHTS Eagles
ONE OF US Abba
ONE ON ONE Daryl Hall & John Oates
ONE STEP BEYOND Madness
ONE STEP FURTHER Bardo
THE ONE THAT YOU LOVE Air Supply
ONE THING LEADS TO ANOTHER Fixx
ONE TOKE OVER THE LINE Brewer and Shipley
ONE TRACK MIND Bobby Lewis
1–2–3 Len Barry
1–2–3 Gloria Estefan & Miami Sound Machine
ONE TWO THREE O'LEARY Des O'Connor
1 2 3 RED LIGHT 1910 Fruitgum Company
ONE VISION Queen
ONE WAY LOVE
Cliff Bennett & The Rebel Rousers
ONE WAY TICKET Eruption
THE ONE WHO REALLY LOVES YOU Mary Wells
ONION SONG Marvin Gaye & Tammi Terrell
ONLY IN MY DREAMS Debbie Gibson
ONLY LOVE Nana Mouskouri
ONLY LOVE CAN BREAK A HEART Gene Pitney
ONLY ONE WOMAN Marbles
ONLY SIXTEEN Craig Douglas
ONLY SIXTEEN Dr. Hook
ONLY THE LONELY Motels
ONLY THE LONELY Roy Orbison
ONLY THE STRONG SURVIVE Jerry Butler
ONLY THE YOUNG Journey
THE ONLY WAY IS UP
Yazz & The Plastic Population
THE ONLY WAY OUT Cliff Richard
ONLY WHEN YOU LEAVE Spandau Ballet
ONLY YESTERDAY Carpenters
ONLY YOU Ringo Starr
ONLY YOU Yazoo
ONLY YOU Flying Pickets
ONLY YOU Platters
ONLY YOU CAN Fox
OOH BABY BABY Linda Ronstadt
OOH LA LA LA (LET'S GO DANCING)
Kool & The Gang
OOH TO BE AH Kajagoogoo
OOH!WHAT A LIFE Gibson Brothers
OOH—WAKKA—DOO—WAKKA—DAY
Gilbert O'Sullivan
OOPS UPSIDE YOUR HEAD Gap Band
OPEN ARMS Journey
AN OPEN LETTER TO MY TEENAGE SON
Victor Lundberg
OPEN YOUR HEART Madonna
OPEN YOUR HEART Human League
OPPORTUNITIES (LET'S MAKE LOTS OF MONEY)
Pet Shop Boys
ORINOCO FLOW Enya
ORVILLE'S SONG Keith Harris & Orville
OSSIE'S DREAM Tottenham Hotspur
THE OTHER WOMAN Ray Parker Jr.
OUR DAY WILL COME Ruby & The Romantics
OUR FAVOURITE MELODIES Craig Douglas
OUR HOUSE Madness
OUR LIPS ARE SEALED Fun Boy Three
OUR LOVE Natalie Cole
(OUR LOVE) DON'T THROW IT ALL AWAY
Andy Gibb
OUR WINTER LOVE Bill Pursell
OUT IN THE FIELDS Gary Moore & Phil Lynott
OUT OF LIMITS Marketts
OUT OF THE BLUE Debbie Gibson
OUT OF TIME Chris Farlowe
OUT OF TOUCH Daryl Hall & John Oates
OUTA—SPACE Billy Preston
OVER AND OVER Dave Clark Five
OVER UNDER SIDEWAYS DOWN Yardbirds
OVER YOU Roxy Music
OVER YOU Gary Puckett & The Union Gap
OVERKILL Men At Work
OWNER OF A LONELY HEART Yes
OXYGENE PART 1V Jean-Michel Jarre
P.S. I LOVE YOU Beatles

P.T. 109 Jimmy Dean
P.Y.T. (PRETTY YOUNG THING) Michael Jackson
PAC—MAN FEVER Buckner & Garcia
PACIFIC 808 State
PAINT IT BLACK Rolling Stones
PAINTER MAN Boney M
PALE SHELTER Tears For Fears
PALISADES PARK Freddy Cannon
PALOMA BLANCA George Baker Selection
PAPA DON'T PREACH Madonna
PAPA WAS A ROLLIN' STONE Temptations
PAPA'S GOT A BRAND NEW BAG James Brown
PAPAS GOT A BRAND NEW PIGBAG Pigbag
PAPER IN FIRE John Cougar Mellencamp
PAPER PLANE Status Quo
PAPER ROSES Marie Osmond
PAPER ROSES Anita Bryant
PAPER ROSES Kaye Sisters
PAPER SUN Traffic
PAPERBACK WRITER Beatles
PARADISE CITY Guns N' Roses
PARALYSED Elvis Presley
PARANOID Black Sabbath
PARISIENNE WALKWAYS Gary Moore
PART OF THE UNION Strawbs
PART TIME LOVER Stevie Wonder
PARTY Elvis Presley
PARTY ALL THE TIME Eddie Murphy
PARTY FEARS TWO Associates
PARTY LIGHTS Claudine Clark
PASADENA Temperance Seven
PASS THE DUTCHIE Musical Youth
PASSENGERS Elton John
PASSION Rod Stewart
PATCHES Clarence Carter
PATCHES Dickey Lee
PATCH IT UP Elvis Presley
PATIENCE Guns N' Roses
PEACE ON EARTH David Bowie & Bing Crosby
PEACE ON EARTH Hi Tension
PEACE TRAIN Cat Stevens
PEACHES Stranglers
PEARL IN THE SHELL Howard Jones
PEARL'S A SINGER Elkie Brooks
PEEK—A—BOO New Vaudeville Band
PEGGY SUE Buddy Holly
PENNY LANE Beatles
PENNY LOVER Lionel Richie
PEOPLE Barbra Streisand
PEOPLE ARE PEOPLE Depeche Mode
PEOPLE GET READY Bob Marley & The Wailers
PEOPLE GOT TO BE FREE Rascals
PEOPLE LIKE YOU AND PEOPLE LIKE ME
Glitter Band
PEPE Duane Eddy
PEPINO THE ITALIAN MOUSE Lou Monte
PEPPER BOX Peppers
PEPPERMINT TWIST (PT. 1)
Joey Dee & The Starliters
PERCOLATOR (TWIST)
Billy Joe & The Checkmates
PERFECT Fairground Attraction
PERFECT WORLD Huey Lewis & The News
PERFIDIA Ventures
PERSONALITY Anthony Newley
PETER GUNN Art Of Noise & Duane Eddy
PETER GUNN THEME Duane Eddy
THE PHANTOM OF THE OPERA
Sarah Brightman/Steve Harley
PHILADELPHIA FREEDOM Elton John
PHOTOGRAPH Ringo Starr
PHYSICAL Olivia Newton–John
PIANO IN THE DARK
Brenda Russell & Joe Esposito
PICK UP THE PIECES Average White Band
PICK UP THE PIECES Hudson—Ford
A PICTURE OF YOU Joe Brown & The Bruvvers
PICTURES OF LILY Who
PICTURES OF MATCHSTICK MEN Status Quo
PIE JESU Sarah Brightman
PIED PIPER Crispian St. Peters
PILLOW TALK Sylvia
PINBALL WIZARD Who
PINBALL WIZARD Elton John
PINK CADILLAC Natalie Cole
PINK HOUSES John Cougar Mellencamp
PIPELINE Chantays
PIPES OF PEACE Paul McCartney
A PLACE IN THE SUN Stevie Wonder
PLAY ME LIKE YOU PLAY YOUR GUITAR
Duane Eddy & Rebelettes
PLAY THAT FUNKY MUSIC Wild Cherry
PLAYBOY Marvelettes
PLAYGROUND IN MY MIND Clint Holmes
PLEASANT VALLEY SUNDAY Monkees
PLEASE COME TO BOSTON Dave Loggins
PLEASE DON'T FALL IN LOVE Cliff Richard
PLEASE DON'T GO Donald Peers
PLEASE DON'T GO KC & The Sunshine Band

PLEASE DON'T GO GIRL New Kids On The Block
PLEASE DON'T MAKE ME CRY UB40
PLEASE DON'T TEASE Cliff Richard
PLEASE HELP ME, I'M FALLING Hank Locklin
PLEASE LOVE ME FOREVER Bobby Vinton
PLEASE ME POSTMAN Carpenters
PLEASE MR. PLEASE Olivia Newton-John
PLEASE MR. POSTMAN Marvelettes
PLEASE MR. POSTMAN Carpenters
PLEASE PLEASE ME Beatles
PLEASE TELL HIM I SAID HELLO Dana
POETRY IN MOTION Johnny Tillotson
POETRY MAN Phoebe Snow
POINT OF NO RETURN Expose
POISON Alice Cooper
POISON ARROW ABC
POISON IVY Lambrettas
POLK SALAD ANNIE Tony Joe White
PONY TIME Chubby Checker
POOL HALL RICHARD Faces
POOR LITTLE FOOL Ricky Nelson
POOR MAN'S SON Rockin' Berries
POOR ME Adam Faith
POOR SIDE OF TOWN Johnny Rivers
POP GO THE WORKERS Barron Knights
POP LIFE Prince & The Revolution
POP MUZIK M
POPCORN Hot Butter
POPEYE (THE HITCHHIKER) Chubby Checker
POPSICLES AND ICICLES Murmaids
PORTRAIT OF MY LOVE Matt Monro
PORTRAIT OF MY LOVE Steve Lawrence
PORTSMOUTH Mike Oldfield
POSITIVELY 4TH STREET Bob Dylan
POUR SOME SUGAR ON ME Def Leppard
THE POWER OF LOVE Frankie Goes To Hollywood
THE POWER OF LOVE Huey Lewis & The News
THE POWER OF LOVE Jennifer Rush
POWER TO ALL OUR FRIENDS Cliff Richard
POWER TO THE PEOPLE John Lennon
PRECIOUS Jam
PRECIOUS AND FEW Climax
PRETEND Alvin Stardust
PRETTY BLUE EYES Craig Douglas
PRETTY BLUE EYES Steve Lawrence
PRETTY FLAMINGO Manfred Mann
PRETTY LITTLE ANGEL EYES Showaddywaddy
PRETTY LITTLE ANGEL EYES Curtis Lee
PRETTY PAPER Roy Orbison
PRETTY VACANT Sex Pistols
THE PRICE OF LOVE Everly Brothers
PRIDE (IN THE NAME OF LOVE) U2
PRIDE AND JOY Marvin Gaye
PRINCE CHARMING Adam & The Ants
PRINCESS IN RAGS Gene Pitney
PRIVATE DANCER Tina Turner
PRIVATE EYES Daryl Hall & John Oates
PRIVATE INVESTIGATIONS Dire Straits
PRIVATE NUMBER Judy Clay & William Bell
PROBLEMS Everly Brothers
PROMISED LAND Elvis Presley
PROMISES Eric Clapton
PROMISES Ken Dodd
PROUD MARY Creedence Clearwater Revival
PROUD MARY Ike & Tina Turner
THE PROUD ONE Osmonds
PROVE YOUR LOVE Taylor Dayne
PSYCHEDELIC SHACK Temptations
PSYCHOTIC REACTION Count Five
PUBLIC IMAGE Public Image Ltd.
PUFF THE MAGIC DRAGON Peter, Paul & Mary
PUMP UP THE JAM Technotronic Featuring Felly
PUMP UP THE VOLUME M/A/R/R/S
PUNKY REGGAE PARTY
Bob Marley & The Wailers
PUPPET ON A STRING Sandie Shaw
PUPPY LOVE Donny Osmond
PUPPY LOVE Paul Anka
THE PUPPY SONG David Cassidy
PURPLE HAZE Jimi Hendrix Experience
PURPLE RAIN Prince & The Revolution
PUSH IT Salt 'N' Pepa
THE PUSHBIKE SONG Mixtures
PUSS 'N BOOTS Adam Ant
PUT A LITTLE LOVE IN YOUR HEART
Jackie DeShannon
PUT A LITTLE LOVE IN YOUR HEART
Annie Lennox & Al Green
PUT YOUR HAND IN THE HAND Ocean
PUT YOUR HANDS TOGETHER O'Jays
PUT YOUR HEAD ON MY SHOULDER Paul Anka
PUT YOUR LOVE IN ME Hot Chocolate
PUTTING ON THE STYLE Lonnie Donegan
PUTTIN' ON THE RITZ Taco
PYJAMARAMA Roxy Music
QUARTER TO THREE Gary U.S. Bonds
QUE SERA MI VIDA (1F YOU SHOULD GO)
Gibson Brothers
QUEEN OF CLUBS KC & The Sunshine Band

QUEEN OF HEARTS Juice Newton
QUEEN OF THE HOP Bobby Darin
QUESTION Moody Blues
QUICKSAND Martha & The Vandellas
QUIEREME MUCHO (YOURS) Julio Iglesias
R.O.C.K IN THE U.S.A. John Cougar Mellencamp
RABBIT Chas & Dave
THE RACE Yello
RACE WITH THE DEVIL Gun
RADANCER Marmalade
RADAR LOVE Golden Earring
RADIO GA GA Queen
RAG DOLL Four Seasons
RAGAMUFFIN MAN Manfred Mann
RAGE HARD Frankie Goes To Hollywood
RAGS TO RICHES Elvis Presley
RAIN Status Quo
RAIN ON THE ROOF Lovin' Spoonful
RAIN OR SHINE Five Star
THE RAIN Oran 'Juice' Jones
THE RAIN, THE PARK & OTHER THINGS Cowsills
RAINBOW Marmalade
RAINBOW VALLEY Love Affair
RAINDROPS Dee Clark
RAINDROPS KEEEP FALLIN' ON MY HEAD
Sacha Distel
RAINDROPS KEEP FALLIN' ON MY HEAD
B.J. Thomas
RAINY DAY WOMEN #12 & 35 Bob Dylan
RAINY DAYS AND MONDAYS Carpenters
RAINY NIGHT IN GEORGIA Brook Benton
RAMBLIN' MAN Allman Brothers Band
RAMBLIN' ROSE Nat 'King' Cole
RAMONA Bachelors
RANDY Blue Mink
RANKING FULL STOP Beat
THE RAPPER Jaggerz
RAPPER'S DELIGHT Sugarhill Gang
RAPTURE Blondie
RASPBERRY BERET Prince & The Revolution
RASPUTIN Boney M
RAT RACE Specials
RAT TRAP Boomtown Rats
RAVE ON Buddy Holly
RAWHIDE Frankie Laine
REACH FOR THE STARS Shirley Bassey
REACH OUT I'LL BE THERE Four Tops
REACH OUT OF THE DARKNESS
Friend And Lover
READY WILLING AND ABLE Doris Day
REAL GONE KID Deacon Blue
REAL LOVE Doobie Brothers
REAL LOVE Jody Watley
REAL WILD CHILD (WILD ONE) Iggy Pop
REALLY SAYING SOMETHING
Bananarama/Fun Boy Three
REASONS TO BE CHEERFUL (PT 3)
Ian Dury & Blockheads
REBEL REBEL David Bowie
REBEL YELL Billy Idol
REBEL-'ROUSER Duane Eddy
RED BALLOON Dave Clark Five
RED DRESS Alvin Stardust
RED LIGHT SPELLS DANGER Billy Ocean
RED RED WINE UB40
RED RIVER ROCK Johnny & The Hurricanes
RED ROSES FOR A BLUE LADY Viv Damn
RED RUBBER BALL Cyrkle
REET PETITE Jackie Wilson
REFLECTIONS Diana Ross & The Supremes
REFLECTIONS OF MY LIFE Marmalade
THE REFLEX Duran Duran
REGGAE TUNE Andy Fairweather-Low
RELAX Frankie Goes To Hollywood
RELEASE ME Little Esther Phillips
RELEASE ME (AND LET ME LOVE AGAIN)
Engelbert Humperdinck
REMEMBER (SHA-LA-LA) Bay City Rollers
REMEMBER (WALKIN' IN THE SAND)
Shangri-Las
REMEMBER ME Diana Ross
REMEMBER ME THIS WAY Gary Glitter
REMEMBER YOU'RE A WOMBLE Wombles
REMEMBER YOU'RE MINE Pat Boone
REMINISCING Little River Band
RENT Pet Shop Boys
RENTA SANTA Chris Hill
REQUIEM London Boys
RESCUE ME Fontella Bass
RESPECT Aretha Franklin
RESPECT YOURSELF Bruce Willis
RESPECTABLE Mel & Kim
RESURRECTION SHUFFLE
Ashton Gardner & Dyke
THE RETURN OF DJANGO Upsetters
RETURN OF THE LOS PALMAS 7 Madness
RETURN TO ME Dean Martin
RETURN TO SENDER Elvis Presley
REUNITED Peaches & Herb

REVEREND MR. BLACK Kingston Trio
REWARD Teardrop Explodes
RHINESTONE COWBOY Glen Campbell
RHYTHM IS GONNA GET YOU
Gloria Estefan & Miami Sound Machine
RHYTHM NATION Janet Jackson
RHYTHM OF THE NIGHT DeBarge
RHYTHM OF THE RAIN Cascades
RICH GIRL Daryl Hall & John Oates
THE RIDDLE Nik Kershaw
RIDE Dee Dee Sharp
RIDE A WHITE SWAN T. Rex
RIDE CAPTAIN RIDE Blues Image
RIDE LIKE THE WIND Christopher Cross
RIDE ON TIME Black Box
RIDERS IN THE SKY Ramrods
RIGHT BACK WHERE WE STARTED FROM
Maxine Nightingale
RIGHT BACK WHERE WE STARTED FROM Sinitta
RIGHT BY YOUR SIDE Eurythmics
RIGHT HERE WAITING Richard Marx
RIGHT ON TRACK Breakfast Club
RIGHT PLACE WRONG TIME Dr. John
RIGHT TIME OF THE NIGHT Jennifer Warnes
RIKKI DON'T LOSE THAT NUMBER Steely Dan
RING MY BELL Anita Ward
RINGO Lorne Greene
RINKY DINK Dave 'Baby' Cortez
RIO Duran Duran
RIP IT UP Bill Haley
RIP IT UP Orange Juice
RISE Herb Alpert
RISE & FALL OF FLINGEL BUNT Shadows
RISE TO THE OCCASION Climie Fisher
RIVER DEEP MOUNTAIN HIGH Ike & Tina Turner
THE RIVER Ken Dodd
RIVERS OF BABYLON Boney M
THE ROAD TO HELL (PT. 2) Chris Rea
ROAD TO NOWHERE Talking Heads
ROBERT DE NIRO'S WAITING Bananarama
ROBOT MAN Connie Francis
ROCK & ROLL MUSIC Chuck Berry
ROCK & ROLL PART 2 Gary Glitter
ROCK 'N ROLL Status Quo
ROCK 'N ROLL WINTER Wizzard
ROCK AND ROLL HEAVEN Righteous Brothers
ROCK AND ROLL MUSIC Beach Boys
ROCK AROUND THE CLOCK Bill Haley
ROCK ISLAND LINE Lonnie Donegan
ROCK ME Steppenwolf
ROCK ME AMADEUS Falco
ROCK ME GENTLY Andy Kim
ROCK ON Michael Damian
ROCK ON David Essex
ROCK STEADY Aretha Franklin
ROCK STEADY Whispers
ROCK THE BOAT Hues Corporation
ROCK THE BOAT Forrest
ROCK THE CASBAH Clash
ROCK THIS TOWN Stray Cats
ROCK WIT'CHA Bobby Brown
ROCK WITH YOU Michael Jackson
ROCK YOUR BABY George McCrae
ROCK'N'ME Steve Miller Band
ROCK-A-BEATIN' BOOGIE Bill Haley
ROCK-A-BILLY Guy Mitchell
ROCK-A-HULA-BABY Elvis Presley
ROCKARIA Electric Light Orchestra
ROCKET Mud
ROCKET 2 U Jets
ROCKET MAN Elton John
THE ROCKFORD FILES Mike Post
ROCKIN' ALL OVER THE WORLD Status Quo
ROCKIN' AROUND THE CHRISTMAS TREE
Kim Wilde & Mel Smith
ROCKIN' AROUND THE CHRISTMAS TREE
Brenda Lee
ROCKIN' CHAIR Gwen McCrae
A ROCKIN' GOOD WAY Shaky & Bonnie
A ROCKIN' GOOD WAY
Dinah Washington & Brook Benton
ROCKIN' PNEUMONIA & THE BOOGIE WOOGIE FLU
Johnny Rivers
ROCKIN' ROBIN Michael Jackson
ROCKIN' ROLL BABY Stylistics
ROCKIN' THROUGH THE RYE Bill Haley
ROCKING GOOSE Johnny & The Hurricanes
ROCKIT Herbie Hancock
ROCKY Austin Roberts
ROCKY MOUNTAIN HIGH John Denver
RODRIGO'S GUITAR CONCERTO DE ARANJUEZ
Manuel & His Music Of The Mountains
ROK DA HOUSE Beatmasters/Cookie Crew
ROLL AWAY THE STONE Mott The Hoople
ROLL OVER BEETHOVEN Electric Light Orchestra
ROLL OVER LAY DOWN Status Quo
ROLL WITH IT Steve Winwood
ROLLIN' STONE David Essex
ROLLING HOME Status Quo

ROMEO Mr. Big
ROMEO Petula Clark
ROMEO AND JULIET Dire Straits
RONI Bobby Brown
RONNIE Four Seasons
ROOM IN YOUR HEART Living In A Box
ROOM TO MOVE Animotion
ROSE GARDEN Lynn Anderson
THE ROSE Bette Midler
ROSES ARE RED Ronnie Carroll
ROSES ARE RED Mac Band
ROSES ARE RED (MY LOVE) Bobby Vinton
ROSIE Don Partridge
ROUND AND ROUND Jaki Graham
ROUND AND ROUND Perry Como
THE ROUSSOS PHENOMENON E.P.
Demis Roussos
RUBBER BALL Marty Wilde
RUBBER BALL Bobby Vee
RUBBER BULLETS 10CC
THE RUBBERBAND MAN Spinners
RUBY BABY Dion
RUBY TUESDAY Melanie
RUBY TUESDAY Rolling Stones
RUBY, DON'T TAKE YOUR LOVE TO TOWN
Kenny Rogers & The First Edition
RUDE BUOYS OUTA JAIL Specials
RUMORS Timex Social Club
RUN AWAY CHILD, RUNNING WILD Temptations
RUN FOR HOME Lindisfarne
RUN JOEY RUN David Geddes
RUN RUN RUN Jo Jo Gunne
RUN TO HIM Bobby Vee
RUN TO ME Bee Gees
RUN TO THE HILLS Iron Maiden
RUN TO YOU Bryan Adams
RUN, BABY RUN (BACK INTO MY ARMS)
Newbeats
RUNAROUND SUE Dion
RUNAWAY Del Shannon
RUNAWAY BOYS Stray Cats
THE RUNNER Three Degrees
RUNNING BEAR Johnny Preston
RUNNING IN THE FAMILY Level 42
RUNNING SCARED Roy Orbison
RUNNING UP THAT HILL Kate Bush
RUNNING WITH THE NIGHT Lionel Richie
RUSH HOUR Jane Wiedlin
S-S-S-SINGLE BED Fox
S.O.S. Abba
SABRE DANCE Love Sculpture
SAD EYES Robert John
SAD MOVIES (MAKE ME CRY) Sue Thompson
SAD SONGS (SAY SO MUCH) Elton John
SAD SWEET DREAMER Sweet Sensation
SADDLE UP David Christie
THE SAFETY DANCE Men Without Hats
SAIL ON Commodores
SAILING Rod Stewart
SAILING Christopher Cross
SAILOR Petula Clark
SAILOR Anne Shelton
SAILOR (YOUR HOME IS THE SEA) Lolita
THE SAINTS ROCK 'N' ROLL Bill Haley
SALLY Gerry Monroe
SALLY G Paul McCartney
SALLY, GO 'ROUND THE ROSES Jaynetts
SAM Olivia Newton-John
SAME OLD LANG SYNE Dan Fogelberg
SAN ANTONIO ROSE Floyd Cramer
SAN BERNADINO Christie
SAN FRANCISCAN NIGHTS
Eric Burdon & The Animals
SAN FRANCISCO (BE SURE TO WEAR FLOWERS
IN YOUR HAIR) Scott McKenzie
SANCTIFY YOURSELF Simple Minds
SANDY John Travolta
SANTA BRING MY BABY BACK TO ME
Elvis Presley
SANTA CLAUS IS COMIN' TO TOWN
Bruce Springsteen
SARA Fleetwood Mac
SARA Starship
SARA SMILE Daryl Hall & John Oates
SATISFIED Richard Marx
SATURDAY IN THE PARK Chicago
SATURDAY LOVE Cherrelle & Alexander
SATURDAY NIGHT Bay City Rollers
SATURDAY NIGHT AT THE MOVIES Drifters
SATURDAY NIGHT'S ALRIGHT FOR FIGHTING
Elton John
THE SAVAGE Shadows
SAVE A PRAYER Duran Duran
SAVE IT FOR ME Four Seasons
SAVE ME Dave Dee, Dozy, Beaky, Mick & Titch
SAVE THE LAST DANCE FOR ME Drifters
SAVE YOUR HEART FOR ME
Gary Lewis & The Playboys

SAVE YOUR KISSES FOR ME
Brotherhood Of Man
SAVE YOUR LOVE Renee And Renato
SAVED BY THE BELL Robin Gibb
SAVING ALL MY LOVE FOR YOU
Whitney Houston
SAY A LITTLE PRAYER Bomb The Bass
SAY HELLO WAVE GOODBYE Soft Cell
SAY I WON'T BE THERE Springfields
SAY I'M YOUR NO. 1 Princess
SAY IT AGAIN Jermaine Stewart
SAY IT ISN'T SO Daryl Hall & John Oates
SAY IT LOUD-I'M BLACK AND I'M PROUD
James Brown
SAY SAY SAY Paul McCartney & Michael Jackson
SAY WONDERFUL THINGS Ronnie Carroll
SAY YOU WILL Foreigner
SAY YOU, SAY ME Lionel Richie
SAY, HAS ANYBODY SEEN MY SWEET GYPSY
ROSE Dawn Feat. Tony Orlando
SCARLETT O'HARA Jet Harris & Tony Meehan
SCHOOL DAY Chuck Berry
SCHOOL IS OUT Gary U.S. Bonds
SCHOOL'S OUT Alice Cooper
SCORPIO Dennis Coffer & The Detroit GU
SCOTCH ON THE ROCKS
Band Of The Black Watch
SEA OF LOVE Honeydrippers
SEA OF LOVE Marty Wilde
SEALED WITH A KISS Jason Donovan
SEALED WITH A KISS Brian Hyland
THE SEARCH IS OVER Survivor
SEARCHIN' Hazell Dean
SEASIDE SHUFFLE Terry Dactyl & The Dinosaurs
SEASONS CHANGE Expose
SEASONS IN THE SUN Terry Jacks
SECOND CHANCE Thirty Eight Special
SECOND HAND LOVE Connie Francis
THE SECOND TIME AROUND Shalamar
SECRET AGENT MAN Johnny Rivers
SECRET LOVE Kathy Kirby
SECRET LOVERS Atlantic Starr
SECRET RENDEZVOUS Karyn White
SECRETLY Jimmie Rodgers
THE SECRETS THAT YOU KEEP Mud
SEE EMILY PLAY Pink Floyd
SEE MY BABY JIVE Wizzard
SEE MY FRIEND Kinks
SEE SEE RIDER Eric Burdon & The Animals
SEE THE DAY Dee C. Lee
SEE THE FUNNY LITTLE CLOWN
Bobby Goldsboro
SEE YOU Depeche Mode
SEE YOU IN SEPTEMBER Happenings
SEE YOU LATER, ALLIGATOR Bill Haley
SELF CONTROL Laura Branigan
SEMI-DETACHED SUBURBAN MR. JAMES
Manfred Mann
SEND FOR ME Nat 'King' Cole
SEND IN THE CLOWNS Judy Collins
SEND ONE YOUR LOVE Stevie Wonder
SENSES WORKING OVERTIME XTC
SENTIMENTAL LADY Bob Welch
SENTIMENTAL STREET Night Ranger
SEPARATE LIVES Phil Collins & Marilyn Martin
SEPARATE WAYS (WORLDS APART) Journey
SEPTEMBER Earth, Wind & Fire
SERIOUS Donna Allen
SET ME FREE Jaki Graham
SET ME FREE Kinks
SEVEN DRUNKEN NIGHTS Dubliners
SEVEN LITTLE GIRLS SITTING IN THE BACK SEAT
Avons
SEVEN LITTLE GIRLS SITTING IN THE BACK SEAT
Paul Evans & The Curls
SEVEN SEAS OF RHYE Queen
SEVEN TEARS Goombay Dance Band
SEVENTH SON Johnny Rivers
SEXCRIME (NINETEEN EIGHTY FOUR)
Eurythmics
SEXUAL HEALING Marvin Gaye
SEXY EYES Dr. Hook
SHA LA LA Manfred Mann
SHA LA LA LA LEE Small Faces
SHA-LA-LA (MAKE ME HAPPY) Al Green
SHADDUP YOU FACE Joe Dolce
SHADOW DANCING Andy Gibb
SHAKE IT UP Cars
SHAKE RATTLE & ROLL Bill Haley
THE SHAKE Sam Cooke
(SHAKE, SHAKE, SHAKE) SHAKE YOUR BOOTY
KC & The Sunshine Band
SHAKE YOU DOWN Gregory Abbott
SHAKE YOUR BODY (DOWN TO THE GROUND)
Jacksons
SHAKE YOUR GROOVE THING Peaches & Herb
SHAKE YOUR LOVE Debbie Gibson
SHAKEDOWN
Bob Seger & The Silver Bullet Band

SHAKIN' ALL OVER Johnny Kidd & The Pirates
THE SHAKIN' STEVENS E.P. Shakin' Stevens
SHAMBALA Three Dog Night
SHAME Evelyn 'Champagne' King
SHAME ON THE MOON
Bob Seger & The Silver Bullet Band
SHAME, SHAME, SHAME Shirley And Company
SHANG–A–LANG Bay City Rollers
SHANNON Henry Gross
THE SHAPE OF THINGS Yardbirds
SHARE THE LAND Guess Who
SHARING THE NIGHT TOGETHER Dr. Hook
SHATTERED DREAMS Johnny Hates Jazz
SHAZAM Duane Eddy
SHE Charles Aznavour
SHE BELIEVES IN ME Kenny Rogers
SHE BLINDED ME WITH SCIENCE Thomas Dolby
SHE BOP Cyndi Lauper
SHE CRIED Jay & The Americans
SHE DRIVES ME CRAZY Fine Young Cannibals
SHE LOVES YOU Beatles
SHE MAKES MY DAY Robert Palmer
SHE MEANS NOTHING TO ME
Phil Everly & Cliff Richard
SHE WANTS TO DANCE WITH ME Rick Astley
SHE WEARS MY RING Solomon King
SHE WORKS HARD FOR THE MONEY
Donna Summer
SHE'D RATHER BE WITH ME Turtles
SHE'S A BEAUTY Tubes
SHE'S A FOOL Lesley Gore
SHE'S A LADY Tom Jones
SHE'S A WOMAN Beatles
SHE'S GONE Daryl Hall & John Oates
SHE'S GOT CLAWS Gary Numan
SHE'S JUST MY STYLE
Gary Lewis & The Playboys
SHE'S LEAVING HOME Billy Bragg
SHE'S LIKE THE WIND
Patrick Swayze (With Wendy Fraser)
SHE'S NOT THERE Zombies
SHE'S NOT YOU Elvis Presley
SHE'S ON IT Beastie Boys
SHE'S OUT OF MY LIFE Michael Jackson
(SHE'S) SEXY + 17 Stray Cats
THE SHEFFIELD GRINDER Tony Capstick
SHEILA Tommy Roe
SHEILA TAKE A BOW Smiths
SHERRY Four Seasons
SHERRY Adrian Baker
SHINDIG Shadows
SHINE A LITTLE LOVE Electric Light Orchestra
SHINING STAR Earth, Wind & Fire
SHINING STAR Manhattans
SHIP OF FOOLS Erasure
SHIPS Barry Manilow
SHIRLEY Shakin' Stevens
SHOO–BE–DOO–BE–DOO–DA–DAY
Stevie Wonder
SHOOP SHOOP SONG (IT'S IN HIS KISS)
Betty Everett
SHOP AROUND Miracles
SHOP AROUND Captain & Tennille
SHORT PEOPLE Randy Newman
SHOTGUN Jr. Walker & The All Stars
SHOTGUN WEDDING Roy 'C'
SHOULD'VE KNOWN BETTER Richard Marx
SHOUT Tears For Fears
SHOUT Lulu
SHOUT (PT. 1) Joey Dee & The Starfiters
SHOUT TO THE TOP Style Council
SHOUT!SHOUT!(KNOCK YOURSELF OUT)
Ernie Maresca
SHOW AND TELL Al Wilson
SHOW ME THE WAY Peter Frampton
SHOW ME YOU'RE A WOMAN Mud
THE SHOW MUST GO ON Three Dog Night
THE SHOW MUST GO ON Leo Sayer
THE SHOW Doug E. Fresh & The Get Fresh Crew
SHOW YOU THE WAY TO GO Jacksons
SHOWER ME WITH YOUR LOVE Surface
SHOWING OUT Mel & Kim
THE SHUFFLE Van McCoy
SHUT UP Madness
SHY BOY Bananarama
SICK MAN BLUES Goodies
SIDE SHOW Barry Biggs
SIDESHOW Blue Magic
SIGN 'O' THE TIMES Prince
SIGN OF THE TIMES Belle Stars
SIGN YOUR NAME Terence Trent D'Arby
SIGNED SEALED DELIVERED I'M YOURS
Stevie Wonder
SIGNS Five Man Electrical Band
SILENCE IS GOLDEN Tremeloes
SILENT NIGHT Bros
SILENT RUNNING (ON DANGEROUS GROUND)
Mike + Mechanics
SILHOUETTES Herman's Hermits

SILLY GAMES Janet Kay
SILLY LOVE SONGS Paul McCartney
SILLY THING Sex Pistols
SILVER DREAM MACHINE (PT. 1) David Essex
SILVER LADY David Soul
SILVER MACHINE Hawkwind
SILVER STAR Four Seasons
SIMON SAYS 1910 Fruitgum Co
SIMON SMITH & HIS AMAZING DANCING BEAR
Alan Price Set
SIMON TEMPLER Splodgednessabounds
SIMPLE GAME Four Tops
SIMPLY IRRESISTIBLE Robert Palmer
SINCE I FELL FOR YOU Lenny Welch
SINCE YESTERDAY Strawberry Switchblade
SINCE YOU'VE BEEN GONE Rainbow
SING Carpenters
SING A SONG Earth, Wind & Fire
SING BABY SING Stylistics
SING ME Brothers
SING OUR OWN SONG UB40
SINGING THE BLUES Guy Mitchell
SINGING THE BLUES Tommy Steele
SINK THE BISMARCK Johnny Horton
SIR DUKE Stevie Wonder
SISTER CHRISTIAN Night Ranger
SISTER GOLDEN HAIR America
SISTER JANE New World
SISTERS ARE DOIN' IT FOR THEMSELVES
Eurythmics & Aretha Franklin
(SITTIN' ON) THE DOCK OF THE BAY
Otis Redding
16 BARS Stylistics
THE SIX TEENS Sweet
SIXTEEN REASONS Connie Stevens
SIXTEEN TONS Frankie Laine
'65 LOVE AFFAIR Paul Davis
SKA TRAIN Beatmasters
SKINNY LEGS AND ALL Joe Tex
SKWEEZE ME PLEEZE ME Slade
SKY HIGH Jigsaw
THE SKYE BOAT SONG
Roger Whittaker & Des O'Connor
SLAVE TO LOVE Bryan Ferry
SLEDGEHAMMER Peter Gabriel
SLEEPING BAG ZZ Top
SLEEPY SHORES Johnny Pearson Orchestra
THE SLIGHTEST TOUCH Five Star
SLIP AWAY Clarence Carter
SLIP SLIDIN' AWAY Paul Simon
SLOOP JOHN B Beach Boys
SLOW DOWN John Miles
SLOW HAND Pointer Sisters
SLOW TWISTIN' Chubby Checker
SMALL TOWN John Cougar Mellencamp
SMALLTOWN BOY Bronski Beat
SMARTY PANTS First Choice
SMILE A LITTLE SMILE FOR ME Flying Machine
SMILING FACES SOMETIME Undisputed Truth
SMOKE FROM A DISTANT FIRE
Sanford/Townsend Band
SMOKE GETS IN YOUR EYES Platters
SMOKE ON THE WATER Deep Purple
SMOKIN' IN THE BOYS ROOM
Brownsville Station
SMOOTH CRIMINAL Michael Jackson
SMOOTH OPERATOR Sade
THE SMURF SONG
Father Abraham & The Smurfs
SNAP YOUR FINGERS Joe Henderson
SNOOKER LOOPY
Matchroom Mob With Chas & Dave
SNOOPY VS THE RED BARON Royal Guardsmen
SNOOPY VS. THE RED BARON Hotshots
SNOT RAP Kenny Everett
SNOWBIRD Anne Murray
SO ALIVE Love And Rockets
SO COLD THE NIGHT Communards
SO EMOTIONAL Whitney Houston
SO GOOD TO BE BACK HOME AGAIN Tourists
SO IN TO YOU Atlanta Rhythm Section
SO LONELY Police
SO LONG BABY Del Shannon
SO MACHO Sinitta
SO MANY WAYS Brook Benton
SO MUCH IN LOVE Tymes
SO SAD (TO WATCH GOOD LOVE GO BAD)
Everly Brothers
SO YOU WIN AGAIN Hot Chocolate
SOCK IT TO ME–BABY!
Mitch Ryder & The Detroit Wheels
SOFTLY WHISPERING I LOVE YOU Congregation
SOLDIER BLUE Buffy Sainte Marie
SOLDIER BOY Shirelles
SOLDIER OF LOVE Donny Osmond
SOLEY SOLEY Middle Of The Road
SOLID Ashford & Simpson
SOLID GOLD EASY ACTION T. Rex
SOLITAIRE Andy Williams

SOLITAIRE Laura Branigan
SOME GIRLS Racey
SOME GUYS HAVE ALL THE LUCK Rod Stewart
SOME KIND OF LOVER Jody Watley
SOME KIND OF SUMMER David Cassidy
SOME KIND OF WONDERFUL Grand Funk
SOME LIKE IT HOT Power Station
SOME OF YOUR LOVIN' Dusty Springfield
SOME PEOPLE Cliff Richard
SOMEBODY HELP ME Spencer Davis Group
SOMEBODY TO LOVE Queen
SOMEBODY TO LOVE Jefferson Airplane
SOMEBODY'S BABY Jackson Browne
SOMEBODY'S BEEN SLEEPING
100 Proof Aged In Soul
SOMEBODY'S WATCHING ME Rockwell
SOMEDAY Glass Tiger
SOMEDAY Ricky Nelson
SOMEDAY WE'LL BE TOGETHER
Diana Ross & The Supremes
SOMEONE Johnny Mathis
SOMEONE ELSE'S BABY Adam Faith
SOMEONE SAVED MY LIFE TONIGHT Elton John
SOMEONE SOMEONE
Brian Poole & The Tremeloes
SOMEONE'S LOOKING AT YOU Boomtown Rats
SOMETHIN' STUPID Nancy & Frank Sinatra
SOMETHING Shirley Bassey
SOMETHING Beatles
SOMETHING 'BOUT YOU BABY Status Quo
SOMETHING ABOUT YOU Level 42
SOMETHING BETTER CHANGE Stranglers
SOMETHING ELSE Sex Pistols
(SOMETHING INSIDE) SO STRONG Labi Siffre
SOMETHING IN THE AIR Thunderclap Newman
SOMETHING OLD, SOMETHING NEW Fantastics
SOMETHING SO STRONG Crowded House
SOMETHING TELLS ME Cilla Black
SOMETHING'S BURNING
Kenny Rogers & The First Edition
SOMETHING'S GOTTA GIVE Sammy Davis Jr.
SOMETHING'S GOTTEN HOLD OF MY HEART
Marc Almond Feat. Gene Pitney
SOMETHING'S GOTTEN HOLD OF MY HEART
Gene Pitney
SOMETHING'S HAPPENING Herman's Hermits
SOMETHING Beatles
SOMETIMES Erasure
SOMETIMES WHEN WE TOUCH Dan Hill
SOMEWHERE P.J. Proby
SOMEWHERE IN MY HEART Aztec Camera
SOMEWHERE IN THE NIGHT Barry Manilow
SOMEWHERE OUT THERE
Linda Ronstadt & James Ingram
SOMEWHERE, MY LOVE
Ray Conniff & The Singers
SON OF HICKORY HOLLERS TRAMP O.C. Smith
SON OF MY FATHER Chicory Tip
SON–OF–A PREACHER MAN Dusty Springfield
SONG FOR GUY Elton John
SONG FOR WHOEVER Beautiful South
SONG SUNG BLUE Neil Diamond
SONGBIRD Kenny G
SOONER OR LATER Grass Roots
SORROW David Bowie
SORROW Merseys
SORRY I'M A LADY Baccara
SORRY SEEMS TO BE THE HARDEST WORD
Elton John
SORRY SUZANNE Hollies
SOUL MAN Sam & Dave
SOULFUL STRUT Young–Holt Unlimited
SOUND AND VISION David Bowie
THE SOUND OF SILENCE Bachelors
THE SOUNDS OF SILENCE Simon & Garfunkel
SOUTH STREET Orlons
SOUTHERN FREEEZ Freeez
SOUTHERN NIGHTS Glen Campbell
SOUVENIR Orchestral Manoeuvres In The Dark
SOWING THE SEEDS OF LOVE Tears For Fears
SPACE ODDITY David Bowie
SPACE RACE Billy Preston
SPANISH EYES Al Martino
SPANISH FLEA Herb Alpert
SPANISH HARLEM Ben E. King
SPANISH HARLEM Aretha Franklin
SPEAK LIKE A CHILD Style Council
SPEAK TO ME PRETTY Brenda Lee
SPECIAL BREW Bad Manners
SPECIAL LADY Ray, Goodman & Brown
THE SPECIAL YEARS Val Doonican
SPEEDY GONZALES Pat Boone
SPIDERS & SNAKES Jim Stafford
SPIES LIKE US Paul McCartney
SPILL THE WINE Eric Burdon & War
SPINNING WHEEL Blood Sweat & Tears
SPIRIT IN THE SKY Norman Greenbaum
SPIRIT IN THE SKY Doctor & The Medics
SPLISH SPLASH Bobby Darin

SPLISH SPLASH Charlie Drake
SPOOKY Classics 1V
SQUEEZE BOX Who
ST. ELMO'S FIRE (MAN IN MOTION) John Parr
ST. VALENTINE'S DAY MASSACRE E.P.
Headgirl
STACCATO'S THEME Elmer Bernstein
STAIRWAY OF LOVE Michael Holliday
STAIRWAY TO HEAVEN Far Corporation
STAIRWAY TO HEAVEN Neil Sedaka
STAND R.E.M.
STAND AND DELIVER Adam & The Ants
STAND BACK Stevie Nicks
STAND BY ME Ben E. King
STAND BY YOUR MAN Tammy Wynette
STAND TALL Burton Cummings
STAND UP FOR YOUR LOVE RIGHTS Yazz
STANDING IN THE ROAD Blackfoot Sue
STANDING IN THE SHADOWS OF LOVE
Four Tops
STANDING ON THE CORNER King Brothers
STAR TREKKIN' Firm
STAR WARS (MAIN TITLE)
London Symphony Orchestra
STAR WARS THEME/CANTINA BAND Meco
STARDUST David Essex
STARMAKER Kids From 'Fame'
STARMAN David Bowie
STARRY EYED Michael Holliday
STARS ON 45 Starsound/Stars On 45
STARS ON 45 (VOL 2) Starsound
START Jam
STARTING TOGETHER Su Pollard
STATE OF SHOCK Jacksons
STAY Maurice Williams & The Zodiacs
STAY Hollies
STAY AWHILE Bells
STAY IN MY CORNER Dells
STAY ON THESE ROADS A–Ha
STAY OUT OF MY LIFE Five Star
STAY WITH ME Faces
STAYIN' ALIVE Bee Gees
STEAL AWAY Robbie Dupree
STEP BY STEP Eddie Rabbitt
STEP INSIDE LOVE Cilla Black
STEP OFF (PT. 1)
Grandmaster Melle Mell & Furious Five
STEPPIN' OUT Joe Jackson
STEPPIN' OUT (GONNA BOOGIE TONIGHT)
Tony Orlando & Dawn
STEREOTYPE Specials
STEWBALL Lonnie Donegan
STILL Bill Anderson
STILL Commodores
STILL I'M SAD Yardbirds
STILL THE ONE Orleans
STILL THE SAME
Bob Seger & The Silver Bullet Band
STOMP! Brothers Johnson
STONE LOVE Kool & The Gang
STONED LOVE Supremes
STONED SOUL PICNIC Fifth Dimension
STONEY END Barbra Streisand
STOOD UP Ricky Nelson
STOOL PIGEON Kid Creole & The Coconuts
STOP Sam Brown
STOP AND SMELL THE ROSES Mac Davis
STOP AND THINK IT OVER Dale & Grace
STOP DRAGGIN' MY HEART AROUND
Stevie Nicks/Tom Petty
STOP STOP STOP Hollies
STOP THE CAVALRY Jona Lewie
STOP!IN THE NAME OF LOVE Supremes
STORM IN A TEACUP Fortunes
STORMY Classics 1V
THE STORY OF MY LIFE Michael Holliday
THE STORY OF THE BLUES Wah!
STRAIGHTEN OUT Stranglers
STRAIGHT FROM THE HEART Bryan Adams
STRAIGHT UP Paula Abdul
STRANGE KIND OF WOMAN Deep Purple
STRANGE LADY IN TOWN Frankie Laine
STRANGE LITTLE GIRL Stranglers
STRANGER ON THE SHORE Acker Bilk
STRANGERS IN THE NIGHT Frank Sinatra
STRAWBERRY FAIR Anthony Newley
STRAWBERRY FIELDS FOREVER Beatles
STRAWBERRY LETTER 23 Brothers Johnson
STRAY CAT STRUT Stray Cats
THE STREAK Ray Stevens
STREET DANCE Break Machine
STREET LIFE Roxy Music
STREET LIFE Crusaders
STREET TUFF Rebel Mc/Double Trouble
STREETS OF LONDON Ralph McTell
THE STRIPPER David Rose & His Orchestra
STRUT Sheena Easton
STRUT YOUR FUNKY STUFF Frantique

STUCK IN THE MIDDLE WITH YOU
Stealer's Wheel
STUCK ON YOU Elvis Presley
STUCK ON YOU Trevor Walters
STUCK ON YOU Lionel Richie
STUCK WITH YOU Huey Lewis & The News
STUMBLIN' IN Suzi Quatro & Chris Norman
STUPID CUPID Connie Francis
STUTTER RAP (NO SLEEP 'TIL BEDTIME)
Morris Minor & The Majors
SUBSTITUTE Liquid Gold
SUBSTITUTE Who
SUBSTITUTE Clout
SUBTERRANEAN HOMESICK BLUES Bob Dylan
SUBURBIA Pet Shop Boys
SUCU-SUCU Laurie Johnson
SUDDENLY Angry Anderson
SUDDENLY Billy Ocean
SUDDENLY LAST SUMMER Motels
SUDDENLY THERE'S A VALLEY Petula Clark
SUDDENLY YOU LOVE ME Tremeloes
SUEDEHEAD Morrissey
SUGAR AND SPICE Searchers
SUGAR BABY LOVE Rubettes
SUGAR CANDY KISSES Mac & Katie Kissoon
SUGAR DADDY Jackson Five
SUGAR ME Lynsey De Paul
SUGAR MOON Pat Boone
SUGAR SHACK Jimmy Gilmer & The Fireballs
SUGAR SUGAR Archies
SUGAR TOWN Nancy Sinatra
SUGAR WALLS Sheena Easton
SUKIYAKI Taste of Honey
SUKIYAKI Kenny Ball
SUKIYAKI Kyu Sakamoto
SULTANA Titanic
SULTANS OF SWING Dire Straits
SUMMER War
SUMMER (THE FIRST TIME) Bobby Goldsboro
SUMMER BREEZE Seals & Crofts
SUMMER HOLIDAY Cliff Richard
SUMMER IN THE CITY Lovin' Spoonful
SUMMER NIGHT CITY Abba
SUMMER NIGHTS
John Travolta & Olivia Newton-John
SUMMER NIGHTS Marianne Faithfull
SUMMER OF '69 Bryan Adams
SUMMER OF MY LIFE Simon May
SUMMER SET Acker Bilk
A SUMMER SONG Chad & Jeremy
SUMMERLOVE SENSATION Bay City Rollers
SUMMERTIME Billy Stewart
SUMMERTIME CITY Mike Batt
THE SUN AIN'T GONNA SHINE (ANYMORE)
Walker Brothers
THE SUN ALWAYS SHINES ON T.V. A-Ha
THE SUN AND THE RAIN Madness
SUN ARISE Rolf Harris
THE SUN GOES DOWN (LIVING IT UP) Level 42
SUNDAY GIRL Blondie
SUNDAY WILL NEVER BE THE SAME
Spanky & Our Gang
SUNDOWN Gordon Lightfoot
SUNGLASSES AT NIGHT Corey Hart
SUNNY Boney M
SUNNY Bobby Herb
SUNNY AFTERNOON Kinks
SUNSHINE Jonathan Edwards
SUNSHINE AFTER THE RAIN Elkie Brooks
SUNSHINE GIRL Herman's Hermits
SUNSHINE OF YOUR LOVE Cream
SUNSHINE OF YOUR SMILE Mike Berry
SUNSHINE ON MY SHOULDERS John Denver
SUNSHINE SUPERMAN Donovan
SUPER TROUPER Abba
SUPERFLY Curtis Mayfield
SUPERFLY GUY S'Express
SUPERMAN (GIOCA JOUER) Black Lace
SUPERNATURAL THING PART 1 Ben E. King
SUPERNATURE Cerrone
SUPERSTAR Carpenters
SUPERSTITION Stevie Wonder
SUPERWOMAN Karyn White
SURE GONNA MISS HER
Gary Lewis & The Playboys
SURF CITY Jan & Dean
SURFER GIRL Beach Boys
SURFIN' BIRD Trashmen
SURFIN' U.S.A. Beach Boys
SURRENDER Diana Ross
SURRENDER Swing Out Sister
SURRENDER Elvis Presley
SURRENDER TO ME Ann Wilson & Robin Zander
SURROUND YOURSELF WITH SORROW
Cilla Black
SUSPICION Elvis Presley
SUSPICION Terry Stafford
SUSPICIOUS MINDS Elvis Presley
SUSPICIOUS MINDS Fine Young Cannibals
SUSSUDIO Phil Collins
SWAYIN' TO THE MUSIC (SLOW DANCIN')
Johnny Rivers
SWEARIN' TO GOD Frankie Valli
SWEET AND INNOCENT Donny Osmond
SWEET CAROLINE Neil Diamond
SWEET CHERRY WINE
Tommy James & The Shondells
SWEET CHILD O' MINE Guns N' Roses
SWEET CITY WOMAN Stampeders
SWEET DREAM Jethro Tull
SWEET DREAMS Air Supply
SWEET DREAMS (ARE MADE OF THIS)
Eurythmics
SWEET FREEDOM Michael McDonald
SWEET HITCH-HIKER
Creedence Clearwater Revival
SWEET HOME ALABAMA Lynyrd Skynyrd
SWEET INSPIRATION
Johnny Johnson & The Bandwagon
SWEET LITTLE MYSTERY Wet Wet Wet
SWEET LITTLE SIXTEEN Chuck Berry
SWEET LOVE Commodores
SWEET LOVE Anita Baker
SWEET MARY Wadsworth Mansion
SWEET NOTHIN'S Brenda Lee
SWEET PEA Tommy Roe
SWEET SEASONS Carole King
SWEET SOUL MUSIC Arthur Conley
SWEET SURRENDER Wet Wet Wet
(SWEET SWEET BABY) SINCE YOU'VE BEEN GONE
Aretha Franklin
SWEET TALKIN' GUY Chiffons
SWEET TALKIN' WOMAN Electric Light Orchestra
SWEET THING Rufus Feat. Chaka Khan
SWEETER THAN YOU Ricky Nelson
SWEETEST SMILE Black
THE SWEETEST TABOO Sade
THE SWEETEST THING (I'VE EVER KNOWN)
Juice Newton
SWEETHEART Franke & The Knockouts
SWEETS FOR MY SWEET Searchers
SWING THE MOOD Jive Bunny & Mastermixers
SWING YOUR DADDY Jim Gilstrap
SWINGIN' SCHOOL Bobby Rydell
SWINGING ON A STAR Big Dee Irwin
SWISS MAID Del Shannon
SWORDS OF A THOUSAND MEN Ten Pole Tudor
SYLVIA Focus
SYLVIA'S MOTHER Dr. Hook
SYSTEM ADDICT Five Star
TAHITI David Essex
TAINTED LOVE Soft Cell
TAKE A CHANCE ON ME Abba
TAKE A LETTER MARIA R.B. Greaves
TAKE FIVE Dave Brubeck Quartet
TAKE GOOD CARE OF HER Adam Wade
TAKE GOOD CARE OF MY BABY Bobby Vee
TAKE GOOD CARE OF YOURSELF Three Degrees
TAKE IT AWAY Paul McCartney
TAKE IT EASY ON ME Little River Band
TAKE IT ON THE RUN Reo Speedwagon
TAKE IT TO THE LIMIT Eagles
TAKE ME BAK 'OME Slade
TAKE ME HOME Phil Collins
TAKE ME HOME Cher
TAKE ME HOME, COUNTRY ROADS
John Denver
TAKE ME HOME TONIGHT Eddie Money
TAKE ME TO THE MARDI GRAS Paul Simon
TAKE ME TO YOUR HEART Rick Astley
TAKE ME WITH YOU Prince
TAKE MY BREATH AWAY Berlin
TAKE ON ME A-Ha
TAKE THAT LOOK OFF YOUR FACE Marti Webb
TAKE THE LONG WAY HOME Supertramp
TAKE THESE CHAINS FROM MY HEART
Ray Charles
TAKE YOUR TIME (DO IT RIGHT)(PT. 1)
S.O.S. Band
TALK BACK TREMBLING LIPS Johnny Tillotson
TALK DIRTY TO ME Poison
TALK OF THE TOWN Pretenders
TALK TO ME Stevie Nicks
TALKING IN YOUR SLEEP Romantics
TALL PAUL Annette
TALLAHASSEE LASSIE Freddy Cannon
TAP TURNS ON THE WATER C.C.S.
TARZAN BOY Baltimora
A TASTE OF AGGRO Barron Knights
A TASTE OF HONEY Herb Alpert
TEACHER Jethro Tull
TEARDROPS Shakin' Stevens
TEARDROPS Womack & Womack
TEARS Ken Dodd
THE TEARS I CRIED Glitter Band
TEARS OF A CLOWN
Smokey Robinson & The Miracles
TEARS OF A CLOWN Beat
TEARS ON MY PILLOW
Little Anthony & The Imperials
TEARS ON MY PILLOW Johnny Nash
TEDDY BEAR Red Souvine
TEDDY BEAR Elvis Presley
TEEN ANGEL Mark Dinning
TEEN BEAT Sandy Nelson
TEENAGE IDOL Ricky Nelson
TEENAGE RAMPAGE Sweet
A TEENAGER IN LOVE Dion & The Belmonts
A TEENAGER IN LOVE Marty Wilde
A TEENAGERS ROMANCE Ricky Nelson
TELEFONE (LONG DISTANCE LOVE AFFAIR)
Sheena Easton
TELEGRAM SAM T. Rex
TELEPHONE LINE Electric Light Orchestra
TELEPHONE MAN Meri Wilson
TELL HER ABOUT IT Billy Joel
TELL HER NO Zombies
TELL HIM Hello
TELL HIM Exciters
TELL IT LIKE IT IS Heart
TELL IT LIKE IT IS Aaron Neville
TELL IT TO MY HEART Taylor Dayne
TELL IT TO THE RAIN Four Seasons
TELL LAURA I LOVE HER Ray Peterson
TELL LAURA I LOVE HER Ricky Valance
TELL ME SOMETHING GOOD Rufus
TELL ME WHAT HE SAID Helen Shapiro
TELL ME WHEN Applejacks
TELSTAR Tornados
TEMMA HARBOUR Mary Hopkin
TEMPTATION Everly Brothers
TEMPTATION Heaven 17
TENDER LOVE Force M.D'S
THE TENDER TRAP Frank Sinatra
10538 OVERTURE Electric Light Orchestra
TERRY Twinkle
THANK GOD I'M A COUNTRY BOY John Denver
THANK U VERY MUCH Scaffold
THANK YOU (FALETTINME BE MICE ELF AGIN)
Sly & The Family Stone
THANKS FOR THE MEMORY Slade
THAT GIRL Stevie Wonder
THAT GIRL BELONGS TO YESTERDAY
Gene Pitney
THAT LADY Isley Brothers
THAT OLE DEVIL CALLED LOVE Alison Moyet
THAT SAME OLD FEELING Pickettywitch
THAT'LL BE THE DAY Crickets
THAT'S ALL! Genesis
THAT'S ALL YOU GOTTA DO Brenda Lee
THAT'S LIFE Frank Sinatra
THAT'S LIVING (ALRIGHT) Joe Fagin
THAT'S MY HOME Acker Bilk
THAT'S OLD FASHIONED Everly Brothers
THAT'S ROCK 'N' ROLL Shaun Cassidy
THAT'S THE WAY (I LIKE IT)
KC & The Sunshine Band
THAT'S THE WAY I'VE ALWAYS HEARD IT
SHOULD BE Carly Simon
THAT'S THE WAY IT IS Mel & Kim
THAT'S THE WAY LOVE IS Ten City
THAT'S THE WAY LOVE IS Marvin Gaye
THAT'S WHAT FRIENDS ARE FOR
Deniece Williams
THAT'S WHAT FRIENDS ARE FOR
Dionne Warwick & Friends
THAT'S WHAT I LIKE
Jive Bunny & The Mastermixers
THAT'S WHAT LOVE WILL DO
Joe Brown & The Bruvvers
THEME FOR A DREAM Cliff Richard
THEME FROM 'A SUMMER PLACE' Percy Faith
THEME FROM 'GREATEST AMERICAN HERO'
Joey Scarbury
THEME FROM 'MAHOGANY'(DO YOU KNOW
WHERE YOU'RE GOING TO) Diana Ross
THEME FROM 'SHAFT' Isaac Hayes
THEME FROM 'THE LEGION'S LAST PATROL'
Ken Thorne
THEME FROM DIXIE Duane Eddy
THEME FROM DOCTOR KILDARE
Richard Chamberlain
THEME FROM HARRY'S GAME Clannad
THE THEME FROM HILL STREET BLUES
Mike Post Feat. Larry Carlton
THEME FROM M*A*S*H* (SUICIDE IS PAINLESS)
Mash
THEME FROM NEW YORK NEW YORK
Frank Sinatra
THEME FROM S'EXPRESS S'Express
THEME FROM S.W.A.T. Rhythm Heritage
THEME FROM THE APARTMENT
Ferrante & Teicher
THEME FROM THE DEER HUNTER (CAVATINA)
Shadows
THEME FROM THE THREEPENNY OPERA
Louis Armstrong
(THEME FROM) VALLEY OF THE DOLLS
Dionne Warwick
THEN CAME YOU Dionne Warwick/Spinners
THEN HE KISSED ME Crystals
THEN I KISSED HER Beach Boys
THEN YOU CAN TELL ME GOODBYE Casinos
THERE ARE MORE QUESTIONS THAN ANSWERS
Johnny Nash
THERE BUT FOR FORTUNE Joan Baez
THERE GOES MY BABY Drifters
THERE GOES MY EVERYTHING
Engelbert Humperdinck
THERE GOES MY EVERYTHING Elvis Presley
THERE GOES MY FIRST LOVE Drifters
THERE I'VE SAID IT AGAIN Bobby Vinton
THERE IS A MOUNTAIN Donovan
THERE IT IS Shalamar
THERE MUST BE A WAY Frankie Vaughan
THERE MUST BE AN ANGEL (PLAYING WITH
MY HEART) Eurythmics
THERE THERE MY DEAR
Dexy's Midnight Runners
THERE'S A GOLDMINE IN THE SKY Pat Boone
THERE'S A GHOST IN MY HOUSE R. Dean Taylor
THERE'S A HEARTACHE FOLLOWING ME
Jim Reeves
THERE'S A KIND OF HUSH Herman's Hermits
THERE'S A MOON OUT TONIGHT Capris
THERE'S A WHOLE LOT OF LOVING Guys & Dolls
THERE'S ALWAYS SOMETHING THERE TO
REMIND ME Naked Eyes
(THERE'S) ALWAYS SOMETHING THERE TO
REMIND ME Sandie Shaw
THERE'S NO ONE QUITE LIKE GRANDMA
St. Winifred's School
(THERE'S) NO GETTIN' OVER ME Ronnie Milsap
THESE BOOTS ARE MADE FOR WALKIN'
Nancy Sinatra
THESE DREAMS Heart
THESE EYES Guess Who
THEY DON'T KNOW Tracey Ullman
THEY JUST CAN'T STOP IT (THE GAMES PEOPLE PLAY)
Spinners
(THEY LONG TO BE) CLOSE TO YOU Carpenters
THEY'LL BE SAD SONGS (TO MAKE YOU CRY)
Billy Ocean
THEY'RE COMING TO TAKE ME AWAY HA-HAAA!
Napoleon XIV
A THING CALLED LOVE Johnny Cash
THINGS Bobby Darin
THINGS CAN ONLY GET BETTER Howard Jones
THINGS WE DO FOR LOVE 10CC
THE THINGS WE DO FOR LOVE 10CC
THINK Aretha Franklin
THINK OF LAURA Christopher Cross
THIS CORROSION Sisters of Mercy
THIS COULD BE THE NIGHT Loverboy
THIS DIAMOND RING Gary Lewis & The Playboys
THIS GIRL IS A WOMAN NOW
Gary Puckett & The Union Gap
THIS GIRL'S IN LOVE WITH YOU Dionne Warwick
THIS GUY'S IN LOVE WITH YOU Herb Alpert
THIS IS IT Adam Faith
THIS IS IT Melba Moore
THIS IS MY SONG Petula Clark
THIS IS MY SONG Harry Secombe
THIS IS NOT A LOVE SONG Pil
THIS IS TOMORROW Bryan Ferry
THIS LITTLE BIRD Marianne Faithfull
THIS MAGIC MOMENT Jay & The Americans
THIS MASQUERADE George Benson
THIS OLD HEART OF MINE Rod Stewart
THIS OLD HEART OF MINE Isley Brothers
THIS OLE HOUSE Shakin' Stevens
THIS ONE'S FOR THE CHILDREN
New Kids On The Block
THIS TIME Troy Shondell
THIS TIME (WE'LL GET IT RIGHT)
England World Cup Squad
THIS TIME I KNOW IT'S FOR REAL
Donna Summer
THIS TIME I'M IN IT FOR LOVE Player
THIS TOWN AIN'T BIG ENOUGH FOR THE BOTH OF US
Sparks
THIS WHEEL'S ON FIRE Julie Driscoll/Brian Auger
THIS WILL BE Natalie Cole
THORN IN MY SIDE Eurythmics
THOSE LAZY CRAZY DAYS OF SUMMER
Nat 'King' Cole
THOSE OLDIES BUT GOODIES
Little Caesar & The Romans
THOSE WERE THE DAYS Mary Hopkin
A THOUSAND STARS
Kathy Young With The Innocents
THE THREE BELLS Browns
THREE STEPS TO HEAVEN Eddie Cochran
THREE STEPS TO HEAVEN Showaddywaddy
THREE TIMES A LADY Commodores
3 x 3 (E.P.) Genesis

THRILLER Michael Jackson
THROW DOWN A LINE Cliff Richard
THROWING IT ALL AWAY Genesis
THUNDER IN MOUNTAINS Toyah
THUNDER ISLAND Jay Ferguson
TICKET TO RIDE Beatles
THE TIDE IS HIGH Blondie
TIE A YELLOW RIBBON ROUND THE OLD OAK
TREE Dawn
TIE ME KANGAROO DOWN SPORT Rolf Harris
TIGER FEET Mud
TIGHTEN UP Archie Bell & The Drells
TIGHTER, TIGHTER Alive & Kicking
('TIL) I KISSED YOU Everly Brothers
TILL Tom Jones
TILL THE END OF THE DAY Kinks
TIME Craig Douglas
TIME (CLOCK OF THE HEART) Culture Club
TIME AFTER TIME Cyndi Lauper
TIME DRAGS BY Cliff Richard
THE TIME HAS COME Adam Faith
TIME IN A BOTTLE Jim Croce
TIME IS ON MY SIDE Rolling Stones
TIME IS TIGHT Booker T. & The M.G.'s
TIME OF THE SEASON Zombies
TIME PASSAGES Al Stewart
THE TIME WARP Damian
TIME WON'T LET ME Outsiders
TIMES OF YOUR LIFE Paul Anka
TIMES THEY ARE A–CHANGIN' Bob Dylan
TIN MAN America
TIN SOLDIER Small Faces
TINA MARIE Perry Como
TIRED OF BEING ALONE Al Green
TIRED OF TOEIN' THE LINE Rocky Burnette
TIRED OF WAITING FOR YOU Kinks
TO ALL THE GIRLS I'VE LOVED BEFORE
Julio Iglesias & Willie Nelson
TO BE A LOVER Billy Idol
TO BE OR NOT TO BE B.A. Robertson
TO BE WITH YOU AGAIN Level 42
TO CUT A LONG STORY SHORT Spandau Ballet
TO KNOW YOU IS TO LOVE YOU Peter & Gordon
TO LOVE SOMEBODY Nina Simone
TO SIR WITH LOVE Lulu
TOBACCO ROAD Nashville Teens
TOCCATA Sky
TOGETHER Connie Francis
TOGETHER P.J. Proby
TOGETHER FOREVER Rick Astley
TOGETHER IN ELECTRIC DREAMS
Giorgio Moroder & Phil Oakey
TOGETHER WE ARE BEAUTIFUL Fern Kinney
TOKOLOSHE MAN John Kongos
TOKYO MELODY Helmut Zacharias Orchestra
TOM DOOLEY Kingston Trio
TOM DOOLEY Lonnie Donegan
TOM HARK Piranhas
TOM–TOM TURNAROUND New World
TOMBOY Perry Como
TOMORROW Sandie Shaw
TOMORROW'S (JUST ANOTHER DAY) Madness
TONIGHT Kool & The Gang
TONIGHT Ferrante & Teicher
TONIGHT I CELEBRATE MY LOVE
Peabo Bryson & Roberta Flack
TONIGHT I'M YOURS (DON'T HURT ME)
Rod Stewart
TONIGHT SHE COMES Cars
TONIGHT TONIGHT TONIGHT Genesis
TONIGHT'S THE NIGHT (GONNA BE ALRIGHT)
Rod Stewart
TOO BUSY THINKING ABOUT MY BABY
Marvin Gaye
TOO GOOD TO BE FORGOTTEN Chi-Lites
TOO GOOD TO BE FORGOTTEN Amazulu
TOO HOT Kool & The Gang
TOO LATE FOR GOODBYES Julian Lennon
TOO LATE TO TURN BACK NOW
Cornelius Brothers & Sister Rose
TOO MANY BROKEN HEARTS Jason Donovan
TOO MUCH Bros
TOO MUCH Elvis Presley
TOO MUCH HEAVEN Bee Gees
TOO MUCH TIME ON MY HANDS Styx
TOO MUCH TOO YOUNG E.P.(SPECIAL AKA LIVE)
Specials
TOO MUCH, TOO LITTLE, TOO LATE
Johnny Mathis & Deniece Williams
TOO NICE TO TALK TO Beat
TOO SHY Kajagoogoo
TOO SOON TO KNOW Roy Orbison
TOO YOUNG Donny Osmond
TOO YOUNG TO GO STEADY Nat 'King' Cole
TOP OF THE WORLD Carpenters
TORCH Soft Cell
TORN BETWEEN TWO LOVERS Mary MacGregor
TOSSIN' AND TURNIN' Bobby Lewis
TOSSING AND TURNING Ivy League

TOTAL ECLIPSE OF THE HEART Bonnie Tyler
TOUCH ME Doors
TOUCH ME (I WANT YOUR BODY) Samantha Fox
TOUCH ME IN THE MORNING Diana Ross
TOUCH OF GREY Grateful Dead
A TOUCH TOO MUCH Arrows
TOWER OF STRENGTH Gene McDaniels
TOWER OF STRENGTH Frankie Vaughan
TOWN CALLED MALICE Jam
TOY BOY Sinitta
TOY SOLDIERS Martika
TRACES Classics 1V
THE TRACKS OF MY TEARS Johnny Rivers
THE TRACKS OF MY TEARS
Smokey Robinson & The Miracles
TRACY Cuff Links
TRAGEDY Fleetwoods
TRAGEDY Bee Gees
THE TRAIL OF THE LONESOME PINE
Laurel & Hardy
TRAIN OF THOUGHT A–Ha
TRAINS AND BOATS AND PLANES
Burt Bacharach
TRAMP Salt 'N' Pepa
TRAPPED Colonel Abrams
TRAVELIN' MAN Ricky Nelson
TRAVELLIN' BAND Creedence Clearwater Revival
TRAVELLIN' LIGHT Cliff Richard
TREAT HER LIKE A LADY
Cornelius Brothers & Sister Rose
TREAT HER RIGHT Roy Head
TRIBUTE (RIGHT ON) Pasadenas
TROGLODYTE (CAVE MAN) Jimmy Castor Bunch
TROUBLE Lindsey Buckingham
TROUBLE MAN Marvin Gaye
TRUE Spandau Ballet
TRUE BLUE Madonna
TRUE COLORS Cyndi Lauper
TRUE FAITH New Order
TRUE LOVE Bing Crosby & Grace Kelly
TRUE LOVE WAYS Peter & Gordon
TRUE LOVE WAYS Cliff Richard
TRULY Lionel Richie
TRYIN' TO GET THE FEELING AGAIN
Barry Manilow
TRYIN' TO LIVE MY LIFE WITHOUT YOU
Bob Seger & The Silver Bullet band
TRYIN' TO LOVE TWO William Bell
TSOP (THE SOUND OF PHILADELPHIA)
MFSB Feat. The Three Degrees
TUBULAR BELLS Mike Oldfield
TUFF ENUFF Fabulous Thunderbirds
TULIPS FROM AMSTERDAM Max Bygraves
TUMBLING DICE Rolling Stones
TUNNEL OF LOVE Bruce Springsteen
THE TUNNEL OF LOVE Fun Boy Three
TURN AROUND LOOK AT ME Vogues
TURN BACK THE HANDS OF TIME Tyrone Davis
TURN IT ON AGAIN Genesis
TURN THE BEAT AROUND Vicki Sue Robinson
TURN THE MUSIC UP Players Association
TURN YOUR LOVE AROUND George Benson
TURN! TURN! TURN! Byrds
TURNING JAPANESE Vapors
TUSK Fleetwood Mac
TWEEDLE DEE Little Jimmy Osmond
TWEEDLE DEE TWEEDLE DUM
Middle Of The Road
THE TWELFTH OF NEVER Cliff Richard
THE TWELFTH OF NEVER Donny Osmond
THE TWELFTH OF NEVER Johnny Mathis
20TH CENTURY BOY T. Rex
TWENTY FIVE MILES Edwin Starr
25 OR 6 TO 4 Chicago
TWENTY FOUR HOURS FROM TULSA
Gene Pitney
TWILIGHT TIME Platters
TWILIGHT ZONE Golden Earring
THE TWIST (YO, TWIST)
Fat Boys/Chubby Checker
TWIST AND SHOUT
Brian Poole & The Tremeloes
TWIST AND SHOUT Beatles
TWIST AND SHOUT Salt 'N' Pepa
TWIST OF FATE Olivia Newton–John
THE TWIST Chubby Checker
TWIST, TWIST SENORA Gary U.S. Bonds
TWISTIN' THE NIGHT AWAY Sam Cooke
TWO FACES HAVE I Lou Christie
TWO HEARTS Phil Collins
TWO KINDS OF TEARDROPS Del Shannon
TWO LITTLE BOYS Rolf Harris
TWO LOVERS Mary Wells
TWO OCCASIONS Deele
TWO OF HEARTS Stacy Q
TWO PINTS OF LAGER AND A PACKET OF CRISPS
PLEASE Splodgenessabounds
TWO TRIBES Frankie Goes To Hollywood
TYPICAL MALE Tina Turner

U GOT THE LOOK Prince & Sheena Easton
THE UGLY DUCKLING Mike Reid
UM, UM, UM, UM, UM, UM
Wayne Fontana & The Mindbenders
UM, UM, UM, UM, UM, UM Major Lance
UN BANC, UN ARBRE, UNE RUE Severine
UNA PALOMA BLANCA Jonathan King
UNCHAIN MY HEART Ray Charles
UNCHAINED MELODY Righteous Brothers
UNCLE ALBERT Paul & Linda McCartney
UNDER PRESSURE Queen & David Bowie
UNDER THE BOARDWALK Drifters
UNDER THE BOARDWALK Bruce Willis
UNDER THE BRIDGES OF PARIS Dean Martin
UNDER THE MOON OF LOVE Showaddywaddy
UNDER YOUR THUMB Godley & Creme
UNDERCOVER ANGEL Alan O'Day
UNDERCOVER OF THE NIGHT Rolling Stones
UNEASY RIDER Charlie Daniels Band
THE UNFORGETTABLE FIRE U2
THE UNICORN Irish Rovers
UNION OF THE SNAKE Duran Duran
UNITED WE STAND Brotherhood Of Man
UNTIL IT'S TIME FOR YOU TO GO Elvis Presley
UNTIL YOU COME BACK TO ME Aretha Franklin
UP AROUND THE BEND
Creedence Clearwater Revival
UP ON THE ROOF Drifters
UP THE JUNCTION Squeeze
UP THE LADDER TO THE ROOF Supremes
UP UP AND AWAY Fifth Dimension
UP UP AND AWAY Johnny Mann Singers
UP WHERE WE BELONG
Joe Cocker & Jennifer Warnes
UPSIDE DOWN Diana Ross
UPTIGHT (EVERYTHING'S ALRIGHT)
Stevie Wonder
UPTOWN GIRL Billy Joel
UPTOWN TOP RANKING Althia And Donna
URGENT Foreigner
USE IT UP AND WEAR IT OUT Odyssey
USE ME Bill Withers
USE TA BE MY GIRL O'Jays
VACATION Connie Francis
VACATION Go–Go's
VALENTINE T'Pau
VALERIE Steve Winwood
VALLERI Monkees
VALLEY OF TEARS Fats Domino
THE VALLEY ROAD Bruce Hornsby & The Range
VALOTTE Julian Lennon
VEHICLE Ides Of March
VENTURA HIGHWAY America
VENUS Shocking Blue
VENUS Bananarama
VENUS IN BLUE JEANS Jimmy Clanton
VENUS IN BLUE JEANS Mark Wynter
VICTIM OF LOVE Erasure
VICTIMS Culture Club
VICTORY Kool & The Gang
VIDEO KILLED THE RADIO STAR Buggles
VIENNA Ultravox
VIENNA CALLING Falco
A VIEW TO KILL Duran Duran
THE VILLAGE OF ST. BERNADETTE
Andy Williams
VINCENT Don McLean
VIRGINIA PLAIN Roxy Music
VISIONS Cliff Richard
VIVA BOBBIE JOE Equals
VOICE IN THE WILDERNESS Cliff Richard
VOICES CARRY 'Til Tuesday
VOLARE Bobby Rydell
VOLARE Dean Martin
VOODOO CHILE Jimi Hendrix Experience
VOULEZ VOUS Abba
VOYAGE VOYAGE Desireless
THE WAH–WATUSI Orlons
WAIT Robert Howard & Kym Mazelle
WAIT White Lion
WAITING FOR A GIRL LIKE YOU Foreigner
WAITING FOR A STAR TO FALL Boy Meets Girl
WAITING FOR A TRAIN Flash And The Pan
WAITING FOR AN ALIBI Thin Lizzy
WAITIN' IN SCHOOL Ricky Nelson
WAKE ME UP BEFORE YOU GO GO Wham!
WAKE UP LITTLE SUSIE Everly Brothers
WALK AWAY Matt Monro
WALK AWAY FROM LOVE David Ruffin
WALK AWAY RENEE Four Tops
WALK AWAY RENEE Left Banke
WALK DON'T RUN John Barry Seven
A WALK IN THE BLACK FOREST Horst Jankowski
WALK LIKE A MAN Four Seasons
WALK LIKE AN EGYPTIAN Bangles
WALK OF LIFE Dire Straits
WALK ON BY Leroy Van Dyke
WALK ON BY Dionne Warwick
WALK ON THE WILD SIDE Lou Reed

WALK ON WATER Eddie Money
WALK RIGHT BACK Everly Brothers
WALK RIGHT IN Rooftop Singers
WALK RIGHT NOW Jacksons
WALK TALL Val Doonican
WALK THE DINOSAUR Was (Not Was)
WALK THIS WAY Run D.M.C.
WALK THIS WAY Aerosmith
WALK WITH ME Seekers
WALK–DON'T RUN Ventures
WALK–DON'T RUN '64 Ventures
WALKIN' C.C.S.
WALKIN' BACK TO HAPPINESS Helen Shapiro
WALKIN' IN THE SUNSHINE Bad Manners
A WALKIN' MIRACLE
Limmie & The Family Cookin'
WALKIN' TO NEW ORLEANS Fats Domino
WALKING AWAY Information Society
WALKING IN RHYTHM Blackbyrds
WALKING IN THE AIR Aled Jones
WALKING IN THE RAIN Modern Romance
WALKING IN THE RAIN Partridge Family
WALKING ON SUNSHINE Rocker's Revenge
WALKING ON SUNSHINE Katrina & The Waves
WALKING ON THE MOON Police
WALKING THE DOG Rufus Thomas
WALL STREET SHUFFLE 10CC
WALLS COME TUMBLING DOWN! Style Council
WAND'RIN' STAR Lee Marvin
THE WANDERER Status Quo
THE WANDERER Dion
THE WANDERER Donna Summer
WANDERIN' EYES Frankie Vaughan
WANNA BE STARTIN' SOMETHING
Michael Jackson
WANT ADS Honey Cone
WANTED Dooleys
WAR Bruce Springsteen
WAR Edwin Starr
WAR BABY Tom Robinson
THE WAR SONG Culture Club
THE WARRIOR Scandal Feat. Patty Smyth
WASHINGTON SQUARE Village Stompers
WASTED DAYS AND WASTED NIGHTS
Freddy Fender
WASTED ON THE WAY Crosby, Stills & Nash
WATCHING THE WHEELS John Lennon
WATCHING YOU WATCHING ME David Grant
WATER WATER Tommy Steele
WATERFALLS Paul McCartney
WATERLOO Abba
WATERLOO SUNSET Kinks
WATERMELON MAN Mongo Santamaria
WAY DOWN Elvis Presley
WAY DOWN YONDER IN NEW ORLEANS
Freddy Cannon
THE WAY I WANT TO TOUCH YOU
Captain & Tennille
THE WAY IT IS Bruce Hornsby & The Range
THE WAY IT USED TO BE Engelbert Humperdinck
WAY OF LIFE Family Dogg
THE WAY OF LOVE Cher
THE WAY WE WERE Barbra Streisand
THE WAY WE WERE/TRY TO REMEMBER
(MEDLEY) Gladys Knight & The Pips
THE WAY YOU LOVE ME Karyn White
THE WAY YOU MAKE ME FEEL Michael Jackson
WAYWARD WIND Frank Ifield
(WE AIN'T GOT) NOTHIN' YET Blues Magoos
WE ALL FOLLOW MAN. UNITED
Manchester United Football Club
WE ALL STAND TOGETHER Paul McCartney
WE ARE DETECTIVE Thompson Twins
WE ARE FAMILY Sister Sledge
WE ARE GLASS Gary Numan
WE ARE THE CHAMPIONS Queen
WE ARE THE WORLD USA For Africa
WE BELONG Pat Benatar
WE BUILT THIS CITY Starship
WE CALL IT ACIEED D. Mob
WE CAN WORK IT OUT Beatles
WE CLOSE OUR EYES Go West
WE DIDN'T START THE FIRE Billy Joel
WE DO IT R & J Stone
WE DON'T HAVE TO TAKE OUR CLOTHES OFF
Jermaine Stewart
WE DON'T NEED ANOTHER HERO
(THUNDERDOME) Tina Turner
WE DON'T TALK ANYMORE Cliff Richard
WE GOT LOVE Bobby Rydell
WE GOT THE BEAT Go–Go's
WE HAVE A DREAM Scotland World Cup Squad
WE LOVE YOU Rolling Stones
WE TAKE MYSTERY (TO BED) Gary Numan
WE'LL BE TOGETHER Sting
WE'LL BRING THE HOUSE DOWN Slade
WE'LL NEVER HAVE TO SAY GOODBYE AGAIN
England Dan & John Ford Coley
WE'LL SING IN THE SUNSHINE Gale Garnett

WE'RE ALL ALONE Rita Coolidge
WE'RE AN AMERICAN BAND Grand Funk
WE'RE READY Boston
WE'RE THROUGH Hollies
WE'VE GOT TO GET OUT OF THIS PLACE Animals
WE'VE GOT TONIGHT
Kenny Rogers & Sheena Easton
WE'VE ONLY JUST BEGUN Carpenters
WEAK IN THE PRESENCE OF BEAUTY
Alison Moyet
WEAR MY RING AROUND YOUR NECK
Elvis Presley
WEDDING BELL BLUES Fifth Dimension
WEDDING BELLS Godley & Creme
THE WEDDING Julie Rogers
WEE RULE Wee Papa Girl Rappers
WEEKEND IN NEW ENGLAND Barry Manilow
WELCOME BACK John Sebastian
WELCOME HOME Peters & Lee
WELCOME TO MY WORLD Jim Reeves
WELCOME TO THE JUNGLE Guns N' Roses
WELCOME TO THE PLEASURE DOME
Frankie Goes To Hollywood
WELL I ASK YOU Eden Kane
WEST END GIRLS Pet Shop Boys
WESTERN UNION Five Americans
WET DREAM Max Romeo
WHAM RAP Wham!
WHAT Soft Cell
WHAT A DIFF'RENCE A DAY MAKES
Esther Phillips
WHAT A DIFF'RENCE A DAY MAKES
Dinah Washington
WHAT A FOOL BELIEVES Doobie Brothers
WHAT A MOUTH Tommy Steele
WHAT A WASTE Ian Dury & Blockheads
WHAT A WONDERFUL WORLD Louis Armstrong
WHAT ABOUT LOVE? Heart
WHAT AM I GONNA DO Rod Stewart
WHAT AM I GONNA DO WITH YOU Barry White
WHAT ARE YOU DOING SUNDAY Dawn
WHAT BECOMES OF THE BROKENHEARTED
Jimmy Ruffin
WHAT CAN I SAY Boz Scaggs
WHAT DO I DO Phil Fearon & Galaxy
WHAT DO YOU WANT Adam Faith
WHAT DO YOU WANT TO MAKE THOSE EYES
AT ME FOR Shakin' Stevens
WHAT DO YOU WANT TO MAKE THOSE EYES
AT ME FOR Emile Ford
WHAT DOES IT TAKE TO WIN YOUR LOVE
Jr. Walker & The All Stars
WHAT HAVE I DONE TO DESERVE THIS
Pet Shop Boys & Dusty Springfield
WHAT HAVE YOU DONE FOR ME LATELY
Janet Jackson
WHAT I AM Edie Brickell & New Bohemians
WHAT I'VE GOT IN MIND Billie Jo Spears
WHAT IN THE WORLD'S COME OVER YOU
Jack Scott
WHAT IS LIFE George Harrison
WHAT IS LOVE Howard Jones
WHAT KIND OF FOOL
Barbra Streisand & Barry Gibb
WHAT KIND OF FOOL (DO YOU THINK I AM)
Tams
WHAT KINDA BOY YOU LOOKING FOR (GIRL)
Hot Chocolate
WHAT MADE MILWAUKEE FAMOUS
Rod Stewart
WHAT NOW MY LOVE Shirley Bassey
WHAT THE WORLD IS WAITING FOR
Stone Roses
WHAT THE WORLD NEEDS NOW IS LOVE/
ABRAHAM, MARTIN & JOHN Tom Clay
WHAT THE WORLD NEEDS NOW IS LOVE
Jackie DeShannon
WHAT WILL MY MARY SAY Johnny Mathis
WHAT WOULD I BE Val Doonican
WHAT YOU DON'T KNOW Expose
WHAT YOU NEED INXS
WHAT YOU WON'T DO FOR LOVE
Bobby Caldwell
WHAT YOU'RE PROPOSING Status Quo
WHAT'D I SAY Jerry Lee Lewis
WHAT'D I SAY (PT. 1) Ray Charles
WHAT'S ANOTHER YEAR Johnny Logan
WHAT'S GOING ON Marvin Gaye
WHAT'S LOVE GOT TO DO WITH IT Tina Turner
WHAT'S NEW PUSSYCAT? Tom Jones
WHAT'S ON YOUR MIND (PURE ENERGY)
Information Society
WHAT'S THE COLOUR OF MONEY ?
Hollywood Beyond
WHAT'S YOUR NAME Don & Juan
WHATCHA GONNA DO Pablo Cruise
WHATCHA SEE IS WHATCHA GET Dramatics
WHATEVER GETS YOU THRU THE NIGHT
John Lennon

WHATEVER I DO (WHEREVER I GO) Hazell Dean
WHATEVER WILL BE WILL BE Doris Day
WHATEVER YOU WANT Status Quo
WHEELS String–A–Longs
WHEN Showaddywaddy
WHEN A CHILD IS BORN (SOLEADO)
Johnny Mathis
WHEN A MAN LOVES A WOMAN Percy Sledge
WHEN DOVES CRY Prince & The Revolution
WHEN FOREVER HAS GONE Demis Roussos
WHEN I FALL IN LOVE Lettermen
WHEN I FALL IN LOVE Donny Osmond
WHEN I FALL IN LOVE Nat 'King' Cole
WHEN I FALL IN LOVE Rick Astley
WHEN I GROW UP (TO BE A MAN) Beach Boys
WHEN I LOOKED AT HIM Expose
WHEN I NEED YOU Leo Sayer
WHEN I SEE YOU SMILE Bad English
WHEN I THINK OF YOU Janet Jackson
WHEN I'M DEAD AND GONE McGuinness Flint
WHEN I'M WITH YOU Sheriff
WHEN IT'S LOVE Van Halen
WHEN JOHNNY COMES MARCHING HOME
Adam Faith
WHEN JULIE COMES AROUND Cuff Links
WHEN LOVE COMES TO TOWN
U2 With B.B. King
WHEN MY LITTLE GIRL IS SMILING
Jimmy Justice
WHEN SHE WAS MY GIRL Four Tops
WHEN SMOKEY SINGS ABC
WHEN THE BOY IN YOUR ARMS (IS THE BOY
IN YOUR HEART) Connie Francis
WHEN THE CHILDREN CRY White Lion
WHEN THE GIRL IN YOUR ARMS IS THE GIRL
IN YOUR DREAMS Cliff Richard
WHEN THE GOING GETS TOUGH, THE TOUGH
GET GOING Billy Ocean
WHEN THE SWALLOWS COME BACK TO
CAPISTRANO Pat Boone
WHEN WE GET MARRIED Dreamlovers
WHEN WE WERE YOUNG Bucks Fizz
WHEN WILL I BE FAMOUS Bros
WHEN WILL I BE LOVED Everly Brothers
WHEN WILL I BE LOVED Linda Ronstadt
WHEN WILL I SEE YOU AGAIN Three Degrees
WHEN WILL YOU SAY I LOVE YOU Billy Fury
WHEN YOU ASK ABOUT LOVE Matchbox
(WHEN YOU SAY YOU LOVE SOMEBODY)
IN THE HEART Kool & The Gang
WHEN YOU COME BACK TO ME Jason Donovan
WHEN YOU WALK IN THE ROOM Searchers
WHEN YOU'RE HOT, YOU'RE HOT Jerry Reed
WHEN YOU'RE IN LOVE WITH A BEAUTIFUL
WOMAN Dr. Hook
WHEN YOU'RE YOUNG AND IN LOVE
Flying Pickets
WHENEVER I CALL YOU 'FRIEND' Kenny Loggins
WHENEVER YOU NEED SOMEBODY Rick Astley
WHERE ARE YOU NOW
Jimmy Harnen With Sync
WHERE ARE YOU NOW (MY LOVE) Jackie Trent
WHERE DID OUR LOVE GO Supremes
WHERE DID OUR LOVE GO Donnie Elbert
WHERE DID YOUR HEART GO Wham!
WHERE DO BROKEN HEARTS GO
Whitney Houston
(WHERE DO I BEGIN) LOVE STORY Andy Williams
WHERE DO YOU GO TO MY LOVELY
Peter Sarstedt
WHERE IS THE LOVE
Roberta Flack & Donny Hathaway
WHERE OR WHEN Dion & The Belmonts
WHERE THE BOYS ARE Connie Francis
WHERE THE STREETS HAVE NO NAME U2
WHEREVER I LAY MY HAT (THAT'S MY HOME)
Paul Young
WHICH WAY YOU GOIN' BILLY Poppy Family
WHILE YOU SEE A CHANCE Steve Winwood
WHISKY IN THE JAR Thin Lizzy
WHISPERING GRASS
Windsor Davies & Don Estelle
WHITE CHRISTMAS Bing Crosby
WHITE HORSES Jacky
WHITE LINES Grandmaster Flash/Melle Mell
WHITE ON WHITE Danny Williams
WHITE RABBIT Jefferson Airplane
WHITE ROOM Cream
WHITE SILVER SANDS Bill Black's Combo
A WHITE SPORTS COAT (AND A PINK
CARNATION) Marty Robbins
A WHITE SPORTS COAT King Brothers
WHITE WEDDING Billy Idol
A WHITER SHADE OF PALE Procol Harum
WHO AM I Adam Faith
WHO CAN IT BE NOW? Men At Work
WHO FOUND WHO Jellybean
WHO KILLED BAMBI Sex Pistols
WHO LOVES YOU Four Seasons

WHO PUT THE BOMP (IN THE BOMP, BOMP,
BOMP) Barry Mann
WHO WILL YOU RUN TO Heart
WHO'LL STOP THE RAIN
Creedence Clearwater Revival
WHO'S CRYING NOW Journey
WHO'S HOLDING DONNA NOW DeBarge
WHO'S IN THE HOUSE Beatmasters
WHO'S JOHNNY El DeBarge
WHO'S LEAVING WHO Hazell Dean
WHO'S MAKING LOVE Johnnie Taylor
WHO'S SORRY NOW Connie Francis
WHO'S THAT GIRL Eurythmics
WHO'S THAT GIRL Madonna
WHO'S ZOOMIN' WHO Aretha Franklin
WHODUNIT Tavares
WHOLE LOTTA LOVE Led Zeppelin
WHOLE LOTTA LOVING Fats Domino
WHOLE LOTTA SHAKIN' GOIN' ON
Jerry Lee Lewis
WHY Anthony Newley
WHY Carly Simon
WHY Donny Osmond
WHY BABY WHY Pat Boone
WHY CAN'T THIS BE LOVE Van Halen
WHY CAN'T WE BE FRIENDS? War
WHY CAN'T WE LIVE TOGETHER Timmy Thomas
WHY DO FOOLS FALL IN LOVE Diana Ross
WHY OH WHY OH WHY Gilbert O'Sullivan
WHY? Bronski Beat
WICHITA LINEMAN Glen Campbell
WIDE BOY Nik Kershaw
WIDE EYED AND LEGLESS
Andy Fairweather–Low
WIG WAM BAM Sweet
THE WILD BOYS Duran Duran
WILD IN THE COUNTRY Elvis Presley
WILD ONE Bobby Rydell
THE WILD ONE Suzi Quatro
WILD SIDE OF LIFE Status Quo
WILD THING Troggs
WILD THING Tone Loc
WILD WEEKEND Rebels
WILD WEST HERO Electric Light Orchestra
WILD WILD WEST Escape Club
WILD WIND John Leyton
WILD WORLD Maxi Priest
WILD WORLD Jimmy Cliff
WILDFIRE Michael Murphey
WILDFLOWER Skylark
WILDWOOD WEED Jim Stafford
WILFRED THE WEASEL Keith Michel
WILL IT GO ROUND IN CIRCLES Billy Preston
WILL YOU Hazel O'Connor
WILL YOU LOVE ME TOMORROW Shirelles
WILL YOU STILL LOVE ME Chicago
WIMOWEH Karl Denver
WINCHESTER CATHEDERAL
New Vaudeville Band
WIND BENEATH MY WINGS Bette Midler
THE WIND CRIES MARY Jimi Hendrix Experience
WIND ME UP (LET ME GO) Cliff Richard
WINDMILLS OF YOUR MIND Noel Harrison
WINDY Association
WINGS OF A DOVE Madness
THE WINNER TAKES IT ALL Abba
WINTER WORLD OF LOVE
Engelbert Humperdinck
A WINTER'S TALE David Essex
WIPE OUT Surfaris
WIPEOUT Fat Boys & Beach Boys
WIPEOUT Surfaris
WIRED FOR SOUND Cliff Richard
WISHFUL THINKING China Crisis
WISHIN' AND HOPIN' Dusty Springfield
WISHING (IF I HAD A PHOTOGRAPH OF YOU)
Flock Of Seagulls
WISHING I WAS LUCKY Wet Wet Wet
WISHING ON A STAR Fresh 4
WISHING ON A STAR Rose Royce
WISHING WELL Free
WISHING WELL Terence Trent D'Arby
WISHING YOU WERE SOMEHOW HERE AGAIN
Sarah Brightman
WITCH QUEEN OF NEW ORLEANS Redbone
THE WITCH Rattles
THE WITCH'S PROMISE Jethro Tull
WITCHY WOMAN Eagles
WITH A GIRL LIKE YOU Troggs
WITH A LITTLE HELP FROM MY FRIENDS
Young Idea
WITH A LITTLE HELP FROM MY FRIENDS
Joe Cocker
WITH A LITTLE HELP FROM MY FRIENDS
Wet Wet Wet
WITH A LITTLE LUCK Paul McCartney
WITH ALL MY HEART Petula Clark
WITH EVERY BEAT OF MY HEART Taylor Dayne
WITH OR WITHOUT YOU U2

WITH YOU I'M BORN AGAIN
Billy Preston & Syreeta
WITHOUT LOVE (THERE IS NOTHING)
Tom Jones
WITHOUT YOU Johnny Tillotson
WITHOUT YOU Nilsson
WOLVERTON MOUNTAIN Claude King
WOMAN John Lennon
WOMAN IN LOVE Barbra Streisand
A WOMAN IN LOVE Frankie Laine
A WOMAN NEEDS LOVE (JUST LIKE YOU DO)
Ray Parker Jr. & Raydio
WOMAN, WOMAN Union Gap Feat. Gary Puckett
WOMBLING MERRY CHRISTMAS Wombles
THE WOMBLING SONG Wombles
WOMEN IN LOVE Three Degrees
WON'T GET FOOLED AGAIN Who
THE WONDER OF YOU Elvis Presley
WONDERFUL CHRISTMASTIME Paul McCartney
WONDERFUL LAND Shadows
WONDERFUL LIFE Black
A WONDERFUL TIME UP THERE Pat Boone
WONDERFUL WORLD Herman's Hermits
WONDERFUL WORLD Sam Cooke
WONDERFUL WORLD BEAUTIFUL PEOPLE
Jimmy Cliff
WONDERFUL WORLD OF THE YOUNG
Danny Williams
WONDERFUL! WONDERFUL! Tymes
WONDERLAND Big Country
WONDERLAND BY NIGHT Bert Kaempfert
WONDEROUS STORIES Yes
WOOD BEEZ (PRAY LIKE ARETHA FRANKLIN)
Scritti Politti
WOODEN HEART Joe Dowell
WOODEN HEART Elvis Presley
WOODSTOCK Matthews Southern Comfort
WOOLY BULLY Sam The Sham & The Pharaohs
THE WORD GIRL Scritti Politti
WORD UP Cameo
WORDS F.R. David
WORDS Bee Gees
WORDS GET IN THE WAY Miami Sound Machine
WORDS OF LOVE Mamas & The Papas
WORDY RAPPINGHOOD Tom Tom Club
WORK REST & PLAY (E.P.) Madness
WORK THAT BODY Diana Ross
WORKING IN THE COAL MINE Lee Dorsey
WORKING MY WAY BACK TO YOU Four Seasons
WORKING MY WAY BACK TO YOU/FORGIVE
ME, GIRL Spinners
WORLD Bee Gees
THE WORLD IS A GHETTO War
A WORLD OF OUR OWN Seekers
A WORLD WITHOUT LOVE Peter & Gordon
WORST THAT COULD HAPPEN Brooklyn Bridge
WOT'S IT TO YA Robbie Nevil
WOULD I LIE TO YOU? Eurythmics
WOULDN'T CHANGE A THING Kylie Minogue
WOULDN'T IT BE GOOD Nik Kershaw
WOULDN'T IT BE NICE Beach Boys
WRAPPED AROUND YOUR FINGER Police
THE WRECK OF THE EDMUND FITZGERALD
Gordon Lightfoot
THE WRITING ON THE WALL Adam Wade
WUTHERING HEIGHTS Kate Bush
XANADU Olivia Newton–John/E.L.O.
Y VIVA ESPANA Sylvia
Y.M.C.A. Village People
YA YA Lee Dorsey
YEAR OF THE CAT Al Stewart
YEARS MAY COME, YEARS MAY GO
Herman's Hermits
YEH YEH Georgie Fame
YELLOW BIRD Arthur Lyman
YELLOW RIVER Christie
YELLOW SUBMARINE Beatles
YES I WILL Hollies
YES SIR I CAN BOOGIE Baccara
YES, I'M READY Barbara Mason
YES, I'M READY Teri DeSario With K.C.
YESTER–ME, YESTER–YOU, YESTERDAY
Stevie Wonder
YESTERDAY Matt Monro
YESTERDAY Beatles
YESTERDAY HAS GONE Cupid's Inspiration
YESTERDAY MAN Chris Andrews
YESTERDAY ONCE MORE Carpenters
YING TONG SONG Goons
YO–YO Osmonds
YOGI Ivy Three
YOU AIN'T SEEN NOTHIN' YET
Bachman–Turner Overdrive
YOU ALWAYS HURT THE ONE YOU LOVE
Clarence 'Frogman' Henry
YOU AND I Eddie Rabbitt/Crystal Gayle
YOU AND ME Alice Cooper
YOU AND ME AGAINST THE WORLD
Helen Reddy

YOU ARE Lionel Richie
YOU ARE EVERYTHING Stylistics
YOU ARE EVERYTHING Diana Ross/Marvin Gaye
YOU ARE MY DESTINY Paul Anka
YOU ARE MY SUNSHINE Ray Charles
YOU ARE SO BEAUTIFUL Joe Cocker
YOU ARE THE SUNSHINE OF MY LIFE
Stevie Wonder
YOU ARE THE WOMAN Firefall
YOU BEAT ME TO THE PUNCH Mary Wells
YOU BELONG TO ME Carly Simon
YOU BELONG TO ME Dupress
YOU BELONG TO THE CITY Glenn Frey
YOU BETTER SIT DOWN KIDS Cher
YOU BETTER YOU BET Who
YOU CAME Kim Wilde
YOU CAN CALL ME AL Paul Simon
YOU CAN DEPEND ON ME Brenda Lee
YOU CAN DO MAGIC America
YOU CAN DO MAGIC
Limmie & The Family Cookin'
YOU CAN GET IT IF YOU REALLY WANT
Desmond Dekker
YOU CAN'T CHANGE THAT Raydio
YOU CAN'T HURRY LOVE Supremes
YOU CAN'T HURRY LOVE Phil Collins
YOU CAN'T SIT DOWN Dovells
YOU DECORATED MY LIFE Kenny Rogers
YOU DIDN'T HAVE TO BE SO NICE
Lovin' Spoonful
YOU DON'T BRING ME FLOWERS
Barbra Streisand & Neil Diamond
YOU DON'T HAVE TO BE A BABY TO CRY
Caravelles
YOU DON'T HAVE TO BE A STAR (TO BE IN
MY SHOW) Marilyn Mccoo & Billy Davis Jr
YOU DON'T HAVE TO GO Chi–Lites
YOU DON'T HAVE TO SAY YOU LOVE ME
Guys & Dolls
YOU DON'T HAVE TO SAY YOU LOVE ME
Elvis Presley
YOU DON'T HAVE TO SAY YOU LOVE ME
Dusty Springfield
YOU DON'T KNOW Helen Shapiro
YOU DON'T KNOW ME Ray Charles
YOU DON'T KNOW WHAT YOU GOT
(UNTIL YOU LOSE IT) Ral Donner
YOU DON'T MESS AROUND WITH JIM Jim Croce
YOU DON'T OWN ME Lesley Gore
YOU DRIVE ME CRAZY Shakin' Stevens

YOU GAVE ME LOVE Crown Heights Affair
YOU GIVE GOOD LOVE Whitney Houston
YOU GIVE LOVE A BAD NAME Bon Jovi
YOU GOT IT Roy Orbison
YOU GOT IT (THE RIGHT STUFF)
New Kids On The Block
YOU GOT IT ALL Jets
YOU GOT SOUL Johnny Nash
(YOU GOTTA) FIGHT FOR YOUR RIGHT
(TO PARTY) Beastie Boys
YOU GOT WHAT IT TAKES Marv Johnson
YOU GOT WHAT IT TAKES Dave Clark Five
YOU GOT WHAT IT TAKES Showaddywaddy
YOU HAVEN'T DONE NOTHIN Stevie Wonder
YOU JUST MIGHT SEE ME CRY Our Kid
YOU KEEP IT ALL IN Beautiful South
YOU KEEP ME HANGIN' ON Kim Wilde
YOU KEEP ME HANGIN' ON Supremes
(YOU KEEP ME) HANGIN' ON Vanilla Fudge
YOU LIGHT UP MY LIFE Debby Boone
YOU LITTLE THIEF Feargal Sharkey
YOU MADE ME BELIEVE IN MAGIC
Bay City Rollers
YOU MAKE LOVIN' FUN Fleetwood Mac
YOU MAKE ME FEEL (MIGHTY REAL) Sylvester
YOU MAKE ME FEEL BRAND NEW Stylistics
YOU MAKE ME FEEL LIKE DANCING Leo Sayer
YOU MAKE MY DREAMS Daryl Hall & John Oates
YOU MAY BE RIGHT Billy Joel
YOU MIGHT THINK Cars
YOU MUST HAVE BEEN A BEAUTIFUL BABY
Bobby Darin
YOU NEED HANDS Max Bygraves
YOU NEEDED ME Anne Murray
YOU NEVER DONE IT LIKE THAT
Captain & Tennille
YOU OUGHT TO BE WITH ME Al Green
YOU REALLY GOT ME Kinks YOU SEE THE
TROUBLE WITH ME Barry White
YOU SEND ME Sam Cooke
YOU SEXY THING Hot Chocolate
YOU SHOULD BE DANCING Bee Gees
YOU SHOULD HEAR HOW SHE TALKS ABOUT
YOU Melissa Manchester
YOU SHOWED ME Turtles
YOU SPIN ME ROUND (LIKE A RECORD)
Dead Or Alive
YOU TAKE ME UP Thompson Twins
YOU TAKE MY BREATH AWAY Rex Smith
YOU TALK TOO MUCH Joe Jones

YOU TO ME ARE EVERYTHING Real Thing
YOU TURN ME ON Ian Whitcomb
YOU WEAR IT WELL Rod Stewart
YOU WERE MADE FOR ME
Freddie & The Dreamers
YOU WERE ON MY MIND We Five
YOU WERE ON MY MIND Crispian St. Peters
YOU WIN AGAIN Bee Gees
YOU WON'T FIND ANOTHER FOOL LIKE ME
New Seekers
YOU WON'T SEE ME Anne Murray
YOU YOU YOU Alvin Stardust
YOU'LL ANSWER TO ME Cleo Laine
YOU'LL LOSE A GOOD THING Barbara Lynn
YOU'LL NEVER FIND ANOTHER LOVE LIKE MINE
Lou Rawls
YOU'LL NEVER KNOW Shirley Bassey
YOU'LL NEVER STOP ME FROM LOVING YOU
Sonia
YOU'LL NEVER WALK ALONE The Crowd
YOU'LL NEVER WALK ALONE
Gerry & The Pacemakers
YOU'RE A LADY Peter Skellern
YOU'RE ALL I NEED TO GET BY
Marvin Gaye & Tammi Terrell
YOU'RE DRIVING ME CRAZY Temperance Seven
(YOU'RE) HAVING MY BABY Paul Anka
YOU'RE HISTORY Shakespears Sister
YOU'RE IN MY HEART Rod Stewart
YOU'RE MORE THAN A NUMBER IN MY LITTLE
RED BOOK Drifters
YOU'RE MOVING OUT TODAY
Carole Bayer Sager
YOU'RE MY BEST FRIEND Queen
YOU'RE MY EVERYTHING Temptations
(YOU'RE MY) SOUL AND INSPIRATION
Righteous Brothers
YOU'RE MY WORLD Cilla Black
YOU'RE NO GOOD Linda Ronstadt
YOU'RE NO GOOD Swinging Blue Jeans
YOU'RE NOT ALONE Chicago
YOU'RE ONLY HUMAN (SECOND WIND)
Billy Joel
YOU'RE ONLY LONELY J.D. Souther
YOU'RE SIXTEEN Ringo Starr
YOU'RE SIXTEEN Johnny Burnette
YOU'RE SO VAIN Carly Simon
(YOU'RE THE) DEVIL IN DISGUISE Elvis Presley
YOU'RE THE FIRST, THE LAST, MY EVERYTHING
Barry White

YOU'RE THE INSPIRATION Chicago
YOU'RE THE ONE Vogues
YOU'RE THE ONE THAT I WANT
John Travolta & Olivia Newton–John
YOU'RE THE REASON I'M LIVING Bobby Darin
YOU'RE THE VOICE John Farnham
YOU'VE GOT A FRIEND James Taylor
YOU'VE GOT ME DANGLING ON A STRING
Chairman Of The Board
(YOU'VE GOT) THE MAGIC TOUCH Platters
YOU'VE GOT TO HIDE YOUR LOVE AWAY Silkie
YOU'VE GOT YOUR TROUBLES Fortunes
YOU'VE LOST THAT LOVIN' FEELIN'
Righteous Brothers
YOU'VE LOST THAT LOVIN' FEELIN' Cilla Black
YOU'VE MADE ME SO VERY HAPPY
Blood Sweat & Tears
YOU'VE REALLY GOT A HOLD ON ME Miracles
YOUNG AT HEART Bluebells
YOUNG GIFTED AND BLACK Bob & Marcia
YOUNG GIRL Gary Puckett & The Union Gap
YOUNG GUNS (GO FOR IT) Wham!
YOUNG HEARTS RUN FREE Candi Staton
YOUNG LOVE Donny Osmond
YOUNG LOVERS Paul & Paula
THE YOUNG NEW MEXICAN PUPPETEER
Tom Jones
THE YOUNG ONES Cliff Richard
YOUNG PARISIANS Adam & The Ants
YOUNG TURKS Rod Stewart
YOUNG WORLD Rick Nelson
YOUR LOVE Outfield
YOUR LOVE IS KING Sade
(YOUR LOVE HAS LIFTED ME) HIGHER AND
HIGHER Rita Coolidge
(YOUR LOVE KEEPS LIFTING ME) HIGHER AND
HIGHER Jackie Wilson
YOUR MAMA DON'T DANCE
Loggins & Messina
YOUR MAMA DON'T DANCE Poison
YOUR PRECIOUS LOVE
Marvin Gaye & Tammi Terrell
YOUR SONG Elton John
YOUR WILDEST DREAMS Moody Blues
YUMMY YUMMY YUMMY Ohio Express
ZABADAK Dave Dee, Dozy, Beaky, Mick & Titch
ZIP–A–DEE DOO–DAH
Bob B. Soxx & The Blue Jeans
ZOOM Fat Larry's Band
ZORBA'S DANCE Marcello Minerbi